of them along the garden's downhill edges so that their vines
could spread outside onto the sifted rock and gravel border.
   Bert planted the seeds ᵗⁿᵈᶤᵛᶤᵈ┄ ┄
turnip seeds which he sprir
after they sprouted. The g
not need aisles (from the s
all space was planted. See
the seeds with a layer of s
recommended); not thick en
floated up some of the seed

Despite being tiny, the turnip seeds sprouted well and
quickly, and grew vigorously. The beans, all varieties, also
sprouted well and big initially, but were slow growing second
leaves. The lentils sprouted well but grew slowly. The chard
sprouted slowly (as Suzanne had warned) but quite well. (She
had suggested pre-soaking seeds. But when planting, Bert was
in that area only one day.) Not many broccoli seeds sprouted
and they grew slowly at first, but eventually became the biggest
plants. The pumpkins sprouted very slowly but grew long vines.
   For protection from small creatures, the screen door (after
patching a few rips with other screening sewed on) was mounted
horizontally on corner posts ± 2 ft high. The sides were
covered by loose screening hung vertically, with tops tied to
the door frame, and bottoms anchored with rocks. When harvesting, we temp removed the rocks and curled up the side screens.
   Some turnips seemed too close together. We soon thinned
them by snipping with sizzors (pulling might disturb neighbors'
roots). That is also how we did a little weeding.
   We also soon harvested some chard leaves, but sparingly so
as (we hoped) to not seriously injure the plants (which, Suzanne
had said, could survive a few yrs and then reseed themselves).
   The broccoli was very slow producing flower buds (the part
usually eaten), and the buds were small, so we also ate the
leaves (which, cooked, taste about as good as the buds).
   The beans were slow flowering and producing pods (perhaps
because the screening excluded bees which, Suzanne reported in
Ab #10, are needed for pollinating). The pumpkins grew big
yellow flowers, but most did not develop into pumpkins.
   Though the netting was a barrier to most insects, it would
not deter deer (which often ravage the gardens of rural settlers
in this area); maybe not even rabbits. To hopefully repel
animals, and as future fertilizer, we poured pee around the
garden, putting most on the uphill sides.
   We set several mouse traps, some within the screening,
some in crannies under big rocks outside (to not catch birds).
But we did not catch any nor see evidence of mouse damage.
Something (sow bugs ?) ate small holes in some leaves. But we
noticed very little damage by wild creatures - which pleasantly
surprised us. Nor did many weeds grow.
   For watering, after trying various ways, we used a squeeze
bottle, refilling it from jugs in which we hauled water from a
small pond we'd dug ± 50 yards away. We tried to water early
mornings every 2 or 3 days (depending on temperature and amount
of sun), but sometimes missed because of trips away. We simply
squirted the water onto the top screening and let it spray
through. About four gallons per watering.
   By mid Sept our summer camp got sun too briefly each day
for solar cooking to be practical. So we moved to our new
winter camp. (There we continued solar cooking until much
cloudy/rainy weather began in mid Oct). Before leaving, we

harvested most of what remained.

Broccoli: We cut off and cooked all leaves and buds, except for a few old leaves past their prime, and a few small new shoots that might continue growing.

Turnips: On most, the leaves had withered; we harvested the roots. Biggest was orange size; most were plum size (small for turnips ?). By the time we got around to cooking them, some had partly rotted where there had been insect infestation. The remainders of those, and the others, tasted okay.

Chard: We harvested some leaves but left many in hopes the plants would survive the winter.

Beans: Only a few pods had developed. Most pod covers were tan (dead). Damp when picked so, to dry them, we put them in a pail with dry newsprint (from a recycling center).

Lentils: No pods had developed.

Late Sept and early Oct were quite warm and sunny except for a few showery days. Then in mid Oct came a few cold days. Frost warnings on weather radio. I don't know how cold the garden got; we were not there then. Then, through early Nov, mostly cool cloudy rainy/showery days.

On 9 Nov, Bert made a day trip to our summer-camp area to fetch things. He briefly inspected the garden. The frost had killed the pumpkin vines but left two immature pumpkins, the biggest orange size. The bean and lentil plants were dead. The broccoli had grown vigorously, putting out many new leaves and, on one plant, buds which had flowered. The chard was still growing. The few turnips we had left still had green leaves. We hope they survive the winter and next year produce seeds. Bert, lacking time and weight capacity, did not harvest anything.

In early Dec, shortly before an arctic air mass moved in with temperature below 20°F, Bert did a final harvest of leaves and shoots of broccoli, but left a few blossoms in hope they might produce seed. I removed the beans from the pail, hulled them, and was pleased that most were dry and looked good. All four varieties. But not many more harvested than were planted. Enough for only one meal. Tasted fine.

Conclusion: Harvests were not near enough to compensate for our labor. But we learned - and may do better next year.

The garden got several hours of sun on fully sunny days from late May until late July - the period when the sun goes higher in the sky than the tops of nearby bushes and small trees. But overall, the spot apparantly does not get enough sun for seed or root crops to produce much. Also, the screening reduced sun intensity. So, next year, we will grow only plants with edible leaves: turnips; broccoli; chard (if it survives winter); kale (another cabbage relative) if we get seed; parsley (thanks again to Suzanne). But not lettuce, because we forage much wild gosmore (Hypochoeris radicata) a lettuce (and dandelion) relative that is probably more nutritious than domestic lettuce. (This year, we harvested gosmore all winter near our base camp, despite the Dec freeze.) Holly & Bert

I survived by foraging wild foods and dumpster diving.

And by working odd jobs where I could. After leaving my parents' home at age 17, I was on the road for ten years, living out of my backpack. I developed a taste for traveling lightly. I seldom stayed more than two nights in one place. I went to various political events and alternative gatherings.

As a single woman, I had no problem getting rides. I've been to every U.S. state and Canadian province, most of Mexico, and all of Central America; but not much farther. When south of the U.S. border, I stayed far away from tourist destinations and so was always seen as a novelty and was fed by the locals in the small towns I hitched into.

After a while I grew tired of always being on guard among strangers, and having to trick or coax at least one man a day to avoid rape. (Believe it or not, I've never been raped or beat up.) I got enough money to buy an old broken-down van and began to live in it. I got books from libraries and learned how to fix it. I even replaced an engine. (It had a cracked head.)

I learned: if all the world's earnings were divided equally, each person would receive $6 a day. But more than 80% of earth's people live on less than $2 a day. I tried to. But that was impossible while having a van. And I never camped near enough to a town to bike there and back. But living on $6 a day was fun: requiring creativity and meaningful thoughtful activities. For 17 years now, I've lived on $5-$6 a day. I drive very little, not only to spend less, but to contribute less to fuel-related deaths and destruction.

As for companionship, having a partner has never fit with my lifestyle. I have sweethearts here and there. I've gone to Rainbow gatherings since 1978. I no longer love them as I once did, but I still get lots from them.

I have a desert 'home' I return to each winter. I've been there nine winters so far; no one has found it yet. I have to hike two miles to reach it, and 2½ miles to backpack water. But I love it: 360° views with no neighbors. It is perfect for my needs: so quiet and peaceful; beautiful because my time is my own to invest in qualities I want.

To build it, I bent cattle panels between boulders. Inside is lathed and stuccoed. Outside is covered with plastic, then rocks and recycled 'windows' or glass, and stuccoed between rocks. I've invested about $200 into it.

(In a sharply-focused color photo, her abode resembles a rock outcrop. Terrain seems to slope gently. Waist-high bushes with sparse foliage; patches of cactus; no trees visible.)

During other seasons I live in a small vehicle. I removed all seats except the driver's. Kitchen in right front. Cupboards along one side in back. I sleep with my feet between the driver's seat and kitchen. The car is cozy; does not need heat.

In early spring I carry in all my supplies to my campsite and don't go back out (except for a trip to a gathering) until I leave in the fall. I take a shovel and hand-rake for building a a road to where I'm camping. I cover my vehicle's tracks behind me by replanting trees and bushes, and spreading grass seed I gather or buy. For crossing creeks, I have two 7-foot-long steel ramps (custom made, $50). I try to find camp-sites on the far sides of creeks. (Few folk will cross creeks and get wet to go exploring.) After each crossing, I remove ramps and meticulously repair the creek's sides, to leave no trace of my passage. Rockann (pen name given by H&B, so readers may refer to article)

Silicone caulk plus thinner seam-seals tent; waterproofs pants.

Before bicycling from Tucson to Seattle last summer, I needed to seam-seal my tent. I dislike the pricy containers of seam-sealer that dry up so quickly. So I tried using D.A.P. 100% silicone caulk (±$3.50), thinned with a solvent. (Gasoline or paint thinner will do. I didn't try alcohol.) After it dried, I dusted the seam with corn starch to lessen the sticky feeling. One tube of caulk will waterproof MUCH fabric, and

I've stored caulk for more than a year without problems.

I also tried coating the inside of nylon pants. Applying two thin coats with a brush seemed to work well. I didn't take those pants with me to Seattle, so I don't yet know how long the coating will endure. Lauran, March 2009

Experiences with two different bicycle-assist engines.

The first engine I told about (in May 06 DP) is a 23cc two-stroke. I still have it. 7000 miles to date.

This past summer I purchased a 35cc four-stroke, slightly heavier, same drive system, different sounding, no mixing of gas and oil. I thought it might be better because 4-strokes are cleaner burning than 2-strokes; and there is 'talk' of eventually outlawing 2-strokes because of emissions.

For the 2-stroke I had a pretty good system for mixing oil and gas, so I didn't find non-mixing to be that great a convenience. The 35cc engine definitely could pull the weight all day with an easy cruising speed of 25 mph - though I find 22 mph more congenial for safety.

A disadvantage of the 4-stroke: I had to change the oil. Not a big job, but something I didn't need to do with the 2-stroke. I also needed to check oil level - though it NEVER needed topping off. To change the oil, I removed the engine from the bike (a 5-minute job), tipped it upside down into a suitable container, let it drain, then remounted the engine. Total time: less than ½ hour. I preferred to do this near a gas station to which I could take the oil. Once I simply took the engine into the gas station and asked if I could pour the oil into their waste barrel. They were fine with that.

The 4-stroke engine performed well except at altitudes above 7000 feet (Colorado). Trouble starting, fouled plug, very rough idle, etc, due to engine not getting enough oxygen. The 2-stroke has an adjustment for altitude. I talked with the owner of the 4-stroke business. He told me to send him the engine when convenient and he'd put an adjustment screw on the carburator. When they sell to someone living at high altitude, they put in different jets. I am one of only a handful of people who use these engines for long hauls through different altitudes, so I tend to expose these problems.

I hauled a Burley trailer weighing 60-80 pounds, depending on food and water load. Going up mountain passes, I needed to pedal to assist the engine. But that is well within my strength level. (I'm 52; in good shape compared to most women my age.)

I like both engines, though I slightly prefer the 2-stroke. It doesn't go as fast (which I don't care about) but is peppier: responds faster, which is nice. It also can be put in any position without problems. Eg, when I camp at night, I often go into trees/brush, etc. That may require putting the bike under fences, or laying it down so that car headlights don't shine on my reflectors and reveal my location. Two-strokes are designed to be run in any position. Whereas 4-strokes must stay fairly level. Users have reported: if a 4-stroke is tipped past a certain angle, oil gets into part of the carburator, requiring work to clean it out. I was aware of that, so I kept the engine level. But there were times when I was put at risk or inconvenienced more than I like.

I was told the 4-stroke would get as good or better gas mileage than the 2-stroke, but it hasn't. I averaged 180-200 mpg with the 2-stroke and 140-160 mpg with the 4-stroke.

The 4-stroke has a lower throatier sound - a bit more

6

tolerable. But the 2-stroke sounds better than some 2-strokes. Their db levels are about the same. A personal preference issue.

I looked at cargo bikes. But for my needs they seem big, awkward, extra heavy, cumbersome. I often need to get the bike off into brush. A cargo bike would be more of a hassle.

On a trip in Idaho, I found and purchased a Raleigh that isn't made anymore. It's a cross between a comfort bike and a recumbent. I REALLY LIKE IT. Pedaling it uses slightly different muscles, more glutes and hamstrings. When I sit on it, my feet are flat on the ground. Its wheel base is slightly longer. I am AMAZED at how much nicer it rides on a dirt road. Much smoother, less bumpy. I don't know how much this is due to the longer wheel base or to the type of tires. I haven't put the engine on it as I love riding it as is.

I also like its seating position. Riding long distances on conventional bikes with my head facing up and forward, puts an awful kink in my neck. I suffered a very painful herniated disk two years ago. I'm not sure that extended bike riding caused it, but I don't think it helped. This new bike lets me sit more upright with little or no kink in my neck. The pedals are slightly more forward than on a conventional bike, but not as far forward as on a recumbent. The one thing I'll change: its wide-berth comfort-bike seat. Because of the slight angle of the pedals, there is nothing behind my butt to push against when pluggin' up hills. (Not much of a problem here in Tucson, but Seattle was another matter.) I need a seat with a small back, maybe 3-4" high. I may design it myself, or see if any type of modified recumbent seat would work.

If you go into a bike shop, a current model, "Electra Townie", is much like it, I think. Lauran, March 2009

(Comment) I wonder what type of handle-bar you use on a conventional bike. Or, how you position the hand grips. I HATE a bar that droops; requiring me to sit hunched over - and then strain my neck to look forward. I want to sit upright. When climbing hills, I often stand on the pedals. (This is with a 2¼-speed bike. Typically, one speed won't stay in gear well.) Yeah, more wind resistance. Not a big drag at my 10-15 mph cruising speed, but I suppose it would be at 25 mph. B & H

My wife and I car-camped in Nashville for five years.

At night we parked free, behind a brake place, in exchange for night-watch services. (I found that opportunity by distributing hundreds of fliers to businesses, delivering them before the businesses opened. Very few responded.)

At the brake place, we had to drive away each morning by 6:30 when they opened. During summers we usually drove to a park and stayed there until after dark. We then drove back to the brake place and parked in the alley behind it. We typically ate supper at K mart, then went to a library until 9:00, then returned to the brake place, got into our car, and went to bed. We slept in Geo Metros by removing the front seat, adding a foam-rubber mat, and sleeping longways.

Leaving each morning always felt good, because we had beat the system out of rent; enabling us to afford a decent car, and to save money - with which we eventually bought an old 30-foot travel trailer and fixed it up (report in March09 DP). During our 5 years car-camping we saved thousands on rent, and had our freedom - but nothing is perfect. Our car costs $500 a month, including car payments, insurance, gas, etc.

I sang and played guitar in bars. (Report in Ab#9) When

not playing, I usually kept my music equipment in storage units.
But when I came home at night, the storage unit was closed, so
I had to leave my equipment outside the car.

A few times, people tried to rob us while we slept. A man
tried to steal my guitar from my car, but I woke up and ran
him off. A female sneak thief tried to steal my wife's purse
by reaching inside the window, but my wife woke up and gave her
hell. So we got a dog and chained it to the bumper to warn us.
Late at night, kids sometimes woke us by throwing rocks at us.
Mexicans tried to steal the car. The neighborhood was racially
mixed, and some blacks tried to make us pay them protection
money, but we never did. In winter nobody bothered us much,
but in summer kids and Mexicans roamed at night. We were
hassled 4 or 5 times a year. I did not have a fire-arm, but
I kept a baseball bat or crowbar or heavy wrench handy.

Once, as I drove off, I heard something dragging under my
car. I stopped and looked. It was a man who had passed out.
I called an ambulance, but he got up and ran off.

In Nashville, to sleep on business property, you need
written permission from the owner - to show the cops when they
come and wake you, which they will eventually. After you
explain what you are doing, the cops will tend to leave you
alone - unless new cops take over that beat; then you can
expect to be bothered again. Cops' reactions to us ranged
from helpful, to feeling sorry for us, to distainful. If any
gunshots sound nearby at night, cops may question you. We were
never arrested but always lived in fear of the law and outlaws.

In summer, fleas and mosquitos could be bad. In winter at
night, we needed plenty of quilts over us. However, Nashville
seldom gets colder than 20°F.

The library helped us get through many days and nights.
Library people are nice here. Downtown, they are quite tolerant
of the 'homeless'; many come from the mission. The library
never gets new books, but the magazines are current. I'd never
steal from the library as they are the only free thing here.

Nashville is quite dead at night; not as much happening
as you might expect. It is a work-and-go-to-bed town - the
buckle of the Bible Belt. It is a rich man's town. It tries
to copy LA and NYC. Nashville has poor areas right next to
rich areas. East Nashville is poor-to-middle-class; probably
the friendliest area. West Nashville, Franklin, Beele Meade,
Brentwood, Bellvue are rich and snobby. The rich and some
middle-class whites won't hardly speak to the poor. If you
drive an old car through a rich area, the police will be called.
Nashville is 25% black. Some blacks are prejudiced, but most
are friendly if you are. Blacks and whites bond against Mexs.

Broadway, famous for country-music dives, now runs off the
poor. Costs $12 to park and $3 for a beer. The middle-class
young go there, but poor rednecks are not welcome. How ironic;
country music was originally the music of poor whites.

Rooms rent for $400 a month. Apartments, $600 up. Trailers,
$135-$150 a week. No rent control. Most people here put their
money into cars and housing, and don't have much else. No state
income tax, but TN has one of the highest sales taxes in U.S.

Nashville now has a "quality-of-life" ordinance, so the
cops can harass and fine the poor. They want the poor out of
sight. But sleeping in cars on city streets is not illegal
here yet. There is a tent city downtown on the river. Some
intolerant people wanted to run them off, but the mayor let it
stay. 50,000 people were unemployed in 2009. 6000 'homeless'.

Nashville ranks third in U.S. for violence against the homeless. Car-camping is stigmatized here. I never let straight people know that I car-camped. So why did we car-camp HERE ? We grew up here and knew people. Would I ever car-camp again ? Not in Nashville. I have been here too long and done all that a poor person can do here. But I might in a much bigger city. It would have to be a place with many music jobs. But during this depression, I doubt that there is such a place.

Advice if car-camping. Keep tools with you and learn to fix your own car. Use window tint; don't use curtains, they would be a give-away. And do not leave bed covers visible in the car during daylight. Or, get a van with no windows and you can park most anywhere, as long as no one sees you get in and out. (But I've heard that such a van may attract attention some places; eg, parked on a street in a residential neighborhood.) If woken by someone at night, do not respond unless you are sure it is the cops. (If you don't respond to a would-be thief, he may break in. Or, if legally parked on a street with a vehicle in which you are not visible, why respond to cops ? If you lay still (don't rock vehicle) they won't know anyone is inside.)

Go to bed early and get up early before locals can see you. Before parking on business property overnight, get written permission from the owner. Keep a big wrench for protection. (Not illegal.) Stash your money away from the car, in case you are robbed. If you need warm places to spend time during cold weather, look for stores with delis, such as K-mart and Krogers.

Keep a low profile and enjoy your freedom from rent. You can move around nightly and enjoy the adventure. Enjoyment depends on attitude. Make a game out of hiding your lifestyle from the public. They think it is a moral crime to be poor. So build up your savings - then you can laugh at them. Car-camp until you can do better. If 'better' is not better, you can go back to car-camping. Or ?

I know people who live in the woods near the interstate. They sell firewood at the exit. They do not bother to own cars. They built a cabin and use a propane heater. They get by on $40 a week. They seem rather happy. Marty Brown, 2009 & 2010.

A do-it-themselves village near Portland of houseless people.

I heard an hour-long discussion about "Dignity Village" (DV) on OPB's "Thinking Outloud", 26nov09. DV has existed 8 years. DV is situated on asphalt pavement near Portland's airport. A prison and golf courses are near by; not much else. DV is 40 minutes by bus from downtown Portland; a big problem for DV residents who have jobs or are seeking them.

DV presently has 60 residents/members. Apparently most are men. A few are couples. No kids mentioned. When DV began, most residents lived in tents. But now most have 8-by-10-ft cabins. Some have wood stoves inside. A few have photo-volt panels on roof for elec lights and devices. None have running water or grid elec. Apparently most cabins were built by their original occupants. There are toilets outside (like those at construction sites ?). DV has a "common room" with wood stove wherein the discussion was conducted. On cold winter nights, a few houseless non-members are allowed to sleep in it.

The site was provided by Portland city. Residents pay $20/ month, which goes for insurance the city requires. Legally, DV is a "non-profit corporation". On-site management and maintenance is by DV residents elected to their positions. Several were interviewed. One, the gate-keeper, said that residents are not allowed to bring alcohol or illegal drugs into DV. Police have visited DV once a week, average - a high rate for a village of 60. Mostly in response to calls from DV.

DV wants to construct a shower/toilet building with water and sewerage hookups, but needs $14,000 merely to pay for the permits and inspections required - the charge for ANYTHING legal built in Portland ! The $14,000 does not include the costs of actual construction or hook-ups.

DV has had various micro-businesses: candle-making; a hot-dog cart; an e-bay store; firewood sales (more scrap wood is donated to DV than it uses): total, $1500/month. These may be businesses conducted by/for DV; not including members' individual activities. Some gardening is done in pails and raised beds. (All ground is asphalt covered.)

Interviewees included several-year residents, a recent arrival, an ex-resident who remembered DV's founding. But the person who got the most radio time is not a DV resident. Her main job: administering Portland's ten-year program to "end homelessness". She is also city liason with DV; she collects info about the people in DV. Her line: Though DV is commended for doing as well as it has done (maybe the best such effort anywhere in U.S.), "we" want to get all "homeless" people into conventional housing that is affordable. (Ha ha ! With $14,000 required to merely get a permit ? Fat chance. But SHE has a well-paid position.) She said, "Children belong in a house with electricity and running water."

Electricity and indoor plumbing are relatively recent inventions. They are costly luxuries, not necessities. Our ancestors got along without them, and most people in the world still do. I am saddened and angered when some people want to force their preferences onto others.

Also said on the program: There are 1600 houseless people in Portland. Their rates of addiction and mental illness are no higher than among low-income people with houses. Poverty is the main cause of houselessness. Holly

To sleep warm during cold weather, use plenty of covers.

Most sleeping bags are rated optimistically even when new, and their effectiveness declines with use because stuffing gets compressed and voids develop. Presently, sleeping INSIDE our winter base camp, where seldom colder than 50°F, we are using one old rectangular sleepa (opened out as a quilt) inside a cover bag to help keep it clean and together, plus a quilt. When much colder inside than 50° (20° or colder outside, seldom), we add a third quilt (quite thick sleepa opened out). Under the covers, we usually sleep nude except for knit caps and (on Holly) long thick socks. We have a 4th sleepa in a pail near by, in case of extreme cold, but haven't had to use it. (Only a few times a century does w Oregon get colder than 0°F.)

If occupying a semi-buried shelter long, what is under us is less important for warmth than what is over us, because the ground will gradually warm. We presently have barely enough foam (open-cell on top of closed-cell) for cushioning. (We've more foam stashed, but other things have had backpack priority.)

Some years ago, Lazlo Borbely, car-camping in WV, wrote in DP that, when colder than 40°, he slept with his head under the covers. 40° may be my approx threshold. If 50°, when I get into bed, to warm up I usually keep my head under for a few minutes and may blow exhaled air toward my feet. But after CO_2 accumulates to cause hard breathing, my head comes out.

Whereas when colder, the ventilation is greater (depends on the difference in temperature as well as thickness of covers) and my head stays under (though more air leakage around head than around body). I also wear a second knit cap. Bert

Use ground as floor ? Or insulate floor from ground ?
Which is better for warmth during cold weather ? That depends on the site, soil, depth of floor, occupancy.
We have used the ground as our floor, covered only with plastic film plus maybe thin foam and linoleum. That is simpler than insulating the floor, and is usually as good or better for warmth IF the shelter is underground or earth-sheltered deep enough that the floor is several feet below the depth to which the ground usually freezes (if it does).
Insulating floor from ground may be desirable IF the floor is at or close to the surface.
As insulation, soil is much less effective PER THICKNESS than are fluffy or porous materials that entrap air, such as dry moss, loose leaves, crumpled newspapers, feathers, foam. (The still air is what insulates; the moss (or ?) merely serves to keep the air quite still.) But soil can insulate effectively if SEVERAL FEET of it is between the inside and the cold; ie, if the floor is quite far below frost level. (Exception: where soil is very porous (eg, loose gravel) and cold rain or snow melt percolates through. In that case, the water could be diverted by plastic tarps on the surface around the shelter. But insulating floor from soil might be easier.)
If ground is floor, what will the floor temperature be during winter ? Unless there is water flow, many feet underground the soil temperature remains close to the average year-around outside temperature, because the soil stores heat (or cold) and many feet of it insulates effectively. Where we are, deep soil is 50° to 60°F, depending on slope and elevation. (South-facing slopes are warmer than north slopes; moderately-high slopes are warmer than valley bottoms and high altitudes.)
When in winter we return to a well-insulated partly-underground shelter that was vacant for several weeks, the floor will typically be ±50° and the inside air close to that temperature - desirable if outside air colder. After one night occupancy, the floor will not have warmed much and the inside air may warm to only 60°. But if we stay several weeks, our body heat (and cooking, if done inside) will gradually warm the floor to ±60°, with the inside air typically fluctuating between 60° and 80°, depending on outside temperatures (typically lows of 30° and daily highs of 50°) and our activities. Generally coolest at dawn and warmest late afternoon. (Some data in March 09 DP.)
If insulating floor from ground (I never have), I'd use a floor material that will store much heat and thus help warm the shelter during cold periods. Barefoot Architect book (review in Ab#10) suggests dark-colored stones or ceramic tiles. But damp soil stores more heat per weight (because of its water content) and is generally more available. I'd put plastic film above and below it to confine the moisture. The insulation under it must support the weight of the soil plus the occupants and their equipment. I might try alternate layers of plastic film and scavenged styrofoam chips (used for packaging; they don't have many other re-uses). I'd reserve foam SHEETS for walls/ceiling.
Raised wooden floors are desirable only in special situations: on flood lands where the floor must be above high water; on very steep slopes where terracing would be difficult; on

permafrost; in earthquake zones for a structure built to 'dance' over the ground (suggested by Barefoot Architect).

(Raised wooden floors began as status symbols centuries ago when only the rich could afford them. Peasants had dirt floors, covered at most with straw. Back then, no plastic film or linoleum or automatic-machine-made carpets. When they became available, floors could have been made better without becoming more costlier. But no - building codes were imposed which required complex floors along with many other non-essentials. That made houses much more expensive, forcing house dwellers to work longer hours and pay more taxes.)

"Earthquakes don't kill people. Buildings kill people."
    Recent earthquakes in Haiti and Chile prompted us to review our seismic situation. Odds of a big quake off Oregon's coast within the next 50 years, raised to 80% after researchers found that the fault slips oftener here than farther north.
    Crustal plates gradually move relative to each other. But edges may hang up. The force increases until it overcomes the resistance and the edge breaks loose. That's the quake. The more time since the previous quake, the greater the force that may build up, and the more violent the quake.
    During the past ten thousand years, intervals between giant quakes here ranged from 200 to 800 years; average 300 years. The last giant quake: 310 years ago - accurately known because the tsunami swept all the way to Japan and was recorded.
    The fault is only 75 miles from the coast. A tsunami would smash ashore in a few MINUTES. Coastal residents are being warned: if you feel the ground shake, IMMEDIATELY head for high ground. DON'T WAIT for evacuation instructions. Past tsunamis here were as high as 40 feet, sediment deposits indicate.
    Our base camps are high enough and far enough inland (± 10 miles) that even a 100-foot tsunami would not reach us. Most years we are ON the coast no more than a few days, and our temp camp is usually up on some hill, so that is not a big concern.
    A quake's effects inland depends on type of soil. Safest, solid rock. Riskiest, deep sediments, esp if soaking wet - as they often are here during winter. The sediments will slosh about, like liquid in a pan that's jolted, thus amplifying the movement. Thus valley bottoms are usually riskier than higher ground. Portland and the Willamette Valley is at high risk. Also risky, steep slopes which may avalanch, esp road cuts.
    Because Oregon hadn't had big quakes recently, most bridges and buildings are not as sturdy here as in Calif. So, minimize time in schools, stores, offices, libraries, multi-story apts, etc; esp those built before 1995, which was when past earth-quakes were discovered. I've read: the wood-frames of most houses are resistant, but plaster and sheet-rock may crash down, furnishings be tossed about, conduits ruptured, and escaping gas be ignited by a pilot light or electric spark. Barefoot Architect has some advice re quakes we've not seen elsewhere.
    Our new winter shelter SEEMS fairly safe. No big trees near. A ± ten-foot-bank is on one side. It is stabilized by old tree roots and by new trees and bushes as they grow. So I don't expect a MASSIVE land slide. The bank sheds dirt and a few rocks, esp when the ground thaws after a hard freeze (one in Dec 09). I left a two-foot space with a ditch between the bank and our shelter's surface: wide enough to crawl through to remove fallen dirt. So a quake may only fill the ditch.
    One change: We had many jugs of water inside, setting

quite high. (Ceiling ± 4½ ft) We'd put them there because they
stayed warmer, and because not much floor space, and because
they might freeze outside. But if a quake upsets our shelter,
those jugs could come bombing down. So now, we leave most jugs
outside. We bring in a few to warm up, a day or so before
needed. If freeze forecast, we bring in all - despite clutter.
    During winters we cook mostly with propane, usually once a
day. After cooking, we turn off the tank's valve, mainly to
reduce leaks, but also for safety in case a quake ruptures the
connections. The stove is inside; the tank is in the antiway.
    We've read: the N Amer region most at risk is the Ohio
Valley and adjacent areas. That area has several major faults
and deep sediments. A quake there two centuries ago, was so
powerful that in Boston, ± 1000 miles away, churches were shook
enough to ring their bells. No seismographs then, but estimated
magnitude: 8.0 to 9.0. (An 8.0 quake is 30 times as powerful
as Haiti's 7.0. A 9.0 quake, 900 times.) Another quake is
overdue. The early 1800s quake killed few people because few
people lived there then. But a quake there now could demolish
buildings in an area hundreds of miles across and kill or injure
many millions. A book, "8.5", dramatizes what may happen.
Though fiction, it is well-researched seismically, I've heard.
    The few radio reports we heard about Haiti (we don't listen
much) described destruction and death, but didn't mention what
a geologist said years ago: "Earthquakes don't kill people.
Buildings kill people." Haiti, quite far south and surrounded
by ocean, has a warm mild climate. So why were so many risky
buildings built ? Why not more use of tents and other soft
lightweight shelters.? Haiti also gets hurricanes. What would
withstand BOTH, yet be economical ? STRONG tents ?
    Animals behaving strangely sometimes give advance warning,
perhaps because, before a VIOLENT movement, the ground may creep
enough to open deep cracks, letting unusual odors to surface.
Most mammals can smell much keener than can humans. B & H

Since getting my first vehicle, I've lived with a kitty.
    Cats are quiet, bury their shit, and provide for themselves
where there are trees they can climb to protect themselves.
When in a desert lacking trees, I keep my kitty inside at night
and lay a trap-line of 15 little head-snappers around our camp.
If I wake early enough to beat other critters to my prey, I
typically harvest 4 or 5 mice. Keeps kitty fat. Rockann

Preventing and responding to animal attacks.
    Each year, nearly 5 million Americans are bitten by dogs,
and a 4th of the bites require medical attention. Of 500,000
emergency-room visits prompted by bites; approx: dogs, 90%;
cats, 8%; rodents, 2%. I've never encountered aggressive dogs
in the wilds, but have been charged by many dogs when on roads
and streets and sidewalks. I fought them off with sticks and
rocks, or outran them on a bike. So, the most important
preventive: minimize time near the abodes of people who keep
unchained dogs. I've never encountered an aggressive cat. I
assume most cat bites are inflicted on people who handle them.
    Once, years ago, I encountered a rat in a storage tent who,
instead of fleeing, stood its ground and bit the stick with
which I attacked and killed it. We then discovered: it was a
male trying to defend its mate and young who had a nest in the
tent. (Brave, but their choice of nest site was a fatal mistake.)
    If bitten, the most effective treatment: "Immediate and

vigorous washing and flushing with soap and water, detergent, or
even water alone." (If a snake-bite suctioner is at hand, I'd
then try that.) Then "apply either ethanol (eg, booze) or tincture or aqueous solution of iodine, or povidone iodine" (if at
hand; if not, I'd use isopropyl alcohol or diluted bleach
(though more toxic) or hydrogen peroxide (though less effective).

As for rabies: 19 cases in U.S. from 2000 to 2006 of which
18 fatal, caused by: bats, 13; raccoon, 1 in VA; mongoose, 1 in
PR; transplanted organs from one donor, 4. Bats are the only
rabies reservoir in Oregon. Foxes often acquire rabies from
bats, and rabid foxes may attack humans. In OR, 2000-2008, of
animals tested who were rabid: bats, 93 of 905; foxes, 6 of 25;
dogs, 0 of 337; cats, 0 of 738; other, 0 of 258. In OR,
rabies prophylaxis strongly recommended if bitten by fox or bat,
unless animal can be caught and tested and is not infected.
"However, prophylaxis should not be undertaken lightly", because
costly (mean, $3700) and time consuming. In 2000, a survey of
11 u-associated ERs, found that prophylaxis administered
"inappropriately in 40% of cases". (from CD Summary, 26may09)

To stop a charging bear, a can of hot-pepper resin with
compressed air is more effective (92% of time) than a fire-arm
(75% of time) said a BYU biologist (Outdoor Life, Mar09). Why ?
Not said. But in May09 Backpacker, "Most canisters produce a
visible 30-foot cone of spray", whereas gunshots must be accurate,
and even then, the bear may reach you and maul you before dying.
"Aim for the bear's eyes and face, and pull the trigger when the
bear is 40 feet away. As soon as the bear is disoriented, leave
the scene as quickly as possible." On average per year, one
person is killed and 12 injured by grizzly attacks. "Out here
(in WY) we have many times more black bears than grizzlies, but
we have fewer encounters with blacks. Blacks are scared of
humans because they are hunted; grizzlies are not", said an elk
hunter (in OL) who was injured and probably would have been
killed if his companion (dad) had not killed the grizzly "with a
single well-placed arrow". The federal "bear recovery coordinator" disputed that, saying: "Bears are not taught anything by
being killed." No. But the bears who AVOID humans are more
likely to pass on their traits to offspring. Either that
official is ignorant - or wants more money thrown his way.

General advice for defense against big predators: If with
companions, stay close enough to each other that a predator who
sees any of you sees all of you. A predator is less apt to
attack a PACK of creatures who appear defensive than a loner.
For defense, unless you are a fast-draw expert, you can get a
spear or staff into action quicker than a gun or pepper spray;
important esp against cougars because they often ambush. (Advice
not seen elsewhere: When on a road, we usually walk on the
downhill side, thinking that a cougar waiting in ambush will
likely be on the uphill bank so that it can leap farther.)

If a predator is encountered, stand tall, look big. Maybe
open coat or raise knapsack over head to look bigger. Don't
stare at it. Slowly back away. Speak in a low voice. Ie, act
differently than its usual prey. DON'T turn and run. That will
likely prompt a race you will LOSE. If attacked, fight back
aggressively with whatever is at hand. Bert & Holly, Oregon 973

Pet animals are the source of many deadly/crippling diseases.
Especially in young children. (CD Summary, 5aug08, 19aug08)
(Comment) I hope toy makers develop robots that are more
appealing to kids than are puppies (etc) - AND are not toxic.

Prions contained in dirt are very infective.
   Prions are mis-shapen proteins that cause brain-destroying
diseases (eg, mad cow). "Prions linger in soil for at least 3
years by binding tightly to clay and other minerals." Prions
get into soil when an infected animal dies; also from
urine and saliva. Animals often swallow hundreds of grams of
soil per day when eating plants, drinking muddy water, and
licking the ground to get minerals. (Sci News 11feb06,21july07)
(Comment) Though probably more of a problem with domestic
animals, esp animals concentrated in feed lots, some wild
animals get prion infections. When foraging plants growing
close to the ground, esp where animals frequently graze, I'd
wash plants thoroughly. Boiling doesn't deactivate prions. H&B

Mysterious malady cured by discontinuing treatment.
   Bert noticed a tiny sore on the edge of the web of skin at
the rear of his arm pit. I examined it, saw nothing, but felt
a minúte swelling. A bite? Or a pimple starting ? I dabbed
on a little tea-tree oil but did not cover it.
   The next day, the spot, still slightly sore, was redish.
I dabbed on more tea-tree, then covered it with a small piece
of aluminized-plastic food-wrap, taped on, to slow evaporation
of oil. But the tape did not adhere well to the edge of skin.
   The next day, a penny-size area was now red and tender.
Before Bert sacked out, he had me dab on more tea-tree; then
lay with his arm snug against his arm pit to hold in the oil.
   The spot got no further attention for a few days, but Bert
continued to notice tenderness. When I again inspected it, I
saw an irregular maroon-colored area with abrupt boundaries,
approx one by two inches, all tender when touched. It seemed
to be spreading ! But what was IT ? And why the strange
shape and bruize-like color ?
   Bert finally guessed that the tea-tree was irritating the
tender skin in his arm pit. The irregular shape was where his
arm had fit snugly against his arm pit and confined the oil.
   Now, approx a month later, the skin looks and feels normal.
What caused the original sore ? Maybe mechanical irritation.
One night had been unusually cold. Instead of fetching another
quilt, Bert had slept with sweaters on. Maybe, during a deep-
sleep period, a seam had pressed long and hard against his skin.
We've not noticed bad effects of tea-tree on other skin.
But we put it only on a small area and seldom more than 24 hrs.
   The moral of the story: You don't have to go to pricy MDs
who prescribe pricy drugs and very costly surgery, to suffer
bad side effects. You can do it yourself, cheap. Holly

How to distinguish hyper-hydration from dehydration.
   Though drinking too little water is much more common than
drinking too much, either is harmful. And some of the symptoms
are similar: dizzy, tired, vomiting, shakes. Nor is frequency
of drinking a reliable criteria. During hot dry weather, one
may drink often, but sweat out more water than is ingested
without noticing because the sweat quickly evaporates. Dehydration is also common during cold weather, esp at high altitude,
because of moisture lost by breathing hard to get enough oxygen
while working/hiking vigorously to help stay warm, and because
of reluctance to drink cold water. Symptoms that differ:
   Too much: Urinating often and much, and the urine stream
appears colorless or very pale. You might also notice water

sloshing in your belly. If too much, quit drinking. Maybe eat
a little salty food. Stay warm. Note STREAM: urine that looks
colorless in a narrow stream, will look yellow in a container.
    Too little: Urinating seldom and little, or not for many
hours, and the stream is quite yellow. Urinating might also
be irritating. If too little, drink more WATER (NOT "sport
drinks"; their sugar/salt is dehydrating.) Or, if no water,
maybe eat edible succulant plants you KNOW WELL, that are NOT
sweet, salty, bitter, or other strong taste. Stay cool.
    If hot, whether or not dehydrated, get out of the sun.
Remove clothes. (Except, if no shade, loose clothes, opened,
might reduce heating.) If no shade, rig some from clothes or
whatever is at hand. Eg, ball up a small garment, set it on top
of your head to maintain an air space; then drape a big garment,
preferably white or light colored, loosely over it. Or, if
sticks and twine available, rig a parasol (shade umbrella) or
mini roof. If enough materials, form two layers with an air
space between. (A single layer will get hot and radiate heat,
esp if material dark.) Unless without water and close to source,
postpone travel until evening or (cooler) very early morning.

Potassium is as vital as protein for building/retaining muscle.
    In people over 65, muscle mass correlated with the amount
of potassium in their diets. "The body converts protein and
cereal grains to acid residues. Excess acid triggers breakdown
of muscle into compounds that ultimately make ammonia which
removes the acid. Potassium-heavy diets, being alkaline, can
buffer those acids without scrificing muscle." Fruits and
vegetables are rich in potassium. Science News, 29mar08
    (Comments) I read elsewhere that some grains (eg, millet)
don't have acid residues. (But we tire of millet faster than
other grains we have eaten. I don't know why.) And that some
fruits (eg, plums) have an acid residue.
    Safer to get potassium from food than from mineral supple-
ments. Too much potassium is toxic. A balance of potassium
with sodium and other minerals is needed.
    Getting enough potassium may be a problem for people in
northern climes who live off the land year around, because their
diets may be mostly meat. It has been a problem for us some
winters, because our diet was mostly grains, esp wheat. (This
winter, luckily, gosmore (Hypochoeris radicata) has remained
plentiful near by, though we wonder about the effects of eating
so much of IT. We've also eaten legumes and tomato paste.) H&B

To reduce risk of breast cancer, do NOT wear bras.
    And gently massage breasts daily, starting nearest the arm
pit, suggests a New Connexion article. Reason: Unlike blood,
which is circulated mostly by a heart, lymph flow depends on
body motions. If circulation is hindered by a bra or by not
moving enough, carcinogenic toxins (both natural and human-made)
accumulate in tissues. (But, while massaging, if you feel any
lump, DON'T massage it - and seek further diagnosis.)
    I read previously, in Naturally, that breast cancers are
very rare in cultures where women don't wear bras. But possible
co-factors: more movement; less junk foods; more babies
starting at age ±20, who are breast-fed.(epidemiologists say).
    People tend to blame chronic illnesses on things they CAN'T
control, such as unlucky genes or pervasive environmental
pollution. Though those are likely co-factors, the most
important causes are often things that people CAN control. H&B

Ab

c/o Lisa Ahne, POB 181, Alsea OR 97324. #9 Dec 2009.
$2 for big-print copy until all sold; $1 for tiny
print. Ab discusses how and where to live better
for less. Ab, an ab-apa, encourages readers to send
pages ready to copy (text 16x25 cm or 6.3x10", black on white,
on one side of paper, compact). Usually published UNedited.

WOOD STOVE for MAD HOUSER HUTS in CHICAGO

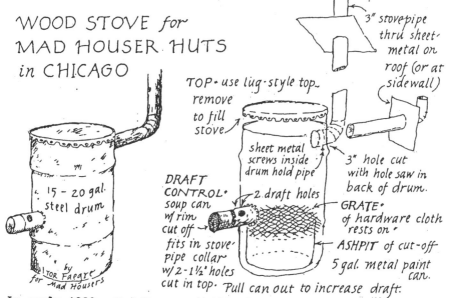

3" stovepipe thru sheet-metal on roof (or at sidewall)

TOP· use lug·style top. remove to fill stove.

sheet metal screws inside drum hold pipe

3" hole cut with hole saw in back of drum.

DRAFT CONTROL· soup can w/ rim cut off → fits in stove-pipe collar w/ 2-1½" holes cut in top. Pull can out to increase draft.

2 draft holes

15 - 20 gal. steel drum

GRATE· of hardware cloth rests on ·

ASHPIT of cut-off 5 gal. metal paint can.

by TOR Faegre for Mad Housers

In early 1990s, Mad Housers built ultra-low-cost houses and
gave them to houseless people. 6x8x8 ft, no elec or running
water, not to code. But occupants preferred them to official
shelters that were so regimented that residents could not hold
a job. In Jan 09, Tor wrote. "Mad Housers are no longer in
action, though I think about a revival." For more info:
Tor Faegre, 1600 Ashland, Evanston IL 60201. 847-869-1969

I choose comfort over appearance.
      I wanted to sew cuffs onto a long-sleeved sweatshirt whose
arms were too short. Conventionally, seams are sewen with the
raw edges and stitching facing inwards. But when such a seam
is pressed against the skin, as does the cuff seam when I'm
writing and my wrist is pressed against a table, there can be
irritation, even soreness. So I chose to face the seam's raw
edge outward. Feels better. Julie Summers, OR 973, Jan 09

For foot comfort and health, change footwear often.
      And don't wear the same ones again for a week. There is
not any best kind or brand. Boots, shoes, tennies, mocs,
sandals, thongs, and various hybrids all have good qualities -
and bad ! Wear any one everywhere or long and it will rub a
spot raw, or collect thorny debris, or not block sharp objects,
or not keep feet warm, or not let sweat evaporate.
      We don't buy footwear new. We make mocs from discarded
truck innertubes. We've found many tennies in a thrift-store
dumpster, and got some dress shoes at a church give-away.
Sterilize in a laundry drier, or by sunning in a clear plastic
bag on a hot day. (170ºF kills harmful microbes.) H & B

Thank you for the DP and ABs. I notice DP is becoming more focused;
and absorbing extraneous but interesting material is for AB to do. good
stuff. I agree with you about choosing a place based on climate/terr-
ain and likeminded folks. Personally I would - or might - have ended up
in the south but the culture was too psycho. And summer heat was awful. The terrain and winters were more to my liking.

Religion: while we do have our crazies in the NE they are fewer than
in most other areas Ive travelled. NE religion is traditionally very
personal, not something to bludgeon others with, despite puritan heritage. My own background is that of a seeking Christianity, not dogmatic.
The problem is religio fascism in times of unrest, i.e. nativist Father
Coughlin types. Desperate people seem to either organize(Argentina in
the 90s, midwest farmers during foreclosure sales in 30s, miners since
the 1870s) or cling to insane theology. .

Anyway I live here cause I like it. 12 years so far. I have hitched·
extensively, camped illegally, walked and biked much, and only once
interacted with cops when my car headlight was out. But I am White, and
Black friends tell a different story. Maine is 98% white.

Old time Skills: where do OTS leave off and new skills begin? To start
with I think useful to talk about attitudes, then develop particular
skills or tool proficiencies, observation techniques, from there.

Patience: OTS, or post oil skills (POS), rely more on human energy and
natural process (the flow of a river to move a boat). Walking takes
time. The use of some tools can be dangerous in the hands of inexperienced, impatient users.

Familiarity: with ones abilities, limits, with others one is with, with
ones environment, with tools/gear one uses, and so forth.

Ability to make do: Not needing to have everything be 'ideal', being
able to make and mend with whats at hand. Some connection with familiarity. One friends old truck (1966) was simple, he was familiar with,
and we fixed it numerous times with rope, wire, once a plywood washer
to facilitate holding axle on, once a rope to hold driveshaft. Ability
to improvise, do without, conserve.

Of course these are all vonu skills too.

In terms of actual skills, I would start with knife and axe craft. Many
books on the subject incl. _The Axe Book— which is excellent.
With these two tools one can get fuelwood, clean out animals/butcher,
cut poles for shelter, make other tools, crafts, etc. A good axe is
hard to find, old ones best, 3# with no marks on the poll (opposite to
the blade). A poll struck with steel i.e. to drive a wedge, will deform
head, ruin axe.   A good knife can be found at Woodcraft (woodcraft.com)
which carries the line of Frost swedish laminated sttel knives/wood
handles, thse are inexpensive ($10) and very good. I like the medium,
wide blade.   Cant recall if a sheath is included, sometimes in stores
they will come with a thermoplastic sheath. The axe rough   shapes,
the knife refines. Made a bucket yoke with these 2 tools yrs ago,
also new tool handles, spoons (yeah, I know, not necessary-but nice)
toggles for coat closure, and with a hand saw, a frame for a 24" buck
saw blade. Your experience with the h'ware store bowsaw is sadly typical of the state of tools today. One must either buy expensive custom
tools or (as I do) haunt the used tool sellers (many here). I will send
drawings/instructions for bucksaw if you wish, it is portable and sturdy
but not as handy as bowsaw or as compact. Also, induction hardened teeth
on a saw of the Swede-style can be sharpened with a diamond file. not
easy though.

Thanks to Chris Withemi for his piece. Good to hear how children can/
do grow up freer.

Here we have some locally organized buying clubs for bulk foods. Comes
from Assoc. Buyers, etc. Decent. Much agglomeration happening w/bulk
food buying as United gobbled up the little guys.

ANDREW IN ME, FEB 09. NOTE: "NE" HERE MEANS NORTHEAST (NOT NEBRASKA).

(Thoughts) Andrew advises, be familiar with your own abilities.
YES ! For that reason, I do NOT want an axe. An axe is too
dangerous unless the user is skilled with it. I would not use
an axe enough to develop and maintain skills. An axe is easier
than a saw to resharpen, and is faster for some tasks IF one
is skilled. But I'll make do with saws and knives.

Holly and I have quite a few knives, here and there,
bought cheap at yard sales, etc. Most are not the best but are
adequate for our tasks. A few have broken but we have spares.

Apr/Oct 1981 DP has plans for a bucksaw frame. I've never
made one. A few times I've used a broken piece of bow-saw
blade without frame. Not very efficient, but light and compact:
adequate if not much sawing needed. Andrew says: be willing
to make do, vs insisting that everything be ideal. YES !

About attitudes. Often more important than how skilled
someone is, is what they DO with whatever skills they have.
Years ago, DP got a letter from someone who said he knew HOW
to build. He said his problem was, finding WHERE to build.
He was seeking a county where he could build a conventional
cabin with conventional conveniences (eg, a drive-way) without
getting hassled about permits and building codes.

We don't know of such a place. Though some counties and
states are PRESENTLY not as bad as some others, they may change
ANY TIME and become as bad or worse - and require that existing
structures be expensively brought up to code - or demolished.

He may have been an itinerant carpenter, in s CA winters,
n CA summers. If so, he was probably more skilled with tools
than I am. I build things, but not very many. And I've never
apprenticed, or taken courses, or diligently studied a manual
and practiced techniques. If he watched me build, he could
likely show me ways to use a tool more efficiently and thus do
a task faster and better. None the less, I had built comfortable shelters for Holly and me, whereas apparantly he hadn't
for himself. Why ? Because I am willing to build and utilize
shelters of kinds and in ways that don't attract hassles.

But I still wonder why he hadn't. In Oregon (and many
states ?) small buildings (8x12 ft max ?) don't require permits.
Does CA not allow them ? Or not allow sleeping in one ? Or
was he fixated on building something bigger ? I don't know.

Regarding familiarity with abilities of self and others.
Seems to me, that is gained mostly by DOING - and quite often
making mistakes. Gauging that a repair, though not ideal, is
probably adequate, comes from making other repairs, some of
which sufficed, some of which didn't.

Holly and I like having our own junk piles. Most items
will never be used, but some will - and we can't predict what
will and what won't. We scavenge much from impromptu (illegal)
dumps beside logging roads; some from recycles and dumpsters.

Regarding tools and materials. What can be accumulated
now that may become valuable and tradable during future
conditions - which are NOT predictable ! I'd avoid high tech,
except for things I want to use SOON. Dmitry Orlov (reprinted
in Ab#6) suggested buying and storing photovoltaics. But pv
prices have trended downward, and may decline greatly when a
cheaper manufacturing process is developed. So, unless demand
increases SOON, pv bought now is likely to lose value.

The future can NOT be predicted well. Many wild cards.
Any preparations will likely be needlessly early - or TOO LATE !
Thousands of people make and publicize predictions. A few are
right on, partly BY LUCK. Only 6 predicted this depression. B&H

Comments on the tribode: a structure for living on the ocean.
      The tribode may work in reasonably protected waters but
it is wacky. It will be tough to resell. D.S. in FL, Nov 08

      A 60-foot-tall structure on the water will draw the
attention of both local authorities and the USCG. The USCG has
a rep even among 'normal' boaters as being thuggish, and a
'weird' boat, let alone structure, seems to bring it out more.
I know of two boats here declared unseaworthy and 'grounded'.
      Carbon fiber is extremely pricey and toxic (epoxy bonds
it). It's also UV-sensitive; needs paint or other UV blocker.
      The structure is quite top heavy, and I'm not sure the
splay of the legs makes up for it. A center of gravity 40 ft
up, compared with a boat's COG which is below the waterline.
The tribode seems more suited to calmer waters, where swells
are more common than breakers. Andrew in ME, Feb 09

      Your write up was interesting, but, as you said, it's not
"a complete, detailed, proven design ready to build." Is that
as far as you will go with your idea ? Or will you provide
detailed plans ? If so, how soon ?
      Have you built anything similar to a tribode ? What ?
How much have you lived out on the open ocean (not just in a
marina) and where and when and in what ?
      Your pen name suggests that you are involved with aircraft.
Have you designed, built or flown seaplanes ? Salt water
wrecks equipment not built to withstand it. Even a cabin 32 ft
up will get some salty particles. Bob, CA 908, Feb 09

      I like the idea of homes that are mobile without depending
on roads for mobility. I also like the idea of each family
being independently mobile (vs leasing living space on a cruise
ship.) But I wonder where and how a tribode dweller could buy
more supplies at reasonable prices; a problem for a family
living in a remote wilderness or even an isolated small town.
      It was a problem for boat dwellers (whose reports were in
the bulletin of the Seven Seas Sailing Assoc, SSSA, who swapped
with DP years ago). Though the Caribbean has many independent
island nations, for boats in that area, the best places to buy
more supplies and replacement parts were Puerto Rico and Virgin
Islands, as well as U.S. mainland. Go there and you will
likely have to deal with USCG and other officials. Bert, Mar09

Reply to D.S. in Florida. Ease of resale depends on numbers.
If as many people want tribodes as want boats of a certain type,
resale will be as easy. I'd build a tribode now only if I
wanted to use it for a long time.

Reply to Andrew in Maine. USCG, I agree. Tribodes are not for
U.S. waters nor for any coastal waters. For shallow waters I'd
favor something like that boat with legs that could raise
itself out of the water. (Mentioned in March 09 DP.)
      Stability. I assume you had not seen my "limits" (on
"Tribode" p.8). They may assauge your doubts. The CG of an
empty tribode is ~ 16' above sea level. When inhabited the CG
is lower unless the cabin is heavy loaded which I warn against.
      Some boats have CG below the water line. Some don't.
Mono-hull yachts with deep heavy keels do. But their heavyness
reduces yielding when struck by waves. That increases stress,
which requires more strength and even more weight and cost.
Most multi-hull boats are light-weight shallow-draft with most
of their structure and volume above the waterline. Their CG

is lower than a tribode's but their hull spacing is much less.
      The price of ultra strong fibers will come down as patents
expire and as new kinds increase competition. If building now
I might use carbon fiber on the booms where stiffness is very
important, but I'd use fiberglass on floats and cabin.
      Yes, epoxy is toxic but has been used many years and safe-
guards are well developed. (Fiberglass particles are hazardous
too. They can behave like porcupine quills and penetrate flesh.)
      Yes, epoxy is UV sensitive. On a tribode instead of paint-
ing I might wrap most parts with a plastic film that blocks UV.
Films are easier to replace than are paints. Wrapping isn't
practical on most boats because of their complex shapes.

Reply to Bob in Calif. How far I go with the idea depends on
how much interest it arouses. I haven't yet built any vehicle
or structure for salt water use. Before offering plans I would
build a tribode and rigorously test it, and live in it on
stormier waters than I recommend frequenting with it.
      Yes, salt water can wreck equipment. Salt water is not
especially harmful to most plastics. Less so than to metals.
Any wetness can harm wood. Fiber-reinforced wood seems the
easiest materials for building a prototype for testing the
configuration, but probably not for large-scale production.

Reply to Bert in Oregon. I'm not familiar with SSSA. But my
impression is that most boat dwellers use the ocean only for
travel to lands that interest them. There they dock, moor, or
beach. While sailing they cannot easily obtain supplies.
      Tribodes are for ocean living, not mainly for travel. I
agree that a family living isolated on the ocean would have the
same problems as on land. But I doubt that many tribode
dwellers would live isolated. There are easier ways to be
isolated for anyone who wants that. The advantage of tribodes
is that their dwellers can congregate without having to go into
ports, and they can easily change neighbors when they desire
that. For vehicle dwellers on land, somewhat similar is The
Slabs in southeast Calif. But that will continue only as long
as government agencies tolerate it.
      A congregation can attract supply boats or, if big enough,
ships that act as department stores, perhaps making circuits of
several tribode groups along with small islands. On land there
are mobile merchants who go to small towns and offer merchandise
not available locally. Ave Dave, OR 978, May 09

      (The first 6 pages about tribodes were in the original Ab#7.
We now offer all (so far) 10 pages (5x8, quite big print)
separately for $2. I hope to obtain 2 more pages about it or
related topics. (12 pages are easier to bind than are 10 pages.)
What other mobile structures exist or are contemplated for
RESIDING on (or above or under) deep water in mid ocean ? The
Ab#7 reprint contains everything in the original issue except
the tribode: 16 pages originally, now tiny print, $1.)

"20,000 Nations Above the Sea" is an article in July 09 Reason.
      It talks about an organization to promote the idea of
seasteading. It is run by Patri Friedman, son of David and
grandson of Milton Friedman. Patri formerly worked for Google,
has connections with Silicon Valley money people and has gotten
some financing from them. Jim Stumm (in Aug09 The Connection)
      I found Reason in Corvallis city library and briefly read
the article. The group seems to be thinking of building islands,
not mobile structures. Bert   Ab #9   Dec 09   Page 5

Our experiences buying dry foods, including wheat from growers.
    Until recently we did not search for growers. Nearby
stores sold the foods we wanted at affordable prices.
    When Bert and I first came to this area nearly 30 years
ago, there was a funky co-op that emphasized nutritious foods
and that minimized their expenses. It sold 50-pound bags of
organic hard red wheat for ± 20¢/pound. Other stores charged
almost that much for non-org hard red wheat. So we chose org.
And wheat became our biggest source of calories; replacing rice
(the grain most pesticided). We bought non-org lentils, beans,
oatmeal, popcorn, millet, sunnies, etc, because we ate much
less of them and, for them, org cost much more than non-org.
    At that time, what was "organic" was a matter of trust
and reputation. So, the extra cost of org was due only to
more field labor or less yield; not to hoop jumping.
    That all changed. The co-op gradually became fancy, pricy,
hypy; and emphasized very-costly highly-processed more-
tempting-but-less-nutritious foods, bought by affluant but
deluded folks who seemed to believe that anything "organic" was
healthful. It no longer had space"for extra 50# bags of wheat.
    Also, organics became certified: growers had to fill out
forms and pay for inspections, etc, which raised costs. Also,
rich folks were discovering organics faster than growers could
switch, which bid up prices. So, we quit buying organic.
    For a while we bought most dry foods from a small local
wholesaler. For 50-pound bags, non-org hard red wheat, ± 18¢/
pound; other foods ranged from 25¢ to 45¢. The wholesaler did
not get much walk-in trade; the store was small and crowded,
difficult to get around in. Then the owner retired. The new
owner enlarged and remodeled. But apparently sales increased
less than did costs. A few years ago he went out of business.
Now, no nearby wholesaler (we know of) sells to walk-ins.
    We had food reserves, so no immediate problem. We hoped
to find and pool purchases with someone local who was buying at
wholesalers in Portland (± 150 miles away). So far we haven't.
We don't have a motor vehicle. Nor do most local friends. Nor
are they buying 50/25-pound bags when here. Most are in this
area only in summers when wild berries and greens are abundant.
    Winco is the only nearby store that stocks many dry foods.
(Winco has stores through-out Northwest. Headquarters in Boise.)
Winco buys 25-pound bags to fill their bulk bins. They sometimes have extra bags they will sell. But the bags are not
setting out; you need to find a stocker. Nor do they sell bags
for less than bin price; despite that reducing wastage, and
saving plastic bags and stocking/clean-up labor. Some prices
reasonable: eg, oatmeal 42¢. Some prices weirdly exorbitant:
eg, 70¢ for non-org hard red wheat when growers were getting
only 10¢. Whereas unbleached white flour was 30¢ and cracked
wheat 35¢, despite needing more processing. Why ? Probably not
demand: Winco has only one bin of each (vs 7 bins of oatmeal).
Is their buyer corrupt: eg, paying a high price to a relative
who grows wheat ? Or lazy ? Or over-worked and lacks time to
find a low-priced source ? We don't buy wheat from Winco !
    Years passed and our reserves dwindled. Then we learned
of a friend of a friend who was buying white wheat from a local
grower to feed chickens. We got a sample. Direct from the
combine, it included many wild rye-grass seeds which have sharp
barbs. But after grinding, the fragments were too small to be
a threat. The bread tasted fine. And 95% of whole kernels
sprouted, indicating good condition. So we ordered 400 pounds.

Price, 11¢/pound, which was what big buyers in Portland were then paying growers for wheat the buyers exported to Asia.

When the wheat arrived we noticed a bad smell the sample hadn't had. We hoped the odor was extraneous, picked up during storage or transport. Baking might remove it. But baking did not: the bread tasted bad. We tried lengthy aerating and even washing and then solar drying/parching before grinding and baking. That lessened but did not eliminate the bad taste. Adding spices (esp basel) masked the taste. Also alarming: only a third of the kernels sprouted. A few were brown and soft, obviously rotten. Those we could pick out before grinding. But many more kernels had brown tips. The grower offered to refund if we returned the wheat. But we had already backpacked it to our storage. Nor did we have much else to eat.

What may have happened. The wheat had been in the grower's silo several years. (He didn't grow wheat every year.) During summers, most of the wheat gradually warmed. But wheat close to the concrete foundation remained cool. Moisture migrated from warm wheat to cool wheat on the bottom - which became damp enough to start rotting. (Either that, or the silo had not been cleared out between harvests, and the bottom wheat was very old.) When we bought, not much wheat remained in the silo. The sample wheat had been barely high enough to remain dry. But the 400 pounds included much low-down rotting wheat.

Some advocacy groups claim they encourage and have info about local food growers. Most such groups did not respond to our quiries. Ten Rivers Food Web did. They suggested only one grower. He was experimenting with organic red wheat. He asked $1/pound !! Xanthippe Augerot of Ten Rivers, in Feb09 Sentient Times (Ashland), said that grains are no longer grown in the Willamette Valley (± between Portland and Eugene), partly because "food system infrastructure" had been lost. Did she not know that much white wheat is still grown here ? Or did she not know that wheat direct from combine is edible after grinding and baking ? ("Infrastructure" not needed.) Or does Ten Rivers shun non-organic growers ?

Local animal-feed dealers were asking 20¢ to 34¢/pound for white wheat. One said, their wheat was not for human consumption but didn't say why.

We told everyone we knew that we wanted to buy up to 1500 pounds of white wheat (we eat ± 500 pounds/year) and would pay 50% more than the Portland price. Via word of mouth we finally learned of and contacted a large-scale white-wheat grower who was selling some locally to poultry raisers. (Saved him hauling the wheat to Portland.) This year's harvest. When tested, 97% sprouted. He had one silo not treated with an insecticide after harvest. (Most wheat is treated. The insecticide is short lived, but we haven't learned what it turns into and if that might be toxic.) He asked 8¢/pound, the Portland price then, but we payed him 12¢ because we had widely offered 50% more than Portland and we didn't want to stint him. Also, the extra 4¢ seemed trivial, compared to prices asked by stores and feed dealers. I assume the wheat is direct from combine. (Most growers don't have cleaners.) No rye-grass seeds but quite a few tiny black seeds, angular. (Might be a buckwheat relative.) If the dough is risen long or solar baked (slow) the bread tastes sweet, almost like cake. We don't know why. No other wheat we've used, produced sweet-tasting bread.

(We bartered the remaining 300 pounds of deteriorated wheat to a chicken grower. The chickens eat it.)

We haven't yet found good sources of other dry foods.
Two Ab/DP readers in nw OR separately suggested Azure Standard.
I quiried by mail. No response. A friend found them on www.
They don't divulge prices to non-members. Another Mtn People ?
    Winco's lowest-priced legume has been split peas, 52¢.
Lentils, our taste favorite, also more protein than peas and
pintos, 70¢+. So, this autumn we are eating much bread, not
much legumes. We are foraging much gosmore (a lettuce/dande-
lion kin) and chantrelles. Hopefully they balance aminos.
    Regarding "organic". Pesticides migrate. All foods have
some, org hopefully less. Fruits and vegies are the crops most
pesticided. The fruits and vegies we eat are mostly wild. So,
despite eating non-org grains, we probably ingest less toxins
than does someone who eats only org but spends much time in
cities or on roads. Our incomes are each around $400/year.
(We don't keep records.) We spend over half for food. To buy
org staples, we'd have to spend more time commuting through
and working in environments that are more polluted or stressful
or dangerous than the woods where we usually live.
    Tips to buyers. Many newspapers print prices paid growers,
both for white wheat in Portland and for high-protein red wheat
in Mpls. Price is per 60-pound bushel. Eg, $6/bu = 10¢/pound.
Oat prices are printed too. But, unlike wheat hulls which are
removed by combines, oat hulls require steaming. To make oatmeal, the oats are then rolled and dried. Ie, oatmeal sold for
human consumption is NOT raw. So, expect to pay more for oatmeal than what growers are paid for oats. Unlike whole wheat
flour and wheat germ, which soon get rancid unless refrigerated
or vacuum packed, oatmeal keeps a year or longer if cool.
    Capital Press, a weekly ag paper (Salem), covers Northwest.
Some libraries get it. (Similar pubs elsewhere ?) For legumes,
it reports both prices paid growers and prices asked by big
dealers which are ± 50% higher. Do beans (etc) direct from
combines still have pods/stems/dirt and require further cleaning ? Even cleaned beans may include a few pebbles.
    To buy direct from growers, best be flexible. Find out
what is grown locally in COMMERCIAL quantity and learn to make
use of that. West of Cascades, white wheat. In interior West,
red wheat. In east-central areas, corn. In parts of Northeast,
buckwheat. Expect to buy at harvest time or soon after. (Most
growers don't retain harvests long.) To interest commercial
growers, be prepared to buy hundreds of pounds and to pay cash,
and to buy at their farm at a time convenient for them.
    Bring your own containers unless told otherwise. For
grain from a silo that had a ± 1½ ft sq door at the bottom,
pails were easier to load than were big sacks. The farmer
scoop-shoveled the wheat into our pails (4 gal, held ± 25 lbs).
    For storage, if concerned about infestation, instead of an
insecticide I'd use dry ice (solid CO_2). Approx 2 ounces CO_2
per gallon storage. Eg, ½ pound per 4 or 5 gal pail; 6 pounds
per 55 gal barrel. Put CO_2 in bottom, fill with grain, place
lid on LOOSELY (else may explode). CO_2 is heavier than air so,
as it evaporates, it will seep up through the grain and push
the air out. AFTER the CO_2 evaporates (bottom no longer cold),
put lid on tightly. If dry ice not available, if container is
air tight, any insects will consume the oxygen (producing CO_2)
and die before eating more than a 1000th of the grain. Cooking
will sterilize their remains. In a cool dry air-tight container, wheat will keep 15+ years; likewise lentils. Other grains
and beans not as long (but some short-grain rice good at 5 yrs).

Advice for touring musicians, esp any who may perform in hotels.
I spent 15 years on the road as singer and guitarist,
mostly at hotels and clubs. I've performed in 40 states and
Canada, but mainly in Midwest where most of the opportunities
were. Most Midwest hotels want country music. Hard rock and
rap won't work in hotels - you must keep the volume down. Long
hair and beards are taboo: look like a businessman. Never say
anything on the mic that could be taken two ways. Comedy is
hard to pull off: most listeners will think you mean it.
If possible I would not use agents for road tours. They
send you long distances for little money and don't care if you
lose; and you must go where they send you if you want to call
yourself a professional musician. If a hotel fires you during
a gig and won't let you finish, the agent always has a replacement ready to go who has been out of work; a hazard in an
over-crowded field. Sometimes non-union local acts will steal
a gig from a touring performer by going in cheaper, esp if a
club has been unhappy with the acts the agent has sent them.
Pay your agent even if he strands you. Agents are in
touch with each other via computer; word gets around about who
stiffed one out of a comission or booked a room without paying.
Always go meet your boss before you start work. Rules
vary with the hotel. They won't tell you the rules, even if
you ask - until you violate one. Some like you to mix with the
guests, but may want you to be discrete if you date any.
Others forbid mixing. If you date your boss, be nice - and
realize the power structure. One manager fired me for dating
lower-class girls from a local honky tonk. She did not want
that kind in her hotel. Another manager accused me of pimping
and fired me - because I let my date go into the bar and talk
to men. Always stay with whoever you pick up for as long as
you are there. Do not put anyone down; they will go to your
boss or call your agent with lies about how you abused them.
If you dress below the hotel's standards when not on
stage, that can get you fired. Always wear a shirt when room
service brings a meal, and always tip them. Never forget to
pay your room tab; they can arrest you. Never ask for or
offer dope. Hotels are extremely straight-laced; they tend to
suspect that all performers are dopers or boozers. Never
forget that you are a hotel employee and part of a corporation.
You are expendable and easily replaced. Hotel law is fairly
complicated, and in most cases they got you because the touring
performer does not know the law. Hotels never cheated me out
of the dollars I sang for, but may not let one finish their gig.
While touring I usually earned $400-$500/week plus my room.
When a room was not provided, I often considered moving into a
van for that gig. But usually I was in the Midwest when it was
way too cold. If I could have stayed in warm climates on tour,
and fixed my own cars, I would have cleared much more money.
If you hit the road, be sure to have reserve cash. I've
had engines blow up and had to buy the first car I could afford.
I sold a really good guitar for $25 to get bus fare home.
I sold blood to get home. A country band in Colorado fired me
one cold December without paying me what I'd earned. With only
$100 I went on to Los Angeles. A relative had to Western-Union
me money to get home from there. At age 22, I did not know
about missions, street people, or Travelers Aid.
I might have been happier playing taverns and rock clubs
for younger people when I was their age. Rock clubs were much
more fun. But hotels paid more. I missed the wild women of

rock; though in hotels you can meet classier women.
    I'm from Nashville. When my agent didn't have a gig for
me, I'd visit Nashville, just to be around people I knew -
after being a stranger in every town. At age 35, my agent
finally stranded me in Nashville, and I had to make a living
where there is little if any pay for live music. I really did
not want to perform here. But, having long hair and a rock-n-
roll attitude, I could not easily get regular work. The only
singing job I could find quickly was on lower Broadway, a block
of country-music dives famous to tourists. Pay: $20 for 5 hrs.
    In Nashville the older country fans hate the recent rockin
country, and the rockers think country is watered-down rock.
When I play bars, I have to sing both country and rock.
    If you come to Nashville and try to make it in music, be
prepared to work a day job for many years as the song writers
do. Music Row hires only young people to go on the road as
stars. The music biz is winner take all. A very few make
millions; many has-been stars end up bankrupt. Playing here
is not much fun; people do not respect musicians. Karaoke has
replaced live bands in many clubs. (Drunks singing off-key and
out-of-time made me hate karaoke.) As of 2009, 50,000 people
were out of work here. Marty Brown (Marty's report about
trailer living was in March09 DP; and a report about car
camping in Nashville will be in spring 2010 DP.)

Beg Big Bully ? Or shun Big Bully ?
    Governments have various programs called "welfare". They
are actually make-work programs. The work consists of learning
the rules and keeping the records needed to fill out forms.
This is work that lawyers and accountants are PAID to do. Like
most dealings with governments, such work is RISKY. If you err,
you may be fined or locked up. Ie, the hoops to jump through
are razor sharp and red hot !
    Someone (not in Ab/DP) disagreed, saying ±: "I have
obtained several kinds of welfare and I've never been prosecuted. Bureaucrats are lazy. Unless you try to con them out of
big money, you are unlikely to be prosecuted. Of course they
publicize the few cases they do prosecute. Media give a
distorted picture of what is happening. Ignore scare stories."
    I agree that big media distort; we seldom read or hear
them. But when something bad happens to one of the ±50 people
we know personally, we pay attention. Eg, Pluma's ordeal.
    Pluma lives in Tennessee, in a small cabin she rebuilt.
It has a wood stove and running cold water and grid electricity.
Comfortable and affordable - but not up to code: no frig, and
the only hot water is from a kettle on the stove. After giving
birth, Pluma's sister stayed with Pluma. The sister applied
for "welfare" and gave Pluma's address. "Social" workers came
to check, pretended to be friendly, and left. Two hours later
they returned WITH COPS and snatched the 2-day-old baby from
the arms of its mother who was breast-feeding it ! Reason
given: the baby's surroundings. (More in April 2000 DP)
    The most wide-spread "welfare" program may be food stamps.
Years ago, Holly tried to obtain them, unsuccessfully.
Recently, when food prices soared, Holly tried again. With the
help of a librarian, she went as far as looking at the application form on internet. No further. The form required that all
income be listed. We have very low incomes by U.S. standards
(a bit below average by world standards). Most years, under
$500 each, we think. (At that level, record keeping is not

worth the time.) Money comes from many sources. If Holly estimated income and offered no proof, the well-paid food-stamp bureaucrat, who can't imagine anyone living so cheaply, would likely assume Holly was lying and refuse her. Holly might also be one of the relatively few charged with fraud.

Even people who do manage to obtain food stamps, may gain only slightly more than the value of their time spent keeping records, etc. The big beneficiaries of that and other gov "welfare" programs, are the well-paid administrators.

Obtaining "welfare" may be worthwhile for people who have appropriate talents and situations, and who enjoy lawyering. Sadly, the people most in need of welfare are generally the people least able to jump through the hoops !

RIDDLE. Believe it or not, one gov program really does help many low-income people including us. No hoops to jump through. Curiously, "welfare" is not its announced or main purpose. Oregon was maybe the first state to enact it. Many states now have it. What is it ? Answer at end of next item.

Political slysense. When be daring ? When be steadfast ?

I can think of 3 reasons to vote. I. You live in a small town with only ±20 voters, where one vote is quite likely to decide a local issue. II. You need to pacify nasty neighbors who insist that everyone vote. III. You are often stopped by cops; and when you fish out your drivers license, if the cop also sees your voter card, he might treat you better - else you will vote against more money for police.

None apply to us. And, to register, we'd have to lie about where we actually live. And we'd get put on a gov list.

I confess: I sometimes hope that a political candidate or party will lose. That is like hoping for no rain tomorrow. But I don't spend time praying to Mother Nature - or voting.

In U.S., two political parties, Democrats (D) and Republicans (R) share a duopoly of power. Though each is worse on some issues, overall I rate them equally evil. D pretend to help low-income people. At the city/county level, D may be not quite as bad as R on average. But at state and federal levels, D are worse. D not only try to tax low-incomers directly ("Social Security", compulsory medical insurance, sales taxes*); but D put high taxes and myriad regulations on high-middle incomers (small/mid-size food wholesalers; specialty stores selling tents, pv, led lights, bike parts, etc; dentists, doctors, etc) that increase their costs and reduces their competition - which results in them raising their prices.

Least evil ? Generally a D president or governor (G) with an R-majority congress or legislature (L). Oregon had that for a while. L refused to pass most laws that G wanted, and G vetoed most laws that L did pass. In a lobocracy (rule by big lobbies), that may be the best that can be hoped for.

This can affect what I do, because disputes on top can trickle down and result in less enforcement of contraversial laws. That may be a good time to undertake major dwellingway changes; because, while learning a new way, goofs are likely that may attract Big Bully's thugs. Bert & Holly, Oct 09

* Oregon 1990s. The teachers union wanted more tax money. In L, only 1/3rd of R but 2/3rds of D voted for a sales tax. (L barely passed it but voters rejected it 3 to 1.) Sales taxes penalize low-incomers more than high-incomers. Evidence (Sci Am, July 2004): WA gets most revenue via a sales tax. It robs low-incomers THE MOST. AK, DE, MT, without state sales taxes,

rob low-incomers least. NH and OR, too, are lesser robbers.
     Answer to riddle. Payments for empty drink containers.
Simply collect them and take them to a store that sells those
brands. No records to keep. No hoops to jump through.

Is the U.S jumping out of the emergency room into the morgue ?
     Most Democrats in Congress support a law that requires
everyone to buy medical insurance, even healthy young people
who are unlikely to need medical care and who usually have low
incomes. Their payments would subsidize insurance of people
who are sicklier - often because of unhealthy behavior; eg,
having consumed much junk foods, alcohol, tobacco, etc.
     Such a requirement is in essence a head tax: robbing from
everyone the same amount regardless of income. A head tax
penalizes low-income people even more than does a sales tax.
So, again, Democrats, who pretend to help "the little guys",
are trying to ROB the little guys. (Yeah, gov might give
insurance to very low incomers. But, as with other "welfare",
you must prove you have low income. Risky work !)
     The federal system would be like what Massachusetts has
had, which copied the German system (originally enacted by the
Nazis ?). In a radio interview, a doctor who works in a MA
hospital serving low-income people, said that those laws were
originated by insurance executives. She also said: the MA
law has been a disaster - and the federal law would be worse.
     If the law passes, Holly and I will ignore it. In MA, 5%
of residents are known to still lack med insurance. The actual
percent may be much higher, because the people missed by
counts are also the people most likely to lack insurance.
     Politicians pushing the German system on the U.S., call it
"health insurance". That label is FRAUDULANT. NO WAY can you
insure HEALTH. You can't even insure that you will receive med
treatment. The insurer, whether corporate or governmental, may
refuse to provide it for various reasons - and often does.
     Pushers of the German system claim: everyone is morally
obligated to buy med insurance because, regardless of present
health and healthy practices, a freak accident or illness might
cause them to be taken to an emergency room and, if they lack
insurance or sufficient savings, someone else must pay.
     But it is the GOVERNMENT that requires public hospitals to
treat all comers. So, any moral obligation is the GOVERNMENT's.
The gov should pay, and pay out of general revenues, NOT with
an unfair tax on low-income people who are living healthily.✱
     Furthermore, I doubt that hauling people to emergency
rooms helps much. Many die before arriving, or despite treatments - or from infections acquired in hospitals. Three of
many ways to save MORE lives and health, and save money too:
     I. Vehicle accidents are the biggest killers and maimers,
counting YEARS of life and health lost. So, reduce use of cars
for commuting (which, per mile, may be the most dangerous
travel because drivers are often rushed, or tired, or bored, or
distracted by cell phones, etc). Reduce commuting by encouraging camping at or near work places on work-week nights, and
rescheduling work to provide longer weekends.✱
     II. Soft drinks (cola, pop) may be the single biggest
cause of degenerative diseases, not only because they lack
vitamins etc, but because their sugars are absorbed too fast
for bodies to cope with well. So, reduce consumption of them.✱
     ✱ If the gov needs more taxes to reimburse doctors and
hospitals for unpaid services, fairest would be taxes on soft

drinks and higher taxes on car fuels and alcoholic beverages.
III. Public schools may be the biggest spreaders of
infectious diseases, not only to pupils, but brought home to
babies whose immune systems are not yet potent. So, abolish
those day-jails, and offer more learning via web, TV, books.
A radio program we happened to hear, described the high
administrative costs of med insurance presently - but made no
mention of other enormous cost raisers such as:
Malpractice lawsuits cause care-providers' liability
insurance to be very costly. Mexico's different legal system
may be the biggest reason why costs there are much lower.
(Dental work I've had in Mex seemed as good as in U.S.)
High-middle-income people, including doctors and dentists,
pay high taxes. (They are the main tax cows. Big corporat-
ions and the very rich largely avoid taxes by setting up
elaborate tax shelters that others can't afford.)
The medical mafia restricts the supply of MDs by limiting
admissions to medical schools, and by requiring pre-med training that is padded with "liberal arts" courses (no more useful
to a doctor than to a sales clerk, waitress, barber, etc).
The med mafia and subservient officials prosecute non-MD
care providers or unreasonably restrict what they can do.
Many surgeons perform unnecessary and risky operations.
Likewise, many chiropracters perform unnecessary manipulations.
Pharmaceutical companies promote pricy patented drugs with
doubtful benefits and harmful side effects.
Med researchers paid by those companies, and the med mafia,
bad-mouth (and, in Europe, outlaw) low-cost herbs that are
often as effective as prescription drugs and less harmful.
The med mafia and subservient media emphasize MEDICAL care.
That is one reason why many people neglect diet and lifestyle
changes that could prevent or cure degenerative diseases.
Myriad gov regulations and taxes greatly increase costs of
almost everything. That prompts most people to work long hours
at high-stress jobs, and to not get enough sleep, etc.
That, in turn, causes many people to perpetually postpone
doing the things they want. Then, when their health finally
fails, they desperately try to prolong life. (I've read, on
average, 3/4ths of a person's life-time medical expenses occur
during their last year of life, and half during last month !)
Real reforms would greatly lower medical costs AND
increase health. But don't expect them from Big Bully.
Insurance is the flip side of gambling. The difference:
instead of hoping to win big, the insurer hopes to not lose big.
Like gambling, insurance can be addicting. The addict craves
more and more security. But complete security is impossible.
Insurance is least costly to administer, and claims are
most likely to be paid, if the insurance is for happenings not
arguable. Before planting a crop, a grower may sell the harvest
for a set price per pound. The grower thereby insures receiving
that price (unless buyer goes bankrupt). But most other kinds
of insurance are rife with arguable uncertainties. For medical
insurance: pre-existing conditions, present condition, age,
occupation, hobbies, suitability of treatments, etc, etc !
Canada's system is supposedly not as bad as the German
system or the present U.S. system. Yet, many Cdns are refused
effective treatment in Cda. (Some go to U.S. and pay for it.)
I doubt that any med-insurance system could work well.
Many critics of the German system think it would function
so badly in U.S. (because of cultural differences; eg less

obedience) that it would be replaced by the Canadian system where the gov pays for all treatments out of general revenues.

Pushers of the German system may say: "Young people should not object to subsidizing old folks, because the young will someday be old. They will then be subsidized."

That is unlikely. The system will almost certainly change before then. Regardless of who then pays and how, fewer treatments will become affordable as real incomes in U.S. continue their decline toward world levels. (This assumes that, as in the past and now, little or nothing is done that actually reduces medical costs.) Effective treatments will be reserved for people who are likely to continue living (and paying taxes) for many years. Even wealthy retirees who can personally pay for treatments, may have to go abroad to get them - if allowed to. Some sociologists have advocated killing everyone at age 80. That may become the policy in some nations. In the U.S., more likely, the med system will dispense sedatives and pain-killers to ailing seniors. If you want something more when you get old, prepare to do it yourself or with friends. B&H, Oct 09

How Lauran cured or alleviated various health problems.

After reading some health and fitness books, I decided I needed to find out how many calories per day I was eating. Without changing my eating, for ten days I recorded my food intake. I was shocked to discover that I was eating only 700 to 900 calories most days; occasionally 1000 or more. That was far too little for my activity level, which included much biking and walking and an exercise regime. Seemingly my metabolism had dropped into a "low" state to accomodate my habits. As a result, I had only moderate energy and, believe it or not, I had bulges of fat I was battling.

I started eating more food. That was difficult: took me ten days to raise my intake to 1500 calories consistently. (For my energy expenditure, 200-400 MORE calories/day recommended.)

Within two weeks I began losing weight. And it was FAT I lost. Two pounds per week for several weeks until I stabilized. I had more energy than I'd had for years, and felt great.

Many Americans have the opposite problem. But for the few who may be undereating, I mention my experience.

My food costs almost doubled. I live on $5000 per year. $3000 of that is spent on food. (Yes, I keep a budget. Numbers are becoming good friends of mine.) I'd like to spend less for food. I'm experimenting with approaches that cost less yet provide enough calories. A difficulty: I had to quit eating grains and beans because they raise my blood sugar. I did just discover that if I soak spelt until it sprouts a tail about $\frac{1}{4}$" long, I can eat that grain with no rise of blood sugar. It tastes great to me, and is opening up possibilities.

Some years ago I read about a 14-year-old boy with a split personality. In one personality he is physically normal and healthy. In the other personality he has diabetes-1, requiring insulin injections to stay alive. Recently I read of a 30-year-old woman who had that same split. These stories fascinate me from the perspective of personality/moods affecting physiology.

Some books coming out talk about the personality types of people prone to some diseases. Years ago at a function in Atlanta, the woman sitting next to me was a nurse. I asked if she had observed any patterns of personality and disease. She almost popped out of her chair with a bright "Oh my yes !" At her hospital, for efficiency, they put all cancer patients on one floor and all patients with digestive problems (liver, gall bladder, etc) on another. None of the nurses wanted to work on that floor because the patients were angry or bitter or loud or opinionated, and generally difficult. She said, there seemed to be truth in the saying, "He has a lot of gall." Whereas the cancer patients were all very "NICE". Easy to please, never rocking the boat, "sacrificing themselves for others" types.

Our culture puts much emphasis on external variables with respect to health and disease. Only recently are we looking more closely at inner variables, like stress, attitude, personality; variables we can personally influence more.

I suffered a herniated disk two years ago that was very painful. I went to a chiropractor. She recommended all sorts of expensive things for me to do - which I could not afford. I just needed to know what was wrong. She diagnosed it based on my symptoms and was very concerned for me. I asked lots of questions so I could pursue my own approach - and get my money's worth. Chiropractors are cheaper than doctors but still too pricy for me to consider for long-term care. But they can be a good source for muscular-skeletal diagnosis.

She mentioned that some people with my condition show damage on xrays yet suffer no pain; while others show no damage to the body but suffer terrible pain. A baffling situation. But maybe not in light of the power of consciousness.

One of my symptoms was losing feeling in my left arm and some fingers. The supposed cause: a nerve pinched by the herniated disk. That causes the arm to feel weak, you then use it less, you then lose muscle and ARE weaker.

After that visit I came home and tried to hoist myself between two countertops in the kitchen. The lack of feeling in my left arm made it crumple under my weight. I told myself, this was an illusion. I KNEW I was still strong; I still had muscle. Only the feeling of strength was gone. I tried for three days until I could support my weight between the countertops. I also started hanging from the clothesline cross-piece to stretch the muscles of my arm, neck and back.

The pain was terrible in my neck. But if I continued to think I was weak because I felt that way, I would become weak from inactivity. Took me four months to become totally without pain and to have full range of motion. For most people in our culture, surgery plus years of pain killers are the options.

I have read that some people who have a painful inflamed tooth-root (for which dentists recommend a root-canal) can instead use their mind to deaden the infected root. The body then absorbs the dead tissue, leaving the tooth without pain, infection, or any root tissue. I wonder if you may have done this to that molar you wrote about in DP. Lauran, AZ 857, Mar

(Comments) Diet and weight. Strange ! We've read of people whose digestive systems were unusual in various ways. But we have not heard of anyone with experiences similar to yours.

Blood sugar. Adding vegetable oil to grains/beans may slow digestion. (To not degrade oil, apply after cooking.) Have you tried that ? Have you tried sprouting wheat ?

Personality and diabetes. Was personality affecting pancreas ? Or was pancreas affecting personality ? Or was something else affecting both ? Possibly the pancreas was episodic: putting out enough insulin for a while; getting exhausted; shutting down for a while to recuperate; etc. If so, the effect on the brain was probably not as simple as

the blood level of insulin determining personality; else an
insulin injection would switch personality. The endocrine
system is complex: many hormones interact with each other and
interact with the nervous system.
    Variables. Some externals (people dealt with, stressful
work, food obtained, home environment) may be easier to change
than are some internals (feeling stressed, personality, etc);
depending on the individual and their situation.
    Xrays and pain. Xrays are blurry (dental xrays I've seen).
They don't show fine detail. So, no big surprise if painful
damage does not show, or if damage that does show doesn't hurt.
    Infected tooth root. Mine, an upper molar, resulted in a
boil on the gum through which pus (?) oozed occasionally.
Tooth usually not painful unless chewed on hard. But one week
it became painful. We deadened the pain by liberally and
repeatedly applying clove oil diluted with veg oil, and by
massaging the gum and wiggling the tooth to hopefully work the
oil down to the root. (A friend who had a dentist, asked him
to prescribe penicillan over the phone, but he wouldn't.)
I decided to remove the tooth. Holly tied a strong string
around it. I spent a whole day vigorously wiggling the tooth
to loosen it, and repeatedly tugging hard on the string. The
tooth didn't come out. But the pain went away. And gradually
so did the gum boil. Maybe the clove oil killed the microbes.
    Now, years later, the tooth is still there and is function-
al. I chew on it. No pain. The dental mafia's line seems to
be: a root infection cannot be cured except by removal or root
canal, and, if left, may have serious consequences such as
heart infection or jaw cancer. But, though the body's disposal
of microbes and removal of dead tissue may be slow, apparently
that can happen. Tooth removal may often be a good idea. But
dental advice should be tempered with the realization that the
dental schools and organizations have a vested interest in
encouraging people to frequent dentists. An individual dentist
may be sincere, but merely parrot what s/he learned in dental
school. (The same is true for MDs and other professionals.)
    Tooth removal is safer than root canals, according to a
root-canal pioneer who later changed his mind. Replacement of
a tooth may become simpler, better, cheaper. Meanwhile, if you
lose many teeth, buy a food grinder.
    Do most U.S. dentists now push root canals instead of
removals ? Root canals cost much more than removals (esp if
people remove their own teeth, which many do, though I wasn't
able to). Coincidence ? Mexican dentists, after drilling out
as much decay as they can easily, may try to sterilize any that
remains and then fill or cap the tooth. Sometimes that fixes
the tooth; sometimes it doesn't. If not, remove the tooth.

Allergies are often mis-diagnosed on basis of blood tests only.
    Half of children diagnosed with allergies, didn't have
them. Wrong diagnoses prompt families to needlessly buy
special foods that are costly. (from NPR, March 09)

I live near a National Forest in Japan. I eat dandelions.
    Which dandelion relatives are best to eat ? Misa, Nov 09
(Reply) Of plants with dandelion-type flowers, hairy leaves
usually less bitter than smooth leaves, at least to Bert
(tastes vary). None of that <u>Tribe</u> known to be poisonous. (But
beware tansy ragwort, yellow flowers but different shape.)

Ab c/o Lisa Ahne, POB 181,Alsea OR 97324. #10, May 2010
$2 for big-print copy until all sold; $1 for tiny
print. Ab discusses how and where to live better for
less. Ab, an ab-apa, encourages readers to send
pages ready to copy (text 16x25cm or 6.3x10", black on white,
on one side of paper, COMPACT). Usually published unedited.

Small plastic storage bin converted to experimental cold-frame.
    I cut the bottom off at a slight angle with a hacksaw. I
planted lettuce seedlings in a flower bed outside my apartment
(in Idaho) and placed the "cold-frame" around them, angling the
top towards the sun. At first, I left the top open. When the
weather cooled, I placed fabric row-cover over the top. When
snow and cold began, I put on the bin's transparent lid. The
lettuce grew really well; I harvested it before extreme cold
came. In its place, I planted mâche seedlings. Mâche is cold-
hardy; it should
survive the winter
fine and provide
fresh salad greens
by early spring.
Dan Murphy (from
Juniper #11 wnt09;
gardening reports
& environmnt thots.)
www.juniperbug.
blogspot.com

(Comment) Sometimes we find discarded plastic bins which we
salvage. Some have cracks. So, with luck, a cold-frame can be
made without cutting up a bin still good for storage. H & B

Long-time southern Ohio gardener copes with Oklahoma climate.
    (April 09) I have worked myself to exhaustion in my
garden (near Oklahoma City). But I'll get food from it.
    (June) I'm back (after a month away). Weeding and weeding
and weeding. I'm planting more vegetables. They grow fast
here. Two zucchinis are about ready to pick. Been hot and not
much rain - I have to water. I fear the water bill.
    I am ordering Skyfire garden seeds to try myself and to
share. Mom in Las Vegas likes tomatos, but too hot there for
standard varieties. And my neighbors across the street love
tomatos, but their backyard has a 6-ft privacy fence that makes
it too hot. Skyfire has 20+ varieties that are drought and heat
tolerant. Tomatos don't have to be staked. One year I let them
run and put straw under them. I lost some but got more fruit.
    (July) My bean vines are lush and have many blooms but no
pods, because no bees. Wasps fertilize the squashes; all of
the cucurbit family are doing great here. (Never in Ohio) The
tomatos and carrots are not doing well. But I've learned what
to get in early and what to plant in the shade of taller plants.
I've had to water some, but now we are getting rain. Hail
twice. No tornados nearby, but I make good use of my shelter.
    I walked around the neighborhood with chard, collards,
kale, squash. I gave them away and made new acquaintances.
    Potatos and sunflowers put unfriendly stuff into the soil,
so don't plant them near other vegies. (Black walnuts do, too.)
    Carrot seed is viable for approx 10 years, lettuce seed
for 2 or 3, onion seed for only one. Bean seeds will survive
many years if kept cool and dry. (Beans are grown in north/

central states. I doubt that any are hybrids.)

     In a Russian documentary I saw, women stuck small seeds on
narrow strips of toilet paper with flour-and-water paste. An
easy way to plant tiny seeds and not waste any. Suzanne

(Comment) The pasting can be done during winter when gardeners
are not as busy as in spring. Here (w OR), humidity usually
high, winters esp. If seeds PASTED on, I fear they will absorb
enough moisture to rot - before paste dries. Instead, I tried:
cut strip of newsprint ±3" wide; prefold it to crease; open
it; put thin streaks of white glue* ⌒‾‾‾‾‾‾
at ±1" intervals; fold, thus forming small pockets; let dry
THOROLY; insert a seed into each pocket (tweezers helped);
fold flap over ⬤▬▬ . That held seeds adequately. I 😖
planted during late-Feb showers. 4 of 11 wheat seeds grew.
* Home-made flour-water paste cheaper. May be strong enough.

Some of the ways that Suzanne earns money and cuts costs.
     I have relatives and friends nearby. All of us shop yard
sales and buy things for ourselves and each other. We give
WHEN we get; NOT on birthdays and holidays. My extended
family frequently swaps furniture: "musical chairs".
     My son teaches at a college. They give or throw away what
they no longer use. He got me a folding table, 2½ by 9 feet.
I set it against the wall in a bedroom and, for once in my life,
I have a sewing room. (Formerly I used the dining room table.
That messed up the whole house.)
     My daughter-in-law phoned in a panic: her friend needed a
skirt for her daughter. I whipped out two skirts, matching,
for both daughters out of material I already had. I didn't ask
for money but she insisted on giving me $20. So my sewing room
is paying off. And I'll probably get spin-off referrals.
     I love pants made of sweaters (on front of Ab#8). I made
myself one four years ago. I used all black sweaters; even so
it looks funny. I made another for my son-in-law who is
seriously crippled with arthritis, but my daughter informed me
that he would never wear anything that looks funny. So I gave
it to a tall friend. She, like me, is trying to save money.
     I made a down comforter (quilt) for my bed out of coats I
got for a few dollars at the Salvation Army. They came apart
with seams intact, so no down leaked out.
     I'm trying to get more (music performance) jobs. Some
nursing homes have cut their activity budgets: I've lost two
jobs, but I'm finding others here and there. My jobs are
closer to home than when I lived (in a small city) in Ohio.
Most are 5 miles or less, one way. That saves time and gas, so
I can charge less. I play free for the Salvation Army senior
center, and they give me fresh produce that is donated to them.
I am amazed at what many people don't want.
     I turned off the hot-water heater, because I got a free
membership at a nearby YMCA I often go by on my way to stores
and jobs. There, I have a warm shower and a pleasant swim.
     Reducing cooling costs. I brought my sheets of styrofoam
out here, cut them to fit these windows, and glued aluminum
foil on the pieces for the south and west windows. I open
windows after dark; close them when the sun rises. I run the
air conditioner for myself only if 100°F+ forecast; only for
an hour in the morning while the attic is still cool, then turn
it off. When more than four poeple are here, I use it plus a
box fan which, with the dry air here, boosts the cooling effect.
If alone, I use only the fan.   Ab #10   May 2010   Page 2

The Barefoot Architect: for building with what is available.
This 710-page-5x8 handbook, by Johan van Longen, has thousands of drawings that show how to build houses, bridges, windmills, water heaters, pumps, stoves, silos, lathes, solar driers, distillers, and much else; mostly out of natural and recycled materials. The title honors ancient builders who "mixed adobe by treading mud with their bare feet." "This manual does not propose rigid rules for building, but instead shows many ways", thus offering many choices. Excerpts:
"When using alternative, non-conventional building techniques, you should employ quality-control testing, especially when fabricating critical structural elements." (from intro.)
"Locate the bedrooms more or less towards the east side so that the occupants wake up with the rising sun." p.24
"Immigrants often build in their new homeland the same type of house they had before ... a common mistake. Before designing, observe how local people build their homes." p.38
"Often large windows or glass walls are used to frame scenic views. However, sooner or later the pleasure of looking out of them is exhausted and the view is ignored." p.61 (Big windows are structurally demanding, and can lose much heat.)
Because "hot air always rises ... ceilings in cold regions should be lower than in hot regions" for comfort. p.273
"A quick way to protect the underground bases of wood posts is to scorch their outer surfaces in a mild fire until they are blackened." p.339
"A wooden house with well-crafted joints can be built loosely connected to the ground. During earthquakes, this type of house 'dances' over the ground but does not collapse. All the joints must be braced." p.362
"Doors and windows should not be close to each other nor to corners", to not weaken walls. "During earthquakes the walls crack and the corners are the first parts to fall." p.399 (I wonder if this applies mostly/esp to heavy walls that don't much resist pulling apart, such as walls built of stones or adobe bricks.) "It is worth building strong corners and walls to strengthen the house in case there is no time to exit in an emergency." (Various ways to reinforce corners are shown.) "In a disaster situation such as flooding or landslide or earthquake, inhabitants are often trapped while attempting to save their valuables." To avoid this, "build a small secure area" strong enough to survive a disaster, and keep valuables there. "Usually houses do not collapse with the first tremor, but the door is often unopenable since its frame is bent. In unstable zones", make the door frame of thicker wood. (Or ? Make door flimsy enough to push through - and burglar-proof the yard ?) "Many people do not wake up at night to leave. Hang a bell in the bedroom that rings at the very first tremor." p.401
"A shingle roof must have a slope greater than 15° to prevent winds from lifting up the shingles." p.455
"Part of the floor can be built to absorb and store heat" of sun coming through a window. Use materials that absorb heat, such as dark-colored "stones or ceramic tile. Prevent heat from escaping through the ground" by insulating floor from the ground. p.276 (Is an insulated floor better than using ground as floor ? Depends on climate. Discussed in spring2010 DP.)
A round-bottom pot heats water more efficiently than a flat-bottom pot. p.570 (Seems to me, best shape depends on amount of water, area of flame, shroud on pot if any, etc.)

"In areas where water is scarce, for bathing use a vaporizer: a container with pump that sprays water out like a cloud of fine drops. These drops penetrate the surface of the skin. This cleans the skin very well and soap is not necessary." p.639 (Shown is what I call a "spray bottle". The fine drops may penetrate and loosen DIRT on skin. If they penetrated the SKIN, that could cause infections. A translation error ?)

A section is devoted to each of 3 climates: humid tropics, 82 pages; dry tropics, 46pgs; "temperate" (cold winters, hot summers), 26pgs. However, most of the other 547 pages (design, materials, construction, water, etc) are climate-related or seem to be; requiring me to often shift focus and sometimes guess re climate. I'd prefer 3 smaller books, each about a single climate, despite duplicating info (±50pgs ?) useful anywhere. Smaller books would also be handier HANDbooks when building.

The houses suggested are quite big: eg, 6x8m(19½x26¼ft) with 5 rooms. In U.S., they'd be priced at $100,000 or more. Not for purchase by the 80% of earth's people (including us) who have incomes under $2 a day. Could they be home-built in the time remaining after growing food or earning the money to buy food ? Construction seems complicated and labor intensive. Eg, notching posts, beams, rafters where they join, p.451 and 479. But I am accustomed to the abundances here of used hay twine and various kinds of wire, free at recycles. They may be scarce in some countries. (2 pages about processing sisal fiber, which can be used to tie parts together. p.340)

Several home-made machines are described, which were actually built and used by some people, somewhere, some era. Eg, the "monjolo", a water-powered see-saw grain mill, p.544. But, recalling problems I've had with devices that SEEMED simple, I suspect monjolos were built and maintained by semi-specialists. If I built one, I'd expect to do MUCH tinkering.

Inaccuracies: "Angles" p.692. The "30°" layout actually yields 26½°. May not matter much if inclining a roof or solar heater, but could if other uses. INSTEAD use a 4-to-7 ratio which yields 29.7° or 15-to-26 which yields 29.98°. "Maps", for solar-heater slopes, p.697. Eg, Dublin shown at same latitude as Seattle. Dublin is actually ±5½° (480 miles) farther north.

Some info is not as extensive as I'd like. Eg, insulation values, p.681. A single layer of 4mm-thick glass is valued at 1; 200mm of earth at 40; etc. But not listed: TWO layers of glass (or transparent plastic) with an air space between.

I noticed a description that is not complete: a home-made battery for welding, p.534. Doesn't say what metals are put in salt water to yield electricity. (I recall reading: any two different metals may yield some elec, but some combos yield more, or higher voltage, than do others.)

Despite these complaints, we do much appreciate this book. It contains a great wealth of ideas and info that can inspire and inform do-it-yourselfers. Review by Bert & Holly

Translated from Brazilian edition by Carina Rose, 2008, $18 cover price, Shelter Publications Inc, POB 279, Bolinas CA 94924; http://www.shelterpub.com. A Spanish edition, Cantos del Arquitecto Descalzo, 1991, in Mexican libraries. Portugese (Brazilian) editions, Manual de Arquiteto Descalço, 1997-2004; for sources of it, and workshops: http://www.tibarose.com

Shelter Publ also has: HomeWork, Handbuilt Shelters: yurts, caves, tree houses, tents, thatched houses, glass houses, nomadic homes, river boats, and more. 256 pages, 1000+ photos, 300+ line drawings; 9x12", 2004, $27. Ab #10 May 2010 Page 4

Responses by Andrew to topics in Ab #9.

Re: Finding WHERE to build. Here in Maine you can build under 100 sf (eg, 10x10 or 12x8) without any paperwork. BUT, if you want grid electric, phone, etc, you have to file 'intent to build' so town can tax. But I know of a few landowners who have unreported buildings, in the woods. Tax assessors here-and-now generally don't snoop but assume that what they see is what there is. I wonder if there are any outlaw builders in the northeast who have done partially-earth-sheltered, rot-resistant-wood buildings (as in Shelter, p.151) - which would seem necessary during our cold winters. Semi-hidden, too.

I, too, have junk piles; can't hurt, might help. As for investing in tools and materials for the future, I don't. I only have those tools I know how to use, and a few spares. Buying high tech stuff or highly visible items could make you more prone to being robbed. Best to look poor and broke so as to not attract unwanted attention. I favor being aware that the future may well be rough, but obsessing over it is probably counter productive. Enjoying life, eating well, keeping in shape, and developing skills are what I try to keep foremost.

Good piece on wheat. In summer I eat grains; in winter, potatoes plus more fats and some meat when weather is cold enough to seriously sap strength and energy. This works for me; maybe not for all, or for warm-climate dwellers.

Tribode. After re-reading all ten pages, I still have serious misgivings. I. Carbon fiber is strong but it does not bend - it breaks. Ie, not resiliant. I've seen big thick-walled CF masts on sailboats destroyed by storms off Maine coast. CF bike frames must be junked if 'laid down' in a wreck, whereas steel frames can still be ridden. Reason: damage to CF may be imperceptible. CF is used much for making things lightweight to race with; not for long-term durability. II. Tribode hulls are very slender; waves will likely break THROUGH the tribode structure. Whereas a boat will ride atop waves (usually - though even big sailboats can 'pitchpole', ie, go end over end.) III. Few ocean areas are: free of storms and traffic, AND mostly warm, AND free of threats by govt & pirates.

(Comments by Bert) Earth sheltering will reduce wind chill. But, other than that, I doubt that PARTIAL earth sheltering will reduce chill much in cold climates, because the ground near the surface will get almost as cold as the average outside temperature. For earth to insulate much, I think you need to build COMPLETELY underground, with the ceiling well below the depth to which the ground freezes. Soil is a poor insulator PER INCH, but effective if MANY FEET are between the interior and the cold. Reports about two underground homes in: Buffalo NY, 6 ft under, Mar09DP; Nantucket MA, Sep04DP. The Buffalo home had earth walls; only the roof needed carpentry. That simplified construction. But unless soil is tough or reinforced by many roots, an earthquake could collapse the shelter. A fault-zone map shows one near Montreal. How far away are you ?

Re future. Yes, obsessing over it is probably counter productive, partly because the future can NOT be forecast well. It may NOT be much like the recent past, or trending the same way - or much resemble any other specific prediction.

Re investing. We try to maintain a several-year supply of those dry foods that store well, and some materials (esp those now free in recycles/dumpsters; eg, used hay twine, plastic wrappings, clothes) for personal use (tho might trade).

Re appearance. Looking poor and broke seems wise if seen by robbers, but maybe not if seen by cops. When police want to arrest "suspects" to gain favorable publicity, poor people are prime targets because they can't afford lawyers. When going into public, Holly and I try to look "ordinary": clean and neat (but not stylish; here, many people aren't). I walk briskly as if going to work. I wear a SMALL knapsack (common here). If acquiring more than fits into it plus one quite-big shopping bag, I try to arrange pickup by someone who has a car.

Re dry foods (update to Ab#9). Jim in nw OR sent Azure Standard (A) prices (THANKS) of some foods I'd bought at Winco (W) in Jan 2010. Price per pound of non-org; A, 25-pound bag; W, bin or bag: split green peas A36¢ W56¢; (whole green peas A31¢); lentils A51¢ W77¢; oatmeal A39¢ W42¢. (Organic, A: split green peas 104¢; lentils 129¢; oatmeal 67¢. A org, W non: flax A138¢ W56¢.) Thus, for non-org, A prices ± 2/3rds of W except for oatmeal. (Oatmeal seems to be one of Winco's lures to attract shoppers who, W hopes, will also buy pricy items. Most of W's lures are name-brand junk-foods which W brags about pricing lower than do other stores. But I praise Winco for NOT accepting credit cards (which not only include fees that raise prices, but forbid the giving of discount for cash). Whereas the co-op, which claims to promote the best interests of members and community, DOES.) We will try A. But, when A receives our order for ±500 pounds of low-price staples and NO pricy items, will A be "out of stock" (as was Mtn People) ? I don't know A's range. But if you are in mainland U.S. and paying much more than the price above, you can probably do better.

Re carbon fiber. Much thanks for your report. CF's limitation seems important, not only for boat builders, but for anyone thinking of building or buying anything that uses CF.

Re tribode. I reread description. Ave Dave (AD) seems aware of CF's characteristics. On p.4: "The boom sections must be straight and stiff and must be mounted so that they take mainly compressive force. The less bending force the better. They are probably formed with carbon fiber or other very strong, stiff synthetic.... I use wood in the floats and cabin because they are necessarily subject to bending stresses."

(To AD) Have you considered the force of a wave breaking against the lower portion of a boom ? Seems to me, that would tend to bend it. On p.8, "Limits", you specified max wind speed and tilt by waves that a tribode could withstand, but did not mention waves BREAKING against sections of a tribode.

(To Andrew) Does "break THROUGH" mean that the waves would go above the floats ? If so, waves would impact the booms and cables but then move into empty space (unless the waves were tall enough to hit the cabin 32 feet up).

(To Andrew and AD) Is pitch-poling a threat to a boat that is sea-anchored ? Or only for a boat moving against waves ? I assume, if a storm came, a tribode (or boat) would sea-anchor and remove sails. But might waves get both steep enough and have a length that wrenched a tribode's 32-ft-long float off of its boom ? If so, ? better if the float penetrates waves instead of riding atop them ? Would it ?

In Ab#9, AD wrote: "Before offering plans I would build a tribode and rigorously test it, and live in it on stormier waters than I recommend frequenting with it." I think that is wise with ANYTHING, on sea or land, that is new/different and big or powerful or sharp enough to be dangerous.

If you want to do something on the sea, do it pronto.

Pierre of The Connection spoke at a recent "seasteading" conference. Some of his comments (from TC#314 Dec 09):

"... Events adverse to the seasteading concept have been happening for the last forty years and are continuing.... So in my opinion it's important to get as much activity going out at sea as soon as possible, the better to weather whatever comes along.... At the conference, it seemed that most of the good ideas were centered around medical facilities of some kind or other. But whatever the best opportunities turn out to be now, it's important to get going pronto. Eg, if Paddy Roy Bates hadn't been successful as a radio pirate, he wouldn't have been in position to establish Sealand.

"With that in mind, I was particularly impressed by Mikolaj Habryn's presentation on "shipsteading." He had a lot of hard numbers, missing from most of the other talks - and on brief reflection, the reason is obvious: ships are actually out at sea operating every day, while the other concepts are only ideas. He said a cruise ship could be had for under ten million. Allowing $10M for the ship, $10M to repurpose it, $5M for incidentals, and the usual start-up fudge factor of two, a shipstead venture could probably get going for about $50M - a lot less than any realistic figure for alternatives.

"Another talk that impressed me was that of Jorge Schmidt on the legal aspects. A ship in motion enjoys a much more permissive legal regime than a stationary ship, or any kind of platform, floating or anchored to the bottom...."

(Comments by Bert of Ab/DP) Repurposing. Holly and I have not lived on the ocean. But we and other Ab/Dwelling-Portably participants use things for tasks other than what they were built for. Some vehicle dwellers advise: Don't modify a van much. Only put in things (bed, stove, sink, table, whatever) that you can remove easily. That minimizes initial cost and labor. That also leaves both the vehicle and its furnishings more versatile/valuable for other uses.

This may apply to a cruise ship. Modify it as little as possible. That minimizes start-up costs, and gets you on the sea sooner. That also leaves the ship easiest to resell if/ when you need to change strategy.

What can you do with a cruise ship without modifying it much ? Do cruises - but of kinds and in ways different from cruises offered by others. My impression from ads seen: Most cruises are luxury vacations for rich folks who want to visit world-famous resorts without much effort or hassle. Such people are accustomed to being waited on. Consequently the ships carry nearly as many paid servants as paying vacationers. Such cruises are PRICY. Instead ? A few ideas - combinable:

Cut costs by hiring only a few pro ship commanders. Other work is done by many of the passengers. Shifts are short (not onerous): clean-up, food service, lookouts, and (?). Being at sea, the management can be more creative than can land-based competitors who are constrained by Big Bully's myriad regulations. Prices can be lower, and appeal to the many people who can't afford luxurious living on sea OR land.

Shun resort cities where, along with exotic foods and entertainments, passengers may get exotic diseases and exotic hassles (eg, be jailed with serious charges trumped up - and ransomed !). Instead, anchor off uninhabited islands and visit them with suitable small boats. Or rendezvous in mid ocean with other cruise ships that have different ethnics, foods, entertainments. Let passengers switch ships if desired.

Become a cruise college. Make use of the environments (ocean, ship) by offering training in oceanography, marine biology, navigation, ship design, etc. Traditional universities are riddled with pressure groups that not only demand high pay, but require courses not relevant to the skills that students are trying to learn. A ship-borne college might hire only a few top facilitators and let most of the teaching be done by the students themselves. A student may take a course one year and teach it the next, thus refreshing/reinforcing learning.

Pierre mentioned medical facilities. How about cruises for people needing lengthy recuperation. Eg, people with diabetes-2 who want to ameliorate it through diet and exercise (instead of insulin injections which can worsen it), and who DON'T want to be tempted by the junk foods pervasive on land.

Sizes. Regardless of founders' hopes and words, if "sea-steading" is done on a ship or big structure, I expect the resulting community will more resemble the remote company towns than the homesteads of two centuries ago. Though most company towns may not have been as bad as union organizers portrayed them, they didn't offer very much freedom.

So, a case can be made for having family-size residences and businesses. Easier to change neighbors or move to a different floating community; thus less social friction and less agitating for restrictions/regulations.

But what about shelter costs ? A big ship provides more space per hull surface than can anything smaller. However, smaller sea-shelters could be mass produced, reducing construction labor. What are the numbers ? How much space does a $10M cruise ship provide, and how much time and money is needed to repurpose it ? What are production costs of smaller shelters with equivalent space, and how quickly could they be built ? I suggest that proponents of various alternatives provide realistic detailed estimates.

(Pierre commented in The Connection #315, Jan 2010. Excerpts:)

The Seasteading Institute (830 Williams Way #3, MtnView CA 94040) ... sees seasteads as "beacons to the world", spreading across the ocean, and similar things ultimately happening on land, as the number of nations in the world proliferates, and competition between them forces them to loosen their grip....

Operating an ocean-going cruise ship is inherently a high-overhead operation.... My gut feeling: the least that a stripped-down cruise could charge would be about half of what conventional cruises cost. This is still too expensive for most people, and too spartan for those who could afford it....

"Smaller sea shelters." People have been working to build the cheapest seaworthy vessels they can for millenia. I am skeptical that any great cost breakthroughs are imminent. It's easy to project low-ball cost estimates; but any boat owner can tell you, they always cost way more than you first think...

(Response by Bert) Many kinds of vessels have been built for many different purposes. A traditional type (eg, canoe) usually gets better or cheaper only when a new material comes along. But new purposes arise, for which new types are invented. Have any vessels been designed and built primarily for DWELLING in mid ocean ? Though I (personally) am not fond of some of the tribode's features, I think the overall concept has merit.

Slavery then - and now. How to cope ?

America has had many forms of slavery. Slaves in the South of African descent have been publicized the most, not because they were always treated the worst, but because the Union won the Civil War and victors write history (at least until it is revised). Abolitionist and Union propaganda featured dire abuses and atrocities. They did occur but were not very common. Southern slaves were generally treated better than were military conscripts of that period - because they cost much more. The price of an obedient healthy adult slave was around $1000 in 1850 dollars ($40,000 in today's dollars ?). Or, if raised, costs included: less work by women while pregnant or caring for infants, and no work by young children. Whereas the only cost of acquiring military conscripts was rounding them up. Because slaves were valuable, plantations often hired free laborers for dangerous tasks. (That was before employers were often held liable for employees' injuries.) Whereas the military reckless-ly expended soldiers' lives and limbs in the Civil War.

Competent plantation owners/managers (and incompetents often went bankrupt or got fired) tried to keep their slaves content so they would be less likely to shirk work or run away. In some regions, running away was quite easy. Owners allowed holidays, held parties, bestowed gifts. (Some owners gave hunting rifles. Apparantly they trusted their slaves more than many officials today trust their "citizens".) Owners paid slaves for extra work or for implements crafted during the slaves' free time - but delayed part of the pay, which was forfeit if a slave ran away or was fined for disobedience. (Notice any similarity to "Social Security" ?)

By the way, slavery was no more a cause of the Union's war on the Confederacy, than were German atrocities against Belgium civilians in World War I a cause of the U.S. joining that war. Both were merely fodder for pro-war propaganda. Lincoln had not been an abolitionist. His famous declaration that freed slaves, applied only to Confederate-held areas, and was motivated by hopes that slave rebellions or fear of them would tie down Confederate forces. Slaves in states that stayed in the Union, remained slaves until after the war.

Some of the other forms of slavery in America, along with conscription: indentured servants, Amerinds forced onto reser-vations, children forced to attend schools, people jailed or put in mad-houses for non-violent acts, people forced to pay taxes. To anyone who claims that taxes on low-or-middle-income people* are not slavery, consider this: In the Old South, some slaves who had valuable skills they could sell, were allowed considerable freedom to live wherever and do whatever they wanted - provided they paid their owners a portion of their earnings. Were those slaves not really "slaves" ?

For a slave in the Old South, the best alternatives were the extremes. Either be exceptionally obedient, productive, diligent, loyal - and hope to be rewarded with better treatment, perhaps including special privileges. Or else, run away; and try to make a living in some wilderness, or reach a territory that did not have slavery (at least not of that kind). There were NO good intermediate ways. A slave who remained but was perceived to be disobedient or surly or lazy, could expect punishment or, if troublesome enough, to be sold to (eg) a prison-like sugar-mill where slaves could be closely supervised and severely punished if they malingered. To replace slaves who died, the mills could buy troublesome slaves cheap - so mill

41

slaves, often over-worked and underfed, rarely lived long.
     Though the details are different, the extremes are still
generally the best alternatives. People who 'stay in the
middle of the road get run over.' **
     Both then and now, for most people freeing themselves, the
biggest challenge is usually, not how to leave nor how to elude
hostiles, but how to maintain themselves. Eg, how to produce
everything needed or else replenish initial supplies.
     Those people that Holly and I know fairly well, are free
in many ways but remain vulnerable in some ways. (Eg, for us,
resupply uncertainties.) How to become more broadly free ?
Though no sure way, some attitudes that may help: Don't get
hung up on one or a few alternatives. Be imaginative, but
focus on changes do-able. (Very unlikely that, during this
century, we could move to another planet or vastly change this
planet.) These topics deserve more pondering in Ab and DP. B&H
*   Giant organizations of all kinds, and billionaires, have
government-like powers or influence. So, taxes on them can be
thought of as transfers from one government to another.
**   When young, Holly and I had independently concluded that
middle-income people were foolish. Most of my older relatives
worked themselves into early disabilities or graves, to buy
stuff they didn't even have time to use much. One exception:
an uncle who mostly did his own things but occasionally went to
distant places where/when temp labor was in demand. He seemed
to enjoy life. He was also my only old relative who remained
healthy into his 60s (at least; we lost contact then). I
decided: unless someone could quickly become rich (and I did
not think I could), better to learn to live well on little.
     My mother's several sibs and their offspring formed an
extended family - though a marginally functional one. At get-
togethers, their favorite pastime was dissing those relatives
(esp in-laws) who weren't there. But they did pass on out-
grown clothes and toys and books. An aunt who sometimes fed me,
helped me learn to read. But I didn't much appreciate her,
maybe because she pushed bible stories. (Even as a child I was
a firm non-believer: Jehovah was too much like Santa Claus to
be credible.) Reading became my favorite winter-time activity,
in the inland northeast where daily highs were seldom above
freezing. (The books passed on to me were mostly 'girls'
stories. Apparantly, only female relatives had learned to
read. Yeah, I got a crush on one FICTIONAL protagonist.)
     The relatives who fed me, were usually too busy working or
recuperating from work to bother with vegies other than what
came in TV dinners. Consequently I often craved greens, even
grass (which I chewed and chewed for the juice, then spit out
the residual tough fibers). The itinerant uncle showed me some
edible wild plants. I often nibbled on them, raw. One was
purslane. (Holly and I have found it in gardens here, but not
in the wild.) Though edible wild plants were quite common in
that area during summers, I do not recall any other relative
utilizing them, except for black-caps (raspberries) which,
along with plenty of sugar, was sometimes made into jam.
Strangely, I liked ragweed pollen, to which many people are
allergic; to me, it smelled and tasted much like orange peel.
When very young, I feared all mushrooms and umbelliferae (which
include poison hemlock). I think I inherited those fears -
I don't recall any warnings. (Yeah, these food memories are
semi-digressions - to fill the page, and lead in to next article)

Some beliefs about the Stone Age are ROCKY.

Summary: During the past ± 10,000 years, most of our ancestors ate much UNrefined grains. Before that, during a SHORT part of the Stone Age, most of our ancestors ate much meat. Consequently, because the high-grain period was more recent than the high-meat period, it probably had more genetic effects on the nutritional needs of most people today.

Elaboration: Some nutrition writers favor high-protein diets. Their arguments go: Our Stone-Age ancestors ate much meat. They did not eat much grain until they developed agriculture ± 10,000 years ago. So, our genes haven't had time to evolve adaptation to grains. They remain adapted to meats.

Most such writers do not define what they mean by "Stone Age". However, one writer was more specific.* "20,000 years ago, people hunted and foraged for their food, eating lean meats, seafoods, and organic (pesticide-free) vegetables and fruits that resemble our modern kale, rose hips, and crab-apples. The diet" was "high in protein, relatively low in saturated fat, and high in non-starchy (low carbohydrate) vegetables and fruits." p.32 "The relative percentages of animal foods vs vegetable foods varied from culture to culture, but, interestingly, no society was entirely vegetarian."

HOW ancient ? Food-remains decay so, presumably, most that were studied were fairly recent. 20,000 years ago may be average. The author seems to assume that what humans ate then, was what they ate AT ALL TIMES prior to agriculture. Really ?

What were our ancestors eating ± 8 MILLION years ago when proto-humans diverged from chimpanzees ? Studies indicate that human genes differ more than do chimp genes from genes of our common ancestors. So, those ancestors probably ate more like how chimps eat now, than like how humans ate 20,000 years ago. Chimps eat mostly fruit when available. But they sometimes hunt: females and adolescents more than adult males; appropriately, they need more protein. They make crude spears from branches, sharpening them with their teeth. (Sci News 3mar07) But they don't secure much meat. They eat the meat raw.

Gorillas genetically diverged a few million years before the chimp-human split. They usually eat mostly foliage. But when fruit is abundant, they eat mostly fruit.

What were our ancestors eating ± 100 million years ago when primates diverged from other mammals ? They ate much fruit and/or foliage. Evidence: those ancestors lost the ability (which most mammals have) to form vitamin C.

RAW meat was/is a risky food for humans, and probably for chimps and most primates; because we lack the strong stomach acids of carnivores; and because we have longer life spans - and thus more time to accumulate and be harmed by parasites.

Fire was domesticated ± 500,000 years ago. How much meat were those proto-humans eating then ? Their brain size was mid-way between chimps and modern humans. Their weapons were superior to chimps' crude spears, but inferior to humans' weapons of 20,000 years ago. So, they likely ate more meat than do chimps, but less than did late-Stone-Age humans.

Our ancestors' diets began to change greatly ±30,000 years ago, after modern humans evolved and developed (eg) accurate arrows (NOT easy to make) and sophisticated traps and fishing gear, along with language able to coordinate complex endeavors. That enabled modern humans to proliferate, spread out, and interbreed with or displace proto-humans.

When humans first arrived in an area, most animals did not fear DISTANT humans, because those animals can run faster than can a human for a short distance. Even today, in areas where humans rarely go, animals don't flee until a human gets very close. Yes, in open country during hot weather, a naked human could sometimes chase a fur-covered animal until it collapsed from heat exhaustion. But often, the animal, faster at first, would get far enough ahead to hide successfully. Did such chases usually burn more calories than they yielded ?

When humans first arrived, they were few and the animals plentiful. And the animals, fearless of a human at arrow range, were easy to kill. Thus, ± 20,000 years ago (earlier in some places, later in others) began a PEAK era of hunting, trapping, fishing - and meat consumption. As big animals were hunted to extinction or evolved fear of distant humans, humans did more hunting/trapping of small animals and foraging of wild vegetables. But meat continued to be a major source of calories in many cultures until agriculture developed.

Prior to agriculture, how much grain was eaten ? Our ancestors probably preferred fruit and meat and succulent vegies when available. But often they were scarce. Wild grass seeds were sometimes abundant, and some can be harvested and prepared with Stone-Age tools. Certainly, grass seeds were utilized; else domestic grains would not have evolved.

Mature grass seeds are one of the few foods easy to store in savanna/semi-desert areas where modern humans are thought to have evolved. So, grass seeds may have first been emergency rations, eaten during famines. Then, as harvest techniques improved, grass seeds were utilized more. Then, maybe one spring after a benign winter, someone tried sprinkling left-over seeds on bare earth deposited by a flood. Then, grass seeds began to evolve that were easier to harvest. At first, horticulture was probably only an occasional diversion. (Seems unlikely that large-scale agriculture began suddenly.)

High-protein advocators argue that ± 10,000 years has not been long enough for humans to evolve the genes needed to thrive on high-grain diets. If true, the period of high meat consumption was probably not long enough either. And the high-grain period is more recent, so its effects are probably greater.

Another argument of high-protein advocates: Thousands of years ago, two "genes, which predispose a person toward celiac disease, were relatively common among humans."

HOW common and among WHICH humans ? Were most of the tested remains from people who had inhabited Europe during the ice ages and who, like arctic peoples recently, of necessity hunted and fished much more than they gathered plants ?

"During most of human evolution, these genes posed no disadvantage, because people rarely consumed grains."

During most of human evolution, EVERY type of food was probably scarce in most places much of the time. Most of our ancestors got enough to eat only by consuming MANY types.

"The situation changed about 10,000 years ago when people began cultivating gluten-containing grains.... The incidence of many diseases skyrocketed.... Archeological evidence indicates significant post-gluten increase in birth defects, osteoporosis, arthritis, rickets, dental enamel defects, infertility, child mortality, and disease and death at all ages."

Due mainly to gluten intolerance ? Or due to various adverse effects of increasingly dense populations in grain-cultivating areas ? Eg: more spread of infectious diseases;

more famines because of dependence on fewer foods; less food variety for most of the people as gatherer-hunter bands of a few dozen were displaced by nations of many thousands. In them, the rulers likely hogged most of the fruits and meats and favorite vegies, while the peasants ate mostly grain.

Furthermore, each ancient ag society was at first limited to the FEW grains and beans (etc) native to its area. Whereas N Americans today enjoy MANY kinds that originated all over the world. And, we know more about nutrition. Eg, grains need sprouting to yield vit C, and fermentation (yeasting) to yield absorbable vit B3. So, the deficiencies of ANCIENT high-grain diets, are not necessarily reasons to shun grains now.

(To learn gluten-intolerance's importance: In ancient ag societies, were diseases less where the main grain was gluten-free (eg, rice) than where the main grain contained gluten (eg, wheat) ? Or were diseases about as common ?)

Each human alive today is carrying a unique mixture of genes from thousands of different ancestors living in different environments and eating many different diets. So tolerances vary. Eg, gluten-containing grains cause serious digestive problems (celiac) in approx 1% of people. Eg, a high animal-protein diet, increases cancer risk in many people (Sci News 25oct08; book "China Study" summarized in Ab#6). But, considering our ENTIRE evolutionary past, I think that, for MOST adult humans, a high-grain diet is healthier than a high-meat diet. H&B

* Feed Your Genes Right, Jack Challem, 2005. I chose this book to quote because it seems BETTER researched and more specific than other pro-high-protein books I've seen. Of course, the sources are early 2000s or older and do not report discoveries since then. The only two Stone-Age refs to sci journals: Am J Clin Nutr, 2000, 71:682-92; Euro J Nutr, 2000, 39:67-70.

I've also read three 2008 issues of Challem's newsletter. (Recommended. www.nutritionreporter.com Ask a library to subscribe. $33/yr/ten in 08. POB 30246, Tucson AZ 85751.) It did not promote particular diets other than reporting on the effects of vitamins, etc. Did Challem change his mind ? Or, did publisher slant book to obtain meat-industry support ? Eg:

"Vegetarian foods, like beans and nuts, provide incomplete proteins in that they lack one or more of the essential amino acids. For this reason vegetarians must eat complementary proteins, such as legumes and brown rice...." p.66. WRONG. All beans and nuts and grains (that I know about) contain ALL essential amino acids. Some do not contain optimum ratios. Eg, corn, the least-balanced common grain, contains (as I recall) 30% less lysine than optimum. Consequently, more of corn's other amino acids can be utilized as protein (rather than like carbs) if (eg) a lysine-rich legume is eaten within few hours.

"Celiac disease is an inherited intolerance of gluten, a family of related proteins found in wheat, rye, barley, and many other grains." p.180. BIASED. No mention there of rice and other grains that do NOT contain gluten.

Finally, advocating ANY specific diet for EVERYONE, contradicts the book's title and theme: "Feed Your Genes Right."

Bert and I eat mostly plants - for convenience, not ideology. We also kill and eat animals that become nuisances. Recently, a pack rat that invaded our storage tent. Young, tender, tasty. (Some are not as tasty. A possum - yuck !) (For rodents, taste depends more on feed than on species.)

To breed or not to breed ? Broad eugenic policies harmful.

Some diseases are often inherited. Ie, an illness may be much more common in an extended family than among the general population. This has long been known. Recently discovered: the genes whose variants cause or contribute to some diseases.

With many of these diseases, someone will develop it only if BOTH parents provide the variant gene. If only one parent does, the variant may be advantageous - which explains why the variant is not weeded out by evolution. Eg, sickle-cell anemia. If one parent provides the variant, the child's red-blood-cells have normal shape - and are more resistant to malaria than if neither parent provides the variant. But if both parents provide the variant, the red-blood-cells are sickle shaped and and do not flow well through narrow blood vessels.

A genetic disease may be caused by a variant gene forming an enzyme that does its job less well. Eg, if its job is transforming molecules of a proto-vitamin into the active form, the enzyme might not grab onto as many of those molecules as they pass by. Such a disease may be ameliorated by ingesting more of that proto-vitamin. The book, Feed Your Genes Right (Jack Challem, Wiley, 2005), has quite a few case histories of inherited diseases ameliorated by appropriate nutrition.

If/when genetic determinations become inexpensive, a prospective parant can learn which potentially-harmful gene variants s/he has (most/all people probably have some) and choose a mate who does not have those variants.

Most traits result from MANY genes PLUS environmental factors. Some outstanding individuals had parents who were similarly outstanding. But many had parents who were ordinary or even "inferior" by contemporary standards. Similarly for plants. To breed a superior (in some way) variety, one method: work with open-pollinated plants, select a few with the trait desired, propagate them, select among their offspring, etc. Another method: hybrids. A superior plant may result from cross-breeding parents BOTH of which are inferior.

Broad eugenics, whether due to government decrees or conformist fashions, would produce a quite uniform population. Expect fewer morons but also fewer geniuses; and, most important, fewer individuals with freaky talents that may be vital in the decades ahead. Also, there's an advantage of a large population: the more people, the more freaks. Holly & Bert

If you would like to give birth, don't be quick to assume you are genetically unfit merely because some people disapprove of some of your traits. Be esp wary of psychiatrists (many of whom are appropriately called "shrinks": their treatments kill neurons - shrink brains). They are prone to label someone "mentally ill" merely because s/he doesn't conform.

I heard a radio interview with Temple Grandin. When young, shrinks said she had "autism". Though less capable some ways than most other people, she was superb at learning what animals felt/needed and designing/building compatable equipment. She also wrote books and became quite famous. Thereupon, shrinks said, she had "high-functioning autism". (Were those shrinks "high-functioning idiots" ?)   Holly

Soon after we met, Holly served notice that she didn't want children. Her reasons: taking care of babies is much work; compatability of parents and kids is a gamble; and, regardless of parents' hopes and plans, the end products, adults, will likely be much like most of the people already on earth.

Supplement to Ab and Dwelling Portably, March 2010.

June 87 MP(DP) is enclosed (if that doesn't increase postage).
FREE, because some portions are blurry. Thrifty Prints
(Baraboo WI) goofed, but then made better copies. We seek a
low-price printer with reliable quality, the closer the better.

I attribute my dental health mostly to diet.
I had my teeth examined and cleaned for the first time in
13 years. I had much tartar but no cavities. The dentists
were amazed. I eat well - very little sugar and NO SODA DRINKS
(which contain phosphoric acid). Andrew in Maine, Feb 2010

Iodine and Chlorine only kill Giardia, not Cryptosporidium.
I read that about the water-disinfecting tablets. So
unless you are absolutely certain that your drinking water
source is safe, boil, filter, or use a new UV-light gadget.
If you filter, beware cross contamination: don't touch pickup
and discharge hoses together, or touch both with same hand.
(Comment) If you are in an area for a while,   David in MI, 09
you can probably find or develop a safe source. (Suggestions
in May 08 DP.) If you must sterilize, heat is more reliable
than filtering or UV. You don't need to boil, 170°F suffices -
obtainable if sun, with reflectors and transparent shroud - but,
to be sure water is hot enough, you'll need cooking thermometer.

Pure magnesium chloride is available from Get Tanked acquariums.
gettankedaquariums.com   Bill in cyberspace, 2009

I believe: feet must be able to flex around in the cold.
So I wear good sox and put wool insoles in boots, but buy
boots a bit big. Works good. I rotate footwear, though not as
often as you recommend (in Ab#9). I have 3 pairs of rubber
boots for winter (needed here), and many cheap sneakers for
                                         summer. Andrew, Feb
My chosen vehicle is a 2001 Dodge minivan.
I removed all the rear seats. A great way to haul - whatever. I'm not wealthy but my modest pension lets me camp in
wonderful places. I moved from Michigan to Oregon 5 years ago
and will never go back. I've grandchildren here - retirement
is terrif for me. Years ago I was a DP subscriber but let it
lapse when I moved abroad for 3 years. Recently I came across
your book at Powells in Portland. What a blast from the past.
I have always agreed with your lifestyle. Joe, OR 971, 2009

Years ago, old step-vans and buses were great units to convert.
But now they are conspicuous and 'targeted'. Clean-looking
small vans and motorhomes aren't hard to find. The big rigs
can be found in the Sun Belt when spring comes and widows want
to head home - minus rig and memories. But vans and smaller
less-conspicuous motorhomes have advantages. Few people with
the big rigs ever travel as much because of poor mileage and
lack of suitable squat spots. Al Fry (More by Al about RVs
and his experiences with them in Living Mobile. Availability?)

My dog and I are house/property sitting long-term.
We are in southeast Tennessee on a chilly plateau. The
house must be occupied for insurance coverage. It is lonely
up here but the furnished house is warm and comfortable. I must
climb a tall oak tree for a cell-phone signal. The owner pays
all utilities. Everyone except 4-wheelers respects the private-
road/no-trespassing sign at the turnoff. For food money, I
help a friend maintain his rental properties. Jimmy in TN, 09

Should Ab/DP include only well-proven devices and techniques ?

Your pole/plastic shelter designs are tried and proven. And other unconventional LAND-based dwellings/dwellingways written about in DP are generally things people have tried or currently practice. And being on the ocean in a decent boat with a good crew, is as safe or risky as any other undertaking one is prepared for and/or skilled at. But I get a sense that some suggestions in Ab/DP for OCEAN-based dwellings are by people with only theoretical knowledge who do not understand and appreciate the realities of living on the ocean.

On land I've survived for days virtually naked. Whereas the ocean is inherently hostile to humans. Without a boat you will soon die from drowning or exposure. Also, the ocean plays havoc with gear, structures, metals of all kinds. Eg, plastic wrap on a float will wear off quickly. Andrew in Maine, Feb 2010

(Response) No human will survive for days virtually naked - in Maine IN WINTER. Most of N Am is, at times, inherently hostile to humans who lack shelter (clothes being portable shelter). Our long-ago ancestors were tropical. We lack thick fur.

Each pole/plastic shelter we build is UNTRIED - because it is different from every other shelter we've built - because each is tailored to the site and every site is different.

After having built many shelters, variously configured for various purposes and sites, we do have a sense of what is likely to endure long enough to achieve what we want. But almost all have been west of Cascades - relatively mild. We've little or no experience building shelters in the inland north, desert south-west, etc. Nor, usually, do we put many details in DP, because they would not much help anyone else - because their resources and needs and site will differ from ours.

A Metronome group experimentally built a "Hillodge" during winter, inspired by our write-up in Apr92 DP. Its roof was not steep enough. Snow accumulated, sagged the roof, and had to be repeatedly cleared off during the night. Our write-up had not sufficiently emphasized the importance of roof slope: possibly because, the year or two we'd used a Hillodge, no snow.

For Metronome, the snow accumulation was merely a nuisance. Also, their motorhome parked nearby was backup. (In Metn#10, $2)

Repeatedly, we and others in DP caution: if trying anything new/different, have a backup easily accessible. (Eg, Sep04 DP, p.3) This applies to the ocean, too. Ships carry lifeboats. Sailboats heading for the same area often travel in groups.

I'm not convinced that a somewhat-different kind of ocean shelter is inherently much more dangerous than a somewhat-different kind of land shelter. With EITHER, builders would be foolish if, immediately upon completion, they headed alone, with no backup, to a remote land wilderness OR remote OCEAN area.

Holly and I know very little about the backgrounds of most Ab/DP authors. We prefer articles by people who have considerable experience doing what they write about. But we take what we can get. With ANY info from ANYone, USER BE WARY ! The author may omit an important detail (especially if writing from memory), or the reader may misinterpret something, etc.

Re ocean vessels, at least those of family or small-group size, my impression is: most designers/builders are experienced only with traditional types, because such boats sell the most. Reason: presently, most moderate-size boats are used for sport (racing) and recreation and status; not for dwelling long on the ocean. And most buyers value tradition. Eg, in most boat races, an odd configuration would be as unwelcome as would be a

cheetah in a dog race. So, any break-through likely will come
from someone outside the field. And, yeah, the prototype likely
will need changes before it performs reliably - if it does.
     Holly and I much appreciate the specific doubts about
specific equipment/techniques/proposals that you and others
have expressed, because they may lead to improvement or
replacement, or avert disasterous consequences. But Ab/DP/LLL
will continue to publish some untested ideas,as well as
widely-verified info and long-followed instructions. B & H

I plan to leave my job and squat on some family-owned land.
     It is in nearby mountains. I am building a small cabin,
and planting a garden, and raising some capons and rabbits.
My present job (sales) is ridiculous and awful. I welcome the
advice of stressless individuals and free thinkers.
     Tom Hodgekinson, a Brit, offers some good advice, I think.
He has several books, his own magazine "The Idler", and hosts a
a website: http://idler.co.uk/ Brian, PA 185, Feb09

(Addendum) A friend looked at site briefly and reported: Tom
advises: don't seek status. He also believes most Europeans
lived better during medieval times (±475-1450) than recently.

Google "Jeff Jonas". His thinking may help DP readers.
     Re "recession": Where we are, the people are used to hard
times. However, number of food boxes distributed around here
is up 50% as of last month. Michael, AZ 853, March 09

I came across a huge database of do-it-yourself information.
     13 gig file size. Google cd3wd.com   D.S., FL 322, Jan2010

Tennessee now requires gov photo ID from EVERYONE buying beer.
     Luckily I found a store that ignores this bad law. Jimmy

A copy-ready page for Ab can also go into The Connection.
     We are previewing in TC some of our Ab pages to get
additional/quicker comments. (TC publishes 8 times a year.)
If you'd like us to put your Ab page in TC: to get in quickest
send us TWO copies. Ab's format (text 16x25cm or 6.3x10") is
okay for TC if on 8½x11 paper with at least ½" margins left and
right and ¼" top and bottom. But, unlike Ab, no cut-and-pastes.
     Our current subscription to TC (extends through Jan 2011)
lets us put in 4 pages per issue. We seldom have 4 of our own.

Wanted: clippings and net-printouts with info for Ab and DP.
     The only periodicals we have recently received regularly:
American Survivor, CD Summary, Living Free, The Connection,
Wild Foods Forum, Zine World. No big-circulation publications.
     For several years we got Science News. But we let our
subscription expire in late 08 because SN had changed. SN no
longer prints much health info do-able yourself. Instead, SN
now mostly features elaborate procedures that will become
available (if at all) only after many more years of development.
Ie, medical pie in the sky, by and by, priced very high.

Items I saw ads for that might be useful:
     Woodburning Trail-stove, mass produced version of the old
coffee-can stove, sometimes called rocket stove. $25, 2 pounds,
burns sticks and twigs. trail-stove.com
     Udap's Bear Shock, portable electric fence encloses 30x30-
foot area, 4 pounds, 6000-volt shock, runs 6 weeks on two D-cells.
$300. udap.com Expensive. Instead you could run a standard
elec fence off a car battery (indefinitely with pv tricklecharge)
     Trick birthday candles, won't blow out. David in MI, 2009

Is vitamin D from sunshine healthier than vit D from pills ?
    Michael Mogadon, MD, thought so in 2001 when he wrote a
book. Though the vitamin may be the same, its transport by
blood differs. From skin, it is carried by protein. From gut,
it is carried by fat - which may contribute to artery clogging.

What percent of ultraviolet-B is absorbed by the atmosphere ?
    On a typical early-summer day near noon when sun is very
high in sky (except in/near arctic) ? Knowing that, absorption
on other dates at any latitude is easy to calculate.

Source for acrylic (or?) FILM that resists UV yet passes UVB ?
    Use film for winter-sunning mini-shelter. (On internet,
a friend found only sellers of thick acrylic SHEETS.)

Do MDs and millionaires die younger, on average, than others ?
    I read that years ago, but seek confirmation. Info very
pertinent re effectiveness and advisability of most med care !

What care do Nimh batteries need that NiCd don't need ?
    A clerk at Radio Shack (which sold BOTH) said: unlike
NiCd, Nimh deteriorate if left discharged. Garrity recommends
cranking their light at least monthly. Also heard: a fully-
charged Nimh can't tolerate a continuing trickle charge.

How much more energy-per-weight does Li-ion store than Nimh ?
    Than lead-acid ? What special care does Li-ion need ?

What simple vessels may be good for mid-ocean dwelling ?
    A few years ago, Zalia sent a photo and a note about a
small boat she'd designed, built, used. (We put it into a
Supplement, but not DP then, hoping for more details.) Simple
to build. 3 sections bolted together. Mid section rectangular,
open, held 2 people. Front and back sections
tapered in depth, foam filled so unsinkable.
    Could an ocean abode be built that way ?
Eg, ± six 8-foot-cube mid-sections, identical
except for deck fittings; tapered front and back sections,
identical except fittings. It'd be simpler to build than any
ocean-going craft I've seen or read of, including tribode. It
would roll more than a tribode, but could contain a pivoted
flywheel-stabilized inner room. Info/ideas welcome for other
fairly-simple mobile craft for DWELLING long on deep water.

What ocean areas far from land are usually quite placid ?
    Ie, rarely have violent storms, at least some seasons ?
Usual weather ? What months ? Approx latitude/longditude
extent ? Or, what book has this info ? (This question is
especially to anyone who proposes an ocean dwelling.)

How durable/reliable are pepper-spray bear-deterrants ?
    Supposedly more effective than guns for stopping charges.
But a gun can be test-fired occasionally to verify it works.

CHORD EASY, short version (12p.5x8) is FREE to any library.
    IF ordered BY LIBRARIAN. (Else $1.) If public access is
doubtable, tell location, and hours, and who can simply walk in.
(Of course, we hope readers will then order the full version:
5th edition, 60 songs, 64p.5x8, $6.) In a Zine World review,
Clint said, "This is AWESOME. If more artists were familiar
with what Chord Easy is teaching, popular music would be a lot
more interesting." CE c/o Lisa Ahne, POB 181, Alsea OR 97324

Each float is kept upright by stays from its outrig to its boom mid joint or (on lead float) to a spar directly above its center. (If the bottom end of a boom kept a float upright, that boom section would get bending force whereas the stays exert only compression.)

Boat hulls are painted with toxic chemicals to keep barnicles from growing on them. Tribode floats can be protected by wrapping plastic film around them. They have shapes easy to wrap, unlike most boats. If barnicles adhere to the plastic, hot water will detach.

ACCESS. If the cabin will be only a residence and light work place, I'd build the aft room's bottom to also be the hatch. (The bottom instead of deck so what when open the hatch is near level for easy passage and is somewhat sheltered from rain.) The hatch's inner end is hinged to the bottom frame. The outer end is supported, when open, by two stays to the deck above and, when closed, by latches.

Extending out and up from the room's aft corners are two spars. Their upper ends join and are braced by a stay. They hold a hoist. Safety netting extends from hatch's sides to the deck frame and from hatch's outer end to the hoist spars. A rope ladder goes to the deck.

To go from the cabin to the deck, open the hatch, walk out onto it, twist the ladder a half turn, step onto it and climb to the deck.

To haul up supplies or to descend, don a safety harness, open hatch, and unclip ladder and outer safety net to put them out of the way. If electric, the hoist can be operated either from the aft room or by remote control while riding it. If manual, I'd mount it so that the rider operates it. When the load comes up, swing it over the hatch (or deck if wanted there) and slacken the hoist.

I'd use a hoist mounted aft only for loads under 400#. For a heavier object I'd put a hoist under the center room and operate it from a net beneath cabin. I'd work on object there (not inside).

STOCAT is an open catamaran, 32' long, width optional. Its two floats are identical to the tribode's floats. It is often tethered to the tribode's booms' mid joints. It can carry supplies that exceed the cabin's capacity. To access them, position the stocat beneath the cabin's hoist. Most supplies may be in watertight containers on top of the stocat's floats. To avoid rain or sea spray, hoist a container up and into the cabin and open it there. Supplies can also be carried on top of the tribode's floats but access is not as easy. Only liquids could be carried inside floats and be easily accessed.

I'd join the floats with stretchy stays forward and aft plus a cylindrical beam that inserts into sockets on the outrigs. Unlike the tribode's booms, the beam's ends keep the stocat's floats upright which imposes bending force. The outrigs bolt to the floats, same as the tribode's floats' outrigs, but the sockets are horizontal instead of angled up. This way of joining the floats allows them to pitch independently and to a lesser extent yaw independently. This way they are stressed less than they would be if rigidly connected.

A hoist on the stocat can raise any of the tribode's or stocat's floats for maintenance. (A stocat float is raised by trying to lift a heavy bag of sea water on the opposite side. That tips the stocat.) I'd mount the hoist on the beam so that it can be slid over to either float. The hoist is braced by two stays to that float, one forward, one aft, and by a stay to the opposite outrig.

A stocat also provides space for activities that are best done close to the water. Netting extends between the floats.

If not burdened with supplies, the stocat can be used separately as a boat propelled by outboard motor or sail. To not need a mast or rigging, use a triangular sail. Attach each bottom corner to a float and hold up the top corner with the hoist.

SAIL. For sailing the tribode down wind or cross wind I'd use a
single triangular sail as big as 30x30x30'. It is curved to better
catch the wind. Its top corner is fastened to the high forward joint.
From each bottom corner two guys go, one aft, one forward, to sheaves
mounted on low joints and from there to control. I'd usually control
from a net between cabin and high forward joint. (Control from inside
requires more sheaves plus holes for the guys.) The four guys angle
the sail to make best use of the wind. To deflate sail, the control
person slacks guys and bundles sail into a pack bag. The guys remain
threaded through the sheaves for easy respreading of the sail.

To travel upwind I'd use electric outboard motors on the aft
floats, powered by wind generators mounted on the aft mid joints, and
by photovoltaics on the floats. Though probably not as fast upwind
as a sloop rig, that provides easier control and enables travel
directly into a wind whereas a sailboat must tack from side to side.

AEROCABIN. More streamlined than the view-cabin described on page 3,
it is for a tribode that remains where hurricane winds may occur. The
top view and center room (drawings 3, 5, and 6) are like the view-
cabin's, but the outer rooms' decks slope at the same angle as the
outer rooms' bottoms and the joints are more rounded.

A tailplane keeps the aerocabin's front slightly lower than its
rear so that any lift is negative. (Otherwise, swells would sometimes raise the front and a 100 mph gust then may create enough lift
to raise a near-empty tribode and tumble it.) A 100 mph wind's drag
on aerocabin will be ~ 300 pounds and on the booms, spars and stays
~ 500, not enough to seriously affect a tribode's stability.

For a tribode unlikely to encounter winds over 70 mph, I prefer
a view-cabin. Better vision ahead and toward sides. (The aerocabin
may need mirrors outside.) Simpler structure because joints are not
rounded. Simpler hoist. (On aerocabin I'd want the hoist streamlined or retractable, to not mess up the cabin's air flow.) Outer
decks are nearly level and thus easier to walk on. When the cabin is
floating (not yet on tribode), outer decks are farther above water.

Either cabin is for activities needing only light equipment.

LIMITS. When the wind is fierce, open the hatch a little to reduce
pressure inside the cabin and thus reduce outward stress on deck and
bottom. (Hurricanes rip off the roofs of tightly closed houses.)

For least stress, keep the tribode and its floats parallel to the
motion of the biggest waves, using a small quickly-deployable sea
anchor on leading float's bow or wave rectifiers (hinged flaps that
resist motion one way) on the trailing floats' sterns. The stays that
position the floats are stretchy which lets the floats wiggle in
response to waves instead of rigidly resisting.

For stability, keep the center of gravity (CG) low by storing
most supplies on a stocat tethered to the tribode or on the tribode's
floats. Unless the cabin is heavy loaded, CG is highest (16' above
sea level) when the tribode is empty. For waves alone to capsize an
empty tribode, they must tilt it up to 55° (steep). That would
require a wave over 50' high that also has a length that puts the
trailing floats in a trough when the leading float rides a crest. If
simultaneously hit by a 100 mph gust, the critical tilt is ~ 34°.
A 153 mph gust alone may capsize an empty tribode that lacks a sea
anchor or tethered stocat.

Structurally I'm designing for a 115 mph wind with a safety
factor of 3. (Wind force $\propto V^2$, so 200 mph may cause damage.) I would
not keep any tribode where/when the wind might exceed 115 mph.

Stability can be increased by attaching a big deeply submerged
sea anchor to leading float. For least stress use a stretchy cable.

Tribode   Page 8

Message Post

Portable Dwelling Info-letter
POB 190, Philomath, OR 97370
February 1990   One issue $1   Six issues $5 cash; $5½ check

Primitive Trap for Birds Does Not Harm Them

My great grandfather used
this during the depression to
help feed his family. It will
catch quail and many other
ground-feeding birds - a
dozen or more at one time.
It does not harm them;
the birds not wanted can
be released.

slope

The trap is made of sticks. Birds feed
down a slope to the entrance, come up thru
the hole, and when ready to leave always
look up and go round and round the sides,
over the small board,
hunting a way out.

A portable version
can be made of
hardware cloth (wire
mesh). It's a box about
20" long, 12" wide and 8" high.
An 8" long tunnel leads in from the
entrance. When trying to leave, the birds go up and over the
tunnel. Roger, Alabama, November

small board   bait
bait

Tools Useful When Camping - Part I

Air Force Survival Knife. Use to shave, cut, shape wood.
Use butt to hammer stakes, small nails. Attach sharpening
stone to back of sheath with epoxy glue. Use pocket to carry
flint or magnesium stick.

Hammer/axe/nail puller combination. Made in Taiwan.

Machette with 12" or 18" blade length. Good one made in
El Salvador. Cut/chop brush and small trees. Dig holes in
ground and ice. Use for defense. 8-10" machine file resharpens.

Small files for resharpening. Small stone, arransan(?)
type, fine-medium grain. Sharpens sizzors, knives, chisels,
etc., even razor blades.

Bow saws. Use to cut trees, trim dead wood. Buy a good
one with an extra blade.

Pulley and rope set. Useful for picking up or dragging
heavy objects.

Additional tools for bikes: chain tool, pressure gauge,
tire tools, air pump, patch kit, 6" adjustable wrench, and
valve tool helps in basic maintenance.

Additional tools for small engines: socket tube wrench
for spark plugs, gap & wire tool, 120 volt neon tester with
clips (checks spark safely when cranking), and 4" adjustable
wrench helps in basic maintenance.

For appliances, generators, batteries, bulbs, radios,
etc., a basic VOM can be used. Also check line voltages. If
utility is lowering them ("brownouts"), that can damage
electrical items hooked into the line. Wildflower, CT, April

A Way to Do Errands in Town

My mother, a confirmed city dweller, insists it's cheaper
to use the bus plus occasional taxis than to own a car. She
rents a car for the day once or twice a year to do a well
planned list of errands in hard-to-get-to places.   Anne, CA

● This book has 164 of MP/DP's 316 pages done during 1990s.

Message Post

May 1990 #26   One issue $1

Portable Dwelling Info-letter
POB 190, Philomath, OR 97370
Six issues $5 cash; $5½ check

Head Strap on Flashlight Leaves Both Hands Free

I sometimes hold a penlight in my mouth
but not when hiking. (I might trip and
ram it against my teeth or into my
throat.) Instead, to my pen-light
I tie a rubber strap (cut from an
inner tube) or a piece of elastic.
The penlight goes along the side
of my head above my ear and the
rubber strap goes around my head.
Julie Summers, Oregon, March

To Revive Weak Batteries

I rub each end vigorously back
and forth on a taut piece of cloth
(such as on my pants when my thigh is
bent). If an erasor is handy I first
clean the ends with it. Both these actions
remove invisible corrosion. If a flashlight is seldom used,
this cleaning before each use brightens the beam.

Warming batteries next to my body, inside my clothes or
sleeping bag, also helps. Don't heat with flame - batteries
may explode if they get hot enough. Julie Summers, March

Tools Useful for Camping - Part II

Vise grip pliers. I carry two 5 WR size in my traveling
tool bag (old camera case). I use them to grip nuts, bolts,
and nails; to cut wire; to clamp wires to battery terminals;
as vise; as handle for 6" saber saw blades, sewing awl needles,
and xacto razor blades. I prefer the name brand.

Rachet head. I prefer one with a magnetic socket that
takes various ¼" hex-based bits, including screwdrivers (for
Phillips, straight, hex, tork, etc.) and drills (for wood,
plastic and light metals). Also, with a ¼" adapter, it can
drive sockets (for nuts and bolts, metric and standard).

Paramedic sizzors. These have their handles at an angle
to the blades so your hand stays out of the slit. They can
cut canvas, screen, light metals, leather, rubber, etc. Buy
them at local medical supplier. Beware of cheap imitations.

Folding shovel. In addition to digging holes, removing
fire ash and preparing garden beds, by sharpening one side it
can be used as an axe or for defense.

Web belt, alice harness, or alice pack. These military
surplus items are useful for carrying machette, shovel, and
other tools. Wildflower, CT, April & Oct. (Part I, in Feb'90
MP, mentioned survival knife, hammer/axe combo, machette,
files/stones, bow saw, pulley, and bike & small engine tools.)

No Special Tool Carried for Pocketknife Sharpening

In the woods I can usually find a rock or pebble that
suffices. It needn't be flat, merely without bumps. In town
I use any convenient concrete edge, such as a step or low wall.

On a regular sharpening stone with uniform fine grains,
I move the blade edge-first, to avoid getting a feather edge.
But on a rock with rough grain, or on concrete, I move the
blade edge-last so that it can ride up over any protruding
grains: better a feather edge than a knick.

Hand holding a small stone for sharpening can be dangerous - keep eyes and mind on your task. If unsure of yourself, try to use a rock heavy enough to stay in place by itself, or wear a stout glove. Julie Summers, Oregon, March

Pump-Spray Bottles and Squeeze Bottles Have Many Uses

I use pump-spray bottles to spray cooking oil on pans, kerosene on rusty bolts, light oil on gears, ammonia on pests (including any two-legged types), and sterile water or hydrogen peroxide on wounds, scrapes and cuts. Various sizes, from very small to two-quart, are available in discount, hardware, and drug stores. Wildflower, Connecticut, October

(We use squeeze bottles as water dispensers when washing things that won't fit under a Portable Faucet. We find many discarded (originally contained shampoo, flavorings, etc.) Squeeze bottles are even simpler and lighter than pump-spray bottles, and better when a stream is wanted. Pump-spray bottles are better when a fine spray is wanted. Holly & Bert)

Degradable Plastics Waste Money and Hinder Recycling

Some plastic recyclers have stopped recycling bags because degradable bags get mixed in and cause problems. We've called for a boycott of degradables. (Degradable materials are also less reusable. Once you have something, the best disposal is to reuse it yourself. Better than recycling, which requires collection, transport, sorting, cleaning, refining, etc.)

When shopping, the best thing is to bring your own reuseable bag. If you don't have it along, then choose either paper or plastic, depending on which you can recycle or reuse. Jeanne Wirka (condensed from Nutrition Action, April 1990)

Fire Black Need Not Be Removed From Pots

If you wish, you can go thru the coating-the-outside-with-soap-before-cooking routine to ease soot removal from a pot which is used over an open fire. But I find it much easier to simply wash the pot's inside and leave the outside alone. I let the pot air dry, then double bag it in a couple of large bags. (I like the large plastic bags used at supermarket checkouts. Paper bags are bulkier and tend to fall apart if they get wet.) I close the bags tightly with a couple of rubber bands. The bags keep the pot from soiling other things in my pack. Julie Summers, Oregon, March

We Use Skunk Cabbage Quite Extensively in Our Cooking

But as a flavoring agent, not as a main course. It imparts an excellent flavor to rice, noodles, or stews. It is dried and saved for use. When harvesting the heart, bring the leaves home and wrap your cheese in it to age. I learned these uses from a friend who learned it from Nisqually Indians with who he grew up. Gary Cropper, POB 864, Snoqualmie,WA 98065; July

After 15 Years Storage, 95% of Wheat Germinated

I reported (in June'89 MP) a sprouting test of 12-year-old wheat. Recently some even older wheat gave an even higher rate of germination: 371 out of 392 kernels showed sprouts ¼" or longer after four days. (A random sample of 400 had been counted out but 8 were broken or crushed and not included in test.)

This wheat, purchased in 1974, was not sprouted as it normally would be for eating. Instead, after soaking about 12 hours, it was drained, then distributed on a cotton cloth which was rolled up and placed on its side in a small plastic

container left open. The cloth was kept moistened.
   Thinking that the different sprouting method or the warmer
temperatures (later in spring) might be responsible for the
greater germination, some of the 1978 wheat was tested with
that method and 86% germinated (versus 76% with earlier method).
   Why did the 1974 wheat sprout better than the 1978? Was
the 1974 wheat actually younger? (The dates are when we
purchased; we don't know when the grain was grown.) Or was it
stored better (cooler) prior to our acquisition? Or was it of
better quality for stor age (higher in vitamin E)?
   Both kinds were stored by us in similar conditions: in
sealed metal containers with no special atmosphere (as I
recall), outside, in shady areas. Carl DeSilva, OR, July

Raw Watercress May Contain Liver Flukes
   Liver flukes are parasites of ruminants (cattle, sheep,
goats, deer, elk) and occasionally of humans. Aquatic snails
are the intermediate hosts. After leaving the snail, the
fluke forms a cyst around itself. This form is found on vegetation or in water. Barely visible to the naked eye (small
pin-point tan colored spots), it can be identified only thru
a microscope. Humans have reportedly become infected by eating contaminated watercress. Cooking should destroy the cysts.
Gary Zimmerman, DVM, Col.of Vet.Med.,OSU; May'89 (reply to JS)

Poison Oak Most Dangerous if Smoke is Breathed
   The letters in Message Post (Sept'86, Feb'87, June'87,
June'88 & Dec'88) are interesting.
   The mucus membranes of the mouth, esophagus, stomach and
intestines are less penetrable to the oil than is the surface
skin. That is why Robin got a rash on his/her anus - the oil
came out in the feces and caused a reaction on surface skin.
   Julie's point (that if anaphylactic shock were likely,
manufacturers wouldn't sell the oil over the counter) is good.
   A bigger danger is breathing the smoke of a poison oak
fire into your lungs along with tiny droplets of the oil. In
my research that is the only cause of death I have heard about.
   For people who are highly allergic to poison oak, I suggest
eating a small piece of mango skin every day - then every week.
It has the same oil as poison oak. My son, just back from
Australia, mentioned "mango rash" around people's mouths.
(Have you heard of anybody dying from eating a mango? I have
not, so I think it would be safe to eat a little skin.) The
oil does not degrade, so you can dry the skin and it will keep
for years. To keep up a tolerance, it is necessary to continue
to expose yourself to the oil, or your sensitivity will return.
   In my book Poison Oak & Poison Ivy (reviewed in May'82 MP),
I tell the possible risks - because Jon Seaver is right: "You
oughta know something of the risks you face." Sandra Baker, CA

We Had a Lot of Trouble With Ticks Last Spring
   One visitor got Lyme disease; we aren't sure from her home
ticks or from ours. The best control measure for us has been
to keep the grass cut short wherever we spend much time.
   We got some info on non-pesticide control and traps from:
Bio-Integral Resource Center, POB 7474, Berkeley, CA 94707.
It cost about $3½. Please put everything you can find on
ticks in Message Post. Anne Callaway, California, March

Cat Flea/Tick Collars Worn on Ankles Repel Ticks
   Nancy Sturhan, in WA, wore them over her work boots but
under her jeans. (Sci.News,29April'89)

Large Tents are Versatile

Our group lived and worked in southern Nevada for 12 years before moving to Washington. During that time we accumulated equipment for manufacturing almost anything we might want (as well as lots of just plain stuff) and hauled it north in old travel trailers. After arrival we needed storage for the stuff so that we could utilize the trailers. We spotted an ad for 16x32' military tents and bought two. As we get more permanent facilities constructed, we'll move the equipment in from the tents and set it up, but that'll take time.

Meanwhile we're getting our biosystems started. We've got 52 diary goats, 32 steers, 9 sheep, 2 cows, chickens, rabbits, and a pony. All these critters require space and storage, and the tents have played an important part. We're doing our milking and our intensive bottle feeding in an 18x52' we call the barn tent, and we have a second large tent that we're setting up to handle meals during the summer. Additionally we've picked up a few 16'-wide octagonal tents that are handy for various purposes.

The tents allow us maximum versatility in layout, both within the tent and in the selection of a place for the tent. There are a hundred ways to lay out a barn, milk parlor or workshop, and with the tents, we don't have to be locked into any one way. We're constantly shifting things around to meet our current needs or the latest insight into how things can be done better. For example, because of the embryonic state of our electrical system, we presently cluster our pens and facilities. Later we'll be able to spread out into a more dispersed format. When we no longer need the tents for year-round operations, we plan on using them for gatherings we will host from May until September, and for hay and equipment storage fall and winter.

A surprising side effect is the image the tents convey to visitors. So many people have enjoyed the M*A*S*H series that a group with lots of army tents is not all that strange. On the other hand, it is a different setting. Windward operates by the consensus process which differs from the competitive system in subtle but powerful ways. If people are in surroundings that resemble what they are used to, on a fundamental level, they presume that "things" work in the usual ways. In unusual surroundings, that presumption isn't so strong. Walt Patrick The Windward Foundation, POB 51, Klickitat, WA 98628; (509) 369-2448; March
(Notes from Windward describe their daily activities. Sample $2. (22p.8x11))

For Fire Safety, Make Exits Easy

In 1967 two children died when unprotected interior foam insulation caught fire in a garage where they were playing. "There was just no chance of getting to them", said their father. "When the insulation was burning, the flames were so red hot you could hear the fire roar."

Though plastic on fire will sometimes go out when blown on (unlike wood), under certain conditions polyurethane foam (even "non-burning" types) has a "very high flame spread, high early heat output, and produces large quantities of dense black smoke.... Ironically, flame inhibitors usually increase toxic gases or greatly increase amount of smoke." (Refried Domes, review on page 8.)

Most other plastics burn, including polyethylene (bags, tarps) and styrofoam (packing, cups), as do most natural materials (straw, leaves, thin wood.) Most materials that won't burn (adobe, rocks) are heavy and dangerous in earthquakes. So, the best advice may be:
Be careful using flames. And build your shelter so all occupants can get out quickly if it does catch fire.

The safest entrance covering may be a curtain which you can simply duck under or pull up. (If wind's a problem, anchor the lower corners with elastic straps.) A zipper may jam. So may a door if warped by heat, or in the smoke a child might not find the latch. B & H

Ventilation Vital Where Flame Used

In answer to Anne's question, use of any flame appliance (including catalytic utensils) in an enclosed space mandates absolutely reliable ventilation. Carbon monoxide poisoning may manifest as either acute poisoning (one exposure produced symptoms) or chronic (you lose neurons to hypoxia, your children become intellectually stunted). Also, children raised in homes with flame appliances therein, seem to fall prey to more frequent respiratory infections, and to more often develop asthma. This problem may be more pronounced with wick appliances which, I imagine, provide less complete combustion than a mantle can. Jon Seaver RN, Michigan, March

Always Use a "Full-Spectrum" Light

if you use fluorescents. It warns the iris to close so the retina is not "burned". Paul Doerr, Calif., November

Kenwood Amateur Radios Fail in Salt Air

Our Kenwood 140-S has been repaired five times in the year we've owned it, and has never worked for more than 14 days. Kenwood personnel have advised that their radios, even properly and professionally installed, are not suitable aboard boats. Fred & Lori (from Dec'89 Seven Seas, address on page C)

Skate Usable on Rail or Road?

I'm looking for a skate/scooter I can use for cross-country travel, going between cities on railroads, then using side roads/streets to detour around rail yards. Any made? Or kits? Or plans?

One foot rests on the skate, the other pushes (like with a skate board). When one leg tires, change off.

The skate may have two main wheels, front and rear, and two or four auxiliary wheels which flip down for rail use (to keep the skate on the rail) and up for road use. I'd like main wheels that are fairly large (kiddy bike size?) for low resistance and so they don't catch in holes, and rubber tired for quiet operation (to hear approaching trains).

Yurt Spacious But Hard to Find Places For Near City

We have lived for most of five years in our 16-foot yurt.
We are now a family of six. The largest group we've had in
our yurt at one time, for a party, was 22 - 14 children and 8
adults. It was crowded but everyone had a lot of fun.

We've never had any trouble entertaining friends during
good weather as long as we are in a place where the owners of
the place want to join in the party (i.e. we have the same
circle of friends). We just throw a barbeque party, pull out
the guitar, and sit around and sing.

While living in a house last winter, all of us were home-
sick for our yurt - except for our oldest boy because he
likes cooking with the electric kitchen gadgets. Once I read
that some Mongolians obtained a castle in which to live.
They put their animals in the castle and pitched their yurts
outside the wall. Now I feel the same way.

The hardest part of portable living has been finding
places to put our yurt where we are welcome. We have always
traded work for a camping site, but it's never been easy to
find people who want that, so we are frequently stuck someplace longer than we want to be, or forced to move by circumstances we're not responsible for. It would feel much more
comfortable if we were the ones to choose to move on.

We can't get too far from the Bay Area because that's
where my husband works (8 days a month) to feed us all (four
children). Otherwise we'd head for the wilderness. As it is
now, I think we are going to try living out of our VW bus in
the city this summer. We've been able to stay off welfare for
3 years and don't want to get back into that again.   Anne

Inner City People Pleasanter to Camp Near

We never had any hassle until we moved to this more-rural
area last year. The houses are mostly on 3+ acre lots. We
had a chores-for-rent exchange with friends who own vacation
property here. But someone complained to the building
inspector, and we had to take our yurt down. Fortunately we
were able to use the house for the winter, because the owners
never come here then. The neighbors said they hadn't
complained, so we think it was the meter reader, mail man, or
fire inspector - all of whom have been here.

In retrospect I see we didn't pay enough attention to
camoflage. The yurt is covered with blue tarps - perfect for
the city where every few houses there's some junk under a blue
tarp. But here in the future, we'll use camoflage or dark
green tarps, and we'll hide the yurt from view of the driveway
(it was already hidden from neighbors and from the street).

This past year has been our first experience camping
rurally. The previous four years our yurt was set up in the
city (San Francisco Bay Area) in various friends' back yards.
Although we really appreciate the beautiful trees, clean air,
peace and quiet, etc., we've found the inner city people
easier to live with. It would seem that with so much space
the country folks would not notice us so much. But the city
neighbors were much more live-and-let-live types.

I'm coming to the opinion that the more people own, the
more they get locked into the social pressures which don't
let them do what they want with what they own. In other
words, they don't really own their property; it owns them.

Everyone we know has a house and privately or not so privately wonders what's wrong with us that we don't have one too.
I'm always glad to get your newsletter. It encourages me just

to know there are others like us out there facing similar
problems. Anne Callaway, California, September & March

Yurt Survives Strong Wind and Heavy Snow

Last winter we experienced hurricane-force winds in the
yurt. The whole structure was moving and distorting. Things
hanging from the rafters were swinging for 24 hours. But the
yurt stayed put. It was tied down to six tent pegs - nothing
special. My husband threw two extra ropes over the clear
plastic we use to cover the opening in the ceiling. (The clear
plastic slides off for ventilation, using ropes attached by
Lexan clips to the plastic. The Lexan clips work very well.)

A few ropes had to be tightened, a few pieces of plastic
pushed in under the leaks, and the blankets we use to insulate
the ceiling had to be pushed back in place in a few spots,
then we were back in business again, good as new.

Around the neighborhood there were fences blown down,
porches blown off, windows broken, screens blown away, plus
lots of broken branches. Next door there were circular marks
worn in a wooden fence by dead weeds whipping back and forth.

This winter was the first time we "camped" in snow. That
big storm in February dumped three feet of wet, sticky snow
on this area. The yurt handled the weight - no problem. But
a wickiup-shaped tent collapsed.

Lots of trees and branches fell due to the heavy snow
build up. The top of a tree (8" diameter) fell and crushed
our entryway tent set-up. It brushed against our oldest boy.
He wasn't hurt, but pretty scared. We believe that even that
large a branch wouldn't have hurt anyone inside the yurt,
though it would wreck the tent. Our yurt is strong. (We
built it using Chuck & Laurel Cox's plans for the frame, and
covered by lashing on old blankets and cheap plastic tarps.)

The entry porch needed a new plastic cover, but the PVC
pipe arches just sprang back into shape once the weight was
removed. We had no choice about where to put the tent on this
property, and knew it was too close to the trees for comfort.

Except for this deep snow, we've found the colder, drier
weather in the Sierra foothills more comfortable than the
warmer, damper winters near the coast. The deep snow was just
plain hard work shoveling paths. Rain goes away by itself,
but leaves all that mud. Anne Callaway, CA, Sept. & March

I May Soon Be Living in a Tipi With a Young Child

Or perhaps in a twipi, a yurt, or a wickiup - investigating possibilities. I'm also interested in connecting with
other portable shelter dwellers. Chris White, 157 Woodland
Avenue, Lexington, KY 40502; November

Suggestions for Adding Insulation to Portable Shelter

I live in a canvas yurt and also a dome. This is my
fourth Oregon winter coming up and I'm not looking forward to
the cold and dampness - tho it usually isn't bad enough to get
me back into the suburbs. I have thought about lining the yurt
with wool felt - though I haven't gathered that much together
yet. I'd like to see other yurt set-ups. Jao, OR, August

(Reply) Any lining material will help insulate. Even plastic.
If there isn't much wind, I believe several thin liners would
insulate more than would one thick liner. On the other hand,
if the yurt is buffeted by wind a lot, then something heavy
like wool felt might insulate more. Try to space the liner(s)
½" to 1" from the yurt (and from each other) for most warmth.

Quite often I find a lightweight white foam, sort of closed cell, about 1/8" thick, thrown out at furniture stores (used to pad shipments). Several layers of it gives good insulation on a ceiling or wall (but not on a floor - we tried some once for bed padding and it soon crushed paper thin.) It also tears easily, so I'd cover it with something tougher.

I wonder if you've tried suspending a tarp above the yurt and extending out a foot or so beyond it. By keeping the rain off the roof, it might make the yurt drier and warmer. Space the tarp a few inches above the yurt's roof. (If just layed on, it will hold moisture in the yurt's roof.) Bert, Sept.

Techniques for Working and Walking in the Rain

For working I wait until it lets up and wear as few clothes as possible. It's a lot easier to dry wet skin and warm up, than to take off piles of wet clothes that are hard to get dry again in wet weather.

For walking I prefer the good old umbrella. It doesn't make you sweat and it's not noisy like a raincoat or poncho. It's also faster to put on, so to speak. I wish there were a way to make an umbrella since they are so fragile and not always available in stores. Anne Callaway, Calif., September

Condos Condemned

Condominiums combine all the worst features of owning a home with all of the worst features of apartment life, with the unique and added annoyance of a "condominium board" consisting of little tyrants who call tow trucks on other people's cars in in the parking lot and write official-sounding "notices" about having "scruffy-looking" guests.

Condos were the biggest fast-buck scam around for someone with the money to buy a building, sell it unit by unit, and then get the hell out with the money. Some condo high-rise buildings along Chicago's lakefront strip were built as quickly as possible during a construction frenzy about 25 years ago, and built so close to the lake that huge waves were crashing through the lobby windows during a period of high water levels a few years ago. The cracks in these cheap concrete struct- ures are now becoming more and more evident, and I have seen them weaken to the point that shoring crews were holding up the corners of a building with huge jacks and timbers while they patched it up. What an investment!

A person would be out of their mind to buy a home in this city, as doing so would place them squarely in the crosshairs of politicians looking for more and more tax dollars from fewer and fewer working people. Property taxes are rising all the time, and the homeowner is being milked dry; largely to support the sort of people who are going to lower the value of his property until he will only be able to get out at a loss.

Of course, a property "owner" actually only rents his property from the government, which can seize it for failure to pay taxes. And an apartment dweller is actually paying as much as a homeowner, in many cases, except for a down payment.

As I look around me, I notice how society "conspires" to keep us chained down to rent or house payments. Did you notice how, as more women started working, the price of everything increased to the point that it now takes two people working full-time to support the same household that one person could support before? Of course, people with too much "disposable income" could be dangerous, because they'd be able to lift their noses from the grindstone long enough to see what was happening around them. J. Wieser, Illinois, January

Message Post

Portable Dwelling Info-letter
POB 190, Philomath, OR 97370

July 1990   One issue $1   Six issues $5 cash; $5½ check

When Walking a Bicycle That Has a Flat

A partly or fully deflated tube and tire will gradually rotate on the rim. But the valve stem is held by its hole in the rim and cannot follow. This may eventually tear the valve stem from the tube, resulting in an unpatchable leak.

valve stem at
bad angle

rotate tire and
tube this way to
reposition valve
stem

To avoid this, I can carry the bike, of course. But that will be tiring if I'm going a long distance with a loaded bike.

If I decide to walk the bike, I first transfer most of the load, if necessary, so it rides on the unflat wheel. Then period- ically I stop and check the tire, and if necessary rotate the tire and tube to put the valve stem back in its proper unstressed position. This is easiest if the tube is deflated as completely as possible and the wheel is off the ground. With one hand I hold on to the rim and push, while with the other hand I jiggle and pull the tire in the opposite direction. Then I move my hands a few inches along the rim and do the same thing. I repeat, working my way around the wheel, until the valve stem is perpendicular to the rim. Julie Summers, 1986

valve stem at
proper angle

I Intended to Bicycle Around Last Summer

But rides with friends and hitch-hiking seemed to happen easier. I haven't got a real touring bicycle yet. I like the new lightweight mountain bikes (except for the prices). Aarran, British Columbia, March

Some Day I'm Going to Have a Fold-Up Bicycle

It will pull a fold-up trailer carrying a fold-up boat. I saw your ad in Messing About in Boats. Paul, NH, March

A Friend and I are Leaving Home to Travel the USA by Foot

Julie and I have back packs, sleeping bags, and a small tent. Jenn, New York, February

Walking Plus Occasional Taxi Saves Money

My car was getting old and I was spending a lot keeping it in shape. So I got rid of it. I live four miles from town and found walking wasn't bad at all and I feel so much better. I usually walk in, stay over night with a friend, next day do what I have to, then go back home. I can always take a taxi when I bring groceries back, if I don't catch a ride.

I'm still planning to get a tipi but not sure when. I have to get new flooring on my deck this year. That's where I'll put my tipi. I want to get a good one as I would like to live in it for 8 or 9 months a year. Until I get one, I'll use my camper and the two tents I have. Gloria Orr, NY, April

Camping Out Near Towns or in Large City Parks

The piece about using a camo net (June'87 MP) is good. Other ideas in this field? Ellis Weinberger, Exeter, U.K., Apr

I Am Reducing My Possessions to Travel Lighter and Faster

I have a mini van so I want to condense what I have to fit
in it. It's 6 cylinder so could pull a small storage trailer
like a U-haul. I am contemplating tipi living in a community
during June and July, and am trying to decide how.

I plan to keep two file cabinets (letter size, 2 drawer),
which I will use with a board across the top as my work
station. I make jewelry and don't know if my gold and
sterling silver wire will be protected in a tipi. (I know how
clothes are hung up inside but that's all.) Samie, AL, April

On the Road Three Months

Enjoying the excitement of new horizons, places to explore,
and interesting, friendly folks. Few mechanical problems; most
I can deal with. Gas our major expense, at 5-7 mpg. Overnight
stops not difficult: we use reststops on the freeway (except
Calif.); mall parking lots (dark corner), industrial areas and
church parking lots in town; any out-of-the-way spot. High-use
agricultural areas are most difficult. One contact with police
was positive - brake lights out, guided us to nearby church
parking lot. Travel slow (40-50) and make lots of stops for
food prep, exercise, exploring, junk stores. When we meet new
folks, we tell them we are looking for homeschoolers interested
in community and simple living, and they generally refer us to
friends with similar interests.

Food is a bit tricky for us, as we are vegetarians without
refrigeration. We stock up on organic vegies at the co-ops,
and store them in insulated areas low in the bus. It has
generally been cool enough (Jan-Apr) to get away with this.
Sometimes we must resort to mainstream produce. We haul lots
of grains, beans and dried fruit in square 5 gal buckets. We
stock up on bulk foods through Nutrasource in the northwest and
Tucson Co-op Warehouse in southwest. We cook on a propane one-
burner (would like two) and our "tin" wood stove. Use a dishpan. Water in plastic 5 gal (spring water when available, or
hook our purifier to public water). No plumbing in our bus.

To bathe we heat water and sponge it, visit hotsprings
often (have done considerable research on locations). We dig
holes or roll rocks to poop; plastic bucket with lid for town/
emergency use.

We make sure the boys, who are very social, get plenty of
time with other kids. We trade off with other parents whenever possible. When in town, we visit parks. Our land search
and homeschool interest connects us with people. We never pass
a bulletin board, especially in co-ops, peace centers, used
bookstores, country stores, etc., without looking at it.

So far, we like the Gila National Forest best, especially
the southwest section. Silver City is a great small town with
alternative schools (including high school), co-op, small university. 3.3 million acres of forest are nearby, including the
Gila Wilderness Area, inhabited for thousands of years, now
saved from development. The canyons are filled with the
presence of the ancient ones. Jai, New Mexico, April

I'd Like to Retain a Low Rent Home While Traveling

Do you have any advice on this? I'm presently renting a
room in a large home (I'm a Humbolt State University student),
but will be away overseas on a low budget journey across
Africa for at least a year. I'd like to have a "home" to come
back to when I return. I'm particularly interested in small
cabins, trailers, etc. I lived in a disabled VW van (no
wheels) for two years. David Buck, CA, May

Message Post

October 1990   One issue $1

Portable Dwelling Info-letter
POB 190,   Philomath, OR 97370
Six issues $5 cash; $5½ check

Hands-Free Magnifier Holder

In the 1990 Nature Company's catalog, is a stand which holds a low-power magnifying glass and alligator clips. It allows hand-free viewing of objects, which is very helpful when dissecting flowers to identify them or when removing a splinter from one's own hand. But rather than spend $15 (plus $4 postage) and encourage unnecessary use of resources, I came up with this free-from-salvaged-materials version.

rubber straps

The stand is improvised from a piece of drift wood, sculpture, book end, or whatever you have available. (I used a piece of junk machinery.)

For the arms I used clothes-hanger wire. (If my magnifier were heavier, I'd double the wire.) To bend wire at sharp angles, I hold it with pliers. After positioning the pliers, I move the wire **well away** from my face, and direct my force so that, if the pliers slip, nothing will move towards my face. Particularly if the wire is long, I'm careful not to whip the distant end into my face. I hold that end down with my foot.

A clothes pin, spring metal clip, or alligator clip is fastened to the wire arm with a rubber strap cut from a blown innertube (discarded at bike shops). Julie Summers, OR, May

I Would Like to Live Simply and Portably in the Wilderness

I am just beginning to learn the techniques of survival, so any help and references (human preferred) would be appreciated. I am a 43 year old woman. I saw your ad in Great Expeditions. Valerie Morgan, P.O.Box 9, Lion's Head, Ontario, Canada, NOH 1W0; August

We Are Selling Our Home and Plan to Travel Awhile

This is a **very** new experience for us. I saw your Home Education mag ad. Mary Aschenbrener, Wisconsin, July

Next Year, I Plan a Road Trip Across the U.S.

And maybe into Canada. I've got an old jalopy and very little cash. I'm originally from the D.C. area. Elio, VA, Aug

Comfortable Compact Car Camping.   Part I: The Car

The last three summers, I've taken 12,000-mile-long trips with a friend, including one to Alaska and the Yukon, and another up the spectacular Dempster Highway over two mountain ranges and two ferry crossings to Inuvik, North West Territories. On both trips we camped out almost every night. I'd like to pass along tips and ideas from these trips and from many years of similar ones.

On our first trip, we had a used Volvo station wagon. This was very nice in terms of comfort and space. But the new Toyota Corolla hatchback we had on the later trips had almost as much room, twice the gas mileage, and was just as comfortable. A back seat that folds **flat**, doesn't have large wheel

bases and doesn't have a space between it and the front seat,
is preferable. Check for good clearance under the car, and if
you carry a canoe, look for a roof with gutters and solid hooks
under the car in front and rear for tie downs.

Service the car before you go, making sure the tires are
in good condition (including the spare), the fluids are all
topped up and you have new oil and air filters. If your car
is foreign made, you may want to take extra filters as it may
be hard to get non-US-made ones in some areas. Take time out
on a long trip to have it serviced again after 4,000 or 5,000
miles. We've never needed (or taken) extra gas, fan belt,
etc., or special tools, but make sure your jack is intact and
you know how to use it, and take your car manual and registration. A screwdriver for tightening loose screws, some glass
cleaner and rags or paper towels for wiping windows, and a pair
of pliers for all sorts of things, completes your tool kit.
Artificial sheepskin seat covers are great both for keeping
cool in the summer and warm in the winter.

Our only addition to car care equipment was a large
sponge, a necessity after thousands of miles on muddy dirt
roads when no commercial car wash was available. And rain gear
and waterproof boots came in handy when the car wash was a do-
it-yourself high pressure hose!

If you are traveling with a "significant other" who is not
a close legal relative, consider each of you getting a Medical
Power of Attorney (technically, Power of Attorney and Temporary
Guardianship) for the other. Then in case of a serious accident, there will be no hassle about hospital visiting, granting
permission to operate, etc. Finally, check that your car
insurance covers out-of-state accidents and Canada, if you
plan to drive there. Jan Brown, Massachusetts, 1988 & 1989
(This article was published in Women Outdoors Magazine, v8n4,

For health, minimize exposure to solvents.
Kerosene is not used as widely as formerly, but should
still be avoided. Dr Hulda Clark found many of the alcoholics
in her clinic had a build up of beryllium from kerosene fumes
of lamps previously used by the patients. Beryllium in the
body causes depression by blocking normal pleasure centers.

Since lead was replaced by even more dangerous gas
additives in California, hundreds of people have gotten toxic
illnesses. Other states seem to have less toxic gasoline.
Beware of breathing gas fumes continuously.

Most shampoos now have traces of propyl alcohol (same as
rubbing alcohol) in them, and Clark found it in all breast
cancer cases she treated. It slowly erodes and accumulates.

Almost all other solvents and additives commonly found in
potions, lotions and cleansers bring on health problems.
Clark's "Cure for All Diseases" is a testament to living
without the usual packaged and processed products.

Most houses with their rugs, upholstered furniture, and
other bacteria catchers are invitations to sickness. Persons
who can adapt to a simple living plan have a much better
chance for health. Al Fry, Idaho, April

Spit trick for silicone glue application.
Apply glue to item. Insert finger in mouth to moisten.
Spread glue with finger. Silicone won't stick to wet finger.
Water also works but not as well, and spit is always handy.

I don't think silicone is too toxic. The seams of fish
tanks are sealed with it, and tropical fish die if you look at
them sideways. Double Dorji

Message Post

Portable Dwelling Info-letter
POB 190, Philomath, OR 97370
Jan. 1991 #27   One issue $1   Six issues $5 cash; $5½ check

Spots a Few Miles Apart Have Quite Different Microclimates

We are only ten miles from last winter's spot. But we've had heavy frost every night for weeks, while our former neighbors had only one frost. We've seen 21° three mornings. This is unexpected. Last summer was much hotter here than at our former spot "up the hill" (1000 feet higher).

The cause may be: we are camped on a ridge within a little valley. The valley bottom often gets frost.

This winter so far has been much colder than last. Today (Dec. 15) was our first snow. The boys were disappointed as rain soon melted it. 3 miles away and 200' up, 4" accumulated.

Fortunately we have plenty of warm clothes and a good propane heater. (Wood heat would attract attention.) Anne, CA

My Family and I Now Live in TWO Tleantos

The new one is presently about 400 miles south of the first one. We migrate between, not so much for winter warmth (the southern spot isn't much warmer then), as for a sunnier spring and to be closer to the couple whose kids we board.

The new tleanto is much like the original (Sept'85 & Sept '86 MP) except longer: 36' total. (Actually there are two separate frames joined end-to-end with covers overlapping.) It contains two insulated rooms plus some uninsulated areas.

Usually two adults and three small children live in it; on occasion two additional adults. During the coldest weather for warmth we all crowd together into one room. (One morning I measured 22°F outside, 30° within the outer shell, and 48° in our room.) We don't want a heating stove with the fire hazard, fumes, smoke, work. During milder weather we spread out. The tleantos are warmest where there is little wind.

For ceiling insulation, I replaced the leaves with sheets of flexible foam, which are quicker to put on and easier to keep in place. I am now gradually replacing the foam with bubble plastic (as we find it) which has not been bothered much by animals (whereas the foam becomes nests if not protected). We take down each tleanto when we leave for the season, to avoid mouse/rat infestation.

Another change: I angle the south wall with the top farther out than the bottom, so the sun doesn't reflect far. (Once we were careless and attracted a hunter who was on the slope below. Luckily, he was friendly.)

I have now lived in tleantos for most of five years and am quite satisfied with them. Wanda, California, August & Nov.

To Prevent Condensation, We Lined Our Yurt Ceiling With Plastic

Layer of plastic, lots of blankets, then the roof. It worked well last winter. Anne, California, August

Two Pails Together Protect Long Objects

Round plastic pails are made in various widths. So a wide pail can be placed, inverted, over a narrow pail to protect objects too long for a single pail. The pails probably won't seal airtight, but will keep out rain and rodents. Last fall we stored some things this way. The pails fit so firmly that strapping didn't seem necessary. However a racoon or larger animal could probably work them apart. Bert & Holly, Oregon, November

Materials Worth Accumulating for Long-Period Camping

These items are cheap when found new "on special" or used at garage sales - or free when found in dumpsters. Whereas they may be expensive or unobtainable if you're rushed.

PLASTIC PAILS for storing other things, and for use at a camp kitchen. In-store bakeries often sell them, 50¢-75¢ each. Unless free, check that lids and rims fit well and are undamaged. (Lids that are notched to open, may have excessive cuts that extend to the lid's top, sever the gasket, or even penetrate the pail. Also pails are sometimes badly scarred inside or even holed by sharp utensils used to dig or scrape out frozen contents.) Clean before using, outside as well as in, to remove any food remnants/odors which might attract animals. Larger containers, such as 55-gal barrels with heads that come off, are also useful, but harder to find, cost more per capacity, and harder to transport, especially by backpack or bike. So, before acquiring anything that needs protection but won't fit in one or two 5-gallon pails, we think thrice!

PLASTIC JUGS. Milk/juice jugs are fine for storing, but too flimsy for reliably hauling water. Bleach jugs (discarded at laudromats) and various other jugs are sturdier. Read label; but also sniff inside for unfamiliar odors. (The jug might have been reused for toxic chemicals that linger. Bleach seems to rinse out.) We put only wash water in a jug for a month or more, before using for drinking water or (after thoroughly drying) for storage of rice, beans, etc.

SHEET PLASTIC (polyethylene) for tarps and tents. We use both clear and black (and white if we find it), either new (on special) or salvaged (furniture store discards).

TWINE for tying out tarps, rigging clotheslines, etc. Much twine is discarded by many stores, but most of this is clear/white - okay inside but deteriorated outside by sunshine. Black, orange or pink twine, used for hay bailing, is more durable outside; black is best.

RESILIANT FOAM, for floor padding and mattresses. At rug store dumpsters, we sometimes have our choice of scraps of new foam or large sheets of old foam. The latter, removed during remodelings, smells of cigarette smoke, etc., so we place plastic over as well as under it. The least desirable foam is the kind that looks like fruit cake, with various colored fragments stuck together. It's heavier, lumpier, weaker.

CLOTH remainders and remnants. Some discount fabric shops sell unpopular patterns for 50¢ a yard or less. Piece together to form top tarps. Dark, drab blacks, greys, browns and greens "visually pollute" least. Synthetics are more durable in wet; cotton in sun; acrylic withstands both quite well. Netting, such as old window curtains, is useful for blocking bugs.

Not included above are items most readers will already have for short camping, hiking, car travel, or indoor living; such as lighters, flashlight, water sterilizer (iodine crystals or tincture), knife(s), needle & thread, utensils, etc. H & B

Footwear Made from Salvaged Materials is Warm and Dry

While sewing up snow pants from used rain coats (the executive type), and felting mittens from fleeces being thrown out at a Barter Faire, I devised an alternative to $90 Sorvel boots: I made a felted boot slip-in with cuff, which goes into vibram-soled galoshes; with gaters made from raincoats.

Since that moment, both Jai and I have not been tempted to buy things we wanted but could not afford. Going beyond recycling, we just don't bring the stuff in! Even our food comes in bulk bags we reuse. Beguin Z. Lapwing, WA, December

Aluminized Mylar "Space Blanket" Reduces Heat Loss

If suspended above you, it will reflect back 80% of your
body heat, adding to your warmth. It will also add to your
safety if ever a helicopter with an infrared sensor is night-
stalking you. Above the mylar, suspend camo netting or an
improvised burlap "shaggy". Wildflower, Connecticut, July

Bedding in the Bush

Cheap sleeping bags provide plenty of warmth if two or
more are used together. (A single cheap bag loses much heat
out its sewen-through seams; but with two together, most seams
are offset.) Cheap (light) bags are more versatile, easier
to dry, and not much heavier than is one expensive bag.

Synthetic (usually nylon) covers and liners are the most
durable in a damp climate; we acquire cotton-covered bags only
if free. A bag with defective zipper is usable as a quilt.
Blankets seem heavier for the warmth; we acquire only if free.

Used bags (or blankets) we seal up in pails for a few
months or put through a hot dryer to kill any vermin (details
in 1980m MP). We may leave extra bedding stashed in pails
near places we travel to often, rather than carrying it along.

At base camps we use several layers of foam under us.
But it's bulky and heavy, so when light camping, we take only
one thin piece and build a bed out of springy weeds.

When we camp together, we put opened sleeping bags over
us as quilts. On top we place an old sheet (if we have one)
to collect most of the moisture. The sheet is faster to dry,
less to rot if it doesn't dry, or lighter to carry along.

Our bedding would not favorably impress the staff of
Outdoor Fashions magazine, but it keeps us warm and comfy.
                                                      H & B, OR

We Often Have Large Quantities of Laundry to Dry

We let it drip outside for a day, and then hang it inside
for heat from the stove, lantern, or heater to finish off.
But this causes a lot more condensation on the walls. Our
yurt has some insulation. Maybe we need more.

We have the walls arranged so the condensation runs off
into the dirt, instead of dripping on our heads, which isn't
too bad. But we'd rather not have it at all. Anne, CA, Dec.

We Like Simple Showers Very Much

For simplicity, water conservation, and reliable temperature control (especially important for children who could
scald themselves with fauceted showers). A little practice
was needed before the motions became easy. Half-gallon jugs
with handles are easier for me to hold than are quart/liter
bottles lacking handles (as most do). If only gallon jugs are
available, I fill just half way for myself, less than a fourth
for the oldest child (who usually bathes herself; the younger
ones don't yet). Wanda, California, August

I Live on a 30' Houseboat in the Delta of Northern California

My neighbors include ducks and lots of other river-rats
(that's what we boaters are known as). We fish for crawdad,
catfish, etc. It is very easy to get 300 or 400 crawdads in
one hour using a slice of beef heart. No, they do not eat it;
they just grab on and hold. You can bring in 3 or 4 each time
you cast (sometimes just one). This is a great place to live
and fish. I'm looking for others, women especially, that like
boating and fishing. I'm 45. Richard Arndt, 333 Tuleburg
Levee #2, Stockton, CA 95203; September

● Most addresses and prices in here are out of date.

The Past Five Summers I Horse Trekked in the Pacific Northwest

I have two horses, both for riding and packstock. I have trekked, mostly solo, in the Coast Range, Cascades, and central and eastern Oregon. The High Plateau is where my heart belongs.

The sun and warmth and long days and fresh green make for easy living during summer. But I don't know enough yet to make it all year around in the backcountry. Another obstacle is a certain lostness in my loneliness. I would like other people (a tribe, so to speak) living a nomadic "horse-way-of-life" along with the appropriate philosophies and techniques to move lightly on the land.

This spring I plan a short trip back to Germany, to see my folks and to look at some alternative ways of living going on there. An old buddy is part of a group of 500 people who are about to start an "eco-village" in what was East Germany.

Upon coming back, I will move my outfit to a basecamp in the Ochoco's (east of Prineville), then drift from there over to the Steen Mtns, and later back north towards the Hell's Canyon of the Snake River. But I'm totally open to rerouting, as long as I'm able to make out a spot to spend the winter at.

I'm presently living in a camper with tarp-porch extension in the backyard of friends and do housesitting here and there. That is okay but it keeps me too far from the earth.

Other crafty skills include saddle and leathercraft, fine woodworking (for 15 years - trained in Germany), spontaneous street and vaudeville theatre performer, and photographer with equipment for both 35 mm still and 16 mm movie. I am currently producing a couple of slideshows about the use of horses in wilderness: one about backcountry access by alter-abled riders; the other about high plateau places for trekking and long camping.

I have found that grainsacks, as well as army surplus duffel bags, make excellent horsepacking gear.

The single one-front-foot hobble with 20 feet of soft rope to a screw-in stake (as sold in department stores for stake-outs of large dogs - but don't use the little dingy swivel to tie the rope to!) is the best way to allow for controlled grazing of the stock. Mine are rolling and resting and moving "free" on that device each morning and evening feed. I just have to be in sight.

Over night, the hitchline strung between two solid points well above horses' heads, does the job, without any entanglement.

On Forest Service land, I like to make contact with the FS people and offer myself as a volunteer. That way, I'll get accepted when spotted and usually left alone when dropping out of sight. To private landowners, I say I'm a backcountry photographer. Works well - and is part of the truth, too. Eberhard Eichner, POB 23433, Eugene, OR 97402;   February

Info Wanted About Native American Living on the Oregon Coast

I noticed Julie's review in MP #27 of "Tillamook Indians of Oregon Coast". I'd like to learn more about living there and about foods and shelters there. Is it true that coastal Native Americans had a high standard of living compared to other groups? I'm currently living about half time in a small 30-year-old trailer in the woods east of Florence, and the rest of the time with a combination of truck/camper/bicycle mobility.

Also I like the idea of "confluential" living or "flowing together". As a way of relating, this seems to come closest to having the best of all worlds with the least structure, exposure, and other costs. Roy, Oregon, January

I Am Newly Moved Into a Converted Bus-Camper

Ms C. M., Arizona, November

I Have a Chouinard "Megamid" Tent

It's 9x9' and weighs 3 lbs. I've used it extensively in rain, snow, very high winds, and desert. In spite of having no floor (use poncho or tarp if you want), my only weather-related problems were during extreme downpours and blowing powder snow.

The original center pole was weak. They now have a beefed-up pole that should not fail. A design fault not corrected is the #5 coil zipper. When this fails you can get by with the full-length velcro flap, but you may want to replace it with a #7 coil zipper. (The tent gets stuffed into a sack smaller than a football, which could break teeth off a toothed zipper.)

Also this tent is too expensive. It could be made much cheaper at home. I'd like one twice as large (18x 18'). Do you know anyone who can make this? The ripstop nylon used in my original tent, is also used in cargo parachutes that take huge loads, and so should be satisfactory. Henry, AZ, Aug.

(Comment:) To withstand as much wind or snow load, a tent twice as large must be stronger. How much heavier? With the span of the fabric double, it's strength must be double - requiring twice as much fiber per area and thus twice the weight per area. And there's four times the area, so the fabric might weigh 8 times as much. This assumes it never flaps in the wind. If it flaps, loads are even greater (Bert was told, when doing the twipi). Also the center pole must be stouter (16 times?). So, if your 9-foot tent weighs 3 pounds, expect an 18-foot tent with the same configuration and able to withstand the same wind, to weigh between 24 and 48 pounds. Of course, if you'll never be in that strong a wind, then the fabric in your 9-footer might be adequate. (Bigness costs! Elephants need stockier legs, proportional to body size, than do mice or spiders.) B & H

Comments on LLL's Shelter Plans

WOODLAND TENT. This is the only one of your plans I've built, a 15x9x9.

Structurally, it's been okay so far except that set up is slow because of the many tie-outs to adjust.

Shelter-wise it's kept out the rain. Sometimes there's a little condensation inside. I haven't covered the entrance to try to keep out insects, but instead just hang netting over my bed.

My biggest complaint is, the plastic roof reflects any open sky to any passer-by. Where that's undesirable, the tent must be completely covered by foliage or by a cloth over-tarp, which nullifies its light-passing advantages.

TWIPI. This seems rather complicated for what it is: essentially just an insulated roof over a hole in the ground.

Both the twipi and the woodland tent have steep roofs - to shed snow, you say. But, as you also point out, is to invite rodents to foul them. If they are taken down, they don't need to shed snow. (While you're there, you can keep brushing it off.) Could they be simplified, or other features improved, by dispensing with the steep roofs?

BUG FREE. Net tents are fairly inexpensive to buy. So collecting and piecing together old curtains doesn't seem a wise use of time, unless you need a different shape than what's for sale. Even then, it may be cost effective to buy a roll of netting. Dave Drake, OR

(Reply:) Regarding the twipi, roof insulation is very important. That's where, otherwise, the most heat will be lost. As for covering "a hole in the ground": well, the earth is there so why not use it, assuming it's firm enough, well drained enough, easily dug, and environmentally tolerable. Where it's not, a twipi isn't recommended. (Also see comments in Sept'85 MP, p.5.)
Bert

Comments on Arches Used for Storage

Regarding Dave Drake's idea (in June'89 MP) for assembling a storage structure out of plastic arches. Plastic no heavier than that in trash cans will deform under load and not provide weather-proof and perhaps not even mouse-proof joints. Corrugating the plastic crosswise (like road culverts) would help stabilize shape, but not enough I think. To obtain weatherproof joints would require heavier gauge material, and/or a more complex shape with ribs, and/or fastenings at many points. If such arches were manufactured, I suspect the unit cost would be more like $50-$100 than $5-$10.

Regarding Dave Stewart's idea (in August'89 MP) for forming arches out of plywood sheets glued together. As soon as the clamps are released, the plywood will partially unbend and assume an intermediate shape. And each arch will be shaped differently (wood not being a uniform material). Better, I think, to glue together the arches out of individual veneers (plywood plys) - a technique used for boat building. But even then, a stable, consistent shape will require ribs - as does a sizeable boat.

The boat comparison is useful because, what is wanted is much like the hull of a long narrow boat turned upside down (tho simpler because of constant cross-section). Boat hulls have to withstand water, waves and organisms for long periods. So any technique good for boat hulls might also be good for storage arches. Luke Hoppingmole, Oct.

Sexicosas Use Materials Efficiently

If building a portable dome, storage container, den liner, or snow-cave liner out of sheet materials such as plywood or fiberglass-foam sandwich, the sexicosa is a shape worth considering. Not one of the regular geometric solids, the sexicosa (short for sexicosahedron - 26 faces) consists of 18 square faces and 8 equilateral triangular faces.

If a sexicosa with 4-foot edges is built from 4x8' plywood, 11 sheets are needed, with only 2½% scrap. Whereas domes with all triangular faces have 10% to 20% scrap (according to Refried Domes). Furthermore, the sexicosa's "scrap" will be two strips 8'x6¼" which will almost certainly find uses. 24 of the faces (6 triangles and all 18 squares) are sawn directly; two of the triangles require

one join each (as shown →).
If that's not feasible, 12
sheets will be needed, with
11% scrap. The resulting
dome will be approx 9.6 feet
diameter with 557 ft^3 volume.

    For comparison, an 8-foot
cube would require 12 sheets
of plywood and provide only
512 ft^3 volume. Furthermore,
its edges and faces are twice
as long, requiring, for the
same strength, much heavier
plywood or more reinforcing.

    A model sexicosa can be easily
made by cutting two pieces of card stock
as shown (below left), folding along the
dashed lines (scoring them first with a
dull edge helps), gluing/taping each tab
to its adjacent edge, and then joining
the two halves together. (Two 8½x11
sheets suffices for a model with all
edges 2¼".) The finished model shown ⌐
↓

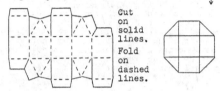

Cut
on
solid
lines.
Fold
on
dashed
lines.

    The card model is stable. A strut
model will not be stable because, as
Lloyd Kahn said, "triangles are necessary for stability." To stabilize, add
two diagonal bracing cords to each face.

    Ordinary plywood is weaker on the
diagonal than parallel with the grain.
If strength per weight is important, I
would reinforce each square face along
the diagonals by gluing on fiberglass
ribbons. Some marine plywood includes
plys with grain on the diagonal.

    As with any structure built of
sheets, the edges must be joined very
well along their entire lengths to reinforce each other. Openings will weaken
a sexicosa less if thru the triangular
faces than if thru the square faces.

    Many of the problems of all-trian-
gular domes are shared by sexicosas:
e.g., difficulty roofing by conventional
techniques. So, with any structural
form, think and test! Is it right for
your application? Don't just fall in
love with a "sexy" shape. Luke, NW, Oct.

Portable Housing IS Efficient

    (The following is in response to
Refried Domes, reviewed in May'90 MP
p.8, which said: "Portable housing: bad
idea. Once you build a floor (there are
no portable floors), install plumbing
and wiring and road or paths, it's very
inefficient to move the building.")

    We've lived in portable housing for
over ten years and we disagree.

    A floor for our 9-foot-diameter
"Thing" costs no money and requires one
hour to one day of labor (depending on
how steep and rocky the site is). We:
1) clear, level and smooth the soil;
2) lay down a vapor barrier (we use big
plastic wraps found in furniture store
dumpsters); 3) lay down something soft
and insulative such as moss, leaves or
salvaged foam (from rug store dumpsters);

4) lay down another vapor barrier;
5) lay down rugs or whatever we'd like
next to us. All but the soil is portable.

    Plumbing and wiring we don't have.
They, and the heavy appliances they feed,
may be truly labor saving for a laudromat, restaurant, or big farm. But we
can live more efficiently without them.

    Consider water, for example. For
cooking and washing we catch rain. For
drinking we backpack water from a spring,
often in the course of hikes for other
purposes. If we piped water, we'd not
only need plumbing; we'd probably also
need a filter, a pump, and power. If
you are far from existing utility lines,
a pump is expensive to connect, or
complicated to power with a windmill or
PV system. Besides initial costs, there
is maintenance, repair, and eventual
replacement. Also freezing protection:
keeping a heater going if you're away
during winter. (Pails we can just
empty.) Labor saving? I doubt it.

    The same holds for most electrical
appliances. Compared to simpler, lighter
alternatives, they might save some time
when you use them. But add up all the
costs and they're usually labor wasting.

    We aren't against all high tech.
But we only want what's truly beneficial;
not expensive, encumbering toys.

    As for roads and paths, we don't
need them. Our dwelling is small and
light enough to backpack (in pieces).

    Regarding efficiency, the bottom
line is: How much time do you have for
what you enjoy - versus time consumed by
household chores and by outside employment (including not only time at work,
but also time spent training for,
searching for, primping for, commuting
to, and recovering from work). By this
measure, for us portable housing is
highly efficient. Holly & Bert, OR

Exchanges Backwoods Child Care

    I now have a baby girl - and a new
companion. Also, for 8 or 9 months a
year, we have been hosting two somewhat
older kids of another couple who live
and work in an urban area.

    This has been a good arrangement
for us, financially and otherwise. We
are paid about as much as a conventional
boarding school, but have much lower
expenses. Also, on most weekends, the
other couple relieves us; sometimes
taking their kids with them; sometimes
staying here and caring for ours along
with theirs while we use their car.

    Of course for this to work, the
adults must agree on how kids should be
treated, the hosts must get along with
the kids, and the kids with each other.
No major problems, so far.

    One attraction for the parents:
their kids are less exposed to other
kids, who might have serious diseases
without showing symptoms, and who often
have crazy attitudes picked up from TV.

    During summers, the other kids live
with their parents, and we with our
child live at our northern tleanto or
travel with friends. (We no longer
have a car of our own.)

    My former companion and I broke up.
He grew bored and restless living in the
boonies, even though originally he had
been the one most keen for it. Also, I
wanted kids before I got any older
whereas he wanted to wait. Wanda, Aug.

Comfortable Compact Car Camping. Part II: The Tent

My friend and I are back from our 12,000-mile summer
camping trip to Inuvik, North West Territories. Instead of
turning left as Dawson City and going into Alaska as we did
the summer before, we turned right and drove the spectacular
Dempster Highway over three mountain ranges and two ferry
crossings of the Peel and MacKenzie Rivers. We camped out
almost every night. I'd like to pass along tips and ideas
from these trips and from many years of similar ones.

For sleeping take a roomy tent with a waterproof floor
that comes up a foot or so and a fly that extends almost to
the ground. On previous trips we took an Eureka Sentinel
which we liked as it has two doors. One tarp under the tent,
and another on the floor inside, give extra moisture and
puncture protection. Tuck the edges of the outside tarp
under the tent so they don't collect rain. Bring the edges
of inside tarp up around your air mattress and sleeping bags.

Free standing tents are much easier to set up than those
requiring stakes. If you need stakes, invest in some 6"
spikes from a hardware store; they are the only kind that will
penetrate packed gravel sites. You'll need a hammer to drive
them in. A little piece of string tied to the tent loops can
then be wrapped around each nail to hold the loop in place.
If you use regular tent stakes, a stake-puller really helps.

Have a roomy stuff bag in which all this will pack easily.
Take some spare large trash bags for wet tarps and fly. (Often
you can dry them in a few minutes on your car at lunch.)

On previous trips, for daytime comfort we also took a
screen tent. A cheap one will do. It goes up in ten minutes.
Be sure to take plenty of 6" spikes to hold it down. You can
put the screen tent over a picnic table and cook and read, bug
and rain free in the evening. Or you can set it up anywhere
with your folding table and chairs inside, or even put your
sleeping tent inside so that it doesn't get wet in a downpour.

On our latest trip, instead of separate sleeping and day-
use tents, we tried a Camel model 2510 Sahara cabin screen tent
that performs both functions. We found it very satisfactory.
The 8 x 10' sleeping area has two full-length zipper doors and
two large windows that zip closed from the inside. It
provides ample room for two cots and could sleep 3 or 4 women.
The floorless 6 x 10' screened area has enough room for two
tables and chairs. It sets up easily in about 10 minutes and
weighs less than 30 pounds with steel poles. This tent will
not withstand driving rain or gale winds, but it held up well
in the moderate weather we experienced.

Camel's latest catalog (5988 Peachtree Corners E, Norcross
GA 30071) lists a new 2500 model for $249 which has a smaller
screened area and a less desirable feature of the cabin windows
closing from the outside (not good when it starts raining
after you are in your sleeping bag). But Gander Mountain (Box
248, Wilmot, WI 53192) says they have "plenty" of Model 2510
for just $150. Jan Brown, MA, 1988 & 89 (previously published
by Women Outdoors Magazine, v8n4,v9n1,v9n4. Address on page A.)

Simple Lean-To Comfortable During Fall Travels With Pickup

For just one night during fair weather, I dispense with
shelter. But if camping in a spot for some time, I build an
open-faced lean-to. This is basically a canvas tarp stretched
sloping from overhead to ground. With a fire in front, I've
been comfortable in weather lowering into the twenties at
night. Gary Cropper, POB 864, Snoqualmie, WA 98065; December

A Friend Lives Outdoors the Year Around

He normally sleeps, under a polythene tarp and in two
sleeping bags, about 5 miles outside town. At that distance
he doesn't get hassled. He tried a camoflage net but found it
too bulky. Water is the single most important thing to carry,
he says. His biggest problems are money, boredom, and loneliness. Others living this way in U.K. are welcome to write him
c/o Huskisson,13 the close,Babrakam,Cambridge. Ellis, UK, Dec.

I Spend Summers in a Tipi and Winters in a Sailboat

I've been living this way, summers in MI, winters in FL,
full time for 4 years. Before that it was a pickup camper for
3 years. Maintaining cars and trucks was costly, thus the
boat. Yet tools and supplies for the boat also add up.
In Florida I was given a bicycle, then a 40cc Honda. The
motorcycle is costlier, but faster, more fun, and easier. (I'm
disabled with Guillian Berre syndrome, contracted while with
Peace Corps in W. Africa. Previous travels included 'Nam and
all over the Pacific with the U.S. Navy.) Harv Henry, MI, Sept.

Inexpensive Living Along the Sea of Cortez

No papers are needed north of San Felipe and there's no
time limit. Anything can be taken across the border into
Mexico except lumber. ($20 bribe gets it across too. Or it
can be carried in a house trailer which are seldom inspected.)
Land can be leased for $35 a month (payable yearly), for
ten years with another ten year option. You can tow a trailer
south to put on your lot, or build a shack.
Brakish water is usually available for a $150 set-up fee,
and fresh water is 25¢ a gallon or $7 for a 50-100 gal. tank.
Disadvantages: In summer, 120° during neep tides (when
no tide stirs the wind). Fairly frequent sand storms are
bearable but will drive you inside. There's little theft
except food, booze, money, and (I suspect) solar panels and
batteries. Don't believe the bandito stories!
Once you are there, options show up. Many Mexican families can provide things you need economically. Lee, CA, Aug.

Photovoltaic Lighting System Utilizes Cheap Used Batteries

Replying to Anne: Flame appliances are probably safe to
use during summer as you'll be using them less (longer days)
and with better ventilation (summer warmth).
For winter lighting I use a small (12x12") ARCO solar
panel, a 7-watt compact flourescent bulb, and an old car
battery. The solar panel has a diode built in and is self
regulating so no other gizmos are needed. All can be carried
on an old pack frame. (Keep battery upright to not spill acid.)
Pluses: Quality light without flicker. No fumes or flame
and thus safe with kids. The panel and bulb are long lasting.
Minuses: High initial expense (panel $85, bulb $20; in
1987 from Backwoods Solar Electric, 8530 Rapid Lightning Ck Rd,
Sandpoint,ID 83864). Battery must not freeze. Battery is
heavy and bulky. You need a sunny day to have a "sunny" night.
I can get 3½-4 hours of light on a charge without drawing
down the battery all the way. Such use eventually ruins a car
battery. A deep-cycle battery would last longer. But, in fall
I can buy a used car battery from a junkyard for $10 and, come
spring, turn it in for $5 salvage. Why spend more for a longer
life battery which I don't use and can't maintain in summer?
I supplement the flourescent with candles. They are cheap,
easily available, and give off little fumes. I also use them
when I snow camp in winter. Rob, ID & VT, June

Avoid Dust if Cleaning Out Old Buildings

Histoplasmosis is a strange disease spread by air-driven spores released from dried, dusty bird feces. It enters the lungs, causing flu-like or even tuberculosis-like symptoms. From the lungs it travels through the blood to other body parts. It damages eyes most, scaring surfaces, often causing blurred or double vision and, if untreated, eventually blindness.

Many a victim had recently converted an old chicken house or barn to living quarters, or renovated an attic previously occupied by pigeons or bats. Not much is known about the disease, but I suggest wearing protective clothing and a good dust mask, and keeping dust to a minimum. Al Blanche, NY (condensed from Nov'90 Rural Network Advocate; addr. page C).

Dairy Goats Are Not Very Portable, We've Found

To set up their pen and house and feeding was almost as much work as moving the whole rest of our camp. Also, last time we had to move right when they were due to kid. Though the milk tastes great and is probably healthier, powdered milk is much less hassle. Anne Callaway, California, August

Many Recently-Made Victor Mousetraps Have Poor Springs

They are weak even when new, and soon slacken until useless. Did the company fear that somebody might carelessly let their pet hurt its paw - and then sue them for a million dollars? Or did they figure that if they built flimsier mousetraps, the world would beat a path to their door to buy replacements?

We are buying replacements. But not Victor. Others we have tried, McGill and Enoz, have stronger springs and seem generally better built. McGill bait pans won't hold hard bait such as corn. Reshaping with long-nose pliers helps. H & B

Efforts to Stop Nature's Aerialists

I assumed most outdoor people knew about those cones or discs on the lines which tie ships to docks. They keep rodents from tightrope walking onto the ship. But a tip I saw (not in MP) to hang gear up, failed to mention a guard on the rope.

Actually I've never seen a mouse or rat walk on a rope; only evidence that they had - and on very narrow cords. They might not get to a newly suspended line the first night, but given days or months they probably will. And they chew not only food and nesting material; they also chew for sport - anyway so it seems. (Rodents' teeth grow continually and will become too long if they don't chew, I've read.) Julie Summers

(Comment:) We have a regular cotton clothesline strung across our tent. I placed our bread in a plastic grocery bag and hung it from a hook in the middle of the clothesline. The mice walked down the rope to get to the bread.

Next, I fashioned a guard by drilling a hole in a pie plate to receive the hook. The mice simply jumped onto the pie plate and slid off onto the sack of bread. When they were done they dropped to the floor. One evening I watched the whole performance by candle light - they had gotten bold!

Perhaps a rigidly fixed, larger guard would work: rigid to prevent sliding off and bigger to "shadow" the whole bag. But someone gave us a metal bread box which works great.

Mice also went for the styrofoam sheets we put in the ceiling for insulation. They were chewing it up and taking it away. So we threw it out and are back to just blankets. Anne

Message Post

Portable Dwelling Info-letter
POB 190, Philomath, OR 97370

March 1991   One issue $1   Six issues $5 cash; $5½ check

Bracken Fern is Edible and Delicious in Fiddlehead Stage

Pick them by snapping off the fiddleheads (like asparagus, it will break above the fibrous section of the stem). Place them in a pot and cover with hard-wood ashes. (You can use baking soda but you may need to treat the ferns two times before the astring-ent quality is gone.) Pour boiling water to cover the ferns. Let the ferns sit until the water is cool. Drain (can you dye wool with this water?) and rinse off all the ashes. Now cook: simmer in water seasoned with soy sauce and honey until most of the liquid is gone. Or dry by spreading on baskets in a shady, breezy place. Reconstitute by soaking in warm water with a pinch of salt for 3 hours.   Anne Schein, California, January

(Comments:) Bert likes fiddleheads of bracken raw (after rubbing off the fuzz), but not so much cooked (plain boiled - has not tried your recipe). He hasn't noticed any astringency. Difference of tastes? Or difference of ferns there and here? I (Holly) don't like the taste of bracken raw or cooked (at least not plain boiled).

An article in March'81 Coltsfoot and June'81 MP, mentioned reports that eating bracken (Pteridium aquilinum) was linked with stomach cancer, but did not say how mature or fresh was the bracken. Were fiddleheads defuzzed and eaten promptly as an occasional salad or pot herb? Or were mature fronds cut and dried as hay, and fed in large quantity to livestock? (Many edible greens become toxic as they wilt.)   H & B, OR, March

"Edible" Mushrooms Can Cause Allergic Reactions

Quite often I eat wild mushrooms, including morels, puff-balls, chantrelles, and corals. Recently I was given a large amount of chicken-of-the-woods, a mushroom I had never eaten before. I ate it with relish but, afterwards, suffered from stomach illness. This experience reinforces the warning to eat only small quantities of a new mushroom (or any new food), even though it is listed as, and positively identified as "edible". Gary Cropper, POB 86, Snoqualmie, WA 98065; December

The Trick to Cooking Rice Fast is to Soak It Like Beans
Lee Mauck, California, January

We Are Building a Solar Cooker as a Homeschool Project

We are using Joseph Radabaugh's design. It is made by nesting cardboard boxes, so it is not weatherproof. My guess is that careful covering with aluminum foil could prevent damage by rain and damp. Our cooker will have a plexiglass door. I bought the book, Heaven's Flame ($5 from Radabough, POB 1392, MtShasta, CA 96067) after reading a review in Home Power. Anne Schein, California, January

More About Nature's Aerialists

Mice have sometimes eaten food that I suspended overnight in a backpack 12 feet off the ground. I suspect they ran up the rope. The food had not been well sealed (zipper left undone, bags not tied, etc.). I've had no problem with bears though. Aarran Rainbow, British Columbia, December

I Have Lived in Vehicles and Tents Most of My Life

When I was 18, I left home and went to Europe with a
large canvas rucksack on my back, a sleeping bag, a train pass,
and very little money. I slept in vacant barns, fields, youth
hostels, and trains or train stations. I've also backpacked a
lot in the mountains of California and Oregon.

However, I prefer living and traveling in vehicles,
because the freedom I enjoy most is the freedom of travel.
I've had two VW vans (too Spartan), a pickup with camper (too
tight), a house-truck - a house built on a 16' long flatbed
truck (comfortable, but drew too much attention because of all
the wood), and now a raised-roof school bus painted blue.

Unlike cars, buses are very simple to work on. And if
you have a Chevy or GMC bus, most pickup and car engine parts
are the same - and cheap! We carry a spare fuel pump, water
pump, spark plugs, points, distributor and starter (all
rebuilt, or gotten off an abandoned Chevy somewhere).

I converted my rigs to run on non-polluting propane.
I got giant truck tanks for $10 and a carburator for $10,used.

The bus has two solar panels, two deep-cycle batteries,
12 volt lights and a propane light. I easily wired it for
110 volts and 12 volts with used, heavy extension cords.

The bus has a full kitchen with double sink, cabinets,
stove/oven, propane RV refrigerator, and Paloma instant hot
water heater. A plastic utility washtub/sink (30x30" by 14"
deep) has above it a shower curtain on a track for a shower
(total cost $20). The water tank is 80 gallons. Most came
from yard sales, swap meets, or, used,at RV service centers.

I have (and sell) Multi-Pure water filters. This filter
removes all bacteria, giardia, and chemicals. It has an
inexpensive cartridge inside. We don't get sick down in
Mexico any more. And when we fill our tank with city water,
it takes out all the chlorine and bad taste. We also got a
hand pump for it that goes backpacking with us, to pump water
out of puddles, lakes or streams.

I got eight sliding RV windows with screens for $45.
Scrap linoleum went on the floor and cheap, thin indoor-out-
door carpet went on the ceiling. Two bus seats and a piece of
nice birch plywood scrap makes the dinette. (You can reup-
holster bus seats with a screw driver, a staple gun, and any
scrap materials.) The bus has a propane furnace. I have a
sign shop in the back for making money on the road.

I added up the time we (3 kids, 2 adults) have lived in
the bus off and on over the last 6 years and it totals 2½
years. We don't register it; we just buy a $5 trip permit
when we go traveling - usually to Mexico.

I'd like to communicate with other vehicle dwellers.
Prem Dhanesh, 332 Otis St., Ashland, OR 97520; Jan. & Febr.

(Question:) With a trip permit, what do you do about insurance? I've heard that the cops require insurance. B & H

Cooperative Bus Would Tour Craft Fairs

I like the idea of confluences: communities without
leaders. Specifically, I'm interested in a cooperative bus.
Divide it into individual (or family) sleeping compartments,
and into common kitchenette, dinette-lounge, and workshop
areas. Make the rounds of craft fairs. (There are hundreds.)
Each person has their own art/craft project, and also helps
promote   recycling, bus living, confluences, etc.

I've seen retired school buses, still running, for sale
cheap - some under $1000. (But better have at least one

person along who's a mechanic.) Write me if you are interested.
(But don't print my address.) Dale, North Carolina, February

(Comment:) Seems to me that a cooperative bus would need a
manager - making it a mobile community, not a confluence. (For
the difference, see Jan'91 MP p.5.) However, if the members
stay light (able to drop off easily), I think you could avoid
most of the problems of a settled community (where members who
grow disgruntled can't easily leave). B & H, OR, March

Comfortable Compact Car Camping. Part III: The Furnishings

I invested in a Thermarest mattress (full size, standard;
not 3/4 or Ultralite). When the mattress is deflated and
rolled up, secure it with a webbing strap with a fastec buckle.
American Camper's 26x72" folding cot was fine. (They also have
one that is padded, with which a separate mattress isn't needed.)
In the summer you'll only need a light weight sleeping bag.
You may be able to pick up one in a salvage store for under $20,
and Campmor (Box 997,Paramus, NJ 07653) and other mail-order
stores have some good buys on new ones. If it gets really nippy,
wear a hat, socks, and polypro underwear to bed. (A wonderful
hat of angora/wool blend that packs into nothing and is incredibly soft and warm is made to order by Karen Sue Van Tine (Star
Rt Bx 14,Penobscot,ME 04476.) Recently I discovered that a hooded sweatshirt is even better than a hat for keeping warm on
chilly nights - it doesn't slip off! If traveling in style,
take your favorite pillow along. (Or use your life-jacket.)
We've found the Gadabout folding chair from Sporty's
(Clermont Airport,Batavia,OH 45301), which is the same as the
Anywhere Chair from Thos. Oak (901 Main St.,Salem,VA 24156),
expensive but worth it because it is durable, light weight,
comfortable, and very compact when folded. A good, small folding table is even harder to find. We have used a dandy one
made by American Camper (available in many sporting goods stores,
they say). It folded down to 3x24x24", yet could be raised to
a comfortable 28" for cooking, with an area of 24x48". CO-OP
America (2100 M St.,NW,#310,DC 20063) has a folding table well-
built of oak. L.L.Bean (Freeport,ME 04033) has one with adjustable legs. Many companies carry roll-up tables.
For lighting, there are a number of options, from "nothing"
in the high Arctic with its long hours of summer daylight, to a
fancy flourescent lantern powered by four 6-volt batteries if
you like to read a lot at night. In any case, you'll want a
couple of Tekna flashlights for your car and tent, preferably
with long-lasting lithium batteries and bulb, and at least a
Coleman Peak 1 lantern (with spare mantles and a durable plastic
lantern case) for the dirty dishes you've left too late.
Jan Brown, MA, 1988 & 89 (previously in Women Outdoors Magazine)

Cooking on the engine of a vehicle.

For several years my main job has been driving a cab,
and I have become quite adept at cooking on the engine block.
I wrap food in aluminum foil and place on top of or around the
engine. While driving, a large stew usually cooks in a little
over an hour. (On long trips, my customers have been amused
when I told them I had to get dinner off the engine block
before it caught fire.) I have also tried the old trick that
hobos did with campfires: punch a small hole in canned food
and place on the engine block. Unfortunately, this is
difficult with a moving vehicle because one must find a place
to wedge the can without interfering with the engine.
When placing and removing food, I wear industrial work
gloves. Be very careful: escaping steam can burn badly.
There is a book on the subject: Manifold Destiny. I've
only read reviews, but it sounds pretty good. Kurt Wettstein,

Traveling By Train in Mexico

I always go regular first class. Around $25 gets me to
Guadalajara. There is also a primera first, which has beds by
reservation only and is nicer, and a third class which is more
crowded (you may not get a seat) and pretty skungy after a
couple of days. The train takes a day and two nights. Venders
get on and off selling delicious food. It's never made me sick.

The train leaves Mexicali (near CA) or Nogales (near AZ)
at 10 p.m., but people get in line before lunch. Your gear will
hold your place while you wander around and nobody will steal
it then, but watch it when you are on the train.

Getting from the border (called"la liñe"in Mexico) to the
station is a project. The distance is about 5 miles. A taxi
is $10; a bus only 5¢-15¢. But I've never found a bus that
goes directly to the train station. Instead I keep asking
"Donde 'sta auto bus central" to find a bus going to the bus
center, and then ask "Donde 'sta estacion de tren" to find a
bus that goes there. You can walk from the bus to the train
station, but they are two very long blocks apart.

The train arrives in Guadalajara at 8 or 10 p.m. From
there you can get a bus or train (second class) to Mexico City.
(You are unlikely to get a place on a first-class train.)

Take the bus back home. Catching the train is not unlike
a cattle stampede - after waiting hours for it to arrive. To
get directed toward the border, ask "Donde 'sta la liñe."

Yes, solo females can do it (without Spanish). Just don't
try to say "no" and be cute at the same time. Lee Mauck, CA

Senseless About Homeless

"Homeless in America" was the cover article in the Dec. 17
1990 issue of *Time* magazine. One photo shows a sleeping box,
made by telescoping together several cardboard cartons, which
looks snug and warm. On the same page a headline claims:
"After a decade of despair, Americans are finding solutions
that work - tailor-made, cost effective, time tested."

Yes, indeed! A sleeping box, built by the user out of
scrap, is certainly tailor-made, cost effective, and time tested.

However, sleeping boxes are not the kind of solution that
reporters and officials have in mind. The kind of solution
they want, are programs that train the homeless to earn rent
money (and help officials advance their careers).

What would happen to those who don't want or can't win
steady jobs? One hint. According to *Time*, releasing people
from mental institutions who had "no place to go", was a
"stunning social blunder."

In San Francisco near city hall, some folks built
"a second city of cardboard condos, clogged with traffic of
shopping carts through makeshift living rooms, outfitted with
easy chairs." They were evicted by the mayor.

But the mayor has a remedy for homelessness. "If you give
me the money, we have a chance to end sleeping on the streets."

True. If you give the mayor the money, you can be sure
the mayor won't be sleeping on the streets!

Politicians and officials cause homelessness when they
interfere with people's efforts to build what they can afford.

Poor folks around many Latin American cities manage to
shelter themselves (when the cops leave them alone). And
dumpsters there aren't so rich with reuseable materials as are
dumpsters in the U.S. Bert & Holly, Oregon, February
(Thanks to Aarran for sending us the clipping.)

Message Post

May 1991 One issue $1

Portable Dwelling Info-letter
POB 190, Philomath, OR 97370
Six issues $5 cash; $5½ check

Years Ago, I Made a Tent Out of a Parachute

I bought the 19-foot (as I recall) diameter chute inexpensively from a surplus store. Most of the cords had been cut off, but enough length was left to form peg loops.

For the center pole, I bought a large 2-3" diameter bamboo pole from a supplier of commercial fishing boats and cut to 12'.

To waterproof the chute, I put it in a bucket with some Thompson Waterseal and then hung it out to dry.

A slit served as a door. (There wasn't Velcro then; I would use it now.) Inside, under the chute's air-spill hole, I rigged a collector and siphon for rain water. The hole still allowed hot air to escape. Even so, sunshine made the chute hot inside. (With another, I'd have peg loops one foot long, in addition to the short ones, so it could be rigged above the ground, like a circus tent, to let in the breezes.)

To erect it, I stuck a peg in the ground, tied another peg to it with about 10' of cord, and drew a circle. The edges of the chute were pegged to this circle. Then I inserted the center pole. Usually it had to be raised with rocks or lowered by digging a trench to get the proper tension. Perhaps a pole of plastic pipe sections would have been easier to adjust.

Slack in the fabric went wild in the wind, but uncoated ripstop is quiet and the tent never blew down. Henry, AZ, March

I Am Looking for Inexpensive Portable Housing for Summer

I would like something bigger and more stable than most tents, but yet capable of being taken down, folded up, and put in the back of a station wagon. Maybe a tipi, yurt, or portable geodesic. But except for one dome I saw in Real Good's catalog, I have no idea where to acquire one. After June 1, you can reach me c/o Oesterreich, Rt 1 Box 55, Harris, MN 55032.

I want something mosquito proofable (I will be in MN on a friend's land), big enough to stand up in, and without metal supports. (I can enjoy storms if not worried about being struck by lightening.) Donna Berry, Minnesota, April

We Lived in Tipis at 9000 Feet Elevation for Twelve Years

My four sons and I spent 3 to 6 months a year in them. The boys are all on their own now, and the tipis are old and leak like sieves. I'm working on a yurt - hope to move in this summer. Jerry, San Juan Mtn Bikes, POB 777, LakeCity, CO 81235; Feb.

Insulated Gravel Floor in Dome Lessens Humidity

To reduce living expenses and impact less on resources, I am using a Shelter Systems' 18' LightHouse dome.

I set up the dome between two live oaks near Santa Rosa. It gets afternoon sun but is protected from the wind. The last few days it experienced several inches of rain with high winds (50 mph in unprotected areas). I am pleased with its performance.

To reduce humidity, I created an insulated pea gravel floor system.

dome

bender board
4 ml plastic
6 ml plastic
5" pea gravel
5" shredded redwood bark

After setting the dome on cleared ground, I put two yards of shredded redwood bark over a plastic vapor barrier on the ground. Inside I ran 3½" bender board up against the poles and used 50 pn nails where needed to keep the board in place. The bottom plastic was brought up over the bender board to prevent outside rain water from getting it wet. Then I put another layer of plastic over the bark, and spread four yards of pea gravel on it. This plastic, too, was brought up over the bender board to prevent outside water from getting into the rock. As I spread the rock, I made sure the bottom fabric of the dome was folded in so I could shovel rock over the bender board and fill up the space between board and dome. This also holds down the dome all the way around (except at the doors).

The gravel absorbs humidity slowly and then lets it off when the weather is dry. So far I've had no mold.

As a floor, the gravel is fine so long as care is taken when preparing and eating food and when entering with boots not cleaned. To cover the gravel, I am experimenting with $1.50 a sq yd carpet padding made from recycled acrylic sweaters.

For a clean sleeping and meditation space, I set up a 10' dome inside the big one, and put a carpet on its floor.

I have a MacCracken (Alturas,CA) solar distiller which gives drinking and cooking water. I am still plugged into the grid for washing water. I will convert to a solar-powered pump system if the year-around creek is not too polluted.

For hot water, a simple passive collector hung on the garden fence, works noon to five on sunny days. I am experimenting with radiant floor heating by running black pipe thru the pea gravel under the inner bedroom dome, but so far the heat exchange is not enough to make a difference. Maybe after I build the greenhouse, that will heat the rocks 10° or so.

For pee, I built a urinal pit which does not cause smell or pollution. My next two projects will be an underground grey water system that automatically waters the roots of a food growing bed, and, the most difficult, a compost toilet producing night soil for garden use.

For night light, I use a solar lantern (Real Goods, $110) which works great. My only other electrical device is a Walkman with rechargeable AA batteries. Randy Riis, CA, March

(Comments:) For a floor, did you first try just bare dirt with plastic covering? Did adding the bark and gravel to the floor noticably reduce humidity? For setups more portable or remote, I wonder what other materials would have a similar effect. (Bark and rock are plentiful some places but not others. Where we are now, the rocks are weak and soon crush into muddy sand.)

I believe we get a similar effect during cold weather when we bring in jugs of collected rain water (to keep them from freezing and bursting). Our dwelling, which is small and insulated, warms quickly when we come inside, and warms further when we cook or the sun shines. The jugs remain cool for a while, moisture condenses on them, runs down their sides, and forms little puddles beneath, which we occasionally sponge up and add to the kitchen waste water for disposal outside. (With some elaboration, we could set the jugs in a trough that would automatically drain outside.) But the jugs further crowd our 9' diameter dwelling, so, as soon as the weather moderates, they go back outside. Bert & Holly, Oregon, March

More About Simple Drainage Systems

To dispose of waste water and pee, we sometimes use a large funnel (actually a narrow-mouth plastic jug with the bottom cut off - which can be used as a bowl or plate) feeding into a hose

(or bike innertube, or several, depending on length wanted).
     Compared to a drain bucket (in Oct'90 MP, p.2), a funnel
seems easier to connect and less likely to leak - assuming I
find hose just a little larger than the mouth of the funnel/jug,
so that the funnel fits snuggly inside the hose. Also, with
the funnel, there is no problem of a residual remaining in the
bottom and not draining. What advantages has the bucket?
Faster pouring? Bert, Oregon, October

(Reply:) We use a big bucket because the six of us use lots
of washing water. Also boy power doesn't have very good aim.
     We installed a piece of ¼" hardware cloth over the top of
the bucket to catch debris that could plug up the hose leading
away from the bucket. It also catches the silverware and jar
lids our 11-year-old leaves behind in the dishpan. Anne,CA,Dec.

The Simple Shower Was Helpful Recently When the Pipes Froze
     My mobile home had no running water for a few days, yet I
still had a hospital expecting me to be there and in the
hygenic condition of an emergency-room nurse.
     Two 2-liter pop bottles, filled with water from the tea
kettle to provide the desired warmth, served me nicely. One
provided enough water to soak and lather, and the second
provided a luxuriously thorough rinse. Standing in the tub
took care of the run-off. My kids also thought it fine.
     Regulating the flow with the caps was tricky the first
couple of times. If this was an ongoing situation, I would
secure duplicate caps, and perforate the duplicates with a
fine nail, to provide a shower head I could turn off by
setting the bottle down. Jon Seaver, Michigan, March

(Comment:) When showering, we simply remove the cap and tilt
the bottle to regulate the flow. (I tried it with the cap on
loose and didn't like it as well. I didn't try perforating
the cap.) The illustration in the June'87 MP (and 1987-88
Summary-Index) may be misleading because it shows the bottle
completely inverted. With the cap off, that would occur only
when the bottle was almost empty. Do other readers prefer
cap on? Or cap off? Holly & Bert, Oregon, April

Comfortable Compact Car Camping.   Part IV: The Water
     Some campgrounds have only one pump for all the sites, so
we've found a three-gallon water pail is very handy. Collapsible
plastic water containers are not as good as they are hard to
clean. Also handy, if there is a tree to hang it from, is a
bag that zips open at the top for filling and has a spout at
the bottom. What did not work? A collapsible bucket. Empty
or full, it collapsed!
     We assume that the water supplied in a campground is safe
to drink (if in doubt, boil) but nevertheless it may have
suspended dirt particles or an awful taste from chlorination.
A First Need filter will cure the first fault and a little lime
juice will take care of the second.
     Most campgrounds don't have showers; those that do often
have very little dry space, so a washbag that opens up and can
be hung from a hook or over a door is very useful. For non-
shower days, a pot of water is fine for a sponge bath. Or, if
we camp on a sunny day in good time, we use our Solar Shower;
first placing it in the sun to warm up, then attaching it to a
secluded tree with the handy webbing strap. This is often a
good time to string up the clothesline too, and catch up on the
underwear. Larger soiled clothes go into a big ditty bag for
a laundermat stop every few weeks. Jan Brown, MA, 1988 & 1989
(previously published in Women Outdoors Magazine (addr. on p.A))

Home-Made Berry Comb

Red huckleberries (Vaccinium parvifolium) were prolific here last year.
Tho fairly sour, they are pleasantly
fruity (like pink lemonade).

However, picking them is tedious
for me. So I made a berry comb with
attached cup. Using a nail held with a
vice grip and heated in a flame, I
melted matching holes in a large coarse-
toothed plastic comb and in a squat one-
pound margarine tub. Then with heavy thread I laced them
together. The straight comb pulled the tub into an oblong.
I removed some teeth from the comb until the spaces between
were 3/16 inches. (I got the idea from a photo of an eskimo-
made berry picker, which looked like a wooden-burl cup with
metal-wire teeth added.)

In a timed test, the comb was no faster than picking, but
did provide variety. I wonder if speed would increase with
practice, or if speed depends on the kind of bush. (I don't
know what berries the eskimos were gathering.) Julie Summers,
OR, June

Comfortable Compact Car Camping. Part V: The Kitchen

In the past we often took lots of freeze dry food - and
found we returned with it. The U.S. and Canada are loaded
with supermarkets and farm stands, so there's no reason not to
"eat fresh". Some homemade granola and pancake mix, powdered
milk and minute rice, a plastic lime or lemon, some dried
apricots and Baker's semi-sweet chocolate (which doesn't melt)
is about all we take now. In Canada, a delight is supermarkets with "bulk" produce sections. Probably they are meant
for large quantity buyers, but no one seemed to object when we
purchased minute quantities to refill our spice and drink
containers. Recent additions to our larder were hearty Magic
Pantry boil-in-a-bag dinners (in Canadian supermarkets), maple
syrup crystals for pancakes (from Walnut Acres), and Uncle
Ben's Rice in an Instant (better than the usual minute rice).

Almost all our kitchen and food gear goes into two milk
crates. They are durable, easy to carry, and don't collapse
in the rain as do cardboard cartons.

In one we put three small nesting pots (a larger serving
as a lid for a smaller), a small frying pan, potholders, three
metal plates, two plastic cups and two plastic drinking
glasses, a two-cup plastic measuring cup which serves as a
mixing bowl, a small plastic shaker for mixing milk, and the
silverware and utensil bag. This is easy to make: just fold
up a square of nylon, sew in some pockets, and secure it with
velcro or a sewn-on shoelace. It contains forks, steak knives,
tea and soup spoons, a sharp folding knife from Early Winters,
sandwich spreader, vegetable peeler, slotted cooking spoon,
metal spatula, can-opener, pot lifter, scissors, tongs,
plastic scraper, small wisk, and a gadget that sparks when
squeezed to light the stove. In addition, we take one larger
pot for cooling wine, rinsing dishes, washing hair, and
storing wet bathing suits, tarps and washclothes.

The other crate contains paper towels, plastic bags,
toilet paper in a Ziplock bag, garbage bags, dish towel, empty
plastic containers for left overs, three ditty bags with cord

locks, and our staples. The ditty bags can be open mesh so you can see what is inside, or color coded. One is for washing up: liquid soap, a sponge cloth and a scrubber; one is for drink mixes in labelled plastic bottles (instant coffee, cocoa, tea, etc.); one is for a selection of our favorite spices, also preferably in small, labelled plastic bottles.

We also take a small cooler which keeps perishables like butter, salad makings, and a small bottle of cooking oil, (no ice; you can only buy it in too-large quantities); and a small insulated bag (L.L.Bean or Early Winters) in which we pack lunch after breakfast so that we needn't unpack the car at noon.

Unfortunately, the stove we have used for many years is no longer available. (Its two burners ran on propane, available in any hardware store, and it has a griddle, all of which packs into a lightweight double "roasting pan" which can be used for baking and dishwashing.) A Coleman two-burner stove is probably the best current bet because of its reliability. L.L.Bean, Famous Cookware and Store 64 have griddles that fit this stove, and you can probably find an inexpensive roasting pan that will fit over the burners - recommended for an in-tent bath or for washing dishes. Jan Brown, MA, 1988 & 1989 (previously published in Women Outdoors Magazine, addr. on p.A).

We Use Gallon Milk Jugs With NO CAPS for Our Simple Showers
We call it "jugging". Works fine.

Most of our plastic pails have come from health food stores. We paid $1 or $2 each. Friends have given us some in which bulk laundry detergent is sold - at Cost Co I think. Many of our pails have labels indicating baking supplies - e.g. artificial raspberry filling. Anne Callaway, CA, May

Sources for Hot Water When in City or Traveling
If washing clothes at a laundromat lacking a sink, the washing machine can also furnish hot water for a simple shower. When the machine starts filling, open the lid momentarily and place a bowl under the inflow, close the lid to restart the flow (which will stop while the lid is up), then open again and empty the bowl into the jugs or bottles to be used for showering. Repeat until the jugs are full. The water inflow remains on until the washer fills to a certain level, so I don't believe this affects the laundering.

Another source (if you don't mind free-loading - or are a customer) are the rest rooms at a McDonald's. (Many public rest rooms have only cold water.) To fill a jug, you may need a cup or small bowl that will fit under the spigot.
B & H, OR, Nov.

How Large Were Indigenous Groups?
Indigenous peoples tribes (both nomadic and more rooted communities), that lived in relative balance and survived quite well, were usually made up of several dozen and upward to a few hundred folks. Bands/clans of a dozen or less were almost unheard of, other than short-term hunting and gathering parties. Usually when you found groups of less than a dozen, unless they were going about the larger clan/tribe business or going to visit other clans/tribes, they were the outcast that simply couldn't get along with other folks for long, or they were living in environments so desolate that the

local ecology simply could not support a larger group. In fact, when folks were living closer to nature you normally found nuclear families of a dozen or so - and those were parts of an extended family/clan/tribe of several dozen to a few hundred, with size largely depending upon what the ecological balance could support. Rainbow Hawk, New York, May

(Comment:) To clarify: a <u>band</u> is a group that lives and works together; a <u>tribe</u> is everyone who shares a heritage and who considers each other "my people".
  Among nomadic foragers/hunters, the <u>band</u> might be as small as one nuclear family (mama, papa, and kids) or as large as two dozen. I don't recall reading of <u>nomadic</u> bands much larger (other than some pastoral peoples which are relatively recent). A larger band would need more territory for sustenance and would have to forage farther from camp or move camp oftener, and thus be less efficient. Also, a band of two dozen probably includes ±8 able-bodied adults and adolescents of each sex (the rest being small kids, the lame, and the very old) - the most efficient size for many kinds of work and group hunting. (That is why, today, ±8 is also the size of most sport teams, most military squads, and most task groups.)
  A nomadic <u>tribe</u> may number from several hundred to many thousand. But they all congregate (if they do) only for special occasions. I have read that the Paiutes of the Great Basin usually roamed as nuclear families, but gathered into larger groups occasionally to round up rabbits and for social functions. (Some might call their environment "desolate", but I imagine most of <u>them</u> liked it.)
  <u>Settled</u> communities were often much larger, primarily for military reasons. People who want exclusive use of much fertile land, must be able to defend that land against all comers, or become the subjects of some gang who can. To coordinate the larger number and to suppress disagreements, requires authoritarian organization. (Moving apart, an option for nomads, is not practical for settled folks.) That also seems to hold for those present-day intentional communities that last.
                                                              H & B

Avoiding Wrenching Experiences
  Some frown upon grabbing trailside vegetation to assist a climb or prevent a fall. But I presume most hikers do it, at least in emergencies. For least trauma to both plants and people:
  Try to select sturdy, non-brittle plants that will take your weight without breaking.
  Apply force in line with a branch. Do not bend it far.
  Keep aware of your arms' range of movement. (Try moving them now.) They cannot bend far back - without tearing something. Consequently you must keep facing (more or less) toward each handhold. E.g., when going downhill, your body must either keep facing uphill, or else must pivot as you pass each handhold. Julie Summers, Oregon, 1990

Hat Can Be Used as Pocket
  If you need a pocket but are without one, or the ones you have are covered up, keep your hat in mind. Its shape, stretchiness, and how tightly it clings will limit its capacity, but most hats will accomodate at least note paper and a pencil.
  The voyageurs used their long stocking caps for various odds and ends; and Thoreau used his crown-and-brim hat for what he considered an ideal vasculum (plant collecting container) - with just the right humidity. Julie Summers, OR, November

Message Post

Portable Dwelling Info-letter
POB 190, Philomath, OR 97370

November 1991 $1 per issue   Add 50¢ to check/mo under $10

Two Lean-Tos Together Provide More Shelter

During the fall, when temperatures are invigorating yet pleasant and I'm not yet ready to be completely enclosed, I find open-faced lean-tos sufficient for my needs.

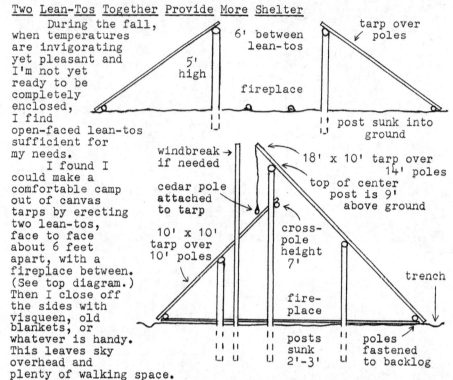

6' between lean-tos

5' high

tarp over poles

fireplace

post sunk into ground

windbreak → if needed

cedar pole attached to tarp

18' x 10' tarp over 14' poles

top of center post is 9' above ground

10' x 10' tarp over 10' poles

cross-pole height 7'

trench

fire-place

posts sunk 2'-3'

poles fastened to backlog

I found I could make a comfortable camp out of canvas tarps by erecting two lean-tos, face to face about 6 feet apart, with a fireplace between. (See top diagram.) Then I close off the sides with visqueen, old blankets, or whatever is handy. This leaves sky overhead and plenty of walking space.

I have used this shelter exclusively in eastern Washington where rains are generally brief and soils absorbent.

In a wetter climate I would overlap the leantos. (See bottom diagram.) This would give full rain protection yet allow the smoke to escape. Also this requires fewer supporting poles. When there is no fire, a moveable flap closes the smoke outlet to reduce heat loss. Total floor space is 16' by 10', and space at 5' height is 6' by 10'

Ideally, I would erect this shelter where there are natural windbreaks to the north, and face the smoke outlet that way. If not possible, a windbreak must be constructed (shown).

The top tarps and the sides would be doubled for protection. Various materials could be used. Light colored tarps are preferred, for increased light within and also because of the solar-oven qualities of olive drab. Some adjusting may be required to achieve proper draft for the smoke outlet. Not shown is crossbracing which I would add for extra support and to keep the visqueen from flapping and being destroyed by wind.

With the various lean-to arrangements, there are possibilities of being able to walk into the woods, axe in hand, and build them from available materials. The chief advantage I see over a tipi, is no exposure of poles to the rain.

I like a shelter that includes a suitable source of fire heat (preferably wood), especially in a wet climate. If using an open fire, I stick to non-sparking deciduous woods such as alder. Cross poles may be hung in the rafters for smoking fish

and meats. If using a wood stove, I carry a small piece of plywood thru which a round hole has been cut wider than the stove pipe, plus a metal collar that fits between pipe and plywood, and install this someplace on the upright side walls.
I am of the Metis people from Canada. Traditional shelters have been the tipi, the lean to, and the wigawam - a round dome-type shelter made from bent willow sapplings. These have stood the test of time. Each was designed for a different purpose: the tipi for nomadic plains travel, the wigawam for forest dwelling (the frames are left standing to be returned to from time to time), and the simple open-faced lean-to for lightweight travel. Gary Cropper, POB 864, Snoqu. WA 98065; Feb.

Comfortable Compact Car Camping. Part VI: The Other Equipment

A third milk crate (in addition to two kitchen crates) holds items we seldom need to take out of the car: the backup Peak 1 stove, lantern and mantles, directions, extra fuel and matches in a waterproof container; string; trowel; a pocket hammock; a 15' cord with clothes pins in a ditty bag; a Solar Shower; the First Need Filter; and a small pair of pruning shears - useful when a shrub stalk is in just the wrong place.

We each have a day pack with camera, film, binoculars (pocket ones fit nicely in a small ditty bag padded with foam rubber), pocket knife, Kleenex in a Ziplock bag, bandana, hat with visor, sun screen, bug dope in a small leakproof metal box, and Wash 'n Dris. Wallet, keys, etc., can also go in the day pack, or, as has proved handier, in a purse along with sun glasses. If you smoke, a metal bandaid box covered with contact paper, makes a fireproof ashtray to carry.

What clothing you take obviously depends on the weather. The Times World Weather Guide, Pearce and Smith, gives high and low temperatures, humidity and precipitation each month for various cities throughout the world. We have found that a large ditty bag or duffle for uncrushables and a small suitcase for crushables provides ample room for each person. Along with dress up clothes, the suitcase contains extra and exposed film, a sewing kit, address book, traveller's checks, first aid supplies and medicines. We got along fine with just boat mocs for driving and at campsites and sneakers for swimming in unknown waters.

Catalog stores: L.L.Bean (Freeport,ME 04033) is notable for quick service and a special women's sport catalog. REI (Box C-88125,Sea.,WA 98188) gives dividends to members. Wearguard (Hingham,MA 02043) features inexpensive, sturdy work clothes. SI (Box 3796,Gardena,CA 90247) has good buys on used military clothes. Bass Pro (1935 S.Campbell,Sprfld, MO 65898), Ramsey (Bx 1680, NJ 07653), and Campmor (Bx 997, Paramus,NJ 07653) have many standard items at lower prices than the fancier catalogs. Don Gleason's (Bx 87,Nhmtn,MA 01061) has many spare parts and accessories. James River Traders (Hampton,VA 23631) and Lands'End have some good buys on clothing. And worth getting just for its luscious layout is Patagonia (Bx 86,Ventura,CA 93002). Jan Brown, MA, 1988/89 (previously published in Women Outdoors magazine, addr.on p.A)

For Obtaining Hot Water from a Washing Machine

Most washers have a push-in switch at the bottom of the lid door. You can often reach it while the lid is up, allowing you to hold the jug while it is filling if the water isn't too hot. Ken Scharabok, August, Ohio

More Items Useful for "Out There" Repairs

I buy hot glue sticks in bulk packs. They store well for years. When heated with candle, etc., can seal holes in pails, bottles, boats; glue solid surfaces together; mend wood; etc.

Plastic zip/stop/lock ties, commonly used to bundle wires together or to an object, also serve to fasten wire frames together (such as a fish trap) or fasten poles together for a structural frame. They are a good substitute for wire in corrosive areas like salt-water boats. I buy assorted sizes.

Acrylic clear nail polish is useful not only for coating your finger nails to protect them when working dirt or cement, but also for waterproofing cord bindings, coating cracked wire insulation against short circuiting, coating soldered wire joints against corrosion, coating (dry) fingertips (twice) to obscure prints, and fixing pinhole leaks in plastic sheets.

I also take a Portasol butane-powered tool ($40-$60). With interchangeable heads, it provides a soldering iron, hot knife, hot air blower, and torch. I use it to solder wires, thaw frozen locks, start fires, cut plastic, and seal plastic. Burns 30-90 minutes. Refillable. Wildflower, CT, 1990

Bye Spy: Tips for Staying Free and Effective

As police agencies target more and more activities, many people feel their only choices are slavish conformity or paralyzing paranoia. However, my compatriots and I accomplish most of what we want, in relative safety, by apply three rules: (1) Seem small and unimportant. (2) Trust only those closely involved with you. (3) Minimize time in dangerous situations.

The police might like you to believe that they watch every move, listen to every conversation, and study every letter. But they can't. They can pay close attention to relatively few. They will choose you only if you are an easy target or if they consider you and your group especially important.

Keeping groups small and numerous, or thoroly decentralized, not only increases your safety, but by "cluttering the field" reduces risks for everyone.

Who are important in the eyes of inquisitors will vary from agency to agency and year to year.... Whether or not an activity is explicitly illegal does not matter very much because thousands of vague laws grant police broad powers. The announced reason for suppression may not be the chief reason - as with marijuana....

In the coming decade, the activities targeted will probably include low-cost ways of living. Requiring less income, they reduce tax collections and threaten all those who have grown dependant on Uncle Sapsucker. Back in the 70's, there was more redirection (or co-option) than prosecution: the mass media publicized a few fashionable "alternatives" (such as $100,000 "homesteads") and some self-reliance trivia (such as making your own handkerchiefs), while largely ignoring options offering big savings. But in the 90's, with fewer people affluent, redirection may not suffice. If it doesn't, expect overt attacks.... (Only relatively large groups) will probably be infiltrated. Lesser groups and individuals will be monitored if they can be easily; else ignored.

Distinguishing between infiltration and monitoring: An "infiltrator" is someone who devotes much time to penetrating one specific group or activity. A "monitor" is someone who attempts to track a number of groups or individuals without devoting much time to any one. A large part of monitoring is collecting and correlating information publicly available.

But making sense of the data and weeding out disinformation usually requires reports from persons on the scene.... The one trait all monitors possess (as long as they remain monitors rather than infiltrators) is an unwillingness to devote much time to one target.... This brings me to rule 2: Trust only those closely involved with you. Looked at another way: either be very close to someone, or else very distant. Try not to mess with mister or ms in-between. Looked at yet another way: a few steady companions are usually worth more than many occasional friends....

Without limiting myself to existing companions, I cannot avoid in-between relationships entirely. So I minimize them by developing new relationships rapidly and by ending unproductive ones promptly and completely. I.e., either come in or go out. Don't loiter in the doorway....

Unlike monitors, infiltrators may be impossible to spot. A top-notch one may be hired and trained to penetrate one specific group or activity, and may devote years to gaining trust.... Intelligence agencies expect losses and lapses. Against an important target, they may send several agents unaware of each other and cross-check reports. No way can a targeted group prevent infiltration and still function well. But, because deep-cover agents are costly, relatively few groups can be infiltrated. That brings me once again to rule 1: Seem small and unimportant. I say "seem" because, what matters is not how much impact your work actually has, but what your enemies believe....

A group's optimum size will depend on the activity, but seldom will exceed a dozen near-full-time members. If larger, advantages of scale and specialization may be lost in higher overhead, even if the group should escape infiltration.

Finally, rule 3: minimize time in dangerous situations.... You can best judge what is riskiest for you.

Advice to dress and act inconspicuously, is well and good. But no matter how careful you are - accidents happen! I've had very few encounters with police, which I attribute, not to great ability at blending in, but to my spending little time where police are common. Most places they frequent are dangerous in other ways as well. E.g., highways: one survivalist seriously injured himself in a wreck while driving hundreds of miles to attend a survival workshop.... (Reprinting welcome if this notice is included.) Frieda Linkbetter, 1991 (much condensed)

How Do You Avoid Annoying Marijuana Cultivators?

Those paragons of free enterprise are reputedly more willing to be violent than formerly. I learned to be streetsmart as a medic in Detroit. Backpacking infrequently, I suspect I've yet to become "trailsmart". Jon Seaver, MI, March

(Reply:) We steer clear of any cultivation or structure, unless there are clear signs of welcome or of long abandonment. Tramping through a garden or picking the plants will naturally infuriate the gardener, be the crop marijuana or marigolds.

We've seen only two small patches of marijuana (many years ago). Both were on low land near water. So, in hilly country, most cultivation can probably be missed by staying high.

Though a few cultivators may plant booby traps or stand armed guard, I suspect that attacks on innocent hikers are rare, and that the problem has been much exaggerated by big media in collaboration with drug hunters anxious to justify their jobs.

On the west coast, most serious cultivation seems to be indoors or farther south (in CA). (Most summers here are too cloudy to produce potent marijuana, we've heard.) Perhaps readers in northern CA will comment further. Bert & Holly, OR

Dwelling Portably

(formerly Message Post) #28
POB 190, Philomath, OR 97370

April 1992 $1 per issue   Add 50¢ to check/mo under $10

MY CHILDREN AND I WERE IN OUR TENT DURING A THUNDER STORM

The lightning struck so close we saw light even with our
eyes closed. I kept everyone away from the poles and we had no
trouble. Once in a tipi with Native American friends during a
night-long ceremony, lightning struck just outside. Everything
went blue. The man next to me was leaning on one of the tipi
poles and felt the current go down the pole.

The Plains Indians weathered the most violent storms in
their tipis. I suspect they kept away from the poles.
Laura Martin-Buhler, The Gentle Survivalist, Utah, August

SEVERAL LAYERS OF OLD CARPET INSULATE THE ROOF OF OUR YURT

They make a big difference when the sun beats down. The
yurt is now slightly cooler inside than is the air under the
shadiest nearby trees. The yurt can support the extra weight.

My husband found the carpet in a dumpster behind a carpet
store - the manager was glad for him to take it. To get the
smell out, I had to bake it in the sun and spray it with a
bleach solution. Anne Callaway, California, August

TEMPERATURE AND HUMIDITY AFFECT TENSION OF RIPSTOP NYLON

It stretches when cold and wet; contracts when hot and dry.
During a cold rainstorm, a nylon tent slackens, and will flap
and jerk until you tighten it. But don't forget to loosen it
afterwards. I did one morning and went hiking. The afternoon
sun drew it tighter than a drum. Henry, Arizona

SIMPLE DWELLING IS COMFORTABLE IN MOST WEATHER

The Hillodge is designed for
portable living year around on
steep slopes. A clear
front wall, combined ≫➤

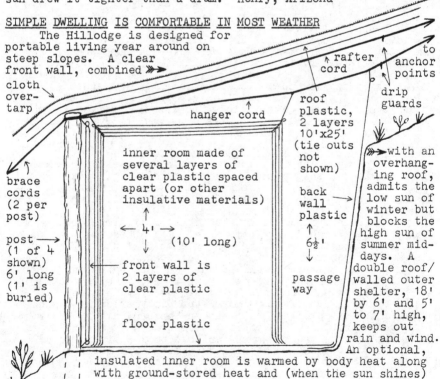

cloth
over-
tarp

hanger cord

↑ rafter
cord

to
anchor
points

drip
guards

roof
plastic,
2 layers
10'x25'
(tie outs
not
shown)

inner room made of
several layers of
clear plastic spaced
apart (or other
insulative materials)

back
wall
plastic

≫with an
overhang-
ing roof,
admits the
low sun of
winter but
blocks the
high sun of
summer mid-
days. A
double roof/
walled outer
shelter, 18'
by 6' and 5'
to 7' high,
keeps out
rain and wind.
An optional,

brace
cords
(2 per
post)

← 4' →

(10' long)

post →
(1 of 4
shown)
6' long
(1' is
buried)

front wall is
2 layers of
clear plastic

6½'

passage
way

floor plastic

insulated inner room is warmed by body heat along
with ground-stored heat and (when the sun shines)
solar heat. (Heating stove not needed in mild

climates.) Materials cost $30 to $60 in 1991.

The frame consists of only four posts, each with 4 cords. Each post sets up independently, minimizing readjustments.

The roof consists of two sheets of plastic 10 x 25' (the commonest size) uncut, which are simply layed upon the frame and tied out. An optional overtarp of cloth or light matting will extend the life of the plastic and reduce visibility.

The front wall and one end are formed from one 10x25 sheet of clear plastic, folded double. (Tips for erecting on page 3.)

I BOUGHT AN 8 x 10 x 6 DOME AND PUT IT UP ON MY LAND

I will use it this summer. It includes a tent, rain fly, poles and stakes, which all fit in a small bag. It is easy for one person to carry and to put up. I got it instead of a tipi because it has a floor. I almost bought a "Mountainshelter" but it was too expensive. After reading Henry's comments (p.4) I am glad I didn't. I did buy their stove but found it cheaply made and feel I wasted money. Gloria Orr, New York, June

OUR PARTTIME NEIGHBOR HAS AN 18-FOOT DOME FROM SHELTER SYSTEMS

She had trouble with rain coming in at the doors. (I don't know if she followed the advice in the manual.) Left unoccupied for a few weeks last November, the dome was flattened by 6 to 8 inches of wet snow. Most of the plastic pipes and connectors were broken, but the fabric appeared undamaged. Moral: never leave a lightweight dome unattended. Anne Schein, CA, Jan.1991 (Shelter Systems' catalog cautions that snow must be removed.)

I USE BLUE CLOSED-CELL FOAM ON TOP OF OPEN-CELL FOAM

It blocks the cold and keeps both foams from pancaking. I haven't slept on closed-cell foam by itself. There are at least two grades of blue closed-cell foam. I get the better grade but, even so, it starts thinning after a month or two (less quickly if used together with open-cell foam) losing insulation and cushioning value. Lee Mauck, CA, Feb. 1991

COMPARTMENTED AIR MATTRESSES ARE NOT VERY DURABLE

I had one with tube inserts which developed pin-hole leaks and went flat. Samples in the store did too. You can carry spare tubes but that runs up weight and cost. Lee, CA

OUTER COVER PROTECTS AND NEATENS WORN BEDDING

Ragged blankets, quilts, and sleeping bags used as quilts, provide good insulation. But I don't like their looks nor the way my fingers and toes snag their holes - and enlarge them.

To cover, I make a simple envelope, joined at top and sides, open at bottom. It's a foot longer than the bedding to allow for creep-up at the bottom. For material I look at garage sales and for discontinued styles in fabric stores. Some sheets have pretty patterns; white ones can be dyed.

The bedding is held in place within the cover by ball ties at corners and top center: bunch all layers over a wad of rag and secure with a rubber band. Easily removed for washing.
Julie

EXTRA CLOTHES AND BLANKETS SERVE AS CUSHIONS

That way they remain useful, rather than taking up storage space. And the frequent movement discourages moths. I sewed cushion covers out of heavy cloth I found. Paul Doerr, CA

WE ARE MOVING INTO AN 18' DOME-TENT ON FIVE WILD ACRES

We first thought of a yurt but couldn't find any 18'+ ones for less than $1300. Laurel & Charles, Texas, Jan.

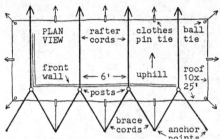

PLAN VIEW	rafter ←cords→	clothes pin tie	ball tie
front wall	← 6' →	uphill	roof 10x 25'
	←posts→		

brace cords
anchor points

TIPS FOR ERECTING A HILLODGE

I prefer southerly slopes during fall and winter, and easterly slopes during spring and summer (for morning warmth).

For a site, choose a 10 by 25 foot area clear of high bushes or trees. Uphill must either be steep, or else have fair size trees to provide elevated anchor points for the rafter cords. (Avoid large trees dangerously close.) Downhill ideally has no trees or tall bushes close enough to block light. Level and smooth a 6' by 18' terrace.

Only shallow post holes are needed, because cords will brace the posts. I round and smooth the top of each post so that it won't puncture the roof plastic. Carving a groove close to the top helps to keep the rafter cords in place.

Seldom are anchor points for rafter cords ideally located. I use whatever are available and then reposition each rafter cord with an auxilliary cord pulling sideways. I run separate cords for hanging things on, rather than use the rafter cords and sag them.

If the rafter cords must fasten to trees (because uphill isn't steep), I tie to the bases of branches (rather than around trunks, to avoid bruising), and then brace to logs, roots, or bases of bushes (to avoid bending the trees).

For the roof, black plastic will outlast clear, especially if no cloth overtarp. To tie out the plastic, I use 1½-2" diameter ball ties on the corners, but spring-clamp clothespins on the sides (where ball ties might form rain-collecting pockets). Where clothespinning, I roll the edge of the plastic a few times around a straight twig, ¼" diameter a few inches long; clamp to the roll; then tighten the grip by wrapping a narrow rubber strap around the clothes pin. I tie the tie-out cord through the clothespin's spring.

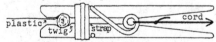

I stretch the roof's upper layer tauter than the lower layer, to form ±1" air spaces between. For an overtarp, I use any old drab-colored cloth, pieced together. Because the plastic is waterproof, the cloth need not be.

On the uphill side, just inward from the edge of the plastic, I wrap a piece of string or strap around each cord, so that any water running along the cord will drip off there rather than inside.

I ball-tie the front wall plastic to the posts, bottom as well as top (rather than just set rocks/dirt on the bottom), for reliability and to save time moving.

I cover the back wall and floor with plastic, to block moisture and confine any loose dirt or leaves. Odd/holed/salvaged pieces may be used, overlapping as necessary. For comfort and appearance I add mats, rugs or drapes.

An insulated inner room can be built in various ways out of many different materials: anything that can be kept in position and will provide several inches of loft. We have used our Hillodge only during spring so far, and thus have not needed an inner room. When I build one I plan to use several layers of clear plastic for sides and top, suspending them ¼" to 1" apart with a succession of ball-ties-with-tails. Such can be made by tying a bulky knot in a short length of cord. To erect, wrap the top layer of plastic over the bulky knot and tie the suspension cord around the base of the bundle, letting the tail hang through. Then tie the tail to the next layer of plastic in a similar manner. Etc. How I build the ends of the inner room will depend on the materials at hand.

If a 6 by 18' Hillodge is not roomy enough, rather than enlarging, I would build additional shelters near by. (Leveling a site for a Hillodge twice as big would disturb 8 times as much dirt.)

Limitations of the Hillodge: The roof is not steep enough to shed snow, nor strong enough to support an accumulation, and therefore should not be left up and untended when heavy snow is likely. The plastic roof and front wall may not take gales. The frame is not well suited for areas which are both flat and treeless. The outer shell includes seams that will admit insects unless carefully chinked. (A bug net can be hung in inner room.)

Tho the frame, roof, and most walls are simple, the end closures are irregular - and are left for the builder to work out. (Detailed instructions would not only fill many pages, but might take longer to read and understand than to invent for yourself.)

Comparing the Hillodge with Wanda's Tleanto (in Sept'85 and Sept'86 MP):

The Tleanto's roof is steeper and stronger, and thus can shed snow or support an accumulation. The frame is self supporting, not requiring high anchor points; thus is not restricted to steep hillsides or edges of groves. The front wall is higher, providing more solar heating and more light inside, especially high up. If south facing, a Tleanto does not need a cloth overtarp to prevent reflections of the sun.

The Hillodge's frame (only 4 posts) is much simpler and lighter. The rafters are cords instead of poles, and thus are not hazardous if they break. The roof slopes the same direction as the land, and thus is less intrusive and less buffeted by wind. The inner room can be placed at the front, with a full-height passageway behind it. For the same width of terrace, it has more floor space. B&H

REPORT ON THE "MOUNTAINSHELTER"

In the Jan. 1991 issue, I evaluated the 9x9' Chouinard "Megamid" and asked if there were similar tents twice as big.

I found one: a Mountainsmith 8-man "Mountainshelter". It has an oval cone shape with floor diameters of 14 and 18'. Like the "Megamid", it has an adjustable center pole, coated ripstop nylon, and no floor. It weighs 9½ pounds, and the 8¼' pole breaks down into four sections, easy to backpack. The zippers are heavy duty YKK coils and should hold up well as long as you don't try to stuff the tent into too small a bundle.

However, while living in it this past fall and winter in the mountains of AZ and NM, I discovered major problems.

For some reason the fabric's coated side is out, rather than in. So, unlike the Megamid where condensation droplets inside run harmlessly down the smooth walls to the eaves, in the Mountainshelter they adhere to the fabric's rough inside until a breeze shakes them loose and they rain on everything. Consequently, when breaking camp, you have to wait for your sleeping bag to dry.

The Mountainshelter has two windows. But they are less than a sq. foot each and are covered with a heavy duty mosquito netting, which not only reduces air flow, but being white clouds the view.

The stove-pipe vent near the apex is made of a Kevlar fabric that resembles plastic-coated fiberglass cloth. Being near the apex it experiences much stress and stitches in it pull out easily. I have glued and then sewn on a patch of coated nylon packcloth to prevent pulling away from the edges, but have left the hole open as an air vent.

The folding stainless-steel stove sold for the tent ($170), is so small you must fuel it with twigs every 20 min. They also sell for $85 a propane stove. But you can get one with nearly as many BTUs from Walmart for $15, which is also lighter and more compact.

The 6" pegs supplied with the tent are inadequate for anyplace but a lawn in fair weather. I've tried a number of commercially available pegs and presently prefer 10" Durapegs for most situations. These pegs alone will not hold with high winds and either water-saturated soil or the gravelly sand common in southwest mountains. To reinforce them, I tie a piece of 1/8" braided nylon cord around each peg, and tie the ends together to form a 4" loop. Another peg can then be put through the first peg's loop, bracing it; and then a third peg in its loop cord, etc. This may be over kill, but is better than having your tent blow down during a freezing rainstorm on a pitch black night. The loops also aid removal of pegs from hard or frozen ground. The tent's original loops are rather small, so to them I have tied 4" loops of cord.

The tent has some two dozen peg loops and you might think it would be a beast to erect. Not so. One person can do it in 15 minutes, even in high winds. Stretch out the tent along the long diameter and temporarily peg it at both ends. Then move each end in 2' toward the center and drive the pegs in. Next pull each end of the short diameter out until taut, then in 1½' and peg firmly. You now have the base held at four points and can insert the center pole. Then, starting next to the short diameter and alternating sides, stretch the loops out and peg away. (A method such as this would also probably be a good way to erect a parachute tent like the one I described in the May 1991 issue.)

A final problem of the Mountainshelter is the price: $600 list. I bought mine through REI for $500 and will get a 10% member rebate on that. Henry, AZ,Mar'91

EARTH FLOORS WARM AND COOL NATURALLY

During hot weather, the ground takes heat from the air above; during cold weather, it gives heat back. Where we live is usually mild, with extreme cold and heat infrequent and brief. If we lived where subfreezing temperatures persisted many months, we would insulate not only our shelter, but also the earth around it for several feet (perhaps with mulch or extra snow) to keep the frost from creeping in under us.

Shelter Systems also likes earth floors. "Being on the ground is warmer than being on a deck (wooden platform) unless the deck is heavily insulated - because of cool air flowing under (the deck). Earth floors are incredibly inexpensive compared to decks, they save trees and are easier to construct. (On a sloping site) make a level area with a ditch around the uphill side for drainage. On a flat site, raise an area above the surrounding ground to insure that water will flow away." Add plastic as barrier to vapor and dirt. H & B, OR

PORTABLE DWELLINGS SAFER IN EARTHQUAKES

A best-selling prehistoric novel begins with an earthquake. The ground cracks open, a woman falls in, and the ground closes again - while her daughter watches in horror. A few people may have died that way, but many more are crushed by collapsing buildings or trapped in wreckage which then burns. As a geologist said after one major quake: "Earthquakes don't kill people. Buildings kill people."

Portable dwellings are generally much safer in quakes, both because they are flexible and bend instead of breaking, and because, if they do collapse, there is less weight to hurt anyone. "In the days following the 7.1 quake in Santa Cruz in Oct.'89, our neighbors find more security in a flexible 'LightHouse' (portable dome) than in their damaged home", writes Robert & Catherine Gillis in Shelter Systems' catalog (see p.C).

Places like California and Japan are lucky in a way, because the frequent quakes relieve the stresses before they become extremely large. According to geologic evidence, the northwest gets colossal earthquakes every 1000 years or so (not very regular) much more severe than the quake that wrecked San Francisco. These are often accompanied by waves hundreds of feet high smashing the coast. Other "earthquake free" areas may also. (No one knows yet.)

Animals acting oddly, strange odors, early tremors, sometimes give warning.
April 1992   H & B

FREE RV PARKING IN SOUTHEAST CALIFORNIA
"The Slabs" is the remains of a military base on the east side of the Salton
Sea about 50 miles north of the Mexican
border. During winter several thousand
people live there in various rigs. You
can camp without vehicle if you like but
it's rough. Winters are mild: dates
grow around there. Summers are often
hot (120º sometimes), sometimes humid
from irrigation and the Salton Sea,
sometimes sand storms. Few people stay
the entire summer. Lee Mauck, CA,Feb'91

MORE ABOUT CAMPING IN BAJA CALIFORNIA
There is abundant free camping once
you know where to go. Be discrete and
take your time. If no one is around, it
is free. There are various little roads
off the highway to the Sea of Cortez.
At one spot camping may be $7 a night,
while expensive motorhomes 100 yards
away are parking free because they knew
a road that led to government land.
Some people out in the country can
advise you on what is free. I don't
think you can get this info in town.
The main difficulty is getting fresh
water. You can buy it for about 25¢ a
gallon and then have to get it to your
camp. Second-class buses are cheap,
clean and safe, and stop anywhere.
Without papers you can go south as
far as San Felipe on the Sea of Cortez
and a few miles past Ensenada on the
Pacific. The U.S. and Mex. governments
are negotiating for an open border, but
presently, bringing computers, TVs,VCRs,
etc. into Mexico is a hassle. If you
cross the border during commute hours
and don't look like a tourist, you probably won't be stopped.
Just as you get street wise, you get
Mexico wise. Cops are creeps but bribe-
able - they just want their cut. Unless
you are arrogant you can't get into much
trouble. Working for money is a crime:
if caught you get deposited on the U.S.
side of the border and the cops keep
what you had. Mexicans know poverty and
have an eye for it but are not hostile
toward it as in the U.S. Lee Mauck

GETTING DENTAL WORK IN MEXICO
During the past 20 years I've had 8
teeth crowned by four dentists in Mexican border cities; most in Tijuana.
Three of them did work that lasted,and
seemed honest; one did poor work,and
lied. (On average, bit better than U.S.)
The dentists themselves seem to net
about as much as north of the border
(and seem about as well trained and
equipped). But lab work such as crowns
and bridges costs much less, and overhead is lower - legal liability especially. In 1989 for an alloy crown I paid
$70 U.S. (a gold crown would have been
$170). A U.S. dentist asked $350 for
gold. (I now have four alloy crowns.
They have given no trouble; however the
oldest is only 8 years; whereas my oldest gold crown is 30 years.)
Get recommendations from people who
have had the same kind of.work you need.
If lacking recommendations, ask dentist
(or any skill-person in any country)
what they do most of, before saying what
you need. Tho most dentists will do
crowns, some do many more, and not only

get better at them, but also faster and
may charge less. The average Mexican
border dentist probably does crowns
better than the average U.S. dentist
simply because of doing more of them.
Unless fluent in Spanish, seek English
speaking dentists (in border cities where
available). A Spanish-only dentist is apt
to quote higher, to allow extra time for
the language barrier. Dentists expect a
50% deposit; U.S. currency seems welcome.
With dentists anywhere, do get a firm
quote, making sure it includes everything. Before getting a root canal,
obtain second and third opinions. (In my
experience, if a tooth doesn't hurt, it
doesn't need a root canal.) Chal, CA,Jan.

DENTAL SELF HELP AND MORE HELP
For a temporary filling (if an old
one falls out) I keep myrhh handy. Heat
it until it becomes a sticky sap, then
apply it to the tooth where it hardens
once more. It's also antiseptic. It
won't work long, but will protect the
tooth until you can get further treatment.
Dental prices are much lower in Mexico. If looking without personal recommendations, you are as apt to find a
good dentist there as here. A U.S. con-
sulate or embassy will provide a list of
dentists they think competant, but who
may charge more than the local norm.
In the U.S., universities with dental
schools provide low/no-cost work done by
students supervised by teachers who are
some of the best in their field.
Rainbow Hawk, New York, August

FOR IMPROVISED FILLING OF CAVITY IN TOOTH
Tamp in a ball of wax or pine resin.
Wildflr.
CONIFER RESIN NATURAL BANDAID
Spread on small wounds, it keeps out
dirt and bacteria. I've found it soothing and it may even promote healing. In
Plants With A Purpose, Richard Mabey says
resin (pitch) may be antibiotic to fungi
and bacteria. Thin, somewhat runny pitch
seems to sooth more than the thick, gummy
kind. After applying pitch, I dust it
with fern spores, ashes, or flour -
whatever is handiest, to keep it from
sticking to things. I've used pitch from
hemlock (Tsuga) and doug-fir (Pseudotsu-
ga). Young trees with thin bark often
have small pitch-filled blisters. Julie

AMERICAN INDIAN MEDICINE
Virgil J. Vogel's book extracts from
the vast literature on Indians. Altho
ineffective against introduced diseases
such as smallpox, "Indian treatment of
externally caused injuries (such as bites
and fractures) was usually rational and
often effective." Vogel, a historian,
"renders no judgement on efficacy...."
To poison ivy, various Indians applied
Grindelia robusta (tarweed), Astragalus
nitidus (milk vetch), Lactuca canadensis
(wild lettuce) juice, Impatiens biflora
(jewelweed) leaves, Lepidium virginicum
(Virginia peppergrass), Fagus grandifolia
(beech) bark tea, Rhus glabra (sumach)
poultice of leaves or berries.
Vogel surveys only 200 plants (ones in
USP/NF). The Cherokees alone used ±800.
1970, 584pp, $29 in'86, University of
Oklahoma Press, POB 787,Norman,OK 73070.

TIPS FOR SEEING BETTER AT NIGHT

People can see surprisingly well in dim light after their eyes become accustomed: allow ten minutes or more. If using a light briefly, keep one eye closed (I was amazed how dark-adapted it remained). Look near, rather than directly at an object. If observing a large area, keep eyes moving.

To prepare, avoid carbon monoxide (cigarette smoke especially) which decreases oxygen to eyes; avoid alcohol; get good nutrition (particularly vitamin A) and adequate rest. Minimize time in bright light during the day, to conserve the eyes' chemicals for night use. (From Sept'91 Directions; see p.A)

EASY-TO-MAKE CANDLE LANTERN DOES NOT BLOW OUT

Furthermore, it directs the light away from you and thus does not blind you. And it keeps your hands warm. Any can with a shiny inside may be used, but a 3-pound coffee can is the best size. It does not get overly hot, and it is easy to light in a wind because you can put your whole hand inside with a lighter or match.

About an inch from the original bottom of can, punch a hole into which the candle will fit snugly. Insert only an inch of it into the can. Readjust as it burns down. "Plumbers" candles work best for me. If all you have is a smaller can, use a much smaller candle. Make the handle out of wire.

This lantern is also great for late reading, because it may be placed close to the text with you behind and no light in your eyes. The can acts as a reflector, giving more light than you might expect. Paul White, WA, April & May 1991

VENTILATION IS VITAL WHERE ANYTHING IS BURNING

Responding to Jan'91 issue: Just because "the fumes don't smell bad" does not mean they are safe to breathe. What do you suppose is the "black deposit" collecting on the mantles? It isn't CO_2, it isn't water, and it doesn't belong in your lungs.

Though an alcohol lamp might produce only CO_2 and water if perfectly adjusted, any imperfection causing incomplete combustion will produce carbon monoxide, which is not only poisonous but also explosive. (Ask any firefighter about flashover.)

I urge you to VENTILATE when using ANY flame OR catalytic appliance. Ideally, air for burning comes directly from outside and goes directly back to outside, Check frequently that intake duct and chimney are airtight. Jon Seaver, R.N., MI

KEEP EXHAUSTED LIGHTERS TO USE AS SPARK GENERATORS

After a disposable lighter runs out of fuel, remove the metal shield, and use to ignite tinder or propane appliances.

Dry sawdust mixed with dry lint (clothes driers are a source) provide good tinder. Store in an airtight container until needed. Wildflower, Connecticut, February 1991

DISPOSABLE LIGHTERS CAN CORRODE - AND MAY BE HAZARDOUS

Tho not as vulnerable to moisture as matches are, a lighter left a few days in a damp raincoat pocket became inoperable. The nozzle corroded shut, the flint corroded stuck, and much of the sparker wheel's purposely rough surface rusted away.

While repairing, the flint and spring shot out - with amazing force! Moral: don't point lighter at anything hurtable.

Lighters removed from wet within a few minutes and allowed to air dry did not corrode. When drying, don't subject a lighter to much heat: treat it like the bomb it is. Julie, OR

STICK WITH STUB BRANCH HELPS WASH CLOTHES BY HAND

I sit on a log (or covered pail with cushion) next to a 5-gallon pail of laundry, and agitate with one hand at a time. To minimize back bending and detergent contact, I use an L-shaped stick about 2 feet long (5/8" diameter is strong enough without excess weight) with a 4-inch-long branch-stub flush on the end that goes in the wash. For easier gripping, I enlarge the handle end by wrapping with a strap or rags. Julie Summers, Oregon, March 1991

BULKY CLOTHING CAN BE WASHED BY WALKING ON

Prepare a tub-size hole in the ground, removing any sharp projections. Line with plastic. Place in it a sleeping bag, etc., and soapy water. Let soak, then agitate by walking on. Add more water to rinse. Most cheap sleeping bags may be washed this way. Paul Doerr, California, February 1991

SOME MILK JUGS HAVE SCREW CAPS THAT SEAL WELL

One kind of cap has no gasket to wear out, but rather an inner lip molded out of the cap's plastic. These continue to seal well over time. I prefer them for portable faucets (LLL plans) on which leaky caps would be undesirable. (I collect strays I find, as spares for any missing or broken.) Julie

JUGS THAT DEVELOP LEAKS CAN BE MADE INTO SINKS AND TRAYS

The 2½ and 5 gallon rectangular narrow-mouth plastic jugs, discarded by restaurants and bakeries, are handy sizes. I use intact jugs for water hauling and storage. But in time, some spring leaks. Cut in two vertically, the leakless half can be used as a sink or dish drain; the leaky half as storage tray.

FUNNEL MADE FROM VINYL DRINK BOTTLE FITS MOST ONE-GALLON JUGS

The two-liter size with a long neck fits down in well, and is wide enough to pass grain. (Suggested by Kurt Saxon.) The cut-off bottom can be used as a cup or bowl. To fit into jugs with narrow mouths, I file off the threads. Julie, OR

DURING HOT WEATHER I USE PAPER BAGS FOR CARRYING BREAD

The paper (unlike plastic) lets the food dry out, thus preventing mold. If the bread gets rock hard, it can be softened with water before eating. Julie Summers, Oregon

POPCORN POPPED WITHOUT OIL KEEPS WELL

It does not mold, nor go rancid. Because of its bulk I tie it outside of my pack, or compact by grinding it. Plastic bags will keep it dry. If ground, I eat it like granola with raisins, nuts, sunflower seeds. Because popcorn stores well, I reserve it for last, and eat perishables first. Julie, OR

COVERING BERRIES WITH JUICE PRESERVES THEM FOR SEVERAL DAYS

Picking just before eating is best for taste and nutrition. But sometimes I have a surplus of blackberries, raspberries or huckleberries and no refrigeration. If nothing is done, some berries are moldy the next day. To prevent mold, immediately after picking I juice enough to cover the rest and store in the coolest place available. I use a 10x12" drawstring bag, made of fine-weave nylon curtain fabric, to hold back the seeds while squeezing out the juice. The pulp can be soaked in water and squeezed again to yield berry-ade, which I drink promptly (seems to sour faster than berries). Julie

Dwelling Portably

(formerly named Message Post)
POB 190, Philomath, OR 97370

Sept. 1992 $1 per issue   Add 50¢ to check/mo under $10

HOW IS A STOVE INSTALLED IN A TENT?

How far from the walls is it placed? Does the chimney go
out the sides or out the top? How is the outside part secured?
Where do you get a non-combustible collar, and how do you keep
the liner and tent from touching there? If you use a spacer
between liner and tent, what is it made out of?
        I am making a tent that a hammock can be hung in. I will
let you know how it turns out. Bob Barker, WA, March

A FRIEND DID THIS:

Where tent would be, dug
pit for a small wood stove
plus a trench for the flue pipe.
The pipe was buried with 6" of
dirt between it and the tent's
wall. The outside chimney was
supported with 3/4" iron pipe.
The surplus canvas tent in
northern Canada was heated all
winter this way. Wildflower, July

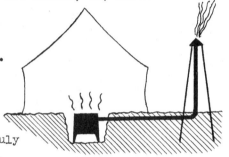

MORE INFO WANTED REGARDING COLD WEATHER LIVING

It seems most of you are living in moderate winter
climates. Here it is nearly zero every night for a month or
more. Scott Shaward, New Mexico, January

COMMENTS ON VENTILATION AND BURNING APPLIANCES

Whenever a stove or lantern is used inside, the oxygen
for combustion must come from somewhere and the end products
of combustion (chiefly CO_2, H_2O vapor and - if combustion is
incomplete - CO (the silent killer) and any of a host of
potentially carcinogenic substances) must go somewhere.
        True enough, the solution is to provide ventilation in
excess of the needs of the appliance plus any occupants.
When faced with the necessity of using a stove inside a tent
in mountaineering situations when providing adequate ventilation is difficult because of weather - and this is a common
situation - and your life depends on getting snow melted, etc.,
then a stove which is least likely to generate deadly carbon
monoxide will be safest. Water vapor and CO_2 are normal
byproducts of human respiration and pose not the extraordinary
risks associated with CO which, without warning, can cause
unconsciousness and death.
        Alcohol produces less heat per fuel weight than does
petroleum (including white gas, kerosene, butane). That means
that alcohol will be considered as a fuel in situations where
weight is critical only if the devices that burn it are, by
design, more efficient. Designs which rely on minimal moving
parts (operator adjustments) to obtain efficient combustion,
will tend to be safer in the situations described above.
        Be aware of factors that can compromise the efficiency
and safety of alcohol-burning stoves such as Trangia, Optimus
or Westwind. One is burning a fuel other than ethanol or
methanol. Another is burning a fuel contaminated with other
chemicals. The color of the flame (it should be blue, not
yellow) and the absence of soot accumulation on bottoms of
pots are good indications of efficient combustion. Robert, VT

SUGGESTIONS FOR GATHERING AND SELLING ALUMINUM DRINK CANS

I find that a mop handle, with a right angle "hook" (with threads) screwed into the end, is perfect for retrieving drink cans from dumpsters. Barbeque tongs are good for retrieving cans from regular garbage containers. Any rest area is a great collecting place during hot weather when people drink a lot. When you go to sell them, the best prices are given by metal dealers rather than recycling centers which in turn resell them to a metal dealer. Tumbleweed, Desert SW, Oct.

IDEA FOR CONNECTING REMOTE LIVING WITH CITY JOB

To put together and mail the May'90 MP, I hiked and biked over the mountains to a close-to-city camp site (where I had left stashed a sleeping bag, tarp, etc.) I stayed several days and, from there, made two one-day trips into the city (picking up the printed MP, putting it together at my camp, then returning to the city to mail).

I wonder if a family who has a steady business or employment in a big city, but who would like to live far out in the backcountry, might do something similar. One family member drives to the city several times a month and, each trip, works several days straight while sleeping in the vehicle. Other family members remain at their base camp. (In our case, Holly did. I went to the city camp alone.)

Of course this assumes a vehicle is needed for work (else would not be economical), and that the work can be performed in spurts. Bert, Oregon, November 1990

WHERE CAN YOU CAMP WHILE GAINING EXPERIENCE?

Do you know of anyone selling a plot of land really cheap that would be exempt from taxes? I think that I would first have to start in a tipi or something that is on land of my own, before I could entertain the idea of nomadic living. Brenda, CA, Febr. 1991

(Reply:) If you want to camp (or park) in one place for a long time, I suggest renting or swapping services (such as caretaking) for land, at least at first. I recommend not buying land, at least until you gain experience with your new dwellingway (whatever it may be), because, until you have experience, you won't know what kind of land or what area is good for what you want to do, or even if you will want to own land at all. I believe you could find suitable swap arrangements in various areas of northern CA and the northwest; maybe in southern CA. You may have to do quite a lot of advertising or looking around to find a situation you like. Place ads in places (stores, rural shoppers, etc.) frequented by rural property owners. Bert, Oregon, April 1991

SLEEPING ON STYROFOAM SHEETS IN WINTER

That is the most comfortable I've ever been at 0° F. Reflects body heat. Paul White, Washington, April 1991

ANY PLASTIC BOTTLE CAN SERVE AS A HOT-WATER BOTTLE

All it needs is a tight-closing cap. If my feet are cold when I go to bed, it warms them fast. Otherwise they may remain cold for hours. Holly, Oregon, December

TOOL MAKES COLLECTING MATERIALS FROM DUMPSTERS EASIER
       To a mop handle 4 to 6 feet long, tape to one end a magnet
from a speaker - for picking up metal hardware, and tape to the
other end a 10/0 fishhook (with sharp point cut off) for pulling
materials to you. Saves climbing into bins that might be
hazardous to be in. Wildflower, Connecticut, September

SQUARE PLASTIC JARS MAKE GREAT STORAGE
       I have some that Japanese seasoned seaweed comes in. They
are durable, light weight, and don't waste space as round
containers do. They hold 3 to 4 cups. A disadvantage is they
don't collapse as the contents are used, like a plastic bag
would. The seasoned seaweed makes a great snack. Lee Mauck,
                                                          June
HOW TO GET RID OF THINGS AND HAVE THEM TOO
       As living and storage space become more expensive, a
clutter of advice on reducing clutter has appeared: "If you
haven't used it in two years, throw it away." "Destroy it
before throwing in the waste basket so you won't be able to
change your mind." "Throw out everything you don't really
need." These kinds of suggestions can best be discarded
because they ignore the crucial factor: comparative costs.
       If holding on to something costs you little (in money,
time, or emotions) there is no reason to throw it away. In
fact, disposing of some things may cost more than keeping.
       For written items, consider putting them on microfiche.
That way they take up negligble space. For other items,
consider getting some 5 gallon pails (free or cheap at many
in-store bakeries). Fill them with what you don't really need
but don't want to destroy, go for a ride, and cache them in
the boonies. If you never go back, little is lost; if you do,
they might still be there. Julie Summers, Oregon, April

MORE USES FOR OLD INNER TUBES
       Float self or equipment over water.
       Float basket, bucket or net inside to hold crabs, clams,
or fish while catching more.
       Tractor tire tubes roped under wood platform form a
raft or support a small dometent (an expedient houseboat).
       On shore, if lined with plastic sheet, bag or poncho,
an inflated tube forms a basin for washing clothes, dishes
or feet, or as a small bin for veggies and fruit. Wildflower,
                                                          July
BIRD NETTING CAN BE USED TO COVER PLASTIC TENTS OR TARPS
       Weave various natural materials into the netting to
conceal the plastic or to protect it from the sun. A 14'
by 14' section costs about $10 in New England garden/nursery
outlets. Wildflower, Connecticut, November 1991

FORGET YOUR COOKING UTENSILS? DON'T WORRY!
       Many foods can be cooked directly on coals. The coals
keep the food above any dirt or gravel, and the ashes brush
off surprisingly well. The secret is to wait until all flames
are gone before cooking. Also, remember that the food will
become more susceptible to burning toward the end of cooking,
as water content is· reduced, so pay closer attention then.
Drier foods, like toast, require closer supervision than do
moister ones, like potatoes or steak. Julie Summers, Apr.'91

Dwelling Portably
(formerly named Message Post)
POB 190, Philomath, OR 97370

Dec. 1992 $1 per issue   Add 50¢ to   check/mo under $7

I BUILT A WIGWAM

I use it for rendezvous, Renaissance
Faires, and Pirate get togethers. It is 8'
by 10', and 8' high - giving plenty of head
room so I don't have to hunch over. Eight
people have slept in it. It has stood up in
some strong winds.

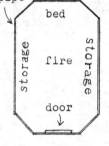

I use dome-tent poles and PVC pipe for
framing, and blankets and tablecloths for
cover. I put carpets on the floor. All
goods and bedding is stored in chests around
the sides. I have hung lamps on long hooks
from the frame. I even have a smoke flap,
so I can have a fire inside like in a tipi
if I want. I can partition the inside by
hanging blankets.

The whole thing lashes together in an
hour. 1. Put together PVC-pipe floor frame
(stake down). 2. Fit dome-tent pole arches
into holes drilled in pipe. 3. Weave dome-
tent side poles in and out of the arches
and lash in position. (Looks like a basket
upside down.) 4. Put on covering (any kind
you want). It comes apart in half an hour
and folds up into a small bundle that goes
in one chest.

Instead of poles and pipes, you may
use bamboo or branches - dug into ground.

I am looking for additional information
on wickiup, wigwam and yurt construction.
Lani Tucker, California, April

IMPROVISED COVERING KEEPS FEET AND LEGS WARM AT NIGHT

If your sleeping bag is marginal for warmth, but you have
extra clothes, use a sweater to insert your legs into. If one
sleeve is roomy enough to accomodate both legs, you can fold
the garment in half and invert one sleeve into the other. This
doubles the insulation, and keeps both legs together, reducing
exposed surface area and hence heat loss. (Mittens are warmer
than gloves for the same reason.)

Keep the garment zipped or buttoned as it normally would
be, and enter from the waist end, with the sleeves extended
away from you. To keep feet from protruding, I close the
cuffs with multiple turns of rubber bands.

This idea comes from One Day in the Life of Ivan Deniso-
vich, by Alexander S. Izhenitsyn (Bantam, 1963). Ivan, a
Siberian work camp prisoner in Stalinist Russia, slept with
his blanket and coat spread on top, "and both his feet tucked
in the sleeve of his jacket." (It is an extraordinary book,
showing how extremely harsh conditions can become taken for
granted, and how people build a life around them.) I got to
try the idea the very same week I read about it, during some
unseasonably cold spring days. Worked nicely. Julie Summers,

Is there anything non-toxic that will repel biting flies?

I have tried every suggestion I've heard: oils of pennyroyal and lavender, citronella, garlic juice. The pennyroyal
seems to repel crawling creatures, but the flies still bite.
Lavender seemed best, but the flies still bite, maybe less
often. Any ideas will be immediately tested ! L.N.Smith, WI

Dwelling Portably

(formerly Message Post)   #29
POB 190, Philomath OR 97370
May 1993 $1 per issue   Add 50¢ to check/mo under $7

How to Simple Shower in winter more comfortably.

Here's how we now bathe during cold weather. (1) Start
water heating. (2) Inside our inner (insulated) tent where
warm, soap up one part at a time. Rub each part until dry
before soaping the next part. (3) When water is the hottest
that will be comfortable, partially fill several plastic jugs.
(4) Wearing only thongs, carry jugs outside, along with
towels. (5) Rinse from the top down. (6) Dry off.

Advantages: less time outside; less time wet all over; no
fumbling with soap outside (and sometimes dropping in dirt).

(The soap-and-rub-dry technique was discovered by Mar at
age 7 as a magic trick. Soap on skin becomes invisible when
dry. Add water and get suds "from nowhere".) Wanda, CA, Jan.

Simple Shower saved energy and time - even in house.

Two years ago, Holly and I care-took a big old country
house for a month during the winter holidays. The electric
water heater was close to the kitchen sink, but far from the
bathroom. So, instead of running the shower faucet until warm
water finally came through, I simply filled a jug at the
kitchen sink, carried it to the bathroom, and Simple Showered.

This not only saved electricity, but saved me time. Also,
with a jug, easy to get the temperature you want before
undressing and wetting. (Holly opted for long hot soaks in the
tub: something we don't have at our camps.) Bert, OR, Dec.

Three-sided reflector solar heats water faster.

I made mine from polished aluminum sheet,
but a cut-down cardboard box covered with
aluminum foil works fine. It can warm jugs for
Simple Showers. Brother Bat, AZ, August

Jugs tested for solar heating water.

The four one-gallon plastic jugs were:
clear (milk/juice); white (bleach) painted
"dull" black (but somewhat shiny) on one side
(which faced sun); dark brown (syrup?); dark
brown, set in front of used, crinkly aluminum foil 18x18"(like
reflector shown except no bottom), and both covered by one
clear, used plastic bag. All were full; outsides dried off.

The jugs were set tilted (for best sun angle) on pieces
of bark in hazy sunlight at 11:20 AM daylight time, April 19.
Air 55°, light breeze. All water 46°. (We were still at a
winter camp-site on a south slope where the sun did not rise
completely clear of trees to the east until 11 AM. The jugs
had been outside beneath a tarp overnight. If not testing,
we would have taken water from inside: water 61°; air 69°.)

At 1:50 PM (after 2½ hours), sky half covered with thin
clouds. Air 63° in shade, breezy. Water (after shaking each
jug to equalize): clear 74°; black & white 76°; brown 80°;
brown in bag 84°. The jugs were repositioned for best angle.

At 4:20 (after 5 hrs total), sky bright overcast. Air 59°
calm. Water: clear 84°; b&w 86°; brown 88°; brown in bag 101°.

Comments: This was a mediocre day for solar heating -
but therefore good for testing. On a clear day with an early
start (or with water from inside), water just in a brown jug
(without bag or reflector) gets too hot for comfort (over 110°)
and needs cold water added. On this spring day with the sun
high in the sky, the bag probably helped more than did the

vertical reflector (which is best suited for mid winter when the sun is low). A bowl-shaped reflector set under the jug might have helped more. Holly & Bert, Oregon, April

I use flat-bottomed steel bowls for boiling water or food.
They don't tip and spill like a regular bowl. I also use to dig in sand or dirt. Pet shops sell: pt & qt sizes. Wildflwr

I cook and eat from the same pot. Saves dishwashing.
I use coat-hanger wire to make a handle around pot or metal cup. I like 8-oz metal spice shakers (from restaurants): a screw-on top keeps bugs and ashes out. Eugene Gonzales, Jan

A nylon stocking can be used as a large tea bag.
Place bulk tea or ground coffee in the end, tie off, and boil all. Keeps the grounds out of the pot or cup. After use, discard grounds, wash stocking, and reuse. Wildflower, March

Experience with various camping equipment.
While working and living for a year in a south Miami warehouse, and for 6 months in a van in northern Georgia, I used:
Coleman multi-fuel stove, new. Excellent, no problems. I used it twice a day for 6 months on Coleman fuel and 6 months on kerosene. Coleman fuel easier but too expensive.
Thermarest Camprest mattress, new. Excellent but costly.
Solar AA battery charger. About size of cigarette pack, holds four cells. First one was stolen at warehouse. Second one I've used for 6 months. Adequate.
Solar/battery/dynamo-powered AM-FM radio, bought through Emergency Essentials Co., Utah. 120 cranks of dynamo gives an hour of listening. Reliable, but cranking is noisy.
Igloo 36-qt Koolmate thermo-electric cooler, new. It can plug into a cigarette lighter. After 4 months continuous use at warehouse, I had to replace motor. Since then I've learned to do without a frig. I now use it for storage and to sit on.
Sunshower, 5 gallons, new. Direct sun heats cold water in 2-3 hours. I've had two. The first one, $15, was slashed while heating water on the back of the warehouse. The second one, a $10 imitation, I keep on the roof of my van when heating water. Eugene Gonzales, Georgia, August

Various combination tools tested.
The Leatherman(TM) combo plier tool had better knife blades, screw drivers and file; and cut "10" fence wire easiest.
The SOG(TM) had poor file and screwdriver, knives hard to resharpen, poor grip as pliers, and pinched hands cutting wire.
Both SOG and Gerber are expensive, yet not worth having. Also beware of poorly-made Leatherman look-alikes. Wildflower

I use a plastic fresnel lens for reading small print.
Sold for telephone books, it is cheap, light, flexible, and nearly unbreakable. And, being big (8½x11), it will start a fire any day unless thick overcast. L. Smith, WI, October

I carry at least three sealed containers holding lighters.
Or matches. That way I always have one that is dry when needed. I also recommend learning alternative methods using fresnel lens, flint, etc. Wildflower, Connecticut, January

Underground fire could heat a winter camp.
   Wildflower's stove set-up (in Sept
'92 DP) reminded me of a drawing I
once saw. It showed how dwellings
were heated in northern Korea
during the bitter winters.
   From an underground fire pit
at one end, tunnels fanned out
under the floor and came together
in a chimney at the other end.
The tunnels were made by digging
trenches and covering with rocks and earth.
   Advantages: Because the earth floor stores heat, a fire
is needed only occasionally (rather than continually as it is
if heating air). Also, the fire can be outside of and away
from the dwelling: less fire hazard and fumes, and no inside
space taken up and soiled by ashes. David French, SD, Nov.

I lived in the wilderness for 4½ years.
   I had three different campsites in Tennessee. I built
shelters mostly out of materials at hand, stretching plastic
over bent saplings. I ate game I snared or shot with a 22
rifle. I grew "spot gardens". The wildlife got about half,
but that was okay because I harvested them too.
   I've stored beans, rice, noodles, yellow cornmeal, wheat
flour, brown sugar, and coffee in five-gallon plastic buckets
that have garbage-can liners placed in them and then tied off
twice. After putting the lid on, I place the whole bucket in
a garbage bag, then bury about two feet below ground level.
I've had no problems yet.
   I did all my cooking over a Dakota hole - below ground
level so the fire did not show, and burned only dead, dry
hardwood giving almost no smoke. One hole lasted two years.
   I've tried many sleeping bags. My Warmlite Stephenson
bag is the best. Tim Leathers, Florida, January

(Comment:) I read somewhere that colored garbage bags are not
recommended for food because they are made from recycled
plastic that might be contaminated. Bulk food stores often
give/throw away clear food-grade bags that foods came in. H&B

The easiest way to cook over a fire: BOIL EVERYTHING!
   Forget about broiling, baking, or frying. With boiling,
food is less likely to stick or burn, coals aren't needed,
and less time is spent over the fire. The pot can be hung
above the fire with a wire to a tripod or tri-rig (lines to 3
trees): the most stable way I've found to hold a pot. Heat
can be varied simply by raising or lowering the pot.
   Suppose I have rice, roots (eg, carrots), greens (eg,
nettles or lambsquarters), and meat. I put rice, roots
coarsely cut, and water in pot. (If measuring, I use 1¾ cups
of water per cup of rice. Or I may just put in ample water
and be content with soupy rice.) When the water comes to a
boil, I add chunks of meat (as big as chicken thighs). After
the water comes back to a boil, I reduce heat to a simmer -
by raising the pot. In a few minutes I turn over the meat.
After about 15 minutes I add the greens and increase the heat.
The greens need steam only a few minutes. Then I remove the
pot from the fire, put it in a paper bag (to confine soot),
cover it with sleeping bags, and let residual heat finish the
cooking (in about an hour). Now I can relax or do other
things until dinner is ready. Julie Summers, Oregon, January

Keep supplies in more than one place.
       If living or moving about in one area, I suggest caching
excess goods, extra food, and emergency kits in your local area
but away from your home or usual camping spots - in case of
sudden eviction for any reason. Even people with legal title
to a house or land, or with permission to camp, are being
forced to leave suddenly for various reasons; or, if away, are
not able to return. Wildflower, Connecticut, January

After something unusual happens, be more cautious.
       An accident analysis by the National Speleological Society
discovered a pattern: deaths during scuba dives happened, not
because of one mistake, but as the result of three or four.
       I suppose the first goof disturbed and distracted the
victim, leading to FURTHER errors.
       After one blunder I try to be extra cautious, perhaps by
slowing down or taking time out. To counter guilt I remind
myself: "Life IS dangerous." "These things DO happen." Also,
"No gain without goofs." Someone who NEVER makes a mistake, is
either kidding self, or else being TOO cautious - thereby
missing opportunities and learning experiences.
       A triumph or stroke of luck is also a time for extra
caution, because of distraction, albeit by GOOD feelings. Julie

A small squeeze bottle can be used for personal defense.
       Filled with household ammonia, it will stop most four and
two legged predators. One should not kill, but one should be
able to stop another from killing. Wildflower, CT, April 1992

Succession of rinses removes skunk odor.
       I reached back in memory 20 years to help a friend whose
puppy got "skunked". First a wash with tomato juice, then a
shampoo and water wash, then a rinse with a gallon of water
containing a shot glass (1 oz) of ammonia, and finally a rinse
with plain water. Very good results. Brother Bat, AZ, Dec.

Further technique for tick removal.
       After grasping close to its head with tweezers, I twist
and pull SLOWLY, so the tick knows it's in trouble and will
let go. (If jerked out, the head is left.) Tumbleweed, Oct.

The most effective and least-toxic control of head lice.
       Sheila Daar, at BIRC, recommends use of hot water,
shampoo (preferably coconut or olive-oil based), and a
specially-designed metal-toothed comb that removes both nits
(eggs) and adult lice. Only if the infestation persists
should an insecticide be considered. Not only can an insecticide applied to the scalp be absorbed into the bloodstream,
but lice have become resistant to many, such as lindane.
       Launder headgear or bedding in hot soapy water and place
in a dryer where the high temperatures will kill any lice
stages that survive the washing. Plastic sleeping pads where
children nap can be wiped down with a solution of household
bleach or ammonia. In schoolrooms, store hats, hooded clothes
and pillows in separate cubbies. (A 24-page booklet on topic,
$6¼ from BIRC, POB 7414, Berkeley, CA 94707; (510)524-2567)

Always wipe from front to back, especially if you are a woman.
       So that bacteria from anus is not transferred to genitals.
This is especially important in places where water may be
scarce and washing of clothes and body infrequent. Julie

Tleantos, too, need tending during snows.
        In your comparison of Hillodge and Tleanto
(Apr'92 DP p.3) you said, "The Tleanto roof
is steeper and stronger, and thus can shed
snow or support an accumulation."
        Correction: The Tleanto will
support a few inches of snow - or
shed it. (To shed wet, sticky snow,we
have to shake fly.) However, as the
snow sheds, it accumulates between the
roof and uphill and, if not removed, would
eventually sag the coverings or break the ceiling poles.
        Removal is not easy. You must squat uphill (and try not
to slide down onto the roof) while throwing the snow OVER the.
tleanto and downhill, or else out beyond the ends. (Throw snow
uphill and it will slide back down.) We use a pot to throw it.
(A shovel might cut the roof.) This has been tolerable
because heavy snows are not frequent where we have been living.
        Your Hillodge might actually be better for snow removal
because, with some massaging, I think the snow would slide off
on the DOWNHILL side. If we ever live where poles are hard to
get, we may try a Hillodge. However, I like the Tleanto's
tall window-wall which lets in plenty of light. A Hillodge
might be bright enough while the plastic is new, if there is
no growth downhill. But how is it when the plastic gets
grungy or bushes grow up? Wanda, California, January

Experimenting with tarp/tent structures in Appalachians.
        At present I am house-sitting a rural barn/house so I can
work on my van. For privacy, I have a camp-site a few miles
away. There, I made an A-tent by tying a cord between two
trees and hanging over it a 9x11' tarp. I closed off both
ends with plastic and duct tape.
        Inside I pitched a pup tent (found in the trash).
I lined it with a "space blanket" attached with duct tape to
the pup tent. Two plastic tarps cover the ground. I sleep
in a 10° hollofill sleeping bag ($50 new) on a Thermarest
Camprest. I had cold feet until I discovered putting the
sleeping bag foot end inside my jacket (M-65 army, with liner)
and zipping jacket up. With the combination of layers, I'm
comfortable at 35°. I expect to test in colder weather soon.
        For cooking or heat, I use left-over sterno from the
restaurant's garbage bin - about one can a day. (Unbelievable
waste at those ritzy places.) Also left-over candles for light.
        My job as cook is winding down and will end Nov 1.
Camping has enabled me to save lots of money, so I may not
work again for a while (even tho I have a part-time job offer
in town). I want more time for experimenting and having fun
in the woods. Eugene Gonzales, Georgia, October

Which materials best for shelter: natural or synthetic?
        Some portable dwellers use plastic. Others: criticize.
Considering esthetics, utility, and environment:
        I don't like the feel of plastic sheeting - the way it
clings to my skin if I contact. However, I like the way
plastic sheds rain yet passes light. So I use it for portions
of a shelter I seldom have to touch.
        An enclosure made ENTIRELY of natural materials, such as
thatch or leaves, is dark inside. That may be tolerable
during summer when one wall can be open or we can work outside.
But not during the cold, wet days of winter. Therefore, we
make at least one wall of an all-weather shelter from plastic.

What natural materials pass light? Oiled animal skins do
- poorly. Some Eskimos use sheets of ice: ice soon melts here.
I've not tried to make glass out of native materials. (BOUGHT
glass seems as artificial as bought plastic, besides being
heavier, more breakable, and more hazardous if it breaks.)
Polyethylene (most plastic sheeting) has been used for
several decades to hold fruit juice, milk and distilled water -
without bad health effects we've heard of. Anyway, we don't
eat off our plastic walls. Plastic can burn, but so can most
natural materials. Rocks can't, but are dangerous in earthquakes. Plastic is not very durable, especially in sunlight.
It breaks up into flakes - no uglier to me than bones or hair.
As for environmental impact, quantity counts. ANY house
that costs $100,000 uses MUCH resources - whether the walls
are logs or plastic. (Logs may be natural, but power saws
and logging trucks aren't.)
Most plastic presently comes from petroleum, but could be
made from such materials as saw dust or fallen leaves (we've
heard), and probably will be when the oil wells run dry. Anyhow, a plastic tent uses less than a motorist burns in one week.
Environmentally, cotton cloth may be worse: grown with
insecticides, and soaked in fungicide and waterproofing for
outdoor use. Even so, I'd choose cotton in dry climates
because it withstands sunlight longer. But where wet much,
even with fungicide, cotton eventually rots.
Many people still living in houses/apartments can no
longer afford them and need quick and easy alternatives.
Natural materials may require too much time or skill.
By the way, folks who prefer houses should be grateful to
portable dwellers: WE aren't pushing up prices of building
sites or existing units by bidding against them! Holly & Bert

I have been living in my tipi for a year.
But I've had difficulty keeping rain out. Nomadics, the
maker, says: DON'T waterproof. Also, the natural-fiber ropes
rot in the rain we get here. (I'm in the wet western part of
the Columbia Gorge; not in the dryer east.) Sherilyn, March

I have added a canopy to my pyramid tent.
The sides are held by poles.
During good weather, it provides
shade. During inclement weather,
poles are lowered and it becomes
a storm shield. It could be easily adapted to other
structures. Brother Bat, Arizona, January

For shelter, I prefer tarps.
They are lightweight, cheap, waterproof, versatile, easy
to replace, and come in many colors. I've used them in all
kinds of weather and places - while climbing, bicycling,
canoeing, camping, etc. Also, they can cover other gear while
packing or biking. And, if bright colored, they can signal
an airplane in an emergency. David French, South Dakota, Nov.

A small shelter is easy to make from thatch.
Thatch can be formed from many kinds of vegetation (grass,
boughs, fronds, some leaves). It can be supported and held
together by various means. It provides insulation. And, if
steep enough and properly overlapped, it will shed rain. I use
it when manufactured materials are not at hand. Some tips:
For support, take advantage of any natural formations
that are safe. A small tree partially fallen and sturdily

hung up, can be the ridge pole of an A-frame. A large tree-trunk lying on the ground can hold up and form one wall of a lean-to. A big bush with branches bent over can provide the ribs of an arc hut.

Build a simple shape. A lean-to or A-frame is best for shedding rain. An arc hut is warmest. Also consider what materials are available: straight, stiff sticks are good for an A-frame; curved limber branches for an arc hut's ribs.

Make your shelter tiny at first: just large enough to crawl into. (You may add on later as you have time.)

Angle roof steep to shed rain. The more irregular or porous the thatch, the steeper the roof needs to be.

Thatch from the bottom up if working from outside (or top down if working inside), overlapping so that each row of thatch will drain onto the OUTSIDE of the row beneath.

If you have some waterproof material but only a small amount (plastic bags, large leaves), put it over the peak - the place where any leaks will be the most serious.

Bushcraft, Richard Graves, Schocken Books, 1973, shows some simple ways to thatch. (In print? Try libraries.)

On a spring trip, when a ride failed to show, I hiked to where I had cached a sleeping bag and tarps several years before, but could not find them by the half-moon light in a shady forest. I built my shelter at the base of a tree that had large low branches still alive, using one branch (left attached to tree) as a ridge pole. A recent heavy snow had broken off many doug-fir boughs which I used for thatch. I hooked a branchlet of each bough over the ridge pole; tip end down. Snuggling in, I slept quite warm (except for cold feet) in just the clothes I was wearing. (No rain fell to test my nightime thatch work - just as well.) Bert, OR, Apr.

A rain poncho is easy to make from a large plastic bag.

Just cut a slit near one corner for your face.

Or, with a sheet of plastic, fold it in half and ball-tie the edges together in a few places, leaving an opening for your face.

If you have a rain jacket but lack a rain hat, a triangular piece of plastic (or a square piece folded in half diagonally) can be used as a kerchief. Tie under your chin. In my tests, it got clammy but kept the rain off. Julie Summers, OR, 1991

Experience with various Gortex garments.

I have camped, climbed, packed and bicycled for years.

A pair of mittens were fine: kept rain and snow off hands.

An overparka was okay: big enough to allow air to circulate; but moisture did build up now and then.

A bivouac sack worked ONCE in a snow blizzard while climbing the Tetons. Every other time, even with vent open, moisture collected inside and "rained" - wetting my sleeping bag. David French, South Dakota, November

Hammock helpful. Suggestions for using.

I slept in a hammock in Florida to avoid ant bites and wet cold ground. A tarp over it gave rain protection.

A net hammock is difficult to get in or out of. To make easier, I line with a strip of rug or a foam pad. With that I can get in even when wearing a sleeping bag. Wildflower, CT

My watch cap stays in place better if I fold cuff to INside.

I fold in front only, to keep cap out of my eyes. I let back and sides hang down to warm ears and neck. Julie

Ball ties keep socks up.

When hiking, some socks work their way down
my ankles until they disappear into my shoes and
become uncomfortable wads. My quick and easy
solution does not cut off circulation nor require
wearing garter belts or long pants, and saves
otherwise sound socks from the rag bag. The
result looks much like the little pom-poms at
the back of low-cut tennis/golf socks.

At the back of my ankle, I insert
a ball between skin and sock - a little
above the shoe top to allow slack.
Then I gather the fabric around the ball and hold it with
multiple windings of a rubber band. For a ball, I trim a
3/4" diameter piece of styrofoam from discarded packaging
materials. Styrofoam is light, firm, and easily shaped.
Lacking it, I use acorn, small tree cone, or wad of leaves.

During wet weather, I often wear plastic bags inside
my shoes but over my socks to keep them dry (for a while).
I ball-tie the bags along with the socks. Julie Summers, OR

Hints for easier hand sewing:

Use a piece of thread no longer than your reach, so that
you can pull it taut after each stitch with just one motion.

To lubricate the thread so it goes thru easier and twists/
tangles less, pull it over some wax such as a candle stub.

If thread still twists, hold the garment up every few
stitches and let needle and thread dangle so it unwinds.

When mending clothes, a glass jar can be used as a darning egg. The smooth curved surface deflects the needle,
helping to direct it out of the fabric where desired. Julie

Detergent and fasteners found in laundromats.

If I run out of detergent or am traveling light, rather
than buy overpriced little boxes from a laundromat's vending
machine, I check the trash both inside and out back. I often
find containers with considerable residue. After pouring out
what I can, I rinse to get out the rest.

I also find many discarded garments. Even clothes not
worth mending often have good zippers and buttons which I
salvage for replacing broken/lost ones or making new garments.
                                                        Julie

Motor oil containers often found alongside roads.

Those with caps on usually still contain a tablespoon or
more of clean oil. I transfer oil to a small plastic bottle
(attached to my bike's basket by a rubber strap) for cleaning
and lubricating the drive chain and other parts. Julie Summers

Packframe with added support holds bucket easily.

I bought an external frame at a flea market
for $3. At the bottom, using the same hardware
that attaches the straps, I mounted a U-shaped
support piece cut from an aluminum chair.
I braced it using $\frac{1}{4}$" nylon rope with metal
rings on each end. They slip over the
frame's tips. A bucket can be set on the
support. The bucket protects its contents
better than a bag does, and is also useful
at camp. Eugene Gonzales, Georgia, January

I carry two compasses - so I have a spare.

One, fairly large, I use with maps. The other, pinned on,
I use for general navigation. Wildflower

Dwelling Portably

(formerly named Message Post)
POB 190, Philomath OR 97370

Oct. 1993 $1 per issue   To check/mo under $7, add 50¢

Candle formed in jar provides wind-proof light.
   I use a one-pint jar with lid. I place a
stick across the mouth of the jar, and from it
suspend a wick so it barely touches the bottom.
Then I half-fill the jar with melted wax.
After the wax cools, I trim wick to 3/4" high
and put on the lid. I carry matches in jar.

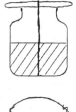

   To melt wax safely, I use a double boiler.
The wax goes in a 64 oz juice can with wire
bail, which sets on 2" of small rocks placed
in the bottom of a #10 (3 lb) coffee can
partially filled with water. A small fire
beneath the coffee can heats the wax without
scorching or igniting it.

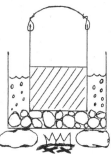

   A double boiler can also be used to melt
and refine fat for making soap, or to melt
resin for use as glue, etc. After melting,
pour and filter into a clean container.
I make a filter by removing both ends from an
empty can and wrapping and tying wire screen
over the bottom end. Wildflower, CT, Oct.90

With flames or candles, always have a fire extinguisher handy.
   I found out the hard way that a WD-40 can is a happy
camper's nightmare if punctured near flame. Eugene, Jan 1993

(Comment:) I recommend thinking in advance about simple AND
RELIABLE ways to cope with a fire in various situations.
   I recall once (in a bus at a gathering, not in a tent)
seeing a frying pan catch fire. On the wall near the stove
was an impressive-looking fire extinguisher. It was applied -
and didn't work! Quickwittedly, someone grabbed the pan and
carried it outside. Nothing got burnt except some bacon.
   Most small fires can be smothered with a towel (preferably damp) or rug or any heavy garment. If outside, a few
shovelfuls of dirt may suffice. On an oil/grease fire, soil
or garments is better than water. Water may splatter it.
   With any flammable fluid (many lubricants, solvents,
paints), best not use it in any enclosed space, even if no
flame. Static electricity could ignite it. Holly & Bert

If your car burns oil, use synthetic oil.
   It doesn't smoke, which will save you hassles by the
'clean air police'. Mobil One is now down to about $2.
   If I need a vehicle and come across a good-running older
vehicle, I buy it. It has been running good to last this
long and thusly may keep running. My last vehicle was a '71
Toyota Corona Delux. I paid $200 for it and drove it 26
months. One day it just quit running while going down the
road. I sold it for $50 (and had 30 callers!). I got a $575
'74 Ford pickup. It runs good, and hauls my trailer too.
Insurance is only $107 for 6 months. It has a 302 and is
easy on the gas. David French, South Dakota, December

Don't go to jail for old traffic violations.
   Judges jail people who have priors on the books. With a
little effort, priors can be erased. Write to your state
motor vehicle department for a listing of traffic-violation
courts that still have charges against you. Al Fry, ID, Febr.

March 1994

drawing
is by
Amanda
Lewis,
Minx
Comix

Dwelling Portably
P.O. BOX 190-FFF,
Philomath,
OR. 97370

$1 per issue

Trailer useful for storage - and living in.

For $400 I bought a 25 ft trailer. I gutted it except for the bathroom. Originally I got it for storage, it being much cheaper than a rental storage. However, the first year I used it for 5 months during summer as a base to come home to while camping around the area. Savings in rent and utilities more than paid for the trailer.

Now I live in my trailer full time. I have propane for heat, a solar panel for electricity, and a large queen-size bed for comfort. The bed is built 25" above the floor so I can store almost 40 12x12x12" boxes underneath.

Used construction-office trailers can be had for $500-$700. They are not filled in like a regular travel trailer, letting you build inside what you want.

A 5 gal tank of propane lasts about a week. I use it mostly for heating. David French, South Dakota, December

Suggestions for washing.

I bathe about once every 3 days. I put 3 gals of water in a 5 gal bucket. I heat up 2 gals of water on my propane stove and add it to the 5 gal bucket. I use a cup to pour the water slowly over my head. I wash my head and use the suds to wash my body. I use biodegradable soap - Dr. Bonners. This system has worked well for me for 1½ years.

About once every two weeks I go to a truck stop to use their shower. For only $1 I get a hot shower one hour long. Most truck stops I've seen have showers. I've used them when bicycle touring too.

Instead of WASHING my clothes every time, often I just rinse them. This extends the time between washings by two or three times, and saves on soap too. To rinse, I put them in a 5 gal bucket, fill with water, mix them up with a broom handle. I then let them sit over night and ring out the next day. I've been doing this since 1984.

If you can find old silver spoons, buy them. The silver kills germs. So, to clean, I just wipe off thoroughly. I have one I've been using for 2 years. David French, SD, Dec.

Gatherings: experience and recommendations.
I got back from trip south 3 hours ahead of the recent snowstorm - lucky! I was to two regional Rainbow gatherings, one in Florida, and other in Georgia. At both, I encountered "the law"; a lot of nice people; some bozos; and some good memories. Recommendations:
Do come with proper gear, including flashlight and/or lantern, toilet paper, and extra food. Do remember this is held in "primitive camping" areas. Use a light at night on dark trails. Otherwise you might end up lost like some "nightwalkers" did (and they were local people). No matter how dead a plant looks, toilet paper is safer.
Nights get cold. The warmer your sleeping bags, the happier you will be in the morning.
Tools and supplies to bring: water; bulk food for kitchens; extra cookpots; tarps (12x20' and larger); cord and rope; GI folding shovel; bow saw and extra blade; machete (or ax) with file; 5 gallon pails with lids (numerous uses); kero lanterns and extra fuel. "Extra" is better than "not enough".
Leave the pills, drugs, alcohol, and hostile ego at home. Nobody is perfect. Don't expect it.
Do try to help set up, run errands, cleanup! If you pack it in, pack your trash out.
Expect "courtesy checks" by local law as you enter or leave, for valid ID, sobriety, etc. Wildflower, CT, March'93

(Comments:) We generally recommend bringing and preparing your OWN food. Large field kitchens can have problems with diseases - and egos. However, if you will be eating at a kitchen, do bring food or money for them, and help out.
Scrutiny by people who will fine you, jail you or shoot you if you don't do what they tell you to: that I would NOT call a "courtesy check". (Next we'll be hearing about "courtesy robberies" and "courtesy rapes".)
Why should gatherers travel hundreds or thousands of miles, and spend thousands of dollars for fuel and food, enriching local businesses - only to be hassled - or worse? Let's stay away from such areas, and do our gathering where we are welcome, or where no one else is around.
Rainbows are not the only gatherings being harassed. We have heard of arrests at primitive rendezvous for wearing feathers that were FOUND (discarded by the birds). We have heard of fines at sci-fi conventions, completely enclosed in hotel suites, for "indecent exposure" though no one had complained. We have heard of road blocks in resort areas.
Perhaps this is a time to forgo national gatherings (or to hold them in exile), and only gather locally, with people we trust, in areas where we will be alone (and maybe have ham radio link-ups between gatherings).
We have long been supporters of gatherings including big Rainbows (and have gone to quite a few). But we will not go to or encourage gatherings where we must kowtow to the police (or to anyone else). We can find better things to do. H & B

Suggestions for low-impact backpacking.
Avoid popular areas. Avoid holidays and weekends. Travel and camp in small groups. Buy gear in subdued, earth-toned colors. On a short excursion, bring foods that require no cooking. When traveling cross-country, use rocky or timbered terrain as much as possible. Allow right-of-way to horses. Look at and photograph, rather than pick or collect.

Seek ridge-top or timbered campsites (but not near trees big enough to injure if they or their branches fall). Choose well-drained and needle-strewn or sandy campsites; avoid leveling or digging hip holes or tent ditches. Use existing fire rings (or, better, don't use fire). Gather downed, small firewood from timbered areas outside camp; never cut standing trees, living or dead. Stir ashes with water, hand test, then sprinkle aside or bury. Camp, wash, brush teeth and dispose of waste water at least 200 feet from water sources. Wear soft shoes around camp and avoid trampling vegetation. Bury human waste and fish entrails 6" deep and at least 200 feet from drainage areas. Bury toilet tissue with human waste or burn in pit. Camp as quietly as possible so others can also savor the solitude. Leave radios at home. Save bright colors and loud noises for emergencies. Pick up all litter. Pack out non-burnables. (Adapted from "Without a Trace", Pacific Northwest Region USFS, 1985)

Suggestions for more enjoyable trips.

Don't choose it as a time to give up caffeine. Tufts U. Diet and Nutrition Letter, Feb'91, says going off "cold turkey" can result in a severe headache and other symptoms. They advise cutting back one cup every few days. This applies to caffeine soft drinks as well as coffee.

To avoid constipation: drink plenty of water, and eat high-fiber foods such as carrots. Coarsely ground whole wheat is even better. On long drives, take a 10 minute break every two hours and walk around. That will stimulate peristalsis.

Writing "after-action" reports can make future trips more enjoyable. Make it a family or group affair. To stimulate thought, ask questions such as: What went right? What went wrong? What did I take that I didn't use (and will omit next time)? What didn't I take that I wished I'd had? What do I wish I had done differently? Julie Summers, Oregon, 1992

Springing snare needs dry wood.

Many outdoor people are familiar with the springing snare. However, a word of advice. The trigger should be made of hard "dry" wood. Green wood has resin "sap" that can become sticky, making the trigger hard to spring once the animal has been snared. Tim Leathers, FL, May

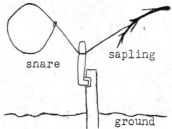

I'm experimenting growing vegetables.

Mostly in very poor, gravelly soils. So far I have been successful with various varieties of kale, as well as peas, greenbeans, potatoes, and husk tomatoes. I've also tried many varieties that haven't grown. However, by composting small spots at a time with leaves I gather (and with everything at all compostable), and growing in raised hills, I've found some recent success. The raised hills concentrate more soil in one spot, and also make watering much easier during the severe dry spells we have been having of late. I simply poke a hole in the center of each hill, and pour a jar of water into each hole. I use wood ashes to adjust the PH balance of acidic soils. Last season I got some squash for the first time. This year my hopes abound. Gary R. Cropper, Washington, March

The Dakota hole.

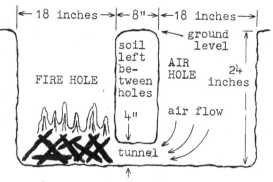

This burns hotter and is more easily regulated than an open fire, due to the air shaft which feeds air from the bottom. If dry hardwood is burned, there is little smoke; and, being underground, the fire is less visible at night.

Dig two holes 18" diameter by 24" deep, leaving 8" of dirt between them.   Then burrow a 4" diameter tunnel between them.

Build your fire in the bottom of one hole. Regulate the air flow by partly covering other hole. CAUTION: this fire can burn hot enough to ruin a pot. Tim Leathers, TN, May & Dec.

(Comment:) This seems much better than an open fire, yet is simple and without the problems of a wood stove (which is nasty to carry and, if thin metal, soon rusts through). B & H

Some ways to suspend a pot.

Setting a pot on rocks isn't too satisfactory. The pot can slide off and spill, its height can't be changed easily, and refueling the fire under the pot (which is where you want the fire) will be difficult if the pot is in a hole.

With the Dakota hole, I might make slots in the ground on each side of the hole, then place a stick across the hole and in the slots. The slots keep the stick in place. The stick should be stout enough not to burn if the fire momentarily blazes high (and preferably damp or green) and clean of dirt or loose bark (which could fall into the pot if the cover is removed). I would suspend the pot with wire that goes over the stick and attaches to a cord. I tie several loops in the cord. One loop goes over a small stump, a low stub-branch, or a stake. I change the pot's height by placing a different loop over.

Or, I would rig 3 cords to form a Y (if seen from above), tying them out to trees. The cords join in a ring above the pot. The wire/cord from the pot goes up thru the ring and then outward, and one of several loops hooks over a stub branch. This allows pot to be raised completely out of hole.

For suspending a pot above an open fire, Julie Summers suggested (in June'84 MP) a tripod and hanger stick, which allows the pot to be moved sideways (by moving the tripod) as well as up or down (by placing a different crotch over the joint of the tripod - see pic on next page). However, with some solar cookers and maybe with the Dakota hole, the tripod would be in the way unless very large.

With any system, rig the pot before lighting
the fire. Bert & Holly Davis, Oregon, April

Some alternatives to campfires.
    In the media, an open fire is supposed to
indicate outdoor know-how. But in reality, an
open fire may indicate a LACK of know-how. An
open fire wastes time, wastes fuel, produces
smoke, and may be dangerous. Smoke is bad to
breathe - and alarming. Even smoke from a safe
woodstove can invite hassles, because it can't
be distinguished from a beginning forest fire.
    We usually live in well-insulated shelters
or mild weather. Only once during the past ten
years did we need a fire for warming ourselves.
Therefore this article will concern cooking. Alternatives:
    Don't cook. While light camping during summer, we often
go for days, sometimes weeks without cooking. Instead we eat:
raw berries we forage; dry foods we cooked previously, such
as popcorn, biscuits/crackers/hardtack, pinole; ready-to-eat
foods such as bread or tortillas we buy if camped near cities.
    Use barbeque pit in a park. An option when in a city.
    Solar cook. Though not possible year-around here, we
now often do so in summer - the very time when fires are most
risky and alarming. Some proven solar-cookers are cheap and
fairly simple to build, and semi portable - light but bulky.
(We will soon test another that is very portable.)
    Cook on a portable propane stove. We now do so when at
a base camp - about 8 months a year. By using insulative
cooking techniques (see Sept'84 MP p.5; now part of Feb'85m)
we burn less than two 5-gallon tanks per year. Refills cost
us $6-$7½ per tank. Be sure to get a stove and fittings that
connect to 5-gal tanks (not the little canisters). Some
people favor kerosene or gasoline stoves. But propane seems
less smelly and may be safer. Principal disadvantage:
propane tanks are heavier. But we use too little to fret.
    Cook with charcoal. We would if we lived too remote for
backpacking propane. We may anyway some day. Charcoal can
be made, we've read, by heating wood in a closed but vented
container. (By condensing the fumes, wood alcohol and other
chemicals can be collected.) We would make charcoal in
quantity during the wet season (when no fire hazard) at a
site away from our base camp (so no odors there) and near
plentiful down wood which we would gather in advance during
the dry season and tarp. IMPORTANT: have adequate ventilation
with ANY combustion, especially with charcoal because its
fumes are odorless (we've heard).
    Make a lightweight woodstove out of a 3-or-5-gal metal
can (see Jim Burnap's design in Sept'84 MP p.1; now part of
June'84m). Or buy a portable stove. Or form a stove or
equivalent (eg, Dakota hole) out of earth. Compared to an
open fire, a stove is easier to ignite, needs less tending,
burns hotter, can burn damper wood, produces less smoke, uses
less wood, and is safer. The smoke outlet should include a
metal screen to stop sparks.
    If necessary to build an open fire when the woods are
dryish, the safest place is probably close by a creek in the
bottom of a narrow canyon, where the ground is wet and the
air calm. Clear surface debris from several yards, pre-soak
the soil, dig a pit for the fire, and keep the fire small.
The safest time is usually just before dawn when things are
cool and damp from dew. Afterwards drench whole area. B & H

A wild salad green that is widely available.
   The new leaves of gosmore (Hypochoeris
radicata) are a welcome treat during winter
and early spring when few fresh foods are
available. Gosmore is also called
"Chinese lettuce", and is related to
lettuce (Lactuca sativa). When young,
gosmore leaves taste to us much like
some cultivated loose-leaf lettuces:
bland or slightly bitter (but not
unpleasantly), depending on the
individual plant or the growing
conditions. Later, gosmore plants
that get much sun become quite bitter,
while plants in the shade may remain
palatable through summer.
   Unlike many wild greens which
taste acceptable at first, but after
a few minutes grazing become
unpleasant or irritating, gosmore
continues to please us. Some days we
eat several dozen leaves (each ± ½ by
2 inches), picking just one leaf from
each plant, and eating immediately,
after wiping or washing off any rain-
splattered soil. (Haven't tried cooking.)

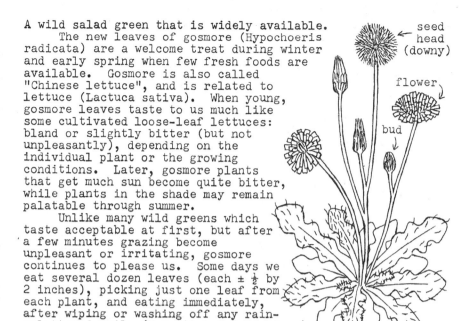

seed
head
(downy)

flower

bud

   Gosmore is also called "false dandelion", and is related
to dandelion (Taraxacum officinale). Like a dandelion,
gosmore starts as a rosette (flat, circular cluster) close to
the ground of pinnately-lobed-or-toothed leaves with milky
juice that are basal only (none on the flower stalk); then
produces yellow blossoms which mature into downy seeds spread
by wind. But gosmore leaves may be hairier ("cats-ear" is
yet another name) and the flower stalks are tougher, often
branched, and can grow taller (up to 2 feet).
   One more look-alike relative of gosmore is hawkbit
(Leontodon nudicaulis). It often grows with gosmore and we
may have foraged them together without distinguishing them.
   All the plants mentioned above, and several others with
dandelion-like leaves, belong to the chicory tribe (a botan-
ical subdivision of the daisy family (compositae)). I know
of no members that are poisonous. However, at least one
more-distant relative is: tansy ragwort (Senecio jacobaea)
which also bears yellow daisy-like flowers. But compared to
gosmore, dandelion and hawkbit; ragwort's leaves are more
divided and raggedy, and some leaves are on the flower stalks
which often grow taller (to 4') and more branched.
   Plants can be most easily identified while blooming.
Patches could be marked then for harvesting later. With an
unfamiliar GREEN plant, sample just a tiny piece at first,
chew and spit out. If irritating to mouth, reject. If not
irritating, wait a few hours before trying more. (Don't do
this with mushrooms. Some deadly mushrooms taste fine.)
   Gosmore "is especially abundant west of the Cascade
Range, from Canada to California; perhaps the most conspicuous pasture and roadside weed during summer" writes Ronald
Taylor in Northwest Weeds. Fortunately for us, gosmore is
also common on some forested hills in open/semi-open spots,
especially on north slopes where the ground was disturbed by
logging. Several species also grow in the east, and in Europe
to which it is native. Gosmore is perennial, but some species
are annual. Holly, Oregon

We eat raw greens AS WE PICK.

We don't collect them to later make a salad, because, unlike some cultivated salad plants such as head lettuce and head cabbage which were bred partly for keeping qualities, most wild greens start wilting as soon as they are picked and produce toxins not found in the fresh plants.

Also, eating one leaf at a time, we immediately taste any unpleasant and possibly poisonous look-alike, which we might not notice if mixed up in a salad.

Very few mammals collect greens to eat later. One that does is the sewella (Aplodontia rufa), a rodent that actually makes hay. But apes and monkeys graze as they go, we've read.

H & B

Foraging wild edibles saves us much money and time.

We are not purists. When one of us gets to a store (not often), if (eg) cabbage is on sale at 19¢ a pound, we usually buy some - provided we don't have to carry it far before eating it (it's mostly water). But when cabbage is 69¢ a pound and other vegies even higher, or when we are far from stores, we eat only wild greens.

"But you can't survive on just greens - you aren't cows" we hear. "What do you eat instead of potatos?"

We eat rice, popcorn, wheat, corn, oatmeal, flour - all of which we buy. But, if bought in bulk, grains are cheap; and being dry, are light and keep well. Fruits, vegetables and meat are what are expensive to buy and troublesome to keep. So foraging those foods can pay off big. Holly & Bert

Rotting vegetation produces some heat.

Under tent floors or stacked alongside mini-shelters, straw or similar 'rottables' can be more effective than is passive insulation. That is a little-known secret for keeping pipes and water containers unfrozen during cold weather. A few inches of compressed straw above and below the water line will provide just enough heat to do the trick.

If I needed a cheap warm shelter, I'd build a tiny straw or hay-bale shack. Better than a tent any winter day. Al Fry, ID, Feb.

Considerations when chosing insulative materials.

In farming areas, hay sometimes gets damp and moldy (not good as animal feed) and can be purchased cheaply. In some cities during fall, huge quantities of leaves can be easily collected from lawns and sidewalks, etc. (Property owners even pay for removal.) But in most woods, leaves are difficult to gather in quantity. Where most trees are conifers, leaves are scarce. But even where plentiful, fallen leaves may be intermixed with bushes, vines and fallen branches.

So, if a material is heavy or bulky, I would use it only if it is easily obtained AND CLOSE to a good camp-site. (Hay bales or leaves are no bargain if you need a pickup to haul them to the mountains, or a rented site to camp near them.)

If leaves ARE abundant and close, I might build a sturdy framework out of interwoven branches, cover that with something to keep fine particles from sifting in (old drapes, often discarded, may be good; plastic is fair but will puncture), pile the leaves over and around (at least a foot thick, preferably thicker - they will compact), and lean more branches to hold the leaves in place. (I haven't done this much.) If rain or snow-melt is likely, suspend a tarp a few inches above (so that moisture in the leaves can escape).

If I plan to live in it long, I would make one side (the side with least foliage) out of many layers of clear plastic to let in light. Bert & Holly, Oregon

Report on Shelter Systems' dome-tent.
Ours has been in continuous use for two years, set up in a shady spot. The cover is still good. The insect net ripped long ago. The wall seams tend to open up and have to be often fooled with: we have to readjust the clips before a rain.
On the whole, this tent has been worth the cost for us. The 3 boys use it as a separate bedroom, so that our main tent is less crowded at night. Gives the parents some privacy.
Anne, CA

Our tipi lasted only five years of summer-only use.
It was waterproofed (cotton canvas?). Now sticks poke right through it. Jai Loon, Washington, July

Durable fabric salvaged from no-longer-inflatable building.
It was a military-surplus blow-up hospital, which can be purchased cheaply if the bladders get leaky, but may be difficult to find. The rubberized nylon usually lasts 15 or 20 years. With a treadle sewing machine, I made a 15-foot tipi which I use for socializing during summers. Al Fry, ID

Strong fabric can be salvaged from discarded sails.
If you happen to be near a sailboat storage area, check the dumpbins now and then, especially at the beginning and end of the sailing season. Many boaters replace their sails every year or two, and the cloth may still be good enough for resewing into tents or tipis. (Many sails are polyester.) Discarded tarps and ropes are also found. Wildflower, CT,

Legality of salvaging from dumpsters.
Amy Dacyczyn, who phoned several police officials, said (in The Tightwad Gazette, July 1993), "dumpster diving is' generally considered to be legal with the following except- ions: -- If the container is on CLEARLY MARKED private land, behind a fence or locked up. However, most dumpsters in 'semi-public' areas such as parking lots are fair game. -- If the discarded items are outside the dumpster they should not be taken. -- If you make a mess. Leave a dumpster site cleaner than you found it." A deputy district attorney in Santa Clara, CA, where many people rummage for high-tech discards, told Amy: "By putting items in a dumpster, the companies have abandoned ownership.... The idea that people are stealing is not a prosecutable case." (sent by Julie)

How to prevent unraveling of synthetic fabric.
I pass the edges through a candle flame, which melts the ends of the threads and sticks them together. When I do this I wear sunglasses. They prevent the temporary vision loss I otherwise get from looking into the flame, and might guard against long-term eye damage. Julie Summers, Oregon, January

How to render canvas tents and bags water-resistant.
One method: Measure 3 cups soybean oil and 1½ cups turpentine. Mix well, then paint on outer surface. Allow to dry fully before use. Only for articles used only outdoors.
Another method: Rub soft wax onto surface of cloth.
What waterproofing do you recommend? Wildflower, CT
(Reply:) In June'87 MP p.11, Dennis reported on "RainCheck", which worked fairly well on some materials, not others.
We often use NON-waterproof cloth as a top tarp, with a plastic under tarp. (Most waterproofers smelly (and toxic?)).
If waterproofing doubtful, pitching a tarp STEEP helps.

Golf cart converted to trail cart.

I found a second-hand golf-bag cart at a yard sale. By removing the bag and adding a surplus military pack-frame, I now have a rugged "all terrain" handcart for bulky items. Wflr

Choosing portable dwellings easy to find places for.

The smaller, lighter and more backpackable your dwelling is, the more places it will fit. On the other hand, the better equipped (and presumably larger) your dwelling is, the further you can live from settlements and the more territory you have in which to find places. What will be optimum?

For a remote over-winter camp, Holly and I may carry in 10 to 20 backloads, which includes much of the food we will eat. For a summer camp, which may be near a city or a good foraging area, we may carry in only two backloads initially (one trip by the two of us), but may add to it gradually.

Width of a structure is more crucial than length, at least around here where forests and brushlands are usually on slopes, often steep. A long, narrow structure (eg, 6x25') can be sited easier than a round or square structure (eg, 12x 12') with the same floor area, because long, narrow terraces are easier to find or to prepare than are short, wide ones. A long, narrow structure will also be brighter, assuming most light comes from the downhill side, and warmer when sunny.

Height is also important, especially if much wind. A low structure need not be as strong and thus can be built lighter. It will also be warmer, at least at night or on a cloudy or windy day. It will also be less visible and therefore less likely to provoke complaints or hassles.

For year-around living in the maritime northwest, our favorite user-built shelter is presently the Hillodge (long description in April'92 DP). In flatish interior desert areas, we might like a Twipi (described in LLL packet), though we have not had much experience with Twipis nor deserts.

For summer-only use, a much simpler and lighter shelter will suffice. If little wind, just bug net and plastic tarp.

Unfortunately, quite a few novices see a big, spectacular tipi, yurt or dome at a gathering or trade show, fall in love with it, and buy it - WITHOUT having a good place to put it. They wind up in a friend's backyard or some farmer's pasture, which usually leads to problems. A big tipi (etc) can be nice at a gathering for a council or concert on a rainy day. But for living in, we much prefer smaller shelters.

If we need more room, we cluster several small shelters. For winter warmth, we live mostly in just one of them which we insulate, and use the others mainly for storage. For a project requiring much space, we erect a temporary tarp - or wait until summer.

Any backpackable structure is easier to site than is any vehicle, except perhaps in some dense cities and intensively-farmed areas which might allow temporary parking on streets but have no unused lands. We don't have experience with vehicles since a little car-camping while traveling, 15 to 20 years ago. But our impression is: the smaller and more ordinary-looking a vehicle is, the more easily it can be parked. Hank and Barb Schultz, MP/DP founders, wrote (in Sept'82 MP p.2) about living out of and sometimes in a pickup with canopy which they insulated (not a big camper).

(In the early 1980s, they also wrote several articles about chosing shelters, which are in the Light Living Packet (or, if you prefer bigger print, set #W). Any later info?)

B&H

Tips for making a comfortable bed without a mattress.
I dig a hip hole that is actually a TRENCH - the whole width of the bed, so that I can turn over freely. If I have only a little padding, I place most of it under my hips because that is where I bear heaviest. Julie Summers, Oregon

Bed and storage in van made from footlockers and plywood.
Living in a van can be a pain for lack of storage space. I purchased four military-surplus footlockers, covered all with a piece of 3/4" plywood, topped with a foam mattress. I now have a comfortable bed with storage space under it. And, I can easily remove all and temporarily store outside, if I need to haul bulky items in the van.
Another footlocker I made into a standing storage-locker with door by adding a few shelves. Wildflower, CT, July

Connecting remote living with city jobs.
My husband goes to the Bay area (a 2½ hour drive) for two days every other week, to do his gardening jobs there. He sleeps in his truck, parked at a friend's house.
One acquaintance lives in Oregon and spends every other week washing windows in San Francisco. Another lives in northern California and works two weeks per month as a lawyer in Los Angeles. Anne Callaway, California, June

Cellular phone useful though not reliable.
There is much static and service often cuts off in the middle of a call, even though we have an auxilliary antenna.
We tried recharging by plugging into a vehicle at night, but that was inadequate. Now we have a 12-volt deep-cycle battery that we get charged in town. (Someone goes often.)
The phone is EXPENSIVE to use, but worth it since both my husband and oldest boy use it to schedule yard work and odd jobs. Many people won't bother to hire someone they cannot reach by phone. Anne Callaway, California, June

Gasoline Coleman lanterns are cheaper to fuel but break easily.
The old Coleman-fuel type was more reliable.
By calling the 800#, we get replacement generators fast, but we would rather they not break. We cope by always having an extra gasoline lantern. Anne Callaway, California, June

Our James washer works great but is too fragile.
It has broken many times, requiring welding or replacement of parts. We may be partly to blame: our muscleman teen does the laundry and he overloads the machine. Anne, CA, June

Some rural landfills do not discourage scavenging.
They are like free hardware stores. Al Fry, Idaho, Febr.

Tips for avoiding trouble with rural settlers.
Someone in the southeast wrote that people there tend to be inquisitive, hostile to unconventional dwellingways, and likely to call the police. The same is true of some people in the northwest - and probably everywhere.
Most house-dwellers are too busy working to earn money to pay their rent or taxes (and to pay for the vehicle they need to commute to work - etc.), to give much mind to what goes on beyond their immediate neighborhood. However, SOME people ARE nosy and, like the dog who didn't want a bone but didn't want anyone else to have it either, would be hostile to us if they could, even though we are no threat to them nor do

they covet our lifestyle. We avoid trouble by avoiding them.
    We try to look conventional when traveling. Often we
bicycle. Bicycling is common here, else we wouldn't stay here.
    We generally avoid any short, dead-end road that has
houses along it. Some people in those houses may be
acquainted with everyone who lives on that road, and will be
curious about anyone else they see repeatedly.
    When leaving any road to go into the woods, we do so
where and when we are out of view of houses and motorists.
    For long-period camping (more than a few nights), we
choose areas that are not near any road and not easy to hike
through. Generally our areas are steep, tangly or both.
(Western Oregon has many such areas to choose from.) We avoid
areas due for logging or thinning.
    At our long-period campsites, we don't build open fires,
keep noisy animals (or any animals), cut down trees, or do
anything else that might attract attention. H & B, OR, April

Various comments on places and dwellingways.

    Many people in the east seem to believe that the west is
mostly empty. True, there are large areas with almost no
people. But these are mostly deserts. There are such areas
in EASTERN Oregon (far from where we are), in much of Nevada,
and in parts of CA, AZ, NM, UT, WY, ID and other states.
But to find large WOODED areas that are unpopulated, I
I believe you must go to Alaska or northern Canada.
    WESTERN Oregon is not trackless wilderness. On the
average it is as heavily populated as are most eastern states.
Though it has many unsettled areas, these are relatively
small (none much larger than 10x10 miles), are traversed by
logging roads, and are surrounded by farms, villages and
some big cities. However, we have portably dwelled here for
15 years without any serious problems. A few times we have.
been hassled on roads and in cities (probably less than are
most people because we spend little time there). We have
never been hassled in the woods.
    Sometimes we hear from people who would like to live
conventionally (in a house, or at least a large house trailer)
but to do so cheap. Western Oregon does not seem good for
that (at least not where we have been). (For more about western Oregon, including the weather, see April'92 DP p.5.)
    We don't know of any place in the U.S. that is good for
conventional dwelling. There are some semi-ghost-towns out
on the plains where houses can be PURCHASED cheaply, sometimes for no more than back taxes. But TAXES there are as
high as anywhere (we've heard) - which may be one reason the
houses were abandoned. (Someone who wants a high-taxed dwelling, had better move somewhere they can make lots of money.)
    We have heard of parts of Mexico where land can be rented
or leased inexpensively for trailers ($35/month, Lee reported
in Jan'91 MP p.10). I don't believe a U.S. citizen can BUY
land in Mexico unless married to a Mexican citizen.
    Last winter was exceptionally cold and nasty in the east,
someone wrote. The northwest was somewhat milder than usual,
with no heavy snow. No prolonged cold where we were (in the
hills), but the cities (in the valleys) were often colder.
Some days, even in January, were sunny and warm enough by noon
on our south slope to sun bathe (70°?),while the weather radio
reported Eugene still foggy and 28°. Bert & Holly, OR, April

We welcome more reports, especially on shelters and equipment.
    Payment: subscription/extension (or ?). What are you
using? In what conditions? How is it performing? May 1994

Dwelling Portably

(formerly named Message Post)
POB 190, Philomath OR 97370
July 1994 $1 per issue   To check/mo under $7, add 50¢

Panniers fit on bicycle along with crate.
The rack on my new bicycle has a
metal hold-down spring. Therefore, in
the cloth band that joins the two panniers, I recessed the rear for fitting
under the spring, and made a hole for the
lip of the spring to go through. The
tabs attach to the bottom of the plastic
milk crate. Some racks are different, so
measure and modify accordingly.
Bob Barker, Washington, May

recessed

tabs   hole   tabs

PANNIERS, TOP VIEW
← aft   forward →

plastic
← crate
← lip
of spring

← tab

STARBOARD VIEW

I am leaving for the Amazon in two months.
Do you have any advice on rubber
boots, mosquitos, etc? A water distiller
would be neat. Any suggestions?
I think Stephenson builds the best
tents and sleeping bags, and Fabiano the
best mountain shoe. For stoves, I think
propane is best. Who builds the best
backpack and survival suit? George Malben
NV, June

Al Fry's Tipis.
Tipis are fun and tend to draw nice
'real' people to you. But most tipis are
temporary playthings: the light-weight
cloth turns to sun-rotted rags in a few years.
I use heavy rubber-coated nylon canvas, which is said to
have a 20+ year life. I salvage it from surplus military
blow-up hospitals. Buying new cloth to make a tipi, would
cost much more than what I charge for a completed tipi. 14'
diameter is $395 plus $20 shipping. Color grey. I use heavy
industrial sewing thread and heavy straps for tie down.
I feel that the 14-foot size is best. Larger sizes are
more difficult to set up, heat, carry, and find poles for.
To find your poles, you can go into an area where over-
crowding and shade cause trees to grow long and slender. If
that isn't practical, use a section of conduit pipe as a
joint for shorter pole sections. Measure the pole length to
match the tipi height and allow plenty of extra. Using a nail
or notch to insure your rope won't slip down the pole, will
save a hassle later. 12 poles are recommended for spiritual
reasons. The front draft flaps are adjusted through the use
of a couple of extra skinny poles - in the traditional manner.
Stake the tipi down or sooner or later you will probably
find the wind moved your tipi elsewhere.
If you are going to winter in a tipi, you should insulate
the interior with old carpet foam, etc. Running a stovepipe
up through the draft hole is a lot smarter than breathing the
nasty smoke all winter. Use fiberglass curtains and tin to
make a fireproof exit hole for the pipe. For the floor, you
can use a layer of plastic topped with rug padding and rugs.
For leaks, use silicon rubber glue and patches to re-sew.
If you can't do it with a needle and thread, get a tent-and-
awning outfit or upholsterer to. Decorating tipis can be fun
and most libraries have books with Indian symbols and tipis.
My tipis may have a few designs to cover up glue blemish areas
in the re-used canvas. Al Fry,Box 2207,Garden Valley,ID 83622

I sold my boat and moved into an older log-cabin.
The main reason was insufficient living space on the boat
for me and my 4-year-old son. Also, I have garden space behind
the cabin. Living on the boat was best during summer and fall;
winter was not very comfortable. But I would consider living
on a larger boat. Aarran Rainbow, British Columbia, May

City lacks low-cost housing that is legal.
When the Centennial Car Camp for Homeless People closes
at the end of May, where are the campers going to go? All
alternatives are either expensive, distant, or illegal.
Several people plan to move their trailer into a private,
commercial campground 20+ miles south of Eugene. The cost,
$230 per month, is quite low compared to most housing, but not
for someone trying to live on $270 per month disability.
Others intend to use recreational campgrounds. Most have
stay limits of 14 days and are at least 50 miles from Eugene.
The Homeless Action Coalition and the Forest Service have
prepared a brochure for "homeless and financially distressed"
people, which lists various rules, regulations, helpful hints,
and nearest resources: available at social service agencies.
The most viable choices are, unfortunately, illegal.
These include: living in a vehicle and parking on the street,
usually in a residential neighborhood; living in a vehicle that
is parked on private property (in a friend's driveway or back
yard, or on rural land); or living in a friend's garage or
storage shed. What makes these choices reasonable for many
people is that the laws are rarely enforced.
The Eugene Police have a comparatively benign policy:
they don't bother someone who is sleeping in a vehicle, unless
they have been in the area more than 24 hours; and then they
issue warnings, requiring people to move, before issuing
citations. Even less often enforced are the zoning laws,
which regulate how many unrelated adults can live in a building
or prohibit people from living in vehicles on private property.
Literally thousands of people are living in these kinds of
situations. If these laws were fully enforced, the numbers of
"visible" homeless would probably quadruple.
The local waiting time for subsidized low-cost housing,
is about 2 years for someone disabled; even longer for others.
What can we, as a community do? (1) Support proposals for a
permanent year-around car camp. Although no one likes to see
homeless people "forced" to camp; building, maintaining and
staffing indoor shelters costs 15 times as much per resident.
(2) End discrimination by adding homelessness to Eugene's
anti-discrimination ordinance. Wayne Ford (from Other Paper,
Spring1994)
Low-cost hay house hassled by city officials.
Jim Simon and his son live in a house made of hay bales.
The squat one-room building measures 8x15 feet. It sits in
the backyard at 1038 Mason Street in Victoria, BC, surrounded
by poultry and gardens. Simon, 50, has lived here since the
courier company he was managing went out of business in 1991.
At first he camped out in a tent. But after spending a
"summer in Eden" as he put it, he was not keen on wintering
in the dim and dismal room he could afford to rent on UI.
So - why not a bale house, similar to what pioneers built
on the praries? $40 worth of hay and two weeks later, Simon
had a home. It was small but it was warm. Best of all, it
was cheap: less than $400 total including the two-by-fours
and plastic sheeting for the roof. And since then, $325 a
month rent for the space.

For shower and toilet Simon visits the main house, but
otherwise lives quite independently, cooking on a small propane
stove that doubles as a source of heat. A garden hose is
coiled beside the camper-size stainless steel sink in corner.
Were he allowed to stay here, Simon had planned to stucco
the place and put on a permanent roof. According to a report
by the Canada Mortgage and Housing Corporation, hay bale houses
are surprisingly resistant to fire if the walls are mortared
properly. Some built in NE 90 years ago, still stand strong.
1038 Mason is also the address of Brett Black, known to
many as Victoria's urban farmer. In the damp days of spring,
his garden is a profusion of green, broken by a purplish splash
of flowering rosemary. To many folks, it is a needed reminder
of what is real and pungent amidst the asphalt and upward
growth. But others find it a little too pungent. City bylaw
officer Dan Scoone says he had several complaints from people
upset about extra buildings (including a camper and chicken
coop) on the property. He told Black to get rid of the straw
house. Black says, the city will have to deal with Simon
directly. "It's specious, really - when you look at all the
illegal suites in town." In 1991, Black had to battle city
hall to keep his 100 chickens. He won. But two years later
he was battling again, this time fending off a proposal to
rezone the property and put up 27 condominiums selling for
$109,000 each. Linda Cassels (from Monday Magazine, May 1994,
thanks to Aarran)

Hostility of local people prompts camper to leave.
For nearly four years, I lived by myself in a wall tent
with a wood stove, and an abandoned VW Minibus on blocks, in
the woods on 40 acres owned by a friend in western New York.
It was beautiful from May through September, but got pretty
cold in winter with -20° wind chills and tons of snow.
For a while I was not bothered much and I did pretty well.
Last summer, however, I started to have problems. In August,
loggers who were cutting my friend's land, deliberately
crushed some of my firewood storage piles. I sued and won
$60 in small-claims court. In Sept., another logger who was
cutting up the crowns, bent a retaining bolt for the road chain
so badly that I had to hammer it to straighten it out and
refile the threads to reinstall it.
On December 5th, I came under a hail of gunfire from
across a brook ravine about 400' away, from the property of an
absentee landlord. Bullets were striking into trees 20 feet
from me and I later found some bullet holes in my tent. I got
into my car and drove to the nearest pay phone and called the
sheriff's dept. Two cars arrived quickly and they flushed out
two gunmen who had assault rifles. They claimed they were just
target shooting. Though this is considered reckless endangerment under NY law, they were not charged nor were their weapons
confiscated. That prompted me to move away, though I may go
back. I did win a small claims judgement of $304 against one
of the gunmen, and a hearing against the other is scheduled.
Also, whenever I left my campsite, someone would enter
the rear of my tent. The front is locked and the sides are
staked down, but the rear sod cloth is held down by a 10-foot
2x4 weighted with several heavy rocks. Someone kept removing
this though nothing was ever taken. I suspect nosy neighbors
and/or police. I interpret all of this as a concerted effort
by the locals to drive me out of the area. Lather, NY, May

(Comments:) (1) I would move out of an area before logging.
The faller has plenty on his mind (how to drop the trees so

they don't smash on each other, and are easy to skid) without also worrying about not hitting my camp. (2) I would not sue for something so minor. If the faller was to blame (he may not have been in this case), I would ask him to fix my wood piles or to pay me to do so. If he refused, the most I might do is circulate a report to woodlot owners in the area, suggesting the faller was incompetent or careless.

Being hauled into court may have infuriated the logger - far more than the $60 damages. The faller probably had local friends. The tent break-ins may have been a search for illegal substances for which they could prosecute Lather. Presumably nothing was found, whereupon they resorted to guns.

General advice: When moving into an area, don't start or escalate a feud with long-time residents. They are probably more numerous and better organized. If someone damages property, don't quickly assume they did it deliberately, and do try to settle directly, without involving police or lawyers.

If, even so, a feud develops, do move. Bert & Holly

Supplies worth storing for barter or personal use.

As money becomes worth less each day, one wonders what to buy now for use or swap later. Some "survival experts" suggest gold or silver. But such metals are useful only if traded for any currency still afloat. Worth stashing for later trade: salt (especially in areas far from ocean); butane lighters (store 10+ years; longer than paper matches); tools (metal files, saw blades, taps, dies, drill bits - in oilcloth in air/water-tight containers); plastic bags and sheets; hot glue sticks; quality duct tape; aluminum foil; candles; soap bars; pens and pencils; paper goods (in vac-sealed plastic); iodine crystals (for disinfecting or water sterilizing).

Items to cache but NOT trade: ammo, powder and primers (buyers might use them on you); food (buyers may raid you later for more); books (even if not used now, future generations may need them; store in vac-sealed plastic); vitamins and pain relievers (if gone bad, may harm customer, resulting in deadly revenge!); spare parts for your equipment; solar electric panels (costly now but later worth more for power-on-tap).

Some guidelines for other items: Is it difficult to obtain even now? Is it difficult or impossible to make yourself now if not later? I know I will be able to salvage metals, plastics and wood from the ruins and abandoned automobiles about the area. But intact equipment or critical parts may be difficult to find. Wildflower, Connecticut, April

(Comments:) We've had vitamin C tablets turn brown (bad?). We now buy pure ascorbic acid powder (Bronson) which seems to have kept well a few years so far. (No experience with other vitamins.) We've had stickem on plastic tape either harden or come off after a few years. (Haven't used duct tape much.) I also wonder about pens. (I'd bet on pencils.) Supposedly most paper contains acid and self destructs before many generations. Better to borrow books and copy onto acid-free paper? H&B

A woman walked across the U.S. eating (drinking) only grass.

Her method was to juice wild grasses. (She didn't say which ones. Perhaps any.) The machine is heavy (2 or 3 lbs) but grass juice is very nutritious. You just can't digest the cellulose as can a cow or goat. Also the silica will wear your teeth down. I tried garlic juicers and hammers on grass and found them useless for extracting juice.

I loved the article on gosmore. Tumbleweed, CA, May

Dwelling Portably

(formerly named Message Post)
POB 190, Philomath OR 97370
October 1994 $1 per issue   To check/mo under $7, add 50¢

To join two lines.

This hitch is
much faster than
splicing, and does
not weaken the ropes
or cords as much as
does an ordinary joining knot.
Testing, I joined two thin monofilaments with this hitch
and three times I pulled until one broke. It did not break at
the hitch. Whereas a sheet bend reduces the strength to 60%.
This hitch holds even slippery plastic cords, provided
they are about the same diameter and stiffness, and reasonably
flexible. I do not recommend for stiff, large-diameter monofilament or wire. Another limitation: the big lump formed
may jam if the rope feeds thru a block and tackle.
To form, wrap each line around the other five times or so.
Then feed each end thru the middle. Work snug.
Some books call this a blood knot. I think of it as a
double-ended pipe hitch. Hank Schultz, 1986?

Out of the rent race and into the woods.
When I told my mother about my plan to move out of my
Flaggstaff apartment and into a tent, she wept. Her son, the
college graduate, was soon to be homeless. "You have no idea
what hardships you will face," she said. She was right. Until
then, my only camping experience was a few weekends as a young
Boy Scout. Nonetheless, I was determined. At 27, I was an
aspiring writer whose biggest problem was simply finding time
to write. I figured that if I didn't have to pay rent, I could
spend less time working at a "real job" and more time working
on my not-too-profitable writing.
Environment was another concern. My tent, unlike conventional dwellings, would be constructed and put in place without
the need to cut down any trees. Also, living in a tent would
force me to use less water, gas and electricity.
In August 1992, I sold most of my possessions, put a few
things in storage, bought a tent, a sleeping bag and some other
gear, and put my theory to the test. I pitched my flimsy
little tent in the woods near Northern Arizona University.
Every morning, I packed up my tent and stuffed it, along
with all my other camping gear, into the four large saddlebags
on my mountain bike, trusting the tiny locks to deter thieves.
I spent most of my days at the library, where I could plug
in my portable typewriter instead of relying on costly batteries. Later, when I found out about the university's computer
lab, I sneaked in and did my writing on a computer.
In September, I began driving a school bus part time. To
shorten my commute to the bus barn, I moved my campsite to a
spot in the woods just east of town along a quiet stretch of
Route 66. At this secluded spot, I left my tent set up even
when I was gone all day, as I often was. I spent many of my
off-duty hours typing or reading in the warm employee lounge
at the bus barn. My evenings were often spent on a bench in
the mall, my typewriter on my lap.
As winter approached, I invested in a slightly larger and
much sturdier tent. I also bought a warmer sleeping bag, which
when wrapped around my summer bag, helped keep me warm on sub-
zero winter nights. When I was not in my sleeping bag, my

propane lantern, hanging in the center of my tent, kept me surprisingly warm. Of course, the use of any gas (or other combustion) appliance within an enclosed space is extremely dangerous. I kept my lantern at least a foot from anything that might burn, and left the roof vent open to avoid asphyxiation.* I also kept a fire extinguisher in my tent.

The cold was just one of the challenges. Winter storms, some with winds gusting to over 40 mph, might have blown my tent away but for its wind-shedding shape and the many pounds of gear inside. Heavy snows were also a threat. When falling copiously, every few hours I went out and brushed the tent off to avoid being crushed. Later, I strengthened the tent by attaching guy lines to several surrounding trees.

Riding a bike in the snow was another challenge. However, I found that as long as the snow was not too deep for automobiles, it was not too deep for a healthy man on a bicycle. Fortunately, I was near a road that usually was among the first to be plowed. But getting my heavy bike from my tent to the road when the snow was knee-deep, was a struggle. Often, I simply stashed my bike behind some trees near the road.

One benefit of the snow was that I could always tell whether anyone had visited my campsite while I was away. Only once did I find the telltale tracks of a stranger, who got to within 50 feet, where my tent was clearly visible, before turning around and retracing steps. The only theft, of a shovel and small propane tank, happened weeks later, after the snows had melted and heavy rains had washed away any tracks.

Although my friends knew about my homeless lifestyle, I was careful not to tell my co-workers. They might not understand. I might even lose my job. What would parents think if they learned that homeless men were driving school buses.

To keep clean, I often used showers in university locker rooms. Sometimes, I paid for a shower at an RV camp or youth hostel. Occasionally, I would shower at a friend's place. To keep in touch, I rented a post-office box and a pager.

I made it through the entire school year without losing my job to paranoia. Over the summer, I found a new job across town, and have moved my campsite closer to it.

Though I have not achieved much success as a writer, I am having too much fun to pack up my tent. The only thing that might prompt me to, is the realization that few women take a homeless man seriously. But then, few women took me seriously even when I lived in an apartment. In any case, I'm hoping there is a woman out there somewhere with Helen Keller's outlook on life: "Life is either a daring adventure, or nothing." Dan Frazier (shortened from The Arizona Republic, 9 Dec 1993).
                              * I never slept while lantern on.
I am looking for people who want to live along a river.
Preferably somewhere with a hot springs. I have a tipi.
Lisa Armstrong, Arizona, June

I need an inexpensive temporary shelter for a few years.
About 400 sq ft. What tents or domes do you offer? Alan,
                                            CA, August
I have completed my first year in a yurt.
I am very interested in what works and what doesn't.
                              Robert Sanders, NM, Aug.
Where to go and what to do.
After high school I took a year off to figure that out. I discovered that I do not want to conform to the "get a job, pay the bills, and die" mold. I am looking for contacts with other young people who have been able to resist the brainwash.
Tanya Vincent, Nova Scotia, June

I made a strong, light-weight tent pole for bike touring.
     I have been using it for five years. It consists of three
sections which join together. Each section is 16" long, of $\frac{1}{2}$"
schedule-40 PVC pipe. I plugged the bottom end of the bottom
section so it doesn't sink into the ground. I put union fittings on the other two sections for joining the sections.
     I drilled a hole in a cap and installed a bolt 1$\frac{1}{2}$" long
$\frac{1}{4}$" diameter with threads sticking out. Then I glued the cap
onto the top end of the top section. The bolt fits grommets on
tarps and tents. When disassembled, I keep the sections
together with a velcro strap. David French, SD, July

Mr Tuffy tire liners nearly eliminated bicycle flats.
     I have gotten only 3 flats in 5 years. One was from a
thorn in the side of the tire, another from the inside due to
an old tube, and the third from a staplegun staple. D. French

Many states now have less money for game wardens.
     Also for park rangers and other state officials, accord-
ing to friends who camp. The result: less chance of harassment and more peace of mind for people living or walking in
these mountains, including the Ozarks in n. Arkansas and s.
Missouri, the whole state of Tennessee, and North Carolina,
Kentucky and West Virginia. Also, no reports of gun-happy pot
growers shooting at campers. (They are learning!) Tim Leathers
                                                   TN, Sept.
Are second-hand yurts available?
     Or has anyone built their own from sapling wood or
scraps? In an old DP I read that Anne Callaway in CA built a
yurt. I would like to correspond with her, or with anyone
with info on yurts. While in OR this winter, we visited the
yurt builders near Eugene. New yurts seem expensive to us.
     We have lived in various tents and vehicles in cities and
wilderness areas; a couple of summers in canoes in Alaska (we
will do more of that), and a couple of winters in Mexico.
     Now we are living in ne Washington part of the year. We
bought some land because I am an avid gardener, and the
community garden seemed befret with politics and petty bicker-
ing. But we have refrained from building a permanent dwelling.
We live in an old Airstream trailer when necessary. Pat Evans,
                                                       WA, July
I have been looking for yurt plans for years.
     I notice that Anne Callaway built a yurt using Chuck and
Laurel Cox's plans. Where can I obtain these? Frank Stephenson
                                                     VA, June
More van living, travel and working in the east.
     At the resort in Georgia where I had worked, the owner
got greedy, wanting too much for rent. So in April I left.
     Driving northward, I slept overnight in a truck stop, and
showered outside in a secluded campground, using my sunshower.
     I drove the 100-mile-long Skyline Drive thru Shenandoah
National Park. Entry $5, speed limit 35 mph, and campsites
$10 a night. But beautiful scenery, especially in VA, despite
the rain and cold. I saw many deer and groundhogs, all tame.
     Then came Murphy's Law: a flat tire, a clogged carburator
and a shorted condenser. Not expecting trouble with my new
engine, I had left all my spare parts in GA, so had to buy some.
     Toll booths, at least in PA, now check that seat belts
fastened, ask for ID, and check tires for wear, etc.
     Upon arrival in NY state, I became extremely ill, either
from apple seeds I had chewed (I usually swallow whole) or from
water out of a brand new garden hose (which tasted awful but I
swallowed some before noticing). I needed 4 days to recover.

Some old friends said they could not find work. Nonetheless, I was offered my old job back, with a raise, starting
immediately. Typically, I do great in a new place until I get
a negative attitude, usually from other people.

I am working on the landscape and also do a little of
everything: pressure clean, recycle beer bottles, wash dishes,
clean up, carpentry, etc. I think the owners prefer someone
who will do all kinds of work. I usually work 8 AM to 6 PM.

The owners gave me permission to park my van behind the
restaurant. It was a great spot, off the main road and
complete with a spring. However, cops came around 9 PM and
told me camping was illegal. Rushing to move in the darkness,
I got stuck. The same cops returned at 10 PM and helped me
get unstuck. They only checked my tag, which was current.
They must have known my GA drivers license had been suspended
because they did not ask for ID. They searched my van and
found a pipe containing half a joint of pot which they dumped
out. They implied they knew all about me, but said I was a
"nice enough guy". I said I would not be any trouble. The
cops said they had hassled me only because a neighbor, 100
feet away, had complained - twice.

In retrospect, I had felt too secure at my site and had
shown obvious signs of camping, such as hanging my laundry out
to dry. If I had been as clandestine as I usually am, I think
I would have been okay. Also possibly, I could have met the
neighbor immediately and maybe made friends.

Now I park in the parking lot, shower upstairs from the
restaurant, and hang my laundry INSIDE my van even though
drying takes longer. I have been laundering in a 5 gallon
bucket. For an agitator I use a ski pole that has a plastic
thing on the end. I tie 18" pieces of strong line to my
buckets for more easily drawing water or tying onto branches.

I get to eat free at the restaurant. The only expenses
I expect are batteries for my radio and postage stamps. I
will use my bicycle for local transport.

I ran an extension cord to my van to operate a light,
heater and radio. Most evenings I write letters and listen
to shortwave. (One night I heard someone named "Wildflower"
call a talk show. I wondered if the same "Wildflower" in DP.)
Though only 50 miles from New York City, the moon and stars
here are beautiful. Eugene Gonzalez, NY, October

We have been living in our home-made pickup-shell.
Also, house sitting when phriends are away, and just
winging it. Stevyn & Kelly Prothero, Iron Feather, CO, June

My wife and I were almost ready to start living in our van.
And possibly land squat in Oregon or n. California. But
a legal problem took much of our money. Also, we are expecting
our first child in Feb. We are not giving up; we will just
have to wait until we save a little money.

We are vegetarian and non-authoritarian. Do you know any
families we might hook up with? Tree Frog, California, August

I am thinking of moving into a 26' travel trailer.
Instead of paying apartment rent, I would be putting the
money toward owning something, plus have the mobility.

Although my little Toyota pickup won't tow the 4200 lb
Airstream I am considering, I figure I can locate a tow vehicle
when I desire to move it. Jim Wirth, California, September

Trailer living, travel and working in the west.

In Sept. 1992, my partner and I sold almost everything we had accumulated (a HUMONGOUS moving sale!) and bought a 32-ft travel trailer and an older (1976) truck with guts enough to tow it. Since then we have traveled in OR, NV, ID, AZ and UT. Sometimes we have made enough bucks to allow us the luxury of a small, cheap RV park; sometimes we've gotten by on ingenuity.

We lived on the east slope of Donner Pass (10 miles west of Reno) at 6900' altitude, during the worst winter the place had seen in 20 years (and trailers ain't insulated worth a damn). Some mornings were 28° INSIDE. We refused to waste propane heating the trailer while we slept.

Next we went to eastern Oregon at Malheur National Forest where I got a caretaker position at a summer conservation and scout camp for the season. It meant free rent and electricity and free meals (we are vegetarians).

From there, to Idaho. McCall is very pretty but it is a tourist spot. Deb got a fine job as Director of Nursing at a nursing home, but the administrator made the job too stressful.

Off we went again, this time with no job prospects. We stayed in Kingman AZ for awhile and really liked the high desert. But employment didn't materialize. Prescott AZ is very nice, but becoming overpopulated since a major magazine named it THE most desirable place to retire IN THE U.S. The cost of living wasn't too bad, but Deb found herself in another intolerable working situation.

Our next stop was Panquitch/Bryce Utah: very pretty country there close to Bryce Canyon. Great hiking and photography. We lived a month in a small RV park until it became obvious we would not get hired in that area unless we became Mormons. Running low on funds, we moved to a free campground while learning of job opportunities elsewhere. I hooked up a single solar panel (bought in Prescott) to light the trailer inside. We lived there April and May. Because of the 8000' elevation the Forest Service would not turn on water until mid June, but we found a wonderful spring. We showered every other day using our solar shower bag. Showering outside was fairly comfortable SOME TIMES. But many mornings were under 30°, and many afternoons the wind would pick up or clouds would accumulate. Often we had thunderstorms. There was no sewer hookup, and to avoid using our toilet and holding tank (odors inside even the newer units can be annoying), we would dash for the pit toilets not far from our site. Astonishingly often no other campers were there, even on May weekends, when many days reached the mid 70's. Utahns must be awful wimpy. But that allowed us to sunbathe nude without offending.

Now we are almost full circle from where we started near Donner Pass, except we are 44 miles farther east and 2000 feet lower. We are at an RV site at Pyramid Lake, on the Paiute Native American Reservation, and we are hooked to the grid. All utilities (except the small amount of propane we use) are included for $150 a month. And we have the view of a 21 x 9 mile lake surrounded by some pretty high peaks. The lake temperature is about 70°, great for swimming. Deb has a $40,000 per year position with a non-profit home health care corporation. I am caring for all else in our lives. I write environmental and human interest stories for publication, and am still seeking employment. We expect to stay here until we get some old debts/obligations paid off. Then we will once again be seeking a place in the woods where we can live with the land in a more native-like style. Wayne Packwood, NV, July

75

I once believed I would lead a "van revolution".
    With the restrictive housing and building codes, it may
be that portable housing is the only answer for those who do
not wish to devote their lifetimes to their housing needs
                                        Charles Wilson, VA,Aug
I seek tips for living cheaply in a small roomette.
                                        Dave, Quebec, Aug.
Much land is vacant and suitable for microhouses.
    Many churches own land surrounding their structures which
could hold small temporary buildings called "microhouses".
The church would provide basic utilities while the microhouses
provide shelter. Any unused space could be gardened.
    With shelter, food and basic sanitation needs met, people
could then seek productive work as well as help the church with
everything from cleanup to fund raising. A win-win action.
    To build microhouses, materials can be donated or recycled
from construction leftovers, and labor volunteered by seniors,
unions and other groups. Young people as apprentices could
learn useful trades. Examples of other places and uses:
    An older couple builds a microhouse in their backyard as
a hobby shop. Later, crippled by arthritis, they are cared for
by a young mother with 2-year-old who lives in the microhouse.
    In a small town, the owners of a big lot put a microhouse
on it for an elderly former farmer who tends their garden.
    A father laid off from his middle management job, does
appliance repair in his backyard microhouse. As business grows
he builds another microhouse for a part-time helper.
    My vision of the future: Instead of millions of people
homeless, I see many microhouses in backyards, woods and
forests - and everywhere there is a small space and some love.
What would bring this about? Just the willingness of good
people to build a simple shelter and make it available to those
in need. Bill Kaysing, Holy Terra Church, PO 832, Soquel CA
                                        95073;(408)4624176
(Comments:) Microhouses will be more acceptable if they are
portable - easy to move if an arrangement does not work out.
Also, portable microhouses can be taken into forests without
constructing driveways (which disrupt soil and trees).
    If the whole microhouse is too big to carry easily, I
would assemble it by bolting or lashing together sections that
ARE small enough to hand carry over steep or rough ground.
    I assume microhouses would have many different designs
using whatever materials are abundant locally: eg, straw huts
in hay-growing areas; adobe or cob where there is good clay;
wickiups along willow banks; pole frames in those woods where
there are many skinny trees. However, one general point:
    Most small cottages, trailers, and large tents we have
seen, tend to be imitations of big houses, with little windows
on every side. All these windows not only complicate construction, but most of them usually face trees or other buildings,
making them almost worthless for illumination. And the one or
two windows that do face sky are too small to admit much light.
    Instead, make ONE wall mostly window, at least from knee-
height up, and face it toward the most open sky. Build all
other walls solid. Big houses need many windows because they
have many separate rooms. Little houses don't.
    For economy, light-weight, insulation, and no breakage,
the window could be formed from several layers of clear
plastic. For UV resistance, use plastic sold for greenhouses.
Such a window can also serve as door and vent. Use rubber
straps to hold the lower corners down and to sides. Open simply
by raising the plastic. Easier and safer than doors. B&H, OR

Dwelling Portably

formerly named Message Post
POB 190, Philomath OR 97370

May 1995 $1 per issue   Add 50¢ to check/mo under $7

Candle lantern easily made from plastic jug.
   Cut off the upper portion of a one-gallon
milk/juice/water jug, leaving handle intact.
   Place short candle (2" to 4" long) in
jug, centering it beneath the opening. Add
gravel, sand or dirt one inch deep around
candle to hold it upright. Tilt and gently
shake the jug to make sure the candle will
stay upright. (If it doesn't, add more gravel,
pack dirt firmer, or use a shorter candle.)
   This lantern can be set on the ground or
carried about. Usable even in light wind,
because the jug shields the flame, and the
gravel weights the jug. The gravel also protects the plastic
bottom when the candle burns down. Wildflower, CT, 1993

(Comment:) We wondered, if the jug was tilted would the flame
melt or ignite the plastic? But we used it several times with
no problem. (Compared with a different lantern on page 5) H&B

For storage of long items, consider PVC pipe.
   It is widely available in diameters up to 4", and with
some hunting (at irrigation or building supplies) as large as
6", maybe even 8". (Common length is ten feet?) Put a glued
waterproof fitting on one end and a screw cap on the other.
   PVC pipes cannot be sensed by metal detectors, provided
you don't store metal items in them. (If you do, consider
planting diversionary stashes of scrap metals.) Jon Seaver, MI

Desirable features if buying a travel trailer.
   Two axles provide better load distribution; and a flat
tire won't dump the trailer sideways. Common-size car tires,
14 or 15 inch, are cheaper and easier to replace than special
trailer tires. 18 to 25 feet long: the smaller the trailer,
the easier it maneuvers, and the less wear on the tow vehicle.
   If you gut the interior, you can build in a very efficient
use of space. (For that, I'd look for a trailer that is extra
cheap because damaged or shabby inside.) Otherwise you are
stuck with the tight fit of the original floor plan.
   Add a photovoltaic solar panel for electrical freedom.
   I have a pickup and a 25-foot travel trailer in which I
have been living since 1989. David French, South Dakota, Dec.

More about the Baja California border area.
   A few miles north of San Felipe, 75 x 100' lots can still
be leased for $35 per month; for parking a trailer or building
a cabin or house. Though you can sell your structure, the land
still belongs to owner. Lease renewable every 10 to 30 years.
   There are great buys on big old trailers and houses along
that coast: $3000 plus lease. Water can be bought from trucks.
   Summers are very hot and humid with sand storms, salt, no
shade. If you go away, robbers break in and take booze, money
and food, but not items needing electricity (which they lack).
   Beware of El Dorado where everyone "wins" a piece of land
with a country club on the beach. You will be miles from the
country club on crummy land where they want you to build house.
   Many people buy prescription medicines in Mexico at great
savings, without border hassles. The California Pharmacy in

Algondonas, just across from Yuma AZ, can provide prescription.
    I now go to Mexico only during days: for dental work, $5
blankets, and great street tacos. I've never gotten sick eating
Mexican-style food, but have from American-style food in Mexico
(eg, cake with whipped cream) even in snazzy restaurants.
    You cannot legally work in Mexico doing anything that any
Mexican is capable of doing. The reality is: on a job you get
promised, but may never receive, a work permit. You get paid
and everybody is happy, but no job security. Teaching English
privately is possible. (Only Mexicans teach in public schools.)
                                                Double Dorje

Vehicular camping near Yuma Arizona/California
    If you have a remote source of income such as retirement
or disability benefits, I recommend the BLM's Long Term Visitor
Areas (LTVA). LTVA includes many thousands of acres from Yuma
to Quartzite - even a hot springs (soaking only; no soap).
You can stay in LTVA with only a tent, car and ten-gallon water
tank (fill up free at RV store). Or buy a camper without truck
for $500 and pay someone $25 or $50 to move it. The "Green
Meanies" (rangers) may make you live in specific areas, and are
often arrogant and hostile if they suspect you are poor and,
though camping legally, not there on vacation. $50 per winter.
    Or, the Indians will rent you space on the bank of the
American Canal for the price of a fishing license ($60/year).
Places get broken into if left for the summer, but Christian
Center, about 18 miles north of Yuma on S24, will store
anything on wheels for $10 per month. They generally have 5 to
15 rigs for sale. For more information, ask campers you see;
especially ones with funky rigs.
    A few guys live along the river in the tules.
    Thousands of people are here during winter (7 or 8 months:
Sept - April). Most are old, honest but rigid, and tsk their
tongues at longhairs. Bible belters abound.
    Winter temperatures are typically 65° days; rarely as low
as freezing nights. (Clue to mild winters: date and orange
groves.) Sand storms may last hours or days but are survivable.
Double Dorje, California, December

I recently developed a bikeshelter.
    It consists of an 8 by 10 foot heavy nylon tarp over a
parked and secured bicycle. It can be set up in less than five
minutes with a bike specifically equipped for this: front wheel
brace, kickstand, parking brake, flippable rear basket (my own
design). It withstood a 35 mph wind.
    I plan to use it on long bike tours. The only disadvantage
- it looks 'dorky' and I may be snubbed by some cyclists with
high-fashion high-dollar stuff, who sleep in $200 one-person
tents while leaving expensive superbikes out in the rain.
    Another improvisation is a face shield for nasty weather
made from a 2-liter vinyl bottle which attaches to my helmet
visor. I have spent 9 years learning how to use non-bike gear
with bikes, including military surplus, ag items, and household
stuff; and found that I don't need expensive equipment to enjoy
bicycling. Randy Wyatt, Backroads Bicycling, Kansas, December

General rules for easier and safer trekking.
    The path of least resistance is usually safest and fastest.
Follow a path instead of breaking trail. Go around instead of
over. But also know when to go the hard way.
    Cliffs are too dangerous. Usually there are ways around.
    If you must cross a river, do so where the water is wide
and shallow. When I have to wade, I probe each step with a

stick. Even in slow-moving clear water, depth can be deceptive.

A raft can be improvised from two or more inner tubes lashed together with poles and covered with blankets or tarps. When not in use, deflate the innertubes by removing valves from the valve stems; then put valves back in and cap.

Crossing frozen water is best avoided. On running water, ice is thinnest and most risky in the middle of the river.

I prefer to travel from daybreak until noon or two p.m. People notice me less then, because either they are not up and about or else are busy. Also, this allows me ample time to set up a comfortable camp, forage, do chores, and play.

To travel and not be seen is almost impossible. However, to be visible but not noticed is quite easy. In populated areas, I wear the customary clothing, am clean and neatly groomed, and maintain a happy face with a bright smile and kind word. If a busybody confronts me or questions me about my presence, I keep walking while maintaining an ongoing chatter about anything. That soon discourages them. Guy Hengst, Ind.

Bivying in snow country.

A snug shelter can often be made at the base of an evergreen tree that has broad low limbs. Under the tree the ground may be bare, while beyond the tree snow accumulates. A snow bank a foot or two deep will normally turn the wind and blowing snow. Such spots may be 20° warmer than are exposed areas. Guy

A naturally warm-and-cool shelter that needs no poles.

The Snugiup is a small enclosed dugout formed entirely of earth and plastic. Thus it can be built even in areas that lack timber such as deserts and brushlands.

The roof and front wall are insulated by air spaces between the layers. The other three walls and the floor are mostly soil, and act as natural, automatic heaters-coolers; absorbing heat on warm days and giving it back during cold spells. In western Oregon winters: when occupied, inside is typically 65°; seldom below 50° even when 15°F outside. (We've not had any weather colder than that to test it.)

The roof is flush with the ground, which minimizes wind forces and facilitates concealment.

The roof will not support much snow, but may allow snow to slide off, depending on steepness of roof and the type of snow.

Materials cost $10 to $20. Erection requires an hour or so, NOT counting site preparation which may take several days (but can be done in advance of use).

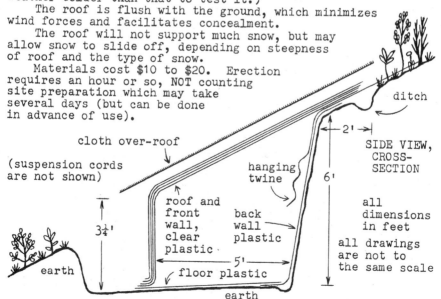

cloth over-roof

(suspension cords are not shown)

ditch

hanging twine

SIDE VIEW, CROSS-SECTION

2'

6'

3¼'

roof and front wall, clear plastic

back wall plastic

all dimensions in feet

all drawings are not to the same scale

earth

floor plastic

5'

earth

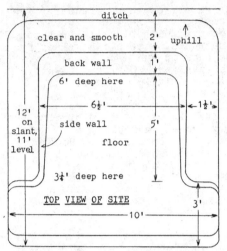

```
              ↑    ditch        ↑
    clear and smooth       2'  ↑ uphill
         back wall       1'
      ┌─ 6' deep here ─┐
       ├──── 6½' ─────→ ←─ 1½'
12'
on       side wall      5'
slant,
11'       floor
level
      3¼' deep here
      TOP VIEW OF SITE         3'
      ←────── 10' ──────→
```

Suggestions for building a Snugiup.

Construction is easiest on a steep slope. For winter, a south-facing slope will be brightest and warmest. For summer, an east-facing slope will warm during mornings and cool during afternoons. An ideal site has much foliage overhead, but little foliage downhill.

The Snugiup's walls require firm soil that will not collapse. Avoid soils with much sand or gravel. Roots are desirable for reinforcement though they will slow digging. Digging is usually easiest when the soil is somewhat moist. Early spring may be a good time to prepare a site for use the following winter; and allows time for soil instability to maybe show up. CAUTION: build and live in a Snugiup (or anything) at your own risk! We make no guarantees and assume no responsibilities or liabilities.

For a site also consider: can the dirt be disposed of easily and inconspicuously.

The illustrations assume a uniform slope that rises one foot for every two feet level distance. Most slopes don't. Furthermore, less digging is needed where a depression or irregularity exists. Therefore, modify to suit your site.

To prepare site, clear an area 10 by 12 feet. If much rain expected or if the soil does not drain well, shallowly ditch along the back (uphill) side of clearing.

Dig out the portion shown. Slant the walls, especially the back wall, to reduce risk of slumping. (Don't make the walls straight up and down.) Round all corners. Remove any rocks protruding from walls and tightly pack their holes with moist dirt. Cut off roots flush with wall. (Don't try to pull them out.)

Slope the floor slightly downhill. If ground water expected, ditch around.

If the site is left vacant for long, the walls will be eroded less by frost or dryness if covered with plastic.

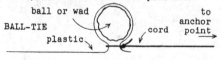

```
        ball or wad ⌒            to
BALL-TIE           (   )         anchor
        plastic             cord  point →
```

To erect, hang pieces of white or clear plastic over the walls, holding in place with ball-ties going to bushes/ logs/rocks beyond the cleared area.

Hang lengths of twine on the back wall (for suspending light-weight items when the Snugiup is occupied).

Form the roof and front wall from a piece of clear plastic 10 by 12½ feet. (If the plastic comes in rolls 10 by 25 feet, simply cut in half.) Anchor with ball-ties along sides and back. (Do not put ball-ties along front of roof, because they would form puddles.) Let excess length lay on the floor.

Suspend a second 10x12½ piece of clear plastic ½" to 1" outward of the first. If possible, tie its anchor cords to different bushes than hold the first layer, so that tension on one layer does not slacken the other layer.

Add additional layers as desired for insulation. (For summer use only, two layers are probably enough; for winter, four or more layers may be desirable.)

Cover floor with plastic. Add rugs, drapes as desired for comfort or decor.

Entry is by raising the front wall plastic and ducking under.

Where not much foliage is overhead, if shade during summer or concealment from air are desired, form an over-roof from appropriately-colored cloth 10½x10½ (need not be waterproof). Suspend it about 6" above the roof plastic. Put its front (downhill) edge so as to block direct sunshine during summer when the sun is high, but to admit sun during winter when the sun is low in the sky.

If extremely hot and sunny, add a second over-roof of white or reflective material, suspending it 6" above the plastic and 6" below first over-roof.

The Snugiup is small inside: floor 5 by 6 ft; height 3 to 6 ft. Therefore most belongings must be kept outside in stashes or under tarps when not in use.

Hints for building a longer dugout.

If you want the inside bright while the roof is shaded, the dugout must be narrow up-down the slope. Make it long only across the slope.

Rafters will be needed every few feet to hold up the roof. Poles supported by posts may be used. The rafters must go up-down the slope. (If put crosswise they would form puddles.) Also will need strips of carpet, moss or other insulative material to space roof layers apart.

For more ideas and explanations, see Hillodge in Apr'92 DP, which is similar in shape though not as sunken.   Bert

Two candle lanterns compared.

A lantern made from a 3# coffee can was described by Paul White in Apr'92 DP. Advantages: If inside shiny, more light goes to front. Less light in eyes. Metal won't melt or burn. Easier carry (weight directly below hand). Lighter (no gravel). Shelters flame from rain.

Advantages of jug lantern on page 1: Easier to make (plastic softer to cut and precision not needed). Candle may be any diameter (whereas can-lantern needs candle that fits snugly in hole). Easier to set down (candle not protruding below). Jug includes handle.

Overall preference: when hiking, can lantern; at camps, jug lantern.   H & B

Living aboard a boat.

Live on a boat? Don't be ridiculous. Might as well live in a camping trailer - there would be more room. Of course, going fishing in a camping trailer is difficult, but you wouldn't have to put up with the wind whistling through your neighbors' shrouds, the waves rocking your boat, the sea lions barking, and the herons caterwauling after dark.

I have been living on boats since April 1992. This has long been a dream of mine. Fulfilling it hasn't been easy.

Living on a boat is not for everyone. Actually, it's for hardly anyone. For instance, you've got to get used to the thought of being afloat all the time - even when sleeping. Think it would be great to enjoy those cool summer breezes each night? Well it is, except when they become cold, chilly winds in fall and winter - often accompanied by a downpour and occasional gale.

Speaking of winter: ever try to heat a boat sitting in near-freezing water? Very few boats have central heating systems or thick layers of insulation. Most marina slips have inadequate electricity, and few if any have natural gas piped from shore. Many boats are equipped with diesel heaters however, and some even have bottled-gas catalytic furnaces which do a fine job of heating.

Living aboard requires special skills like finding a nook and cranny for all the things you really want and need to have around. Few boats of any size have much free storage, especially hanging lockers (closets to you landlubbers). Don't expect me to wear a different outfit every day: I just don't have the space. Summers I wear nothing but a T-shirt, slacks, and dock-siders.

Enjoy large-screen television? Forget it if you want to live on a boat. Many of the permanent residents of this marina don't even own televisions, but if they do it's usually a small one. Besides, there's no cable service. And many video stores won't rent to someone who doesn't have a street address.

Which brings up check-cashing and identification. My checks are imprinted with my mailing address and telephone number, but cashiers always want to know my street address. When they learn I live on a dock in the bay I start getting those quizzical glances. And the Department of Licensing won't issue a license to a post office box - they want to know where to come and get you.

Live cheaply on a boat? The purchase price of a livable boat starts at around a thousand dollars a foot, and goes up from there. Every year it has to come out of the water to repaint the bottom (at $100 or more per gallon of paint), replace anti-corrosion zincs, and clean barnacles off of the propulsion system. Any wood above the water line must be stripped, cleaned and revarnished - not just for appearance, but to prevent corrosion from the sun and rain. Mooring lines, halyards, sheets and sails must be replaced due to wear and the effect of ultraviolet rays. BOAT is an acronym which means: Break Out Another Thousand.

Last year I noticed an older cabin cruiser in the shipyard undergoing a major refit. It was large, probably 45 foot overall. All the surfaces were stripped down to the bare wood and some planks and ports were being replaced. After many months in drydock it was launched last fall and suddenly appeared at the head of my dock. I watched as a young man and his obviously pregnant wife moved aboard. They were soon joined by a tiny black kitten and a furry Husky puppy - then a brand new baby. They were fulfilling their dream.

Within a few weeks however, a small tragedy struck: the wiring on the boat, inadequate for the demand placed upon it by several electrical heaters, caught fire. The inexperienced skipper, in violation of Coast Guard regulations, didn't have any fire extinguishers on board. Luckily, several Fire Department engines arrived and quickly extinguished the fire. The family moved off of the boat temporarily, and a large pile of singed and smoke-damaged clothing and other possessions appeared on the dock.

The puppy soon grew so large that it could no longer safely lounge on the aft deck without falling overboard, and had to be confined, alone most of each day, inside the enclosed bridge.

One sunny day the young skipper slipped the lines and ventured out into Port Gardner and points beyond, only to return from the expedition with obvious signs of a hostile encounter with a creosote-coated piling. A few days later a "for sale" sign appeared. Apparently living aboard had lost its appeal.

Myself, I live on a boat for many reasons. For one thing, how many people are surrounded by a moat? To get to my boat, one must have a key to the barbed-wire reinforced gate or be willing to swim in the chilling waters. A security guard walks past my boat several times daily, on the lookout for suspicious activity. The parking lot is well lighted and patrolled. The handful of other people who live on my dock watch out for my boat as I do for theirs. When an inexperienced skipper ties his boat up too loosely, someone will step forward to fix it, seeking neither recognition nor compensation.

We are a neighborhood and have interests in common beyond simply a love of boating. We are concerned with the water quality in the marina - after all we live there. Many of us are bird-lovers and environmentalists concerned with preserving the natural habitat of the harbors and wetlands, and especially with enhancing the fish and shellfish population in the bays because we enjoy viewing, gathering and eating them.

My best friends live on other boats nearby. They come over for chili; I go over for coffee. We share meals, boating tips, stories of successes and failures.

Last summer I took a sabbatical to restore my old wooden boat, arising each morning to row my dingy out into the bay to gather crabs or clams, and trolling for trout on the way in. Fresh trout or smelt for breakfast, crab salad for lunch; clam chowder for dinner on stormy days - that's heaven. Each day the sunset seems to out-do itself.

Doug Lewis, © March 1994; Washington

Piñon nuts are nutritious; but robbing pack rats hazardous.
    All pines have edible seeds, but nuts large enough to be
worth gathering are produced mainly by: Pinus edulis (needles
in twos); P.quadrifolia (fours); and P.monophylla (needles
singly). They grow in many areas of the southwest.
    The nuts are in hard dark-brown shells found within the
cone, with one shell under each cone scale. Some shells
contain no seeds, and professional pickers have ways to tell.
    The seeds are collected in late August or Sept by picking
the almost-ripe cones and roasting them to release the seeds.
An easier method, if there are not many squirrels, is to
simply wait until the seeds fall and gather them from the
ground. Not every year does an area have a large crop.
    Some people collect pinon nuts from pack-rat dens. However
an old Indian legend is confirmed by recent evidence: most
people who died from Hanta virus had collected nuts from pack-
rat dens. Pack rats commonly get Hanta virus (as do many
other rats and mice) and their storage areas are filled with
infected feces. Transmission is thought to be by breathing
dust from feces. (from Christopher Nyerges, Coltsfoot, Nov'94;
and Donald Kirk, Edible Wild Plants, Naturegraph, 1970)

Crawfish are abundant in streams of many areas.
    After gathering, I purge them by placing in a bucket with
extremely salty water. After a few minutes the crawfish will
shit. I then take them out, rinse off, and cook. Tim Leathers

Marigolds are natural bug repellants.
    I have found that rubbing marigold blossoms on exposed
skin repells most insects very well, and seems to slow down
even ticks. A potted marigold of a short variety can be
transported easily. Guy R. Hengst, Indiana, September

Selecting clothes and equipment to be inconspicuous.
    Choose clothes in styles you can wear daily and equipment
you can use daily. And wear and use them daily. You will
learn which are useful and which are junk. You will become
handy with them. You will replace them when they show heavy
wear. And you will always be ready, even on a date.
    Camo clothes look very macho, but earth-color clothes in
combination blend well, cost less, are less conspicuous when
worn on streets, and don't set in closets when you need them
miles away. Don't wear white clothes; not even underclothes
which are conspicuous when hung to dry. Stores carry jock
shorts and T-shirts (etc) in black and dark green.
    Carry three sets of clothes: one to wear; one clean; and
one to wash, or washed and drying. Sort clothes and gear into
bags with different colors and textures, for easy finding in
light (by color) or in dark (by feel).
    Instead of a bunch of pouches or packs, I wear a fisher-
man's vest which has about 20 pockets. The weight is better
distributed and the bulk isn't as obvious.
    Two cheap rectangular sleeping bags, one light, the other
medium or heavy, provide three temperature ranges. For cold
conditions, put one inside the other. For additional warmth,
wear a cap to bed: balaclava is best, and is also a mask -
hiding light skin at night. Also wear socks and long jons.
    Do not get synthetic sleeping bags. Turning over in them
can be heard for half a mile, especially if the enemy has a
sound magnifier. Paul Doerr, California, June

(Comments:) Dark clothes also dry faster than white if hung in
the sun, because they absorb more heat.

In this climate, cotton sleeping-bag covers and liners soon rot and rip. We prefer synthetics. At a distance their rustle sounds much like foliage, wind and water noises. For military patrols bivying, the noise might be a concern. But for everyday living in the woods, the noise seems trivial compared to other sounds. The most unnatural, distinctively-human noise is metal striking metal: a pot against a stove; a lid or spoon against a pot; a fastener against a pack frame. For stealth, minimize metal (also glass). Carve a wooden pot lid. Use wood or plastic spoons. Put metal tools in separate cloth bags, etc.

Also conspicuous is the human voice. Better to whisper. Very conspicuous is music. Listen only with earphones. H & B

Spotting people from the air is difficult, even with infra-red.

As the National Guard OH-58 helicopter swept over sugar cane fields cloaked in darkness, searching for five escapees who had tunneled out of a Glades prison; the pilot said, that without good tips, spotting someone who doesn't want to be found "is like finding a needle in a haystack."

From 500 feet above the ground, the surreal images the pilots see through their goggles and on two small monitors cover an area half the size of a football field. At that distance, a herd of cattle shows up as white dots on the screens. A person could squat among them and be easily mistaken for a cow. And "a hubcap laying all day in the sun might look suspicious." Flying the chopper costs $140 an hour.

Equipment on the chopper's underside picks up slight temperature differences and converts them into a black and white image. Though it can't show what is inside a house, it can tell if one room is even 3 degrees warmer than another. Monika Gonzalez, Jan (from <u>Directions</u>; and <u>Palm Beach Post</u>)

Defenses against large animals.

The most dangerous animal is man. Next, in my experience, moose (but I've not dealt with grizzlies or boars). If threatened by a moose, keep a sturdy tree between you and it.

If using a stick, staff or spear for defense, keep hold of it and jab, stab or swat - never throw. If alone, I prefer a 6-foot whip in one hand and a 3-foot inch-diameter stick in the other. If with another person, one wields the whip and the other a 4½-to-6-foot staff or spear. Remember to give the creature a way to escape. It almost always will.

At night, the biggest danger may be your own fears. Most sounds are made by creatures you could hold in one hand. To avoid large intruders, camp or bed down in a spot requiring an effort to reach. Be clean and odorless (no garbage), be quiet, and do not allow a light to show. Guy Hengst, Indiana

Preparing sites and simple shelters for winter use.

I lived nomadically for three years in Kentucky around two lakes and one year in northwestern Minnesota. For me, winter was the best season: generally quiet and tranquil, with no flies or mosquitos and with few recreational people about.

The key to easy wintering is preparation. From late spring (after the rains) through early fall (until deer season), while exploring and foraging I also scout and prepare many camp sites and caches to use later.

I find excellent sites along abandoned fence lines, hedgerows, briar patches, and rose thickets. To prepare, I crawl into the thicket and, working from the center outward, cut canes at ground level and push them out until I have a big enough clearing.

Usually I want three chambers: a main chamber with length 1½ times my length, width equal to my length, and tall enough to kneel upright with several inches of clearance overhead; a sleeping chamber slightly larger than the most people that will use it; an entryway between main chamber and outside.

I set a cache near each site or in the entryway. It typically includes: a complete change of clothes or a thin blanket; matches, tinder and kindling; candles; fish hooks and line; dental floss; ten pounds of unground wheat and two of rice; bouillion; salt; baking powder or soda; sharp knife; fork; a 3-pound coffee can to cook in; at least one tarp. Most of this stuff I get free or for pennies. I store in a 5-gallon (or larger) plastic jug or bucket-with-lid. (Most metal containers disintegrate in one or two seasons if buried here.) I bury with 8" of dirt over the container.

I usually also have two or three large caches somewhere in the area from which I draw most of the year. These are as out of the way and as difficult to find as I can make them. (Yes, once I hid one so well that I never found it.) These hold most of my food, equipment, and seasonal clothing.

When I move to a site, I erect within each chamber a clear plastic tarp, held up by a few saplings which I bend to form arches. Then I lay ground tarps in the main and sleeping chambers, fastening their edges up a few inches to provide fairly waterproof floors.

The only insulation is the thicket itself, and the only heat sources are bodies and candles. A candle or two quickly warms the main chamber, and can heat water to a boil for cooking if not in a rush. I have never built a fire in a shelter. Too dangerous. To reduce condensation and heat loss, I leave boots, outer clothing, and firewood in the entryway and do not heat it. When entering, I close off the outside before opening the interior. I have a second exit.

Frequent moves reduce problems with mice, rats, lice and other vermin; and with becoming noticed by busybodies. Rarely did I stay in one place longer than a week or two. Exceptions: during the fall gun season for deer (the most dangerous time), I stayed down and well hidden for two months; and during the spring rains I stayed put about one month.

During winter, when not raining or snowing I spent most time outdoors: exploring, fishing and hiking about with other people. The exercise generates heat; therefore I wear several layers of lightweight clothing which I remove as necessary to prevent sweating. I take with me: extra clothing; some food; a tarp; and fire makings. (Only once was I cold or worried - 7 miles from shelter in a blizzard that lasted two days.) Evenings and rainy or snowy days, I spend in a shelter reading, talking, playing, and making stuff. Guy Hengst, Dec.

Tips for increasing privacy and security in the wilderness.

Before choosing a camp site, walk around it from different angles and at different distances. The harder your camp is to approach, the less likely someone will find it. Climb hills, climb trees, scan the area. Consider visibility from the air.

Don't camp in favorable hunting and fishing areas.

Never create paths or leave trails near your camp. Approach your camp from various directions; not the same way each time. Don't let your wandering become routine: stay aware of where you are and what way you are heading.

Be careful not to break limbs, turn over stones, or drop anything. When approaching your camp, move slowly and stop every 20 paces or so to look and listen for anything unnatural.

Think about how you can blend your camp into the surrounding terrain. Camo netting can be bought or made. Cover shiny objects or put them where the sun will never reach them.

Avoid or minimize fires at camp. Large fires are easily seen at night. Smoky fires are easily seen during the day.

Noise such as gunfire, barking dogs or chopping wood draws attention. Do any hunting away from camp and try for one-shot kills. (I prefer to snare or fish.) Rig equipment so it can't make noise. Eg, tie down anything that could blow around.

Having a dog around just for company isn't smart. You have all of the outdoors and the wild creatures to entertain you.

Keep anything valuable or incriminating well hidden. Try burying plastic buckets with tight-fitting lids. Tim Leathers
TN, Febr.

Additional security tips, especially for newcomers.

If new to the wilds, or in a kind of terrain new to you, expect mistakes at first. To minimize the consequences:

Best stay elsewhere during hunting seasons. (Sporting-good stores have schedules.) Chances of encounters then are much greater than at other times, and may be with people armed and trigger-happy. Autumn is also when many people enter the woods to gather mushrooms, firewood, and holiday decorations.

Keep important ID and most valuables well hidden (eg, in a buried jar). But have a little money and ID on you. (Otherwise robbers might assume you have a cache and threaten further.)

If living in a vehicle, move frequently - at least weekly. If not, use it briefly to bring in supplies, then QUICKLY get it AWAY (sell or store). Do light trips by bus/bike/hike.

If digging or brush-cutting much at a site, the best time is late winter, so spring growth soon helps cover disturbance.

Generally, foresters don't want unnecessary enemies (who could do much damage) and won't hassle unless something seems to threaten their property. You greatly improve your odds, both of not being discovered, and of not being hassled even if discovered, if you: don't smoke; don't make fires; don't cut trees; don't have power tools, pack animals, or a dog. B & H

What dangers seem likeliest in woods where we have been.

Poke eye with branch. (Wear safety glasses with top and side shields, or helmet with face plate - little kids espec.)

Step into unseen hole and break leg. (Where you can't see the ground, move slow and probe ahead with foot or staff.)

On wet slope, slip, slide, and possibly impale on a sharp stump. (Lean close to slope and keep hold or dig hands in.)

Chilling, because of change of weather or activity. (Take enough warm clothes. Also learn how to make an insulated "cocoon" out of leaves, moss, grass, ferns, boughs, etc.)

Carbon monoxide in tight enclosure. Sneaky and deadly! (Ventilate well if ANY combustion, even candle or catalytic.)

Collisions on back roads where vehicles are not expected.

The back country is probably the safest place to be.

We publish the foregoing to help DP readers take sensible precautions. But we don't feel threatened. The media gives a false impression by featuring the few assaults and accidents in the bush while largely ignoring many calamities elsewhere.

Bert and I have backpack camped almost continuously for 15 years without any hassles or serious injuries. (We had one minor theft - from a temporary stash near a road.) Most mishaps we hear of, occur to people traveling on roads, living in or with vehicles, or camping in city parks.

May your times be interesting - but not TOO interesting.
Holly & Bert

Dwelling Portably
formerly named Message Post
POB 190, Philomath OR 97370
October 1995 $1 per issue   Add 50¢ to check/mo under $7

Controlling water flow when showering with jugs.

On a spare cap that fits my bleach jugs, I installed a small shower head. That seems to give better control and coverage than just loosening the cap. I also drilled a 3/16" vent hole in each jug handle to allow the jugs to "breath" as the water drains. When a jug is empty, I transfer the shower head/cap to another jug. Two half-gallon jugs are adequate for a good shower. If extra water is required for extra people, I heat it in a solar shower bag and refill the jugs from that.   Brother Bat, Arizona, May

(Comments:) Did you try simply removing the cap? That is what we do and we have no difficulty controlling flow. (Did we at first? We don't remember. But any learning came quickly, requiring at most a few showers.)

Does the solar shower bag heat water faster than does a dark-colored or black-painted jug? Holly & Bert, OR, Oct.

More about the "Silly Shower".

I fill a yoghurt container with warm water and put it on my head upside down. Unless you are a skinhead, your hair will allow air to enter and water to trickle out all around the rim. Jai Loon, Washington, January

Portable shower enclosures.

REI sells one with inflatable frame, 30x30x65", 8¼ lbs, for $24 plus shipping. That is less expensive and lighter than Bivouac Buddy, which was $159 and 13 lbs (reviewed in March'89 MP/DP). But REI's lacks a holding tank (the water drains directly onto the ground) and thus can't be used in a room where you don't want to wet the floor.

For use outside to block wind or view, a piece of black plastic will do as well as REI's enclosure, and is lighter and much cheaper though not quite as easy to rig.   Holly

Technique for comfier showers also improves hand washing.

A first-grade-teacher friend complained that her kids used far too much water and soap when they washed up before lunch. I told her about Wanda's suggestion (in May'93 DP). Now she walks around the room and gives each kid a squirt of soap. They rub vigorously to make the soap disappear, then go rinse. Not only does that save water, but my friend thinks they also get their hands cleaner. Laura LaBree, WA

Orchard sprayers are portable and have many uses.

I love mine for showering; with a sink; and for better flushing a portable toilet. It is easily pressurized with its hand pump. The spray is adjustable. For frequent use, industrial models are far superior to garden-store varieties.

If used on food, I'd get a stainless steel model, remove lube, and replace with mineral oil. NEVER use on person or food a sprayer previously used with chemicals.   L. Smith, WI

I have been catching a dozen crawfish a week.

I catch them in the lake at the resort where I work, near NYC. I made a trap out of chicken wire and baited it with kitchen left-overs. The crawfish go around the trap

trying to get the bait, enter a funnel-shaped end, and get
stuck inside. Or maybe they get lazy with all that food to
eat and decide to stay. The door is for removing them.

This week, though, I found the door open and no crawfish
inside. Maybe a fisherman took them. Or maybe the muskrat
I see swimming around in the mornings.

I am catching muskies on topwater plug (rapala 11S(?))
and spinner/minnow combinations. I bought a fishing license
($35 if out of state) due to warnings from friends about
enforcement. Eugene Gonzalez, New York, May

Keeping qualities of edible oils.
The cooking oil I've found most durable is Cannola. To
me, it has no taste. It seems to handle high heat well.
I've had corn oil go bad. Brother Bat, Arizona, May

(Comment:) A pint of cannola oil we bought in bulk at a
large-volume co-op, went bad soon after purchase, developing
an increasingly strong fishy smell and taste. Several
previous batches had kept okay. We have never had corn oil
go bad, neither refined nor unrefined. The latter is the
oil we buy most often. Holly, Oregon, October

The three rock wok stove.
I developed this at my own personal
cooking fire. It keeps a rounded cooking
vessel squarely seated - no rocking, no
spills. A small, economic, controllable
fire underneath works best.
Regulate heat by pulling out or
pushing in 3" diameter or smaller fuelwood. No more than 6" clearance between
wok bottom and ground is fine. Scooping
a bunch of large glowing embers under,
works nicely also. Peter Bridge, Utah

Portable heat pack does not work.
The "ReHeater" brand, re-usable,
3x6" that I spent money on is totally
worthless. What's more, ReHeater Inc of
Gardena CA seems to be out of business,
so I can't even complain. Brother Bat

I live outside six months or more a year.
I am on some property I have. I live in a tent, haul
water in buckets, and have no electricity. I prefer to
live this way.

When cold, I burn small votive candles in my tent and am
impressed how warm it can get. The candle is in a small glass
container, which I feel is safer.

This year I put up a small strawbale shed for fun and
storage, and plan to build another for living in. I know
this option isn't practical for many of your readers, but
strawbale structures are really inexpensive, warm, quiet, and
easy to build. Laura LaBree, Washington, June

Sheer curtains are an inexpensive source of bug netting.
You can find them near free at any resale shop or yard
sale (people are happy to find someone who wants the darn
things). With a little sewing, you can custom make an
enclosure any size you need. To make it really bugproof,
velcro closures at door and window work well and are also
easy to sew on. Joyce Pierdinock, Herbal Voices, MI, June

(Comment:) We use curtains as netting and like them. However, we have been in a few places where there were tiny gnats (no-see-ums) which could get through. LLL has a paper, "Bug Free".

Mosquito repellant used before and after bite.
    If a mosquito bites, right away I touch or spray the spot with Cutters repellant. Itchy bump won't develop. Apparently Cutters breaks down a substance that humans are allergic to, which mosquitos inject to keep the blood from clotting. Other brands may also work. Double Dorje, Arizona, May

A complete covering of white prevents bee attack.
    I took a course on beekeeping. The less you look and act like a brown or black bear (the bees' arch enemy) the safer you will be. Bees, including killer bees, do not attack white. That is why bee keepers wear all white. Even a black pen top showing in your shirt pocket will invite a sting. My white dog was stung last year - just above her beady little brown eye. Bees go for my hair, which is brown. A net kept folded in your pocket can be retrieved to cover your head.
    "Killer bees": the name is an exaggeration, but they are incredibly hostile and very territorial. Their hive may be small, eg, a water meter box. They can pick up the vibration of you walking. Their territorial limit is said to be 50 feet - much farther than the limit of domestic bees. Ie, you can walk nearer to a hive of domestics without being attacked.
                                        Double Dorje, June 1994
Best defensive tactics against stinging insects?
    If I get too close to a bee hive or wasp nest and anger them, and some come at me, should I run away or stand still?
    Last summer I disturbed some wasps or hornets. Being on a fairly good trail, I ran, heading INTO the wind (blowing 5 ? mph). As long as I ran fast, I could stay ahead of them. But when I slowed for obstacles they caught up, at which times I batted my hands in the air at them. I had to run maybe half a mile before they gave up the chase. None seemed to land and I got no stings. Maybe they didn't really want combat. (There were only about a half dozen, so casualties would have seriously depleted their family.)   Bert, Oregon, November

(Reply:) I've heard that you are supposed to act like a flower. Don't flail. Stay calm. But personally, I'd run.
                                            Double Dorje
Comments on snake bite treatments.   Dec
    Most pit vipers are not lethal to otherwise healthy adults. If prevention fails, probably the best course is to seek professional medical attention. In the meantime, I suggest gentle local wound cleansing with mild soap and water, & minimal exertion (to reduce spread of venom and extent of tissue damage). Ie, I would personally do as much nothing as possible until antivenom could be administered.
    Some studies have shown that cut-and-suck treatments increase injury. Likewise ice treatment. I'm not aware of studies of electrical therapy. Jon Seaver, Michigan, Oct 1994

(Comments:) There is a high-vacuum extractor (discussed in March'91 MP/DP; sold by REI for $11 plus shipping; maybe also by Campmor and other dealers) that supposedly extracts most of venom WITHOUT cutting. Supposedly cutting, not sucking, is what often increases injury. A suction stronger than mouth is supposedly needed to extract most venom.

Yurts; housing restrictions; BLM land.

I would like more progress reports from people who build yurts or live in them. What did you use for struts; cover; yoke; ropes; etc.? I've heard some people use Sears snow fences for sides and roof.

A second-hand yurt was sold in the Illinois Valley of sw Oregon, summer 1994. I don't know price. New yurts I've seen were gorgeous and well designed but cost thousands and are technically not legal. Yurts may be great in Mongolia where nomads are legal, but here a yurt is too bulky to move easily without a car or yak.

With any kind of shelter, the big problem is finding a place to live legally. Building permit requirements make a home unaffordable whether it is a house or a yurt.

A great folly or oversight of this age, is homelessness and landlessness in a world and country with so much land. I or most any homeless person can build a house or yurt, and manage a garden. Instead, many of us are on a "death march". Even in the face of declining health, we must keep moving.

BLM land is pretty good for free camping, and there is plenty of it, but it is all but invisible. Boundaries are never marked. Exact locations are word of mouth. The maps that BLM sells are crap.

The sweet and gentle manners of rangers and park keepers change to arrogance and hostility the moment they suspect they are dealing with a poor person who is there legally but not on holiday - just deadly serious about staying alive for a few months before moving to another site as seasons change.

Double Dorje, AZ, May

(Comments:) Yes, the fantastic cost of houses and the lack of legal alternatives is insane, especially so considering the many low-cost (or free if scavenged) building materials available. Obviously, except possibly in Tokyo and a few other over-crowded cities, "homelessness" is not a housing problem but a LEGAL problem: created by building inspectors, big contractors, politicians, lawyers, and police - and by some "environmentalists" who want 90% of population to die.

(Of course there are many different "environmentalists". We think that what we do helps the environment. But we find obnoxious the rich hypocrites who, while living luxuriously themselves, claim that the planet or an area is overpopulated and try to deny others living space. A few years ago, thousands of them flew in jet airplanes (burning much fuel and injecting a stew of chemicals into the thin stratosphere) to Rio de Janeiro (a big, crowded city) where they no doubt ate heartily (in a land where many go hungry) while pontificating about conserving resources and reducing pollution. If they had been sincere, they could have stayed home and conferenced via internet.)

However, Bert and I don't let the lack of a house get us down. You and we and most houseless people have more and better sheltering options than our ancestors thousands of years ago when (eg) windows, if any, were oiled animal skins - or ice. We sometimes worry about rangers or building inspectors: our ancestors worried about hostile tribes.

Is lack of a house more life-threatening than is a house? More houseless people may die from chilling (those who don't know how to improvise insulation). But more housed people die from housefires and earthquakes, and from auto accidents commuting to work to pay for their houses.

Bert and I get house-sitting offers we pass up. And when we accept, we do so because use of a pickup is included,

or so we can be in/near a city for a while; not because we
want to live in a house. Our own shelters are smaller than
yurts and quite crowded, but are more comfortable than were
most houses we have sat. Eg, in winter our shelters stay
quite warm naturally (partly because they are small) whereas
most houses require stove tending. Holly & Bert, Oregon, Oct.

The criminalization of homelessness.
        In California where an estimated million people are home-
less, eight municipalities recently passed anti-sleeping
ordinances. The city of Berkeley now forbids loitering within
one block of laundromats, parks, and recreation centers; and
has considered outlawing the carrying of more than one
shopping bag ! Santa Cruz arrests people who sit on a sidewalk, even if only there waiting for a ride or bus. San
Francisco spent 450 police hours and $11,000 during 1993 to
arrest 15 people for begging.
        Why? "Visible poverty does discourage shoppers -
especially those out to spend discretionary dollars that they
could just as easily spend elsewhere. No one wants to run a
gauntlet of panhandlers to get to a boutique...." In New
York City, ad campaigns say that shoppers "have every right
to be selfish and annoyed." Celine-Marie Pascale (from Utne
Reader, Sept. 1994; sent by Guy Hengst)

(Comments:) Why don't all those "selfish and annoyed"
shoppers simply say "no" to panhandlers? If they did, the
panhandlers would soon quit. Refusing beggars, is less hostile
than are anti-loitering laws, which not only threaten many who
are not beggars, but may arouse sympathy for beggars.
        This article, like most of the slick media, follows the
official line that "homelessness" is the cause of panhandling.
That encourages shoppers and merchants who don't like beggars,
to persecute everyone who lacks 'proper' housing. Most "homeless" we know don't beg. And not all beggars are "homeless".
        Perhaps the anti-camping and anti-sleeping laws are an
attempt to goad the "homeless" into real crime, such as
robbing to get rent money, so that frightened citizenry will
support hiring more police and building more prisons.
        Some consequences that officials might overlook:
        Any city that prohibits shopping bags, knapsacks, or
bike baskets, etc., threatens many thrifty, energy-conserving
shoppers who bicycle or bus, or park a car one place while
running short errands on foot; and makes a mockery of
environmental preachings to conserve fuel and reduce pollution
by driving less.
        Any city that prohibits napping in vehicles, threatens
many shoppers from the hinterlands who do one multi-day trip
rather than many one-day trips; and makes a mockery of safe-
driving preachings to stop and sleep when tired.
        We say: Don't shop in such a city. Or shop less often.
Remember that most shopping is discretionary, especially if
you live in the boonies. If we had to, we could make just one
supply run a year, perhaps hiring an unemployed person with
pickup or van to help.
        Some victims launch boycott campaigns to encourage
reforms. Even just posting a few dozen copies of a well-
worded warning, can upset merchants, who will then lean on
the politicians and police. If doing that, some tips:
        Warn; don't just complain. Most people are too busy to
care much what happened to YOU. But if THEY feel threatened,
they will try to avoid the threat.

Make many people concerned. Eg, while taking cardboard from a dumpster to shade her parked, well-loaded bike, a friend was questioned by police and asked for ID (not for her riding or for taking the cardboard, but because she "looked suspicious"). In retaliation, she composed a poster (which we helped put up within a 50-mile radius) which not only related her experience, but said she had heard that many motorists, especially people with pickups and vans (which includes big shoppers) as well as bikes, were often hassled there for petty or imagined violations.

Target a specific place. Eg, the poster's heading, in very big print, was: "AVOID DOWNTOWN CORVALLIS". Our friend did not know for sure that police were worse downtown than elsewhere in the city; or worse than police in Eugene, Albany, Newport, etc. But merchants in each city and neighborhood are in competition with merchants elsewhere. Though people can't easily stop buying, most can easily go to an outlying shopping center instead of downtown, or, if from out of town, to a different city.

After that poster, there seemed to be less hassling. H&B

Students choose autos and camping over dorms in Corvallis.

Are you tired of high rents? Or living in that roach hotel? Or dealing with the landlord from hell? Or of lugging boxes up three flights of stairs? OSU students have done everything from set up house in old civil defense shelters to camping out at Avery Park and the fair grounds.

After hearing rumors that some graduate students live in their offices at OSU, I managed to contact one person who was doing it. The setup is plain and simple: a foldaway army cot, a few personal belongings, a box of clothes, and toiletries adorn the shelf above the desk. How not to get caught? "Well, I know the exact timetables and days the janitors come, and when they come I just leave the office. They've never seen me sleeping in here. Sometimes I feel just like a rat living this way, but it's cheap, and I'm here all the time anyway, working on my research. When I first came here, I couldn't find a place that was affordable. I didn't want to pay a lot to live in a dump, so I tent camped fall term. Then, in winter, I moved in here as it was pretty wet and cold." The student plans to return to tent camping in the spring quarter. Favorite spots to camp? "Personally, I like behind the baseball field by Parker, but the fairgrounds are okay, too. Less hassles there."

Another student has been living out of his vehicle since spring of 1993. Why? "I wanted to conserve resources and not just monetary ones. I was only sleeping in my apartment so it was a waste of space." After an investment of about $1000 including building a "topper", his truck became home sweet home. "The first night was pretty scary. I would walk up and down the street looking for people that would attack my truck," he laughs. "Eventually, I got used to it. I just light a candle to read before I go to sleep." A senior in Environmental Science who also works two jobs, he has a busy schedule. Having facilities isn't a problem as he discovered Dixon Recreation Center (which is open only to OSU students, and ID is checked by a full-time receptionist). "Dixon is great. I just rented a locker for the whole term." His pad is 8x5': big enough for a bed and to store all that he owns. What to do when company visits? He laughs, "It gets pretty crowded. I usually visit people at their house." As for hassles from security, he says to date he hasn't had any

problems. "I also don't always park at OSU. I park in the
surrounding neighborhoods, in front of people's houses. I
change locations a lot." Would he recommend this lifestyle
to others? I really love it a lot. It's not a bad lifestyle
at all. Next time I want a bigger truck though," he laughs.
Laura Tesler (from Daily Barometer, April 25 1995

Mobile bed and storage.
        During my bachelor days, I traveled hither and yon in a
full-size pickup with cap on the back, and slept on it in a
folding army-surplus "D-ring" stretcher which has latching
hold-open bars. It is equivalent to a skinny, low canvas cot.
When not in use, it folded into a 7 ft by 6 inch package that
fit in one corner of the pickup bed. Jon Seaver, MI, Oct 1994

Last summer I lived in the woods along the McKenzie River.
        I camped more or less traditionally. I commuted to work
on the Eugene bus system. Friends of mine are headed to Baja
over the holidays, so I am interested in info on camping
there, for them. Kent Jones, Oregon, October 1994

More about living in van and working at resort near NYC.
        I was able to park close to an electric outlet, so I am
using an electric heater (ceramic) for warmth, and six 4'
fluorescent lights to grow stuff inside the cab section.
I closed it off with mylar curtains, and covered the windows
with foil and then a tarp to keep light in and for insulation.
        However, I am not content here. Too many people around
for me to "be myself". Also many petty rip offs. Also toxic
waste dumps nearby. Also NYC is 50 miles away, and a
potential danger. This summer I plan to travel to North
Carolina where friends with a nursery business have offered
me work. Next winter I hope to stay in southwest Arizona,
which might help my arthritic pains. Among other trades,
I have carpet installation tools and sometimes work as a
helper for $50-$100 per day. Eugene Gonzalez, NY, May

I live in a blue Chrysler mini-van for the time being.
        It has a tiger print steering wheel cover and a disco-
ball. I inherited it from my grandma last year. Although
I do not expect that she intended for me to LIVE in it, I'm
sure she would be delighted that it is being put to good use.
        I am sort of sick of people staring at it, though.
Punks hate it cuz it looks like a familymobile-bourgeous-
dream of the hip '90s, and everyone else thinks I am gonna
unload the two kids and the ski equipment from the back.
And when they see a bed in there -- ! Sue, NJ, April

My three children and I are living a mobile lifestyle.
        At present, we are in a car with a utility trailer. Fran
                                                          CA, June
I was living in a Subaru Turdmobile station wagon.
        I just got a Ford 138 WB van. It will be like a mansion.
                                                          Ed, NJ
I used to live in a truck box.
        Friends called it the coffin because it didn't have any
windows. Vince, Ontario, April

I will soon move into my "new" 1955 Spartan trailer.
        Info and ideas on space saving and energy independence
are welcome. Sue Harrington, Colorado, March

With trailer housing, you can avoid a disaster.

Some environmentalists want to forbid rebuilding in flood-prone areas of the Midwest, wildfire zones of California, and other regions that are frequently devastated. This would reduce the social cost of repeatedly providing disaster aid.

I suggest a more moderate approach: rebuild with a cluster of trailers which are individually small enough to be towed out of danger by the homeowner's car. I envision trailers that have two doors, one at each end. A covered connector fills the gap between the doors of several trailers, which together provide enough room even for a large farm family.

The cluster might be shaped like a wheel. The connector is a central "hub". Each trailer attached to it is a "spoke", providing each individual with a private room. The kitchen and bathroom could be either in the "hub" (if large) or in a "spoke". If still more space is needed, one or more peripheral connectors would join the far ends of "spoke" trailers to "rim" trailers, which could be connected also to each other.

This arrangement would occupy more land than a traditional house, but the vacant wedges between "spoke" trailers would have their uses. They would form play areas for small children that mothers could easily supervise; garden party areas with more privacy than a back yard; courts for outdoor games; etc.

Advantageous side-effects: Grown-up children could tow their trailer with them when they leave home; they needn't buy a house. Empty-nest parents would not be stuck with an overly-large house, nor with taxes on the value of its empty rooms. Ailing parents could more easily receive home care. Their children or other relatives could tow a trailer over and attach it, and thus be on hand for assistance without feeling either trapped or in the way. Visitors who brought their own trailer could also be present but out-of-the-way. Communes could be quickly assembled and, if discord arises, disassembled. Roger Knights, Washington, April

(Comments:) Other advantages: A home can be purchased gradually, trailer by trailer, as a family grows (or as possessions accumulate), and as finances allow, without going into debt. Unfinished trailer shells can probably be mass-produced and delivered at a much lower cost per space than a house built on site; and probably less even than can a mobile home (which, being much bigger, is expensive to haul far, and therefore is usually manufactured locally in small quantities). Each shell provides shelter immediately, and can be finished and turned into a bed room, kitchen, work room, or whatever, as the purchaser has time.

One disadvantage compared to a house: The trailer cluster has much more outer surface for the same inside space, and therefore more heat loss, or gain, or much more insulation required. This is a problem only if a family insists on heating or cooling their entire home. If, eg, during winter they are willing to crowd together in one trailer which is well insulated, and leave the others uninsulated and unheated to use as storage or during mild weather, it is economical.

(That is our usual arrangement, but with tents instead of trailers. One well-insulated tent is our cold-weather core dwelling. Other tents/tarps, notinsulated, provide storage and mild-weather expansion space.)

For a flood-threatened farmer in the Midwest, where winters are long and very cold, I wonder if a large, well-anchored houseboat would be better than a trailer cluster, and maybe just as safe. H & B

Travel-Trailer Homesteading Under $5000.
    In this 65 page book, Brian Kelling describes how he set
up and equipped a travel trailer to live semi-permanently in
the San Luis Valley of southern Colorado. Usually sunny and
cool at 7500' elevation, "we average 50 nights a year in which
the temperature gets below zero" F. With only 7" of rain/snow
yearly, Brian hauls in water with his pickup. A photo shows
only low desert growth nearby,but trees on a mountain far away.
    His costs included $2195 for 5 acres, $1200 for a used
21-foot trailer, $825 for electricity (solar and generator),
and $575 other. Not counted, was his pickup and power tools,
that Brian considers essential. Land taxes were only $52 per
year. Not mentioned is trailer's license, if required.
    "A travel trailer (vs mobile home) is the best, because
they're cheap, give all the comforts of home, and are easily
transported by ordinary vehicle." Mobile homes are legal in
his county. Travel trailers are not, but are tolerated by a
lenient building inspector. (That could quickly change!)
    Brian includes tips and some instructions with diagrams
for choosing and setting up trailer, and skirting bottom; and
for installing a septic system (the longest chapter!) and
other equipment. "Slipping the upper (stove) pipe down over
the lower pipe ... is the way it is usually done, and I did
this when I first installed my (wood) stove. However, this
allows condensation and creosote to flow freely from the
joints, making a mess all over the outside of your trailer,
and sometimes inside. Some people (especially in Europe)
reverse the pipes, as I have done. This makes any liquids
flow all the way back down into the stove. If you do this,
make sure the 45 degree elbow out of your stove is a solid
piece, not adjustable.... Another possibility is to install a
piece of aluminum inside the joint where the 45 meets the
straight piece. Make it long enough so the liquids drip into
the stove (diagram in book). Don't use a regular piece of
metal (for this)... I tried, and it rusted out."
    Most of Brian's choices seem sensible. A few exceptions:
    Flush toilets may be desirable in places that have both
abundant water and dense population (such as London in England
which is where they were invented). But not out in the
boonies where you must build your own septic system. (There,
shallow burials, widely distributed, are much easier, and are
less likely to contaminate ground water.) And not in a place
where water is scarce. Using a flush toilet in a thinly-
populated desert where water must be brought in, seems insane!
    Piped water makes sense if you use much water (eg, for a
farm) and have a flowing source (creek or spring). But not
where you must first haul it in. Especially not in a cold
climate. "Travel trailers aren't really designed for winter
living... Water pipes in them tend to run in odd-ball out-of-
the-way places, and during extremely cold weather (below zero)
I have sometimes had them freeze...."
    The propane frig "costs less to operate than the cost of
ice". But where nights are cold, most kinds of food can be
cooled enough to keep several days simply by exposing the food
at night and then insulating during the day. Of course, this
won't suffice if someone insists on keeping frozen goodies.
    Despite such criticisms, we recommend this book to anyone
considering an RV, to help learn of the problems and some
solutions. (Review by Holly & Bert of Dwelling Portably.)
    (1995; Loompanics, POB 1197, Port Townsend WA 98368; $8 +
$4 p&h; ISBN 1-55950-132-4. 292p.8x11 catalog of 800 bks,$5ppd
or free with order.

Dwelling Portably
formerly named Message Post
POB 190, Philomath OR 97370
December 1995 (will be reprinted as part of the October 1995)

Shocking way to protect a vehicle.

There was an item in Mar'94 DP (now part of Oct'93) about
parking a van in rough inner-city neighborhoods to avoid cops
(who don't enter much? or are too busy when they do?) and
then electrifying it to repel anyone else. We wonder if the
writer has actually done this.

Imagined scene: a gang of kids comes strolling down the
sidewalk, playing around. One shoves another, who falls
against the van. ZAP! (How to make enemies and start wars.)

To avoid that, the van occupants could turn on the shock
only if someone was trying to break in. Possible problem:
most people have deep-sleep periods when not easily aroused.

I think the electricity could be shorted out by tossing a
chain or metal cable over a bumper or trailer hitch. Electric
fence chargers have problems in wet weather if even a tree
falls across. But the burglars might not think of that, or
might not have a chain along. Bert and Holly, October

(Reply:) I do electrify my vehicle. As you surmise, it is
only turned on when I'm aboard at night, parked, and sleeping.
It generates pulses, rather than a continuous output, so it
won't grab someone so he can't let go.

It is fairly easy to set up with a farm fence charger.
It might not be compatable with modern computer ignitions.

You are correct about grounding it out, but that will
sound an alarm, allowing occupants to take other measures.

At night, my truck is parked in abandoned gas stations,
deserted factory districts, or remote highway rest stops.
In those circumstances, I assume that anyone who touches my
vehicle IS an enemy. The least I will do is drive off.
The cab is protected with Kevlar armor and Lexan windows.

So far, the worst that has happened is, a couple of rocks
thrown at the truck after an attempt to break in. The
attackers were surprised when they discovered that the
windows could not be broken.

Electrifying vehicles is not new. The idea was pioneered
in the 1960s to keep mobs from overturning riot-control
vehicles. I have been experimenting with the idea since I was
a kid after seeing the movie "20,000 Leagues Under the Sea".

There are some parallels between Captain Nemo (in the
novel, not the movie) and my thinking. After a partially
disabling accident, the state and the insurance companies
cheated me. When one sees how the laws are used to disempower
the ordinary citizen, one becomes an 'outlaw'. The stories in
Oct'95 DP of hassles at Kauapea Beach and elsewhere infuriated
me. I guess there isn't enough real crime to keep the storm
troopers busy. That is why I park overnight in the most crime
ridden (lawless) parts of the city. I can defend myself from
criminals who are not in uniform. L.Smith, Wisconsin, Nov.

Criticism of the SRT-1 Survival Rescue Tool.

It is an imitation of the real thing, on a par with
Chinese reproductions of U.S. Army gear. Badly cast. You
would be lucky to cut through a few branches with it. The
author of the report (in April'92 DP) certainly can't have
tested it very rigorously.

Carrying it in an urban area would probably get you
arrested. It would be considered "brass knuckles". L.Smith

Low-cost trailer parks are shutting down, stranding many poor.

Life hasn't been easy for residents of Olivia Mobile Home Park in Everett WA since it closed last June to make room for a planned mall. Only a handful found space in other parks.

Mark Gordon wasn't among them. He sold at a loss his 1973 14x46 Lamplighter mobile home (bought 5 years ago for $3000), and purchased a 1972 Dodge Tradesman van for $600. With nowhere to go, he squatted for a while on the site where his trailer once stood. Behind the van, under a clear plastic covering propped up by 2x4s, is his "living room". An oil-stained tarpaulin hangs on one side to keep out the wind. A blanket, tossed over what used to be his front steps, serves as a table. He uses a toilet in an abandoned trailer nearby.

Unemployed for 6 months, Mark, 33, last worked as a quality-control inspector at a metal-plating plant. He has been unable to find a new job because prospective employers have no place to reach him. "I have no address. I have no phone. I just keep filling out applications."

Movers told Sharmi Daniel that her 1972 Greatland mobile home would fall apart if they tried to lift it. So she left it behind. Junk or not, it was home - and affordable. Before moving to Olivia, apartment rent had cost $78 more per month than her $546 welfare income. She has also been a traffic flagger, teacher's assistant, and a dancer in a club.

After eviction, the Daniels moved to a campground ten minutes away by canoe on an undeveloped island in the Snohomish River. With a 6-year-old son, they spent most of summer in a tent. Sharmi's daughter left to live with her father in another part of the state. "It's really embarrassing for any 12-year-old girl to have to live like Robinson Crusoe", Sharmi says. Sharmi caught pneumonia after a week of rain. The family bathed in an icy river.

Wallace Barnett, Olivia's owner, says the park had become run down. Maintenance and taxes made it unprofitable to operate. However, he says he felt bad for the tenants and, as a humane act, left the park's water on.

Never popular with nearby homeowners, trailer parks have nonetheless been important enclaves of affordable housing for America's poor and elderly. Building of trailer parks first boomed during World War II to provide housing for workers flocking to defense jobs in cities. Early trailers were narrow, uncomfortable, and flimsy; and quickly took on a negative image, which persisted even though later models were bigger and better built - and called "manufactured homes".

Mobile home parks, especially older ones with cheap rent, are at risk. In WA since 1989, 22 parks have closed and 34 more will soon. Other states are losing similar numbers. Some are being closed or condemned as their aging sewers and streets deteriorate. But many, such as Olivia, are destroyed to make room for stores and parking lots. Their sites, on the fringes of cities out of sight of other houses, are the same locales favored by discount retailers. Joseph Pereira (much condensed from Wall Street Journal, 15 Nov 1995)

(Comments:) For the Daniels, a jug shower (Simple Shower) using hot water, would be much more comfortable than an icy river. (I assume they had some sort of stove for cooking.)

We would like to inform houseless people about the jug shower and other techniques for living comfortably without expensive, elaborate equipment, but don't know how to reach most of them. Many would not want our entire dwellingway. (Eg, we are too remote for daily commuting, and even those

unemployed may hope their luck will change and they can resume
profligate living.) But some techniques may be useful.
    Housed people, too, can sometimes benefit. Their houses
may stop functioning. Recently, high winds in Oregon knocked
out electricity in some areas for long periods, and houses
with electric pumps were without running water. Some people
became so desparate (or smelly?) that schools put up signs:
"showers open to the public after school hours".
    Some 12-year-olds would love to live like Robinson Crusoe.
But kids who go to school, become very fashion conscious,
because, if they are different in any way, other kids will
pick on them. Many kids may not only be happier but also
learn more if they do NOT go to school. (There are many
resources for learning at home, such as F.U.N. listed in OBP.)

I roam in a 1974 Dodge Long Van.
    My habitat is north of San Francisco, routes 1 and 101
along the ocean. Robert Di Falco, California, November

I am going on the road this summer in my Toyota with camper.
    I could use some suggestions. Sharina, Texas, March

12-volt electric bunk warmer.
    It is a pad you sleep on rather than under. Inside a
cheap rectangular sleeping bag, it is highly efficient, being
on about 30% of the time. A bunk-size model draws about four
amps, so you need an auxillary battery for overnight use.
But no carbon monoxide danger, no open flames, and no extra
fuel to store. With it, I have no fear of -20° temperatures.
    I've had one about 3 months, bought for $43 from Back-
woods Solar Electric (8530 Rapid Ltn Ck Rd, Sandpoint ID
83864). Also check local truck stops. Electro-Warmth maker.
                                        L. Smith, WI, Nov.
(Comment:) In cold weather, we use more than one sleeping
bag, either one inside another, or opened up and spread on
top. Seems easier than hauling around an extra battery and
worrying about keeping it charged. Holly and Bert, OR, Dec.

Tips for fishing and for obtaining fishing equipment.
    When fishing with bait, pools are easier than running
water. Where a stream widens into a pool, fishing is usually
best near the inlet. Drop live bait into the moving water to
drift or tumble into the pool. Bobber optional. No weight.
    In a pond or lake, fish near the edge of the water or in
vegetation (such as cattails or reeds) using bobber and bait.
Or fish near a sharp drop off without bobber.
    Water levels in most impoundments (man-made lakes) are
greatly lowered in winter, exposing much of the bottom. You
can then harvest many expensive lures and other equipment
simply by walking. Most plastic lures will look new after
swishing in some soapy water. A few may need rubbing.
    During low water is also a good time to study the shape
of the bottom. Or drag out some brush and tie it down, to
encourage fish to congregate there when water is high again.
    Braided line is cheap. Buy 40 lb test or more. Brand
is not important. To make it float (a plus) wax with a stub
candle. Buy the best monofilament. Seldom will you need
more than 10 lb test. 100 yards should last years, if used
as 6-foot leaders added to braided line for fishing with pole.
Store in dark, on original spool, with a little talc powder.
Guy Hengst, Indiana, August

Dwelling Portably

formerly named Message Post
POB 190,   Philomath OR 97370

May 1996 $1 per issue   Add 50¢ to check/mo under $7

Simpler, more versatile bug bar.

Instead of forming a box-
like enclosure ("Bug Free", LLL),
I now simply sew netting (such as
salvaged curtains) together into
a flat sheet. Five yards on each
side is ample for one person,
adequate for two or three. The
shape need not be a perfect
rectangle: ie, if one curtain is
a little longer, I leave excess
(to avoid trimming and hemming).

With a crayon or grease pen
(a felt pen might damage fabric),
I mark diagonal lines from each
corner inward at 45° angles (half
the right angle). To suspend, I
attach four ball ties, placing one
tie along each line. (To form a ball
tie, wrap netting over some roundish
object or a wad of leaves, and tie
between the object and the rest of
the net. Drawing in May'95 DP.) If tied near the corners,
the enclosure will be wide but low; if tied further in, higher
but narrower.   Julie Summers, Oregon, December

Wintering in a Snugiup.

In mid November I built a shelter like the one in May'95
DP (also shown in 1995-96 Summary-Index) and have been living
in it since. I used six plastic liners and two roofs. The
top roof is cloth; the under roof is clear plastic. Most days
the shelter stays warm enough to wear just a T-shirt and watch
cap, or nothing. During one freeze I had to wear more, but
stayed comfortable. This is with no stove. The shelter has
stayed dry except for a little condensation on the front wall.

One problem: rain formed a puddle on the roof which had
to be dumped frequently - a nuisance, especially at night.
As instructed, I tied the roofs only at the sides and back;
not in front. (Would Shelter Systems' clips be better?) My
roof is not as steep as yours (because the slope is not as
steep) which may be why a puddle formed. To eliminate it,
I put three poles under the roof (but over the liners), spaced
two feet apart, oriented up-down the slope.

Another problem: not enough light inside when heavy overcast. (Fine on sunny days.) Downhill is not entirely clear:
a few tree tops protrude into "my" sky. To get more light,
I rerigged the top (cloth) roof so that on cloudy days I can
undo two ties and flip it back half way, uncovering the clear
plastic under-roof. (If a low-flying aircraft comes over,
I can flip the roof back down in a few seconds. But on cloudy
days, most aircraft stay above the clouds.)

Another problem: muddy water splashed onto the front.
I greatly reduced that by laying fir boughs (blown off tall
trees on the next hill by a strong wind) on the ground in
front. (I also made a bough foundation for my bed - comfy.)

I cook over a fire, quite far from the shelter, down near
a creek so I have plenty of water. About once a week I cook a
big pot of rice or spaghetti and lots of popcorn. Between

cookings I first eat the rice (lasts a day or two) and then popcorn - plus nuts, sunnies, raisins, sauces/seasonings, and vitamins. I have not found much to forage (a few wild carrot tops). Come spring I will search further.
  For next winter, I plan to get a propane cooking stove and put it inside my shelter - which I want to enlarge. I've not decided whether to widen it (which will require more poles and larger plastic), or to make several shelters the same size and interconnect them with tunnels. But how to line the tunnels so I don't get muddy crawling thru?   Emtu, Oregon, Febr.
  (Comments:) With any structure, if the roof is not steep, irregularities will collect rain. Shelter Systems' clips would bunch the plastic less than do ball ties. Clothes-pin ties would bunch it even less. To form, roll edge of plastic a few times around a $\frac{1}{4}$" diameter stick, grip with a clothespin, and strengthen grip by wrapping rubber strap around jaws. Thread tie-out cord through spring of clothes-pin. (Drawing in April'92 DP.) Clothes-pin ties are usable only at edges. (Fine for a tarp or Snugiup but not for a dome.)
  A larger shelter will be chillier, unless you close off part. Interconnecting several small shelters sounds interesting, and eases the avoiding of trees and disposing of dirt. I don't know a simple way to line tunnels. (I can imagine plastic held up by wands (flexible branches) steadied with cords. But not real simple. For safety, keep tunnel narrow, close to the surface, and arch ceiling. Bert, Oregon, April

Aborted test of a manufactured tent.
  Seven years ago, to learn how the "other half" camps, we bought a Stansport dome tent, made in Taiwan, $30 on sale. Since then, it was never at hand when we could have used it to advantage. (For summer travel, we take just an insect net plus a dew tarp - which weighs less and admits more light.)
  Finally, last summer, we were able to test it. It set up quite fast and easily, 20 minutes first try, by fitting the segmented wands together and inserting into sleeves.
  But the tent STANK, probably from fire retardant. We did not move in, but left it set up and open to air out. Several MONTHS later it still stank, not quite as strongly. We wondered if scrubbing with a strong detergent would help, but did not have time. So back it went into storage. It easily stuffed into a 5-gallon pail after removal of the aluminum wands.
  I won't blame the manufacturer: I suppose the fire-retardant was required by some government agency. (I wonder if it was the same stuff required on childrens' pajamas until found to cause cancer ! (I'd rather take my chances with fire.)
  How was the tent otherwise? Like many commercial products, it seemed to have good detail design and fabrication, but poor overall concept. The fabric near the bottom was olive. But the upper portion and fly were off-white - conspicuous, yet not passing much light through the two layers of woven material.
  (A better configuration would be a semi dome with one big vertical window under an overhang. Make the window out of transparent plastic and the remainder out of olive cloth. When setting up, face the window toward the most open sky.)
  Light is not a problem if a tent is used only for sleeping. But even a summer trek may include cold rainy days when you remain inside. I suspect that chief executives of most camping equipment manufacturers have not done much camping. Bert and Holly

I saw a 30-foot yurt at The Slabs, east of Salton Sea.
You can still camp there free, year around, in anything you can tolerate. There are no facilities; just miles of sand and greasewood. Catfish in a canal near by. A grocery store four miles away in Nyland (a one-horse town).
The weather is pleasant from October until mid April. Many hundred come then, most with vehicles. Some incinerate their poop but some don't so there are flies. In summer the heat is extreme. Double Dorje, California, May 1995

If you care-take, take care not to get taken.
Some situations advertised, offer "free" use of a mobile home in trade for 25 hours of work PER WEEK. Outside income would be needed to pay for food and other supplies.
Actually, considering the fantastically expensive rentals these days, such an offer is not surprising. Translating into dollars, 25 hours a week at minimum wages is about $400/month: a typical rental for a mobile home with site and utilities.
But 25 hours per week is a huge chunk of your life.
The solution, is not to complain about greedy landlords, but to become more independent. Learn how to live comfortably without elaborate structures and utilities.
If you can provide your own shelter, you can find better deals. Many landowners who would like help, don't have spare mobile homes (or converted chicken coops), nor a spot to which a mobile home could be hauled. But they may have steep wood-lots where a tent (or?) can be put and not be in their way. For just a tent site, 5 or 10 hours PER MONTH is reasonable.
Some positions advertised are in "remote" areas. If only living space is offered, we're not interested, because FREE space is easily found in remote areas. When we house sit, we do so in or near a city for access to shopping or temp jobs.
H & B

Need portable dwelling space? Consider a burned area.
Forest fires are destructive but also beneficial. For ten years or more after, there will be lush growth, because the ground gets more sun and the ash neutralizes some of the forest soil acidity. This gives animals more cover and forage.
Most people avoid a burned area because it seems ugly or because the dense brambles impede hiking. But this provides privacy for us living light. Guy Hengst, Indiana, Sept 1994

(Comment:) After a burn there may be salvage logging and then replanting. I'd wait until that is done before moving in. Clear-cuts, too, develop lush growth, but often slash is burned some months later, so WAIT until replanted.

Tips for accessing cities from far away.
Any suggestions for living without a car in areas too far from town to bicycle for supplies? Hitchhiking is dangerous even for a male, and I'm female. Even cycling is too danger-ous here, as the main highways are the only routes to town.
Jaye, Washington, Dec.
(Reply:) We often had the same problem. Some possibilities:
To reduce the number of trips, reduce the weight by buy-ing mostly dry foods such as grains and beans. 50 pounds of brown rice will nourish you much longer than will 50 pounds of potatos (which are mostly water). The rice will also keep much longer (if kept dry), is at least as nutritious, and cheaper (per nutrients; not per pound). Avoid canned foods and beverages, which are not only heavy and costly, but often less nutritious than what you can prepare from dry ingredients.

Try to forage most salads. We also take vitamin C.

   To further reduce trips, buy dry foods in quantity, a few
hundred pounds at a time. (Check wholesale grocers, as well as
asking for discounts at natural food stores.) Then, rent or
borrow a vehicle, or hire someone with vehicle to help you
transport. (Check ad boards for move/haul offers.) You will
also need to get (eg) pails with good-fitting lids for storing.

   Bicycle to town very early on a Sunday morning when most
roads have little traffic, stay for a week at a temporary camp
near town, and return the next Sunday. Best during spring and
early summer when daylight hours are long. To allow a pre-
dawn start and to shorten the ride, stash your bike and some
bedding near a paved road, hike there a day or two before, and
depart from there. Also stash bedding in pails near your town
camp (to avoid hauling it back and forth on your bike).

   There might be trucks coming your way fairly regularly,
delivering to country stores, resorts, ranches, etc. One might
be willing to drop off supplies, or pick up a pail you stash
close to a highway pull-off. An independent trucker might
even give you rides. (Company trucks have insurance hang-ups.)

   On main highways there may be Greyhound or other buses.
Though expensive, they are affordable if you don't use them
often, and are cheaper than owning your own car.

   Holly and I have hitchhiked some: most often me (a male)
alone, but also together (including a few long trips to CA),
and sometimes Holly alone. Our worst experiences: a very few
rides with people intoxicated or driving recklessly. Holly
was asked for sex a few times but, though she declined, never
forced or threatened. Some women who hitch try to look like
men. But, unless able to appear so even when in the car,
might be better to look like a woman so you will have many
ride offers from which to choose. Turn down rides with two or
more men together, and with anyone who seems intoxicated.

   If possible, locate near people with similar needs who
are willing to run a few errands for each other when they go
to town: eg, post and pick up mail, and buy small items whose
needs were not anticipated. They might even share rental of
a vehicle once a year to transport most of their supplies.
Unless you know someone VERY well, better not direct them to
your base camp. Arrange sites to meet or leave parcels at.

   A possibility we haven't found desirable, but which might
suit some: camp near a rural resident who goes to town fairly
often and will give rides in exchange for occasional house-
sitting or a little work. Likely problems: nasty neighbors;
trips not scheduled in advance; different values, resulting in
each party considering the other incompetant or crazy. Also,
the settlers may feel they are being turned into chauffers,
while the nomads may feel they are being turned into serfs.

Simple, cheap, high-energy travel/trail snack.

   I make "cheapola" by mixing sweet molassas with dry oatmeal (the finer the meal the less I have to chew). Cheapola
tastes as good to me as do most commercial granolas and candy
bars yet costs only 1/6 as much (eg, oatmeal 35¢ and molassas
70¢ per pound at bulk food stores) and may be somewhat more
nutritious: more fiber; less fat; less processed; less stale.

   Some people add nuts, sunflower seeds, raisins, brown
sugar, dried coconut, cut-up fresh fruit, etc.

   Some stores don't carry molassas in bulk (and prepack-
aged little jars are pricy). If so, I may snack on just dry
oatmeal (not bad) maybe with brown sugar. Bert and Holly

"Raw" oatmeal has been cooked

Recently I've been buying 50# bags of rolled oats from a wholesale grocer. (Formerly I bought smaller quantities from a bulk bin at a natural food store, but switched when they raised prices.) These particular oats taste very good. They were bagged by Grain Millers in Eugene. I phoned their 800 number.

A man in their lab said: after hulls are removed, oats must be heated to 212° F to inactivate enzymes that would otherwise cause rancidity in 8-15 days. The oats are again heated for rolling.

After proper heat treating, oats have a nutty flavor. (I used to wonder why "raw" oatmeal tasted so much better than other grains.) Oats are high in oil: 8-15%. Vs, wheat 1%; walnuts 50%.

Rancid oats taste bitter/acrid, and cause a burning sensation in the throat. Some oats that sat in the lab 8 months after heat treating, still tasted good. Coarse-ground might keep no better than quick-cooking oats. Oats easily pick up odors. Eg, some shipped in a truck with residual perfume, were refused by buyer.
Julie, Dec

Sources for cheap or free equipment.

Most metal buyers have scrap bins that often contain bargains. I have bought stanless steel buckets, electric fry pans and other items by the pound at a small fraction of the original cost.

Big-city thrift stores trash or give away unsaleable items. If your cause sounds worthy, you can get trailer-loads. Al Fry, Idaho, 1994

Useful Reuse.

There seem to be two approaches to utilizing discards: devise special projects; or, keep a junk pile.

The projects approach can lead to creations like chain-mail vests from drink-can snap-top-rings (seen in book Re/Uses) - artistic but not too useful.

I prefer to wait for a need, then try to fill it from my junk pile. In the past month I have made: a replacement handle for a pot lid, from the case of an exhausted ball-point pen; circular knitting needles, from other exhausted pens (joined with cord); a pump-drill flywheel, from a typewriter-ribbon spool wound with strap cut from a bike inner-tube (for weight); rubber bands, from other inner tubes; moccasins, from a truck innertube; plastic gaskets, from margarine tubs; an awl, from a piece of bone; a desk-caddy addition to hold my sizzors, from a small carboard box that staples had come in.

My junk "pile" doesn't take up much space. The non-bulky items fit into a 5-gallon container - itself a discard that formerly held vegetable oil, with the top cut off for access (because it had only a narrow mouth) and holes cut to accept a cord handle. Julie Summers

Propane Notes

In this 11 page 8½x11 booklet, David Smith tells how he made heaters for various craft projects (kilns; heat treating metals; glass blowing) mostly from discarded household appliances.

Smith discusses tools, fabrication, connecting, adjusting, testing, safety; and lists sources for burners and parts.

"This or a regular stove should burn with a blue cone-shaped flame. If it's yellow, burners and ports are clogged or need adjustment. Pipe-cleaners work well for unclogging gas ports." If you use too much air, you lose heating power. "Start with a flame that's slightly orange and increase the air flow until the flame turns blue. In some furnaces there is an increase in the sound of the burners at this point."

"Regulators provide about 30 pounds output pressure from 80 pounds pressure in the tank. Typically regulators are set for a given pressure by a screw which adjusts the pressure a spring places on a diaphragm inside.... Tightening the screw DECREASES the pressure. Usually you will not need to adjust the pressure...." However, for supplying a Bunsen burner, designed for low-pressure natural gas, "a standard propane regulator will produce an output of less than a pound by replacing the spring with a stiffer spring...."

Smith does not use a sparker. "The spark might not come at the correct time and the electronic sparking units tend to wear out after about a year. I got the best results using a pilot flame to light the main burner." Some of Smith's heaters require continuous pilot lights.

(Reviewers comment: But a home cooking stove doesn't. On it, a pilot is unnecessary, wasteful of gas, and dangerous: a gust or momentary pressure drop could extinguish the pilot light and fill the shelter with an explosive mixture that any spark (static, or an appliance turning on/off) could ignite. On our stove, we use an exhausted propane lighter as a sparker.)

"I started working with propane when cleanup day provided me with free materials. I went around collecting all the old propane regulators, valves and gas lines from equipment I could find at the curb. I even picked up several tanks still filled with propane, though discarding (them) is against the law. I took apart an old gas stove for the valves and burner assembly...."

"Propane safety information. If any propane tank starts leaking, you must get it outside, into the open air, at once." "Check for leaks with a soap and water solution sprayed on. NEVER use a flame...." "Don't leave propane cylinders in a hot area, like a closed car. Keep your car ventilated when transporting." Don't transport in the trunk. "Paint white or silver. Dark colored cylinders can overheat in the sun...." "Store and use propane cylinders outside, or in well-ventilated shed separate from house or main building."

Criticisms. Though some items are repetitive, others left us wondering. "Compression fittings are not recommended because they are more subject to mechanical harm.... I feel better with flare fittings" (but no illo to help reader identify the two types). And the only two illos have kinky lines. (Does the jet really have little steps? Or is that merely how the computer draws?

1992, Cybernetics Design, 88 E. Main St #457, Mendham NJ 07945-1832. Order # 16719. $9 ppd in 1995. Revu by B & H

There's Something About a Train, #3.
This collection of freighthopping stories is informative and entertaining. Some are by women and most are recent (early 1990s). Includes a map of U.S. "main lines" from Rand-McNally Handy Railroad Atlas; and 14 book reviews.

Rail maps are not designed for hobos. "Neither show Roseville (just east of Sacramento), yet it is the biggest yard in the western states...." But maps do show what companies serve what routes, which is important. Eg, if in L.A. and heading north, go to the Santa Fe or Southern Pacific yards. Likewise, if heading east, try Union Pacific yard.

"Topographic maps show in detail the layout of rail yards. Topos can be found and xeroxed in map rooms of most university libraries...." But some are old.

Finding a train going where you want to, may be difficult. "I woke up thinking the train had ridden south all nite. Unfortunately, it had taken a turn east in Portland and headed back up to Pasco."

New freighthoppers (at least) depend on railroad employees for train info. Fortunately, many are helpful. "The yard workers, the brakies and switchmen and the like, are sometimes friendly, usually cooperative... They won't turn you in.... I think that bulls (security guards) must give the yardworkers shit, and so the workers don't like them...."
"The shop is where the mechanics of the yard hang out. I've found the shop to usually be a pretty safe no-bull zone."

"The tower is the tall, narrow,white building, found in most train yards. Its height enables any person at the top to have a full view of the train yard. Telephones, radios, camera monitors (and hobo haters) are in them... We put our backs to the wall and inched past...."

"It was the edge of winter, and this time I was gonna be prepared with COVER-ALLS, mechanic-style. They are loose and warm and you can pass as a guy in them."

"Car selection is important - the train might not stop for six hours. You want a good hiding place, and not where cargo will squish you. Trains do this slamming thing, which you can't hear coming and you have to be ready for all the time. Underneath a semi-truck, good in decent weather; ends of a grain car, good;"tween intermodals,ok but no hidin.

"Empty boxcars are your best bet for concealment, and bulls do not care so much if you ride them." Nothing to steal.

"It's preferable to get on before the train moves out, but as often as not you will have to catch it 'on the fly'. Boxcars are difficult and dangerous; grain cars, piggy-backs, and gondolas (long rectangular car with short walls) are much easier cuz of ladders that are just a big step from the ground. Look way ahead, make sure you won't stumble on anything while running alongside, concentrate, match your speed...."

Beware of some container cars, a few gondolas, and spiners (a kind of piggy-back) which don't have floors.

"When you move around, always hang on and not too close to the doors of boxcars - trains jerk a lot. Sitting on the edge of a boxcar opening with your legs hanging out is dangerous and could prompt a train stop and unhappy visit from a pissed-off train engineer. Always

jam a spike or piece of wood in the sliding track so the door won't slam shut (and lock you in). Never stand between two rail cars. Always look both ways before crossing tracks, in yards especially, as single cars can be moving silently. When possible, sleep sideways near a front wall or with your feet to front in case of sudden braking...."

"In general, it is better to ride near the middle or rear of the train, as cars near the front are those most likely to be dropped off...." "When your train stops in big yards, be prepared to hop off on the side not being monitored, until the bulls are thru checking...."
(Many more tips and cautions in book)

"The older non-punk freight hoppers were mostly homeless white males who traveled from town to town picking up food stamps.... They were very dumb, very racist, and hard-core misogynists." The younger, punk freighthoppers traveled summers, but usually had a home or squat to return to.

"Reno supposedly has some of the harshest anti-homless laws in the west. You can be arrested for walking the streets just looking homeless, hitch-hiking, or hopping freights...."

An article in Oct'81 MP(DP) said, "hitching is quicker but freights are more thrilling." But much depends on appearance. "Some people still score good rides but I don't - being somewhat weird looking and punked out...." One author thinks freighthopping is safer than hitching and maybe even driving.

One criticism: a third of the space occupied by photos most of which didn't print well or add much information.

1995(?), 87p.8x11, $6ppd, Hobos From Hell, POB 2497, Santa Cruz. CA 95063

Personal Defense Weapons

This book, by J.Randall, briefly introduces types, functions, history and selection. Not a training manual.

Desirable traits of a weapon: likely to be with you; unobtrusive; likely to disable assailant long enough for you to flee; easy to use; hard to snatch away; legal and acceptable to you and society.

Punching can hurt the deliverer as much as the receiver. Brass knuckles provide hand protection plus increased impact, but are illegal. A substitute: "C" link, made for joining chain/rope. Made in various sizes. Use as key ring.

From a high-powered slingshot with $\frac{1}{2}$" or larger ball-bearing ammo, "a shot to the head ... can kill and a hit anywhere else can be extremely painful."

A bullwhip excells at scaring off dogs. 8 to 12 feet. Shorter won't snap loud; longer not practical.

Steel-capped shoes are inconspicuous (some look like regular shoes); enable you to kick hard; difficult to disarm.

Other weapons discussed: firearms; knives; canes (if age justifies, good for jabbing); night sticks and heavy flashlights; tear gas (effect unpredictable); electric zappers; bow and arrow (good for home defense); martial arts weapons (impractical); steel clipboard.

"The best way to defend yourself is to avoid having to do so ...(by) being able to look mean, serious, and prepared...." Because the eyes can reveal fear, do not maintain eye contact.

To strengthen your hands' grip, punch and resistance to injury, Randall recommends squeezing a solid rubber handball.

As for 'iron hand' traning, he says, "By the time my hands became formidable weapons they ceased being good for much else.... Yes, you can break bricks but be unable to tie your own shoes."

How we dispose of feces when inside.

This topic is slighted in publications, because foraging and eating foods is more glamorous than what happens at the other end. And most of what little is written, assumes you are outside in pleasant weather with no one else nearby. But what do you do in bitter cold? Or when there's 6 feet of snow? Or at a gathering where your tent is near many other people and far from a stinking, fly-infested community latrine?

When Bert and I began living in the woods, we soon devised simple solutions. And we assumed everyone else had too, and that the subject was not worth discussing. We learned otherwise when we reviewed (in Oct'95 DP) a book about trailer homesteading. The author was in the middle of a desert and had to truck in water from miles away. Yet, with much labor and expense, he installed a flush toilet and a septic field !

Anyhow, here is what Bert and I usually do when inside during winter. We have only one small insulated (warm) room, typically 10 ft diameter. We also usually have a plastic shed adjoining or nearby, which is not insulated.

For me, the urge to defecate comes suddenly, with only a few seconds warning. If I have to wait, I'm uncomfortable. As compensation, what comes out, does so quickly, in less than a minute. So I shit inside. (Yes, in view of Bert. He is welcome to watch, but doesn't seem interested.) The smell soon dissipates, especially if a drape is raised.

Bert is different. The urge comes gradually. But he takes longer to get everything out - maybe ten minutes. So Bert usually goes to the shed to shit, so that he does not occupy much of the floor (and interfere with my activity) and smell up our shelter a long time.

Regardless of where, our procedures are about the same: put a few pieces of paper on floor/ground; bring a pee bowl within reach; remove any bottom clothes; squat over the paper; defecate; wipe; fold/roll the paper up around the shit; put in a container outside; squat over the water-catch basin; wash crotch; wipe off excess water. Further tips:

Shit-on/wrap paper. We often use slick paper from catalogs or magazines which has no other re-use. We may put an 11x17 sheet on the bottom with two two 8½x11 sheets criss-cross over it.

Pee bowl. Presently a plastic 4# yogurt container with snap-on lid.

Wiping. We prefer brown paper with no printing on it. We get much from 25 -50# bags that grains/beans come in.) We've also used news print. We never buy special wipe paper. We crumple/ crinkle each piece to roughen it for better wiping. For hygiene, I wipe from front to back. If I will also wash, I may use only two pieces. If water is scarse, I may use 20 pieces, spitting on every third to provide some washing.

Disposal. We temporarily store the shit packages in a one-gallon plastic detergent tub we keep outside on the coolest side of our shelter. Putting a little dirt in the bottom may reduce odor. When full, we empty into our narrow-hole (±8" diameter) latrine, somewhat smooth the surface by pressing with a log or rock, pour pee over it to repell animals that might dig it up, and cover with an inch of dirt. When near full, we cover with 6" or more of dirt and tamp firmly. (Privies and wide-hole latrines were invented before contagious diseases were understood, and are poorer than narrow-hole latrines in every way but one: they're somewhat easier to dig.)

Water-catch basin. (Also used with jug-faucet for washing hands or dishes. See, "Running Water Anywhere", LLL.) This is presently one half (vertically cut) of a 5-gallon syrup or salad-oil jug, previously used for water storage, which sprung a leak in its other half.

Washing. I hold a squeeze bottle in one hand and squirt water onto my pubic hair. The water runs down and off into my other hand which splashes the water onto my anus while simultaneously rubbing. (More technique involved than I realized until I observed myself just now.) I also rinse after peeing, but that only requires squirting.

Bert and I have never lived IN a vehicle (vs car camping). But if we did, I think we would defecate just as we do now. Except, if I was sharing a bus with a large number of people, I think I'd like it to have a small room with a snug-closing door, an electric fan vented outside, and a waterproof tub-floor - so it could also be used for jug showers. Holly & Bert, Oregon

Common Poisonous Plants & Mushrooms of North America, 324pp 6x9,215 color photos

Nancy Turner and Adam Szczawinski describe over 150 plants, both wild and cultivated. Each entry includes photos, common name, species, family, description, occurance, toxicity (to animals and people), treatments (most assume hospitals), and notes. Plus a 19-page index (lacks entries such as "saponin" and "thujone"), and 99 references.

Children under 5 are "most vulnerable to accidental poisoning." (Elsewhere I read that during weaning, children necessarily fear new tastes less.)

The N.Am. plant most violently toxic is water hemlock (Cicuta spp.), It is mistaken for parsnip, carrot, celery.

The fiddleheads of bracken fern contain "high concentrations" of carcinogens and thiaminase (destroys vit. B1). Even though risks to humans "have not yet been fully established", it "should no longer be used." Ostrich fern (Matteuccia struthiopteris) fiddleheads safe.

All parts of nightshade (Solanum dulcamara) are toxic. Yet Adam recently found its leaves in a restaurant salad.

Comfrey contains liver-damaging alkaloids. But those who gather it should distinguish from more-toxic foxglove.

Many ornamentals are extremely toxic. At least remove flowers of such plants as castor bean and lantana - which develop fruits attractive to children.

As antidote to Indian hellebore, death camus, and water hemlock, B.C. natives eat lots of salmon oil.

1991, $55+$4p&h in'92. Timber Press, 133 SW 2nd Av #450, Portland OR 97204

We do most of our cooking over a one-burner propane stove.
The one-pound cylinders cost $2½. You can save money by
refilling them yourself from a 20-pound tank which costs $6-
$7 to refill. Use an adapter you buy or make, and, to refill
the small cylinder, turn the 20-pound tank upside down.
A Coleman stove comes along as back-up. I use Amoco
Silver (used to be called "white gas") in all Coleman units.
Never had any problems, but you got to be careful. Seldom do
we cook in the van, but I keep a fire extinguisher there anyway. Frank Dolan, West Virginia, Oct
(Comment:) There is also an adapter for connecting a 20-pound
tank to a stove made for the little cylinders, but it costs
$12 new. (Not seen used.) Better to buy a stove made for 20-
pound tank plus regulator. Check RV salvage yards.
If a camping trip is so short that a one-pound cylinder
would suffice, better to leave the stove behind and take
ready-to-eat foods (pinole, popcorn, cookies, etc.). H & B

How to withdraw water from a bucket without contaminating it.
I installed a small spigot about one inch from the
bottom of a 5-gallon bucket. Thereby, after I fill the
bucket, the lid stays on and the contents stay clean. I am
not repeatedly dipping into the bucket, risking contamination. The spigot makes hand washing easy. The lid must be
on loosely for the water to run freely. Laura LaBree, WA,
June
(Alternative:) After sediment settles, we transfer the entire
contents at one time via funnel to plastic jugs. We half-
empty bucket by dipping with a clean bowl; then slowly pour
the remainder. As we use water, we take it from the jugs.
For washing hands, utensils and vegies, we partially
fill our "portable faucet", which is an inverted jug, filled
through an opening cut in the former bottom. To "turn on",
we twist the cap, thus loosening it and letting water out
through it. (See LLL paper, or Oct'81 MP(DP).)
Advantages we see for Laura's method: Less transfering
of water. Buckets are easier to clean than are jugs (which
gradually collect a grungy film on the inside).
Advantages we see for our method: Simpler equipment –
no spigot to procure or hole to drill. Jugs are more
plentiful (and expendable) than are buckets. Holly & Bert

When using a jug to shower, we REMOVE the cap.
Some people try just loosening the cap. But that does
not let much water out of an UNcut jug. (A jug used as a
faucet has a filler hole cut in the former bottom.) Holly

A child's inflatable wading pool makes a dandy tub.
Use both for bathing and for washing clothes. But it
will withstand only cool or warm water (not hot). Guy Hengst

Van remodeled to provide more storage space.
I am now living near the Pisgah National Forest in
western North Carolina. Luckily, my 25-year-old van broke
down near the home of friends. It is on blocks with the
engine out (clutch problems) and covered with a tarp. The
camper top is up so I have standing room. For a porch,
I put a wooden pallet by the door. I am re-doing the inside.
I got rid of the built-in sink and refrigerator. Easier
to wash dishes in a 5-gallon bucket or in my friends' house.
And any stuff that needs cooling, I keep outside.

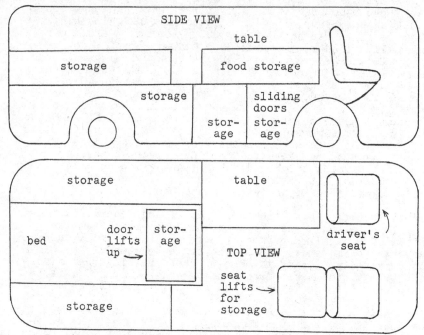

SIDE VIEW

table

storage

food storage

storage

sliding doors

stor-age

stor-age

storage

table

bed

door lifts up →

stor-age

driver's seat

TOP VIEW

seat lifts → for storage

storage

        I extended the sleeping platform using ½" plywood, and
have storage under the bed area. Now, all my things can be
stowed away without jamming and breaking anything.
        The van had a closet on one side that ran from the floor
to the roof and completely blocked the long window on the
passenger side. I cut it at window height and installed the
cut half on the other side. Now I have an extra big window
and a much more efficient storage area on each side of my bed.
        The only materials I had to buy new were two 4x8' sheets
of plywood, plus 20 small L-braces for attaching. I reused
everything else, especially the pre-laminated. It looks good.
        One of my best ideas: have sliding doors instead of
swinging ones, so I don't have to move things to open doors.
        I am plugged into electricity for my 75-watt light, corn
popper for boiling water (etc), and a portable shortwave radio.
        I am living on wages earned last summer, and some days I
help my friends with their landscaping business.
        The weather here in the mountains has been okay the past
few weeks. One snow flurry left one inch which melted by noon.
Nights 30-40°, days 50-60° a few to 70°. I am writing this
during a rainstorm that's lasted 12 hours so far. Eugene
                              Gonzalez, NC, March
I have traveled many miles while van camping.
        East of the Mississippi, I get reasonably secure over-
nights in county hospital parking lots. And nobody has ever
bothered me at river or ocean "put-ins" for fishers with boats.
Boat ramps are usually quiet spots and sometimes in early
morning you can get a fresh fish just by asking. Only one
unpleasantry: a broken window and petty theft in New Orleans.
        We often carry an old, battered aluminum canoe. Nobody
wants to steal it, and with it we get to places often overlooked, such as the headwaters of the Green River and a
stretch of the Colorado. The canoe is good for fishing, too.

We take along a weather radio and a small world-band
radio. They keep us posted - and entertained: CBC and BBC are
often funny, sometimes even on purpose. Frank Dolan, WV, Oct.

Selecting a vehicle for dwelling in.
Holly and I have little first-hand experience (some car-
camping 20 years ago) but we get many reports from others.
For simply living out in the bush for long periods, a
vehicle is a poor choice. Much better is some sort of backpackable or temporary shelter. It will be more comfortable,
especially during cold or hot weather, because it can set
directly on the ground (or, better yet, partially sunken)
which moderates temperature. It will be safer, because it can
be carried away from roads without leaving conspicuous tracks.
It will be cheaper. It will be less trouble, without the
legal problems (insurance, registration) or maintenance
problems (keeping battery charged). A vehicle may be helpful
occasionally for scouting and for hauling in supplies, but is
best used promptly and then disposed of.
The only reason to dwell in a vehicle, is because you are
moving frequently. Maybe you are traveling. Or maybe you are
in a city and parking on the streets.
For traveling, consider a vehicle you already have, if
any, because you may soon tire of travel. Or, you may
discover an area where you want to linger. People who live in
one place for many years, especially in a small town, get
starved for travel and believe they can never get too much of
it. But, like with any hunger, feeding brings satiation.
If you have a sedan, camping along side will probably be
more comfortable than sleeping in it. During mild weather,
all you will need is a sleeping bag or two, a foam pad, and a
small tent with ventilation screened against insects. For
easiest set up, get a tent that is self supporting - not
needing tie-outs. Weather-proofness not too important: in a
heavy rain or strong wind you can retreat to the car.
If buying a vehicle, sedans are generally cheaper than
pickups or vans in comparable mechanical condition. A fairly
big car may be best if fuel costs will be minor. (If you pay
$500 for the vehicle, spend another $500 for insurance and
licensing, and then drive it 2000 miles; even at 10 miles-per-
gallon, fuel will cost only $250 - one fifth the total.)
If price isn't crucial, and if spending much time in the
backcountry, I'd choose a pickup with canopy (NOT a big camper), because they have more ground clearance. Also, pickups
are common in the bush and don't attract much attention.
For use mostly in cities, I might choose a van, for more
room, a more weather-proof shell, and so I could move around
inside without going out. The fewer windows, the better,
because you may want to block them for insulation and so that
people can't see in and light inside can't shine out.
Unless with a dozen or more people, I'd not get a bus,
because it won't go as many places and because it is more
conspicuous. For 8 people traveling together, I'd get a van
but only ride in it, and set up separate tents for sleeping.
In these "interesting" times, when many folks are
suspicious or resentful, especially of anyone who has more
leisure or seems to be enjoying life more, the best vehicle
for living in may be one that does not look like it is being
lived in. Preferably not new, but not too shabby either.
Even people who can afford a $50,000 motorhome should
consider: it will be a tempting target for robbers - **AND
COPS.** And if police find one speck of an illegal substance

(which might have been tracked in; or planted by the police
themselves) or if they want to claim they SUSPECT the vehicle
is being used for something illegal (they need not PROVE anything), they can confiscate the rig, everything in it, and any
bank accounts too (so the victims will not even be able to
hire lawyers to fight back). And the police share in the loot.
     We have read idylic tales of motor nomading in big rigs.
But these stories seem to be from 20 or more years ago when
police maybe did not have as much power. Or, maybe the stories
were written for commercial RV magazines (which exist to sell
RVs and accessories) and left out the bad news.
     Don't buy any vehicle unless you are at least able to do
routine maintenance and minor repairs - or unless you have
loads of money. If not, hitch/bus/fly to your destination,
then buy a used bicycle for local travel.
     What I've said about hunger for travel, applies equally
to hunger for settling. Don't buy any land, at least not
until you have lived in an area for several years. Some folks,
after seeing a few beautiful sunrises over the mountains and
sunsets over the ocean, are sure THIS is where they want to
live forever; forgetting they might have once felt the same
about some other place. Realtors love such people.   H & B

Some engines seriously damaged if timing belt breaks or slips.
     The valves will collide with the pistons ! 1981 to 1992
engines at risk include all: Acura, Alfa Romeo, Daihatsu,
Honda, Hyundai, Mitsubishi, Nissan, Sterling, Volkswagon,
Volvo. Plus: Audi V8, diesel; BMW 2.5-2.7L; Chrysler Corp.
Medallion 2.2L and Mitsubishi built; Fiat 1.3-2.0L; Ford
Escort 1.6L, 2.3L diesel and Mazda built; Infiniti 3.0L; Isuzu
all except 1.6L; Mazda 2.0L diesel, 2.2L, 3.0L; Peugeot 2.2L;
Porsche all 4 & 8 cyl; Suzuki 1.3L DOHC; Toyota 2.2L, 1.5L,
1.8L, 2.4L diesel; Yugo 1.1L. (from J.C.Whitney 1995 catalog)
     What a crazy way to design engines. A friend said it's
done so the valves can be bigger or open wider, for more air
flow and thus more power at high RPM. But makes little
difference at normal speeds. I'd avoid those models. Bert

What's wrong with $750 bicycles?
     Many are not fixable with ordinary tools. Thus, to the
$750, add the cost of special tools - also their weight.
     Expensive bikes are more attractive to thieves. And, if
stolen, much more is lost. My $10 or $20 bicycles are less
likely to be stolen. And, at that price, I can afford to have
several, stashed in various locations. If one does get ripped
off, I'm not out much. Julie Summers, Oregon, December

LED lights, used on bicycle and in camp, conserve batteries.
     I like the flashers for riding at night, because I can
usually see well enough to ride without a light but cars may
not see me. I use a red light in back and a yellow in front.
     The yellow light can also be turned on steady. It is
perfect for peeing at night or finding things in my pack. It
attaches with a clip to my collar for hands-free use.
     The two AA batteries last 300 hours flashing and 60 hours
steady - much longer than in an ordinary flashlight. The LED
light bulbs are rated for 100,000 hours. Mine is Vistalite,
bought from Bike Nashbar for $12, but I assume they are sold
by most bike stores. Chris Soler, Washington, November

Rubber strap expedient fix of bike tire with bad bulge.
     Wrapped around tire and rim. After 50 miles, showed wear.
                                                    Bert

Dwelling Portably

formerly named Message Post
POB 190, Philomath OR 97370

December 1996 $1 per issue   Add 50¢ to check/mo under $6

Blowtube turns balky campfire into healthy blaze.
Take an old tentpole section, or piece of
thin metal tubing. Flatten the exhaust end
to increase pressure. Place a handful of
small sticks on last night's faintly
glowing embers. A slow puff of air
through the tube aimed at the
embers, makes the fire burst into
life. Bridge, Utah, July

(Comments:) I have rejuvenated fires just by blowing with my
mouth. But if doing it often, a tube is nice for keeping
your face further from the fire and for getting the breeze
right where you want it. Other sources of tubing: discarded
aluminum lawn chairs; rolled-up paper (maybe dampen exhaust
end to resist fire); hollow stalks. Bert

Cow-tongue cactus may alleviate painful joints.
Growing in Texas and Arizona (and maybe elsewhere), it
looks like a chain of cow tongues each licking the next. And
each pad is about the size of a cow tongue. Use a new bud
(new pad; not the fruit) when about 3" long. Imbibe some each
morning for about four days. Takes that long to act. Seems
to "grease up" the joints. An old Native American man told me
this remedy. Double Dorje, Arizona, 1995

(Question:) To prepare, Dorje suggests: put some in a jar,
refrigerate 24 hours, drink off the liquid (what oozes out?
or is the bud soaked in water?), refill jar, and repeat.
I wonder if this is done so the thorns need not be removed
from the bud. Can people who lack refrigeration just eat it?

Oxalis grows prolifically in the Pacific Northwest.
And Nancy Turner and Adam Szczawinski mention oxalis
(Oxalis spp., wood sorrel (another name for it) family) as a
lemonade substitute, in Edible Garden Weeds of Canada.
So I tried it. I picked a few handfuls of leaves and
stems, put in a pot, covered with water, and boiled about 5
minutes. The water had hardly any taste. The cooked greens
tasted sort of like spinach. Thinking I'd used too much
water, I repeated, using two cups oxalis and only ¼ cup water.
After boiling 5 minutes, the water was a beautiful dark pink.
It tasted very tart so I only sipped it. With sugar it might
have tasted like lemonade. I did add sugar to the leaves and
stems which then tasted somewhat like rhubarb.
Nancy and Adam say, "The leaves are also a tasty addition
to soups and stews and, like the leaves of sheep sorrel (Rumex
acetosella), make a superb sauce.... They are also said to
make a delicious dry wine." Kirk, in Wild Edible Plants of
the Western US, says, "The leaves and stems may be eaten raw."
However, I hesitate to eat much of the plant in any form
because of the high oxalic acid content.
In appearance, oxalis resembles clover, and along with
white clover and black medic, is a shamrock (trefoil) - the
emblem of Ireland - indicating it grows there also. Each stem
is a few inches long and ends in three heart-shaped leaflets,
which are often somewhat folded along their central veins.
Julie Summers, 1987

109

Another simple way to dispose of feces when inside.
       Compared to your system (May96 DP), ours is just as
effective and even more simple. We use two buckets. At least
one, the toilet bucket, has a close-fitting lid. The other
bucket holds a ready supply of dirt, gathered in summer when
dry, and the clods are broken up.
       A little dirt is first put in the toilet bucket to
furnish the bacteria needed to break down the feces. After
each deposit, a little dirt is sprinkled over the feces and
wipe paper. A squirt or two of water will wilt the paper and
cut down on the amount of dirt needed. This process is
repeated until the bucket is full.
       Then either: the bucket is emptied into a trench or hole
and covered with at least 6" of soil; or the bucket can be
tightly closed and a third bucket put in its place. In 3 to
6 months (depending on weather), the feces will be turned into
soil, and can even be used as the covering. Alma Schreiber,
                                                 CA, June
(Comments:) The chief advantage I see for your system: paper
to hold/wrap the feces is not needed. The chief advantage I
see for our system: bulky pails are not needed inside where
we have little space. (Our insulated shelter only ± 9' D.)
       Something not mentioned. Do you have a toilet seat that
sets over the pail? Or do you place blocks on each side to
raise your feet, and squat over the pail? Either would work.

Alternatives to flush toilets.
       Flush toilets are a poor joke. They gobble up water.
And if not warmed enough in northern winters, they crack.
       I put efficient RV potties in all my mobile homes and
living quarters. In colder climes I use the kind that does
not need flushing tanks.
       On lots without a $2500 septic system, I simply pull in
a portable outhouse that looks just like the rental units.
This keeps inspectors at bay and is usually legal with a
little ingenuity - like you are gonna build soon and are
working on the foundation. I pick these up from the rental
places when they get too banged up to rent. ($100 up.)
I scrounge the wheels or trailer cheaply.
       In many counties, out houses are still legal. But
building inspectors will seldom tell you that they are.
       I once lived next to a gypsy camp where most of the
population only spent the winter. Very few were legal.
When harrassed too far, they would simply pull their trailers
away for a few months. In summary, you don't need to conform
if it is not affordable or to your liking. Al Fry, Idaho, 96

I am in a large 'wild' guava orchard in Kilauea.
       I squat to pee or poop. I poop near my camp in a hole
I dig, cover with soil and leaves (becomes fertilizer), wash
anus with pee, and clean with water or leaves. Most
third-world bush folk do likewise.
       I bottle-bathe frequently by pouring quart or gallon
jug of clean cool water over my naked body. Very invigorating now. I wash face, feet and hands in cold water to wake
up or clean up.
       This mini camp is only sleeping/dreaming space. During
rains I hang a space-sheet-tarp over my bush hammock. During
storms I get wet. Wild chickens forage and crow nearby.
       Acclimatizing to nature is the simplest way to be warm,
bug free or immune, energetic, and happy wherever we are.
                                       Micheal Sunanda, HI

Parents with unusual lifestyles should take precautions.
With the current trend to persecute those whose beliefs
or lifestyles are different, especially in the Bible Belt
parents are in danger of being accused of child abuse or
molestation, having their kids seized, and going to prison.
I read in publications I receive: Over 50% accused of
child-related crimes are innocent. Of those in prison, over
75% never saw their court-appointed attorney other than the
only day they went to court. Over 98% were coerced by the
state and their lawyer into taking a plea bargain instead of
going to court. Two gentlemen who arrived here in prison
the past month, are nomads but not for the next 10 or 20
years. They had a choice: plead guilty; or have their
wives arrested and their children forced into foster care.
If you think you are safe because you have never had any
problems or you have never been spotted by the law, remember:
it only takes one trip to the emergency room and then, unless
you pay cash right there, the police and state are involved.
I recommend: Never put your kids in school. Never take
federal or state money to support your kids. Never let
churches or religious groups know how you live. If changing
lifestyles, always relocate at least several hundred miles
from your last sedentary residence. Never stay in one camp
more than a couple of weeks, and move on immediately once the
authorities become aware of you. Keep your licenses in order.
                                        Guy Hengst, IN ,Feb.
(Comments:) Thanks for your recommendations. Others: Keep
school-age kids out of public view during school hours. And
when in public view, try to look fairly conventional. To
make dressing up less unpleasant, don't go to populated
places often, and, when you do, beforehand try discussing
them as if they were costume parties. (In a way they are.)
If you go to an 1840s-style rendezvous, you will probably
have a better time if you, too, dress that way. Likewise
if you go to a 1990s city or public campground.
As for never staying in one place longer than 2 weeks.
If living in a vehicle, that is probably wise. (If parking
on the streets, moving several times a day may be wise.)
But if in a secure backpack camp, and you have not been seen
by anyone; moving less often will be safer, because each move
to and preparation of a new camp might attract attention.
We would like more info on the cases you know about.
How were the people living? What brought the police?
We have no kids of our own. But we hear from quite a
few parents, and we know of no arrests or child seizures due
to unusual dwellingways (which is not to say there aren't
any). However, most families we hear from are in the Pacific
states. Hasslings may be worse in some other areas.
Overall, portable dwellers who home/un-school, seem to
have fewer problems than do house dwellers who send their
children to school - and then discover their kids are being
turned into fashion hounds (expensive!), tube boobs, and
junk-food-junkies; or, if they resist, are despised and
tormented by the other kids, and maybe beaten up or worse.

Your zine seems to becoming more passive as issues go by.
Yes, I could shave off my beard, never be nude outside
a bathroom, and never express a contrary opinion. Don't go
to Rainbow gatherings: you'll just be hassled. Don't defend
your property (electrify your vehicle): you might antagonize
someone. What next? Don't live in the woods: someone might
think you are the Unibomber.

There is a point where rights unexercised become rights revoked. It's one thing to maintain a low profile because one is doing something quasi-illegal (squatting). It's another thing to blend in at any price. I have a friend who won't order books (ANY books) from Loompanics because then he might end up on a government "list". I told him, if we all got on as many lists as possible, then the lists would be useless for profiling anyone, or even for rounding up people.

Where would Blacks and Gays be now if they had never asserted themselves? Certainly more persecuted than they are now! The Amish have done pretty well at resisting public schooling and state-required registration of outhouses.

You don't need to be Freud to see that bigots and religious zealots are basically insecure. So they want to force everyone else to conform. That will ease their self doubts. Well, I don't intend to encourage their persecutions by always "lying" low and lying (denying) what I really am.

I haven't been lynched yet. If I am, I insist that you dedicate an issue to me as a martyr to the cause. L.Smith, Febr.

(Reply:) I don't think DP has become more passive. To the contrary, the Oct95 issue had perhaps the most activist article yet: about how one portable dweller, without great effort, launched an apparently-successful boycott of a city.

One problem with Standing Up For Your Rights. You can't really do that, unless you have a bigger and better arsenal than the cops and are willing to shoot it out. You are depending on the police and prosecutors not being as nasty as they could be. On one hand, if you have plenty of money for lawyers or if (eg) the ACLU happens to take an interest in your case, you might get an evil law overturned. On the other hand, the cops may decide to make an "example" out of you to deter other non-conformists. They beat you up, then charge you with "resisting arrest" - and your court-appointed attorney advises you to plead guilty.

Trying to defeat someone at their own game, is usually not wise. If a bull charged you, would you lower your head and counter-charge? Or would you climb a tree or hop fence?

Even if you are willing to become a martyr, most people aren't. By using boycotts, we can fight back without becoming martyrs. Blacks made effective use of boycotts. So did Gays (against Colorado when it passed an anti-Gay law). If we avoid a particular area, or if we earn and spend less generally, less taxes are collected. That hits politicians and police where they are vulnerable: in their wallets. Also, merchants will become unhappy and (better than you or I could) pressure the police to desist. Of course, a boycott by DP readers alone won't have great impact. But word gets around. We don't say, avoid all Rainbows. We do say, hold Rainbows only where people are friendly, or where there are no other people. Bert and Holly, Oregon, November

Rural deputies claim many people hide in the back country.

Clyde McLain, undersheriff for Crook County, told this story. "The sun was just going down over the rimrock and another deputy and I were heading back to town in an unmarked rig over this little dirt road. All of a sudden I looked up and saw a guy standing in the trees up ahead watching us. He was dressed in brown, camouflaged in the trees, and had a gun strapped to his hip." The deputies stopped and talked with the man, who turned out to be a benign fugitive, merely fleeing the company of other people.

McLain says some of the juniper-covered ravines and pine-lined mountainsides of eastern Oregon are dotted with little hideaways sheltering such solitary folk, living without electricity or telephones or nearby neighbors. Some, he says, are the law-abiding type, wanting only to be left alone. But others are hiding from the law. "There was one ranch out near Paulina in the middle of nowhere, and I can remember how eerie it was. As soon as you drove in, just for a split second you'd see 20 or 30 people. And then you'd see nobody."

A survey of law-enforcement agencies around the state, produced a chorus of agreement with McLain's view that it's easy for a fugitive to vanish into secluded mountainsides. (from The Oregonian, 1996; sent by James)

(Comments:) Why did all those "fugitives" stand up in plain view when an unknown vehicle drove in? And do they even exist? We spend most of our time in the woods, in areas more attractive than Crook County (which is far from any city), and we encounter few other woods dwellers. Maybe McLain just wanted his name in the paper, and would like more taxpayers' money to "protect the public" from "fugitives".

Furthermore, we and people we know are "fugitives" only from absurdly-expensive housing (though we also like living in the woods because they are attractive). I doubt that remote woods attract many desparados because, my impression is, most real criminals crave excitement. They'd get bored.

The original article, which included the line, "... back country is filled with reclusive souls like the Unabomber...", is typical of the sleaze delivered by the major media. Viewers and readers beware. Bert and Holly

An igloo or snow cave is more comfortable if lined.
The snow is fair insulation, but keeps the inside from getting much warmer than the snow's melting point (and if it does - drip, drip, drip). Insulations I've tried are either bulky to carry (foam) or tedious to gather (leaves). Other suggestions? (no name on this, which got separated)

Recently I designed a solar-powered knock-down pyramid.
I am also attracted to dome homes. Ross McKenzie, BC, June

Mud is an interesting building material.
Though not light or portable, in some situations it is inexpensive and easy to use. We built a 20-foot post-and-beam circle with shed-roof low to the north. We filled the low north side with 2-foot-thick mud walls and the high south side with windows. Three of us were very comfortable during our long, cold northern winter. On sunny days the door was open, and most nights the fire was allowed to burn out.

Mud could be used on a smaller scale in the woods. If carefully done, it could be very discreet and leave no obvious scar. Cob Cottage Co., Box 123, Cottage Grove OR 97424, offers courses on building with mud. Jai Loon, WA, 1996

(Comment:) In most situations (obviously not in a swamp or where drainage is poor), for a small structure I prefer to make a dug-out of some kind. (Eg, Snugiup, May95 DP) That way the walls are of undisturbed soil which may already be naturally reinforced with roots, instead of disturbed soil which may need reinforcement. A dug-out does require more digging, but if small that is tolerable. Bert, Oregon, Nov.

Handy bike panniers easily made.

These are more widely available, easier to load, more durable,
and easier to keep out of wheels
than are feed bags (in LLL
paper, "My two-wheel
Truck"). Also more
versatile: off the
bike I use them to
fetch water, launder,
and hold things.

These are squarish,
flexible, 5-gallon,
plastic containers of
vegetable oil or soy sauce,
thrown out by restaurants
and bulk food stores.
I prefer the lightest weight.
(Some have thinner plastic
than do others.) For easiest
washing, I like to get them
before they have sat around
so long that the oil hardens.

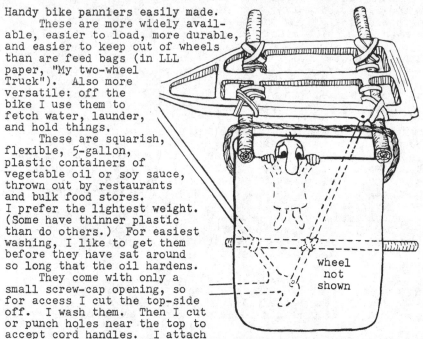

wheel
not
shown

They come with only a
small screw-cap opening, so
for access I cut the top-side
off. I wash them. Then I cut
or punch holes near the top to
accept cord handles. I attach
each end of the cord by passing it thru the hole in the
pannier, and (not shown) up around the lip of the pannier and
tie to itself. I leave extra length so I can adjust the
height of the pannier after it is on the bicycle.

For hanging the panniers, I permanently lash two sticks
to my bike's rear rack, at right angles to the wheels, about
pail's width apart, and far enough to the rear to keep the
panniers out of the way of my heels when pedaling. I lash
the sticks to the rack's UNDER side, so they don't raise what
is on top of the rack and make the bike less stable. Make
lashing strong enough to take weight of the loaded panniers.

The pannier's handle slips over the sticks. To secure
handle, I tie its ends to the rack, or pass rubber straps
(cut from old inner tubes) around the sticks outboard of the
handle, front and rear (which may also hold on a top load).

I also lash sticks to the bike frame parallel to the
wheel (shown), to keep the panniers out of the wheel.

These panniers are not easy to cover (because their
handles interfere). Therefore, if rain likely, I prefer square
4-gallon plastic pails with snap-on lids. But they are heavier
and slightly smaller. (The square (viewed from above) pails
wobble less than do round pails.) Julie Summers, Oregon, Dec.

Tent camping and working in southern Appalachians.

My stay with friends ended because of driveway improvements and inlaws visiting. I'm now working at an "exclusive
resort community" and have a wonderful campsite in the woods
nearby. I am using a Eureka Timberline 2-man tent. I sleep
on my Thermarest Camprest in an old sleeping bag ($5 at yard
sale). Outside my front entrance is a huge rock formation,

over which I put a camo tarp to form a miniature porch.
I've found many useful items in a nearby dump, including
a hibachi over which I cook dinners with oak firewood (less
smoke). I use plastic 4-pound peanut jars to store things.
For pee I use a one-gallon Chlorox bleach jug. That brand
has a wider opening (more comfortable). I empty 30 feet from
camp. Does pee scare away animals? A few bears are around.
I make $8 an hour and work 25-35 hours/week. On the
mountain side I build railroad-tie structures 60x40', which
are filled with dirt to form level sites for RVs. Hard work.
In June, nights were 45-60°; days 70-85°. Now in late
autumn, nights 30-40°; days 50-60°. Eugene Gonzalez, NC, Dec

Tent liner-ette improvised from large bedsheet.
When some unexpectedly-cold spring weather caught us in
under only a plastic tarp, I rigged a double-bed-size sheet
across the head end of our bed, suspending it with four ball-
ties (like the insect net shown in May96 DP).
With heads inside the sheet-tent, our breathing raised
air temperature 10-15°F over the near-freezing outside, allowing us to use bare hands for (eg) writing and sewing without
discomfort. Our lower bodies remained warm in sleeping bags.
Enough air filtered through the sheet for ventilation.
Moisture from our breath dampened the sheet, but did not annoy
us because we touched sheet only when we reached outside. B&H

Further report on the Stansport model-723 dome tent.
We used it for a month last summer. The smell seemed
less (see May96 DP) maybe because we were in it mostly at
night when cool. With a net top beneath a built-in fly, and
a double door (one netting; one fabric), ventilation ample.
When closed, with two inside maybe 5-10° warmer than outside.
As a bug barrier, the tent was fine - even better than
our home-made net-tent because of sewen-in bottom. The
zippers (which we'd had doubts about) survived frequent use.
Though most days dry, a few were very rainy. The built-
in fly shed fine. But much water came in the trough-like seam
where sides and bottom joined. (We carefully kept ground tarp
from protruding beyond sides.) To cope, we suspended a large,
clear-plastic tarp above the tent. (If simply layed over, it
reduced ventilation, causing condensation inside.) But the
tarp with its tie-outs, nullified the self-supporting tent's
chief advantages: quick set up; and no lines to trip over.
                                                        B&H
South slopes warmer, but beware if steep enough to slide.
For winter campsites, I prefer south-facing slopes. The
steeper, the warmer when sun, because the light spreads over
less ground. Also, downhill trees less likely to block sun.
However, if very steep, snow or wet soil may slide. A
mostly-treeless patch extending up-down, in an otherwise-
forested area, may indicate former (and future?) slides.
(Some spots are treeless because soil thin. Sign: bedrock
protruding. If rock firm, spot maybe safe unless much snow.)
How steep is too steep? That depends on soil and snow.
I'm wary if more than one yard rise per two yards on slope.
                                                        B&H
Dwelling in a bus in Toronto.
From June 1992 until Oct 1995, I lived in a full-size
(35') Chev school bus. I spent one year in New Orleans, and
two years, including one milder-than-usual winter, in an
industrial area of downtown Toronto. Another winter was
too cold to live in my bus, so I stayed with friends.

The bus, which had not been on the road for two years, cost $1300 Cdn. I also bought furnishings I installed.

In Toronto, I fortunately found a parking spot that was near attractions of the city, but also had open space, trees, birds and animals.

Finding my urban oasis took some asking around. The property was practically abandoned. I discovered who the owner was, and wrote a letter explaining the advantages of me being there as a guard. Unscrupulous container trucks often dumped illegally in the area at night. Anyway, the owner let me stay, and then I never heard a thing.

I lived alone there, tried to be as discrete as possible, and didn't have many visitors. I kept the entrance blocked. I was on a deadend street and few people came there except for hookers turning tricks in cars. Though I don't object to their trade, I encouraged them to go elsewhere because many are addicts and hang out with Bad guys.

Metal is a good conductor of heat, so warming my "tin shack" was difficult. Accumulated snow would melt off the roof. I bought a propane RV furnace (forced air), insulated the floor with "Reflectix", covered the windows with plastic, and formed movable partitions by hanging thrift-store curtains with velcro, so when extremely cold the heat could be concentrated in a small area.

I slept warm and cozy in a quality sleeping bag with blankets piled on top. But getting out of bed was uncomfortable.

I experimented with a cheap, silver, heat-reflecting "space" blanket, and it helped. You are supposed to suspend it above you somehow.

I cooked on a propane camp stove. Propane is clean burning, relatively cheap, and widely available. I had a 100-pound tank. A friend with car helped me fill it - ± monthly in winter.

There happened to be an accessible city-water tap nearby, so about once a month I made 5 trips with a shopping cart and filled my outboard tank. From it, with an RV hand pump, I filled a low-cost water-filtering pitcher (Brita).

For cleansing, I collected rainwater into another tank, and used a standard easy-to-find car-windshield-washer pump (with switch, foot operated), some low-cost vinyl tubing, and jerry-rigged a spout beside a used stainless-steel sink. The sink drained directly under the bus. The pump's low flow was enough to wash dishes, vegies, face, etc. I bathed at a nearby public swimming pool.

My "porta-potti" toilet was adequate for one person and occasional visitors. To control odor, baking soda (sodium bicarbonate) proved most effective. I emptied it about twice a week in a nearby vacant lot, going at night to not be seen. I just poured out the contents and let the sun and rain dispose of.

Often my only night-time light was a candle, though I worried about carbon monoxide - deadly if vents shut tight.

Building the interior while living in it was frustrating at times. Best do as much as possible before moving in - otherwise you'll be living in a mess. Some knowledge of carpentry and metal working was needed, though this can be learned. Some ideas are in a 1970s picture book, Roll Your Own Home. Check libraries for others, eg, RV maintenance.

Moving a big bus down the road can be expensive. A bus/truck repair manual and mechanical abilities help. Even if you can't do a repair, you can diagnose. A repair shop is less likely to rip off someone in the know. Also consider step-vans, such as UPS and bakeries use. They are easier to park. Inside they are shorter but often higher.

I was never assaulted or burglarized. At first I worried, but gradually I relaxed. Toronto is a fairly safe city. Of course I kept the door locked, and when I went away I covered the windows. Potential thieves would be detered by the oddness, and by not knowing how many were here or if we had weapons or an attack dog. Other security measures might be: motion detectors that trigger a quiet alarm, or a camera; posted signs warning of dogs or electronic surveilance; or   SECURITY VEHICLE.

One problem was height. I am six feet, and the ceiling inside was barely six feet in center, less at sides. Installing flooring for more insulation would further reduce height. This was one reason I eventually moved out.

In Oct 1995 I sold the bus and moved to Japan to be with the love of my life, a Canadian woman here on an English-teaching contract. I too now teach English, and we plan to stay until July 1997. Fred Spek, December

Most RVs are built to remain heated.

Freezing ruins all lines in RVs and trailers, including Airstreams. Some RV suppliers now carry a new plastic pipe that does not split when frozen. When I get an RV, I promptly replace all metal lines with rubber or plastic.

If without commercial electricity, to get running hot water is more trouble than it's worth. Al Fry, Idaho, June

Complex RV appliances are not reliable.

I once had a motor-home with a lamp, stove, oven, heater, and "instant" (no tank) hot-water heater, all propane.

The lamp and stove both had simple, manually-operated valves - and worked fine. The other appliances had thermostat controls and pilot lights - and all were perpetually troublesome.

The hot-water heater had additional problems. The main burner often blew out the pilot light, which required going outside to relight - in the middle of a shower! Also, an unexpected freeze cracked the tubing, causing a fast leak in an inaccessible spot.

Even house-size appliances are not reliable, I've heard. RV appliances are generally worse, because they must be smaller, cheaper, and (most important) fewer. To build something that is BOTH complex AND reliable, requires mucho engineering, which is affordable only if building millions (or if charging millions and selling to the government).

So, yes, DO do things simply. When you count maintenance, a (eg) jug shower using water warmed on a stove, is more convenient than a complicated "convenience". Chal, California, Dec.

More on RVs in May96 and May95 DPs.

Portable electric systems.

This is an update/summary of past articles, including Rob's in Jan91 and Hank's from Feb82 through Sept84 MP(DP).

If your base camp is remote both from power lines and motor vehicles, and if you want more electrical gear than a seldom-used flashlight or radio, you probably need a rechargeable battery plus a photovoltaic panel. (Other power sources: pedal generator; backpacking battery to where a charger can plug in.)

I still know of only two kinds of rechargeable batteries available: lead-acid and nickel-cadmium (nicad). Both contain toxic metals and corrosive liquids. Both produce explosive gases, especially if recharged rapidly. Both are easily damaged.

Lead-acid, especially, needs much care. If fully discharged, or if left long without recharging (they self-discharge), lead-acid batteries are ruined or seriously damaged. Even with the best of care, their life is only a few years. (Don't be confused by names given to varieties. Eg, "gell-cell". Any rechargeable battery bigger than a flashlight and less than $100 new, is probably lead-acid.)

Nicads are not damaged if not kept charged, and are generally longer life, but are very expensive. Even used nicads sell for several times as much as new lead-acids with equivalent capacity.

So, before buying, be sure you really need an electric system. For an occasional night light, a candle or even a propane lamp will be easier. (Yes, they are hazardous. But so are batteries.) To minimize use, during dark hours do things (eg, talk) not needing light.

Next, if such terms as amp-hours, volts and diode are like Greek to you, acquire some knowhow. Read Hank's series, or look for books in libraries.

If my system was very remote, and if I could afford them, I'd buy nicads. They are usually much less grief than are lead-acids. Otherwise, like Rob did I'd get used auto batteries. Though not tolerant of deep discharges, they are cheap, widely available, and (barely) light weight enough to backpack.

Suppose your system will be used mostly in winter when daylight is short. Each autumn, buy a used auto battery ($10-$15) from a dealer, or from a motorist who is buying a new battery. (Many do every few autumns to avoid winter problems.) The battery may no longer reliably start a cold engine, but should be near-fully charged (test all 6 cells with hydrometer) and be capable of holding a charge. (If, with no load, it self-discharges in only a few days, return it and get another.) With fair care, the battery will probably last the winter. If, then, you are away all summer and the battery is untended, it will self-discharge and be ruined. No big loss. Come autumn, trade it in (the metal is still valuable) on another.

A photovoltaic panel will cost $20 to $500, depending on size. Size isn't critical. But the panel MUST have at least 35 solar cells, wired in series, to generate enough volts (17 or so) to recharge a 12-volt battery.

(This assumes a system with battery. If powering equipment DIRECTLY, get a panel with about twice as many cells as volts needed. (Eg, 18 cells to power a 9-volt radio.) More may burn out radio.

The size needed, depends on your equipment and your sunshine. Some books tell how to calculate. Or you can buy a small panel and try it. If not big enough, add another. (Panels with same voltage can be paralleled.) Better a panel too small than too big. If too small, you can't use your equipment as you'd like. But if too big, fast over-charging may damage the battery as well as generating explosive gases (unless a regulator added: more cost/complication).

You will need a blocking diode (one-way valve) unless the pv panel has one built in. The diode prevents battery discharge back thru the panel at night.

Frequently check battery with hydrometer. (A cheapo, with little balls that float or sink, is $1-2 at auto stores/depts.) When half discharged, shut off equipment until battery recharges. (Don't wait until (eg) lights dim. That will damage lead-acid battery.)

Radios take little power, tape player somewhat more, TV much more - especially color TV. Forget electric hot-plates, heaters, clothes driers, etc.: they need MUCH too much power to be practical.

If using a light several hours each night, a LED may be desirable, despite cost, because of efficiency and reliability. (Fluorescents are also efficient, but probably brighter than needed in a small shelter, and not too reliable.) If using a light seldom, ordinary small 12-volt incandescent bulbs (in auto stores) are cheap and adequate.

IMPORTANT. For safety, keep battery OUTSIDE your shelter, but near (to not lose much power in wires). Shelter from rain and sun, but ventilate space so explosive gases don't accumulate. B & H

Electricity in a bus.

I rigged a simple 12-volt system using a 100-amp-hour deep-cycle lead-acid battery (aka RV/marine). It looks like a regular car battery, but is designed to be discharged further, and may have different-looking connection posts. A car battery could be used, and they are cheaper and easier to find, but won't last quite as long. Keep a lead-acid battery warm, as they put out less power when cold. (The reason car batteries are so big, is for starting an engine when cold.)

Don't expect much power from just one battery. My loads were modest: a small stereo with AM/FM, cassette, CD; 8-watt fluorescent light ($15 from Canadian Tire), but the tubes can't take frequent switching on-and-off for long; the fan in my RV furnace; a windshield-washer pump used for water; and a 5-watt keyboard amplifier.

To recharge the battery, I bought a 22-watt (1½ amp full-charge current) amorphous photovoltaic solar panel. In winter it wasn't always enough, so I reluctantly ran an extension cord to the adjacent building to power a 12-volt battery charger. The cord also powered a 120vac heater I kept on hand for occasional comfort, or emergencies. I had to run the bus's engine occasionally, which also recharged some. Fred

Practical candle craft, and tips for easier use.
     Candles are inexpensive, convenient light sources. I do
not like candle light for reading, but it's fine for cooking
and eating. CAUTION: burn only where ample ventilation.
     I buy candles at yard/rummage sales. I seldom pay more
than 25¢ for a big one (pound or more).
     If a broad (eg, 3") candle burns long, a big pool of
melted wax forms and may either drown the wick or spill over
the side. To avoid that, I alternate two or three candles:
I burn one until only a SMALL pool forms, then light another
and extinguish the first to let its pool harden. But just in
case wax spills, I set candles on a plate or pie pan. Any
spilled wax usually pries off easily after hardening.
     If a chunk of wax lacks a wick, I gouge a hole (with a
narrow, pointy knife; though drill bit or hot nail works too)
and insert a wick. Experts say, don't leave much air space
around the wick; so, if the hole is overly large, I stuff wax
shavings in beside the wick, and I may drip wax from a lit
candle onto the wick to "prime" it. In any case, as soon as
the new wick is burning, it melts wax that fills in the hole.
     Some broad candles come with thin wicks that burn little
craters in the wax until the flame is surrounded by wax walls
that shade it. I insert (as above) a stouter wick alongside
the original, or distribute thin wicks and burn one at a time.
     An easy way to make a candle from small scraps of wax:
put them in a shallow clear-glass jar and insert a wick
between them. As the wax melts down, I add more pieces.
I keep the level of wax near the top of the jar, so the flame
doesn't heat the glass enough to crack it.
     For wicks, I experiment with various cotton strings from
my collection. Some work better than others. If too thin, I
twist a length, then fold in half and let it twist itself into
a 2-ply cord. To make thicker yet, I repeat to get 4-ply,etc.
     I have also made candles from various animal and
vegetable fats, and wicks from thistle or cattail down. I may
form a wick by rolling the down between my hands and doubling
(as above). (Tricky because these fibers are short.) Or I may
mix the down with soft fat, glom onto an 1/8" diameter stick,
and insert the stick as a wick into fat. If the fat is liquid
I put a few pebbles around the stick to hold it up. Collect
plant down when you find it: may not be in season when needed.
     To extinguish a candle, I prefer using a metal bottle cap
as snuffer. (Blowing may spray wax or leave a smoking wick.
Pinching wick between moistened fingers may scorch fingers or
get wax on them. Julie Summers, Oregon, November

I have been treating my engine with Slick-50.
     I began at 70,000 miles. Now 217,000 miles and no major
engine repairs on my 1981 Ford 6 cylinder. Under $20 when on
sale. Steve Ronalter, Connecticut, May

Synthetic oil is the best thing to put in an oil can.
     Fans on RV heaters will seize up in a few months using
the usual auto oils. Two-cycle oil is next best for holding
up under heat. Al Fry, Idaho, April

I keep an extra key tied in the laces of my shoe.
     That way I avoid a major disaster if I lock myself out of
my car while shopping, laundering, hiking or gold panning.
Tumbleweed, CA, May   (Comment: A few times my shoe lace has
broken without me noticing until I had walked many yards. I
would tie the key so it hangs down into the shoe. H&B)

Equipping a vehicle for dwelling in.

Keep it simple. Don't install plumbing. Put in only what you can easily remove. That way you can use the vehicle for hauling, or use the equipment separately at a remote camp.

For a bed, plywood supported by crates may be warmer than the floor, and provides storage space beneath. Bedding used for backpacking should also suffice in a vehicle, except you may want more padding: wood is harder than most soils.

Though ready-to-eat foods are abundant in cities, in the back-country an ability to cook can increase food variety and reduce cost. A propane stove is usually best. (Campfire smoke could attract hassles.) Get one that connects to a 5-gallon tank. (Not to the little cans. The fittings are different.) May96 & Dec96 DPs tell simple ways to defecate inside.

H&B

Bathing while camping in a city.

If without a vehicle, you may be on undeveloped brush-land, such as a river flood-zone during dry season, where you can shower with a jug (or whatever contraption pleases you). But if living in a vehicle, brush-lands may not be near by.

You might join a gym. But if in a city mainly to earn and accumulate money, you don't want to fritter it away.

In a van or bus, consider rigging a portable shower enclosure (eg, like March89 DP). You will need a big strong pan or tub to stand in and to catch the water, and a shower curtain (which may be rigged out of plastic) to intercept splatter. If your vehicle is too low to stand in, can you shower okay while sitting, squatting or kneeling?

Some public rest rooms have hot water. (McDonalds did.) Take along (eg) a cup for filling jugs. (Jugs won't fit under most faucets.) Holly & Bert, Oregon, December

Lives out of pickup more than in it.

Responding to John and to H & B in Dec96 DP. Yes, we still have our pickup with insulated canopy. But it is too small and usually too crowded with equipment to really live IN. We sometimes sleep in it a few nights when traveling or in cities. But   usually we live OUT of it - using it as a mobile closet while doing most activities in our tent.

A few times I cooked in it (while Barb was elsewhere), but had to shift things around to make room.

Our original canopy was home-made, mostly of wood, with insulation built in. Despite frequent repaintings, the wood eventually deteriorated. I replaced it with a manufactured canopy, insulated with flexible foam held on by contact cement (which dissolves some materials - test), and inside that, plastic as a vapour barrier. The cement does not hold long (especially if pickup left parked in hot sun), so I have re-glue occasionally, at which time I also replace the plastic (which gets grungy). The pickup bed, too, has foam and plastic linings, layed in and duct-taped at sides. Hank & Barb

NM, January

Instead of fixing my van myself, I phoned a dealer.

I thought they would have all the parts and know-how needed. I said the van was old and described all its ills. The dealer said: no problem, bring it in. But after I paid $120 (double what should have been) for towing 50 miles to Asheville, the dealer refused to work on my van because of its electrical problems. So then I had to have it towed to mechanics who were willing. Three repair shops and $700 later it is running. I will wait until January to get insurance and new plates, because my rates drop then - to $135/6 mo. Eugene

Living out of a car in Appalachian cities.
    You can live lightly and enjoyably in West Virginia. But
not secretively in the mountains. At least not with a car.
    I tried, beginning in 1982, but found it difficult. Rural
residents and hunters spotted me faster than any search by
police or chopper might. Even at night, if moon and not too
cloudy, they saw my shiny metal before I could see or hear
them. Suspicious of my wayward esconced vehicle, they reported
their find and deputies soon arrived to run me out. I got so
anxious that every time a bird landed on my car I relived a
horror-movie scenario. So I opted for blending into urban
confabrications. I have now lived out of my car continuously
for eight years plus some summers previously.
    In Wheeling, my home town, I easily made friends. After
locals knew my plans and trusted me, I was in. At first, cops
checked me out. But when satisfied, they left me alone.
Sometimes they even offered advice on better places to park.
    During my first year at WVU in Morgantown, everyone
checked me out. After that they treated me fine, except for
two WVU security guards who took a dislike to me, ran me out
of buildings and parking lots, and issued trespassing citations.
I complained to others on the force including the captain,
and the harassment greatly diminished.
    For warmth, at temperatures below 45°F I sleep with my
head inside sleeping bag - completely covered.
    To add insulation at night, I cut cardboard to fit and
put several layers inside the windows. This also prevents
frost from forming inside (which must be scraped off in the
morning before moving).
    Don't start the engine for heat. That not only wastes
fuel, but rapidly wears cylinders while oil is cold.
    To keep out insects when windows are lowered for ventil-
ation, I cut fine-mesh hardware cloth (25¢/foot) to fit, and
used magnetic strips (craft stores) to attach.
    To keep rain out of lowered windows, vent-shades must
reach all the way down the forward diagonals. (Most cover
only the top.) A local sheet-metal business made me some
awnings (working on them when business slack) in exchange
for feedback. Also, J.C.Whitney sells some (four/$45).
    While juggling in the park, I met a man who ran a salvage
yard and used-car lot. Since then, whenever my car needed
work, I visited him and he provided tools and advice to fix
mine while he worked on his clunkers. In return, I sent him
students looking for bargains. We have kept quite a symbiotic
friendship over the years.
    I earn extra income doing clinical and pharmacological
research for a local drug company. Travelers can to, provided
they have a phone number or local address.
    I seldom use or want a computer, television, or phone.
I make calls from pay phones. I prefer interfacing with real
people. I also learn much from books; and from journals,
magazines and newsletters I receive by mail. I get BBC via
radio, and carry oldies cassettes.
    I keep a permanent po box in Wheeling so my moves do not
interfere with my mail, and I rent a storage unit where rent
is cheap. (In Wheeling, you can buy a house for a song.) My
unit is over 30' tall. I built four levels of free-standing
shelves. (Lighter stuff goes on top.) A big unit does not
react so drastically to day-night cooling cycles. (A small
unit, especially a tin building, can over-heat and spoil
things including electronics unless located in a sheltered
spot.) So that is how I am heavy but light.

For the 23rd straight year, WV had the lowest crime rate in the U.S. (FBI) and Wheeling was again the lowest city. Only 5 murders in WV last year (most by out-of-staters). WV is among the poorest states and has high unemployment, which shows that poverty and crime don't necessarily go together. Laszlo Borbely, WV, December
(Comment:) Some Chambers of Commerce, I read, pressure local police to under-report crimes to the FBI, to make a city look good to prospective industries. So be skeptical of all statistics.

Living out of a car in New Orleans.

After completing degrees in Bio, Geo, Chem, and Physics at WVU, in Dec 1993 I drove south, just ahead of the worst winter in history. I had heard of jobs in Houston, but decided against Texas because police there often arrest single males to charge with unsolved crimes. Though transients and loners commit fewer crimes than do gregarious locals, prosecutors prey on them because they lack the connections and dollars for defense against bogus charges.

I stayed in New Orleans four months, living out of my car in high-crime neighborhoods. (The cops ran me out of up-scale neighborhoods, and threatened to jail me if they caught me there again sleeping in my car.) Almost every store had security guards at check-outs. Parking in wrong or risque places often elicited warnings or advice.

I met many locals including Cajuns selling door-to-door, enjoyed talking with them, and learned much. One fellow was sleeping in abandoned buildings without a sleeping bag. Temperatures dipped below 30°F occasionally. Then, just before spring, I read he perished from hypothermia. Only 40 years old.

I did not bother to rent a po box or beeper. I might have used a mail box at a vacated abode, driving by to pick up, though I'd try to get permission.

Seems 25% of population has left New Orleans due to dwindling jobs and much crime including 458 murders a year. As vacated homes are looted of appliances and construction hardware, neighbors get scared and move in turn. Due to heat and humidity, uninhabited dwellings succumb to mold and termites - often within a year. Laszlo Borbely, WV, Dec.

Travels With Lizabeth, by Lars Eighner

I was surprised to find dozens of books on homelessness in OSU's library. This was the most recent, spanning 1987 to 89, and perhaps the best. Lizabeth was the author's canine companion.

While Lars was living amidst a bamboo patch in Austin TX, fraternity boys cut some for party decorations. This exposed another squatter's tent to view of a hill-top mansion. The lady there had a wild imagination: the one 4x7' tent became, to her, half a dozen 6-man tents and the one occupant a well-armed para-military troop. The police rounded up the occupant and Lars (forcing Lars to walk, barefoot as he was, over the sharp bamboo stubble), and showed them to the woman. But the woman insisted an army was still in the bamboo. To satisfy her, the city sent in bulldozers and destroyed all the bamboo.

Though some homeless are alcoholic, drug-addicted, or insane, Lars thinks the numbers are greatly overestimated. "People who do not want to help, blame the homeless for being homeless."

"The purpose of welfare systems is not to help poor people, (but) to provide jobs for social workers and bureaucrats." 1993, 271 pages, Saint Martins, NY. Reviews in this issue by Julie Summers.

Government agencies seize children.

In response to Guy Hengst, Dec96 DP: I know of cases where, with no evidence of abuse, state "welfare" workers and cops took kids from families that were camping out; or were vegetarian, nudist, slept together, refused to immunize, or gave their kids freedom that someone claimed was "neglect". That happened to my family twice. We worked to get our kids back by proving NO abuse or neglect.

Two mothers I know had babies stolen because of home water-births. Took months to get them back, by which time bonding was broken. You never hear of these cases in the media.

A big threat, are laws that allow kids to be seized because of an anony-mous complaint, without requiring that the informer first confront the accused in court. In these state-kidnapping cases, children have no civil rights, and neither do parents unless they hire expensive lawyers.

Yes, schools train fashionettes, media addicts, treat pigs, and money hounds - afraid of raw nature. I am a homeducation teacher and partime parent. Homeducation is legal now and risks are minimal except in fascist regions that hate free families. Know the politics of any area you stay more than few days.

I usually like to meet any neighbors, especially if I'm with or near kids, to show I am responsible even though nude, natural, playful, and camping for free.

The recommendations of Guy and of Holly & Bert were mostly negative. Invisibility is good. But too much fear and caution can ruin a natural-camping experience, playing, and fun. Peaceful solutions to family wars are deeper than politics, hiding, or diets. We need to clarify our goals, values and needs (feelings) about children. Michael Sunanda, Family Peace Games, Hawaii, Dec.

Child "protection" has become a racket.

Favorite targets are low-income mothers who can't afford lawyers to fight the thefts of their children.

State social services get $4000 from the government for every child they put into a foster home. They keep 75%, and are not responsible for what it's spent on. Payoffs to police are common.

Child abuse cases are big business. For men to even be alone with under-age girls, is getting dangerous. One neigh-bor girl has sent four men to jail so far. Only two got off - after spending thousands to fight her false charges.

I am aware of families who have unpapered kids that get home taught, so that is still possible. Tom Van Doren, ID, Dec.

Cattle the most dangerous big animals. Probably because they are common, and are less afraid of humans. Be wary.

I cut firewood with an antique pointcut pruner.
#120, made by N.K.Porter, Everett MA for pruning apple trees. With a vise-grip-like mechanism, it easily cuts 3" thick oak branches, without the noise of an axe. (Safer too.) It folds to 18" long. Eugene Gonzalez, North Carolina, Dec.

Sewing flesh is easier with suture needles.
Sold by vet supply houses for about 50¢ each, they are curved and have sharpened blade-like points. If you get a deep cut, they can save a $200 doctor bill. I use hydrogen peroxide to sterilize silk thread, needle, and wound; and put Bentonite clay over the wound to allow faster filling.
I have a fight-happy dog I have to sew up often (after subduing by sitting on him). Tom Van Doren, Idaho, December

Silicone caulking is good for waterproofing sewen seams.
Buy caulking that has a 20 or 40 year rating. A tube usually costs less than $10 and will last years. Spread thin with finger for most flexability and endurance. Guy R. Hengst
IN, 1994
Learning more about sealants.
In summer 1996 I phoned the Locktite Corporation tech advice number (1-800-562-8483). They said, their Black Rubber sealant is softer and more flexible than their Black Plastic. Both cure when the solvent evaporates.
Silicone cures by reacting with air. It can withstand 400°F, whereas rubber only tolerates 300°. (Sea-level boiling water 212°.) Silicone also has good moisture resistance and therefore is well suited for window caulking.
Locktite also has a clear vinyl sealant; itself vinyl.
I've used the Black Rubber and Clear Plastic to seal seams on vinyl upholstery repairs, and rain gear I made. The Black Rubber did not become brittle and crack (especially in cold weather) as did the Clear Plastic, and maybe adhered better. The Black Rubber also adhered well (for years) to a bike seat, where it was smeared over stitches in a flat surface; but poorly in the crevice of a rainjacket seam - eventually peeling out.
I have used silicone caulking on rubber boots, applying it over the stitching of a sewn repair, but it did not stay waterproof long. Julie Summers, Oregon, November

During winter, drink ample water - 2 or 3 quarts a day.
When cold air is warmed, either by a heater or by inhaling, it becomes drier and absorbs moisture from your lungs. (That is why a vapor cloud forms when you exhale.) Most sore throats and sinus problems can be prevented or alleviated by ingesting more fluids. Guy Hengst, Indiana, 1994

Fishing, hunting, and gardening in southern Appalachians.
Fishing is a 15-minute walk from my camp. Or when my friend isn't working, we use his canoe and motor to a lake. Smallmouth bass are biting on 4" "Power Slugs" (brown and pumpkinseed colors best) from Berkely (not CA) with a tiny split-shot sinker 18" above bait to keep it submerged 1-2 ft.
I started a garden but small animals ate the seedlings.
While I was away for a few days, mice gnawed their way into my tent. Later, rats gnawed more holes. Sometimes at night I sit quietly at my tent entrance and kill rodents with a Wrist Rocket slingshot using .32 cal (9mm) buckshot. (I've had the slingshot 20+ years and am good with it.) I am overcoming an aversion to eating rodents.

I am also practicing with a compound bow, 50-60 pound draw, I bought for $115, plus $45 for sight and $60 for arrows. After getting over the fear of the bow string thwacking my cheek and nose, I have become accurate to 40 yards. But only once have I seen deer tracks nearby. The locals use dogs to hunt deer and boar, so the big game are skittish. Eugene, NC

Hawksbeard: another wild salad plant of the chicory tribe.

In May94 DP, Bert and I wrote about gosmore (Hypochoeris radicata), a wild green related to lettuce and dandelions. Last spring, in a recently replanted clear-cut, we came upon what we thought was a variety of gosmore, though the leaves were smoother, tenderer and generally less bitter - tasting very much like cultivated open-leaf lettuce. We ate handfulls of the leaves almost every day.

When we returned in mid summer, the plants had gone to seed and the leaves had dried up - unlike gosmore which is a perennial. A friend identified as rough hawksbeard (Crepis setosa). We have seen no mention of edibility, but we ate hawksbeard in quantity and suffered no ill effects.

Hawksbeard, gosmore and several other members of the chicory tribe (subdivision of daisy family) have (at least during spring) a rosette of basal leaves and then (if enough sun) yellow dandelion-like blossoms. But, unlike dandelions, the flower stalks branch and (in our experience) the leaves are less bitter. However, bitterness depends much on growing conditions. Generally, the more sun, the more bitter. All of these plants are tastiest before flowers develop. That makes identification difficult. So use caution. (Beware of tansy ragwort, a distant, poisonous relative with yellow flowers but more intricately divided leaves including leaves on the flower stalks (not just basal). Holly Davis, OR, Aug.

Don't swallow "concentrated energy" hype.

I've seen ads for "survival capsules" or "energy bars" which imply that a few pills or tiny wafers each day will furnish all essential nutrients. Nonsense! Though they might provide vitamins, such tidbits can't possibly furnish enough energy. A resting adult needs about a pound of carbohydrates per day; an active adult two pounds or more. Else s/he will lose weight, probably feel weak, and eventually starve. (Fat contains 2 times more energy than does carbohydrates, but eating mostly fat is not healthy.) Holly & Bert, Oregon, Dec.

Three compasses have stopped working, maybe from jostling.

I wear them around my neck and seldom take them off. The most expensive ($35), a Silva, lasted less than a year. Eugene

"Out There" Repair Kit

In a tobacco can, paint can, or Tupperwear container (etc.) with 12-16 fluid oz volume, I carry such items as: hot glue sticks, candle stubs, small Bic lighters, epoxy mix, super glue, small rolls of tape, plastic "snap" gasmets(?), small rolls of wire (10' each), small plastic clothes clips, spring paper clips, zip lock ties (4-6"), eyeglass screws, a few nails, assorted needles, assorted safety pins, razor (safety) blades, 2x2" sheets of sandpaper, assorted patches, rubber glue, rubber bands, rosin solder, vinyl glue, waxed floss, pack frame pins, tweezers, clear nail polish; with a Swiss (Victronix) "Champ" or Leatherman "toolbox" with various blades, files, other tools.

With these I can mend torn-off straps, broken eyeglasses, ripped clothing and pack bags, cracked water bottles, broken tent frames, and many other things. "Too heavy to hike with?" I would rather carry a little extra than abort a trip. Wildflr,

Dwelling Portably
formerly named Message Post
POB 190, Philomath OR 97370
December 1997 $1 per issue   Add 50¢ to check/mo under $6

How to make a small, smoke-free fire.

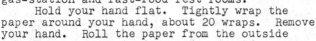

top view

Because I'm locked up I'm forced to witness
much stupidity. But I've also seen ingenious
improvisations. In here, any fire must not
draw the law's attention - and they're walking
around. So this fire would also be useful in
a populated area if you want to heat a cup of
water without smoke. The fuel is single-ply,
white, unscented toilet paper such as is in
gas-station and fast-food rest rooms.
     Hold your hand flat. Tightly wrap the
paper around your hand, about 20 wraps. Remove
your hand. Roll the paper from the outside
toward the center to form a "doughnut". You end up with a
ring with outside diameter 3½"-4", inside 1½"-2", ht 1½"-2".
     Set the "doughnut" on the side with the most irregular-
ities because it needs to draw air through the bottom. At
least, if setting it on a flat surface, make sure its bottom
is not perfectly flat. Light the center. It burns with a hot
flame, almost smokeless. To heat water, most folks here use
a drink can, holding it with a 12" piece of string.
     The only problem is extinguishing the fire. If you are
not quick and thorough, you will produce lots of smoke. Most
people here flush it down the toilet while still burning.
I guess dumping a pail of dirt on it would work. Lance Brown

My philosophy for survival: fit in; be invisible.

     What could be more different and offer more freedom?
Anyone can be a baglady. But to be a baglady and not have it
show, takes genius. For diversion I camouflage the baglady
me and portable-ize my dwelling, making it simple and easy to
maintain. And I work on my arrogance. I observe little
creatures: wasps don't get caught in spider webs. D. Dorji

I have fifteen acres here I am taking care of.

     I seem to be doing all right. I don't have a well yet,
which would make local officials unhappy if they knew, so
I keep them diverted. I'm from Los Angeles. When I get this
chunk paid off, I'll move back to the West Coast. Donald,ARK

I have been living portably for a few years.

     In tree houses, a school bus, and other ways. Soon, my
friends and I will build an earthen ("cob") cottage out in
some Oregon woods. Lee, Oregon, August

Tips for evading tracking dogs.

     In the turbulent times ahead, the government may decide
to round up nonconformists. Dogs that have been trained to
track and attack escaped prisoners, would likely be used.
The Texas Department of Criminal Justice now has 3500 track/
attack dogs trained and ready to go. As an unwilling guest
of the State of Texas, I spent 2½ years working with these
dogs and have learned many of their weaknesses.
     A human constantly sheds billions of minute skin
particles. Bacteria break down the particles and emit odor.
Though these bacteria thrive most in warm, moist areas such
as armpits and crotch, they are present on the entire body.
     These skin particles drift in the slightest breeze, so
the tracking dogs usually run 3 to 10 feet downwind of a

trail, parallel to it. The skin particles continue to drift until something catches them such as wet grass or leaves.

Heat, direct sunshine, wind, and low humidity favor the fugitive. The bacteria rot faster in the heat. The dogs are running with fur coats on and they don't sweat. The wind will scatter your scent over a large area and the low humidity will dry the grass and ground so there is no moisture to catch your skin particles that emit your scent.

Fog, cold, calm, drizzle/rain, clouds, dew and frost favor the dogs. Anything but a heavy thunderstorm will not wash away your scent. Moisture on vegetation will hold your scent. The dogs will stay cooler and have more endurance.

Most of the tricks you hear about for evading dogs are bogus. Putting pepper in your socks or behind you won't work because dogs don't run in your exact path. Nor do modern tracking dogs keep their noses to the ground; they run and sniff 8 to 10 inches in the air. Sure, you might incapacitate one or two, but they track in packs of six to ten.

What does work is a patch of fresh asphalt paving, but only if the whole pack gets a noseful. Fresh creosote railroad ties are also good. Any hard surface such as gravel roads or railroad beds will tear up the dogs' foot-pads and stop them. The easiest way to stop dogs is to keep them away from water. On a hot summer day they won't last 90 minutes without water. That fur coat is hot !

Do change direction frequently and irregularly. Make your turns sharp and approx right angles (90°). If you have time, overshoot your turns by ten yards or so, backtrack, and then turn. This will slow the dogs down but not lose them. Make lots of sharp turns, traveling at least 30 yards between turns, but not in a straight line for more than 5 or 10 minutes. I've timed my travel over a path, and then the dogs tracking me, and if I kept my corners sharp, the lengths of my segments varied, overshot and backtracked now and then, and walked a fair pace, I always gained time on the dogs. Also good is to walk toward an object that is obvious to the dogs, such as a building, woods or water, then backtrack exactly, and make a sharp turn.

Don't get in a pattern. I've seen dogs tracking someone who did 50-yard segments and 90° turns over and over. The dogs figured out what the pattern was and just intersected the corners, so the fugitive covered more ground than did the dogs.

A good dog handler will counteract most of your maneuvers, but each one will buy you time. If you change directions, change patterns, walk steady so you don't tire, don't panic, and pick terrain that doesn't hold your scent (hard dry), you can gain time until you lose the dogs for good. In wet grass, dogs can track you for 6 to 8 hours. In a dry field that has been plowed or harvested, dogs can track you less than 4 hrs.

If you get in the habit of following creeks, the dogs will run the creek bank, knowing that if they lose you, you'll be back. Likewise if you follow fence lines, ridges, or valleys. If you trend in one direction overall, you may find yourself boxed. Don't get in any habit: be unpredictable. Remember, you must outwit not only the dogs but their handler.

My own escape was semi-successful. I got all the way to Tennessee; then was busted because of a stupid mistake.
© Lance Brown, 1996 (originally in <u>Walter</u> <u>Mittey</u> <u>Papers</u>)

(Further tip:) At first, count your steps so you will know how long you are making each segment, to vary them. After a while it'll come automatically.

How track-attack dogs are trained.

At 6:30 am on a typical day, the Dog Sargent (S) arrives at the kennels. The Dog Boys (B), inmates who take care of the dogs, have been there two hours washing the pens and doing other chores. The S sends one B on a "puppy track" - a short track about 1½ miles long without much "work" on it, for training dogs 7 or 8 months old. "Work" consists of turns such as "stairsteps" ⋏⋀⋀⋀⋀⋁ and "boxes". "Not much work" means making the stairsteps 75 yards or longer and boxes 150 yards or so.

The S sends another B to lay out a full-sized track of 4 or more miles for training older, more-advanced dogs. The S tells B what pastures to go through and points to reach. (Eg: "work your way through the bull pasture to the lee woods, weave through the woods, and work your way to the windmill..." Sometimes B will leave the kennel on foot; other times he is driven to the starting point.

The S will run the puppy track while fairly "hot" - less than an hour old; and the full-size track when ±2½ hours old.

On the full-size track, the S takes the dogs to within a mile or so of where the track starts. Then he gets the dogs to "drag": run in front of S's horse in a left, right, left, right sweeping motion, with the sweeps about 150 yards long and about 40 yards between sweeps.

Eventually the dogs hit the scent and take off baying. The track is now about 3 hours old. Three-fourths of the time, the dogs take off in the correct direction. If they go the wrong way, S will try to turn them around by hollering at them. If they don't turn, he will start them again.

For the first 200 or 300 yards, the dogs overshoot badly and lose the scent a few times. But then they get "locked on". Before, they were looking for any human scent, but now they are tracking a specific person. That person can now cross the path of others and the dogs will search for his scent. They still overshoot, but not as badly.

Near the end of the track, B is supposed to wait 200 yds from his final destination until he can hear the dogs. Then he rushes to his tree or roof or shed, and puts on his "pack suit" to fight the dogs. When the dogs hit the "hot tail end", their baying becomes more frenzied - they know they are close.

Even though they are trained to fight, the dogs are not overly big or violent. I think they could be discouraged.

On one track I made, I followed a large ditch for more than a mile. The ditch was 12 feet deep and 25 yards wide with a small stream down the center. It was choked with willow, bloodweed, cattails, etc. Beside the ditch was a 50-yard-wide strip of 5" grass and then hundreds of acres of knee-high corn. The pattern I ran: down the center of the ditch for 150 yds; out and do a 150 yd box in the grass; back into the ditch for 150 yds; out and do a box on the other side; etc. I tried to walk in the water as much as possible and felt proud, thinking I'd fooled the dogs.

Wrong! From my waiting point I could see the whole ditch. The dogs headed for me like they were on rails.

Another day I did almost the same thing, but on a creek 30 feet across in places and chin deep. I ran 9 boxes off the creek. After following them the dogs decided: "Too hell with this. We'll keep running on this side and he'll come back." But I didn't. Took them an hour to decide they had lost me and to back track to where they re-acquired my scent.

If I ran an irregular pattern with overshoots and sharp

turns, the dogs ended up covering much more ground than I did. Whereas if I ran a "lazy" track with gradual turns, the dogs didn't overshoot and they gained time on me.

On one hot sunny day, 95°, I went from a creek up into plowed ground, crossed into a pasture, and ran sort of "loose" work: stairsteps about 75 yards and boxes 150 to 200 yards. From the creek to a water hole was about 3/4 of a mile. In that distance, two of the dogs overheated and had to be carried to water. For this reason, most of the training tracks were around water, or from waterhole to waterhole. Lance Brown, TX, July

Story of an escape from prison.

One Sunday night in November I was in bed asleep. At about 10 pm the police woke me and told me to go to work. There had been an escape from another prison 15 miles away. The police put 8 dogs, 2 horses, and us Dog Boys on a trailer. I was there to feed dogs and horses, and keep the dogs from fighting. They sent us to a pasture where we unloaded. They "dragged" the dogs some. I sat in the trailer and watched. At sunrise we went to an area near the prison.

As I learned later, three inmates had gotten into the boiler room of the prison, tied up the inmate who worked there, and knocked out the power. From there they cut through the first fence and climbed over the second.

There, one escapee twisted his ankle. So he went to some nearby trailers where the police lived and hid under one.

The second escapee ran 200 yards to the highway, crossed it, and hid in some extremely dense woods, about 35 acres.

The third escapee also ran to those woods, skirted the edge of them, then took off running down the highway.

The dogs got to where the escapees went over the fence and took off baying after #2 and #3. When the dogs got to the highway, one got hit by a car and the others scattered in confusion. Early the next morning the dogs found escapee #2 in the woods. The police assumed the others were also there.

From the feds they borrowed a Blackhawk helicopter equipped with infra-red, used to spot illegal immigrants. By now there was a wall of police around the woods. The Blackhawk went over and detected two heat sources. All that day we Dog Boys sat around while the police tried to get the prisoners out of the woods. They sent teams in, but they returned empty handed. Finally, with the Blackhawk controlling from the air, a line of police, shoulder to shoulder, walked through the woods. A medium-size doe came running out, soon followed by a good-size wild boar. So much for heat sensing. They wasted two days in the woods.

That night escapee #1 got caught when he came out from under the trailer. Escapee #3 got clean away. Lance Brown, TX, July

(Question:) Might tracking dogs be used to find "homeless" people camped in such places as big, undeveloped city parks?

(Reply:) Virgin ground is a must for tracking. I'd say no other foot traffic for at least 24 hours, mainly for the initial pick-up and lock-on to scent. When training, I've seen dogs try to lock on to a previous day's track, instead of the new track. Dogs are most effective where very few people are on foot.

I don't think dogs would be used in city parks. Too much chance of tracking someone like the mayor's kid and biting. I've seen dogs used one at a time on a tether, but that is not as effective and there would still be too many "wild goose

chases". I'd say they'd more likely be used on rural squatters. Lance
(Comments:) The dogs you worked with were trained to attack
whoever they ran down. But other dogs, used to search for
lost persons, do not attack (I hope). So they could be used
in city parks without endangering the mayor's kid. But, as
you say, too many trails. Seems like most rural areas would
also have too many trails. Some remote areas don't, but have
millions of acres of bush to crash through.

Anyhow, 90% of nonconformists probably live in urban
areas. Of the 10% who are rural, I expect 9/10ths could be
netted simply by going to their known addresses about 2 am.
The remaining 1% would likely be ignored during a mass round-
up (except for any prominant "trouble makers"), because the
government would be busy dealing with the others (millions?).

According to Tracking Dog (review in June 89 DP), the
oldest trail that dogs can track is about 3 days (less under
hot, dry conditions). So, in a situation where dogs might be
used, another way to elude them would be to leave more than
3 days before the dogs arrived. Holly & Bert, Oregon, Dec.

Jerry-rigged electric water heater for urban nomads.
The "stinger" requires 120-volt electricity so its
usefulness is limited, but it is simple and light. Parts
needed: a short electric cord; a small piece of wood (two
wooden matches, or a popsicle stick); some string or thread;
and two small pieces of steel (each about 2" x 1/2" x 1/16").

Place the wood between the metal pieces so they don't
touch, but leave some open space between the metal pieces
because electricity traveling through the water is what
produces the heat. Tie each wire to a metal piece.

Place in a non-metalic container of water so that most
of the metal pieces are submerged, and plug in. Within
seconds, water near the metal will bubble. In about three
minutes, six ounces of water can be heated to boiling.

The first few uses should be with a container and water
you can discard, to remove coatings and impurities from the
metal. After a few uses the steel should look rusty but the
water stays clear. Use glass or plastic container (NOT metal)
and don't touch the metal pieces or water while it is plugged
in. (I once saw an idiot test the water temperature by
sticking a finger in. He pulled it out fast !) Lance Brown

Turbine ventilators are more effective than RV-type vents.
Powered by the wind, they are frequently seen spinning
on factory roofs. The smallest fits on a 6" diameter stack;
ball about 10" diameter. Consider getting one if your shack,
vehicle, or underground bunker lacks sufficient ventilation.

If on a vehicle, install the ventilator so it can be
easily removed, and the end of the stack covered with a
plastic coffee-can lid. Don't drive with the ventilator on
the roof. L. Smith, Wisconsin, July

I currently live on a bus.   Nicky, Arizona, March

I live in my pickup.   Kelly, Kansas, October

Another possible use of trailer housing.
    I am somewhat skeptical about the usefulness of trailers
for housing to be evacuated in an emergency. "Mobile" homes
that set for long become progressively less mobile as various
extensions are built on and as the tires go flat, etc. Take
a walk through any trailer or "mobile" home park, imagine you
have a tow truck, and ask yourself: how quickly could I move
them all? For midwest flood lands, seems better for farmers
to put homes and important buildings on high ground, and
commute to their riverside fields.
    However, trailer housing seems fine for seasonal or
annual moves for which there is plenty of time. As well as
the traditional migrations north and south, there are environmental incentives for mobility. Oregon (and probably most
states) has a growing conflict between preserving nature and
providing homes. A state-wide law prohibits new construction
on farm and forest land. But one result is absurdly high and
rising costs of conventional housing.
    Though that increases sales of Dwelling Portably, not
everyone is willing or able to live in tents hidden in the
woods (commuting problem) or in vans parked on streets
(privacy problem - and if many did, the streets would jam).
    So, how can people live on (eg) farm land without inter-
fering with the crops? Maybe in trailers. Most fields lie
fallow part of each year, or every few years. So, park
trailers in a fallow field during winter. Then, in spring
when ready to plant, move them to pasture (if not used during
summer), or to marshy areas (that were too wet during winter),
or to mountains (that were too snowy during winter to commute).
The trailers must be fairly self-contained (no water or sewer
lines). But, no problem: compost kitchen and human waste and
fertilize the fields - thus benefiting the crops.
    On forest lands, after an area is clear-cut and replanted,
partial shade will benefit the little trees. So bring in
housing then (maybe not trailers with wheels, but just boxes,
moved by the same equipment that moves big logs around). The
boxes also serve as a sort of mulch, suppressing some of the
weed growth that competes with the trees for water. Then,
when the trees get big, move the boxes to a younger site.
    Of course, to do this legally would probably require
changing the laws: beyond the realm of most DP readers. But,
if anyone happens to have an in with some politician or big
media person, you might suggest this. Bert and Holly, Nov 97

Legal exemptions would make more rentals available.
    Jim Turner, a small-scale landlord discouraged by too many
bad tenant encounters, suggests what he calls a no-cost way to
provide not only affordable housing but domestic "mentorship"
for the needy: exempt owners who rent out rooms within their
own homes from landlord-tenant laws. Then they would not
have to give 30 days notice and undertake eviction proceedings
to get rid of crazies and deadbeats, nor meet building-code
standards for new rentals. "Overnight, you'd open up 200,000
to 300,000 units of housing," predicts Turner.

Should small shelters also be portable?
    The need for lightness drives Dwelling Portably people to
use materials (tent fabrics, sleeping pads, insulation, etc.)
that requires petroleum industries and don't burn or decay
without problem products. So what, since DPers use way less
than do conventional householders? Also, DPers tend to
scavenge or buy used, and use thoroughly what they buy;
instead of buying new stuff on impulse that soon goes
into attics.

Great. But someone still needs to develop alternatives, and those in small-but-not-backpackable shelters are in the best situation to do so. They are also better able to experiment, and draw on history for ways of using natural materials. They are also in a better position to affect environmental consciousness and policy in their communities than are those who are always moving on. Pluma, Small Shelter Council, TN 376, August
(Comments:) You assume portable dwellers are always moving on. Holly and I do most of our moving around within a home range 50-to-100 miles across (somewhat like traditional nomads). We might stay as long as 6 months at a winter base camp, and then several weeks each at a succession of lighter camps during the warmer/drier season, but seldom moving far.

Though DP folk vary, more seem to move mostly within home ranges, than move on and on never to return.

For experimenting and developing alternatives, portable dwellers seem better situated than are small-but-stationary dwellers. Both lack room inside. But, for projects needing much space, portable dwellers can temporarily move during summer to where outside space is abundant; while stationary dwellers are limited to what is close by. Likewise if special equipment is needed. And, for affecting community policy, if portable dwellers try something that stirs up more antagonism than is tolerable, we can move away until the hostiles cool down and forget about us. Whereas stationary dwellers live in perpetual fear of officialdom. They dare not "make waves" - else building inspectors or truant officers (etc) may notice them and come harass. Historically, most innovations were initiated by relatively-mobile artisans, traders, fishers, etc. Peasants, rooted to their spots and beholden to their lords, were last to change.

Socially, a big advantage of dwelling portably, is the ease of moving away from unpleasant neighbors. Though a stationary dweller may initially select a neighborhood for compatability, it may not remain compatable. People change, or are replaced. This is one reason why even people with big dwellings often strive to be portable: rent instead of buy; or sell one house and buy another. And look at some of the monster RVs on the road. So, if a shelter is to be small, why not also make it portable?

By the way, plastics don't require petroleum industries. They can also be synthesized from (eg) methane (producable by compost piles) or alcohol (I've read). Plastics are presently produced from petroleum only because petroleum is cheaper. (That will change as oil fields run dry.)

Also, synthetic end products are not always the most harmful. Petroleum-burning vehicles are nasty polluters, but replaced even worse polluters: horses. Between 1900 and 1930 in New York City, infectious diseases greatly declined, especially tetanus and tuberculosis (and this happened long after discovery of how diseases spread, and improved sanitation (mid 1800s), and before antibiotics were commercially available (mid 1900s)). Probable cause? Most horse-drawn wagons were replaced by motor vehicles, greatly reducing fecal dust and flies. Tetanus microbes breed in horse dung (which for some reason is much more dangerous than cow dung).

Holly and I usually use natural materials for framing (wood poles, instead of aluminum or PVC pipe), partly because they grow where we live (transportation only a few yards). But for windows and moisture barriers, we prefer plastic.

If natural materials are heavier, they are environmentally

better only if they occur at the site. Eg, a thatch hut is
fine if the thatch grows close by. But not if someone must
drive several miles to harvest it. That would burn more
petroleum than goes into a plastic tent.

Comparison of portable showers: suspended versus hand-held.
    May99 DP described an upright-jug faucet. Similarly, to
make a shower, punch several holes and plug with golf tees.
    The one real advantage of a suspended shower (either this
one, or the devices sold): both hands are left free - a big
advantage when scrubbing hands, vegies or dishes; but not
important when washing your body.
    Advantages of a unaltered hand-held jug (to shower,
remove cap): Does not need tree with strong limb above and
clear ground beneath. (Often hard to find.) Allows showering
in patch of sunshine. Control flow simply by tilting jug (vs
manipulating tees). Can use same jug to haul/store water. H&B

Vets use ethyl cyanoacrylate "super glue" to close wounds.
    A formulation for humans is coming. Meanwhile, though
super glue is NOT labeled for wound closure, weighing risks
vs benefits, one might decide to have some for an emergency.
                                                          Jon
Pot with pail provides convenient wash basin.
    I use a 2½-gallon pail, with rope tied to handle for
easy dipping, to fetch and store water. I also keep clean
utensils, plate and cup in it. A deep, sturdy, flat-bottomed
aluminum pot is my wash basin. After filling from the pail,
I set the pot into the top of the pail where it fits snugly
whether level or tilted. Along with cleanser and towel, the
pot with pail sets on the step of my van. Thus I can easily
reach it to wash my hands without entering the van and
touching door, sleeping bags, etc. A MUST when working on a
vehicle while living in it. I use bandanas to wash and dry
kitchen stuff, changing them daily.
    On previous trips I didn't give much thought to cleanli-
ness (I don't like washing dishes) and got sick a few times.
    I also cook in and pan gold with the pot. Eugene Gonzalez,
                                                NM, Oct 1997
Simplified toiletry also diagnostic.
    Though temporarily living in an apartment, I remain
sensitive to waste. Eg, instead of the toilet (which needs
much flush water), I urinate into a cup and pour it down the
sink. I need only a little water to rinse the cup, and that
cleans the sink as well. Instead of toilet paper, I clean
myself with a thin rag and then rinse it. Dries between uses.
    Added benifits of peeing into a cup, are seeing and
smelling my urine. I am learning to use it as a diagnostic
tool. Too dark, not enough water; too sweet, too much sugar
(any form); too sour, too much acid producing foods.
    Simple-living people need health awareness different than
people who can afford expensive treatments. I appreciate
readers' experiences maintaining health; as opposed to
ignoring their bodies until they become sick.
    I have noticed that usually (not always) before getting
a cold, I ate too much sugar for several days. My first
symptoms are very faint - in the nose, throat connection.
Formerly, I ignored them - until too late. Now I immediately
swallow about 4000 mg of powdered C, and go to bed a little
early. I wake up fine.
    More people (mostly older women) break hips in toilet-
sitting cultures than where people squat. Doctors blame muscle
weakness, and believe squatting keeps muscles toned. I now
squat, even when using toilet bowls. Since doing so, I have

not had hemorrhoid troubles, which had bothered me for years.
By the way, when baking I mix into the dough about one teaspoon of vitamin C per loaf. Retards mold growth. Laura, WA 981, Sept

How much vitamin C and how often?

Al Fry (in Dec97 DP) is only partly correct when he says 200 mg is all the body can use and any more is wasted. Linus Pauling recommended taking 90% of bowel tolerance, which for me is a whopping 9 grams. Pauling cited numerous studies. Eg, men who took 500 mg a day almost never contracted prostate cancer, and had much fewer urinary tract infections.

I find my point of diminishing returns and balance that with my budget. When finances are good, I take 500 mg a day. Otherwise, I bite the tablets in half and settle for 250 mg. If I feel a cold coming, I take an extra tablet or two.

On my generic vitamin C, bottled by Park Taft, it says: "Vitamin C often darkens in color; this does not affect the potency." Lance Brown, May

(Comments:) Al Fry said, "at one time". I take a dab of vitamin C powder (maybe 200 or 300 mg) two or three times a day (except during blackberry season when I get plenty naturally). Supposedly better than taking all at once. Neither Bert nor I have had infectious illnesses for many years. (Why? Usually good nutrition? Generally low-stress dwellingways? Or being around many other people only during summers when flu (etc) at minimum? Maybe all of above.) H&B

Vaccinations and potential consequences.

The cynics (mentioned in Dec96 DP) who counsel "get everyone else to vaccinate their children but don't vaccinate yours", have grasped the concept of "herd immunity": a disease will spread only if there are enough susceptible hosts within a population. If few of your neighbors are susceptible, you are not likely to get exposed. On the other hand, you may face sanctions from the health or child service folks, which may change your assessment of risks vs benefits.

My wife and I are both registered nurses. She is an infection control nurse where she works. I have been a fire-department EMT in Detroit, an ER and ICU nurse, and nursing supervisor. Our children are vaccinated per health department recommendations. Of course, we live in a small town, and our children are in the local school system and therefore exposed to whatever the children of negligent parents bring to school.

I second Holly and Bert: do your homework. Consider the costs and benefits of your alternatives, and act according to your best judgement. Remember that adverse reactions to innoculations are very very rare. During 20 years in ER and ICU, I have never even spoken with anyone who has seen a reaction. On the other hand, I do not get influenza vaccinations, though my wife accepts them each year. Jon Seaver, MI 488, Jan

(Comments:) This and other health topics are occasionally discussed in DP because risks for portable dwellers differ from risks for settled folks. On one hand, people who live in vans and go round to many gatherings each year, may be even more exposed to infections than is Jon and his kids. On the other hand, people with secluded backwoods dwellingways have much less exposure to most diseases (but possibly more to some such as hanta and Lyme). Most portable dwellers of both kinds may be less threatened by child "protection" folks: the van dwellers because they may move on before a kidnapping can be organized; the backwoodsers because no one knows they exist.

Therefore health, not law, is likely to be the chief concern.
Adverse reactions are easily identified as such only if
they occur soon after vaccination; not years later. Seems
like health problems among children and young adults have
increased. Causes? Junk food? Legal drugs? Illegal drugs?
TV watching? Environmental pollutants? Fast long-distance
travel (which brings exotic microbes)? Vaccinations? But
vaccinations are certainly invasive and should be undertaken
with caution. (A flier came for "The Immunization Resource
Guide", Diane Rozario, 2nd ed 1994, 60p."oversize", $12 ppd,
Patter, POB 204, Burl.IA 52601. "Detailed reviews of over
60 books" on the topic.") Holly & Bert, Oregon 973, June

Across the border in Mexico I managed to secure Claforan IV.
It is needed to treat third-stage Lyme disease, which
usually requires self-treatment as doctors don't seem to care.
                                                Michael, July
Recipe for a herbal tea believed to boost immune systems.
Ojibway or essaic tea, which supposedly cures some
cancers, was mentioned in Dec96 DP, but not proportions of
the herbs. Laura Martin-Buhler (Gentle Survivalist Oct98)
uses as a preventive: 6½ cups burdock root (Arctum lappa);
16 oz sheep sorrel (Rumex acetosella) powdered; 1 oz turkey
rhubarb (Rheum palmatum); 4 oz slippery elm bark (Olmus
fulva) powdered; distilled water (quantity not mentioned).
Stainless steel pot, strainer, funnel, utensils. Cooking
time not mentioned. This makes enough "for several days".
Laura keeps the prepared tea in her refrigerator.

Experience sprouting various legumes.
I read both LLL's instructions and a Readers Digest
back-to-the-land book, and then pretty much came up with my
own method. Lentil sprouts were easy. But I couldn't get
garbonzo, pinto, or soy beans to grow well. I rinsed three
times a day, just as I did with the lentils, and they did
grow for a while, but always rotted before very big.
Mung beans are my favorite sprout, but neither of two
local health food stores carry the dried beans. I wonder why.
A store clerk said, soy sprouts are harmful. I was
surprised because I've seen soy sprouts mentioned both in
LLL's paper and in The Farm Vegetarian Cookbook. James Dawson
                                                CA 954, July
Increasing the storage life of eggs.
Preparing for 4 months of camping this summer, I coated
eggs, both raw and hard-boiled, with water glass: sodium
silicate, available at good pharmacies. I haven't kept fresh
eggs, coated and refrigerated, past 60 days. I have eaten
hard-boiled eggs, coated and refrigerated, kept as long as 120
days. Water glass sealing of eggs dates back many years.
                                                Brother Bat, May
A trick for opening screw-top jars with stuck tops.
Wrap a belt around the jar lid, put a stick or ruler in
the "crotch" of the belt (between it and the side of the lid)
and pull. Works much like those tools for loosening stuck
oil filters on cars. Laura, Washington 981, September

Oh, the thought of being able to camp and enjoy open places.
Listening to the wind; the sweet smell of it; the fire
burning down to embers; the starry sky; frogs singing for
mates and birds calling out. For five years I've been locked
up and surrounded by people not of my choosing. I'm hoping to
go to a half-way house in June 99. Samuel Tucker, MI 498,June

Dwelling Portably

May 1998 $1 per issue

formerly named Message Post
POB 190, Philomath OR 97370
Add 50¢ to check/mo under $6

How to keep drawstrings centered permanently.
Annoyed by drawstrings on sweatpants,
hoods, or parkas pulling out or getting
lopsided? There is a simple remedy. Arrange
the drawstring so equal length is on either
side. Then, at the midpoint of the drawstring,
sew a few stitches through drawstring and
garment. This does not interfere with
snugging up and tying the drawstring. Julie

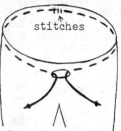

Quick and ugly foam booties.
No pattern; no sewing; very simple. For each foot use two
pieces of foam: one the size of your foot's sole (or a little
larger); the other roughly a yard (or meter) square. Set the
small piece in the middle of the large piece, set your foot on
the small piece, gather the sides of the large piece up around
your ankle, and tie a cord around the bundle. Bulky but warm.

I have been sleeping on Thermarests for many years.
Some I've had ten years; some five. The $100 mattress, "top
of the line", stays inflated for many months. I put it on the
bottom of my pile of three. The other two, each 2" thick, I
inflate a little every night to keep them (over) inflated.
I love them. I wish they were wider, but 26" is tolerable and
they are exceptionally light. Double Dorji, Arizona, April 97

Materials at hand form simple seats that add camp comfort.
I used to think chairs were effete. Chairs certainly aren't
necessary: I can sit or sprawl on the ground, stoop, or stand.
But some sort of raised seat makes many tasks more pleasant.
I've never bought a camp chair, nor built any of the complex
designs I've seen in camp-craft books. I like to minimize
possessions that cost much money or time - things I must carry
with me or protectively store. I've found I can quickly improvise
comfortable seats from natural materials at hand.
There may be stumps, logs, or rocks I can use with little
modification. Or I may pile up big pieces of thick bark from old
stumps or fallen trees. (The bark, resistant to rot, separates
easily after the wood rots.) Or I may be able to support a chunk
of bark or a log on other logs, earth mounds, or other indigenous
features. At one camp, I hung a slab of bark from a slanting tree
to make a swinging chair - my favorite seat so far. Julie, Oregon

I plan to live in a tent at a nudist camp.
While attending massage therapy school in Tampa. Much cheaper
than other housing. I had almost given up the idea until I read
DP. Though I may not want to live out in the woods, I think DP
will help me live more cheaply and simply. I tend to have very
different ideas from what is the norm in the Deep South, so mostly
I keep quiet about them. Lory, Alabama, October

Upholstery remainders become a ten-by-twenty-foot wall tent.
I'm camping on private land with the run of near 600 acres,
in addition to 12 acres I share with my landlord's business. I'm
next to a pond in which I swam until October when it got too cold.
For $80 I bought 300 yards of upholstery material from a
factory that builds furniture. All roll ends or flawed. Most
pieces only a yard long, but plenty are 2 to 7 yards long. I will
sew the tent on a treadle sewing machine I ordered from Lehman's.
Meanwhile I'm living in a quickly deteriorating Wal-Mart
wall tent. I put a tarp over the top and as a windbreak, which
greatly extended the tent's life - else I'd be back under a tarp.

Since the end of July I've been splitting my time between my job and getting ready for winter. Short periods of intense activity as I acquired the funds for the next item needed, with long periods of inactivity between.

(Later.) I completed my tent. Unfortunately the temperature dropped before I could waterproof it, so I am dependent on the over-tarp/canopy for rain/snow protection. Most modern upholstery materials consist of a relatively durable fabric with a rubberized backing to which exterior latex enamel will adhere well for full waterproofing. I did paint some small pieces to test, and they are in much better shape than the exposed rubberized backing is.

To waterproof, add 2½ cups of water to a gallon of exterior latex enamel and apply with a 3-inch brush made for latex enamel.

Sewing tips: Use the 'Jeans' weight 'sharps' number 16 needles and size 50 or 60 polyester (dacron) or nylon thread to sew the tent. (Cotton thread will soon rot.) Guy R. Hengst, IN,
Oct & Febr

Evaluation of some widely-sold dome tents.

The June 97 Consumer Reports reported on tents and sleeping bags they had tested; about 20 of each. CR's "advice is mainly for casual campers (who camp near their vehicles) rather than serious backpackers who need ultra-lightweight compact equipment", and for people who camp only for short periods.

"After a summer outside, most tents were ready for the trash - victims of the sun's ultraviolet rays. That's because nylon (used for the roofs or walls) ages rapidly in sunlight." The only tent with "very good durability"in sunlight was Eureka Space III, a big cabin tent and, at $560, the most expensive.

Spraying the tents with Fabric Guard 303 retarded sun damage (how much not stated). One 16-oz can, $10-$15 (800-223-4303) does small dome; 4 cans big tent. Other brands tried,didn't work as well.

None of the tents blew away in a 22 mph wind, though the rain fly on a Coleman Sundome ripped.

CR tested two types of tents: cabins and domes. Of the two, domes seem the more useful to most DP readers because they can be erected quickly and are fairly light. (If staying in one place long, when erection time and weight aren't important, you can probably contrive a shelter better than any of the tents here.)

A large dome weighs 11 to 15 pounds; a small dome 7 pounds. After take down, a small dome is compact enough to backpack. A large dome is roomy enough for three; a small dome for two, says CR. Some manufacturers claim twice that many can fit in.

Features to look for: shock cords linking the segments of each pole; clips or brackets (rather than fabric sleeves) to attach tent to pole; seam sealant included with tent (apply it first time you set tent up); floor material that extends part way up walls; a rain fly with a peak over doors and windows (on some, the fly blocked window); at least one round (on top) window with a storm flap secured by a zipper with 2 pulls; FINE-mesh screens on door, windows and ceiling vents, to block gnats.

Of large dome tents tested, the 3 best, according to CR, in order: L.L.Bean Family Dome L377 $230; Eureka Sunrise 9 $230; Sierra Designs Mondo 5CD $500. All 3 rated excellent for rain protection (after seam sealant applied), and good+ for most other qualities EXCEPT durability in sunlight. Of the cheaper domes, Greatland (Target) Northridge 918093 $120, was generally good+ (except durability). LEAST durable: Coleman Sundome 9160E101 $135.

Good-to-excellent (except durability) small domes: Eureka Tetragon 7 $120; Coleman Sundome 9260D707 $70. NOT acceptable: American Camper Alpine 3 46471. Poles snapped while just setting.

Evaluating sleeping bags, CR found nylon covers and liners more durable than cotton; hollow-core fibers no warmer than ordinary polyester (but warned against half-poly half-"unknown-textile-fiber" mixes, which clump when washed); down warm and light, but absorbs moisture easily and difficult to dry. Manufacturers' temperature ratings were not accurate and generally

135

optimistic. "Our thermal tests of 8 bags rated from 0° to 40°
revealed only a 12° spread." (For full details, seek in library.)

(Comments:) To resist sunlight, instead of an expensive spray
(and how long before it flakes off?), I suggest setting the tent
in a shady place. If no natural shade, erect above it a cotton
canvas tarp, or an over-roof formed of poles/branches/ferns/straw/
leaves. Of course that will reduce light. But when brightness
important, best not use a solid-fabric tent. Buy or make an all-
net tent (eg, see May96 DP) and suspend a clear plastic tarp above.
    For go-heavy-and-stay-long camping, we recommend using 2 to 4
cheap sleeping bags, one inside or under the others. Cost less,
and easier to wash and dry than one arctic-rated bag. If you
sometimes use a sleeping bag as quilt, opened out, make sure its
zipper extends across the bottom. (Some mummy bags don't.) A
used bag of unknown history can be disinfected in a hot laundry
drier. Critters such as lice can be killed simply by enclosing
in a plastic bag for a month. Holly & Bert, Oregon, January

Further report on the Stansport dome tent.
    I reported in May 97 DP, the bottom-side seams leaked much.
Later, stuck inside the box, I found "Stansport Tent Tips" which
say: "... the sewing necessary in all tent fabrication can cause
water leakage.... We strongly recommend that the new tent be
erected before it is used and all seams treated with either Stansport seam sealer #344-F or Stansport silicon spray #DC-86."
    But Stansport did NOT include their sealer with the tent,
costing a customer time and delay to purchase separately. More
important: why didn't Stansport apply the sealant before shipping? Compared with sewing, the extra labor would be trivial.
My guess: because the sealant would separate from the seam when
the tent is folded for packing. (CR did not say if they erected
their test tents more than once.) If Stansport applied the
sealant, they'd get blamed. Whereas if the customer does, s/he
may assume s/he did something wrong. The basic fault is a seam
that needs sealing. (For a design that doesn't, see May95 DP.)

I made a very nice "space blanket".
    I affixed aluminum foil to a comforter I salvaged from a
dumpster. It needed 2 cans of Elmers spray-on glue and some
touching up after the first night's sleep, but I'm quite pleased
with the results. Kurt Wettstein, Illinois, December

How long-distance sport backpackers minimize weight.
    Ray and Jenny Jardine of LaPine Oregon have finished their
third through-hike of the Pacific Crest Trail, Mexico to Canada,
in a record 95 days. To average 33 miles a day, they carried
homemade gear weighing only 8½ pounds, not counting food.
    Ray's 28-ounce 8x8' tarp is roomier, lighter, better venti-
lated, and better rain protection than are most tents. It has
withstood 60 mph winds, and has no zippers to jam or poles to
break. Ray sewed 2 pieces of 1.8 oz urethane-coated nylon together along what becomes the ridge line, seam sealed, and added tabs
and reinforcements where lines attach. $15 plus 4 hours sewing.
    For a ground-sheet they use a trimmed 4-layer space blanket
($15). Even though it gets poked full of holes, it doesn't pass
too much moisture. Pack, and running shoes go under it as pillow,
which also keeps the shoes from freezing. They look for cushy
campsites that haven't been compacted by other campers, but also
carry pieces of closed-cell foam cut to torso width and length
($15). Though not enough insulation for sleeping on snow, the
Jardines find some bare ground almost everywhere, even in winter.
    Believing that a sleeping bag's under half is not very
insulating, they made quilts, each 79x58", 3 lbs, from synthetic
insulation sandwiched between 1.1 oz breathable nylon. $17 +
8 hrs sewing. One side white; one black. In sun with black side
up, "it'll dry within minutes."

They usually sleep in all their clothes for warmth and
mosquito defense. A piece of netting sewen to the head-end of the
quilt provides face protection. If weather too warm for the quilt,
they wear a nylon jacket and pants, and apply repellant to face.
All this goes in a 12-oz knapsack they made from 1.9-oz coated
nylon, with shoulder straps of Cordura-coated nylon and Beva Lite
#2 foam. With such light loads, frame and waist belt not needed.
They buy polyester dress shirts and light-weight nylon socks.
For those who sweat a lot, Ray says plain old polyester is better
than high-tech wicking fabrics, and in rainy conditions dries
faster. They make lycra shorts, Thermamax pants and shirt, and
fleece and nylon jackets. Each costs about $8 and 4½ hrs sewing.
For rain they carry umbrellas, lightened by removing springs
and trimming handles. In deserts the umbrellas, covered with
(aluminized?) mylar to reflect sun, provide shade.
They carry a basic model Swiss Army knife, no soap, no
deodorant (attracts bears, says Ray); floss and shortened toothbrush but no toothpaste. Total cost: $135 per person.
But Ray warns: "Hiking with minimal equipment requires much
greater proficiency. Until you have that, always carry backup
items. Always prepare for the worst that nature can throw at you."
Tina Kelley (Seattle Times 97/6/26,shortened; sent by Roger Knight)

Bicycle panniers strengthened by adding cord around bottom.
My original design (May97 DP) had the support cords attached
only to holes in the panniers. Recently, while carrying a very
heavy load, one of the holes ripped out. To repair, I cut a new
hole further down. I also tied an auxillary cord, to the support
cord and around the bottom of the pannier, to take much of the
weight. A rubber strap, horizontally around the pannier, helps
keep this cord in place. Julie Summers, Oregon, July

Mount pannier-support sticks over or under the bicycle's rack?
If the sticks are put on top, the lashings that hold them to
the rack can't stretch and possibly break under load. David French

(Reply:) I had said, I put the sticks under the rack, so they do
not raise a load placed on top. I now think the effect on stability
may be negligible. But something I didn't mention: sticks under
the rack, leaves the rack's spring clamp (if any) usable. Also,
the rack's top is left flatter, for better support of some loads.
If the lashings have enough wraps, they won't stretch or
break. The extra weight of lashing seems negligible. Julie

Report on self-stick patches for innertubes.
I bought an Advent Speed Patch (tm) kit for $2 at a local
bicycle shop in August 1997. Distributed by Service Cycle Supply,
Commack NY 11725. The kit contained 6 patches 1x1", and one
piece of sandpaper that size, in a mini-ziplock bag.
I used one in Sept. It held okay even though a bit of one
corner,where backing and patch had separated, did not adhere. The
backing seems to separate easily at the corners, just from moving
around in the package. After noticing this, I transfered the
patches to a plastic 35mm film can.
A more expensive brand was packaged in a hard plastic box.
The store clerk thought that only under very wet conditions
(heavy rain) would a patch with separate cement be more apt to hold.
I've had opened, carefully-recapped tubes of cement dry out -
discovered only when needed to fix a flat! Thus the appeal of
self-stick patches. But I don't know how long they will stay good.
Both kinds are over-priced - considering I find all the inner
tubes I need (including some with no leaks) in bike-store dumpsters.
But a patch kit is lighter and less bulky. I usually carry both:
one extra tube; and a patch kit (with both kinds of patches). Julie

Porcupine(?) bit tires of bikes stored over winter in woods.
Many punctures. Good to have extra tubes in critter-proof jar.

Acorns are high in energy and many other nutrients.
Oak trees grow from Maine to California, yet few people know
how to make acorns edible. The best way: shell, then cover with
warm (but not boiling) water. Let set. When the water becomes
brown, change it. Repeat until the water stays clear. Maybe 5
changes over 2 days. (The tannic acid is what makes acorns bitter
(and would cause a belly ache) and turns the water brown.) Then
(eg) grind them and make acorn pancakes - or experiment. Lance

Almost every wet area grows some cattail.
Young green shoots can be steamed, boiled, mixed in stews,
or eaten raw in salads. The cattails themselves (top portions of
stalk) are excellent in spring when tender. The roots are a
typical tuber that can be baked, boiled, or added to a main dish.
One thing that worries me about cattails is their ability to
thrive in polluted areas and filter pollutants from water. In an
emergency that might not deter me, but for day-to-day consumption
I'd select plants growing in relatively clean water. Lance Brown

More about wild salad plants of the Chicory Tribe.
I've noticed that several "false dandelions" seem less bitter
than true dandelion (Taraxacum officinale); enough so for the
leaves to be palatable and even delectable raw, at least during
winter and early spring, and in shady spots later. I wondered if
the difference was due to species or to growing conditions.
This February I came upon what I think is gosmore (Hypochoeris radicata) and dandelion growing side by side in a spot which,
then, was getting little sun. The leaves looked quite different:
gosmore had little or no indentations; dandelion had indentations
half their width, and were longer and less fuzzy. No flowers, so
identification not certain. Gosmore tasty; dandelion too bitter !
(Correction to May97 DP.) Last summer we returned to the
same area while the hawksbeard (Crepis setosa) was blooming. We
found that, unlike gosmore or dandelion, hawksbeard DOES have some
leaves on the flower stalk as well as basal leaves. The hawksbeard
was much less prolific than the summer before, being crowded out
by various perenials, indicating it is an EARLY pioneer. Holly, OR

Ramen-noodle soup-mix provides cheap no-cook snack.
I crunch the noodles some, add half the seasoning pack,shake,
and eat. The left-over seasoning I use with dinner; or save.
Ramen noodles contain much sodium (especially the seasoning)
so I would not try to live off them. But an occasional snack is
tolerable, because I don't often eat salted foods or add salt.
I've seen these soups on sale ten for $1. (If each 3 oz, ±
53¢/lb.) Not as cheap as some bulk foods, but much cheaper than
chips which is what I'd otherwise snack on. Lance Brown, Texas

(Comment:) I've also eaten these after moistening with warm-to-
hot (but not boiling) water sun-warmed in a jar or jug. Quite good.

What device do you recommend for cooking food in a car?
A friend and I plan a road trip, summer 1998. We won't be
able to start a fire every evening, and would like to be able to
cook inside (after we tire of eating cold snacks).
We plan to shower at beaches and parks; wash our clothes in
laundromats and dry on a string in the car.
If we need cash, we plan to stay in a town a few weeks and
get jobs. What skills should I learn for easy employment? I've
been a store cashier; also baby sat, washed dishes. Anne, NY

(Reply:) I've never cooked inside a car, and don't know what if
any device would work well. If all you want is a little hot soup
or drink, there are 12-volt emersion heaters that plug into a
lighter socket. Though more efficient than hot-plates, they do
take much electricity. Maybe okay if driving much, heating little.

Personally, I'd rather cook outside. Some waysides and city
parks (which are usually free unless overnighting) have barbeque
pits. Collect some firewood enroute in case woods near barbeque
are picked clean. I've heard that fast-food shops have a rapid
turn-over of employees. Bert and Holly, Oregon, January

Leaky fuel joint almost caused disaster.
      I've used my MSR-XGK stove
thousands of times without mishap.
Then last night after refueling I
didn't tighten down the fuel bottle.
A few drops leaked out and caught fire.
      At first I wasn't sure which way
to turn it to tighten the connection.
But to loosen it would be disasterous.
So I quickly took the stove outside where I shut it off.
      A few burning drops landed on the floor of my van but soon
went out. A few drops landed on my legs and also went out, but
today I notice blisters. Ouch !
      The XGK does not support a pot well. Its "legs" swing around
too easy (on mine anyway). So I use an old auto license plate
(with plastic previously burnt off in a fire) bent around the
burner for pot support. If the pot is small, I put a Backpacker
adjustable grill under it. Eugene Gonzalez, Arizona, October

Hot springs may spread diseases, but can be disinfected.
      In my area there are half a dozen natural, free, hot spring
pools I have used for years. Last year several were contaminated
by outside visitors with new hybrid virus strains to which I
lacked immunity. I picked up sinus, throat and other ailments
repeatedly. Now I take sterilization iodine (available from vet
and stock suppliers) and treat pools I suspect. Al Fry, Idaho

I hope to join or start a kayaking community.
      We would live on the coastlines of the Americas, migrating
seasonally. I like caravans, but not piling into pickups and
driving around. Not cost effective. Rolf Hardiek, Utah, Nov

Two old Solar Showers developed leaks around the fill holes.
      I discarded, and bought a new one at K-mart for $10. Eugene

(Comment:) Have you tried using unaltered plastic jugs for showers?
(Remove caps.) For years we've used nothing else. Jugs work fine
and save buying (or making) and storing unnecessary gadgets. The
first few showers may seem awkward, until motions become easy.

In a trailer, how to install plumbing so it does not freeze.
      May97 DP said, "Complex RV appliances are not reliable."
      SO TRUE. I gutted my trailer and threw out all the original
appliances. I put in a simple stove and a gravity-feed water
system. I put all my plumbing (plastic) INDOORS, with removable
sections for clean-out and repair, connected with flexible
(rubber) fittings. I sloped the pipes more than usual, to have
quick, complete drainage so no water remains in them to freeze.
      Last winter, my neighbors' new $40,000 trailers froze up.
Not mine, even with outside temperatures to minus 80oF.
      On very cold days I sprinkled some salt down the drain.
Helped prevent freezing. Last winter I used 12 lbs table salt.
      I engineered my drain system so my waste water flushes my
toilet. Saves much water. By mounting bath tub 6" above floor.
      If wintering in snow country, add a foot+ to the plumbing
vent sticking above the trailer's roof. Otherwise, snow will
cover vent and vacuum-lock plumbing, causing it not to drain.
Happened to my neighbors last winter.
      If buying a trailer, look for an older model with twin
I-beam frame and two axles. David French, South Dakota, May97

(Comment:) Put salt down a drain only if the plumbing is plastic or tile. Might corrode metal. If using much salt, look for non-food-grade (sold for industrial uses). Cheaper than table salt.

When rebuilding a van or bus into a motorhome:
        For framing, instead of wood I use slotted steel to which I can easily bolt. Bolts and nuts hold more reliably than nails/screws, and allow easier transfer to a future vehicle.
        I "module" everything for easier changes or replacement.
        I color-code wire and pipe systems for easier maintenance and fixing. I prefer "marine grade" electrical and plumbing parts because they are designed for long life in rough environments.
        Before refitting a vehicle, make an accurate drawing of its floor space, and maybe even build an interior model with modules to scale, to find best arrangement and avoid costly mistakes.
        I use bungee cords and small nets to secure loose objects, which otherwise become flying missiles during a "very sudden stop". (Once a heavy mug went through my windshield.)
        Even if the vehicle seems large enough to live in, carry along a large tarp or tent to provide extra space when parking in the boonies at one spot for quite a while. Even a modest dome tent serves to reserve a space when away a few days. A tent also provides personal shelter when the vehicle is in a repair shop. (Saves renting an expensive motel room.) Wildflower, CT, Febr

I am not homeless. My HOME is homeless.
        So says Guinea Apollos. She lives in a 1964 school bus, purchased 3 years ago when her income could no longer pay the rent of a small San Francisco apartment. She equipped the bus with stove, sink and spice rack; and brightened it with family photographs, potted plants, crocheted afgans, and window curtains.
        Although Guinea is as poor as many of the thousands of homeless on the streets, she believes her bus sets her apart. Some officials agree. They are considering a project that would stop the grim cat-and-mouse game that Apollos and many like her play with police. The city may build campgrounds in the port area, far from residential neighborhoods, where hundreds already park. Showers, toilets, laundries, a community room, and social and health services would be provided for car dwellers, who would be responsible for maintenance and security. With homeless shelters filled every night and hundreds more sleeping parks or business doorways, pressure is mounting on officials to do something.
        Sleeping in vehicles is presently illegal in SF between 10 am and 6 am. But typically, police move people or tow cars only if residents complain. One day last month, police ticketed 58 vehicles parked along one port-area street and later towed 17 of them. A few days after the sweep, some had already returned.
        Mike Waters, president of a charter-bus company whose bus yard is there, periodically asks police to move the campers along. "We've seen the street lined solid with campers, trucks and cars. They like to park here because they can get fresh water from our spigots. Most seem harmless, but some have dogs who chase my employees." Waters opposes building campgrounds. "I think it will be a waste of taxpayers' money. Some of these people have psychological problems and belong in supervised care. The others probably wouldn't have anything to do with such a place." Mary Curtius (from Seattle Times 10/22/97; sent by Roger Knight)

Life on the streets of downtown Eugene.
        When 14-year-old Olivia arrived in August, the mall seemed better than her mom's house. Mom drank and Mom's boyfriend was abusive. Olivia had much to learn and learn quickly. Her first night was tough. She didn't know where to sleep. A young girl asleep outside was an obvious target for sexual predation. Or if a cop found her, she could be locked up - it's illegal to sleep outside or in a park after 11 pm. The "mall rats" (other kids)

told her green, newspaper-recycling boxes were good. That's where
Olivia slept her first night. She removed some papers, flattened
the cardboard boxes, climbed in, and covered herself with papers.
   The veteran mall rats also told her which restaurants, such
as IHOP, would let you stay all night, until the 5 am breakfast
crowd came in, if you paid 99¢ for a bottomless cup of coffee.
   Olivia learned where to snag free food boxes (Catholic Community Services, St Vincent de Paul, Looking Glass); where to clean
up (public restrooms downtown); and how to get around town (LTD
central bus station). Above all she needed safety; provided by
other mall rats who looked out for her - her street family.
   The true mall rats were kids who had nowhere else to live,
and were able to get along with each other. Kids who didn't -
who refused to share food when they had it, stole from the other
kids, or narked to the cops - were ostracized, sometimes beaten up.
They wound up back with their parents, in foster homes, or jails.
   In July, life on the streets had seemed attractive, not only
to teens from bad homes, but to wanna-bes, rebels and thrill-seek-
ers to whom a teen-only world, without parents and responsibilites,
seemed preferable to the drudgery of school and rules. But by
December the number on the mall had plummeted along with temperature.
   Homeless runaway teens are becoming more visible. The North-
west's relatively mild climate and grunge image are attractive.
Brett Campbell (condensed from Eugene Weekly, August 1997)

States vary in regulation of home schoolers.
   Low-regulation states do not require parents to initiate
contact with officials: ID, IL, IN, MI, MO, NJ, OK, TX.
   High-regulation states require parents to send notification,
test scores and/or professional evaluation of progress; and may
require corriculum approval, parental qualification, or home visits
by officials: ARK, MA, ME, MN, ND, NV, NY, PA, UT, VT, WA, WV.
   Intermediate regulation states: those not listed above.
   Recently, on standardized tests, 5400 randomly-selected home
schoolers averaged 80; compared to 50 by state-school students of
similar ages, races and wealth. (0 to 100 scale.) NO correlation
between regulation level and achievement level. Now ± a million
home schoolers in America. Brian Ray, Home School Research Inst.,
                                            Salem OR, 1997?
Fix-a-Flat caused tire to thump.
   Fix-a-Flat is goopy-glooey stuff in a pressurized can used to
temporarily seal punctures. You are supposed to later have the
tire fixed at a service station. Instead, I plugged the leak
myself but used too much Fix-a-Flat (2 cans). A "thump" developed
and got progressively worse. At first I thought a brake cylinder
had seized and tried to fix it. But the thump remained. I finally went to a VW specialist who found the problem. Eugene Gonzalez

I sleep in my car under tule netting.
   I drape it over me if there is even one fly or mosquito
inside. I also use it to barricade each open window: I open the
door, drape the netting around the outside of the door, over the
top, and back out through the window; then close the door. That
leaves a gap between layers at the bottom, but few if any skeeters
find their way in. Won't stop gnats. 59¢/yard at fabric stores.
                                                        D.Dorji
I use spring shades as window covers and awning on my car.
   I have one for every window. I don't want to look up from
my bed and see a face, cop or otherwise, leering at me.
   While parked, if a window is open for ventilation, I lay a
spring shade on roof, overhanging window, as awning. I anchor by
setting a bean bag, rocks, or food cans on top of it.
   A spring shade goes from dish size to window size in one
swoosh and weighs only a few ounces. Auto stores/depts sell for
about $7. Cardboard would work, but not be as light nor fold so
neatly. Double Dorji, Arizona, June

Dwelling Portably

October 1998 $1 per issue

formerly named Message Post
POB 190, Philomath OR 97370
Add 50¢ to check/mo under $6

I have taken the first steps to a more mobile and free life.
I purchased a used van in good condition: ideal for the
open road. Also, I have been using only a pager with voice-
mail for the past two years, instead of a home phone. And, to
top it off, I have been receiving job offers in my chosen
field (a fast food) from people I know who will pay me under
the table. Bill, New York 139, June

More about trailer housing on Mid-west flood-plain farms.
In response to your objections (in Oct95 and Oct97 DPs):
Farmers would place fewer attachments on their trailers than
do trailer-park residents; knowing that emergency mobility was
why they chose trailers instead of permanent houses. And
mortgage insurers could restrict attachments. To avoid tire
problems, put run-flat or solid-rubber tires on trailers.
Even without such measures, a farm's six-trailer home
could be made ready to move in half a day at most, and moved
to high ground in another half day. In most floods that would
be quick enough, because there are usually days or weeks of
warning: true of the Upper Mississippi floods a few years ago.
Your suggestion that farmers commute to their fields from
homes on high ground, is common in Europe and might be good in
many flood-plain situations here. But trailers would be a
better choice where: (1) Severe floods are rare, and are
preceded by long warnings: consequently infrequent trailer
moves would be less burdensome than daily commuting.
(2) Unattended farm equipment or animals may be stolen or
vandalized. (3) No high ground near by to commute from (as
in the upper Midwest). (4) The family prefers a home with no
close neighbors (instead of in a cluster of houses on hill).
Trailers could be phased in naturally AFTER a flood, as
on-site emergency housing for victims. This may already be
done sometimes. (Long after a flood, the ground is too wet
for conventional rebuilding. Or infrastructure was destroyed,
as in Central America after the recent floods.) So victims
could/should be encouraged to continue living in trailers.
Trailer housing would also be advantageous in beachfront
areas subject to storm surges - the most damaging result of
hurricanes. Warning time is usually ample. Roger Knights, WA

Isolation did not foster individuality.
Pitcairn Island, a speck in the Pacific, is famous as the
refuge of the sailors who in 1789 mutinied on the ship Bounty.
Today it is inhabited by 38 descendants of those mutineers
and their native Polynesian spouses. The island has no autos,
sporadic electricity, and only a few simple appliances. No
ships dock there, though some pause to trade for mementos.
Is Pitcairn an idyllic haven? No, says Dea Birkett in
"Serpent in Paradise". Much on the island appealed to her:
the islanders' physical skills, good looks, and courage;
their pleasant demeanor; their curious language (a patois of
Polynesian and 18th-century English); their religious
devotion (they are 7th-day Adventists); and their friendly-
ness to her. But after several months she began to see that
envy and rivalry existed on Pitcairn as elsewhere, that
everybody watched everybody else, that gossip was the most
popular pastime, and that individuality was impossible in so
small a place. Not without some regret, Birkett had herself
ferried out to a passing freighter and headed home to London.
(from Parade 22Nov98; sent by Roger Knights)

With a bicycle, is a sidecar better than a trailer?
Responding to December 1997 DP, page 7: yes and no.
With a sidecar you can sit on a bike without having to
balance it. While underway you can reach into a sidecar for
goodies, or to adjust an auxillary motor or engine. You can
add a top cover and sleep in it or on top. A brake cable can
reach the sidecar but not a trailer. A sidecar can't fishtail
or jacknife as can a trailer.
On the other hand, a trailer is cheaper, easier to start
with, narrower, and tracks directly behind the bike.
As for forces sideways due to bike not tilting: no
problem with 20-inch wheels. Kids are rough on bikes, yet
I've repaired hundreds of bicycles and never seen a 20-inch
rim bent by side forces. Even better are 20-inch BMX wheels.
More spokes, thicker spokes, and wider and stronger rims.
I've used many on trailers I've built for people. The only
rims I've seen bent by side forces, were 26-27 inch, and they
only with forces of a 300-400 pound load. If bent, you just
kick them and they snap back into shape.
I have been in third-world countries and seen many
bicycles with sidecars. David French, South Dakota 577, March

(Comments:) For items accessed while moving, a small handlebar basket suffices me. Why can't a trailer be covered as
easily as a sidecar? Or slept in? (Maybe make it just big
enough for head and body, with pull-out extension for legs.)
For abrupt stops, have brakes applied by springs after
pulling a release cord? Disadvantage: must stop and dismount
to release. But mostly used on long hills, and emergencies.
All our bikes (old) have 26-27" wheels. I've seen no
adult-size bikes with 20" wheels, except folders. Big wheels
have less rolling resistance. (Enough less to matter?)
Yes, with a trailer, jackknifing might be a problem. But
with a sidecar, might spins be a problem, set off by unequal
braking? Eg, after partly missing a puddle, the sidecar rim
is wet while the bike rims are dry.
In a third-world city I might prefer a sidecar.   If
most traffic bicycles and moving at bicycle speed, the width
is not as hazardous. And, with many petty thieves, a sidecar
would be less easily stolen from at stop lights. But on North
American streets and highways, I believe I would prefer a
trailer. Makes me a slimmer target. Holly & Bert, OR 973

I plan an extended bicycle trip of the U.S., Mexico, Canada.
I will leave between September and December. How can I
make money along the way to keep me going? (How do I parlay
my skills into successful bartering or day labor, for food,
shelter or cash? Will I get a good reception doing this?)
How do I learn to dwell more portably? (Currently I do
lots of camping. I also stay with other cyclists.)
How do I meet up with like-minded people? (I've done
several long tours, mostly skirting the cities in favor of
rural places, and have met nice farmers, Amish folk, laid-back
suburbanites, etc., but no real counterculture people like I
imagine read Dwelling Portably. Jerome, OH 452, June

(Reply:) If you camp for free and eat economically, you
should not need much money. One summer, Holly and I biked
several hundred miles to a Rainbow gathering in northeastern
Calif, and made more than enough money picking up drink cans
along the way. (5¢ deposit in OR. Now in most states?)   We
ate mostly bulk foods (much dry oatmeal); some bread and marge.

Departing in autumn, you will encounter cold weather (unless you winter in southern Mexico), and the additional insulation may reduce portability. You might TRY (best test beforehand) using only one light sleeping bag, augmented over and under with leaves, moss, crumpled newspapers, or whatever, gathered locally. What you have been doing to meet people, sounds effective. DP readers are very varied. No one method of meeting people will work with all. Bert & Holly, OR 973

I lived on my bicycle for three months during summer 1985.
Saved much money on rent. Had fun too. Washed at the river, and when I went swimming in the lake. (Dr Bonners soap works well in cold water.) David French, SD 577, 1997

Lives in and travels with trailer from Midwest to Southwest.
After retiring, I traveled to Yuma AZ and spent the winter there. In the spring I returned to MN and SD where I have ties. This Midwest summer has been strange. My little travel trailer suffered a hail storm in MN. Only cosmetic damage - the skin looks like a bad case of cellulite, but the insurance company considered it a total loss and paid off the loan, so in essence I got a free trailer.
I plan to return to Yuma in September, leave my trailer there, and drive on into Mexico in December with my canine companion. My son lives in Mexico City, so I plan to get as close as common sense allows: the pollution there is horrid. I've done research on retiring in Mexico, and talked to friends.
Incidentally, there were a number of Oregonians in Yuma. I hate to say so, but they seemed red-neck. Maybe it was their age, or maybe it was me. I wouldn't want to live among them. Supposedly, Oregon is beautiful. But what about the political/ social climate? Are some areas friendlier than others? That is true of Minneapolis and Rapid City. I guess us non-traditionals just have to nose around to find our place. Vardo,
SD 577, July
(Reply:) I can't say from personal experience (our contacts are either too selective and unconventional, or too fleeting). But based on statistics we've read (eg, Abapa Freer), per capita, Oregon has more social/political non-conformists of most types than does any other state. Hippies, punks, gays, greens, reds, libertarians, pagans, atheists, whatever.
Us non-conformists are not evenly distributed. Most are around Portland (biggest city); Eugene, Corvallis, and Ashland (university cities); and some coastal areas. The rest of Oregon may be more like Idaho than like the above places.
If you live in an area where there are many non-conform- ists, the upside is: you are more likely to find people like yourself. The downside is: some narrow-minded people feel threatened by all the "weirdos" around - more so than where non-conformists are scarce and may be regarded more as curiosities than threats. (South Dakota?) Holly & Bert

I found a nice place in an otherwise-uncampable area.
It has picturesque scenery, remarkably friendly people, and will let you stay there occasionally in a tent or RV in exchange for some work. It has a sweat lodge, features trading events, and is non-profit, dedicated to wildlife. For info: Silverado (or Belle Santos), POB 5434, Bisbee AZ 85603.
Michael, OR 970, July
I have been living homelessly on the East Coast a few years.
Soon I will be moving to the Pacific Northwest; toting a backpack with all that I own in it. Eric, VA 229, February

Dwelling Portably

formerly named   Message Post
POB 190,   Philomath OR 97370

May 1999 $1 per issue   Add 50¢ to check/mo under $6

I use a Sierra Designs "Flashlight" tent.
      I have had three since 1983. My first two, the smaller
model, are still in use by friends. I now have the larger
model. I sewed a 4" extension on the edge of the fly so as to
cover the tent's seams. Recently I tried ironing on tarp tape
over all the bottom seams. So far the tape is holding well.
(Seam sealant is expensive, toxic to breathe, and a hassle to
apply.) I've had good experience with these tents. But I take
time to care for them and I keep them out of direct sunlight.
      Many years I traveled by motorcycle or bicycle, living
outside 6 months or more per year, mostly in drier, eastern
Washington. But I've also used the tent in wet climates and,
with my modifications, it does well. Laura LaBree, WA 981,Nov

Bike rack made from branches.
      This autumn, at a yard
sale, for $5 I bought
an old 3-speed. It
had sat unused for
years in a garage and
both tires were
deflated, but it was
otherwise ride-able.
No basket or rack.
It had a step-thru
("girl's") frame,
and while playing
with sticks to rein-
force the top, I
realized that two
sticks, criss-crossed,
and extending back-
wards, would also
provide a rack.
      For the two main
sticks, I used ± 5/8" diameter

green willow branches, because they were prevalent where
I was. For the other sticks, smaller diameters. (I prefer
western red cedar (Thuja plicata) when available, for its rot
resistance. I also prefer dry wood, for lightness. But green
wood will gradually dry.) I did not peel because I liked the
bark's color for camo when stashing bike, and I lacked time.
      The main sticks were curved, so I mounted them bowing
outward in the rear for greater rack-width. (I later replaced
them with straight, aluminum ski poles I found in a dumpster,
which were lighter. Both worked fine.)
      Later, I sawed off the front extension, because if bulky
objects were put on it, they interfered with steering. Also,
the rack not turning along with the handlebars, visually
disconcerted me (though I might have become accustomed).
      I lashed the rack together and to the bike with rubber
straps cut from discarded (holey) bike innertubes. Multiple,
tight wrappings gave a very strong joint. Time allowing, I
may cover the joints with duct tape. Otherwise sunlight will
deteriorate the rubber. Julie Summers, Oregon 973, Sept 97

Tip for cutting innertube into straps with uniform width.
      I first cut along seam, then in half, and half again until
narrow enough. (Halfing easier than cutting narrow off wide.)

When lifting a bicycle over a fence.
Goes easier if the handlebar or front wheel are fastened
so they can't pivot. Safer, too, so the handlebar won't pivot
unexpectedly and poke an eye. I tie twine to the down-tube,
at the point closest to the front wheel. Then I loop the
twine around the wheel-rim and tube a few times and tie again.
If encountering many fences, to save time I might leave
the twine permanently fastened to the down-tube. Julie, 1996

Shifting gears on a three-speed bike.
If shifting from low to medium
is unreliable, try this. Shift from
HIGH to medium, and then adjust the
indicator rod so its shoulder is flush
with the end of the axle (seen through
an observation hole in the sleeve part
of the axle nut).

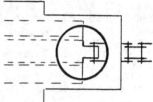

Then, whenever shifting to medium,
always go FROM HIGH. (If in low, go first to high, then med.)
The reason: There is a spring that gets compressed when
shifting down, and expands when shifting up. I guess it
weakens with age or rust and does not expand the same each
time. But when compressed, it necessarily moves the same each
time, and hence returns to where it was adjusted.
When I am done riding, I leave the gears in high, to
release compression on the spring. Julie Summers, 1992

Loading a bicycle for stability.
Put heavy items low and toward the center. I strap (eg)
grain sacks in the triangular frame section, if they are
narrow enough to not interfere with my legs. I put next-dense
items toward the front of panniers; somewhat lighter objects
rearward; and lightest bulk (sleeping bags; foam) on rack.
(This assumes the panniers cannot swing. If they can, I put
only light things in them.) Water bottle and in-route food go
in handlebar basket along with excess clothes as removed. Be
sure straps don't dangle where they could catch in wheels.
If you wear loose long pants, strap bottoms snug so they
can't snag on something and prevent putting a foot down. H & B

Don't be blinded by a bungee.
If the bungee is stretched, and you lose your grip or the
bungee breaks: WHAM ! No telling where the hook will go.
Instead of bungees, I use rubber straps, doubled to provide
loops. There is usually a projection to put the loop over.
(If not, I may permanently mount a strong hook.) Julie, Dec.

I love to bicycle, but fear for myself when on the road.
One year, when camped in eastern Washington, I rode 34
miles (round trip) to town once a week. Several times I was
almost killed by unyielding motorists. Laura, November

Suggestions for safer bicycling on roads.
Well-known precautions include: being visible (bright/
light-colored upper-body clothing); wearing helmet (cheap at
thrift stores); riding single file; riding slow or walking
where gravel ; not arguing right-of-way, especially with
anything bigger; checking tire inflation and wheel fastenings
often; and avoiding busy streets if there are bike paths or
low-traffic byways. Some less known or less heeded:
Never ride faster than you are willing to crash. A tire
may blow, an axle break, or a deer dart out unexpectedly.

A long down-grade before an up-grade tempts me to let bike gain speed. Risky! On a two-lane road lacking wide paved shoulders, avoid double passing. Ie, do not get passed simultaneously by over-taking and oncoming vehicles. Anticipate passings, stop, and get off of pavement. Also be wary when on curves or summits where an overtaking vehicle cannot see what is oncoming. Some cyclists believe they have as much right to the road as motorists and refuse to get off: forcing overtaking vehicle to either slow to bike speed, or try to squeeze by. That is not only dangerous, but angers motorists who then may agitate for anti-bike laws.

Bert rides some highways I won't, by alternately sprinting and resting. During pauses in traffic he sprints; then when the next "convoy" comes along, he gets off and lets it pass.

If you must stop (other than briefly to let traffic pass or to check bike), get completely off the road and OUT OF SIGHT. Don't be a "sitting duck" for motorized predators, uniformed or other-wise. A stopped vehicle (of any kind) is an easier, more tempting target than is a moving vehicle. (Last summer, on a secondary road, Bert and I stopped for a mid-day snack, well off the road but visible from it. We were not on posted land nor near any building. We were clean and "decently" dressed (not bikini weather). As we stood by our bikes eating/drinking (not smoking), a county cop drove in and began interrogating us: "Where you coming from?" Where you go going?" After his first questions, we mostly ignored him and busied ourselves putting away lunch remnants. Maybe that was a good tactic: at least he soon left. Why did he accost us? We were easy prey: already stopped where he could park off the road. (Stopping ON that stretch of road would be hazardous: no shoulders; few pull-offs; many blind curves.) He may have hoped we were affluant sport-cyclists (many use that road) who would pay a fine no matter how wrongful, rather than go to court. But when he got close, he saw our old bikes and non-snazzy clothes. (Local police don't like to fill jails with poor "hobos" who can't pay fines.) That was the first time either of us have been hassled in over 20 years.)

The safest time to travel is usually very early Sunday mornings, especially in late spring and early summer when days are long. Few motor vehicles, no/little frantic commuting-to-work traffic, and most police are sleeping after scoring on party-goers the night before. Next safest: early Saturday morn. H&B

Camping with horse and milk goat.
Horses aren't for everyone. They are BIG strong animals and can easily panic. For beginners I recommend donkeys.

I've worked with horses most of my life and spent long periods in the back country with one or more pack horses.

One horse can carry 150 lbs: enough for a very plush camp. I usually have along a cast-iron skillet and dutch oven. I prefer wool blankets to nylon sleeping bags, and a horse easily packs all the wool I need. By eating mostly whole grains and foraging greens, I can stay out months without trips to town for supplies.

Move the horse often, to not over-graze one spot. I use a 50' picket rope. If necessary, I can hide my camp, horse and all. During the day I keep the horse in woods or brush; then, after dark, put it in open pasture to graze.

I don't get hassled in National Forests because I keep moving. And most Green Meanies like horses. The only place I've ever been hassled was on a state beach in California; and there only because I was still in camp at noon. I could have avoided trouble by moving early. But I recommend staying out of California no matter how you travel.

In populated areas, I've camped along the edges of highways. A horse changes people's attitudes. Many strangers are friendly and helpful, offering pastures for grazing, back yards for camping, and gifts of hay. On the road, people stop and give me money. I've taken long bicycle trips and never had that happen.

I live in a horse-drawn wagon-camper during cold weather. I mostly park it on a friend's private property. I don't like using it on highways because car drivers are crazy and in a big hurry. But I know quite a few folks who do.

I often have a milk goat along. She forages as we hike and turns brush and leaves into a high-protein drink. A goat can't walk as far or as fast as a horse or human. But I do more wandering than treking and am willing to wait for the goat as she's got the lunch with her. A milk goat can't be used as a pack goat, as she needs all her energy to make milk. I've found that one horse plus one goat work well, and keep each other company if you need to leave them briefly.

I hope more people use horses as their main transportation. The oil-burning-auto lifestyle is most damaging of Mother Earth. Dancing Bear, ID 834, Jan.

Two kinds of police at Mexican border.
The regular U.S. Border Guards were polite and efficient, and did not seize or damage the anti-biotics I had bought in Mexico (which, though legal in and manufactured in U.S., are almost imposs-ible to obtain in U.S. (because U.S. MDs, fearful of serious side-effects that could bring law suits, won't prescribe?))

But also at the border were specially assigned police, probably all from the Drug Enforcement Agency though they often wore uniforms of various other agencies including Forest Service. All looked similar: wiry males, tobacco-stained, and contageously nervous. And all were trouble: sticking dirty knives into sterile factory-sealed packages.

I have heard the DEA may be withdrawn. Meanwhile, best remain in Mexico while taking any medicines bought in Mexico. Michael, Oregon 970, December

Be careful with ID and credit cards.
Do not carry them on your person, especially not where you might be robbed. If you have only cash, the robber will take it and hopefully let you go. But if you have credit or bank cards, the robber has an incentive to kill you so you can't report the theft while he, or an accomplice who resembles you, cashes them or makes purchases. (I've never seen store clerks examine ID carefully. If they did, ID would be seldom usable, because most people's looks change too

147

much.) Also, if the robber is "wanted", he may desire your ID so he can impersonate you if he meets cops.

If driving, keep your drivers license hidden in the vehicle where you can get it if police stop you and demand it. But not on your person. Likewise with a credit card: retrieve only when you arrive at the store. (We recommend not having credit cards. They incur high charges, and encourage impulse buying and excessive consumption. H & B)

Some cities and states try to require carrying ID. But such laws have been ruled unconstitutional when appealed. Police would like everyone to carry ID so they can process subjects faster, levy more fines, and improve promotion prospects. (The police might also like everyone to be tatooed with a number, like in Nazi slave-labor camps.) The police don't much care if more people are murdered as a consequence: in fact, the more crime, the better for police - as long as most ~~sheep~~ citizens respond by voting more funds for police.

I've heard, some airlines require ID, even on domestic flights. Boycott them.

Most foreign nations require ID for admission. I would not go there, at least not for recreation. If interested in some far-away place, I can learn more easily, quickly, economically and safely through books, zines, recordings and videos than by actually going there for a few weeks. Or, if I seek live novelty, I am more apt to find it nearby because I can better search nearby. Most major cities and some smaller ones have ethnic neighborhoods, stores, festivals, etc.

However, if you must travel abroad, keep your passport and other important papers hidden next to your body. Also carry small bills in a wallet or purse for surrendering to a robber.

If stopped by police, make sure they ARE police before giving them anything important. Gangsters often impersonate police. When you check their ID by phoning their (supposed) headquarters, look up the number in a phone book. (Do not merely call a number they might give you.) Steve, New Mexico 880, November

Helping lost children survive.
A child can get lost anywhere. I live in a small town on a cul-de-sac where everyone has several acres. One morning, a young girl who lives some distance away, became lost and wandered to within 50 yards of my neighbor's house, only to die at the gate to the yard. To help avoid such tragedies, have each child:

Wear red or orange outer garments.

Carry a whistle. It takes less energy and can be heard farther than a voice.

Carry a clean trash bag. And teach: If becoming cold or wet, put bag on over head, after making hole for face.

Once you know you are lost, hug a tree. If you stay in one place, you'll be found quicker and can't be injured by falling. If scared, hugging may calm you.

If at night you hear a sound, yell at it, but remain where you are. If it is an animal, you will scare it away. If it is a searcher, you will be found. (Fears often cause children to run.)

Hundreds will search for you. Do not fear them, or feel ashamed of getting lost. (Some kids, afraid of strangers or men in uniform, or of parents' wrath,

hide and don't answer calls.)

Try to pick a tree to hug near a clearing. If you have spare energy, make a big SOS in the clearing out of broken shrubbery, rocks, or by dragging foot. Whether or not you do, when you hear a low-flying aircraft, go out into the clearing and lay down, outstretched, to look bigger from above.

For retention, make these teachings into a game. Ken Larson, GA 301, 1997

(Comments:) I like the trash bag idea but have doubts about some others.

Among thick foliage, which absorbs high frequencies, a voice may be heard farther than a whistle. Also, around here, a common bird call sounds identical to many whistles. Teach: call or whistle in groups of three.

Red does not show well in twilight or dense woods. Wear orange or bright blue (which, unlike orange, can't be mistaken for autumn foliage). Or maybe best: blue bottom with orange top.

Hundreds will search? Don't count on that unless you're a VIP. Even if they do, foul-ups may delay search many hours. (Instances reported in Signpost zine.)

Do not fear? Most kids are taught to fear strangers, and such fears may also be instinctive. Unrealistic to expect an abrupt change of feelings.

Hug a tree? May be best if weather is warm or if child has ample clothing. If not, the child may die from chilling before being found. (Would tree-hugging have saved that young girl?) Also, a tree with big dead limbs is dangerous in wind, and a lone tree or tree taller than nearby trees is dangerous in lightning. Instead, I would equip the child with bright ribbons ALL THE SAME COLOR (which can be cut from worn-out plastic shopping bags) and teach: During daylight, keep moving and try to find your way to other people. But, as you go, tie a ribbon every 20 paces or so. Under each ribbon, form an arrow (can be just >) with foot-rub or broken branch, to show direction of travel. Searchers are much more likely to cross such a trail than to happen upon a motionless child; and once they do, they can easily follow it to the child. Also, that helps child detect if s/he is walking in circles.

City and Suburban Survival: Tom Brown's Field Guide (with Brandt Morgan, 1984, 266 p., Berkley, 200 Madison Av, NY 10016)

"No amount of insurance can guarantee that we won't lose our homes or jobs, but if we know how to fend for ourselves, we will be able to enjoy our lives whatever the outward circumstances."

"Some survival situations are so dismal that if we stop to consider all that is left to endure, we will be overwhelmed by despair.... The only way to get through, is one moment at a time."

In crises, many people make wrong choices. Eg, many die in fires because "they were too modest to leave the house without their clothes. Don't be afraid to act boldly."

You can slip a few pages of flattened newspaper "inside a meagre jacket (front and back) to create a weather break..." For sleeping, a newspaper spread over the body serves like a blanket.

"Good heat insulators ... contain a lot of dead air space that can trap and hold the heat." To increase insulative qualities of paper or other thin material, crumple, or put in separated layers. "Even fir springs can have a tremendous warming effect (within clothes) if you tie off your cuffs to keep the stuffing in."

As umbrella, Tom suggests: "Take a cardboard box (found in dumpster) ... and hold it, spread flat, over your head...." "Many other useful shelter items can be found in dumpsters and alleyways. Boxes, packing crates, plastic sheeting, and other untainted debris can be used in much the same way as furniture to form a protective shelter." Eg, a hut made of mattresses.

"There is no way for the human body to warm a whole room, much less an entire house. If it's cold and you have no additional heat source, make a small shelter - the smaller the better" - within the house if it is warmer than outside. But never have flames of any kind inside a mini shelter.

"Almost any open flame can be made more efficient by enclosing it in a metal container. Instead of quickly escaping, the heat ... collects and radiates through the walls of the container, casting its warmth in all directions. This is what stoves are all about." If making one from a coffee can, "to create draft, punch holes around sides at both ends...." The heat from 3 candles may be enough to boil a cup of water.

To make "canned" fuel, roll up a strip of corrugated cardboard (as wide as a tuna-size can is high) and fit it snuggly into can. Pour in paraffin, leaving $\frac{1}{4}$" of cardboard sticking out for lighting. (Review by Julie Summers)

A way to dry a small quantity of kindling.

When the whole world seems wet and I plan to build a fire later that day, I gather some tinder and kindling (for least damp, I look under leaning trees or logs), put loosely in an extra T-shirt (or wrap in paper), and place inside my upper garments next to my body. In a few hours (if not too wet or too much or too big chunks) my body heat will dry it.

To ignite still-damp kindling, I place a candle beneath for a few minutes. Conserves lighter or matches. Once a fire is well started, it will burn quite wet wood. To partially dry, I place the next pieces near the fire.

Body heat can also dry (eg) cap or mittens.   B & H, Dec

Butane lighters survive wetting well.

They are temporarily disabled, but okay after drying out. Some lighters I had stored a few years still work fine. Whereas "waterproof" matches, after long storage, light unreliably or not at all. They seem to absorb moisture.

All butane lighters I've had, worked fine except for ones with the confounded "child-proofer". But it can be pried out.
Julie, Oct

Brief suggestions for building a winter shelter.

Designs in past DPs include: Tleanto, Sep85; Hillodge, Apr92; Snugiup, May95; Twipi, LLL. However, I usually tailor shelter to site, rather than follow plans exactly.

Choose a site sheltered from: wind and lightning (avoid ridge tops); water (avoid gulch bottoms; flood plains); big animals and people (avoid houses, campgrounds, cow pastures, easy-hiking terrain; also read May95 DP). Generally best: south slope (for solar heating) but not near top (windy) or bottom (cold sink). If possible, prepare site before hunting season, but wait until after hunting season to move in.

Cut as little vegetation as possible. Digging is usually easiest when soil is moist but not soppy. In this area, best done the previous winter or spring.

If rain or snow expected soon, erect roof first. If you will depend on rain water, think about how roof can catch it.

Use mostly materials occuring at or near site. If you will only sleep in the shelter, all natural stuff may suffice. Otherwise, I'd also use plastic: for window; and perhaps an under-roof to intercept leaks and sifting debris.

Make one wall entirely or mostly of plastic and face it toward the most open sky. (That is simpler, and better for light, than are little windows all around.) Hang plastic vertical or (if reflections might attract attention) with bottom further in. At least 2 layers spaced ½" to 1" apart.

For the other walls, and ceiling, use anything fluffy that can be easily contained. Eg, bags of leaves or moss; or inner and outer wattles (interwoven branches) with insulation between. CAUTION: don't put weight where could fall on you !

In most areas, the best floor is earth: smoothed and packed, and maybe covered with semi-stiff plastic (eg, lino-leum): easier to wipe than is limp plastic. Earth stores heat (or cold) and warms a shelter in cold weather (and cools it when hot): much more comfortable than a raised wooden floor. If water seepage may become a problem, ditch around.

For warmth, the best entrance is from below, so heated air (which tends to rise) does not escape when hatch opened.

If using combustion inside, be very careful, not only to avoid setting the shelter on fire, but to provide enough ventilation. (Carbon monoxide is sneaky and deadly. People have been killed by candles in air-tight tents. However, every site-built shelter of ours has been leaky enough for candles and a propane stove without extra vents. A bigger problem has been mosquitos infiltrating during warm weather. We often need an insect net hung inside, at least at night.)

If in an unfamiliar environment or type of shelter, have a back-up shelter handy. Bert & Holly, Oregon 973, January

Blockage of trailer's heater nearly kills movie actress.

On location near Reno, Jenny McCarthy was in her trailer. "My heart started palpitating.... I got dizzy. I was nauseous and started convulsing. Everything was going black."

She collapsed to the floor but managed to crawl to the door, open it, and tumble out. Oxygen was administered in the ambulance. The hospital released her later that day. The doctor said, the convulsions indicated she was near death.

The crew had taped plastic tightly around the trailer's bottom to keep the water pipes from freezing. That blocked air circulation to the heater. Carbon monoxide built up and seeped into the trailer. (From 29 Dec 98 National Inquirer, sent by Roger Knights)

My dog and I live in a 1979 Chevy van.

We are relatively safe and comfortable on 3 acres of wooded residential property on the fringes of Chattanooga. By being here, we provide some security for the owner's two vacant houses. But I'm free to go away for long periods. I have enough privacy to be nude when temperatures permit.

My only source of income is occasional climbing for a tree-care service. My casual employer reaches me via phone with answering machine located inside one of the houses.

I could move into the house for more living space. But I am happier in my little box on wheels. Everything is within reach, and the small kerosene heater makes the inside toasty even on the coldest nights. Jimmy, Tennessee 374, February

I have lived year around in my 26' Nomadics tipi over 4 years.

I plan to relocate out west. Paul, VA 228, Feb 98

Live cheap and portable. Have nothing government can seize.
    I have lived on a farm since I graduated in 1971. Took
me until last year to pay it off. All 640 acres. I worked
night shifts and day shifts and farmed, and had a wife and
family. It seemed to make sense: my ancestors had done it
and I was trained to.
    Now I am 45 and look back with an emptiness. I'd wanted
to camp and travel and maybe even sail a boat to taste the
variety and wonders of the world. Instead, all those years
were spent complying with government farm programs: do this,
do that; plant this, plant that. Once you have a big stake
you can never leave. You will not own it; IT WILL OWN YOU.
    I encourage DP readers to stay small. Limit possessions
to things that are portable and concealable. I have become
defensive because of a bitter divorce I never wanted. But
because of money and possessions I was forced to play the
game. Roger, Kansas 677, November

I have been living "primitively" off and on for ten years.
    For the past 7 months, I've been in the Kiamichi Mtn
Wilderness Area on the Oklahoma/Arkansas border in Ouachita
Mtns. No electricity or running water. Sharon, AR 719, June

Backwoods nomadics: problems; solutions.
    Here are questions Bert and I are asked. Our answers
apply to OUR way of life. What works well for us here, will
not necessarily work for someone else, somewhere else, or in
a different portable dwellingway. (There are many kinds.)
    Do you gather/hunt most food? Or buy? Income sources?
    Sometimes we forage much; sometimes little; depending on
season and opportunities. We forage mostly fruit (berries) and
salads. Most calories come from purchased foods. Grains cheap
if bought in bulk. Occasional short, low-pay jobs suffice.
    How do you handle medical emergencies? Snake bites, etc?
    We have not had major traumas. Minor injuries we treat
ourselves. We do have (eg) "Ship's Medicine Chest and Medical
Aid at Sea" on microfiche for consultation. But we emphasize
prevention: hike carefully to not break limb or step on snake;
avoid constipating diet that might cause appendicitis; and
sleep/rest plenty to keep immune system potent. Prevention is
more important than response, because even someone living next
door to a hospital will die if injured badly enough. In a few
cases I might die while a house-dweller could be saved. But
overall, most house-dwellers are much more at risk. Eg, they
commute daily in frantic rush-hour traffic, to pay for their
houses and for the vehicles needed to commute. Each year,
traffic accidents kill MANY more people than do snake bites.
    How often do you move? And how? Only with backpack and
bike? Or motor vehicle too? Do you lug typewriter along?
    We move quite often (maybe 5 or 10 times) during the warm
dry season when we need only light equipment; seldom during
winter. Like some traditional nomads, we move mostly within a
home range ± 50 miles across, where we are not far from cached
supplies. We own no motor vehicle, but sometimes borrow,
rent, share or hire one to (eg) bring in much food supplies.
    Our typewriter remains with winter-base-camp equipment
and thus may move only once a year and only as far as our base
camp moves (seldom far). If we will be away from the base-
camp area most of the summer (usually), we pack away things
that rodents could damage: into plastic pails, trash cans, or
barrels. (The plastic barrels (olives or pickles were shipped
in) are stronger and seal better than trash cans, but aren't
as available and don't have as wide openings.)

Do you camp alone? Or with a group? How big? Clumped or spread out? If spread, do you visit? Hold gatherings?

Sometimes we camp alone; sometimes with others, depending on proximities and activities. If with others, we spread out, with camps ± a mile apart for easier tolerance of differences. We don't visit each other's camps (apt to annoy) nor try to gather everyone together (difficult). Each pair of families who wish to interact, choose a spot to meet at or to leave/pick-up items lent/swapped/bought-for. For us, winter is better than summer for interactions (other than chance meetings at events), because we have more free time then, and because we move less often and know farther in advance where we may be. (Most winters, some fairly mild dry days here.) Population unpredictable. (Sometimes zero: all are elsewhere.)

H & B

A simple home-made washing machine.

Salvage a 5-gallon pail with lid. Cut a hole in lid big enough for the handle of a plunger (a rubber bell-shaped device sold for unplugging drain pipes). Add plunger, clothes, water and soap (or whatever you wash with). Close lid. Voila ! Patricia MacKenzie, NY 130, February

(Comment:) Instead of plunger, may use any smooth stick with fork on end in pail. (Julie's tip in Apr92 DP.) The lid with hole (new idea) prevents much splashing of water out of pail.

To pour into a narrow-mouth container.

One way to avoid spilling: use a funnel. But suppose the opening is narrower than the funnel's spout. Or suppose you don't have a funnel along when (eg) you are hiking and want to pour some iodine solution from your crystals bottle into your canteen.

Fortunately there is a neat way. I suppose chemists use a glass rod to guide the flow. I use a grass stem or twig; or finger if opening is wide.

Hold stem vertically. Place bottom of stem into the container receiving but without touching its opening. Place the lower lip of the source in contact with the stem. Pour slowly. The water will flow along the stem. Julie Summers, 1997

Another way to make a faucet from a plastic jug.

Poke a pin-hole near the bottom. Fill with water. When ready to wash hands, loosen the cap. The weight of the water will force a small stream through the hole. When done, tighten the cap. If the cap is airtight (if leaky, add a plastic liner), the water will stay inside the jug. David French, SD

(Comments:) Compared with Julie's inverted-jug faucet (in LLL Packet), advantages we see for this upright-jug faucet: Hands don't touch spout. If spout is above the bottom, any debris may settle to the bottom and not interfere with flow or stoppage. (With inverted jug, debris may get between lip and cap, causing leak.) Cap-thread size doesn't affect flow. (With inverted jug, thread size critical; new milk jugs have threads too fine.) A jug is easier to tie to a tree or pole when it is upright. Unscrewing of cap isn't critical. (With inverted jug, if cap is unscrewed too far, it comes off and dumps all the water.)

Advantages we see for an inverted-jug faucet: The jug need not be strong. (A milk jug, left full of water, was collapsed by a vacuum after a slow leak developed.) The flow stops immediately when the cap is tightened. (With upright jug, the flow continues until a vacuum builds.) Flow rate is more easily adjusted. The jug is easier to clean (if filler hole big enough for hand).

A naturist park with portable dwellings.
(This is fiction. Any similarities to real places is not admitted.)

Valley View Park is located part way up Maple Mountain near Varied Valley, 50 km (30 miles) from Central City.

To minimize initial costs, property taxes and building-code hassles, Valley View has only portable structures.

The facilities dome, 16 meters (or yards) diameter and 5 m tall, consists of an open geodesic framework on which are layed various covers. On hot days: reflective tarps overhead and on the west for shade, with insect netting on other sides. On cool days: clear covers toward sun, with insulation on other sides. At night: complete insulation.

The dome contains: small pool; salad garden; communications center (phone, fax, etc); library (mostly fiche); frig (solar powered); and the Eatery.

The Eatery's fare is free to members but rather monotonous: plenty of rice, oatmeal, popcorn, and beans (etc) and seldom much else. The vegetarian menu minimizes cost, frig space, and clean-up. Members may bring any foods, including meat, into park for own consumption.

Though residence varies with season, the park is the usual home of more than half its members, and a weekend/holiday haunt for most of the rest. A shuttle van, towing a trailer with bike racks, drives down and up the mtn twice a day (which is a long tedious climb for a cyclist), connecting in the valley to bike paths and a city bus line. Once a week or so, the van goes all the way to the city for items too big for bike or bus. Few members own motor vehicles: parking space is scarce and NOT free.

Residents set up various portable dwellings in wooded or brushy areas of the park. With food and facilities at the dome, little personal space is needed. Bitter cold is rare. When it comes, some members take their bedding to the dome and crowd in. With the dome heater going full blast, and the pool emitting stored warmth, the dome almost always remains above freezing.

To allow disturbed environments to heal, the park is divided into two zones. One year, camping and hiking are limited to the first zone; the next year, to the other; with some overlap for moving.

Nudity is encouraged within the dome. At its portal, any clothes worn outside are removed and left outside, and a shower is required. The dome is usually warm enough for naked comfort. (The more-active or less-heat-tolerant occupants often need dips in the pool.) But in the dome, as elsewhere, clothing is optional, except: only garments that are kept inside may be worn inside. That helps keep out vermin, dust and associated pathogens; and minimizes pool water filtration and changes.

About half the members are women; more than at most naturist parks. As inducements, women join free. Men pay nearly a thousand a year: high, but with most everything else free, no one needs steady employment. Most of the funds buy food supplies for the Eatery. A few members garden and provide seasonal fresh vegetables, or do maintenance, instead of paying money.

Some women use Valley View only as a free campground, and never go to the dome where they would have to shed their shrouds. Some nudist members resent "subsidizing textilists". But most tolerate that, expecting those women will eventually either be tempted enough by the dome's freebs to overcome their inhibitions, or will leave.

(This is the first of two parts. In next issue: Valley View's youth-oriented synergistic competitor & how it differs)
H & B

More than a tick about ticks.
Lyme is a devastating disease and difficult to cure. To avoid infection, discover ticks before they bite (best) or soon after (next best). Disease transmission usually requires several hours. Here is what we now do if hiking or working outside during tick season.

To best detect ticks, wear as few clothes as possible. Choose light color so ticks will show. (Ticks I've seen were dark: brown or reddish brown.)

Carry any bedding or extra clothes enclosed in plastic bags.

Promptly investigate any irritation. View through a hand lens. (Some ticks are pinhead size.) If hiking solo, have two mirrors for viewing all body parts. Frequently stop, remove any clothes, and inspect body carefully, both seeing and feeling. Check lumps. Unlike most scabs and moles, ticks when attached can be flipped from side to side. Inspect clothes, turning inside out.

At end of hike, remove any clothes, inspect body extra carefully and, if possible, shower BEFORE entering camp area or any dwelling. If you don't have time then to scrutinize clothes, put them in plastic bags until you do have time. Best not enter any shelter while wearing clothes you have been hiking in, without first inspecting them.

Kill any tick by burning, or by crushing between rocks. (Tick is tough.) Don't get its body fluids on you.

If a tick bites, remove promptly by grasping with tweezers, improvised tweezers (from stick) or fingernails close to its head. Try not to squeeze its body. Pull gently and maybe twist a little to hopefully remove in one piece. (Dabbing with oil or hot match did not budge ticks we tried that on.)

Suck wound using a short pipe or (eg) film can with hole in bottom.

Wash wound with (eg) iodine solution, hydrogen peroxide, or soap and water. (I don't know how much sucking and washing help, but they seem worth doing.)

With hand lens, inspect wound for any remaining head parts. Dig out with sterilized pin or thorn.

Not all tick bites are noticed: be alert for symptoms regardless. Michael, a former lyme patient, says: only a third of cases show a bulls-eye rash. More common: stiff neck; flu-like cold that doesn't go away. Lab tests for lyme are not reliable. If symptoms, promptly seek antibiotics (eg, minocycline). MUCH easier to cure early.

I've read, nudists get fewer tick bites. Nudity helps several ways:

Ticks are easier to see on most skin than on most clothes (at least on skin lighter colored than the ticks).

You need only inspect your body; not also clothes with many irregularities.

Ticks are easier to feel crawling on you, if no clothes clinging to or rubbing you (but ticks crawl slowly and do not tickle much, so also look for them.)

Ticks are easier to feel with your fingers if clothes are not in the way.

You can more promptly check a sore if clothes removal isn't necessary.

Ticks usually crawl around looking for cover before biting. Clothes are cover. A tick may eventually bite regardless. But the more it crawls around looking, the more likely you are to discover it before it bites.

When hiking nude (except shoes and sunshade hat), Bert and I have seldom if ever been bitten. Ticks get on us but we find them before they bite. When wearing only shorts, most bites have been under the shorts.

During 25+ years of camping and hiking, mostly in the West, Bert and I have found maybe 100 ticks on us. Most (maybe 80 of 100) before they bit (and this was before doing everything suggested above). Of those that bit, most were felt quickly - some before they got firmly attached. With one exception (a juvenile), all ticks were discovered before they had fed long enough to bloat. The ticks included all stages but mostly adults. We encounter most during warm months. But this year, Bert found one on a mild late-Dec day.

For clothing, some authors recommend tight fits, apparently hoping ticks won't crawl under them. Such clothes are not comfortable hiking or working. I prefer loose fits, so I can feel inside clothes easily and remove clothes easily. A light forest green looks natural yet contrasts with ticks.

As for repellants, anything toxic enough to dissuade a tick, I'd rather not have on my skin. Also, repellants won't stay on long, especially in hot weather when sweating or showering.

Be kind to lizards. I've read, the California fence lizard has something in its blood that not only safeguards the lizard from lyme, but also disinfects the tick. (Range? Other lizards? I don't know.) But that may be why lyme is less common in West than East. (However, other tick-borne diseases lurk in West - and East.) Holly & Bert, OR 973, Jan

Grandmother's bug repellant.

She mixes: 1 oz white tyme oil; ½ oz each of lavender, citronella, patchouli and cade oils; 8 oz any clean vegetable oil. She may bottle in little vials, or mix with 2 gallons red cedar shavings and put in small plastic bags.

To keep out mosquitos and flies, put a few drops in little tea light candles, or near a light bulb or other warmth.

For roaches, do like for mosquitos, and also use roach baits.

For ants, follow their trail to where they are entering. Block their path with a heavy line of oil.

For fleas, put a big handful of the cedar shavings under pet's bed-padding.

For moths, put some cedar shavings in cloth bag and hang in closet.

Spiders couldn't care less. (Maxine's Pages, Crystal Rain Research Agency, GA)

Cedar: Tree of Life of NW Coast Indians, Hilary Stewart, 1984, 192p., 47 photos, ±600 drawings (clear,accurate,detailed), Douglas&McIntyre,1615 Venables,BC V5L2H1

Cedar so permeates NW coast Indian culture, "it is hard to envision their life without it." Red cedar (Thuja plicata) is lighter green than conifer companions. Mature trees contain thujaplicin, a fungicidal oil that resists rot. A fallen tree may remain sound for a century. Because its "loose, cellular structure creates air spaces," it insulates better than do hardwoods.

The wood was made into totem poles and dugout canoes; or split into planks for boxes, chests, and huge houses.

Bark was harvested from trees "about 2 handspans wide". Only during spring and summer, when sap was running, could the bark be removed, in long, vertical strips. (I remove bark only from fallen trees. Some fall naturally, especially beside streams where their roots get eroded. Some are left behind after commercial logging. Removing bark from a live tree kills or injures it - depending on how much of the circumference is removed.)

UNseparated bark was used as bark boards (a popular trade item - threading with salmonberry sticks prevented curling), storage boxes, cooking pots, canoe bailers, and emergency canoes.

For other uses, inner and outer bark were separated with knife, then pulled apart. The bark might first be bent every 4 handspans to crack the outer bark, which made separation easier.

For baskets, mats and rope, inner bark was separated into layers and split in width: eg, 1" wide for coarse matting or 1/16" for fine baskets. To split with speed and precision, 2 razor pieces were set in a wooden handle. (NW Indians had iron-tipped tools (of unknown origin) for centuries before Capt. Cook came in 1778, but apparently they were scarce.)

For quality clothing, inner bark was softened by shredding: fully dry bark was pounded, then twisted. Oil on the hands helped soften. Clothing of yellow cedar (Chamaecyparis nootkatensis) is tougher than red; thus more valuable.

Withes (branchlets) were used as fastenings. Twisting made them flexible. For quick use in the woods, the withe was twisted right on the tree, with bark left on. Better: heat withe; remove bark; reheat; then twist. Split withes were used for lashing, sewing, rope.

Cedar roots, split one to 8 times, were used to make coiled baskets which were often waterproof. Roots were straighter in rock-free soil. About 15 feet from base of a big old tree, a woman dug down with a digging stick, 2 feet or more. All women made baskets, but the most expert were spared some household tasks so they could devote more time to their craft.

Formerly, and still in Britain, all conifers were collectively called pines. When early explorers spoke of NW coast Indians using "pines", they meant red or yellow cedar. Review by Julie

Dwelling Portably

formerly named Message Post
POB 190, Philomath OR 97370

August 1999 $1 per issue   Add 50¢ to check/mo under $6

Holders improve access.

I use holders with multiple compartments (also called caddys) for kitchen utensils, craft tools, and art supplies. Those that revolve are nice. I've bought them inexpensively at garage sales, and even found a perfectly good one in a dumpster. But I wanted more than I was finding, so I began making my own. My home-mades don't rotate: duplicating that feature seems not worth the effort.

I make them from discarded plastic bottles. Ones with square cross-sections fit together without the gaps that round bottles leave. Clear film canisters hold small items. In cities, I find bottles at recycle centers or in recycle bins behind eateries; in the boonies, at impromptu dumps.

I cut the tops off with scissors. Then wash. Then punch holes for joining. I use a paper punch or revolving leather punch. Where punches can't reach, or when I'm without them, I use a narrow-bladed knife. But cutting flexible plastic is tricky. An alternative: melt holes with a hot nail, held with pliers or vice grips and heated over a candle or stove. Finally, I fasten the cut-off bottles together with twist ties, string, or rubber straps.

I prefer several small holders to one big one. Easier to pick up and move, and fewer compartments to search thru.

These holders are so helpful and easy to make, I even construct them when light camping if I expect to be at one place more than a few days. Julie Summers, OR 973, 1996

Bivy/storage boxes desired, especially for sleeping in cities.

A bivy box is big enough to sleep in when the top is raised, but closes quickly and then is weather proof, mouse proof, and very low profile. Closing takes much less time than does taking down a tent and stuffing bedding into pails. Easy close-up is especially advantageous when camping on remnant brushlands in urban areas, where a tent left set up is likely to be seen and vandalized.

A bivy box is light enough to transport as a bike trailer (lash on wheels and hitch) or to backpack empty. Or it may stay cached, semi buried, with only the top above ground. If slept in, to avoid condensation the box must be insulated. Even for storage, insulation is desirable; else moisture will concentrate on inside top or bottom (depending on temperature).

I've looked at big plastic boxes (for carrying/storing tools in pickups). About $17 on sale. But not big enough and not insulated. How weather and mouse proof I don't know.

Then there are tent-trailers, made to be towed by vehicles as small as big motorcycles. They expand for living

in, and close up for towing. Much too big for human-powered
transport (lightest a few hundred pounds). But that type of
structure might be miniaturized.

If foam ice chests are made giant size, they might
serve after strengthening the outside with fiberglass.

A wooden box would not be good. Ordinary wood quickly
rots when in contact with soil, and mice eventually chew
their way in - assuming the structure doesn't warp enough to
let them simply stroll in. Fungicide-treated wood is available but may be toxic to humans as well as to fungus.

Maybe best: something of molded plastic, mass produced
for other uses, that could be adapted. Bert & Holly, 1997

(Comments:) Insulating any shelter is pretty easy. 4x8 sheets
of ½-inch-thick insulating board sell for about $6. Available
faced with aluminum (which blocks moisture). With foam core,
it cuts easily with razor knife. I've used it in trucks.

Or, to insulate a tool box, maybe "bubble wrap"?

I believe very cheap coffins are made - for cremations.
But I think they are only heavy cardboard.

Perhaps some sort of shipping container would do. L.Smith
WI, Apr 98

Henry David Thoreau wrote of bivy boxes.
I used to see a large box by the railroad, six feet long
by three feet wide, in which the laborers locked up their
tools at night; and it suggested to me that every man who was
hard pushed might get such a one for a dollar, and, having
bored a few auger holes in it, to admit the air at least, get
into it when it rained and at night, and hook down the lid,
and so have freedom in his love, and in his soul be free....
You could sit up as late as you pleased, and, whenever you
got up, go abroad without any landlord or house-lord dogging
you for rent. Many a man is harassed to death to pay the rent
of a larger and more luxurious box who would not have frozen
to death in a box such as this. (from Walden, ± 1850; sent by
L. Smith)

A new hotel concept for rucksack tourists.
The cabins of modern Danish ships accomodate four people
in 85 square feet (eg, 8½x10'). Two-tier bunk beds are
arranged so the upper ones fold away. They provide real
comfort, including private bathrooms, but without pretensions.

My idea is for a hotel on the same lines, in the city
centre where visitors most want to be. The small floor area
allows prices to be low even in an expensive part of town.

The walls and ceilings of the units would be made in one
piece by spraying fibre-reinforced cement into moulds. The
resulting shells would then be bonded onto floor slabs of
reinforced concrete, and outfitted before being taken to site.

Managers are of the same social group and ages as the
guests, who they treat as equals. They are friendly but
without acting as servants. Each manager has charge of a
section and, within limits, runs it as own business. The
managers are the only permanent staff, minimizing costs
during slack seasons. When the place fills, a manager may
pay guests to help with the cleaning and other work. Thus,
the availability of help is proportional to the need for it.

I have researched this idea in depth. Unfortunately,
the public health rules make it unworkable. Nicholas Saunders
(from Institute for Social Inventions, London; sent by Roger
Knights)

I seek information about freighthopping and nomadic living.
Willis, Georgia 311, November

A naturist park with portable dwellings - Part 2.
        120 km (70 miles) away across the valley, nestled between
two hills, is Bushy Gorge Park: the synergistic competitor
of Valley View (described in May99 DP). Some differences:
        Valley View is mostly families, with adults 25 or older
plus their young children (few teens or early 20s), and Valley
View does not stress body shape or muscle power (it includes
some heavies). In contrast, Bushy Gorge is mostly singles,
13 to 25; with few younger than 10 or older than 30. Though
there is no age limit, male members must pass, initially and
annually, fire-fighter fitness tests - quite a few pull-ups,
push-ups, etc. (Waivers, given mostly to new young applicants,
require members' unanimous consent.) As men approach middle
age, most either can no longer pass the physical, or they lose
interest in the youth-oriented activities. Women need not be
athletic (though many are), but most of them, too, eventually
lose interest. A few stay on - often in house-mother roles.
        Valley View is open to visitors only a few days each
year. Bushy Gorge is always open, but confines visitors to a
separate area. Members may visit visitors, but not vice versa.
        Valley View allows alcohol and some other drugs "in
moderation". Whereas Bushy Gorge, to avoid "underage" hassles,
absolutely bans alcohol, tobacco, and other restricted or
illegal substances. But, conveniently, the park is bordered
by public land, and what happens there is of little concern.
        Valley View is usually quite quiet. Bushy Gorge is often
noisy, with live concerts weekends, or stereos blasting.
        Not surprisingly, aging members of Bushy Gorge often move
to Valley View. And, not surprisingly, Bushy Gorge occasionally "raids" Valley View (tacitly ignoring visitation rules)
and lures away its young with tales of the fun going on at
Bushy Gorge - far from domineering parents and other old fogies.
                                                         H & B
What abode will you abide ?
        There seem to be conflicts of interest. Holly/Bert's idea
of dwelling portably is what you can carry on your back into
the woods. Whereas for me and many readers it is: what can
I drive - and live in ? Perhaps we are as fascinated with
vehicles as the Indians were with horses.
        But obviously, from the letters DP receives, not every-
one wants to endure years of wage slavery to buy a factory-
built RV. Anyhow, they are built to be used only two weeks
a year; not lived in. The ones I've examined were shoddy,
sloppy, and not well thought out.
        I think there is a niche DP could fill: between using a
vehicle to just transport camping gear (pickup truck), and
building a rolling house with flush toilet and generator, etc.
        My interest: how to live out of a vehicle simply and
cheaply. My vehicle just serves as a shelter. The exterior
is deliberately drab, to elude rogue D.A.'s seeking plunder,
and, more importantly, to avoid theft by unofficial criminals.
        Laws are easily circumvented; especially laws concerning
vehicles. L. Smith, Wisconsin 532, 1997

(Reply:) This conflict of interest arose soon after DP (MP)
began. The decision then (in Feb85 MP): MP is primarily about
portable (backpackable) dwelling, but many of the techniques
are also useful to people living other ways.
        Anyhow, I wonder how fillable your niche is. DP has had
short articles by various people on how they outfitted their
vans, but not much detail. Detailed plans may not be worthwhile, because every make of van has different dimensions. B&H

(Comments:) Quite a few write that they wish to live out of a van or school bus, and then ask how. Of course, this is somewhat silly. Who knows what facilities they want, versus portability. And it does smack of the "ask the expert" syndrome so prevalent today. How will any new ideas be generated if all we do is copy someone else? What happened to Yankee ingenuity? Maybe what they really want is a fully-equipped RV, but they don't have the funds. But, still, I will encourage them.

My own rig just grew out of sitting in an apartment and thinking: I'll need storage of food and clothes, room to lie down and sleep, and perhaps a light to read by. Trying to keep it simple is harder than imagining ways to do it. I now realize I will never make it to the Salton Sea with four golf cart batteries aboard (240 pounds) - which are only powering two 8-watt fluorescent lamps, a blender, and a radio. Ah well.

I am writing this at the harbor in Milwaukee. It is deserted nights and weekends, and I have a nice view of the waters. Soon I'll be leaving for the beautiful shores of Lake Superior, far from the summer tourists up from Chicago.

L.Smith, Apr98

Chilly sleeping bags chill desire to camp.

In spite of our good intentions, we brought civilization with us: cooler, dehydrated foods, medicines, creams, deodorants, state-of-the-art sleeping bags, and reading material. Still, we reminded ourselves, few people of our age would sleep in a flimsy tent in the cold mountain night.

This campground is developed, yet has a remote feel, with trees, boulders, meadows and logs between the widely-spaced campsites. On this spring day, only 10 other campers are in an area with spaces for 75. There is a narrow, fast-paced river with falls, and wildflowers fill the meadows.

The animals are quirky. The ground squirrels are cute, with their glossy tabby fur coats: eating seeds and nuts from their little front paws; or standing on their hind legs staring at us. But they scamper obnoxiously close. Barry spent lunch time scaring them off with a stick, or throwing water at them. At times he was almost surrounded by those shrewd scavengers. While we were both busy elsewhere for a moment, they gnawed a banana and chewed on a unopened soup cup on our picnic table. One persistant fellow crept up to the woodstove and gnawed open my USED tea-bag. He shook out the tea, tried to chew it, then threw it down disgustedly.

At noon, warmed by the bright mountain sun, we talk bravely of future camping trips: how we'll streamline the food supply from overly-complicated cooking of scalloped potatoes, to instant or dehydrated soups and stews.

Around 3 p.m., the sun is already sinking behind other nearby mountains and I'm cold. I briskly walk to our tent-cabin, where lay two inviting sleeping bags on their hunks of foam, with colorful rugs, blankets and pillows placed around them. I quickly change into long-johns.

At 7 p.m., with dinner finished, Barry starts the bon-fire. I sit before it with wine. Barry pops Jiffy popcorn.

One hour later the scene changes. After dousing fire and blowing out candles and lantern, we lay shivering in our sleeping bags, anxiously listening to the night sounds. The full moon hovers above and casts white eerie shadows through the thin tent walls. I toss and turn.

Two hour later, awakening from crazy, frightening dreams, my heart is beating madly. I have to pee again, so I go through the procedure of putting shoes on, unzipping the tent, stepping outside, and rezipping. I spot an animal. Seeing me, it freezes. It is large; cat-size. It has a bushy tail (no, not a skunk.) A red fox? It hesitates, then scurries behind a boulder. I hurry back to the tent.

More shivering, tossing and turning. The night creeps slowly forward. Finally, we squint our eyes at the approaching pink dawn. My head pounds as Barry scuttles over to the stove to boil water for tea and coffee. I pull up the sleeping bag, absolutely frozen. But the morning performs her magic show, with bird choruses widening in the crispy fresh new day. Ironically, the most lovely early morning I've ever seen. Now I lean forward my exhausted shivering body and sip grateful gulps of sage tea.

Later, after the day warms, we sleep like zombies for a few hours. We've made up our minds to enjoy this day: do some hiking and cook a nice dinner - then raze the tent and head for home BEFORE the shivering terror-filled night comes.

Until now, the few campers here have given each other a wide berth. But, right as we finish our fry pan of cheesy potatoes and tofu dogs, a pickup backs into the NEXT campsite. The two occupants immediately hook up their CD player AND television. As we pack our gear, we are treated to a blasting sports report, plus hooting and laughing.

As we pulled out, heaving a sigh of relief, at the gate we notice a new sign: "Warning - some ground squirrels are contaminated with fleas which carry BUBONIC PLAGUE."

We have come to the conclusion that campers we're not. Nature is a bit too hard on our aging bodies.

EPILOGUE. It's 7:30 p.m. I put down my book for a moment to view the golden setting sun out the screen windows of our beloved tent-cabin. We will probably leave it up here in our BACKYARD all summer. (From "Notes from Campsite 30", Essay #8, © 1998 by phyllis hordin, CA 921

(Comments:) Many things are difficult at first. MOST people have unpleasant experiences the first time they camp (or do anything very new).

To sleep warm, use two or more sleeping bags if necessary. They need not be "state of the art" (unless you are a competition trekker who needs to eliminate every ounce possible). Cheapo bags are fine. Just have ENOUGH.

For convenience, keep a pee bowl (or jug) in your tent.

To avoid obnoxious animals, DON'T go to developed campgrounds. Animals there have learned to scavenge. Far from human activity, we are seldom bothered by creatures bigger than mice (which are easily trapped).

Yes, do simplify food supply and preparation. Even in our winter base shelter, with jug faucet and sink, and propane stove on 5-gal tank, and where our two bodies usually keep inside air above 60°F, we seldom use the stove oftener than once a day. When light-camping during summer, we may cook only once or twice a week. Holly & Bert, Oregon 973, May

TVP is one of the mainstays of my diet.

Texturized vegetable protein is dehydrated soy protein. Available in most food co-ops in several sizes, from flakes to chunks. Light weight, and cheap: ± $1 per pound.

I've been totally vegetarian for 24 years. I don't know if it has improved my health, but it hasn't harmed it. L. Smith

(Comment:) At times we have bought whole soy beans. Much cheaper than TVP. Roasted, they have a pleasant nutty taste.

But HARD - not easy to chew. They can be ground along with
wheat to enrich bread. At first, soy improves the flavor.
But after a few weeks, DELETING soy improves the flavor. Is
there something in soy our bodies don't want much of? H & B

Santa Claws leaves us a high-protein Christmas present.
     In January 1998 we found the deer on a water trail, only
a quarter mile from our winter base-camp. From the marks, we
think a cougar ambushed it. (Suppose I had come along before
the deer?) Quite fresh. (One day old?) Only liver and part
of one hindquarter had been eaten. We took all we thought we
could eat before it spoiled (cold spell, fortunately), but
left some for the cougar in case it returned.
     We don't hunt much. We don't like harming animals that
aren't harming us, find hunting boring, and think a steady
high-protein diet is unhealthy for most adults. But, like our
ancestors, we happily scavenge. One risk with road-kills and
predator-kills: you don't know if the prey animal was sick.
So cook thoroughly. And, at least with mammals, don't eat
brain or spinal cord (mad cow (etc) disease, which, we've
read, cooking does not inactivate). Holly & Bert

Someone came seeking an Easter dinner. It was not a bunny !
     The first sound of our visitor: gentle rustling of the
curtains at one end of our shelter. Not loud. A chipmonk or
lizard ? But, peering through the translucent plastic, Bert
glimpsed something big ! No guns on hand. We grabbed knives.
     The creature moved out of sight and circled our camp -
amazingly quiet. (Except for a small terrace in front, our
shelter was surrounded by thick brush.) Finally the animal
stalked across in front, profile silhouetted against the sky,
only a few feet away. Four footed. Much bigger than a coyote
but smaller and leaner than most bears. And bears are usually
NOISY. So are dogs. A cougar? The same one?
     We both growled, deeply. It took off. No sign of it
since. Why did it come? We had not recently eaten meat.
But I had been menstruating. Had it smelled me ?
     Since then, when hiking solo, we carry wooden spears
(which are also useful as staffs in some spots). When hiking
together (attack less likely against two), we carry knives.
                                             H & B, May 1998
(Comment:) I was reluctant to publish these two reports,
because they are NOT typical experiences. Bert and I have
camped full time for over 20 years, and part time before that,
and have not had any other close encounters with big animals.
We don't want DP to become like the sensational "adventure"
magazines which feature the freaky. However, anyone who lives
in the bush (or anywhere) a long time, will sooner or later
have some UNusual experiences. Holly & Bert, Oregon 973

Don't scavenge vending machine discards - unless desperate !
     (In response to Laszlo Borbely's article in Dec97 DP.)
I've been in the vending business off and on for 20 years.
Venders buy only the cheapest meats, bread, and other foods.
A small vender buys his food from a kitchen distribution
center. Refrigeration from the kitchen to his facility, and
from his facility to the machines ? Maybe, sometimes - if
not inconvenient. But usually, just throw in a cooler - and
by the time the driver reaches his last stops, the food is
warmer than your mother's heart.
     Health safety switches, that prevent vending if the
cooling fails, are often bypassed. Expiration dates on food
are usually coded; if not, they're made illegible with a
drop of paint thinner. L.Smith, WI

Dwelling Portably

November 1999 $1 per issue

(formerly named Message Post)
POB 190, Philomath OR 97370
To be reprinted as part of Aug

I have been using canvas shoebags as caddys for years.
   I usually hang them on walls. Each consists of twenty
6-by-4-inch pockets, fairly well reinforced. Unlike vinyl ones,
canvas bags are repairable. Skilled sewers might make their
own out of heavy cloth.
   A shoebag is very portable, because you can roll it up,
tie the ends, and transport without losing anything.
   I got the idea from Carl Franz books: On and Off the Road
Cookbook; or People's Guide to Mexico. L.Smith, WI 532, August

Cyclists use newspaper as wind-break.
   During mountain stages of the Tour de France, helpers and
fans wait on summits and offer flat newspapers to riders, who
stuff them in their jerseys to help keep upper body warm during
descents at speeds over 50 mph.
   During the 21 years I lived in n. Cal, I carried a spare
paper for crisp morning commutes. Worked well. Dave Parish, FL

I freighthopped several times during the 1970s.
   West of the Mississippi; sometimes alone, sometimes with
a male companion, once with a female companion.
   Talking to frequent "hoppers" is the best way to glean
info. I was told which cities were most dangerous to go into,
either because of the railroad "dicks", or because more of the
people going there were desparate and willing to give you a
shake or a sore head to gain your goods.
   Many of the hoppers had alcohol problems, but not in a way
that alarmed me. Most were helpful, witty, knowledgable, and
more than willing to share info, food or spirits (both kinds).
Some hoppers were migrant workers. I was there for the "fun of
it" and to experience some areas that are rarely visited except
by trains and wildlife.
   I suggest, walk to the nearest train yard and just watch.
See who's who. If you spot someone about to hop, ask a few
questions. Follow your instincts: if you question someone's
character, be friendly but move on quickly - you will live
longer. Many railroad employees such as brakemen and engineers
were friendly and helpful when I asked which direction a train
was going. One railroad dick in Reno even took me to breakfast. But I suspect my being a woman accounted for his
kindness, as he had a stiff reputation among the hobos. The
railroad dicks can make your life unpleasant, and there were
several stories of physical abuse by some of them.
   That was 25 years ago. Maybe some particulars have
changed. Ask around the yard: that is the best way to learn.
And don't ride mail trains unless you have great faith: they
go recklessly fast. Once was enough for me. Laura LaBree, WA

(Comments:) We have never hopped. Once I was tempted to. I
was in s. Cal hitching north, not getting rides, and saw a
freight go slowly by. But I felt I did not know enough.
Getting on and off (especially) can be dangerous if one does
not know how (as can many things).
   For campsites in cities we generally avoid "hobo jungles"
near railroads, not because we dislike hobos (those we've met
we liked fine), but because hobos are a target for cops.
   May 96 DP included a detailed review of a book about
freighthopping, by Hobos From Hell. Various peoples'
experiences, most recent, with some detailed advice. B & H

How dangerous is camping?

Traveling and camping for extended periods has long appealed to me, but I have yet to do much of it because of all the contradictory reports I've heard about cougars. Do they ever come into your camp? What do you think would be enough protection if camping in remote areas of the Coast Range?

Also, could one be arrested if a forest worker came across a campsite that seemed like it had been there for months, in a National Forest or on timber company lands?

Krista, OR 973, Oct

(Reply:) We do not get media, so I don't know if many attacks by cougars have been reported. Two years ago, a cougar came very close to our shelter. We both growled, which scared it off. (Account in Aug99 DP.) We have had no other close encounters in the woods with big animals or hostile people in over 20 years. If meeting a cougar, advice I've heard: look big; stand tall; never run. And, when hiking, observe carefully: cougars like to ambush their prey.

Since our encounter, we keep spears (just sharpened poles) at camp and often hike with them. (They are also useful as staffs.) Enough protection? I don't know.

A gun may provide better defense at a camp. And it has much longer range for hunting. But, while hiking and possibly BEING HUNTED by a cougar, maybe not. A gun can't be gotten into action as quickly as can a spear, unless it is carried in hands, loaded, safety off, with finger on trigger. And, if carried thusly, it is dangerous: without hands free to grab, stumbling is more likely, and any jolt could cause discharge. Also, a gun is more delicate and needs much more care, and is expensive to buy or time-consuming to make. (A spear requires only a few minutes whittling.)

For safety at camp, see articles by Tim Leathers, Guy Hengst, and us in May 95 DP. If discovered, I suppose arrest is possible. But the usual procedure, I've read: post warning to move within a specified time (24 hours? 2 weeks?); then, if the camp remains, steal or vandalize the equipment. The campers might also be fined IF caught.

If not experienced camping, you might consider trying to make an arrangement with a private landowner and camp on some not-too-remote wooded or brushy acreage while testing your equipment and gaining skills and confidence, and so you can more easily obtain anything additional you need.

When camping (or doing anything), keep in mind the relative risks. Even if someone camps only 20 miles from a city and goes there only once a month, I suspect the biggest danger by far is from traffic during those monthly trips. B&H

How we dispose of kitchen waste in the woods.

First and foremost, at the end of each meal, we EAT every edible remnant that is too perishable to keep or too small to be worth saving. Then we wipe plates and pots with (eg) bread, or lick; then pour in a little drinking water, rub with a clean finger, and drink.

If people from another dwellingway saw us clean up, they might assume we are fanatic conservationists or else are from a land of chronic hunger. But our biggest reason: any edible remains will attract hungry creatures we would rather not have around: flies, mice, rats, bears.

Food parts we don't eat (peels, shells, bones, bad parts of apples, etc), we carry far away and place under bushes.

Relatedly, pee or wash-water containing menstral flow, we pour slowly on the ground (being careful not to splash), let it soak in, then pour over it Bert's pee to mask any odor.

Cattail down too clumpy to be good insulation.
    I read it is warmer than goose down, so I tried it.
I stripped the dry down off cattail stalks in the fall and
stored it in a tightly-closed plastic pail for a few years
until using it to repair a garment that had lost some of its
original goose down.
    I tried to tease the cattail down apart with my fingers,
but it didn't separate easily. Then I used a pair of wool
cards (which are like broad wire brushes). That fluffed the
down quite well. But after filling the spaces in the garment,
the cattail down clumped together. Shaking the garment did
not unclump it. To eliminate spaces between clumps and thus
insulate effectively, would require a dense filling using
much down - and be HEAVY - undoing the advantage of down.
    I also tried the cattail down as pillow stuffing but
found it relatively hard - less comfortable than cut-up small
pieces of poly foam. Julie Summers, Oregon, March

In damp cool and cold weather I prefer wool.
    Keeps me more comfortable than any other fibre I know of.
And it does not lose its warmth while I rest, like the
synthetics (plastics) do. Guy Hengst, Indiana, October

Is Baja for you?
    Come to Mexico only if you are interested in Mexico, love
the people, and know Spanish or are willing to learn it.
    Mexico is a foreign country. Americans are guests here.
If you do not befriend Mexicans in a sincere, respectful and
generous way, you will not be able to afford to live here and
probably won't like it. Desert conditions in Baja are harsh
and services are few, which makes people all more dependent on
each other. You will be able to live simply here only with
the good-will of the locals. Anonymity is almost impossible.
    The only Americans here worth associating with, are also
doing this. If you are able to do this, you will be enriched
and rewarded by the experience. If not, stay home: do not
visit Mexico - or other countries either.
    If you want to leave the USA, start today by befriending
people of color and other cultures on THEIR terms.
    I live far south of the border and plan to move even
further south, as does most everyone who is halfway hip.
Near the border are gringos - and the military.
    I think many DP-types might be able to hack it here.
But you must scout it out and make friends and contacts. And
you can NOT make it without help from the locals. You got to
want to mix in.
    You must be very healthy and totally insane to survive in
this desert during summer. I love it. It is tranquil - no
Americans. I see the tide is nearly high again so I'm off for
a swim. I got stung by a Manta the other day and temporarily
lost my desire to swim when the tide is way out.
    I can't tell you how to cross the border; I haven't done
it for many years. (I recently read that officials want to
charge $15 to everyone who crosses the border more than 15
miles, but I don't recall the details.)
    Yes, dental care is cheap and good. But I am astonished
that anyone would drive 1000 miles for it. Would you save
anything? (I had a pretty good experience at the dental
school in Portland in the early 1990s.)
    To live cheap and simple here, you must love the people
and want to go native. Otherwise Mexico will suck you dry.
Luz, Baja, June

(Comments:) Your advice to Americans regarding Baja, sounds much like the advice to city people in back-to-land magazines: move to a settled rural area or small town in America only if you like the people there and are willing to mix and conform.

Good advice, I expect, regarding places and ways the writers have lived. But the writers tend to make sweeping generalizations, and assume everyone will live like them.

Bert and I sometimes live on the fringes of rural areas, and do so without having much or anything to do with the local settlers. Sure, a few might be congenial IF we could associate without getting involved with the others. But usually we can't, so we don't try.

This is not to disagree with you regarding where you live. I can't imagine why any American would want to go into a Baja desert merely to live in seclusion, well-hidden from the locals, when they can do that in an American desert without having to cross the border. But when you suggest that anyone who lacks your attitudes and mix-in abilities should not visit **ANY PART OF** Mexico - or any other country either. !?! Not even Tijuana or Mexicali? How about Mexicans - or Americans visiting San Diego or Portland? I assume you don't like those places. But should NO ONE ?

As for dentistry, millions of Americans including many DP readers live within a hundred miles of Mexico, and many more migrate to near-border areas during winter for sunshine, visiting friends, earning money, or buying things unavailable where they summer. If they need teeth repaired, why not hop over the border? Save money and time too(vs U.S. dentists).

You say the desert climate is harsh. So is most any climate to someone ill-prepared for it. (Western Oregon has mild temperatures compared to most of the U.S. But, to someone lacking equipment or improvisation skills, the long cold rains can be deadlier than the colder snows further inland, because staying dry is more difficult.)

Personally, I don't mind heat if there is some shade (or I can rig some) so I don't sunburn, and plenty of water for frequent showers (or dips or swims), and if I don't have to wear clothes. Which brings up: I've heard many Mexicans are even more hostile to nudity than are many Americans (though SOME Indians are quite different from Hispanics that way).

Local friends may help. But I expect they will respect and like someone more if s/he does not need help often. H&B

Can a trailer be protected from thieves and vandals?

I am moving to Alabama where I was offered a teaching position. Many trailer parks are there. But I've heard: no way to stop people from breaking in and destroying or stealing everything; depending, I guess, on how they feel about you or the value of your stuff.

The problem seems global: people in San Diego talk about being ripped off repeatedly. This makes me hesitate to buy a trailer. How do your readers overcome such vulnerability, especially singles who leave their trailers and vans unoccupied while they work or shop? Angela Lakwete, CA 921, May

DWELLING PORTABLY prices as of 2009: 2 samples, $2.
Future issues: big print, 3/$6; tiny print, 6/$6.
Past issues, tiny print only: 2/$2, 6/$5, 14/$10.
Postpaid to U.S. if cash or if check is $5 or more.
NEW ADDRESS: DP c/o Lisa Ahne, POB 181, Alsea OR 97324
Email via: juliesummerseatssensibly@yahoo.com

Index

Dwelling Portably

formerly named Message Post
POB 190, Philomath OR 97370
April 2000 $1 per issue   Add 50¢ to check/mo under $6

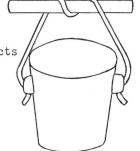

Stick makes cord handle more comfortable.
Without it, the cord digs painfully into my hand. The stick must be LONG or the cord will slip off.
The cord may be on several light objects bundled together as a hand-carry, or on a pail. I often find pails lacking handles, to which I attach cords. Also, I often remove wire handles (easy with vise grips) and replace with cord for lightness and quiet. Julie Summers, OR 973, April 1999

Plastic bottles make good eyeglass cases.
Lighter weight than cases sold - and FREE.
Some lotion bottles are ideal size. I cut off enough of the top to BARELY fit the glasses in (so they don't fall out). Or, if too wide, I put a rubber band around it. Julie, 1996

Steel bread boxes are rodent-proof food-storage containers.
I often find them in thrift stores. Bruce of BC, May 99

All-metal ammunition boxes good for storing electrical gear.
Look for ones with good gaskets, and levers that pry the lids closed tightly. Put gear inside with a drying agent. The contents are relatively safe from water, animals, fire if not intense, and EMP from a nuke weapon (or close lightning strike?) because the metal shields contents. Paul Doerr, 1991

Wear gloves when handling watch batteries.
Touching them with bare fingers may put sweat on them which can gradually discharge them and shorten their lives.
I prefer lithium watch batteries. They still work in sub-zero cold where other batteries conk out. I had a cheap Casio wrist watch with a 5-year lithium battery. Bruce of BC

Cheap, light way to sharpen blades; even stainless.
Buy a variety pack of silicon carbide sandpaper (five 5x11" sheets < $5). Place paper FLAT on (eg) wood block. Stroke blade against grit, just like with a sharpening stone. Don't press too hard or the grit will quickly wear out. (Silicon carbide is very hard but BRITTLE.) Use coarse grits (eg, 80) for removing much metal; then fine grits (over 200) for honing. The finer the grit, the keener the edge. (Cutting oil did not help, and it unglued the paper.)
For convenience, glue sandpaper to one end of a wood block. Use remainder of block as handle. If stuck on with rubber cement, worn-out sheets easily replaced. Silicon carbide is so labeled on package or sheets. Usually black. Greg DeLoach, ME 040, June

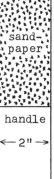

sand-
paper

handle

← 2" →

Before you use force, remember of course:
Always steer clear, of all that is dear:
Your eyes and your nose, your thumbs and your toes;
Your forehead and chin, your thighs and your shin.
Make sure all your body parts are clear before applying force with any tool, especially sharp ones such as needles, awls, knives, saws. Ask yourself where the tool will go if

your stroke is longer than expected or the tool slips off your material or goes all the way thru. Especially when using awl, knife or screwdriver to pierce with, assume it will go thru the material and beyond. Make sure it will go harmlessly into space, or a work surface - NOT into your palm or thigh ! A lacing needle, or awl used to tighten a knot, will keep going the way you are pulling if lace breaks or awl slips. Pull in a safe direction, or brace elbows to limit stroke. Julie (?)

For one year I lived in a cellar in Toronto.
My friend was opening a small cafe, so I asked him to let me occupy 150 ft^2 of the basement. A small south-facing window opening to a sidewalk grate, let in some light and provided an emergency exit. I cleaned out some junk, then put up a simple 2x4 wall with locking door. I sound-insulated the wall and ceiling so I could practice on my sax - and not hear footsteps overhead. I spray-painted the walls with white latex, and put some found carpet on floor. (City folks throw out good stuff.)
I used the cafe's washroom, but urinated into wide-mouth bottles and sometimes just poured into the floor drain (to city sewer). For showering I used another bathroom, above the cafe, though sometimes I went to a public swimming pool.
I prepared simple meals on an alcohol camping stove, and had a small bar frig. Eventually I made a deal with the cafe and swapped dish washing and clean up for food.
I set up a small desk for writing, and could play my horn, listen to music, or watch a small TV. Rent: $75/mo. The building owner was pleased: my work had improved the basement.
I was renovating a school bus to live in (see May97 DP). When done, and agreed year over, I moved. Fred, Ont., March 99

Advantages of various kinds of insulating boards.
Caution: the half-inch thick aluminum-faced insulating board (in Aug99 DP), is a type of fiberglass. When cut or rubbed, it releases particles which are harmful to breathe. Also, when wet, its insulating value is almost zero.
Another rigid insulation available is blue board. Designed for underground use, it is impervious to water (it even floats). It is a type of styrofoam, so particles are not harmful. I am familiar with 1" and 2" thicknesses. Laura LaBree, WA 981, Oct

(Comment:) Unlike styrofoam, fiberglass does not melt, or burn and emit toxic fumes. That may be why it's much used in home construction (building codes). But no reason to use it where fire unlikely or where occupants can easily escape. B & H

Duct tape and first-aid tape can be re-rolled.
I carry duct tape in my fanny pack for expedient repairs of tents, packs, shoes, bikes, etc. But an economy roll is big and heavy. So I re-roll some onto (eg) a stick. Julie, 1996

How many window layers ? More not always better.
The more layers (spaced $\frac{1}{2}$" to 1" apart), the greater the insulation but the less light passed. Also, the less condensation on inner surface. But condensation not always bad.
Most winters we have two layers and, with two occupants (and no heater), our 10-ft-D $4\frac{1}{2}$-ft-high inner shelter is usually 60 to 65°F (and hotter when sunny or cooking). So far, this winter has been mild, so we've had only one layer. Result, 5° cooler, and more condensation (which collects in a trough and has to be sponged up every two days). But clothes dry faster, and mold stopped growing on the typewriter case. Bert
April 2000

More on winter shelters.
May99 DP had tips
on site selection
& prep, window
direction,
floors,
entry.

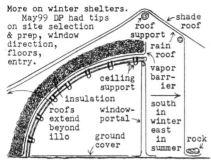

shade roof
roof support
rain roof
vapor barrier
ceiling support
insulation
roofs extend beyond illo
window-portal
ground cover
south in winter
east in summer
rock

Here I'll discuss the shelter itself.
Though I've necessarily drawn a particular shape, what is best will depend
on site, use, builder, and materials. A
partially underground structure, with
roof flush with the ground surface (such
as in May95 DP), will be more sheltered
from wind, less visible, and warmer
during cold spells (because of heat from
more earth surface exposed). However,
digging may be impractical: ground froz-
en, solid rock, weak soil (sand), no
drainage (swamp), or too little time.
To minimize transport, use mostly
materials abundant nearby.
Though a single part may do more than
one thing, I'll discuss: ceiling support,
vapor barrier, insulation, and roofs.
Ceiling support might be branches
interwoven or tied together to form a
partial dome. Most branches are curved,
and may be more availdble than straight
poles. Conifers (eg, cedar, fir) are
more durable than most broad-leaf trees.
If sheltered, may last ten+ years. Mid-
age dougfirs may have dead lower branches still sound. Drawback: pitchy.
However, for a dug-out, straight poles
are easier to use. Lay across hole with
ends₄extending at least a foot beyond.
A small shelter might not need frame.
Vapor barrier might be strong enough.
The vapor barrier keeps moisture (of
breathing and cooking) out of insulation.
Otherwise, during cold, vapor condenses:
adds weight (danger!), lessens insulation, and eventually drips on occupants.
Common polyethylene plastic is fine unless more strength is needed for (eg) a
ceiling with no frame, or wide gaps. If
you dislike buying plastic (which causes
more to be made), look in furniture
store dumpsters for shipment wrappers.
(Stores generally love people to take
them; else they quickly fill dumpster.
The store may have more inside: ask.)
If plastic holey, overlap wrappers.
For insulation, use anything fluffy
or foamy that is ABUNDANT nearby. (But,
fiberglass hazardous.) Bubble plastic
passes light, but I've not found much.
I find thin white foam (pads shipments).
Too weak and squishy for mattress, but
okay for insulation if nothing heavy
will rest on it. To reduce amount needed,
sheets might be spaced apart with (eg)
dfir cones or styrofoam chips. If chips
abundant, use to loosely fill plastic
produce bags, then nestle bags together.
(If loose, chips can blow.) Or suspend
a few sheets of plastic ½" to 1" apart.
(See Apr92 DP) Remember: stilled air is
what insulates; not the solid material.
April 2000

Natural insulations: moss, leaves,
hay. Gathering and hauling laborious,
but can be done gradually after shelter
is erected. If below freezing, snow can
help insulate but needs other insulation
under it; else shelter will remain cold
and will gradually melt the snow.
In a dry climate, the roof might rest
directly on the insulation. Otherwise
I'd suspend it above; else puddles may
form and compress insulation, or seep
through small·holes. In illo, the rain
roof, which might be a big clear plastic
tarp, is supported by poles or ropes
(which are fastened to trees or braced-
poles at the side - not shown).
The site may include trees or bushes
with live branches extending over the
shelter. If not, and if the shelter
will be left up during sunny seasons,
a shade roof will protect the rain-roof
plastic from sun; and reduce visibility.
Any dark cloth will do. Acrylic resists
both sun and rain. (Some, in partial
shade, has lasted us 20 years.) B & H

Rustic Retreats: build-it-yourself guide.
David and Jeanie Stiles provide brief
instructions and diagrams for 26 diverse
structures including: bowers, huts,
small houses, cart, and cabin raft.
Diagrams are generally clear and well-
chosen for conveying much info briefly.
Tools, safety and joints get 7 pages.
"Without electric power, the most difficult job: ... boring holes." Battery-
powered drill suggested. "The most
important hand tool is a crosscut saw
with Teflon coating or a stainless steel
blade and ten teeth per inch." If it
binds, "spray the blade with silicone
sliding compound or rub it with soap."
25 tools listed in order of usefulness.
"Thousands of accidents on ladders
every year." Make sure legs are level
and stable (but not mentioned: side-
bracing tall ladder with cords). Never
climb to top or above spot it leans on.
Nails "must be used perpendicular to
the expected force. Use only galvanized
nails and, if necessary, drill a pilot
hole to avoid splitting." "Screws have 3
times the holding power of nails. Bolts
are the best fastener because they
provide a permanent clamping force...."
I question some of their post
joints. One they call "strong",
I call "less weak". And, to
attach a beam part way up a
post, they recommend notching   beam
both members, which is extra
work, and weakens them. I say,
better to simply fasten beam to
post (which they call "weak"),   brace
and add brace piece below, thusly:
Windows, doors and roofs get
11 p. Some roofs are encumbered
with chimneys, turrets and skylights, which are complex and
prone to leak. I say, better to
put them thru a wall, beneath a
roof with a big overhang.
For a handcart "capable of moving up
to 500 pounds" they specify used 26"
bicycle wheels. I say: too weak sideways,
especially on rough ground at a construction site. 20" BMX wheels stronger.
Seven different huts get 30 p. Most
are as complex as small houses. Simplest
is a bent-pole hut covered with plastic
and then "camouflaged with twigs, branches, or whatever is handy"; and a

3

lean-to thatched with boughs. "A very crude lean-to can be built in less than an hour using only an axe. However, one that will last more than one season and repel rain may take 2 or 3 days."

"Primitive native shelters": wigwam (3p), tipi (6p), yurt (6p), and stacked log hogan (4p). Canvas covered, except hogan which needs MANY logs.

Tree huts get 12 pages. A few of 15 guidelines: "Never design your tree hut first and then try to find a tree that fits. Let the tree suggest to you what the design should be." "Make safety your first consideration." "Allow for flexibility in the joints so the tree can grow and move with the wind." "You can nail or screw into large trees without causing much damage." Eek! ANY metal put into tree may cause you to be cursed when, long after hut is gone and tree dead and down and being cut up, someone's saw hits a forgotten nail !

This book inspires thinking about a wide variety of shelter shapes and construction techniques, though not always the most simple and reliable.

Bibliography describes 23 books, 2 periodicals, 6 catalogs (Campmor, Bean, Defender (marine), Silvo Hardware, Woodcraft, Harbor Freight Tools).

1998, 159p.8x11 (much white space), many diagrams, 2 color photos, $20 + shipping?,ISBN 1-58017-035-8. Storey Books, Schoolhouse Rd, Pownal VT 05261. Has 11 other home do-it-yourself books. 1-800-441-5700; www.storey.com   (B&H)

Making Bentwood Trellises, Arbors, Gates.
Also from Storey, Jim Long's book is about decorative structures. But the techniques can also (eg) form a shading over-roof at a semi-permanent camp-site.

"Bentwood projects ... can be made from a vast variety of woods. The main requirement: use green, flexible limbs for the arched parts." Cut "no more than 24 hours before you begin.... Wood loses flexibility quickly." Not fully restored by soaking. Before you cut, decide on a design and list the arch pieces needed.

Jim discusses good and bad traits of 29 eastern trees, including toxicity and invasiveness, in 15 p. Most rot in 2 or 3 years, except: bald cypress (Taxodium distichum), but hard to find and often short and stocky; eastern red cedar (Juniperus virginiana), but sap slightly sticky and needles mildly irritating; and osage orange (Madura pomifera). Not mentioned but we have used: western red cedar (Thuja plicata). It has relatives elsewhere (also called arborvitae).

"Settlers moving west in early 1800s took osage orange cuttings" and planted them "in rows spaced every 3 ft, then allowed to grow together into a dense hedge that was cut every 3 or 4 years... Impossible for cattle or people to penetrate hedge due to the tough, dense limbs and the short thorns along them."

"As the wood dries it will lose its flexibility, so don't try to reshape.... Joints that are wired will need to be retightened after shrinkage occurs."

Jim also tells (in 4p.) how to form a living arbor by training live saplings/bushes/vines. That takes much longer as they must grow, but endures. Of the ten plants suggested, hemlock (Tsuga) and holly (Ilex) have foliage year-around.
April 2000

Designs for 22 bentwood and 9 other trellises, 6 gates, 13 fences, 4 arbors get 96 p. Jim then suggests vines for climbing them, and, finally, devotes 10 p. to recipes for teas and cakes to ingest while admiring your handiwork !
1998, 158p.8x9 (much white space), 14 color photos, many diagrams. $20 + shipping? ISBN 1-58017-051-X. (addr to left)

Report on Ero tent and a moss hut.
Last autumn we were temporarily in an area where we had little equipment and didn't want to build anything elaborate.

Holly had found a used dome tent in a dumpster; in good shape except poles missing and hole melted in netting. The floor showed no wear, indicating little use. Made in China for Ero Industries, Morton Grove IL 60053; sold by FredMeyer. 60x92x38"; floor 4.5oz reinforced polyeth, walls 1.7oz nylon taffetta. Much like the Taiwan-made Stansport (see May 96 & 97 DPs) except the door zipper was less convenient (⊥ instead of ∩ routing).

One problem: the top was net, with a fly (hooked-on tarp) suspended above, giving much ventilation whether wanted or not. (Done so someone can't asphyxiate self with candle, causing lawsuit?)

I salvaged slender branches from a fallen cedar and, by lashing two together with thin ends overlapping, made poles long enough to erect tent - with difficulty: I had to add side bracing cords to stabilize. (Maybe branches were less stiff than original poles.)

But the tent alone with its unstoppable ventilation, gave little warmth. Okay at night when huddled under sleeping bags. But not for frosty early mornings when we wanted to do things inside while waiting for outside to warm up.

An old moss-covered maple had fallen nearby. That inspired me to build a moss hut around the tent. I did not trust the tent to support the moss (it barely held up itself !). So, over the tent, I made a squat tipi-like frame (from little alders in need of thinning), and layed moss on that. I had to repeatedly chink thin areas and sags. (I used MUCH moss.)

To reduce ventilation, and keep our breath moisture out of the moss, I covered the tent with plastic; except the door on which I hung several burlap bags which we raised to enter. When we wanted light inside, we replaced the burlap with plastic. To keep dew and rain off the moss, another tarp went over it, extending to the ground on 3 sides, but tied out in front to form an antiway in which we could remove rain wear and keep water and pee containers.

After ALL THAT, we were comfortable. One cold mid-Oct dawn, outside measured 29°F, inside 60°. Quite dry after moss added. (With tent alone, condensation on walls trickled down into our foam pads, becoming wet spots.) Minor gripes: moss fragments fell on us and bed when we went in or out; tent walls sagged. YKK Winnebago plastic zippers all worked at first, but outer one soon failed.

Despite having a level site and all items within 200 yds, project took ± 30 hours. Worthwhile for a two-month stay? Probably not. But educational. Bert

Our backyard tent rotted in the sun !!!
We set up a smaller tent, but keep it covered during day. Phyllis, CA 921

Free parking for live-in vehicles ?
    Many community parks allow free camping, usually boondock-
ing (no piped water or power), but sometimes with limited hook-
ups. Some fed lands allow boondocking, but usually charge.
    My husband and I spent $3 total for camping fees during
our first 3 years on the road as full-time RVers. That was
for one night in a NM park on the Mex border. Coleen Sykora
                                  (from Workers On Wheels #24)
(Comments:) My impression: communities that offer free camp
sites are generally in long-depressed areas (eg, Great Plains)
where chambers of commerce try desparately to attract retirees
or anyone who will spend money. (Years ago, DP got a brochure
from a highway assoc in s.Nebraska listing free camping there.)
    In western Oregon, though there may be possibilites we do
not know about (not having a motor vehicle, we are not keenly
attentive), the only campgrounds we know of close to cities
are not free. (And we've heard of people ticketed for sleeping
in vehicles parked on streets.) Farther out, there are many
graveled logging roads, negotiable by most pickups and vans,
and some sedans. (But I'd not take a motorhome.) Many of the
roads, espec close to cities, have locked gates (more now than
20 years ago) and are posted against motor vehicles (though
motorcycles often bypass gates): often good for hikers and
bicyclists. Most gravel roads are occasionally patrolled by
police or timber-company security (depending on whose land:
some areas are a checkboard). There are many dead-end spurs
where one can park away from the main road. B & H, OR 973

Protecting a trailer against thieves and vandals.
    Replying to Angela in Nov99 DP: many things can be done
to make a trailer safer. Most cost less than $50 and are sold
by building supply stores. Old trailers are less-easily made
safe than mid-1970s and later, because built differently.
    First: install an interlocking hinge protector. This
keeps door from being jacked open, or pried open with crowbar;
because the hinge locks from the hinges, not the door handle.
    Next: add lock guards that go over door next to handles.
Door knobs and dead-bolt locks also worth adding or changing.
    Also good: reinforce door frame with 2x4s nailed into the
wall. This helps prevent jacking a door open. (A burglar can
use a car jack to force apart the frames on each side of a
door. After half an inch, the door will just swing open.)
    Windows, too, need attention; especially any near ground
level. Bolt on Plexiglas, Lexan or other coverings that are
difficult to break. If caulked, they also add insulation.
    Home security systems can be bought and easily installed,
and you can subscribe to a monitored alarm system. There are
other possibilities, but these will get you started.
    Remember: even a fort will not keep burglars out if the
occupants don't do their part. Lock your doors, get to know
your neighbors, and tell them what you would like them to do
if they see anyone but you go into your trailer.
    If someone is strongly determined to get in, they will.
But with some thought and a little work, you can make breaking-
in too difficult to tempt a casual thief. Steven Cleveland,
                                            TN 377, Dec
(Comment:) Instruct your neighbors CAREFULLY. If (eg) a
friend arrives before you do and enters with your permission,
you don't want someone over-reacting and calling the police !!
                          April 2000

5

Be wary of distant job offers, especially at campgrounds.
    If seeking work, I'd only go to areas where I wanted to
spend time whether or not I found jobs. Then, while there,
I'd check out what was available. If I found a camping
facility I thought I'd like, I'd stay there a few days to get a
feel of the place and to learn what work they might need.
    I've heard many horror stories about people who accepted
far-away jobs and spent much time and money traveling to them,
and then were unhappy. Coleen Sykora (from Workers on Wheels)

For quick earning with little expense, consider cab driving.
    I can almost always get a job immediately, anywhere in
the country. Drivers often quit, and cab owners are anxious
to keep their equipment rolling.
    After 6 months, a driver will usually start to 'burn out'
and not put in as many hours. That's okay: if you've worked
hard and not spent much, you'll have enough money to move on.
    I just quit the best deal I ever had: 38% of meter plus
owner paid gas. I did so much business I couldn't handle the
stress. But I now have enough to live modestly for two years.
    I usually lease a 24-hour (single shift) cab and sleep in
it, bathing at public facilities. Generally, if one is
working hard, the owner gives you a lot of leeway.
    You will need a valid drivers license with good record,
and a sense of direction and ability to rapidly learn your way
around. Cab driving is a good way to scout a new area, and
gain information and interesting experiences.
    I buy a map and (if available) a cab-drivers handbook.
The handbook tells the city's numbering system, and the map
shows lakes, rivers, railroads which break up the system.
    Alas, driving is becoming increasingly competitive and,
in big cities, regulated. Also, some cities are dangerous,
even if one knows the streets well. I advise: small towns,
or working-class suburbs adjacent to big cities. Depressed
areas are actually good places to make money as many people
there can't afford cars. You'd be surprised how many people I
take to welfare offices. Waitresses and bartenders often tip
well, because THEY depend on tips. Las Vegas is, by universal
acclaim, the best place to earn big bucks. As with anything,
ask the old timers - which will be easier after one has
'hacked' a few times. Kurt Wettstein, IL 606, March 99

Are freight trains more dangerous than highway vehicles ?
    (Responding to Laura's report in Nov99 DP:) One of my
uncles worked many years as an engineer (train driver). He
told about folks trying to hop freights. Of how they were
injured trying to get on, and of hassles by railroad security.
Ever since, I've stayed far away from moving trains.
    Hopping may be a thrill for some folks. But I'm content
to walk, hitch, or get rides other ways. You are correct that
known hobo camp-sites become targets of police. Steven, TN377
                                                         Dec
(Comment:) Someone in Hobos From Hell (review in May96 DP)
thought railroads were safer than highways, at least for going
long distances. Though getting on and off a moving train is
risky, while on,you are relatively safe, provided you (eg)
avoid cargo that might shift and crush you ! Yes, railroad
security can be nasty. But so can highway police. These days
with ANY mode of travel, do it only if you have a STRONG
reason to, and KNOW what you are doing !!!
    To anyone considering hopping, I strongly recommend the
Hobos From Hell books (review, at least) for safety tips. B&H
                       April 2000

I spent summer in the police states of Florida and Louisiana. The Florida Marine Patrol stopped my slow boat on a slow day. After I was interrogated and my boat searched, and cited for no life preserver on board, I was "free" to go if I would wear a state-loaned life jacket. (I wonder how the REAL natives (Creek, Apalach, Seminole) survived for centuries without life jackets in their canoes !) Which is the least policed of the 50 police states ? I want to move somewhere and be left alone. I've been living car-free for almost a year. Jimmy, TN 374, Jan

Be wary of "welfare agencies", especially if you have kids. A family consisting of mother, father, and two children age 4 and 6, had been living in their van, going from day job to day job. A local church announced a food bank for needy folks. But, when the family asked for food, the church turned them in to police. The children were taken into custody by child "protection services" and the parents were arrested for "child endangerment." The parents are now out of jail and trying to get their kids back, so far to no avail. Steven, TN 377, Dec

Pluma Beyer (who edits/publishes Green Pathfinder) lives in a 12x12 ft cottage she built. The cottage has electricity, stove, sink, and running cold water; but no frig. Hot water is obtained by heating on the stove.

After giving birth, Pluma's sister was staying with Pluma. Social workers visited, supposedly to make sure the baby was well cared for. They pretended to be friendly, and left. Two hours later they returned with police, snatched "the two-day-old baby from the arms of its mother who was successfully breast-feeding ,it", and took it to foster care. They cited the baby's temporary surroundings. Several months and one court hearing later, the baby had not been returned. Pluma reports, "I am astonished at how social workers lie." TN 376

(Comments:) Social workers have an incentive to lie ! In May 97 DP, Tom Van Doren in Idaho reported: "State social services get $4000 from the government for every child they put into a foster home. They keep 75%, and are not responsible for what it is spent on." Also in May97, Michael Sunanda reported on kids snatched from people he knew. And we've read many horror stories elsewhere. Tips for avoiding trouble in Dec96 DP. Though most portable dwellers less jeopardized than rooted folk (either hard to find or quick to move), best avoid roads and public places (except maybe summer when many kids about).

After any suspicious encounter, promptly move on. Local news item: A 15-year-old boy was playing basket-ball. Needing to pee, to save time he went into bushes. An 8-year-old girl saw him and told her mother who called police. They arrested him, charging child abuse. He was convicted of exposing himself and is now in a juvenile prison with a sex crime permanently on his record. Steven Cleveland, TN 377, Dec

(Comments:) If the boy had immediately left the scene, he probably would have been well away by the time the police arrived. (But maybe he didn't know he'd been spotted.) When we visit cities, we often use bushes, not only to pee, but for jug showers, and to temporarily stash and later retrieve big items we don't want to lug around: all activities a law-n-order fiend might consider offensive or suspicious. Of course, we use (eg) undeveloped park areas where few people go. But accidents happen. If spotted, we quickly leave the area.
April 2000

How to live during tough times ?
Recently, many readers have asked this or similar questions. Some say the USA (USSA?) is now a police state. And police are not the only threat.

Is a portable dwelling safer than a house or apartment ? That depends on particulars, as there are many options.

During our 20-odd years dwelling portably, Holly and I have had very few scary encounters; and no arrests or fines, serious injuries or illnesses, or major property losses. Because we did things right? Or mostly luck? Anyhow, for what they're worth, our suggestions.

Minimize travel on roads. Besides bringing hassles, vehicles destroy more years of life and health than does any other menace. (Cancers mostly kill those who have already lived long.)

Recreate near home. Instead of big, far-away gatherings, seek local picnics, etc. For distant fellowship, maybe hold many the same day and link by radio.

If you must travel on roads, ride-share with careful drivers. Keep windows clear (no stickers or dangles) and all lights working. Carry spare bulbs for promptly replacing any burn-outs.

For rest stops, park away from public roads. If bicycling, you might go into some bushes. If motoring, pull into a shopping-center parking lot (where cops seldom hassle unless complaint.) *5/99p3

For long stays, seek private land where you can park (with permission) out of sight of roads and neighbors.

When employed, try to find shelter close to work. Some companies allow employees to park overnight or camp on their lot, and use water and electricity. (Advantages to employer: workers are more available for unexpected rush over-time jobs, and their presence deters burglars.) When choosing a job, pay attention, not to the supposed pay rate, but to how much you can CLEAR after all living costs are paid. *6/88p7

Though a motor vehicle is sometimes useful, ownership is a costly nuisance. If you must have, pick a common one that won't attract attention and that has parts widely available. *5/96p11

Backpackable dwellings are much easier to hide. *5/95p9-12, 5/94p10-11. But, if remote, will re-supply be a problem? Think about various ways to. *5/96p3

Don't expect to find one dwellingway that combines all the advantages of several different ways. Eg, as roomy as a house or big dome, mobile as a 4WD, portable and low-cost as a small tent, and secure as a dug-out. You must choose. However, contrary to beliefs of folks whose only camp-out was an ordeal, physical comfort is quite easily obtained, though may require learning how. *9/84.

Regardless of dwellingway, generally be quiet and unobtrusive. Do anything noisy either in a remote TEMPORARY spot and leave immediately, or in a sound-proof chamber. (Underground? *9/86p5)

Store at least 6 months food. 6 YEARS is better if you expect to remain in the same area. *9/85p1, 6/88p3. But hide in several places to protect from thieves both private and official. (Now law: when an emergency is declared in an area, anyone caught with more than six-months food is eligible for 15 years in prison, REGARDLESS of when purchased!)
April 2000

Cut costs. Expensive possessions and activities not only attract robbers, but take much of your life to pay for.

Don't train for jobs or start businesses that need licenses.

Get your dwellingway in good shape before having children. Have kids only if you(all) can care for them full-time. (Sticking them in schools forces them into a clash of values between other kids and you, that will likely make them AND YOU miserable.) Keep school-age kids unseen during school hours. *12/96

Don't give up hope. Police states don't last forever. (The 70-year USSR lasted unusually long.) Unless reformed, they eventually bring themselves down by fouling their economy or environment, and alienating supporters. Ordinary people can hasten change by avoiding taxes and fines, and spending less. Eg, a boycott of recreational travel would not only save lives and reduce pollut-ion, but cut the profits of oil compan-ies, auto makers, airlines, and giant resorts - and THOSE folks will get atten -tion if they tell the cops: "lay off" ! Bert & Holly, Oregon 973, January
* DP issue and page with more on topic.

Safety for a woman or child alone.
Best be hard to find. But maybe your camp is temporary and you don't want to spend much time hiding it.

To deter two-legged predators, you might simulate being with other people whose return you expect at any moment. Eg, when a second sleeping bag is not needed for warmth, lay it out to suggest an additional bed. And, beside it, put sweater, jeans, and boots much larger than yours. (If big enough to wear over yours, they'd also give extra warmth.)

Against four-footers I suggest, first a spear, which can be just a sharpened pole of a tough wood (test), light enough to move fast. Jab, DON'T throw. (If you throw, it's GONE!) Also see Nov99 and May95 DPs. Holly & Bert.

Be wary of big, dead, high limbs.
Even a small branch can kill or maim if it falls far enough to gather speed. A hard-hat or helmet can save your head from light blows but not heavy ones.

Though limbs and whole trees often fall during winter storms, they also fall on warm summer days when carpenter ants, termites, and fungi are active.

Be alert for breaking sounds above: you may have time to dodge. Also be aware, if you grab or bump a tall slim tree that bends, it may knock something loose high up.

Best not camp near big trees. If you must, choose the base of a straight live conifer (eg, fir, pine) with many large limbs near ground that may intercept branches falling from higher up. Even a plastic tarp adds some protection. (Though weak, it will stretch and absorb energy.) Camp on SIDE (not top or bottom) of narrow valley. (Less wind.)
(B&H)

Choosing pack frames for comfort.
In summer 1999 Outdoor Explorer, Mike Randolph, though writing for rec hikers, gives some advice good for all.

If you hike mostly on trails or easy terrain, choose an external frame with "a high pack bag, which enables the wearer to stand up straight and helps

8

the frame ... transfer the weight onto hips." Also, "inexpensive, and cool in hot weather because the frame keeps the pack bag away from your back." "If, however, you scramble up mtns and need lots of flexibility," pick an internal frame. Mike prefers bags with drawstring closures. "Zippers eventually wear out."

Not addressed: how easily can pack bag be removed when frame is used for hauling (eg) pails and boxes, and how well does it endure such use? Extrastrong "freighter" frames are made.

To stow map, compass, sunglasses, etc, Mike favors a pack bag with many external pockets. But they won't help when the pack bag isn't on. I prefer pouches on the waist belt. Or, on a smooth trail, I sometimes wear a small knapsack in front as well as an external frame in back. I can access knapsack's contents without removing anything. Also, the weight in front improves my balance. Drawback: I can't easily see my feet and where they step. To keep the knapsack's straps from slipping off, I put it on first, with the frame's straps over.

For comfort, seek a frame with "hip belt that hugs the sides of your pelvis without creating any gaps. When you have the pack on and it's loaded down, the angle of the hip belt is not right if the belt is tighter at bottom than at top." "Firm foam preferable...." Shoulder straps should "meet your (shoulders) at a comfortable angle."

"Be wary of stores that carry only one style of frame, and of zealous salespeople who recommend a type of pack before asking the mágic question: 'what kind of hiking do you plan on doing?'" But the proof is in the wearing. "If possible, borrow a friend's pack, fill it up, ánd take it for a test hike."

Almost any frame will eventually cause sore spots. Not mentioned: if with others, swap loads occasionally, so weight bears on different spots. Or, if carrying in stages, taking one load part way and then going back for the next, use two+ different frames, alternating.

Also not mentioned: building your own. Plans for a simple triangular frame of branches in LLL. Merits, besides being buildable when needed: potentially light -er; easily folds for rides or storage. But loading for comfort takes longer, espec with big hard items like pails.

Polyprop clothing preferred to wool.
(Re March & Sept 84 DPs): I've used polypropelene Boy Scouting, and it kept me dry and warm where wool did not. I make sure new boys' parents get it for them. Steven Cleveland, TN 377, July

Good wicking helps prevent blisters.
California College of Podiatric Med study: runners in cotton socks got twice as many blisters, three times as big, as those wearing acrylic. Dampness blamed: not wicked away as well by cotton as by acrylic or wool. Julie Summers, 1990

Vapor barriers, sweat - and odors.
Stephenson (see p.5) sews vapor barrier liners into sleeping bags, and sells vb undershirts ($25-$30 + ship). He challenges readers: "do a test. (If) you are wearing an undershirt, one or two insulating shirts, and a warm jacket: replace the undershirt with a vb shirt.

(Lacking a proper one, use a plastic bag with holes cut for head and arms.) Don't put the jacket back on and you will notice you are as warm as before.... The vb shirt reduces loss of humidity and thus reduces evaporative cooling at your skin...." I'm now trying that and, yes, I need one less sweater. But I put on the plastic bag, not next to my skin, but over my undershirt, because yrs ago:

I was bivying in a city and had only one thin sleeping bag. So I used a big plastic bag as a liner. It was not comfortable next to my skin, clinging to me when I turned over. But it did add warmth. However, after 2 days, despite daily washing of feet and arm pits (but not liner), my whole body and the liner got stinky - much like feet can smell.

Stephenson claims, a vapor barrier reduces odors because of "quick sensing and thus avoidance of sweating, plus blocking of air circulation that causes sweat to turn rancid." What I found, ABSENCE of circulation was what caused odor build up. (Feet stink; not hands.)

(Later.) I've now worn the plastic bag during 7 days, with the same upper-body garments. Only arm pits washed. No unusual odors. Maybe the cloth between skin and plastic allows enough circulation. (However, bag's neck and arm holes enlarged, compromising test.)

I plan to repeat sleeping-bag test, but with a cloth liner INSIDE plastic.

Stephenson's vapor barrier is not a smooth plastic but a "flannel-like soft fabric". Assuming no clinging, perhaps it alone allows enough air circulation. Stephenson claims: "easy to clean with a wipe of a damp cloth (soap or detergent okay if needed)." B & H, February

More about ticks. (Also see May99 DP)
If wearing clothes, smooth fabrics, such as windbreakers, are better than knits. Harder for ticks to grab onto.

If wearing long pants, tuck into socks, so that any ticks that get on feet must crawl up the outside of pants and might be spotted before reaching skin. But ticks may grab on elsewhere.

Any clothes should be light colored, for easier spotting of dark ticks.

If you cut your fingernails short, and seldom carry POINTED tweezers, you might leave parts of a few nails long enough to use as tweezers. Grab tick as close to your skin as possible.

Permethrin "repels 82% to 100% of ticks", but is toxic and absorbed thru skin. If used, apply only to clothes and let dry before wearing. Ditto DEET. An early DP tip: wear cat flea collars on boot ankles. But won't stop ticks above.

Larval ticks feed on mice. To deinfest an area, scatter tubes of cotton balls dipped in insecticide. (Eg, Damminix) Mice use cotton to make nests.

A former lyme patient says: few MDs can/will diagnose or cure lyme (which requires high doses of antibiotics for months). For lyme specialists, plus treatment info (latest only on internet: some librarians can help): www.Lyme.org

The map, from Yale U of Med, shows "lyme risk" by county in ne. Only other mod-risk county: Mendocino CA. But a county may be "low risk" either because ticks few or not infected, OR because humans are seldom outside. Within an

April 2000

area, risk depends on habitat, espec mouse numbers. A backyard or park may be more hazardous than a remote mtn. H & B, Jan

moderate risk →

low risk ↙

high risk →

Store bicycle off ground ?

In May98 DP, Bert reported that a porcupine punctured tires of a bicycle left in the woods. To prevent animal damage, hang bike on tree branches. Bruce of BC, 1999. (Comment:) Good idea where feasible. Unfortunately where we were, no tree suitable for hanging was also where it would get winter sun (desirable for keeping dry and thus minimizing rust). Also, unless hung VERY high, a hanging object is more visible.

Many years we've left bikes over winter in woods, protected only by tarps, with no damage. We were hoping to stay lucky. That winter we didn't. Bert & Holly, OR 973

Folding bicycles are handy but expensive.

In Nov 1998 I bought Car-I-Bike's "Urban" 5-speed at Cruiser Bob's in Oceanside CA for $270. Under 30 pounds with a factory kickstand. No problems so far.

I found the Urban takes about the same effort as a full-size bike. Maybe a bit more on hills. I pulled a trailer shopping, but not up any serious hills. (But a trailer is no fun on hills even with a full-size bike.) I would not use it for loaded touring (only 5 speeds), but I did a comfortable 80 miles in one day out of Seattle with a daypack.

It's best feature: when folded, there is room for it almost anywhere, so I can take it with me to use at a campsite, in town, wherever. Cruiser Bob says, you can stuff it in a bag and carry it on a bus. I also test rode a Dahon but found it way too flexible. Ken Gilbert, WA 982, Nov

Bicycles with 20" wheels have some advantages for adults.

They fit easily inside trunk, shell or van. Though not as compact as folders, they cost much less. Often found at yard sales. Tires and tubes are cheaper than for 26" wheels. Spokes are shorter and much stronger. BMX one-speeds are built for abuse. But extra-long seat post needed. Ken, Nov

Small bike handy, not speedy.

I'd had trouble fitting a full-size bike into some vehicles. So, when I saw a 20" "kiddy" bike free at a yard sale, I took it. It lacked a seat but was otherwise okay and seemed sturdily built.

Fortunately, I had a seat and a LONG seat post among my parts collection. The post's diameter was a little too small, but with a shim of drink-can aluminum, it fit passably. When I raised the seat high enough, only the recommended-minimum 2" was within the bike's frame. But the bike's sissy bar, when positioned high and angled forward, reached the (regular,

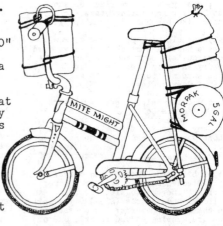

April 2000

not banana) seat, to which I lashed it as added support.
Unfortunately, with the shim and the lashed sissy bar,
the seat won't easily lower for transport. But the high-rise
handlebars swivel down after loosening one nut, and that
alone allows the bike to fit in some small cars.
The sissy bar plus the sturdy rear fender provides a
fairly good rack, to which I lash a load with rubber straps.
And the dip of the high-rise handlebars is just right for
holding a 5-gal pannier (see May97 DP), which I attach to
rings I lashed to the handlebar near the hand grips.
I don't ride fast on this bike. It has only one (low)
speed; and, with the short wheel base, small wheels, and high
me, a pot hole could literally throw me for a loop. Also,
the short cranks give little leverage for climbing hills.
But, otherwise, it handles nicely.
If getting a 20" bike, remember, it won't be a bargain
at any price if you must buy expensive parts to make it
usable. Seat posts are costly at bike shops. On one full-
size bike, I used a wooden branch as seat post, but don't
yet know how well it will hold up. Julie Summers, November

Crab trap easily made from salvaged items.
Find: hoop (eg, bike rim, bike tire stuffed to stiffen it,
flexible branch bent round and lashed to self); fishing net
(in trash cans near fishing boats); 2 or 3 pound weight; rope;
bait (eg, fish heads or guts). Tie: piece of netting to hoop,
weight to center of net, and rope to hoop in 3 or 4 places.
Place bait on net. Lower to bottom of water. Wait. After
crabs have found bait, pull up. Herbert Diaz, CA 956, 1996

Improvising a fishing reel.

Fasten a weight (a spark
plug is easy to tie to) to one
end of the fishing line (often
found in trash cans on fishing piers, sometimes WITH HOOKS
(be careful !). Attach hooks to the line near the weight.
Bait is easy to find. (Many people throw away left-overs.)
Tie the other end of the line around the neck of a jar,
bottle or drink can that has smooth parallel sides. Then,
starting at the neck end, wind the line around the bottle,
trying not to overlap turns except for the first few. (You
want the line to easily slip off the bottle.)
Hold the neck of the bottle firmly in one hand. With
the other, throw the weight to where you hope the fish are.
Most fish are one or two pounds and can be easily pulled in
with a 6 or 20 pound line. Herbert Diaz, CA 956, 1996

Discarded music strings usable as snare wire.
In a musical-instrument-store dumpster, I found brass or
bronze guitar strings, in good condition. Bruce of BC, 1999

Don't get scalded by steam from a hot pot.
It's no fun anywhere, but in the back-country away from
medical help, it's worse. When lifting the lid, first raise
the FAR side while keeping the NEAR side resting on the pot,
so the lid will deflect steam away from you. Also, do not
peer in immediately. Let initial blast dissipate. Julie

A better reminder than a string around my finger:
A clothes-pin dangling from my hair onto my forehead.
When an easily-burned food is cooking, the clothes-pin reminds
me to check, even if I'm doing other things. Julie Summers
April 2000

Be careful when selecting and instructing companions.
Bert asked what led to my recapture after I successfully
escaped in Texas (eluding pursuing dogs, described in autumn
97 DP) and traveled to Tennessee.
I was with a friend and his wife. I was confident she
knew my situation and understood that she should not talk
about me. But she told some of her friends that I had escaped
and they told others, etc, and the story reached the police !
Lessons: If you can possibly do something by yourself,
do it alone even though it may be more work. The fewer people
who know about your business, the better. Never assume
another person sees the situation as you do: "everyone is
logical unto himself." While there is nothing wrong with
traveling or dwelling in two-somes or more-somes, make sure
every member of your party knows all the do's and don'ts -
even the obvious. Lance Brown, Texas, August

Social workers DO often lie.
(In response to the report in April 2000 DP), Pluma is
right. It has been my experience that social workers would
rather tell lies - to justify their jobs and their seizure of
children, than to tell the truth and risk being reprimanded
or told by a judge they were wrong to take a child.
Supposedly, the goals of the social workers and judges is
re-unite the child with its birth parents. In actuality, with
institutionalized foster care, very few parents ever get their
children back unless they go through all kinds of hoops.
The social workers have way too much power and authority.
And, as Pluma found out, attorneys and the law are stacked
against unconventional child rearing. Steven Cleveland,
                                          TN 377, Feb
How do "wild" families deal with education/socialization ?
An unconventional lifestyle that children are born into
and grow up with, is not exciting and idealistic to them, as
it was to their parents. For the children it is just routine,
and, often, something to be rebelled against. That was the
main reason for the demise of the Kibbutz movement in Israel.
You touched on some of this in DP. (In Aug-Nov 99 with part 2
of "a naturist park with portable dwellings" ?)
I also understand people's need to keep their family's
business (and their family) "on the D-L" because of hassles
from the Kulturpolitzei. **Alan, NY 140, April**

I like the Spyder clip-on knives.
Military guys call them "tick" knives. There are various
styles. My favorite is the Endura, fully serrated. These
knives are light, rugged and easily accessible because of the
clip. When new, they are almost too sharp. I purposely broke
the tip off mine so I would not have to be so careful: I use
the knife to eat with. I've had one since late 1980s. Eugene

Dwelling Portably   Aug/Dec 2000

I am interested in living on a house boat.
Or in an old summer house. Maybe on Hog Island or
Prudence Island across from Newport. As a first step, I
bought an air boat and pump.
The article about welfare and families with children (in
April 2000 DP) is true. Churches often squeal on people.
Churches treat me badly, perhaps because I am big and smart
and have Indian in me. Social workers steal. They prey on
the weak and retarded. They pressure you to put their name on
your bank account so they can withdraw funds - leaving you no
money for food. One social worker told me she can get me on
SSI - IF I pay her and her lawyer. (Have you heard about
this ?) People shouldn't depend on welfare or SSI if they
want to live free.
I live communally. We collect aluminum cans (5¢) and
deposit bottles, trash-pick used clothes and stuff, sell and
hustle at flea markets, barter, borrow, gamble, get free food
at churches, and buy price-reduced bread, fruit and vegies.
I often cook spaghetti and beans. Elaine, Rhode Island, July

I am still living on a boat.
My fifth winter without space heating. John, WA 981, Oct

A dairy goat, plus foraging, can nourish.
In Jan 91 MP(DP), Anne Callaway wrote: "Dairy goats are
not very portable, we've found. To set up their pen and house
and feeding, was almost as much work as moving the whole rest
of our camp.... Powdered milk is much less hassle."
Maybe that's true - IF you don't count the hassle of
going to town to buy powdered milk, and the hassle of getting
a job to earn the money. Also, if you ignore the environmental and social damages inflicted by commercial milk
producers, dehydrators and transporters - and the war-making
paid for by those industries' taxes.
"Goat walking is one of the few ways that a group of
people can live without making war on life", says Jim Corbett
in Goatwalking, Viking, 1991, a book I highly recommend. Jim
tells how to select the proper goat and train her for range
milking, and how to supplement her milk with foraging. "With
a daily supply of three or more quarts of milk, you won't need
to worry about protein and calories; but sources of vitamin
C, iron, copper, manganese, and fiber must be added."
Goats are one way to survive the collapse of society.
After your food reserves are eaten, goats will still feed you.
Bear, Idaho 832, May
(Comments:) Goats are the only domesticated animals (we know
of) that might be able to move through the steep and brushy
woods where we usually live. But I wonder how much milk a
goat could produce here. Good browsing/grazing areas are
small and scattered. (In your May99 DP article you cautioned:
a goat producing milk could not also carry loads. Would
traversing very rough terrain, even without a load, be a no no
?) I also wonder about winter. Even in western Oregon, where
farm animals can graze almost year around (snow infrequent),
they also receive hay. Does your goat find enough winter
browse in Idaho ? (You bought feed for a pack llama.)
Another advantage of goats over cows or horses: their
hoof prints are almost identical to a deer's, and thus won't
arouse curiosity (but might attract a deer hunter). But is
noise a problem ? Can you train goats to remain silent ? Or
do you surgically mute them ? Holly and Bert, July

December 2000

(Reply:) Quoting Corbett: "Quick-witted, social and educable, with a capacious, high-speed digestive system, a thorn-chewing mouth, cliff-climbing hooves, and a relatively undiscriminating appetite for low-grade roughage, goats thrive on a wider range of plants and in more varied terrain than any other large herbivorous mammal.... Because goats will readily admit human beings into herd membership, they can be managed and moved without fences, corrals, hobbles, tethers...." Not necessary to move pen, house and feed, as Anne did.

"In canyonlands or other rough country, goats are at home on cliff faces where humans can follow only with difficulty."

You **CAN** pack females. But better to pack neutered males so females' energy all goes into milk production. During winter here in cold snowy Idaho, I do feed hay - because ranchers will still trade me hay for dead pine trees (fence material). And I still buy food for myself in stores. But with the goats as partners, I'm prepared for the day when I can no longer get either hay or groceries. Goats milk more in summer than winter, and if dependent solely on wild browse in winter, might not milk much if at all. But during summer, I make and store cheese. Corbett tells how. I've found solar drying is the best way to preserve - learned from an old Nat Geo article on Mongolian nomads (fellow goat herders).

A happy, secure goat is very quiet. I have bells on mine to help keep track of them. Bells also serve as night-time alarms: if anything chases them, I'm awakened by the clanging - a consideration here where wolves hunt at night. Some goat packers say Nubians are noisy and don't want them. But I milk a Nubian whose milk is rich and sweet. She cries a bit just prior to milk time, to hurry me. If a goat is scared, trapped, or separated from its herd, it will make noise. But I could NEVER see a reason to surgically mute them.

A goat's track is similar but not identical to a deer's - a herder must learn the difference to track lost goats.

When I camp the goats share my tarp shelter. They are trained to stay off my bed and to pee outside. A squirt gun will teach a goat its bounds: they don't like water. However, if herd/herder bond strong, they can be trained to wade creeks.

Bear, ID 832, August

(Comment:) I believe Anne was living in urban/suburban areas. Without a pen, keeping goats from ranging onto neighbors' land and eating gardens or rousing dogs, might be difficult. B & H

Yes, there is a law authorizing confiscation of food.

Though, to find it, you must wade through reams of legalese. It is part of the anti-hoarding/profiteering act. It applies only after an area has been declared a disaster zone. To date it has been enforced: in flooded parts of the Mississippi Valley several years ago; in San Francisco after the earthquake; and even here in Lenoir City when we had our tornado. The law reads: anyone with over 6 months of food in their home is a hoarder regardless of when the food was bought or put up. Your food can be confiscated. You may also be fined and imprisoned. The law was passed in reaction to a group in Houston who, after a tropical storm, bought up all the ice and resold it for $10 a bag. Bureaucrats said they feared that, after a disaster, some rich man might buy up all the food in an area. Class-action suits have been launched against enforcers of the law including the Federal Emergency Management Agency, and are still being fought through the courts. Steve Cleveland, Tennessee 377, July

December 2000

More about tents used in the California Sierras.

The North Face tent was a tadpole model, two-person, 4½ lbs. It is great for long pack trips where weight is a concern. I took it along on an 80-mile round trip into John Muir Wilderness Area, to Puppet Lake and back. My hiking partner liked it very much (and bought one after we got back). North Face uses what they call a no-hitch pitch system on many of their tents. The poles stay together on the tent, making it easy and fast to set up. That is nice if the weather worsens and you need to set up camp fast - which I've done many times with this tent. Cost about $100 in 1996.

The Eureka was a geo-desic #4 dome tent that sleeps four. Large and roomy, and totally wind and waterproof when closed, it is designed mainly for bad weather. It is not easily set up in wind by one person; it really needs two. It is sturdy: I spent several days and nights in it during a storm that dumped 3 feet of snow. The tent handled that fine.
                                        John Atkins, CA 960, July

(Addendum:) Campmor's New Year 2001 catalog lists no "Tadpole". North Face "Slickrock", free-standing, "3-season", floor 4½x7½, center ht 3½', 4½ lbs, $240. Eureka "K-2 Extreme", "geodesic design", "4-season", floor 7½x9', center ht 3½', 10 lbs, $300 on sale. (Prices plus shipping.) Bert

Report on tents, based on 30 years experience.

All tents, are a compromise between comfort, weight, and cost. I've lived in a tipi (comfortable but heavy); an 8x10' canvas wall tent (more portable than tipi and comfort comparable;. but need a stove if you want a fire inside); a yurt for a few days (very comfortable, but need a stove, and difficult to move); many nylon dome tents (light weight, but can't have a fire inside, and sun rays destroy in a year or two).

These days, when not in my wagon, I use a plastic-tarp lean-to, an army-surplus bug net over my bed, and a fire in front of the lean-to with a pile of rocks behind the fire as a heat reflector. As I age, I become more and more a minimalist.

I'm spending the winter 50 miles from the nearest town, on the edge of the Frank Church wilderness area - the largest and least explored in the U.S. outside of Alaska. I'm training two horses to pull my wagon, But I hesitate to take it on highways. I just need to be mobile on forest roads. I plan to spend next summer exploring hot springs. Bear, ID 832, May

I camp on an island in Maine.

I live there 7 months a year in a large green tent. The tent sets on a poly tarp that covers a thick mat of twigs and leaves. That keeps the tent's inside drier, I hope. (The site is wet.)

I use 4 big plastic containers to store food, tools, clothes, and

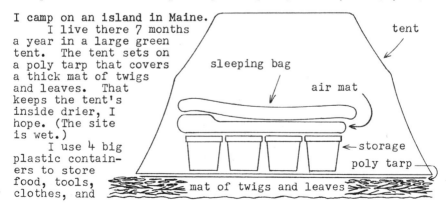

tent

sleeping bag

air mat

←storage

poly tarp

mat of twigs and leaves

books. On top of them, an air mattress and sleeping bag
provide comfortable seating and sleeping.
    I work on and in boats, which enables me to spend five
months a year in the caribe/tropics. There I use a 6x4' kid
tent and a 3x6' air mat. Total cost: $38 at a big box store.
With a nice floral bedsheet I thrifted, I sleep well. Off the
ground, I found no need for a sleeping bag. David, February

(Comments:) Is the air mattress in Maine just a hollow shell?
Or does it also contain foam ? The latter provides more
insulation. In May98 DP, Double Dorji, who had used a stack
of three Thermarest pads for ten years, reported favorably.
    Does your tent include a fly (tarp) suspended over it ?
Or a liner within ? We've found they add warmth and dryness.
    I wonder if your containers are the long/wide squat
"totes" we sometimes see on sale at hardware stores. How well
do they close ? How durable ? (We've been using 4-gal plastic
pails, which are okay, but not as stable a foundation, and
more tedious to open if accessing many things.) Bert & Holly

I lived aboard a sailboat for seven years.
    Back in the 1970s, my husband then and I spent months at
a time living in the Bahama islands. We found little to
forage on land. But fish was free for the taking. We learned
to salt dry fish. I ground wheat kernels for bread, and we
supplemented with brown rice and freeze-dried and canned foods.
Fresh foods on the islands were and are very expensive.
    It was a grand adventure but, like anything else, not
entirely "free". You must maintain the boat, and purchase
maps and other needed supplies. You can certainly get by
without such accessories as self-steerers, but some gadgets do
make things easier. Depends on your values and budget.
    Many tricks made life easier. Eg, rain catchers on
canopies can supply fresh water for drinking and, when plentiful, other uses. But I remember drought periods when, after
bathing only in salt water for weeks, I would have adored a
fresh-water shower.
    From what I hear, living aboard and cruising is more
difficult now, and not as safe, but can be done. Read up
first. And do it only if you've already spent much time on a
boat, because you will need courage and expertise. Lynn,
                                                OR 970, Dec
Frequent showers cool comfort while working hard in heat.
    A few years ago, Bert and I helped with a hay harvest in
interior Oregon during 90-degree temperatures, racing rain
forecast for the next day. The hay had been cut and bailed
by machinery, but loading the bails onto a flat-bed truck and
then into the hay loft was manual. During the hottest hours,
we showered every 15 or 20 minutes.
    Water there was plentiful. But if showering merely to
cool, or to rinse off dust (without soaping), a quart is
ample. I feel better drinking moderately and pouring water
on me for cooling, than gulping huge amounts and sweating it
out. Furthermore, I can rinse with water I would not drink
without sterilizing. (To quench thirst, I prefer plain water
to sweet drinks. Then, a half hour after drinking, I may eat
fruit to replenish sugars and salts.)
    At the haying, I introduced jug showers. (Previously
the family had used a hose - which was out of the way.) To
shower, remove jug's cap. The narrow mouth plus appropriate
tipping regulates flow. Some people, accustomed to piped
showers or tub baths, have difficulty at first maneuvering the
                        April 2001

jug and getting the flow where they want it. However, with practice, the motions become automatic. If a full jug is too heavy, use several partially full. (For more about simple showers/baths, see esp LLL Packet or Set, and DPs: June87 p.1, Mar89p.1 (now in Dec88), Jan91p.3&8, May93p.1, May97p.7, May98p.8, Aug 00p.1)

During the hay harvest, everyone worked nude but for shoes, gloves (for grabbing bails by their twine), and (during mid day) sun protection. Except: a near-teen girl who drove the truck, wore clothes, maybe to avoid skin-to-seat contact. (As I recall, she showered nude a few times, though usually she just wet her head.) A neighbor's house was within binocular-viewing distance, but no one seemed concerned.

Being nude not only exposes more skin for cooling, but makes showering easier. No need to remove clothes - or get them wet and have them bind. (Wet shorts or slacks are especially uncomfortable.)

Also, when warm, nudity is more healthful. Men's genitals need to stay cooler than their bodies: that's why they hang out. Pants and undies not only promote genital cancers, but cause more birth defects due to mutations of sperm than do all nuclear activities combined (we read in a fallout-shelter book). And, for women, bras are now thought to be the main cause of breast cancer. Bras constrict lymph flow, interfering with excretion of toxins. "Breast cancer is epidemic only in cultures where bras are worn. Where there are no bras there is little breast cancer, despite high levels of toxins in the environment and a poor diet."
(from Naturally, summer 1996)

To protect head, neck and shoulders from sun, Bert and I wore bill caps with short capes attached. They were not too satisfactory; when hoisting bails, the cape often flopped to one side, uncovering a shoulder. Other people wore wide-brim hats. Holly & Bert, OR 973, 97& 01

Free city has hot summers; mild winters.
Slab City spreads across the desert a few miles east of Salton Sea near the foot of Chocolate Mountains in southeast California. Within ill-defined borders, squatters live in vehicles ranging from $300,000 mobile palaces to junkers that can't budge - and in tents.

Thousands dwell there from October thru April. A hundred or so remain year around. Summer temperatures can exceed 110° day after day. Frequent baths or showers help cope with the heat.

Most residents are seniors living on pensions. But there are younger people, too - some too broke to live elsewhere. One extended family of 30 including kids, living in old trailers, now shun highways after being told to pay $1500 for insurance and smog device.

Most residents live individually. But there are a few organized groups, RV clubs mostly, including one composed of ±200 singles. Residents communicate on CB channel 23.

The main street is a flea market with diverse merchandise. Many of the conversations are in Spanish.

Slab City got its name from concrete slabs poured in 1942 as foundations for army buildings. They are treasured as level and comparatively-dust-free camp-sites. There's still an aerial gunnary range nearby that disturbs the quiet.

The county would like to regulate Slab City and charge fees; claiming the squatters benefit from (eg) fire protection while paying no taxes. (But they do pay taxes indirectly when they buy from area businesses.) However, the state owns the 640 acres and, last we heard (early 2000), the governments had not gotten their graft together.

Residents haul in their own water from a freshwater spring near the salty Salton. They also haul out their own wastes, and generate their own electricity if any. Many RVs, large and small, have one or more photovoltaic panels. (From Out West 1995(?); Time 17Aug98; Double Dorji; Phyllis Hordin.)

Travels and troubles with a motorhome.
In March 1997, I departed my Asheville NC home, driving a recently-purchased 1981 motorhome. With me was my dog and cat, and a little money from the sale of my house. I had read much (though not yet learned of DP) and talked with people about how to travel economically. My goal was to backpack and hike a lot. I was perhaps as well-informed as someone can be who has not actually done this. But, as I learned, you have to actually do something to learn what you really need to know - and you usually learn the hard way !

I learned that older motorhomes require tremendous upkeep - my small capital did not last long. Perhaps most important I learned: "What you own and what you owe, owns you." I knew this about houses. But only after I was out there on my own, did I realize that my 23-foot RV was owning me just as much as my house had. I wanted to go places off the beaten path, but worried that my vehicle might not be able to - or might, but break down and maroon me with no money for repairs. Chronic worry does not add up to a fun time.

By spring 2000 I'd run out of money, having had horrendous mechanical troubles. My replacement engine warranty turned out to be worthless, because a warranty is only as good as whoever gives it. After that new engine imploded, I should have stopped, found a place to park, and gone to work. But I was in the middle of nowhere with an RV full of stuff I'd collected. And, by then, seemed like I'd replaced every dang part. So I replaced the engine AGAIN, which cost my remaining funds. Next ? I got two flat tires at once. I had to call someone to send me money. Fortunately I knew someone who did, else I might still be sitting there in an immobilized vehicle. But I did not like having to ask. At nearly 60 years of age, I do not have indulgent parents willing to foot the bill.

After that, I thought I had already experienced the worst that could happen. WRONG ! Flat broke, I arrived in Beaverton OR one cold night, parked my vehicle, and went to sleep. I was awakened by my dog barking frantically and licking my face. I could not breathe - I was seconds from dying of smoke inhalation - the furnace had set the motorhome on fire ! The dog and I managed to tumble out the door just as
April 2001

17

flames engulfed the interior. I could not get back in to save my cat or anything I owned.

The fire department arrived. My dog and I watched as they tried to extinguish the fire. Hopeless ! The RV burned to the axles, destroying everything I owned except the sweat pants and T shirt I was wearing. No shoes.

After receiving a small insurance settlement, I rented an apartment and bought work clothes. Presently I have an (ugh) real job while living in an (ugh) real apartment in a Portland suburb. Not thrilling, but it is how I will finance my next adventure and replace some of my losses. I bought a Toyota pickup and had installed a small canopy - which is beginning to look like a camper's den. Slowly I am replacing camping equipment so, when I do take off I will have a good-quality tent and other gear, and not be huddled under a leaky tarp somewhere - which isn't fun for me. For a while, I will have to satisfy myself with short trips, but that's okay. Before going to bed, I read books about hiking - and dream.

Advice to those preparing for mobility: Go as small and light as you possibly can. (Read Travels With Charlie and Blue Highways for inspiration.) Even if you have mechanical skills (I didn't), replacing tires and other parts can be very costly. Don't set off in an unreliable vehicle: be in the best possible shape mechanically, and have a reserve for maintenance and the inevitable repairs. OR be prepared to work when you need' replenish your coffers - which may be easier said than done. (I met a delightful young couple living out of their van who needed jobs but had no "interview clothes" nor money for even a brief stint at local hostel.)

Everyone's situation is different, so figure out, IN ADVANCE, what the worst-case scenario FOR YOU might be - because that may happen. If you have (eg) $2000, will you travel on the first thousand and then look for work while you still have a thousand in reserve ? Or will you keep going until you spend it all ? If the latter, are you willing to accept whatever happens ? If so, I hope all you have is a backpack. If you are able to live comfortably that way, WONDERFUL, because you can nearly always get by if you don't have stuff that needs money to operate. Lynn, Oregon 970, November

How to keep pickup-bed contents drier ?

My pickup has a bed liner. And the canopy was installed with a felt liner that is supposed to help. It probably does, but not enough: everything kept in there is continually damp. I don't look forward to camping in or living out of this space. What have others done - other than move to Arizona ? Lynn, OR, Jan

(Reply:) We've not had a pickup. Maybe readers who have, will advise. Meanwhile, tips based on other shelter experience.

Any heat source that does not add moisture, will help dry. Eg, if you often park where a household electric extension cord will reach, a small incandescent bulb (60 watts, Hank Schultz said he used; in Mar89 DP) may warm your canopy space and dry it. Place bulb inside canopy, but NOT touching anything it might scorch or melt.

If the canopy has a window, park the pickup so the window faces the sun. (That will work better in Arizona.)

Unless the felt liner is quite thick ($\frac{1}{2}$" or more ?), it won't provide much insulation. If there is a narrow air space ($\frac{1}{4}$" to 1" optimum) between liner and shell, that will help insulate. If the space is much wider than $\frac{1}{2}$", placing additional insulation between liner and shell should help. Eg, the white flexible shipping foam often found in furniture-store dumpsters.

IMPORTANT. The liner should have a vapor barrier on its inside surface. (Ordinary felt doesn't.) Else moisture will diffuse through the liner, condense on the shell when outside is cold, eventually wet the liner, and won't be easily removed by ventilation.

If you haven't already, you might try living in that space for a few days to learn the effect. Our experience with well-insulated shelters (but on the ground or sunken; we've not been on a platform above ground), has been that, especially during mild cloudy/rainy weather, our presence reduces dampness, despite the moisture emitted by our breathing, cooking, bathing. Ie, our body heat dries the shelter more than our moisture dampens it. To achieve this, the shelter needs enough ventilation to let moist air out, but not so much that most heat is lost. Try varying amount of ventilation. Bert & Holly

Selecting a portable dwelling area.

This is for people with backpackable or improvised dwellings. (Those who live in or beside motor vehicles have different capabilities and problems.)

Where will you obtain supplies ? Even if you are able to live entirely by foraging/fishing/hunting/trapping, or by grazing a dairy goat or by cultivating small plots, you may learn that (eg) patrolling your trap line, day after day in all weather, though interesting at first, eventually ceases to be fun. Also, a high-protein diet (likely during winter when plant calories are scarce) may cause long-term health problems. If near a coast, subsisting mostly on shell fish may be easy - but risky. Filter feeders accumulate toxic heavy metals, even in unpolluted waters. (All oceans contain some.)

Unless you will dwell where you grew up and, luckily, are already well accepted by the natives, I suggest locating within easy hiking or bicycling (or kayaking ?) range of a city or urban cluster that has at least 25,000 people within its trade area. In small towns (except some resort and highway communities), someone unfamiliar will arouse curiosity, especially if they show up repeatedly. Also, a city has more stores, usually including a wholesale grocer or co-op or feed store that sells 50#/25# bags of grains.

Some people locate far from any city, hoping that fewer folk will traipse through the woods and possibly blunder into them. In our experience, the important distance, is not to a city, but to the nearest settlement or road. A spot only a few miles from a city, but with those few miles roadless and rough, will probably be less frequented than a spot far from cities but close to roads
April 2001

or rural residents. This assumes contemporary economic conditions when (eg) avid hunters, many of whom would rather drive than hike, often drive far to reach grounds not recently hunted. If gasoline become very expensive or scarce, driving distance may matter more. For us, an ideal city would have no outlying farms or diffuse suburbs. Ie, where the shops and houses end, the wilderness begins. Western Oregon cities do have outliers, but also some sizable forests or brush areas fairly close.

For chosing a site WITHIN an area, see especially DPs: May99p.5; May95p11& 12; May94p.10; Sept86p.1.

How will you earn money to buy supplies ? Cities are where most of the money is. Even people who work in woods mostly commute from towns and cities, and are hired by companies with personnel offices in cities. So, a city may be your best bet. Earn money as fast as possible and live economically while earning it. (Many people become addicted to (eg) costly foods or housing and spend money as fast as they earn it, dooming themselves to perpetual wage-slavery.) Try to sleep close to work. Maybe your employer will let you sack out on the premises. Spend spare time at no/low cost activities such as catching up on reading at libraries.

How will you transport supplies without a car.? Some suggestions in May96 DP, p.3. Unless you have a sizable group, a 4-wheel vehicle will probably be more trouble to store, maintain, insure, and license, than it is worth for occasional hauling. If you must use a vehicle, generally cheaper to borrow or hire than to own. Or possibly buy the cheapest heap you think will go the distance, do the haul, then promptly dispose of it. Bert & Holly, January

Scooter test report.
Inspired by DP's discussion (Dec 00), I borrowed a scooter for a test ride. Sturdy (steel?) construction; 25(?) lbs; wheels about 7" diameter, 2" wide. Two hand brakes. Plus one foot brake actuated by pushing down on the rear fender with one foot. Not foldable, but easier than a bicycle to fit into a small hatchback car. In good condition.

I was able to get on and go, and feel in control and stable immediately. I rode about 2 miles one way on a paved road that had mild rises and dips, somewhat more up than down. I did not know legalities, but felt more at ease riding on the left side so that I could see any oncoming traffic and get off the road for it. Then I rode ½ mile on smooth gravel, which the scooter handled well.

I had better balance when pushing with my right leg, but was able to trade off. My muscles tired much quicker than they do on a bicycle. Because I was using muscles I don't use much when bicycling or walking ? Wearing a heavy knapsack didn't help. But even when I removed it (for the gravel test), my legs continued to tire quickly.

On the level, I needed a series of 4 pushes to build up enough speed for a glide, and then got about a 4-second glide. I did not seem to go much if any faster than walking. (This puzzles me because, when I walk, skateboarders and roller-bladers outdistance me.) Downhill

(not very steep or long), scooting was faster than walking but maybe not as fast as bicycling. Uphill I walked. This test lessened my interest in scooters. Anna Li, OR 973, January

Cheap push-scooters are made in China. They do not impress me. Like Paul said, their small wheels easily catch in holes, cracks and ruts, and trip the riders. Some kid scooters I've seen up close, had poor welds or were too heavy. Bruce of BC, January

At home on the roam.
Before traveling in town or country, by foot or bike or auto, I go over this check list and select items to take. (Seldom if ever do I take everything on the list.) It has evolved over many years because, while traveling, I note usefulness of items I do have, and note other items I would LIKE to have had.

I try to be as well prepared as possible within limits of weight and bulk and costs, vis-a-vis likelyhood of needing. (I can't be ready for every contingency. Sometimes I just have to improvise as best I can.) The more multipurpose an item, the better. Eg, bar soap may be used for body, clothes, hair (and shaving); and as deodorant.

I offer this list as a guide to help others make their OWN lists, which they should tailor to THEIR individual needs.

CLOTHING. Rain: waterproof jacket with hood (or poncho; better on bike but not thru brush); pants; mitten covers; plastic bags (to protect items in knapsack, and as shoe-liners). Sun: bill cap with skirt; light-weight long-sleeve shirt. Rocks/thorns: shoes/boots. Cold: socks; mittens; dicky; sweaters; cap; vapor-barrier shirt; sweat pants; wind breaker; insulated vest or hooded jacket. (Extra clothes are cheap insurance.) Bugs: head net. Prudes: tee shirts (double as towels); pants/shorts.

SHELTER: clear plastic rain tarp with tie-out cords already on; bug bar; sleeping bag; pad; sheet; (tee shirt stuffed with extra clothes form pillow); twine; rubber straps (from innertubes).

TOOLS: knife, small saw; clippers; pliers; trowel; work gloves; knapsack or packframe; compass; hand lens; mirror; binoculars; watch; air thermometer; duct tape (small roll off big roll); small scissors; mouse trap; fishing line/hooks.

NOURISHMENT: canteen (used plastic drink bottle); water treatment (iodine crystals and water in small bottle); food (more than when sedentary); vitamin C; berry-picking jug (gallon plastic wide-mouth with shoulder strap, can be packed with food, also used to wash clothes); assorted plastic bags; pot, or foil as improvised pan; wire for use as a fire-proof pot hanger.

FIRE: flame maker (butane lighter/ matches/ magnesium/ large flat plastic lens); wax (for igniting damp kindling).

ILLUMINATION: flashlight; spare cells; candle. (Can usually find jug or can to make lantern to shield candle from wind. If not, use berry jug.)

GROOMING: bar soap; safety pins; sewing kit; comb; nail clippers; menstral sponge (and date of last menses).

INFORMATION: field guides to plants; other reading material; maps; pencils/
April 2001

pens; paper; crayon/felt marker (for
hitching and other signs); stamped envelope (to notify someone if delayed);
money (including phone coins).
    BICYCLING: sun/wind glasses; helmet;
panniers; pump; tube-patching kit (with
an UNopened cement; or self-stick
patches); adjustable wrench; 3 tire
irons (or spoons); screw driver (on
knife); heavy plastic scrap (to line
tire if big hole - inaddition to duct
tape); spare tube (stays tied on bike);
spare brake pads; lube oil (motor oil in
reused small plastic bottle); rags;
generator light (attached to bike);
black plastic for covering parked bike.
    MEDICAL: sun screen; chap stick;
toothbrush; floss; adhesive tape (to
make band-aids, etc); foam (to pad
blisters - see LLL paper); tweezers (for
thorns and ticks); snake bite kit if in
rattler country. Additional kit for
long trip: medical thermometer; oral
antibiotics; large gauze bandages;
sutures and/or butterfly bandages;
sterile scapel; povidone-iodine;
elastic bandage; more tape. (I don't
include aspirin or other pain killers.
Seldom do I want them, and they soon
deteriorate and become harmful.)
Julia Summers, OR 973, 1991 and 2000

Poison oak (and ivy) update.
    Leaves are thornless and in groups of
three (except on poison sumac, which
grows in the East). Leaves' shapes and
colors vary; often shiny. Grows as a
bush in the open, as a climbing vine in
woods, and as low undergrowth hard to
spot among other plants.
    Poison oak has no leaves during
winter, but twigs are distinctive (here
at least): light brown (most other
shrubs have green or dark brown twigs);
dull texture (most twigs shiny); branch
alternately (leaves on maples and most
honeysuckles branch opposite); tips
about 1/8" thick (most tips thinner).
    Merely brushing against the plant
supposedly won't cause rash IF foliage
not damaged. The toxin is sequestered
in resin canals within stems and leaves
(else it would react with the plant's
own tissue) and released only when plant
parts are crushed or broken. Or burnt -
the smoke is harmful to breathe.
    The toxin takes 20 minutes (say some)
or an hour (say others) to penetrate
skin deeply enough to cause rash. To
remove, some say, wash with soap and
cold water as soon as possible. (Hot
water may spread toxin.) Others say,
wash IMMEDIATELY with anything moist.
If no soap, gently rub repeatedly with
lots of plain water, damp dirt, pee, or
crushed leaves. (But careful: don't use
poison oak !) Sandra Baker (review in
May82 DP) rubbed on DRY dirt to hopefully absorb the toxin.
    Tecnu, sold specially for removing
toxin, is effective but no more so than
washing with soap and water, according
to dermatologist Dr Scott Serrill (in
Albany Democrat-Herald 9July2000).
    If you can't wash soon enough, Dr
Eric Weiss (in Men's Journal 6/99) says
gasoline (? !) or paint thinner will
dissolve the toxin and halt a rash up to
6 hours after contact. Rub on with a
clean rag, then wash off.
    Avoid contact with contaminated
clothes until they can be washed.

    If a rash forms, it will remain
until new skin grows, in about 20 days.
After the toxin is washed off, scratching will not spread the rash.
    Trying to develop immunity by eating
a little, or buying toxin-containing
pills, is dangerous. Better for any
damage to be on your OUTSIDE than INSIDE.
                                  H & B
Plants of the Pacific Northwest Coast:
WA, OR, BC, AK. Andy MacKinnon and Jim
Pojar, editors, with 8 other writers
including ethnobotanist Nancy Turner.
539 pgs 8x5, ±20 oz; 1100 color photos.
1000+ line drawings and silhouettes.
    Each entry describes one or more
related species and includes a range map.
Usually two entries per page. Many
entries include uses for food, medicine,
and construction. Many plant names are
explained. Has index for common and
scientific names, but none for uses. My
only other gripe: some species' families
are not mentioned. Regardless, this is
THE BEST field guide I've seen - and at
a reasonable price. Sample entry:
    COOLEY'S HEDGE-NETTLE ● Stachys
cooleyae.
    GENERAL: Perennial from rhizomes;
stems erect, leafy, mostly unbranched,
square in cross-section, bristly-hairy
on the angles, 70-150 cm tall.
    LEAVES: Opposite, deltoid or heart-
egg-shaped, long-hairy on both sides,
stalked, coarsely blunt-toothed, 6-15
cm long.
    FLOWERS: Deep red-purple, hairy, 23-
40 mm long, stalkless; sepals united in
a tube, the lower lip 3 lobed; 4 stamens;
4-lobed ovary; several to many in open
terminal clusters.
    FRUITS: 4 nutlets.
    ECOLOGY: moist roadsides, clearings,
thickets and open woods; common at low
elevations.
    NOTES: Taxonomists are not unanimous
about the distinction between Cooley's
and Mexican hedge-nettle. In fact,
Calder and Taylor (1968) maintain they
are all Stachys cooleyae in our region.
● The odour given off by hedge-nettles
when bruised is pungent, fishy, and
rather unpleasant (tho they are of the
mint family). ● The reddish-purple deep-
throated flowers are attractive to
hummingbirds. ● The Saanich made a
spring tonic by steeping the crushed
rhizomes in hot water. The Green River
and Puyallup people used the plant for
healing boils. The Quiliute made a
steam bath to cure rheumatism by putting
the leaves in an alder tub with hot
rocks, sitting in the tub, and covering
themselves with an elkskin or bearskin.
● The Haida of the Queen Charlotte
Islands apparently used to chew the
young stems of this plant, sucking out
the juice and discarding the fibre. The
Quinault sucked the nectar from the
purple flowers. Other northwest coast
groups did not consider it edible. ●
This "nettle", which often grows along
hedge rows, was first described from
Nanaimo on July 18, 1891 by Grace Cooley,
a professor from New Jersey. Stachys
means 'a spike' (as an ear of grain) and
refers to the inflorescence. (Despite
sharing the common name "nettle",
Stachys is not closely related to Urtica
(stinging nettle). Unlike Stachys,
Urtica is not in the mint family.)
                              April 2001

A few tidbits from other entries:
"Nettle" comes from Indo-European ne
meaning to spin or sew, "reflecting the
widespread use of nettle (Urtica) as a
source of thread."

"Nightshade" came by error. "An old
herbal describes the narcotic Atropa
belladonna as a solatrum, or soothing
painkiller. In translation this was
mistaken for the words solem atrum,
meaning black sun or eclipse."

Self-heal (Prunella vulgaris) has
long been used by aboriginies and Europeans alike, for healing purposes.
"Prunella is from the German die Braune
or 'quinsy'" (inflamed tonsils), which
the plant was used to treat.

The leaves of wintergreens (Pyrolas)
"contain acids that are effective in the
treatment of skin eruptions..." Oil of
wintergreen does not come from Pyrolas,
but from another member of the heath
family, false wintergreen (Gaultheria
procumbens), a salal relative.

Birch resin contains zylitol, a
disinfectant now sold as a natural tooth
cleaner. It also contains terpenes, and
"Athabaskan Indians were reported to
chew birch gum much as Andean people
chew coca leaves." The sap is used to
make syrup, soft drinks, beer, and wine.

Some say "the red huckleberry (Vaccinium parvifolium) was created by Asin,
the monster-of-the-woods, and that those
who ate the berries lost their reason
and were carried off to the woods."
However, "They were popular and were
eaten fresh by all coastal aboriginal
groups within range of the plant."

The Saanich dried leaves of vanilla-
leaf (Achlys triphylla) "and hung them
in houses to keep" flies/mosquitos away.

"Several species of Polygonum were
called 'smartweed' or 'arsmart' in the
old days, because of the irritating
effect of the leaves. It is not clear
why species in this genus were used
medicinally on the human hindquarters,
but they were, for everything from
poultices for external bleeding to
treating piles and itchy skin diseases."

Before the flowers matured, the
peeled sweet young stalks and leaf stems
of cow parsnip (Heracleum lanatum) were
eaten by many aboriginal groups. But
care should be taken to not confuse it
with violently poisonous water-hemlock
or poison-hemlock. However, cow parsnip
contains furanocoumarins, which can
cause rashes and persistent blisters
after handling the plant and then exposing your skin to sunlight. Giant cow
parsnip (H. mantegazzianum), known from
Strait of Georgia area, is apparently
more phototoxic than H. lanatum.

The central pith of fireweed (Epilo-
bium augustifolium) was eaten by the
Haida and other aborigines. French
Canadian voyageurs ate the plant as a
pot herb. "The leaves are rich in vitamin C; can also be used to make a tea."

1994; Lone Pine Publishing, 1901 Raymond Ave SW, #C, Renton WA 98055. 800-
518-3541. $20+$3 p&h in 2000. (Canada:
206, 10426-81 Ave, Edmonton AB T6E 1X5.
800-661-9017. $27+?p&h). Revu by Julia
Summers

Store-bought herbs seldom effective.
They may have been grown in poor soil,
sprayed with pesticide, picked at the
wrong time, heated, or left in the sun
too long (which destroys active ingredi-

ents). Much better to get fresh herbs
and process yourself. Evidence shows
that raw foods and herbs raise immunity
levels and prevent (eg) cancer.

We are surrounded by natural healers
that are free. Many tree saps are
better than expensive wound lotions. (If
sap too thick, dissolve in booze.) I use
aloe vera and comfrey on burns. Cayenne
peppers increase circulation, and have
been successfully used on many diseases.
Lobelia tinctures, if made from good
seeds with booze (eg, vodka) and vinegar,
have knocked out pneumonia.

To judge potency, smell the herb. If
no smell, not effective. Al Fry, ID 836,
1998?

Garlic oil cures my earaches.
It is cheap and effective. I extract
a few drops from fresh garlic cloves and
put in the painful ear, repeating if
pain persists. Bruce of BC, 2000

Homemade ear-drops for "swimmer's ear".
Mix equal amounts of rubbing alcohol
and white vinegar, lie on your side, and
put a few drops in the ear. This creates
an acid environment that eliminates the
bacteria which cause the irritation.
G.S.Stevens (from Men's Journal 6/99)

Garlic treats various infections.
Stevens says, for a cold or sore
throat, sip garlic soup. For a cut or
scrape, mash a fresh clove and rub on,
then cover with a bandage.

Honey, too, has antimicrobial properties.
Apply to wounds, burns, abrasions.

I clean my teeth with a twig.
For removing incrustations, a plain
twig plus much rubbing works about as
well as anything, I've found. (Pumice,
toothpaste, or baking soda don't seem to
help much.) I reshape the tip various
ways, using a knife, as needed to fit
between my teeth.

Use only twigs from bushes/trees you
know are not poisonous. (A few woods are
very toxic. Eg, oleander, which grows in
southern Calif and much of South.) Bert

Root fillings now thought harmful.
George Meinig, DDS, a root-canal
pioneer, changed his mind after seeing
much evidence that root fillings often
cause serious infections of heart, lung,
joints, kidneys, stomach, eyes, and
other organs. To warn, he wrote Root
Canal Coverup in 1993, updated 96. (226
pages, $20 + p&h, Bion Publishing, 323 E.
Matilija 110-151, Ojai CA 93023.)

Teeth are not solid. They contain
tiny tubules. Body fluids normally flow
from blood vessels in a tooth's root
outward through the tubules, nourishing
the tooth. Filling the root blocks this
flow. Then, normally-aerobic mouth
bacteria that get into tubules, turn
anerobic and produce dire toxins.
Neither immune-system cells from the
blood nor antibiotics injected into the
blood, can reach those bacteria to kill
them. But the toxins (being very tiny
molecules) reach the blood and travel to
other body parts where they may cause
"degenerative diseases".

Not everyone is so affected. Some
have immune systems able to cope with
the toxins, at least until they suffer.
April 2001

What kinds of pails are best for what ?
    Storing food ? Shedding water ? Sealing air-tight ?
                                                  Bruce of BC
(Reply:) For unsheltered storage, we prefer round 5-gallon
pails with rubber gaskets on lids, and NO pouring spouts
(which might crack and leak). Check that rims and lids are
in good condition, with no breaks, and no cuts taller than
needed to open. (Some food-handlers slash ruthlessly) Those
pails sometimes seal air tight, but don't depend on it.
    For extra protection, we may put a small tarp over each
pail, with a clump of dry paper, moss, bark, or leaves
between lid and tarp, to bow up the tarp so puddles don't
form and leak through any punctures in the tarp. (We do NOT
suspend a tarp ABOVE a group of pails. Rodent residence !)
    For storage within a shelter, we prefer 4-gal squarish
pails because they fit closer together. Also for transport
because, on pack frame, their weight is closer to our backs,
or, in knapsack, the flat surface is more comfortable. H&B

How can I get pickle-smell out of a plastic pail ?
    I found a neat pail with a tight lid that formerly
contained pickles. Lynn, Oregon 970, January

(Reply:) I don't know of any quick way. The smell of our
pickle pails SLOWLY lessens with time and use storing books
or clothes. The stored items pick up the odor but lose it
when exposed to air or (with clothes) washed.
    Storing water in a container, with occasional changes,
seems to help. Eg, a former peppermint-shampoo jug we've
used for rain-water storage for ten (?) years, is now ALMOST
ODORLESS. Because the water picks up the smell/taste, we put
in such jugs only water for washing.
    With some onion barrels, we tried: scrubbing with hot
detergent solution; setting open several days in hot sun;
stuffing with crumpled newspapers and leaving in for a few
weeks. None helped much. Holly & Bert, Oregon 973

Tips for getting food free or cheaply.
    Fast-food outlets often discard large amounts of unbought
still-good food each night when closing. Find out the closing
time of one close by, and politely ask the manager if they
have any cooked left-overs they are about to dump. Usually
the manager will be glad to put unsold food to good use and
let you have it free or for a dramatically reduced price.
    The owners or managers of some independently-owned
restaurants will swap meals for dishwashing, cooking (unless
local laws require handler's permit), or other needed services.
    I have used both these approaches when I didn't have
money, or simply wanted to save money. Jane Johnson, NY 100,
                                                          Dec
(Comment:) I have seen left-overs set on top of dumpsters
for people to take. Perhaps worth checking if going by an
outlet already closed. But keep in mind that most prepared
foods spoil quickly, especially those containing meat, milk,
eggs, or concoctions that include them (eg, mayonaise).
    For dumpster diving tips, including tales of some
fabulous hauls, see Lazlo Borbely's article in Dec97 DP. H&B

Your eating choices intrigue me. I'd like more details.
    Especially your avoiding canned foods, yet using a stove
only once a day. I eat from cans little compared to most
Americans but I do like canned peaches and tomatos. Laura,
              April 2001   WA 981, Oct 99

(Reply:) We preferably eat fresh foods, mostly wild, when available. We try to obtain a variety but aren't fanatic. Eg, during blackberry season, we may eat only berries all day until evening meal. And during spring, if near a good patch, nettles are our chief cooked green vegetable. During winter, we eat mostly stored grains and beans, various kinds, sometimes sprouted, cooked once a day for the evening dinner with the remainder consumed the next day. Cooked starches keep at least 24 hours if cool (under 60°?) we've found. Dry unoiled popcorn keeps much longer. (We don't have a frig.) Holly & Bert

Holey pot becomes portable fire pit.
   I found a big old pot with holes in its bottom. I set it on rocks to let air through the holes. With a grill set on top to hold a pan, it works well for cooking.

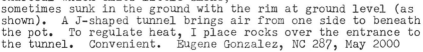

   I use the pot various places: sometimes on my porch, burning charcoal which emits little smoke; sometimes sunk in the ground with the rim at ground level (as shown). A J-shaped tunnel brings air from one side to beneath the pot. To regulate heat, I place rocks over the entrance to the tunnel. Convenient. Eugene Gonzalez, NC 287, May 2000

(Comments:) The sunken arrangement is somewhat like the Dakota Hole, shown in May94 DP (and 94 Summary-Index). Advantages I see of using a pot as hole liner, instead of building a fire directly in the hole: keeps the sides of hole from slumping into the fire (especially a problem if soil sandy/gravely); less fire hazard, especially if the soil contains old roots, because the fire does not directly contact the soil.
   Advantages of an air tunnel narrower than the fire hole: may be easier to form; easier to partially block off air flow. Advantage of two symmetric holes (as in May94 DP): air hole and fire hole can be interchanged if wind reverses direction. For most air flow, put air entrance up wind and (if ground slopes) downhill from fire hole. Bert & Holly, OR 973

"Stinger" water heaters are used in prison here.
   To heat water for soups, teas, coffee. They are safe if you don't spill water on yourself or put your finger in the water while the power is on. A meal can be cooked by putting food in two plastic bags, one inside the other, and submerging in a 5-gal bucket of water heated with stingers. (To make a stinger, see Dec97 DP.) They are also made commercially: 200, 300, 500-watt sizes. Herbert Diaz, CA 939, July

Why we have no telephone.
   A friend gave us a phone that hooks to a car battery and an antenna. But it seems to be a party line. Without lifting the phone, we hear others talking. When we tried to use it, there was so much static we couldn't hear well. And the bill shocked us: must have charged us for all calls crossing it.
   We had a phone in our car, but too much static here. We had to drive a half mile for it to clear up.
   Some visitors have come with cell phones that worked fine. But they need to be plugged in all night. We can't: no electricity on this plateau. Betsy and Jim Frazier, Widow's Mite Mission, AZ 860, June (from Another Look Unlmt.)
   (Puzzle:) Near a valley camp, many vehicles went up a logging road, then soon back down. (Explanation:) They went up to get cell-phone reception. B&H   **April 2001**

Dwelling Portably

formerly named   Message Post
POB 190,   Philomath OR 97370

Sept 2001 $1 per issue   Add 50¢ to check/mo under $6

Living underground with secret entrance and rooms.
    I am seeking info about that.   Joseph, IL 606, March

    I'd like to live COMPLETELY underground; so well hidden
that someone could walk across my home and not spot it.
    Have you heard any more about the underground home on
Nantucket Island ?   Al, New Mexico 880, May

(Reply:)   A 4Dec98 AP clip, reprinted in Living Free #111,
told a little more.   "There is a skylight, and a small
entrance hidden under dead branches." "The dwelling is heated
with a small stone stove."   Discovery was by a hunter who
"found a stovepipe sticking slightly above the ground." A
stovepipe is easy to conceal, so I assume the hunter was
attracted to it by smelling or seeing smoke. (The builder was
interviewed by the Boston Globe which might contain more info)
    So far, our experience has been with sunken-but-not-
completely-buried base-camp set-ups such as the Snugiup in
May95 DP. A wide window protrudes above ground for light,
ventilation and access, and the over-roof is some mix of cloth
and woven branches - not dirt.
    Someone might get within ten yards of such a structure
without spotting it, but could not walk across it.   Natural
obstructions, perhaps added to with dead conifer branches and
maybe live briars and brambles, discourage anyone from getting
close. One time a mushroom hunter came within ten yards of
ours, apparently without spotting it.   But an experienced
searcher looking for hidden camps, who got that close, might.
    Living completely underground seems more difficult.   If
you do much more than sleep in a buried chamber, you will need
artificial lighting.   For an electric light, a photovoltaic
panel that recharges batteries may be as difficult to conceal
as is a window. A gas lantern will produce fumes.   B & H,

More about Wendy's earth-sheltered home in Vermont.
    The only portions that protrude above the earth are the
greenhouse and the peak of the addition.   The addition has a
metal roof;   the rest of the house a sod roof.
    You asked (in DecOO DP) if I hid my house from inspectors.
NOPE. My town only requires building permits, not inspections.
But every time the town re-does its property-tax list, we get
checked out.   For ten acres plus the house
and outbuildings, I pay about $600/year
tax.   That is cheap for Vermont.
    Folks who believe they can't
legally build a house for less
than $100,000, might be
pleasantly surprised here.
I know people who started
very small and added on,
or built cheaply.   My
daughter is building
a 16x24' cabin.
The materials and
roofing come to
$2000.   Totally
furnished and
insulated,
it should   earth   earth

addition

sod roof

green-
house

not cost more than $5000.
My inexpensive house provides space for books and sewing stuff, and starting garden plants in spring, yet leaves time and money for travel south during winter. Wendy, VT 056, Apr

(Comments:) Much thanks for the further information.
I'd be very reluctant to spend even $5000 for something a government controls, because, if I do, I'm on their hook. Some year, the tax accessor may say, eg: "The rules have changed. Now you must install a flush toilet with septic system." That may cost a few thousand more. And, I must either obey, or lose the $5000 and considerable time I've already invested. If I obey, then I invest even more, and am even more on their hook next time they demand something. That makes me a slave !
But maybe $5000 is small enough to you that you don't feel hooked, and could walk away without major regrets if demands became excessive.
Holly and I invest quite a few hours and a few dollars in a base camp - which we could lose if a hostile found it (though no one has). So, the basic issue: how much is someone willing to risk - or how much abuse will they take ?
Because I am in earthquake country, I do not want a sod roof or anything heavy above me. (But a thin mat of branches, berry vines, moss, and fallen leaves is okay.) You are probably far enough from the Mississippi Valley to survive the next big quake there. (See below.)
Holly and I have many books and sewing items, most of which are stashed in pails here and there. They may be safer from rot and rodents (and inspectors) than if in a house, but not as accessible - and keeping track of what-is-where is a chore. So, our way, and any way, has its pros and cons. B & H

Potentially the greatest natural disaster of modern times.
The Mississippi Valley Seismic Zone consists of at least six fault systems that dwarf those in California. Because of their size and resonant rock, an earthquake could devastate large areas of MO, KY, TN, MS, AR, IN, IL. Moderate damage could extend to OH, LA, VA, NC, SC. A series of 8-plus size quakes in 1811-12 were so strong that church bells in Boston were shaken hard enough to ring. Though that quake affected a thinly populated area, a similar event today would kill and injure millions. Most seismologists expect one or more such quakes this century. (from Peter Hernon's book, "8.4", review
by LiveFree(IL)
More people can be housed in existing buildings.
There are many large houses here, built when families were bigger, with unused rooms that could be rented out. Also, ordinances could be expanded to allow owners of single-family homes to add an apartment within or attached to their house or garage. Legalizing such accessory units provides a quick and effective way to add affordable housing. The Seattle region needs tens of thousands of them. Doug Kelbaugh (much condensed from Seattle Times, 20Apr97; sent by Roger Knights)

(Comments:) Bill Kaysing made a similar proposal in Oct94 DP. I am glad that idea finally got into big media.
But, though helpful temporarily, seems better long-term to minimize occupancy of heavy buildings, at least in regions known to suffer severe earthquakes. Instead, turn a house into a resource centre time-shared by several families. Use its plumbing, washer,freezer, stove, etc; but sleep in tents.
September 2001

More idiotic temporary housing by a government agency.

The state of Washington is getting into the labor-camp business, spending an estimated $1.2 million to house about 750 cherry workers in state-purchased tents on public land.

The new plan is to erect at least three camps with as many as 50 tents at each camp. Each tent sleeps up to six workers on cots. The camps would be set up in succession, following the harvest around the state, with no one camp operating more than 21 days. Growers would pay a fee of $15 to $20 per worker per night. Workers also would pay $3 each per night to use the camps, or $10 for a family.

The state plans to hire a 24-hour staff for the camps, which would have trailers with showers, toilets, and cooking facilities. Water would be trucked in and sewerage trucked out. State prisoners would move and set up the tents.

An official called the program "an experiment" to determine whether growers and pickers would use centrally-located camps. Pickers tend to shun housing far from the orchards because they are expected at work as early as 5 am.

Every year, about 38,000 migrant workers, picking every-thing from berries to tree fruit, are homeless for the harvests. The cherry industry is most affected because of its brief, labor-intensive harvest. Many workers have been sleeping on riverbanks, in their cars, or in woods. Lynda Mape
(from Seattle Times, 10Apr00)

The state's first emergency tent camp for migrant cherry pickers opened Monday - just as the cherry season was coming to an end. It will be open for 21 days. The cost of 50 military-style tents was $800,000 - about $16,000 per tent. The per-unit cost will be spread over a number of seasons IF the state can find what it has yet to find: a permanent place to put the camp. (from Seattle PostIntelligencer, 16July00)

Saga of Chicago's Mad Housers.

The homeless are everywhere, and because there are so many, they often gather together to create communities. These "shanty-towns" are beginning to appear in major cities. They are usually hidden, but those who look carefully will find them - on vacant lots, in old factory areas, along river edges, by railroad tracks, and under viaducts.

While searching for potential sites, I came across many wintertime camps. A carpenter by trade, I marveled at the ingenuity of some constructions. People built with whatever they could scrounge: construction debris, milk crates, discarded furniture, old carpet. It is wonderful how society's cast-offs are turned into good habitations.

But many people, lacking decent tools and materials, have difficulty constructing even modest shelters. That is why Mad Housers became involved. The Mad Housers built ultra-low-cost houses and gave them away. The houses were small (6x8x8'), had no electricity or running water, and were not up to code.

By late spring, 18 were spread along railroad tracks, creating a new village in the heart of Chicago dubbed "Tranquility City" by its residents. Soon the huts were transformed by proud owners from raw spaces into homes. They painted walls, put up shelves, cleaned up yards, and planned to plant gardens. As word spread, the residents were encour-aged by (eg) railroad workers who tossed bags of food and clothing from passing trains. The media, sensing a good story, started to tell the tale of Tranquility City.

But, as media coverage grew, city officials became alarmed. They did not want a third-world city growing within

September 2001

sight of sleek Loop office towers. Inspectors showed up and summarily declared the houses unsafe. We hoped that media coverage would protect the houses: dramatic images of residents standing with folded arms before oncoming bulldozers would not be welcomed by politicians. But the city did not use bulldozers. Instead, city officials promised to give the 18 residents public-housing apartments if they would vacate their houses. One by one, the residents accepted.

Of course, officialdom's favors to those few, delayed public-housing availability to others, and did nothing for the thousands of homeless still on the streets.

The city argues that it provides shelters for the homeless. But city shelters are a poor solution at best. Many homeless prefer the streets to the strict regimen of city shelters; especially those who have jobs that conflict with shelters' hours. ALL hut residents I spoke with, found the huts a better solution than the city's shelters.

Thereafter, Mad-Houser-built houses were put in inconspicuous places and their locations were kept secret. Tor Faegre, IL 602 (who reported in Jan00 that Mad Housers are no longer active but may be revived (from Heartland Journal; winter 93)
I welcome info on turning a cold shoulder to the system.

I'm a squatter, though right now I'm sleeping in the belly of the beast. Squat for life - live free. Randy, TX 782, March

Napping in city parks and airport terminals.
Many urban residents use public parks to read, picnic, play ball - and to nap on blankets on the grass. So can backpackers and travelers, discretely, during the day or early evening. (At night, either parks are closed or sleeping is illegal.) However, obvious camping gear, such as tents or sleeping bags, will probably bring hassles.

Many travelers sleep in airport lounges while waiting for ongoing flights. If you have typical air-travel gear, you are less likely to get hassled. Jane Johnson, NY 100, December

(Comments:) In Feb90 DP, Cowboy, a homeless-resource-person in Los Angeles, wrote: "At night I walk the streets with my notebook. I sleep in the daytime in the park with a big cowboy hat over my head to keep the sun out of my eyes." I wonder if many urban nomads tend toward night activities because sleeping spots are more available during days.

Backpacks, too, may bring hassles. In Abapa Freer, someone reported seeing police hassle a man with a backpack who was sleeping on a park bench in Eugene. And, many years ago, while waiting for a bus beside a park in downtown San Diego, Holly and I saw police arrive and begin hassling people with packs. (We left promptly - before the police got to us.) I expect a big suitcase would have the same effect.

In a park there may be bushes which, though not big enough to sleep in, are adequate for hiding a backpack and other items not carried by most park users. The main risk: a busybody might see you hide your things and tattle. B & H

Places to park a car while napping.
Several friends of mine have successfully used train and bus parking lots. Station officials and police realize that people may sleep for hours in a car waiting to pick up a friend or relative. Jane Johnson, NY 100, January

I lived in a van for two months and may do it again soon.
Jen, CA 941, December   Sept 2001

Effective treatment of chronic lyme was not obtained in U.S.
Despite spending $26,000 and 25 years going to 110 MDs.
Finally, Michael traveled to a Mexican pharmacy across
from Douglas AZ. For $390, he bought enough Claforan I.V. to
"break" the disease (though he needed follow-up drugs for
several years to kill remnant Borrelia and prevent relapse).
Treatment of third-stage lyme is complex, requiring a
special diet and oral antibiotics to thin out the Borrelia
before taking intravenous drugs. Otherwise, (eg) Claforan I.V.
may kill so many Borrelia so suddenly that their die-off
neurotoxins paralyze the heart. Allergy tests are also
needed. (Claforan is chemically similar to penicillin.)
The only reliable treatment info Michael found: "Rutgers
University Co-op Extension Paper on Lyme's Disease", ten
documents available at www.lymenet.org . H & B

More about Mexican-border medical services.
I asked the Chamber of Commerce in Douglas AZ which Mex
pharmacies had English-speaking pharmacists, and which clinics
could install catheters. In 24 hours they obtained that info.
The Mexican pharmacy required a few days to obtain the
large amounts of medicines I needed. Each of three 10-gram
bottles of Claforan I.V. cost $130. (Cost in the U.S.: about
twice as much IF you could buy it. You can't, but if you
could, professional administrations would be required, costing
tens of thousands.) In Mexico, catheters cost about $8 each,
installed. For twice as much, the clinic will administer the
dose with a doctor or nurse present. If taking high doses
once a week, clinic administration is probably preferable to
doing it yourself without equipment such as a bottle stand.
But if dosing every few hours, as I was, clinic administration
would be inconvenient and expensive.
Regardless of who administers, best do it in Mexico.
Otherwise you must carry medicines across the border. I did -
and DEA special agents stuck dirty knives into factory-sealed
packages of sterile medicines. (The regular border guards,
polite and efficient, occasionally delayed me a few minutes
while checking the drugs against a list.) Michael in Oregon,
                                                        Oct 00
More about seeking services in Mexico.
I have lived in Mexicali part-time for the past 5 years,
while working on a documentary project and pursuing business
interests. When I first came I could hobble along in Spanish.
Now, after a total of about 4 months there, I am fluent: I can
read a newspaper, listen to the radio, and have discussions
beyond the "Where's the bathroom?" level. I have an ability
with languages, but, more importnat, when in Mexico I hang
with Mexicans, not Americans. For a while I had a Mexican
novia (sweetheart). A so-called "sleeping dictionary" helps.
Be aware that I'm an extremist: few of your readers
would adopt my lifestyle just to save a few bucks on a crown.
When I first arrived, I lived in a 10x10' tin shack among the
bar-girls and pingos that hang out in the old downtown area.
The latter thought of me as prey until I disabused two of them
of that notion. Those folk were the subjects of my photo-
graphic work. And who is more believable - some timid camera-
toter who goes home every night to a hotel room, or someone
who lives where the action is ?
If you are hanging with the locals, one of them would
probably help you find decent medical or dental care at
affordable prices. That is not as good as being able to speak
and negotiate for yourself, but it's better than being limited
                    September 2001

to English-speaking practitioners, especially if you have little money. Even if you lack local friends, resourcefulness helps. If you can gesture, speak a few words, and count enough to negotiate, then why not give it a try ? Stay in control, just as I hope you would in the U.S.: shop around, get a second opinion, and remember that you are the customer.

My little successes include getting a crown for my novia for less than she could find it for, and renting a 1000-square-foot bodega (cellar) for $100 U.S. per month and converting it to living quarters. The same landlord later rented me a hacienda (estate) for $100/month just to keep it occupied.

But let's be practical. If you're only after inexpensive medical or dental care, then seek out an English-speaker. You will pay only a little more - and much less than in the U.S.

But if your interests run deeper, then settle in and enjoy life in Mexico. Michael Trend, Nevada 891, May

My daughter and I plan a road trip to Montana this summer.

Heather, who dropped out of school in second grade and was an unschooler for ten years, will be working for the Student Conservation Association at Glacier National Park. I went to college for forestry at University of Montana in Missoula, and want to see what it's like out there now. Heather and I have camped out in southern U.S. and Mexico most winters. Now we will have a chance to camp up north. Wendy, VT 056, April

I live in Belgium, run a distro, and assist anarchistic groups.

Dwelling portably seems interesting. But isn't an address a problem ? Here, you have to have an ID card, and tramping is against the·law. Peter, Bruges, Belgium, May

(Comment:) Belgium sounds horrid. (France is too, last I heard, requiring registering with police if you move or are away from home overnight.) But how much are the laws enforced? Is it really any worse than the U.S. ?   Bert & Holly

Expedient backpack.
With a little twine, you can transform ordinary pants into a pack. You can do the same with a long-sleeve shirt. (Sent by John Atkins)

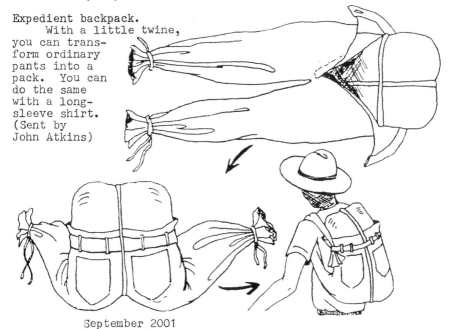

September 2001

For water I now use a large MSR Dromedary bag.
It holds 2 or 3 gallons. To heat water, it can be hung in the sun like a Solar Shower bag, but is much stronger. It has heavy-duty grommets for easy carryng or hanging.
To water plants, I added a 3-foot length of 3/8 or 1/2 inch clear vinyl tubing on the nozzle end (just pokes on easily), and attached straps to the bag so I can wear it on my back. I hold the tube in my hand to direct the flow. Eugene, NC 287, May

Catching menstral flow - or puddling through.
Commercial tampons and pads are costly, and contain ingredients questionable for health. Cloth pads are a nuisance to wash. Moss may have dirt/grit in it, and sheds.
I tried making paper pads, with newsprint inside and brown paper from food bags outside (so the newsprint doesn't contact me), but they weren't very absorbant nor comfortable.
At times I have used clean rags and discarded after use. But I don't always have a surplus. Nor do I like keeping used rags around until they are dry enough to burn.
I bought sea sponges at an art supply store, cut tampon-size pieces, and attached strings. But insertion was uncomfortable (as are tampons that lack Tampax-type inserters).
Finally, I sewed together two of the largest sea sponges, forming a 7x4x1" chunk, and used that as a pad, held in place by panties. Depending on flow, I rinse the sponge once or twice a day. (I seldom have a heavy flow.) Sea sponges seem amazingly absorbent and, unlike fabric, rinse easily in a few changes of water. Then I squeeze out as much water as possible (wringing would tear them). Unfortunately, drying requires 24 hours or more. If used wet, a sponge absorbs my flow, but dampens what I'm sitting on. I could buy more sponges and use them in rotation, but they're expensive. Sea sponges aren't very durable: mine started tearing after only a few months. I reinforced by sewing back and forth and all around. (I should have done that before using.)
Polyurethane foam is supposedly quite inert, so I cut a chunk off a cushion and tried it. It absorbed my flow, but wasn't as comfortable as the sea sponge - and more apt to cause a sore at the top of my butt cleft. Julie Summers, 1999

Simple electric heater also circulates air.
(In Apr 01 DP, Lynn asked how to reduce dampness within a pickup canopy.) If you are often able to plug into commercial electricity, mount a 100-watt light fixture on a plywood base. Remove tops and bottoms from two #10 cans (2# coffee), and solder together to form a chimney. Place the chimney around the light fixture and mount it 2 or 3 inches above the plywood, which provides a gap for circulation as the heated air rises.
D.L.Smith, FL 322, May
(Comments:) If you lack solder, you can punch holes near the cans' rims and wire them together.
The cans will get hotter and induce more air circulation if their insides are blackened (to absorb instead of reflect light.)

I have never had the lid blow off my potty pail.
But, when warm, it does leak enough to have an odor.
Bill Fargo

If honeybees scarce, provide nests for solitary bees.
Their pollinating will increase yields of fruits/berries, wild or tame. In a fir block ± 4x6x24", drill thru-holes of various sizes, 1/8 to 5/16", spaced 1/2" apart. To seal holes, mount a board on back, using screws. Once a year remove board and clean holes. Paul Doerr, CA 945   Sept 2001

Dwelling Portably

March 2002 $1 per issue

formerly named Message Post
POB 190, Philomath OR 97370
Add 50¢ to check/mo under $6

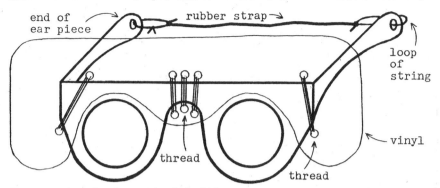

end of
ear piece

rubber strap→

loop
of
string

vinyl

thread

thread

Eye guard made from vinyl bottle.
   The biggest threat in the woods and brambles we frequent,
has not been animals (neither 8 legged (spiders), 6 legged
(insects), 4 legged, 2 legged, or no legged (rattlesnakes)),
but branches that can poke eyes. Ordinary sunglasses are not
adequate, because often my head is bowed, watching where I am
stepping, which allows twigs to intrude above my glasses.
Safety glasses I've seen were little better. They included
side guards but nothing above the frames.
   I cut plastic from a 2-liter drink bottle, bored holes in
it with an awl (or strong needle, or a nail or wire sharpened
to a fine point), and sewed it on using strong thread.
   Made several years ago and worn whenever I hike, the
guard has endured well. Minor problems: the vinyl, though
clear initially, was soon clouded by abrasive dirt wiped off,
slightly reducing peripheral vision; and it has a bit too
much curl and touches my forehead - irritating if worn many
hours. When I make another, I will use flatter plastic.
   To help hold glasses on when moving through brush, or in
a gale, I melted small holes in the tips of the ear pieces
(using a fine nail or big pin, held with pliers, heated with a
candle), tied string (or several strands of thread) through
each hole to form loops an inch or so long, and then tied a
light rubber strap (cut from bike inner tube) between the
loops. (Easier than tying the strap directly to the ear
pieces.) The strap goes around the back of my head. Bert

In summer 2003 we will travel the country.
   We are searching for the perfect place to start a punk
farm. We are seeking new friends all over, to help make our
journey a little easier and more exciting. Christopher and
                                        Danielle, PA 180, Oct
(Comment:) I wonder if there is any good (forget "perfect")
place to start a farm of any kind. Especially if you lack
experience and money. Land that is cheap to buy will generally
be far from jobs. But you will probably need jobs, not only to
pay property taxes and other overhead expenses, but to pay for
the vehicle you will need to commute a long distance to a city
where you can find jobs ! Result: more expense, more stress,
more danger (driving), more pollution, more resource consumption, less free time, and maybe even less fresh foods (because
of less time to garden) than if you lived in a small or middle-
size city. Christine of Slug & Lettuce, who searched a few
years ago, concluded that rural living was a snare and delusion.

We use a non-prescription tetracycline for infections.
Fish-Cycline: a hundred 250mg capsules, under $10.
D. Smith, FL 322, August
(Comment:) We've read: tetracycline becomes harmful if kept
long past its expiration date (marked on package), whereas
penicillan loses potency but doesn't become harmful.
With antibiotics as with food, cold storage can prolong
life. Generally the colder the better: deterioration rate is
roughly halved for each 10°F drop in temperature. So, even
storing in a buried pail (typically 50° to 60°, depending on
site and depth), rather than in a warm room, can double or
quadruple the time that the substance remains useful. H & B

I am saving up to buy a van.
I want to get out of here and take some trips. Clayton,
CA 932, Aug.
Car Living Your Way:
Stories and practical tips from over 100 people who been
down the road. This is A. Jane Heim's second car-living book.
(Her first was reviewed in Apr 00 DP.) It includes items from
her first book and from DP (with many DP writers mentioned),
but also much that is new.
"I am happy with my Ford Explorer ... which is going
strong at 200,000 miles. The seats fold down in back and I
can stretch out. The windows are tinted. And snow is not
going to stop me with four-wheel drive."
"The main problem I had with the (Dodge) van, and heard
of others having too, was that fumes from the engine would
quite often enter inside. I worked hard at sealing things up,
to no avail.... So, while not nearly as stealthy as a van,
I think that a pickup with camper is probably preferable."
"... In Mexico, have a car that is not cosmetically
perfect on the outside. Don't get too fancy, whether it be
your car or the way you dress. You are less likely to be
molested or robbed.... Make sure the car has had good
maintenance and is a make for which parts are readily
available. I prefer a Dodge or Ford because the engines and
running gear are so interchangeable from year to year."
"For added privacy, most states allow solar film on the
side windows only. A night-driving hazard on front and back."
"I cook on an alcohol stove (non pressurized), light
mostly with candles", and shower with "a 2-gal pump-up garden
sprayer.... No solar panels on the roof to be smashed by hail,
or water lines to freeze in a cold spell, or propane tanks to
explode if in a crash. Funny that nearly every RV has a
propane stove and frig, but if you use propane on a boat you
can't get insurance because of explosion danger."
Phil Johnson's 1973 Dodge Dart Swinger "is well planned
and well organized." While visiting his sister, though her
half-million-dollar home was "full of all kinds of material
goods,... she was always coming out to my car to borrow
important things she couldn't find in her house - stamps,
sewing kit, markers."
"Don't stay in single-business parking lots. A strip
mall is better - everyone assumes you are associated with one
of the other stores." "Truck stops are nearly always one-
nighters. I never met anyone that made (one of) them a
regular living spot," because that would not be tolerated.
"... Police are generally fearful of strangers (as are
the residents they serve), so it was better if I spent my
March 2002

nights in locations that were outside town limits, or in parking lots that had late-night business activities, or on properties that belonged to someone I knew. Because I was a member of the local Junior Chamber of Commerce, I got permission to park on their property with the understanding that I would act as an informal watchman. A small-town park was right next to it, so I had a public bathroom to use. There I stayed for a year or so."

At bed time, "Joyce suggests getting in your car and staying there.... Use a bottle for a call of nature so you do not have to go out in the middle of the night."

"There is a law against 'residing' in a National Forest. You are supposed to be vacationing. After talking with forest rangers, I understand this rule is hard to enforce." "In Colorado, anyone caught sleeping more than 14 days in a 30 day period faces up to a $5000 fine or 6 months in jail. This is to discourage resort workers in Steamboat Springs from living in Routt NF, 'taking prime spots away from tourists'."

Wherever she went, including a party at an elite country club, Jane found people who lived in their cars at times - including some who had plenty of money but did not like motels.

Each August, a high official attends hot-rod expositions in Reno, during which the city's population doubles, crowding facilities. Instead of paying $100 a night for a hotel room, he lives in his hot rod - but uses hotel pools free. "I always take a white towel (that) looks like a hotel towel. In the early morning, I get out of my car in my bathing suit, walk in, put down my towel, and jump into the pool. You can't do this at the same hotel each day; you've got to change hotels. In the afternoon I take my blankets and pillow and go to one of the public parks to nap.... I sleep by day and cruise by night.... You can't appear to be a vagrant. You walk with an air about you as if you own the place. You have clean clothes. You have an appearance of professionalism and quality about you. I never get hassled in the public parks...."

"I was a starving homeless person with two adorable sons, aged 6 and 8. We lived in various Disney World hotel parking lots, and found ways to crash the parks and restaurants daily. A bit nerve-wracking for me but a riot for the boys. They enjoyed car living so much they tried to persuade me to revert to this lifestyle a year or two later."

"... I've noticed a number of trucking families that live on the road. Mom and dad take turns driving, and the kids ride and play in the sleeper." Most are owner-operators contracted to household-goods movers. "Household-goods loads are light so you can have a really big sleeper." Also, "the delivery schedules tend to be less demanding so you won't have to run 30 or 60 hours straight.... The kids are pre-school age, or they are 'homeschooled' on the road...."

"At least 10,000 hippies live in or around the New South Wales (Australia) town of Nimbin. Most live in the 62 communes surrounding the village, but others live in tepees, tents, vans, campers.... 'It is a very tolerant, accepting community. That means we've also got junkies, alcoholics, mad people.' Tourists have discovered this 'colorful spectacle'. Their money presents a Faustian dilemma to townsfolk whose lifestyle is founded on eschewing materialism."

Lists, with some descriptions: 40 products and resources; 77 books; 28 periodicals; 29 media articles or shows. Index. 257 pages 6x9. 2001. ISBN 0-9649573-3-7. $22 + $4 shipped first class. A.J.Heim, Touchstone Adventures, POB 177-dp, PawPaw IL 61353. (Review by Holly & Bert)

March 2002

Home-made fly paste did not catch flies.
A house I sat had many flies in the kitchen. Not wanting to swat (tedious; messy; nik-naks in the way) nor spray, I got a formula for fly stickum. (A reference librarian found it in a Readers Digest book, "Back To Basics: How to Learn and Enjoy Traditional American Skills".) Mix one egg yolk, tablespoon molasses, tablespoon black pepper. I dabbed onto 3 jar tops, and set on window sills. Result: in a week, one dead fly (and it might have died of other causes and fallen in: I also killed flies by trapping between a sheet of paper and window. Through the paper I could see where the fly was. I tried to press hard enough to disable without squashing, but sometimes squashed.) Julie Summers, Oregon 974, December 2000

To stay healthy, get plenty of rest and sleep.
According to Science News 14July01, a century ago American adults averaged 9 hours sleep daily; today they average less than 7. Sleep-short people may use insulin less efficiently and become diabetic. (I've read elsewhere) if rest/sleep not enough, toxic wastes that form in cells during activities, do not get cleared out. Also, to get going and keep going, sleep-deprived people take drugs. Coffee, the most popular drug, contains caffeine and other potent chemicals, plus tars formed by roasting. Whether or not very harmful directly, coffee harms indirectly by suppressing urges to sleep or rest. And coffee no longer suffices: stronger drugs are sought. Most are legal, but that doesn't mean they are harmless.
Like rest, exercise is beneficial in moderation. But an excess can harm. People who (eg) win marathons seem super-fit, but may hurt their health long-term (I've read).
Sad, the number of fairly young people (40s, 30s, even 20s) who suffer heart attacks or cancers. Caused by longer work hours (with two jobs now needed to pay for the same life-style that one job paid for in 1970) and a more frantic work pace ? Or by more pollution ? (And, the more hours worked, generally the more exposure.) Likely, multiple causes.
Some medical spokespeople claim that Americans are living longer than ever. But they are talking about life expectancy AT BIRTH. Intensive care enables more premature and defective babies to live. But ADULT life expectancy ? There was a big gain from 1800 to 1900, due to learning more about infectious diseases, leading to better hygiene; and a lesser gain from 1900 to 1960, due to developing more antibiotics. But since ?
(To understand how statistics can mislead, imagine a place where half the babies die soon after birth and the other half all live to age 80. Average life expectancy: 40 years. Then, baby care improves, only 1/4 die, and the others live to age 80. Average life expectancy: 60 years. Finally, only 1/8 of babies die. Average life expectancy, 70 years. Obviously better for mothers, and for babies who would other-wise die. But people who survive infancy live no longer.)
Many forms of portable dwelling, because they require less work to pay for, allow more rest, less pollution, better nutrition, and more compatable exercisings. Thus they can improve and prolong health. Holly & Bert, OR 973, November

Drinking enough water greatly reduces cancer risks:
(breast 79%, colon 45%, bladder 50%), and eases 80% of joint and back pains. A 2% dehydration (barely enough for thirst) impairs short-term memory. 75% of Americans are chronically dehydrated. I should drink a gallon a day (16 8oz cups) at my weight (210 lbs). author unknown (from recycle bin)
March 2002

Dwelling Portably

or Shared, Mobile, Improvised
Underground, Hidden, Floating

June 2002 $1 per issue   POB 190-d, Philomath OR 97370

Copper wire: the best thing since rubber straps.
     I wrote an LLL paper, "How to Hold Your World Together",
about the many uses of rubber straps (cut from discarded innertubes). But sunlight or oil deteriorates them. Eg, lashings
on my home-made bike racks rot in a few years. Covering with
duct tape extends their life, but costs money and extra time.
     I found a good alternative: copper electrical wire. Much
gets discarded when buildings are remodeled. I prefer
strands 1/16 to 1/8 inch thick. (The fine wire within the cords
of discarded appliances is too flexible for most structures.)
Copper wire is more flexible than steel wire, enabling tighter
joints. Aluminum is lighter but too weak for most of my uses.
     Most wire I've found has an outer plastic casing with
several separately-coated wires inside. To remove the casing,
I prefer a knife with a straight cutting edge that comes to a
point (versus a curved cutting edge). I may leave the coatings
on the individual wires. They are less likely than bare wire
to mar the bicycle's paint.
     In addition to lashing things together, I've used copper
wire (both with and without the plastic coating) to make guards
on thrift-store kitchen knives. That facilitates strapping one
into a sheath I wear on my belt when hiking. (A guard also
keeps hand from sliding onto the blade if jabbing.) I also made
a magnifier holder (described in Oct90 DP): two thicknesses of
1/8" wire bent easily yet is stiff enough to hold shape once
bent. Wire may also be formed into a small "cage" to hold a
pretty pebble - to be worn as a pendant. Julie Summers, Dec

Steel wire is good for making pot handles.
     Sometimes we find a pot, free at a
dump or cheap at a thrift store, from
which the handle has broken off without rupturing the pot. A pot lacking
handle is desirable for cooking with
solar heat using a clear shroud, or
on a well-controlled flame (eg, gas
stove) using an insulative shroud.
(A long side handle would get in way
of shroud.) Drawback: need pot holders or thick cloth to move hot pot.
     However, if wanted, a handle can be formed from stiff wire
such as coat hangers. Various types of handles are possible.
Here I've shown a swing handle (bail), which is useful if
hanging the pot over a fire. Wrap wire around pot and twist a
little to hold it on. Form "ears" (small side handles).
Another piece of wire becomes the handle. Fasten it to the
ears, loosely enough so that it can swing down close to the rim
for storage or if using a shroud. Holly & Bert, OR 973, Jan

We live on our boat three and a half months a year.
     We are very comfortable, as it contains everything we need.
We cook with propane and have a gas frig. A diesel generator
powers lights and VHF radios, and tools my husband needs for
boat work. We dig for clams on nearby beaches, set crab and
prawn traps, and jig up a flounder or cod or halibut at times.
(We have sports fishing licenses.) We also fish commercially,
but the seasons are very short now and fenced in with miles of
red tape and extra expenses. I'm 65 and my husband 75, so we
probably won't play that game much longer. My husband also has
two ex-seine boats he is turning into live-aboards. Eleanore, BC

More about nomadic dairy goats.
Answering questions asked by Kurt. Yes, a doe needs to be bred and have kids to produce milk. She can then be milked for two years before she needs to be bred again.
I sell my kids to the local Mexican farm laborers. I have a problem with Kurt's (and many other meat eaters') attitude. If he eats meat bought from Safeway, someone kills those meals for him. The animals live in pens up to their knees in shit, are injected with growth hormones and antibiotics, and never experience kindness or love. Why is it okay to eat them, but not eat an animal you raise in a kind manner, slaughter without fear or trauma, and process without polluting the environment ?
Holly's suggestion to buy a milking doe and trade her in, is one answer. But she still has kids, some of which will be eaten by someone.
Any dairy breed will fit into a nomadic lifestyle. Avoid individuals who are very high producers. Some goats milk up to 3 gallons a day and those mostly have poor udder attachments - and too much weight to carry around. Choose goats who milk 3 or 4 quarts per day. Good feet and leg joints are important in any animal who is expected to walk to its food rather than having its food carried to it. Males make good pets or pack animals but must be neutered at one month of age so they don't become smelly and ornery. Bucks are ornery only if mistreated.
I don't know if grazing goats on public land is legal. I move camp every few days, which keeps the impact on the land low, keeps fresh food in front of your animals, and keeps you ahead of slow-acting federal employees. Bear, Idaho 832, Dec

Giant biting flies trapped and killed by tarp set-up.
One summer we were camped on a cattle ranch infested by inch-long biting flies. Most summers we live in light-weight minimal shelters - often just an insect net under a plastic tarp. But that summer we were still in a winter shelter, not having had a reason to move. (With ventilation, it was cool.)
Attracted by our odors, the flies came toward the front of our shelter and flew in under a clear plastic over-tarp. A net curtain prevented them from entering the shelter itself. Smart as they are (compared to other flies), the big flies got confused by the clear plastic. Encountering it and feeling trapped, they flew toward the sun which was behind the shelter. That brought them between the over-tarp and the dark-colored insulated roof - which the sun made HOT. In front, the over-tarp was a few inches above the roof. But, toward the back, the tarp rested on the roof. Struggling toward the light, the flies wedged themselves between tarp and roof. Hundreds exhausted and solar-cooked themselves - quite by accident. (We had not arranged roof and tarp in hopes of catching flies.)
I've thought about fabricating a biting-fly trap that could mount on the exhaust vent of a shelter. It would be a boon, not only to portable dwellers, but to people raising animals. (Anything like that already manufactured ?)
The stinky-jar traps, containing rotting meat as bait, catch many dung flies and yellow jackets, and some carrion beetles (which are beneficial and should not be caught), but few if any biting flies and mosquitos. Bert & Holly, 2000
Dwelling Portably   June 2002

36

Suggestions for preventing and treating animal bites.
Most victims are small children. The vast majority are bitten by pets: their own, or friends' or neighbors'. Most others are bitten by "cute" wild animals they try to feed or pet. To help prevent, don't keep pets, don't take small kids to visit people who do, and don't otherwise encourage contact with animals - at least until your kids are mature enough (8 or 10 ?) to clearly understand that an animal is not a toy or an oddly-shaped human, but is a very different creature with its own perceptions and urges. If a small child wants a pet, provide something inanimate that's soft and cuddly. And shun movies/videos/shows/books that portray animals unrealistically.
If bitten, wash wound immediately and thoroughly with plenty of water and soap. Generally leave open. (Don't suture) If infection develops, it will probably do so within 12 hours. If it does, take oral antibiotics (eg amoxicillin/clavulatate - if not allergic). Keep wound elevated. Severe pain may mean that teeth penetrated a bone, joint, or tendon. (Cat bites often do.) If much pain, or if any swelling or inflamation does not lessen within 24 hours, or if animal seemed rabid, seek further advice (desirable in any case). (15July01 Patient Care, in p.o. recycle bin)
When is treatment for rabies advisable ?
Rabies is a disease of mammals, mainly bats and carnivores such as raccoons, skunks, foxes. It's almost never found in squirrels, other rodents, rabbits. In U.S., wild animals are more likely rabid than are dogs or cats, many of which receive protective vaccinations. Rabies is extremely rare in humans. But if someone exposed waits until symptoms develop before obtaining treatment, the disease can't be halted and death sure.
The rabies virus penetrates any mucous membrane (need not be broken), or broken skin. The virus is fragile and can be washed away with soap and water and inactivated. However, if it has penetrated, death can be prevented only by administering rabies vaccine plus rabies immunoglobulin.
Who should get them ? Consider type of contact and local prevalence. Eg, when rabies has been reported in area wildlife, someone bitten by a raccoon should undergo treatment. On the other hand, transmission is very unlikely when a squirrel scratches the pants of a park visitor and does not break the skin. Cases between these extremes pose problems. Abnormal behavior of an animal is a warning sign. But the only sure way to know, is to study tissue from its brain. If the animal can't captured and observed or autopsied, the decision is anguishing. During the past 20 years, no untreated bite victims developed rabies from doubtful exposure. But a Texan bitten by a bat, who rejected treatment, developed rabies.
Some victims reject treatment because of cost: $1000 to $2000. (How much in Mexico ?) Others hesitate because they've heard that injections are painful and cause severe effects. This was once true, but not of treatment available in U.S. the past 20 years. Laurie Lewis & consultants (from Patient Care) 15July01)
(Addendum:) I read elsewhere that people who enter bat-occupied caves or buildings, sometimes get rabies without being bitten. By getting bat saliva or urine into eyes, nose, mouth, or into a pre-existing scratch ? Encouraging bats to nest nearby might not be wise. As insect eaters, birds may be safer. Humans are less closely related to birds than bats and share fewer diseases.
Dwelling Portably   June 2002

Tuberculosis a threat in crowded, poorly ventilated buildings.
Between 11/00 and 11/01, 17 active and 53 latent cases were
discovered at a Lane County (Eugene) homeless shelter. Of the
17, 16 were male, 16 U.S. born, 14 white non-Hispanic. Ages 23
to 59, median 48. None HIV (AIDS) positive. Microbes identical;
evidence that infections happened at the shelter.
Since a 1994 TB outbreak, skin tests have been required of
shelter residents and, if positive, other tests, and treatment.
The shelter has beds for 250 transient men, 90 men doing work
for the shelter, 60 women, and 11 staff.
In Oregon as a whole, TB has declined, from a high of 50
cases per 100,000 population in early 1950s, to 4 per 100,000
in late 1990s. (from CD Summary, 18Dec01)

(Comments:) This accents the importance of providing your own
shelter and not depending on institutions - and the evil of
officials who outlaw and police who hassle people sleeping in
cars or parks. TB, still very common and a major killer world-
wide, is only one of many diseases that spread anywhere that
people are close and enclosed. The most common may be flu.

No matter how nomadic I am, before preparing food I clean up.
I wash hands and work surfaces with soap and water, scrub
my nails, rinse with a drop of bleach, and then lemon juice if
available. Lemon juice can kill most hepatitus, I'm told, which
is why clams and oysters on half-shells come with lemon wedges.
For most of my life I've had extremely limited cooking and
sanitary facilities. I learned the hard way not to be dirty.
Never let trash or dirty dishes sit around after a meal. Lisa

Wild Child: Girlhoods in the Counterculture.
This book is by women whose early years were unorthodox.
Editor Chelsea Cain says: "Hippie kids grew up the products of
a great experiment. As with any scene, there were good parents,
and bad parents, and everyone's experience was not the same.
But these parents were all trying something different....
"How successful were the hippies at insulating themselves
from the mainstream culture, and what influences could they
not escape ? What aspects of the counterculture have their
children embraced as adults, and what have they rejected ?..."
Most if not all the authors are writers/editors/performers
quite well known in literary circles - which may be how the
editor found them. They now live in cities and have
conventional dwellingways. Thus they are not representative
of ALL women who had unusual beginnings.
Some tell only about their earliest years. Others also
describe growing to maturity. One says nothing about her past,
but promises her baby an American Dream childhood. Some
provide cryptic poems or prose (which I've ignored). Some
recall their girlhoods fondly. But most are put-down-ish.
Several dwelled in vehicles or other unusual abodes when they
were children; others had conventional homes with some
"hippie" trappings. Most or all attended public schools at
times. Childhoods full of snubs and taunts from other kids,
may explain why most grew to reject their parents' ways.
(The following excerpts are heavily edited to shorten.)
"Fear of a Bagged Lunch." I was born on the kitchen
table in a tiny cabin in rural PA. A midwife and my dad
composed the entire birthing team. It was a glorious moment
for my parents, that October day in 1972. They were both 25
and growing most of their food, raising goats, and making
dairy products. I slept with my parents until I was 5, drank
goat milk, and peed in an outhouse. Photos of me show a
naked girl-child, smudged with dirt and smiling like crazy.
June 2002

When I was a year and a half, my parents loaded everything we owned, which wasn't much, into a green 1952 Chevy truck and moved across country. My dad had built a miniature house on the back of the truck, and into this they packed our meagre belongings, our two dogs, and our goat....

Everything we possessed had been made by my parents or bought second hand. When I wanted something we couldn't afford (which was often) my parents would do their best to build or sew it. In third grade, I lusted after pin-striped jeans - and my mother valiently sewed me stiff, ill-fitting pink denim jeans (which fell off during a ferocious game of Red Rover). We lived my parents' hippie dream in various New Age communities: in WA Skagit Valley and, later, Sedona AZ.

When I was six, we traveled across the country again, this time to Ithica NY. I entered an "alternative" school. When I expressed an aversion to math, my first-grade teacher replied that I didn't have to do it if I didn't want to. Years later, my 7th grade teacher would wonder why I still didn't know my multiplication tables. (So what ? Calculators were cheap by then. Or, if high tech was taboo, slide rules.)

My isolation intensified when we moved to Beantown WI. My parents had two folk-musician friends there and wanted to start a band. We were a complete anomaly: my mom still made most of our clothes, and a wood stove was our only source of heat. My parents were pagan, and our "bible" was a combination of I-Ching, Tarot cards, and Seth channelings. Obscure lifestyles or any sort of difference can seem threatening in a small town - and we were misjudged accordingly. People saw my parents and immediately assumed (incorrectly) that we did drugs.

At school, my bagged lunches amused the hot-lunch kids. They had never seen home-made wheat bread, blue corn chips, tofu, natural licorice. And so again and again - the pointing finger, the gaping mouth and the inevitable comment, "What IS that ?" I tried to defend my family's organic choices. But my words were wasted - because the food looked different, which made it weird, which made ME weird.

In high school, my friends rebelled by stealing their parents' cigarettes, skipping class, and getting stoned at lunch. I rebelled by becoming a cheer leader and class president. Thankfully my parents were patient enough to let this wild stage run its course, as I pranced through my teen years in disguise - my bangs curled high and immobilized with hair spray, my lips glimmering with shell-pink lipstick, my jeans rolled tight to my legs, my Keds whiter than white.

My friends went to college and became vegetarians. I went and became a meat eater. The natural foods craze held no sense of independence or contained rebellion for me. I felt more insurgent satisfaction from eating a hamburger or a slice of chocolate cake. So even now, as an adult who enjoys eating healthy foods and is surrounded by a community that sanctions rather than punishing this choice, I am still guilty of occasional secret trips to fast-food restaurants.   Rain Grimes

"Seeing Belize." I was 7 and Shelly my sister was 5 when, in 1974, we spent five months in the village of San Antonio. My mother had been there before, during the summer that Shelly and I spent with our father. Her older brother was doing research on Mayan agriculture and she'd helped construct and plant his experimental raised-bed system.

Little is conventional about my mother. We'd stayed in a Canadian commune, a Greenwich Village apartment, a tree house, a teepee, and a white Dodge van. My mother thought nothing of taking us out of school to go to Belize for the winter.

Our house in Belize had an old-fashioned palm roof that let in the breeze. On hot days the school teacher's wife, whose new house had cement-block walls and a tin roof, would come over, sit on the steps with us, and list the drawbacks of a tin roof: hot in sun; noisy in rain. Our roof never leaked, even during the rainy season when mud washed through the streets in waves and people ran about with cardboard pieces over their heads.

Nearly everyone in San Antonio kept pigs. In the morning we'd see blood on their ears where vampire bats had fed during the night; everyone slept with windows closed. Many pigs ran loose, rooting through garbage and corn husks along the street and getting into people's gardens. At night and in the heat of day, they slept under our house, the only one on stilts. We could hear them snuffle and grunt below us.

Shelly and I came in one day and found our cousin lying face down on the floor. He'd found a knothole and was peeing through it. We were thrilled: the path to the outhouse was overgrown and I had seen snakes there. Why go there when we could pee through the floor ? Our mother put a stop to it.

The muddy green Rio Hondo was slow moving, with trees and vines draped over its banks. We bathed in it near our house. Shelly and I were the only kids with bathing suits: other girls wore old cotton dresses; the boys swam in shorts.

We ate rice and beans - for breakfast, lunch, dinner. Sometimes there was an egg; sometimes a friend brought a fish from the river. Shelly and I craved anything that wasn't rice and beans. Sometimes, as a treat, our mother bought us corn-flakes. We ate them in handfuls without milk, and could empty a box in half an hour. Shelly also liked sweetened condensed milk, which she drank directly from the can.

We walked to school, barefoot but with neatly combed hair. Kindergarten, first and second grades met in a whitewashed room with the same teacher. The day began with the ringing of a huge bell in the school yard. We found our places at the low wooden desks, then stood together to recite the Lord's Prayer and to sing the national anthem: "Oh Land of the Gods by the Carib Sea, our tran-quil haven of dem-o-cra-cy."

English is the official language of Belize, and though everyone in the village spoke Spanish or Mayan at home, school was taught in English. It's an English slightly different. "Don't vex me now", the teacher said when a student misbehaved. In the U.S. I'd struggled hopelessly over phonic worksheets; but in Belize, because of my English, I was the star pupil. It was in Belize that I finally learned to read. The texts were Dick and Jane primers, yellow and cracked. In Belize, Dick and Jane read like fantasy. Spot, their pet, did not resemble the lean mangy dogs who fought and copulated in the dusty streets.

The price of cane had shot up and all the young men and some of the old men had switched from farming corn to cane. They worked land that they carved out of the jungle and leased from the government for a few pennies per hectare. The cut cane went to a sugar refinery in nearby Orange Walk. After my uncle and his family returned to MN for the spring semester, my mom worked in the cane fields. She was the only woman who did, except for an occasional wife or daughter who helped out for an afternoon. She got up before dawn and waited by the general store with the other workers for a cane truck to come by. She loaded, standing on a board over the back wheel of the truck and passing great bundles over her head. Sometimes there'd be ants swarming on the cane. She made maybe six dollars a week (± $25 in 2002 dollars ?). Now, when I ask her why she did it, she shrugs. "I wanted to make some money, and see what it's like."

No one in San Antonio had much money. Two families were

rich enough to own generators. One of them had a TV. They watched it religiously in spite of the picture being barely visible.

Our house had two rooms, furnished almost entirely with hammocks. From the start I loved the feeling of being suspended and at the same time held tight. At night we lit brittle, dark-green mosquito coils under our hammocks. They burned for about 8 hours with a strong, unpleasant smoke.

Nostalgia is a funny thing. Those months in Belize were among the most vivid in my life, and I remember them with an ache of longing. But, at the time, it was a world too raw, too strong for me. And when, the following year, my mother announced that we were returning to Belize, I shook my eight-year-old head and refused to go. Carin Clevidence

Seal Press, Seattle; 1999, 186p.5x7, $16 cover price. (Revu
by Anna Li)

How can hammocks be made comfortable for sleeping ?

Bruce of BC wrote: "Homeless people spend lots of time in all types of weather, including damp rainy weather. I am sure they would sometimes appreciate a hammock to keep their bodies elevated off of damp or insect-ridden ground."

In past DPs, several people said they had tried sleeping in hammocks but found them uncomfortable. Others mention using hammocks, but did not tell how they achieved comfort.

In Sept83 MP(DP), Judy Brueske told how she rigged a hammock from an old floor-to-ceiling curtain (fairly easy to find at yard sales or dumpsters). She advised: "The difference between a crummy hammock and a luxury job is not so much in the materials used, as in the DIMENSIONS (she's 5'3" and uses cloth 8x8') and in the ANGLE at which you hang it"(she hangs it deep, with lots of slack). She doesn't use spreaders. She didn't say whether she usually sleeps in it, or merely lounges in it briefly.

Duration affects comfort. Eg, on sunny days, city people lounge on the grass in parks during lunch breaks with only a towel under them. But I doubt that'd be comfy for all night.

Bruce sent instructions (from Earth Garden magazine) and a list of twine sources. I said that Judy's method seemed "much easier than making or cheaper than buying a knitted hammock...."

Bruce replied: "Can anyone, including convicts or disabled, really make their own hammocks from bedsheets ? (Also), a knitted hammock may have many advantages compared to a hole-less type."

Availability of materials varies. Sometimes we find old drapes; sometimes lots of discarded hay twine.

Julie Summers replied (to what I'd said): "A knitted hammock may be lighter than a cloth hammock, and dry faster. But I doubt it is cooler. A few years ago, I lounged several hours in a big knitted hammock with about one-inch mesh. I needed cushions under me. Otherwise the cords dug into me uncomfortably."

I wonder if hammock comfort depends on preferred sleeping positions. I sleep mostly on my sides, only briefly on my back. Bert sleeps mostly on sides-toward-front, sometimes on sides or sides-toward-back; seldom on back. Conventional hammocks may be most comfy for people who prefer sleeping on their backs.

I think I read that tropic peoples who routinely sleep in hammocks, make them WIDE - and lay in them cross-ways.

Seems to me, a hammock's main advantage: no need to clear and level ground, which might be rocky, hard, frozen, snow covered - or a swamp with no dry ground. Main disadvantage: need trees suitable for suspending. Advice needed from people who spend most of their sleeping hours in hammocks. Holly & Bert

We are grounded here in San Jose for a month.

We were vehicularly nomadic but I lost my license. Rent prices alone are enough cause to live portably. Joshua, November
June 2002

Dwelling Portably
or Shared, Mobile, Improvised
Underground, Hidden, Floating
September 2002 $1 per issue   POB 190-d, Philomath OR 97370

Ways to cut twine when you lack a knife.

At a county fair where I was selling my crafts,
I went to the hay storage to look for twine. Two
young girls came to fetch hay for their animals.
They did not want a whole bail, but lacked a knife
to cut the bail's twine. Resourcefully, one girl
picked up a loose piece of the same twine,
and, using it like a wire saw, she pulled
it back and forth across a spot on the
bail's twine, severing it in a few
seconds. Anna Li, Oregon 973, November

(Addendum:) A way I've used: Find a rock
with a sharp edge. (Or, if only rounded rocks,
to make a sharp edge, break a rock by hitting it with a bigger
rock.) Lay cord over edge and pound it with another rock.   Bert

Selecting and lashing poles to build structures.

I use small diameter poles, seldom more than four inches
thick. Thicker poles are too heavy to handle easily without
complex rigs or several helpers. I avoid long unsupported
spans that would need thick poles. Eg, with four-inch poles,
I want supports not more than seven feet apart.

Because we like sun, and DON'T like to be under big trees
that could fall on us, we usually live in areas that have been
clear-cut within the past 10 to 20 years, or in rocky areas
where trees are stunted. Consequently, poles must be carried
from neighboring areas that have older trees - another reason
to use light-weight poles. I look for groves, maybe 25 to 40
years old, that include some tall spindly trees which are dying
because of shade by bigger trees. I prefer trees that have
died within the past year and not yet rotted (sign: some
needles hang on but have turned brown), or that will die within
the next few years (live foliage only at top, and bigger trees
within a few feet). This avoids conflicts with whoever is
growing the trees commercially. Also, such trees no longer
have branches along most of their height, minimizing trimming.

I prefer conifers (eg, doug-fir, hemlock, spruce, pine,
cedar) for durability. However, they exude pitch, so, for
inside structures that will stay dry (rot less) and may be
touched frequently, I use broad-leaf trees such as maples. For
posts that touch or penetrate the ground, I use cedar if I want
the structure to last much longer than a year.

Though removing bark will reduce weight and may increase
durability (bark may shelter boring insects), I seldom remove
it except from interior wood where flaking bark would annoy.
If a tree still has strong branches,
I do not immediately cut them off
flush with the trunk. Instead,
I leave stubs a few inches long
which could facilitate fastening
or hanging things. Later, I trim
off stubs not needed, or in the way.

To lash together two poles
that cross each other, I wrap the
twine quite a few turns over and
under, pulling each turn tight. Then I
wrap around those turns to further tighten
them. (Some call this a "square" lash. But
it will be square only if the poles are

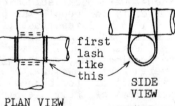

PLAN VIEW

first
lash
like
this

SIDE
VIEW

then
like
this

the same diameter and cross at right
angles. Better name: parallel lash,
because, in plan view, turns are
parallel to poles.)

   To join poles that
must swivel, such as
a tripod whose legs
come together for
carrying, I lash as
shown here. (Called
a "sheer" lash.)
   The poles are usually green or
moist and will shrink as they dry.
If the joint must stay tight, I add a
tightening wrap of rubber straps (cut
from discarded innertubes). Light
ruins the rubber in a year or two. If
I want longer life, I then wrap the
joint with strips of black plastic,
quite a few layers, tying frequently
as I wrap. Light gradually ruins the
plastic, but the inner layers will
last many years. (What would endure
both light and rot ? Cedar bark ?)
   For twine I usually use synthetic
hay cord. We find it discarded where
hay has been fed and along rural roads.
It does not rot and it endures partial
sun for several years. If limited to
natural materials, I'd try vines. Some
are very strong while alive, but weak-
en in a year or so. Vines can't take
knots. Use several clove hitches ?
   We've not sought great durability.
Though we might return to the same
site seasonally for a few years, we'll
eventually stop using it because of
too much shade if for no other reason.
   I dis-recommend nailing. Weak; apt
to split poles unless drilled; noisy.
   (For more about fastening poles,
and for calculating diameters needed
with various loads and spans, Vonulife
1973 recommended, (DP sells for $2.)
esp if building something heavy enough
to injure if it collapses. VL is 30
years old, but the techniques probably
haven't changed in millenia.) Bert

Five tents tested in windy mountains.
   All were advertised as "expedition"
models. Three were big, heavy-duty
geodesics, weighing 8 to 10¼ pounds,
capable of sleeping 3 people. The
North Face VE-25 and Walrus Eclypse
did well; the Moss Olympic failed.
   To save weight, some "four-season"
tents are designed to flex: yield to
the wind and spring back. In 1981 four
of us "were holed up in a VE-24 (VE-25
sans vestibule) on Tibet's Xixapangma.
Brutal winds crushed the tent and its
occupants into the floor with every
gust. When winds subsided, tent popped
back up. That went on for days."
   But the Moss: "A gust of 50 to 55
mph hit. The windward sidewall folded
nearly in half; the ridgepole bowed
under; then one of the leeward poles
snapped in two. Its broken edge punctured the vestibule which then ripped."
Not repairable in those strong winds.
   Two light-weight (3 pound, two
person) tents did well:
   The Stephenson Warmlite survives
high winds and snow loads by not
resisting. "If you leave the tent
alone in a heavy snowfall, it'll just
sag in the middle until the load hits
the ground. Nothing breaks or rips,
it just yields." One drawback of the
R2: screened vents small. "With all
vents open and one person sleeping
inside, on a dry dirt platform in a
low-moisture area, condensation was
considerable, especially on the
single-layer door. I'd hate to be
stuck inside on a hot day in mosquito
areas." (2SR has screened windows.)
   The Chouinard Pyramid achieves
lightness by having no rain fly, bug
screens, floor. Good as emergency
shelter in summer thunderstorms.
Four people can squeeze inside. "You
won't be comfortable but you won't get
wet." The shape isn't roomy "but with
most of the surface close to ground,
it's very stable in high winds. The
beefy, single center pole shivers and
sways with the wind, but it doesn't
break or let the tent collapse." Eric
Perlman (from Backpacker 3/88; sent by
                          Bruce of BC)
(Comment:) These models may no longer
be made, but may show up at yard sales
or outdoor-club swap meets. If the
Moss is cheap because of its poor rep,
it may be a good buy for gentler use.

Further report on a small dome tent.
   We bought a Stansport #723 over ten
years ago ($30 on sale). We've used
it only during summers - a few months
total so far. We protect it from sun
either by setting up where shady, or
by covering with cloth (or, at one
gathering, with cardboard). Between
uses, we remove poles and store fabric
in a plastic pail. It has so far
endured our gentle, infrequent uses.
Problems (also see May96,97,98 DPs):
   Scary chemical stink (fire retardant?) dissipated after several years.
   Light-color fly (built-in top tarp)
admitted some light but was difficult
to conceal. We painted it with dark
drab green exterior latex housepaint
thinned with water. That may also slow
sun harm but adds weight.
   Leakage, esp near bottom. At first
we blamed lack of seam sealing. But
applying a sealant (which maker didn't
furnish) did not help much. During
rains, seepage wets anything that
contacts tent. The fabric is fine-
weave nylon (not ripstop) and is not
coated. Even when no rain, lower sides
dampened by condensation. (Inside top
stays dry, thanks to insulative space
between tent top and fly.) If more than
dew or brief drizzle expected, we
suspend a 10x12½' piece of clear plastic above (NOT touching) tent (with
extra length in front). But that adds
to set-up time, and the tie-out cords
encumber movement around the tent.
   I wonder if all single-wall self-
supporting tents have a wet problem.
If the built-in fly is small, it does
not shield the whole tent. If it is
big, extra poles or other complications are needed to support it.

This summer the Stansport has supported, not only itself, but also a heavy, sometimes-wet cotton drape layed over it as sun screen. It hasn't experienced snow load or strong wind.

We like the Stansport better than the Ero (report in May99 DP). Stansport ventilates through a net layer that is part of the door and can be closed by a separate zipper when not wanted, whereas Ero ventilates through a net ceiling that can't be closed.

I don't like either tent's zipper configuration (∩ on Stansport; ⊥ on Ero) because it must be kept zipped to exclude flying insects, requiring an unzip for every access of things outside. I think I'd prefer a ⊔ zipper, so the door will drape closed and need zipping only if there is much wind or many crawling insects. Bert, October

Dome tent versus bug net plus tarp.
Advantages of a small self-supporting dome tent: quicker set up; no tie-out cords to encumber movement around it; somewhat warmer IF vent can be closed; better protection from rain and from crawling insects, esp when windy; blocks view of any prudes.

Advantages of an insect net plus a clear plastic over-tarp: admits more light; less weight; no hard/sharp poles to transport - and replace if they break; easier egress (if no floor); much simpler to fabricate if making it yourself (for how to, see May96 DP). Set-up can be quickened by rigging net and tarp together, but won't be as quick as a good dome tent.

With either, I recommend a plastic ground tarp, to keep tent bottom or mattress cleaner. If tent, the tarp should not extend beyond its sides; or if over-tarp, the ground tarp should end well inboard of its sides (else it will collect rain). Bert & Holly, Jan

How to keep mattresses drier.
If using porous padding such as open-cell foam, leaves, straw, or boughs; put two-thirds of layers under the tent floor but on top of the ground tarp; and only one third tween you and the tent floor. Or, if no floor, use two tarps under you: one on the ground, and one between layers of padding two-thirds of the way up.

This will keep water vapor (from breathing and sweating) from diffusing all the way down through the padding and reaching a temperature near ground cool enough to condense the vapor.

If using closed-cell foam, or open-cell entirely sealed within plastic, condensation may not be a problem. B&H

More reports about plastic tote bins.
A few years ago, I was given four 21-gal Rubbermaid bins. I first used them to store grain. They worked fine.

Last winter, I used one as a water trough for the horses. It worked fine until it got very cold - maybe 20° below. The plastic got brittle and could no longer endure being kicked and bitten by the colts. I repaired a big crack in the bottom by melting it together with a spoon heated red hot.

When traveling last summer (see Mar 02 DP), I used two bins as panniers (pack baskets) on one of my horses by rigging a sling out of old car seat belts. The bins held folding shovel, axe, horseshoeing tools, etc (hard, heavy objects). They got smashed into trees, and once dropped 3 feet when the horse snagged her saddle on a low tree and broke a cinch. They withstood all that. Bear, ID 832, Jan

Rig for mounting barrels on horses.
A "pivot point" lets barrels hang straight whether going uphill or down; whereas ordinary pack boxes tilt. And on "a deep trail where ordinary boxes would drag", the barrels rock up out of the way. Designed and sold by Ken Wegner of K&S Saddlery in Spinaway WA (s of Tacoma), the rigs are made of nylon seatbelt strapping and brass.

As barrels, Ken suggests Rubbermaid garbage cans. They are "soft enough that if you run into a tree, they bend and come back out. And if you do destroy one, you just buy another for $10." Kathy Peth (from Cascade Horseman, May01; sent by Anna)

Choosing a bicycle to carry luggage.
If a bike hauls weight other than its rider, tire cross-section is very important. A tire is a rim protector. It is also a suspension part. Luggage is dead weight; unlike a rider it has no hands or legs to act as springs. At every bump, it pushes down hard. A 125-pound rider with 30 pounds of luggage is harder on a bike than a 200 lb rider with 10 lbs of luggage.

The tire's air pocket is what protects wheels and cushions bumps. So if you carry non-rider weight, get the fattest tire that fits the frame. A tire narrower than 28x1½ or 26x1.25 is likely to damage the wheel.

Also important, if using panniers, is length of chainstay - the tube that connects rear axle and pedal crank. Mountain, hybrid and most cyclo-cross bikes are long enough. Most recent road bikes, which are racing designs (even those falsely touted as "sport touring") are too short. 16½" from bottom bracket center to rear axle, is minimum for heels to clear panniers.

Almost all mountain bikes work well for hauling as long as the rider is comfortable with the hand positions that flat handlebars allow. Mtn bikes have rigid flames that won't flex much when carrying extra weight, and rims wide enough for a tire that will support the loaded bike and cushion rider well. (If riding on pavement, non-knobby tires roll easier and quieter than knobbies.) Some racks are made for attaching to shock forks. Mtn bikes with frames 14" or less often need customizing and special hardware to mount a rear rack. As on any bike, threaded holes in the frame's rear dropouts (where the wheel clamps in) are necessary for rack attachment. (Desirable but not necessary. I've lashed a rack's struts to the chain stays and seat stays with rubber straps. See (eg) May99 DP.)

Hybrid bikes fit 32c to 45c tires that will support weight and absorb shocks. Most hybrids have rack and fender eyelets and some have shock forks. Don't attach front racks to bikes that have rigid aluminum forks.

Most so-called road bikes made since 1990 lack room for tires wider than 700x25c, and have short chainstays and non-steel forks. Frame strength isn't a problem but wheel strength may be. I wouldn't pack luggage on wheels with less than 32 spokes, esp with a 700x25c tire. David Feldman (from Oregon Cycling, 8/01)

In-line skates for transportation ?

I had hoped that skating would be faster than walking, for mobility in a city to which I ride in a vehicle that can't easily accomodate a bicycle.

I bought a pair at a yard sale for $10. At thrift stores I bought wrist, elbow and knee protectors: $3 total. I wore my bike helmet ($2 at a thrift store previously). To protect my tailbone (and neck - they're connected), I put foam in my underpants. After a few falls I also wore a piece 1½x15x 17" over my butt, outside my clothes, crudely tied to waist and legs.

I'd watched a video, Let's Roll, 5 months before. It was encouraging and covered some basics, but not how to fall - a VITAL skill ! I read 5 books about skating. The best was Inline, William Nealy, 1998, 201p., Menasha Ridge Press, AL (with hilarious cartoons). It had the most about falling. Next best, and more concise: In-line Skater's Start-up, Doug Werner, 1995, 159p., Tracks Pub, Chula Vista CA.

I kept a record. After 24 hours total on skates during several weeks, I don't fall often, esp if not trying anything fancy. But I don't do well on rough surfaces. I tried skating on a typical asphalt highway and could not - my skate would stick and I would have to catch myself from falling forward. Part of the problem: the highway was narrow and busy, confining me to the right edge (in OR the legal side for skaters, who are considered "vehicles" by police). On a surface equally rough but with almost no traffic, I was able to skate with difficulty - because I could zigzag more. I had to exert much force to get any momentum; and I continually feared the skate sticking and tumbling me before I could catch myself.

On smoother streets I was able to skate easier. A patch of ultra-smooth concrete was a dream - I felt graceful. But smooth surfaces are few. (And when I went back to asphalt, it seemed more difficult than before.)

Timing myself on 1/8 mile of fairly smooth asphalt with a slight grade:

both up grade and down, my skating speed was about the same as a brisk walk (6 mph ?) and only a few seconds faster downhill than up. Bicycling quite fast, upgrade was 2½ times faster than walking or skating; downgrade 3 times faster. Walking and bicycling took less energy than skating. I skated 10 minutes while wearing a 10-lb knapsack. No problem. But I don't think I'd feel steady with much more, at my present skill level.

On smooth concrete when wet, I had no control - and doubt anyone would. One book said: when it starts raining, take off your skates. Another said skating was possible.

For now I've given up skates for transportation, but plan to practice more and will report. I hope more-experienced skaters will too. Anna Li

Winter wanderings in a pickup camper.

Two weeks ago I was in Vermont, huddled by the wood-stove as below-zero temperatures froze the garden solid. Now, my daughter and I are in Florida at the Ortona Lock and Dam on the Okeechobee Waterway near Ft Myers. On one side is a cattle pasture dotted with cabbage palms and spreading oaks. On the other side is the lock. As we watch, watercraft cue up and go thru: immense barges, yachts, canoes. My daughter has been out there in her 17' sea kayak she built last summer. With her are manatees, otters, an alligator.

We are seldom bored. My daughter has her roller blades and kayak. We swim in pools, keys, and the ocean. We have snorkeling equipment we use in the keys or in (eg) Salt, Alexander and Juniper Springs in Ocala NF. We write in our journals and work on articles. We read things brought from home and trade while on the road. We stop at libraries; sometimes score a temporary card, sometimes borrow one; or just sit and read. (When short of cash, stick your hand between cushions. We often find something.)

We have a 1989 Chevy Cheyenne half-ton truck with a beat-up camper on it. Driving from VT to FL costs about $150 for gas. We camp free in parking lots of Wal-marts, Kmarts, and truck stops.

National Forests now charge for sites that used to be free: $4 per night; or $40 for a year's pass. Big Cypress Preserve has free campgrounds.

When we get to an area, to learn of local events, we pick up the free weekly paper, a daily paper, and any interesting tourist info at the chamber of commerce. Often there are discount coupons for attractions. We also converse with folks and learn even more that way: Sometimes we are invited to homes or churches, or told about off-the-beaten-path opportunities. Other snowbirds or full-time RVers are also good info sources.

During summers I grow and sell vegetables in Vermont. The season is short, leaving winters free for travel to warmer places. At home I make fruit leathers, dry fruits and veggies, and save up garlic, onions, shallots, potatos, carrots and squash from my garden. We take with us enough food for months. We eat the fresh and heavy stuff first. As we travel we glean just-picked fields, and get food from campgrounds and folks we visit. This campground has all the oranges, grapefruits, kumquats you can pick. Heather has eaten two gallons of kumquats in three days ! Don't overlook dumpster diving. We get much perfectly good food that way. Marines practice in our favorite national park, and in two weeks we got over 500 pounds of MRE's (meals ready to eat - canned in plastic/foil pouches) from dumpsters. Check after weekends. We've snagged still-frozen cases of food and cans not opened - left by Boy Scouts. (WHY didn't they take them home ? Waste !)

I bought our camper for $300 years ago. On our first trip to Arizona, we had to rebuild the overhang, which almost broke off enroute. A couple of years later we faced reality and cut most of the overhang, leaving only a foot. The camper is 8 ft long, barely fitting in the truck bed with the tailgate closing up behind it. The tailgate folds down to become our back porch. The camper has a built-in stove/oven and a propane furnace.

We now have staggered bunks, with storage under each. I keep a leather seat cushion on a porta-potty so it doubles as a seat. We sit on that and the lower bed and use a wooden tray table between us for eating and playing cards. Three big cupboards hold food and utensils. Next to the stove is a counter with the dishpan. A 5-gallon water jug sets on the floor. We have totes of clothes, toiletries, candles, medicines and other items. Under the bed is a HUGE food storage container, two ice chests, a pressure clothes washer, and a footlocker of books. Up front, between us on the seat, is a storage organizer containing snacks, wet-naps, maps, and other stuff needed while driving. Heather's kayak goes on the roof and her backpacking tent at the foot of her bed. Wendy Martin, VT 056, 2000
(Comments:) Wow. What fabulous food finds ! (Holly and I have scored freebees but never such huge amounts.)

Re porta-potties. I might want one if I often entertained guests accustomed to flush toilets. But I've heard a pp can be a nuisance to empty and an expense for chemicals. In the woods we bury. In a city, if no toilet handy, we wrap well and dispose of as garbage. (No worse than disposable diapers.) May96 DP tells how to defecate simply, almost anywhere. B&H, OR 973, Febr

Wild Child: Girls In Counterculture.
(These book exerpts much shortened.)
"Our Mail Truck Days." In 1969 my father was arrested for an anti-war protest and sentenced to two years in prison. He had become increasingly

focused on political work, and his arrest meant my mother had no help caring for me. She was furious at him and fury made her feel free.

She met Jim who had embraced the counterculture but not on political terms. They soon made plans to head across the country in Jim's truck. A platform bed stretched across the width of the van, and a hinged half-moon table folded down from the wall and perched on one leg. We ate sitting cross-legged on the mattress. The walls were lined with bookshelves, fitted with bungee cords to hold the volumes in place. On a shelf behind the cab was our kitchen: a two-burner propane stove, a tiny cutting board, and a ten-gallon water jug. Jim covered the metal floors with Persian rugs and hung a few ornaments on the wall. Jim bought a small wood stove and bolted it to the floor near the back wall. The smokestack jutted out the side of the truck, the hole weather-sealed with a tin pie plate. A friend wired in a stereo system, and mother sewed heavy denim curtains that velcroed to the window frames for privacy at night. The engine on those snub-nosed trucks bulged into the cab and was housed by a metal shell. Jim covered it with a piece of thick foam, which would be my bed.

In spring 1970, we packed essential belongings and set out on a year-long journey. Thrills of travel sustained me for a while, but I was a difficult age (4) to be rootless. I played with other kids for a day at a campground or city park; then we drove on. After a day on the road, mother tucked me in on my foam bed, warmed from below by engine heat. Lisa Michaels

"Water Baby". In late May 1970, my parents successfully crossed the Canadian border. They had driven all day, anxious to reach the British Columbia island of Sointula. Mom was 7 months pregnant with me, her first of two children. They were traveling in a GM panel truck, altered with a blowtorch to create plexiglass skylights above where their heads rested on the sleeping platform. Underneath it lay all their possessions.

Sointula was founded by Finnish immigrants in late 1800s who started a commune before communes were cool. Altho their dream faded, it has never been entirely forgotten. Then along came hippies to start a new way of living. They were mostly city folks and had no idea how to relate to the locals or even that they should.

Mom said she didn't know what hard work was until they left the city. Photos usually show her bending over a baby, or dishes, or a row of weeding in the garden. Sometimes she is singing with a band on the front porch.

Mom's parents were excited about the coming birth, but knew nothing of the "home" part. Mom thought it best to spare them anxiety and suggested

Sept 2002

46

they come a week or two after my due date. But, as a well-grounded hippie child, I came when I was ready. Altho I did not arrive in June, my grandparents did. Grandma took one look around the ten-by-ten-foot room (a converted sauna) and KNEW: the eye drops and gauze, the Whole Earth Catalog with birth section earmarked, the Basic Guide For Midwives open on the kitchen table, the piles of fresh linen and buckets for extra water.

Dad delivered me; grandma coached him. When mom's afterbirth didn't come out right away, dad was afraid to push her belly too hard and hurt her. Grandma told him he better, and he did.

Growing up on Sointula was in many ways grand. There were no locked doors and I had the whole forest, beach and ocean for a playground. Zoe Eakle

(Though these excerpts are positive, most authors rejected alternative lifestyles. Comments in June 02 DP.)

Editor, Chelsea Cain; Seal Press, Seattle, 1999, $16 cover price, 186p. 5x7. (Review by Anna Li)

Health advice: 2000 BC to 2000 AD.

2000 BC: Here, eat this herb.

1000 AD: That herb is heathen. Here, say this prayer.

1850 AD: That prayer is superstition. Here, drink this potion.

1950 AD: That potion is ineffective. Here, take this antibiotic.

2000 AD: That antibiotic no longer works. Here, eat this herb.

(from Nutrition Today, 3/01)

Why We Get Sick. (A Darwinian View)
This book explains why our bodies function - or fail. It is especially insightful for portable dwellers who selectively adopt prehistoric ways enhanced with contemporary tools. Though Randolph Nesse MD and George Williams PhD don't offer much HOW-to, they prompt readers to think about WHAT-to and, especially, what NOT-to.

Why do we have seeming "flaws, frailties, makeshifts? Why do we crave the very foods that are bad for us ?

"Evolution does no sensible planning." It proceeds by slightly modifying what it already has. This results in some trouble-prone arrangements. Eg, in vertebrates, food and air tubes intersect, allowing choking. And optic nerves pass in front of sensors, shading them. (Whereas in squids' eyes, nerves pass behind sensors.)

Because of humans' big brains, fetal heads fit through pelvises only with difficulty. "This explains why human babies have to be born at such an early and vulnerable stage of development, compared to ape babies."

Every major structural change brings problems. "Walking upright enables us to carry food and babies," but because of inadequate adaptations, predisposes us to (eg) back pain, gut blockages, hernias, vericose veins, swollen feet.

"Sitting for hours at a time on chairs or benches in classrooms is unnatural. Nothing of the sort was ever demanded of Stone Age children."

Hunter-gatherers must be able to spot distant edibles and threats. Arctic natives "were seldom nearsighted when first contacted by Europeans. But when their children began attending school, 25% became myopic" - the same percent as among Americans. Why ? Eyeball growth is controlled, not by genes alone, but also by neural feedback. If often looking too close to focus, the brain prompts the eyeball to grow longer. To prevent myopia, the authors suggest using very big print in childrens' books. (I doubt that would help much, because books must be held close to turn pages easily. Simpler: wear reading glasses)

Sudden infant death syndrome is up to ten times higher in cultures where babies sleep apart from their parents instead of in the same bed.

In the Stone Age, "you were born into a nomadic band of 40 to 100. It was a stable social group." You knew everyone in the band and their genetic and marital connections. "Some you loved deeply and they loved you in return. If there were some you did not love, at least you knew what to expect from them, and you knew what everyone expected of you. If you occasionally saw strangers, it was probably at a trading site, and you knew what to expect of them too.

"Despite great variation, social systems were constrained by economics and demography... Groups that had to gather their food from within walking distance, remained small. No chief could control enough food, wealth, or people to build pyramids or cathedrals.

"Natural selection clearly favors being kind to close relatives because of their shared genes. It also favors being known to keep promises and not cheat members of one's group or habitual trading partners in other groups. There was, however, never any individual advantage to altruism beyond these local associations. Global human rights is a new idea never favored by evolution during the Stone Age....

"Individuals may be viewed as vessels created by genes for the replication of genes, to be discarded when the genes are through with them.

"Natural selection has no mandate to make people happy, and our long-range interests are often well served by aversions." Eg, nausea and food aversions during pregnancy evolved to impose dietary restrictions on the mother, thereby lessening fetal exposure to toxins when most vulnerable (first few months). The fetus is a minor nutritional burden then, so a healthy woman can afford to eat less. She usually prefers bland foods "without the strong odors and flavors of toxic compounds....

"Women who have no pregnancy nausea are more likely to miscarry or bear defective children" because they are more apt to eat harmful foods. Unwisely, many doctors attempt to alleviate symptoms. "Pregnant women should be extremely wary of all drugs, both therapeutic and recreational....

"Colds bring many symptoms children dislike: runny nose, headache, fever, malaise. Acetaminophen (eg Tylenol) can reduce or eliminate some of these symptoms." Traditional physicians are likely to recommend it.

"Fever is unpleasant but useful. It is an adaptation shaped by natural selection to fight infections." In one study, children with chicken pox who were given acetaminophen, averaged about a day longer to recover than those who took sugar pills. (More important: did they also incur more complications such as pneumonia ?)

Why aren't we normally hotter ? "Fever has costs as well as benefits. Even a moderate fever (103°) depletes nutrient reserves 20% faster."

Taking (eg) aspirin for a fever is not ALWAYS bad. "Each condition needs to be studied separately and each case considered individually."

Malaise, too, helps us. By deterring unessential activity, it favors immune defenses and tissue repair.

Distinguishing defenses from defects can be vital. Totally block a cough "and you may die of pneumonia."

By 1970s, iron lack was proven to inhibit infections. "But even now, only 11% of physicians and 6% of pharmacists know that iron supplements may" worsen infections.

"The majority of kidney stones are composed of calcium oxalate." For years, doctors told such patients to reduce calcium intake. However, a study shows that low-calcium diets INCREASE kidney stones. "Calcium binds oxalate in the gut so that it cannot be absorbed." If too little calcium is eaten, some oxalate is left free.

Why such medical ignorance ? One cause: "pervasive neglect of evolutionary science at all educational levels," due to religious opposition.

"The body is a bundle of careful compromises. Stronger stomach acid helps digestion and kills bacteria but aggrevates ulcers."

Microbes are "sophisticated opponents. We have evolved defenses to counter their threats. They have evolved ways to overcome defenses or even to use them to their benefit."

Pathogens can evolve rapidly, because of their fast reproduction and vast numbers. How they change will depend on conditions. They may not become more benign. "A rhinovirus (cold) that does not stimulate abundant secretion of mucus and sneezing is unlikely to reach new hosts." If more than one Shigella strain is in a host, "the one that most effectively converts the host's resources to its own use will disperse the most progeny before the host dies....

"If disperal depends not only on a

host's survival but also on its mobility, any damage to the host is especially harmful to the pathogen. If you are so sick from a cold that you stay home in bed, you are unlikely to come into contact with many people that your virus can infect...."

Fatal diseases lurk in hospitals. "People who are acutely ill, do not move around much, but hospital personnel and equipment move rapidly." Pathogens are spread by inadequately cleaned hands, thermometers, eating utensils. "Diseases may rapidly become more virilent" because the pathogens don't need mobile hosts.

"Mosquito-borne infections are generally mild in the mosquito and severe in the vertebrate. This is to be expected because any harm to the mosquito would make it less likely to bite another vertebrate." But (eg) malaria does not need a mobile vertebrate. In fact, experiments with mice and rabbits show: "a prostrate host is more vulnerable to mosquitos."

In the Stone Age, most ills were caused by worms, and by protozoa born by (eg) bugs. Most bacterial and viral infections require rates of personal contact only possible in dense populations.

Our bodies evolved during millions of years for lives spent in small groups hunting and gathering. "Those conditions ended a few thousand years ago (for most people) but evolution has not had time since then to adapt us to" present conditions.

"Life on a primitive farm or third-world village may be as abnormal" as are offices, classrooms, fast-foods.

"During almost all of human evolution, it was adaptive to conserve energy by being as lazy as circumstances permitted." Energy was a scarce resource and could not be wasted.

This book refers to Timothy John's "With Bitter Herbs They Shall Eat It" (reviewed in May93 DP). "Our dietary problems result from a mismatch between tastes evolved for Stone Age conditions and their likely effects today. Fat, sugar, and salt were in short supply through nearly all of our evolutionary history.... In the Stone Age it was adaptive to pick the sweetest fruit available. What happens when people with this adaptation live in a world full of chocolate eclairs ?

"When every household had to make its own wine ... in small vessels and with primitive equipment, it was not likely that anyone would have enough for heavy daily consumption...."

"Paradoxically, the increased food production made possible by herding and agriculture, resulted in nutritional shortages...." About 1500 years ago, some tribes "abandoned hunter-gatherer lifestyles and started growing corn and beans. Compared to earlier skeletons," the farmers are on average less robust and show B-vitamin lack.

"There is great wisdom in our innate tendency to follow the seemingly arbitrary dictates of culture. The rituals of many societies require that corn be processed with alkali before it is eaten." Though Stone Agers did not know that doing so balanced the amino acids and freed niacin, they or their ancestors observed that eaters of unprocessed corn more often got pellegra. (But many contemporary rituals were crafted by governments/churches/corporations, not to help US but to help THEM. Beware !)

"Nectar is an elaborate cocktail of sugars and dilute poisons." It evolved as an optimal trade-off between the flower's need to repel the wrong visitors and attract the right ones.

"Toxin molecules in sufficiently low concentration will be quickly taken up by receptors" on liver cells and rapidly detoxified by enzymes. "If we overload our body with so many toxic molecules that all processing sites are occupied, the excess circulates through the body, doing damage...

"There is no such thing as a diet without toxins. The diets of all our ancestors, like those of today, were compromises between costs and benefits.

"Human diets expanded after fire was domesticated" because heat detoxifies many of the most potent poisons.

Artificial pesticides are a special hazard because some "are extremely different chemically from those with which we are adapted to cope.

"Since the invention of agriculture, we have been selectively breeding plants to overcome their evolved defenses. Most wild species of potato are highly toxic, as you might expect, given that they are an otherwise unprotected, concentrated source of nourishment. A new variety of disease-resistant potato was recently introduced that did not need (artificial) pesticide protection, but it had to be withdrawn from the market when it was found to make people ill. Sure enough, the symptoms were caused by the same natural toxins that had been bred out.

"Toxin manufacture (by a plant) requires materials and energy, and the toxins may be dangerous to the plant. In general, a plant can have high toxin levels or rapid growth but not both. Rapidly growing plant tissues are usually better food than stable or slowly growing structures." Spring's first leaves are relished by bugs.

"It takes such elaborate processing to turn acorns into human food that we wonder if the tannin may be too much even for squirrels. (8% kills rats.) Perhaps it leaches out when acorns are buried. If so, the squirrels are processing as well as hiding food.

"The Pomo indians of CA mixed unprocessed acorn meal with a certain kind of red clay to make bread. The clay bound enough tannin to make the bread palatable. Other groups boiled acorns to extract the tannin. Our enzyme systems can apparently cope with low concentrations of tannin, and many like its taste in tea and wine."

Domestic animals and plants were bred to be tender, non-toxic, easily processed. "The mainstay foods of the Stone Age would seem to us inedible or too demanding of time and effort. Many wild fruits, even when fully ripe, are sour to our tastes, and other plant products are bitter or have strong odors." (I disagree. Many wild berries are as sweet as most domestic fruits, and nettles and some other wild greens are as tasty as garden greens - though not as seductive as candied cherries or pumpkin pie !) Random House, 1994, 289p, $13 cover price. (review by H&B)

Should I taste unknown green plants ?
Many people, including me, taste leaves or fruits WITHOUT swallowing. I chew a tiny piece and hold in my mouth a minute or so. If it tastes bad or burns/numbs/stings, I spit out and keep spitting. But suppose it tastes bland - or nice. Then what ? Some people swallow a tiny portion. If no bad effects within 24 hrs, they may eat somewhat more. And so on.

Ray Vizgirdas, in Wilderness Way v5n2, condemns this. He points out that water hemlock (Cicuta) smells and tastes good to many people, yet a piece of root "the size of a marble may kill you within a half hour." Some other plants' poisons are cumulative and thus can't be assayed by sampling. And most of the toxins in lupines "are excreted by the kidneys. One must eat a lethal dose at one time to die." Ray advises, eat only plants you've positively identified as edible.

Except for fruits, I agree, partly because most plant parts won't provide enough energy to sustain me if I'm famished. Leaves contain vitamins but few calories (and I'll probably be able to identify before developing a vitamin deficiency). Most roots are tough to dig. Most wild seeds are tiny and difficult to separate out.

However, with an unknown plant, although I don't SWALLOW it, I may TASTE it - to reduce the number of plants I must identify. Most plants taste awful to me. So, tasting saves me much time otherwise spent keying.

As for fruits, in this area at least, the only wild fruits that taste good to me are edible. (I deliberately tasted a baneberry, one of the few poisonous berries, and didn't like it) And fruits are rich in sugars which provide energy, and vitamin C which humans need frequently. Holly & Bert

Water: easy out-flow abets in-flow.
Chronic dehydration (body too dry) is believed to be a major cause of cancer, joint pains, memory and vision loss, over-eating, and lack of pep; perhaps because removal of toxins (which all body tissues produce during normal activities) is slowed.

70% of Americans are chronically dehydrated, I've read. One cause: a weak sense of thirst (which is not felt until 2% dehydrated - I suppose because dehydration was seldom a problem for primate ancestors who usually got enough moisture from their food: mostly shoots and fruits rich in water, and healthier than often-contaminated streams and ponds). But, in present society, the biggest cause may be: not wanting work, play, or sleep interrupted by trips to toilets.

To minimize inconvenience, keep pee jugs/bowls handy. When inside, I have one within a few feet. Even when we sit a house, I use a pee jug, to save me time as well as saving the owners water and electricity. For men, liquid detergent bottles have good-size openings and are not easily mistaken for water/juice jugs. For women, 64-oz plastic bowls are low enough to squat over and wide enough to reliably intercept flow. Use tight-fitting lid.

Pee frequently. Letting urine set long in you, may harm bladder.

To decide how much to drink, I do not rely on thirst alone. If I feel irritation when I pee, or if I've not had an urge for many hours, or if my pee looks dark, I drink more.

Water is best drunk between meals: at least 2 hours after and 1/4 hour before eating. (If drunk with meals, it dilutes digestive secretions.)

Sweet fruits or drinks may not relieve thirst and might increase it. On one hot 60-mile bike trip, we took scant water, thinking we'd pass some. We didn't. We ate many blackberries, which lessened thirst but did not provide enough moisture. When we did reach water, we drank MUCH (slowly) - but that night I hallucinated.

According to MDs Clark Cobb and Rahul Khosla in 7/01 Patient Care; "During heavy exercise in a hot environment, most people should drink 16 to 32 ounces (2 to 4 glasses) of cool water each hour. Water is just as good if not better than sport drinks. Do not take salt tablets." (If needing salt, will likely crave salty foods.)

Cold, too, increases water needs, because cool air becomes drying when warmed by lungs. High altitude further increases water needs because of more breathing in the thin air. B&H, March

Buying at wholesale grocers.

Though Bert and I sometimes buy (eg) ramon noodles on sale at retail stores, most of our food purchases are at wholesalers. In western Oregon, we have recently payed about 25¢ a pound for oatmeal and popcorn and under 20¢ for red wheat, buying 50-pound bags. Brown rice was over 30¢ and (we've read) is more pesticided than other grains, so we now eat less. Recently, lentils were much cheaper (±30¢/pound) than other beans, and they cook faster, so we bought hundreds of pounds. Prices vary, depending on harvests.

Whereas, if noodles on sale are $1 for ten 3-ounce packets, that is 53¢ a pound. Not really a bargain. Also, when we get to cities, we are usually too busy to want to chase sales.

A decade ago, we were able to buy 50-pound bags of organic red wheat at a local co-op for under 25¢/pound. But now, the co-op not only marks up more, but no longer stocks extra bags - because they "need" the space for more shelves of (eg) "organic" cookies and candies. (Sad story. They began as a small, simple, funky, volunteer-run shop selling basic foods and some locally-grown produce - but now differ from Safeway mainly in hype. That seems the fate of any organization that grows big enough to need a full-time employee or a professional manager - because one yuppy who buys pricy processed junk, profits them more than do 10 customers like us.) If you want organic grains and local sellers are pricy, consider buying from THEIR source - if your group has enough storage for a truckload.

Most grains we buy are grown elsewhere: eg, popcorn in IA and wheat in MT. People in central U.S. can likely buy for less than we do - esp if they can buy direct from growers. (Weather here is chancy for grains. Some feed-store corn (±10¢/lb) included moldy kernels. A nuisance to pick out.)

Most sizable cities have wholesale grocers. I look for ones (also called institutional grocers) that cater to restaurants, bakeries, schools, etc, because they have the big bags. (Some sell cases of small packages to retail stores - which are not bargains.)

A few wholesalers, pressured by retailers who fear losing trade, say they don't sell "to the public". I ignore that - and briskly walk in like I'm a business person who's been there before, know where I'm going, and do not have much time. (Don't pause and ask.) If questioned, I might say I have (eg) a popcorn stand at the fair, or am a cook at Camp Cukinuki. Seldom am I refused - they want my money. Of course, I pay cash - and carry.

Bert and I together spend ± $400 a year for food. (Total expenses ± $600 a year; not including DP which costs and earns under $1000/year.) H & B

Solar pre-cooking can save fuel.

Here and in much of North America, sunshine is often too brief (because of morning clouds, or hills or trees) to rely on solar alone. However, on most summer days and some days year around, water can be heated to 170°F or hotter. That will greatly reduce fuel needed to finish cooking, esp if (eg) rice soaks in the water while it is heating: very worthwhile if using (eg) propane or alcohol that must be bought and backpacked. 170 is also more than hot enough to kill disease organisms in drinking water. (163 is supposedly hot enough, but thermometer might not be accurate.)

Time needed to get water hot can be shortened by keeping the water inside overnight (if your shelter is insulated) or under a pile of leaves or (eg) extra clothes. Bert & Holly, March

Solar cooker easy to pack and store.

This reflector-type cooker is esp for portable dwellers at mid latitudes (most of N.Amer). Its main advantage over similar designs: folds to 8½x11": small enough to fit into a 5 gal pail: important where its materials will rot or lose shine unless sheltered.

Covered with 12-inch-wide aluminum foil (standard size); little scrap. Accomodates pot up to 10" diameter.

I built ours out of non-corrugated cardboard from recycle bins. (Stiff pieces best.) Hinges and reinforcements of Tyvek, a super-strong paper (from used "Express Mail" envelopes). White glue. About 6½ feet of foil. Total cost under 25¢. Tools: pencil, ruler, sizzors, knife, clean flat surface at least 2¼x3 feet.

The cooker consists of eight 8½x11 panels hinged together. (If bigger sheets available, less gluing needed.)

CONSTRUCTION. (Read through to "use" before starting.) Cut bottom side panels as shown on right, leaving tabs. Cut slots in back side panels. I reinforced tabs and slots and fold lines by gluing Tyvek onto cardboard. For best adhesion, apply glue to blank sides (if one side has printing).

Ω Cut a Tyvek piece 7x9", fold into a Ω shape 9" long with "feet" 1" wide and glue to (what will be) non-reflective side of top panel.

Cut foil slightly larger than the cardboard. (Eg, 9½x12" to cover an 8½x11 panel) On top of the LEAST shiny side of the foil, put a panel (or multi-panel section), centering so the foil extends about ½" beyond all edges. (Except: I trimmed off foil that would cover tabs.) Fold foil up over the edges of the panel. (I did not glue foil to cardboard. I did sticky-tape to non-reflective sides in a few spots to help hold.)

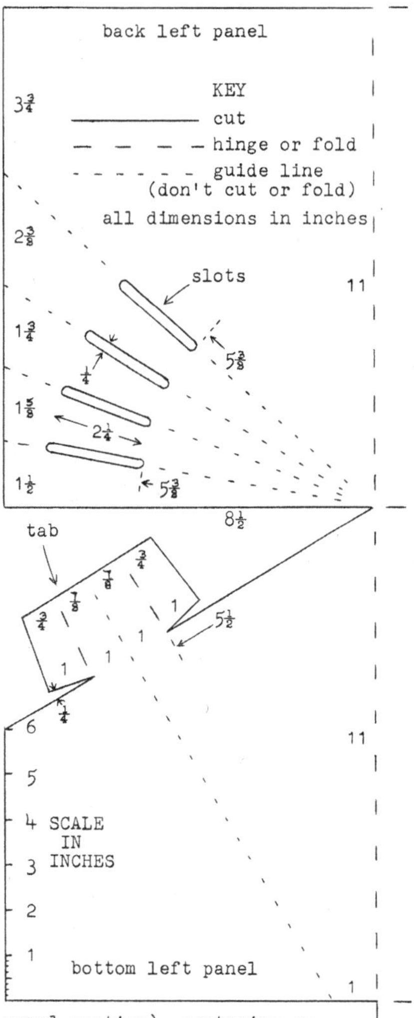

back left panel
KEY
cut
hinge or fold
guide line
(don't cut or fold)
all dimensions in inches
3¾
2⅜
1¾
1⅝
1½
slots
11
5⅜
¼
2¼
5⅜
8½
tab
¾
⅞
⅞
¾
1
1
1
1
5½
¼
6
5
4
3
2
1
SCALE IN INCHES
11
bottom left panel
1

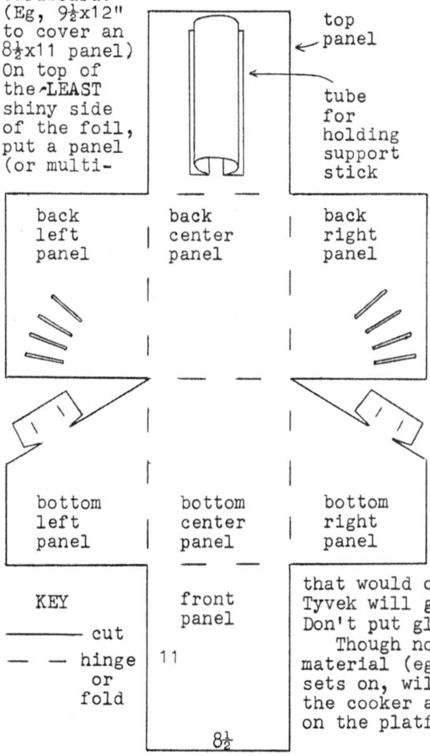

top panel
tube for holding support stick
back left panel
back center panel
back right panel
bottom left panel
bottom center panel
bottom right panel
front panel
KEY
cut
hinge or fold
11
8½

Place panels, reflective sides down, about ¼" apart (to allow fold-up room). To hinge panels together, cut 18 pieces of Tyvek about 2x4" (2 for each 8½" join; 3 for each 11" join). Before gluing on, trim off folded-over foil that would otherwise be covered by Tyvek (so the Tyvek will glue to the cardboard, not the foil). Don't put glue on the hinge/fold lines.

Though not essential, a 2x3-foot piece of flat material (eg, plywood), to be a platform the cooker sets on, will faciliate turning the cooker (because the cooker and the props that adjust it can all set on the platform and turn with it).

September 2002

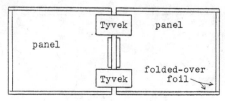

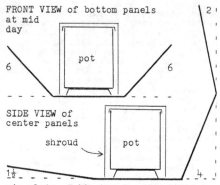

FRONT VIEW of bottom panels at mid day

SIDE VIEW of center panels

shroud → pot

USE. I cook or heat water in a spot sunny for several hours. Place platform level and non-tipsy. Or, if no platform, level and smooth ground.

Connect each bottom side panel to a back panel by folding in edges of tab, pushing tab through slot, and then partly unfolding tab. If sun is quite high: eg, near mid day from April until mid Sept near 45° latitude (eg, near Portland, Minneapolis, Montreal, Milan, AlmaAta, Vladivostock, Christchurch), I put each tab into the third slot from the bottom. During the same period near 35° latitude (eg,near Santa Barbara, Albuquerque, Memphis, Charlotte, Algiers, Beirut, Tokyo, Capetown, Sidney, Buenos Aires), I'd use the second slot. At latitudes 25° or less (eg, Miami, Honolulu, Calcutta), I'd use the first slot. If at 55° or higher (eg, Prince George, Edmonton, Edinburgh, Copenhagen, Moscow), or late in day or season (sun low in sky) I'd use the fourth slot. Ie, the lower the sun, the higher the slot.

Set the cooker's bottom center panel on the platform. Hold up the top panel by inserting into the tube a 2-foot-long stick. Place (eg) rocks against the bottom of stick.

I set an uncolored glass dish, 5"D, 1" high, upside down, on the bottom center panel, and set pot on dish - to insulate pot from panel. Or, 3 small clear glasses or jars. Last choice: chunks of bark (will block a lil sun).

Don't use a pot that has a long side handle. (It would get in way of a shroud). For the greatest heat, the pot and lid should be dull black.

Turn cooker and adjust panels to reflect most sun onto pot. Slant the back panels by placing objects under the back side panels, or against the non-reflective side of the back center panel. Adjust top panel by moving the stick that holds it up. Raise front panel by setting something under it, or lower it by raising the platform.

The shroud should be enough larger than pot to provide a narrow air space (½" to 1") between them for insulation. A transparent jar or pail will be most convenient. Next best: oven bag. If using an ordinary plastic bag, try to keep it from touching the hot pot. The bag may be kept extended by inserting a few bent, limber twigs.

TESTS. On 6 days of late summer at 43° latitude 600 ft altitude, I heated 8 cups of water. I used a slightly rusty "tin" can, 6¼Dx7" (8 cups filled it 5" deep) because I happened to have a transparent plastic jar that fit it well as shroud. Lid made from aluminum pie plate. I blackened can and lid in a fire. (Black adhered to can, not lid)

I adjusted cooker once an hour but left tabs in third slots all day. At 1:30 (sun highest), as shown above. Early and late in day, I set center back panel steeper, top panel less steep, front panel horizontal or below.

During all tests the water got hot enough long enough to cook almost anything. (I didn't cook because can had soldered (lead?) seam, and because the tests were too long.)

The last test, Sept 8, got hottest despite lower sun, because sky had no clouds. Strong breeze in early PM. At 9:00, when sun rose above trees, test began: air 55°F, water 49°. 11:30,162°. 12:00, 177° (now steaming). 12:30,187°. 1:30 (local solar noon), 202°, air 87°. 3:00, 208° (hottest). 6:00, 195°, air 66°, sun going behind trees, test end. A cup of water evaporated. Its cooling effect prevented boiling. (A pressure cooker would have gotten hotter.)

On Sept 2, when sky mostly/partly cloudy until 3:30, water 170° at 2:00, max 197° at 4:00. 185° or hotter for 3 hours. (Plenty hot enough to cook - typical simmer 182° on a gas stove.)

COMPARISON. A decade ago, we built a window-box-type cooker out of cardboard, insulated with crumpled newspaper. We cooked with it almost every day during July and early Aug. We had no candy thermometer to measure temperatures. As I recall, it got steamy hot though not audibly boiling. It needed adjusting less often than does our reflector cooker; and had few parts to adjust. But it required a high sun (or else tilting the whole box, which would complicate pot support). Biggest problem: VERY BULKY - much too big to fit in any container we had. Sheltered only by wrapping in plastic, moisture and mice ruined it in one winter.

COMMENTS. Some may wonder why we want to solar cook, living as we do where wood is plentiful. Solar is safer: no chance of starting forest fire or of producing smoke (which can cause alarm and attract hassles, even from a safe wood stove). Also, with solar, less chance of scorching food. Also, we might be able to cook inside, where we definitely don't want smoke !

September 2002   B&H

Dwelling Portably

or Shared, Mobile, Improvised
Underground, Hidden, Floating

May 2003 $1 per issue   POB 190-d, Philomath OR 97370

Update on Rubbermaid storage bins used as horse packs.
A horse fell on one, cracking it along a corner. Also,
the lids are cracking; maybe sunlight has weakened the plastic.
However, they were free, and I got two summers use as packs,
and can still use them to store 'junk' at my base camp.
I spent most of the summer training horses on a light
wagon, but did manage a three-week trip into the wilderness to
visit hot springs. Bear, ID 832, Oct

Cook stove made from one-gallon paint can.

I read about this on the internet and
made one to use on a recent camping trip.
I punched a 4x2" hole near the bottom as
the main air inlet, and many small holes
(nail size) on the opposite side near the
top. At first I did not have enough holes:
the fire almost died when I put a pot on
top. So I gave the stove a "face" by
cutting "eye" and "ear" holes. I dubbed
it "Fire Monster". Use a large nail and
light hammer. After punching the holes,
hammer out the dents.

Feed fuel mostly through the top, but
small pieces can go through the eye/ear
holes. I put leaves/paper in first, then
pine cones and small pieces of wood, then
anything burnable that fits. As a starter
perhaps a candle stub. Light it through
the mouth. As an air blower, I used a
piece of bamboo with a $\frac{1}{4}$" hole in the fire
end. Blowing into the 2" end creates a
strong air stream that gets a fire going quickly. I kept the
fire end damp so it wouldn't burn easily. Don't cook food on
the first fire, and stand back while the old paint burns off.
Careful ! I burned my fingers trying to reposition the
stove. Leave the bail handle on and use a stick to move the
stove. For stability I put stones in the bottom.
To slow the fire, turn the face away from the wind. I was
able to slow it enough to simmer. But the stove seems best
for boiling. Fred Spek, Ontario M6J, Sept

I use propane for heating and cooking.
A small refillable one-gallon bulk tank (much smaller/
lighter/handier than the standard 20# 5-gallon tank) lasts me
for months. U-haul locations fill propane tanks and have no
minimum (this is rare). I pick slack times.
My stove is a one-burner designed for the disposable
bottles. But I use a "Mr Heater" 90° elbow/adaptor and leave
it attached to the tank between refills. It is very stable
for cooking. For heating, it will warm my tent or pickup
shell in a minute or two, even in freezing temperatures. So,
in the evening, I turn it on and off several times. In the
morning, I stick one arm out of my bag, turn the propane on
full so I can hear it, light a 'strike anywhere' match, and
get a small 'poof' as the stove lights. (Takes practice to
not get a big poof !) In a minute or so my space is warm and
I get up. (I have never gone back to sleep after lighting the
stove. Fumes could be deadly. Ken, WA 982

Benefits of foraging and gardening.
     I lived on 45 acres once. Though there was a pond,
cattails, rose hips, and many blackberries, I could not gather
enough wild food to feed my family. I had to buy, and plant.
     Hunting/gathering takes ALL your time. That is why
horticulture was developed.
     This week I put in early garden stuff: spinach, onions,
peas, lettuce. I have a row of broad-leaf dandelion and
winter cress. Those greens are full of vitamins. Indoors
I've started the cabbage family and tomatoes, peppers, squash.
I buy seed for 10¢ a package at Walgreens. For a few kinds
I have to pay more at specialty stores. But, all in all, my
garden pays. A bonus: people stop by, look over the fence,
and comment. We share what we have and what we know. Suzanne,
(Comments:) Interesting that you are   OH 451, Mar 02
cultivating dandelions. Edible weeds are hardier than
domestic vegies and seem a better bet for nomadic gardeners.
They taste about as good and have more vitamins than do most
domestics, though fewer calories than (eg) potatos. I've read
that some "weeds" were formerly cultivated. Did they lose
status because they were EASY to grow ?!
     If growing weeds, best to encourage those native to the
area. A few years ago we were given some amaranth seeds
gathered from garden weeds. We planted. They sprouted but
soon died. Wrong soil ? Not enough sun ? Too dry ? Most
garden weeds here are from eastern N. America and need summer
rains or else irrigation, as do the domestic vegies.
     Foraging does not fully feed us, even during summer.
Plenty of vitamins but little fat. However, we do forage most
of our fruit and vegies; which are expensive to buy, heavy to
transport (mostly water), and difficult to store (without
great loss of nutrients). We buy mostly grains and other
edible seeds; which are cheap in bulk, light weight per
calories, and easy to store.
     We've known people who bought or built rural "homesteads",
thinking they could grow all their food. But, though they did
produce some, they also had to buy food - in most cases more
than we do, because of lack of time due to needing jobs to pay
the taxes, and pay for the cars needed to commute !
     Some anthropologists say that early hunter-gatherers had
MORE leisure than did horticulturalists; perhaps because the
latter were more easily preyed upon through taxes and
conscriptions by lords or through robberies by raiders.
Agriculture displaced hunting/gathering, not because it took
less time, but because it took less land. A problem for
contemporary foragers: most of the lusher areas are now
occupied by farms and cities. Holly & Bert, OR 973, February

Living lightly in the Chicago area.
     I manage to scavenge most of my food. I am leery of food
straight out of garbage cans. I spend much time cutting off
the better portions and discarding the rest. I douse with
tumeric or curry, esp if drying. Tumeric kills viruses and
bacteria and arrests rotting. It apparently kills bugs.
     I also salvage most clothing and much else. I never walk
the streets when I can walk the alleys. Anything that won't
fit into a sealed locker or foot-locker should probably not be
taken. I've made money selling salvagings: eg, $5000 on two
boxes of signed first-edition books that someone left in an
alley. To learn value, I check references in libraries.
     My experience being homeless in Chicago. The cops don't
need you - and they expect the same. Ie, if you don't look
                 Dwelling Portably   May 2003

well heeled, your safety is not their concern. Cops generally
won't bother you if you are minding your own business. But
they do take a dim view of exercising your 2nd amendment
rights - including knives over 3 inches. At first I was
somewhat worried, sleeping day time in parks on the near-west/
northwest side. But no one bothered me. After 20 years
experience, I've learned to avoid groups of homeless as they
draw the wrong kind of attention. Aggressive beggars and
drug addicts are slowly closing down one of Chicago's best
services: showers in the Public Park District.
     I just walk in like I belong there and bathe myself and
and my clothing (which I leave on) with a bar of laundry soap.
Okay for hair, too. After wringing my clothes, during summer
I put them in a mesh bag to dry naturally. During winter I
carry them in a plastic bag to a laudromat and use the driers.
When I was driving a cab, I'd put them on newspapers below the
dash board, open the windows, and turn the heat on full blast.
Fashion concerns aside, one needs only one change of clothes.
     Backpacks don't seem a problem, but I carry an innocuous
book bag. Sleeping bags or bed rolls do seem to draw attention.
Walking railroad tracks is an excellent way to travel.
Northern tier railroad personnel seem almost nostalgic about
hobos. Under land-grant laws, railroads have virtual
sovereignty over their right-of-ways and stations. Trespass
involves city police only if they are called in. However, not
all police know this. My only hassles have been by drinkers.
     As I tend to work a circuit, I have a series of places
where I deposit my finds. Bridges and overpasses provide my
roofs and windbreaks during inclement weather. One problem:
the heavy pesticide spraying, esp in the South. Of course,
I gather and plant far off the right of way. I don't even
sleep in areas that have been sprayed. Goats and other animals
should not forage in those areas. Kurt, IL 606, March 02

Encounters bear with cub while hiking.
     I heard sounds of claws scratching on a tree. I followed
the sounds toward their source. I spotted a small cub approx
25 feet up in a slim jackpine. I was 20 or 30 yards away.
I immediately turned and started running away (mistake) down
into a gully that emptied onto a railroad track. I glanced
back and saw the mother black bear trotting toward me.
     As I ran, I took off a small daypack and dropped it on
the ground. It contained donuts and baked buns (my snack for
the day). I thought the bear might smell them and stop. When
I got to the railroad and riverbank, I felt safer. Much of
the ground there is covered with big boulders which bears have
difficulty traversing. I waited two hours before going back
and retrieving my daypack. It was still where I had dropped
it and the food inside was untouched. Apparently the bear had
stopped after advancing only a few yards in my direction.
I guess she felt I wasn't much of a threat (and she wasn't
very hungry). Over time, I've read many reports of bear
attacks and maulings of innocent hikers and campers.
     I often see black bear scat and even tracks in this area.
But bears haven't molested the small amounts of dry foods and
tinned foods I leave at ground level. One rule: I NEVER cook
or eat meat or fish at my base camps. Those odors are much
more attractive to bears than are odors of (eg) beans or rice.
                                          Bruce of BC
Food I put out for my cats attracted rats.
     Also ants. A factory near where I put it, said not to.
I now feed my cats on an abandoned lot I cleaned up.
I planted some seeds there. It is beautiful outside. Elaine,
              May 2003   RI 029

Long-tolerated hut dwellers finally hassled.
For 12 years, Thelma Cabellero and Besh Serdahely have
lived in a home-made hut built amongst the branches of a
sprawling oak tree halfway up San Bruno Mountain south of San
Francisco. The hut masterfully blends tree branches with
building materials salvaged from dumpsters. The roof is a
patchwork of plastic panels held together with cords and clips.
The couple met and fell in love at a S.F. homeless
shelter in the late 1980s and set up a home in some bushes by
the Caltrain tracks before discovering their present site....
San Bruno Mountain Watch, an environmental group that has
fought commercial development, want Thelma and Besh to stay.
"They have always been good stewarts. Because of their efforts
Owl Canyon has no invasion of broom, fennel, hemlock."
Their home looks out on San Francisco Bay, freeways,
power lines, and other apparatus they don't need. Thelma
said, "We have the trees and the sunshine and the sky."
Occasionally the couple hike into town for supplies;
mostly beans and bread. Other times they snip away at the
non-native plants, tend their compost heap, haul water from a
nearby spring, and relax by reading cast-off books, playing
Monopoly and working crossword puzzles. Steve Rubenstein
(from San Francisco Chronicle 4Sep02; sent by Herbert Diaz)

Lynnwood criticized for ban on living in cars.
Lynnwood's code-enforcement officer, Peter Van Guisen,
said the law, approved last month, was passed to prevent
transients from living in cars they park in front of parks or
homes, often using the shrubbery as bathrooms. Car camping
has especially been a problem, Van Guisen said, at Gold Park,
a wooded, city-owned lot at Highway 99 and 200th St SW, across
from the Labor Ready temp agency, a magnet for the homeless.
The lot is also adjacent to condominiums whose residents, Van
Guisen said, complain they often can't walk through the park
without stumbling across makeshift camps.
The ordinance prescribes jail terms of up to 90 days or
fines of up to $1000 for people caught living in their cars.
It particularly targets people who have "camping paraphernalia"
including tarps, sleeping bags, cooking gear in their cars.
Laws like these irk "homeless" advocates who say that
Lynnwood is just passing its problems on to Seattle and other
cities. Seattle's city council proposed a similar ordinance
a few years ago but dropped it under pressure from activists.
Some cities, including Seattle, ticket cars that have
been parked in the same place longer than a specified time.
However, car dwellers get around those laws by moving frequently. Catherine Tarpley (from 5/7/01 Seattle Times)

(Comments:) Many vacationers carry "camping paraphernalia" in
their vehicles because they plan to stop at (eg) National Park
campgrounds. They may be more threatened by laws such as
Lynnwood's than are poor car dwellers. Because, these days,
most police are, first and foremost, revenue sources. So,
regardless of a law's intent or their formal instructions,
police are encouraged to issue citations to people who can and
will pay fines, rather than to people who are likely to end up
in jail, costing the city government money.
I wonder if homeless advocacy groups could form potent
alliances with travelers' organizations such as AAA. AAA
lists towns where police operate speed traps, and urges
motorists to avoid them. Laws that prohibit sleeping in
vehicles are much worse than speed traps. Such laws not only

rob; they ENDANGER by discouraging sleepy drivers from
stopping and napping.

Seattle officials agree to stop hassling tent city.

Tent-city residents now have the right to put their 100-
person encampment nearly anywhere - a big back yard, church
property, commercial parking lot - so long as (eg) their camps
are at least 20 feet from a neighboring lot and hidden from
view by an 8-foot-tall buffer. Tent city may stay in one spot
for up to 3 months. Neighborhoods cannot veto. Only one tent
city is allowed. Tent-city residents are elated that officials
have stopped insisting that tents are substandard housing.

Tent city, which has moved 27 times in its two-year
history, has spent much of the past year in church parking
lots. Those lots became havens from the threat of city fines
after city officials acknowledged that federal law may be
viewed as allowing churches to ignore land-use codes by
insisting that welcoming the homeless is part of ministering
to the poor and integral to their religions.

(Summary of events. Parts were reported in 9/01 DP)
March 00. A tent city with 20 residents begins on
undeveloped land in Seattle, with tolerance by owner.

Jan 01. Now numbering 100, tent city leaves El Centro de
la Raza after a 6-month stay. Officials had ordered El Centro
to eject tent city. El Centro refused. Officials threatened
to fine El Centro, and rejected its application for a permit.

Apr 01. Officials decide to not fine a Ballard church
for hosting tent city, citing fed court rulings.

Sept 01. King County Superior Court Judge Thomas Majhan
rules that the city was wrong to refuse a permit to El Centro.
The judge said, the military, scouts, and disaster-relief
groups all have histories of establishing safe tent cities.
City officials appealed, but rather than risk losing, which
could throw housing laws into doubt, they conceded.

March 02. Tent-city and Seattle officials sign agreement.
How tent-city residents beat the system, is a story of
persistence, pushiness, good legal advice, and alliances with
churches that made hosting tent city part of their ministry -
and backing city officials into a morally-difficult corner.

That tent-city residents have won anything, is close to
a miracle. They are out of work or under employed. They are
construction workers, often injured, without training to do
something else. They have some money, but not two months
rent. They are hiding from husbands who beat them. They are
mentally ill. They are divorced. They didn't get that job on
a fishing boat that they came to Seattle hoping for.

Gary Gibson, a tent city resident 10 months, says the
group has succeeded because of its record as a quiet, safe
neighbor. Anyone who comes in drunk or disorderly is expelled.

Seattle deputy major Tom Byers said, "My feels are
profoundly mixed. Is it a victory to win the right to sleep
in a tent in the rain ?" City Council President Peter Stein-
brueck, has begun to see things differently. "Why is a tent
settlement worse than a mat on a floor in the basement of a
church ? Talk to the folks who are there. They're happier.
There's self determination. There's strength in that...."

But some other city council members are expected to try
to outlaw tent city, at least on non-church sites, by
requiring plumbing and other facilities that tent city could
not provide. How the council will vote is not known.

Complaints of homeless advocates regarding Seattle's
officially-approved shelters: too few for the thousands who

need shelter; no private spaces for couples to sleep together; no segregation of potentially dangerous residents; requiring residents to be in by 10 pm and out by 6:30 am, which prevents night employment, and forces people with nowhere to go onto streets in cold and wet weather. Beth Kaiman (much shortened from 14 & 28 March 02 Seattle Times, sent by Roger Knights).

(Comments:) Officials and media, whether sympathetic or hostile, blatantly ignore an embarrassing fact: the main cause of homelessness is the lack of low-cost housing - which is POLITICALLY CREATED by the myriad zoning laws and building regulations that greatly increase costs of legal structures. Instead of changing their policies, officials campaign for more tax money to provide government-managed housing. But most anything a government does, it does clumsily at exorbitant cost (eg, those WA state camps for migrant harvesters, reported in 9/01 DP). So the result is a token project that benefits only a few people who are able/willing to jump through all the hoops - and then spend ten years on a waiting list. But, hey, such projects provide some high-pay jobs for administrators !

When the homeless move in next door.
    The three months that tent city spent on the hill beside Lake City Christian Church, tested the depth of convictions of its neighbors. One took a homeless woman to dinner, while another itched to call the cops. One said she would welcome another tent city, while her neighbor began locking her car in her driveway. Kathern Carlstrom lives closest to the former site. Like many, she was bothered that the church did not notify neighbors before the tents went up. But she told me how polite the tent city residents were. They even cleaned up around the bus stop, and two men did some edging on a steep hill in front of her property. "I look out now and miss their tents. I hope their weeks here allow some of them to move up."
    But another neighbor, Virginia Arnoux, said: "I am glad they are gone." Though she is a church goer, taught to help those in need, she said that a friend who works with the homeless told her that "tent-city people don't want jobs and don't want to help themselves." Nicole Brodeur (Seattle Times 7/8/01

(Comments:) The many campers near that temp-work agency in Lynnwood (p.13) refutes the claim that tent dwellers don't want jobs. But probably, most don't want to work 40 or more hours a week steady - and have rent take most of their earnings !
    Those house-dwellers who hope the "homeless" will "move up" (ie, get high-pay jobs so they can afford houses) seem unaware that, if the homeless do, they will bid up housing prices even higher - causing some present house renters to find THEMSELVES homeless. Anyone who has a house (or apartment), is benefitted by people living in tents, cars, bush huts, etc - because those people are not competing for that house. Likewise anyone who has a high-paying job, is benefitted by people who live economically, because they are not competing for that job.

Survey of urban campers who live in Vancouver.
    The city has become home to hundreds who sleep on beaches, in doorways, under bridges, in cars, and in dozens of other mostly-hidden places. "Urban campers are most readily found near densely populated areas, fast-food outlets, laundromats, and liquor stores - the same areas that appeal to many single people", says Judy Graves, who has spent several years doing walkabouts at night with teams of people to count urban campers. "The shelterless do not distribute themselves evenly across the city. They look for alcoves, bushes, trees, landscaping, underground parking lots, unlocked public buildings, and wash-

rooms." Some sleep on porches or garages in Kitsilano, with the home-owner's permission. Many said they lived outside because they had no income, and they either didn't qualify for welfare or had given up applying for it.

However, Graves found much fewer urban campers in Vancouver than in Toronto. In Vancouver "we have to really search to find many people sleeping out." Whereas "in Toronto, as we knelt on the pavement talking with one person, we could always see the next 2 or 3 we would be talking with. In most blocks there were 3 steam grates, and someone slept on every steam grate. In shop doorways, as many as 8 under-age youth slept closely side by side." Graves thought the difference may be due to BC building more "social"(subsidized) housing.

At least two-thirds of those that Graves and companions found, had severe addictions to alcohol or other drugs. Frances (from 22June02 Vancouver Sun, sent by Bruce of BC)

(Comments:) The difference between cities might be due to topography and climate. North of Vancouver are extensive forests. Whereas a land-use map shows mostly farms around Toronto. Also, Toronto has much colder winters. In January, a steam grate may seem better than a tent in the bush.

As for the two-thirds that supposedly have severe addictions. Addicts are more easily found, because they are likely to fall asleep on the nearest bench or lawn, instead preparing a hide-out. So any such survey will be biased. (The article failed to mention that.)

Though Holly and I camp mostly in remote forests, over the years we have also spent quite some time in/near cities. As far as I know, our camps were never found. Partly luck, I suppose. But also because we spent time and effort finding and preparing good sites, and because we went further into the brush or out of town (not wanting liquor or fast foods). B & H

Where can I build a small cabin without getting hassled ?
Preferably some place where I can obtain work. I've found plenty of info on HOW to build, but none on WHERE to build. I just want a base to work from during summers.

Do you live on vacant land ? Doesn't that bring hassles? If you know anyone who has built not to code and gotten away with it, please let me know what county. How is Sonoma co. ? Shane, CA 922, 1998. (I replied immediately, and put reply in a Network Supplement, but not DP, hoping for more info.)
(Reply:) For non-hidden dwellings that are not to code, I read a few years ago: the most tolerant county in CA was Humboldt (Arcata, Eureka). I don't know if it still is.

You say you have plenty of info on HOW to build. Even more important is WHAT to build. A conventional cabin is tall and has an unnatural shape (difficult to conceal) and needs truckloads of materials that are nailed together (difficult to haul in and assemble without attracting attention). Bert

Many people live in tents and vehicles on Prudence Island.
Also in abandoned houses. The island is across from Newport and Portsmouth. Ferry round trip, $5. I plan to go there this summer. Elaine, Rhode Island 029, April 02

How do you stay warm during winter ?
My tent (small dome) is okay in summer but was often too cold the one time I tried camping during winter. Eve, CA 950
(Reply:) We build small, low, WELL INSULATED shelters. Sept
Some designs in 5/95, 4/92, 9/85, 5/99 DPs. However, best to form the shelter to the site, rather than trying to find or reshape a site to accomodate a particular design. B & H

While living in Portland, I have been eating free food.
    In season: Je-Jy cherries; Jy-Ag-Sp blackberries; Jy-Ag
plums; Sp-Oc-Nv-Dc apples. Also, some charities put out free
bread (past pull date; stores/bakeries donate) each week. You
just go and get what you want. Zalia, OR 972, December 2002

(Addendum:) Here (100 miles south) our free fruit this year:
My-Je salmonberries (but seldom got filled); Je-Jy redberries
(Vaccinium parvafolium, shaped like blueberries, tarter but
much tastier if sweetened); Jy black-cap raspberries; Ag-Sp
blackberries. No apples (in abandoned orchards) this year,
due to hard freeze while blooming. Fortunately we dried quite
a few redberries. So, most mornings this winter, I make a
little redberry-ade by soaking the berries in water a few
hours, adding vit C powder and a SMALL amount of sugar. I do
not know if natural vit C survived the drying, but the berries
add bioflavenoids which enhance vit C. Holly & Bert, Dec 03

In Iceland I discovered a wonderful light-weight trek food.
    Dried paper fish, white fillets. At first they feel like
paper in your mouth. But they puff up with saliva - and are
darned good. They supposedly taste better with margarine, but
I don't approve of margarine so I didn't try. Icelandic
cowboys carry them easily in pockets. Lisa Falour, France, 03

When boiling pasta by the sea, try using salt water.
    If the water is clean, it imparts an enjoyable sea-salt
taste. And salt water cooks foods faster. Drew Feuer, July 03

(Comment:) Also, it has a better balance of minerals than does
refined salt. Eg, potassium and lithium, as well as sodium.
But also wee amounts of toxic heavy metals. Holly, Oregon

Ramen noodles need not be cooked to be tasty.
    I was on a bike trip and didn't want to cook. So I got
HOT water from a campground bathroom, mixed it with noodles,
waited, checked, waited. After 20 minutes the noodles were
ready to eat. Since then I've never cooked ramen noodles.
    Soy protein (TVP) mixed with ramen noodles provides a good
ready meal, tasty and nutritious. TVP takes on the flavor of
whatever you add it to. 37% protein. $2 to $3 per pound.
    I get hot water from store bathrooms, convenience-store
coffee/tea counters (where I ask first), and by solar-heating
water in a GREEN 2-liter plastic soda bottle. I also use the
bottle for showers. Zalia, traveling, March 03

Gatorade bottles, used as canteens, never leak.
    I used to buy "camping" bottles. But they always leaked.
Then, in 1998, I took a Gatorade bottle on a bus trip. Though
it got bashed and sat on, it never leaked. Since then I have
used them everywhere. They also store dry foods well. Zalia

Bottles form low-drag float.
    Many objects float.
This float's advantage:
streamlined: often desirable
where water flows or a boat moves.
    Collect three empty smooth-sided plastic bottles the same
size. The straighter their sides, the better. Two need caps.
(If lacking, close by wrapping ends with pieces of plastic held

on by rubber bands.) From the third bottle, cut off the top
and bottom. (The top can be used as funnel to fill jugs. The
bottom as bowl.) Slit lengthwise the cylindrical middle piece.
Bore or punch small holes in it. Place the two whole jugs
together, bottom to bottom. Fit the cut piece around them to
hold them in line. To keep them from slipping apart, tie a
string between their necks and to the holes in the cut piece.
Two-liter bottles will float up to 4 pounds without much drag.
    One use: fishing if lacking a casting rod, or where over-
head branches prevent casting. If you plan to stand in mid
stream, tie a cord to the float's upstream end. If you will
be on the bank, tie a long slender pole. The pole can be
longer and more flexible than an ordinary fishing pole because
the float supports the far end. To the float's downstream
end, tie your hook. Bert, Oregon, September 2003

Floating island built from 250,000 plastic bottles.
    Richie Sowa, a skilled carpenter, 49, left his native
England 6 years ago. Soon after, on Mexico's Yucatan
peninsula, he began gathering thousands of bottles, putting
them in sacks made of strong fish netting, and weaving the
sacks tightly together. Local kids helped collect bottles.
    Now 65 by 54 feet, the island holds a 4-room house, sand
beaches, and lush vegetation including palm trees. The
house's roof collects rain for fresh water; and holds a photovoltaic panel for electricity, and what looks like a parabolic-
reflector solar cooker. The 5-foot-thick foundation of bottles
is topped by a bamboo and plywood floor holding, in places, a
two-foot-thick layer of soil. Richie plans to grow his food.
    The island gets bigger as Richie adds bottle-filled sacks
to the edges. He is also thickening the layer of bottles to
float the island higher above the waves. "I scuba dive so I
can check the underside regularly." The island has survived two
hurricanes. He seeks a woman to share it with. It is presently
moored 40 yards from the mainland, off Puerto Aventuras.
    Local authorities gave permission to build, to encourage
awareness of trash reuses. Richie hopes his feat will inspire
others. "This proves you can use the garbage from consumer
overspill to create land for people to live simple lives in
great surroundings." Richie, who earns money as musician and
artist, sometimes takes tourists to his island and their
donations help cover costs. Chris Pritchard (from National
Enquirer 5Nov02 and Sun 8Oct02; sent by Roger Knights)

(Comments:) I think the plastic bottles (designed to withstand
acid drinks) and the fish netting (designed to withstand sea
water) may have a long life, sheltered from sun. But I wonder
about the bamboo and plywood. I also wonder if the island,
which weighs 60 tons, can withstand towing in open ocean to a
new site; in case officials change their minds or impose
taxes and restrictions that Richie finds unacceptable. B & H

More about Prudence and Hog Islands near Providence.
    On the back side of Prudence Island are blue berries,
pear and apple trees, and rocky Indian Springs. Hog Island is
next to Prudence. The ferry won't stop there because the dock
isn't safe. Some squatters had trouble with the summer-home
people. A man washed up dead. One must be careful and self
sufficient. I tell homeless people how to make tents, heat
water and cook on tin-can stoves, shower using jugs, and live
in boats and cars. Many are rough and dirty. Elaine, RI, 02

Cleaning and fueling Coleman Pressure Lamps

Many vans and RVs have Coleman lamps. Upkeep can be cheaper and easier than most people suppose. Coleman-made replacement mantles cost half as much in Mexico.

Premium unleaded gasoline works as lamp fuel at less than half the price of name-brand white gas. Only it doesn't burn as clean. After a couple months of nightly use, unburned gunk may block fuel flow through generator (the tube between the mantles). Symptoms: balky fire-up; higher pump pressure needed to maintain brightness; dim. Instead of an expensive replacement, clean generator. That can solve many problems.

You need pliers, a knife, and two small wrenches.

Loosen the two generator-securing nuts all the way, and remove generator from lamp.

From the tube bottom, slide out cleaning needle rod.

With knife, scrape carbon deposit from all around rod until brass is shiny. Careful: needle wire tip breaks easily.

Remove top orifice piece from tube: screw out with pliers.

Now, to burn gunk out of tube, with pliers center tube over a stove burner or set into campfire coals. Remove it as soon as yellow flames stop shooting out its ends (in ± 2 min).

After it cools, re-assemble all parts, being very careful to center cleaning wire when re-inserting it into tube center, so it doesn't hook on to the capillary spring inside.

Light up and see the difference. Bridgey, UT, May 02

Candles versus LED lights with batteries recharged by sun.

At first I used candles at night. But I found problems: fire hazards of open flame and tipping over; uses up oxygen (and emits toxic fumes); often flickers; most candles don't burn right because wicks too thin for wax; heavy to carry along; costs $5 to $6 PER MONTH - thats $60 to $72 per year.

So 3 years ago I changed to LEDs, fed by NiMh AA's ($8 for four 1600-mah at Walmart), recharged by a small 5-watt 12-volt photovoltaic (PV) panel ($20 used). The AAs also power a tape player and cell phone. I use a yellow LED most: for reading and writing; most chores; bicycle front light. I use a white LED for area lighting and some chores.

Total weight less than a few candles. Total investment $78, and no more costs until my NiMhs need replacing in a few years. (NiCds I tried got bad 'memory' in 6-18 months.) Zalia

(Comments: $60+ a year for candles ? Wow ! Do you stay up late most nights ? Back when we used only candles (and wax lamps) we may have burned them 2 hours average per winter night for 5 months a year. (Very seldom during summer: we usually go to sleep when dark.) Buying at yard sales and thrift stores, as I recall we spent only a few dollars a year average. We bought paraffin (home-jam-canners use) as well as candles. Most candles were remains of decorative craft gifts. They did not burn well: wax broad, so flame melts a crater and then flickers - and illuminates only ceiling. But wax usable in lamps (see Sep84p.4, Oct93p.1, Sep04p.1 DPs). Recently, by luck, Holly found a few pounds of warped or broken candles in a thrift-store dumpster. She also bought 2 pound-packs at Dollar Tree: each $1 for ten candles 6x$\frac{3}{4}$".

Flames seem to flicker mostly if deep in narrow jars or craters. Our shallow wax-lamps (1$\frac{1}{2}$x$\frac{1}{2}$") seldom flicker.

For the past 7 years we've also used LEDs and rechargable batteries: a winter-base-camp system with PV, and two flashlights (one home-made from $3 LED). Many problems (see May97 p.4&5; Dec97p.8&9; May98p.11&12; Oct98p.3; Nov99p.8; Mar02p.11 DPs). Connections corrode; need cleaning often. Much testing.

There are many alternative ways to move things.
Once, while working on a tug boat, the marine engineer asked me to help carry a heavy, greasy, irregularly-shaped chunk of machinery. I assumed we would both just grab hold and struggle away. But the engineer, being of Philippino descent, knew a better way. Wisely, he found a 2-by-4 and lashed its middle to the machinery. Then we each took hold of an end of the 2-by-4. That made our task much easier, and kept us clean.
Different cultures have different ways. Some people often carry objects on their heads. Some drag them. Some use stretchers. All those ways work. There are backpacks, and big messenger bags. There are one-wheel wheelbarrows often used in rural environments, and two-wheel hand carts commonly used for deliveries and salvaging in cities.
Some of the old photographs of Chinese laborers building railroads in the West, illustrate ingenious ways of moving stuff around. Noticing how different cultures do things, can help us develop more techniques; enabling us to better solve a wider variety of problems. Drew Luna Feuer, NY 120, July 03

Auto seat belts make excellent pack-frame straps.
They are easy to scrounge (eg, at auto salvage yards ?).
I put them on several frames I made from hardwood slats bolted together, like shown in Jaeger's book, Wildwood Wisdom (reviewed in May93 DP p.7). For packing heavy, hard, irregularly shaped objects, they are easier to use than are many aluminum pack frames. Al Fry, Idaho 836, 2001 ?

Simple water pre-filter easy to make.
Loosely drape 9 layers of white cotton flannel (or, in an emergency, T-shirts) over a pail. Tie cord or elastic strap tightly around the rim of pail to hold cloth in place. Pour water into the cloth. Let it drip through. This removes particles larger than 5 microns (1/200 millimeter) in diameter. Once a week, wash the cloth with soap. Rinse well. Zalia, Feb 03

water — strap — cloth — filtered water — pail

(Comments:) This is for removing sediments from water prior to sterilizing with iodine or chlorine. If not removed, the iodine may mostly react with the sediments instead of killing any microbes. I don't believe this will reliably remove microbes; certainly not viruses (see May 03 DP p.2).
Some sediments will settle out of water in a day or so. Others (especially organic sediments) will not settle.
If boiling water, first removing sediments is not necessary for sterilization, but may improve taste or reduce the amount of chemical contaminants.
Zalia designed several variants. The above is the simplest to build; but not the easiest to use if filtering much water (because the cloth must be removed to extract the filtered water). Other variants: a pail with a faucet near its bottom; a short length of big-diameter pipe with a catch basin under it. Holly & Bert, OR 973, February 04

Some local thrift stores have an end-of-month sale.
Clothes are only $1. I stock up then. Zalia, OR 972

A kerchief is a very versatile garment.
Uses include: water filter for removing mud and insects; nose/mouth air filter; washcloth; towel; carrying bag; dew collector (drape over bush at night); neckerchief; hat for shade; woman's bathing-suit top (need two); bandage; splint holder. Can you think of 5 more uses ? (Sent by John Atkins)

(Comment:) A spare T-shirt has the same uses and is better for some (carrying bag, shade hat, towel) as well as providing a change of clothes. But it is slightly bulkier and heavier.

A moving vehicle, plus bucket, can serve as washing machine.
I use this method when on a boat or when traveling in a vehicle. The vibration and rocking provides agitation. All you need is a bucket with a tight-fitting lid, water, soap, and a way to secure the bucket so it doesn't tip over or slide about. I just tie the bucket in place on my truck's bed or boat's deck. In a few hours, the grime will be removed.
However, when on the road, I may splurge on a laudromat if I have many dirty clothes and am spending a few hours in some small town where I can do a load for a dollar.
Soap is usually available in the bathrooms of fast-food restaurants and truck stops. If the dispenser is empty, check cabinets/cupboards. Drew Luna Feuer, NY 120, July 2003

(Comments:) Vehicle-as-agitator was mentioned in an early DP. But NOT mentioned was how to RINSE. In my experience, wringing between rinses is much of the work when hand laundering. In the woods, if doing multiple pail loads, or doing other activities at the same time, I may hang the clothes and let them drip for an hour or so, instead of wringing. In a vehicle, I couldn't do that. Also, if the clothes are rinsed in 3 changes of water, and each rinse goes for a few hours between stops of the vehicle, washing AND RINSING would be practical only on a long trip. So, enroute laundromats are attractive. But on a boat voyage ? Probably plenty of time - and lots of water - and no mid-ocean laundromats !
If using a laundromat, check their trash for discarded detergent containers. We sometimes find cardboard boxes that had gotten damp on the bottom, with much detergent stuck inside. And any liquid detergent bottles that have not already been rinsed, can thereby yield a fair amount. Bert & Holly

What is more economical when driving up a long hill ?
Run the engine fast and use a low gear ? Or lug the engine in high gear ? Many trucks have a vacuum gauge, and it's a rule of thumb that high manifold vacuum, which occurs during high-rpm part-throttle running, means better economy. Low-vacuum readings mean high fuel consumption.
Engines generally consume least fuel at or near their torque peak. For most big V8 truck engines, this is around 2500 rpm. So trying to stay somewhere between 2000 and 3000 rpm is a good target. But both carburetors and fuel injection will richen the mixture at wide-open throttle (WOT) to prevent engine knock and keep temperatures down. So, for most fuel-efficiency on long up-grades, use the highest gear you can pull with the engine around 2500 rpm that doesn't require WOT. (From Popular Mechanics, Apr 2000, sent by Roger Knights)

I have a small pick-up with a camper shell.
St Louis summers are hot and buggy; winters are cold. I am a 44-year-old nurse working in a small urban hospital. I don't want to rely on my grown children. I need $10 worth of your best advice for urban survival. Maureen, MO 631, 2002
Dwelling Portably   April 2004

Wintering in the West on wheels.
     Travel rigs should be small and light to not guzzle gas.
There are hundreds of small Toyota-powered mid-1970s Chinooks
around that are ideal. Few are worn out, because motorhomes
tend to be driven less than are cars and trucks. Police seldom
bother them, unlike the psychedelic-painted vans of the 1960s
and 70s. Toyota makes engines that last and last. Dual wheels
have just been a pain for me. They cut mileage and pick up
more nails. If needed for more weight, a larger tire is better.
     Baja Mexico has much shoreline. While there I get my
teeth fixed for cheap. As in most places, there are good and
not so good dentists. One higher-dollar dentist in Tijuana
attracts clients from all over the world.
     Hot springs on both sides of the Salton Sea are fun but
overcrowded. I put a little iodine in them to make sure I do
not pick up any bad bugs. East of Camp Verde AZ is an old
wintering spot the Mob used back in the 1930s. It is on the
E. Verde River, next to a hydroelectric station, and has a
small hot springs in a cement tub. While you soak, you can
look at the big carp floating around in the river. The Mob had
another spot in the mountains south of Elsinore CA, but this
hot springs has been commercialized, and that area has few
squat spots. The San Francisco hot springs are at the eastern
edge of NM below Megollon. The big pool is only luke warm, but
there are smaller pools near by that are hotter. While you
soak, you can sometimes see mountain sheep cavorting on the
ridge. I met a nomad hanging out there who financed his travel
by filling his big trailer with drink cans found along the way.
     Magollon was a mining district. I always carry a metal
detector and gold pan in such areas. Rock shops have good
books on sniping, and metal detectors. I once washed up an old
safe. A friend comes up with nuggets quite often in certain
areas. Another seems to find stashed hoards and rich gold
deposits by dowsing. Of course, much more money has been spent
on speculation than has been produced by mining. And each
issue of Calif Mining Journal tells of Forest Service assaults
on small-time miners.
     One character I knew, made good money in a rocky canyon
area collecting pretty fireplace rock he sold to builders.
(Most cities now have landscaping-rock outfits that are doing
great.) A few weeks ago, a girl friend and I were snooping
around an abandoned mine and came up with iron pyrite and gold
ore that would be gorgeous fireplace rock. Later we found
many pounds of ore that was almost solid silver crystals.
Silver City ID had rich ore like this, and when I was a kid,
some pure silver chunks were still lying around old cabins.
     If traveling north from San Diego, I stop over at Harmony
Grove, 5 miles west of Escondido. This is a high-energy
vortex spot that makes the hair on my arms stand up. It is a
mecca for psychics. There were ancient writings here from some
advanced culture of the past, but the huge rocks got stolen in
the 1990s. Half way up Rawson Road in Morongo Valley, there's
a different kind of vortex. It is an interdimensional portal
and at certain times some bizarre things happen in the area.
The whole badlands area north of Indio has little valleys with
smaller other-dimensionals running around.
     Further north, the military bases have "whackenhut" guards
that are nasty to curious people. One guy told me he got in an
old tunnel and ran across a newer tunnel that carried high-
speed underground trains hauling goods between bases.
     Each year I see more locked gates and "keep out" signs all
over the West. If worse comes to worse, I sometimes just

explain to a property owner that I would like to squat a while (cleanly). I am seldom refused. Parking in front of a house is safer than on the outskirts of towns that are patrolled by police. Al Fry, Idaho 836, January 2004

How to squat in an empty house.
Who owns empty houses ? Many government departments do; mis-management and bureaucratic delays can cause houses to remain unoccupied many years. Private developers leave houses empty so they can make a fast buck, or to keep rents high by limiting available housing. Wealthy individuals own houses they may use only occasionally. Deceased estates without living relatives, are administered by the Public Trustees office, which may take many years to settle their fate.
Finding empty houses is generally quite easy: an unkempt look; mail oozing out of mailbox; overgrown garden; power off (check the electric meter); broken windows and doors.
You should always knock on the door before entering or prowling around the house. Sometimes old people are living in their home without maintaining it well. Then take a closer look. Is there thick dust inside ? No obvious signs of occupation ? Are any floorboards missing ? Are the electric and gas meters still there ? How many rooms ? How is the overall structure ? You need to know what to bring to fix it.
Try to find out who owns the property, so you will know who to negotiate with if necessary. In Netherlands at least, only the owner or agent of owner (who can be but is not necessarily the police) can legally evict you or ask you to leave; not the neighbors, nor the police without direction from the owner. The neighbors may know who owns the house. Quite often your first contact will be with the neighbors, who you will eventually have to contend with anyway; best present yourself as honestly and openly as possible. The land-titles office is another way. Their system may seem mind-boggling, but it provides info on recent transactions and proposed developments. The staff are quite helpful and you can't be denied info though you may have to pay for some.
The best time to check out houses is during daylight on a weekday; less conspicuous, and you can see more. Best to first just look; don't bring tools such as crowbars that police could use as an excuse to arrest you for breaking and entering. Getting in is generally quite easy: often through broken doors or windows previously forced by other visitors. Vandalism often indicates vacant houses; the local kids may use the place. As well as making it quite easy to just walk right in, that can be a good argument to use with the owner for letting you live in the house rather than leaving it empty. As long as you don't damage the property, you are not illegal. If you do break something accidentally, then leave immediately and return after a lapse of several days.
A few hours to a few weeks may pass before the owners realize that someone is occupying the house. Use this time to make the house livable. Try to keep the house occupied constantly at first, or until you can come to some agreement with the owner. If after a few weeks you have heard nothing from the owner, you can start to get more comfortable; it is harder to evict well-established households than people who appear to be just using the place to crash in.
First thing to do is change the locks and secure the house. Most barrel locks are easily replaced by using a few tools (screwdriver, hacksaw, pliers). Deadlocks may have to sawn off and replaced totally; these cost more but are more

secure. Door and windows that can't be immediately repaired, can have wood or chipboard nailed on them for security.

If the water is off at the taps, find the main and turn it back on, after checking the pipes. If the water was turned off because water rates were not payed, go to the water authority and pay off some. If plumbing isn't intact, hoses and clamps can be used for at least temporary plumbing.

Get electricity and gas on as quickly as possible. If the wiring is okay, you have a legal right to have electricity connected, but may have to pay a security deposit. You may be asked to show proof that you are leasing; just say you are living there and have a right to services. It may not be a good idea to tell them you are squatting. If electric wiring or gas pipes are damaged or broken, get someone who knows what they are doing to fix them !

As a squatter, you have almost no rights. But if you are threatened with eviction, there are things you can do to postpone eviction or even negotiate a settlement that allows you to stay. Try to talk to the evictors; evictions have been stopped at the last moment. Quite often you will be told lies, or at least bent truths, as to the history and future plans for the house (demolition, renovation, etc) in an effort to get you to leave. If you are asked by the owner or owner's agent to leave and you don't, you can be arrested for trespass.

Ways to resist eviction: Get friends and other squatters to come around when eviction is due; people showing support can stall eviction. Leaflet or door-knock surrounding houses; try to get some local community support. Talk to the media, though be careful as the media may not portray you and the issue favorably; alternative media, local papers, noticeboards, etc, best. Visiting and perhaps protesting outside the offices of owners can sometimes cause them to back down.
(From http://squat.net/archiv/squatbookl/index.html , sent by Bruce

(Comment:) When cleaning up dust, be careful to not breathe any. Eg, wear dust mask. Dust that includes rodent or bird feces may carry serious diseases. (See Jan 91 DP, p.12)

Living on a floating island in New York City.

For the past 25 years, Mario has lived in Mill Basin, a backwater of Jamaica Bay. At first he stayed on a friend's house barge, then on an old house boat by himself, and now on a 2000-sq-ft floating island made of old docks roped together; presently moored 60' behind Macy's in Kings Plaza.

Mario sleeps in a 200-sq-ft wooden hut with a woodstove and copper cookware, and two storm windows. He gathers firewood from the shoreline. "If it's free, it's for me." Elsewhere on his island are tomato and pepper plants growing in pails, a tiki bar, and a tanning area for when women friends visit. Kelly, 30, says Mario's island is a "riot". "I get seasick so I can't go out on deep water. But there, the water's calm."

Mario has many friends in the area, some of whom live on boats in the marina. Many never leave the basin. Ray, 45, a retired fireman, says, "It's so relaxing being on the water." About Mario's island: "You should see this place in summer. It booms. Guys bring their boats, blast their radios." Another friend says, "There's something about him. People just go to him. You go down, you bullshit about your life. He tells you what's going on. He don't look like much but he's a very smart man." Ray explained why Mario gets to live on his own island. No one else does. "No one else tries. At first, King Plaza tried to throw him out. They couldn't do it.

Dwelling Portably   April 2004

Everybody came: police, harbor patrol, coast guard. Everybody likes Mario. We are trying to get him a mooring permit."

Of Cuban ancestry, Mario was born and raised in Florida. He left home at 14 and landed in the Bronx. For a while he had an incense shop in NYC but "lost the place". Then he cooked "at a restaurant in Flatbush." Then he worked for a friend lobster fishing, but only for a few years because it is "too rough and not enough - no way to make a living." Now he fishes some. Using for bait little black crabs he finds under rocks on shore, he goes out in his small outboard boat an hour before high tide, and drops a line in the basin "near the wooden poles where the black fish feed on the barnacles." He sells some to a Chinese fish store. He keeps a bicycle on shore. Toni Schlesinger (Village Voice 12Dec00, sent by Drew)

Lone woman is only resident of forgotten Maine town.

Hibberts Gore is home to Karen Keller, 50, who lives on 640 acres overlooked by surveyors and mapmakers and unclaimed by any county, deep in the remote reaches of Maine's vast wilderness. She was not discovered by officials until she filled out a census form. "I love it here. The first time I laid eyes on this place, I knew, this is for me." When she first moved there 15 years ago, Keller was married. But the couple split and she decided to stay.

She lives in a cedar-shingled A-frame house, hunts deer with a bolt-action rifle, grows vegetables and fruit, hauls water from a well, chops firewood, and cooks her meals on a wood-burning stove. She is coping with her manic and depressive episodes - without the help of drugs or the stress of main stream life. When she's feeling upbeat, she roams the fields, climbs bridges, cleans, plays with her cat and dog, and walks, walks, walks. "It's like tripping naturally on speed." When she's down, she toughs it out by making herself get out of bed and do one chore. (from Examiner 17July01, from Roger Knights)

Backyard sheds now popular as offices and bedrooms.

Backyard sheds traditionally house lawn mowers and trash cans. But in the insane CA real-estate market, where many families can't afford bigger homes, gussied-up sheds are housing people. At The Shed Shop in Fremont, sales of "room-addition alternatives" have tripled in the last 5 years. Instead of spending big bucks for a traditional addition, and living with sawdust for months, homeowners hire the firm, or rivals like Tuff Shed, to build customized wooden-shingled backyard structures. Sizes range from 4-by-8 to 12-by-16 feet; average price $3100. Construction takes only a day or two. Customers then add insulation, dry wall, carpeting, electricity - or hire contractors to. Most building codes ban plumbing.

Most customers use the sheds for home offices, art studios or hobby areas. But some space-starved families use them as spare bedrooms or guest rooms - even though most building codes prohibit sleeping in them. Daniel McGinn (Newsweek, 29Sept03)

Philosopher has camp site that is both sylvan and urban.

For the past 17 years, Donald Kearney, 61, has lived rustically in the middle of Boston. He lives in a self-made tent in the woods near Jamaica Pond, less than a mile from the middle-class Brookline home where he grew up. Though he has enough money, he has little desire for more than a plastic tarp for a room, several heavy blankets, and the 11 newspapers he reads every day and then uses to insulate his tent.

Like Henry David Thoreau whom he has long admired, Kearney

loathes government and social conventions such as paying rent
and concealing opinions. "Living outside with nature means
living in the most intimate way." Raised by a Jewish mother,
and an Irish father who played horn in the Boston Symphony,
Kearney calls himself a Lepre-Cohen. "It is peaceful, no one
bothers me, and there's no better place to read than under
natural light." One of the hard-core homeless who refuse to
sleep in city shelters, Kearney and about 300 men and a few
women live outdoors year around, surviving the coldest nights.
   Though Kearney's home is concealed by a thicket of oaks
and pines and hemlocks, the property owner knows he is there.
But "as long as he takes care of the environment and himself,
we let him live his way." Kearney does not reveal his exact
location in the large stretch of woods; he doesn't want more
visitors. A few times, thieves have stolen his blankets.
   Though Kearney spends much time alone in the woods, he
goes downtown nearly every day, dining in soup kitchens,
speaking out at rallies and lectures on college campuses,
attending classical concerts, and collecting newspapers. He
also visits friends: other homeless people he buys food for and
talks politics with. Occasionally he ventures to Watertown
to see his sister, who hosts him for holidays such as Passover
and receives his subscriptions to several Conservative
magazines including National Review and Weekly Standard. Social
workers who know Kearney say, that unlike most soup-kitchen
patrons, he helps wash dishes and mop the floor after meals.
   His sister, an Ivy-League-educated accountant with her own
business, isn't sure how her brother ended up so differently.
He doesn't do drugs or drink, she says, and with a trust fund
left by a wealthy aunt, "he can certainly afford an apartment.
I just think he genuinely likes living in the woods."
   Kearney began sleeping outdoors when he was young and went
to camp in Maine where, as a gifted clarinetist, he won awards
for his chamber music. Over the years he sought more isolation,
living for months at a time in NH's White Mtns and ME woods.
David Abel (from Boston Globe, 3Dec02, sent by L.Smith)

(Comments:) Note the author's derogatory labeling of Kearney
as "homeless", though, inconsistently, elsewhere refers to
"his home". Ie, if you have a home that officials and the lap-
dog media don't approve of, you are "homeless". (Next, will
people who live in unapproved ways, be called "lifeless" ?)

Make sure any lamp wick is ALL natural fiber.
   Burn a bit at one end. If only fine ash remains, it is
probably natural. If a hard lump remains, it is partly or
entirely synthetic. Much string that looks like cotton, is
actually part polyester for strength.
   Recently I prepared a replacement wick for a wax lamp
(see Sept 04 DP p.2) from string (that had sewen shut a grain
bag) that LOOKED like cotton (fuzzy). But, in the lamp, it
burned and melted away in less than a minute. Holly, Febr 04

A tiny fan will greatly increase a wood-stove's efficiency.
   Or, if electricity is not available, sheet-metal baffles
around a longer chimney. Air-tight stoves are the only kind
to buy. If you make a stove, allow a foot of space above the
door for smoke collection. Al Fry, Idaho, 2001 ?

Wet boots can be dried by filling them with warm sand.
   Usually they will dry overnight. Al Fry
Dwelling Portably   April 2004

Tick-borne diseases: a pound of prevention - or a TON of cure.
Compared to other arthropods (including insects), ticks
are more often infected and more likely to transmit an infection. And some tick-borne diseases, especially Lyme, can be
very difficult to diagnose and cure. I read several books
from a library. By far the best was "Everything You Need To
Know About Lyme Disease and Other Tick-borne Disorders" by
Karen Vanderhoof-Forschner (Wiley, 1997, 249p.6x9, $15 cover
price). But the title exaggerates: much is NOT known.
Karen learned about Lyme the hard way. Infected by a tick
while pregnant, the disease spread to her fetus (though MDs
assured her that did not happen with Lyme). After various
mis-diagnoses and inadequate treatments, Karen finally got
effective treatment and slowly recovered - but her son died.
Consequently she founded the Lyme Disease Foundation to pool
the considerable but scattered knowledge.
"Ticks transmit more kinds of micro-organisms than any
other arthropod, including mosquitos", perhaps because of their
mode of feeding and relatively long lives. Almost everyone in
the U.S. is at risk, including a city dweller who uses parks.
Lyme has been vastly under-reported for various reasons,
and some other tick-borne diseases even more so. Karen
estimates that over a million U.S. residents are infected. In
CT, one person out of 29; in RI, one in 42; NY 59; NJ 93; DE
107; WI 124; PA 159; MD 267; MN 309; MA 330. However, infection rate varies from area to area within a state: in the worst
areas, a third of the population may be infected; and some
states not listed may have places with much Lyme. Though south
eastern and south central states do not have much Lyme, other
serious tick-borne diseases are common. Ticks are much more
common in eastern than in western North America; the reason
may be that ticks need a moist environment year around.
"Owning a pet, especially a cat, puts you at increased
risk." Though dogs seem to get more ticks, a cat may be more
likely to bring a tick to a human, because cats groom themselves more/better than do dogs. Eg, a cat picks up a tick
outside, comes in, grooms itself, and removes the tick before
it gets firmly attached - which then gets onto a human. Whereas, a tick that gets onto a dog is likely to remain on the dog
until fully fed. However, for that reason, a dog may be worse
than a cat for increasing the tick population. (My conjectures)
Not mentioned by books: if you have an animal, either keep it
in or leave it out. Don't let it in and out.
Ticks "tend to live in close proximity to potential hosts.
This frequently places them in the dense overgrown area between
a manicured lawn and a forest." A tick doesn't move more than
ten feet under its own power, but may be transported long
distances by animals, especially birds. A tick rarely climbs
higher than 3 feet above ground, and cannot jump or fly.
Ticks typically seek prey by climbing upwards on vegetation, waiting until a prey brushes past, and then grasping it
with one set of legs. However, larvae may actively seek prey
instead of waiting. Most ticks prefer non-human animals: esp
deer, mice, chipmonks, rabbits, dogs, birds; but will feed on
whatever animals are available.
For protection, all advice I've read seems inadequate.
Most authors say: wear shoes (not sandals), socks, long-sleeve

pants and shirt; light colored. Tuck pants into socks and shirt into pants. That way, a tick that gets on your foot must crawl up the outside of clothing to reach bare skin. But how likely are you to spot a tick on clothing which probably also has on it stickers and bits of debris ? If you don't spot the tick until it reaches your neck, it will likely get into your hair where it will be more difficult to see and to remove. Also, long clothes not comfortable/healthy on hot days.

In CT, the state with the most Lyme, almost no nudists get tick-borne diseases. From that, a researcher concluded that ticks don't bite fully-exposed skin. Unfortunately, not true. "Most likely, the nudists simply had more opportunities to examine their own bodies and the bodies of companions, making them more likely to spot and remove crawling ticks."

In our (H&B's) experience, ticks bite bare skin much less often than covered skin. During tick season we usually have bare legs. If ticks seldom climb higher than 3 feet, they most often grasp legs. But we've had few bites on legs. Most were on bodies; some on arms. In many instances we were bitten after coming inside, often at night. I suspect the ticks rode in on our clothes, then crawled around until they found skin covered by clothes or bedding. So perhaps the most important precaution (which none of the authors suggested): Remove outside clothes before coming inside. Leave outside clothes outside. Carefully inspect before coming inside. While inside, wear only clothes that never go outside.

"One of the most effective pesticides is permethrin, which is a synthetic imitation of natural substances called pyrethrum found in chrysanthemums and other flowers." Sold in most garden shops. Soldiers apply it to their uniforms and find that it lasts through several launderings. Permethrin kills, within minutes, ticks and most other arthropods that contact treated fabric. It has little toxicity to mammals, because it is little absorbed and rapidly inactivated. Occasionally people report local irritation. Although registered as a possible carcinogen, it is believed not toxic after it dries. Do not apply to clothes while wearing them, and do not touch the clothes until dry. "A good idea is to treat one special outfit and then wear that whenever you go outside." However, permethrin is not a repellant, which means that a tick that grasps bare skin and doesn't then wander onto fabric, could bite.

(Is permethrin really better than the natural substance ? Or is this another case of a corporation slightly altering a substance so they can patent it and charge more ?)

To remove a tick, Karen says, "it is almost always better to wait until you can secure the right (fine-pointed) tweezers, especially if it is only a matter of a few hours." But elsewhere: ticks who "are systemically infected" in salvary glands as well as mid-gut, "may be able to transmit the pathogen in only a few hours." (Ticks with only a mid-gut infection, may need 24 to 48 hours.) So, I might wait a few MINUTES, but NOT HOURS ! If lacking fine-pointed tweezers, I can usually improvise an adequate substitute in a few minutes. Most tweezers have points that are too broad, and would squeeze the tick's body, spreading its fluids. Do not use; or sharpen.

Grasp tick as close to skin as possible. Gently pull straight back, away from skin. Do not twist tick.

If mouth parts remain in the bite, should they be left ? Or removed, which may require digging with a needle ? Authorities disagree. After removing tick, apply antiseptic to bite and tweezers, and wash hands thoroughly. "Alcohol or Betadine" suggested by one book. [Other possibilities (I don't

know relative effectiveness): soap and water; iodine water
solution or tincture (which you might have for sterilizing
water); eucalyptus or tea-tree or other very-pungent oil;
hydrogen peroxide; chlorine bleach, maybe diluted (not good
for you, but tick diseases much worse); conifer resin; tart
(acidic) berry juice; urine; booze (ethyl alcohol is much
less toxic to humans than is isopropyl "rubbing" alcohol).]
    Place tick in closable container. If you will send it
to a lab for analysis (cost $25 to $60) "you must keep the
tick alive." A few grass blades or moistened tissue in the
container will suffice for a few days. Make sure the lab will
test tick for all pathogens known to be in area where bitten.
    If a tick remained attached more than two hours, or if
attachment time not known, some of the MDs who are knowledgable about Lyme (most MDs aren't), recommend taking oral antibiotics immediately, without waiting for symptoms. "On the
one hand, you may be taking $20 worth of medication unnecess-
arily (and possibly getting bad side effects). On the other
hand, you may be avoiding a nightmarish scenario that involves
$30,000 worth of intravenous medicine... Given the early
dissemination of the Lyme bacterium throughout the body and
into the brain, I think that waiting for a telltale rash is"
foolish. 67% of Lyme patients with an early rash, already had
the infectious spirochete in their spinal fluid.
    Four weeks of doxycycline or minocycline, long-acting
members of the tetracycline family, are commonly recommended.
They are well absorbed on an empty stomach and thus can be
used at a low dosage, and some of those drugs reach the
central nervous system. Also effective against some other
tick-borne diseases including relapsing fever, tularemia,
ehrlichiosis, Rocky Mountain spotted fever. "Not recommended
for pregnant or breast-feeding women, or for children under 8."
Possible side effects: yeast infection, nausea, blurring of
eyes, dizzyness, liver and kidney disorders, intracranial
pressure (simulates brain tumor). Avoid dairy products, iron
supplements, antacids; they interfere with absorption.
    If we (H&B) lived in an area with much Lyme or other
bacterial diseases, I would want antibiotics ON HAND, so I did
not have to wait until I could get to a doctor and drug store.
Also, an ignorant or timid MD might insist on time-consuming,
expensive tests before prescribing. A friend who knows an MD
could probably procure antibiotics easier than I could. Or,
in Mexico, antibiotics can be purchased without a prescription.
Animal-feed-store antibiotics, such as fish-cycline, are a
possibility, but might not be absorbed as well or reach as
many organs. Anti-biotics are perishable; store in the coldest place available. They don't help viral diseases; eg, flu.
    As with other spirochetal infections such as syphilis and
relapsing fever, the first symptom is often a local skin rash,
but it is not always present, or can be overlooked, esp on
dark-complexioned people. Don't confuse a rash with the
inflammation at the bite that usually develops within a few
hours but starts to disappear within 24 hours. The rash does
not develop so soon, and it lasts longer. "Early dissemination is characterized by flu-like symptoms such as headache,
stiff neck, mild fever or chills, swollen glands, muscle ache,
and fatigue. Often the symptoms are not unduly alarming, and
many people do not seek medical attention." The early symptoms may go away on their own. "But if the underlying infection has not been treated appropriately, the disease can
progress, sometimes within a month, sometimes not for a year
or longer, to late-stage dissemination, when damage to multiple

body systems can occur (and) the disease is securely lodged in the body, difficult to diagnose and much harder to treat."

How sick and what symptoms, depends partly on what strains or microbes. On Shelter Island NY, "60% of black-legged ticks studied were infected with more than one strain of Borrelia burgdorferi (Bb)", the Lyme microbe. In CT, 20% of patients with Lyme also had at least one other tick-borne disease.

"There are many strains of Bb, and a drug effective with one may not work on another" (esp if not treated early).

Though ticks are the main carriers of Bb, it can also pass via placenta (pregnancy), raw milk, sex (at least among mice), blood transfusion, and getting urine of an infected animal on cuts, eyes, mucus membranes. Biting flies and fleas suspect. Mosquitos can become infected but because Bb can live only a few hours in a mosquito, transmission is unlikely.

As of 1997 there was no reliable test for Lyme. In its absence, most U.S. MDs won't prescribe the powerful drugs needed to cure Lyme after it disseminates. In 1992, the average cost of treating Lyme disease was $62,000 per person, and half the costs were incurred BEFORE diagnosis !

Ticks spread at least 8 other serious diseases in U.S.:

Rocky Mountain spotted fever (RMSF), a rickettsia. Despite name, 60% of cases in east. Tick can transmit within a few hrs. Onset sudden: high fever, rash resembles measles, 3-8% fatal. Tetracycline or doxycycline or chloramphenicol.

Ehrlichiosis, a rickettsia. Mostly in se and s central. Symptoms, none to severe; resemble RMSF; 5% fatal. Quite a few kinds of ticks transmit. Tetracycline or doxycycline.

Babesia microti, a protozoa. Mostly coastal and n midw. Like malaria; some strains deadly. Clindamycin & oral quinine.

Tularemia, a bacterium. Mostly s central and sw to CA. Many kinds of ticks cause half the cases. Also biting flies, drinking contaminated water, touching infected animals or eating their under-cooked meat. In over 100 mammals; some birds, amphibians, fishes. Painfully swollen lymph glands. Streptomycin or gentamycin or tetracycline or chloramphenicol.

Relapsing fever, a spirochet related to Bb. Mainly w and sw. Spread by soft ticks often in old cabins, mines, caves. Can transmit within 15 minutes. Tetracycline or doxycycline.

Powassan encephalitis, a flavivirus. Mostly e N. Amer. Also spread by raw milk of infected goat. No antibiotic for it.

Some of these diseases are carried by the same ticks that carry Lyme; therefore a single bite can transmit more than one. Except soft ticks, all adult females in U.S. have a circular black or dark shield on the front portion of their back, with the rest of back red-brown or brown. Ticks other than Ixodes also have various white markings on their backs. Ixodes don't. Adult males have all-dark backs. Unlike mosquitos, males bite. But the adult female is most apt to spread disease because it must feed before it can lay eggs, and it feeds longer.

The black-legged tick, Ixodes scapularis, in e and midw N.Am can transmit Lyme, babesioses, granulocytic ehrlichiosis, Powassan encephalitis. The western black-legged tick, Ixodes pacificus, looks identical and transmits same diseases, but only 1% of them carry Lyme, vs 30% of their eastern relatives.

The lone-star tick, Amblyomma americanum, in se as far n and w as RI, IA, TX, is a major carrier of tularemia and monocytic ehrlichiosis and maybe other diseases. White spot on back of adults. "Aggressive and seeks out humans to bite."

Several Dermacentor species (dog ticks), the most common ticks in N.Am., spread RMSF, monocytic ehrlichiosis, tularemia and probably others. Chalk-like markings on adults' backs.

Dwelling Portably   April 2004

Dwelling Portably

or Shared, Mobile, Improvised
Underground, Hidden, Floating

Sept 2004 $1 per issue   POB 190-d, Philomath OR 97370

Portable dwelling myths and realities.

Many people believe that living without a house (or a big
RV) must be arduous and uncomfortable. That attitude is
fostered by some wilderness-experience providers who dare you
to take their training to prove how tough you can become.

Camping doesn't require exceptional fortitude or strength.
Before Europeans came, millions of Amerinds camped full time.
(Only a few tribes built permanent lodges.) They included small
children, pregnant women, elders, injured. (Tips for learning
how to camp comfortably are on page 3.) Holly & Bert, Jan 04

I want a tent that is warm in winter and easy to set up.

In a few hours at most. Thanks for your reply (in May 03
DP p.16), but I don't have time to try to build something.

What is the best 4-season tent I can buy? Or what features
should I look for ? I'd like enough daylight inside to read and
write. (I go to classes 3 days a week, and work freelance many
nights and weekends, so I prefer to stay in camp on free days.)
High enough to hang clothes, and sit comfortably in a chair.

I can't afford to rent solo, and I don't like sharing a
space. (My work provides more than enough relating to people.)

Also, I need a good rechargable flashlight for following
trails and at camp. (My present flashlight is bright enough,
and I can set it down and then point beam where I want it, but
its battery is costly and doesn't last long. Eve, CA 950, Aug

(Reply:) I don't know of any tent for sale that meets your
requirements. (If any reader does, please write.) "4-season"
means: you can stay ALIVE winters, but during extremely cold
weather you may be COMFORTABLE only when in bed.

IF you have or can easily buy replacement poles for your
present dome tent (in case poles don't survive the following),
you might try: Remove its fly (top tarp) if it simply clips
on (if not, leave it on). Spread over the tent a big thick
(insulative) quilt, or maybe two rectangular sleeping bags
opened and zipped together. Above, erect two (for less dew)
tarps, big enough to reach to the ground on 3 sides and
provide some rain-sheltered space in front. Space them one
above the other, not touching each other or the quilt. If the
quilt blocks ventilation, DO NOT USE ANY FLAME INSIDE.

Or, if buying a "4-season" dome tent, look for one with
strong poles (probably more than 2); ie, a tent rated for high
wind or accumulated snow, so the poles will support insulation
layed on top. But I doubt that such a tent will admit much
light. (For features I'd like but haven't found, see p. 7.)

For hanging clothes and keeping most equipment, I'd get a
second tent. Some car-camping tents are tall enough and somewhat portable. Then rig big tarps, overlapping, above both
tents for extra rain shelter and for dry passage between tents.

I've seen ads for rechargable flashlights: some plug into
the grid; some set in sunshine to solar charge; some you
shake for a few seconds every few minutes. I don't know how
good. Also see Dec 03 DP, p.4,5,6. Bert, OR 973, Sept 03

Low/no-cost lamp is easy to make.

Materials: empty tuna or catfood
can; cotton cord or other NATURAL
fiber (synthetic burns stinky); thin
stiff wire with insulation removed;
candle-remains; extra empty can.

Braid
wire
around
wick.

Then
shape

like
this.

Assembly. To stiffen the cord, braid two thin wires around it. (Ordinary string will soon put itself out by slumping into the liquid wax puddle that develops.) Then shape wick as shown, so one end sits straight-up, self-supporting inside the tuna can. Top of wick should not stick above top edge of can. Melt wax in other can and pour into tuna can over centered wick. Fill nearly to the brim. Let cool and harden. Your new lamp is now ready for use.

When wax level gets low, causing too much flame, add pieces of wax. When I use at camp, I set lamp on a flat rock, to reduce risk of knocking it over.

Brijji, UT, May02 bridgepeter@yahoo.com

(What Bert did.) Had no tuna can. I used a tiny aluminum pan $1\frac{1}{2}$"D $\frac{1}{2}$" high. (It had been one of a dozen mini-lamps - also called "votive" or "tee" candles. As the wax burned away, I'd added more. But its wick, too, had gradually burned away and in a few hours got too short.)

For a new wick, I used loosely-twisted cotton cord, 1/12 inch diameter.

The first wire I tried, a paper clip, was too thick. After a bit of wick that protruded above the wire burned away, the flame went out. I suppose that wire conducted away too much heat.

The next wire, copper, fine hair size, was too thin. Cord not stiffened enough.

Somewhat thicker copper wire, coarse hair size, did fine. Stiff enough, yet not so thick it snuffed the flame. Steel wire might be better: stiffer per thickness. But none here thin enough.

To wind wire onto an 8-inch length of cord, I tied thin string to ends of cord and suspended it quite taut. I twirled cord between fingers while moving wire along; then reversed to spiral other way. The cord was long enough to make 3 wicks. I dripped melted wax from a candle onto the cord near where I would cut, to make sure wire did not unravel when cut. Also, waxed wicks light easier.

I shaped the stiffened wick as shown, except circled twice to provide spare length. I set it in the tiny pan, put chunks of wax around it, and lit. As the chunks melted, I added more until the pan was nearly full of melted wax. The wick got tilted but still burned okay.

The wick burns away much more slowly than on original mini-lamps - and most candles. Because the wire's conduction cools it some ? When, after a week, it got too short, I raised more, grasping it low (scorched part fragile), using improvised wooden tweezers. (Metal tweezers stuck to wick, because their conduction solidified wax near wick.)

Total work appreciable, but overall easier/better than what we'd done previously: lay wick on sloping side of a clam shell. It needed more frequent adjustments, and often went out or flamed too high. Thanks Brijji !

Julie Summers described a lamp somewhat like Brijji's in Sept84+DP p.4. She threaded hollow woven cord such as some shoelaces onto stiffish wire coiled like Brijji's. She burned tallow and various oils as well as wax. (I don't recall trying. Maybe we had no hollow cord.) More on candles in May97p.6 & Oct93p.1.)

This kind of lamp needs more careful attention than does a candle set in a secure non-flammable holder. It is more dangerous if knocked over because more of the wax is liquid; and, if wax burns low, the entire wick may catch fire.

Mounting solar panel on travel trailer.
To not have the fumes and fire hazard of candles, I built a 12-volt lighting system. A 35-watt PV panel recharges a used auto battery. (More in May 97 DP.)

Instead of drilling potentially-leaky holes in roof, I glued on the mountings with Barge cement and regular clear silicone caulking. Has held for over 4 yrs thru high winds and severe winters.

I first cleaned the roof. After gluing down the mounting, I also put a thick layer of silicone ON TOP OF the mounting foot. I applied silicone to an area 3 times as wide as the mounting foot, so the silicone has more surface to stick to. David French, SD, May 98 (Was only in Net Suplmt then, hoping for more info about the mounting feet.)

(Thought:) Why not just bolt panel onto a wood frame (eg, two 2-by-2s glued to plywood cross pieces) slightly longer than the trailer is wide, drilling bolt holes in the 2-by-2s as needed ? Then, hold the frame on roof with ropes from 2-by-2s down the sides of trailer and tied to frame. Put something soft and not slippery (closed-cell shipping foam) between plywood and roof to cushion.

That seems more reliable. (How long & well will cement adhere to the roofing tar ?) Also, frame with panel is easily removed when traveling, if hurricane, if hail, etc. Also, frame can be tilted so PV intercepts more rays. (Panel flat on roof not good in winter when sun low.) B

Living in vans and travel trailer.
I lived in an outfitted mini-van for over a year. Then the two of us lived in a larger van for 6 months. We had a king-size bed, propane heat, cook stove, and solar electric system.

Though we were comfy, we wanted more space and facilities. So we saved until we had enough money to buy a 1982 Shasta 16-foot travel trailer we tow with our van. It more than meets our needs.

Some folks buy big expensive RVs they must finance - but lose them to the repo man if they are layed off work. That is why we waited and saved, and chose a low cost used trailer we could buy outright.

For money, we prefer to wait until our funds run low; then get a job and save like mad until reserves build up; then camp until our funds get low again.

Places to park. If you are self-contained, construction sites are good; often you can live free with electric and water and sewer hookups provided, in exchange for your presence providing security. Similarly, industrial sites and equipment enclosures. We recently site-sat a truck rental place. No pay, but parked free. Sometimes you find an employer who will not only pay for day work, but let you stay as night watch.

I presently work for a transit system part-time. We sometimes over-night in their lot; also at Walmart and other shopping centers. On weekends we're at campgrnds: drain tanks; charge battery.

Usually we winter as caretakers at a private campground after they close. They pay only $15 per week, but not many chores to do: in autumn we winterize the plumbing; in spring we get everything running again before leaving.

Some summers we camp-host at state parks; usually for 2 or 3 weeks, but a park may want you to commit longer. Some remote parks give small stipends, but usually no pay. However, we get a site, electric hookup, pool use, and other amenities free. All we did was check the rest rooms twice a day, and alert the park staff to any problems. Parks also take seasonal workers and pay quite well. Check with park offices.

We've seen more and more van dwellers here. John & Rose Ward, PA 174, Aug 2003

How we go to and from cities.

Most of our camps, though remote from settlements, are within 60 miles of DP's po box. If friends are camped nearby and happen to be going through there, they may be able to bring our mail to a stash shared. If so, we might stay in the woods many months. Otherwise we go once a month or so, and shop then too.

For travel on highways, we bike, bus, hitch, ride-share; depending on season, weather, road, distance, and what is available. To find ride-sharers, I may hitch back in late afternoon when many commuters go home, and ask ride-givers if they go regularly. If hitching, I always offer a $ or 2 to help pay costs. For ride share I offer more, because driver must commit to time and place.

We bicycle to a ride meet or bus stop, or all the way if city near. We leave bikes stashed near a paved road, and may also have a temp campsite and gear there so we can hike there the day before and rest a night before traveling on.

Bike trips longer than a few miles we do only on early Sunday mornings when traffic is light, during late spring and early summer when dawn comes early.

We bicycle mostly on paved roads. Gravel is riskier, wears tires faster, and not much faster than walking. B & H

Learning to dwell portably with comfort.

Some people try to do too much too quick. Perhaps inspired by a movie or book, they hike many miles into a wilderness with a single backpack load of gear and grub, and then try to live off the land. Most soon hike back out - IF able to. A few, better prepared or unusually talented, survive uncomfortably for a few months or years, but grow dissatisfied and eventually leave, saying: "Been there, done that."

Bert and I learned gradually: first day hikes, then summer weekend backpacks into nearby woods, then summer camping for longer periods. Any time the going got unpleasant, we'd head for other shelter where, after drying off and warming up, we'd ponder what went wrong and how to do better next time.

The biggest problem with our bit-by-bit approach, was finding energy and time while still employed (sporadically; fortunately neither of us worked steady full time) and renting (various cheap rooms and out-buildings with improvised furnishings - probably "substandard",but codes seldom enforced unless complaints).

We had read quite a few books and they helped, but most were broad (to sell widely); not focused on one area.

Neither of us had "outdoor survival" training. Most such courses teach how to stay alive until rescued or until you find your way home - which IS IMPORTANT, but not much help learning to camp as a way of life. If you seek, try to find some that deals with the climate and terrain where you expect to live. Check nearby colleges. Some offer rec courses (no credit) open to outsiders.

Some readers assume that portable (backpacking) dwellers live much as do vacation trekkers: each morn, pack up all gear, carry it in one trip to the next site, and set up camp - day after day. NO - that's not what we do.

Though we sometimes go on long treks, or visit cities where we stay a few days, we live mostly at base camps where we may remain (except for short trips away) a few weeks to a few months.

General advice. At first for backup, remain close to familiar shelter. Go slow, stay observant, be thoughtful. As you see things, ask self: how could that be dangerous - or useful. H & B

Experiences camping in northern BC.

I've been in one place since late Oct. When I moved here, I didn't have enough time to build a proper shelter, so I made a lean-to (resembles a bimini on a boat) out of ten-foot-long pieces of black pond-liner. (Last year, I saw a road-construction forestry crew using it around a culvert. I went back after hours with my freighter pack-frame and EMT shears and some rope, and cut pieces out of scrap left behind.) It feels and looks very tough - hail proof, much stronger than my toughest tarp, which I have to double up to keep me completely dry during the heavy downpours here.

Under the plastic I stretched a piece of barbless fencing I found, from which I hang clothes to dry. The fencing is also handy for keeping bedding and other gnaw-able materials suspended where pesky ground critters can't easily reach them. The plastic and fencing are tied out to live deciduous trees.

Under the lean-to, I made a bough bed 8" thick, beside a big dead-fall log which provides a windbreak. 1000 yards away is a brook running year around.

The terrain here consists of a series of terraces. In the valley's bottom is a river; above that a cliff; then a terrace on which is a public road; then another cliff, and then a 50-yard-wide terrace on which I'm camped. Above me is another cliff and terrace. My camp is near the back of the terrace for less wind and more seclusion from the road.

I've seen deer and rodent tracks in this area, but animals don't bother me. No humans have come near. But I do fear people finding my camp and stealing or vandalizing. I'm too close to the road to have fires or make noise. After the snow melts, I'll move to a higher level for spring and summer. Bruce, Feb 2002

I moved my camp 50 yards to a higher elevation. Took a full day. I'm now even closer to year-around water. May 02

One day around noon, a domestic dog ambled through my camp. In less than 3 minutes it disappeared into nearby woods not to be seen again. No sign of owner. That prompted me to move yet another 100 Sept 2004 yards, going higher, still in same area. Also, during hot weather, the creek I'm near still has small pools whereas the lower part of the same creek goes dry.

I am camped beside a small cliff off which sound bounces, so I don't hammer or make other loud noises on still days.

So far, at my higher site, the only visitors have been chattering squirrels and local birds. Black bears have long been out of hibernation: I've seen their scat and tracks. But they've not bothered what little dry and tinned food I've had at ground level. I NEVER cook or eat meat or fish at my camp. Those odors are quite strong and more attractive to bears than are rice/beans/lentils. Jy 02

I had thought my latest camp was high enough and far enough from the road to be secure from human intruders. Wrong ! In early August, on separate occasions, two mushroom pickers discovered my camp. They had spotted some of my white and colored buckets. I got face-to-face contact with both who were apparently alone. One was Native-American, about 30, quiet but friendly. I felt he wasn't likely to steal my belongings. The other was Caucasian, 30ish, wearing bright white T shirt, blue jeans; short hair. He didn't look like a mushroomer; more like a nosy undercover cop. However, I will stay here the rest of winter.

This summer was nice: humid but with lots of sun. Many berries. Chinook fishing great. But August was tough for me financially so I didn't go moose hunting with my brother. He lost his 20 year job at a local sawmill because of the lousy economy and mismanagement. He is still bitter. No other job skills.

I pick wild mushrooms in the fall. But I haven't made big dollars: prices low past 8 years because of world-wide economic slump; weather too damp or dry and areas over-picked. Now, local native bands want to charge picking fees !

This area has many logging roads. Most go uphill, winding, for miles, but don't connect with other logging roads. Many are blocked to keep out unwanted motorists. I hike along some to check them out, but fear meeting bears. Sept

So far, all my camps have been within 2 or 3 miles of civilization. I use adult-size bicycles with carrying racks for transport. I don't stash bikes at my camps. If I did, I'd probably hang them from tree branches to keep ground critters from nibbling tires or valve stems or seats. Lately, some have been discovered and had tires slashed. So I have many bikes and keep them in various places as backup in event that one gets stolen or vandalized, or breaks down.

I go to town every 2nd day. I salvage from dumpsters, pick up mail, search internet on library's computers, visit thrift/2nd-hand stores and job banks. On weekends I often stay at camp: cook; wash clothes; tidy up; sew broken gear; saw firewood, etc. Keeps me busy.

Mushroom pickers are here again. Many have annoying habits: defecate without burying; litter; vandalize; steal; raid my provisions. I stay away from one of my camps on weekends because the pickers come in groups of 2 or 3 then. I'll be glad when the season ends, and when kids
Sept 2004

go back to school in early Sept. The woods will be quieter then. Bruce, Aug03

(Comments:) In woods here, we've had no unwanted human encounters, and less vandalism and stealing than you report. Because we are usually further from settlements ? Because these woods are more difficult to hike through ? Luck ?

The drawback of living remotely or in difficult terrain: going to a city is quite an expedition. Consequently, we go much less often than you, and don't have time there to access internet, etc.

How we choose and prepare camp sites.

Holly and I have dwelled portably for nearly 25 years. Though sometimes we camp on river floodlands during dry season, undeveloped city parks, railroad right-of-ways, and overgrown vacant lot, 90% of our living has been at long-term sites in forested mountain areas.

We may live at a good base-camp site seasonally for several years; using different sites different seasons. At each site, we may stash some equipment, stored in pails/totes/barrels, rather than move it all. (Duplicates are often cheap at yard sales and thrift stores.)

Except maybe in summer, we prefer sites that are high enough to be above the cold air that collects in valley bottoms during clear still nights, but far enough below ridges to avoid high winds and lightning. (When scouting, we may climb mountains to view surroundings but we don't live on mountain tops.)

For winter, we like a south-facing slope with no trees tall enough to block the low winter sun. During spring, we prefer a spot within easy hike of nettle patches and other edible greens. During summer, we prefer an east-facing slope for morning sun and mid-day shade, that is near many berries, and perhaps within hiking range of a creek with swimming hole and fish, or the ocean. For autumn we might camp on private land posted "no hunting" if working for owner; otherwise dense conifer forest with little browse attractive to deer and elk. (We prefer autumns for temp jobs. Less competition because pro harvesters are busy with commercial crops, and most kids are back in school; and cooler but mostly dry.)

Our typical base camp is 10 to 60 miles from the nearest city; at least a mile from any settlement; at least 1/4 mile from any paved or graveled road; at least 100 yards from any much-used game trail (or we may reroute a trail).

For winter and spring use, for max sun (when it shines), we may choose an area that was clear-cut a few years ago, and now has bushes and small trees big enough to discourage hunters (can't see deer before deer smell or hear them), and brambly enough to keep other hikers on trails; but without growth tall enough to shade our site.

I may scout and start preparing such a site soon after logging, but not move there for several years. For least digging, I look for a natural hole (formed centuries ago when a big tree fell, uprooting, then rotted. I remove remaining slash (else it will entangle as vines grow and be more difficult.) I might lay long branches across the hole interweaved, for vines to grow upon and form a natural over-roof. But I leave clear exposure to a sun-facing window.

I decide where I want trails, clear slash (left from logging) off them, and distribute slash on unwanted paths.

Other possible winter sites: places where poor or shallow soils stunt trees; steep slopes recently thinned that might have spots still sunny because, by luck, no tall trees close down slope. CAUTION: very steep slopes are prone to landslide ± ten years after logging, when old roots rotted and new roots not yet deep.

Most winter/spring sites need shaping. I prefer to do that in the early spring prior to the winter we will move in; the soil is softer (damp), and spring growth of vines will help cover dirt piles.

We stop using a winter site when the trees grow tall enough to block the sun.

Time scouting and preparing a good winter/spring base camp might total 100 hours or more, but is spread over many weeks and is thus quite congenial.

Moving a base camp requires much more than one back load. Assume we move in summer to an area we've not lived before and do not have supplies stashed. In the first load we might carry: tarps, insect net, sleeping bags, pad, canteen, knife, small saw, trowel, and ready-to-eat food for a few days, packed in wide-mouth plastic jars which, when empty, can hold water. We prepare a temp site, choosing a levelish spot we can clear and smooth quickly. (Seclusion not very important if we won't be there long.) From there we scout for water and a better site.

In the next load, we typically bring cooking utensils and more food, and bow saw and shovel to prep the better site.

If we move during winter, we go to a site previously prepared at which we have supplies stashed. B & H, Jan 04

More about hidden underground home.

Doug Underwood (one of his chosen names) says he has been a nature lover since he was a boy in Binghamton NY. Born about 1960, one of 7 children of a judge, Doug often sought solitude on the banks of the Susquehanna River. "I had imaginary friends - Indian spirit guides who would show me secret places where I could escape adults' peering eyes."

When Doug was 20, his father died. Doug dropped out of college and became a carpenter. In the 1980s he moved to Nantucket, a 57 sq mile island about 20 miles off the southeast coast of Cape Cod MA, where his family had often visited during Doug's childhood. Many wealthy people vacation on Nantucket, causing it to have some of the most expensive real estate in the northeast. During summers, landlords "charge $300 a week for a room in a basement." Working as freelance carpenter and painter off and on, Doug became a familiar sight to permanent residents as he bicycled around the island wearing a small knapsack, to jobs and shops, and sometimes pausing at the tavern for a beer.

Doug made a small underground abode, then, after hard thinking, decided to build a larger home. After much scouting he chose a spot with sandy soil on land owned by the Boy Scouts, near an estate owned by TV newscasters.

"I planned everything - the logistics were huge. I figured out exactly how many studs I'd need, how many sheets of insulation." Some items he found at old camp sites around the island; some he bought. He carried the materials on his back hundreds of yards into the woods.

He worked stealthily, often at night. While digging the 8-foot-deep hole, he covered it during daylight so it would not be seen from the air. Installing walls and roof took a weekend. Total cost: 6 weeks labor and less than $150.

The finished structure "is easy to heat, easy to cool. It is basically stormproof, bombproof, and the wind blows right over you." It includes a main room 8 by 8 feet; two anti-ways; a skylight; and a small cellar where food and drink can be kept cool.

Furnishings include: a queen-size loft bed, hinged so it folds out of the way when not in use; pine paneling; floors of Belgium stones he found; a wood-burning stove made of stone; a kitchen sink; a plastic tube attached to a jug of warm water for showering, with a plastic curtain drawn to confine splatters; and a home-made portable toilet. Shelves of books and music tapes line the walls. A cinder-block-size battery provides electricity.

Few people venture into that area. Trails through thick underbrush seem to lead nowhere. In winter, temperatures sometimes drop to 12°; and in summer, ticks bearing Lyme disease are active. Doug routed paths so they led away from his home. And he made 4" blocks with bottoms carved like deer hooves, which strap to his feet. "Like walking on stilts." If snow less than 4" deep, they leave tracks that look like deers'.

Even on a moonless night, Doug found his way without flashlight, moving past bayberry bushes, blueberry patches, scrub pine, and fallen dead trees, thru matted twigs and branches. Arriving at a jumble of dead branches concealing a small rise in the earth, Doug set aside some branches and lifted a hatch to enter his home. "Each path is a separate dance, which I memorized."

Doug lived there 8 years. Only a few close friends visited, including his mom who was pleased to find it clean and neat. But many islanders heard rumors.

In Nov 1998, Jack Hallett, a local man, while supposedly crawling on hands and knees looking for deer sign, saw a stove pipe protruding a few inches above ground. He told a police officer. Early the next morning, they went there and encountered the startled occupant. Doug invited them down for coffee.

After they left, Doug alerted the island's NTV channel 13 and told why he lived as he did. For a while, Doug was a celebrity, interviewed by major media. Doug used the exposure to criticize some islanders for turning an environmental gem into an overdeveloped resort. That did not endear Doug to those islanders.

The police thought Doug was on the newscasters' estate, and ordered him to vacate in 4 days. Then it was learned he was on Boy Scout land, and the local leaders decided to let him stay. But (perhaps threatened with fines if they didn't evict), they changed their minds, and got a ruling ordering Doug out within 30 days. His home was then destroyed. Sept 2004

Richard Ray, a health inspector who visited the home, said, "Many people would be envious of his living conditions." But in court, Ray claimed the home had 23 health code violations including with toilet, heating, ventilation.

Doug's achievement polarized island residents. "I'm either a folk hero or a vagrant. They either like me or hate me. I've lost friends over this, but I've made a lot of friends, too." Some call Doug a tax-dodger who wants the benefits of year-around Nantucket living without helping to pay for "good" government. But Dr.Tim Lepore, med director of the hospital, says that's nonsense. "He's not driving (a car) crazy; he's not contributing to congestion. He works and he goes home. He fits in very easily." Lepore offered Doug space in his back yard for a new underground home.

Doug, who said he had homes hidden elsewhere, including in Catskills near NYC, and CO and HI, left Nantucket for a while and lived, he said, in a home he'd built behind a waterfall on the Delaware River in PA. But Doug returned a year later, drawn back by "an intense spiritual attraction." Also, many houses being built, so Doug's skills much in demand.

Doug says, most islanders now accept him, but that an unswayed minority still regard him as an outlaw. (From Boston Globe 3Dc98 and 6Je01, and Long Island Newsday 2May99; MUCH THANKS to L.Smith for getting these via internet.)

(Comments:) The newspapers differed as to how Hallett discovered Doug's home. Neither tale seems likely. Doug was very careful with construction and trails, so I doubt he would leave a stove pipe easy to see or bump into, or light a fire in daytime when smoke might be visible, esp in Nov when days short and nights long.

Hallett's tale may be a cover story. My guess: "concerned citizens" heard the rumors and complained to police. Police learned who Doug's friends were, picked one they could intimidate to show them.

What Doug did after discovery: alert-the media quickly, seems wise. Officials then had more difficulty misrepresenting Doug. Even so, they tried to malign him by claiming that 6'4" Doug had assaulted or threatened people. That may have been exaggerations of minor spats in taverns.

The news reports, like most media, were to entertain; not how-to. I put in the little they gave, and tried to fix obvious goofs and fill in a few blanks.

The reports gave Doug's official name. I've not used it in case Doug has moved and prefers that notoriety not echo.

I suspect that Lepore's offer was merely a gesture. If Lepore did let Doug build on his land, Lepore might be fined or sued for code violations.

Hide-outs behind waterfalls provide dramatic scenes in movies, but do not seem desirable for living in. I wonder if Doug hoped to send any hostile pursuers on a wild waterfall chase.

Doug's ability to memorize a trail so well he can follow it in total darkness, is a talent neither of us have. Even with a flashlight, I have difficulty because surroundings look different in light beamed from me than in light from sky overhead. My feet may feel a main trail, esp if wearing mocs, because soil is packed firmer. But, if dark, I often stray, bump into things, and then wonder which way I strayed. Bert & Holly, OR

Suggestions for hiding a camp.

Make use of what occurs naturally in your area. Here there are many steep, bramble-covered slopes where hiking is difficult except on roads and trails: where humans don't go unless they have strong motives. If you live where slopes are slight and woods open with little undergrowth, concealment may be more difficult but perhaps you can be more remote. (Eg, maybe you could ride mtn bikes through the woods - not practical here.) Or, if you have deep snows that remain for months, that may hinder - but also an advantage for hauling in a year's supply on a sled. Likewise, deserts and swamps and rocky outcrops all pose problems - and offer advantages.

Generally avoid unique places: the only grove of trees on an otherwise treeless plain; the only dry mound in a swamp; the only island in a lake; the only known spring in a desert (better to collect and store occasional rains); a hot spring (except where many hot sprs); a choice fishing or hunting spot.

Route any trails around your camp; not to it. Don't end a trail abruptly; continue it to a plausible destination (eg, spring, fruit tree, view spot); one you go to occasionally so that portion of trail continues to get wear.

To get from a trail to your camp with out causing visible wear, look for any natural objects. Any boulders you could step on ? Any branches you could go arm over arm along. If bringing many back loads to (re)supply a camp, may be best to prepare a temp trail. Tie vulnerable vegetation out of the way; bring everything in; then re-naturalize. Put back vegetation; remove any that got damaged.

We often use staffs to assist trail access. Its print is much smaller than a footprint and, if carefully placed in among ground debris, not conspicuous. An expert stilt walker might be able to leave no footprints at all. We are not that adept, but a staff enables us to step further and more irregularly without losing balance. A staff (provides a third leg) is also helpful for hiking on steep slopes that lack hand holds, for crossing rivers, and for fighting off any cougars, bears, wolves, or whatever, (though not had to - so far). Make staff strong enough to take all your weight and long enough to reach the ground on your downhill side when on a slope.

Mocassins are better than hard-soled shoes in most woods here. They not only disturb the ground less, but are safer on side slopes (less apt to sprain ankle) and give better footing on most logs and boulders. Rubber mocs made from truck innertubes (see Packet or Set R) are less slippery than leather mocs.

The lower your shelter, the less visible; also less prone to wind damage, and warmer. For a long-term camp, we usually dig out enough to put roof flush with the ground. One time, mushroomers got within ten yds without noticing it.

For camo, at least in these woods, black or brown or dark grey are better colors than green. Human eyes are very sensitive to shades of green; no wonder, our ancestors had to distinguish edibles.
Sept 2004

Our variously green pails and totes and barrels, though much better than white or red, do not blend well here. On other hand, green outer clothing is less apt to be mistaken for a deer.

Clear plastic tarps may be visible a long distance, esp in winter when many bushes and trees are leafless. Black plastic is quite visible if sloped; it reflects sky. But it's not as visible if hung perpendicular to ground. Note: if on slope, on downhill side hang the plastic like ⌐⌐ ; not like ⌐⌐ .

Best for concealment from the air: many evergreen trees/branches above; next best, an over-roof of dead branches with vines growing on it; next best, cloth with a varied pattern of moss and fallen leaves on it, which may be less visible than camo cloth. (Spotting from air not likely unless there's an open fire or something else conspicuous. I've read of plane crashes, with survivors trying to be seen and many planes searching - without success.)

Do noisy activities elsewhere; maybe in the bottom of a steep, crooked canyon or at a temp camp. (Twice we've heard noisy parties on neighboring mountains, playing loud music audible for miles. The party lasted a few hours; then, promptly, everyone went away.)

Don't cook when you think people or big predators are nearby. Odors can drift far, esp downhill on calm eves.

If, despite your precautions, someone comes near your camp, don't assume (s)he saw it. Very few hikers are looking for campers. Most are looking for mushrooms, saleable greens, deer, trees, survey marks, whatever. They see only what they are looking for unless something unusual attracts their attention. Your imperfectly concealed camp will be more visible to you than to most others because you know what to look for.

If you are quite sure someone HAS spotted your camp, may be best to greet them, be friendly - and try to ascertain their motives and likely behavior. Exception: if you think they're hostile, get away promptly if you can without being seen. Better to let your camp be ransacked than to confront them. Keep valuables in safe cache; not setting out.

Don't camp close to a concentration of careless campers who might provoke a mass round-up. (We read of one along a NV-CA river a few years ago.) If dozens comb area, they will find most camps.

Learn about all the backwoods activities in the area. Even though you have more enjoyable and profitable ways to spend your time than (eg) gathering greenery that will become wreaths at some rich guy's funeral and then into trash; may be wise to do some, to learn what gatherers seek and where they go. Buyers will show you what they want, and suggest places to look. During autumns we like to be within hiking range of our winter site, to pick any edible 'shrooms as soon as they arise. (Some years we gather and eat $300+ worth at retail. Usually can't get them to a buyer easily enough for selling to be worthwhile.) Be sure to identify mushrooms VERY WELL before eating. Some good tasting ones are deadly for humans, though some other animals eat them without problems.

Sept 2004

My dream tent for winter camping.

Arc-shaped (like a quonset hut), it's supported by (maybe) 5 flex poles that intersect each other for bracing. (Arc tents that have only 2 poles, need tie-outs of ends.) Possible pole placement: (Know a better way ?) Fabric not shown.

end view   side view   top view

Side-walls/ceiling have tough outer fabric to withstand hail and falling branches. Maybe not waterproof. (Coatings seem not durable, esp on cloth exposed to weather.) When rain or sun protection needed, black polyethylene film (common plastic), cut to proper width, is layed over tent and clipped to rings along tent's bottom. Non-bunching fasteners (like clothespin ties, see 1995-96 Summary or Ap92DP) connect clips to the plastic - which may not survive long but is cheap and widely available. The plastic extends a few feet beyond tent's entry end and can be tied out to provide somewhat-sheltered space there. The tie on one corner is easily reclipped high for entry and exit.

The ceiling/side-walls have (maybe) 6 liners, spaced approx 3/4" apart for insulation. The next-to-inner liner is a vapor barrier to keep moisture (from breathing and sweat) out of the outer layers. (NEXT to inner, so human contact does not soil or damage it.) The INNER liner is removable for laundering.

The floor has 4 layers, all but one removable. On the ground is a plastic tarp, separate from tent, to keep tent's bottom clean. Next is a tough rot-proof fabric, sewen to tent. Next a foam pad; either closed cell, or open cell sealed within plastic. (It's in addition to any pad with bedding.) The floor's top layer is cloth; tough but easily washed. The foam insulates the inner layer from the ground enough to prevent condensation.

One end of tent is all window; at least two layers of transparent plastic, UV resistant; flexible but stiff enough to remain unwrinkled and thus easily wiped off; maybe polyester. The window usually faces the brightest, most open sky. The panes zip to the tent, and are removed: for backpacking (better rolled than folded); for cross-venting during hot weather (net window substituted); and to replace. (Likely the first parts ruined by UV.) The ceiling overhangs window a few inches and window slants inward, to minimize rain splatter. The slanted window also reflects sky into the ground instead of across the valley.

The tent's other end is for entry and ventilation. It has 6 lightweight porous curtains spaced apart; one is netting. The curtains can be zipped completely closed to block wind or crawling bugs; or, if few breezes and bugs, hung closed without zipping bottoms, with enough slack to crawl through or reach items outside; which eases access and reduces zipper wear. Curtains removable for max venting or to wash. (People brushing under them will gradually soil them.)

Inside is maybe 6½' long, 4' wide, 3' high: roomy for one; comfy for two to sleep but not do much else. Outside, 7¼ by 5 by 3¼. Maybe 25 pounds total; 15 pounds without poles, window, floor-pad.

side view, cross-section

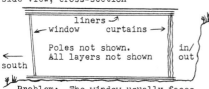

```
          liners ⌐
  ⌐ window        curtains →

  Poles not shown.              in/
  All layers not shown          out
south
```

Problem: The window usually faces down slope for max light. But, if it does, the tent needs a terrace at least 9' broad (7½-long tent plus 1½' stand-up space at entry end). Unfortunately, most terraces are narrow. May need to dig a trench into the bank. Putting window on side of tent would ease siteing, but greatly complicate this tent.

I'd like, attached to tent, a big 6+' tall fully-enclosed anti-way for doffing outside clothes and as rain-sheltered storage. Best shape and size depends on site and weather, and therefore is best designed and rigged by the user.

Cost ? The many layers need careful sewing. Even if made abroad in quite big quantities, my guess: $1000+ at retail. But only a month's rent in many places.

Not worth trying to hand-make one or a few for ourselves. So, until such a tent is for sale, we will continue to winter in wikiups we rig out of plastic plus whatever is available near site.

Most of our wikiups are roomier than this tent and thus better at a base camp we occupy continuously for many months. But our wikiups require much time to set up and take down (and if left up unattended, mice soon move in); whereas in an hour this tent could be set up, or taken down and stored in a barrel. Bert

Totes are not insect-proof.

The lids do not fit tightly enough. Small red ants nested in a 20-gal tote holding solar reflectors. Not damaged only because ants didn't use them. Trash barrel lids, too, seem not tight enough.

Most pail lids do. We've stored food, clothes, papers in many rain-sheltered pails for many years without damage.

The only rodent penetration was of a plastic trash barrel full of jars and bags, left over winter at a summer camp site. Oddly, the hole (big enough for a small rat) was near top. Did rodent get locked in, and gnawed to get out ? Holly

I use many 20-litre buckets for storage.

Ones with good-fitting lids. Also, medium-size totes. Dried foods I keep in 3-foot-long steel ammo cans. Bruce

Water storage during freezing weather.

Some 5-gallon water jugs froze solid. I now use gallon milk jugs, filled only half full. Half full so if they do freeze they are less apt to burst. Milk jugs so if they do burst they are easily replaced. However, I try to prevent freezing by keeping them out of the wind behind natural barriers such as big trees and boulders. Bruce of BC, 2003

I prefer pots with solid steel handles.

Riveted on. Bakelite plastic handles eventually crack or are melted by too hot a campfire. Or worse, the screws come loose repeatedly. I prefer folding handles but they are harder to find.

Cast iron is too heavy.

I buy my cookware and most of my equipment at thrift stores. Shopping tip: many items that don't sell at weekend garage sales, get donated to stores on Mondays. They are usually put out for sale by noon. Bruce of BC, 2002 (Comment:) Pots that have lost their handles have advantages. Though more difficult to move while hot (need heavy gloves or rags), they fit better under a transparent shroud when solar cooking, or insulate more compactly in bed after a brief simmer. And more compact to transport or store. Sometimes cheap or free at yard sales, thrift-store trash, unofficial dumps along logging roads.

If pot has a handle, I prefer welded. If it breaks off, it will probably leave the pot entire, whereas a riveted or bolted handle may leave holes that leak.

The pots we use for solar cooking.

The ideal pot is dull black, inside and out. None of our pots are. Some got darkened while cooking over fires, but more grey than black, and wears off.

I found two pots in a fussy 2nd-hand-store's trash. One small (3 cups), shiny black outside and in (teflon); no lid.

Other pot is mid-size aluminum, black teflon inside, Bert painted outside. (No free/cheap black paint. Bert mixed soot scraped off stove, with oil poured off of white paint.) Needs 2nd coat. Paint survived solar cooking but wouldn't fire.

Solar cooking equipment.

Three summers ago, Bert designed and built and tested a reflector-type solar cooker. Consisting of 8 aluminum-foil-covered cardboard panels, it folds to 8½" by 11" for transport and storage. (5 illos and instructions in Sep02 DP. This illo shows panels assembled, prior to setting up.)

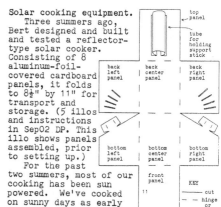

For the past two summers, most of our cooking has been sun powered. We've cooked on sunny days as early as mid April and as late as late Oct, but mostly during the sunniest months which here have been July, Aug, Sept. Thus, year around, about one-third of our cooking has been solar - well worth it given problems and costs of other heat sources.

We soon learned: one reflector cooker isn't enough. Bert made a larger 8-panel, identical except scaled up: 13¼" x 17" panels covered with foil 18" wide.

Bert also made a 3-panel "corner" reflector (see May93 DP or Summary) with panels 14x14" (size of some cardboard on hand). Though not as potent as 8 panels, it sufficed to cook on hot clear days. But mostly it provided hot water that reduced cooking time on the 8-panels; both a second batch that same day and, by insulating over night, the first batch the next day - helpful because

Sept 2004

81

many mornings are cloudy until noon.

Though the 3-panel concentrates sun less than does a properly-set 8-panel, it does not need adjusting as often.

To heat and store water for cooking, we used a gallon narrow-mouth brown glass jug I'd scavenged (had aloe vera extract). We didn't want to heat cooking water in plastic because, not only does near-boiling water weaken most plastics, but heat may greatly accelerate leaching of any toxins out of plastic.

For insulating water overnight, Bert lined a 6-gal plastic pail with plastic foam: rigid foam top and bottom; flexible packing foam rolled up around the sides; into which the jug fit snugly easily. (A wide-mouth gallon jug might fit, with foam, into a 5-gallon pail.)

Concentrated sun had changed the (vinyl?) bowl, used as shroud when first testing, from transparent to whitish. Luckily I'd found many big scraps of transparent plastic (polyester?) in Kinkos' dumpster (used to laminate). Somewhat flexible but stiff enough to hold a shape, and thus easier to put on and off a pot than is an oven bag (which we would have used otherwise). From it, Bert made various-size shrouds that fit our pots. It has endured sun well. After a while it delaminates, becoming slightly less clear but more insulative.

Bert stapled together ends of side-piece to form cylinder, then fastened on top piece. Some fastenings did not hold well. Our final way: bend ends of tab to insert into slot. Number and exact size of slots/tabs depends on diameter.

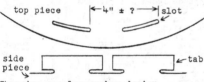

top piece   ←4" ± ?→ slot

side piece   tab

Choosing a solar-cooker design.

The main reason Bert designed our 8-panel reflectors rather than using SCR's CooKit design: an 8-panel folds smaller and thus stores easier. Also, it may be more effective in autumn when the sun is not high here. (CooKit is mainly for tropics where mid-day sun always high.)

SCR (p.B) sells two CooKit versions: one, foil and cardboard, won't take rain; one, foil and plastic foam, endures rain but crushes easily. With either, foil gradually loses shine. If/when a more durable CooKit is made, we may buy one to test along side our 8-panels.

Last summer, Bert added a 9th panel to our small 8-panel (a "fore panel" is attached to the front panel). It boosts power during high sun (near noon from mid May thru July) but helps little when sun low. Conversely, the top panel helps much when sun low, but not when sun is high. If in tropics, we might not want a top panel, because its hold-up stick takes time. (CooKit has no top panel.)

The big-8 accomodates a larger pot than does the small-9, which is why Bert made it. If pot small, big-8 is more tolerant of azimuth. But big-8 needs more materials and stiffer panels, gets more wind force, and won't fit in 5-gal pail (will in 10-gal tote). If adjusted

Sept 2004

frequently, small-9 should heat a small pot as fast as does big-8. Holly, OR

Tests compare solar reflectors.

I used 3 identical one-gallon jugs full of water; plastic, deep blue (not best color but I wanted identical jugs). NO SHROUDS. Jugs' bottoms insulated from reflectors by ¼"-thick styrofoam.

Started 1:30 on 22July02, water 85°. Left caps slightly loose to vent steam. Ended 3:30. Water 150° on big-8; 135° on small-9; 130° on 3-panel. Big-8's jug evaporated cup of water; others little.

Because big-8's jug got hotter, it lost more heat, so big-8 did better than temperatures indicate. Small-9 had more panels. Why was big-8 best? Big-8 was newer (in use a month, vs 5 months), so its foil was shinier. Jug was too big for small-9: parts of jug were beyond area getting most sun. 3-panel did almost as well as small-9, despite less area and less concentration of sun, probably for both reasons above.

Reflective areas: big-8, 1785 sq in; small-9, 841; 3-panel, 588. Approx ratios: 2.8 to 1.4 to 1.0.

To learn effects of shine loss, on 10Sept03 I tested side by side, heating blue jugs, the original big-8 and a new big-8 same size. In 3 hours, 60° water heated to 152° by new, 142° by old. Bert

How solar and flame cooking differ.

With flame (wood or propane), heat comes from below, so the food cooks from bottom up. Even in an oven where all air nearly the same temperature, a bread heats more on bottom where covered by pan than on top where evaporation cools.

With our solar reflectors, heating is usually greatest on top where both direct and reflected rays shine, whereas the bottom gets only reflected rays. The lower the sun, the less the difference, because fewer rays shine on top and more reflect in onto bottom. Also, the higher the pan, the less the difference, because more space between bottom-center reflector and pan lets in more rays. By setting pan on clear glass jars 3 inches high, we were able to cook breads quite evenly without turning them over.

When cooking in water, we completely cover the food; else food above water may scorch before food in water cooks.

With nettles and other greens, we heated water nearly to boiling (at least 170°) before putting in greens. The hot water instantly wilts the greens which are then easily stirred down into water.

Bert and I cook bread differently. Regardless of heat source, he sprinkles flour on pan, and then around edges of bread, to prevent sticking; and uses low heat because he fears burning.

Whereas, when cooking with propane or wood in an aluminum pan with patina (a tough thin coating that develops), if I get pan hot enough or cook long enough, a bread usually comes free as the crust forms. (If dough very moist or getting sour, sticking to pan is more likely.)

When we switched to our solar rigs which provide only low heat, at first I cooked bread like Bert does. Then I tried spreading a thin coating of oil on pan (with finger). The bread tasted better to me, so I kept using oil, even

though for health I prefer to cook without oil (which heat may degrade). But
even with oil, I sometimes had to shake
pan vigorously, or invert and knock it
on something, to jar the bread free.
   With solar, I form dough approx one
inch thick - slightly thicker than with
flame so I need not tend as often. Bert
forms loaves thicker. Sun-cooked bread
tastes different than flame-cooked. Does
the top, cooking before middle, seal in
volatiles that otherwise evaporate ?
   I tried frying pans and teflon-lined
pot; covered and uncovered; loaf's top
sprinkled with dark poppy-seeds, or not.
None affected cooking-time much. What
did: sun height. In mid summer near
noon, a loaf cooked in approx 1½ hours.
Later in season, 2 or more hours needed.
   I made a few cakes (moistish bread
dough with molasses and cinnamon added),
cookies, and blackberry pies (thin layer
bread dough; then berries 3 deep; then
another thin dough). All cooked fine.
Peanuts, soybeans, sunflrs toasted fine;
never burned (unlike with flame) ! Holly

Report on one day of solar cooking.
   (No two days quite the same.) 1 Aug
02, 45° latitude, solar noon 1:30.
   9:15. Set gallon 60° water heating in
brown glass jug with shroud on 3-panel
reflector. Sky partly cloudy until noon.
   12:40. Water in jug 150°. Used two
cups to start one cup lentils cooking in
small stainless pot with lid and shroud
on small 9-panel. Also used some water,
diluted with cool water until "warm to
wrist" (100°?) to mix with flour and
yeast to start dough rising we will bake
tomorrow. Refilled jug with cool water.
Jug water now 110°. Again on 3-panel.
   1:12. Started cooking coolish dough
(made from flour ground in early morn
and yeast-risen today), approx 1½" thick
in aluminum frying pan sprinkled with
flour, with cover and shroud, on big 8-
panel. Pan set on jars 3" tall.
   3:35. Air between bread and cover
190°. Tasted small bit from center
interior. Not as done as we like.
   4:24. Air 220°. Bread done. Removed.
   4:29. Water in brown jug now 160°.
Moved to (now vacant) big 8-panel.
   4:32. Lentils 195°. VERY done - soft,
as Holly likes. (I like firmer) Removed.
   5:58pm. Water in brown jug now 183°.
Put jug with water into insulated pail.
   8:30am next morn. Water in insulated
jug 119°. (Air about 55°.) Bert

Solar reflectors' problems and fixes.
   To better hold top panel's support
stick, I lashed its bottom to a bowl
(cut-off plastic jug) into which I put
rocks. The lashing goes through holes I
bored in bowl's side. The stick needs
a small fork or lump at its bottom; else
it may slide up out of the lashing.
   Play of the support stick and Tyvek
hinges let wind gusts flap the top panel
back and forth, esp on big 8-panel.
   The only structural failure so far:
on my first big-8, a Tyvek hinge holding
center back panel to center bottom panel
tore; weakened by repeated foldings when
putting rig away. (I'm surprised it tore
instead of ripping off the cardboard.)
For big-8s, I'd like stronger hinges.
   For my first big-8, I lacked enough
stiff cardbd. Some pieces I stiffened

more by gluing on other pieces, cross-
laminating. (Cardbd stiffer one way than
the other.) Even so, the panels often
warped as heat and humidity changed;
but were easily bent back approx flat.
   I made the new big-8 out of old 1/8"
plywood I found. Portions had rotted,
but much was sturdy enough for panels.
Much stiffer than cardbd. Design change
of tabs: instead of flaps that fold out
to hold tab in slot, I put a hole in
each tab through which a peg goes.
Because paneling is thicker than cardbd,
it needs bigger gaps between panels to
allow folding, and panels must be folded
in order; else hinges get over-stressed.
   Because the bigger reflectors have
bigger problems, I probably won't build
more unless cooking for many people. For
our largest pot now, the small-9 is big
enough though not as fast as a big-8.
   The small-9's fore panel needs frequent adjustments; else its reflection
misses the pot. I probably won't fasten
a fore panel to future reflectors. If I
want one temporarily, I'll set an extra
reflector in front of the front panel.
   Breezes sometimes flipped the front
panel over onto pot, partially shading
it. I tied on a little tray on which I
set rocks, to limit panel's motion.
   When I made the first reflector, I
didn't glue foil to cardboard, because
I thought white glue wouldn't adhere to
foil. Instead, I folded foil over the
edge of cardbd. But the foil sometimes
came loose, esp near the hinges where
only tabs of foil folded over. So, when
repairing, I tried gluing edges. Held
better than expected.
   So, when I made the new big-8 I glued
all foil edges (glue seams ½" wide). On
the edges not joining other panels, I
folded foil over the edge and glued foil
to the shady side. But on edges joining
other panels, I glued foil to sunny side.
That enabled me to use one long Tyvek
hinge (glued to shady side) on each
joined edge. Simpler and stronger. So
far, the glue has held as well to sunny
as shady side. (I thought heat might
weaken it.) If I build more big-8s, I
will make panels 13.9" by 18" to utilize
full width of foil, and glue all edges
of foil to sunny sides of panels.
   3-panel reflector. If each panel is
joined to the other two, they can't fold
for storage. But if not all joined, the
back panels will blow over unless held
by something. So I added a second bottom
panel. Each bottom panel is hinged to a
back panel, and the back panels to each
other, but the bottom panels not joined.
To set up, I place one bottom panel
under the other. The pot then anchors
the whole rig. I partially covered the
under panel with left-over foil scraps,
which adds reflective power if back
panels set wider than a right angle. The
best angle depends on width of the pot.
   All aluminum foil is not manufactured
equal. Our first reflectors were made
with Reynolds. But I didn't have enough
for the second 3-panel, so I bought
another brand, 18" wide, 37½' long for
$1 at a dollar store. The box says
"heavy duty". But it is thinner than
Reynolds, and got wrinkled more when
rolled by factory. Worse: a moist jug,
set directly on the foil, corroded it
enough in two hours to lose shine. Bert
      Sept 2004

If panels not 8½x11". panel mac 1/8
To build the big-8, in in mac
instead of recalculating inches mm mm
all measurements (in Sep 9¼x12 27.7 3.5
02 DP), I made a special 12x15¼ 35.9 4.5
ruler with each "macro- 13½x18 41.6 5.2
inch" (mac) equal to 18x23¼ 53.8 6.7
17/11" (39.3mm) and each
1/8 mac equal to 4.9mm. (Check: 11 macs
= 17 inches.) I then simply made all
measurements in macs. This works ONLY if
a panel's ratio of width to length is 8½
to 11. Above are some other sizes that
use 12" and 18" wide foil efficiently. B

The Encyclopedia of Edible Plants
of North America. Francois Couplan's
prodigious work includes approx 4000
species of 850 genera. However, many
are tropical plants found only in s FL.
Not for identification; no descriptions.

Genera rated "A1": tasty, healthful,
easily gathered and prepared; and abundant throughout N.Amer: Urtica (nettle),
Quercus (oak), Stellaria (chickweed),
Chenopodium (lambs qter), Amaranthus
(pigweed), Malva (mallow), Brassica
(mustard), Raphanus (radish), Rubus
(blackberry), Sonchus (sow thistle),
Taraxacum (dandelion).

Couplan says the young leaves of
Hypochoeris, a relative of lettuce and
dandelion, "can be eaten raw. They are
crisp and have a pleasant flavor, exempt
of bitterness, and make very good salads."
But, inconsistently, he rates it only D1
(not very edible). Where we are, H.
radicata (gosmore) is much less bitter
than dandelion. But species may vary.
Perhaps Couplan wrote his praise before
he encountered one less tasty - and
revised his rating but not his praise.

"The very young tops of Salsola kali
(russian thistle) are tender, salty and
edible raw. The plant soon becomes woody
and spiny and turns into well-known
tumbleweeds blown by the wind for miles.
Rich in many minerals." The seeds, too,
are said to be edible.

The leaves of most Dodecatheon
(shooting star) species "are one of the
best tasting salad ingredients to be
found in the mountains" near the West
Coast. The flowers, too, are edible raw.
Papaver (poppy). The young basil
leaves of several species, formed before
the plant blooms, are excellent raw.

"Many of the Chenopodiaceae have the
ability to grow on saline soils from
which they derive a salty taste."

"The young shoots of Pinaceae (pine
family, including also firs, spruces,
hemlocks, doug-fir), rich in vitamin C,
are excellent raw, added to salads and
other dishes." But some other conifers,
including arborvitae (red cedar), some
junipers, and especially yew (easily
mistaken for hemlock) are toxic.

Oxalis (wood sorrel). "The leaves,
flowers and young fruits of various
species are edible raw." However, "all
species contain oxalic acid and potassium oxalate... People subject to arthritis, rheumatism, gout, asthma and kidney
stones should abstain." Also, regular
ingestion for several months can inhibit
the body's absorption of calcium.

The leaves of Oxyria digyna (mountain
sorrel, arctic and high mtns) are edible
raw or cooked. They contain oxalic acid,
but "it can be eliminated by boiling in

a change of water." (Also true for more-
common Oxalis (above) ?)

"The very young fronds of Pteridium
aquilinum (bracken fern), picked while
still tender before they have started to
unroll, taste very good" but should be
either thoroughly cooked, preferably
with change of water; or else soaked for
24 hours in water with wood ashes. When
raw, they contain a carcinogen and a
vitamin-B1 destroyer. Members of the
first scientific expedition to cross
Australia from north to south (1860-61)
died from beriberi (vit-B1 lack) after
feeding on a thiaminase-rich fern,
nardoo (Marsilea drummondii). This fern
was commonly eaten by aborigines, but
only after soaking in water which rids
it of the heat-resistant thiaminase.

"The tender young leaves of maple are
good raw or cooked. They are rich in
sugar. The seeds are edible but often
bitter" which can be eliminated by
boiling in a change of water. Maple sap,
for making sugar, is most sweet and
plentiful when, in early spring, "warm
sunny days are followed by very cold
nights" (common in northeast). Climate
is more important than species of maple.

The sweet aromatic juniper "berries"
(fleshy cones) are a well-known condi-
ment. But too big a dose, or continuous
long use, can irritate the kidneys.

"The sweet taste of licorice is due
to ... a saponin 50 times as sweet as
white sugar.... If used regularly over a
long period of time, it can be a cause
of hypertension (high blood pressure)."

"In moderate amounts, the essential
(odorous) oils of crucifers (mustards,
cresses, cabbage, etc) stimulate the
appetite and activate digestion. But big
doses strongly irritate mucous membranes
and cause digestive or urinary problems."

Pods and seeds of various lupines
(legume family) have been eaten, but
"contain toxic alkaloids which must be
removed by boiling in water."

"After peeling off the bitter outer
layer, the inner part of the stem of
Arctium (burdock) is one of the best
vegetables; tender, crunchy, sweet, with
a delicate artichoke flavor. It can be
eaten raw or cooked in various ways. The
new unfolding leaves are edible raw" but
soon become very bitter. "The roots are
good raw or cooked, have a pleasant
artichoke taste and a sweet flavor due
to inulin" (up to 45%), a sugar easily
assimilated even by diabetics. Best when
fresh. Sold in NYC markets as "gobo"
(Japanese name) "for quite a high price"
but can be picked free in nearby empty
lots. Harvest after their first growing
season, in fall or winter - before the
flower stalk develops.

"The cambium layer of Alnus rubra
(red alder) was eaten by Indians."

California Indians often preferred
bitter acorns, as they keep better (due
to their tannin) and are more abundant
than sweet acorns. Tannin is soluable
in water. To eliminate, chop up acorns
and boil "in several changes of water
until bitterness"gone and water clear.

Pine nuts "are very nutritious. But
they turn rancid rapidly and must be
stored in an airtight container."

"Bitter almonds (Prunus amygdalus)
and their essential oil have been used

to flavor desserts. However, this can be dangerous as 30 to 50 kernels can kill an adult if ingested at one time." Humans can detoxify hydrocyanic acid, which is also in plum and peach pits, apple seeds, and many other fruit seeds, but only in small amounts, gradually.

P. emarginata, bitter cherry. "The pulp is thin and sweetish. Local Indians removed the kernel from the stone, crushed it, leached out the cyanide with running water, and ate the result as a mush, or dried it for later use."

Beans contain much iron (more than lentils, known to be a good source).

The seeds of lima (Phascolus limensis) and some other beans "contain cyanogenetic glucosides which yield by hydrolysis toxic hydrocyanic acid." It "can be eliminated by boiling the seeds in water for a long time. But it's not destroyed; merely transferred to the water which should be discarded." Poisoning due to improper cooking, is quite frequent.

"Raw beans (and beans newly sprouted) contain a toxin, phasine, which causes serious digestive disorders (sometimes fatal) by inhibiting enzymes and destroying red blood cells. Prolonged cooking (but not simple drying) eliminates this toxin. Bean sprouts must not be eaten raw until leaves are green....."

More toxic warnings about cultivated than wild species, but probably only because more is known about them.

Kudzu, Pueraria lobata. "Young leaves, flowers, unripe pods are edible raw or cooked." In Japan, roots are gathered in fall and starch extracted by grating, soaking in water, filtering, letting starch settle, pouring off water, drying, and crushing into powder. Much valued for nutrients and easy digestibility. In southeast U.S., commercial harvesting could benefit "the producer, the local rural people, and the native plants oppressed by this aggressive invader."

A common error: "The proteins (in grass-family cereals) are incomplete: that is, they don't have all essential amino acids." No. They have all, but (eg) corn has only 2/3 the ideal amount of lysine. So, unless eaten with something rich in lysine such as legumes, portions of other amino acids are not well used. Couplan, French, uses some British English. Eg, "saccharose" vs "sucrose".

1998, 512p., Keaten, 27 Pine St, Box 876, NewCanaan CT 06840; $20. Revu, H&B

Plants and Animals of Pacific Northwest.
In this book, Eugene N. Kozloff describes approx 300 plant species and 100 animals. The 123 line drawings and 321 color photos are helpful to all who wish to learn the area's flora without delving into technical works with keys. Few mentions of edible and other uses. Some tidbits I found most interesting:

"Any delicate trailer (stems tend to sprawl) with square stems (and usually also downward-directed hooks on the corners) and with leaves arranged in whorls, will almost certainly be a Galium. If you pull the plant across your hand, you will notice that the hooks make it cling...." Common names 'bedstraw' and 'cleavers'. (Cleavers grows, sometimes abundantly, in many places around here. We (H&B) often eat the young growing tips (stem with leafs)

raw in spring. (More in June 89 DP.))

Yerba buena, Satureja douglasii, is in "the same genus as the kitchen herb called savory or basil-thyme" and is "a low creeper of the mint family... rarely missing from an oak woods." Also in dry conifer forests. Kozloff doesn't mention, it makes a mintish-flavored herbal tea.

Kozloff says salal berries, Gautheria shallon, "taste something like huckleberries marinated in a dilute extract of fir needles"; and serviceberries, Amalanchier alnifolia, are "neither sweet nor juicy." I've found both very varied. Some of both were sweet and delicious.

Pacific dogwood, Cornus nuttalli, "ordinarily has a single trunk." To help identify in winter, branches bud as whorls of four though all may not develop, whereas maples branch in pairs. Also, "as branches grow outward, they curve upward." (In spring, big showy white flowers open before or with leaves. Wood is fine-grained, dense, hard when dry; used for salmon-harpoon foreshafts, shuttles for weaving, bobbins, tools and "dogs" (skewers), hence name. Root-bark tea widely used as quinine sub to treat malaria. Berries eaten raw or cooked.)

1976, 270 pages, $15 in 1986 (ppd?), U of WA Press, POB 85569, Seattle WA 98145. Review by Julie Summers

Many wild herbs yield tasty seasonings.
I have learned to enjoy the natural flavors of most wild plants I eat; salt or other seasonings seldom desired. But some other foods I like to spice up. To them I add a herbal mix I blend myself.

Seaweeds provide mostly potassium chloride instead of sodium chloride (table salt). Almost any fresh, non-rotting seaweeds can be collected, dried, powdered, and used as salt. They taste like table salt but milder. WARNINGS: Never eat any that are not fresh or that have foreign growth on them; or gathered near where sewage is dumped into ocean.

The leaves of all Atriplex species can be dried, powdered, and used like salt. Commonly called "saltbush" due to high mineral content and salty flavor. I've also tried burning dried Atriplex leaves and using the ash, but prefer the flavor of the unburnt leaves.

Related to Atriplex is Chenopodium, a genus of the Goosefoot family. Best known is lambs quarters, a nutrient-rich spinach relative found world-wide. All species edible; flavors vary slightly.

Many other herbs, though not salty, are tasty. Choose strong-flavored herbs so that you need only small amounts.

Most members of the mustard family are excellent cooking spices: shepherds purse, wild radish, sweet alyssum, water cress, and the rockets, as well as those called "mustards". No members are toxic. (Watercress may have liver-fluke eggs. We cook. Cooked flavor quite bland.)

The leaves of many wild sages, dried and powdered, can be added sparingly.

Though not salty, licorice-flavored fennel seeds may be a good addition.

Wild and cultivated onions, garlic, leeks, chives, ramps are best fresh.

Never use any wild plants for food or spices you've not positively identified. Christopher Nyerges (shortened from Gentle Survivalist of a few years ago) Sept 2004

Easy-to-make tool cleans the insides of jugs.

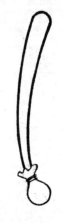

A dirty film gradually develops in water jugs.
It grows algae and (?). Ordinary brushes don't reach
well inside narrow-mouth jugs. To make scrubbers that
do, I bend a piece of wire in the middle to form a
handle, and lash a wadded rag or piece of soft foam to
its ends with rubber bands or cord.

I like to have three scrubbers. For two, I use
coat-hanger wire. It is fairly stiff yet can be bent.
One scrubber is quite straight for cleaning a jug's
bottom. The second is curved to reach portions below
the handle. The third scrubber, made from more-
flexible wire and with a smaller wad, is for reaching
into the handle. With some difficulty, I have been
able to clean all jug handles encountered except for
newer bleach jugs which have tiny openings at top. H&B

Jug showers versus spray showers.

Three writers have recently said they prefer spray showers,
including at least one who has also used jugs. But none said
why. Back in May 82 DP p.1, Julie Summers said she sometimes
showered with squeeze bottles - to use less water.

Carefully-applied squirts from a squeeze bottle may rinse
more efficiently than do less-easily-controlled gushes from a
jug. A fine spray from (eg) a window-washing bottle might be
most efficient of all. However, I think an orchard sprayer,
such as the rig shown in Feb 04 Supplement, would be LESS
efficient, because the flow is less controllable.

If rinsing is more efficient (by whatever means), it will
probably be SLOWER, and you will be wet longer. That is
tolerable or even desirable in hot weather. But when cold, I
like to get rinsed as quickly as possible, even if I use a
little more water. Usually we have enough water. If not, I
wash a few high-priority parts and postpone the rest. Next to
hands and crotch, the parts I wash most often are feet and
lower legs because any hike gets them muddy. For them I often
use a squeeze bottle, because it is easier to handle than a
gallon jug and I don't need much water. (Also see LLL "Simple
Shower", and DP May93 p.1, Oct95 p.1, May96 p.1, May97 p.7,
May98 p.8, Aug00 p.1.) Holly & Bert, Oregon 973, Dec 2004

Some potato-chip bags have shiny reflective insides.

They are more durable and remain more reflective than
aluminum foil. Useable for solar cooking. I sometimes find
such bags in dumpsters. Lauran, Arizona 857, May 2004

RV-type propane equipment better than lighter-weight gear.

If buying propane equipment, get refillable tanks. One-
gallon tanks are made (in case 5 gal is too much to backpack
to a remote temp camp). With the tank, you will need a
regulator (a disk-shaped thing that screws into the tank), a
LOW-pressure stove (like used in most RVs), and a hose or tube
to connect. Shun the little cans and the stoves that fit them.
They are not only more expensive (per propane) but also more
hazardous and wasteful because high pressure feeds the stove.
Also, I've heard the stoves' tiny holes are prone to clog up
and impossible to clean. If at a camp too briefly to want RV-
type equipment, solar or fire cook, or bring ready-to-eats.

Don't drive with engine running too slow.

I purchased "How To Keep Your VW Alive, for the Complete Idiot". Good book. It answered many questions. And I learned I did things that sent my engine to an early grave. At gatherings, I was referred to as "lug head". I thought it meant I was often working on my van. But, no, it referred to my lugging the engine. Near the campground, I drove at low RPM to make less noise and not disturb the other campers. But quietness not worth ruination. 3000 rpm best for my VW. (I'd been driving at 2000-2500.) Eugene Gonzalez, NC 287, December

I prefer tents that are tall enough to stand up in.

For me, squat tents are not worth the lesser price and weight. I'd thought I'd seldom stand (true), and lower would heat easier (true), and the occasional crouch to dress or exit would be no big deal (false). Could be my age - 55. Ken, WA 982, June

(Comments:) Other advantages of low shelters (of any kind): less likely to be crushed or toppled by wind, and less unwanted ventilation during winter storms; easier to conceal; a hunter's stray missile may go over, not thru.

Ways to obtain stand-up height in a squat shelter: dig a hole in the middle; build a small dome (might be pop-up) on the roof. Most of our shelters have not had stand-up room.

Bear damages and scatters items in an unattended stash.

When moving base camp, I left a pile of remainders near the former site, awaiting further sorting and salvaging. Mostly old plastic tarps and various plastic containers. Nothing valuable. No food. I returned a year later - and found the stuff scattered. Pails had been tossed ten yards. They had claw marks on them. My guess: Some rodent had nested in the pile. Then a bear came along, smelled the rodent, and swatted things helter-skelter in a frenzy to catch rodent. Bert

Methods of processing acorns.

Oak trees grow throughout the world. Over 200 species include deciduous and evergreen trees and shrubs. All oaks are easily identified by their acorns which are nuts set in scaly caps. The tons of acorns that fall to the ground every fall are mostly discarded by gardeners. How sad. In a world with frequent food shortages, it seems wise to learn about an abundant food that was eaten by many of our ancestors.

The tannic acid in most species of acorns makes them too bitter to eat raw. Humans are rarely if ever poisoned by them because no one with normal taste would eat an acorn raw. S/he would just spit it out. But tannic acid is easily leached out.

A quick method. Put two pots of water on the fire. While they are heating, begin removing the shells from the acorns. This can be quite a task if the acorns are still somewhat fresh and not dried out. I have set freshly-collected acorns into the hollow of a rock, hit them with another rock, then easily removed the shells. I put the acorn meats into the first pot, and continue removing shells until I have enough.

Let the water and acorns in the first pot boil for about 15 minutes, or until the water looks dark. Pour off that water but not the acorns, pour in hot water from your second pot, add cold water to the second pot, and put both pots back on the fire. Again let the first pot boil for 15 minutes or until the water gets brown, then change water, etc. Repeatedly boiling and changing water will remove the tannic acid in 45 to 60 min. Occasionally take out an acorn and taste it. After the acorns are no longer bitter, I change water and boil once more just to

make sure. You can then add wild vegetables and other items.
   Though quick, boiling removes much of the flavor and oil
of the acorns. Slower methods are better for nutrition and
taste - and don't require metal pots and fire.
   Neat but not quick. Shell the acorns and leave them
whole. Put them into a mesh bag. (An onion bag
is suitable if it doesn't have any holes big enough for the
acorns to slip through.) Place the bag of acorns in a flowing
stream, secured so it does not drift away. The running water
will leach out the tannic acid in 2 to 7 days, depending on
species. (Various quicker methods that use cold or warm water,
require grinding the acorns. Described in original article.)
   Acorns are 65% carbohydrates, 18% fat, 6% protein. Their
flavor is somewhat like graham crackers but highly variable.
   Though the leaching removes most of the tannic acid, a
little remains. If you start eating many acorns frequently,
add a pinch of charcoal to your acorn products. That will
neutralize the tannic acid. Christopher Nyerges (much shortened from Wilderness Way v6n4, sent by Bruce of BC)

(Comment:) Many edible plants contain some tannic acid. They
include thea (ordinary tea, esp if boiled long), coffee, some
grapes and wines, and (I suspect from the taste) artichokes.
According to the authors of "Why We Get Sick" (reviewed in Sep
02 DP), humans can detoxify small amounts of tannic acid.
Also, many people seem to like the taste (an indication that,
as with many substances, small amounts may be beneficial even
though large amounts are toxic ?).

Be careful if gathering mushrooms to eat.
   Many species of wild mushrooms grow naturally in our area.
Some are delicious, but many may not be edible, and a few have
potent toxins that can permanently damage organs - or kill.
   ACCURATELY IDENTIFY each and every mushroom as an edible
species before eating. Despite folklore to the contrary,
there are no simple tests that will distinguish edible from
poisonous species. Many edible species have toxic look-alikes:
learn what these are and don't rely only on photographs or
drawings. When in doubt, throw it out !
   Never eat any mushrooms raw. Cooking improves flavor,
digestibility, available nutrients; and eliminates some toxins.
However, cooking will not eliminate all kinds of toxins and
will not make poisonous mushrooms edible.
   When trying a mushroom species for the first time, eat
only a teaspoon full and wait at least 24 hours before eating
any more - even if other people have eaten the species without
problems. You may have an allergy to that particular species,
just as some people are allergic to shrimp or strawberries.
Keep a whole uncooked sample in a cool place in case you later
need to confirm identification. Do not consume alcohol when
first trying a mushroom. That may intensify allergic reactions. Also, some Coprinus with alcohol cause discomfort.
   Do not eat spoiled/moldy/rotten mushrooms.
   Do not eat fungi growing on ornamental trees. The fungi
may absorb toxins in the wood. (A recent illness in Eugene
was caused by eating Laetiporus growing on black locust.)
   Be careful where you collect edibles. Mushrooms can
readily pick up chemicals from the environment. Avoid lawns
where fertilizers or pesticides might have been applied; the
sides of busy roads; near old dump sites. Cascade Mycological
                                                        Society
(Comments:) Mushrooms were esp bountiful here this
autumn. We ate many, mostly chantrelles. From Sept thru Nov,
         Dwelling Portably   April 2005

we probably averaged at least a pound a day, each. We heard
that chantrelles were selling for $6 to $9 a pound in stores,
and gatherers were getting $4-$5. But we were too remote for
selling to be practical. A few times we had slight nausea or
louder-then-usual ear whistling (indication of toxin ?) which
soon went away. We were not eating any other suspect food.
But the symptoms did not correlate much with amount eaten. On
a few days when we ate several pounds and nothing else, we had
no adverse symptoms (other than not feeling peppy - mushrooms
are not high in calories). Was the cause a little rot or mold
we failed to trim off ? Or had one of the mushrooms grown near
a poisonous specie and absorbed a little of its toxin ?
    We usually cooked them alone, so that remaining silt
(impossible to clean perfectly) dropped to the bottom of the
broth and did not contaminate other food. We put in little or
no water, because the mushrooms quickly exuded ample broth.
    Mushrooms are richer in B vitamins than most vegetables.
But we wonder how well they digest. Though we tried to chew
them thoroughly before swallowing (not easy, because they are
slippery), our feces became voluminous. Holly & Bert, Dec 04

More about Mexican border opportunities and problems.
    Algodones (west of Yuma) exists to take care of gringo
dental and medical problems. Small town, many English-speaking
dentists and MDs, laid-back border crossing. I don't know much
about hotels and camping opportunities there, but Yuma is not
far away. Michael Trend, AZ 853, 2 June 2004

    Since May, Nogales police have arrested 12 Arizonans
during an enforcement effort targeting people suspected of
buying tranquilizers or painkillers without Mexican prescriptions. In Sonora state, an American prescription must be shown
to a Mexican physician who will rewrite it, for it to be legal.
"We won't go back to Nogales, said Karen Tafoya, 54, of
Apache Junction AZ. "We've gone to Algodones and always felt
very safe." Several other Phoenix-area residents said they
have not encountered problems in Algodones. They say pharmacies there cater more to their needs and rarely require
prescriptions, so they are shifting their business to there.
    Noe Ramirez, an employee of Farmacia Algodones, said no
arrests are happening in Algodones because it is in Baja,
whereas Nogales is in Sonora, and the prescriptions laws differ.
(from yumasun.com 25June04, sent by Michael Trend)

    I drove from Mexicali to San Luis Rio Colorado today. When
I crossed to AZ, I got asked for ID for the first time in ages.
Evidently, border officials are now supposed to ask for ID from
everyone who crosses. I don't know how thorough the checks
will be, or for how long. Michael Trend, 20 July 04

    Algodones caters more to gringos than does Mexicali, so
prices tend to be higher. Michael, 12 Oct 04. (Recent prices
of Michael's dentist in Mexicali: crown $125, cleaning $25,
fillings $30-$50, extractions $30. "She can get along in
English, and is connected with a great endodontist who is
virtually bi-lingual." Also see DP Dec03 p.7, May 03 p.4,
Sep 02 p.12, June 02 p.6; Sep 01 p.14, Apr 01 p.7, May 99 p.3.)

Suggestions if driving in Mexico.
Don't drive at night. Dusk and dark are the worst times for hitting black cows and brown burros.

Mexico has fewer accidents than U.S. or Canada, and most are fender-benders. During 4 months in Mexico, Liz and I saw only one accident; whereas during 6 days in Texas we saw two, including a high-speed collision that destroyed two cars and several people (two ambulances in attendance). I would rather drive in Mexico than the U.S. Most Mexican drivers are very good defensively. They survive by remaining aware of what goes around them; always on the lookout for the unexpected.

Mexican drivers seem to do as they please. Laws are used only in law courts. Because, under Mexico's Napoleonic Code, you are assumed guilty, it seems laws are made to be broken.

Newer buses often display a 95 km/hr sign. Any good bus driver knows that is the minimum speed expected. No one stops at railway crossings. They merely reduce speed, look, and keep going. Some crossings are topes (speed bumps) in disguise.

Every village has at least one pair of the dreaded topes, 10 to 15 cm high, approx a metre wide, and usually all the way across a road. They can be of concrete, blacktop, bricks, or shiny steel hemispheres. If you don't slow to a crawl, they will tear your suspension apart. As warnings, there MIGHT be official highway signs showing 2 or 3 bumps, or handpainted boards (probably put there by local victims) saying TOPES. Other indications that topes are near: "40 km/hr maximo" (almost certain); "65 km/hr maximo" (probable); sounds of trucks accelerating; sign with village name; rocks piled on sides of road (to prevent going around topes); people selling items on side of highway (they stand where vehicles go slow).

On highways, when a truck in front of you turns on his left signal light, it means it is safe to pass if you are not being passed and you are quick. Whereas, in cities when the same driver signals left, it means he is going to turn left. Sometimes drivers forget where they are or forget to signal.

Highways are well marked, with numerous directional signs at intersections. And there are lots of km-to-go signs - except when you are low on gas. Getting lost in cities is easy; just follow your map or rusted detour signs. Mexicans don't take down detour signs - maybe they will be needed again. If you get a map, get a good one that shows all of the streets. Don't worry about being able to read the street names; you won't find the faded street signs because they've been painted over, fell off, or are hidden behind trees.

Canadian and U.S. auto insurance is of no value south of the Mex border. You don't need insurance in Mexico but it is a gamble: save money and drive carefully, vs have an accident and go to jail. The first time we went to Mexico, we got Mex insurance; the second time we didn't bother. John & Liz Plaxton (from "RVing in Mexico & C.Am", Faraway, 1996; sent by Bruce)

(Comments by Bruce:) Starting from Kelowna BC, John & Liz visited Mexico in 1994/95, in a Class C Motorhome, and on a 305 cc motorcycle. Before going, they'd had only 20 hrs of Spanish lessons and no understanding of Spanish phonetics.

After reading Michael Trend's short letter (good tips) in Ab #3, I looked at guide books available. One of the best was Lonely Planet's "Mexico", 8th edition. It had articles on cycling, train travel, hostels, lesser-known cities/towns, and other info not in Frommers and other big-name guide books. Also recommended: "The People's Guide to RV Camping in Mexico" Carl Franz; Travelers Guide to Mexican Camping" Mike and Terri

Dwelling Portably   April 2005

Church; "Nothing to Declare" (woman travels alone)Mary Morris.
Mexican beaches are considered public property. You can
camp for nothing at most of them, but security non-existant.
Cabanas are basically huts with palm-thatch roofs. Some
have dirt floors and nothing inside but a bed. Others have
electric lights, bug nets, frig, fan. Rentals, $10-$35 U.S.

Hitchiking and busing in Mexico.

I had reached San Francisco before realizing that I had
forgotten to bring my passport. I called my roomates in
Portland, but their search was unsuccessful, so I entered
Mexico without it. Just across the border, I tried to get a
tourist visa. The immigration officer would not accept my
drivers license. He wanted a passport or birth certificate.
Finally he accepted a photocopy of an expired passport (which
I had along because it showed me with long hair). 90-day visa.
I met up with Andy a week later in Xalapa, Veracruz. We
planned to hitchike through Veracruz, then to Chiapas (Andy's
plan) or to Yucatan (my plan). Andy nixed my plan by inform-
ing me that the Yucatan Penisula was, not the endless jungle
I had imagined, but a hot dry plateau. Though this was my
third year in Mexico, I had never read far enough in any
travel guide to rid me of my misconceptions.
Andy and I bussed to the edge of Xalapa. For hitching,
we picked a bad fake-out spot where we thought people were
pulling over for us only to realize they were turning onto a
gravel road 50 feet past us. I was strumming my jarana,
hoping people would be more likely to pick up a musician.
Four hours passed before a semi-truck heading for the
port of Veracruz picked us up. The truck had poor suspension,
bouncing us up and down on the bed behind the driver and
co-pilot. He asked me to play a song, but I was jerked around
so much that my hand kept missing the strings. Three hours
later, we got off at intersection with south-bound highway.
It was early afternoon. We had chosen to avoid the four-
lane behemoth, and were on a two-lane highway that rolled down
the coast. No rides ! At sunset I decided that all the
stories I'd heard about ease of hitching in Mexico were bull.
It's not any easier than in the U.S. It's just wait, wait,
wait, ride, wait. Fortunately there is a difference between
the U.S. and less-affluent countries. In the U.S., if you find
yourself on I-5 at sunset halfway between nowhere and somewhere,
you are stranded. You can sit in an all-night gas station
drinking coffee and asking customers for rides. Or you can
sleep in a field next to the highway. Whereas in Mexico, where
busses are most peoples' transportation, you can flag down the
next one and keep traveling - until your money runs out.
I'd been on that highway before and knew that it came to
the beach about 30 km ahead. So I suggested we bus it, spend
the night on the beach, and resume hitching in the morning.
At sunrise, we swam in the brownish-blue water of the Gulf
of Mexico before returning to the highway. The day was hot and
there were no trees for shade. We waited 5 hours for our first
ride, with a quiet friendly grain salesman in a VW bug.
Unfortunately, he was only going 60 km. The area we passed
through, Los Tuxtlas, became an incredibly green patchwork of
plantations: coffee, tobacco, banana. Our next ride was with
an old man who just pointed at the back of his truck and said
get in. It was a tall wood-slat-sided truck; the kind used
to haul pigs or a heap of used tires. After we were in back,
he seemed to forget about us. He stopped along the way to chat

with people in small towns. He even stopped for dinner at a
restaurant without bothering to let us out. Sometime after
dark, I had to jump from my sleeping bag and move out of the
way as he hoisted a refrigerator into the truck with us.
    We landed inside the city of Coatzacoalcos late at night.
By then, I was tired of hitching and frustrated with our snails
pace, so I told Andy I wasn't about to spend 3 more days on the
side of the highway just to save $12 bus fare. He wanted to
keep at it, but that also meant finding a place to sleep for
the night, so he gave in and we hopped on a bus toward Palenque.
(From a zine by Skot, ±2002. The author may be Michael Cabello
who had a long report in Apr 01 DP. From Chile, bi-lingual.)

A short freight hop as a learning experience.
    I chose the evening of Thursday, 4 July 03, to embark on
an adventure in the spirit of those who, for me, are some of
North America's greatest heros: the truly tough men and women
who sleep under bridges, work for minimum wages - and think for
themselves. My home town, Peterborough, is on a hundred-mile-
long branch line of the Canadian Pacific that goes from Toronto
in the west to the end of the line at Havelock in the east.
Enough volume is shipped to warrant an out-and-back train from
Toronto almost every day. There is no set schedule, but for a
few weeks prior to my trip I had payed close attention to when
trains were moving and in what direction. I had Friday off
work, and thus had time to ride a train and return home in time
for work Sat morning. Late Thursday night seemed a good time
to catch an eastbound, and I knew from experience that trains
travel very slowly through Peterborough, especially at night
when they don't whistle for crossings. If nothing came during
the night, I would wait until noon, sleeping near the tracks.
    At 11 pm I bicycled downtown, locked my bike at a grocery
store near the old station, and wandered around for a while,
finally settling down on a bench by the river to read (always
bring a book). When I became sleepy, I checked the most obvious
spot first: in the bushes near a bridge. TOO obvious. The
cardboard that I could barely see in the dark was already
occupied by some other tramp, who was invisible until I was
almost sitting on him. A quick apology and I was on my way, to
what turned out to be a better spot, near the station, which
would allow me to climb the train from the old platform. So
it was that I fell asleep in the bushes beside Jackson Creek,
across from the station, my bag tucked under my arm.
    I had slept about an hour when my rumbling ride came
along. As I stood up I saw the three bright lights of a freight
engine. It was moving very slowly and I was close, so I stayed
where I was until the engine units passed. Then I ran across
the small bridge to the station platform as the train was
passing it, grabbed a ladder, and climbed. Did I use one hand
or two ? Which foot went first ? Did I get on the grainer
platform from the side or the back ? I don't remember. I did
it all instinctively, making me think I was born to do this.
    An auto was at the first road crossing (about 25 metres
from my catch point), and the driver likely saw me settling in,
but that did not worry me. As we rolled across the Otonabee
River bridge, I became aware that I was on the 'wrong' end of
the grainer - where all the air brake equipment is; the result
of my 'just get on the damn thing' haste. And it was the FIRST
car behind the two engine units, causing me to worry that the
car might be set off at a siding. But I had not known what cars
might be behind. Fortunately, the train went unbroken.
                    Dwelling Portably   April 2005

Freight hoppers say that most rail workers are friendly, and Peterborough and Havelock seemed unlikely to have bulls. Even so, I hid inside the cubby hole with some old rags as we crossed the swing bridge over the Trent-Severn Canal. The railway usually sends someone by road to turn the bridge just before and after the train passes, which allows boats to pass through most of the time. I did not want to be visible to the bridge swinger. Turned out, this was not a problem.

As we rolled past the siding at the east end of town, the train's slow speed made me think it might drop off cars. So I wore my pack and leaned out the side of the car, watching for anyone to climb down from the engine. I repeated this a few times during the trip; I was prepared to bail out if it seemed like anyone might see me. Finally, the train picked up speed.

I settled in for the ride and relaxed. The floor of the grainer was a safe spot to leave my bag, with no worry of it bouncing out onto the tracks. The compressor made a pretty good seat, although I wasn't sure how safe it was to leave my feet down among all the steel bars and lines.

I had wondered how loud the train would be. My only previous experience was riding a flat car for three days in Mexico (with the bull's permission). Noise had not been a problem there. But down by the wheels between two empty grainers, earplugs are a great asset. Every once in a while I took them off to hear the roar and clatter of steel.

The urban fog of light was left behind, revealing a cloudless night full of stars. Farms went by at 30 miles per hour, seeming fantastic. Grade crossings flash by, some lit, others dark. The whistle wails regardless. We cross rivers. The old grain elevator at Indian River siding stands somberly in the dark, a reminder of days before trucks. And out from behind it, like a fire on the horizon, the moon is climbing orange and crescent through the trees. As the train slows once again, I climb to the top of the car to take in this festival of light: to the left, the Big Dipper and Belt of Orion. Out in front, the trees illuminated by the headlights. They light up a power line suspended across the track; reminding me that being up that high is not a good idea, although that line had ample clearance. As the train swayed from side to side, I climbed back down to the safety of the platform.

The only town on the way to Havelock is Norwood. We barely slow: apparently the residents don't mind the sounds as we whistle and roar past, crossing the main street on an overpass. Soon after, highway 7 curves in parallel to the rails. Little traffic: a few late-night trucks. One passes, slightly faster.

We slow as Havelock approaches. As the train comes to a stop for the brakeman to throw a switch, I disembark. No sense riding into the yard; though little chance of being caught.

I settle down in some long grass. I hope a train will leave for Toronto early in the morning. That would provide a good opportunity for photos; I didn't take any at night. But the crew slept until ten, then bumped cars around for an hour, then headed north to the mines at Nephton. Fortunately I got a ride home with an acquaintance working in Havelock. Sloth (www.northbankfred.com/sloth2.html , sent by Bruce of BC)

Personal rail-vehicles are much used in Columbia.
Some railroads have stopped running trains but, like in U.S., the tracks are often left in place. Two sizes of rail-vehicles were shown on Mexican TV.
A small one holds two people. A long pole is used to push

it along. It is light enough for two people to remove it from
the tracks if it meets another rail vehicle.
    A big one can carry 8 people or considerable cargo. It
rides on 4 metal wheels. To propel it, a motorcycle is mounted
so its rear wheel rests on the track. A 125cc engine suffices
because it travels slow, 15 or 20 mph max. It has the right-
of-way if it meets a smaller rail-vehicle. If used as bus,
fare for a 20-mile ride is about $1 U.S. Herbert Diaz, CA 939,
                                                        Sep04
Rides unicycle in places where bicycles can't go.
    Tom Acevedo starts at the foot of Mary's Peak southwest of
Philomath and wheels all the way to the top; then all the way
back down. "It's called the 'evil trail' because there are
lots of rocks and tree roots, and most of it is steep." Even
some mountain bicyclists fear it. Tom unicycles every day,
rain or shine. "I go out in McDonald Forest mostly and also on
the Bald Hill path and the trails in Peavy Arboretum" When he
is at the coast, he unicycled on the sand at the edge of the
water. He has also unicycled with groups in the woods behind
Fall City, in Sierras, in Utah, at Lake Tahoe. "We get on the
internet to find one another and then agree where to meet."
    Tom, age 50, has a desk job at Hewlett-Packard. He says
he was out of shape physically when he began. "At first I'd
practice for 15 minutes and then have to take a nap. I'd go
along the 3-foot-high fence in our driveway, ready to reach out
and grip it to steady myself. You do fall off when you're
learning - and afterwards too" although far less often, Knowing
how to fall is important. Protective gear helps prevent
injuries or at least lessen impacts. High-top boots provide
ankle support. Velcro keeps leg "armor" in place from ankle to
above knee. Elbow guards slip over the arm and fit snugly.
Gloves have padded leather palms. On top is a helmet.
    Tom has 5 unicycles plus parts for more. Why so many ?
The tire size determines the speed. Each tire size is for a
specific use and terrain. The bigger the tire, the shorter the
cranks. If too short, you can't stop yourself easily.
    The 36-inch-diameter 2¼-inch-wide Coker pneumatic tire is
for level trails. It can go faster than a person can run. But
Tom tries to keep it under 15 mph (it has brakes) so that he can
dismount by slipping forward off the seat and running.
    "This next one is my favorite. It's got hydraulic brakes,
a Yuni frame, and an inner tube in the seat for more comfort.
It has a 26" tire that is 3" wide. It is for mountain trails,
and can go through gravel and on grass and in places where
bicycles can't go. I can hop around on it like you do on a pogo
stick." And he does. Gloria Clark (Northwest Senior News, Aug
(Comment:) This article was much more informative than was 04)
the one from Atlantic Monthly in April 04 DP. Apparently the
wheel is direct drive, like on old-time high-wheel bicycles.
No gears. To change speed range, you change unicycles ! B & H

I lived on the water for 18 months - free.
    Free boats. (I even turned down a 35-foot motor boat.)
Free mooring - friends let me tie up to them. I like being on
the water. I met the Floating Neutrinos (who crossed Atlantic
Ocean in a boat built entirely of salvaged materials). They
make rafts, boats, docks out of free recycled materials. I've
done it too, and so have others. Basically: Get materials
that float (foam, plastic bottles, etc). Encase them (in fish-
nets, scrap wood, etc). Build on top of it. Zalia, OR 972
            Dwelling Portably   April 2005

Choosing a boat for transportation or living on.
Select your boat for the type of activity you intend, the kind of water in which it will operate, the speed you will require, and the sleeping/cooking accomodations you will need. Keep your needs in mind when you look at or discuss boats.
Three general types of boats: open boats with no accomodations which may be used for fishing or water skiing; semi-enclosed boats with minimal accomodations for two people; fully-enclosed hulls you can live in. Visualize your trips. How long will you be on the water ? How many people aboard ? Thorough planning increases your chances of filling your needs.
Long-distance sailboats are designed differently than powerboats. They have slow displacement-speed hulls. For ocean crossings, a sailboat with auxillary engine and adequate accomodations is generally best. Endurance races across oceans have involved both monohulls and multihulls. Much can be learned from these demonstrations of strong hulls and stronger crews, but don't choose a boat designed for racing unless racing will be your primary activity.
Most sailboats are sloop rigged, because one mast is less expensive than two. However, for long-distance cruising, some owners prefer a ketch rig (two masts) because, when wind speed increases, they can furl (roll in) the mainsail and proceed at optimum speed without excessive heel (tilt).
The longer the boat, the more comforts it can accomodate, but the more expensive it will be to buy and operate. Where will you keep your boat ? What are the fees ? If the dock is in a shallow waterway, the boat must be shallow draft. Deep-keel ballasted sailboats are often restricted to deep water-ways that have no bridges that would slow access to the ocean.
A fishing boat for protected waters is usually a small open boat with helm (controls) in the center or at bow so that most of the deck is open to walk around on while boarding a fish. But if going well offshore to fish, you will want a different hull. Suitable boats usually have part of the forward half fully enclosed and watertight so that water blown aboard will be deflected and not swamp the boat. A deep V (high deadrise) power boat is probably best for ocean fishing.
If you plan scuba diving, the aft deck should have a transom (swim) platform or a sloped ramp for easy access to the water. Secure storage must be installed for air bottles, regulators, wet suits. The forward half usually contains helm, seating, galley, head. Arthur Edmonds (from summary/ad for book "Buying a Great Boat", Bristol, off internet, from Bruce)
(Comment:) Used boats, usually in need of repairs, are some-times offered cheap or free because the owners have no place to put them. However, regardless of price, a boat (or any item) is no bargain if it is not what you need. Holly & Bert

Some rivers are suitable for secluded houseboats.

The floodlands and bayous of the Mississippi River and its larger tributaries comprise thousands of acres, mostly uninhabited and perhaps unowned. Many other rivers in at least 20 states include such areas. Rarely traversed by humans; the only visitors are hunters, fishers, trappers, surveyors and engineers working on the river, biologists studying the plants and animals, an occasional posse, some adventurous explorers, and refugees from the rat-race.
Rivers frequently change course, devouring old land and creating new land that is unregistered and perhaps unknown. Boundaries are usually vague. A close study of county records

and maps may reveal bits of land that nobody owns or that have
been forgotten. Or, you might find a sizable mud bar left by
a flood or channel-change, transplant willows and bushes onto
it, seed it with edible weeds, riprap the up-current end with
rocks so it won't wash away in the next flood, A new island !
    Many sloughs are perfect for living: deep enough for big
fish to lurk, and for mosquitos not to breed; and with enough
level fairly-clear land for a garden, plus gathering grounds
for wild fruits, berries, nuts, greens, etc.
    Lost and wild animals live in those lands: horses, mules,
cows, goats, fowls that have wandered or been abandoned, or
lost from shipments or swept down the river and never found.
If the creatures give birth, the young grow up feral and not
owned. Some big predators live there and are seldom hunted
because travel is difficult. Snapping turtles grow as big as
wash tubs and can grab an adult bird swimming on the surface.
In some places are alligators and alligator gar big enough to
kill a cow or human. Ocean sharks sometimes swim up fresh-
water rivers for hundreds of miles, and may remain in fresh-
water lakes. Reportedly seen in remote places are 3-foot-tall
red-furred primates that live in small families. They are
primarily vegetarian and very secretive.
    The riverbanks and floodplains are littered with debris
from many floods: logs, planks, boards, boxes, small buildings,
entire walls of houses with doors and windows, boats, chicken
coops, pianos, light machinery attached to work tables, and
anything else that will float. A shanty boat or small cottage
can be built and furnished entirely from free findings.
    A raft can be built by lashing together logs or timbers.
For more floatation, lash empty sealed 50-gallon drums under it.
To replace lost caps, drive wooden plugs into holes. Tar or
paint the timbers and drums heavily and often to prevent rot
and rust. Also tar the drums inside after thoroughly drying
them, by pouring in thinned hot tar and rolling the drums
around. Build a deck out of boards, and on that build a shack
or rig a tent. Leave part of the deck vacant for sunning and
fishing, and for maneuvering the raft.
    At first, furnish your floating home with anything close
at hand. Then, as you have time, search for better furniture.
Walk along the high-water marks, indicated by small stuff
deposited in bushes and tree branches which catch an amazing
variety of items including many clothes. Look in the trees
where high water may leave chairs and tables. Look in backwater driftwood piles for heavier objects which may be half-
buried in mud. Metal objects heavier than water will be on the
bottom, often in bedrock cracks or whirlpool holes where they
were left when the swift currents that were rolling them, slow.
If you can spot the natural eddies and backwaters of the
various water levels, you will discover frequently replenished
treasure troves. But test mud and sand before stepping on it.
Some that looks solid will suddenly drop you in over your head.
When exploring a new bar, esp one under water, carry a long
long pole to arrest your plunge and help you scramble out.
    A shantyboat, carefully situated and tied among the bushes,
may never be seen even by boaters. Keep your home small and
unobtrusive, either naturally weathered or painted a drab color.
Don't attract attention. Most people won't bother you even if
they find you. Don't leave obviously illegal items in sight.
Check laws before hanging fish, crayfish, turtle (etc) traps.
    Many river people use a big rock as an anchor. Do not
anchor in the current: waterlogged tree trunks may roll down

the bottom and roll over your anchor line, pulling your craft
under water if your anchor line doesn't break first. The
water level will rise and fall, and could deposit your boat on
land. Listen to weather and water-release reports on radio.
There are several ways to move if you want to. Use sweeps
(very long oars) which can be just wide boards bolted to 2-by-
4s which are mounted on 4-by-4s attached to the sides of boat.
Or, in shallow water, you can pole. If the bottom is rock
or gravel, shod one end of pole with sharp-pointed metal. Or,
if the bottom is mud, attach a flat board: hinged on the end
and braced so it opens to give broader traction when pushing,
but folds when the pole is pulled from the muck.
    Or, walk along the bank pulling the boat by ropes attached
to bow and stern. If moving upstream, a pull on the stern rope
steers the boat away from the bank; a pull on the bow rope
steers the boat toward the bank. Even pulls on both ropes keep
the boat moving. A few minutes practice will teach you.
    For low speeds and short distances, a motor is probably
too much trouble. Fuel, repairs, noise, licensing, rules.
    Controlled drifting is usually safe IF you know what is
ahead. Drifting when unaware, as from a broken or cut anchor
line at night, can be very dangerous. You can be tipped over
by an obstruction, stranded in mud, set on a bar, tangled in
down trees, wrecked in rapids, or swept over a dam. Useful to
have a government-survey river map.
    The water will probably be contaminated. Boiling will not
remove toxic chemicals. Nor will iodine or chlorine. A
reverse-osmosis filter will clean anything, including ocean
water, and is even better than distillation. Read carefully
the spec sheet that comes with the filter. Paul Doerr (much
condensed from Doe #49, 2002)
    (Comments:) Many years ago, Paul traveled on his boat all the
way from the East to the West Coast. Paul did not say how much
and how recently he has lived on floodlands or bayous.
    What does a river dweller do when a flood comes ? Perhaps
if the flood isn't sudden, as the river rises and nearby land
is submerged, s/he can keep moving the boat away from the
increasingly swift currents in main channels; then, as the
flood recedes, do the reverse - though might get stranded. B&H

Trouble in Seattle's "Jungle".
    For a while, Franz Dyduch considered the homeless camped
near his house, in the densely-wooded strip known as The Jungle,
to be his neighbors. He fed their dogs and drank beer around
their campfires. But in January the relationship began to sour.
His home was burglarized weekly. When his daughter admonished
the campers, she was pelted with rocks, and one morning she
found human feces outside her dad's door. She attributes her
84-year-old father's fatal heart attack in April to the stress.
"We've had homeless people who've been delightful neighbors for
years, but they were different from the trash that harassed
them and chased them out ... and took over." Others reported
seeing open drug dealing, needles on school playgrounds.
    The anger peaked in August with a series of burglaries.
One resident came home to find a strange woman in her living
room, filling bags with loot. The two fought before the
burglar fled into the Jungle. Outraged neighbors armed with
baseball bats descended on the Jungle but left without fighting.
    Shannon Mills lost birth certificates, passports, check-
books in a burglary. Worried about being the victim of
identity theft, she joined a neighborhood group that organized

citizen patrols. She makes a distinction: the homeless people are "not the ones breaking into our houses and stealing our stuff. It's the criminal element that are ruining The Jungle."
The Jungle has inspired controversy and brief hassles for a decade. But a rising volume of complaints prompted the city to launch a sustained assault. The estimated 80 Jungle residents were given 24 hours notice to leave. Then state crews mowed acres of underbrush to expose encampments. New roads are being cut and graveled through The Jungle, allowing police cruisers to patrol the area.
A similar assault in 1998 provoked noisy protests. But last month's eviction came as a surprise. Rev. Rick Reynolds, director of Operation Nightwatch, sees it as evidence of a "meaner mood" in tolerant Seattle. "I'd like to know where they're supposed to go. They're not going to be able to (find space) in the shelter system, and most don't have resources to rent apartments. The pattern in big cities is: who can be the meanest and shove them onto someplace else."
A city liaison person claimed, "This is not a campaign on the homeless. We wouldn't even be here if they treated the environment and the neighbors with respect."
Joe Doney lived in The Jungle in the mid 1990s during another city assault. He found a cohesive community of people who took turns guarding each other's belongings. The city is "swatting the beehive. They are scattering the people."
Last week, a handful had returned to the section north of Beacon Avenue South. Complaints from neighborhoods abutting I-5 green space to the north are on the rise, including the foot of Capitol Hill and University District.
A police sargent said, the police are stretched too thin to issue reams of trespass violations. There have been "home-invasion burglaries. That's the type of crime we go after. Trespass is way way down the list." Jonathan Martin (from Seattle Times 19 October 2003, sent by Roger Knights)

(Comments:) The problems mentioned are mostly CAUSED BY GOVERNMENTS that criminalize drugs (as well as low-cost housing). Most burglaries are to pay for drugs. If drugs were legal, addicts could get enough money by (eg) collecting drink cans.
I read: a century ago, before the War On (some) Drugs, heroin was sold by drug stores; price about the same as aspirin. But there were FEWER addicts than now, because there were not huge profits and strong incentives to hook more people.
Solutions ? Don't expect governments (which are, first and foremost, giant terrorist gangs) to do much if anything that is truly helpful. Instead, avoid or minimize time in big cities and other places exposed to bullies (whether in uniforms or not). Spread out, and have as neighbors only compatables.

Some Wal-Marts no longer allow over-nighting in parking lots.
Many Wal-Marts long had an unofficial policy of letting RVs and others   over-night, assuming that stay-overs will buy stuff. We suspect the privilege is rescinded because of abuse. We saw a rig pull in, drop its levelers, open the awning, unhook a towed car - and leave to shop at another store ! Others park by the front door and hog several spaces. Others stay out of the way but seem to live there permanently.
Some Wal-Marts are in shopping centers not owned by Wal-Mart. They never allowed over-nighting. RVers who tried, were chased off by security thugs or, worse, had their rigs towed.
When we want to stay over at a shopping plaza, if there isn't a mall manager, we try to ask the manager of the lead

store. If they say "no", we simply go to another place. But they almost always say "yes", as they're not often asked. John & Rose Ward (from Living Mobile 3-04)

We have lived in various RVs and buses.
Now Millie and I are busy converting our third bus. Soon it will be our full-time rolling home. We have loved and used alternative energy systems for many years.

Our previous bus-home didn't have much: just two medium-size solar panels, a charge controller, and three big truck batteries. It worked fine in our situation then. But, if you are going to spend much time in the boondocks and want to be really comfortable and self sufficient, you need more.

For our new bus, we have a hefty array of four Uni-Solar panels (two 64 watt, two 22 watt), an Air-X Southwest wind-power generator, a solar hot-water pre-heating system, a composting toilet, a grey-water purification system, two solar air heaters, dual inverter system, solar oven, and other things.

We chose this system, instead of a typical mass-produced RV, because we like to travel but also like to be able to squat and live comfortably in one spot for a couple of months at a time. Our ideal situation is renting or land-sitting a place out in the country, which is usually quite a ways from the nearest RV dump station and electrical plug-in.

Millie and I don't like to stay long in campgrounds. That gets pretty expensive. More important, campgrounds are often noisy. We prefer being out in the country somewhere pretty.

A more important reason for our many alternative energy systems: we expect RISING COSTS for camping. Not just camp-ground fees, but also dump station fees and propane costs. Dumping your holding tanks will get more expensive: many septic systems are overloaded; many cities and rural areas are having a problem handling all the sewage.

Electricity costs are rising too. WHEN (not if) California or other state has major black-outs/brown-outs again, the state will care more about its voters and their TVs and air-conditioners than about transient RVers. We can expect new legislation penalizing so-called recreational use of electricity in campgrounds during an emergency. We might be charged outrageous fees - or might not even be allowed to plug in.

Rather than bitch and moan after the fact, we can do something about it now. By adding a composting toilet to your rig, you avoid the hassle and growing cost of dumping a black-water tank. By having a realistic hybrid solar/wind system, you only plug in when you want to, not out of need. For water conservation, add a rain water collection system.

Upgrading our system is easy in our bus - in comparison to a "normal" house where they sometimes have to knock down walls and split open concrete floors. Forward thinking helps.

With our new systems, we only have to replenish propane, water, food. Our bus carries at least a month's supply of food at a time, and we never camp far from a water source. We are able to purify water from a stream or creek.

We will pre-heat our water using a solar system, which cuts propane consumption amazingly. We can use this water directly or, if we want it hotter, send it through our ten-gallon Atwood RV Hot Water Heater. When the sun is out, even in winter we can bake and cook using our Global Sun Oven. We have a Danby Consul Propane frig/freezer; efficient.

To warm our bus, we have a wall-mounted catalytic propane heater and a little stainless-steel wall-mounted Dickenson

wood stove. It doesn't take up much room but is big enough to
heat our bus. It gets out the condensation that builds up in
a well-sealed RV that uses propane as its main heat source.
   We will add a solar air heating system. They are easy to
build, or you can buy pre-made. They are basically a rectangular box that is layered and covered with a suitable clear
plastic or solar glass. They can either be mounted permanently
on a vehicle's exterior, or designed to be taken off and stored
for the summer. They work by thermal convection: taking air
from inside the vehicle and passing it through the box where it
is warmed by solar radiation. They quickly pay for themselves.
   A system like ours isn't cheap. So far we have $8500
invested. But this kind of system allows you to camp comfortably in the middle of nowhere and be as self-sufficient as
possible. You can put such a system together a piece at a
time. But, if you can afford it, do it all at once. A big
retrofit job can get messy. Michael and Millie (Sent by Bruce,
off internet but no web addr. The Mobile Homestead, POB 6584,
(Comments:) Amazing - all the stuff they think Sitka AK 99835)
they need to be comfortable. Some seems sensible: the solar
items if they usually park where there is sun. A composting
system may be worthwhile if someone is stationary enough to
garden (see Ab #4). But carry it around on a bus ? Sanitary
disposal of human waste is usually quite simple - especially
in the middle of no-where (see May 96 DP).
   Michael and Millie expect grid electricity to become very
costly or hard to get. But propane, along with diesel fuel
and gasoline, will likely become even more scarce and costly.
There are more and easier ways to generate grid electricity
than to extract or synthesize liquid and gas fuels. B & H

The "heat-resistant silicone rubber cement" is a special type.
   (It was mentioned in April 04 DP, p.10.) It's called
"RTV Silicone". Sold by auto parts stores and auto section of
Walmart, etc. Comes in black, red, blue, clear. Zalia, Apr04

Hubbards Shoe Grease waterproofs leather well.
   I've used it on hunting boots and other leather gear.
Made in U.S. from pine tar and other ingredients. A small can
lasts me a long time. Bruce of BC, 2004

Some shipping bags useful for temporary storage of big items.
   Or even as giant sleeping bags. They have a thin paper-
like material covering a p.u.c. plastic bladder type bag.
Sizes 3 ft wide by 6 ft tall, and larger. I have occasionally
seen them left in empty box cars with air trapped in them.
They have small air valves somewhere on the outside. Just
don't get caught by a bull (cop) trying to salvage them. Bruce

Aluminized-plastic "emergency" blankets at a dollar store.
   $1.25 Cdn, made in China. I've also found tools, hard-
ware, magnifiers, reading glasses, even eyeglass repair kit.
(Question:) Were they the kind with aluminum that Bruce
easily rubs off the plastic ? Or more durable ? I'd like to
try such material on solar cookers in place of aluminum foil.

I find many uses for disposable plastic gloves outdoors.
   Such as picking up greasy or sooty things around camp.
Although not as tough as latex or nylon disposables, they are
adequate for many jobs. I go through many pairs a month.
At a dollar store I bought 60 pairs for $1.25. Bruce of BC

Dwelling Portably

or Shared, Mobile, Improvised
Underground, Hidden, Floating

Sept 2005 $1 per issue   POB 190-d, Philomath OR 97370

Clothes pins have many uses besides hanging clothes.
Eg: clamping glued pieces together while the glue hardens;
holding fabric while sewing; temporarily holding a cord in
place (may be quicker than tieing and untieing a knot); hanging
messages on lines where there is no bulletin board; holding
open a curtain or drape; closing plastic bags containing things
I want to access often, or quicker than a rubber band allows;
serving as extra hands while doing complex tasks.
        I keep several clothes pins within sight in my living/
working area, so they are accessible, and so they may remind me
that I have what I need. Julie Summers, 1999

(Addendum:) If a stronger grip is needed than the clothes
pin's spring provides, after I put on the clothes pin, I wind a
thin rubber strap (cut from innertube) or long rubber band
several times around clothes pin between its pivot and jaws.
        I sometimes do this when tieing out a plastic tarp, to
grip its edge without bunching it (as does a ball tie, and to a
lesser extent the grip-clips sold). I roll the tarp several
times around a twig, grip that with a spring clothes pin,
strengthen grip with a rubber strap, then put the tie-out cord
through the spring. (Illo in Apr92 DP or 95-6 Summary). Bert

Vise easily improvised using a stump.
        This can firmly hold an object being worked
on, such as wood being carved or metal being filed.
        Select a stump a few inches in diameter that
is still firmly anchored in the ground (roots not
yet rotten). Split its top downward a few inches
by sawing, or by tapping with a small log on the
back of a strong knife. Spread the split with
some kind of wedge (thick knife, chisel, sharply
rock, carved stick). Insert into the split, the
object to be gripped. Remove the wedge. Tighten
the grip by winding a rubber strap many times
around the stump. (If no elastic strap, strong
cord can be substituted. To tighten, insert a
stick between one loop of the cord and the stump,
and twist the loop of cord.)
        If the object is narrow, the strap can be below it (as
shown). If the object is wide, to keep it in the split while
working on it, may be necessary to put the strap above it; in
which case, before winding on the strap, wrap a cord tightly
around the stump below the bottom of the split to prevent the
split from extending downward and weakening the grip. Bert

Northern Bush Craft, by Mors Kochanski.
        "This book is not simply a manual on wilderness camping or
survival, but rather discusses the basic existence skills that
allow you to live in the bush on an indefinite basis with
minimal dependence on technological materials and tools."
Unlike primitive-skills books devoted to stone-age methods, this
book emphasizes early iron-age methods, especially use of a
steel knife and axe. This 2nd edition is profusely illustrated
with over 300 line drawings and 34 color photos (the latter
sensibly grouped in back, minimizing printing costs).
        I highly recommend this manual to anyone who, after long
careful preparation, plans to move far back into the northern

Alberta wilderness or similar forests and seldom if ever come out. (A broad belt of Northern Forests with similar climate and plants and animals, extend across Canada and curve south into U.S.)

Much of the contents are not too relevant to people like us who are usually within a few-days hike/bike of a sizable city. However, almost anyone will find info that is useful at times. One risk: some readers could get so fascinated by bush crafts as art, that they neglect methods that are less impressive but more practical in their situations.

Of most interest to us, was the chapter on saws, the book's shortest (10 pages). "The saw and axe are complementary." The axe is more hazardous, "requiring experience and constant attentiveness to use safely" - esp dangerous after dark. Whereas a saw may be used by a blind person for many jobs. "The axe takes weeks of constant use to master, whereas the saw requires a few hours...." Most of the work is done with the saw; the axe is back-up. Limbing is easier with the axe. "Wedges are easily made and pounded in with an axe. The axe is more versatile" and is chosen if limited to one tool.

A saw "can fall and section a tree with a fraction of the exertion" an axe requires, "and with greater convenience in confined or awkward situations, such as cutting in dense growth or above the head. With the assistance of wedges, a saw can fall a tree in directions impossible with an axe alone.... The saw can make squared ends ... or boards with a minimum of waste." A hand-powered saw is quieter than an axe. "The axe is more durable.... The cutting edge can be maintained with locally-found natural stones." A saw blade is comparitively fragile.

"A saw frame (of a bow saw) should be heavy enough to keep its blade under considerable tension." Function and durability should not be sacrificed for compactness and portability. "All saw blades should have guards to prevent cuts.... Using a saw above the head puts sawdust in the eyes.... Keep the eyes closed enough to help the eyelashes exclude the dust."

"A gently used saw will stay in working order for a long time.... Use (only) the weight of the saw at first.... As you become more skillful, you may apply downward force with the wrist of the hand holding the saw. When you can use the saw smoothly and unconsciously after having developed a sensitivity to its cutting action, you will know how much force to use to make it cut even faster.... If too much force is used, you will tire quickly. Any technique that adversely affects tooth arrangement should be avoided, such as twisting, kinking, bending, heavy pushing or pulling or downward force." Cutting close to the ground so that dirt gets into the cut, or sawing sandy driftwood, will quickly dull a blade. Sharpening gets 4 pages.

Axes get 34 pages. "The full-size axe with a handle length of about a metre is the safest as it normally deflects into the ground before reaching any part of the body." The hatchet, or short-handled axe, though the most portable, is the most dangerous. However, Mors tells how to use hatchet least riskily.

Tree falling gets 12 pages. Falling is dangerous, esp if tree is bigger than a foot diameter or crowded or dead or leaning. Many cautions given, including some I don't recall in "Professional Timber Falling" (review in June 1989 DP).

Knives and knife-sharpening get 26 pages. Knives are versatile. Eg, by bending a wrist-thick limber tree, a sharp knife can cut it in one stroke. Many tips are given for efficient use and safety. Some of the techniques shown seem risky to me unless one is very skilled and careful. Not mentioned: jury-rigging a vise to hold the wood (see p. 1).

Dwelling Portably   September 2005

Fire craft gets 60 pages. "When all else fails, fire is the simplest means of providing comfort and warmth against cold and wet in the Northern Forests. If you were dressed in the old European tradition, with numerous layers of fluffy wool adequate to deal with bitter cold, you would likely be wearing about 9 kg (20 lbs) of clothing. If you were unable to dry your clothing out, within 5 days you would be carrying 6 kg more weight of accumulated frost. The efficiency of your clothing would be so impaired by this frost build-up you could die of hypothermia within a week." Not mentioned: wearing a vapor barrier to keep body moisture out of the clothing. A big plastic bag, with holes cut for neck and arms, may suffice. For comfort I wear it over the inner layer; not next to skin.

"When you stop moving in cold weather, the first thought should be to light a fire. Your hands should not be allowed to become so numb that fire-lighting becomes difficult...." Bow drills get 14 pages, flint and steel 4 pages, matches one page. (Not mentioned: propane lighters; big flexible plastic lens, which can ignite even damp tinder quite quickly - but you do need some sun.) Kindlings get 10 pages; fire arrangements 7 pages. For most uses, esp for warmth with an open-fronted shelter, Mors prefers a fire with logs laid parallel. However, if the only fuel is long poles and you lack a saw or axe to cut them, or if a fire is wanted only for cooking, cross the poles in a star array and light them where they cross. Pot support gets 8 pages; cooking 12 pages.

Fire safety gets 5 pages. "A common, though unnecessary practice, is to ring open fires with stones", believing that "the stones confine the fire and make it safer; yet many forest fires are in fact traced to such fireplaces." When the fire is extinguished, "stones that are not moved aside can harbour hot spots... There are, however, justifiable uses of stones in a fire: to store warmth in a closed shelter; to support pots when no other means are available." Not mentioned: rocks provide a low wind break, so that gusts are less likely to scatter glowing embers. With any fire, unless roots are removed from soil or the soil is very damp, combustion may spread through underground roots that act like fuses.

Making cord from natural materials gets 12 pages. "The time and effort in making a cord should be matched to its intended use. A quickly and crudely made grass rope will do as a lashing in shelter building. A carefully and precisely twisted bow string may take hours to make."

Shelters get 34 pages. Most are open-fronted, used with a fire in front. To be effective, "the occupant must sleep parallel to a fire that is as long as he is tall. The back of the shelter must be near enough to the fire to be warmed by it" and very close to occupant to prevent cold air infiltrating between occupant and shelter. "The bed, the fire, and the wind must be parallel to each other" so that the smoke blows away instead of blowing or eddying into the shelter.

"The proper management of a fire in front of an open shelter demands constant attention resulting in relatively short periods of rest.... Whatever needs to be warmed must be positioned close to the fire and exposed directly to the radiation. Any warmed air rises, providing little warmth...."

"The conical shelter is very efficient. It provides a large floor space in relation to the amount of cover required. The shape allows for standing room in the middle, and an easily heated low overhead volume. The design is stable in wind and useful in heavier forms of construction." Also, unlike a dome,

a cone has no flat area on which rain could puddle and then
drip through any leak; and, if big sheets are available, a cone
can easily be efficiently and snugly covered by wrapping.

"Birch bark makes an excellent cover that is reasonably
portable. It can be peeled almost all year around." Processing
birch bark gets 12 pages. Formerly, most Northern Forest
nomads used tanned hides. Felt mats were popular in some
places. "Hair or wool covers have a good reputation for being
rot resistant, insulative, rain deflective, light and durable."
Also common: "mats woven from various weeds". "In Lapland,
natural cover materials were replaced with canvas in summer and
horse blankets in winter. Now, such covers are made of durable
woven polyethylene." That was the only mention of plastics.
Plastics may have disadvantages in Northern Forests: easily
melted or ignited; not very durable; not easily repaired;
some kinds brittle when very cold. But why didn't Mors discuss
them ? Perhaps, as a Wilderness Living Skills Instructor, Mors
often leads expeditions of people who don't like the look of
plastics, especially in a wilderness setting.

Enclosed shelters get only 7 pages. Most are snow caves.
Any enclosed shelter is warmest if the entrance is well below
the sleeping level so that warmed air does not escape when the
entrance is opened. The final "ideal shelter, difficult to
achieve with wilderness materials", has a cover that is
"portable with a reflective inner lining, opaque to vision but
translucent to day light." What material ? Not said.

Useful plants of the Northern Forests get 60 pages: paper
birch, alders, white and black spruces, lodgepole and jack
pines, balsam and subalpine firs, poplars, quaking aspen,
willows, saskatoon, red osier dogwood. Ribbed baskets get 4 p.

Moose get 18 pages; varying hares 12. Anatomy, habitats,
habits; how to call, hunt, butcher, tan, and use all parts.

2nd edition 1988, 303 p.5x8, $13 cover price; Lone Pine
Publ, 414-10357-109 St, Edmonton AB T5J 1N3. (Thanks to Bruce
of BC for sending. He says there is now a 3rd ed. Revu, H&B)

I broke a Mora camp-knife blade during sub-zero cold.
I was prying on a big dry log. The knife had cost me
nothing; I'd found it two years before. But, to replace it,
I paid $14 Cdn for a new Frost knife. Both Mora and Frost
(brand) knives, made in Sweden, are often recommended on
survival web sites for value and reliability. Bruce of BC

My Swiss Army knife broke three times.
The first two times I sent it back to Switzerland (lifetime guarantee). But the third time I said "NO" ! Now I use
a stainless steel 'US' military pocket knife. Cost one-third
as much and has not broken. Zalia, OR 972, April 04

The $6 Walmart Multi Tool is not as good as a Leatherman.
But it will do 80% of what a Leatherman will; plus I can
afford to replace it if it gets lost or stolen. I have used
it to do repairs on my bicycle. Zalia, OR 972, April 04

Repairing sails without sewing.
I use heavy dacron or spectra fabric patches, plus 3M
5200 fast cure and 3M 950 seam stitch. Put a plastic sheet
under the ripped area, to work on. Wear rubber gloves. For
big repairs, enlist extra hands. Leave frayed yarns and pin
in place. Then place seam-stick "sutures" across the rip.
Apply thin beads of 5200 close to both sides of the rip

and also about a half inch inside the outside edge of the patch, all the way around. Carefully lay the patch in place, then apply firm pressure with a plastic squeegee. D.Smith, FL 322, (Comment:) Sails must withstand much force. So that method might also do tents and heavy garments. I've read, most sails are polyester, some are cotton. So, before trying to repair other fabrics, I'd test scraps or consult 3M's spec. H & B

Are ice sailboats useful for transportation ?

For a while during childhood, I lived near a sizable northern lake that froze over most winters. I recall seeing ice boats. They went much faster than water sailboats, I suppose because friction of a skate on ice is much less than friction of a hull in water. They may have been used for transportation as well as play. (When not frozen, travel to/from that lake's only city was quicker by passenger boat than by bus, even though the boat was slower, because the road went round about, while the boat went direct.) Bert, Dec 04

Precautions if traveling on ice.

Winter 1997 was a bad time to go onto ice in northeastern U.S. In January, a pair of cousins who drove onto a Maine lake, lost their 4x4 and almost their lives. A week later, a night-time father-and-son snowmobile ride across a frozen pond ended with only the son coming home. Of the approx 4000 Americans who drown each year, half of them do so in the off season. Though falls through ice accounted for only 2% of snowmobile accidents, they caused 18% of snowmobile deaths.

The surest way to reduce your risk is to know the ice. Never rely on appearance alone. Snow can camoflage thin ice, ridges can obscure cracks, open water can resemble ice in the sun's glare. Visual danger signs include slush, cracks meeting at right angles, branches frozen in the crust.

Before stepping onto ice, look for posted warnings. If none, test the ice every 15 feet with an ice chisel. If it doesn't break through, it's probably safe to walk on. Then, to determine if it is vehicle-ready, go out on foot with an ice auger, drilling small holes at 150-feet intervals where you intend to drive. One formula: vehicle weight in tons, find its square root, multiply by 4; equals minimum thickness in inches. 4" for 200 pounds, 6" for 2000, 8" for 4000.

As for when to start checking, forget the calender. In Maine, "I've seen ice in November able to hold a man and a machine, whereas last winter we never got enough ice." Temperatures should be in the low teens or lower for a solid week before you should think about walking on ice.

If you go on the ice, go with a friend, wear a whistle, avoid hip waders or boots that can fill with water, and bring 50 feet of rope. If your friend falls in, "there is nothing worse than standing there and not being able to do anything." If you fall through, remain calm - don't waste energy. You have a few minutes to get yourself out before hypothermia sets in. Tell your partner to back off. If he has a rope, rest your arms over the edge of the ice and have him throw an end to you. If not, have him find a long stick. And carry an accessible knife, screwdriver, or something else pointed to stab into the ice to help haul yourself out. Otherwise, face the direction from which you came (where the ice will probably be strongest), place your arms flat over the edge, rock yourself up and down a few times, and hoist yourself over. Then stay low and slither away fast. Paul Scott (from Men's J, Feb

A line across raging river allowed safer crossing.
      A few winters ago, to help set up and stock a base camp,
I had to repeatedly cross a small but fast-flowing river with
heavy backpack loads. The thigh-deep stream had an uneven
rocky bottom not visible through the silt-laden water.
      During low water of autumn, I had scouted a shallow place
and rigged twine across. I had only hay-twine, used. I chose
unfrayed pieces, not yet cut, or else cut with the knot (from
hay bailing) at one end. I tied them together using the hitch
(in Oct94 DP and Summary) that doesn't weaken twine much.
I tied two lengths of the twine (for redundancy), separately
but adjacent, to trees on opposite sides approx ten yards back
from the banks. I put the twine quite high so that any snags
being swept down stream would hopefully not catch on it.
      Just before crossing, I slacked the twine, so I could
cross a few yards downstream of the anchor trees, to put less
stress on the twine. I removed pants, but left on tennies and
let them get wet. I held the twine on my downstream side so,
if I lost hold, the twine would remain within reach. I kept
my feet spread apart upstream-downstream, and braced myself
fore-aft by keeping tension on the fore twine - facing toward
the anchor tree I was approaching.
      If I had not prepared twine, I might have tied a longer
line to one tree and crossed farther downstream. Bert, OR 973

I use a fishing pole as a bicycle flag pole.
      If it hits (eg) an overhead branch, it gives and bends
instead of breaking - and it is also usable for fishing.
I attach the pole to the bike with hose clamps, or insert it
into an aluminum tube (doesn't rust) attached to bike rack.
I tie on more than one flag, streamer, windsock for extra
visibility and safety. I've used fishing poles this way since
                                                  1985. Zalia
I have caught long rides on tractor-trailer flatbeds.
      I sneak on and hide under tarps that were loose or not
snugged down. I mostly do this at night. I have never been
caught, but I don't do it often. Bruce of BC, 2004

I built a big horse-drawn caravan for $1500.
      My old gypsy caravan, in which I had lived for 14 years,
was only 8 feet long. Over half of that was occupied by a full
size bed. With my daily cheese-making and cooking, it was very
crowded. So I was ready for something larger.
      I already had wagon running gear ($350) to build on. So,
when in March 03 I sold some goats (3 milkers, a buck, 9 kids)
for $500, I invested the money in lumber, plywood, and iron
supports. Later I spent about $600 for paint, trim, insulation,
etc. So I now have a light-weight easy-pulling (rubber tires)
wagon that will house me for many years to come. The horses
and harness are worth about twice that. Thus, for the cost of
a used car, a person could build a caravan and never again pay
rent, license, registration, insurance.
      My new caravan is 12 feet long. With the same size bed,
it has over twice the kitchen area. This spring I am adding a
solar panel and fluorescent lights. Bear, ID 832, May 04

A year caretaking; then back on the back roads.
      In June 2003, I drove my new caravan about 200 miles along
the same route as my 02 trip (see Dec 03 DP). While on the
Salmon River I met a man who needed a caretaker for his remote
ranch. Good caretaking jobs are sometimes hard to find. This
                  Dwelling Portably   September 2005

job found me because of my caravan. People just have to stop
and talk to the weird guy driving horses in the wrong century.
This ranch is the place I've been looking for. It has a
good road to haul hay in on, but is snowed in for six months
every year. It is 50 miles to the nearest store so I plan on
going to town only once every 6 months. My mail box is 12
miles away - an 8-hour ride out and back, so I don't get my
mail very often. In winter the only easy way in or out of
here is by snowmobile, or one could cross-country ski. The
nearest plowed road is 20 miles away over a mountain. A friend
who was fur trapping in the area last winter, brought me my
mail and a few groceries. I have the place to myself most of
the time. The owner was here only four times last summer.
     My new home is 80 acres of creek bottom meadows bordering
the River of No Return Wilderness. It is 15 miles by trail
from the wild and scenic Middle Fork of the Salmon river
(which has 12 hot springs along its shores). My horses and
goats have abundant grazing here, which they share with deer,
elk, moose. I've also seen black bear, fox, coyotes, eagles,
wolves. Caretaking a place this remote is not for everyone,
but if you enjoy nature and don't need to go to town often,
it is ideal. Time to fire up my wood-heated hot tub and sit
back to watch the animals grazing in the meadow. Last evening
there were 12 deer, 9 elk, 8 horses, 5 goats. Bear, May 04
     (Later.) In July I quit the caretaking position. The owner
went back on his word. Rather than deal with a dishonest jerk,
I hit the road. I had been pretty isolated for a year and
needed to see old friends and meet new people, so I headed up
river to the Stanley area where I had lived for four years in
the mid 1990s. Life on the road sure is different than life
on a remote ranch, but fun in its own way.
     7-21. After a week of repacking wagons and shoeing
horses, I got on the road at noon and drove 12 miles down
Morgan creek to the Salmon river. I pastured the horses on an
island away from the roads. Hippies from New York stopped by
camp asking about the local hot springs. They had been to the
Rainbow gathering in California.
     7-22. Drove through Challis and up highway 21 to the
Bayhorse campground. It was about 15 miles of heavy traffic.
The horses did real good except for Ritta, the 2-year-old, who
still does not want to lead on the pack string. She broke
loose and followed along at her own pace, in and out of traffic.
     7-23. Drove 23 miles to Holman creek. This is the worst
stretch of road on the trip. No good place to camp. Even
this spot is not great: too close to the road and not much
feed. Had two flat tires today. First, a tire on the goat
cart was leaking. A very helpful man in Clayton changed it
for me, put on a new tire and tube, and refused payment. Two
miles further a tire on the wagon went flat. I hitched a ride
back to Challis with the rim and bought a new used tire.
     7-24. Moved just a mile to the end of Slate creek road
and camped in an old pasture where the horses have plenty of
feed. After yesterday's travails, we needed a day off.
     7-25 19 miles to Casino creek and camped in the cattle
trap where, 11 years ago, I first saw Mitasunke (My Horse -
Lakotah). She belonged to a fence contractor who was camped
there. I traded one hundred hours of work for her. She is
still paying me for that labor, raising foals and carrying a
pack load in the back country.
     7-26. Day off. I visited with several friends who
stopped by camp. I lived right across the river for 3 years.

There is a big summer house being built in "my" old horse pasture. On the 75 acre ranch that had one house in 1993, there are now eight big summer houses - and no horses.

7-27. Moved just 1½ miles to a spot near Boat Box hot springs. Someone has put a big redwood tub where the 2 ft by 4 ft boat box was when I lived here. The new tub is nice but it takes a lot of river water to cool the 130 degree water to get a soak. More up-river friends stopped by camp.

7-28. Drove 8 miles through Lower Stanley and Stanley (tourists everywhere) to the end of Cow Camp road by Stanley Lake creek. Had my first run in with a federal employee who felt he had to try and bully me. He claimed that I needed a permit to graze my horses on public land. I told him he was a liar and a criminal, and if he continued to harass me I'd see him in court. He left in a hurry.

7-29. Eight miles to Vadar creek rest area. I watched a hundred elk grazing in the meadow across the road.

7-30. Eight miles to Capehorn creek at the end of Bear Valley road. Off the pavement for a while.

7-31. Eight miles over Capehorn summit to Bruce meadows in Bear Valley. This is one of the largest alpine meadows I've ever seen. Elk everywhere you look, and Sandhill cranes filling the air with their weird calls.

8-1. Hiked 3 miles down the creek to Bear Valley hot springs. Large hot pools filled with naked women. Paradise for an old hippie.

8-2. Moved 2 miles up stream to a quieter spot a bit further from the road. This is the road into the head of the Middle Fork of the Salmon river, one of Idaho's most popular white water rivers, so it is very busy and dusty.

8-6. Stayed four days in the last camp and then found a spot just a half mile up stream that is off the road and has lots of feed. Real quiet here. The only noise is the cranes. A pair walked into the meadow by camp. Beautiful birds.

8-9. The horses saw a wolf last evening. I saw them looking at the road into this meadow, but I could not see what they were looking at. But when I went for a walk this morning, I saw a pile of wolf shit in the wheel track I made coming in.

8-10. Drove 5 miles up Bear Valley creek. The feed here is coarse swamp grass.

8-11. Moved one mile to a big meadow with good feed. Camped 100 yards from the road on the creek. This is a side road so the traffic is light. I watched a coyote stalking Little Big Man out in the meadow this afternoon. I think the coyote was over-ambitious. 1100# of horse might be too much !

8-12. My rooster was a big hero today. A hawk tried to grab a hen. The rooster flew up at the diving hawk and drove it off.

8-15. Drove 9 miles to Fir creek and camped ¼ mile from the developed campground. Hiked down to BearValley hot springs for a soak. Right at dark a fool with a trailer full of mules pulled in right next to my camp. I've got four loose horses. I expect to hear fights all night long. Millions of acres of forest and this ass has to camp on my picket line !

8-16. Eight miles back over Capehorn summit. Steep hard pull but the horses did real good. I tried tying Ritta to the pack string. She broke loose twice, broke two halters, two ropes, the rigging ring, and pulled Trisha's saddle off. After that trying day, when I let the chickens out, they went down to the creek for a drink. The white hen drank at the beach where I was watering the horses, but the rooster tried to drink where the bank was two feet high and the water was two feet deep. He jumped off the bank into the water; I guess the creek was so clear that he couldn't tell how deep it was. Sure was funny watching a rooster play at being a duck.

8-17. Two miles down Capehorn creek to where it crosses the highway. The old timer camped next to me packed into this valley and into Bear Valley 50 years ago. He had lots of stories of pack-string wrecks and cattle drives back when the Stanley basin had only dirt roads and no tourists.

8-18. Three miles to Knapp creek at Marsh creek. There is a sheep camp a half mile from me. When the flock arrived at dusk, the colts all freaked out. They had never seen 1000 sheep before. They ran out to the road, then back to mama, several times before I got Trisha and Bob caught.

8-19. Same camp. I went over and had coffee with the Peruvian herder this morning. His boss showed up and I spent the day helping sort old ewes and lambs out of the flock. I enjoy working with sheep. They smell better than cows.

8-20. Same camp. The herder came looking for a lost horse.

8-21. Moved 3 miles to Blind summit at the head of Marsh creek. The sheep owner stopped by to check out my wagon. A Forest Service officer stopped by to visit; not hassle me.

8-23. Four miles to Archer creek at the sheep sorting corrals. Lots of Sandhill cranes along the creek. Cold rain all day. I'm glad I have a wood stove in the wagon.

8-29. Four miles to Marsh creek by the highway. Ritta kicked a truck in the headlight. He was trying to pass us on a narrow part of the road. I'll have to tie her up tomorrow.

8-30. Back on the pavement again. 14 miles to Stanley Lake creek at the end of Cow Camp road. Tied Ritta to the wagon and she threw herself on the road and got road rash on both knees and a hock. I hope she has learned to lead.

8-31. Eight miles to Boat Box hot springs. I took a two-hour soak as soon as I got the horses put away.

9-1. Same camp. I spent all day at the hot springs.

9-2. 17 miles to a friend's mining claim up the Yankee Fork. I need to get off the highway for the weekend. An old crane is at the mine. Osprey have built their nest at the top of the boom. The birds provide many hours of entertainment. As they are alert to threats, they make good watch d̸o̸g̸s̸ birds.

9-5. Three miles to the fish ponds below Ramey creek. These ponds are left over from the HUGE gold dredge that worked the Yankee Fork in the 1950s. The dredge, still here, is now a museum. This river bed was turned upside down and now is nothing but rock piles and holes that are stocked fish ponds. Anyone who wants gold jewelry should see this place. An entire river valley destroyed for greed and vanity.

9-6. Same camp. Lots of fishermen but few fish caught. These stocked rainbows have seen every kind of lure and don't rise. They think food comes in a pail at the hatchery.

9-7. 15 miles to the pasture at the end of Slate creek road. The trip back down river is no fun. The same campsites, the same road. The horses are tired and foot-sore. Paved roads are hard on horse shoes. I'll be glad when back on dirt.

9-8. 23 miles to Bayhorse campground.

9-9. 15 miles to riverside camp by the cottonwood island. Tomorrow I'll be back on Morgan/Panther creeks for the winter.

The wagon trip was about 270 miles. Most days I just moved enough to find grazing for the horses. I met many interesting people and soaked in a few fine hot springs. The wagon worked fine. It is heavy and I need to harness 4 horses on the passes but it pulls easily on level roads. I had no problems with traffic or the law, although one sheriff's deputy

said he'd had many complaints about me slowing traffic. He
agreed that I was legal and no one had cause to complain. Many
people stopped to take pictures and praise my free lifestyle.
    I'm settled in for the winter on a remote ranch on Panther
creek, busy building fence to pay my rent. I'd like to take a
long trip next year, perhaps to the southwest, but I'd like to
find someone to drive my old wagon. Leaving a pile of stuff
stored here is a pain. Many people talk about how they'd like
to live free like me, but so far it's just talk. I guess, when
there is no more oil, then people will have to use horses again.
I'll be ready to teach what I know. Bear, ID 832, May & Oct 04

Are you ready for a mobile chicken farm ?
    Suppose you live in a van, bus, old RV, or horse-drawn
wagon. With a little thought and work, you could have fresh
eggs wherever you travel. For two years I lived in a homemade
camper on a pickup. For most of that time, six hens lived in a
coop on the roof of the cab. Now hens travel with my caravan.
    The thing that makes it possible, is the desire of hens to
roost in the same place every night. They see their coop as
home - no matter that it has moved 500 miles since yesterday.
The only major drawback is that you can't move camp while the
chickens are out grazing. You must wait until dusk when they
go to roost. What do you do on long trips with few stops ?
Feed and water the chickens in the coop.
    If the only place to put a coop is up on the roof, get
banties, as they can fly. My big old hens can only hop a
couple of feet, so their coop is under the wagon.
    A small utility trailer that can be towed by a car or van
could house a goat or two plus a coop of chickens. Turn roadside bushes and bugs into milk and eggs !
    A coop under a rig should have a wire mesh floor so the
poop falls to the ground and fertilizes a new spot every time
you move. A coop on the roof should have a solid floor with
sawdust or old newspaper as bedding and be cleaned weekly.
I think I could make a pack-horse coop and take chickens trail-
riding into the back country. With a calm horse, it would work.
    I can hear you doubters now: "This crazy idea is way too
much hassle." Well, food is never too much hassle when you are
hungry. Once you eat an egg from a free-range hen, you will
never go back to factory-made store-bought eggs. If you can
feed yourself, "they" can't control you by rationing your food.
                                                        Bear
In October, a black bear bit holes in many of my pails.
    Replacing them is laborious. Previously for two years,
I had stored most buckets and totes on the ground. No problem.
    I am now sprinkling full-strength ammonia around tree
trunks in hope the smell will repel bears. I also clothes-pin
garbage bags to clothes lines. Even a slight breeze causes
the bags to rustle, which may scare animals away. Too soon to
know if those repellants are effective.
    I now keep most of my food buckets at one main camp, and
hang them 12 feet up or higher on tree branches with a rope.
I plan to replace the rope system with some sort of metal-cable
crank system for winching buckets up and down.
    I may build a primitive tree house if I find a suitable
tree that is secluded enough. Bruce of BC, February 2004

(Comment:) Physical barriers, such as the cable system you
plan, seem better than odorous chemicals, because the latter
are temporary at best. We haven't had much bear damage, maybe
because most wild areas here are small enough for pesty bears
to roam to folks' gardens - and get shot. Sept 2005

Choosing a tree and means of support for a tree-house.

The higher I go in a tree, the greater my sense of freedom and the farther I may be able to see. However, I also think about ease of climbing up and down, chances of falling, likelihood of injury if I do fall, maximum wind speed the tree may experience, and quality of support for it. Kid's tree-houses are seldom over 10 ft high, to minimize injury if child falls.

Trees are stressed by wind, esp during storms. Trees cope by losing parts of their structure: first leaves, then small branches, then big branches. As each is lost, the tree's wind catchment area decreases, which reduces the force and the risk of the tree blowing over. Adding a tree-house, increases the wind catchment area. In high-wind areas, tree-houses should be in the lower third of the tree, where wind speeds are lower and the wind-force's leverage on the tree's base is less. If wind poses a serious threat, build only a small tree-house and round its sides to reduce its sail effect.

The branches to which the tree-house is attached, must be strong enough to take the weight and wind-force of what they are supporting. Simpler to build on a few strong supports than many small ones. Branch strength varies among species. Generally strong: oak, beech, maple, fir, hemlock. For a one-storey tree-house with four attachment points (one at each corner) and no overhanging parts, minimum thickness is about 8 inches. If more than one storey, or the extra leverage and weight of overhanging sections, 12 inches or more. If your branches aren't this thick, use more attachment points so that the weight is spread among more branches.

If you use two or more branches or trunks or trees to support a tree-house, attachments require extra care. In a strong wind, a tree and its branches will twist and sway a lot. If your house hinders this movement, it could be destroyed. This can happen esp if building across two very long branches, because the wind moves them a lot. Different trees and branches will move differently; supports must be able to cope with that; either have a strong rigid framework or a flexible framework.

Rigid framework. If the branches are not very large, or heavy, you may be able to fasten rigidly to them. The small wind forces can be withstood by the supports and the floor beams. This method is not suitable for large spans or for use between thick trunks. Recommended only on branches 6"D or less.

Flexible (or floating) framework. This is the best choice because very low stresses are created; so smaller, lighter, cheaper wood can be used. However, it may be more complicated. The idea: fix one end of a beam to one trunk or branch, and support the other end on a sliding joint. When the trunks move differently, the support slides across the joint and no big stress is put upon the support or the beam. One such joint is a J-shape metal bracket. The top of the J is bolted to the tree; the hook of the J supports the beam, enabling the beam to slide in one direction. This isn't suitable if the beam may get twisted sideways in the bracket and prevented from sliding. Another way: attach one end of a steel cable to the tree-house's frame and the other end to a higher branch. This is cheap and effective, but be careful how you attach the cable. Suspend it from an eye-bolt fitted to the tree at right angle to the cable and attach it to the support with another eye-bolt. This is important so that, when wind moves the support, the cable doesn't rub away living bark and damage the tree. (From http://www.corbinstreehouse.com , sent by Bruce of BC)

(Comment:) In a windy place if using a bracket, I'd prefer a d shape. The house might tip out of a J shape.

Father and daughter lived four years in Portland forest.

An Australian cross-country runner, scouting routes thru dense woods, spotted a girl and an older man with bushy white hair and beard at a "well-established transient camp" in a remote part of the northeast section of Forest Park. Carved into the ground nearby were two swastikas. The runner and his wife called police at 9:06 am on April 28 and gave the location citing Thomas Guide map, page 565, block G6.

That afternoon, four cops on ATVs searched the slopes for more than an hour with no luck. "We had little to go on."

The next morning, the runner escorted police back, using a compass to lead them on foot through waist-high foliage far beyond marked trails. A police plane flew overhead, but the pilot said the dense fir trees concealed the ground.

After 1½ hours search, they found an elaborate camp dug into a steep hillside about 500 yards above and sw of St Helens road 1¼ miles se of St Johns bridge. Inside a 20x20-ft tarp-covered wood-framed shelter, they found sleeping bags laid out on plastic ground-covering, a makeshift table carved from tree bark, a stove, a large metal pot, a partially burnt log, tools including a hand-saw and rakes, girl's shoes, a doll, a stack of old World Book encyclopedias and other books. Nearby was a rope swing, a tilled vegetable garden, and a creek with a pool shallowly dammed by rocks. But no one was in sight.

Police, armed with rifles and shotguns, stayed around for an hour, keeping silent. "We didn't know who we'd encounter."

As police prepared to leave, a police dog disappeared over a hill. The handler found the dog 50 yards down a ridge, sniffing at a man and girl huddled behind a tree. Immediately police separated them; one cop questioned the girl while the other interrogated the man. The man, Frank, said he was a 53-year-old college graduate and Marine Corps veteran who had served in Vietnam. He said the girl's mother was institution-alized in NH where his 12-year-old daughter, Ruth, was born, and the two now lived on a $400-a-month disability check.

He said, rather than live on the streets and expose Ruth to alcohol and drugs, they had hiked deep into Forest Park and set up their camp. He taught Ruth using the encyclopedias. They went into the city twice a week to shop and to attend church. He said he was a devout Christian and explained that the swastika was an ancient Chinese symbol for prosperity and purity and good fortune before the Nazis had adopted it.

Frank and Ruth told police that the runner was the first person to find their camp during the four years they had lived there - and were stunned that police found them. Their biggest worry was being split up. "Please don't take me from my daddy", the girl pleaded with the cop as they sat on a log talking for half an hour. Police were impressed that the two were clean, well-fed, healthy. Police "persuaded" Frank and Ruth to leave their camp, promised to help find them food and shelter, and said they would try not to separate them. The father and Ruth, leery at first, led police down their zigzagging trail to St Helens Road, carrying some of their belongings in two backpacks. A cop said, "All of us had difficulty negotiating the steep path, except for Frank and Ruth."

Police fingerprinted both and did a thorough national criminal background check which came up empty. A pediatrician examined the girl and found her free of illnesses and tooth cavities and signs of physical or sexual abuse, and as smart as a 16-year-old. After some prodding from supervisors, the sargent alerted caseworkers of the state Dept of Human Resour-ces. Informed that there were no signs of abuse, they allowed the pair to remain together. A homeless outreach worker found them a spot in a family shelter for two nights. But they could not stay there indefinitely. Instead of turning them over to state authorities, the sargent found them a place to live and Frank a job on a horse farm in Yamhill County.

For the past two weeks they have lived in a mobile home. Frank is now mowing lawns and learning to drive a tractor. The two ride bicycles to a nearby church on Sundays. Maxine Bernstein (from Oregonian, 15? May 04; sent by Pam in Oregon)

(Comments:) The police, sensing that the episode would get much media attention, claimed they were trying to help Ruth and Frank, and perhaps actually were more considerate than usual.

Ruth and Frank were lucky that Ruth was not forced into a foster home. The sargent seemed reluctant to notify DHR, maybe because such agencies are prone to seize children on the slightest pretext (I've heard they get paid per kid), and foster homes are prone to abuse (they, too, get paid per kid, so they have an incentive to crowd in all the kids they can get - and some kids will be bullies !).

The Oregonian headlined their front-page article: "Police rescue a father and girl." RESCUE ? !!!!! Ruth and Frank had lived healthily in those woods for 4 years. They did not need or request "rescue". (Big media are seldom more than propaganda. One reason: if they don't "cooperate" with police and other officials, they won't be given "news". Also, their staffs might get traffic fines instead of warnings - etc !)

After a few weeks at the horse farm, Ruth and Frank left and disappeared. They wrote a note to the owner saying they did not like all the media attention they were getting. Now more experienced, hopefully they won't get "rescued" again.

Note that Ruth and Frank were eventually found, not by the police or an airplane, but by a dog. If, upon spotting the police at their camp, instead of hiding nearby and waiting, if they had immediately left, would they have gotten away ? Seems better to chance theft of camping equipment, than to confront police or other dangerous people. Even though someone believes they are "innocent" of any "wrong doing", no knowing how police may construe what they see or what fingerprinting and a "thorough national background check" might show up. (Recently, a Portland man (a lawyer, no less), who had not been out of the U.S. for ten years, was imprisoned because his fingerprints supposedly matched prints left near the train bombing in Spain. Fortunately, Spanish police found the man who had actually left the prints. Did the FBI's fingerprint system goof ? Or were the police 'framing' him ?)

(Based on what little advice we've seen on an ACLU info-card, and in lit from other sources:) If you are with other people and get confronted by police, try to STAY TOGETHER. If questioned separately, any differences in what you say can be construed as evidence of guilt. If the police insist on separating you, or if they question you for longer than a minute and then refuse to let you go on your way, assume you will be arrested, and SHUT UP. Thereafter say only, "I have nothing further to say until I obtain adequate legal information", or words to that effect. Police will usually not tell you that you are under arrest until they put hand-cuffs on you and haul you away, because they want to get as much info out of you as they can before you shut up. Any info you provide, no matter how innocuous it seems to you, may be twisted by police and prosecutors and used against you. When they arrest you, police are supposed to tell you that anything you say may be used against you. Whether or not they do, SHUT UP.

Can orbiting spy satellites spot your camp ? Probably not.
Supposedly they are capable of (eg) reading a newspaper
headline from orbit. But they'd have difficulty finding a
newspaper because, the higher the magnification, the smaller
the area viewed. Testable with a variable power scope.
According to 25May03 "Ask Marilyn" (Vos Savant) column,
"satellites view the entire Earth almost daily at a resolution
of one kilometer and biweekly at a resolution of 30 meters."
That means, something smaller than 30 meters (100 ft) won't be
seen unless it is intense, such as a bright light at night. H&B

Using a shake-light at base camp and on trails.
In Dec 03 DP, I said I'd buy one when the price got under
$10. Well, at a mobile sales (a dealer who travels to small
towns with tools and farm things), John and Rose Ward of Living
Mobile saw new HDC shake-lights (stock #CLFL/38978) on sale at
$5. They bought a few and sent me one (MUCH THANKS !). Made
in China, marketed by Homier Distributing Co, www.homier.com
(no mail address). 6½" long, 1" D except 1½" near light end,
¼ pound (half the weight of our Russian squeeze-light).
Instructions say: If completely drained, 3 shakes per
second for 30 seconds will fully charge the capacitor "which
will give up to 5 minutes of continuous bright light." "During
prolonged use" shake 10 to 15 seconds every 2 to 3 minutes.
Shake with "moderate force" while holding horizontal. "Shaking
too hard may cause damage" as may bumping or dropping.
HDC claims the light is "visible for over a mile" which
may be true. But the beam is too narrow (eg, 3" at one ft) for
most tasks. Immediately after shaking, its beam is brighter
than the incandescent-bulb squeeze-light. But the squeeze-
light's beam is broader (3 times, if set broad; 1½ times, narrow)
and therefore better for following a trail through brush at
night. On trails, the best way I've found to use the HDC:
leave on and shake a few times every few seconds. The shaking
bounces the beam around - which helps illuminate more terrain.
Though most of HDC's light is focused into the beam, the
clear plastic case passes enough light to reduce night vision.
I shaded it by holding that portion of case in my hand.

Unlike present squeeze-lights, a shake-light
can be used solo for tasks requiring two hands.
But for most tasks, the HDC must be set into
something to hold it and spread the beam. I used
a ceramic mug. A chunk of soft foam keeps the
shake-light upright. White cardstock, half way
around behind, holds a cardstock top on which is
glued slightly-wrinkled aluminum foil to reflect
and diffuse the beam. So rigged, the HDC
is approx as bright as an ordinary candle for only
a few seconds after shaking. The light fades
fast at first, then increasingly slower. After
15 minutes, the HDC-as-lantern still gave enough
light for me to (eg) eat without spooning food
onto my lap. It continues to glow dimly for
many hours; helpful for finding it at night.
Experimenting, I shook the HDC rapidly but
gently for 30 seconds - so gently that the
magnet barely bumped its stops. I switched it
on briefly to notice brightness, then shook it
VIGOROUSLY for 10 seconds. Much brighter.
This autumn, for 3 months we've used the
HDC most every night or morn for an hour or more.
No failures so far.   Sept 2005

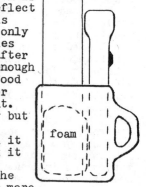

card-
stock

Al
foil

foam

114

Instructions warn: "DO NOT attempt to remove the LED or any internal part", but also claim "water and weather proof", so I assumed its innards were sealed. I noticed the end piece screwed on. Thinking it held only the glass lens, I unscrewed it, intending to remove the lens to broaden the beam. WRONG ! All the innards slid out ! I reassembled with difficulty. The only sealant is a rubber gasket between the lens and an internal tube. So I'd say it is water RESISTANT, maybe as much so as is a plastic pail with a gasketed lid.

A good feature: the switch does not penetrate the case. Instead it is magnetic and actuates something inside. A feature to look for in ALL kinds of flashlights.

The sliding magnet that generates electricity is strong and easily attracts steel objects even through the case. HDC warns, keep shake-light away from tapes, pacemakers, etc.

In Living Mobile 4-04, John and Rose reported on their HDC. "3 minutes of vigorous shaking results in about 6 minutes of usable light, with the light becoming noticably dimmer at the 4 minute mark... The more we use it, the longer it seems to shine. We didn't get even 6 minutes ... when it was new."

We seldom shake our HDC longer than 10 seconds because we are concerned about life of the LED (see next item). Our HDC fades gradually; no abrupt change. Nor have we noticed any change with use. White LEDs are a new product (not yet made the same ?) and individual LEDs may vary. Bert & Holly, Dc 04

Preliminary report on an Eveready "Energizer LED Lantern".
It "folds to put the light where you need it". $3\frac{1}{2}$x$2\frac{1}{2}$x$1\frac{1}{4}$" when folded, 6 oz when 4 AA cells installed. It appears to contain two LEDs (white unfortunately, yellow would be more efficient) which beam most of their light through two small translucent tubes which diffuse it. So, it emits a broad glow like a candle, rather than a narrow beam like most flashlights.

It does not say what kind of AAs, but the package mentions "battery changes" (not recharges) so I assume alkalines. However, because flashlight makers tend to run LEDs at higher power than they are rated for, I installed NiCds. NiCds give only 1.2 volts per cell, vs alkaline 1.5 v). With NiCds, the lantern is about as bright as a candle - adequate for reading or hand-writing if the material is placed close.

When I installed the NiCds, I also stuck in wires at the connections. The wires go to a small socket, so I can recharge it simply by plugging it into our photovoltaic panel.

The little info with the lantern did not say how long the cells should last. I measured 25 milliamps on dim and 50 ma on bright (two settings). That means: new 500 ma-hour NiCd AAs, if fully charged and used until 80% discharged, might last 8 hrs on bright and 16 hrs dim. NiCds lose capacity as they age.

It has been very useful this autumn, because we are able to recharge it some on bright cloudy days when our pv does not generate enough voltage to recharge our main 12-volt system.

Sent by Al Fry (MUCH THANKS) who did not say where he bought it or how much it cost. He noted, "Direct viewing of bulbs is irritating to eyes." Bert & Holly, December 2004

My Brinkman two-AA-cell white LED flashlight is bright.
It cost $12 or $15 at Walmart. It is the only TWO cell LED flashlight I know of. Others require 3 cells, usually AAA. Most white LEDs need 3.6 to 4.5 volts - higher than the 2.5-to-3 volts that two cells put out. Zalia, Oregon 972, April 2004

Charging multiple batteries off of one photovoltaic panel.
         In full sun, our big (1x4') pv panel puts out 17 volts -
ample for charging a 12-volt battery. But when cloudy or
partial shade, it puts out less than 12 volts. The big pv's
cloudy performance is poorer than the small pv on our Casio
calculator which operates in quite dim light. Dim-light
performance of pvs depends on how they were fabricated (and
age ?) - something to check for if buying a pv that you would
like some power from during long cloudy periods.
         Previously, to get something when cloudy, I clipped the
the pv to just one or a few cells of our main 12-volt battery.
This autumn I devised an easier way: I hooked it to other
lower-voltage batteries through separate resistors and one-way
diodes. See below. The "12 volt batt" consists of ten NiCd
cells (originally 20 amp-hours capacity but now, over 30 years
old, MUCH less). The "5-volt batt" are 4 NiCd AAs in the
Eveready lantern. The "3-volt batt" are two alkaline AAs
being recharged, which power our Sony "Walkman" radio/tape-
player ($3 at a thrift store). We play it while sitting doing
inside tasks (NOT while hiking). Voltages are slightly higher
while the batteries are charging or when fully charged.
         We tried the Walkman on two NiCd AAs (2.4 v), but it did
not play. Three NiCds (3.6 v) might blow it. So it needs
alkaline AAs. They warn: do NOT recharge. But none have
blown up - yet. Two "Duracell" swelled and leaked a little.
(We recycled.) No problems with others so far. We have 8 or
so that we recharge in rotation. Some we salvaged from toys we
found at an informal dump along a logging road. Others came
from a pail of discarded batteries for recycle, at a university.
We also tried recharging alkaline D cells (used by a different
radio at a summer camp) with a small pv that puts out 60 ma in
full sun. All leaked - but still worked. To recharge, esp
"non-rechargables", best do it VERY SLOWLY with LOW currant.
         The resistors are to limit current when the pv gets full
sun; else the AAs would be charged too fast and damaged.
Also, the resistors allow the 12-volt batt to get charged. If
the pv puts out 1 amp (1000 ma) at 14 v (voltage limited by 12-
volt batt), the 5-volt batt takes 26 ma and the 3-volt batt 24
ma. The other 950 ma goes into the 12-volt batt. The NiCd AAs
say they hold 500 ma-hrs and to charge 14 hrs at 50 ma max.
         At our present winter camp, even on sunny days the big pv
gets full sun for only an hour or two. More typically, with
cloudy sun or partial shade, the pv puts out 8 volts, in which
case the 5-volt batt gets 8 ma, the 3-volt batt 10 ma, and the
12-volt batt nothing. The 3-volt batt gets some charge when
the pv puts out as little as 4 volts. (Diode loses a little.)
         Recently I found various-size NiCds and a 9 v lithium in
recycle. (Why were rechargable NiCds discarded ?) More later.
                                                          Bert

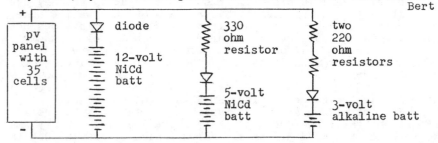

Dwelling Portably
or Shared, Mobile, Improvised
Underground, Hidden, Floating
May 2006 $1 per issue   POB 190-d, Philomath OR 97370

What is wrong with this bridge ?
This drawing is from
"Pioneering" pamphlet #33588,
which came in a boy-scout
magazine. It suggests
activities to "enhance
outdoor skills, especially
knot-tying and lashing"
and "an understanding of
some of the principles of
engineering as they build
temporary structures and
camp equipment" and to
"increase self-
confidence."
The pamphlet
includes some
good info and
ideas. But

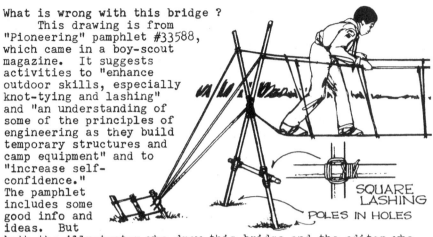

SQUARE
LASHING
POLES IN HOLES

both the illustrator who drew this bridge and the editor who
approved it, deserve to lose their merit-badges. Why? Page 124.

How can nomadic or primitive-living people find one another ?
I know about Rainbow Gatherings, but unfortunately they
are only held once a year, and the only way to find out where
and when is by using a computer (which I don't use).
Most primitive-skills festivals I know of cost money as
well as the time and effort of getting to them.
A common angst with many people who live this way, myself
included, is loneliness. If you've found your soul-mate, you
are one of the rare, lucky ones. Many more of us are the
"freaks" and "weirdos" of our neighborhoods; rarely if ever
meeting people who want to drop out of main-stream society.
Solitude is beautiful, but so is good company. We can be
stronger together. Thoughts ? Resources ? Gumby, NC 275,Jy05

(Comments:) Loneliness is not just a problem for nomads (etc)
but for most people. Though they might live in (eg) similar
tract houses, they differ in important ways and have difficulty
finding compatables. "Mainstream society" is mostly a
statistical fiction. Everyone is a "freak".
Most nomads (etc) have an easier time than most other
people, because we aren't spending most of our lives working to
pay rent. We have more time to find a long-term companion.
For how, seek opportunities fairly near by, so that you
can spend more time in places good for meeting people. Your
area (NC, etc) is culturally diverse, so a long move may not be
necessary. For nearby gatherings, check bulletin boards and
local event sheets. And keep in mind that every popular park
and beach and library is a gathering of sorts.
Don't expect to meet anyone who shares your exact
interests. Be flexible. When Holly and I met, perhaps our
most important commonality was dissatisfaction with the
heavily-promoted options (such as expensive housing, and steady
full-time jobs to pay for it). Bert, OR 973, March 2006

How Rose and John developed their mobile dwellingway.
I (John) don't think that I ever made a singular decision
to live in a mobile dwelling. I built on an extensive camping

experience of over 20 years. After my last house was sold, it
was no suprise to my friends that I moved into my 84 Dodge
mini-van. Some people thought I was nuts, and others wished
that they could do as I was doing.

I was dating then, and one of my litmus tests was, how the
woman reacted to my little home on wheels. Many women look at
a house as a security blanket, and since I didn't have one, I
was not surprised that many of my dates reacted poorly. One
young lady was not bothered by my lack of a fixed dwelling;
she and her folks moved frequently, a la gypsy style, so she
didn't have any problems with my lifestyle. She still doesn't,
as she (Rose) became my wife !

After the minivan quit, we moved into an 86 Dodge full-
size van that had been converted for our nomadic lifestyle.
Though someone living solo in a van can be quite comfortable,
the two of us soon wanted something bigger. But rather than
get rid of a perfectly servicable van, we purchased an 82
Shasta travel trailer that we could tow with the van. Now we
are quite content, and very grateful for our mobile dwellingway. Over the years many people have said that I should
chronicle my mobile life; thus Living Mobile was born as a
way to share knowledge within the nomadic community.

Many in the nomadic life use RV's, though their RV's are
often old. Others use cars, trucks, vans they have modified,
or simply occupied as mobile shelters. I distinguish those who
are mobile by choice, from people who are homeless but would
like to return to "normal" life. John & Rose, PA 174, March05

How did you come to live your choice of dwellingway ?
Did you consciously decide to leave so-called modern life,
or did your dwellingway evolve over a period of time ? Did you
both learn your lifestyle by trial and error, or did you build
on the works of others and maybe have help ? John & Rose

(Reply.) Holly and I learned gradually. We'd both been somewhat outdoorsy tho not into uncomfortable or dangerous feats.

A big "bottom line" for both of us, was the high cost of
conventional housing, esp housing that was comfortable. Before
meeting Holly, I had rented various rooms and structures -
always the cheapest I could find because I considered the rent
money ill spent. Consequently, most were not very comfortable.
Some had no heat; others only an UNvented gas cook-stove.
And some landlords soon kicked me out. I usually payed the
rent on time and I did not smoke or have animals, but I ate and
sometimes cooked (on electric hotplate) in my room. For food,
as for shelter, I believed in spending little money so that I
needed to spend little time working at jobs I mostly disliked.

(I went to restaurants only with dates. Likewise to
entertainment that charged admission. I was generous with
women, at least by my frugal standards, because I didn't find
many who were interested in me - despite my spending much of
my free time looking for them (for which I traveled to beach
resorts or sizable cities, because seldom were there many
women near where I worked). The "litmus tests" were mostly the
women's. I simply tried to get acquainted with every woman I
saw who looked good to me and who did not seem busy or in a
rush or with a man. I am not quick-witted verbally. Though I
tried to be polite, my conversation openers were usually trite/
banal/awkward/contrived - as well as "out of the blue". I got
rebuffed maybe nine tries out of ten. Of the women who at
least talked with me a while, not more than one in ten dated
me. Of those, most did not date me more than once or twice.)

Though I enjoyed travel to/through new places, I hated commuting. So, if I couldn't rent something cheap close to work, I slept in my car (an ordinary sedan), usually parked at my work place with boss's permission - sometimes in climates with winters colder than Oregon's.

The shelters that Holly and I have had while "camping out" have been MORE comfortable and no more crowded than almost all the housing I'd had previously. Exception: one winter camped in the Rocky Mtns while still quite inexperienced. That prompted a move to the West Coast, 25 years ago.

The housing Holly had had before we met, was generally more comfortable than what I'd had - but cost her much of her earnings. And she, too, had had problems with landlords.

As we recall, after getting together, over a period of several weeks we consciously decided that we wanted to live differently than most people lived, though we weren't sure how. We talked about RVs and boats, and looked at a few, but decided they were too expensive if big enough to be comfortable, and too insecure. We also thought about trying to build something permanent in some very remote area, but decided it would be difficult to sustain, and too much to lose if it was discovered or for other reasons became untenable. Holly was even less enthusiastic than I for anything requiring big investments of money or time. So, somewhat by elimination, we arrived at what we have. Comfort is a big thing for us: comfort not only within our dwellings, but minimum DIScomfort while operating our support channels. (I DIS-fondly remember going out on cold mornings and removing snow from my car so I could drive to work, and then having to work out in the cold.)

During a cold spell a month ago, in early morning, 23° outside, 52° inside. By mid-day, 45° outside and sunny (cold days here are often sunny), 65° inside thanks to solar heating. (A more-typical winter morn, 35° outside, 60° inside.) And our heat is free and effortless: our bodies; our plastic-covered earth floor (which stores heat); the sun (sometimes); and cooking in the evening (which consumes 5 gal of propane in 4 or 5 months). Meanwhile, house dwellers who heat with electricity or gas are paying BIG BUCKS. Or, if with wood, spending much time tending the fire and cutting and transporting wood. So - WHO is "roughing it" ? ! Bert & Holly, Oregon 973, March 06

My son and I are now living in an old school bus.
It is about 30 feet long inside. It has a wood-stove, sink, two beds, table - all built in. I parked it on a friend's land. I pay him rent, which includes water and electric hook-ups (plenty of water, but electricity is limited by an extension cord - only enough for lights, radio, TV-VCR).

Long term, I am interested in solar electric in case I unplug from the grid. My bus is wired for 12-volt lights and radio, etc. No phone line; I have a pager.

I bought the bus in Oct 2003 for $2000. I'm working 40 hours a week to pay down the loan I got to buy it. The bus is drivable, but not insured or licensed so it stays put.

Living in vehicles is illegal here, but this is a tolerant place and, if nobody complains, officials ignore it. (They feel: better in a bus than "homeless".) Many other people live in buses and trailers on this island (population 12,000; doubles in summer with visitors and tourists). Rents and house-prices are high. I get plenty of free firewood from a lumber yard, so no fuel bills. (They even cut the wood into short lengths and put it in a free box by the road.)

I heat water on the woodstove in big pots. I like to soak

in a hot bath, and I enjoy long showers. This week I put some
coils of black rubber hose on the roof of the bus and got some
very hot water - enough for a short shower. I am adding a
small water tank to increase volume. I am also working on a
bigger solar system, using recycled solar water-heating panels
(formerly heated swimming-pool water). I found some leaks in
the panels; also, the water pressure here (municipal system)
is too high, causing more leaks.

My 14-year-old son and I dug/built an outhouse, and are
working on a second one. Most people here use septic fields or
a municipal system (which dumps the "treated" sewage into the
ocean). A public health nurse said an outhouse is better than
those two options. Aarran, Saltspring Island BC, June/July 05

(Comments.) Out-HOUSES (difficult-to-move structures over big
pits) may be better than septic fields or municipal systems
(which need many miles of pipes that can leak - or be ruptured
by an earthquake or flood !). But a big concentration of feces
buried deep is likely to pollute ground water. (Unnatural.
What animal digs a big hole and shits in it repeatedly ?)
Better to make small shallow deposits - which are soon broken
down by soil microbes, enriching the soil. To build a portable
rain/snow shelter, lash together poles to form an A-frame and
tie a tarp onto it.

I wonder if your bus also has insulation built in. A bus
dweller in Toronto said his "tin shack" was difficult to heat.
"Metal is a good conductor of heat. Accumulated snow would
melt off the roof." (Long report in May 97 DP.) But Toronto
has colder winters than where you are. Bert

Having a motor vehicle can help in some situations.
A young lady walked into our favorite pipe and tobacco
store and asked to use the phone. The manager pointed to the
pay phone outside. She responded that she didn't have any
money. He allowed her to use his phone. She called several
homeless shelters - and finally found one that had an opening.

The manager later told me that she had lost her job, and
that everything she owned had been repoed. I responded that,
had she at least owned a suitable car or van, even a cheap one,
she would have a place to stay and store her stuff; and would
be better able to find work, even temp work, and to get there.

Personally, I think that to rely upon the kindness of
others, or on homeless shelters, for something that a person
should provide for themselves, is pathetic. Perhaps it has
something to do with the victim mentality, fostered by big
daddy government: you can't care for yourself, but big daddy
will take care of you. This is why I like the DIY of the punk
and nomadic communities. Rose & John, Living Mobile, PA,Mar05

(Comments.) There are good reasons for her to feel victimized.
Big Bully and his accomplices victimize everyone (though some
more than others). Eg, at her former job, how much of her
earnings were taken, directly by taxes on her, or indirectly by
taxes on the business (which partly comes out of what she could
otherwise get payed - her employer won't willingly lose money
or cut profits - at least not for long). At her former apartment (or house), how much was her rent (or payments) inflated
by all the restrictions on building ? However, I agree that
some kind of backup would have been desirable.

But would a vehicle be the best kind ? Costly, not only
in money (purchase, maintenance, fuel, insurance, licensing,
maybe parking) but in time and stress and risk. And, if she
had had one, would it too have been repoed ? Also, living

comfortably in a vehicle takes learning, which takes time. (I was not very comfortable sleeping in a car, because I didn't have the time, or at least take the time, to learn how and to equip it adequately. I regarded it as temporary. Likewise the rooms I rented - and my jobs.)

Nor, would the kind of shelters we enjoy now, necessarily be a good backup for her. They, too, require learning.

The most practical short-term backup for her, might be for her to pre-arrange reciprocal house-sharing with other employed women. Ie, if I can come sleep on your floor, you can come sleep on mine. If the latter doesn't happen, she can give the other woman some money when she gets some. (Most people are unemployed at times, but also earn quite high pay at times.)

Long term, she would probably be better off with a dwellingway that doesn't require much money. Holly & Bert

San Diego police harass occupants of big vehicles.

Every night, Harry Wells slips behind the wheel of his 1976 Itaska motorhome and steers it out of a Mission Bay parking lot, across I-5, and into the hills of Clairemont. Wells looks for a parking space where his motor home won't be a nuisance. Then he sets the alarm for 6 am and he and his wife, Barbara, settle in for a night's sleep.

The next morning, he drives the motorhome back to the bay parking lot before his presence can be detected by residents of the neighborhood. Both the Wells work for temp agencies: Barbara as a nurse; Harry as a telemarketeer.

When the Wells moved into their motorhome last year after a string of bad luck, they joined more than 31,000 Californians living in vehicles. More than 2700 live in San Diego county, angering some house-dwellers. Officials responded to complaints by amping up enforcement of parking regulations in bay and beach lots, which prohibit parking from 2 to 4 am, and by eliminating parking spaces in the bay lots and along Morena Blvd where Wells formerly parked without annoying homeowners.

The changes have sent Wells and other motorhome dwellers into residential neighborhoods to park overnight. Wells said he has been glared at, has had ice thrown at his motorhome, and has been awakened at 5 am and asked to leave. "We're trying to keep a low profile", said Well, 54. "We don't want to bother people." But Chris Rink, chairman of Clairemont Mesa Planning Committee, said motor homes take up parking spaces and that residents worry about who is inside them. "They don't contribute to the neighborhood."

Bay Park resident Mike Vinti said he has called police ten times in the past 18 months about motorhomes parked across the street from his home. While some of the occupants could be homeless, he said many of them are living in expensive new motorhomes. "I feel those people are cutting corners. There are places for them..." But many motorhome dwellers say they can't afford to pay for a permit or to park in RV parks, such as Campland on the Bay - which charges $37-up per night.

Wells, whose only criminal record is a traffic violation, says he doesn't like avoiding police, but he is doing what he has to. When he and Barbara, 56, decided to buy a motorhome and live in it, he never expected it would lead to being harassed. Wells was laid off from his job as a loan processor last June, and the couple were evicted from their rental home in North Park when the owner decided to sell the house. Using what was left of their savings from a disability settlement, the couple plunked down $2300 for the motorhome and moved in, after putting some of their possessions in storage. They also have a Nissan Sentra, which Wells uses to commute to work.

A proposed San Diego ordinance would prohibit parking recreational vehicles on city streets from 2 to 6 am, and for more than 4 hours at any time. Police said, existing rules, which ban parking any vehicle on city streets for more than 72 hours, are difficult to enforce. Santa Barbara limits RV and trailer parking to two hours; Encinitas bans overnight parking of RVs on its streets without a permit. Kristen Green (from 23Je05 San Diego Union-Tribune; sent by Phyllis (thanks)

Thoughts about dwelling in vehicles.

If we were to choose between a house and a motor vehicle, we'd get a vehicle. As long as it keeps running, it can take us places that otherwise may be difficult to get to; and, if we get hassled, we can more easily move. Whereas, in a house you "own" (actually you are just leasing from the government), you are a "sitting duck" for anyone who wants to "get you".

Unless I had a very profitable business that needed a van, I think I'd choose a fairly big hatch-back car. I'd remove the rear seats and install a secure deck under which I would sleep; and (if I lacked a better place) eat, read, write, listen to music on earphones, and sponge-bathe a few body parts. (But I'd shower, and do any cooking and any noisy activities elsewhere.) I'd insulate my sleeping compartment well (easy, because small) so I wouldn't need artificial heat.

The deck would be low enough to not obstruct the windows, and would have stuff on top of it so that its purpose would not be obvious to someone peeking in. With such a vehicle, I think I could park even in neighborhoods lousy with housing-bigots without getting hassled. (These are off-hand thoughts. Experienced vehicle dwellers will probably have better ideas.)

When selecting a vehicle, unless I planned to drive it many miles (which I'd do only if essential for a business), I'd choose something cheap. It would likely not only burn more fuel, but not be capable of going many miles without costly repairs. But those are not big financial concerns if not going many miles. As for environmental concerns: LOW-mileage use of an old "gas hog" consumes less resources and generates less pollution than does manufacturing a new vehicle. Bert

Lew carried all his tools in a van.

So he could do just about any job on site. Small table saw, planer, chop saw, Skill-saw, Sawzall, jig saw, router, and several portable drills - along with other carpentry and plumbing and electrical tools. He did foundation work to cabinet work - and took everything to the job. It's a great idea for a young builder - keep it portable so you can go anywhere in the country. There's a great demand for solo building like this. Lloyd Kahn (final thoughts in his book Home Work, listed in "Off the Beaten Path")

I purchased a small 2-stroke, 25cc, 9-pound bicycle engine.

From www.bikeengines.com. I rode 1100 miles from Tucson to Seattle last fall with no problems hauling 65 pounds of gear on a BOB trailer. Speed depends on load, terrain, wind; but I averaged about 25 mph. I get between 180-240 mpg depending on terrain, load, speed.

The engine installs above the rear tire on the gear side. I installed it in about an hour. It uses a drive ring that snaps onto the spokes, and a belt that goes from that to a gear on the engine. Three gears are available: trail, standard, highway. I ride a lot with loads behind me so I usually use trail gear. But on open flat roads, even with a load, the standard or highway gears result in faster speeds and better gas mileage. Changing gears take about 5 min. The engine kit is designed for mountain bikes with 24-26" tires.

I have really enjoyed this engine. It seemed pricey at $600, but I have since let my truck insurance expire (because I hadn't driven it in a year) which saved me $400 - plus much gas and oil. The engine has saved me money, at least compared to my past habits, and it gives me the mobility I need without the hassle of licensing, insurance, special permits (none are needed in the U.S. unless an engine is over 50 cc). Another web site to check if interested in serious hauling with a bike: www.bikesatwork.com. They have a 8-foot model that can haul several hundred pounds as well as long items. I intend to get their 5' model to haul my tools to the small home-repair jobs I do for money from time to time. Lauran, AZ, July 05

(Question:) How noisy is the engine ? Quiet seems important for safety - hearing approaching vehicles. Even with a good stable rear-view mirror, may not see vehicles soon enough to get safely off the road if no shoulder or if gravel-and-sloping shoulder; especially if winding road.

I wonder, in how many states is riding on the shoulders of freeways legal ? (Was in Oregon.) That seems safer than riding on almost all 2-lane highways. Bert, Sept 05

(Response.) I arrived in Tucson after riding, with bike engine, 2317 miles over 38 days, hauling 55-75 lbs of gear (depending on food/water levels). For the most part I enjoyed myself. The noise isn't bad: it is behind me and on the right, so it "trails" while riding. I do have rear-view mirrors, one on each end of the handlebars. I would never ride without them, engine or no. I focus the left mirror for cars and the right mirror on the load to make sure it is covered and secure.

I do wear ear-plugs while riding, not because of the engine but rather the traffic noise which frays my nerves after a few hours. The ear-plugs don't eliminate sound, but buffer it enough to make it tolerable yet allow me to hear.

I frequently check the mirrors and so am rarely caught off guard by upcoming vehicles. But it does happen (eg, fast vehicle, sharp curve) and is jarring. On this trip it happened less than ten times, as I recall.

I put a bright green neon "wide load" sign on the back of the trailer, partly for visual safety and partly hoping that a little humor might help keep a potentially annoyed driver respectful. I also have on the trailer a 5-foot pole with a red neon flag. Both increase visibility.

I now have just over 4000 miles on the bike engine. Counting the $600 price plus two belts totalling $80, but not gas and oil, the engine has so far cost 17¢ a mile. As for durability, the company said: their longest-running engine to date has 20,000 miles on it, and they have not had any engine failures during the 6 years they have been selling them.

Regarding freeway riding, my understanding: legal only if no other route is available. That is too bad, as I've twice had to take an Interstate and I've felt much safer having so much room between me and vehicles. Lauran, AZ, Jan 06

(Comment.) No matter how visible the rider's flags and clothes, riding thousands of miles on highways seems dangerous. Many motorists, esp drivers of big trucks (who hate to brake because they need much time and fuel to regain speed), feel that roads belong to them. (They pay to use them; bicyclists don't.) Often they try to squeeze by where   isn't room, hitting

the bike or forcing it off the road. Though an engine-assist
bike has the advantage of being on the road less time to go the
same distance, its higher speed increases the time needed to
slow and get safely off the road onto a bad shoulder.
     For long-distance seasonal traveling, I'd try hard to
arrange rides. Many "snow-bird" RVers go south in autumn and
north in spring, and may welcome fuel contributions. If we
spent much time around big cities, I think we could make
connections. Even from the smaller cities we infrequently
visit, we were able to get rides SOUTH the few winters we went.
Coming back north was a problem, partly because we usually
returned in February (because of DP mail obligations), and most
"snow-birds" don't go north before April. So we usually had to
hitch. (Hitching has become very risky now that cops have
hassle quotas and may try to pin unsolved crimes on non-natives
- TX is notorious for that. Hitchers are stationary targets
and thus easier to hassle than motorists.) Holly & Bert

Bicycle trailers, one wheel or two ? My experience:
     The 2-wheel Burley Nomad feels stable while riding and can
often carry more weight comfortably. The BOB's single wheel
tracks beautifully behind the bike's rear wheel and so is the
best choice for trail riding and backwoods going, but is
awkward to back up and park.
     The Burley, even with 100 lbs in the back, doesn't put
more than 11 lbs on the tongue. Whereas the BOB has more
tongue weight per load, and so can be harder on the bike and
you feel it more.
     The Burley, which has a rectangular bed, is easier to load
and manage, whereas the BOB is teardrop shape.
     The Burley tracks a bit to the left, to keep the right
tire out of ditches when on narrow shoulders. On my bike, its
wheels are inside the width of my handlebars, so I can easily
judge where I can and can't go safely. The BOB's width is
about from one pedal to the other. Lauran, AZ, July 05

Venom extractor proved effective on tick bite, but fragile.
     I bought a Sawyer "Extractor" kit at BiMart ($14). When I
attached the smallest cup to the syringe, the cup cracked. The
store exchanged my kit for a new one.   I'd put the cup on tight.
Now I leave it looser. But it seems delicate. Also, it says: do
not get the syringe wet. Durability ? Made in China.
     I used it on a tick bite, after removing the tick with fine-
pointed tweezers. The Extractor drew out fluid and blood. The
bite healed quicker than usual with less redness and soreness.
     Later Bert and I tested, on unbitten skin, the Extractor's
cup with mouth suction as well as with the Extractor. It applied
stronger suction than our mouths could, raising a bigger hickey
in 30 seconds. Also, Extractor suction can be more easily
applied for several minutes than can mouth suction. Recently I
found that, by attaching the cup to the Extractor with surgical
tubing, I can use Extractor in tight places. Holly, Jan 2006

What is wrong with the boy-scout bridge on the first page ?
     The brace ropes at the end are steep, putting stresses
that are unnecessarily high on the support poles and ropes.
The anchor stakes will probably pull out of the ground,
collapsing the bridge and dumping the boy.
     The anchor ropes should be longer and anchored farther
away, so they are not as steep. Also, those little anchor
stakes don't look strong. I'd tie to the base of a big tree.
Or, if none is available, to the base of a BIG stake, deeply
buried, with its TOP braced to the BASE of a smaller stake.
Av Dave, Oregon 978   May 2006

Surviving in the hills and towns of western North Carolina.
During Eric Rudolph's 5 years as a fugitive, despite a
nationwide manhunt and a million-dollar bounty, a hobo came
closer to catching him than did any federal agent.
The search for Eric, accused of abortion-clinic bombings
that killed two people and injured   100, had focused on the
densely-wooded mountainous western tip of NC. Eric had spent
his teenage years there and had returned as an adult in the
early 1990s, supporting himself doing carpentry.
In letters to his mother, written from jail, Eric described
how he repeatedly sneaked into Andrews (population 1600) at
night to scavenge food - even after scores of federal agents
who were hunting him had set up their headquarters there !
Eric describes one mid-Oct foray. "On this particular
night the air was cool, fall having started a month before.
I was hesitant to get out from under my improvised bed, which
was made of leaves and plastic." But he was hungry. He
needed food. Forget hunting. That summer he had found an
easier if riskier way of getting it. Shortly before midnight
he started toward Andrews. "The mountain trail down to the
road was steep and full of obstacles. Traversing it in the
dark without a flashlight was done primarily from memory.
Each step must be calculated and correlated with the surrounding shadows produced by the trees and the general landscape.
Once you get used to the step count and how the trail looks
at night, it becomes fairly easy."
At the road, he paused in a clump of bushes and shrubs
and waited for traffic to subside. Then he headed to "a real
godsend - two big, well-tended gardens right on the way to
town. I had to be extremely gentle with the frozen plastic
(which protected the plants from frost) for across the street,
on the porch of the gardener's house, was my nemesis: a 20-
pound pile of canine crap waiting patiently on guard for the
slightest noise. A sound from the garden would send him into
a rage, forcing my hasty retreat. I tried to make friends by
feeding him (scavenged McDonald's hamburgers), but he would
have none of my bribery. He hated me, and I hated him."
The gardener reminises: "Someone could get a dozen ears
of corn and you wouldn't know it. Now my brother, he got to
missing a lot of tomatoes."
On that night, "everything went smoothly and I proceeded
to bag my take and put it under bushes on the side of the road
where I would retrieve it on my way back."
At Andrews, the road crossed a highway and then a river.
Instead of using the well-lit bridge, Eric waded the river
wearing waders he'd "improvised out of plastic garbage bags
and string." In Andrews, "my first stop was the green garbage
can behind Gibson Furniture" where he often found magazines
and cigarettes. "A little work back at camp, cut the filters
down and wipe the remainder with a clean towel, and you have
nicotine-induced bliss." Then, behind McDonald's, he picked
through the burgers tossed out at closing; and behind the
grocery store he looked through its trash bin. Sometimes he
even went through the cinema's trash for unsold popcorn.
Other nights, Eric obtained hundreds of pounds of corn,
wheat, soybeans from silos. A mix of them, boiled, then
pounded into pancakes and fried, proved to be "a staple that
sustained me for many years." He would climb to the top of a
silo, open the hatch, and scoop the feed into doubled trash
bags (which he'd salvaged, washed, dried). He temporarily
stored the bags of grain in garbage cans he'd previously
stolen and set behind a lone (abandoned ?) building across the

road. "One night I had to wait atop the silo for a few hours as a state trooper set up across the road to lay in wait for hapless speeders. He would race off to catch one, and after writing his ticket he'd return." Another time, Eric thought he had been spotted by a hunter along the creek behind the building. He scurried up a ridge and watched - but the feds didn't come. "For whatever reason, the hunter didn't divulge what happened." To haul the cans of grain to his camp, on Halloween he stole a pickup from a used-car lot. The pickup was found a few weeks later. The owner says, the police "didn't even dust for fingerprints or anything."

A scary encounter happened one night when Eric was searching through trash for materials to improve his leaf sleeping bag. "Right on top was a large piece of plastic perfectly draped over the top of a long rectangular box. I proceeded to fold it up. (Then) the box began to slowly open, like a coffin lid in a vampire movie, and there in the box was the barely visible figure of a human being. My thoughts started racing. Was this an ambush? Did someone see me going through the garbage on a previous night and set this up?" The figure spoke to Eric, in a voice that "came hard - probably damaged by years of alcohol and cigarettes. Suddenly it came to me. 'This is a bum'." Eric replied, then slowly moved away. But Eric worried: "Did he recognize me? Would he run and tell?" (Many "wanted" notices with Eric's picture had probably been posted.) I made my way quickly back across the river, splashing through the cold water." After climbing the far bank, Eric looked back. The person hadn't moved. "But was he just waiting to catch his breath before leaving? Then, after several tense moments, the person lit a cigarette, and every few drags he would let out a few gut-wrenching coughs. After finishing his cigarette, he lifted the lid on his box, climbed back in, and lay back down to sleep." But Eric waited a week before going into that town again.

On a Saturday night in May 2003, Eric went to a grocery store in the neighboring town of Murphy. "A Saturday night is a good night for garbage. I had a pile of bananas already, but thought I could get more and end my fruit drying early this year. Pushing aside my fears, I left my camp."

To cross a bridge, if a car approached he'd have to "hang over the side of the bridge on the other side of the rail", the shallow river 50 feet below. "Finally I get over the bridge and make my way through the field toward the dumpsters. At this point, (to see) what is coming around the sides of the building, I have to rely solely on the sight of (glare from) headlights. So I sit in the field looking from side to side, waiting for the patrol." The cop drives by "usually once an hour, but on weekends, with drunks and teenagers to deal with, his schedule is uncertain. For 3 years I have dodged him; on many a cold night he has come within inches of finding me. One night, while I was hiding in the dumpster at Taco Bell, he got out of his car, went into the dumpster area, and urinated on the dumpster I was hiding in. But on this particular night the cop was the least of my worries. Having to haul 200 lbs of fruit up to camp was on my mind. I run toward the dumpster." But when Eric was halfway there, the cop's car came whipping around the corner of the building with lights off. "This is unusual, for he never (before) turned them off, and this is how I've spotted him coming around the building."

The Murphy police officer had been a cop for less than a year when he spotted Eric and arrested him. Blake Morrison (condensed from 6July05 USA Today)   May 2006

Another method for cleaning a narrow-mouth container.
I fill it about 1/3 full of coarse sand, add a few drops
of soap and enough water to make a slurry, and shake well. With
persistence, cleans even stubborn deposits. Lauran, AZ, 2005

Attaching jug lid with duct tape, makes berry picking easier.
After making sure that the jug and lid
are clean and dry where the tape will adhere,
I firmly press the tape on. (If the tape does
not adhere as well as I'd like, I reinforce by
putting a second piece cross-wise over the
first piece and around the jug.)
Then I twist and scrunch together the
linking part of the tape to create a cord.
The cord must be long enough so that movement
of the lid does not put much force on the
tape where it attaches. Twisting/scrunching
shortens the tape, so allow extra length.
After losing one snap-lid, I did this.
It proved a great convenience when picking,
because I put the lid on and off frequently:
on, when I move over rough ground where I
might fall, or through (eg) rye grass which
can splatter barbed sharp-pointed seeds in
among the berries; off, when I reach the
next berry bush. Also, when I remove the
lid, I can just let it dangle; I don't
have to put it somewhere.
     If I tumble, a snap lid-and-jug is not
as secure as a screw lid-and-jug, but the
lid is easier to put on and off.
     I rig a harness (not shown - an old pant leg, or a strong
bag with straps ball-tied to it, might serve) around the jug
so that I can wear it, leaving both hands free for picking.
                                                              Holly

Eating Nopali cactus - and removing stickers !
     De-thorned Nopali leaves are found in every Mexican
market's produce section. Nopali (prickly pear - Opuntia
polyacantha), a succulent, is endemic to all of the American
West, from Sonora north into BC. Boil in soup; or stir fry
strips; or add diced to salads; or cook with sweetener and
then dry, making candy.
     Smaller northern variants may lack the sweet purple fruit
found on the Sonoran kind, but are good eating. Free for the
harvesting at roadsides, or from public lands (except in
Arizona which has no-picking laws).
     You need to work carefully to avoid the stickers. I use a
long-bladed knife to chop free the leaves, and then two tong-
like sticks to carry the leaves to a campfire for scorching off
the fuzzy thorn tufts. If, despite precautions, you get the
hundreds of tiny hair-like thorns stuck in your hands, smear a
thin coat of white (Elmer's) glue over the affected area, let
dry for 15 minutes, then peel off the glue film with the thorns
all at once. Otherwise, make sure before-hand that those tiny
tweezers are still inside that Swiss knife - and allow 30 min
for picking the thorns out one by one. Brijji, Utah, Dec 04

(Addendum.) Prickly-pear grow in desert areas of BC, like the
Okanogan near Osoyoos and Keremeos. Aarran, BC V8K

Ways we use damaged plastic containers.

Some pails had slits when acquired (caused by too-deep cutting when originally opened) or developed cracks. Others got punctured by a bear's teeth or claws (report in May 06 DP). Some lids had pour spouts which soon broke off. While awaiting better containers, we repaired with duct tape. Our patches endured a few months, even when rained on.

Punctured pails are still useful under cover for grouping small items. Or, a pail or jug with a hole in one side, can be cut in two and its good half used as a basin. Holly & Bert

Huge hasty hazel harvest hardly hearty.

In years past, we sometimes encountered hazel nuts while foraging berries. We picked a few but didn't get enough to excite us. However, the summer before last, we were in the right place at the right time - or so it seemed. Many bushes, some bearing dozens of good-size shells.

The nuts were not yet fully ripe but if we waited, the critters would get them. We picked and picked - many hours. Picking is slow because the husks are almost the same color as the leaves and difficult to spot. Got 15 gal - BEFORE husking.

To dry, each day we set them out in shade, some in net bags, some on old window screens we'd fortuitously found. Each evening we put them away in pails. That went on for a few wks.

To husk, Bert half filled a 10-gal tote and, wearing rubber mocs, tramped on them for ten minutes, picked out the shells and husks that had separated, and tramped on those that remained - again. That wore away the inside layer of the Rubbermaid tote ! After husking, we had maybe 5 gallons.

To shell, we used nutcrackers and pliers - and discovered that the nuts which had seemed plump when unripe, had shrunk: the largest to pea size, most to lentil size. A third of the shells contained no nuts. Hardly worth shelling by hand. (We thought about passing them through the grain grinder set loose, but didn't try.) We still have about 2 gallons unshelled.

Except for blackberries and possibly nettles, none of the foods we commonly forage provide as many calories as we expend harvesting them. But they provide variety: trace nutrients. Calories are cheap to buy and quite light to transport IF in dry seeds such as grains and beans. (We seldom buy canned or fresh foods: not only are they mostly water; they are more perishable and generally more polluted.) Holly & Bert, Feb 06

Participating in Nature: Thomas J. Elpel's Field Guide.

"In order to survive on a particular food source, you have to be able to harvest more calories than you expend. Many 'edible' wild plants require so much effort to harvest that you could starve to death even if you ate all day long every day."

Bitterroot (Lewisia sp.) "The foothills behind our home have small colonies - not enough to justify harvesting. However, I discovered a patch of 1000s of plants 35 miles away. I collected over a gallon of the whole plants during a one-hour harvest in May. Trimming away the vegetation left approx 1½ qts of roots. Pealing off the bitter bark took another 8 hrs ! The peeled roots cook up nicely in a stew. They are starchy, gelatinous, and filling. However, it is important to remove all the red bark. Even a little bit will make the whole stew bitter beyond edibility.... I've since learned that the Flathead Indians test the roots in mid April to see when the bark slips easily.... As with many wild plants, precise timing is the critical factor.... You have to get the roots at exactly

the right time to be able to process them efficiently.
When he started camping, Elpel tried to subsist on foraged
foods - and was usually hungry. Now he also takes food along.
"Much of the wilderness goes unused. People stay on a
handful of well-defined trails leading to a few spectacular
lakes and peaks. The smaller streams, trickles, springs and
ponds are usually unused and unknown.... People rarely wander
off the beaten path except in hunting season, so for the most
part you can have the woods to yourself...."
"In all my reading I found very few shelters that could
be built relatively quickly and still keep a person alive and
comfortable. And those, unfortunately required materials
that were not present in my area...."
"Instead of merely giving you some various shelters for
you to replicate, I want to teach you how to THINK shelter.
You see, every time and place is different, and at every time
and place your own personal goals or objectives will also be
different.... The type of shelter you build, and the location
you choose for it, will vary tremendously depending on the
TIME, the PLACE, and your GOALS. Therefore, every primitive
shelter you ever build will be completely unique, and suited
to the particular conditions at hand...."
Though some other primitive-skills books give more
details, Elpel's advice seems sounder because he tells what has
actually worked for him, including problems encountered. His
specific suggestions are esp applicable to where he lives: in
sw Montana about halfway between Butte and Bozeman.
"I rarely build freestanding shelters like the wickiup.
I use the same principles but I prefer to begin by selecting a
campsite that takes advantage of some natural features of the
environment. For example, in an area with sizable trees, I
look for a big tree that has fallen over, leaving just enough
space for me to crawl underneath, that can be improved upon by
leaning slabs of bark against one or both sides of the tree to
widen the dry space underneath. Slabs of bark are natural
shingles and really easy to use.... Simply start at the bottom
of your shelter and layer the bark up to the top, so that the
water will always fall from one bark shingle to another....
"A tarp or poncho is an easy one piece shingle....
"On winter camping trips I wear sweat pants over my jeans
so" I can easily "stuff grass or other insulation inside...."
"The leaf hut is an excellent shelter in areas where there
is a lot of dead organic matter on the ground, such as deep
layers of tree leaves. The inside is shaped like a sleeping
bag, defined by sticks leaning against a horizontal ridge pole.
This is typically covered over with two feet of leaves, serving
the dual purpose of insulation and shingling.... It stays warm
with only your body heat." But, where Elpel lives, there isn't
enough accessible organic matter for leaf huts to be practical.
"It makes more sense for me to adapt my shelter to the local
resources such as dirt, logs, stone, than to hike 5 or 10 miles
to bring back a huge quantity of cattails." For a temp camp
during cold weather, Elpel often first builds a fire to warm
the ground before improvising a shelter on it.
"Most primitive skills literature and archeological
records are oriented toward bulky material culture like baskets,
pottery, weaponry. By the time you make these, plus your bow
drill set, your shelter, and your tanned hides - you need a
pickup truck to move to your next campsite." Elpel favors
traveling light, carrying minimal tools and supplies.
1998, 198p.8½x11, HOPS Press, www.hollowtop.com; in 2006,
Granny's Country Store, POB 684, Silver Star MT 59751, $25.

(Partial review by Bert, who had time only to read the
shelter chapter (18p.) and skim plants (30p.) before returning
it to a library for a friend. Others: mind (attitudes) 27p.,
fire 20p, cooking 20p, animals 26p, clothing 20p, ecology 16p.)

Different ways for different people in different places.
(Thoughts stimulated by the foregoing book.) Elpel makes
much more use of fire for warmth than we do, probably because
he lives in a colder climate. Also perhaps, most of his camps
are brief, without time for much insulating; whereas most of
our winter camps are used for weeks or months. (At our camp
this winter, with body heat only: during a cold spell, early in
morn, 23° outside, 52° inside; typical morn, 35° out, 60° in.)
Our camps might seem luxurious to Elpel, who often
improvises shelters in small holes. Our shelter, this winter
and most winters, is in a hole, but a big hole (natural, but I
also spent many days digging to shape it). However, our camp
is our home. (We type our zines on a 70?-year-old manual
typewriter.) Whereas Elpel also has a house in town, built by
he and his wife mostly out of natural materials at the site.
(He composes his books on a computer.)
Like Elpel's, each of our camps is different, even though
it may consist mostly of the same materials. (I've used
"wikiup" as a generic term for various kinds of insulated
shelters, most of which were not free standing.) B&H, Feb 06

I spent several snowy winter months in a 5x7x5-foot wall tent.
Made from blue poly tarps. I kept a fire going in a home-
made 5-gallon-can wood stove with a 4" galvanized pipe. The
tent was cozy - and toasty (in the small space the stove had
to be a little too close to my sleeping bag).
Now, years later, I'd think twice before breathing so much
air containing substances that out-gas from heated plastic and
galvanized metal. I'd use less plastic, esp where it is exposed
to heat. Also, I recently read that galvanized coatings contain
much cadmium and other toxic metals; so I'd pay a bit more for
the better stove-blacked pipe and burn it out thoroughly before
closing myself in with it. I think that most toxic building
materials out-gas less as they age. Doug, WA 988, March 2006

(Addendum.) Re out-gassing. That is what we found with a
small Stansport dome-tent we bought 15 years ago. At first it
stunk, probably from a fire retardant (notoriously toxic) that
government regs require. (Aren't you glad that gov protects
you ?!) At first we did not occupy it. Instead, for a few
summers, we hung it (so mice could not easily move in), erected
and opened, in the shade (so that sun would not deteriorate the
nylon). The smell SLOWLY went away. Now we often live in/out-
of the Stansport during summers, and don't notice any odor -
all the more reason to buy/scavenge USED tents/clothes/materials
(we'd bought the tent new), but wise to launder before using.
B&H

Giant blanket, draped over dome tent, added warmth.
Last autumn, our move to a winter base-camp got delayed
(by projects that took longer than expected). During November
we were still at a summer site, living in and out of our 6x7x4'
Stansport tent. Most days were still sunny and pleasant. But
the long nights got cold, often frosty. The tent was within an
open-fronted plastic rain/wind shelter. With both of us in the
tent, typical dawn temperatures: 30° outside, 40° inside -
tolerable for sleeping but not for tasks requiring bare hands.
Years before, we had acquired (from a dumpster ?) a BIG
Dwelling Portably   September 2006

blanket. (Too big for any bed I can imagine. Original use ?)
It had languished, STUFFED (with difficulty) into a 5-gal pail.
(For our bed, we prefer sleeping bags opened out, or quilts -
more warmth per weight.) I draped the blanket over the tent.
It reached most of the way to the ground on all sides. It
warmed the inside at dawn to 50° - tolerable for hand work.
    Would several blankets, sewed into a dome shape, have
provided more warmth yet allowed enough ventilation ? Another
winter, I had covered a dome-tent with a 3-inch-thick layer of
moss (report in Apr 2000 DP), which had kept the inside 30°
warmer than outside. (Last autumn, not time to gather moss.)
    The Stansport tent (made in Taiwan) has held up well -
better than expected. No broken poles or balky zippers - yet.
But its biggest load was that blanket when damp with condensation; no snow load or gale wind. (Longer report in Sept 02 DP.)
                                                        B&H
Cave dweller discovered on militarily-restricted land.
    During his 4 years there, Roy Moore carved out a comfort-
able home. The 56-year-old veteran had solar panels wired to
car batteries for electricity, a wood-burning stove, a bed, a
glass door, a satellite radio, and ten 18-inch-high marijuana
plants growing in soil outside the cave.
    The cave is in Los Alamos Canyon, a quarter mile from
Trinity St in Los Alamos and a half mile from Omega Bridge. It
is well-hidden at the bottom of a steep cliff in a restricted
area belonging to Los Alamos National Laboratory (LANL).
    On Oct 13, a LANL employee spotted smoke and called the
fire department. The deputy chief said, the fire in Roy's
stove, the first of the season, had released a plume of soot
and black smoke. (Presumably, Roy had had fires for previous
winters without producing smoke that had been seen.)
    LANL said, the cave is not near any critical or high
security areas. However, the marijuana prompted someone to
call the Los Alamos police who arrested Roy, charging him
with possession - a felony. Roy pleaded innocent and was
released on $5000 bond. (Jason Auslander, Albuquerque J,290c04)
    Roy then moved to the eastern rim of Pajarito Mtn, an
extinct volcano. His camp, below a ski resort, overlooked LANL
and the Rio Grande valley. Three months later, a Forest Service
law-enforcer asked Roy to move. He then moved in with his
daughter and her boy friend who have a studio apartment in Los
Alamos. There, he baby-sits his grandkids.
    A former computer programmer, Roy quit his job in 1996 and
sold all his possessions, to simplify his life so he could
focus on developing his unifying theory of the universe. He
moved from Amarillo to Los Alamos because of its proximity to
LANL and its dense population of PhDs and deep thinkers. He
has given talks at the Los Alamos library.
    Roy said, during his 3-month stay on Pajarito Mtn, he
enjoyed watching the ravens and deciphering their different
calls, noting how the calls changed as the birds became familiar
with him and learned to associate him with food scraps. Adam
Rankin (25De04 Alb.Jnl.; off internet by L.Smith - THANKS)

(Comments.) No mention of how Roy's second camp was found,
nor of what happened with the marijuana charge.
    Encouraging ravens to come around by providing food scraps,
seems risky. Ravens, and other birds of the crow family, are
especially likely to carry West Nile Virus.
    Media give a biased impression of the risks of dwelling in
ways not approved by Big Bully, because, with rare exceptions,
only people who are discovered, are publicized. My accessment:
                Dwelling Portably   September 2006

Suppose I camp 30 miles from a city and bicycle there once a
month. The biggest dangers: (1) getting hit by a vehicle
while biking; (2) catching flu (or ?) while in the city. B&H

Fires thrive on attention.
Move together pieces of wood that are too far apart, or
spread those that are too close together. A fire tolerates a
void under it but not within it. Fuel should be put on in time
to be adequately dried and preheated.
The cure for a smoky fire is often a matter of proper
adjustment of the wood. If that does not help, the fuel may be
too green or wet. Putting on dry, finer fuel will help burn up
more products of inadequate combustion and the improved thermal
column will carry the troublesome smoke up and over your head
more effectively. Mors Kochanski, Northern Bushcraft (reviewed
in Se05 DP

A "Dakota Hole" cooking fire did not work well for me.
Its configuration was mid-way between Tim Leather's (May94
DP) and Eugene Gonzalez's (Apr01 DP). Bert dug it but then got
busy doing other things, so it was I who tried to cook with it.
The fire was smokier than an open fire. The connecting tunnel
kept getting clogged with fallen dirt and/or ash, but even when
open seemed to not supply enough air. So I soon changed to one
hole with a metal grate over it and the pot on the grate.
Bert now wonders if the pot was too big for the hole, thus
acting like the damper on a stove's chimney. We will try again
when we have more time to experiment. Holly & Bert, Feb 2006

Durability and reliability of various fire starters.
Most storable: a magnesium bar that has an artificial
flint on one side. With a knife, scrape off a small pile of
magnesium shavings as tinder, then strike the flint to put
sparks into the shavings. I had to strike quite a few sparks
before one ignited the magnesium. It works as well now as it
did 23 years ago when I bought it. However, I haven't used it
much so I don't know how many fires I could start before either
the magnesium or flint was used up. (Reports in May82 & Se82 DP)
Propane lighters have worked okay after several years of
storage, but I noticed some corrosion of the flints. Also, the
lighters have quite a few parts that can go wrong.
I bought some Coghlan "waterproof" matches 23 years ago.
I also coated various Diamond matches by dipping both ends in
melted paraffin. After soaking in water as long as 20 hours,
the 2¼" Diamond kitchen (strike-anywhere) matches lit best.
Whereas, after soaking only 3 hours, the Coghlan did not light
until both matches and strikers (not strike-anywhere) had dried
many hours. However, now, after 23 years storage, Coghlan's
still light fairly well; Diamond's not at all. Julia Summers,
(Comments.) More about Julia's match tests in Fe82 DP.   Oc05
The most durable and reliable lighters we have: big (8x10)
flexible plastic ridged-lenses. They can ignite even damp
tinder, and have nothing to get used up and little that can go
wrong. However, you need sunshine - which is not usually when
you want a fire. So, you also need a way to keep an ember. H&B

Further report on solar cooking: our problems and fixes.
(This is an update to reports in Se02, Se04, Ap05 DPs.)
During 2005, like in 04 and 03, we began solar cooking on
sunny days in May, and solar-cooked almost exclusively from
July through Sept. Though Oct included many days with sunny
afternoons, and we had no problem heating water for showers and

clothes washing, the sun was no longer bright enough long enough
for reliable cooking. (During Oct and Nov, still at our summer
camp, we fire cooked on a stove made from tin cans (somewhat
like Fred's in May03 DP). In late Nov, we moved to a winter
camp where we still have propane.)

The biggest change: completing the third big 8-panel
reflector (panels 13x17"). Instead of aluminum foil, I covered
the panels with aluminized plastic from a "space blanket". We
were given the blanket many years ago, but had not used it, and
with our mode of camping, seemed not likely to.) Upon opening
it, I found that a big irregular area in the middle was not
aluminized (which might not have much affected its usefulness
as a blanket because the person would be laying on that portion).
However, I was able to trim enough aluminized pieces.

I also found that the blanket consisted of one layer of
plastic with an aluminum coating (unlike some snack bags which
seem to sandwich the aluminum between two layers of plastic).
So - indecision ! Should I glue the plastic with aluminum-side
out, or plastic-side out ? The aluminum side was shiniest and
the aluminum seemed to adhere well. (I had to rub vigorously
with paper to get any off.) But how well would it withstand
repeated wipings/washings to remove dust or grime - or when
food accidentally dropped on it ? On the other hand, if the
aluminum faced inward, would glue adhere to it ?

I put plastic-side out. Later I put aluminum-side out on
a foam disk that sets under a glass jug for heating water -
and the aluminum came off on the jug !

At first, the aluminized plastic was shinier and tougher
than aluminum foil. But NOT more durable: after two months
use, the plastic began disintegrating, mostly on the bottom
center panel which receives the most concentrated sunlight and
heat. Would the plastic have endured longer if put on aluminum
side out, so the aluminum shaded the plastic ? When I replace
it, I'll try shiny snack bags if I've found enough to cover one
panel; otherwise aluminum foil.

We'd also like a better material for insulative shrouds
over the pots. The salvaged transparent plastic we've been
using, disintegrates after two summers of sun and heat. (We
tried patching with transparent packaging tape, but sun/heat
soon unstuck it.) We are hoping to find, at yard sales or in
dumpsters, small sheet-acrylic aquariums. (Acrylic supposedly
endures sunlight well.) Until we do, we will try oven bags
draped over racks made of wire coat-hangers.

We have not had a really good solar cooking site. For the
past few years, most of our summer camps have been on north-
facing slopes (because foraging is usually better there - south-
facing slopes get too hot and dry) and not far above valley
bottoms. Consequently, any low haze/fog/smoke weakens the sunshine; and distant trees and hills block the sun early morns
and late afternoons, so we may get only 6 hours of sun.

Overall, solar cooking takes less labor than does wood-
fire cooking (counting collecting and cutting wood) and no more
labor than propane cooking (counting buying and transporting
propane), but requires that one person stay nearby while cooking
(for several hours) to reposition the reflectors. What would
help: rotating platforms that automatically track the sun.
They are made (sometimes used with pv panels) but aren't cheap.
                                                          B&H

How to increase storage life of dry foods.
      Keep them dry, and as cool as possible. Rough rule: each
10° drop in temperature halves the rate of deterioration. Eg,
          Dwelling Portably   September 2006

if sunflower seeds can be stored one month at 70° before more than a few become rancid, their life might be 2 months at 60°, 4 months at 50°, 8 months at 40° (typical frig), 16 months at 30° (freezing), 32 months at 20°, 64 months (over 5 yrs) at 10° (typical freezer). In our area, average temperature of a buried barrel with an inch of styrofoam or a few inches of dry debris over it, is 50° to 60°. Coolest on a steep north-facing slope.

For extremely long storage, removal of oxygen from the air in the storage container is recommended. (See article in Ab#2.) Not quite as good: replacing most of the contained air with carbon dioxide from dry ice. (Wait for the dry ice to evaporate before sealing the lid tight; else it may explode !)

Find a hot spring and build your own soaking pool.

Guide books give the locations of popular pools, but they may be crowded or require permits. However, throughout much of the West, many unknown or unpublicized hot springs are free to anyone who finds them. By snooping around the right geo areas (eg, near known hot springs) you may spot the tell-tale (bright green) mossy rocks or, in winter, steam. A few hours work will create a delightful spot for relaxing.

A friend and I discovered hot water bubbling up through sand along a river. We made a pool by laying boulders around a 15-foot circle and scooping away the sand. We added sand bags (made from old Levi pant legs) and a drain pipe. We brought in clay from up the river which, after settling, reduced seepage out through the sand. That gave us a perfect cold-weather pool next to some scenic rapids. While trying it out, a couple of river otters came to see what we were doing.

In earlier experiments I tried metal tubs. But they either got destroyed or were taken out by the Forest Service. Some years ago, a local bath house was torn down after some nit wit slipped on the moss and sued the Forest Service.

Though most pools with substantial flows are safe, much-used pools in (eg) S CA can carry pathogens. I put a dash of vet-supply iodine in them. A few pools have tiny worms growing in the moss. I screen out the moss and put a little soap in the water to deactivate the worms. A long soak in hot water can dehydrate; keep a jug of drinking water handy. A brief dip in cool water will usually restore energy. Al Fry, ID 836, Jan 06

How we dispose of feces, in winter and summer.

During winter when at a base camp with a well-insulated shelter, we usually defecate inside. We shit on several sheets of paper, which also serve to wrap it. (Details in May 96 DP.) We temporarily store it in a pail with lid on, kept outside. When the pail is full, Bert takes it along while foraging or fetching spring water. He empties the pail into some natural depression, well away from our camp and any water, and not within sight of trails, and covers with a little dirt/debris/leaves. We don't dig latrines at a camp where we may remain long, because doing so would disturb much vegetation.

When at a short-term summer camp, we usually dig a narrow-hole latrine (described in a Light Living Library paper). We seldom shit directly into the latrine because it is usually not close and has bushes around it. Shitting on paper is easier.

The only problems we've encountered: During winter, hungry critters often dig up feces, creating a visible mess. (The paper is more visible than the feces, and more durable.) During spring, stinky mushrooms sometimes grow on the feces. Neither problem is serious if the deposits are not near our camps. At some places during summer, the soil, dry then, is very hard.

Dwelling Portably   September 2006

Report on Yukon in northwestern Canada.
    If I had to travel much through the Yukon, I would bicycle,
even though that is time consuming. Hitching is tough there,
though legal and you do get rides eventually. May be, my
attitude and dislike of hitching shows on my face. Companies
like Greyhound bus lines have a monopoly on adult bus fares.
    In 2005 (a rough year for me financially), I traveled out
of town less than in 2004, but I covered many more miles. In
Oct, I and my brother (who drove his pickup-camper) went on a
5-day weekend holiday roadtrip to Whitehorse and back. My
brother is a redneck hunter and drove there to visit a friend
living in Haines Junction. Campground fees are about $13 a
night. We usually parked the pickup-camper on some back road
in wooded surroundings, out of sight of traffic and residences.
    In some ways I find Yukon more appealing than my home area
(in central BC). Much wilder: fantastic fishing, hunting,
camping. And, in summer, 24 hours of daylight. But Yukon is
an EXPENSIVE place to live. Groceries and other supplies cost
much more. I pity some of the people there, such as lodge
owners, who rely on tourist dollars to keep their businesses
open. If you were poor, you would have to be very resourceful
or inventive to survive year around. Most people in Yukon shop
at Whitehorse, a city of 30,000 people, for all the amenities
and services it has to offer. Bruce of BC, January 2006

How to learn more wilderness-survival skills.
    Nothing beats experience. I've attended survival classes
in NJ, NC, VT, ID; most affiliated with Tom Brown's Tracker
School. These classes lasted a weekend to a week, and cost
$800 or more ! They do show you many things but, after the
class, without intensive practice, you're really not much
better than before. For these classes to really be useful,
you need to practice a lot; but, ironically, if you are that
motivated, you don't really need the classes. The best thing
about the classes is having the chance to meet like-minded
people, form friendships, and make connections.
    I think it is better to save your money and buy or borrow
good informative books. Tom Brown Jr's field guides are good
(tracking, wilderness and suburban survival, etc), but intent-
ionally incomplete. Tom believes you learn more by figuring
part of it out for yourself, but this can be frustrating.
Euell Gibbon's books are great for plant info if you can
already identify the plants. For identification, I think
Peterson Field Guides are best, esp the one on edible plants.
Peterson uses drawings, which better emphasize indicator marks.
Audubon is good for identifying trees (bark is hard to draw).
The Foxfire series is interesting/informative, but not always
practical (mountain-man-style living). Newcombs Guide to Wildflowers may be the easiest to use. No field guide is complete.
    Learn about the things around you (ecology is fascinating)
and as for survival skills - practice, practice, practice. Do
not get discouraged; your mistakes are your best teachers.
Go easy, be patient with yourself. If possible, seek people
with similar interests for moral support. How strongly do you
want independence and freedom ? Gumby, NC 275, July 2005

(Addendum.) A good book for this area is Plants of the Pacific
Northwest Coast, MacKinnon & Pojar editors, Lone Pine. It
covers from the Umpqua/Siuslaw divide south of Eugene to the
Kenai Peninsula sw of Anchorage, and east to Cascade summits.
(Despite the wide range of latitude, many of the same plants

occur throughout that area.) Reviewed in Apr01 DP by Julia
Summers who calls it "THE BEST field guide i've seen - and at a
reasonable price" ($23 ppd for 539 pgs 8x5 - subsidized by
Canadian taxpayers ?). Though a beautiful book, with both color
photos and line drawings good for identification, it does not
list many uses. Eg, it includes Hypochoeris radicata (gosmore,
which, second to nettles, is the green we eat most of) and
several of its difficult-to-distinguish relatives, but said
nothing about edibility. For that, good books include Plant
Uses of BC Indians, Nancy Turner; Wild Edible Plants of West,
Kirk. An excellent book for all of N.America is Encyclopedia
of Edible Plants, Couplon (reviewed in Sept 04 DP). H & B

When seeking edibles, evaluate plants plentiful in your locales.
     Plant books tell about many wild edibles in a region. But
if you go looking for all of them, you will probably spend much
time looking without finding many edible plants, because most
grow only in certain habitats. A more productive approach:
first notice plants that are plentiful in places you go and
identify them (easiest when flowering, using a book ordered by
type of flower), THEN check for edibility. Bert & Holly

For nutrition, consider what remains after preparation.
     I was surprised to see an article of mine that was in Sept
1986 Coltsfoot, quoted in Apr 04 DP. I'd written: "Boiling
destroys vitamin C", which is true. The DP author then claimed:
"A more accurate statement would be: vitamin C is destroyed IN
PROPORTION TO light and heat, NOT instantaneously when a food
reaches boiling" (and goes on to cite test data).
     That gives the impression that one is still getting a
significant amount. Linda Clark wrote, in Know Your Nutrition,
1981: "But those who insist we get enough vitamin C in our
foods should realize that, according to a study made in Ireland,
80 percent of the vitamin C in our food is lost in cooking....
Even exposure to the air can cause a loss." George Sherwood,
                                             NY 147, Mar05
Sour about substitute sweets.
     Claim: Unlike refined cane/beet sugar and corn syrup,
maple sugar and honey are safe because they are absorbed slowly.
     Dis: Except for flavors and impurities, maple sugar
consists of the same sucrose that is in cane/beet sugar, and
honey consists of sucrose plus the same glucose and fructose
that are in corn syrup. All are soon absorbed if eaten/drunk
on an empty stomach. Honey contains natural toxins that flowers
put in nectar to deter bugs that dine without pollenating.
(Raw honey may contain microbes that babies' immune systems
can't cope with.) Refined sugar may contain small residues of
toxic chemicals. Neither contain the vitamins (etc) needed to
utilize them. Both are unnatural: 99.999% of our ancestors
(stone-age and before) rarely got concentrated sweets. Thus
humans did not evolve to cope with them. H&B

Our experience with various storage totes and barrels.
     We are now using about 25 totes of various brands. (They
had vent holes under the handles. Purpose ? I covered the
holes with duct tape, inside and out.) None have leaked,
including some setting out with nothing over them. Rubbermaid
lids seem to fit more reliably than do the lids of some other
brands, both because the Rubbermaid lids have taller lips and
because (with the 20-gal size) the sides do not bulge out as
much if the contents press on them.
          Dwelling Portably   September 2006

Dwelling Portably

or Shared, Mobile, Improvised
Underground, Hidden, Floating

Dec 2007 $1 per issue   POB 190-d, Philomath OR 97370

Earthen floors may or may NOT be warming during winter.

Bert wrote that plastic-covered dirt floors have a big
advantage (over raised wooden floors): heat capacity. "They
help warm your home during winter and cool it during summer."

I don't doubt the summer cooling. But winter warming ?
Only if you live where winters are short and not very cold.
Even there, a dirt floor will be warming only when the air
drops below floor temperature which might be 50o. Not balmy !

But where winters are long and cold, uninsulated dirt
floors will be chilling. Packed dirt is a fair conductor.
Your floor will get almost as cold as the soil outside. Here,
soil freezes several feet deep - and this isn't the Arctic.
(We don't have permafrost. Permafrost poses a more serious
problem; not in winter but in summer when the top melts.)

We tried a dirt floor. COLD ! Something that helped:
bank snow around your shelter, deep and wide. It insulates the
ground from sub-freezing air and slows the frost.

What is better: insulate your floor well along with the
rest of your home, and store MANY gallons of water inside.
During the day while the stove is going, the water warms up.
Then at night you can let the fire go out because the water
will give off enough warmth to keep the air above freezing or
at least from going much below freezing - depending on amount
of water and insulation and outside temperature. (Regardless
of how well you insulate, unless your home is tiny you WILL
need a stove. Solar heating ? Not here. Winter days are
short and the low sun (if any) doesn't give much warmth.)

Recycled milk jugs work fine. They are better than one
big tank because they have more surface and therefore take up
and give off heat faster. Also, if not too full, ONE freeze
won't burst them. (I don't fill them above bottom of handle.)
Repeated freezing/thawing may. Mark, Alaska 995, May 2007

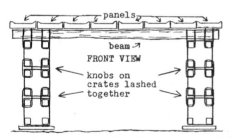
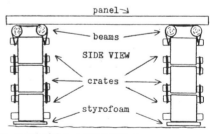

Crates and panels form a versatile portable structure.

A decade ago, we bought the leavings of a family that had
moved away. Some were immediately useful; some we couldn't
use; some were puzzles. We had to take all - but price right.

Among the puzzles were knobby crates and panels of wood,
stiff foam, fiberglass. Parts of a structure ?

Two years ago I got time to play with them. Most needed
repairs; the wood had rotten spots. (I don't know their
history, but I assume they were built for a dry climate - NOT
western Oregon.) I patched those which had rotted least (which
took longer than expected). I'm not sure how the parts were
used, or if I have all the parts, but here is what I did:

Dwelling Portably   December 2007

I lashed together 12 of the crates to form 4 columns, each 3 crates high. I arranged the columns in a quad, setting them on pieces of salvaged styrofoam to insulate their wooden bases from the ground so hopefully they wouldn't get condensation and rot more. Then I set beams between pairs of columns and lashed them to the crates. I used poles as beams. (I didn't find anything beam-like among the parts.) Then I layed panels across the beams, lashing them to the beams and (not shown) each other. Also not shown: pieces of cushiony foam between beams and crates, and beams and panels, to distribute loads.

Result: a gazebo, about 13 by 8 ft, open on 4 sides, but easily covered with netting or several layers of cloth or plastic, depending on weather. The panels, mostly foam, form an insulative roof. But, if rain, a plastic covering is needed to prevent leaks. Inside height, about 4½ ft; adequate for sitting; not standing. (Can be heightened by lashing another crate onto each column, or by digging out the floor.) It is somewhat stabilized by the beams lashed between columns, but would need additional bracing to withstand strong winds.

Advantages, compared to pole/branch-framed structures: Panels are insulative. Crates provide shelves (and totes when moving). May assemble faster. Size can be changed more easily. Saves finding, cutting, trimming poles (if prefab beams are added). Dis: Bulky parts to carry (though quite light), and to store when not in use. Needs level rectangular sites (whereas wikiups can be tailored to space available). With either, winter warmth will depend on the coverings.

I don't know of anything similar manufactured. Feb 1980 MP/DP (in the original first issue no longer stocked; not in the reprint) mentioned a Carry Cabin made in MI that was formed of panels small enough to carry. I've seen/heard nothing about it since. Various lawn sheds are made of sheet metal or wood. But they don't have insulative roofs; and (my impression is) they don't disassemble as easily as this gazebo. (The metal sheds I've seen are held together by many screws.) A few years ago, Rubbermaid made (still makes ?) a small lawn shed formed of plastic panels that fit together easily. Big enough for two people to sleep in, or for storing a few bikes.

I don't recommend hand-fabricating this kind of structure (unless you are a hobbiest who enjoys such work). I suggest molding the parts out of plastic, as are totes and pails - a task for a mid-size manufacturer with appropriate equipment. Choose shapes that are easy to mold, and to ship and store. (I don't suggest this gazebo as a model. Its crates don't nest.) If you or anyone you know works for such a company, please pass on the idea. There is a substantial market for such a product. (Many people can no-longer afford traditional housing.)

What existing things could form structures ? Could milk crates be lashed together into columns and a ceiling ? To insulate ceiling, into its crates put plastic bags of anything fluffy and light (extra clothes; dry leaves; styrofoam chips; crumpled newspapers). For rain protection, suspend plastic tarps above the ceiling, sloping. The space between tarps and ceiling provides an attic for storing LIGHT-weight things.

How available are milk crates ? Do dairies give away damaged crates they would otherwise have to recycle ? Bert

Slope tarps quite steep for rain; even steeper for snow.
And place any rafters up-down the slope. (If cross-ways, they may dam puddles - which will deepen as the plastic stretches - which will further stretch the plastic ...!)

Mongolian Cloud Houses: How to Make a Yurt and Live Comfortably.
About half of this book consists of detailed instructions
with many drawings, for   building a 13-foot diameter yurt like
what the author, Dan Frank Kuehn, built and dwelled in for five
years in northern New Mexico during 1970s. Dan used mostly
native or salvaged materials. Many of his helpful tips are
also applicable to other kinds of dwellings.
   "One way to initially straighten solid wooden poles is to
tie them tightly into a bundle while they are still green,
carefully aligning each pole. When the bundle is dry, the
poles will keep their new shape."
   "If you intend to cut your own poles from the forest,
spend some time looking around in your own neck of the woods
for trees and shrubs that naturally have a straight, vertical
nature. Collect some samples and let them dry."
   "I built (the frameworks of) my first yurts entirely out
of willow poles which were readily available but impossibly
crooked. I've since learned that in Mongolia and Europe,
willow, poplar, ash, hazel, and other woods are specially
chosen varieties, cultivated to grow extremely straight."
   "Johnson grass (which Dan used in NM; it resembles
bamboo) is considered a pest and you should have no trouble
getting permission to cut it; just be sure you are not
transporting its invasive grass seeds with your poles."
   "Cut (poles) as close to the ground as possible and clean
them of branches, carefully working UP the plants so as not to
weaken them at the limb connections."
   For covering, "I used 12-ounce untreated canvas. It's
strong and natural but only practical in the driest climates.
There are other, un-natural but more durable cover options...."
   "Two trenches on the uphill side of the site are necessary:
one (above the back bank) to allow water coming downhill to pass
around the site; and one (between bank and yurt) for water
coming off the yurt itself." (Illo in book.)
   While leveling the site, "if you want raised or sunken
places, this is the time to make them."
   Other topics: dimensions of parts for other sizes; how
Dan would build a yurt differently now; traditional Mongolian
methods; many photos, both of Dan's yurts and of Mongolians
and their yurts; reprint of 1930's kids book about Genghis
Khan; sources for yurts, other nomad homes, supplies, tools.
   Though yurts are more complex to build than are some other
kinds of portable or improvised shelters, they seem well suited
to open areas where a few people may be able to move a small
yurt without disassembling it, and where there are strong winds
but not much snow or rain, and where the native woods available
are mostly slender (eg, 1"D) poles. Comparing with tipis:
"Because of the slope of the roof, a tipi can shed rain and
handle a snow load better than a yurt." "A low ceiling makes
(a yurt) easier to heat, and the short poles fit on or in most
vehicles." If they have the same surface area (and amount of
covering), tipi is 15' high, 18' D base; yurt 10' high, 13'D,
and has a little more stand-up height area. (Illo in book.)
   160 pages 7x10, 2006, Shelter Publications, POB 279,
Bolinas CA 94924; www.shelterpub.com; $17. They also have:
Wonderful Houses Around the World , Yoshio Komatsu and Akira
Nishiyama, 48p.7½x10, $9. Color photos plus cut-away drawings
with captions show/tell how dwellers live.   Homes in Mongolia,
China, Indonesia, India, Romania, Tunisia, Spain, Senegal, Togo,
Bolivia. Some are underground. Book especially for kids.
          Dwelling Portably   December 2007

Latex polymer waterproofs tents effectively.

In my 4-meter cotton tent, during a heavy downpour some visitors remarked that it was like being aboard the Titanic. As soon as the tent's skin got soaked through, it no longer kept out the weather.

I later found and applied an effective product: Kamp-Kote. Now rainwater can even puddle on top of the tent without dripping in. A several-year-long test convinced me: Kamp-Kote works. It is a water-soluable latex-type polymer liquid. Kamp-Kote is ten times better than Scotch 3M, Waterguard, Thompsons Waterseal; also better than similar more-expensive polymer products. About $13 a gallon at outdoor-sports/camping stores. If they don't stock it, they can order it.

You can thin its milky consistency with water for easier application to cloth. It works equally well with natural fibers like cotton canvas, and on many synthetics including nylon taffeta. It dries clear, and, once dry, it does not stiffen cloth nor add noticably to weight. briggi2u@yahoo.com
July 06

Recently-purchased "duct tape" has weak adhesive.

It sticks momentarily but soon peals off. The slight springyness of the tape itself is enough to gradually lift it off of a curved surface or around a bend. The tape peals off even if continually cool. Brands tried: 3M; Tartan (BiMart).

Tape we bought several years ago, holds better. Eg, Tape-It duct tape and SpecTape masking tape. I wonder if the adhesive was found to be toxic and replaced with something weaker.

We use the newer tape only for repairing items we also sew such as clothes. The tape holds the cloth in position for the few minutes needed to sew through cloth AND TAPE. The stitches anchor the tape so that it reinforces the cloth. Holly & Bert

Free water barrels have many uses.

Last month at my mobile home in the woods, my ex-food-industry-sourced polyethylene water drums were showing symptoms of age. After 27 years in the sun, they were cracking and splitting and leaking. Time to find replacements.

Prices have gone up. Eg, commercial sources were selling 30-gallon poly drums for $37 each. But a friendly tip led me to a bottling plant. Coca-Cola plants receive soft-drink syrups in 2-bung poly drums: 15, 30, 55 gallon. Bottlers try to have local recyclers pick up the one-time-use barrels. But when the scrap-plastic-market price is low, the empties tend to accumulate, uncollected, at the loading dock.

Call on your local bottler's manager, offering to help recycle those barrels. They may still have a trace of syrup in them, so rinse well. (Some folks may moan about toxic substances leaching out of fresh plastic - but, hey, it's a plastic world we live in - and those barrels are free.)

There are many uses for them apart from water storage. Make an underground storage cache by cutting open and nesting together different sizes. Or build a huge floating raft by lashing together a hundred barrels with bamboo poles. Or .... ? briggi2u@yahoo.com   July 06

(Addendum:) Though harder to find, there are also barrels with removable tops in which some foods are shipped. Useful for storing things other than liquids. They are much stronger than plastic trash barrels, and they seal better. Bert & Holly

Experiences living in a travel trailer in Pennsylvania.

Last year I learned that our trailer's front framing had gotten wet and dry rotted, causing the trailer's front to bow outward. The RV dealer said that, even if they could fix it, the bill would be about $4000 ! We had bought it for only $1200. So, gingerly, we towed the trailer to where we winter.

This spring, as we were readying the camp-grounds for its May-first opening, a carpenter working there told me he could repair the damage for $100 ! But he had other jobs scheduled until years end. I told him to schedule us then.

Normally we have to leave the camp-ground by May first, and wondered how the trailer would fare on roads in its present condition. Then, the camp-ground owners asked us to stay through the summer months, remaining at our premium site (it is the levelest and closest to the hookups), continuing to pay $15 a week. That change was welcome - but didn't last.

The camp isn't a typical RV park where people come and go. Instead, the camp is rented as a whole by various churches and other groups. Normally, each stays a week or so. But for the last few years, one group has rented the place for 6 weeks each summer. Unfortunately for us, that group's leaders wanted the premo site for their RV. Whereupon, the camp owners, instead of telling them that the site had been promised to us, told us to leave. $$$ were more important to them than integrity !

The trailer towed fine, and we are now set up on a family member's property. Though on top of a hill, we are mostly hidden. But we have no electric, water, sewer connections. We have dry-camped before and found that, by being frugal, we can go 3 weeks, using our trailer's self-contained systems.

We might be here for a while, so we are living in the winter mode: hauling in water; using small kitchen bags and kitty litter in the toilet bowl; and running our generator for electricity. Our gen has a low-amp outlet and a high-amp outlet. After we figured that out, we could sleep in relative comfort as the air-conditioning compressor would work properly. The generator runs all night on 2 gallons of gasoline.

(Later.) The 6-week group has now left. We pondered whether to stay on the hill, or move the trailer back down to the campground. Convenience won out, so we moved.

The guy who offered to fix the trailer, now says he can't do it before next year. So we decided that, next spring, we will look for a better used rig. We'd like another trailer, or an older class C, though we'll consider a well-done school-bus conversion. John & Rose Ward, Living Mobile, PA 174, July
& Aug 06

We live full time aboard our boat.

Very comfortably; very economically. We have had no hassles from the marine patrol this winter, even in the warm clime of southwest Florida. Land dwellers have not been so lucky. Lots of meanness. The police harrass. Also, in northeast FL, an older gent was attacked by two 10-year-old kids, which put him in a hospital. Becky, FL 339, Apr 07

I live aboard merchant marine ships. On ship, I pay nothing.

Off ship, I live in southeast Asia, out in the backwoods boondocks. Even there, I can pick up pocket money by exporting coffee and cocoa beans. Alan, 2006

I am rebuilding a '71 Westfalia Transporter.

I will live in it while searching for land, as a communal venture or on my own. Garner, CA 935, 2007 Dec 07

Exploring railroad tracks can be rewarding in several ways.
Most cities have a vast intricate network extending outward. There used to be many vacant structures along the right-
of-ways, but not with today's economy. However, I find many
places to do gorilla gardening, which is no longer possible
anywhere else in Chicago. Do NOT plant on railroad or power-
line right-of-ways. They are heavily sprayed with herbicides.
Also avoid former wastefields.
While near the tracks, you are close to the fastest and
most discrete method of getting out of town: hitch a freight.
What you want is one empty car in the middle of a bunch of full
cars, so it doesn't bounce around too much. I tend to use only
freight and spur lines, not passenger lines. The workers don't
usually bother me, and less danger of getting run down.
If threatened by a flood or by a hurricane which can bring
a flood, to evacuate my first thought is: get on a rail line
(preferably one on top of a large embankment) and start walking.
A problem, esp if there is a social breakdown: other kinds of
people who do this might be potential marauders. Kurt, IL 606,
2006
Wild ginseng is valuable, but harvest is regulated.
Wild ginseng diggers will trudge deep into the hills of
Appalachia today for the beginning of harvest season. Last
year, 4800 pounds of the perennial herb were harvested (in WV?),
selling for about $300/pound. Some people believe the herb
boosts their energy. (newspaper clipping sent by Herbert Diaz)

Antiseptic/healing oils effectiveness increased by covering.
Tea-tree or eucalyptus oil seems to hasten healing of
insect bites, infected thorn-punctures, pimples. But if not
covered, most of the oil evaporates before it can diffuse thru
our skin. To block evaporation, I cover the oil with a piece
of aluminized plastic cut from a junk-food wrapper. (We rarely
eat junk foods, but we collect a few empty wrappers.) Food-wrap
plastic is not only relatively non-toxic, but it is formulated
to prevent escape of food flavors including aromatic oils.
I hold the plastic on by putting sticky tape around all
edges. (I've mostly used masking tape, without noticable ill
effects. Medical tapes safer ?) One application is usually
enough. If not, once a day or so I remove plastic, apply more
oil (maybe alternating euc and ttree), replace plastic, tape.
H & B
Vitamin D is very important for health.
Over 100 scientific studies show that deficiencies not
only cause rickets (deformed bones), but render people of all
ages more prone to cancer, flu, osteoporosis, tuberculosis, MS,
chrohns, diabetes-1, skin infections, and other diseases.
Some of D's health effects have long been evidenced. Eg,
sunshine prevented/cured tuberculosis; cod-liver oil reduced
infections; people near equator suffered much less MS and
diabetes-1. But until recently there was little formal
research, perhaps because unpatentable natural substances such
as vitamins were not profitable for the medical/pharmaceutical
establishment. And in pop nutrition media, D was long over-
shadowed by vit C, probably because D has a narrower safe range:
megadoses of C are generally safe whether or not helpful,
whereas megadoses of D can harm, esp if eaten, but even if
obtained from sun (sun burn, and more risk of skin cancers).
Physiological effects are numerous and complex. For some,
see long articles in 11Nov06 Science News and Nov07 Sci Amer.
Dwelling Portably   December 2007

Most Americans and Europeans are vitamin-D deficient.
400 first-time moms (half Afro, half Euro) and their babies
were tested by U Pittsburgh. 90% had taken, during pregnancy,
multivits that included D. Half had before. Yet, at birth,
blood of 96% of Afro and 63% of Euro moms, and umbilical blood
of 83% of Afro and 50% of Euro infants, lacked adequate vit D.
A cause of rickets increase in Afro kids. (Sci News, 10Feb07)
In Feb-Mar 2005, blood tests of 420 otherwise-healthy
human females in various north European cities (latitudes 52o
to 60o; N Am equiv, Calgary-Anchorage) found: adolescents, 92%
deficient, 37% severely so; older, 37% def, 17% severly. Nv07
Sci Am

Best obtain vitamin D from sunshine, not from pills.
Because the vit D in pills and foods is fat soluable, it
is carried in the blood by lipoproteins (fat-protein combos)
and may accumulate in artery walls along with cholesterol, and
increase calcium deposits. People who have other coronary
risk factors and who ingest much vit D, may harm themselves
more than help themselves, especially post-menopausal women.
Vit D that is produced in the skin by sun exposure is
carried by proteins (rather than fat) and is unlikely to
contribute to arterial calcification. Michael Mogadon, MD,
from Every Heart Attack is Preventable ,2001, New Am Libr.
(Though major media have recently publicized D's health
benefits, I've NOT seen sunshine's superiority publicized,
perhaps because universities/corporations are patenting
artificial analogs of D they hope you will buy.)
However, if you live where sunshine is absent or very weak
for long periods, and you lack electricity for a special uvb-
emitting lamp, fish-oil or D-pills recommended. One vit D
researcher in Montreal takes 4000 units/day during winter
(which is ten times the official RDA; one-tenth the toxic
amount. There is NOT enough D in "fortified" foods nor in most
multi-vit pills. As for artery clogging, reduce other risks.

Sunshine during childhood prevents multiple sclerosis later.
Health workers who travel widely, have long observed that
MS is rare near the equator but common at high latitudes.
"There's a genetic component to MS but also an environmental
component." (Probably also various dietary components.)
Recent studies "hint that uv rays set a child's immune system
on a normal course for life." Though mostly older folks get
MS, after adolescence sun doesn't seem to help prevent MS,
though it does some other ills. (Science News 28july07)

Too much sunshine is not good for you.
In spite of what sun-worshipers say, ultra-violet rays can
dry your skin terribly, esp as you grow older. The sun acts as
an oxidant. Look what happens to plastics left in the sun:
you can poke a finger through some older tents; a plastic
bottle cracks and crumbles. This same force is at work on your
skin cells. briggi2u@yahoo.com July 2006

How much sun exposure is healthful ?
With sunshine as with selenium, iron, protein, exercise,
and quite a few other things, the optimum range may be narrow.
Recent recommendations I've seen: find out how long an
exposure turns your untanned skin slightly pink; then expose
yourself one-third as long three days a week.
Dwelling Portably   December 2007

Mild exposure directly benefits the skin exposed. So, though a bikini covers only small areas, nudity is better. Except: minimize exposure of face and neck and any other parts that receive much sun during activities when they can't be easily covered or shaded. Change positions frequently.

Complications. Sunshine intensity depends on atmosphere conditions and on sun height (when low, its light goes through more air which absorbs more of the uvb) and on angle of skin to sun. Eg, an hour's exposure that may not pinken skin at mid-day in Dec-Jan nor near sunset any month, may burn it at mid-day in June-July. Dark people (who may need 6 times more exposure than pale people) may not notice pinkening.

Though humans evolved the ability to store vit D for a while, most of our ancestors lived in the tropics and did not need to store enough D to last for several months. Consequently, winter exposure is very desirable when possible. H & B

How to increase sun exposure during winter.
Expose as much skin as is comfortable, except probably not face or neck. If too cold to be nude below the neck, alternate areas: eg, waist-up for ten minutes; waist-down for ten min.

Some ways to increase warmth: Wear insulative head-neck coverings. Stand or lay so that the rays come at nearly a right angle to as much skin as possible. Exercise. Drape a blanket or coat over your shady side. Stand between the sun and something that reflects sun onto you, or that absorbs sun and radiates heat onto you (eg, a broad tree trunk with dark bark). It will also block or slow any breezes.

Build a small portable sun tent, just big enough to lie in (which can also serve as a mini greenhouse). It can be as simple as a lean-to of a plastic that passes uvb. On the back side, put aluminum foil so that you get both direct and reflected sun. Orient ridge east-west.

Ordinary clear polyethylene passes some uv - which is why it soon deteriorates in summer sun. (If used only in the weaker sun of winter, it may last a few years) But I don't yet know how much uvb (needed for vit D synthesis).

Later this winter, we may be in an area where we can build a sun tent - and report. (At our present site, the trees are now tall enough to confine sunshine to spots which move as the earth turns. So, to get much sun, we have to move too.) B & H

Recent wild hazel harvests: fewer nuts but bigger kernels.
A few years ago, we harvested MANY nuts. But, to get them before other animals did, we picked while most were still immature. Drying/curing shrunk the kernels. They tasted fine but most were only lentil size. Last summer and this summer we waited longer - and consequently got fewer nuts. But, after drying, the kernels were bigger: about pea size.

Wild hazels seem to have thicker shells than do domestic hazels. Some can't be easily cracked with ordinary pliers or nut-crackers. Vise-grips crack them ! Bert & Holly

Harvesting tip: the sequence in which plants ripen, varies.
I read that hazels ripen about the same time as black-cap raspberries. Maybe some places some years. Not here recently. Last summer, black-caps were past and we'd been picking blackberries for two weeks before hazels were mature enough. H & B

Prolific "weed" proves to be a nutritious delight.
Following several rain storms, our normally dry, brown,
southern New Mexico desert erupted into acres of green weeds.
As I diligently removed them from our yard, a neighbor happened by - and suggested we eat them instead. Although I have a
copy of Euell Gibbons' Stalking the Wild Asparagus, I had
overlooked purslane. This beautiful "weed" is loaded with
vitamins, omega-3s, and other beneficial nutrients.
Raw, I found it rather uninspiring. We now eat it lightly
steamed. When dressed with garlic, oil, soy sauce, butter, etc,
my husband says it is as good as any of the other greens we
love. I am also pickling it in ACV. I also chop it up and
feed it to our birds, dogs, cats. For recipes, etc, type
Purslane on a search engine and you will find multiple sites.
Gibbons wrote:
"Originating in India
or Persia, purslane has
established itself
around the world. In
America it has found a
congenial home, from
Atlantic to Pacific,
and from Canada to
Tierra del Fuego.
"The wild plant is
a ground-hugging annual

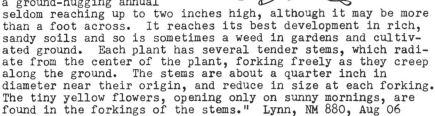

seldom reaching up to two inches high, although it may be more
than a foot across. It reaches its best development in rich,
sandy soils and so is sometimes a weed in gardens and cultivated ground. Each plant has several tender stems, which radiate from the center of the plant, forking freely as they creep
along the ground. The stems are about a quarter inch in
diameter near their origin, and reduce in size at each forking.
The tiny yellow flowers, opening only on sunny mornings, are
found in the forkings of the stems." Lynn, NM 880, Aug 06

What we eat, and how our diets are evolving.
In Ab #6, we will review China Study. Though we question
bits of its advice, we rate that book very important. How much
has it influenced what we eat ? Not much yet: partly because
our diets have long been much like what it recommends; partly
because changes we would like to make, are difficult.
One easy change: no more milk ! Bert was buying ± two
pounds/year of powdered milk. He liked it, along with sugar,
on blackberries, making a sort of iceless ice-cream.
One difficult change: fats. Our biggest source: refined
rape-seed ("canola") oil. (Next biggest: sunflower seeds, some
raw, some lightly toasted, mostly ground; flax seeds, raw,
ground; (we grind them ourselves and eat within a few days);
wild hazels; oats.) Bert calculated: during a month this
summer, 20% of his calories came from rape-seed oil. (He
guesses that 8% came from oils in other foods. Total, 28% -
near the high end of the commonly recommended range of 15-30%.
My consumption might average 20%.) We'd like to replace the
oil with various nuts. But we've not found enough hazels; and
stores seldom sell nuts in shells (because most people no
longer have enough time to remove shells ?). Consequently,
the nuts are not only pricy but often stale, esp walnuts.
Nuts keep better in their shells than after the shells removed.

We eat much fruit; mostly berries during their seasons: ± June-Sept. We forage 7 different berries in quantity, but 6 are of the same genus (Rubus: blackberries and relatives). Some autumns we are near abandoned orchards that still bear apples. Other seasons, our fruit is mostly limited to: canned tomato paste (we eat a spoonful along with vit C); raisins (but less as their price rises along with our doubts about their healthfulness); occasionally scavenged citrus, discarded because of cosmetic defects or small rot spots (easily cut out). A few winters we have found rose hips still on bushes.

We eat much fresh greens, esp during spring and early summer. But most are of only two species. By weight, maybe 70% nettles (Urtica), eaten cooked; 20% gosmore (Hypochoeris, a lettuce relative), mostly eaten raw; 10%, all other greens. In some places we have harvested gosmore year around, but it is most abundant and tastiest in spring. (Picture in May 94 DP.)

During the past few winters, we have been near areas where toothwart (Dentaria) is quite abundant. Toothwart grows for only a month or two, but during times when other greens are scarce. Toothwart came up about New Years in 2006; not until early Febr in 2007. The leaves are small: time consuming to forage many - but we do. Toothwart is of the mustard family and "hot", at least when raw. We eat it mostly mixed with other foods. (Pic in Feb/Apr 87 DP) A relative, bittercress (Cardamine), is sometimes abundant on disturbed soil. Raw, it tastes much like toothwart or watercress; appearance resembles watercress. We haven't noticed bitterness in the plants here.

Greens/flowers that Bert or I eat in small amounts: Cleavers (Galium), raw (pic in June89 DP). Dock (Rumex) cooked. Wild carrot (Daucus) leaves raw, a few year around. (I've read, somewhat toxic. Bert thinks, no more so that celery or parsley (same family); likes taste, hasn't noticed ill effects.) Miners lettuce relative (Montia), raw, very little, else it irritates mouth. Oxalis (Oxalis), raw, little. (Green leaves here year-around, but contains oxalic acid which may prevent absorption of calcium. Oxalic acid also in spinach, chard, beets, chen, amaranth.) Violet (Viola), raw, green leaves year around; pleasant wintergreen taste but tough; not abundant. Ox-eye daisy (Chrysanthemum), flowers, raw; abundant, but more than a few causes an unpleasant taste. Mint (Metha) or yerba buena (Satureja): during summer we pick and dry leaves; during winter we occasionally brew tea. Plants featured in most wild-edible-plant books, such as chen (Chenopodium), purslane (Portulaca), amaranth (Amaranthus) don't grow wild around here. They grow as weeds in some gardens. (A few times we've been hired to weed gardens, and got some. A fringe benefit.)

Occasionally we've scavenged "organic" cabbage outer leaves or other greens discarded by a pricy gourmet food "co-op". But we seldom go to cities. When we do, we are usually too limited for weight to bring home fresh vegies/fruit (mostly water), or too short of time to scavenge much. Also, (eg) just a few gosmore leaves may have more vits than a head of lettuce.

We don't eat much meat; average maybe 3 pounds/year each. Chickens on sale. Eggs (often on sale during spring, but delicate). Seafoods when near the coast. Canned tuna on sale. Wood-rats (which we trap if they invade our shelters). One time part of a cougar-killed deer (report in Nov99 DP). We catch many mice but throw them away: too small to be worth skinning and gutting. We get meat-hungry during blackberry season when the berries supply much of our calories without providing much

protein; seldom other times. We eat mostly plants for health
and convenience: to not get too much protein; to minimize
risk of infection from animal or raw meat, and of cooking odors
attracting big predators; and for easier food storage.
     Most of our calories come from purchased grains: wheat,
oats, millet, popcorn. Most protein comes from those grains
plus lentils, beans, peas, sunnies; also much in nettles.
     Except during blackberry season when we get much vit C
naturally, we take a dab of pure C powder (a heap ± the size
of a lentil) 2 or 3 times a day, with some fruit or greens if
available. (C pills gradually darken as the C reacts with the
binders and (we've read) become harmful.) Other supplements
taken if/when our food may be deficient: B12, E, A (beta
carotene), zinc, calcium (ground limestone), selenium, multivits (mostly for B's). We use maybe 30 pounds/year molasses,
mostly on oatmeal. Bert uses maybe 3 pounds/year refined sugar,
mostly on redberries (Vaccinium). Other than oil and sugar, we
eat almost no "empty calorie" foods. (Minerals in molasses.)
     As it is, what we eat is probably more healthful than what
99% of Americans eat; not because our diets are superb, but
because most people's diets are horrid - including most people
who try to eat only "organic" foods; also most gardeners who
eat what they grow but also buy/make much junk foods.
     A diet that is good for adults is not necessarily good for
children. If we had kids, I think I'd try to provide as much
meat as they wanted (but NOT hype it). If not enough meat, the
youngest children past weaning would get priority. H & B

For solar cooking I use a huge stainless steel bowl.
     It is 15 inches across. In it I put a pyrex casserole
with lid on. To raise the casserole a little above the bowl,
I set the casserole on a trivit or jar lids. I tuck a blanket
around the bowl and cover the bowl with a discarded storm
window. For more reflector area, I add car-windshield
reflectors. They are more durable than cardboard and foil.
     Unless you are among trees you need not move everything.
I have to turn the bowl once or twice. It gets hot enough that
I use pot holders. Wind won't damage it, and spills I just
wipe off. I use the bowl also for laundry and salads.
     I also tried a styrofoam chest. I put fire bricks in its
bottom. I had spray painted the chest's inside and the bricks
black. I covered the chest with the storm window. But the
chest did not cook whereas the stainless bowl did. Suzanne,
                                          OH 451, May & July 06
Update on our solar cooking.
     (Also see reports in Sept 02, May 03, Sept 04, Apr 05,
Sept 06 DPs. Sept 02 includes plans/instructions for making
reflectors that fold up compactly.)
     For hinges between panels, the most durable we've found:
strong denim (cotton) cloth, held on the plywood by carpenters
glue. Tyvek fatigued and tore after a few months use.
     New Reynolds aluminum foil is not as shiny as was the old.
Apparantly produced by a different process, it has tiny ridges
that scatter some of the light. But after the old foil has
accumulated several years of grunge, or abrasion caused by
wiping off the grunge, the new foil is better. Awesome brand
foil, bought at Winco, seems identical to Reynolds. Both are
much more durable than another brand bought at a dollar store.
     The ideal reflector is without irregularities that scatter
                Dwelling Portably   Dec 2007

light. Aluminum foil, despite its ridges and ripples, seems
better than the windshield reflectors I've seen, which were
textured (perhaps so that a reflection won't dazzle a passerby,
cause an accident - and bring a lawsuit !)
   As reported in Sept 06 DP, "space blanket" plastic was
initially shinier and stayed smoother on a panel than doea any
foil we've used - but soon deteriorated. We haven't found
enough aluminized plastic bags (eg, potato chips) to try them.
We doubt that any plastic will long endure the ultraviolet and
heat unless specially chosen for that.
   We salvaged 3 pieces of mirror at a glass shop that also
mounts custom mirrors. Each ± 1x1½ ft, not all the same size.
Ideal reflectors, but heavy and thus difficult to move or
adjust, as well as breakable and with sharp edges.* I want to
compare them with a 3-panel foil reflector, testing side by
side, heating identical jugs of water.   * Metal file smoothed.
   Oven bags have endured quite well as shrouds on gallon
jugs heating water. They become less clear, from scuffing and/
or plastic turning cloudy, but not fragile or brittle - yet.
Other shortcomings: Their wrinkles increase surface area and
thus lose more heat than does a firmer shroud. They tend to
touch the jug or pot in spots, reducing insulation.
   We have yet to live near a really good solar-cooking site;
partly because our sites, scouted and prepared before we began
solar cooking, were not chosen for that. Most of our summer
sites have been on north slopes or had trees nearby that block
early and late sun. But despite site and equipment flaws,
solar cooking has reduced propane use by a third. With better
sites, which we are now scouting/preparing, we expect to reduce
propane use another third. We also save time, overall.
   Even on days too cloudy to completely cook solar (most
days here in winter), we save by pre-heating the cooking water,
or by getting the pot of food as hot as possible before turning
on the stove. Even if the water can only be solar warmed, much
fuel will be saved. (With most foods, more fuel is consumed
heating water and food, than maintaining cooking temperature;
esp if, after a brief simmer, the pot is insulated in bed
(which we do). Also helps: while on the flame, shroud sides
and top of pot with several wrinkled layers of foil (we do).)
   Everything we've tried to solar cook, cooked fine - except
popcorn. Though the air between pot and clear shroud heated to
250°F, and probably hotter inside the pot, no pops. How high
a temperature is needed ?! Makes us wonder about popcorn. B&H

Keep your old Coleman stove and lamp burning bright.
   (Responding to Lisa's question in DP's Apr06 Supplement.)
With these stoves, effective fuel flow depends on pumping
enough air pressure into the fuel reservoir. If you can't pump
enough pressure, check the leather cup-like air gasket, set
inside the pump shaft, secured to the thumb-push pump rod. To
access gasket, lever off the pump-rod cap's retaining wire with
a screw driver - on older models. On yet older models, caps
will screw off. Pull out the rod and gasket assembly. Leather
deforms out-of-round as it dried over the years, allowing a
disabling amount of air leakage. Get a leather treatment
product like you'd use on boots to prevent them cracking. Or
else some animal fat; bacon grease will do. Antique leather
does not like mineral oil or motor oil as well as a plant or
animal product. Using fingertips, thoroughly massage the
grease into the gasket, in a way that tends to reshape the cup

form round and outward, so as to restore a snug fit. Reassemble. If this fix doesn't restore pressure, contact me and we can discuss making replacement cups out of scrap leather.

Coleman no longer stocks replacement fuel reservoirs for stoves. These have to be changed out from a scrap stove. (When faced with a missing stove reservoir, I fabricated a propane-feed adaptor out of metal scrap and a bit of welding. This would not be practical for most folks to try at home.)

Fuel choices. Fumes are an inevitable consequence of combustion. That's why many lamps and stoves come with the disclaimer: "Use only in a well-ventilated area." (Makes you want to go solar.) Any kind of fossil fuel will form carbon monoxide. In addition, virtually all petro-fuels, propane included, have unwholesome additives. Even wood fires, esp if pine fueled, put out unhealthy smoke. I've found 91 to 95 octane auto gas to burn clean enough to be an acceptable substitute for "white gas" camping fuels that fetch 3 times the price. Your choice. Happy cooking, briggi2u@yahoo.com

How I transfered propane from one tank to another.

A few years ago, a law was passed forbidding propane dealers to fill tanks that lacked a new automatic-shut-off valve (asov). The asovs are not only costly, but have had problems, some of which LESSEN safety ! So, something differ- ent and probably costlier may soon be required. Furthermore, BC (all of Cda ? some U.S. states ?) forbid refilling ANY tank that is more than a few years old, regardless of condition.

We payed $20 to exchange one old 5-gal tank for a retro- fitted tank. But we have other tanks we want full, as reserve, and sure aren't going to replace them with asov tanks ! Though we have greatly reduced propane use, and plan to quit using it entirely (or any fossil fuels), at present we like propane as a back-up when other cooking methods are not convenient.

I asked John of Living Mobile if the asov would prevent transfer. He asked a dealer he knew (THANKS) who thought not.

None of the hardware stores I tried, had proper fittings. (BiMart formerly did, but now has only a small rack with few kinds of parts.) So I went to a propane distributor whose main business is trucking propane to dealers and big users. The only person there was a very young woman (looked mid teens) working on accounts. She didn't know about the fittings but tried to be helpful. Together we searched through MANY drawers of hard- ware. No single device was suitable. But, on a bench, left from another job, was a 3-ft length of high-pressure hose; and I found POL (put on left) fittings that could plug into the hose and then screw onto the tanks. Cost: about $12 plus a half-hour search. (No one else came in or even phoned while I was there. Probably lucky. If the proprietor had returned, he might have refused to sell to me, fearing liability if I had an accident.) Only friction held the hose on the POLs. I hadn't seen suitable clamps, nor did the woman know of any. So, back at our camp, I wrapped rubber straps around the hose joints.

I put black plastic snugly around the sending tank to warm it faster, and set it in the sun, upright which seemed safest. I set the receiving tank in a tote and shaded it, and poured creek water in around its bottom to cool it. (If too much water, the tank floated and tipped over.) I screwed on the transfer hose. I opened both tanks' valves. I heard a loud hiss that quickly diminished, then silence. But by almost closing the sending tank's valve and putting an ear close, I could hear a soft hiss: gas still flowing - slowly. (I did NOT open the receiving tank's 10% valve to reduce pressure and speed transfer. If I had, gas would have flowed out and been lost as fast as it transfered.) Hours passed. Along with the gas came much heat (boiling requires heat; condensing supplies heat), so I had to keep replacing the cooling water.

After two days the receiving tank was only half full. Thereupon I set the sending tank upside down so that liquid would flow. That transferred the propane much faster, but not real quick: the rate was limited by how fast the sending tank absorbed heat from the sun, to keep its pressure higher than in the receiving tank. After a few hours the receiving tank was nearly full and no more propane was flowing. But the sending tank still held some liquid. At first I thought the residue was hydrocarbons that had higher boiling temperatures than propane. But later I wondered if the asov, which is to prevent overfilling; when upside down, acted in reverse and prevented complete emptying. So I again put the sending tank upright. Transfer resumed - but slow. The sun was setting, a cloudy week was forecast, and twas mid Sept. So I quit for the year. The gas still in the sending tank, we used cooking.

Learning from that experience, this summer I did much better and refilled several tanks. We were near a spring that had water much colder than the not-very-cool creek. Also, I painted the sending tank's bottom black (up to where the sides are vertical) to absorb solar heat faster when upside down. (If any dealer asks why the black bottom, I will say it helps keep the tank cool - which it does if setting on cool ground.) Also, I solar-heated water quite hot. Then, when the asov stopped the flow, I set the sending tank upright in a tote and poured hot water in around its bottom to keep its remaining propane warm. Those improvements enabled me to transfer a tank-full in one day and to completely empty the sending tank. The last transfer I did, the sending tank emptied while upside down. Maybe the asov did not close. (Tending tanks did not take much time. While tending, I also washed clothes.)

CAUTION. I am now careful to always OPEN the valve on the RECEIVING tank FIRST. One time I opened the sending tank first. Before I could open the receiving tank, the hose blew off the POL ! During the few seconds it took me to close the sending tank's valve (difficult to reach because the tank was upside down) I lost some propane. When I put the hose back on the POL, I wrapped the rubber straps even tighter and used more layers.

Someone who has snow or ice available for cooling the receiving tank, can transfer propane faster. Or safer, because the sending tank doesn't have to be as warm. The best time: late winter when the sun is fairly high yet snow is still on the ground. Even if the air is cold, the sending tank can be warmed by loosely shrouding it with clear plastic, and by putting reflectors around it so as to shine onto it. Bert

A propane automatic-shut-off valve (asov) can be dangerous.
Until a few years ago, most propane tanks had a main valve plus a manual "10%" valve. To fill a tank, the dealer opened both valves. While liquid propane flowed in through the main valve, propane vapor came out through the 10% valve. Though wasteful of propane, that reduced pressure in the receiving tank, which enabled it to fill from a supply tank that lacked a pump. More important: when the receiving tank got nearly full, liquid propane squirted out the 10% valve, signalling

the dealer to quickly stop the filling. (Because, if a tank gets completely full of liquid and then warms, pressure rises much more than if the tank has some vapor space. That is why drink bottles are not filled completely.)

That system was simple and fairly reliable, but hazardous. While a tank was filling, the cloud of propane could be ignited by a smoker passing near by, or by a spark from static electricity or from a loose or corroded electric connection.

To end that hazard, asovs were required. An asov works like the valves on some toilets that stop the refill. But the asovs proved unreliable. Often they jammed close. That happened once with our tank. The dealer managed to free the asov by lifting the tank and dropping it a half-foot onto concrete ! Worse: sometimes an asov failed to close when it was supposed to. Consequently most dealers, no longer trusting asovs, again open 10% valves - re-creating the hazard that asovs were supposed to eliminate. Worse yet: this summer, the last time our one asov tank got refilled, after filling and AFTER the main valve and the manual 10% valve had been closed, when the dealer tried to remove his filler nozzle, propane spewed out of the main opening - and continued spewing. (There is normally only a brief gush as the filler nozzle empties.) The dealer swung the tank various ways, banging it hard against a metal post. That finally stopped the flow. The dealer said, though many asovs stick shut, that was the first time he'd had one stick open. During many years of refilling asov-less tanks we've never had a MAIN valve fail to close. So I blame the asov. I don't know its details, but either it bypasses the main valve or else its failure kept the main valve from closing.

Holly wonders if my refillings might have damaged the asov. Possible. But a valve so easily damaged is dangerous. (I did nothing as drastic as dropping a tank onto concrete or putting it on a mobilhome parked in hot sun (which I've seen).)

An asov is hazardous not only during refilling, but any time the tank is not connected to an appliance with valve.

We hope to find a propane dealer willing to refill the older asov-less tanks. Though illegal, I doubt there is now much enforcement; else dealers would not be opening manual 10% valves which is probably also illegal. Bert

LED lantern is useful though connections are troublesome.
(Also see report in Sept 05 Dp, p.15.) We've used Eveready's "Energizer" lantern during 3 winters, maybe 2 hours a night, average. It requires 4 AA cells. We have mostly used NiCds, 4 of which provide 5 volts. We've also used recharged "non-rechargable" alkalines, which provide 6 volts.

Though our 12-volt light (which contains scarlet and green LEDs) is much brighter, the lantern has the advantage that its AAs get recharged on cloudy days when our PV panels put out too little voltage to recharge the 12-volt battery.

I used the lantern at 6 am one morn to write a first draft of this. I set the lantern on a squat jar and adjusted the LED portion to shine downward. With the lantern 6 inches above the paper, the bright area is about 6 inches diameter. Bright enough for writing; marginal for much reading. Though no brighter than a candle, the lamp emits no fumes, can't start a fire, and is more easily adjusted to shine where I want it to.

Its main problem, like with all UNsealed low-voltage electric devices: the connections corrode, esp the springy negative contacts. They need attention frequently. Usually, twisting the cells in place, back and forth several times, rubs off enough corrosion to restore contact. Bert

A Garrity-Duracell crank-light soon failed.

In May 2006, I bought a "kO23 Powerlight", $10 on sale at Winco. I hesitated: its 3 LEDs are blue-white (we much prefer yellow); its beam is too narrow (3" a foot away) for most tasks; I doubt that it is sealed (I don't see how the crank could be) and thus is prone to corrosion. However, it was brighter than our little Homier shake-light (report in Sept 05 DP), and we haven't encountered bigger brighter shake-lights (which ARE sealed) at attractive prices.

Approx 6x2¼x1¼ inches, ½ pound. Our average use: 3 hours a night during autumn. It needed cranking frequently: though bright at first, it soon faded. (Likewise, our shake-light.) The instructions claim: a minute of cranking yields 30 minutes of light. Well - 30 minutes of DIM light.

Bert experimented, using our solar calculator as a light meter. He hung the light one foot above the calculator and cranked approx 2 turns per second. Number of turns, seconds until the display faded (by then, light quite dim), seconds of light per turn: 5 72 14; 10 121 12; 20 138 7; 40 198 5; (second trial to check: 40 188 4.7) 80 338 4.2; 160 448 2.8. Ie, cranking a few turns frequently, yielded longer light per turn than did cranking many times less often.

Though brighter than our shake-light or squeeze-light, it is less satisfactory on rough trails where I want one hand free to fend off branches and to arrest stumbles, because cranking requires two hands (one to hold light; one to crank). So I must stop often. Whereas, a shake-light or squeeze-light can be activated by the hand that is holding it.

As months passed, the crank-light dimmed more quickly and I noticed less resistance cranking it. Then, in Dec, it failed completely: the light became very dim; cranking did not brighten it, and the crank spun with no resistance, indicating no generation. Bert opened it (which required unscrewing three tiny deeply-recessed phillips-head bolts) and measured some voltages. He thinks the LEDs, generator, battery (tiny 3-cell NiMh) are okay. The fault: a chip that mates gen to battery.

He thinks he might be able to fix it by substituting diodes. But first I'll try returning it to Winco, though I doubt Winco will replace it because they don't regularly stock those lights. (Winco didn't.) The maker offer a "lifetime guarantee exclusive of the LEDs". But mailing it back is not attractive, considering postage and work to package - and prospects the replacement will fail.

A friend who bought one, hasn't had it fail, but I don't think she has used it as much. I heard of another one that broke mechanically but was fixed with a nail.

A friend with internet access checked: www.garitylites. com. It recommends a minute of cranking at least once a month to keep a charge on the battery. That surprised Bert who had assumed that a NiMh like a NiCd (and UNlike lead-acid) could be left discharged indefinitely without damage. Holly & Bert

Shake-lights are the least trouble-prone of existing types.

Better than crank, squeeze, and battery-replacement type lights. Reasons: simple mechanically; can be well sealed, so no corrosion; recharged by the hand that holds it. (Of course I don't claim ALL shake-lights good.) Yellow LEDs best for most tasks. Bert   Dwelling Portably   Dec 2007

Dwelling Portably

or Shared, Mobile, Improvised
Underground, Hidden, Floating

May 2008 $1 per issue   POB-190-d, Philomath OR 97370

A Chinese-style wheel-barrow can be used on narrow trails.
  A housing of poles and sticks, or scrap boards, is built
around a large-diameter wheel. (A big wheel rolls with less
resistance than do the small wheels used on most American wheel
barrows.) Cargo is carried in front of the wheel and beside
it, as well as behind it, which reduces weight on the handles.
A strap runs from handle to handle, looped over the user's
shoulders (or head ?) which takes the weight off
hands and arms. Some wheel-barrows are 3
feet wide and big enough for two
people to haul. (From note
by Andrew, ME 046,
2006)

(Comment)
I like this idea.
Simpler and lighter than
a two-wheel cart. (But on a
bike trailer I'd want 2 wheels for
balance (as does Zalia, next item).) The
sketch Andrew sent showed a ⊏⊤ shape. For our use,
I think I'd prefer a ◁⊏ shape. Lighter, less wobbly, and
the narrow front will hopefully fend bushes aside instead of
hanging up on them. Dis: not much space in front for cargo.
But enough for a small heavy item, to help balance.
  Any kind of cart can be more easily pulled than pushed,
esp on a rough trail, because pulling reduces weight on the
wheel(s) whereas pushing adds to it. This wheel-barrow might
be difficult for ONE person to take through brush where it must
be pushed. But if there are two people, the front person pulls
with a harness and can provide most of the forward force. The
rear person balances and helps lift it over obstacles.
  The wheel needs side strength. (I'd NOT use a 26-inch
bicycle wheel. See discussion in May 06 DP.) If using a
motorcycle or BMX-bicycle wheel: to hold its axle, angle-iron
is easy to lash to the frame, but a front fork may be more
available. The fork would be horizontal and lashed to stout
sticks which lash to the frame. Bert, Oregon 973, Jan 2008

Two-wheel bicycle trailers are best.
  A single-wheel BOB trailer does track behind the bike's
wheels, but has load and balance problems. I use two-wheel
trailers. Much better for balance and load capacity. I have
hauled up to 600 pounds, and sometimes have a wide or tall
load. You can't do that with a single-wheel trailer. Zalia

Some solutions to problems with small tires.
  The tires on small trailers, lawn-mowers, wheel-barrows,
etc, frequently develop flats. I have an old 3-wheeler that
local kids run around on. The tires are cracked and no longer
hold air. Into them I inserted steel-belted thread strips I
cut from old auto tires. I positioned the inserts so that the
narrow bead strips were against the wider supportive thread.

The tires have more drag and less spring than if inflated.
But I'm not going to pay $150 for new tires.
   To make the strips, I snip the steel bead with a grinding
blade, then cut out the strip with a sharp knife. Small narrow
tires may need only one strip. Wide tires need several.
   Large diameter bike tires do require tubes. To prevent
frequent punctures by thorny vines, I either buy super-thick
inner-tubes or else use the tire sealing goop. I occasionally
find thick heavy water hose that I can insert into the bike
tires that I use on garden carts.
   Though I have the usual tire-patch kits with all my rigs,
I find that shoe goo temporarily fixes low-pressure 4-wheeler
tires that get punctured in the outback. Al Fry, ID 836, 06?

More thoughts about springs on carts and other vehicles.
   The fat low-pressure tires on ATVs, not only minimize
sinking on soft ground, but provide some springing on gravel
roads where ATVs often go quite fast.
   I think springs of some kind are desirable on a hand cart
if loping (an easy run, 12-15 mph ?). But springs may not help
much if going slow (1 mph ?). The speed at which springs
reduce forces on wheels and load (including any rider) depends
on how bumpy the road is. A one-wheel barrow can more easily
dodge rocks and holes than can a 2-wheel cart. Bert, OR 973

Elastic cords between pack-frame and load may reduce forces.
   Compared with a conventional unsprung frame, peak vertical
forces exerted by a 27 kg (60#) load were 1/6th as great and
energy consumed was 3/4ths as great. Science News 13jan07

(Comment) The brief report (based on info from frame's designer ?) did not describe test conditions. With a backpack as
with a vehicle, vertical forces partly depend on velocity. I
dislike running with even a light (20#) knapsack. If I must
run, I grab the bottom with my hands to take most of the weight
and to minimize bouncing: ie, my arms act as springs. Whereas
if hiking slow, which I must do on a steep or rough trail: with
a heavy load (80#) the steady pressure on shoulders or head-
and-neck becomes uncomfortable (and prompts frequent brief rest
stops) but I don't notice peak forces. If a trail is smooth
and level enough for fast walking, I notice peak forces somewhat more but they seem less annoying than the steady pressure.
I have backpacked heavy loads for many years, so perhaps I
subconsciously move so as to minimize bouncing. An inexperienced backpacker may bounce more, causing greater peak forces.
                                                        Bert
Backpacking food and other supplies to our base camp.
   Our present winter base is about 2½ miles from a road-
head: ½ mile mostly rough trail somewhat uphill; ½ mile on a
smooth but seldom driven logging road, up and down and level;
1 mile uphill, mostly steep, partly rough; ¼ mile partly rough
some up and down; ¼ mile downhill, mostly steep, to our camp.
   Downhill is the most difficult: slipping is likely.
Though I may wear tennies the rest of the way, downhill I wear
rubber mocs (made from truck innertubes) - less slippery here.
If my load is heavy, eg, two 4-gallon pails of wheat, near the
summit I split the load and bring it down in two trips.
   To carry a heavy load from road-head to camp, takes me ±
5 hours. Ie, I average ½ mph. To go from camp to the road-
head, usually light-weight, mostly downhill, takes ± 1 hr. Bert

The in-route camps we use for city trips have had problems.
We often live at a "winter" base camp from October through
May (8 months a year). Consequently we choose a site and build
a shelter that provides: enough warm space for indoor activities; security for us while there and for our equipment;
sunshine for warmth and light - rainy days often have sun breaks.
   The site that is best in those ways is usually many miles
from cities and quite a few miles from highways. Consequently,
each trip to a city is a minor expedition requiring planning
and preparation - and at least one intermediate camp site.
   A typical city trip. In advance, ready things to go; and
listen to the weather radio, waiting for a mild dry period.
Day 0: pack things to go; bathe. Day 1: hike to an in-route
camp-site near a highway where we have stashed a tent, bedding,
city clothes, ready-to-eat food. Day 2: rest and get ready.
Day 3: hike to the highway and travel to the city by the most
expedient means (options discussed in May 96 DP); do city
things; return to in-route camp. Day 4: rest; select things
to go to base camp (and, if time, read bulky magazines and
books that are NOT going). Day 5: return to base camp.
   Often we don't get 5 good-weather days in a row. If not,
we may forgo rest days. Or, after return from city, we may
remain at in-route camp until the storm passes. Or we may hike
in the rain (but not snow - steep slopes too slippery). Not
surprisingly, we seldom go to cities during winters.
   We have been quite pleased with our winter base camps, but
NOT with most in-route camps. Because the site must be near a
highway yet reachable from base camp, and fairly secure, we do
not have a wide choice of sites. The least-bad site is usually
among mid-size trees (most 2nd-growth forests here) and doesn't
get sunshine during mid winter. Even if no recent rain, bushes
remain wet with dew, or with frost that melts when we rather it
didn't. Also, highways are mostly in valleys into which cold
air collects: when hiking from base to in-route camp, as we
descend we often notice an abrupt chilling of ± 10 degrees.
   For the past few winters, we've used our small Stansport
dome tent as in-route shelter. If we leave it set up, that
saves time and avoids discomfort (bare hands needed to set it
up). Also, we can cover it with blankets or moss for insulation which enables our bodies to warm the inside ± 20°. And we
can suspend plastic tarps over it, which reduces dampness and
provides a rain-sheltered antiway. But if left set up, it is
more visible, and animals might damage it.
   At our present in-route site, we have left the tent set up
with black-fabric over the tarps, and with mouse traps set in
the antiway. A mouse has never gnawed its way into the tent.
Perhaps the fire retardant, whose smell was scary when the tent
was new (report in May 96 DP) tastes bad.
   We usually both go to in-route camp, even if only one of
us will go to city, so that we can haul back more food staples.
Also for warmth: if we split up, neither shelter is as warm.
   At in-route camps, bed covers were a problem. They got
damp from invisible sweat, and could not be dried before leaving. We reduced that problem by enclosing our thickest sleepa
(sleeping bag opened as quilt) into a big plastic bag (from a
furniture store). We fastened the corners to minimize shift of
the sleepa within the plastic. Plastic is also over the foam
padding under us. In bed we wear clothes for additional warmth
and to avoid touching the plastic (which clings to skin and
hinders changing position). The plastic over us is not as

flexible as cloth and does not conform to our bodies as well,
but covers us adequately and adds to the sleepa's insulation.
                                                        B & H

At in-route camps, we plan to use a bigger tent, heated.

We have never used a stove for warmth at any camp.
Reasons: avoid having to cut and haul and shelter wood, and
tend fire; avoid fire risk and smoke inhalation; increase
privacy (smoke might be seen or smelled; heat detected).

Now we are reconsidering. A wood stove could quickly warm
a tent that is big enough for assembling trip things and to
hang damp clothes to dry. Security might be adequate
if the tent is used only briefly and NOT left set up: our
camp-sites are usually in brushy-brambly areas difficult to
hike through by anyone who hasn't figured out the trails.

We would use the site ONLY for in-route camping, so that
few things remain there. (Recently, we used a summer base
camp as an in-route camp also. It offered some advantages but
was over a mile from a highway: a city trip required following
long rough steep brushy trails in darkness with dim flashlights.
And the many things stored there increased security needs.)

For a stove set-up, I like the arrangement
used in Korea that David French described in
May93 DP. The fire is in the ground; the hot
fumes pass through a tunnel under the tent
before exiting through a vertical pipe.
Advantages, compared to a stove in tent: tent
can be smaller and simpler (no stove-pipe
exit) and stays cleaner. The ground gets heated and continues
to warm the tent after the fire goes out. Dis: more complex
site; must go outside to tend fire. After our problem with a
dakota-hole cook fire (report in Sept06 DP), I think I'd want a
small auxilliary burner at the bottom of the vertical pipe to
preheat it so that it sucks the smoke when main fire is lit.

The tent I'd want: fairly big (6x8 ft, 6½ ft high center)
yet compactable enough to easily stuff into a 20-gallon tote;
integral rain fly (over-tarp); sets up quickly. Maybe no
frame. Instead, the tent is held erect by chords that snap
onto pre-arranged anchor rings. I've not seen advertised any
tent that seemed suitable (but, until now, I haven't been
looking hard). Suggestions welcome. Bert, OR 973, Jan 2008

We now use thin-mat black-fabric for camo here.

Black-fabric, also called landscape fabric or weed control,
is sold by garden suppliers during spring. Compared to
ordinary black plastic, its advantage for gardeners: it passes
water and air. I've seen two kinds of black-fabric.

The kind we use is a thin mat of plastic fibers welded
together in many small spots. Compared to ordinary black
plastic, its advantages for us: it is not shiny; it passes
some light. Compared to cloth: cheaper; lighter weight;
more sunlight resistant than most synthetics; doesn't rot as
does cotton. Dis: not as strong. However, even when hung
vertically alone, it withstood quite high winds. Two years ago
a roll 3x50 ft was $6 (4¢/ft sq). Ordinary 3-mil plastic, 10x
25 ft, was $4 (1.7¢/ft sq). Since then, prices of all plastics
(made from fossil fuels) have risen. We haven't found any mat-
type black-fabric wider than 3 feet, unfortunately - we often
need wider pieces and sewing takes time. (Tried welding. Weak.)

Another kind of black-fabric is wider but quite shiny. It
seems to be ordinary black plastic with many tiny holes in it.

In w Oregon woods where there are many old stumps and logs with dark bark or burned black, black-fabric provides better camo than do the mottled green and brown tarps we've seen which seldom match the local vegetation. Bert & Holly, Jan 08

Dwelling in or roaming wild areas, reduces global warming.
Plants respond to increased carbon dioxide by growing faster. And after plants die, some of that carbon remains in the soil. But growth is limited by other nutrients obtained from soil. Humans who frequent wild areas but eat some food grown elsewhere, add nutrients to wild soils. Sci News 15apr06

Whole grains store better than does flour or meal.
This is important to us because we usually buy most of our staples during the dry season (summer) so that we don't have to deal with rain or muddy roads. And, if we can hire a vehicle to help, we may buy enough to last us several years.
Snow-country dwellers may do the opposite: bring in supplies during winter with a snowmobile.
Grains vary in how well they store. Wheat stores well for years, even decades, if kept dry and cool - PROVIDED the kernels are intact. (95% of 15-year-old wheat sprouted, report in May90 DP.) But in whole-wheat FLOUR, the wheat-germ oils soon get rancid. (Notice that stores refrigerate wheat-germ or else sell vacuum-packed jars.) Though wheat-germ is rich in vit E, E is not an antioxidant until converted by our bodies.
Almost all commercial bakers, including purveyors of "organic" breads, buy their flour. Consequently their bread probably contains rancid oil by the time it is sold. Flavorings may mask the taste but don't remove free radicals.
When Bert and I first got together, our main starch was brown rice, boiled. We liked its taste better than white rice; it is less sticky and so doesn't scorch as easily; and we were vaguely aware that it was better nutritionally. Some people have reported storage problems. We had no problems storing short-grain brown rice a few years, kept cool (under 60°F). I wonder if short-grain keeps better than long grain.
Then we learned that rice is the most pesticided of grains. We switched to millet, which is also cheaper. But, though millet tastes fine to us after an absence, we soon tire of it. Does millet contain something our bodies don't want much of ?
We tried wheat boiled: chewier than we like. Wheat slightly sprouted, then boiled, tasted better; but sprouting often isn't practical for us. So, finally, we got a hand grinder and began baking. Usually the only ingredients: flour, water, yeast. Flavor varies: may depend on how long and warm the dough rises. (A few times we got sour dough, unintention-ally.) We prefer and usually eat bread that is still warm, directly off the pan. Holly & Bert, OR 973, January 2008

For identifying wild edibles, mice can be your guinea pigs.
Almost every plant that you observe mice or rats eating, can be good for you to eat. They love to spend hours cracking open pinyon nuts, or else sitting on a stump munching a slab of juicy nopali (a cactus). briggi2u@yahoo.com

(Comment) Rodents eat some mushrooms that are deadly poison for humans. I wouldn't be surprised if the same is true for some plants. Rodents and primates have gone their different evolutionary ways for 150 million years or so.
Dwelling Portably   May 2008

Around here, mice and rats are nocturnal. We see squirrels harvesting doug-fir cones. Seeds edible for humans but TINY.

Calcium-to-Oxalic ratio in green vegetables varies widely.
My understanding. If the ratio is high, the oxalic acid is bound and calcium is left for nutritional needs. Whereas if the ratio is low, the oxalic acid will bind not only calcium in the vegie but other calcium eaten then, preventing assimilation.
In Dec07 DP, I mentioned some vegies that contain oxalic acid. Bert found more info in Apr/June86 DP. Of 22 vegies tested, highest ratios (90:1 - 45:1): collards, mustard greens, kale, cabbage. Lowest (0.20:1 - 0.45:1): swiss chard, spinach, purslane (Portulaca), beet leaves, poke, rhubarb, chen (Chenopodium). Ie, according to the 20-year-old article (any newer contrary info ?), purslane (etc) will NOT provide calcium and may prevent assimilation of other calcium. This doesn't mean that you should shun purslane (etc). Just make sure that, if you eat much low-ratio greens, you get ample calcium elsewhere.
Oxalis is often the only green here in winter. Oxalis was not tested, but from its name and acid taste, I assume it has much oxalic acid. So, when I eat it, I take calcium (limestone flour) with it - enough (I hope) to bind the oxalic and leave surplus calcium. (The article was mainly about miners lettuce (Montia perfoliata), ratio 8.34:1.) Holly, OR 973, Jan 2008

Be careful if eating fruit partly eaten by other animals.
At least, cut away previously-eaten portions. In Bangladesh, nipah virus is spread by fruit-eating bats, and then by kids who collect fruit even if half-eaten and sell to venders who blend fruit into drinks. Purchasers, mostly Muslim, drink the beverage before it can ferment, which would kill the virus. (Pasturizing would, too.) Nipah often causes measles-like symptoms, brain damage, death. Outbreaks of nipah and related hendra occur frequently throughout the bats' range, from the Himalayas to Australia. The Bangladesh strain spreads from bats to people and kills 75% of those it infects. In Malaysia, nipah spreads from bats to pigs to people; in 1999 it killed a third of the 265 people infected. Science News 9june07

Pathogens that infiltrate plants are not removed by washing.
In a lab test, uncut apples were dunked in water containing E coli. The bacteria migrated to the apples' cores. Likewise into unpeeled oranges. Salmonella got into mangos, tomatos, various leaf vegies. Both microbes got into alfalfa sprouts. Bacteria in spinach may have caused the 2006 outbreak that sickened over 200 people, killing 3.
Researchers believe that microbes get into commercial produce from water used to irrigate or spray pesticides. Though bacteria that have evolved to infect animals, don't infect plants as vigorously, they are able to make use of the defense mechanisms of plant pathogens not harmful to humans. The 3-page article suggested: use drinking-quality water for spraying; don't buy damaged produce; get to frig quick.
SN 20oct07, 10nov07
(Comments) Pasturizing will kill the bacteria but will also deactivate enzymes that may help digestion.
The article did not mention wild plants. They seem less risky than commercial produce. But I'd either avoid spots that are popular with animals or else pasturize my pickings. H & B

Plain water was most effective for washing virus off hands.
In a test using norwalk virus, water removed 96%, water
plus an anti-bacterial soap 88%, an alcohol-based hand-gel only
50% - which surprised researchers. Science News 10june06

(Comment) The report did not conjecture why. Though soap and
water is a better surfactant (dirt grabber) than plain water,
it is also a better lubricant. That may have prevented the
hands from rubbing each other as effectively. However, for
removing something oily/greasy (poison oak/ivy toxin ?) I'd
use water AND SOAP if available. Holly & Bert, OR 973, Jan 08

Sand slurry is good for cleaning some containers, not others.
I've cleaned stainless steel cups and bowls with sand and
creek water. Worked very well. Soap not needed. But I don't
recommend sand for plastic bottles. Sand roughens the plastic,
enabling even more scum to grow on it. Zalia, OR 972, Aug 06

Some simple ways to obtain water from the earth.
In my area, water drillers charge $35 per foot. So I
drilled my own shallow well, using an auger and muscle.
Though seldom suggested by back-to-land books, collecting
seepage is simple. Find a slope with water-indicating plants
such as cottonwood and willow. Dig a trench the full length
of the seepage; a foot deep may suffice. Line the trench with
clay to trap the water. Lay perforated septic-system pipe in
the trench. Cover the pipe with gravel. Cover the gravel with
(eg) old carpet or burlap sacks to keep dirt out of the gravel.
At the pipe's upper end, add a clean-out plug. At the lower
end, add a plug and a pipe to the trough or holding tank.
In some places, water veins come close enough to the
surface to be tapped by hand pumps. I once had a girl friend
who could walk along with her palms down and detect not only
where there were veins but how deep they were.
Water can be sucked to surface by a colder temperature.
Some older cultures knew this and built stone spring houses
or water caves at spring sites. Al Fry, Idaho 836, 2006 ?

(Addendum) A few years ago, Holly and I wanted a new drinking-
water source, closer to our camp. I hadn't found a natural
spring so I tapped a seepage. Because of climate and terrain,
my method differed somewhat from Al's.
A nearby creek had a steep V profile with banks ± 30 feet
high. Near the end of dry season (late summer) I struggled
along the creek bed (difficult because of fallen trees) watching for tiny tributaries. I found one. It flowed on the
surface for only a few feet beside the creek. I did not tap it
there because it would be submerged by creek water during the
rainy season. I climbed directly up the bank, far enough to be
above the creek's flood water. I dug. A foot down I reached
saturated soil. The seepage was slow. I widened the hole,
forming a ditch across the slope. I piled the dirt on the
downhill side of the ditch, forming a dam. A little pool began
to collect. I continued the ditch as far as there was seepage,
about 8 feet. The subsoil was clayish (which may be why water
seeped above it) so I did not have to line the ditch with clay.
From a salvaged garden hose, I cut a still-good portion.
I perforated a half-gallon bleach jug. I lashed the jug to one
end of the hose. I covered the perforated jug with synthetic
loose-weave cloth, to admit water but keep out anything that
might block the hose. I placed the jug in the deepest part of
Dwelling Portably   May 2008

the pool and (temporarily disrupting dam) routed the hose downhill. Muddy water trickled from it. I covered the jug and
filled the pool with pebbles gathered in the creek. I covered
the pebbles with plastic to keep out dirt and rain water. I
covered plastic with soil and debris. (Illo in June/Sept84 DP)
       A few days later. Clear water trickled from the hose;
only a spoonful per minute but that was enough. I inserted the
hose into a narrow-mouth 5-gallon jug (salvaged).
       A day later. The jug was full of clear water. I loaded
it into a crude carry basket I had rigged on an old pack frame,
and put an empty jug on the hose. And so forth.
       For several years, seasonally, we've used that water for
drinking and cooking. (For washing, we have a closer source.)
The only maintenance so far: I occasionally blow into the
outlet end of hose to dislodge silt collected around its intake.
After a heavy rain, I wait a week or more before collecting
drinking water, to avoid contamination by surface water.
       This area has water-indicating plants. Horsetail is one
of the best. But the plants apparantly have DEEP roots for
obtaining water during dry season. Once, in a likely-looking
horsetail patch, I dug down more than ten feet. No water !
       I sometimes find a natural spring along the base of a high
steep ridge, or by following down a dry gulch that flows during
heavy rains. But such springs are seasonal: dry near the end
of dry season; contaminated with surface water during heavy
rains; drinkable maybe half the time. Bert, OR 973, Jan 2008

Does sterilizing water with iodine create toxic compounds ?
       Iodine, either tincture or water solution of crystals, has
long been recommended to backpackers as more effective and
less toxic than chlorine. However a report about city water
supplies in 5aug06 Science News, causes concern. The tap water
of most cities contains myriad toxins, formed by reactions of
disinfectants (eg, chlorine, chloramines, ozone) with organic
matter in the water. Over 500 chemicals are formed. The EPA
put limits on a few but rates 50 others likely to cause cancer.
       One is tri-iodo-methane. Might that be formed when iodine
sterilizes water ? Some organics can be removed by settling or
filtering, prior to iodizing. But not any substances dissolved
in the water. Best find or develop a spring you can trust. H&B

More about small engines that mount on bicycles.
       The 25cc 2-stroke engine (that Lauran uses on bike, more
in May06 DP) is standard on weed eaters and is on many small
yard appliances and some chain saws. 21cc-to-25cc are not
designed for sustained loads and don't last very long. 31cc,
up to 49cc (on many road scooters) is better.
       Two-strokes are noisy and put out burnt-oil smoke. A
4-stroke 2-or-3-hp cast-iron engine is better but heavier.
       The drive ring and belt (which Lauran uses) is the best
way I've seen to add power to a bicycle. Most bike engines
use friction on tire, which destroys tire. Zalia, OR 972, 06

Traveling/boarding/working via relays of friendly motorists.
       My idea. The travelers are driven, each night or every
few days, to a place where they can sleep. At each place, a
different vehicle from another area comes and picks them up,
and they start another leg of their journey.
       This is a variant of what was often done during 1800s.
At lectures and church-halls/rectories, travelers arranged to

board with families for a favor/fee/work. Patty, NY 131, 2006

A way that an employed couple may safely park their motorhome.
     If one works nights and the other works days, they can
move back and forth between their employers' parking lots.
The Wells (story in May06 DP) could do this. The husband
works days. The wife, a nurse, can easily find work at night.
I think vehicle living is safer if two people. Suzanne,OH 451

(Comment) Best if every user of the parking lot knows about
the arrangement and approves. Else ? Suppose the woman works
at a place that employs only women. Some "concerned citizen"
may see the MAN in the parking lot - and call police !

Further report about living in a travel trailer.
     Our summer was quiet. Though we got kicked out of the
campground even after the owners said we could stay, we got to
live on a hill top, parked in a clearing within a grove of
trees. The spot was so secluded that the owner called on the
cell phone, asking when we would arrive. He was surprised to
learn that we were already there. Aside from the lack of
electrical and other hook-ups, it was an awesome place.
     We're often asked why we still live in our travel trailer.
We could say, because of the freedom we enjoy. But, being
practical, it is a way to live within our means. A local man
who lives in an old school bus, moved into an apartment for the
winter. We considered doing so, but were shocked by the rents
being asked. From prior experience, we know that many people
in conventional housing, are living way beyond their means,
often on increasing lines of credit. We think, if something
happens, they would soon be on the street. We prefer paying
cash for everything and owning what we live in and drive.
     We never did repair the trailer's framing. If we get
another travel trailer, we'd like a 19-foot. We'd prefer a
driveable, but one in our price range would be a 1970s.
     Some of our readers gave us ideas for insulating. We
filled some windows with styrofoam panels, and have a large
plastic tarp covering the roof. That seems to increase warmth.
But the real proof will be less fuel consumption this winter.
A 20# tank of propane normally last us 2 weeks if used with
care. When we lived in conventional housing, we placed clear
plastic film over the windows on the inside which raised the
temperature 5o or so. But we feel that making the small space
of our trailer too tight would be unhealthy. We do tape the
outside of the windows where the windows open. John & Rose
                                             Ward,PA 174,Nov06
Repair your vehicle south of the border.
     In Mexico, every town and city has countless small work-
shops, going from early morning until late night, that keep old
rigs running. You can get major engine work, transmission
overhaul, and maintenance/servicing for much less than in the
U.S. Parts too, for older Ford and GM, are available cheap
because there is much after-market parts manufacturing.
     My 1992 Ford F-150 pickup slid off the interstate in a
blizzard, then rolled on its side into a hillside median snow-
bank. (Bias-ply tires are not real stable for winter driving.)
The passenger-side door and pickup bed got terribly stove in.
     Last year, near Veracruz, I had all the bodywork done,
including fixing old dents, bends, scrapes, dings collected
through normal use. Then, a nice thick shiny coat of primer
                Dwelling Portably   May 2008

and paint, and detailing and painting the wheels, grille,
bumpers. A beautiful job for $250 total. (The shop accepted
some barter, so I actually paid $200 (in pesos) plus 3 old
wrist-watches.) My road shame turned to road pride. In U.S.,
the same work could cost $2500, because here they don't pull
and hammer sheet-metal so much as replace it with new.
    It helps to talk some Mexican, and to spend time with
different shops to find the best price. Riddle: What is
Mexico's national color ? Answer: Primer ! briggi2u@yahoo.com

(Comment) I would go to Mexico (or other country) only if I
had a very strong reason, or MUCH to do there. If I went, I'd
stay until ALL was done. I'd MINIMIZE border crossing.
    "Jump through the hoops"? The "hoops" are RED HOT.
Border guards are cops. Regardless of how legal someone thinks
they are, any encounter with any cop is DICEY !
    Sneak across ? Regardless of how knowledgable and careful
someone is, accidents happen !
    Mexicans whose businesses require border crossing, are
probably more skilled at crossing than is an occasional gringo
visitor. To fix a vehicle, how about finding a reputable
repair-person who crosses quite often (maybe to buy parts not
available in Mexico) and arranging pickup and delivery ? Of
course, expect to pay more than if driving to the shop. B & H

Outlook can affect odds of surviving the unexpected.
    I became interested in Lawrence Gonzalez's Deep Survival
because the author discovered characteristics that help humans
survive drastic situations. The 2003 book's focus is not on
skills or gear, but on outlook. Many of the stories concern
inexperienced individuals who nevertheless managed to get out
of unbelievable situations. "I remember thinking the jungle
trees looked like cauliflowers", said a 17-year-old girl who
fell out of a lightning-destroyed airplane into jungle, walked
out over 12 days, and lived. A Navy SEAL commander said, "The
rambo types are the first to go." Though the book focuses on
some extreme examples, I think it is, nevertheless, an excellent guide for anyone considering woods life. Especially
interesting: along with calmness, curiosity, non-assumption;
a trait favoring survival is NOT being a rule follower. Also:
know local conditions, and know what you don't know - ie, be
aware that familiar can turn into unfamiliar. Included are
research findings, anecdotes, extensive quotes from eastern and
western Classic Lit. Andrew, Maine 046, 2006

(Comment) I read about the girl somewhere. As I recall she
had no parachute but LUCKILY fell through dense foliage.
    That book may be esp helpful to (eg) someone who has never
been in the woods and has NO interest in any woods, but who is
the sole survivor of an airplane crash in a remote forest. But
to someone CONSIDERING woods life, I suggest: give priority to
info sources that focus on equipment and skills and habitats.
The same holds for anyone considering ANY kind of life, whether
in big city, small town, desert, swamp, ocean, or wherever.
    The difference: preparing for what is expected, versus
responding to the unexpected. Sure, no matter how well you
prepare, you may encounter unexpected threats, and your outlook
could affect the outcome. But, if you have time, best learn
what to reasonably expect, and prepare accordingly. MANY more
people are killed or crippled by fairly LIKELY happenings (eg,
accidents to high-mileage travelers; ill health of junk-food
junkies) than by freak events. May 2008

"BEWARE THE BATS" warns a Science News headline.

Many deadly emerging and re-emerging diseases, including nipah, hendra, sars, ebola, rabies, originated in bats. Not known why. (Because bats are both numerous and may fly far ? And because some hibernate in clusters ?) Also not known why those diseases don't kill bats but kill humans. SN 9june07

Incense and candles pollutes air in churches.

In a Roman Catholic church in Germany, burning candles during a service doubled amount of particles smaller than one μm (the most harmful); burning incense along with candles increased particles 9 times. Amount quicky dropped after candles extinguished but stayed high 24 hours after burning both.

In a Dutch chapel, after candles had burned 9 hours, air contained ten times as many free radicals as by a busy road.

Incense is often used in places other than churches to repel insects or to mask odors. Science News 19aug06

Keep matches and other fire-starters dry.

A few businesses still offer free matches. To protect them from humidity, keep them wrapped at the bottom of a plastic bag. Body heat, too, keeps things dry. Keep bagged matches under your bedding, along with tinders such as dried grass, sage shreds, birch bark. briggi2u@yahoo.com, July 2006

(Comment) Wrapping things in plastic keeps them dry for a while, but water vapor gradually diffuses through thin plastic.

Things beneath bedding may stay dry if the bedding has air circulation under it, such as might be provided by a thick loose mattress formed of conifer boughs. But not if bedding sets directly on the ground or a ground cover. Esp not if the bedding is porous and lacks a vapor barrier (plastic) between sleeper and most layers of bedding. Un-noticed sweat off the sleeper, diffuses through the bedding and condenses on ground.

My experience with a Coleman camping stove.

I acquired a freebie: green case with a red tank into which you pour liquid fuel and then pressurize with a pump integral to the tank. The case had some rust. The tank seemed much used (chipped paint). It held fuel. The pump didn't work.

I reconditioned the pump's leather gasket/plunger with tallow. Now the pump works fine. Thanks briggi (for how-to in ·Dec07 DP). I followed instructions printed on the stove-case and lit burner. The flame was yellow and not well controllable.

Next day I tried again. This time I realized the case's carrying handle had been in the way of the tank seating proper-ly. I moved the handle out of the way. The tank now fit into place properly which extended the carburator tip deeper.

I lit the stove. This time it burned blue, and I could easily turn the flame up or down: better than on my propane stove which tends to go out when I turn the flame very low.

I had planned to buy gasoline (two service stations said their premium unleaded was 92 octane) but decided to first call Coleman: 1-800-835-3278. Surprise ! After waiting ten minutes a real person came on the line and was attentive, knowledgable, responsive. I asked if I could use unleaded gasoline. She said I could if I had a dual tank, which is coated inside so that automotive gas won't corrode it. But my tank was not dual. Also, auto gas has more additives and results in "more mainten-nance"; ie, gunking up the carburator. (A new carb costs $7 to $14 depending on model. Coleman also sells dual tanks.)

Dwelling Portably   May 2008

That convinced me to buy a gallon of Coleman fuel, $6.
Though the Coleman stove's lightness is appealing (I don't like
hauling a **HEAVY** propane tank), lighting a propane stove is
simpler and thus seems **SAFER**. Also, propane is cheaper. Lisa
OR 973

Many people are injured by nail guns.
        U.S. emergency rooms treat 37,000 people annually. Two-
thirds of wounds were to hands or fingers. "Many injuries
occur when a nail gun discharges inadvertently - often when a
safety feature has been disabled for rapid nailing. Also, a
properly fired nail can ricochet off one that's already set,
or run through a piece of wood into a body part." SN 26may07

(Comment) DP readers probably don't use nail guns to improvise
wikiups or outfit vans, but may take temp carpentry jobs.
        I've never used a nail gun. But I've used chain and other
power saws on jobs for others. If a customer wants me to use
power equipment, I want higher pay - which may mean I don't get
the job, because for that much they can hire a skilled carpenter. But that's okay. Better healthy than wealthy. Bert

White LEDs bother people because eyes are accustomed to yellow.
        Sunlight, candles, incandescent bulbs are all yellowish.
After getting used to my white LED lights, I LIKE them. But I
had millions of years of eye evolution to overcome. Zalia, 06

(Response) Though direct sunlight is yellow-white, the sky is
blue. When under open sky but shaded from direct sun, the
light is blue-white. So, eyes have had mega-years exposure to
BOTH colors, though the yellow-white has been brighter.
        Maybe our white LED lights irritate mostly, not because of
color, but because they illuminate only a small area. The
shake-light is focused: fine for spotting a coon in a tree or
for sending morse-code signals across a valley, but not for
much else. The lamp is dim,so it, too, illuminates small area.
        Any white LED has another problem. It consumes much more
power than does an equally-bright yellow LED because: (1) white
LEDs are actually blue LEDs with a phosphor coating that
converts enough of the blue light to other colors to give an
impression of white. The conversion wastes energy. (2) Human
eyes are only 1/4th as sensitive to blue as to yellow, and half
as sensitive to red or green as to yellow. So, a white light
must be more intense than a yellow light to illuminate as well.
        Some dealers claim that white LEDs are "more efficient".
Than WHAT ? Certainly more efficient than incandescents. Also
more efficient than white LEDs of ten years ago. LEDs are
being improved. Yellow LEDs are now used in traffic lights and
turn signals, so I doubt that their development is lagging. B

Many couples break up when building a home.
        Primarily because the job is more complex than it needs to
be. If it were me and I were building a house and I had to
work for a living, I'd look for the simplest method around. My
perspective is that of an owner/builder, not architect or
professional builder. In fact I don't trust experts. (Don't
trust people with initials behind their names.) Pretty much
all the new homes I see being built these days, especially in
the wealthy Bay Area, are disasters.. Lloyd Kahn (in HomeWork :
Hand Built Shelter" (described in OBP) www.shelterpub.com

I do carpentry for friend in exchange for a room. Andrew, ME046

Index

NOTES TO READERS: Numbers 1 and 2 only contained info now
long obsolete. Name changed to "DWELLING PORTABLY" in 1992.

About camping, wandering, living lightly. October 1980 Number 3

Message Post

Published by Hank Schultz, Drawer 190, Philomath, OR 97370.
Subscription, $2 for four issues (about one year).

Simple Shower Convert

Cheers for the Simple Shower.

When I read the description (by Julie Summers in the Light
Living Library) I thought using a jug would be awkward. But I
tried it and find it is a big improvement compared to dipping
out of a bucket and splashing.

I even prefer it to a regular shower (where such is available) because I can get the water to the temperature I want
before beginning, instead of having to keep readjusting knobs -
now too hot - now too cold - wasting water and my temper.

So when in a city I now fill jugs at the sink and carry
them into the bath, rather than fool with the shower controls.

I like half gallon bleach jugs better than gallons because
they are lighter to handle and have smaller openings. I need
one to four jugs ($\frac{1}{2}$ to 2 gallons) depending on whether I'm
scrubbing with soap or just rinsing to cool off, and on whether
I'm washing just my body or also my hair. Pat Rhodes, Cal., May

Whetstone, Knives, Waterproofing Matches, Urinal, Hammock

Being an outdoorsy person I like your pub lots. Wish it
were bigger.

I finally found a sharpening stone that doesn't need oil.
It's "saphire-hard" ceramic, said not to wear. Got it at Huey
& Sons cutlery store in Eugene. (Sorry I didn't get the brand
name.) It's used dry, then washed clean with water and abrasive cleaner (e.g. Ajax). Its only drawback seems to be the
need to apply a lot of force on the blade to get sharpening
action.

Was given a BIG folding lock-back knife. Never could
understand why anyone would want such an ostentatious monster.
But I've found that it's great for whittling, limbing branches,
and anything else where there's much side force on the blade -
takes it better than a small pocket knife yet folds for safe
and compact carrying. With it I made a nifty spatula for flipping flapjacks by shaving a one inch diameter branch thin and
flat for a few inches.

I gave up on match safes. Got some wooden strike anywhere
Diamond matches and dipped them in melted candle butts. Two
stage operation: first coated the head half, placed on a plastic
bag to harden, then dunked the other end. Put a bunch in a 35
mm film canister. Perfect fit. (By the way I've stopped
buying Ohio Match book matches. The striker wears out before
the book is used up.)

Glad to hear you are getting favorable responses to The
Simple Shower. Along the same line there's the Easy Peepot -
another refinement that puts more comfort in camping. It
allows me to pee without bothering to leave my tent and put
shoes on, and eliminates splashing pee off of hard ground.
I use a coffee can, a large plastic food container, or whatever
is surplus and has a tight-fitting lid. Men can use a plastic
narrow-mouth jug.

I carry a portable bidet with me too - in the form of a plastic squeeze bottle. Fill with water. To clean just squirt and towel dry. Eliminates the need for toilet paper.

Do any Message Post readers have experience with sleeping in hammocks? Seems like one answer to hard uneven ground. But they hardly permit turning over so I wonder how comfy they'd be for one night or many nights. Julie Summers

Wire Saw Breakage & Cold Tolerance

A Coughlan wire saw sold by Payless broke after about an hour of use. It first broke at one clamp. I fixed by attaching the blade directly to the bow (branch). 15 minutes later it broke again, this time in the middle. (I was gentle with it --- kept it taut, kinkless, and went slow enough that it didn't get too hot to touch.)

As to speed the wire saw was probably faster than whittling with a knife, but not by much. Took an hour to saw half way through a 10" diameter dry snag.

You (Hank) speculated that your greater cold tolerance is due in part to your build. This seems likely because Eskimos and most arctic peoples tend to be short, not much over five feet, and stocky.

Holly and I notice aclimatization in just a few months. November usually seems colder to us than February, yet actual temperatures are lower in February on the average. Bert Davis, Oregon, September.

Can You Rely on Solar Stills ?

How well do solar stills work? Here's what Mel DeWeese, a search and rescue training officer had to say about solar stills in Woodsmoke #10 (P.O.Box 15754, Colorado Springs, CO 80935; $6 for six): "Oh, by the way, we tested all sorts of solar stills without much results. I know the book says two to three pints per day... not so. By the time you dig a hole with your hands, collect plants, etc. you've used two gallons of water! Besides you need at least two quarts a day...so. We found out, like the Air Force said, that a plastic sheet on the ground over plants collected as much, but not enough...."

Moral: There is much in literature that parrots what was picked up from other literature, that was also parroting. And the original was in error to begin with! Julie Summers, April

Making Tents More Livable

Ann Marshall, writing in the February Signpost (16812 36th Ave. W., Lynnwood, WA 98036; 12 times yearly, $12) suggests sewing pockets inside of a tent for storage of small items. "Pockets made of mosquito netting are really lightweight, and you can see what's in them." To retain waterproofness, apply seam sealer to the stitches afterwards.

Traveler's Toothbrush Mini Case

Make your own from a 35mm film canister or pill bottle -- save money, space, and weight. It balances the scales at 2/8 oz., compared to 7/8 oz. for the full size model. Film cans are available free at many photo stores. Merely cut a slot in the container's lid to accomodate the toothbrush handle, cut a few ventilation holes, and add a retainer cord. Julie Summers, Oregon, Sept.

NOTE TO READERS. Prices and most addresses here-in have changed. Sources that still exist might be on internet.

Make Your Own Sesame Butter

With peanut butter going way out of reason in price, there is a simple substitute that I have used for years. Just use about a third by volume of sesame seeds which are roasted, and grind them up with the unroasted raw seeds. One of the little whirly blade nut grinders health food stores have is great, and a little oil, chicken fat, or honey will smooth it out.

To roast them just use a frying pan and don't burn them. You can roast all of the seeds, but I find it isn't necessary for my taste. Other seeds may also be used but I haven't found them coming as close to the flavor of peanut butter. Al Fry, California, March

Mussels Can Be Poisonous

Don and I enjoyed reading "Summer Idyl" (Light Living Library) which brought back happy memories of beach camping. However the authors failed to mention that mussels and other shell fish are sometimes poisonous. This happens when toxic plankton become abundant in the ocean. The mussels, which are filter feeders, concentrate the toxin. (Apparently they are not harmed by it.)

The poison causes temporary paralysis and, if enough is eaten, can kill by halting breathing though fatalities are few. Cooking doesn't destroy the toxin.

Shellfish are most likely to be poisonous during summer or when there is a red tide, but not all red tides include the toxic kinds of plankton nor is the absence of a red color in the water assurance that shell fish are safe to eat. Outbreaks are more common in some areas than in others. It would be wise to make local inquiries before eating shellfish, especially in large quantities. Jean Apt, Arizona, March.

Mouse Defense

For those who plan to spend more than one night in the same camp, a mouse trap or two may be a boon. (Seems to take the critters a few nights to zero in.) I don't like killing them, however I see no alternative since they can cause a lot of damage. A trap is better than staying up all night trying in vain to swat them. Many things work for bait: peanut butter, sunflower seeds, nuts, popcorn, bread (moistened and molded on), apple, carrot, cheese, etc., but I find a kernel of dried field corn holds up best.

Tying your trap to something will prevent its being carried off by a mouse that gets caught without being killed: or by a predator taking the mouse, trap and all. Tying with an elastic rubber strap may keep a mouse that's caught only by the tail or a leg from jerking loose. For a tie point I drill a hole in the trap at a corner on the end opposite the bait, so as not to interfere with the mechanism.

If I don't know whether I'll be contending with mice or rats, I prefer to have mouse traps. They are lighter, cheaper, and more sensitive. And although a mouse trap won't catch a rat, it can mortally wound it. One morning I found a mouse trap sprung with nothing in it. 20 feet down the path lay a dead rat, bleeding from one ear. If the rat survives, having more brains than a mouse, it may learn not to come around again. Julie Summers, Oregon, February

NOTE TO READERS. Many obsolete items have been removed to make room for more how-to info. Some of the substituted items are not in their original order.

For small tents, double-skin more important than shape.

Frank Ashley's Rag #51, December 1980 (Box 291, Culver City CA 90230, $13 a year) comments on dome tents: "...shapes by themselves do not keep a camper warmer or cooler. Spherical shapes do have the lowest surface area to volume ratio of any shape and can recirculate hot air back around from the top to the bottom of the interior space. However, because volume grows at third power rates and surface area grows at second power rates, this effect is quite insignificant at very small sizes such as in Famous Trails tent. The truth is that a double skin construction system of an inner tent and a rain flysheet, which is designed to trap a layer of air, in infinitely more significant in the control of temperature, i.e., 'warmer in winter and cooler in summer'. Long time readers of this newsletter must realize, by now, that we are not the world's greatest booster of dome type tents...." HS

Free and Easy Domes

Some years ago I scrounged up some redwood strips and fiberglass so decided that some little domes would be handy. I put enough triangular panels together to make three domes and they have been a joy: Being smaller than 100 sq. feet they do not need a building permit in my county. Being set on skids they can be easily moved around on my acre. And being weatherproof they can be used for anything. At the moment I have one as a guest dome, one as a work and printing room, and one set over my septic tank with a toilet (camper type) as a guest toilet and storage room for visitors who pass by. Putting together the triangles with baling wire I secured everything in the most primitive fashion and have yet to have any problems. Printing plates and tin stripping were used to cover the overhead cracks and there are few serious leaks. John Freeman, Calif., Dec.

Making Repairs on Foam

Polyurethane foam (such as mattress pads) can be repaired with a special cement. However it's messy, smelly, expensive, and one more thing to have around. I've found that simply sewing works fine. I use synthetic thread (polyester). No special stitch, just a running one and not too close together (to avoid cutting the foam). Julie Summers, Oregon, January

A foam mattress of ours had lost most of its springiness in the middle where our hips rest. So I cut it in two and fastened the original ends together with contact cement, restoring it. Holly Davis, Oregon, January

Nylon Sheets for Camping

Because nylon is lighter, gives up dirt easier when washed, and dries faster than cotton, we use it for our sheets. We purchased the fabric at the yardgoods store. We have used one set steadily for over 5 years and it's still good! Any raw edges may be heat sealed instead of hemming (move edge through a candle flame). We contoured the bottom sheet to keep it in place. The top sheet is fastened to the sleeping bag (which we use open like a quilt at basecamp) by tying tightly at each corner. (We have recently used polyester to make another set, but don't know yet how it will wear compared to the nylon.) Holly Davis, Oregon, January

Free Leather, Cutting Thongs and Speedy Rivets

I no longer BUY leather. I acquire enough for all my needs FREE by salvaging it from discarded pocketbooks, boots, jackets and coats. Some looks beautiful; other pieces are worn but still strong. (I reject what is weak with rot.)

Alternatively, for about $2 there's the farmer's bundle, about two pounds of scraps (including already cut thongs - some long enough for boot laces), on sale at farm supply and feed stores.

At first appearance a shoe might not look like it has enough leather worth salvaging, but there is actually plenty there for making excellent thongs or laces. Simply cut around and around.

Speedy rivets - two-piece brass rivets - add a professional look to home made articles, in addition to providing some extra strength at stress points (such as where the stitching starts or ends on a knife sheath.) The only tools necessary for installation are a punch (to make the holes) and hammer (to lock the rivet). I purchased mine by mail from MacPherson Bros., 730 Polk Street, San Francisco, CA 94109. Julie Summers, Oregon, January

Disinfecting Small Wounds

Those who live or travel in the bush usually don't have a doctor handy. Therefore it's important to know how to care for minor injuries. Here are questions I sent to the Center for Disease Control, Atlanta, Georgia 30333 and the replies of Dr. William R. Jarvis, M.D., Epidemiologic Investigations Activity.

Question: What is best for washing wounds - superficial ones such as minor cuts, abrasions, blisters, tick bites, and punctures? I have read many recommendations, from soap and water to expensive antiseptic solutions. Have any studies been made?

Reply:"I have limited our discussion to wounds which do not require surgical intervention. As you state, various antiseptic solutions have been recommended for the washing of wounds. I am unaware of any well-controlled study which has compared all the various antiseptic solutions with simple soaps and/or water. Since the major purpose of such washing is to cleanse the wound of possible infectious agents, the vigor with which washing is performed as well as the amount of solution used to dilute out the number of organisms is probably most important. Although the various antiseptic solutions may contain chemicals that may possess antibacterial activity, we would recommend the use of soap and water. In the case of most wounds soap and water is more than adequate to remove the dirt introduced into the wound and to reduce the bacterial count."

Question: I've heard that topical antibiotic preparations (ones applied directly to the skin) are ineffective in combating infection. I wonder if this has been confirmed or refuted by any studies.

Reply: "Topical antibiotic preparations are largely over-used and relatively ineffective. Although these agents do have a role in the medical arsenal, abuse of such agents is certainly not uncommon. For example, such agents are commonly used in the treatment of impetigo, a Staphylococcus aureus skin infection common in infants and children. Numerous studies published in the 1950s and 1960s have shown that topical anti-microbial agents are totally ineffective in the treatment of such infections. However, even today,topical antimicrobial agents are commonly dispensed for the treatment of such infections. The questions that you asked are excellent ones that are commonly seriously discussed among medical practioners. The questions that you have raised are complex ones and abbreviated answers can often be misleading."

Message Post

POB 190 Philomath OR 97370. Next issue, June. $2 for 3 issues

Eating Tules in the Tules

Cattails don't grow near our camp, unfortunately. But a distant relative of theirs does and it's almost as versatile. The tule or bulrush (Scirpus species, Sedge family) grows commonly in the creeks of the coast mountains.

We eat the inner stalk raw, which to me has a pleasant nut-like flavor and a celery-like texture. For a month now Bert and I have been harvesting. We strip down the outer leaves, then snap off the inner stem under water.

Later the immature seed heads are nice tasting though a bit rough to chew. Donald Kirk, in Wild Edible Plants of the Western United States, adds: "The roots are quite starchy and may be eaten raw or baked, dried, or ground into a nutritious white flour. The pollen may be gathered, pressed into cakes, and baked. The seeds may be used whole, parched, ground into mush..."

The local species' leaves are reminiscent of cattail though smaller, but Scirpus acutus, which Kirk illustrates (and is drawn here), has only basal leaves. The stem is tall but not so tall as a cattail's. Locally the flower arrangements are umbels --- many little flowers spreading like an umbrella (whereas a cattail has a spike), but Kirk says the flowers may be in heads, spikes, umbels or solitary spikelets. Holly Davis, Oregon, March

A Backpack for Dropping Off Trains

I would like to hear of any suggestions you have on back-packs. I need one with the following qualities. (1) Large enough capacity for living on the road. (2) Rugged enough to last. (3) With a frame that will withstand being dropped off a train with a full load. (4) Small enough to fit easily into a car when hitching a ride.

The only packs I know of that might work is the Army sur-plus pack with a steel frame and my Jansport Touring Pack 2. The problem with my pack is I have to take the frame off when tossing it off a train.

Is it possible to weld a broken frame?
Mike Cahill, Florida, February.

Partial reply: Aluminum frames can be welded but special equipment is needed. They can also be repaired or reinforced with fiberglass and epoxy resin. Scrape off the paint from the area to be fiberglassed. The Freighthopper's Manual (review further on) says (p.25): "I have found that the squat, army surplus type rucksack can take the shock of being dropped out of a boxcar at 20 mph more readily than the new-fangled oblong outfits such as Cruiser, Kelty, etc. The army surplus packs' tubular steel frames are considerably stronger than aluminum frames and because they approximate a sphere they tend to roll end over end when they hit rather than absorbing all the shock at once. While it is true that the newer types will enable you to carry heavier loads, I also find them topheavy and harder to run with. And while rarely a necessity, running with your pack on can sometimes save you a 24 hour wait for the next hotshot. Dufflebags are definitely out..."   HS

Food Cravings in the Bush

What causes them? Julie Summers asked this in Message Post #3. One possible explanation is offered by Edward Donn in _Pioneer Wilderness Food_ (foregoing review). "Even after eight years of backpacking, I would develop strange cravings after more than five days in the wilderness. I always thought they were caused by the absence of some trace vitamin. After doing some calculations I discovered what was missing: energy. I was starving myself." Elsewhere Donn points up that prolonged outdoor activity consumes more energy and requires more food than people who are sedentary much of the time are accustomed to eat.

Peanut BUTTER is Better

A study (reported on in Science News, October 25, 1980) showed that oil (and possibly other nutrients) is better absorbed from peanut butter than from whole peanuts. Stool analysis showed subjects eating whole peanuts as their principal source of fat excreted "large amounts of dietary fat...(up to one-third in one case)". On the other hand, analysis of the stools of those eating peanut butter and others eating peanut oil "indicated a high degree of fat absorption from these foods, particularly the peanut oil."

For backpackers and others who want maximum energy and nutrition per weight (not to mention cost) it would make more sense to carry a pound of peanut butter than a pound of peanuts whole, in light of the above information. (Reusable squeeze tubes are sold by outdoor suppliers.) Dee Carlson, Ariz., Jan.

The Freighthoppers Manual for North America

This book was written by Daniel Leen and published in 1979 by Capra Press, POB 2068, Santa Barbara, CA 93120; 96 pages, $4.95 paper. The chapters include "Advantages and Disadvantages" (compared especially to hitchhiking), "What to Bring", "Dodging the Heat", "Information" (how to find out where and when to catch the right train), "Picking Your Car", "Getting On", "Easy Riding", "Getting Off", and "The State of the Art - 1978".

"Almost always the first switchman you run into will know everything you'll need to know, but without careful double checking this information you can end up on a train at 2 p.m. that is in fact going where you want to go but will arrive there a day or two after the hotshot leaving the same yard at 10 p.m."

"In any large city there will be a number of different railroad yards, some companies having two or more in the area. Thus you can't just go down to the first one you see and expect to find a freight going directly to your destination...."

"The old standby is, of course, the boxcar.... Empty mail cars ... ride a lot smoother and even have a boarding step at the door.... Flatcars are unsafe as at high speeds you will begin to bounce around and have nothing to hold onto.... Shifting loads and attempting to get off fast moving trains probably kill more hobos than anything besides sterno."

"In conclusion, let me stress: don't try anything that you're not absolutely sure that you can do" (if getting on or off a train while it's moving).

Compared to hitchhiking the author feels that freight hopping is usually faster in the west where large cities are far apart, slower in the east. After reading this book my impression is that travelling efficiently and safely by freight requires more expertise than does hitchhiking. Before trying it I'd reread this book many times or else find an experienced freight-hopping companion. Review by Hank Schultz

LIGHT AND WARMTH: How to Use the Pressure Lantern with Heatshield to Warm Up a Tent.

by Joseph Vetrono

That a kerosene or gasoline pressure lantern, burning gaseous fuel in a fabric mantle, will provide brilliant light in a campsite after dark is well known. That is will provide warmth, sufficient warmth to make a large tent comfortable in inclement weather, may not be so well known. To me, the chief advantage of the pressure lantern in a camp has always been that it extends the useful hours during which activities which require light may be carried on beyond sunset. The considerable heat given off by the powerful generators on such lanterns may be utilized to provide warmth as well, without danger, provided sensible precautions are taken.

The most important precaution is to make sure that the tent is ventilated. If the tent is provided with ventilators, make sure that they are open, and not closed or partially closed by the canvas being folded down over them on the outside. It is probably wise to leave a small portion of the tent door open, too, just to be sure that enough air will get into the tent to keep the lantern burning without producing carbon monoxide. Remember, even a large stand-up tent encloses a very small space, and encloses it much more tightly than any house. A pressure lantern, or any similar burning device, such as a stove, uses up oxygen at a terrific rate, many times over what a person uses breathing, and it will exhaust the air in a closed tent very quickly. Earlier in this century a pair of Arctic explorers were found dead in their unventilated tent with a burned-out Primus stove between them. If sufficient ventilation is provided, however, there is no need to fear using such devices in a tent.

The second hazard to guard against is fire. This is best achieved by making it an absolute rule never to set the lantern down anywhere in the tent while it is burning. In the small, crowded space of a tent it is just too easy to knock it over while turning around, especially if you are moving a bulky article like a sleeping bag. Always hang the lantern from the ridge pole. Then, if you bump into the lantern, it just swings. Be sure to hang it low enough so that the rising column of superheated air produced by the generator does not scorch the tent roof. In this connection, a heatshield provides complete safety and creates additional convection current warmth, as well.

THE HEATSHIELD. A heatshield is very simply made from an ordinary goldpan. Just take any goldpan,✱about 12-14 inches in diameter, and cut a small, rectangular slot in the very center of it. This slot should be about 1/8 inch wide and anywhere between 1½ and 3 inches long, depending upon how the bail handle of the lantern is shaped. If the bail handle has a little bend in it, at the top, to accomodate whatever hook you hang it on, then the slot need be only about 1¼" X 1/8". If the handle is made in a smooth, unbroken curve, you would have to make the slot longer. In that case, you might wish to make a slot shaped like this, instead. The idea is to provide sufficient clearance so that the hook, or snap fastener, upon which the lantern is to be hung, may pass easily under the top of the bail where it protrudes above the heatshield. Where does the heatshield go? Right on top of the bail under snap hook and directly above the lantern itself. (See sketch on next page.)

To make the slot in the center of the gold pan, just draw it carefully at the exact center, then drill several holes, using a 1/8 - 3/16" drill bit, in a line next to each other, and complete the making of the slot with files. It is possible to make a perfect slot in this way. After you have fashioned the slot to just the right size to fit over the bail handle on your lantern, then paint the heatshield to prevent rusting.

The rising column of superheated air from the generator, instead of going straight up uselessly to the tent roof, is deflected outward by the heatshield. The heatshield itself warms up and it, too, diffuses more warmth in every direction. I have used such a heatshield in conjunction with my Coleman Model 127 for many years and it has never failed to give satisfaction..The Model 127 burns kerosene and it is a pity that it is now obsolete, as I think that it is superior to any gasoline burning lantern, as well as safer. The British "Tilly", which also burns kerosene, may still be available from that country. Joseph Vetrono, 6 September 1980

✱(Comment:) I wouldn't cut up a gold pan. A disposable aluminum pie plate or broiler pan should suffice (unless the lamp gets hot enough to melt aluminum, in which case use a piece of scrap sheet steel). Bert

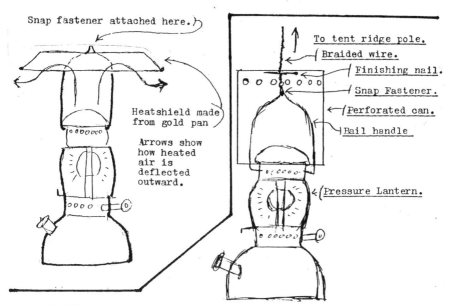

Snap fastener attached here.

Heatshield made from gold pan

Arrows show how heated air is deflected outward.

To tent ridge pole.
Braided wire.
Finishing nail.
Snap Fastener.
Perforated can.
Bail handle
Pressure Lantern.

ADDENDUM: For use in very cold weather, it ought to be possible to rig a heater above the Pressure Lantern, using a fairly large metal can, about 12 inches in diameter and the same in depth.

Just drill a series of $\frac{1}{2}$ inch holes, about 1 inch apart, around the circular base of the can. (But not in the bottom of it.) If no drill is available, just punch holes in the can with a nail. Then drill a small hole, about $\frac{1}{4}$ inch, in the center of the bottom. Turn the can upside down and pass a length of strong braided wire through the hole, tying it around a 6 inch finishing nail (small head) or any similar piece of stiff wire, leaving a sufficient length of suspend the lantern beneath. (See drawing.)

Attach a small snap fastener to the end of the braided wire, twisting the wire back around itself to secure it after adjusting the length so that, when the Lantern is hanging from the hook, the globe with the mantle inside is beneath the lower edge of the can. This is so that you get light as well as heat.

Do not despise such a seemingly primitive stove. I have seen such devices, sometimes heated by nothing more than a candle, give a surprising amount of warmth, even in snow conditions. Joseph Vetrono, 26 Oct. 1980
Copyright 1980, Joseph Vetrono

Economical Footgear

Holly made a pair of mocassins out of a salvaged truck inner-tube using Light Living Library's plans ("Wheelskin Mocassins" by Julie Summers). These mocs are amazingly durable. One pair has lasted over a year whereas I can wear out a pair of tennies in a few weeks. They are also very light, easy to wash, quick to dry, can't rot, and cause less erosion.

Best of all, they are more comfortable in most going than any shoes I've ever worn. Exceptions: coarse gravel roads, pavement, or going down a steep hill when it's wet (the foot slides forward in the moc and the toes jam up in front). On long hikes we also carry tennies and switch off.

For traction, I agree with Julie's comment (MP#10) that these mocs are somewhat better than average tennis shoes. I find them much less slippery than leather mocs. The terrain is a consideration. I prefer mocs to tennies on logs because they allow my feet to shape themselves to the surface and keep me more stable. I'd rather have tennies on a steep slope, especially if there is loose dirt or leaves. Bert, Oregon, February

9

Message Post

POB 190 Philomath OR 97370. Next issue, October. $2 for 3 issues

Tipi Tips

Tipis' long poles can be overcome by using telescoping aluminum pipes locked into place when you raise the tipi. Tipis
work better with a stove (pipe out the smoke flap) because sometimes the smoke flap is hard to adjust with wind changes. Who
wants to smell like pitch? Two years ago I spent the winter
near Boundary Dam, Washington in a tipi with a stove inside.
Tipis withstand snow build up. Don't try to camp extended time
in one less than 16' (too small). 16' is okay for three people
and equipment. Lines can be used to steady them if need be. My
mimus is: they stand too tall and are hard to keep out of
sight. George Pickett, Louisiana, May

I have a 12' tipi so it's easier to heat (less space), small
enough for me to put up alone, and easier to haul and get tipi
poles --- and you can use fewer; 11 poles instead of the usual 18.
I get away with six lodge poles (four --- three tripod and one
lift may be enough) and five 2 by 2's (two for smoke flaps).
Instead of buying expensive canvas to make a lining and ozone,
I bought old sheets and wool blankets at a garage sale. First I
line with sheets and then the wool blankets over top and also
for the ozone, hanging with clothes pins and rocks rolled under
the bottom. Soft wood is smokey so I use a tin stove.
Heather, Texas, May

Storing Bedding at Bivy Camps

To save weight we sometimes leave equipment near a campsite
we expect to return to. Large truck or tractor innertubes serve
to protect our gear, especially bedding, from weather and
animals. Blown out innertubes are thrown away at tire stores.

Cut away the blown section, leaving a long tube. Turn
inside out and wash with soap and water. After it dries turn
outside out. Place rolled up bedding, etc. inside.

With each end of the tube: (A) Fold over. (B) Roll the fold
together. (C) Wrap rubber straps around the roll, using many
turns in order to hold very tightly. The straps can be cut from
the same tube. (Only one end of tube is shown.)

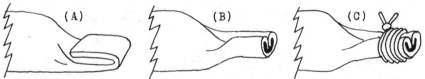

Put the tube in dense bushes or put leaves over it, to protect it from sunlight which will rot rubber. We have stored
bedding this way for several years. A drawback is that the
tubes are rather heavy for the amount they will hold, so we use
them mostly at campsites around cities. Bert Davis, Oregon, May

The Freedome

Being a tent dweller myself now for 10 years, I can relate
to much of your info, news and ideals. I'm enclosing our catalog.

Most of my design work has been with plastic sheeting. The
"clip" is ideal for suspending or joining sheeting of all kinds.

They are available for 65¢ each from Shelter Systems.
Bob Gillis, California, March
    (Excerpted from the catalog:) While most domes are designed
to be rigid and permanent, ours are primarily portable. The
basic triangle used to form the dome has legs of equal length,
making a structure of interchangeable pieces. This means the
dome can be erected very quickly and without complications.
Flexible skins of fabric or plastic are stretched and tensioned
into a taut membrane by the framework, which in turn is held
under compression into connectors. Our patented clip grips the
skin without penetrating or weakening it.
    The frameworks are made of PVC irrigation piping; admirable
in strength, longevity and cost for the task. Should a section
be lost or broken, it can be quickly and cheaply replaced at
your local hardware store.
    For fabric
our Freedomes use
a 5.5 oz. poly-
ester tent mater-
ial. It is very
resistant to UV
degradation, flame
retardant, treated
for waterproofness,
and rot and mildew
resistance. Ten-
sile strength is
167 lbs. warp and
111 lbs. fill.
Color is a light
tan. The resulting structure is an excellent windshield and is
totally waterproof.
    Snow cautions: The Freedome will withstand severe buffeting,
but not great amounts of dead weight. Snow must not be allowed
to accumulate or collapse is inevitable.
    The 16' Freedome encloses a 16 foot diameter, $8\frac{1}{2}$ foot tall
hemispherical space that is roomy enough to do a cartwheel in!
It features two doors and two windows fitted with netting for
ventilation and insect protection. The dome assembles in 20-30
minutes and disassembles in 5-10 minutes. Storage is in two
sacks. Weight is approx 60 lbs. Price, $400 plus $20 shipping.
Options: Tie in floor, $70. Sewen in floor, $90. Liner, $175.
Stovepipe thimble, $9.50.
    Also available: an 11' Freedome, 38 lbs. and $260 basic
price; an 8' Freedome, 18 lbs. and $175 basic price; and port-
able greenhouses. Shelter Systems, POB 308, Carmel Valley CA93924

Bivouac Bag
    Along with my down sleeping bag and my backpack, this is my
most valuable possession. Get one where you don't need stakes
or trees to tie the front up off your face. The bendable wand
system is good.
    Mine's made by Marmount Mountain Works. It was the best I
could find a year ago but to make it better I would suggest
velcro instead of zipper for quicker escape. Not so much gortex.
Seams should not lie on the ground but be on top, like a bath
tub. Heather, Texas, May
    Editor's note: A bivouac (also called bivy) bag is a mini
enclosure for one --- picture a cross between an inflated
sleeping bag and a shrunken one-person tent. Early Winters catalog (free from 110 Prefontaine Place, South Seattle, WA 98104)

Making Repairs When Grommets Pull Out

When the grommets pull out of shoulder straps (or other equipment) one can buy replacements. But it's cheaper and more satisfying (to me at least) to repair the old.

If the hole left by the grommet is wider than the webbing to be installed, reinforce the hole with a piece of fabric that overlaps it at least ¼" or more before sewing on the webbing.

A home sewing machine works if the fabrics aren't too thick. If they are, sew by hand or use a sewing awl. (I've written a Light Living Library article about this handy tool.) Use a match or candle flame to neatly seal the raw edges of all nylon fabric (including the webbing).

So the rings won't rotate, use rather stiff webbing, and "D" rings that are no wider than the webbing. And sew webbing together close to the rings.

Webbing and "D" rings can be salvaged from discarded or second hand camping gear, or purchased from some backpacking stores, leather/harness suppliers, and fabric shops that cater to makers of their own backpacking gear. Julie Summers, April

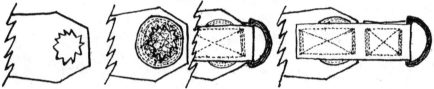

| Shoulder strap with hole where grommet was. | Hole rein- forced with sturdy fabric. | Webbing holding "D" ring sewed in place. | Alternative: mini- mizes thickness that must be sewen thru. |

Bicycling Ease and Comfort

Use cheap army packs for panniers, line with garbage bags. Strap soft frame backpack on top of them. Great to have when you want to ditch the bike and hike.

Bring wool pants, shirt, hat, wind breaker and just get wet if it rains. (Ed. note: Wool retains about half of its insulat- ive value when wet; more than most other fabrics.)

Females, if your pelvic bone jams uncomfortably into the seat, buy a lightweight padded plastic women's seat, remove leather and padding. Figure where your bone hits and cut small hole, enlarging as trial and error shows.

Bicycle gears: New bikes are always sold with worthless gear ratios --- often overlapping and geared for racing and men's muscles. Learn how a gear chart works and figure what you want and replace those gears with lower ones for touring with a load. Heather, Texas, May

Eyeglass Retainer

I drill holes in the lobes of my eyeglass frames and put a thin rubber strap (cut from old inner tube) through them, making an overhand knot at each end to prevent the strap coming out. To tighten or loosen the strap I pull it through the hole. It's a tight fit and friction holds it wherever I want. Now while hiking and rafting I don't worry that my glasses will fall off and break or get lost. A. Copley, California, April

Editor's note: If you don't have a drill you may heat a small nail (held by a pliers or vice grip). If you've never melted holes in plastic, first experiment on a less expensive item such as a toothbrush, and use a very small nail, so as not to melt the whole end off instead of just making a hole.

NOT Wearing Eyeglasses a Handicap ?

I like to wear a pair of safety glasses when hiking where there's tall brush or overhanging branches. Without them I must go slower and even then there's risk of eye irritation or worse.

There are clear "sport glasses" but shop worker's safety glasses may be cheaper and they come with shields on the sides. Holly Davis, Oregon, June

Hitching Hints

Bring large paper bags and crayons to write signs. Get off at a truck stop exit. 18 wheelers can go from east coast to west almost straight through. I was picky my last hitch and refused a few rides till I got one going right past the city I wanted --- a 24 hour ride.

Females: I found wearing a mid length skirt attracted undesirable rides. (I thought pants would be too hot and shorts too showy.) Now I dress in baggy, non-feminine clothes (shorts/pants/T-shirt). Bring a baseball hat to really hide sex.

Now I find rides are all good. People looking close to see an honest face often see I'm female and stop. The weirdos don't look that close. I have never been physically harmed hitching, and have done it for 10 years. I don't encourage anyone to do it unless you feel confident; sometimes I think I've angels who watch over me.

Refuse rides with three or more people unless kids or females. Memorize or write down car license number. Talk to folks before you hop in --- I always pipe out before they do "how far are you going?" Get their vibe and accept or refuse the ride. Heather, Texas, May

Disinfecting Second Hand Clothing and Bedding

Some people hesitate to purchase and use secondhand things such as sleeping bags and garments, for fear of contracting disease. Such fear is not unfounded, however it is easy to render used items safe as new:

Temperatures exceeding 126° F for 10 minutes will kill lice and mites (scabies). This temperature can be obtained by ironing, machine drying on the hot cycle, or washing. (It is recommended[1] that the washing machine temperature be set at 140° F, to insure that the clothes get hot enough.) Dry cleaning will disinfect also.

If the above methods are not practical, an alternative is to isolate the items for a period longer than the parasites can live without a host (person). At 72° F lice can't live longer than a month without a host. Mites (scabies) can't exist without a host more than a couple of days; however holding the items unused for 10 days is recommended[2], to be on the safe side I presume. If one doesn't know if lice or mites are involved, hold for the longer period -- somewhat over a month. Placing the items in plastic bags insures the parasites won't crawl onto other clothes/bedding.

If you suspect diseases other than parasites, "Washing at 160° F for 25 minutes makes all linens safe for reuse; sterilization prior to washing is not recommended."[2]

References: 1) Pediculicides and Scabicides, Dennis D. Juranek, 12 pages, from Handbook of Drug Therapy, 1979, reprinted by USDHEW, Center for Disease Control, Atlanta, GA 30333. 2) The Inanimate Environment, George F. Mallison, 12 pages, from Hospital Infections, 1979, reprinted by USDHEW. Julie Summers, Oregon, March

Mosquitos Not Repelled By Sound

The electronic noise-makers which are sold for chasing away mosquitos do not work, according to an article in the June 1978 issue of Mountain Gazette (no longer published).

Message Post

POB 190 Philomath OR 97370. Next issue February. $2 for 3 issues

Hitching is Quicker but Freights are More Thrilling

Concerning your review (The Freighthoppers Manual, Capra
Press, 1979), my personal experience includes tens of thousands
of miles of each - freights and hitches - both solo and in
teams. Freights are filthy. Freights are definitely more
thrilling, in fact, they are a first degree rush! But they are
rarely if ever faster than hitching for me. I choose freights
for thrills, hitching for speed. Sure, a hotshot may cover a
lot of territory fast, but I maintain that city by city a car
travelling legal speeds will be up to 50% faster than a freight,
and I have never spent 50% of my time in a stationary ride-
soliciting posture on long travels. Although I do have to
recall the ride that let me off on a San Jose freeway on-ramp,
and knowing that those magic on-ramps worth one's hitching
effort are few and far between, I hiked three or four miles
across town to the freightyards and caught the next southbound!
There, that was my two cents on the unbeatable thrill of roaring down the rails with an ear-to-ear grin!
Will Ross, California, September

A Little Portable Faucet at a Big Gathering

"Running Water Anywhere",
designed by Julie Summers (plans
available from the Light Living
Library) has proven a handy
addition to our home-camp. Holly
and I use one many times a day
for washing hands and dishes,
without difficulties.

So, when we went to
this year's Rainbow Gathering, I made several for
public demonstration.
Thousands washed with them
and many commented favor-
ably about them. However
the heavy usage and the
unfamiliarity of most
users caused complications.

Many first-time users
turned the cap too far,
unscrewing it completely and
dumping all the water on the
ground. This happened
despite a large caution
printed on each: "Turn just
a LITTLE !" For a future
gathering I would add some kind
of mechanical stop.

The portable faucets in the
dining meadow were used by many
for bowl rinsing, so I tried to
keep those supplied with water
from a creek considered pure
enough for drinking. But others

(Most of the third
(hind) leg of the
tripod isn't shown
here.)

DO   NOT DRINK
for washing only

TURN JUST A
LITTLE
ON ⟷ OFF

PORTABLE
FAUCET

sometimes refilled the faucets from a closer creek in which
people were bathing. Each faucet carried a warning: "DO NOT
DRINK. For washing only."
    Some little kids didn't understand how to turn the faucet
on and stuck their hands into the water through the fill hole on
top. I solved that (after the first faucet) by cutting the fill
holes small --- about an inch wide. (The small opening would
make cleaning out sediment and algae more difficult --- a problem only if the faucet is used over a long period such as
at home.)
    In general the kids did better than the adults: most kids
read the directions carefully or asked others for instruction,
and then turned gingerly; whereas many a bigger person, without
pausing to read, gave the cap a big twist and --- splosh !
    There weren't conveniently located trees for supporting the
faucets so I built small tripod A-frames. These also allowed
the faucets to be moved easily and frequently so that waste food
from dish washing didn't accumulate in one spot.
    Each faucet was made from a gallon plastic jug and didn't
hold enough water for very many washings. So I collected other
jars and bottles from the trashes, cleaned them, filled them,
and left them by the faucets for replenishing them. But the
storage bottles vanished ! I got more, leashed these to the
frames with cord, and posted "please don't remove" signs. But
still they disappeared. It seems that some people, who had come
to the gathering without personal water containers, couldn't be
bothered salvaging and cleaning as I had done. Out of the thousands not many were bottle snatchers, but enough were to divest
the faucets during the peak inflow. Later, as the crowds
tapered off, some of those departing left their surplus containers at the portable faucets so there were more than enough.
    Supplying and maintaining five portable faucets kept me
going much of the day, even with the unsolicited but welcome
assistance of many users who helped haul water. Yet five hardly
began to fill the hygenic needs of so large a gathering: that
would have required dozens. But they served to demonstrate a
simple device which people could later make for their own use.
    Each bore a packet of Catalogs and a sign; "PORTABLE
FAUCET. 'Running Water Anywhere'. Leaves hands free for washing
and leaves creeks uncontaminated. Provided by the Light Living
Library." Several hundred catalogs were distributed.
Bert Davis, Washington, July

Alternative Sources for Prescription Drugs
    What is a prescription item varies from one country to
another. Antibiotics are sold over-the-counter in Mexico. In
the U.S. antibiotics for veterinary use are sold without
prescription at farm supply stores. They usually carry oral
tetracycline (in powder form). Unfortunately their penicillin
is usually the injectable form (riskier than oral) and is combined with streptomycin (which can cause deafness and kidney
damage, not to mention bacteria quickly get resistant to it).
Julie Summers, Oregon, September

Backpack Birth Control
    Condoms are smaller and lighter than a container of foam
or jelly. And a condom can be reused dozens of times, further
reducing weight and cost. I also prefer condoms because they
are in my body a relatively short time, unlike foam, a pill,
or an IUD, and therefore less likely to be injurious. They
provide excellent contraception if put on before any genital-
to-genital contact begins.

To recycle I wash the condom as soon as convenient. I
partially fill it with water, blow it up a little, and twist it
shut so that I can shake it, which helps clean the inside.
Then I invert the condom and let the water, semen, and air out.
I repeat this rinsing a few times. To clean the outside I let
water run over it, rubbing any adhering secretions with my
fingers. Plain water works best. Soap and hot water deteriorate the rubber.
After rinsing I place the condom, as smoothed out as
possible, on a cloth. After a few hours, when the outside is
dry but the inside still wet, I turn inside-out. (Blowing it
up first may help if the insides are stuck together in places.
If the condom is allowed to dry too long it may become very
difficult to unstick -- just start over by soaking it again.)
Every time the condom is blown up provides an opportunity
to check for defects. I've never had a condom break during use.
When the condom is dry on both sides I blow it up once
more and dust it with corn starch, then turn it inside out and
rub corn starch on the other side. Next, with forefingers on
the inside of the condom and thumbs on the outside, I roll it up.
I put it in a 35 mm film can for protection from light and
abrasion.
Petroleum jelly (vaseline) attacks rubber: water-based
lubricants such as saliva and K-Y Jelly don't. Heat also
affects rubber adversely so store condoms in a cool place. Buy
condoms that are fresh -- look for an expiration date stamped
on the package. When stored in a cool, dark location I've had
condoms remain in good condition well past their expiration date.
Julie Summers, Oregon, April

Forest Fears Unfounded
The woods are full of dangerous beasts, outlaws, goblins
and who knows what, according to old traditions. Remember the
grisly children's stories such as Hansel and Gretel, Peter and
the Wolf, and Little Red Riding Hood?
Julie Summers' story, "Fright in the Night", in Message
Post #6, reminded me that many folk still fear to go hiking, and
would be terrified camping out for a long period. A magazine
editor wrote me that "... fear and paranoia surround the topic".
I've never been afraid of forests, perhaps because my
parents often took me camping and were themselves at ease in the
woods. But for neophytes not so fortunate I'll offer these words.
Don and I have camped in remote places by ourselves, either
in a tent or in a small pickup-camper, most of the eight years
we've been together. During that time our persons have never
been attacked or threatened by any creature bigger than a fly.
Attacks by large animals do occur but they are rare. Risks
are highest (A) in National Parks and other tourist attractions
where bears are accustomed to hand outs or to raiding garbage
cans and (B) on or near farms where there may be bulls. Even in
those environments deaths and injuries are few.
The biggest killer in the outdoors is probably hypothermia
- overchilling - formerly called "exposure". The number two
hazard may be accidents, including falls, cuts, shots, fires and
drownings. Number three is biting/stinging insects, which
sometimes transmit diseases.
There is a grain of truth in the scary fairy tales: I've
read that most unprovoked large-animal attacks are against
children - because children are smaller.
So the "how to survive in the woods" books are worth studying. But, all in all, the woods are safer than cities or rural
areas. Jean Apt, Alberta, Sept.

Bow Saw Transport and Frame Making

In Message Post #3, Bert Davis related that a Coghlan wire saw was slow cutting and soon broke.

I have found a bow saw most efficient for cutting timbers between one inch and one foot in diameter. For lightest transport buy just the blade, and build the frame at base camp out of native wood.

My saw blade (Swedish made but I don't know the manufacturer) is a little more than a yard long and weighs only a few ounces - much lighter than an axe head. It is flexible enough to be wrapped around a five gallon pail, large cooking pot, or even a big bed roll; which allows easy carrying. I first wrap the blade with a strip of tough cloth, rubber or leather so the teeth aren't exposed.

To make the bow I select a branch 1" to 1½" in diameter that curves a little less than the bow will after mounting, so that it will apply tension to the blade.

Cut slots and holes in each end of the bow.

Insert each end of the blade into a slot and anchor with a nail or bolt through the hole.

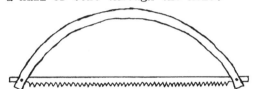 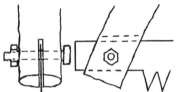

The holes can be made by burning with a hot nail if a drill isn't available. For cutting wood smaller than an inch in diameter, and for cutting wood to make the bow saw, I carry a small stiff-bladed utility saw, about a foot long with 1/8" to 1/16" teeth.

Finding a piece of wood with the proper shape and resiliancy for a bow may not be easy: usually my first attempt is either too limp to hold the blade tautly, too stiff to bend sufficiently without breaking until shortened, or not curved as deeply as I'd like. A more reliable if more complicated alternative is to build an H-frame.

Cut four more-or-less streight pieces 1½" to 2" in diameter, each about the length of the blade, to serve as two Holders and two Braces.

With each Holder make a slot and a hole in one end. Also notch the middle shallowly on both sides. The notches are for keeping the Braces in position.

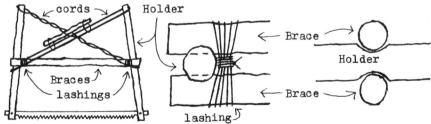

Place the middle of each Holder between the ends of the two Braces, and secure by lashing the Braces tightly together close to the Holder. (I use two Braces instead of one so that they won't apply bending stress to the ends of the blade.)

Insert the blade into the slots in the Holders and anchor with nails or bolts.

Run a cord from the upper end of one Holder to the middle
of the other Holder, and back again so that is is doubled. Tie.
Do the same with the other Holder.
Tighten one cord by inserting a small stick between its
doublings and twisting the cord. Tighten until the blade is
sufficiently taut. Secure by tying the ends of the tightening
stick to the other cord. Charles Long, British Columbia, June

Cotton and Linen Better for Ion-Sensitive People

Regarding Holly's nylon and polyester sheets (Message Post
#4 and #9), I read in the book Secrets of Life Extension that
"Most fabrics (wools, silks, and synthetics) will produce a
static charge when they are rubbed together. Cotton, linen and
hemp fiber are almost the only exceptions. Just the friction of
electrogenic material against the air, or rustling against themselves as we move can trap negative ions around the body and
generate positive ions. Some ion sensitive people have benefited
from wearing only cotton or linen clothing." I assume the same
might hold for sheets for such people. Julie Summers, Idaho, July

Leather Care

Leather that is allowed to dry out will not remain servicable
for as long as leather which is lubricated periodically: be it in
boots, bike seats, straps, or trim on packs/clothes.
Not all lubricants are comparable. According to Jan Vara,
writing in Country Journal, Oct. 1981, neatsfoot oil and silicone
tend to cause too much stretching if over used -- hold it to one
or two light applications per year. (Maybe never on bike seats.)
Mink oil penetrates well while not causing undue stretching.
Apply 2 or 3 times a month, or whenever the leather gets dry
(water no longer "beads" on it).
In addition to lubricating the fibers, oils waterproof to
some extent. For stronger waterproofing, waxes and greases may
be used. (Actually "waterproofing" is a misnomer because some
breathability is desirable -- otherwise sweat will not be able
to exit and you might as well be wearing rubber.)
Because it's cheapest I use tallow, which I render myself
from beef fat obtained free or at small cost from a supermarket.
Cook the cut-up or ground fat in a pan with a few inches of
water on low heat til the fat melts. Strain out the remaining
solids. Fat and water will separate cleanly upon cooling. I've
also used bacon fat obtained free from a cafeteria; a bit
odoriferous. Might attract bears.
If using silicone-containing products such as Sno-Seal, the
seams should be sealed first with a silicone-free shoe polish or
candle drippings, according to Vara who says that silicone rots
stitching.
To condition garment leathers, where the stickiness and dark-
ening created with oils and waxes is undesirable, Vara recommends
Lexol (a trade name for a variety of lanolin, which the dictionary says is a fatty substance obtained from wool). It conditions
but does not impart water repellancy. Sold at leather/shoe shops.
Wetting does not harm leather: it may be washed (buckskin and
chamois may even be washed in a machine) but skip the spin cycle
-- drip dry. Do not use so much soap that all the oils are
removed. Dry at room temperature: never hotter. Excessive heat
can cause irreversable cracking. After drying recondition with
oil if necessary. Julie Summers, Oregon, March

Mosquitos Not Repelled by Sound --- Feedback

In Wilderness Medicine, William Forgey, M.D. says,
"Electronic sound devices that repel these critters have never
worked up North for me, but friends have found them useful in
cave entrances in the lower 48 states." Julie Summers, April

About portable dwelling and long camping. February 1982 Number 8

Message Post

POB 190 Philomath OR 97370.   Next issue April. $2 for 3 issues

Moisture Resistant Matches: Test Results

I get fairly good results waterproofing the large (2¼")
Diamond "kitchen" matches by dipping in melted paraffin. They
live up to the "strike anywhere" claim. The ones I coated with
wax worked reliably when peeled and struck on rough metal.

After three months unheated storage in a damp climate, four
out of five lit. (The failure didn't have much white oxidizer.)

After 20 hours soaking in water three out of five lit. (The
two that failed behaved as if moisture had penetrated.)

The smaller (1 3/4") Diamond "strike anywhere" matches did
not work reliably after coating. Even before soaking only four
out of 20 lit after peeling off the wax and striking on a rock.
Three out of five lit when struck on the dry box striker (wet it
was useless). After soaking only one out of ten lit and that
required a dry box striker. It's not the length of the match
that's important but the amount of chemicals on the head.

I had coated each match completely, including the wood, by
first dipping the head end, allowing to harden, and then the
other end. One drawback of wax coated matches is the dexterity
required to peel: an attribute lacking in cold numbed hands.

I also tested Coghlan's "Waterproof Wooden Safety Matches"
(200 for $1.09 at Payless, four times the price of the Diamond
kitchen matches). They aren't "strike anywhere" - a box striker
is required. After soaking the strikers, both were demolished
by striking five matches. The matches worked reliably after two
hours soaking. Beyond three hours immersion they no longer lit
(until dried a number of hours).

My tentative choice is the large Diamond kitchen matches
with homemade wax coating. I'll reserve firm recommendations
until I see how they perform after longer storage.
Julie Summers, Oregon, December

Quicky Dicky

For cold weather attire some recommend a scarf. However I find the ends
continually unwrapping, getting in the
way, and annoying me. A dicky keeps my
neck warm without falling into everything I'm doing. And I can make a dicky
easily and inexpensively from a worn-out
turtle-neck sweater that still has good
material around the neck. (It might be
the same sweater I make mittens & socks
from. See "Mittens for a Pittance &
Socks for a Song",Light Living Library.)

In two steps my dicky is finished. Cut off as much of the
sweater as desired; then hem or bind. Julie Summers, Ore., Dec.

Reducing Dampness in an Insulated Portable Dwelling

Small insulated shelters, which are warmed only by body
heat and cooking, are often overly humid. Our portable dwelling, The Thing,has had this problem. And others have complained.

The cause is the low rate of air exchange with outside.
Moisture put into the air by breathing, sweating, cooking and

other activities accumulates until it condenses on the coolest surfaces available. Crannies get wet, clothes stay damp and mildew, books mold.

When the sun shines in through the window, that provides enough additional heat to keep The Thing dry, but during winter in the northwest several weeks sometimes pass without much sun.

The problem is eased by reducing the moisture that gets into the air: don't let pots boil vigorously; don't hang wet clothes inside. But even with these measures The Thing is often damper than we'd like.

Recently we found a partial solution that's so simple I don't know why we didn't try it before: open the vents wider while sleeping.

This reduces warmth, or course, so we have to sleep with covers - or more covers. But that's tolerable. I try to wake up a few hours before dawn and close the vents so The Thing will warm up before we get up. (During winter the inside is usually between 50 and 60 F. at dawn, and rises as we get active or cook.)

The humidity is still higher than we'd like, but night ventilation seems to help.

There's an optimum amount of ventilation. Open too widely, so that the inside cools to the outside temperature, and there's no more drying effect (if the outside humidity is 100%, which it is when there's rain or dew). We are presently experimenting, trying to find the optimum.

During cold spells when outside is below freezing at night, we don't have to open the vents; leakage is sufficient. Leakage is greater then because the temperature difference between inside and outside is greater. (I'm not sure why but I think it's because the earth floor, which is only thinly insulated, stores considerable heat.)

Superinsulated houses reduce humidity by means of heat exchangers. Propelled by electric blowers, warm moist air flows outward, cool outside air flows inward, and as they pass each other the warmth but not the moisture is transferred.

I suppose it would be possible to build a small portable heat exchanger if electricity were available to power it. Alternatively, in a breezy location (which we rarely have), the wind might be harnessed by rigging two large funnels; facing one into the wind to ram air in, and facing the other down wind to suck air out. Does anyone know of a passive heat exchanger?

I realize that a small wood stove, fired up once a day or so, would dry us out. But it and its wood supply would take up space, which we have little of. And tending would be a nuisance.
Bert Davis, Oregon, January

Lack of Ventilation Can Kill
        I am enclosing two clippings, both concerning the untimely departure of individuals, who because of carelessness or lack of knowledge, left burning appliances on inside tents which were tightly closed up. One guy asphyxiated himself with a burning candle. Few people seem to realize just how air tight a tent can be when it's buttoned up. Most of the better mountain tents have built-in ventilators, which should be kept open at all times. As for the high intensity pressure appliances, such as lanterns or cookstoves, these will gobble up oxygen out of the air at ten times the rate of a person breathing. In a sealed tent, it just does not take very long for carbon monoxide to fill up the tent, turning it into a lethal gas chamber. Remember also that carbon monoxide is insidious; you just drift off to sleep. Bye!

        I have used kerosene burning pressure lanterns to keep my tent warm and cosy countless times, with no danger at all.

I just made sure that I had plenty of ventilation. Not just the one small ventilator on the back of my large, walk-in tent, which can become partially closed if it collapses a little, but keeping part of the tent door tied open. And I never go to bed for the night with any kind of fire burning inside the tent.
Joe Vetrono, Oregon, November

NEWPORT (UPI) - Siuslaw National Forest rangers, curious why one man had camped in the same spot for several days, opened his tent and discovered the body of a 31-year-old Falls Church Virginia, man.... Authorities said he apparently was asphyxiated after leaving a candle burning.

ENTERPRISE (UPI) - Three hunters apparently asphyxiated themselves in their hunting tent Tuesday by burning two gasoline lanterns throughout the night, authorities said. The men ... had been sleeping in an air-tight tent with a built in floor at campsite 15 miles northwest of Enterprise.... The men were found dead by the four remaining members of the hunting party at about 5:30 a.m.

Bear Report

Our personal experience is similar to Jean's (Message Post #7). We have lived in a tent for most of nearly ten years, and neither we nor our camp has ever been attacked by a bear or any large animal.. This, despite the fact that we routinely cook, eat and keep food in our tent, and occasionally leave our tent unoccupied when away for a few days (tho more often we take everything with us).

On the other hand consider the experience reported by Sherrie Rogers of Port Angeles, Washington in Backpacker Footnotes, July 1981. Their camp was clean, their tent odor-free, and all food was locked in their car, which was only twenty feet from their tent. Nevertheless during the night a bear broke into their car, "in only 5 seconds the bear completely tore the frame around the driver's window...", and wasn't easily frightened off.

Why the difference from our experience? Sherrie Rogers believes the bear that assaulted their car had already been corrupted by previous campers who hadn't put their food away or cleaned up their camp site before leaving.

Sounds plausible. But why hasn't our food-filled tent corrupted some bear? When we move we leave a site spic and span, but sometimes we stay in one spot for several weeks - ample time for a bear to smell us out and become familiar. We've seen bear signs in many of the areas where we've camped - scat, logs ripped apart.

We do keep a firearm. Can a bear smell that, and make a distinction between human-with-gun and human-without-gun? Possible - crows reportedly do, and bears have bigger brains than crows.

Maybe Barb & I have just been lucky. Hank Schultz, Oregon

A Brake for All Seasons

While riding a roller coaster road in a downpour I found my bicycle's front wheel hand brake almost useless, while the foot brake which remained effective saved me. Hand brakes seem to vary; the wet performance of some are better than mine.

In addition to being available on one speed bikes, which most people know about, enclosed hub (foot) brakes are also available on three speeds. (Usually there's a hand brake for the front wheel, in addition to the foot brake for the rear.)

Sturmey Archer currently manufactures the S3C hub, and parts are available for their no longer produced TCW models. **Although new prices are outrageous, I've been able to purchase reasonably a number of used bikes with the three-speed/hub-brake combination.** Julie Summers, Oregon

Does Sprouting Tough Seeds Improve Their Edibility?
        Regarding "War Survival by Camping" (book review in Message
Post #7). I wonder if whole grains and beans that have been
sprouted give sore tongues and loose bowels when eaten in quantity (as did wheat that was merely boiled). I've heard that
sprouting changes the phytic acid in seeds. The phytic acid may
be responsible for the problems. Robin, Oregon, November

Soybean Cooking and Nutrition
        Question: I have read that lysine, an essential amino acid,
decomposes at 255 degrees F. Does this happen suddenly at 255
degrees and not at all at lower temperatures? Or does decompos-
also depend on time? I am concerned because soybeans are a ITION
major source of protein for us, and especially a source of
lysine - grains being low in it.
        We normally cook soybeans either in a pressure cooker which
results in temperatures close to 250°, or by parching lightly
(stopping before they turn brown) and then mixing with grains
and grinding into flour for bread and other pastries.
Holly Davis, Oregon, December
        Answer: We have cooked soybeans under a wide range of
conditions and the lysine content was virtually unchanged....
The decomposition of lysine depends on the food system with
which it is heated. For example, in the presence of reducing
sugars, such as glucose, fructose and lactose, lysine will
decompose or become unavailable much faster than if these sugars
were not present. Soybeans contain no reducing sugars. Time is
an important factor in protein breakdown. It is not instantan-
eous. Roger A. Eisenhauer, Industrial Coordinator, USDA, Agricultural Research Center, Peoria, Illinois 61604, January.
        According to five tests reported by "Full-fat Soy Flour
Extrusion Cooked: Properties and Food Uses" from the Journal of
Food Science, which the USDA sent: Available lysine was the
same (6.2 grams per 16 grams nitrogen) after cooking for 1¼ to 2
minutes at temperatures of 275 and 300 degrees F. Inactivation
of most of the trypson inhibitor (which would otherwise interfere with digestion of protein) required 2 min. @ 275° or 1¼
min. at 300°. However such cooking greatly increased the amount
of rancidity in the oil after an additional 12 months of storage
at 77° F. (up to peroxide values of 213 (meq/kg) oil). This
indicates to me that soybeans should be eaten soon after cooking
and not then stored for many months. Holly Davis, Oregon, Jan.

Feed Corn for People
        It's inexpensive and because it's dried it's a good choice
for packing into a wilderness camp. (If you haul potatoes, on
the other hand, you have to carry a lot of water.) Not surprisingly it's sold at feed stores. (City folk may have to go out
into the country a way to locate a source.)
        A problem with feed corn is that even when pre-soaked for
days it remains "chewy" (some would say tough) after a few hours
of boiling. Pressure cooking helps but even after the time it
takes to cook beans adequately, the corn in with the beans is
still chewy. It's not bad but if you want it soft there's a way.
        The secret is lime. Ordinary hydrated lime available at
farm supply, garden, and feed and seed stores is fine (unhydrated
"hot" lime is said to work also, but I've never found it for
sale). In December '81 I purchased 10# "Snowflake Hydrated Lime"
for $1.95 at a feed and seed store. (The manufacturer is Ash
Grove Cement Co., 1000 Tenmain Center, Kansas City, MO 64105.)
Hydrated lime is used for whitewashing, privies, making pickles,
and soil improvement.

I process the corn in a stainless steel pot (because I don't know if there's any problem using aluminum): 1 part by volume corn, 2 parts water, and 1/16 part lime. (E.g. 2 cups of water and 1 level tablespoon of lime per cup of corn.) Bring to boil. Simmer 40 minutes. Rinse in fresh cold water til it runs clear. At this point the hulls have slipped but the corn is still tough. I either pressure cook it (along with beans for about 30 minutes), or I grind it and make tortillas. (I find I must add some water to the ground corn and knead to get it to hold together.) I break off pieces and roll them out between two sheets of plastic to 1/8" to 1/4" thickness. Then cook on a hot greaseless pan for about three minutes per side. Alternatively the dough may be cooked with additional water as mush (cereal) or made into tamales, or I suppose anything corn meal is used for, such as corn bread.

There are nutritional benefits to treating corn with lime: "The lime makes the niacin in corn more readily available and increases the calcium tenfold." (Nan Bronfen, Nutrition for a Better Life, Capra Press, 1980). Julie Summers, Oregon, January

Hammock Breaks
My inexpensive hammock from Hawkeyes ("Hummocky Hammock", Udisco brand, Message Post #7) broke with my first usage. The nylon, or whatever, may have been in the sun too long before I purchased it. Robin, Oregon, November

Locking Pliers
They do what regular pliers do, but in addition they are capable of locking on to whatever they are holding. Thus you may loosen your grip (or let go completely) without the pliers dropping what's in their jaws.
Another advantage is that locking pliers hold tighter than do regular pliers, because of the compound leverage.
Locking pliers make a good nut cracker because the jaws may be set so they stop at a certain point and don't crush the meats.
Get a sturdy pair - flimsy ones get bent out of shape due to the great forces generated. ("Vice-Grip" is one good brand.) To avoid marring the object held, protect it with a covering: a piece of thick leather, or many layers of rags.
A regular pliers may be made to lock: get them in position, then wrap a long stout rubber strap around the handles. Each additional wrap will tighten the hold; thus astounding pressure can be built up. However they take longer to lock and unlock than the special locking pliers. Julie Summers, Oregon, Dec.

Portable Electric Systems. Part I - What You Need to Know
This article was inspired by work on a friend's electrical system: fixing bad connections (mostly around the battery) and installing a new, larger photo-voltaic panel (solar cells).
Many people are needlessly mystified and intimidated by electricity. I was at one time. I first gained understanding I could use when I added lights inside the canopy of our pickup, as part of outfitting it for overnighting. I had been exposed to electrical theory in a physics course a dozen years before, but that didn't sink in.
Building and maintaining an electrical system doesn't require understanding electronics such as radios or calculators. Both involve electron flow but electrical is simpler than electronic. It's like the difference between a hand pump and an automatic transmission, both of which involve fluid flow.
Electricity is mystifying because it's invisible, and therefore not self teaching the way most mechanical apparatus is.

Someone who hasn't previously seen a bicycle or wind-up alarm clock can figure one out by watching it and playing with it, but could spend days puzzling over an electrical device without making headway. It's necessary to know some theory.

When studying electricity or working on electrical equipment, take the time to build a feeling in your head for what's happening. Don't simply memorize phrases and formulas or try to rely on cookbook troubleshooting. I've known people who could recite Ohm's Law forwards and backwards, or could expound at length about alternative energy, but who were helpless to find a bad connection.

I don't recommend acquiring an electrical system unless you know enough to install it and fix it, or have the time and interest to acquire such skills. (That's good advice with any equipment too costly to give away when it breaks down.) If someone else installs it, it will probably remain mysterious. Electrical systems, especially low-voltage battery ones, are prone to minor breakdowns: troubles that can be quickly repaired by someone with know-how but that can stump the inexperienced. If you can't fix it yourself, you'd do better to rely on combustibles such as propane, kerosene and candles.

An understanding of DC (direct current) is all that's needed for most portable systems. DC means the electricity flows in only one direction around a circuit. DC is simpler than is AC (alternating current) to which most houses are wired.

Automobiles use DC (except for the ignition system, and inside the alternator). For my own introduction to electrical theory, ten years ago, I looked over automotive books at libraries until I found a few that gave clear explanations. Avoid the "Gee Whiz! Isn't Electricity Marvelous" books that tell a little about everything from lightning to computers in 100 pages. Also avoid electrical engineering texts loaded with mathematics (unless you particularly like mathematics). Hank

What Comes Inside In and Goes Outside Out?

Small is sensible. A diminutive dwelling is not only easy to move, but is cheap to build and easy to heat. Our home-built, "The Thing", is backpackable in a dozen loads, cost only a few hundred for materials, and usually stays comfortably warm with just our bodies and cooking.

But there's space in it only for us and for a few belongings that we use daily. Less-used possessions, including most clothes, food stocks, books and tools, reside between uses in one or more adjoining or near-by "plastic shanties" which provide rain shelter but no appreciable warming.

Consequently there's a considerable flow in and out. In winter whenever a cold object from outside comes in, dew condenses on it until it warms to inside temperature. Dew is most noticeable on a large hard-surfaced object such as a pail of water but isn't damaging; we simply set the pail in a large basin to catch the run off. Dew isn't so obvious on absorbent objects such as clothes and books, but could lead to mildew.

To avoid damage, we keep extra clothes, for example, in a plastic bag. When the clothes come in, the bag stays on and closed up until the clothes reach room temperature, so any condensation will be on the bag, not on the clothes.

Going the opposite way, when the clothes go out, the bag is left open for several hours while cooling down. During this time the air will be cooler than the clothes and so will have a drying effect. The bag is then closed, after which for mouse protection it is either hung up or put in a sturdier container. Bert Davis, Oregon, February

Message Post

POB 190 Philomath OR 97370. Next issue, October. $2 for 3 issues

An Even More Portable Faucet

At home I use "Running Water Anywhere" (Light Living Library) but when traveling light I take a plastic squeeze bottle with a cap that has a hinged plastic spout. By holding the bottle between my knees and squeezing them together, I can have both hands free for washing food, dishes or hands.

The plastic squeeze bottle also allows me to shower with the very minimum of water; less than if using a jug. (If I have at least half a gallon of water I prefer to use a plastic jug -- which is faster.)

In poison oak country I carry a squeeze bottle full of water. This allows me to rinse immediately after any brushes with the annoying plant, avoiding or at least minimizing irritation. (A very fine nozzle allows best control over how much water is dispensed, therefore helping conserve it.) Julie Summers, Ore.

More Cargo Space on a Bicycle

The triangular space between the top, down, and seat tubes is an ideal place for transporting tarps, tents and anything else that will lend itself to being draped over the top tube (or suspended directly beneath it on a cord if hanging on the tube interferes with control cables). There are a surprising number of inches to spare before interfering with leg pedaling motion.

After draping on the tarps I secure (and compact) them by wrapping with a rubber strap. Where the strap goes around the slanting tubes it may be necessary to take a few wraps around the tube, to prevent the strap slipping up the tube. Julie Summers, Oregon, March

Putting on the Pump

I've found a good way to secure an air pump to a bike's frame is with two rubber straps, one at each end of the pump; encircling pump and frame. Cheap, easy and when the pump is off there aren't those annoying hooks to catch my pant leg. I attach the pump to the down tube so it's out of the way when I have to pick up the bike by the top or the seat tube.   Julie

Introduction to Long-Period Camping

Why camp for a long time? People we've heard from do so for many different reasons. Enjoy natural surroundings more of the time. Do scientific studies. Work in remote places: tree planting, seed gathering, prospecting, etc. Save on rent when not working. Avoid distractions to creative activities. Release tensions caused by congestion. Reduce exposure to urban hazards. Breathe more fresh air. Get away from the usual routine for a while. View life from a different perspective.

Go to places beyond the range of quick trips. Avoid contributing to crowding and environmental problems in easy-to-reach recreational spots. Save gasoline by going on a few extended vacations rather than many short outings. Spend less vacation time setting up and taking down camping equipment. Have the time to provide more comfortable facilities at camp.

Altho more preparation is needed than for a weekend, in many ways long outing is easier. There's more time: no rush, no strain; if there's a storm just wait it out instead of plunging thru it.

To begin, I'd first get experience camping out in most kinds of weather for short periods. Many colleges, Y's, etc., give courses in outdoor survival: how to keep warm or cool, sterilize water, find the way, select and use equipment, render first aid.

For the first long outing I suggest: Pick easy terrain at low altitude. Don't go far. Do it in summer. Take a variety of food. Do it with just one good friend: the smaller the group the fewer the complications, especially if you're inexperienced. (If you do it all alone, for safety tell someone where you're going and when to expect you back.)

I've rarely had difficulty finding nice camping spots in any mountainous area. Just a few days looking around are usually enough. A local forest service or BLM office may be able to advise which areas to avoid because of crowding or logging in progress. Hank Schultz, Oregon (revised from "What is Long Out?" published by the Long Out Network, 1976 & 1979)

A Woman's Journey on the Appalachian Trail

In North American Anglo society the "vision quest" is not ritualized as it is in various Indian tribes, yet none the less many Anglos design and conduct their own quests. Such may have been the 2100 mile hike of Cindy Ross, this book's author.

I found the narrative an enjoyable read, and the charcoal sketches that accompanied each page beautifully expressive. The book does not contain enough detail to be helpful for planning logistics of a trip.

The author tells of supplementing rations she carried with a grouse (killed with her walking stick), freshwater clams, pokeweed, milkweed, prickly lettuce, dandelion, and plantain.

'Making the best of very little' was done by using sticks to hold her (hair) bun together, large smooth leaves for toilet paper, and baking soda for deodorant and tooth paste.

The account of a nocturnal bear encounter alarmed me. The bruin succeeded in getting food (which had been hung in a tree), then proceeded to paw thru belongings "six inches from my body", relates Ross, who mentioned having only a whistle for a deterrant, which she intended to blow if the beast touched her. Fortunately it didn't.

The author hiked both alone and with partners. She reflected "I think back to other hard times that I found myself in. They never seem as bad when you have someone to share them with -- lighten the load. I approached such encounters light-heartedly, found amusement in them. Alone it is different. Alone I take life so much more seriously. I know now that life isn't to be lived alone."

Published in 1982, 127 pages softcover, $7.95 postpaid, East Woods Press, 429 East Boulevard, Charlotte, NC 28203.
Review by Julie Summers

Bulgar is Inexpensive, Easily Prepared, and Tasty

It's coarsely ground wheat that's been precooked, then dried. Soak overnight in cold water, or less time in hot, and it's ready. Holly

How Many Gears?

In Tom Cuthbertson and Karen Lusebrink's book Better Bikes!
there's a humorous illustration of low gear options: Western
style showing an exhausted rider laboring up a very steep hill on
a lightweight, grotesquely geared bike, vs. the Chinese approach
with rider calmly pushing an unpretentious one speed up the grade.

Because I find pushing a heavily laden bicycle uncomfortable
(probably due largely to having to push from the side and the
resultant twisting forces) I do like a lower gear that enables me
to stay aboard longer when going uphill. And on slight downhill
grades a higher gear means I can pedal without spinning my legs
frantically. So I like three gears. I find any more non-essen-
tial, even tho I know many gears are supposed to allow one,
regardless of terrain, to maintain a steady cadence, which is
claimed to be most efficient.

It's well to keep in mind that a ten speed does not necessarily have any greater range of gears than a three speed -- it
depends on the size of the sprocket (chain) wheels. Also some
ten speeds are heavy. I rode one that weighed more than my three
speed and although it did have an extremely low first gear, its
excessive weight canceled out any advantage. Julie Summers, Feb.

Water Instead of Oil

Don't try this on your bicycle but the trick works in cooking. If you have poultry or fish to cook and no oil you can
"poach" the victuals, viz. cook them in just enough water to
cover the bottom of the pan, not submerge the food. It avoids
sticking, and at the same time tenderizes, giving a succulent
result. It's commonly done with vegetables, but not often
thought of for meat.

Bring the water to a boil, then put in the food (this seals
in the juices, whereas putting the food in cold water and then
bringing to a boil would leach them out). Cook covered at a
simmer. Keep this method in mind when you're out on the trail
with a string of fresh caught trout and no oil. Also good for
the calorie conscious. Julie Summers, Oregon, December

Poison Oak & Poison Ivy: Why It Itches & What To Do

Sandra J. Baker has extensively investigated the subject
and has put together her own evidence, other people's experiences, and lab findings into the best presentation I've seen.

Her book discusses various body coverings for preventing
contact, from clothes to mud. Barrier creams and ointments were
judged "generally unsatisfactory" by one researcher.

She explains how the plant's oil, urushiol, causes an
allergic reaction. Regarding decontamination, "... it is
extremely important to wash the plant oil from your skin as soon
as possible...." because the oil quickly combines with the skin
and then cannot be removed. The pros and cons of various soaps,
solvents, plain water and dirt are discussed. Promptness of
cleaning may be more important than the cleanser employed.
"If I am away from water ... I rub dirt on my skin. The reason
for this is that clays and dirt attract oil molecules to their
surfaces, thereby pulling them from your skin."

Various ways are described for developing an immune tolerance in advance of exposure, such as eating a tiny leaf a day.
Ingestion may cause some outside skin rash (an eruption does not
necessarily occur at the place of contact). But the author has
not personally experienced any internal problems nor did the
clinical studies she's read mention any. However she cautions,
"your body is different from mine..." Alternatively, she gives
instructions for an external "patch method". Still another way:
"accidentally blunder into a plant and come down with a case ...
(which) can make a person non-reactive to the plant for up to
six weeks."

Over 100 palliatives are discussed, from cortisone and cala-
mine lotion to accupressure, skunk cabbage, tofu, urine, and
coolness. Remedies' effectiveness seem to vary from person to
person. The author examines the much debated question of whether
or not the rash can be spread by scratching. "It has been
clinically proven that the blister fluid contains no molecules of
urushiol." She goes on to hypothesize why scratching may spread,
or seem to spread the rash.

Never burn the plant if removing it, Baker cautions. "Tiny
droplets of oil ... can be breathed .... Besides a total skin
breakout, the throat and lungs can be affected and the swelling
that occurs might be very dangerous...."

Published in 1979, 40 pages 6½x8½, this book is $3 postpaid
from the author, Sandra J. Baker, Box 513, Soquel, CA 95073.
Review by Julie Summers

I Now Have a Poison-Oak-Avoidance Computer - In My Head

If you're new to poison-oak country and despair of ever
recognizing the plant fast enough to avoid contact, you may be
reassured to know that after a few years and several breakouts
I subconsciously acquired an "automatic" recognition and avoidance response. Tho not infallible it is a great help. I also
became aware of carriers such as dogs, cats and children who I
stopped petting under adverse conditions. Julie Summers, March

More About Bears

Like Jean (Message Post #7) and Hank (Message Post #8) our
persons have never been attacked by a bear. However at different
times we have had a camp ripped apart during a month's absence,
a food stash on the ground mauled, and a bike seat slashed;
probably by black bears, not grizzlies.

I wonder if hunting might not be a factor. In areas where
bears are frequently hunted, those most likely to survive are
those who stay away from humans and human smells. (Bears like
most ground animals can often smell farther than they can see or
hear.) Whereas in parks and game preserves, with little or no
hunting, bears have no reason to fear humans. Most bear attacks
on people or on occupied camps, I've read of, have been in parks
or along popular trails.

To say that such a bear gets "corrupted" seems to me unnecessarily anthropomorphic. Here is a big, very strong, often
hungry omnivore; accustomed to investigating, ripping apart,
eating and digesting a great variety of animals and plants.
Leaving garbage around may hasten the process, but I see no
reason why park bears, especially grizzlies which are much
larger than humans, wouldn't eventually learn to attack humans'
grub supplies and sometimes the humans themselves.

What's the best tactic if threatened by a bear? There are
many different opinions but all who I've read or heard agree what
not to do: Never run from a bear. A bear, like a dog, is likely
to chase anything that flees from it; and an able-bodied bear can
outsprint any human in most terrain. Charles Long, Calif., March

First Aid For Snakebite

Dr. Thomas G. Glass, this book's author, is a professor of
surgery at the University of Texas Medical School who has treated
over 174 snakebite victims. For first aid he suggests placing
constricting bands above and below the bite, and applying ice in
plastic bags or instant cold packs at the bite site. This keeps
the venom concentrated and inactive, thus "... the extent of
tissue damage is less and much easier to treat" says Dr. Glass.
It also reduces vomiting which can be fatal.

Dr. Glass recommends against routine use of cross-cuts and suction. In 30% of bites no venom will have been injected. In half of the remainder venom will have been injected too deeply to be removed by shallow cross cuts and suction. "It has been my experience that laymen have unintentionally cut large and important nerves, arteries and tendons in their efforts and these errors result in more crippling than the snakebite." Suction by mouth can severely infect the victim.

"Very rarely would a person die within the first few hours after a snakebite, even by a very large rattler.... If one gets to medical care within three or four hours a good outcome from the treatment can be expected", says Dr. Glass.

People "many hours" away from medical care should be prepared, says Dr. Glass, to do more than apply constriction and ice. He does not detail procedures but recommends getting professional instruction in cutting and suction, and excision.

Dr. Glass's case for constriction is convincing, but he leaves me wondering how to achieve proper tension -- tight enough but not too tight.

Antivenin should never be given unless facilities are available to treat the serious side effects warns Dr. Glass: the skin test alone can cause death.

Note carefully that Dr. Glass advocates ice for first aid only, not for long treatment. Immersing an extremity in crushed ice with salt added for several days, as was sometimes done, probably causes cold injury and frostbite, Dr. Glass says.

Although Dr. Glass believes that ice applied as first aid is effective and non-injurious, he mentions opponents of the practice. Unfortunately he doesn't give references to run down.

"... I know that the destructive activity of rattlesnake venom is significantly reduced at temperatures below 85° F.", says Dr. Glass. This makes me wonder if applying cold water (commonly 50° to 60° here in mountain creeks during summer) would help where ice wasn't available.

More info: None of Dr. Glass's patients heard the snake rattle prior to being bitten. Bites of areas covered by ordinary leather boots and shoes did not inject "any significant amount of venom" into the victim. About 1/3 of 168 bites were on fingers or hands and most of those "occurred while the snake or its head was being handled." "I have tried large doses of intravenous and oral Vitamin C for snakebite and it does no apparent good." (Dr. Glass doesn't say how much he administered. Successful treatments of other ills have required grams or tens of grams.)

Although the book leaves me with many questions, it contains the observations of a highly experienced person. (Other authors I've read did not mention their experience, if any.) Published in 1974 with an 1981 update, the book is 41 pages 5½x8½ including 19 color photos. $1.50 postpaid from the author, Dr. Thomas G. Glass, 8711 Village Dr., San Antonio, TX 78217.
Review by Julie Summers

Tips for Staying Healthy at Large Encampments
During seven years of full time camping I've only been laid-up twice. Both illnesses occurred at large gatherings. The worst bout, diarrhea complicated by flu and strep throat, with a fever up to 103, kept me weak and mostly in the sack for two weeks. Many people at those gatherings suffered diarrhea --- some so seriously as to require medical assistance.

Diarrhea and other ailments aren't always caused by contageous organisms --- environment, diet, or mental attitudes are sometimes responsible. But I attribute those illnesses of mine to microbes: I have lived in many different environments, including other gatherings, and eaten widely varying diets (mostly fresh raw vegetables and fruit during some periods, mostly seafoods or mostly whole grains during other periods, etc.) without problems.

Suggestions for reducing risks where hundreds or more gather:

Boil drinking water. Water may appear sparkling clear and yet contain hazardous microbes. Even a creek that's been tested and declared drinkable can later be contaminated by dogs or people. Iodine and chlorine kill most but not all kinds of harmful organisms (e.g. not amoebic cysts).

When washing fruits, salad vegetables and dishes, use sterilized water for the final rinse, at least.

Eat only your own food. Bring your own food. If you want cooked food, cook your own. If individual cooking fires are frowned upon, bring ready-to-eat foods such as granola, hard tack, pinole, nuts, dried fruits. Don't eat foods from large kitchens or dining facilities where there are many helpers. Just one person who is careless about hand washing or who has an open sore can infect many. (Soup or stew that is ladled, boiling hot, directly into your bowl is probably safe regardless; other preparations are risky, salads especially.) At those gatherings where I got diahhrea I drank only boiled water but I ate food from the main kitchen.

If you wish to share food preparation and eating, do so with a few others who have similar ideas and practices regarding health and hygiene. Don't contribute energy (food, labor, money) to a common supply or main kitchen. Besides spreading diseases, large operations provide more opportunities for rip-offs and power-tripping.

Don't partake of passed-around bottles, smokes, snacks, etc. Be careful who you kiss.

Don't spend much time inside large crowded tents or buildings, where germs are easily spread by breathing and coughing.

Make and use your own latrine. Shape the latrine so that after each use the feces can be completely buried. (E.g. "The Narrow-Hole Latrine", Light Living Library.) Camp well away from any latrine that's not so maintained.

Wash hands after defecating and also before preparing food or eating.

Use netting to keep flies and other insects out of food preparation and sleeping areas.

Arrive early and leave early to improve the odds. Most contageous diseases require several days to spread widely.

Keep rested. Avoid prolonged stress, which can reduce resistance to infection. If relaxing is difficult at the gathering, move away a mile or more, every few days, for a full day of recuperation.

Bring and take extra vitamin C.

If you wish to tan, and are light complexioned, expose yourself to sunlight gradually --- just a few minutes the first day. Besides being painful, sunburn lowers resistance to other ailments. Bert Davis, Oregon, March

Giardia and Amoebas Killed by 131o F

I asked the Center for Disease Control how long water must be boiled to kill Giardia and amoebas. Jeffrey R. Harris, MD replied: "Giardia (lambia) cysts are killed immediately at $50^{\circ}C$ ($122^{\circ}F$), and Entamoeba histolytica cysts are killed in one minute at 52° to $55^{\circ}C$ ($131^{\circ}F$).... The boiling point of water on top of Mt Everest is greater than 70 C (158 F)." (According to Bob Young MD in How to Stay Healthy While Traveling, schistosom and amoebas are not killed by treating water with iodine or chlorine.) Julie

Holly's Wild Night

Last winter I only went to town once. I rode my bicycle all the way. The weather was fine on the way in. But returning I had to ride through snow - the only local snow of the winter!

This winter I wanted no more of that. I postponed my trip several times waiting for a period of mild, rainless weather. Finally dawned a morning with the sky mostly clear and a temperature of 42° F. at our home camp in the mountains. The radio reported clouds in the valley and predicted scattered showers during the day with a possibility of more rain that night. Best do it now - or wait for summer, I told myself. It was Friday the 13th, but I'm not superstitious. Bert escorted me to our bike stash and kissed me goodbye.

Ten miles out I got a flat. I fixed it and proceeded on. I reached our near-town bivy site before dark. The sun was long gone and a light drizzle was falling. The air was calm, and surprisingly warm for a November evening - 51° F. I put up a couple of plastic tarps for rain shelter and settled cozily into my sleeping bag. All was peaceful as I dropped off to sleep.

I awoke around eleven to the violent flapping of my shelter and the roar of the wind. Overhead through the plastic I saw trees gyrating nightmarishly. I moved my sleeping bag further under a stout limb of the tree supporting my ridge cord, hoping it would deflect any heavy falling branches. I took comfort in observing that the trees about me didn't seem to be shedding many limbs.

I spent the night retying and rearranging the tarps as they were repeatedly blown out of place by strong gusts, and regretting having camped in such a windy spot. Happily the rain wasn't especially heavy and the temperature remained mild. By dawn I had things well battened down and the wind was easing.

The morning light revealed that my spot had not been exceptionally windy; if anything it had been relatively calm. Some surrounding areas were devastated! Giant doug fir had blown down. Fortunately there had been no large conifers near my camp. When I reached town I learned that I had bivouaced through the worst wind storm in 20 years! Many houses had been seriously damaged.

After several days in town I returned home, encountering limbs and broken tree tops on the roads but no blockages I could not get my bike over or around. Bert was safe and snug but very worried about me - the wind hadn't been fierce at our home camp but he'd heard radio reports of disasters elsewhere.

Moral? In potentially windy weather don't camp near big trees. A lone doug fir or a small group of them seem especially vulnerable to wind toppling.   Holly Davis

Large Plastic Drums Useful for Storage

I have used for storage purposes polydrums sold by Willamette Cherry Growers Inc., 1520 Woodrow St. NE, Salem, OR 97303 (near the fairgrounds). Phone 364-8412. These are large plastic drums with plastic lids, gaskets, and galvanized bands to hold the lid shut. They are about 39" deep and 23" in diameter. The diameter of the opening is somewhat less. My guess is their capacity is about 60 gallons. Most are blue, a few are black.

They are sold for $5 each when they become weakened on the side and bend over, not allowing them to be stacked. The folded drums recover their original shape, and other than silver paint used to mark them are indistinguishable from other drums. They are sold as watertight and include good lids, bands and gaskets. Drums without lids or with breaks are sold for less.

Caution! Check the drums and lids for cracks. Recently I purchased five and after traveling some miles discovered a crack around the top of one drum. I've not tried to return it. Also, check for cracks in the bottom and punctures near the top. Robin

A Handcrank Kitchen Grinder is a Good Survival Tool

Tough vegies and fruits and otherwise inedible things,
small fish and animals with scales and small bones, can all
be ground into burger or dried into leather-rolls. Bones
and cartledge supply needed minerals. Paul Doerr, CA, Jan.

Binoculars as Magnifier

Binoculars can be used backwards to magnify. To do so look
through the objective lens (the big end). What you want to look
at must be at the right distance from the eye-piece lens - which
is very close. Focusing is touchy and the field of view isn't
as large as a regular hand lens provides. Nice to know if you
want to hunt for a sliver and have only a binoculars. Julie

Portable Electric Systems. Part II - Chosing Batteries

Here's a quick introduction or review of some terms:
Amps or amperes (abbreviated a.) is a unit of current - the
rate at which electricity is flowing; like gallons-per-minute
in a water system. A milliamp (ma.) is a thousanth (1/1000) of
an amp; a microamp (ya.) is a millionth of an amp.
Amp-hours (ah) is a unit of capacity - the total amount of
electricity which a battery can hold; like gallons in a water
system. For example a 60 amp-hour car battery if fully charged
will ideally supply one amp for 60 hours, or two for 30 hrs.
Volts or voltage (v.) is a unit of electrical force - the
pressure driving the electricity; like pounds-per-square-inch
in hydraulics.
Hydraulic analogies may be helpful when thinking about
electricity even tho they're occasionally misleading. So every
time I use an electrical term I'll put a water-system analogue
after it in parentheses to aid recall.
For a portable system I'd choose 12 volts (pressure), and
dc (direct current - one way flow - which is what a battery
supplies). The big advantage of 12 volts is that all modern
cars, trucks and motorhomes use it; consequently much equipment
is manufactured that will operate on it.
One disadvantage of 12 volts (pressure) is that much power
can't be wired a long distance efficiently. Either very heavy
wire is needed or else much power is lost. But a portable
system is unlikely to include long lines.
Equipment that can't operate on 12 volts (pressure) includes
household appliances that require 120 volts, and some portable
radios and cassette players that require 6 volts or 9 volts.
Converters(also called inverters) that change one voltage to
another, are widely available (e.g. Radio Shack), but power is
lost in conversion. So when buying anything that may be used
with a portable (or automotive) system, I'd get 12 volt dc gear.
Some 12 volt batteries can be tapped at intermediate points
to supply 6 volts and 9 volts. Modern car batteries can't;
however two 6-volt batteries can be connected together to
provide both 6 volts and 12 volts.
If there will be equipment that uses too many amp-hours
(amount) for flashlight batteries to be economical, I would
begin with a USED car battery. One that will no longer
reliably start a car in cold weather, may yet work fine in a
portable system where there won't be equipment that draws as
many amps (flow rate) as does an engine starting motor. If
such a battery doesn't suffice, at least I'm not out much.
Ask friends with cars to let you know when they need a new
battery, and you can get the old one for trade-in value.
Install battery where ventilation ample. Hank Schultz

Message Post

POB 190 Philomath OR 97370.   Next issue March. $2 for 3 issues

Tipi Living in the Rain

I just moved from the dry west to the Ozarks and haven't found a good way to control the leaks and wet floor in the rainy season. Maybe I'll try a canvas "umbrella" thrown over top of the poles. Does anyone have any experience on staying dry when it's pouring? Heather, Arkansas, June

Hold Your Hats

If like me, you find it a pain under the chin to have to tie a bow there, especially when all fumble fingered from the cold, try this.

The keeper is cut from thick innertube, or from a doubled-over piece of thin innertube. The hole(s) in it must be kept small enough to exert friction which holds the keeper in place.

I find a hook needle handy to pull the cord thru the hole in the keeper. Alternatively I cut the end of the cord obliquely so the point will go thru the hole, plus I may have to poke with a stick.

The knot stops the keeper from coming off. I leave several inches of cord below the knot for grabbing with one hand while the other hand pulls up the keeper.

This kind of keeper can also be used on the draw strings of stuff sacks and on jackets' waist closures and hoods. The keeper can be used on single ends, such as the closures of a jacket that opens all the way down the front, as well as on a pair of ends together. Julie Summers, Idaho, August

keeper

knot

Using Innertubes as Storage Containers, Further Report

In Message Post #6 I described how I use large innertubes to protect bedding left at bivy camps. We had employed this storage method for several years at a number of sites without problems. But this summer I returned to our bivy site near Eugene only to find that something had eaten an 8" diameter hole in the tractor innertube of thick rubber! Fortunately the hole was on the downhill end so not much had gotten wet, and the culprit hadn't bothered the contents. I've read that porcupines sometimes eat tires, and the tooth marks were about that size. Bert Davis, Oregon, July

Short City Job Opportunities

For someone like me, with no skills or trade, a job is sometimes hard to come by. In Norfolk, unemployment 9.4%, jobs were few and far between. Here in Charlotte, unemployment 5.6%, I found two jobs in the first two weeks. First, a job as "boy" at an Arty's Roast Beef; now as a cashier in a gas station/store.

Fast food joints have a very fast turn-over; it's not unusual for someone to work just a few months and go on. If you can run a cash register accurately, you will be able to find jobs as convenience store clerks, which is also a high turn-over job. If you can use a soldering gun, try places that assemble electronic circuit boards. No knowledge of electronics is necessary. I know a few people who rotate through jobs in large nurseries and greenhouses.

By all means use the state unemployment office, which is a crowded hassle and such, but does list dozens of jobs.

Jobs in fast food and as cashiers have advantages, even tho they will start at minimum wage. Since I'm in contact with the public, I've made some friends from among my customers, and that's important in a new town. Also, you can eat cheap, if not free, in a fast food job.

Although I've never tried it, lots of people make money here by mowing lawns, painting houses, yardwork, etc. How much I don't know, but 4 or 5 yards a day, at least $5 a yard, could be as much as a part-time minimum-wage job. In this area, those jobs will end in the winter; as good a time as any to move south!

P.S. I love the irony of riding my bicycle to work at a gas station. Bob, North Carolina, July

Outdoor Work and Living for Economy, Solitude and Aesthetics

I am currently working seasonally as a surveyor. I have done this for the past four years and will probably continue into the indefinite future. I normally work approximately early May to early or mid December.

I have had quite a bit of experience with recreational camping and have also done some long-term camping - once for seven months from mid-Spring to early Winter and again for most of two Winters while attending school.

I began this pattern partly for reasons of economy (I've never quite reconciled myself to paying rent!) and partly for the solitude and aesthetic pleasure afforded by long-term outdoor living. I now feel that I am moving toward a pattern of full-time outdoor living and a decreasing participation in the money economy and its attendant hassles.

However I've found that during long encampments I do seem to crave at least a little human association. In fact, I think that camaraderie, rather than money, is one of the major satisfactions of career-oriented people. Nevertheless I do not feel willing at present to exchange the freedom and flexibility of portable living for the obligations, commitments and mixed blessings of a more-conventional career-oriented life.
Alan Grandstaff, Washington, July

Ten Years On the Road and In the Woods

Ten years ago Barb and I were living and working in the Chicago suburbs. We were both 30. We decided we didn't want to spend the rest of our lives commuting between boring jobs and expensive housing. So we quit our jobs, bought a 4WD pickup, filled it with grub and camping equipment, and headed west.

We didn't have any particular objective except to see more of the continent, live in the "wide open spaces" and try our hands at various kinds of work. Basically that's what we've done.

Gradually our roamings evolved a pattern. During summer we usually work and camp at a mountain resort which has become somewhat of a permanent home altho a seasonal one. Both of us working can clear $3000 in 3½ months in a fair season. We don't earn as much, even for the same time, as we could at regular employment, but we aren't tied down full time and the money is sufficient for our needs.

In fall as the higher elevation cools we move toward the coast to enjoy the lingering warmth. Come winter we sometimes join up with friends and travel south to Arizona or, if our funds are low, remain in the coastal hills. With the arrival of spring we may journey east of the mountains to enjoy more sun.

We have both a 10x12' tent and a pickup with canopy. When camping we live mostly in our tent and use the pickup as a mobile storage shed. A small wood stove, made out of a five-gallon can, heats our tent during the coldest weather. West of the Cascades we seldom need it. (Barb and I seem to be more cold tolerant than most people; whether because of physique or aclimatization I don't know. We are short and stocky which helps conserve heat (less body surface). And we grew up in the midwest which has much colder winters than does the coastal northwest.)

We are also able to sleep and cook in the pickup which we do when pausing in places where we can't conveniently put up the tent. I added insulation to the canopy and pickup bed, more to cut condensation than for warmth. And I built bolt-in cabinets and mountings for our camping equipment. All can be removed in an hour if we need the pickup for hauling.

With a motor vehicle we spend more money than do most purely tent campers, but less than do any house dwellers we know. We rarely drive long distances; moving just a few miles gives a change of scene; traveling a hundred miles in this country can make a big difference.

When we head to the woods we usually stay two or three weeks in one spot. Then we go to town for supplies and mail, and when we return, camp in a new spot, or an old spot where we haven't been for a while. This way we are able to enjoy many different scenes without much extra driving or equipment set-up.

Neither of us wants to settle, perhaps because we've already had our fill of that. Barb grew up on a working farm, the oldest of five kids. I lived in the same suburban house until I quit college at 20.

Rent saving is one reason we like long camping. But perhaps the biggest attraction for us is being able to be alone, where we can behave as we want without having to worry about how other people might react. (This may be important to us partly because the jobs we've held required catering to the wishes of others, sometimes to large numbers of strangers.)

Barb does most of the cloth work, including improving/repairing our tent and making/mending clothes. I do most of the cooking, washing and truck maintenance. Hank Schultz, Oregon, March

Report on Blue Star Tipis
I'm pleased with the quality tipi I got from Blue Star Tipi, Missoula, Montana. They have a material available that's half cotton and half polyester which greatly strengthens the fabric. They were very helpful with my questions and try to please. Heather, Arkansas, June

Freighthopping Hints
Dan Leen's Freighthoppers Manual for North America ($5.45 postpaid from Dan Leen, 6601 116th Av. NE, Kirkland, WA 98033) is a great book to get you out into the land of creosote and steel. If you ever wanted to ride, read this book and go for it. Here's some additional tips I found useful. Take plenty of water. Perhaps the most critical element to making a long ride enjoyable is to have enough to drink. A gallon milk jug or plastic soda bottle works fine. Use gloves. A stout pair of leather gloves that are broken in are best. A cloth pair will do. Wear a mechanic's suit. This is an excellent way to stay reasonably clean and will help cut the wind. Over a wool sweater and turtleneck, it shall help you make it through cold northern September nights. If you can, take a sleeping bag. Mine's a Holofil cheapo that can be machine washed. It helped me survive cold rain, sleet, and wind when I crossed the Rockies on a piggyback. Keep a journal. The folks back home will never believe your stories if you do not. And last but no less important, ALWAYS KEEP YOUR PACK ATTACHED TO YOU even when asleep. Use your gear as a pillow. Getting info and knowing where you are headed is crucial. Rob Burns, Vermont

When Hiking, Always Keep Your "Essentials" WITH You

What they are, vary with terrain, season and personal ideas. A Seattle-based mountaineering club recommends: knife, matches, fire starter, compass, maps, first-aid kit, extra clothes, extra food, flashlight, sunglasses.

I'd add a 6'x 10' thin plastic tarp and cord to tie it out. In many situations that would be more important than extra food -- you can go weeks without eating, but not very long without protection from the elements. And in a downpour without shelter, it would be impossible to maintain, let alone start a fire.

KEEP YOUR ESSENTIALS ON. If you remove your backpack to go on a short exploratory jaunt and become lost or injured, the essentials you left behind will do you no good. To avoid this, I put my essentials in a SEPARATE smaller carrier and never go anywhere without it. The carrier might be a fanny pack, a belt pouch, or even a knapsack that rides atop the main pack but unfastens easily and quickly for separate wearing whenever the main pack is not worn. Julie

Tools that are helpful for removing thorns and splinters.

For crazy hippies who pick blackberries in the nude and other folks who get thorns or splinters, a very handy tool is a splinter forceps. It is a needle-nosed tweezers: one can actually grab hold of the culprit and pull it out, vs trying to dig it out with a needle. Unless the points are very fine and come together well, the tool is of no special benefit, so success lies in obtaining a good pair. Some college student stores carry them, refering to them as watchmaker's tweezers and selling them to botany and entomology students for disection. To sterilize, I heat briefly with a flame. (In 2007, I bought a stainless-steel pair for $6 at the OSU student store. Holly)

Another aid to splinter removal is a ten-power hand lens. It lets you find and SEE what you are doing. When you're not performing surgery, it's great for observing natural wonders such as flower parts. Julie Summers, Oregon

Grooming wild food plants is easier than growing domestics.

Regarding your attempts to grow domesticated vegies in the wilds. First off, I'd not water plants for human consumption with urine or grey-water. This is a new area of research. I think that water is fine for ornamentals, and for for stock forage such as alfalfa or pasture, but I'd stop short of using that water for my food.

About guerilla growing of vegetables in general. I expect you'll have better luck by grooming healthy wild stands of forage food and reducing their competition, than by trying to establish pampered urban vegies in the wild.

However, for an introduction to coaxing the wilderness into civilized vegies, read the Fukuoka book, One Straw Revolution. Getting domesticated plants to grow in the wild is difficult -- needs a unique local solution in every micro-climate. Will Ross, WA 988, January

(Addendum in 2007:) Experimentally in Finland, cabbages fertilized with human urine that had been stored six months, grew bigger and carried fewer germs than did cabbages grown with commercial fertilizer or with no fertilizer. Sci News
6oct07

Pressure Cookery

After 2½ years on Tolfea (our boat) I've finally discovered a method of stove top baking that works. I have tried baking in cast iron pots, which works okay with the proper heat, flame spreader and a bit of good fortune. Unfortunately, charcoal was the usual fare when I used this method.

I have recently been experimenting with pressure baking and am having exceptional results. Pressure cookies were the first experiment. I stacked two round pans with covers inside the cooker on top of the steamer rack. I used salt water in the bottom as there's lots of that available. After bringing it up to pressure, I cooked them 15 to 20 minutes. The end results were delicious and very encouraging.

I now bake yeasted bread using the same method. It takes more water in the bottom of the pot as the baking time is increased. It takes 1 to 1½ hours to cook it thoroughly depending on the size of pan used. I have made custards, cakes, casseroles, etc. and am continuing to find new ways of using this tool.

One day I was cooking beans and just after they came up to pressure I ran out of kerosene. Rather than refuel the stove at that time, I ignored it until later that day. When I came back to finish cooking the beans, to my surprise, they were already sufficiently cooked. I now use this method regularly. Most beans will be cooked after bringing them to pressure for 1 to 5 minutes and then leaving them sit for 2 to 3 hours. Some of the bigger beans take 10 minutes of pressure before they're laid to rest which still means a savings of 30 minutes of cooking fuel.

As stove top cooking and pressure baking unfold, my desire for a conventional oven is quickly fading. The fewer things we have aboard Tolfea, the more time and space there is for living. Miki Gerke (from NOLLA JOURNAL, V3 N9 March'82, North Olympic Living Lightly Assoc.,Box 1073,Sequim,WA 98382; monthly,$10/yr.)

Hopi Cookery and Pueblo Indian Cookbook

Because the recipes utilize much that's dried, such as beans, corn and wheat, these two books are especially applicable for those who backpack their supplies.

Aside from piki (tissue-thin cornbread that needs special skill and cooking stones) no esoteric techniques are called for. There are many uncomplicated dishes that require few ingredients, such as corn and beans, chile beans, tortillas, tamales, hot cakes, gruel, breads, etc.

The books also include unusual recipes such as, in Hopi Cookery, Baked Squash Blossoms, Pinto Beans with Watermelon Seeds, Baked Prarie Dog (the fur is singed off and the skin left on, as with chicken), Yucca Pie, and Culinary Ashes (rich in minerals). Pueblo Indian Cookbook describes Piñon Cakes, Juniper Lamb Stew, and Prickly Pear Jelly.

A valuable lesson these books have for the neophyte cook is that what constitutes a meal needn't be elaborate; e.g., one suggested dinner in Hopi Cookery consists of Whole Wheat Stew (3 cups whole wheat, 1 lb. stew meat, ¼ cut onion, 1 tablespoon salt, and water), bread and a green salad.

To shell piñon nuts Pueblo Indian Cookbook says to roast at 250° F for an hour, shaking pan occasionally, then put between damp clothes while still hot and roll vigorously. Ditto for sunflower seeds except roll lightly.

"How to Dry Greens. 1. Clean and sort greens... 2. Wash greens in cool running water... 3. Spread leaves on drying racks or clean clothes and put in the shade to dry. (Although leaves dry faster in the sun, this process bleaches...) 4. Turn leaves daily. 5. String...or store in sacks or jars.... Things do not have to be complicated to be good. Drying greens is a simple way of preserving them, one that has been practiced by Indians for many generations." (Hopi Cookery)

Message Post

POB 190 Philomath OR 97370.   Next issue June. $2 for 3 issues

Tipi Living During Wet Weather

Answering Heather from the Arkansas Ozarks, she has the right idea to put an "umbrella" over the pole ends. Ernest Thompson Seton described and pictured exactly this in many of his books. The Indians called it a storm cap and it was lifted in place with an extra lodge pole and if windy attached and guyed with some rope lines to the ground. Besides this, any tipi worthy of the name had storm flaps in the front which needed a careful arrangement to adjust the wind so the smoke would draw properly.

A tipi is probably the only tent which can have a good fire burning inside without danger, as the open top gives free ventilation for the smoke from a tiny bed of coals. But for those living in cold or winter weather, it is essential that there be a waterproof liner inside the outer covering to hold the heat. These can be made or bought from tipi manufacturers.

The Plains Indian made an art of living in tipis but too few others have. The best (only?) book on the subject is Indian Tipi by Reginald & Gladys Laubin which sold as a paper back some years ago for $1.65 from Ballantine, 36 W 20 St, New York 10003.

For leaks in any canvas tent, canvas waterproofing can be bought in gallon cans from Sears or others. It can be painted on with a broad brush on a sunny day but needs to air thoroughly before sleeping in it as the fumes from the solvent are toxic until it dries. I have had tents last 20 years or more by using such compounds every few years. It also discourages bugs, rodents.

On wet grounds a tipi or any tent should be pitched on ground with a slight slope where water will not collect in a puddle. Then a small ditch may be made around the perimeter to drain water away, unless you are in the wilderness - then 'ditching' is a no no as it disturbs the soil.   L. F. Barry, R#1, Box 313, Nunda, NY 14517, November

A Tipi Storm Cap

During long continued or heavy rains, a good deal of water may come in the smoke vent or drip down the poles. To prevent this the Missouri Indians would use a circular bull-boat of rawhide on a frame of willows....

For a 12' teepee the storm cap should be about 4' across and 18" deep, made of canvas with a hem edge in which is a limber rod to keep it in circular shape.... The poles should be short and even for this. (From The Book Of Woodcraft & Indian Lore, Ernest Thompson Seton, Doubleday Page & Co., 1913)

Portable Insulated Cabin is Cool as Tree House

This fall, for the first time, I had occasion to set up a modular cabin approximately 8 feet above the ground, instead of on the ground or sunken a few feet as previously.

I was surprised and disappointed to discover that, with two or three people inside, the inside temperature averaged only 10 to 15°F warmer than outside. With surface or subsurface setups this same cabin has provided 25 to 35°F of warming. This is with no cooking or other combustion inside, and with little or no solar heating.

At first I blamed the coolness on the jury-rigged floor
which had many cracks and poor insulation. But caulking cracks
and adding insulation didn't raise the air temperature much.
When on the ground the cabin has no floor in the middle,
except for smoothed earth covered with plastic film and with
about one inch of flexible foam for softness.

I hypothesize that the greater warmth of on-the-ground set-
ups was due to the incoming air getting warmed by proximity to
the earth before entering thru cracks near the bottom of the
cabin. E.g., if the outside air is 30°F and the soil is 50°F,
the air might be warmed to 45° before entering, whereas with an
arboreal setup, the incoming air is close to 30°. I could test
this hypothesis by rigging shrouds or ducts that would circulate
the air close to the ground before entry.

When the cabin is on the ground or sunken slightly, the
lightly-insulated earth floor provides heat capacity but usually
isn't a heat source. I.e., the earth serves to decrease temperature fluctuations inside due to variation of activities inside
or of the temperature outside. But the earth can't directly
increase the inside air temperature because the inside temperature is usually higher than the deep ground temperature. The
earth becomes a heat source only when the cabin is unoccupied
for several days or longer during cold weather, and during such
periods usually keeps the inside temperature above freezing.

I haven't noticed that sunken setups are much warmer than
surface setups; no more than I'd expect because of wind sheltering. When setting up below the surface I leave a several inch
gap between the walls and the soil (the walls aren't designed to
be buried), and with this arrangement the temperature of the
soil at floor level and thus the incoming air temperature may
not be much warmer than when the cabin is on the surface.

This is all rather speculative. But if your insulated
thing-a-ma-jig isn't keeping you as warm as you expected, think
about the air circulation - not only the rate of air interchange
between inside and outside, but how the air flows on its way in.
Charles Long, California, January

Extra Tent Poles Desirable
Next time I buy a tent or bivouac bag I'm gonna make sure I
order a few extra fiberglass poles and the metal connectors
before they break on the trail. Heather, Arkansas, June

For Emergency Fire Starter, Have You Tried a "Vu-Lighter"?
This lighter is available in two sizes and has a clear
plastic fuel reservoir with a button valve to allow fluid to the
wick. They appear to hold fluid for many months (years?) and
can be refilled with standard fluid. Ohio, September

"Unbreakable" Lexan Breaks
Tableware made of Lexan (a polycarbonate resin) has been
billed as "light and unbreakable". First the teaspoon went, the
handle breaking off cleanly during normal use. Then the fork
broke while mashing soft potatoes. The soup spoon followed a
few months later while mixing a paste of nutritional yeast.
The knife I've never used.

In all fairness they had been in daily use for over two
years. While they lasted they washed easily and had a nice feel,
both in hand and mouth. But at about $3 per set I wouldn't
bother with them again. A metal teaspoon weighs only half an
ounce more. Or I can make chopsticks out of branches for stir-
ing and eating solid food, and drink any liquid from a cup, or
the pot. I can get along without a fork. Julie Summers
(2007 update) Polycarbonate (Lexan) leaches a toxic
chemical. Don't use it for/with food or drink.

Ship's Medicine Chest and Medical Aid at Sea

The hiker or camper in wilderness areas sometimes is confronted with medical problems beyond ordinary first aid, where there is neither phone or CB or local ambulance to help. For most problems, the American Red Cross First Aid Handbook is sufficient. But suppose, you are a day or more beyond the reach of medical help. Our merchant marine has this problem and the government required the master of all ships carrying a paid crew to have a handbook and medical supplies aboard. Some such as codein or morphine are prescribed to be used only on radio authority from a physician! But in this one book is emergency treatment for every possible emergency. Yes, even child birth - one of the best books on what to do. Plus heart attacks, cuts, broken bones, etc. For appendicitis, they do not recommend the captain slice open the innards as some TV shows would have the hero do. The chance of a successful appendectomy by a layman is poor; the patient is more likely to live if not operated on. Yes, it does mention VD symptoms and treatment and if some of the prescription drugs for accidents or disease are not at the department store, your doctor can get them with a prescription if he knows you will use them for emergencies only.

This 474 page illustrated handbook is obtainable from the U.S. Supt. of Documents, Government Printing Office, Washington DC 20402. 1978 HEW Pub HSA 78-2024. It deserves to be better known. Review by L. F. Barry ($10.25 pp.,#017-029-00026-6)

Healing Clay for Cuts and Stings

I now always carry a small container of wet clay with me as my only first aid gear. I experienced its excellent healing qualities when I fell off my bicycle and cut my hand badly - an open deep cut on the palm. I wasn't able to care for it for two days except hydro-peroxide. It got swollen and sore. Put a few comfry leaves over it and it didn't do much. So I put damp, soft clay over it, then covered with comfry leaves and then wrapped. Next day was a miraculous healing.

I knew a guy who cut the tip of his finger almost off. They wrapped it in red thick clay and it healed fine.

I've tried the clay alone but it was more effective with comfry over it.

A herbalist friend in Spokane said the clay is more powerful if its made up ahead of time - at least a day. The clay he's had the best results with was: "Bentonite - Aluminum Silicate, gray, amorphous powder 200# mesh, pure". You can find it in the yellow pages under "well drilling equipment" or in ceramic supply shops or from potters. I'm personally not worried about microbes - I would use clay out of a creek.

Clay has a drawing action. Don't think I'd try it on burns, but stings and snake bites seem like injuries it would be good for. Heather Ann, Arkansas, September

Just the Clothes on Their Backs

I have read that survivors of emergencies often have nothing more than what they happen to be wearing. I figure if I always "wear" my knife and magnesium fire starter I'll never be without them. I carry them in my pocket on a lanyard attached to my belt, as an extra precaution against being separated from them. Even if I remove my clothes I can still wear the lanyard. Julie Summers, Idaho, August

Giard House Humor: Don't believe the rumor that water with Giardia can safely be drunk at the time of The Changing of the Giards. They never let their Giard down. Julie Summers

Acorn Processing

In the late summer and fall all over the west, the Indians would go up into the acorn country and forage in large areas while the acorns were ripe and falling. Because the worms were soon eating them, harvest lasted only a couple of months.

In Southern California I have found the biggest acorns and the least worm infested ones around snow line elevation, where the altitude discourages the worm moths. In areas with few acorn trees, the stick rats are usually cleaning up the local crop and their stick nests are often well-stocked by wintertime.

Where acorns were scarce, some Indian tribes would gather unripe acorns over a longer period and let them ripen in various types of granaries. Occasionally, they even treated their elevated stores to a good drying and smoking to kill off the insects and larvae.

It was usually the practice to separate the acorn meats from the shells during the same time the picking was done.

After de-shelling I spread the pieces out, then I pick out the white, good meats by hand, throwing away the dark rancid nuts and hulls. Or I dump the whole conglomeration into buckets of water and skim off the majority of floating hulls with a strainer, and then separate the remaining hulls and rejects by hand.

If you have meats that are clean, you can then run them through your grinder with the setting at a fine grind. But if the acorn meats are wet and bits of shell are mixed with them, then your steel grinding plates should be set so that the thin shells can just squeeze through the plates. Then add water and strain the mixture through some 8-to-the-inch wire screen to remove the bits of shell. Either way try to get the meal ground up as fine as possible.

After grinding I usually soak the meal in several changes of warm or hot water until the bitter tannin is pretty well removed. A little lye can help.

For cooking I prefer mixing the meal with other grain meal, adding sweetening, spices, oil, and making nut and fruit cake or waffles on my teflon iron. Some might prefer using the acorn meal in bread or griddle cakes. In any event, allow almost double the cooking time, unless your meal is very finely ground. Al Fry, California, May

Hidden Tree House Discovered in the Middle of City

It was high-rise living at a very affordable price .... The abode in question was a "well constructed" tree house 40 feet above the ground, wedged between two bushy cedar trees in Washburne Park at 21st Ave. and Agate St. Eugene police and city park officials were called by an unidentified person Friday morning.... It couldn't be seen from the street and police are not certain exactly how it was finally discovered.

Nobody was home. But the foam-pad bed was neatly made up and the amenities of home were at hand....

Nature had provided a perfect ladder with well-placed branches leading to the front door .... A sheet of black plastic coated the roof of the 7x5' structure. But it was all torn down with a chainsaw and a crow bar after the contents were taken....

(Later:) The builder of the tree house ... says the act was "an injustice" and discriminates against people like himself who are hard-pressed economically.... a bearded, 30-year-old man told a reporter Saturday. The man ... asked that his name be kept confidential for fear of being identified by police & fined.

"I bought the supporting beams and used plywood that I had salvaged for the walls" .... Hauling the materials up the evergreens by a rope -- usually during the day -- the structure took about two weeks to complete. The man said he had been living there since October. Passersby didn't pay much attention to his efforts, he said.

"When I completed the platform and sat there for awhile, I realized what a valuable place it was going to be", he said. "It was real beautiful." Police who dismantled the structure voiced surprise over the quality of construction.

The man said he moved to Eugene 10 years ago and has been working seasonal jobs .... Recently he was forced to give up his apartment. "My finances were real low and sometimes nonexistent. I had to eliminate the need to pay for shelter."

He insulated the interior of the dwelling with fabric to keep the weather out and to prevent the light from his candle from disclosing his location .... The inside was "quite warm".

The man invited a friend to stay overnight occasionally. He said he didn't store any food in the house because animals might try to break in. Once, he chased two curious opossums away from the front door. If people were around during the day when he came home, he would climb the trees from a back way, he said.

He was working at a temporary job when police and parks department officials arrived Friday morning, he said. However he knew that some neighbors had discovered the dwelling Thursday night, and he took his valuables to a friend's home.

For now, the man said he is staying with a friend. He plans to continue his simple lifestyle but declined to elaborate .... Tim Talevich (from Register-Guard, Eugene, Oregon, Jan 30, 1983) Thanks to Joseph Vetrono for the clippings.

(Washburne Park is small, only two square blocks, and is surrounded by residences. The unknown builder seems to have become a local folk hero, with radio singers mentioning him.)

Camping Near Eugene
    Bert and I camped near Eugene for a couple of weeks last fall. We were on wooded land, several miles from downtown and a half mile from the nearest house. There was bow hunting and some shooting nearby which made us nervous; otherwise no problems.

We didn't do any cooking while there, partly to save time but also because the woods were still dry and anyone seeing smoke wouldn't know whether it came from a safe camp fire or an embryonic forest fire. We ate fresh fruit and vegetables, raw seeds and nuts, bread, and other foods not requiring cooking. We kept food at our camp, as we usually do. We haven't been bothered by animals larger than rats or mice, which we set traps for.

Our camp was outside the city limits, and the land wasn't posted. As far as I know there'd be no objections to tent camping there without a fire, but probably would be objections to a more permanent structure. I later talked to a hobo who had slept in various places in and around Eugene, and he recommended camping outside the city limits to avoid hassles.

Going into the city from our camp required a good hike and long hilly bike ride. If we returned after dark, hiking was difficult unless there was a moon. We went to Eugene for shopping, looking some things up at the libraries, and recreation. If we had been working, commuting would have been too draining for us to continue our camping arrangement for very long. Holly

Camping Near Santa Cruz
    A lot of land here is posted; or really inaccessible - state or federal parks. Many folks around. The only people camping out here are the traveling beggars, minstrels, and alkies - of course near town. I'm still looking for that place from which I can see the mountains, the bay and the ocean. Dennis Powers, California, September

Message Post

POB 190 Philomath OR 97370.   Next issue Sept. $2 for 3 issues

Kelp Gathering and Sun-Drying

For the past three years a group of us have harvested and dried kelp on an island on the south coast of British Columbia. For a successful harvest you need low tide when you pick the kelp, and dry sunny days to complete the drying.

On a typical day we take the canoe out to a kelp bed, cut off the bulb and put the cut kelp into a clean sack. When we have enough it's time to hang it in the sun to dry. We build racks from split driftwood (usually cedar) placed to get maximum sun and breeze. It's good to do this as a group, because each piece is hung separately. After a day's drying the kelp will be crisp but probably not totally dry. Stuff it into large plastic bags to keep it away from the dew at night. Next morning empty the partially dried kelp on a tarp or plastic sheet to sun-dry during the day. Make sure it's fully dried before storing in air-tight containers. Crush before storing.

I have also gathered kelp from the shore without a canoe and sun-dried it on hot, clean rocks. It's important to keep the kelp away from sand (yuck).

Using the canoe-and-rack method a person can do about four pounds of dry kelp a day. Due to tide and sun you can't work all day, so enjoy yourself. If you've picked a clean and beautiful beach you'll get quality kelp and a deep tan. Don't gather kelp where the water is polluted. I have sold extra kelp (other than my own stash) for $5 or $6 a pound to health food stores and bartered with friends. Aarran Rainbow, BC, February

Keeping Food Cool With Brook or Evaporation

A cold mountain brook is best. Place food in a watertight container and submerge at a shaded spot. But if you have no brook, make a "refrigerator" of heavy felt and a box any size on stilts a few inches high sitting in a dishpan of water. Put perishables on shelf above water, cover with wet felt (if no felt, a heavy bath towel works fine) AND let the bottom edges hang in the water in the dishpan. Place in shade and in breeze. The felt or towel takes up water like a wick, it evaporates and presto the food is kept many degrees cooler. Don't put in sun! Don't let your dishpan run dry. On a hot day, water will cool and evaporate fast. L.F.Barry, NY, March

(Rocks may be substituted to keep the food out of water. And I have used moss in lieu of a towel: during a summer heat wave with 84° in the shade, the temperature of a package of food that was covered with wet moss and hanging in the shade in an onion (mesh) bag was kept at 75° by virtue of evaporation from the moss. Brooks of the area, with water less than 60°, were cooler yet, but none were close to camp. Editor)

Towel
Food in Container
Rock
Water   Dishpan

Keeping Foods Over Without Refrigeration

Having lived without refrigeration for many years, I have learned a number of tricks about how to avoid food spoilage. When I have a left-over such as chili, spaghetti, enchiladas,

cooked vegetables or meat which I want to use for another meal,
I cover tightly and store overnight in the coolest place I have.
If the weather is hot, I heat the left-over TO BOILING the next
morning. This stops any bacterial or fungal growth that may have
started. When I get ready to fix the evening meal, I again heat
the left-over thoroughly before serving. In the winter time, I
can skip the morning heating because my storage area is 40° at
that time of year. I do not keep left-overs more than two days.
    In the cold part of the year, I can keep such things as
deviled eggs and macaroni or potatoe salad for a second meal
but, because it is difficult to heat this kind of food, I make
only the amount we will eat in one day when the weather is hot.
... Home made bread should be cooled and tightly wrapped before
storing. Never make more than a 4-5 day supply at one time.
I haven't lost a loaf of bread in the many years I have followed
this rule. ... cake and pie should NOT be baked in the summer
time unless they can be consumed within 12 hours. Hard cookies
will keep for a week or more if stored in a tight container.
DO NOT make cream pies, puddings, or icing in the summer time.
They are so extremely suseptible to staph contamination, it isn't
worth the risk. I never leave raw meat over-night, winter or
summer unless it is frozen when I get it. If I buy enough meat
for two days, I cook all of it before storing. ... (Grand)Father
Firma (Survival Food Storage newsletter #7, 1982, $4/yr/6 issues,
Box 362, Calico Rock, Arkansas 72519)

Getting the Gas Out of Beans
    For campers beans are a compact, stick-to-the-ribs food,
helping balance the protein of grains. Here's a preparation
method to minimize the gas: Soak the beans until fully plumped
-- 12 to 24 hours depending on variety (small whites take less
time than pintos for example) and temperature (the warmer the
water the faster the plumping -- but don't get it over about
116° F because doing so stops germination and seems to inhibit
plumping). After the beans are fully plumped discard the soak
water, because beans' indigestable complex sugars, called trisaccharides, which are responsible for producing gas, are leached
into the soak water.
    Because sprouting may help further lessen trisaccharides,
time allowing, I let the sprouting process, initiated with soaking, continue by leaving the drained beans sit at room temperature. After four to six hours or so (the warmer the temperature, the shorter the time, to avoid souring) I rinse the beans
with fresh water, add water to cover and cook until tender.
I do not add any sugar because even tho table sugar, honey, and
molassas are bisaccharides, and therefore digestable, unlike
beans' trisaccharides, I find sugar added to beans causes gas.
(Actually I seldom add sugar to any food, period.) I cook the
beans in a pressure cooker, if available, for 20 minutes under
pressure, over flame, then remove from flame and insulate for
three to four hours under blankets, pillows, or clothes to let
residual heat complete cooking.
    Even cooked this way I keep portions small to minimize gas.
If beans still trouble you with gas, you might give lentils a
try. They are legumes, like beans, but non gas forming. They
may be cooked with or without first plumping. To turn them into
a fresh vegetable, sprout for a number of days.
    In the end, don't be worried by a little gas, it's perfect-
ly normal. The average 28 year old man passes gas about 14
times a day, according to the New England Journal of Medicine,
July 29, 1976, as reported in CoEvolution Quarterly, #34.
Julie Summers, Oregon, May

Buffalo Gourd -- the Ultimate Food Root

I first encountered this root when a friend came rushing in all excited about his amazing discovery. It seems he had used his dowsing rod to locate something at the base of a large boulder. After digging down he had brought up chunks of something resembling the flesh of a tubor. But the thing was much too large for a bulb or tubor and it had him in a frenzy. After much huffing and puffing he had a number of football-sized chunks but was still at a loss. After going to the area with him, I quickly spied the dried-up vine of the little-recognized Buffalo Gourd and the puzzle fit into place.

Tho Indians have eaten the gourd seeds and roots for centuries, few people ever realize that the huge vine with white flowers that sprawls over the landscape of certain parts of the southwest is such a prolific food plant. The roots can actually reach up to 50 or 60 pounds and are 50% starch. The only drawback is they must be sliced, soaked in salt water, and cooked in several changes of water to remove a bitter substance. A number of researchers feel the plant should be domesticated and farmed. The seeds are what they feel would make an interesting desertland crop. They contain over 30% oil and 30% protein in most plants. They are like watermelon seeds except for a slight bitterness, and can be roasted (preferably out of shell) and salted, although it's more trouble than it's worth in most cases.

(copied from Kirk)

Harvest any time you see gourds as they do not mould unless opened. The root can be used anytime and is the main food source. Leave part of the root for regrowth. Last time I was through a nearby stand there were enough plants to gather a supply of gourds and seeds. I'll put some in an envelope and send along to readers in the southwest who add a little postage contribution. A. Fry, 22511 Markham, Perris, CA 92370, January

(Kirk in Wild Edible Plants of the Western United States, Naturegraph, POB 1075, Happy Camp, CA 96039, lists Buffalo Gourd or Calabazilla, Cucurbita foetidissima (Gourd Family) and says it's odorous, has a yellow flower and cream-white gourds with green stripes. He says one may eat gourd and seeds but doesn't say anything about edibility of root. However since he says both raw gourd and root when crushed in water "yield a good cleansing lather" I guess they may contain saponins, too much of which can cause diarrhea. I assume the leaching process A. Fry describes would (largely) eliminate them. Editor)

Finding Dropped Objects

Before disturbing the area, drop another object of similar size, shape and weight - but not valuable, e.g., a pine cone or pebble - from where you think you dropped the lost object. Watch carefully where the "finder" lands or rolls. Repeat a few times from slightly different positions. Then search carefully the area where the "finder" landed or rolled, especially any vicinity where it lands repeatedly.

In addition to identifying the most logical place to search, this helps me avoid getting discouraged and giving up since I figure the lost thing is very likely somewhere near where the "finder" stopped. -- Drop it, you'll find it. Julie Summers

Sutures Or Butterflies?

I asked an emergency room doctor if sutures (stitches that go thru the skin itself) had any advantage over butterflies or other methods that tape over the skin only. He explained that because sutures draw the skin together at the bottom, in addition to on top, less scar tissue forms, thus making a stronger, as well as less visible healed place. (Strength is important in places often stretched, such as over a joint.)

Supplies for suturing are sold by Indiana Camp Supply, POB 344, Pittsboro, IN 46167, who also sells Wilderness Medicine by Forgey ($6.95 ppd) and Being Your Own Wilderness Doctor by Kodet and Angier ($7.95 ppd), both of which tell how to suture. Forgey says "If the laceration can possibly be held together (approximated) with tape, by all means use tape ...." Kodet says not to suture wounds that are over 14 hours old. Nor very bruised, irregular or dirty wounds, which almost always become infected. Infected wounds must be left open. Julie, May

Suture / Skin / Suture pulled tight / Underlying tissue (note that suture goes thru skin only)

Commercial Butterfly Bandaid (sterile) with no-stick center

Homemade butterfly cut from tape (not sterile). May be twisted or pinched to make center no-stick

Adhesive tape (sewing goes thru tape only) Edge folded under for strength

SteriStrip (seems like paper first aid tape (breathable), but individually packaged sterilely like a bandaid)

Sutures

Free Lance Writing - For a Living?

For the umteenth time I came upon a magazine article referring to writing as a possible income source for remote dwellers. It's a lovely fantasy: enjoying a pristine existence among the pines, jotting down one's musings, sending them off, and receiving payment by return mail. If that fantasy sustains you read no further. For you realists, here is my experience:

My average yearly gross income over the past three years from writing was $106. Postage was my largest expense, averaging about $20 a year, which gives an idea of the volume of manuscripts/queries I sent out; roughly 75-100 letters/cards. I kept no record of working hours but guess somewhere between 500 and 1000, which translates to between 9 and 17 cents an hour.

In the beginning of my illustrious career I used Writer's Market, billed on the jacket as "Where to sell what you write", which is as optimistic as a guide to Las Vegas' casinos calling itself "Where to win".

Initially I sent my manuscripts to the big slick mags with the attitude I could try the little ones later if the big ones didn't buy. This taught me two things: (1) how to handle rejection, and (2) forget big magazines. (Gambling now and then, I sent this article to Writer's Digest (magazine associated with Writer's Market) with a letter saying "I dare you". My SASE, letter, and article were returned, accompanied by a form reject.)

The little magazines I now submit to do accept a fair number of my offerings. Unfortunately, as far as making a living

goes, most pay little if anything. And I question whether they represent stepping stones to anything more lucrative.
   I assume some do prosper, but very few. Consider the number of aspiring actors, artists, athletes, sculptors or singers, compared to the number actually making a living in those fields. People who want to make money free lancing must compete not only with staff writers, but also with those who find it satisfying to write in their spare time and are willing to take whatever they can get in their eagerness to get published, which creates the epitome of a buyer's market.
   I'm sorry this report is negative. I'd rather write My Golden Pen. But until that happens I look to writing as no more than an enjoyable hobby and all I have to offer is My Pencil Stub. Which is literal. On $86 a year you don't think I can afford to throw them away, do you? By sticking them into the end of an empty felt marker or ball point pen case I can write down to the last inch. First I pull the eraser holder off with a pliers, then I rasp or whittle the stub's unsharpened end to fit. (Do you suppose I could get rich selling rhinestone-studded pencil-stub holders inscribed "Use Stubs - Save Trees"?) Julie Summers, Oregon, February

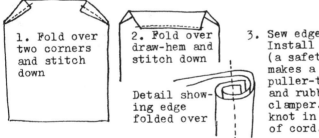

Make Your Own See-Thru Ditty Bags
   They're useful for organizing gear within a pack. Tho costly if bought ready-made, they are very reasonable if home-crafted from second-hand nylon curtains (which also make inexpensive mosquito tents - see "Bug Free", LLL catalog).
   Make the draw-hem wide enough (about an inch) so it will slip freely over the drawcord for easy opening and closing. A thick piece of innertube (or double thicknesses of a thinner tube) makes an inexpensive, light, unbreakable sliding lock for the cord. A small hole is punched in the rubber and friction keeps the "clamper" wherever one slides it. I fold the seams over on themselves so no raw edges are left exposed. (Searing edges in a candle flame may make them easier to handle.) Julie

1. Fold over two corners and stitch down

2. Fold over draw-hem and stitch down

Detail showing edge folded over

3. Sew edge seams. Install drawcord (a safety-pin makes a good puller-thruer) and rubber clamper. Tie knot in end of cord.

"Salt Tablets Are Not Recommended"
   Says the Journal of The American Dietetic Association, Vol. 76, May 1980 "because they frequently cause nausea, vomiting, and gastric distress. Excessive salt intake increases the load on the kidney, and without adequate fluid intake, a state of dehydration can be further aggravated."
   I've read elsewhere they can burn the stomach if swallowed whole. (Easy to understand if you hold one inside your cheek.) Pills also bypass the taste buds, thus eliminating feedback on how much is enough, which makes overdosing easy. Adding salt at regular meals, or carrying salty snacks, would be safer and cheaper -- if needed at all: many people ingest too much salt to begin with. Julie Summers, Oregon, May

Message Post

POB 190 Philomath OR 97370.   Next issue March. 6 issues(2 yrs)$5

A Cheap and Easy Hammock to Make Yourself

Home is where I hang my hammock - at least, I feel I'm really home only when I finally have mine up and am in it! Mayan string hammocks are nice (but expensive/hard to make), but for everyday I made my own from an old floor-to-ceiling curtain. The difference between a crummy, cramped "marine" style hammock and a real luxury job is not so much in the materials used, as in the dimensions and in the angle at which you hang it.

Lie diagonally in your hammock -- using elbow and foot to spread it. The longer and wider it is, the more room you will have to spread around in!

The fabric should be about square, and at least 1½ times your body length - or longer. (I'm 5'3" and mine is 8 X 8 ft.) Sew generous hems on two opposite sides, and run a nylon cord thru and tie in a permanent knot (and don't substitute clothesline, unless you want to crash).

To hang, use additional cords, one thru each loop, and tie to trees (or whatever) with temporary knots. (Try not to get these temporary knots rained on - you may not be able to undo them later.) Allow plenty of leader cord to make adjustments: about 4 feet on each end, plus the amount to go around the tree; tie the tree end as far above your head as you can reach (the further the trees are apart, the higher you'll have to go - you may even want to climb up a bit higher). The angle of hang should be generous (see drawing); the hammock should not be so taut that you cannot spread it sideways.

This is a good angle.

NOT this!

You want to be able to use the hammock for both sitting and lying in. For full reclining, you lie diagonally, using one elbow and the opposite heel for spreaders. I usually hang mine about 6 inches from the ground (when I'm in it), so I can reach things easily, and get in and out easily. To get in, straddle the hammock, spread it with your hands, and sit. To get out, start from a sitting position, one foot on either side, then lean forward and grasp the material in front of you with both hands; it's easy from this position to pull yourself forward and up, and then swing a leg over to get out.

You might think that a hammock without wooden spreaders will cramp the shoulders, or be easy to fall out of. Not true, provided it is long enough and wide enough. The sides will come up around you, and you spread them with your limbs - you are the spreader. Any tough fabric should work okay, with the exception of one that is too slippery. As for falling out --- In southern Mexico babies are often put to sleep in special small sized baby hammocks, where they can swing in the breeze quite securely.   Judy Brueske, Texas, June

<u>Thoughts</u> <u>for</u> <u>Living</u> <u>in</u> a <u>Tipi</u> <u>or</u> <u>in</u> a <u>Tiny</u> <u>Cabin</u>
      Living space in our culture has come to be conceptualized
as only that space defined by the walls of our houses. This
perception generates related restrictive ideas about weather,
activities, our relationship to the Nature Kingdoms, time, etc.
It took me a while, but I have a concept of my living space
which includes outdoor areas near my shelter. And my tipi (or
cabin) is just that, a comfortable shelter. It provides a
limited space, warmth, and dryness, as well as a place to
store a few goods. Much of my daily living is done in the
surrounding area. This includes the spring from which I haul
my water in pails, garden area, woodpile, adjacent field
and woods.
      Obviously, with this expanded living space, many activi-
ties which previously were "extras" or chores are now part of
my daily living in a more integral way. I <u>enjoy</u> splitting and
stacking wood, fetching water, walking my dogs, sitting among
the pines, gathering kindling, picking berries, gardening,
cooking over the open fire, hanging out the wash, etc. All
these activities are elements of my relationship to my living
space.... Earning a living is the only time I now resent
having to spend, and <u>some</u> parts of that are really fun.
Carol Irons, Vermont (condensed from May-June'83 <u>The</u> <u>Log</u>
<u>Cabin</u>, George L. Roberts, RFD #2, St. Johnsbury, VT 05819.
6 issues yearly, $6. Sample $1.)

<u>Polyhedrons</u> <u>Versus</u> <u>Prisms</u>: Which <u>Shapes</u> <u>Are</u> <u>Best</u> <u>For</u> What?
      (In answer to your question) I think that Starplate (R)
connectors are excellent <u>psychological</u> aids for people who
have never built anything on their own, because they simplify
framing, the first step. But what follows, the covering, is
more difficult and trouble-prone with a dome than with a
prism-shaped structure.
      An A-frame, shed-roof, gable-roof, or other prismatic
form, can be mostly covered with one sheet of polyethylene
plastic, without cutting, joining or folding. The ends will
require additional pieces, but the seams will be under shelter
of the roof and need not be leak-proof. Whereas a geodesic
dome has many edges and angles, requiring many seams in the
covering material. Some seams are on surfaces with little
slope and so must be waterproof. (Simple overlapping or
shingling won't keep out <u>blown</u> rain if the slope isn't steep.)
      Prism shapes are also easier to ventilate: the ends up
under the ridge are rain sheltered and so require only insect
screening. Whereas a dome's vents must penetrate rain-shed-
ding surfaces, adding complications. Likewise with the entryway. (A dome can be wrapped with one sheet of plastic but
that provides no ventilation or access.)
      Dome enthusiasts praise geodesic forms for structural
efficiency: domes require least covering materials for a
given volume (if you don't count scraps left over), feature
lightest weight for a given strength, and offer least wind
resistance. All true, but these advantages are paramount only
for large sizes. With a 10 or 15 foot diameter shelter, ease
of covering, ventilating and accessing may be more important.
      Degree of portability is a consideration. If the frame
as well as the covering must be carried long distances (rather
than cut anew at each site), I might favor a dome even for a
small shelter, because its frame members are shorter and
lighter for the same sturdiness and enclosed volume.
      I don't believe that Starplates would be particularly
difficult to use with natural poles. The only extra work

would be forming flat surfaces on the ends for good fit against
the connectors, and drilling the holes. That doesn't seem
formidable, considering that the poles must also be selected,
cut, trimmed, hauled and debarked.

A-frame △   shed-roof ◁   gable-roof ⌂

An A-shape is easy to frame: just 5 strong poles are
required. (Add 4 ground poles if the structure will be lifted
as a unit.) The poles are easily joined by lashing. They may
be but need not be the same length. Also required are four
diagonal brace cords, two on each side. (Or two brace poles.)
If desired, bolt-together connectors, similar to Starplates, could be forged for a prismatic shape. An A-frame
would require six. All would have the same shape if the sides
slope at 60°; otherwise two different shapes will be needed.
(A truncated icosahedron (Starplate dome) requires 11 connectors, all the same shape.)
The comparative advantages I've discussed are inherent
with polyhedral and prismatic shapes, regardless of how the
frames are fastened. I've never worked with Starplates so
there might be other problems I'm not aware of. I have built
a number of prism-shaped structures, both portable and semi-
permanent, lashing the frames. Charles Long, B.C., July

Make Your Own Durable $4 Rain Pants MORE Durable

I have experienced a problem with tearing at stress points.
I think the solution (which I have used successfully in many
cloth items tho not here yet) is to sew on reinforcement
patches prior to joining the areas that will be under stress.
I would use strong fabric, such as heavy nylon, which is also
mildew-proof, for the patches. I make them big so the stress
is distributed over a large area. Note that I sew the patches
on with <u>curved</u> lines of stitches, since the apex of a sharp
angle in a line of stitching creates a point of stress.
I especially recommend curving the ends of the row of top-
stitching on the bib.   I apologize
for this information not appearing in the
original article. Julie Summers, Ore., Aug.

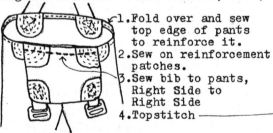

1. Fold over and sew
   top edge of pants
   to reinforce it.
2. Sew on reinforcement
   patches.
3. Sew bib to pants,
   Right Side to
   Right Side
4. Topstitch

Forgetfulness of Cold

While preparing for an outing on days before winter finally sets in, or even after a warm spell in mid-winter, it's easy
to forget how cold it can get later in the day, or with a gain
in altitude, or if one gets wet, or bikes and is therefore
subject to extreme wind-chill. To help compensate for cold-
forgetfulness (which is one example of pain memories fading
with time) I keep a list of things to take which includes garments I was glad to have had on cold days in the past, or
wished I'd had. I also wrote on the list: "Remember that you
don't remember how miserable you'll be if it's cold and you
don't have enough clothes. Extra clothes are cheap insurance."
A word to the once cold... Julie Summers, Oregon, February

Much Survival Writing is Unrealistic

People could survive in the hills on the wild foods that grow there IF they had the skill AND some lead time - which could be up to a year in some areas.

Many survival articles hint that all you need do is walk into open land and get fat. This bull could cost lives.

Anyone who hopes to move suddenly into wild country - and continue to live, should either prepare construction and caches, or arrange to live with someone. Paul Doerr, CA, April

Large Plastic Drums Do Well for Storage Outdoors

An update on the plastic drums that I had written about earlier (MP #8): So far I like them a lot. They don't require painting, they are quiet, and they keep clothes dry throughout the winter even without the gasket that comes with them. I have been keeping a cover over a nest of drums and also am keeping them in deep shade. Deficiencies: a narrower mouth than the middle of the drum, a galvanized band to tighten the top with that breaks sometimes (I've broken two out of ten over two years) and the drums are too wide to go through a narrow doorway. Most of them are bright blue in color. I thought that I should come up with a different band but I haven't done that yet. Rubber straps would probably work but be tedious to use. However I've not had dampness problems even with the drums without bands. Robin Ingrahm, Oregon, August

Organizing Storage Space

Those of us who live in small quarters end up storing many items in bags, boxes and barrels, within which the contents are layered to use the space economically. This can make locating a particular thing a nuisance. I have found a few practices that ease the problem: Items like clothes, fabric scraps, towels, sheets, etc. are folded neatly, rolled and tied. A rubber band makes this a cinch (I cut my own from bike innertubes). Now when hunting for something it's easy to move things around without messing them up and having to refold or leave wrinkled. They may also be stored on end so in any one layer a maximum of items are visible.

Anything I'd otherwise have to stop and puzzle over gets labeled. This is often a bag with more than one item, but may be a single item. Examples: "Summer Socks", "Hats & Mittens", "Leather Scraps", etc. Grouping like things together minimizes labeling. These practices take time in the short term but save time in the long run so I do them. Julie Summers, Ore., May

Finding a Soil Strong Enough for Cave Digging

(In reply to the question in MP #11:) According to the "engineering profession", there isn't any stable soil or rock that doesn't need bracing. All rocks have some type of cracks or fissures, and soil does not have long-term cohesive properties (compressive strength only, no strength in tension).

Anything is possible, though, depending on how "crazy" you are. I do know of an English professor in central Illinois who is raising a family in a tipi and an unbraced dirt cave.

To find a soil that is strong enough for your cave, look for clues in the existing landscape that you are considering building at. If there are steep hills or cliffs existing, then this would suggest a stable soil. Usually, though, these cliffs are held up by layers of rock or intertwined roots.

Don't try relying on dirt as an insulator, it is a poor insulator and it weighs so much that a structure capable of supporting 2' of dirt would put you in debt for 20 years.
Greg Stoewer, Illinois, April

First Aid for Nuts and Bolts With Stripped Threads

I had a bike rear wheel with stripped axle threads. Teflon
tape allowed me to get by without having to replace the costly
axle. The tape is tightly wrapped clockwise (the same direction
the nut will go to tighten) for a number of turns, then the nut
is carefully screwed on.

I had trouble with a loose front fork once on a bike trip.
I didn't have any teflon along but figured a strip cut from a
plastic grocery bag might suffice. I cut spirally starting at
the open end. I wrapped the resulting long strip around the
threads on the fork until the nut wouldn't fit on. Then I
removed just enough plastic so the nut could be threaded on.
I tightened it down and it held nicely. (For redundancy I wrapped a rubber strap cut from innertube on the outside -- around
handlebar stem, fork-nut, head tube and all.) Maybe for sealing
water pipes the teflon works better but I don't know. Teflon
tape is sold in some hardware and plumbing supply stores -- in
rolls larger than I could use in a lifetime. I got a few feet
from a mechanic/plumber friend. Julie Summers, Oregon, May

Channel Lock Pliers: a Favorite Tool

These are also sometimes called
water-pump pliers. The nifty thing
about them is the jaws can be kept
parallel, whether opened narrowly or
very wide, because they are adjustable via the channels (hence the name).

Sometimes a wrench won't work, as on an entirely round
object (e.g., a bottle cap or pipe) or on nuts that have rounded
corners. That's when a channel locks comes in handy. And
because the jaws open wider than any other pliers I've seen,
they'll hold larger objects than any ordinary pliers. And they'll
hold well because the jaws are kept parallel. Channel
locks come in different sizes. Small ones, about
5", are used by some cyclists in their trip tool kits. So far I
have only a larger size, about 9", that I use at home. Their
long handles add good leverage. Julie Summers, Oregon, May

Expedient Brake Pad Replacements: Another Use For Rubber Straps

Mid way on a bike trip through hilly country, I found the
brake pads badly worn. I had no spares. I did have my usual
assortment of rubber straps (cut from discarded innertubes) and
by wrapping a ¼" wide rubber strap around the worn pad, holder
and all, I was able to get by until new pads could be installed.
Fortunately I had foot brakes too (MP#8). Julie Summers, May

If Your Brakes Fail, Remember Your Heel

"Heeling" is something I read about in a letter by Cpt. G.
Kent Anderson in the Oct'74 issue of Bicycling! To execute this
braking technique one puts either pedal in an up position and
with that heel applies pressure to the rear tire. I've tried it
with success, tho not in emergency conditions. Since there's
some danger of getting caught in the wheel I advise caution
when testing this out. I.e., go very slowly and where there are
no obstructions nor traffic so one will be able to watch one's
foot safely. Julie Summers, Oregon, May

Preventing Blisters

Before a hike I cover susceptible toes with one of the
fingers cut from a disposable plastic glove, anchoring it with
tape. Or a piece of 1½" circumference, thin surgical drain
tubing fits tighter and doesn't need tape. A dusting of corn
starch makes it easier to put on. Both coverings are reusable.

For Fun and Money

In response to Alan Grandstaff's letter in Message Post #10:
During the spring and summer I live outdoors. A lot of my
friends are nomads with vehicles and other assorted light
"livers". I carry a tarp or tube-tent for rainy weather, otherwise I sleep outside, in a down sleeping bag on ensolite pad.
I carry an internal frame pack. If I'm in a city or town I stay
with friends while there, but I prefer the wilder places.

I work at various things - kelp gathering, fruit picking,
carpentry or light construction, tree pruning, leatherwork -
whatever comes along at the right time. Much of it is seasonal
casual work, and irregular. At one orchard I picked apples (for
pay) and got a small cabin gratis for a month.

I travel with friends and hitch-hike or share gas. I go to
music and healing gatherings, barter faires, peace gatherings,
draft faires. I also visit hot springs whenever possible. At
one gathering last summer I got admission and meals in exchange
for a few days work.

For food I usually rely on natural food stores, farmers'
markets and fruit stands. I carry some food - bread, fruit,
vegies, but I travel light. I cook over an open fire sometimes.
When I'm with friends we cook soups, make salads, bake bread.
I have lived quite comfortably on dried and fresh fruits, fresh
vegies and bread. I also pick and eat wild berries, abandoned
fruit - keep you eyes open there's a lot of free, natural
munchies out there.

Over the winter I usually find a cabin or live with friends
in a shared co-op. Some winters I move south - I've lived in
Florida keys and south-west U.S. This winter I lived with
friends in south-central BC.

In response to James Rominger in MP#10: If you travel by
vehicle you can bring much more than a hitch-hiker/backpacker
like myself. But walking will get you off the freeway world
into incredible beauty. The Complete Walker by Colin Fletcher
will answer many questions. (Revised 1974 edition is The New
Complete Walker, 485 pages, $11.95 (in 1980) from Alfred Knopf,
455 Hahn Rd., Westminster, MD 21157. Editor)

Your freedom is as unlimited as your flexibility and ingenuity. Keep healthy too. I'd like to hear what others do for
fun and money. Aarran Rainbow, British Columbia, February

Thirst Quenching Tip

Here's a trick I discovered for satisfying one's thirst
when involved in outdoor activities such as cycling, backpacking,
hitchhiking, or anything else which generates a thirst. Try
adding the juice of a lemon to your water jug before you gulp.
You don't need much; a teaspoon of the citrus to a pint will do
nicely. Bottled lemon juice works fine if the fruit is not to
be had. This is a guaranteed cottonmouth cutter and the vitamin
C can't hurt you either. (I've heard that vitamin C tablets
will cancel cottonmouth, too. Any news on this?) The lack of
sugar keeps mucus to a minimum and the tartness will keep your
water bottle fresh. CAUTION: Do not try this with aluminum
canteens! Rob Burns, Vermont, June'82

For Lightweight Knife Sharpening, Throw Away Your Stones

In the article "Choosing a Knife for Backpacking", April
1983 Signpost, M.Hiler recommends "440 grit wet and dry sandpaper, the kind car body repair persons use." Hiler says to use
three inch wide strips, pulled tight over a pan lid or other
flat surface, "using the same motions you would over a stone."

I tried it with garden-variety medium grit paper I had on
hand and it worked nicely, except for cutting the edge of the
paper a few times. I sanded the rest of the blade with fine
paper and it came out shiny-new. Julie Summers, Oregon, May

More on Keeping Food Cool Without a Refrigerating Machine
I have kept food in a plastic pail with lid, placed within a hole slightly larger in diameter and a few inches deeper
than the pail. I put moss on top of the pail to
insulate it from warm air. Temperature in the
hole around noon was 50°F, while the ground beside
the hole was 62°F. The hole was located in moderate shade. Some homemade bread stored this way
showed no mold after seven days, when the last was
eaten. Julie Summers, Oregon, August

Dark Colored Plastic Bags NOT Recommended for Food Storage
An old catalog ('72) of a plastic bag dealer said that
dark colored plastic bags (e.g. green garbage bags) were made
from recycled plastic, some of which may have been in contact
with toxic substances. Therefore they recommended such bags
not be used for food storage. Their newer ('82) catalog lacks
this information. Julie Summers, Oregon, August

Which Edible Oils Keep Best?
Although we have no scientific proof on which to base our
conclusion, we have reason to believe that corn oil is the
best oil for long term storage. It seems to keep well for up
to six months at 72° (unopened). This would seem to indicate
that it could keep for up to a year, or perhaps more, at an
average temperature of 40° F.
Sometimes we get complaints about safflower oil and sunflower oil going bad because of age, but similar complaints
about corn oil are almost nonexistant.
We have read reports of the addition of liquid vitamin E
or wheat germ oil (high in vitamin E) to vegetable oils to
extend their shelf life. One needs to keep in mind that each
time the oil is exposed to air, new oxygen (air) comes in
contact with the oil and can cause further oxidation.
Corn oil is one of our better moving oils and is bottled
throughout the year. However, because of the advantages of
cooler temperatures, your best time to buy and store oil would
be in the colder months. Boyd Foster, Arrowhead Mills (POB
866, Hereford, TX 79045) in recent letter to a friend of mine.

Baking Without an Oven Feedback
Because the temperatures are not as great with stovetop
baking as with regular oven baking, rising persists longer
after cooking starts. Therefore, to prevent over-rising with
its attendant falling, I have found it best to shorten the
final prebaking rising period. In fact if the breads are kept
thin (not over about an inch) I pat them out (from dough that
has risen and been punched down) and place them directly on
the hot pan over heat, where they do their final rising and
cook at the same time.
For sour dough pancakes, unless there's insufficient
sourness, cream tartar or baking powder is unnecessary because
baking soda alone in reaction with the sour dough's acids will
promote sufficient rising. Julie Summers, Oregon, August

Bread Rising and Mineral Availability
Although two spokespersons of the yeast industry could
tell me of no nutritional benefits from rising bread for a
long time, I have since read Raymond Peat, in his self-publish-
ed book Nutrition for Women, lament the cessation of the
practice of overnight bread rising.
I found that opinion supported by an article in Science

News V121 N16, April 17, 1982, that reports Wenche Frølich and colleagues at the Norwegian Cereal Institute "already have shown that the decreased zinc bioavailability of whole flour bread can be overcome by extending the fermentation period when making the bread, 'In this way, the phytic acid will be broken down (to) liberate the zinc for absorption,' Frølich said." (Phytic acid binds essential minerals in compounds called phytates, hampering availability to the body.)

I recall hearing about a study of two neighboring groups, one with a zinc deficiency, the other without. The deficient group ate unyeasted bread, the other group yeasted bread.

I have increased the time I let my dough rise (ferment). I prepare the dough around ten a.m. or earlier and let it rise until around five when I bake it. (I often save part of the dough in a cool place overnight and bake it the next day.) During rising I punch down every couple of hours because I read that eliminates gases that would otherwise inhibit yeast.

To avoid souring from the long fermentation period, I try to keep the temperature of the dough about $70^{\circ}F$, which is lower than for short fermentation. The practice of making a "sponge" may also discourage souring: I mix all the dissolved yeast with only half of the flour but all of the recipe's water (warmed to $100^{\circ}F$ or so). I let this "work" for up to half the total rising time, insulated under blankets if the room temp is cool, in a covered bowl that's over $2\frac{1}{2}$ times the volume of the mixture to allow for expansion. Then I knead in the rest of the flour and set back under the covers. The sponge also seems to activate the yeast better than making a drier dough initially.   Julie Summers, Oregon, May

What Kind of Corn?
I wondered if there were any quality differences between dry field corn sold in feed stores and that sold in food stores. The USDA (Kansas State U, Cooperative Extension Service, Grain Science & Industry, Shellenberger Hall, Manhattan, KS 66506) sent me their pamphlet "Corn Kernel Damage". It includes color photos of mold, rot, and other damage, plus a chart giving criteria for various grades of corn (maize).

All grades may include damaged kernels; they differ only in the percent that may be damaged: e.g. 3% for grade 1, 5% for grade 2, and up to 15% for grade 5. Grade 1 also has least allowable moisture: 14%, compared to 15.5% for grade 2 and up to 23% for grade 5.

The grading standards are independent of who will eat the corn - people or livestock - tho the USDA said in their letter that companies buying for human consumption "usually purchase Grade 1 corn when sufficient quantities are available."

I tested two samples of corn, one from a feed store (10¢ a pound, 80# sack), and the other from a natural food store (29¢ a pound, bulk bin); grades unknown. Results: Percent by weight of broken corn and kernels suspected of damaged germ: feed store 33%; food store 17%. Percent of undamaged-looking kernels that sprouted: feed store 42%; food store 71%.

Conclusion: Regardless of source, corn is likely to contain stuff I'd rather not eat, so I will pick it over before preparing. Regardless of store, I'll carefully inspect a sample before buying. If a costlier corn is of higher quality, my decision will depend on whether I have more time for picking over or more money.   Julie Summers, Oregon, August

Corn May Be Used to Keep Salt Flowing Freely
Fill shaker a third full with dry corn. To reuse the corn with more salt, redry corn with sun or low heat.

Green Outer Clothing Safer Than Brown

For a clothing color that blends well with natural surroundings, green may be preferable to brown because green is less likely to be mistaken for game. (But it's no guarantee - I read of school bus being shot at by one hunter.) Julie

Lamp Mantles Emit Radioactivity

According to Walter Wagner, a physicist who is suing Coleman Company for failure to put warnings on its mantles, these lamps can pose a health hazard. All mantles contain thorium, which is what incandesces and makes such a lamp four times brighter than a wick lantern burning the same fuel.

But thorium is radioactive, slowly decaying into a series of ten radio-daughter elements which emit mostly alpha particles. Most alpha particles are stopped by the lantern's glass mantle or by a person's clothing or skin. But alpha particles are injurious if emitted inside the body. So mantle users should avoid breathing the ash from a mantle or getting any into their food.

Radium 228, thorium's first radio-daughter, poses another hazard. It is given off in the fumes and so can be breathed. And it is biochemically similar to calcium and therefore likely to be incorporated into bones. Children and pregnant women are at special risk.

Most accumulated radium 228 is given off by the mantle soon after the lamp is lit. If a lamp has not been burning for a day or longer, Wagner advises lighting it in an open area and waiting 15 or 20 minutes before bringing the lamp into the home or tent.

Some beta particles are also emitted and these are more penetrating than alpha. Therefore Wagner advises against carrying unused mantles close to the body, such as in a pocket. (Thanks to Ken Scharabok for sending a clipping (published Nov-Dec'82, magazine not noted) which provided this information.)

Ordinary Candles Give Longer Light for the Money

There's a product called an emergency or survival candle that I have now seen advertised (at different prices) in three different places. The price winner is: Indiana Camp Supply, POB 344, Pittsboro, IN 46167. Their price for two candles is $6.50 including shipping. "4-Day Emergency Candles .... Total burning time ... over 100 hours. ICS# 7764."

But is this a good deal? A local drugstore sells 12 inch white, dripless tapers for $2.25/dozen - 18.75¢ each. I burned one to see how long it would last - result: over 9 hours. For $6.50 I can buy 34+ regular candles which altogether will burn for over 306 hours.

These survival candles are compressed and they look durable, so if space is limited, or if you want something to chuck into a knapsack, these might be preferable. But for home use, or where space is no problem, you'll get more for your money with ordinary candles. Jim Stumm (condensed from July'83 Living Free, Box 29 Hiler Branch, Buffalo, NY 14223; sample $1.)

Mouth Suction Versus Suction Cups

I wonder if those who recommend mouth suction in the case of snake bite have ever tried it. I think anyone who does will appreciate the importance of suction cups in a snake bite kit.

Mouth suction seems impossible to maintain steadily for 10 to 30 minutes. It also has the drawback of introducing into the victim's wound harmful bacteria, and can poison the rescuer who has any open mouth sores. Julie Summers, Oregon, May

When Filling Bicycle Tires from Air Hoses

I have often been cautioned by station attendants: use very small bursts; NOT a sustained flow. Though I do consult the hose's built-in gauge, I don't trust it. I stop and FEEL the tire's hardness after each small burst of air. Neither do I trust an attendant with my tires,

"Pant-wraps" for Bicyclists

Each is basically a strip of nylon, about one inch wide, and long enough to go round your ankle or lower leg (about 12"). With a machine I sew a two-inch-long strip of Velcro hooks upon one end, and a five-inch-long strip of Velcro loops to the other. "Pant-wraps" are simple, can be folded, and are more comfortable than metal or plastic pant clips. Aarran,B.C.,July

loops	nylon	hooks

How to Improvise a Miniature Compass

Use any sewing needle. Rub one end on pole of any permanent magnet and the needle will become magnetized. Float on water in glass or cup and it will point north-south. Make a note whether the eye or point points north. Because of surface tension (reason water striders can walk on water) the needle will float if very gently lowered into the water. Rub it in hair to get body oil, or in butter or any grease, and it will float better. So, a few needles in the emergency kit will serve as emergency compass besides having other uses - pick out splinters, sewing, etc. The smaller the better; a large darning needle might not float so well. Lyman Barry, N.Y., June

Prospector's Dry-Camp Shower

Use a square five gallon can with the top cut cut. Any similar can will do. Attach a strong bail of some kind. Use a medium sized nail and punch a hole about $\frac{1}{4}$" from the bottom. Keep this hole small. You want a stream of water not much bigger than a wooden match stick. Whittle a hardwood plug to fit tightly in the nail hole. You half fill the can and let it sit in the sun. Then hang it on the tree and get under. Use the soap sparingly and you can take a shower with about two quarts of water. If you carry it from the creek, or haul it in on your back, bike, or auto you'll appreciate this "dry camp shower" which I long ago got from a prospector's magazine and have since used often. You will be amazed at how good a shower you can get from a stream no bigger than a match stick. And there is something about taking your bath outdoors on a nice summer day that rejuvenates the entire person. Adam,Montana,Apr.

COMMENT: "Running Water Anywhere" (LLL catalog) can also be used for showering. However, like the shower Adam describes, it must be suspended. That's usually not a problem in the low position for dish, food and hand washing, but I often find it difficult to locate a suspension point high enough for showering that's not shaded. Therefore for showers I prefer "The Simple Shower"(LLL catalog). Because it employs a hand-held jug, I don't need a limb to hang it - I can shower in open sun. Its only disadvantage is that both hands are not left free. Julie Summers, Oregon, May

REPLY: The shower you describe is ingenious. For on-the-move it beats the one I use, with the advantage of a regulated stream. My "dry camp shower" holds five gallons and is preferable (by me) for a permanent camp. In summer I take two or three "showers" per day. Whatever method one uses, the ideal is to achieve: great time under water (pleasure) vs a very small amount of water used! Adam, Montana, June

Message Post

POB 190 Philomath OR 97370. Next issue June. 6 issues(2 yrs)$5

Camp-made Clothespins Improved With Rubber Bands
    Horace Kephart in his 1917 classic Camping and Woodcraft
tells how to make clothespins with the split below a node (knob
on a stem from which leaves or twigs may branch). In my
experience it was the exceptional node that didn't
eventually split all the way. I remedied the problem by
wrapping a rubber band tightly around the clothespin's
end. (I make rubber bands free by cutting an old bike
innertube crosswise into rings.)
    I also found beveling the tips allow them to slip
onto the line easier. I like half inch diameter vine
maple for my pins: it's not pitchy like conifer and is
easy to cut with a small saw or knife. Julie Summers

"Half" Towels Save on Washing and Drying
    I cut a bath towel in half, then hem the cut edge.
I have found that a half works as well as a whole one,
for baths as well as hand washing. Pat Rhodes, CA,Jan.

Polypropelene - A Fabric Better Than Wool?
    Wool has long been the outdoorperson's favorite, providing
considerable insulation even when wet. However its position has
been challenged. Bruce Mason, coordinator of the University of
Oregon Outdoor Program, considers polypropelene "far superior
to wool or cotton/wool blends" (personal correspondence). And
writing in the 1983 Free Country Times about kayaking in Nepal,
he says, after a day's wet paddling "Upon reaching camp, I
would simply whirl the wet sweater (poly pile) around my head a
few times, and either lay it out to dry or put it back on. It
would dry in minutes. The same ... for the poly thermalwear.
    "... Cotton no longer makes sense for river camping, so my
sole pair of pants ended up being a pair of Nike nylon wind
pants, the kind joggers wear. They were a fraction of the
weight of jeans, dried quickly and stayed clean. We found that
wearing the wind pants and longjohns on the bottom, and the
poly longjohn top, sweater, paddle jacket (Gore-Tex) and a hat
(poly) on the upper torso, was comfortable in weather down to
about 20°(F). Unlike old-style wool long underwear, the Damart
polypropelene pieces were exceedingly comfortable to wear."
    Poly(propelene) doesn't absorb water. But neither do many
other synthetics. A friend hypothesized that water sticks to
poly fibers less than to other fibers; perhaps for the same
reason that water beads on and runs off a block of wax but
dampens an ordinary brick.
    Plausible in theory, but how's performance? So far only
one polypropelene garment has shown up in free boxes. I've
been using pieces of it to patch other clothes. To test,
I trimmed a scrap to weigh exactly 2 grams, and also cut 2 gram
scraps of wool and orlon. I soaked all in rain water for a few
seconds, squeezed, whirled at arms length for one minute outside on a mild cloudy day, and weighed again. Next I safety
pinned each inside a loose cotton T-shirt next to my skin,
wore for two hours, and weighed once more. Results: (all
weights in grams, accuracy about one-eighth gram)

```
Dry weight before testing:              poly 2    wool 2    orlon 2
Damp weight after whirling 1 minute: poly 5¼   wool 4    orlon 4½
Weight after wearing two hours:         poly 2½   wool 2    orlon 3
```
The wool had the coarsest fibers and loosest weave, the poly the finest fibers, the orlon the thickest weave.

Conclusion: drying speed may depend more on fiber size and weave than on material.

Why did my test results differ from Bruce Mason's experience? Drying speed depends very much on temperature and humidity. (River runners try to pick warm, dry, sunny days whereas my test was during cool, cloudy, humid weather.) I can also speculate that the poly I tested may have lost its water repellancy thru repeated or improper washing.

The present high price of poly seems to reflect novelty status. Until the price comes down I'll stick with whatever good ole second-hands come my way, regardless of material. I'd like to hear more user reports. Julie Summers, Ore. Feb.

Backpack Camp Living for Six Months

Here's how our year went (preparations described in MP#8 p.4). We camped in the mountains of N. Calif. from mid March until late Sept (1982). On the whole it was very pleasant.

Some things went differently than planned. We only moved base camp once. We did go on many backpack trips away from base camp lasting several days. Gold panning - got a few specks. Would need a power dredge to make it pay I think.

The Woodland Tent worked quite well. Heavy rain at times, ran off, no leaks, little condensation. Snow, only light falls which soon melted. Wind rattling wasn't bad; rarely was the wind strong where we were, part way down in a steep valley. A few mosquitos came in, not sure if with us or thru cracks that breezes opened between the entrance covers and the sides. We put netting over the bed.

Setting up our arc tent inside did give a little more warmth but encumbered the woodland tent so after a month we took it out and used it only for trips.

The work part of the year didn't go so well. Burn't up what savings we had travelling and looking for work. Then car camping because we didn't have rent money. Finally connected with fair paying jobs late spring.

After that experience we plan to keep working (if our jobs last) for a year or so and build up a big reserve so we can camp for several years without worrying about money. We are living very miserly to save fast - rented a garage and camping in it (private garage, Rent-A outfits won't allow that).

As fast as we get money we are putting most of it into supplies. When we get a load we wait for a holiday weekend, drive it close to where we'll put our next base camp, and stash it in drums. This will keep us from getting nicked by inflation and also we won't have to truck the stuff in later. (We plan to sell our car and utility trailer just before heading out, so storage won't be a continuing concern and expense. Then for our next work period we'd buy a clunker, etc.) Our next period of mountain camping will begin next spring if all goes as expected.

Eventually we'd like to find a light, simple and quiet way of earning what money we need while camping (chain saws, power dredges, no thanks). Failing that we plan to keep alternating - one year working - several years camping. Craig & Wanda, California, October

Rubber Moccasin Feedback

Since writing "Wheelskin Moccasins" (LLL catalog) I have established some better ways of doing things that makes the task easier and results more durable and neater looking.

I no longer make lacing needles from folded metal. I use the hook needle (Fig.1) exclusively. Its strength and durability in this unintended application pleasantly surprised me. (Conventionally sold for hooking rugs and found amongst sewing notions.)

I no longer use thread in places, but instead exclusively employ $\frac{1}{4}$" wide lace cut from bicycle tubes, going thru 1/8" holes punched with a rotary punch (sold for leather crafters) in the auto or truck innertube rubber of the moccasin proper.

I no longer use knots to secure lack ends, instead at the end of a line of stitching I take a few stitches backwards over the last stitches and may pull the loose end back thru those stitches.

I have found tie cords (over the instep to hold the moc on) that go directly thru holes punched in the mocs tend to tear thru them. Therefore I now sew on an additional piece of rubber for the tie cords to fasten to, thus distributing the force over a wider area (Fig. 2).

I now favor the following design (Fig.3) which lends well to the contours of an innertube, to give a comfortable fit; is easy to make a pattern for - drawing with chalk directly on the rubber, around my foot (wearing whatever socks or foam booties I plan to wear with the moc); requires a minimum of lacing, which wears well because it is slightly up off the ground, accomplished by making the portion of the moc that goes on top of the toes somewhat shorter than the portion under the toes (Fig.3C) Julie Summers, Oregon, December

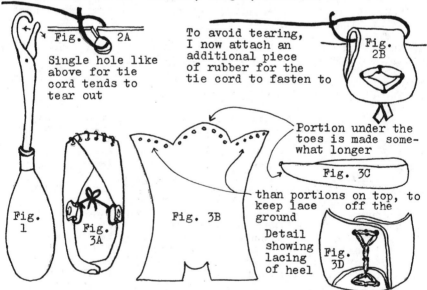

Fig. 2A
Single hole like above for tie cord tends to tear out

To avoid tearing, I now attach an additional piece of rubber for the tie cord to fasten to

Fig. 2B

Portion under the toes is made some-what longer

Fig. 3C

Fig. 1

Fig. 3A

Fig. 3B

than portions on top, to keep lace off the ground

Detail showing lacing of heel

Fig. 3D

The Amazing House Mouse

Can squeeze through openings barely $\frac{1}{4}$" wide. Has feet that walk up walls (unless the walls are very slick). Can walk along a wire like a tightrope walker and can run upside down on mesh. Is a great leaper and can jump one foot streight up into the air. Can jump down from as high as 8 ft. (from The Wild Inside)

How I Catch Menstral Flow on the Trail: Same as at Home

With a menstral sponge, which is a natural sea sponge inserted as a tampon (tho some women use them externally, held in place with a cloth sewn for the purpose). I have used this method exclusively for the past year, since having stopped using commercial tampons after reading in Nancy Friedman's book Everything You Must Know About Tampons (1981 Berkley Books, 200 Madison Ave, NY 10016, 172 pages, $2.50) that "virtually every tampon on the American market" contains "chemically altered fibers". (Even Tampax Regular, claimed to be 100% cotton, contains substances "to increase bonding between fibers or enhance absorbancy".) The problem with these chemically altered fibers is that they "can be so absorbent that they dry out the vagina, causing it to become irritated and sore". Tampons also shed fibers: vaginal ulcers have shown up with "bits of tampon fibers embedded in them". Other ills linked with tampons, in addition to Toxic Shock Syndrome, include rashes, yeast and bladder infections and lacerations from plastic inserters. Since switching to sponges I've gotten rid of stubborn, recurrent vaginal yeast infections.

Sponges are nice for backpacking and camping because they are reusable and therefore take up virtually no space. It's not disasterous if they get wet either. In fact the sponge is purposely wetted prior to insertion to make it more flexible and compactable. It is then squeezed as dry as possible and inserted like an inserterless commercial tampon. I found this somewhat uncomfortable at first but have since gotten used to it. When saturated with blood the sponge is withdrawn (for convenience I attach a pull string of dental floss). When camping I rinse by pouring water from a squeeze bottle held in one hand while kneading the sponge with the other hand, until the water runs clear. Bears are reportedly attracted to menstral blood so in bear country I rinse well away from camp.

I've seen sea sponges especially picked for menstral use sold at some natural and health food stores and a women's book store. Sea sponges are also sold (cheaper) at art supply stores (and art departments in university student stores). Quality may vary more than in the pre-picked sponges but one can do one's own culling in the art store. Julie Summers, Dec.

Sprouts Soaked and Rinsed With Rain Water Grew Poorly

I usually use local spring or creek water to soak and moisten ("rinse") sprouts (alfalfa-fenugreek-mustard-radish; and lentils) and have also used city water without any problems (as I mention in "Successful Sprouting", LLL catalog). Recently I tried using rain water, in part drip-off from oak leaves. (Both rain and spring water tested 5.0 ph on Nitrizine paper). The water became viscous after contact with the sprouts, failed to drain off well, and therefore left the sprouts soggy. As they matured some batches rotted.
Julie Summers, Oregon, December

Soaking in Relation to Phytates

Bargyla Rateaver, writing in midwinter'83 Earthtone #24 says soaking seeds frees their minerals: "When a seed matures, the minerals in it migrate to the outer part, the hard seed coat. They are there tied up in insoluble compounds called phytates, as they are bound to phytic acid. It is only when a seed is exposed to water ... that the phosphatase enzyme can split up the compound and release the mineral from it. ... Buy or make bread with sprouted seeds.... If you use just flour for bread, make it the old-fashioned way, starting

the batter at night, keeping it warm overnight, and adding the
rest of the flour the next morning when you knead it in, punch
down and knead again - even three times. That way the flour
is all moistened." Cereal is soaked overnight too, "but in
the refrigerator so you don't find it full of bubbles (from
bacteria) in the morning when you cook it". Soak beans also.
Julie Summers, Oregon, May

The Alpenglow Portable Solid-Fuel Camp Stove *
     Made of stainless steel, the Alpenglow
should prove more durable than other backpackable wood stoves Message Post has reviewed
(MP#7p.4 & MP#4p.3). It is also lighter
(39 ounces) and less costly ($52.45 postpd.).
     Erected, it's 12½x7½x7 inches and has
a 12" high triangular chimney for draft.
Held together by tabs and hairpin cotters,
it requires "only minutes" to assemble.
It folds to 12½x7½x3/4".
     The Alpenglow is intended for outdoor
use where it is safer and uses less fuel than
an open fire, and doesn't soot up the cookware.
     Unlike other mini wood stoves I've seen, some of which
are even lighter and cheaper, the fire is enclosed, and so the
Alpenglow is potentially adaptable to inside use where the
smoke must be vented. However a chimney extension and maybe
a door cover would be needed. These aren't provided.
     The fuel door is about 3x4". Designed to burn "twigs,
dried leaves, and small pieces of wood", this stove will
require frequent fueling as will any wood stove its size.
"It heats up quickly enough to boil water in 12-15 minutes."
     Sold by VWS Enterprises,Inc. POB 1271, Madison,TN 37115.
Review (from the brochure) by Hank Schultz

For Utility & Economy Buy Kitchen Knives, Not "Sporting" Ones
     M.Hiler in an April'83 Signpost article suggests for the
backpacker a knife with a blade thin enough for paring and
wide enough for spreading sandwich fillings. Sold as a
kitchen tool the price will be reasonable, unlike the same
knife sold at a sports shop. Make your own sheath. Hiler
doesn't like pocket knives because of danger (I assume from
folding) and getting gooped up with peanut butter and jelly.
The double edge of the "survival" knife "makes it as useful
for cutting your thumb as for peeling potatoes" says Hiler.
And hunting knives are too "fat" for food preparation.

Mitten Design Modification
     I have made many things out of old sweaters, and can give a
variation on Julie's pattern ("Mittens for a Pittance", LLL).
One piece. Same ½" around. Same instruction on wrist. But if
the thumb is at its fullest stretch you get an angle that can't
tear out. Each mitten fits either hand - "unihand"?
     Sweat shirts work well too. The waiste band is
usually stretched out too much. But if it is made
snuggish across the widest part of the hand, it hangs
on. Doesn't need hemming.
     And sweaters for infants and young children.
Pattern placement much the same. The neck band can be
reused. The grosgrain on the button side makes both fronts of
the little sweater. Then I hammer on snaps. If there is no
underarm side seam, the pattern body can be place in one piece.
Alma Schreiber, California, June

*NOTE TO READERS. I don't know if this stove or the stove
in #23 is still available, but illos may stimulate ideas.

Soaking and Insulation Shortens Cooking Time of Rice

I find if I soak two cups of rice for 6 to 8 hours, then
cook half the normal time (20 vs. 40 minutes, after coming to
a boil) and insulate under the covers in bed for about three
or four hours, it tastes the same as if cooked over flame the
full time. Whereas if I omit the soaking (or shorten the
flamed period) it ends up raw tasting.

If I cook less than two cups of rice it doesn't retain
heat as long during the insulated period so the time over
flame must be increased or a raw taste results. I suppose if
more than two cups were being cooked, the flamed period could
be decreased. (For other heat saving tips see"Cut Cooking
Costs" LLL.) Julie Summers, Oregon, April

Easy Pressure Cooker Bread

I no longer bother with putting the dough in a cut-down
coffee can, within the pressure cooker. Now I simply place
lumps of well-risen, punched-down dough right on top of beans.
which are not quite covered with water. I leave space around
the sides of the bread for condensation to drip back down.
I cook both beans and bread together for 15 to 20 minutes
under pressure, then insulate in bed under the covers for
about four hours. The bread rises well, tastes delicious, and
surprisingly isn't soggy except sometimes on the edges. Beans
stick to the bread but can be cut off. Julie Summers, April

Portable Electric Systems VII - Experience With Photovoltaics

In 1981 a friend with a portable photovoltaic system
purchased an additional, larger pv panel: an Arco 2 amp (flow
rate). I helped install that panel and I've repaired battery
connections in that system (Part III, MP#10 p.16).

As initially set up, the photovoltaic panels were situated about 30 yards from the battery (NiCad 20 amp-hour)
which is outside of and on the shady side of the shelter.
I connected using 1/16" diameter aluminum wire (what I had).

After installation I wondered how much voltage (electrical pressure) was being lost in the wires, so I installed a
third, light wire in parallel with one of the heavy wires
that was charging the battery. This allowed me to measure
the voltage lost in the heavy wire, which was 0.2 volts.
(Light wire was sufficient for this because it only had to
carry the microamps needed to operate the meter.) Paralleling
the light wire with the other heavy wire, I again measured
0.2 volts. So the total loss in the wires was 0.4 volts,
about 3% of the panel's output.

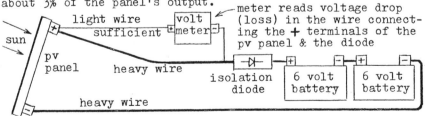

meter reads voltage drop
(loss) in the wire connecting the + terminals of the
pv panel & the diode

The isolation diode shown above acts as a one-way valve.
It allows current to flow when the pv panel voltage (electric
pressure) is greater than battery voltage and thus charge the
battery. But it blocks flow when the pv panel voltage is
lower, such as at night, thus preventing battery discharge.

I measured discharge current of 80 milliamps, twilight,
outside ±35°F. (Joel Davidson wrote that he had measured 130
milliamps reverse current on each of four Arco panels. The
difference may be due to temperature.) So I think an

isolation diode helps more than it hurts (because of its voltage
drop when the panel is charging the battery) here at least.
(It might not in sunny portions of the arctic during long summer
days, with a pv panel that tracks the sun.)
   The first diode I used was a big unmarked unknown one
(probably a factory reject - from a bag marked "100 semiconduct-
ors, 99¢"). It worked okay but dropped 1.3 volts (electrical
pressure) at a current flow of 1.7 amps, which is considerable -
about 10% of the pv panel's output.
   So I bought a new 1N5821 Schottky diode made by Motorola
(thru a local radio parts store which had to special order it).
Cost about $2. Schottky is a kind of diode which drops less
voltage than ordinary silicon diodes.
   As suggested by the parts dealer, I made a heat sink by
twisting six 3-inch-long pieces of 1/16" aluminum wire and slipping three onto each lead of the diode, as close to the diode
body as they'd go. With generous dabs of epoxy I glued these
wires to the diode leads, the diode body, and to each other.
(I didn't want to solder close to the diode for fear of heat
damage to it.) After the epoxy hardened I colored it and the
wires black, using a felt marker. The result looked like this:

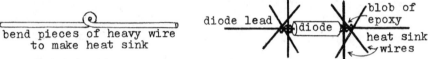

bend pieces of heavy wire   diode lead   diode   blob of epoxy
to make heat sink   heat sink wires

   Put into the pv system, the Schottky dropped only 0.3 volts
versus 1.3 volts dropped by the old diode, a saving well worth
the extra cost. When conducting full-sun current, the Schottky
gets barely warm enough to feel, a sign that my heat sink is
sufficient. The Schottky passes more reverse current than did
the old diode: 20 microamps vs less than one, twilight, 60°F,
but not enough to matter (1/100,000 of the panel's full output).
   The Arco panel doesn't perform as well when cloudy as does
the older 1/8 amp Sensor panel. At 2:30 pm, partly cloudy sky,
no direct sun on either panel, the little panel was still putting one milliamp into the battery, the Arco nothing.
Unplugged, the Arco measured 9 volts. The little panel has 36
cells, versus 35 for the Arco, but that doesn't account for most
of the difference.
   Experimenting, I then plugged the Arco into the battery's
6 volt (electrical pressure) connection. Into that it put a
flow of 25 milliamps. So that would be a way to get something
out of it on continually cloudy days and also give the lower 6
volts of the battery (which has an extra drain, a 6 volt radio)
some extra charge. Cloudy performance of a panel probably isn't
important unless you live where the sky is almost always cloudy
because (with the small panel) 5 minutes of bright sun charges
the battery as much as does 10 hours of cloudy skies.
Hank Schultz, Oregon, Jan. (To be continued)

More On Yurts
   Native or traditional yurts we call semi-portable since
they weigh 500-1000 lbs. We stopped making them since modern
tents are so superior for temporary shelter, and since a
permanent yurt takes less work to build and costs less for
materials than a semi-portable one (strange as it may seem).
William S. Coperthwaite, Director, The Yurt Foundation, Maine

Home is a 12'x14' Greenhouse in the Smokey Mountain Foothills
   I built it for about $80. Earth banking, woodstove for
heat, no elec. or running water. Tim Brown, Georgia, Sept.

Message Post

POB 190 Philomath OR 97370.   Next issue Sept.   6 issues(2 yrs)$5

Tripod Good Pot Support Over Outdoor Fire

I got tired of balancing pots of boiling water and food on tipsy rocks. Now I use a pot that has a bail or make a wire harness for one that doesn't.

To hang the pot from the tripod, I select sticks with several crotches, and cut and lash as shown. Wire is preferred for lashing; cord burns or melts if the flames get high.

The pot height is adjusted by moving the hanger stick up and down, or by moving the tripod legs in and out. If the ground is smooth and hard, I use rocks or logs to anchor the feet of the tripod.

When cooking without water, the pot can be set swinging in a circle to reduce heat and avoid hot spots.
Julie Summers, April

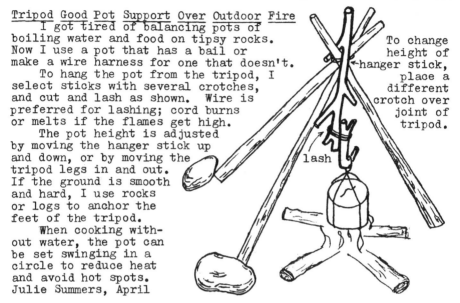

To change height of hanger stick, place a different crotch over joint of tripod.

lash

Camping With Comfort - I - Warm Weather Backpacking

Camping has a reputation as a toilsome, tedious, irksome, aching, grimy activity. This isn't surprising because comfort is usually slighted in favor of tradition, ultra-lightness or economy, if not deliberately rejected for "rugged adventure".

Camping is commonly used: as a way to get rid of the kids for a while (some summer programs); as an initiation rite (old boy & young boy outings); as an endurance test (wilder- ness-as-challenge programs); to encourage improvisation and stoicism (outdoor survival training); to reach extreme places (mountaineering); as a competitive sport (backpackers trying to go as far as possible in a weekend): in financial emergen- cies (travelers short of money); and to fight wars (the Army). None of these applications emphasize comfort.

But camping can be comfortable. We camp almost continual- ly, in part because we are comfort loving (and a little lazy) and don't want the toil and trouble of a house. Some of the things we take if going heavy and staying long:

- A complete insect barrier: either a tent with all vents screened or a net tent used under a tarp. (See "Bug Free" LLL)

- A large plastic fly (top tarp) to suspend above our tent or undertarp. Even if no rain, we like a fly to reduce or eliminate condensation on the underside of the ceiling. (Annoying to get a shower every time you bump it.)

- Plenty of bedding, not only sleeping bags to cover us but also several inches of soft foam to put under us (bulky but not very heavy).

- Plastic jugs, both narrow and wide mouths, for water carrying, water warming in the sun, portable faucets, and simple showers. They are light and they add little to bulk if they are filled with food or small objects on the way in.
- Dry food ready for eating, so we needn't mess with fires (unless we will be staying in one spot a week or longer in which case we may bring a stove).
To this we add an "essentials" pouch (water disinfectant, fire starter, knife, first aid, compass, map, etc.) which, as Julie Summers recommended (MP9),also goes with us on day hikes.
To those who'd rather "rough it" and who reproach us for "trying to take it all with us", I reply: There's a difference between intruding and enhancing - between the portable radio that blares forth alien sounds, and the insect screening that lets us listen to natural sounds without distraction. We'd rather enjoy the wilderness than fight it. Holly & Bert, Oregon, May (Part II will be on portable dwelling year around)

Low-Impact Camping and Spread-Impact Camping
    I believe most Message Post readers already know how to backpack without injuring the environment, so here I'll only summarize recommendations by UO's Outdoor Program: Limit groups to 12 or less. Use trails where they exist. Don't camp on vegetation easily destroyed such as meadows and edges of water. Avoid building fires if possible (bring ready-to-eats or a stove). Select and package food for little waste. Dispose of organic wastes and soap rinsings at least 100 yards away from water. Pack out any inorganic wastes.
    Equally important I think, especially if camping for long periods, is to spread the impact by generally avoiding the few famous wilderness areas and parks which attract many hikers. There are vast stretches of forests and mountains that are rarely visited. During seven years and several thousand miles afoot, Bert and I have met only two people (both hunters) while on hikes from our base camps.
    To recommend any particular areas would concentrate people there and be self defeating. I suggest simply looking at detailed maps (such as small-scale topos, which show every settlement - many libraries have), picking an uninhabited area at moderate altitude that's not been widely recommended, and heading into it more or less at random. Once away from roads and large streams, you probably won't see many signs of people. Holly Davis, Oregon, May

Soaking Time Can Affect Drying Time of Fibers
    Your report in the Message Post (#14) on test of wool, Orlon (acrylic), and polypropolene isn't a valid comparison for several possible reasons. Merely dipping in water might determine the amount of water picked up between fibers, but is not likely to show the effects of long term absorption into the fibers. Wool's popularity stems from short term uses, where fibers haven't had the chance to soak up a lot of water. Once wool is really wet, it's very slow drying out. Wool can ABSORB a lot of water, so is ideal for socks in summer, to soak up the sweat, as long as you change them often. Polypropolene and acrylic Orlon will not absorb any water, so drying time is just the time to dry water between fibers. Try repeating your test with a long soak in warm water, and then compare weight increase.
    Your sling drying test is not a comparison of fiber

material as much as a test of fiber fineness and weave. Very coarse wool will not hold as much water between fibers as will very fine polypro or the thin insulations such as Thinsulate or Sontique. Fine nonabsorbent fiber materials can only wick water if fibers are close and treated to wet easily (and obviously, as your test showed, the design to wick must also have the capability to hold much more water!). Wool wicks water THRU the fibers, not between, so wool can be both water repellent and wicking, as can nylon, but acrylics, polyesters, and polypropolene all must be wetable and very fine fibered to wick. Thus your conclusions on drying speed being more dependent on weave and fiber size should really be that initial water retention is based on weave and fiber size.

You didn't determine drying time: only a test at fixed temperature and humidity, showing weight vs time will do that. And then it would only be valid with identical thicknesses. It's easy to demonstrate that equal DRY thicknesses of polyester insulation, (such as Polarguard or Qualifil) and goose down, saturated with water then dried in identical conditions, will result in the Down drying faster, yet everyone "knows" the opposite is true, simply because of false advertizing, and the fact that a VERY THICK Down bag is known to take a couple of days to dry, while a thin Polarguard jacket will dry in less than a day. 3" of Down will only hold half as much water as 3" of Polarguard, and the retained loft of the Polarguard greatly slows drying. But, if you are careless, and let all the down fall into a big clump, it may never dry. Your test failed to determine actual rate of drying, or what the final equilibrium weight would be ... results could go either way.

There has been so much misinformation put out in advertizing and the idiotic "me too" magazine articles, that I hate to see misleading partial test results published, no matter how well meaning the tester is. Your conclusions at the end are absolutely valid, and show far more intelligence than all magazine writers. But, if you are going to test things and publish results, don't let over-simplification ruin the results. Jack Stephenson, New Hampshire, April

Happy Feet Feedback
In my article "Happy Feet" (LLL 1984 Supplementary Catalog) I neglected to mention that two pairs of socks can help prevent blisters: a thin, snugish fitting pair next to the skin and a thicker, larger pair over them. The idea is to lessen friction between skin and sock by transferring to between sock and sock.

I have found old nylon stockings, cut off below the knee, make a good first layer: lightweight for backpacking extras, and they wash and dry easily. This seems the answer to terrible blisters I was getting on my soles.

For taping the feet to prevent blisters, or over blisters, the rolls of thin, perforated (only apparent when held up to light) adhesive tape (e.g. Johnson & Johnson's "Coach" tape) sold at athletic and sporting goods stores, may wrinkle less and breath better than the thick drug store variety. J.Summers

I'm an Itinerant Tinker and Knife Maker
I've been "on the road" on and off for the last six years. I'm enjoying it but wishing for a greater sense of belonging - not so much to a place, tho a home-base would help, but more to a community of like-minded spirits: fellow-travelers. Maikel, Arkansas, March

Hey Now, Hitchhikers!

This book covers getting and accepting rides, packing, shelter, eating (including over 15 wild plants, tho I'm leery of lead contamination near roads), roadmoney, women on the road (including a 20 p. chapter written by women hitchers), talking your way out of violence, self defense, the law, hitching planes and boats (2 p. each), hopping freights (14 p.), drive-away cars, a 15 p. annotated bibliography, and the results of the authors' questionaire, to which over 950 people have responded including 22% women. (Contrary to media myths, approximately 90% of all hitchhikers surveyed have never been robbed or sexually assaulted.)

The second half is a province and state guide, giving for each: climate, military bases, universities, prisons & mental hospitals (restricted hitching), rest areas, federal land, hitching law and ticketing hotspots, places where long waits, how to get out of cities, jobs, and trains and truckstops (many women get rides with truckers; men less frequently). (This section, 7/8" thick and over half a pound, would be handier for taking along if compacted -- with smaller type.)

Tips for evaluating potential rides: Does the driver pressure you to get in? Is he looking at your sexual parts? Is there evidence of alcohol (odor, bottles, slurred speech)? Ask his destination before getting in or divulging yours, and gauge his response.

Many women will not get into a car that has more than one occupant. "Let's face it, this is the one chance you have to avoid conflict and possible assault without risking anything. Simply refuse the ride. Statistically, women rarely wait over 20 minutes between rides, so why not play it safe? .... People are less likely to try to take advantage of a person they feel is similar to themselves."

"Most people who were robbed had someone drive off with their pack.... When you get out of the car to get your stuff out of the trunk, remind the driver where it is and wait for him to get out first.... One of the best protections against losing anything of value is not to have anything too valuable with you."

"... a study made by psychologists claimed that 'eye contact (with the driver) doubled the number of ride offers'."

The 18 p. "Roadmoney" chapter describes fruit picking, haying, corn detasseling, firewood cutting, resort work, Kelly Girl and Manpower, panhandling, Traveler's Aid, oil fields, tree planting, fishing boats, selling blood, and the carnival - where there are jobs putting up and taking down rides as well as running booths on the midway: "There are over 600 shows travelling North America these days. If you want to find out about their locations, write to Amusement Business Magazine, 1717 West End Ave., Nashville, TN 37203. For a buck and a half, they'll send you the latest schedules."

This book seems thoro, informative, fun to read, refreshingly free of glamourizing, and true to my own occasional hitching experience. Review by Julie Summers

Hey Now, Hitchhikers! 1982, 635 pages, $7.75 ppd. from the authors: Don & Larry Evans, 2211 Menard St, St Louis, MO 63104

When Trying On a Pair of Sun Glasses in a Store, look in a mirror. If you can easily see your eyes, the lenses are probably too light for proper glare protection. (From a pamphlet by Bausch & Lomb.)

Water Sterilization Update: 2% Iodine Tincture Recommended

I found the article by Khan & Visscher ("Water Disinfection in the Wilderness", Western J. of Medicine,122: 450-453, May 1975) and am sending a copy to you. Essentially, their technique using crystals of elemental iodine offers no major advantage that I discern over the use of other iodine preparations. Although they claim that use of 2% tincture of iodine "results in water of less than acceptable palatability," I can think of no reason why use of the crystalline form of iodine should result in substantially more palatable water. Also, they recommend the use of 4-8 gram crystals of iodine, and these crystals (of varying sizes) may be harder to titrate than adding drops of 2% solution or an iodine tablet. Finally, tincture of iodine ... is usually easier to obtain ....

I agree completely, however, with their emphasis on the use of iodine, which kills Giardia cysts (a common cause of diarrhea (among) backpackers), rather than chlorine. CDC continues to recommend the use of iodine, in whatever form, for disinfection of stream water, and, because of its availability and ease of use, I personally use 2% tincture of iodine. Scott D. Holmberg, M.D., Enteric Diseases Branch, Centers for Disease Control, Atlanta, GA 30333, December (Reply to query from Julie Summers. CDC recommends per quart of water: if clear, 5 drops 2% tincture and let stand for 30 minutes; if cloudy or very cold, 10 drops, wait several hrs.)

Sources for Iodine Crystals in Small Quantities?

Altho tincture has the advantage of already being dissolved, the crystals are cheaper (from a good source) and more compact. So we are still looking.

Two mail order sources have been suggested but neither specifies quantity sold. (One was asked twice and refused - he advertises a "lifetime supply" for $5; the other sells a kit weighing ½ ounce including the bottle for $12.50) So I'm not listing them. At present I don't know of a better source than Eugene Scientific, 589 Blair, Eugene, OR 97402 (suggested by Julie Summers, MP13) which sold 125 grams (4.4 oz - would treat ±16,000 quarts) for $35, as of August 1983.

Note: Iodine tablets (tetraglycine hydroperiodide) lose much of their effectiveness within a few days after air exposure. I'd get either tincture or crystals, or boil. Hank

Basecamp Water Supply

Holly and I are presently using iodine crystals (we have not tried tincture) on hikes and at short camps, but prefer not to use iodine steady for a long time in case there are cumulative ill effects. So, at a basecamp where we expect to stay a week or longer, we try to find a spring.

In most of the northwest rain-belt this is easy - just follow a small side creek uphill to its source. (Check another hundred yards beyond where it appears, in case there is surface flow higher up, or a road or other contamination source.)

Some digging out may be necessary to enlarge the flow or to get a pool large enough and clean enough for dipping.

A better collection method, if a piece of old water hose or clean plastic tubing is available: Punch many holes in the bottom of a narrow-mouth plastic jug. Tie a piece of cloth around the bottom on the outside (the finer the weave the better - synthetic won't rot). Insert the hose into the mouth

of the jug (or vica versa) and seal the joint by wrapping a
wide rubber strap around it several times. Dig out as deep
as convenient. Place the jug on its side with the hose down
stream. Cover first with gravel or sand if available, then
with dirt.

Let it flow for a day
or so until the water runs
clear. The hose will
yield a slow trickle - put
a pail under the end to
accumulate. A pail with a narrow opening in the
top will keep out debris; insert the hose.

cloth tied over bottom
jug (holes in bottom)
hose
collecting
pail

After a rain we wait several days before
collecting drinking water, so there is less
surface run off. If the spring is far from our camp, we haul
from a closer creek or collect rain water to wash or cook.

A shallow spring isn't certain to be safe, but it's less
likely to contain disease organisms than a stream. We've
never had an illness we attributed to such water. Bert, Ore.

What Do You Do When You Lose Your Canteen Cap?
I tried whittling a plug from a piece of branch, but
found I got a tighter seal (virtually waterproof unless I
squeezed the bottle hard) by using a plastic bag, folded a
number of times for greater strength, and held on tightly
with many wraps of 3 rubber bands.
(For expedient fixes such as this I carry a supply of
rubber bands & straps, cut from discarded innertubes.) Julie

Plastic Wrapping Not Sufficient for Long Storage of Food
Regarding the suggestion (received by MP but not printed)
to wrap sacks of grain in plastic and store in an unsealed
trash can that's buried: your doubts are warranted.
Polyethylene plastic stops liquid water but not water
vapour. According to data I extracted from a plastics reference book (sorry, don't have title), low density polyethylene
0.004" thick passes water vapour at the rate of 0.35 grams
per 100 sq.in. area, per 24 hours, at 100°F and 90% humidity.
So a 50# bag with a surface area of 1000 sq.in., inside a
0.004" thick plastic bag that's tightly closed, would absorb
about 3½ grams a day, or 2.8 pounds a year. If the grain's
moisture content were initially 10%, it would rise to 15%
after one year and 20% after two years; enough to cause
spoilage. (Commercial grain warehousers try not to exceed 13%,
and recommended maximum for very long storage is 10%.)

At 50-60°F, the subsoil temperature in much of North America, the rate of water vapour transmission is only about one
fourth as much. Using several layers of plastic would further
reduce the flow, provided each layer is completely closed (a
bag). If simply wrapped in plastic with no closure except
overlap, additional moisture might spiral in between the layers. So the grain might keep for a year or two, but thin
plastic isn't sufficient for long storage. Chal Long, Cal. Apr

How Healthful Are Foams?
How do you feel about the healthfulness of being around
soft foam and rigid foam in a close environment? It seems
that whenever I unpack my soft foam from a drum there are
fumes that have accumulated in the drum. Robin, Oregon, April

Portable Electric Systems VIII - More Photovoltaic Tips
My friend has at times used a reflector - a sheet of plywood covered with aluminum foil - with the smaller 1/8 amp (flow rate) panel. Checking, I found the reflector increased the output about 50% in sunlight, only slightly when cloudy.

I recommend checking with the manufacturer before adding reflectors because some panels are not heat-sunk as well as others (e.g., the 2 amp Arco lacks the cooling fins of the smaller one) and overheating might damage the pv cells.

A reader who lives in a wilderness area and is considering photovoltaics, expressed concern that sunlight reflected off a panel might (if the panel were mounted in a tree swaying in the breeze) send a spurious "SOS" to an aircraft and prompt an expensive "rescue" effort.

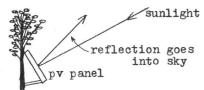 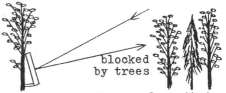

sunlight

reflection goes into sky

pv panel

blocked by trees

To avoid any possibility of this, tilt the panel so that reflections always go toward the ground or into other nearby foliage, not into the sky. Adjust the tilt for when the sun is lowest. Doing this will lose a little power (the panel will put out the most if angled so that its reflection goes back toward the sun). To minimize loss, readjust tilt with season. Hank Schultz, Oregon, April (To be continued.)

Comment Concerning Portable Electric Systems
I doubt that a 1/20 amp photovoltaic panel (MP13) will charge an auto battery during winter, especially a battery too decrepit to start a car. The battery's internal losses would be too much. The small pv might charge a motorcycle battery, which however isn't long lived in my experience. Chal Long

I Don't Have All That Much Confidence in Electronics
A solar cell wrist watch, hanging by a window, died in under 60 days. Rechargable batteries (Dynacell) don't last as long as regular batteries and one was dead in its original package. A Zenith Royal 3000 Transoceanic portable radio works - sometimes. A light meter is inaccurate. Paul Doerr

Bicycle Generator Lights Found Amazingly Reliable
One I've used intermittently for the past ten years with rain and all is still going strong. Since it's attached to the bike there's never a problem of forgetting a light.
The disadvantages are heaviness, dimmer light when going slow, no light when stopped, and since friction is applied to the tire when the generator is engaged, pedaling is harder then, especially noticable when climbing.
Both Union and "Schwinn Approved" SouBite (made in France) brands have worked well for me. Brightness seems to vary with model. For city cycling it's usually not necessary to have a very bright light since the road is illuminated: the light is primarily for being seen. However for country riding, it's desirable to have a beam bright enough to show where the road is and what's on it. Ideally buy only after testing in the darkest conditions in which you plan to be often. Julie Summers, Oregon, April

Portable dwelling and long camping.   September 1984   Number 16

Message Post

POB 190 Philomath OR 97370. Next issue March. 6 issues(2 yrs)$5

Living in a Double-Walled Plastic Tent

The longest I have camped alone is in my present dwelling
place, since mid Feb. Camp is about one-fourth mile from a
gravel road and 3½ miles from settlements. I go to town usually
once a week, so far no longer than every two weeks. Camp is in
a forested low mountain area near Portland.

My shelter is a double walled plastic tent with the back
wall formed by a large half of hollowed out stump. It is
satisfactory, but damp after persistent rains, due mainly to
ground seepage and wet clothes. Insects are kept down by some
well-fed spiders and a screen door in front.

Other camping has been mostly in the form of long backpacking trips, usually alone. One summer I hiked in the San Isabel
National Forest in central Colorado for about 6 weeks. I spent
a week camped on Mt. Elbert at about 13,000 feet elevation and
climbed several other peaks. I have hitchhiked/backpacked from
Redwood National Park up the coast to the Olympic Peninsula,
camping for around a week or two each at different environments
of interest along the way.

Eventually I would like to establish a sustainable wilderness home base and mailing address, possibly in Oregon, and
learn to live mostly on wild foods and gardening; traveling to
nearby differing environments when abundance of wild foods and
supplies is greatest there and/or climate would be preferable.
I would like to maintain contact and not become too isolated,
but still live largely free of societal entanglements.
Dennis, Oregon, June

Can Makes Portable Wood Stove

"Saw the 'Alpenglow' (in
MP#14 p.5) and just had to laugh.
Here is what I have used for a
number of years. Obtain metal
can or box (bread box does fine).
Any size rectangular can works.
Important to allow about ¼ of
can for between baffle and smoke
hole (flue). I use 3" stove
pipe and 8" stoke hole. Rivet
baffle so it can be easily replaced." Jim Burnap, Ohio, April

INSIDE VIEW
baffle
stoke hole
flue
←3/4 of can→ ←1/4→
½"
½"

Jim doesn't mention this, but if there's a removable cover,
I'd position the can so that the cover becomes either the front
or bottom of the stove, and not cut any holes in the cover, so
as not to weaken it in case I want to remove it for cleaning.

Cut flue hole to fit stove pipe. (When cutting I'd err on
the small side, then enlarge if necessary, to get a snug fit.
A sturdy sizzors will cut the cans I've used.) Cut stoke hole.

From sheet metal (could be a piece from another can) cut
and bend a baffle. The baffle fits side to side inside the can
but is one inch shorter top to bottom than the can. Also cut
an L-piece, 1" on each side and as long as the can is wide.

Position the baffle inside the can so that there are ½"
spaces above and below it. Fasten it to the sides of the can.
(Rivets, bolts, sheet-metal screws, and tabs cut & bent from

the baffle (like metal toys are made) are possibilities.) Add two or more lengths of stove pipe.

Jim doesn't specify support. I'd set the stove on a few large, stable rocks, so as not to scorch the ground or floor. Also, if used inside, put a spacer (donut shaped piece) of sheet metal or other non-combustable, between the pipe and the tent, where the pipe goes thru the side of the tent, so the hot pipe doesn't scorch the fabric. (Less problem with leaks when raining if the pipe goes thru a side or end, rather than the roof.) I put metal screen over the outside end of the pipe, to stop sparks. Fire up the stove <u>outside</u>, first time.

This stove can be positioned various ways, Jim says. If I understand correctly, as shown in the first figure, the stove is used both for cooking and space heating, with hot gases flowing both under and over the baffle. If used mostly for cooking, set the L-piece in the bottom against the baffle, to block that opening, so that all the hot gases will flow beneath the top surface on which the pots set. If used mostly for space heating, position the stove on end (figure at right) so that the pipe comes out the top.

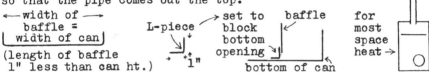

CAUTION! Any stove or flame is dangerous - not only the heat; also sparks, smoke, and carbon monoxide which is odorless and invisible. I'd never leave untended, or go to sleep in a tent with anything burning. MAKE AND USE AT YOUR OWN RISK!

In MP#3 I described stoves I've made, which are even simpler and can use cans of any shape. However I think Jim's would be more efficient, especially for cooking, because of the addition of the baffle. Editing by Hank Schultz, Oregon, May

<u>Learning How to Live Simply in Cold Climate</u>

We came back from living with the Ayta, hoping to be hunter-gatherers here at least part time. We are currently learning how to live simply in cold climate - a couple miles backpack or (earlier, before ice) canoe into this wilderness Maine coast.

With the Ayta, we lived farther in, a couple of hours walk uphill. There were about 12-20 families. They are the pygmies of the Philippines. We read Turnbull's <u>Forest People</u> while there and were amazed at similarities. (Have you read <u>Mountain People</u> for a grim look at the dislocation side of things?)

I've always wanted to know more about the Paiutes and Bush-men. Always thought they were exemplars. Eric Fromm in <u>The Destructiveness of Human Behavior</u> points out how hunter-gatherer groups are almost always peaceful and affluent (because of reduced desires).... David & Barbara, Maine, January

<u>Comments on Humid Portable Shelters and Heat Exchangers</u>

In Message Post #8, Bert asked if there were any portable heat exchangers (ducts so arranged that the outflowing air warms the incoming air without mixing), preferably passive ones. I don't believe a passive heat exchanger would operate, unless it were inefficient, because heat loss is what powers any passive ventilation. No heat loss, no air flow.

In windy locations the wind might be used to push/pull air thru a heat exchanger. Face the intake upwind, perhaps adding a funnel as a scoop. Face the exhaust downwind.

If no wind, a small electric blower would serve. But, considering the weight and cost of a portable electric system, it might be easier to add some combustion heating to reduce humidity. Or it might not, in situations where smoke poses a problem. (I've yet to build either, but I'd rather tackle a heat exchanger than a smoke filter.)

Before making great efforts to lower humidity, consider that around room temperature, a lower humidity will make you feel cooler for the same air temperature - partly negating the benefits of insulation and weather tightness. The reason is that drier air evaporates moisture faster from the skin, and evaporation is cooling. This is one reason some sleeping bags and cold weather clothes (e.g. Stephenson's) employ vapour barriers (coated fabrics that don't pass moisture) next to the skin, so that the air there stays humid regardless of surrounding air. (Another more important reason is to keep moisture from passing into the insulation and condensing, reducing insulation and adding weight.)

A humid dwelling provides somewhat the same effect without having to wear special clothing. So a case can be made for leaving it humid and keeping equipment that humidity would damage inside sealed containers or elsewhere. Chal Long, CA, Apr

Camping With Comfort - II - Portable Dwelling Year Around

A portable abode can be as comfortable as a permanent house - more comfortable if you count the discomforts that financing and maintaining a house entails.

For example, a few years ago we spent a winter camped in "Joe's" woodlot in exchange for some chores. Joe marveled at our ability to "rough it". This gave us many a chuckle on cold, dark, snowy mornings as we lay in a soft bed in our warm, cozy shelter and listened to Joe fussing with his car so he could drive 20 miles to labor all day in a noisy saw mill.

Two months of money-labor during fall had already earned our yearly stake. Joe couldn't consider quitting and dreaded a possible lay-off: taxes alone on his house and 15 acres were more than our total expenses.

Our shelter had a propane stove and lamp, tho not so many conveniences as Joe's house which included wired-in electricity (when a storm hadn't knocked down the wires) and piped-in water (when the pump worked). We had to backpack water to our portable faucets and simple showers, but we preferred that to working steady jobs.

On the other hand, Joe could invite over friends and relatives to admire his "ranch", whereas we had to go elsewhere to congregate. (With an 8 foot shelter, we'd entertain visitors only if we wanted to be in Guinness Book of World Records.)

For camping year around we'd recommend either an insulated shelter or a heating stove (in any climate we've experienced, which doesn't include the southern fringe) unless someone has exceptional cold tolerance. You probably won't need both unless your shelter is considerably larger than ours, or unless you live where there are long periods below zero F.

Choosing between insulation and a stove: An uninsulated tent plus a portable stove will be lighter and faster to set up than an insulated portable dwelling such as a twipi, and so will be less work if you are backpacking far or often. On the other hand, insulation saves you cutting wood and tending a fire, and so will be less work if you spend the entire winter in one spot. Bert & Holly, Oregon, May

A Lamp That's Easier to Make Than a Candle
    A non-electric lamp by whose light I have read whole books,
can be quickly made without special tools or skills. Needed:
    FUEL, such as candle drippings or butts, used canning wax,
tallow, vegetable oil, or used motor oil - NOT gasoline, kerosene (explosive when hot) or oil contaminated with gasoline
(from a worn engine).
    WICK, such as cotton shoelace, string, strip of cloth,or
cardboard.
    CONTAINER, such as shallow tin can, glass jar, or bowl.
    SUPPORT for wick, such as wire, narrow metal strip, metal
tubing or channel or coil, or container with a sloping side
(like an Innuit seal oil lamp).
    Different fuels give different flames. Inside I prefer
wax or tallow. Outdoors I often employ used motor oil (too
smoky, sooty and smelly for inside). Using wax for fuel,
I get about 16 hours light per quarter pound.
    The simplest wick support I've discovered is steel wire,
curved as shown. The wick is threaded onto it - easiest if the
wick is a tube such as shoelace or cord with hollow weave or a
narrow hem. To adjust flame, slide the wick up or down,
or add fuel.
    With solid fuels such as
wax or tallow, when first
filling, instead of melting,
I just put chunks in the   top view   side view
container. Then I light the
wick and, as it burns, push chunks close to it to keep it
fueled, continuing this till melted fuel covers wick's bottom.
    CAUTION! This lamp is more hazardous than a candle or a
regular kerosene lantern. If the fuel is allowed to burn low,
the remainder might get hot enough to explode, the flame may
spread to debris or reserve wick in the bottom, or a glass
container may crack. Therefore this lamp is best not left
unattended. Also, if upset, the liquid or melted fuel and
fire can spread widely (unlike a candle which remains mostly
solid). Keep in mind that water spreads oil/fat fires.
Smother with dirt or heavy cloth. Julie Summers, OR, April

No More Tears Fire Tending
    After cooking on the outdoor fire under the rain fly I'd
be crying. I wondered if swim goggles would help. But a
style-conscious vestige protested, "You'll look crazy - can
you imagine an indian or buckskinner tending their fire in
plastic goggles?" Replied my rational self, "I am a modern
pioneer who (as the ad for Message Post goes) eclectically
interweaves 'primitive' and 'space-age' technologies. I can
stand looking weird if it feels good."
    My feather-light all-clear plastic goggles, which don't
obstruct side vision (sold for racing swimmers at athletic
stores) made the difference between misery and relative comfort.
But, without my eyes warning me, I breathed more smoke. Since
I'd already said to ashes with conventionality, there were no
qualms donning a pollen and dust mask. It helped only if
wetted, and then felt cold and clammy. So I doffed it, and
selectively held my breath.
    I also use heavy leather gloves for handling hot grates and
pots, and for shifting firewood. And I wouldn't go near an
open fire without shoes; for someone I saw who had, it meant
a costly trip to the hospital. Julie Summers, Oregon, December

Patty-cake, Patty-cake
    Patting out thin pan-breads, instead of rolling them, has
the advantage of requiring neither smooth flat surfaces nor
something cylindrical to roll with. By playing at it now and
then over a number of years, I've developed the knack to where
I can get dough as thin as I want. To convey it well I'd have
to show you (video, anyone?) but I can tell you a few 'secrets'
- steps not obvious to a novice watching it done rapidly - that
may speed your learning.
    First of all, the more elastic the dough the better. For
greater elasticity: I use yeasted dough; I get my hand-ground
flour as fine as possible; I let the dough rise a long time
(Message Post #13 discusses long rising); and I use dough that's
on the moist side.
    The next secret regards sticking. To prevent it on the pan
I first get my aluminum frying pan very hot. To prevent it on
my hands I moisten them.
    Start small (it's easier), say with a lump of dough the
size of a small apple. Try to get it only as thin as you can
without problems. Try flattening it between your hands;
pinching the edges or squeezing them between palm and folded
fingers of one hand; pulling on it. Remoisten hands as
necessary. Relax - play - you're not being graded.
    After you develop your own elementary style you can think
about this: For getting dough pizza-thin, it's not just a slap
together motion. There is also a sliding movement of the hands.
As they slide they press together, thus squishing, stretching
and enlarging. There's also rotation as the dough is passed
from hand to hand, so all parts are stretched equally.
    I still can't get corn dough (masa) thin with just my
hands. (Anyone know that secret?) Instead I roll it out
between plastic bags. Julie Summers, Oregon, April

Fireless Cookery
    "Fireless cooking ... is simply a matter of bringing
prepared food to a boil, lowering the heat to a simmer, placing
the pot in a well insulated container, and letting the cooking
process finish with retained heat." Heidi Kirschner, this
book's author, has been a fireless cook for over forty years.
During her childhood in WWI Vienna, the Kochkiste (cooking box)
was an important fuel stretcher.
    Fireless cookery reduces energy consumption "by three to 20
times". For example, Heidi simmers rice only 5 minutes and
quartered potatos only 1-2 minutes. Other advantages include
less time watching the stove, a cooler summer kitchen, and much
less risk of burning.
    The chapter "Making or Buying a Cooker" gives directions
for a cardboard cooker, one of plywood, or an easy-to-sew
portable cooker, stuffed with folded newspapers. "The only
basic rule is that your container be at least four inches larger
in each direction (top, bottom, and sides) than your most
frequently used pot." A two-quart pot is the smallest size
that's efficient, says Heidi, tho she mentions a 1½ quart -
the size I most often use.
    A cooker improvised from a sleeping bag while camping is
mentioned, but the book fails to emphasize the same can be done
anywhere, using blankets and pillows, or even clothes, so
there's no need to wait another meal before trying fireless
cookery. (I've been an under-cover bed-cook for years, tho,
after Heidi's input, I'm placing the pot in a nest of sweaters
before covering with blankets, so there are no large air spaces

thus further reducing simmering times.) Other insulation
possibilities given include hay, shredded newspaper, polyester
fiberfill, and Heidi's favorite - "polystyrene pellets (the kind
used for beanbag furniture)". Pillows of them drape very well
around a pot. For most heat retention, all space around a pot
should be filled with insulation - easiest if the pot has short
handles. Heidi emphasizes that the pot should have a tight
fitting lid, and be filled only 2/3 full (or have 2" head room),
to minimize heat loss thru escaping steam.
    Simmering and insulation times are given for 78 explicit,
varied recipes, including soups, grains, beans, meats and one-
dish meals, vegetables, salads, sauces, breads, souffles,
puddings; plus yogurt making. Insulation times are flexible -
up to several hours is okay, says Heidi (tho for nutrition I
question prolonging the heat). Review by Julie Summers
    Fireless Cookery, 1981, 180 p. $6.95 (not clear if postpaid)
Madrona Publishers Inc, POB 22667, Seattle, WA 98122.

Cactus Apples
    All across the southwest there are cactus loaded down with
fruit part of the year. Altho most varieties are blandly
agreeable, there is a problem with the fine stickers and high
seed to pulp ratio. Indians and Mexicans of the SW used leather
gloves to squish out the pulp or peel the stickery skin. The
pulp could then be squished thru a basket or screen colander to
catch the seeds. Alternatively, when a juicer is available,
simply spear a cactus apple and hold briefly in flame to burn
off the fine stickers, then chop in half, and let modern
technology do the rest.
    The resulting pulp can be dried in the sun for fruit
leather or mixed with other foods to make the mix a little more
colorful and edible. Presently most people mix the pulp with
sugar and make jellies and such from the bright red juice, but
sugar is not particularly healthy as a steady diet. To the
unsweetened juice I add a dash of pineapple juice, or mix with
watermelon for a flavorsome, mineral-rich thirst quencher.
Now if I could just figure out how to ferment agave plant juice
to make pulque I'd have a true ambrosia. Al Fry, Calif., Febr.

Comfrey Contains Pyrrolizidine Alkaloids
as do crotalleria seeds and ragwort. Some rats fed comfrey as
1/3 of their diet developed liver intoxication and eventually
liver cancers. So far there's little evidence of comfrey
poisoning humans or other animals. (From Coltsfoot V2N2 Apr.81)

Harmful Herbs?
    Comfrey is on the list of herbs that the Canadian govern-
ment is considering banning for various reasons. They list it
as "cancer causing". There are 64 other herbs on the list
including aloe (severe diarrhea), burdock (blurred vision),
camomile (dermatitis, anaphylaxis), catnip (stimulant), dock
(diarrhea), hydrangea (stimulant), goldenrod (allergic reactions), jimson weed (stimulant), juniper (irritation of GI
tract), licorice (high blood pressure) and sassafras (liver
damage & cancer causing). Full list and story in Montreal Gazette 8/13/83. (I don't have later word.) Mike Gunderloy,MA,June

Economical Source for Iodine Tincture
    Down here in these hills we buy a 7% solution for use (as
a wound antiseptic) on animals and folks. Our source is
Jeffers Vet Supply, POB 948, West Plains, MO 65775; $3.47 a
pint, $16.69 a gallon,(+ $2 shipping).(Grand)father Firma, Ark.

Share Fire But Not Food When At Big Gatherings

While traveling Holly and I have eaten many different
foods in many different situations, including small potlucks,
with rarely a problem. But whenever we've gone to a big gathering and eaten communally prepared food, we've gotten sick.

We weren't the only ones. I recall one large "healing"
gathering where hundreds were layed up in "Diarrhea City"
(medical aid tents) and numerous others left early because of
illness. For them a festive time came to a miserable end.

Why is gathering size important? Is it simply microbial
roulette: the larger the number the greater the risk of something nasty spreading around? We were careful with water.

Anyway, from now on, we will only eat food we have prepared,
and pass up any affair that requires contributions to a common
kitchen or that charges for meals as part of admission.

Sharing cooking fires is a good idea, to cut down smoke,
hazards and scorched earth. But we'll use our own pots. Bert

Portable Electric Systems IX - More Battery Suggestions

If your radio-cassette doesn't have a socket for external
DC power, or if you don't have a plug that fits the socket, a
simple alternative is to find a branch about the same diameter
as the radio's dry cells, preferably dry wood, Cut pieces the
same length as the dry cells. Bare the last inch or so of the
wires that will connect to the external source. Staple these
to the ends of two of the wooden pieces. Insert the wooden
pieces in the radio in place of the dry cells, making sure that
the positive wire goes to the radio's plus, and minus to minus.

replace [batteries] with [wooden pieces] bare wire
to —   to +

Powering a portable radio or cassette from a battery while
it's being charged is hazardous. If any of the battery's
internal connections happen to break open, the radio will be
subjected to the generator's open circuit voltage (electrical
pressure) which may be much higher than the battery's voltage
(e.g. 18 volts from a photovoltaic panel that charges a 12 volt
battery). That could blow out the radio.

It's possible to make or buy an overvoltage protector (the
details are beyond my knowledge). Other solutions are to not
use the radio while the battery is charging, or switch batteries.

In Part III, MP#10, I mentioned connection problems.
Further report: "Since your last visit two of the aluminum
wires on the battery rusted thru. In each case I cut a piece
of stainless steel fishing leader about half a foot long,
wound it back and forth around the two screws, and tightened
them back down. So far it has worked." 10/83 Hank Schultz, Apr.

Simple Shower TOO Simple?

Hitching last summer, some people who gave me a lift had
been working in the woods for several days and wanted showers.
I told them about The Simple Shower, but that seemed not to
interest them - they continued to discuss such complicated
alternatives as rigging a water tank on their truck's roof.

Somehow The Simple Shower wasn't a shower to them. Maybe
they believed they needed many gallons of water to get really
clean. Or perhaps they think of a shower as a thing that does
it to one, rather than an activity that one does.

Altho The Simple Shower's gadgetry is starkly simple, to
use it well takes a bit of practice: learning how to hold

the jug, pour in the right places, not waste water, and move
hand when rinsing. Julie Summers, Oregon, April

Simple Shower Saved Water and Waiting at Rendezvous
     Backpacking our supplies up the hot dusty road to the
Rainbow Gathering, I came to wayside showers someone had
rigged. The water heater was ingenious: a large barrel
mounted over a fire, with one hose from a spring feeding cold
water in while another hose syphoned warm water out.
     But most bathers were showering directly from the hose,
which required much time with the hose and used lots of water.
Many people were waiting, and the water was coming out of the
barrel not much warmer than it went in. So I found a couple
of empty shampoo bottles in the recycle, filled them from the
hose in just a few seconds, Simple Showered using them, and
was soon on my way. Bert, Oregon, August

The Cart Book
     William L. Sullivan gives detailed plans for garden carts,
dog and pony carts, a push cart, and seven bike carts from
tourer to freighter. One garden and a bike cart have all-
wooden frames. The others use metal pipe, with the option of
bolting, brazing or (strongest) welding. Directions seemed
generally thoro, tho I found one error and some unclarity in
the one plan I scrutinized (p.136).
     In addition to advice on building carts to sell (as Sulli-
van does), entrepreneurs are described who do business from
their carts, including food venders, a sign painter, messenger,
and bicycle fixers. (Tho one bicycle mechanic I spoke with
has since moved into a building and looks back on his cart
days as his "hippy period" when he was willing to work in the
rain for very small profits.)
     There's a survey of cart design, old and new: frame, body,
hitch, and wheels. (A cart with 26-27-inch wheels)"will pull
well with light loads, but taking a heavy load around a corner
is likely to bend the axles (or wheels). The same cart with
20-inch wheels will be able to carry twice the load without
damage. The reason is that bike cart wheels don't tilt on
corners like the bicycle - they stay perpendicular to the road
- so all the weight is thrown against them sideways on a
corner." Sullivan says heavy-duty moto-cross-type wheels
permit loads of 330 pounds. As the book shows with photos,
bike carts can be built to carry 4x8 sheets of plywood.
     In my situation, to minimize things that must be maintained
and stored, I prefer to optimize the freight capacity of a
bicycle alone (see "My Two Wheel Truck", LLL catalog). If
that wasn't a consideration I'd try a cart. This book showed
variety I'd never imagined, thus broadening my horizons.
     The Cart Book, 1983, 274p., $13.50 postpaid, TAB books,
Box 40, Blue Ridge Summit, PA 17214. Review by Julie Summers

A Waterproof Tube Repair Kit and Reliable Cement Container
     Bicycle tube repair kits seem to come in flimsy containers.
The result is that moisture ruins the patch material. I have
found that a plastic vitamin bottle with plastic cap robbed
from a milk jug makes a better container. The tubes the cement
comes in are equally flimsy and often leak dry. I found that
a small plastic bottle, formerly containing typing correction
fluid thinner, could be used. I put a piece of plastic bag
between cap and bottle for extra gasketing. Test your bottle
to make sure it doesn't leak and isn't attacked by the cement.
I also carry an extra for backup. Julie Summers, Oregon, Dec.

Another Innertube Moccasin Design

Inspired by "Wheelskin Moccasins" I've tried another design. Heavy truck tube bottom. Lighter auto tube for top. I made a newspaper pattern first. I used my foot tracing plus one inch or a little more for the upper. Cut bottom larger than the top, and gather bottom to make up-turned toe and sides. Top and bottom must have the same number of holes. Punch holes at least $\frac{1}{2}$" from edge of upper. I used a paper punch and started holes from midpoint of the toe. All lace is $\frac{1}{4}$" thong cut from inner tube with point cut on the end. Back stitch to secure.

I've worn these mocs some this winter and so far I like them. They stay on my feet surprisingly well. Originally I had planned on instep tie but haven't tried it yet. I like high tops to keep ankles covered. The heel is the point that takes most water in. With pads it's not as uncomfortable for short outings. The toes turn water fairly well. The pair I made is large and feels good with pads and heavy sox. Tighter ones might be okay in summer. I made left and right but won't do that next time. I don't tie and untie, just pull on.
Robin, Oregon, April

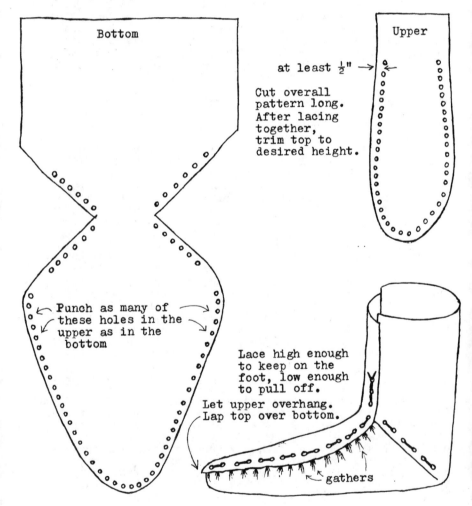

Bottom

Upper

at least $\frac{1}{2}$" →

Cut overall
pattern long.
After lacing
together,
trim top to
desired height.

Punch as many of
these holes in the
upper as in the
bottom

Lace high enough
to keep on the
foot, low enough
to pull off.

Let upper overhang.
Lap top over bottom.

gathers

Message Post
Portable Dwelling Info-letter
6 issues(2 yrs)$5. Sample $1
Number 17   February 1985   POB 190, Philomath, OR 97370

Versatile Knot Update

From Tim Setnicka's book, <u>Wilderness Search and Rescue</u> (reviewed in this issue), I learned that Figure 8 knots are now a favorite with Yosemite SAR. They weaken ropes less than do other simple knots, are unlikely to come undone, are unlikely to be mis-tied, and are easily inspected.

However, for least weakening when joining two ropes, the knot is tied differently than the simple version shown in Light Living Library's 1984-85 catalog.

If both ropes are long, tie a Figure 8 loosely in the end of one rope, then feed the end of the other rope back thru, following alongside the first rope. Then tighten.

Or, if either rope is short, the knot can be tied in both ropes at once, similar to the simple version, except that one long end must be pulled thru the knot (time consuming if rope very long).

Either way, for least weakening of ropes (8% greater strength), keep the first bend in each rope (coming from the long part) on the <u>outside</u> of the knot (as shown) so that the curve is more gradual. (After tightening, the knot won't look quite like this illustration.)

If coming undone could be disasterous, as in mountain climbing, tie off each end around the rope. (Not shown here. Setnicka recommends Double Fishermen's knots for tie offs.) I've never used tie-offs and I've never had a Fig. 8 come undone, but I have not been scaling rock walls either. Hank, OR, Febr.

A Good Rule for Living in a Small Space:

IF IT ISN'T USEFUL, YOU DON'T NEED IT. *(in your pack, van,
IF IT DOESN'T FIT*, YOU CAN'T HAVE IT.   tent, yurt, or ?)
People who stay put tend to accumulate more goodies. Learn to be nomadic and give stuff away. My experience in North America is that stuff comes easily (garage sales, dumps, dumpsters, flea markets, second hand stores) so you never really lack. Aarran

A Van for Living In

I am picking fruit (apples, peaches, cherries) for the next few months, living in a 1970 Ford econoline van. I recommend this style of van. With wide body, I sleep crosswise (approx 6' sleeping length).

For van living I like a large roof rack (for bicycle, spare tire),

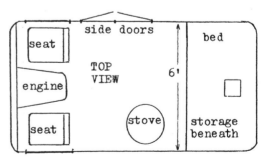

also a roof vent to let out heat or cooking odors. I keep my food in jars and a camp cooler (takes ice or cold water in jars).

I camp in quiet places, sometimes only a night or two when traveling. Presently I'm living in an unsprayed orchard with cherry trees all around. Good eating too! My van was a bargain ($200) - Winnebago owners note. Aarran Rainbow, B.C., June

Wilderness Search and Rescue

Author Tim Setnicka had nine years Search and Rescue experience in Yosemite (home of Half Dome and El Capitan) and rescue is what this book centers on: how to get up or down to a victim and how to raise or lower him, employing ropes and other "technical" equipment, from pitons to helicopters.

Searching is covered in less detail. Because there are more clues than victims, "searchers who look for clues rather than the victim increase the odds of quickly assembling the pieces of the jigsaw puzzle." For example, searchers may travel in circles around where the victim was last known to be, hoping to "cut" tracks or other evidence.

"The U.S. Coast Guard's data ... have shown that people have repeatedly survived far longer than was thought possible. A general rule of thumb for predicting survival is to multiply the time frame felt realistic ... times three." Survival without brain damage has even been documented for a number of persons submerged from 4 to 38 minutes in cold water.

Hints for cold weather comfort and safety include: "Hoods are crucial in wind and cold ..." "Fit any winter boot with a felt or synthetic pile insole to decrease heat loss to the snow ... and insert a dry pair whenever possible ...." For portable stove fuel in winter, "aluminum containers with fresh gaskets are best; some polyethylene bottles are not dissolved by white gas but may be brittle in extreme cold."

SAR for whitewater; caves; ice and snow; avalanches; and field medical considerations got a chapter each. References for further reading included.

Although explanations and illustrations were not always clear to me, I finished this thick volume with the feeling I had a good overview of SAR. And the thought I can avoid a lot of trouble by not climbing rock walls.

1980, 640pp., hardcover, $15.95 postpaid, Appalachian Mtn Club, Five Joy St., Boston, MA 02108. Review by Julie Summers

Fumes of Flare Deadly

A young member of the Santa Clara Valley Gem & Mineral Society helped to find some keys recently. The only light available to use in the search was a flare. No one realized at the time that he had inhaled the fumes of the flare which are magnesium and deadly. The young man became unconscious a little later. The brain damage was so great that he never regained consciousness. (From Treasure Hunters' Express, Sum84)

Living in a Van on the Streets of Manhattan

Here I am with Wanda, my truck. She's a Grumman-bodied 1964 Chevrolet C-30 Step Van that I picked up in non-running and somewhat vandalized condition in May this year for $900. Since then I have resurrected her from the dead and out-fitted her for living, which I now do on the streets of Manhattan. She has a wood/coal burning stove (Skippy Cabin Heater by Shipmate, $135 from Defender, New Rochele, NY), clothes and water storage, a 1000+ volume library, 2 bicycles, a bed, tool storage, and even a sporty brick floor.

Wanda carries commercial plates, which are the way to go as they enable me to park and double park almost at will. I have to move her at least twice a day because I work all night and she wouldn't be safe unattended in her daytime hangout: The Garden of Eden on Eldridge St. NYC 10002, the famous earthwork created by Adam Purple. (See Nat.Geo., Sept84)

I'm starting to see some dollar savings, which will jump when I abandon my apartment completely (now storage, mail drop, phone, shower, roommate), and I'm excited about travel prospects for spring and summer. Rick, New York, December

Second Thoughts About Living in a Van
Here's a little follow-up of my letter, which appeared in MP#17, Feb 85. For any of you interested in living in a van - there are some drawbacks:
- Mechanical failures, especially older vehicles. Tires/ motors/parts can consume your cash. A vehicle is a complex machine: your life may depend on its functioning properly.
- Fuel costs. My Ford van (1970) 6 cylinder, standard, is not easy on gas, compared to European or Japanese machines.
- License, and insurance which in BC is required by law, cost approx $200/year.
- Parking/camping. Can be difficult (at times) to find a good place, especially in built up areas. Vehicle campsites for RVs charge $5 a night and up. In certain areas, police or drunks may be a problem (especially if you like unbroken sleep).
- A standard van is good for sleeping, but during bad weather it can get claustrophobic (if you stay inside a lot).
- I personally tend to overextend myself with a van: drive too much at times, do too much, collect too much, visit too much. Finding a balance is important!
So what is next? I am going to sell my van, and experiment with bicycling/hitch-hiking. A friend rode from Chico, CA to BC and seemed to really enjoy the trip. He also rode back after a month visit here. Aarran, BC, October

Dwelling in a Pickup While Working the Holiday Season
Barb and I both got seasonal jobs this winter. Barb, with two jobs, worked almost continuously except for sleep. We didn't run across any houses for sitting, so we lived out of our pickup. Our sleeping gear was plenty warm and most of our waking time was spent working, so cold wasn't much of a problem. Temperatures were mostly 30s & 40s, with a few days down to 20°F.
Domestic chores are difficult to do in our pickup when both of us are in it. My work ended a couple of hours before Barb's, so I took advantage of the time alone to clean up inside, cook dinner, and prepare next day's bag breakfasts and lunches. When Barb got off, we ate, either in a park or in our pickup, depending on weather, then drove to a quiet street and went right to bed.
We had left our tent and much gear stashed near our last camp site, so we wouldn't have to share the pickup with it.
Barb was able to bathe and change clothes at one of the places she worked. (Both her jobs were clerking and required dressing up.) I heated water on our camp stove in the pickup and took simple showers in a park after work (in the dark - not enough handy bushes there for daytime privacy).
We often bivy in our pickup for a few nights while traveling and don't mind that. Living in it, for a month in a city, isn't so nice. But we prefer that to paying rent - and working longer for the extra money. Our financial mainstay has been summer work at a resort, where we have pleasanter surroundings including our own camping area.
This is the first holiday season in several years that we found much work. Unless you are a "local girl or boy" with connections, holiday jobs can be hard to find except in boom towns. (Barb is a good talker, which helps. Usually she finds work before I do. Once she was then able to get me on.) Hank

Message Post
Portable Dwelling Info-letter
6 issues(2 yrs)$5. Sample $1
Number 18   June 1985   POB 190, Philomath, OR 97370

Iodine Tablets Less Reliable than Crystals or Tincture

We continue to see ads and "news" for various brands of tetraglycine hydroperiodide tablets. The tablets are not only more expensive than iodine crystals or tincture, but quickly deteriorate once the seal on the bottle is broken. "They lose 33 percent of their initial activity when exposed to air for four days." (Kahn & Visscher, West J Med, 1975) (More on water sterilization is in MP17,   MP16,   MP15,   MP13,   and MP10   .) Holly, Oregon, May

Wild Sprouts Update: Mustard Seeds Sharply Flavored

Having the "Wild Sprouts" article (in Light Living Libr.) out has given me lots of feedback. Not everybody likes their food as hot and spicy as us 'born n bred' Southerners! The young sprouts from seeds of the mustard family, including black mustard, peppergrass and wintercress, are very tasty. But some are so sharply flavored that many people will only enjoy eating them raw if they are mixed with larger amounts of blander sprouts, such as alfalfa or wheatgrass. William Chapman, NY

Tip if Backpacking More than One Load a Long Distance

Take the first load only part way, stash it, and go back for the next, etc., rather than taking each all the way. The unloaded strolls back provide more frequent rests. Have each load all put together in one bundle or large bag so it can be put on and off the pack-frame easily. Bert, Oregon, May

Using Plastic Pails for Storage

Barb and I have used ordinary five gallon plastic pails for storage of papers, books, extra clothes, hardware, and (for short periods) food.

Preferred are pails with lids that have gaskets and which don't have spouts (which might leak, or break before the pail does.) Round pails seem to seal better than do square ones.

Plastic pails are occasionally given or thrown away, but most often sold for $1 each. Bakeries have been good sources. Check that the lids fit the pails well; most brands aren't interchangeable.

wood or bark

most valuable things within plastic bags

less valuable outside bags

shroud pail

For storage longer than a few days, I dig a hole just large enough to accomodate the pail, picking a spot unlikely to flood and unlikely to be stepped on by a large animal. Deepen the hole until the top of the pail sets just a few inches below ground surface. (If deeper the pail might leak if the water table rises above the pail during a heavy rain. I've not tried it.) Cover with a few pieces of bark or wood, then ground surface material and leaves.

For extra protection I put the more valuable items, such as papers I want to keep dry, in one or more plastic bags within the pail. Then I put some paper of little value, such as junk mail, in the pail outside of the bag. My hope is that if a little moisture gets in, the low value stuff will absorb it and keep the humidity lower.

It may also help to put a piece of plastic over the pail as a shroud. If there is some air flow into and out of the

pail with changes of atmospheric pressure (i.e. the lid does
not seal perfectly), the shroud supposedly allows less mixing
of air and therefore less entry of moisture. Tie the shroud
down around the pail with cord or rubber strap.
     Any number of animals could chew thru or pry open the
pail. But so far this hasn't happened to us; even the shrouds
(when we've used them) are rarely holed. However we haven't
stored food this way for very long. I wouldn't trust such
storage for anything very valuable. Our experience with this
storage has been in the coastal northwest where frost rarely
goes very deep. I suppose deep freezes might collapse the
pail; maybe not the first freeze but after several. Hank, March

Summers Work in Wilderness; Winters Roam in Mexico
     From June to November, Margaret and I work trail with hand
tools in the River of No Return Wilderness. Although the USFS
provides a small log cabin 30 miles back from the nearest road,
we spend a good portion of our time moving about the backcountry on foot and with portable shelter.
     During the winter we spend several months in rural Mexico,
again in portable shelter. Between places we live in a 30'
trailer that we bought cheap, renovated, and have parked by a
windmill near the Mexican border. We are interested in getting
acquainted with other Message Post people. Rolf Goerke,
Cold Meadows, Salmon River Air Rte, Cascade, ID 83611; April

Twelve Years Experience Living in Many Situations
     I have lived in vans (2), pickup campers (2), a tipi, a
mountain tent for a year in Wash. state, a bus home, in big
cities, along a river in rural areas, back in the tules, and
out of a backpack for many years. Now I live in a cabin I
built on another guy's remote land in Idaho, in exchange for
6 years free "rent" in the cabin with no other obligations.
     Twelve years ago I managed to buy one good quality mtn.
tent, down coat, HD backpack, sleeping bag and hiking boots.
Still have most of them and have lived in/with them under
heavy use for many of those years. Only the boots wore out
sooner. I had one sleeping bag stolen.
     Being "self-contained" was always better than depending
on others for a meal, a bed or a space to be. Most people will
tolerate someone else in their "space" for a day or two, but
unless it feels just RIGHT all the way around, it will only
lead to hassle by stretching your welcome; especially if
hitching and staying in someone's living room.
     College campuses are good for a shower, especially if
you're enrolled, but be low key, go during the "dinner hour",
and take your own towel. The campus library makes a good
evening hangout in colder months. They have pretty good
reference books, maps, music & educational tapes & videos,
films & projectors you can check out (use a viewing room in
the library). Rick, Kootenai Radio, Idaho, February

Salt Tablets Not Recommended
     James Wilkerson, a physiologist at Indiana U ... cautions
against taking lots of extra electrolytes during or immediately
after exercise, particularly since the release of cell potassium into the blood (a mechanism for widening the blood vessels
to aid heat dissipation) as well as the production of sweat
(a fluid that takes more water than electrolytes from the
plasma) makes the blood progressively more concentrated ....
Susan Wintsch (Science 81, June)

Some Tips for Meeting People at Large Gatherings

Choose long gatherings, a week or more, so there will be time to get acquainted or do things together. Some backwoods rendezvous are longer than announced. For example, the Rainbow last year in Calif. was officially July 1-7, but hundreds were at or near the site from early/mid-June until mid-July.

Arrive several days early, so there's time to set up camp and rest from travels before activities get underway.

On notes put a personal logo or emblem that friends can spot easily on crowded bulletin boards. Draw it <u>VERY BIG AND BOLD</u> (the rest of the message can be printed small). (Message Post readers are welcome to use this LLL emblem, suggested by Julie.)

Do things that will bring you together with people who share your interests. Do a workshop or demonstration, or offer a service.

Wear clothes or decorations that express your interests, to stimulate conversations. If your costume goes with something you are doing, so much the better. For example, at the CA Rainbow, a woman wore a dress she had made from cedar bark as she demonstrated how to separate, spin and weave bark fiber.

Leave some time and energy to circulate around to other activities. Don't get completely tied up doing one thing.

Stay well. Sterilize water for drinking and for final rinsing of food and dishes. Bring and prepare your own food. (There are many germs as well as people at large gatherings. Even some people who "never get sick" seem to there.) Get enough rest. Extra vitamin C may help. Have fun. Holly &Bert

Improvising Portable Bulletin Boards

We have been to gatherings where there wasn't enough space for posting information. So, on our way to the Rainbow last summer, we gathered up all the twine we could carry. Lighter than plywood, cardboard or even cloth, it served to make several info boards.

From three poles and three braces I make a tripod. (The braces aren't essential, but allow the tripod to be picked up and moved without the lines slacking and tangling.) Then, starting at the top, I spiral the twine around the tripod, taking a turn around each post in passing. I space the spirals 3" to 4" apart. Then, using rubber straps, I lash the spirals to the posts so they don't slip. (I didn't last summer and had a problem with the twine slipping up the tripod and loosening.)

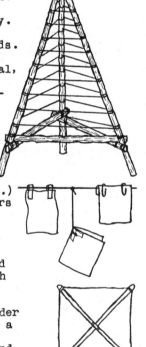

There are several ways to fasten papers to the lines. One way is with two pieces of plastic tape. Another is to fold the top edge over the line and paper clip. More durable, especially with booklets or with papers that need to be flipped to read both sides, is to reinforce one corner with tape, front and back of each page, then punch a hole and tie.

If rain threatens, move the tripod under cover. Or, if there's little wind, I make a roof by tying corners of a square piece of plastic to two crossed poles (like a diamond kite) that go atop the tripod. Bert, May

Gypsies Move Seasonally, Build Furniture, Pave Driveways

I live next to one of the largest Gypsy gathering and living areas in the western U.S. and have a first hand view of how a little ingenuity can keep a person free of the wage and tax merry-go-round. Local Gypsies usually have two lots, one in Chicago and one in the Southern California area. Twice a year they hook their flat-bed trucks to their medium size trailers and head to a more suitable climate.

For money, most build redwood lawn furniture and pave driveways. They pile their chairs or paving materials on their trucks, and in the long run probably make as much as the average blue collar worker, working only when they are in the mood. Knocking on doors eliminates the usual overhead costs. Al Fry, Calif. (condensed from "Living on Wheels" folio, ±7p., $1 from Fry, 22511 Markham, Perris, CA 92370)

I'm Living Like a Queen on a Pauper's Pittance

Finally got "free" late last October ('84), packed my little 18 footer with what gear it could carry, put my two best canine friends aboard, and headed down that open road.... I hit sunny Arizona, loved it, traded in my little trailer for a larger one, found a pleasant, friendly valley 22 miles out of civilization to settle down in. It is a new luxury RV resort, remote, nestled in the foothills of the Superstition Mountains. Luxurious, yes, but I felt I could afford it.

Suddenly my income went down to a trickle.... (But) using my survival instincts and staunch determination, I am still here, living well, and doing it on a little more than $300/mo.

For the most part, I have said goodby to the electric company. I have a couple of photovoltaic panels on the roof of the RV, these take care of a small B&W TV (it only takes 25 watts as opposed to the 57 watts colored TV uses), a couple 12 volt lights and a small fan, etc. I have a kerosene heater for the really chilly nights, but otherwise, a couple of kerosene lanterns provide light and plenty of warmth.

For soups, stews, and many other meals I have a fireless cooker. I put all ingredients together, heat them to boiling on the heater, simmer ONLY ten minutes, pop into Meal Minder, zip it shut, and five or six hours later I have a meal.

I glean delicious salads from the creek. Watercress grows profusely there and is much better than lettuce nutritionally and is FREE. The creek also provides some tasty crayfish. I solar dry a lot of foods to save refrigeration costs. I am learning a lot of other edible foods found in the desert.

Entertainment comes from long hikes up into the mountains, exploring the legends and history of the area or bicycling on the trails. I take advantage of all the "freebies" offered at the clubhouse such as pool games, jacuzzi, pool, library, and once a week, free video movie. Cost of transportation is held down by only twice a month trips into town for necessities. Otherwise, shoe leather or pedalling gets me everywhere else I need or want to go. I'm living like a queen on a pauper's pittance and enjoying every minute of it. Bess, Ariz., Febr.

Small Mobile Units Give More Flexibility

At present I have a 22 foot motorhome made from a large flat-front school bus to live in, a medium trailer to work out of, and smaller vans in various sizes to store things in. This allows me to escape the usual building permits, taxation, etc., and still stay within legal zoning ordinances. My favorite mobile units are large "step-in" vans.

Having more smaller mobile units gives greater flexibility and escapes the dollars-a-mile hauling fees for larger trailers. Gas prices don't really enter the picture because the units are stationary most of the time. I do not license anything I don't drive regularly, and do a little temporary license swapping if I do some short moving.

Snooty neighbors who worry about property values are the first persons who will complain to the authorities about any hint of un-normal life styles. Even if there are no laws broken, this can be a vexation. Tall fences that block the view are often in order. Al Fry (from "Living on Wheels")

Heat May Injure Eyes More than Does Smoke

I am an amateur blacksmith and am aware that one of the most common health problems with retired blacksmiths is eye cataracts. However, they apparently developed by looking into the fire for extended periods while metal heated, and not from fire smoke as Robin from Oregon indicated with elderly Indian women (MP17). I suspect that the Indian women's problem was also glare from the fire, rather than smoke. Ken Scharabok, Ohio, February

First Cold, Then Heat Recommended for Sprains

The mnemonic "chile today, hot tamale" is given by Bob Young, MD in How to Stay Healthy While Traveling. Viz., treat initially with cold (to minimize swelling which can retard healing by strangling circulation) then after 24 to 36 hours treat with heat (which promotes healing by increasing circulation to the area, which now that swelling has been prevented, can handle it). Julie Summers, Oregon

Too Many Electrolytes Spoil the Drink

Numerous marketed beverages claim to replace not only fluids lost thru sweat but also specific electrolytes - usually sodium and potassium. Unfortunately, reports Patricia Beckwith in Sportsmedicine Digest (V3 N5) these athletic drinks are too concentrated and, when ingested, draw body fluids into the stomach to dilute them, delaying rehydration. "... when a normal mixed diet is consumed prior to competition, electrolyte replacement is not necessary." In this case "water is the best and most easily available fluid replacement beverage." (Thanks to Julie for clippings, from Science News August 1981.)

Iodine Feedback: Caution With Crystals

In MP#13, I said the iodine crystals (for disinfecting water) seemed to remain in my one-ounce solution bottle. However, upon closer inspection (the brown bottle is hard to see into) I notice that if the water is agitated, some of the smaller, lighter crystals are swept up into the liquid.

I now pour VERY slowly so as not to stir up the crystals. A clear bottle would probably be easier to monitor (glass, because plastic doesn't withstand iodine).

Large amounts of iodine are toxic but "no fatality from ingestion of less than 15 grams has been reported." (Kahn & Visscher, West J Med May 1975) Because 8 grams TOTAL is the recommended quantity to put in a one-ounce solution bottle, I don't believe the danger is very great. Julie Summers, July

I Am Trying Iodine Tincture Disinfection of Our Well Water

This is for any bacteria in the spring runoff. I would like to set up a tent or tipi in our back 40 this summer and cook outdoors, etc. Diane, Ontario, April

Hominy: The Hull Story
I've been cooking whole corn with cool (slaked) lime as
per the LLL directions and enjoying eating the hominy, but the
kernels still have the hulls on them though the kernels are
puffed and split open. I've wondered if just cooking without
lime wouldn't give the same result so, after a 20 hour pre-
soak at room temperature, I pressured at 15# for an hour, then
insulated for about 4 hours. The corn was about the same as
cooking with lime. I wonder if my lime is different than yours.
Store bought hominy has no hulls. Robin, Oregon, December
   Reply: In my experience corn cooked without lime tastes
differently and never gets as tender as lime-cooked corn.
I, too, use slaked lime (also called cool or hydrated). The
hulls definitely slip off when I rub a few of the kernels
between my fingers to test, after corn and water with lime
have come to a boil and simmered about 20 minutes. Gently
kneading the corn during rinsing may help separate the hulls.
   I wonder if lime, both slaked and hot, may undergo changes
if left long (before or after purchase) in an open or porous
container. The lime I bought came in a paper bag. I immediately transferred it to plastic jars with tight fitting lids
and it has kept okay for years now.
   Store-bought hominy seems larger, lighter and softer than
mine. Perhaps it's made from a white, larger variety of corn,
and cooked longer. Maybe more than the outer hull is removed.
Maybe lye is used instead of lime. (?) Julie Summers, April

Sproutman Defends Alfalfa Sprouts
   "There is a toxic substance called canavanine which is a
natural amino acid toxin in alfalfa seed. It acts as an
oxidant which causes free radicals and kills cells.
   "... All of the testing is done on dry (3 or 4 day old)
dehydrated sprouts. They found ... 1½% canavanine.... What
they failed to do is keep things in perspective. Firstly, they
did not grow the sprouts to their full green leaved maturity.
The toxin exists in the seed but as the seed sprouts and trans-
forms into a green plant the toxins diminish. There are
natural plant toxins in all kinds of seeds....
   "In addition there are natural anti-oxidants in alfalfa...
which counteract any possible effects of the canavanine....
Actually fresh green alfalfa sprouts have an anti-cancer effect."
Steve Meyerwitz (Sproutman), from an interview in The Sprout-
letter #20, Jan-Feb84, $1.75/sample, POB 62, Ashland, OR 97520)
   Sproutman may not be an impartial source, but I haven't
seen conclusive evidence against alfalfa sprouts, either.
I continue to eat alfalfa sprouts. Not as many as I used to,
and I'm more careful to eat only mature ones, but they still
seem like a better bet than say commercial lettuce, and they
are more compatable with portable dwelling. I also sprout
fenugreek seeds along with the alfalfa. Haven't heard anything
implicating them; but then nothing clearing them either.
I also sprout peas and lentils. Julie Summers, Oregon, May

A Survival Kit Worn Almost All the Time
   I wear a hunter's belt pouch with a brass can (about
snuff box size) full of fishing gear, needles, pins, etc.,
a good folding knife (Swiss Army style), compass, magnifying
glass, a match safe, etc. almost all the time. A space
blanket in a packet, some plastic sheet, and some trail food.
Paul Doerr, Pioneer, California, February 1984

Message Post

Number 19   September 1985

Portable Dwelling Info-letter
6 issues(2 yrs)$5. Sample $1
POB 190, Philomath, OR 97370

Preparing to Winter in a Tleanto

We plan to camp in the mountains this winter. We have most supplies cached and are now preparing the site and cutting the poles. We'll wait until late fall to set up and move in.

The Tleanto is a lean-to within a plastic tent. Like the twipi it has two walls (actually 2½ counting the fly).

Our site has a SSW slope (would prefer S or SE but didn't find one with the other nice attributes).

Craig dug two terraces. The larger lower one will be the floor, the upper one the rear support for the roof poles.

We will cover the ceiling with plastic in back but with old sheets in front to let moisture out. On top we will pile leaves for insulation (moss might be better but not plentiful).

The front wall will be four layers of clear plastic spaced apart with some strips of bubbly plastic we found (used for padding when shipping). The end walls will be similar except that the plastic of the east wall will have one corner anchored with elastic straps so that we can squeeze between it and the corner post to go in and out.

The tent will be shaped to match the lean-to but otherwise similar to the Woodland Tent (in LLL catalog), with plastic gathered together to close one end, and entrance covers (cloth top, plastic bottom) over the other.

The lean-to will be 12' long, 6' wide, 5' high in front, 2' high in back. The tent will be 24' long and extends beyond the lean-to to provide an outer room that will

roof beam
fly
cloth
clear plastic
ceiling beam
south
rock
ceiling poles
clear plastic
plastic insulation

(fly is black plastic or cloth - use ball ties to hold out sides)

ground (covering not shown)

be sheltered from the wet but not insulated. Materials, mostly plastic, cost us less than $50. For cooking we have a gas stove (RV salvage, also tank and regulator). The kitchen will be in the outer room, at first anyway, but may try moving it inside the lean-to portion on cold days.

We may put up the tent first for rain protection, with the back side temporarily tied up high for easier working under and for more ventilation while the leaves are drying (if wet).

Our poles are probably stronger than they need be. We didn't try to save on weight because we won't take the poles with us when we leave in the spring - only plastic, cloth and twine. If we come back here next winter we'll use the same poles. If we go somewhere else we'll cut new poles. Poles aren't hard to get here.

We have spent three summers and parts of springs camped around here. This will be our first winter. Suggestions are welcome. Our last mail run will be early November.
Wanda, California, July

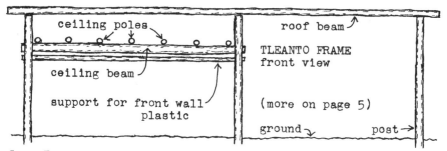

ceiling poles

ceiling beam

support for front wall
plastic

roof beam

TLEANTO FRAME
front view

(more on page 5)

ground   post

Gore Tex Has a Life Expectancy of Two Years,
then doesn't work any more, according to a report in June 1985
Signpost by Ann Marshall, the editor.

Liner Bag Added Warmth but Got Stinky
This summer, while bivying in Eugene for a couple of
nights, I tried using a large plastic bag as a vapor barrier
inside of a light weight sleeping bag.
The liner did seem to add warmth. I don't know how much
was due to higher humidity (because the liner didn't pass
moisture), and how much was due to additional loft (the liner
bag was wider than the sleeping bag so there were many wrinkles).
Though I didn't sweat noticably, after a few hours the
liner felt sticky and clung to my skin, so when I turned over
the liner turned with me. That wasn't particularly annoying.
After the first night I didn't notice much odor. However
after the second night, the liner bag and my whole body stank
- much like my feet do if I wear shoes all day.
I don't know the cause of this stink but I suppose it
might be that the higher humidity or less air circulation
allows bacteria to grow that wouldn't otherwise, and they are
what stink. (Otherwise why should feet smell differently than
hands? They have similar structure and kinds of skin.)
The plastic bag seemed clean before my bivy. (From a
furniture store I think. Might have had cushions shipped in it.)
The first night I wore a T shirt but no pants. The second
evening I showered lightly with water (no soap) before sacking
out, but didn't attempt to wash the bag. The second night I
wore nothing.
I wonder if others who use vapor barrier liners have
trouble with odors developing and what you do about it.
I notice that Stephenson recommends wearing pajamas inside
his vapor barrier lined bags. Bert, Oregon, August.

I Sleep With Socks On
For a long time I resisted wearing socks in bed, thinking
I shouldn't need them. But now I accept them - and no longer
spend half the night with cold feet. I also wear hat and
dicky on colder nights. Julie Summers, Oregon, July

Improvised Hot Water Bottles
A quart bleach bottle with tight fitting cap works but
does not conform to body contours. So I experimented with
using multiple layers of plastic produce bags. I made sure
the inner few bags were free of leaks. I used about five or
six layers in all for strength. I tied each bag shut with
many turns of a rubber band. Tho I was careful not to put
my weight on this container, it was not as fragile as I'd
expected. Its main drawback seems to be lack of easy emptying
and refilling. But it's an option to be aware of, in the

event of certain injuries. When using any hot water bottle, do be careful to cover the container with cloth at first when it's very hot so the skin isn't burned. Julie, Oregon, July

Staying Comfortable During Winter Camping

So far I've been heating my tent with a kerosene lamp. I also use a hot water bottle at the foot of my sleeping bag. The lamp adds maybe 5-10 degrees, but the bottle seems to make a bigger difference in comfort. Drinking a lot of hot tea helps ward off the cold too. I'd rig up a stove like in MP #16 but the shelter's too small. If it gets much colder I'll have to expand it some and put one in.

I think it is possible though to develop considerable resistance to cold by staying continuously outdoors. "Primitive" peoples in cold climes often impressed white explorers and anthropologists with their capacity to endure cold with little apparent discomfort. Though certainly pre- "civilized" white man must have been as well adapted to the cold conditions in native Europe. Possibly going from the tropically heated house to the cold outdoors and back doesn't allow the body's own physiological response to cold to operate. Dennis, Oregon, December

Some Hints for Keeping Warm Without Fire

Add insulation before you begin to feel cold. However avoid insulation-dampening sweat by removing or opening clothing before exercising. Don't smoke (nicotine reduces blood flow to extremities by constriction of vessels). Don't drink alcohol (it increases blood flow to skin, with eventual chilling). Don't jump or wave arms. "The windchill factor is a measure of air movement over your skin; rapid body move- ments always cause some such air movement. If practical, lie down and cover up; then do muscular tension exercises by repeatedly tightening all your muscles so tight that you tremble." (Cresson Kearny, Nuclear War Survival Skills)

"It is very important to prevent heat losses from the head and neck, which have many blood vessels near the skin surface. Heat losses from these vital parts cannot be sensed nearly as well as heat losses from other parts of the body. Furthermore, blood vessels near the surface in the head and neck do not automatically constrict to reduce heat losses, as they do in other parts of the body when heat is being lost faster than it can be supplied by metabolism. So when a person is in the cold, particularly when inactive, he should keep his hands, feet, and whole body warmer by insulating his head and neck very well. (One difficulty in following this advice is that a well-covered head often will feel unpleas- antly warm, even sweaty, before one's body temperature rises enough to increase the warming flow of blood to hands and feet.)

Immersion Rewarms Cold Extremities Faster than Exercise

I use water as hot as I can comfortably stand. Note I'm talking about just cold, not frostbite. When rewarming frost- bitten parts the water temperature is critical: "Higher temperatures (than 108-112°F) produce further damage...." (Medicine for Mountaineering) Julie Summers, Oregon, May

No Advantage of the Alaskan Stove Over a Five Gallon Can

except the metal is heavier and it comes with attachments to burn gasoline, fuel oil, etc. (old mil surplus). Paul, CA, June

Tleanto Versus Twipi

We wonder if you (Bert) thought at all about lean-to shapes when you designed the twipi. The tleanto (p.1) seems to us to have several advantages (we will know better after the winter): admits more light, easier entrance, and simpler to build (fewer poles, no rings).
Esthetically I prefer a twipi, just as I do a tipi over a rectangular tent - round shapes are more natural and pleasing to the eye. But comfort and simplicity come first for us. Wanda, California, July

Reply: Your tleanto looks good to me provided the site isn't too windy. I don't think the outer tent's tall wall will take a strong wind.

The fly and roof may not shed snow (if angled like your sketch). If much accumulates, that will compact the leaves and decrease insulation. That's no problem if there's no snow or if you're there to brush it off as it falls.

The lower portion of the roof may sag enough to lay upon the ceiling. Make sure that the plastic portion of the ceiling cover extends at least that high, else moisture will collect on the underside of the roof, increasing weight and reducing insulation.

Yes, I considered shapes similar to yours. The tleanto will admit more light at your site (south slope, not much shade to south I assume). The twipi provides more light at a site that's level and has high bushes all around. Likewise with entry - depends on the situation. An advantage of the tleanto you didn't mention: it doesn't require soils that drain well (the twipi needs a center hole which, with certain soils and heavy rain, could become a center pool).

On the other hand the twipi has less wind resistance. Also it can shed snow or support an accumulation. I believe that a twipi with a trench entrance would be warmer than a tleanto the same size because you'll lose warm air every time you go between inner and outer rooms.

The twipi requires more poles but they are individually shorter and lighter. (Your ridge beams must be strong and heavy or else you'll need more posts than you've shown.)

A tleanto may be easier to build if built by the designer. But the twipi is easier to explain (because it's symmetrical - all sides identical). That's very important if furnishing detailed plans, which is my intention with the twipi. (But even for it, to give step-by-step instructions that leave nothing to puzzle over, takes lots of time and paper, as I'm learning - 17 pages already written and there may be that many more.) For a builder who wants only a few sketches and hints, there's no problem.

So which is better depends on the situation. Bert, Oregon, August

Hammock Not Very Comfortable for Sleeping

When traveling in wooded country it seems like a hammock would be a convenient bed if the weather wasn't too cold. Just find two trees and sling the hammock and maybe a rain fly and mosquito bar; no ground preparation - moving stones and cones only to find the bumps and hollows are not spaced for comfort.

Awake, I am very comfortable in a hammock - reading, eating, or watching the local wildlife. However when I've tried to nap I've found that my muscles relax and my knees bend backwards and ache. Still, for several years I've wanted to try a hammock for a bed.

Well, it's April Fools night, with a bright gibbous moon high in the sky. Earlier in the evening I tried to arrange my hammock for the night. It took about five minutes just to get the sleeping bag to stay in so I'm apprehensive about the whole operation....

Well, I stayed with it all night and did sleep, though there were some discomforts. My knees did hurt from bending backwards, though not unbearably, and could be relieved by turning part way to the side. Also, my heels hurt from pressing through the bag onto the string of the hammock.

I used a short closed-cell 3/8" foam pad between the string hammock and the sleeping bag.

I had the hammock fairly taut tonight. Next time I'll try it with more slack as per Judy Brueske's instructions in MP#13. I think that it would be a very cold way to sleep if the weather was colder. Robin, Oregon, April

Carcinogens in Mushrooms and Many Plants

"Most hydrazines that have been tested are carcinogens and mutagens, and large amounts are present in edible mushrooms" including the false morel (Gyromitra esculenta) and commercial mushroom (Agaricus bisporus). Some are so potent that as little as half a microgram caused tumors in test mice.

"Plants in nature synthesize toxic chemicals in large amounts, apparently as a primary defense against the hordes of bacterial, fungal, and insect and other animal predators. Plants in the human diet are no exception." So writes Bruce N. Ames in Science V221, 23 Sep 83.

Ames mentions as containing carcinogens: sassafras (flavoring in root beer), black pepper, parsnips, celery (especially if bruised or diseased), parsley, potatoes (especially if bruised or exposed to light), rhubarb, coffee, cocoa and chocolate, tea, fava beans, mustard and horseradish, cottonseed oil and animals fed cottonseeds, lupine and milk of cows and goats that forage it, poison lettuce (and some new commercial lettuces that have been crossed with it for insect resistance), euphorbiacea (some used in herb teas), alfalfa sprouts (but that finding has been contested - see MP#18p.12), alcohol, molds (which may be on or in corn and other grains, nuts, peanut butter, bread, cheese, fruit, apple juice), beets, spinach, radishes, aged meats especially hamburger (because of rancid fats), and all browned foods such as fried foods, bread crusts and toast.

More domestic than wild plants are suspect, but that may only be because they've been tested more. "... no human diet can be entirely free of mutagens and carcinogens ...."

Many plants also contain anticarcinogens. Vitamin E, B carotene, selenium, glutathione, and ascorbic acid (Vit.C) are some.

Gathering and Selling Mistletoe
A couple of weeks before xmas I met a fellow selling
mistletoe in taverns in NW Portland. He said that he gathered
it in the woods, packaged it in bagies, and made the rounds
of taverns, grossing about $50 per evening. He said that the
tavern owners didn't object. Robin, Oregon, February

An Acquaintance of Mine "Lives" in a Car,
at least during the summer, and has a telephone answering
service so he can maintain a small sales operation. Thus he
escapes paying rent while keeping his independence thru
self-employment. Aarran, British Columbia, June

Using Portable, Mobile, and Underground Shelters
For the past five years we have lived most of the time in
a remote mountainous area. There we use a mix of underground
accomodations (ugas) and lightweight portable structures (tents).
The ugas are used primarily as workshops and storages, but
also provide warm spaces into which all of us can crowd when
the weather turns cold.
During mild spells, varying numbers and combinations of
us (4 adults, 5 kids) leave the ugas and set up tents near by,
so that we can enjoy more space, changes of surroundings, and
easy access to the outdoors. (Even during winter there are
usually some mild and not too wet periods, and camping then is
in some ways more pleasant than during summer when there are
many mosquitos here.)
We forage and fish some but also buy supplies (mostly
grains, some of which we sprout). Most summers here are too
cool and cloudy for gardening to be very productive. We maintain a 5-year food reserve (mostly wheat) which, if outside
supplies were cut off, would provide a long grace period during
which to improve our foraging and horticultural capabilities.
That is our way of life for nine months a year during
which we have no contacts with the outside world except for
infrequent trips for mail and (recently) a radio-telephone.
During summers two of the adults (we take turns) and the
older kids travel in a van, going to mountain gatherings, craft
fairs, cities, harvest areas, and anywhere else we fancy. On
those trips we buy more supplies and sometimes earn money, but
the primary reason for the summer travel is to allow contact
with other people, especially for our kids with other kids.
Tho we sometimes pick crops and we sell a few crafts, our
dwelling ways have been financed principally by savings. We
are now trying to develop freelance work that can be done at
our ugas via radio-telephone.
Our dwelling-way philosophy has become: Do with each
structure or locale only what can be done fairly easily. Fill
other needs in other ways. E.g., for secure work/storage
space we have our ugas, for open spaciousness our tents, and
for access to other people our summer mobility.
Trying to satisfy all wants with a single structure,
place, or dwelling way, can lead to much complexity and many
problems: to 'dream homes and homesteads' that never get past
the dreaming stage, or that do but become nightmares to build,
pay for, and care for.
Ten years ago I built a small semi-portable insulated
structure, similar to the twipi in function tho different in
materials and shape. We still use it some but have not
expanded it or duplicated it. We have evolved away from semi-
portable shelters because they are time consuming to put up

and take down, and too bulky even when disassembled to move easily or to put away securely.

Our ugas can't be moved, but they can be quickly closed up and left with little chance of theft or damage. Our tents aren't insulated, but they can be quickly erected to take advantage of nice weather, and then quickly taken down and moved or stored.

For underground adjuncts to portable dwelling, I suggest beginning with plastic drums and buckets (articles in MP#17 and MP#18) or any other sturdy tight-closing containers you are able to buy, before attempting to build something special. Most of what can be done with an underground work- shop can be done more simply tho not as conveniently by accessing storage containers while living and working in a tent temporarily set up nearby. Hopping Mole, Northwest, May

Breathable Fabrics for Rainware. Desirable?

Gore-Tex and other breathable fabrics have been touted for their ability to pass water vapor outward without passing liquid water inward. But there are contrary views:

"Gore has published interesting data that shows porosity, or the 'breathability' of Goretex (when clean) is 5 or 6 times that of Urethane coated fabric, or about 1/3 that of uncoated fabrics. Their tests show that for active hiking the porosity will let out about 1/5 of the sweat caused by overheat, for what they consider a typical condition. The obvious question then is, what happens to the other 4/5 of the sweat? The answer is simple: you ventilate by opening the jacket at top and bottom, and/or remove the excess cloth- ing that is causing the overheat.... Side by side testing of identical design jackets made with Goretex and with Urethane coated fabrics, showed no difference in sweating....

"All the testing by Gore and others has merely proved that the objective of making porous outer fabric was wrong and unnecessary, and that it led to serious problems of lack of waterproofness. We understand that Gore has made signifi- cant changes in Goretex, reducing pore size to make it much less sensitive to the wetting effects of dirts (and also making it less porous).... The question remaining is, why pay so much more for it if it offers no advantages, but still may have problems? ...." Jack Stephenson (from Comfort in Camp, Warmlite Catalog 1980 (see listing on page A).

"Our coated Rainwear fabrics have no 'breathable pores' because we have found that even the tiniest micro-hole can eventually diminish a fabric's impermeability. And we've concluded that none of the 'waterproof/breathable' fabrics that we've tested offer enough breathability to make a notic- able difference in a person's comfort.

"The best way to ventilate, we have found, is also the simplest. We call it the 'chimney' effect.... Cool outside air enters the garment via the bottom edge and cuff. Once inside, this air is warmed by body heat and then rises to escape via the neck. Since warm air can retain more moisture than can cool air, the warming ... vents out moisture....

"Urethane coatings have fallen short of our standards... Wet storage tends to promote peeling and the growth of mildew. Abrasion, too, causes difficulties with urethane-coated fabrics; after one season of hard use, the coating on the wear points of these garments is usually rubbed off...."
(from Patagonia spring 1986 catalog, POB 86, Ventura, CA 93002)

Feedback on Containers for Bike Repair Kits

My tube-repair kit (plastic vitamin bottle with plastic cap) is still doing fine after years. But the cement eventually dried up in my typing-correction-fluid-thinner bottle (MP#16) tho it had remained okay for several months.

Also, I opened a new tube of cement only to find it completely empty, with not even a residue or hint of ever having been filled. A miss at the factory? Its lightness should have clued me. Julie Summers, Oregon, April

Tortilla Suggestions, Lime Source, Cooking Time

I called a nutritionist here about the lime to use in making tortillas. She said don't use the lime from the garden store or feed store because it may be contaminated. So we got some lime (called "Cal") from the Mexican grocery store. It cost 39¢ a pound which I don't consider too bad since one uses so little of it.

I find the length of cooking time for the whole corn changes the taste. One of my boys won't eat the tortillas if the corn is cooked more than two hours. They have a flavor slightly like coffee. Also the trick to flexible tortillas is getting the right amount of water in the dough. Make it as wet as you can and still be able to press it out. Anne, CA, June

Making Seed Milk

In my processing hardware, one of the most important things is my set of separation screens or sieves. My favorite looks like a little wooden drum of about 5" diameter. The sides are around 2½" high and the bottom has course weave cloth attached to the sides with string. These are a couple of dollars or so in Mexico and the design has stood the test of time.

The next time you are prompted to throw out the seeds in a melon, don't. Just grind the seeds and dump the gruel in the seine. As you bang the seine from side to side in a bowl, the seed milk will automatically separate in short order.

If I'm turning out a lot of milk I use a larger screen door screen shaped like a dunce hat. A sewing machine and tough nylon thread will turn these out in seconds. The mesh can easily be squeezed and produce the seed milk faster. Not quite as easy to clean but still simple and fast.

Seed milk can be made from many types of seeds and a little honey or carob flavor will make it a neat treat. Much more nutritious than the stuff that passes for milk in a store. Sesame seeds are great for a close cows milk imitation. Al Fry, California, April

We Make a Delicious Bread by Soaking Whole Grain Overnight,
then grinding it in the Corona Mill. Form into a loaf - no salt, yeast, nothing but a little extra water. Wrap in aluminum foil and pressure cook about 45 minutes. Some times we add ground beans or soy flour to our bread, or maybe grated carrots, but it's always unleavened these days. Easy. Anne

There Are Many People Living Nomadic Lives.
They move all the time. They are owlhooters. They work at various things from prospecting and treasure hunting to lapidary, bounty hunting, collecting antiques and bottles, to doing carpentry, repairs, consulting. Others live as house-sitters, retired in trailer and campers. Some live cheap, get short-time work usually cash to just get enough $ to live. Paul Doerr, CA

Message Post

Number 20

Portable Dwelling Info-letter
6 issues(2 yrs)$5. Sample $1
April 1986   POB 190, Philomath, OR 97370

Camping Out With a Young Child

We camped out with Zak (1½ years old) for about five months this year, 1½ miles from highway, 1/3 mile walk-in to wooded site. It was challenging as he acts like a baby. We learned lots about: emotions, fears, clothing, exploring, fooding, playing, and elimination. Kids naturally imitate us on many levels, including our unconscious fears and feelings.

Clothing and shoes: He seems warm and prefers to be naked and barefoot more than we do.

Bug bites. We let them bite him and put wet bentonite clay on the bites. They seemed to heal fast. There were plenty of bugs. He seemed to get immune to them after a few weeks.

Fears. We recognize them as okay, self-set limits, that we best reflect. We show him something is okay by doing it or touching it. But we accept his feelings. We respect his readiness and unpredictable willingness to test and trust new things. We also let him touch fire, get burned a little, and quickly learn not to. He never cut himself with sharp knives we left open in kitchen.

Elimination. We let naked Zak poop and pee outside anywhere. We covered it with dirt and he copied that. He learned fast to 'go' out of bed. His and our 'going' on arising and after meals is natural and predictable. We usually sleep together.

Fooding. He'd often go berry picking (and poop) before we got up. Or we'd give him fruit or rice-cake before we ate. His awareness of natural food combining (yin & yang) was/is nil. He had his own cloth to eat on, which he'd bring (when hungry) to us.

Exploring. At our camp on small ridge he'd wander around out of sight each day and return. It was safe, tho he'd get scratched, fall, etc., to feel. (Much of the time) he preferred to be with us or near by.

Playing with curiosity - is Zak's main job. We brought toys to our camp: kids pool, balls, geo-toys, etc., but he loves to play with our paper, clothes, food, cats, pillows, sticks, dirt, water. We play with him: carry, tickle, throw, cuddle, massage, tease, chase, laff, and swing him around daily. He loves to be carried. He cries easily but soon returns to playing. He lights our life with fun feeling and ease or mystery of simple needs. Mycall Sunanda, Oregon, Oct.

Shelter Systems' Clips

Besides gathering up less material (than does a ball tie), the clip also allows a perpendicular pull from the center of the sheet without twisting the film. They also function nicely to join sheet materials together.

Materials can be shingled, then clipped together. (That is how we make a) 17' diameter shelter, (which) can be constructed out of a variety of films. It cannot leak, yet because it's shingled it breathes.

Shows inner ring, wrapped with plastic, being passed thru outer ring.

Some sections can be clear to let in light, others dark (opaque) to provide cool shade.

Multiple liners are easy to hang (each part of a clip has holes, so any number of clips can be tied to each other).

Small clips are 60¢ each, large clips $1.20, Basic Shelter plans $5 (review on page 7). Bob Gillis, Shelter Systems, Box 67, Aptos, CA 95001 (408)662-2821; March

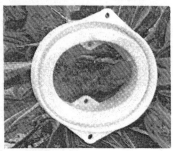

Shelter Systems' Clips Compared to Ball Ties

Bob sent me samples. The large clip, about 4x5", is oval shaped which makes it easy to attach anywhere onto fabric or plastic. The small clip, about 2", is round and one part must be squeezed very hard (Barb needed wide-jaw pliers) to slip over the other part if attaching to the middle of the fabric. (Close to the edge, the fabric can be worked around the parts, rather than slipping one part over the other as shown on page one.)

I tested the clips first with pieces of unreinforced plastic, matching them against ball ties of various sizes, pulling until something gave. The small clip held about as well as does a 3/4" ball tie. (Usually the plastic ripped, close to the clip or ball tie. If the plastic was thin and wet, it sometimes slipped thru the clip.)

I then tried samples of reinforced plastic supplied by Shelter Systems. With the strength of my arms, I could neither rip the plastic or break the clip.

The small clip gathers up the fabric or plastic no more than does a 1/4" ball tie (which would be much weaker than the clip). The large clip gathers as much as does a 1/2" ball tie. So the clips allow the fabric to be stretched smoother, with less puckers and pockets.

(A ball tie is made by bunching the fabric over a smooth pebble or wad of leaves and tying a cord around the neck of the bundle, as shown.)

(A picture on p.2 MP#6 shows how a clip is used to fasten the canopy of a dome to the frame.) Hank

Wintering in a Yurt in the Back Yard

Last year we built our yurt and started living in the back yard. We used Chuck & Laurel Cox's plans for the frame but made our cover by lashing on old blankets and cheap blue plastic tarps. (Their plans have a mistake. They tell you to get much less canvas than you would need to make a tailored cover.)

The insulation is essential when it's hot as there's only one place to put it in our little backyard, so we can't avoid the sun. With just the tarps it would go over 100° on a warm day inside. We roll the sides up to let in the breezes and it's lovely inside.

We have a translucent plastic tarp made from a paint drop "cloth" to pull over the opening in the roof.

We had trouble with leaks at first because the tarps had tiny cracks and holes in them caused by taking them on and off a lot last summer. At least that's the best we can figure because we can't see any holes. So we put another layer of tarps on top of the old ones and no more leaks.

We put it on a platform made of wooden pallets for the wet season since the yard floods in a good rain.

This winter brought a lot more frost than usual. But we did fine without heat - just put on lots of clothes. Our record low inside was 30°F one morning. Sometimes our two-year-old cried because his hands got cold. He doesn't understand how to warm his hands in his pockets. But the two older boys never complained once of the cold. In fact they never complain about any of the tent chores, like they did of the house chores. We even got bad colds during the worst of the cold weather, but everyone got better in the usual way.

We all love our yurt even if it is in a big city back-yard, and we dream of a more pleasant location. But even here we have the sky to admire.

But we have run into an unsolved obstacle: the stove. Everything we've tried makes either my husband or myself sick. Woodsmoke makes me cough, propane makes my husband pass out, and charcoal and alcohol give us both headaches. So we are in a yurt on the end of a long extension cord cooking on a hot plate, which crashes our dream of getting out of here. Does anyone have any ideas about non-polluting heat sources?
Anne Callaway, California, January

Hammock is Not Very Comfortable for Sleeping

My latest string hammock is a Minipak, distributed by EZ Sales & Mfg, Gardena CA. $6.29 at BiMart. 20 feet long (ropes and all), 7 feet wide, 8 oz. "Supports $\frac{1}{4}$ ton."

I am very comfortable in it when awake: reading, eating, or watching wildlife. However when I have tried napping, my muscles relax and my knees bend backwards and ache.

I tried sleeping in it April Fools night. Took 5 minutes just to get the sleeping bag to stay in. I remained in it all night and did sleep despite some discomforts. Turning part way to the side helped my knees. Also, my heels hurt from pressing through the bag onto the string of the hammock.

I had the hammock fairly taut tonight. Next time I'll try it with more slack as Judy Brueske suggested in MP#13.

I used a short closed-cell 3/8" foam pad between the hammock and the sleeping bag. I think it would be a very cold way to sleep if the weather was colder. Robin, Oregon, April

Tips for Vehicle Camping

Park out of view (outa-sight, outa-mind) and don't block any roads or trails. Scope the area out carefully if you plan to stay more than one day.

Keep your vehicle reliable and ready to move on short notice. If someone comes to harass you, promptly move on.

Don't litter the area around your vehicle. If you bring out equipment to make a dinner or whatever, afterwards put everything back in. If staying months, this gets harder as we tend to accumulate useful stuff. Stack it neat, or even under the vehicle, and never accumulate more than you can leave with in one trip. For extended living, consider getting a rental storage unit if one is near.

If someone offers you space to park and you accept, do some work for them - MORE than an even exchange. That impresses them and they will hold a good feeling about you, which could work into a longer term arrangement, a temporary job, or whatever. Offer and DO help them. Rick, ID, Febr.

More About the 12-volt Washing Machine

I have been using it for about one year, purchased through J.C.Whitney. Prior to purchase, my laundry costs were $5 to $7 per week, so payback would be 22 to 30 weeks. It outlived its payback and is still going strong. It's load is limited to 4½ pounds (2 jeans + 2 T shirts + 4 socks), and you must supply the cycles (no pump or solenoids). But it cleans fine and I am able to do other things (cook, write, read, etc) while it runs. Katcha Sanderson (from PV Network News, Feb 1986)

Figure Out Simple AND QUICK Ways

Thanks for the info (in MP#21   and above) on the 12-v washer. Much too small for a family of five. And I know from my Amish hand-agitated washer, that manually changing water - wringing clothes; waiting for it to drain, then refill, etc. - takes much time. That's the challenge with simple systems and family life: time and energy are so limited, compared to before children. So we have to be extra creative. Azima, CA

Tips for Washing Clothes by Hand

Try to wash regularly before soiling "sets". Put clothes in a 5 gal bucket (plastic doesn't rust) with water and let soak several hours. Use pole to agitate/push. Let set. Agitate again. Dump out and let drain. Let soak in clean water. Agitate. Dump out and let drain. Repeat until rinsed. Hang. The soaking softens and loosens the dirt. "Rubbing" needed is usually minimal. Another way to agitate is to use a tub and walk on the clothes. Feet washed free. Paul Doerr, CA

If Driving, Use Road as Agitator.

Take a clean garbage can, secure in the rear of a truck or auto, and fill with dirty clothes and soapy water. Drive to town or wherever on errands. That should yield clean, soapy clothes. Rinsing is up to you. Jon, Michigan, August

Spider Tent

Find a frozen lake to pitch a seasonal tent on its thick ice. Spike, then fasten eight telescopic poles to the hub on top. Whether circular or octagonal, this tent would be suspended. A center pole keeps the height. It prevents excess bounce. A small hole in the floor makes it easy to enjoy ice fishing. A flap on the side barely allows entrance using a rope ladder. If it's freely attached, like a curtain, it revolves in wind. Reached by ski mobile, this warm island is an intricate place. Kned Knowlton, Massachusetts, October

Teaching Natural Living and Eating

This year I taught a class in "Natural Living and Eating" to nine young handicapped and retarded kids. Because I wanted to get away from emphasis on any kind of conventional modern "health" pressure, I got a book about North American weeds and herbs and wild plants, drew the pictures, xerox-copied them, put info on everything they were used for - food, dye, medicine, light, cleaning pots and pans. Jane, Colorado

We <u>Live</u> in <u>a</u> <u>Float-House</u> in <u>the</u> Johnstone Straits.
Our mail is very irregular up here. Eleanore, BC, January

<u>Camping</u> <u>During</u> <u>the</u> <u>Cold</u> <u>Spell</u>
    I was iced in for two weeks because of an icy hill.
I walked to the bus and went to town a couple of times but
didn't try to work for money then.
    I'm now parked in the woods, near an old abandoned farm-
site. I fire the wood stove mornings and evenings. My stove
has a good draft and I bring dry wood so my fire causes
little smoke.
    I sleep with a knit hat on, all but warm nights. In
cold weather or when I'm cold, I use a quart bleach bottle,
covered with a thick sock, as a hot water bottle at the foot
of the bed. Also, sometimes, one in the middle of the bed
next to me. Robin, Oregon, December

<u>Alcohol</u> <u>May</u> <u>Improve</u> <u>Heat</u> <u>Distribution</u>
    When you have surplus heat in one area of body, and are
still cold in another, drink a <u>little</u> alcohol. Works wonders
for heat <u>distribution</u>. But, if you're chilled overall and
still in cold place, <u>don't</u> drink alcohol - improved circulation can increase heat loss rate. A little alcohol will make
warm up in a hot tub much faster. Jack Stephenson, NH, Sept.

<u>Strongly</u> <u>Advocates</u> <u>Using</u> <u>a</u> <u>Liner</u>, <u>and</u> <u>Sleeping</u> <u>Nude</u> <u>Within</u> <u>It</u>
    A liner will make your sleeping bag last much longer,
make washing the bag unnecessary, keep it cleaner and a lot
warmer, without adding much weight. Ordinary muslin makes a
good liner and for winter a very light flannel will add many
degrees of warmth.
    "... if you are dressed in fur underwear inside the
sleeping bag (as did Nansen and Johansen), the invisible
perspiration will condense either on the outside of your
underwear or inside the bag. In either case, when you turn
over in your sleep, you will melt some of the hoar frost, and
that will make you wet. Accordingly the way to keep dry is
to sleep naked. Steffanson's men tried very light pajamas
in the sleeping bags and found they added nothing ...."
(<u>Arctic</u> <u>Manual</u>, Air Corps, 1940)
    Thus I strongly support getting out of sweaty dirty
clothes at night and sleeping nude in a nice clean liner. In
the case of couples, a double sleeping bag with two bodies
will add much warmth in cool weather and it is very simple to
sew up a double liner to fit a double bag. The liner in all
cases should be washed after each trip or, in the case of
longer trips, each week, and aired in sun daily if possible.
Major Lyman F. Barry, New York, September

<u>Nylon</u> <u>Bed</u> <u>Sheets</u> <u>are</u> <u>the</u> <u>Best</u> <u>Thing</u> <u>Since</u> <u>Knit</u> <u>Hats</u>
for sleeping gear. They don't hold dampness like cotton does
and so they warm up fast when I get in bed. Another advantage
was that, on a dry day, they dried so fast that I could wash
them in the afternoon and use them the same night. Before
trying them I thought they would be cold and uncomfortable.
Instead they feel satiny and very luxurious. Robin, OR, Aug.

<u>I</u> <u>Love</u> <u>the</u> <u>Challenge</u> <u>of</u> <u>Warming</u> <u>My</u> <u>Body</u> <u>Outside</u>,
going barefoot and in wintertime by doing various body games.
First you have to overcome the victim-of-cold-weather attitude
.... Dancing and jogging around in circles is invigorating.
I've been camping out alone since 1971 - yoga since 1971.
Mycall Sunanda, OR, Oct.

Be Aware of Bear

Be careful around mountain areas with large wild animals. I love the wildlife as much or more than most, as I live in their midst year around, but I have a number of observations that readers might someday appreciate.

Keep your distance - a big distance from bear or moose. These two animals are incredibly strong and can be deadly. I've seen a "small" black bear turn over a boulder with one swipe of his(her?) paw that I couldn't even move with all my strength. I've seen bears rip apart an 18" diameter stump in seconds, pieces flying 30 feet.

Bears are really fast. I've seen a 500 pound black bear move at 30 mph (i.e. cover 100 yards in 7 seconds) in 6 foot high brush. They mow down small trees and make quite a racket in the otherwise quiet woods. Bears, if they so desire, can always outrun people.

Most wild animals are fairly mellow by nature unless provoked. However some suddenly get angry for little or no apparent reason. Moose are usually very mellow, but in autumn have been known to charge anyone/anything without warning.

I personally believe that one can somewhat disarm anger from some animals by talking gently to them. But this is usually prior to an outburst or a charge by the animal. Once a moose is in a charge, your only hope is to get behind or up a very stout tree.

A lot depends on when you saw/were seen by the animal. Most animals will run away as people approach, but you and he/she may not see each other until you are only a few feet apart! Be nice but by all means be wary! Move away - back off gently and directly away (or toward trees).

I do not see the need of carrying a gun on casual hikes to/from your camp. There are exceptions. When going into wild territory, where people rarely go, is one. When in Alaska or northwest Canada, I recommend you do carry one, always. A shotgun with large buckshot or slugs is best. You must be conscious of the fact that you are entering an animal's territory in some cases, and that they look at you as an intruder, even if you are a gentle vegetarian.

If you are in a dangerous area and do choose to go in armed, be skilled and carry it loaded. At 30 yards a bear can be on you in 2¼ seconds.

I believe you can go into a wild area and enjoy a beautiful, mind opening experience like nowhere else on earth. Just be conscious of the realities of your adventure. Go in for the peace of it but go prepared for the extremes it can sometimes dish out.

We have several moose who winter on our hill. We have many black bears in spring and summer. Deer ravage my garden and orchard every few days and can jump 8 foot fences without any problem. What they don't get, rabbits and little gophers do. We have coyotes in packs of 3 to 10, and an occasional cougar. Rick, ID, Aug.

(Reports and comments about bears also in MP#7 , MP#8 , MP#9 ,MP19)

What Will Scare Away Bears or Dogs?
Will a SuperSound compressed air horn?

Underground Adjuncts to Portable Dwelling
(Continued from MP#19.)

Our experience with underground structures has been entirely in areas with mild winters where frost does not usually penetrate as deep as the structure.

In response to (MP#11p.16 & MP#13p.4) much soil is strong enough for a narrow unbraced tunnel that will be used for only a few years, in my experience. The fact that an open embankment erodes does not necessarily mean that a narrow tunnel will; the bank is more subject to frost. To test, dig a tunnel, only as deep as you can reach without crawling into it, and close it off. Check it in a year.

If digging an unbraced tunnel that a person will enter, I keep it shallow - the ceiling only a foot or two below the surface, so that a cave in won't be very dangerous. Depth will be influenced by soil conditions. Often the top soil with root reinforcement is strongest. Sometimes a clay sub-soil will hold together better than the top soil.

I dig a tunnel as narrow as I can, no wider than 2 feet, for strongest ceiling and least chance of caving. Shape the ceiling like an arch, not flat.

Cover dirt with plastic so that it doesn't dry out and flake off. Close off the tunnel when not occupied so that the walls don't freeze and then spall.

However I haven't found unbraced tunnels, or even artificial caves braced with timbers and lined with plastic, to be very useful. Caving hasn't been much of a problem, but moisture has, and animals can burrow in. You can get around these problems by putting everyting away in strong containers, but if that's necessary it may be easier to just shallowly bury the containers.

We've not tried using natural caves or abandoned mines. Most are damp. Some are unsafe. Most that are easily found, are known to and attractive to spelunkers or rock hunters.

I've heard that plastic septic tanks must be kept full of liquid once buried (and the instructions with one I looked at said so). They aren't strong enough to resist soil pressures for long without equalizing pressure inside.

Whether or not needed for warmth, insulation may be desirable for dryness; else expect condensation on the walls. Put a vapour barrier, such as plastic, between the chamber and the insulation as well as between the insulation and the dirt, so that moisture in the air doesn't pass from ... the chamber into the insulation and condense.

If you build something that you hope to use for several years or longer, access is as important as structure. (If you can't go to your dream den without wearing a conspicuous trail to the hatch, then it affords little more protection against thieves or molesters than would a strong cabin (which is easier to build).) Each solution must be special and personal; requiring knowledge of the area, and imagination. There's a wide variety of good solutions. We've never suffered loss or damage by animals or humans to any completely buried structure or container.

I can't say the same for rented storage space.) Figure out the access and test it before building the structure.

I suggest reading The $50 & Up Underground House Book, by Mike Oeler, which, however, concerns earth-sheltered houses rather than completely underground structures. (The Next Whole Earth Catalog 1980 lists it as 112p. $7 postpaid, Mole Publishing Co, Rt 1 Box 618, Bonners Ferry ID 83805.) Hopping Mole, Northwest, May85

Living on Wheels in New Mexico

I'm in a nice, warm trailer but my only hookup is water. My electric comes from two solar panels and deep cycle batteries. For waste disposal I use two "Blue Boys", one for grey water and one for black water. For toteing them to the dump I devised a hookup to trailer hitch.

There are others here that boondock free, carrying their water, etc. and use generators for power. To conserve battery power I use kerosene lamps which I am writing this by.

My lot fee is only $20 per month which includes the fee for shed I have installed on ranch.

I am living very comfortably and beating the hell out of the high cost of living. It's sure better than being a bag lady on the streets. On a small pension, my income is highly limited.

I ran from a nice home and comfortable living in the city, close to all the amenities. I had an overwhelming desire to be free of high utilities, insurance, property taxes and all that it takes to uphold what everyone expected of you in that "civilized" environment.

My children sit in their nice big heavily-mortgaged homes and call their mother a "crazy rebel". Crazy? I have been smart enough to escape the shackles of dependency on them or anyone and the resentments that invariably accompany it.

I have no monthly deadlines, no collectors hounding me, no streesees or pressures. I have time to enjoy friends and the real meaning of life. (Another letter in MP#18p.10) Bess, NM, January

Tips for Vehicle Camping

Park out of view (outa-sight, outa-mind), and don't block any roads or trails. Scope the area out carefully if you plan to stay more than a day.

Keep your vehicle reliable and ready to move on short notice; if someone comes to harass you, politely move on and don't drag your feet.

Keep a spotless camp around the vehicle; drag it out, make your dinner or whatever, and put it all back in.

Over a longer stay of months, this gets harder as we tend to accumulate useful stuff. Stack it neat, or even under the vehicle, and never accumulate more than you can leave with in one trip. For extended living, consider getting a rental storage unit if one is near.

If someone offers you space to park, by all means go out of your way to do some work for them, more than an even exchange. It really impresses them and they will hold a good feeling about you, which could work into a longer term arrangement, a temporary job, or whatever. Offer and do help them. Rick, Idaho, Feb 85

Wild Harvest: Edible Plants of the Pacific Northwest.

In this book by Terry Domico, a sharp color photo, line drawing, and highly informative text is provided for each of about 40 plants, explaining how to find, recognize, and prepare them, including info new to me, even tho I've been reading about and using plants for many years.

Bigleaf maple, Acer macrophyllum, has edible yellow flower-clusters. Terry also gives directions for tapping and making syrup from this tree.

Regarding giant horsetail, Equisetum species, "In the very early spring ... dig underneath last year's shriveled stalks. The future shoots are encased in brown sheaths ... atop the long rootstalk and ... resemble tubers."

Buttercup, Rannunculus species, contain a volatile toxic agent that can be removed by boiling." Terry uses the roots, cooked 10 minutes with one water change.

From clover, Trifolium species, "a delicious tea can be made from the flower heads. ... The starchy roots may be dug anytime ..."

To pick red huckleberry, Vaccinium parvifolium, faster, "fashion a comb from some headless nails and a block of wood..."

Flowers and buds of Oregon grape, Berberis aquifolium, "are quite edible".

Some of the plants Terry says were "considered edible in many older books but now seem to be toxic" are braken fern (Pteridium aquilinum), skunk cabbage (Lysichiton americanum), and wild peas (beach pea). To those I would add colts-foot (Petasities species), which Bruce Ames in Science Vol.224, May 18, 1984, says (along with comfry) "contain the very potent carcinogenic pyrrolizidine alkaloids that are widespread in plants."

The book covers all of BC, Washington, Oregon and Idaho, and ±100 miles beyond. It has an index with both common and scientific names, and a one-page bibliography. I found it a delight.

1978, 89pp., $6.95 (postpaid?) in 1985, Hancock House, Big Country Books, 1431 Harrison Ave, Blaine, WA 98230. Review by Julie Summers.

(Reviews of Indian Scout Craft and Wildflower Folklore in MP#19p.8 were by Julie)

Wild Ginger Candy Tastes Good

Recently a hiking magazine said that (wild ginger)"cannot be used as a substitute"(for ginger). However, in Edible Wild Plants of the Western United States, Donald Kirk says, "Any of the species (Asarum) have a rootstock that may be used as a substitute for commercial ginger. It may be dried for storage, or candied by cutting it into short pieces, boiling in water until tender, and then boiling the pieces in a heavy syrup."

I've tasted such candy, made by another member of a wild foods class, and found it good - tasting like commercial ginger. Julie Summers, Oregon, February

Shrink or Select? Your Preference?

Here's a vote for the regular print and against the small print. Jim, CA, Oct

Actually the smaller print is easier for me than the larger. Jane, CO, Oct

Alternative Clothes Washers and Driers Sought

I have lived 12 years here in a large plastic "greenhouse" dome tent, birthed three children here. We have solar and propane and wood.

Do you have any info/sources for washers and driers running on propane/12-volts? Or any other wacky system someone has come up with? I have an Amish hand-agitated washer, and the sun and woodstove for drying, but beautiful as they are, it's so hard in the winter for the whole family - so I'm checking around for ideas. Azima Gillis, California, Oct.

Washers: Might find a used electric washer with burnt out motor and replace with some 12 volt dc motor (I don't believe car starter would stand continuous duty, tho I don't know). You'd have to cycle it by hand, because the washer's wiring and controller won't be adequate for the higher current and lower voltage. You could probably wash lots and lots of clothes by hand in time spent tinkering and making adapters. Also you'd need more power than most PV systems furnish.

Driers: Forget all-electric ones - they need much too much power for a 12 volt PV system. I believe that a drier heated by natural gas (commercial ones) could be adapted to propane by adjusting burners, just as cooking stoves can be. But it would burn lots of propane. Hank, Oregon, November

To Reduce Clothes Washing Needed, Wear Thin Outers, Mini Inners

Use outer garments that are a single layer of lightweight nylon (or other synthetic) which is easy to wash and dry. Next to skin, wear cotton bikini underpants, and a cotton T-shirt cut down to cover arm pits and little else; which are easy to wash because small. The idea is for the easily washed outer and inner garments to catch most of the dirt and odors, and keep the warm, bulky, difficult-to-wash in-between garments cleaner longer. Barb & Hank, Oregon, November

Vapor Barriers Sometimes Promote, Sometimes Inhibit Bacteria

On your comments of using plastic vapour barrier liner in sleeping bag (MP#19 p.2): I find it most interesting because we find no change in feet between using no vapor barrier, plastic, or the urethane laminate. But we do notice that if feet are washed well, there is no odor build up on one day, slight the second, bad the third.

In sleeping bags, and vapor barrier shirts and pants, we've noticed a definite reduction in underarm odor, even after a week of wear without washing.

I've suspected that normal vapor barrier shirt and bag liners exclude enough oxygen to stop aerobic bacteric, which are primarily responsible for under arm odors, but, don't exclude enough oxygen to promote anerobic bacteria (responsible for foot odors). Use of plastic sack wrapped around you probably made a much tighter air seal, promoting anerobic bacteria. It'd be a good idea to repeat the test, but after thorough washing to remove any dirt and bacteria.

Incidentally, the odor build up in polypropolene underwear is likely due to similar effect, since it doesn't wick water, and thus holds a layer of water tightly over skin and excludes oxygen. Jack Stephenson, Warmlite, NH, September

Wetwear Improvised from Garbage Bags

There is a wrinkle we use in the ER here where I work that might be useful outdoors, with some adaptations.

(When a total body scrub is needed, the nurse) utilizes

three large garbage bags, as a sort of proximity suit (over
the uniform to keep it clean). One bag is cut to provide arm
and head holes, and each of the other two are delegated to
one foot/leg each. We secure each leg bag with a lengthy
piece of adhesive tape, but I don't see why a person interested in recycling the whole thing couldn't secure them with string
something similar, winding it about the leg/foot like a sandal
of the Roman era. Extra layers of string/tape about the foot
and ankle give the arrangement greater life and traction, and
also serve to minimize the baggy nature of the garment.
    Be warned, however, that all that plastic is very hot,
and you just might get as wet under the plastic as from the
wetness outside. Jon, Detroit MI, January

Naturally Available No-Weight Rain Gear
    Hikers have probably found that hiking in a waterproof
raincoat means you are drenched in perspiration before long,
although protected from rain. I well remember one trip when
the rain came down in buckets and we put all our clothes in
waterproof packs and hiked down from the mountain top to our
parked car, getting in one by one, drying off and putting on
our DRY clothes. Luckily we met no park rangers or others to
be shocked by our nudity. Major Lyman F. Barry, NY, Sept.

Nuclear Radiation from Lamp Mantles Negligible, Claims Aladdin
    In MP#19   Robin asked for further information on the
possible radiation danger from gas lamp mantles.
    Briefly, the Aladdin reply (in Countryside, Nov. 1983)
states that if you were exposed through "... 26 two-day camping trips in one year using two double-mantled lanterns and
four replacement mantles.", you would receive a total body
exposure of 0.03 to 6.0 millirems. This compares to a normal
environmental exposure (cosmic, external terrestrial and
radionuclides in the body itself) of 100 mrem per day. It
also noted that even if you ingested a whole mantle, the
exposure would only be a maximum of 200 mrem. It went on to
note, "In fact, the Nuclear Regulatory Commission, in a
recent review of these (thorium-coated) mantles, concluded
that the small quantities of thorium contained in mantles
creates no unreasonable health risks to the public.
Ken Scharabok, Ohio, September

Aladdin Lamp Doesn't Burn Diesel Fuel Well
    I've been reading of some detrimental effects of winter
darkness on our body and brain chemistry and so, this fall,
I have been supplementing my propane light with the Aladdin.
    I've found that it will burn diesel fuel but only about
2/3 as bright as with kerosene. With diesel the mantle tends
to carbon up more and the wick seems to burn up faster. On
cold mornings the mantle wouldn't glow unless the diesel was
warmed. I've put the lamp on the stove and heated it until
warm to the touch. Diesel is about half the price of kero....
    I've been using the Aladden almost every day. It puts
out so much heat that I now build a fire only on the coldest
mornings and evenings and then only to get the temperature up
to 70°. The Aladdin and propane lamps combined will then
maintain a comfortable temperature with vents open a little.
It looks like $10 (5 gal) of kerosene will last till the end
of Feb. which will make 2½ months. I could do away with
building wood fires for heat if I was willing to burn the
propane heater for 20 minutes morning and evening. Robin,
Oregon, Dec. & Feb.

More About Insulative Cooking

Heidi Kirschner's recipe for cooking yeast bread using boiling water and insulation works great. The recipe is in her book **Fireless Cookery** (reviewed MP#16   p.5).

Essentially, you make a yeast dough. Put the dough in a greased bowl covered with aluminum foil. Put that in a larger covered pot with 5 cups of boiling water. Simmer 30 minutes. Insulate - in our case we bury the pot in a big box of rags and old clothes. She says it will be done in 3 hours, but we always leave it over night and have warm fresh bread for breakfast. It looks a bit funny since there's no crust, but the texture of the bread is so moist and light - much tastier than regular oven bread, in our opinion.

We cook our beans and rice all the time using a "cooker" made of a large round bottom bag full of crumpled sheets of newspaper. The sides are stiffened with cardboard.

Her directions for a cloth bag cooker are unnecessarily complicated. All you really need is a container 4" larger than your pot, in all directions. Wedge the crumpled papers in around the pot. They stay in place well enough when you remove the pot. I did make a round "pillow" filled with crumpled papers to fill in the top of the bag. But loose crumpled sheets would work fine too. The whole thing is made out of scraps I ripped out of old blue jeans. When we move or if something spills - I'll just toss out the old paper and put in new ones. It takes a lot less than one newspaper to insulate my "cooker bag".

I cook breakfast and lunch at the same time. When we get back from where ever we've been, our lunchtime pot of beans is hot and ready to dish up from the cooker. That's wonderful when you've got little kids around. Anne Callaway, CA, Jan.

Lime Feedback

Replying to Anne in MP#19   , to make hominy I use "Snowflake Hydrated Lime" which I bought at a feed/garden store in 1981 at $1.95 for 10 pounds. In 1983 I queried the manufacturer, Ash Grove Cement Co. (who has lime plants in Springfield MO and in Portland OR) about the suitability of their product for cooking with corn.

They replied, "We have sold lime to some commercial establishments for use in corn-cooking, as our product does meet all requirements of Food Chemicals Codex for application in food and drug processes." They also enclosed "Typical Chemical Analyses" of both their Quicklime and Hydrated Lime. No lead was detected in any. Arsenic was 1.63 parts per million (for hydrated lime from OR plant). Fluorine was 0.21 p.p.m. Aluminum oxide was 0.27%. Available calcium hydroxide was 97.51%. Silica 0.24%, etc.   Julie Summers, Feb.

Wheelskin Moccasin Feedback

I was surprised how comfortable the wheelskin mocs were when used while packing heavy loads in the woods. They are also very gentle on the trail and help keep from scuffing up dirt with repeated passes. I've been wearing them all summer while walking in the woods near camp. The design I used (MP#16   ) lets in some dirt and water at the heel. I want to make another pair with a heel more like your design and with smaller lacing holes. I used a paper punch on the first pair. Robin, Oregon, August

Message Post

Portable Dwelling Info-letter
6 issues(2 yrs)$5. Sample $1
POB 190, Philomath, OR 97370

Number 21   June 1986

How to Thin a Skissle - I Mean Skin a Thistle
        First I choose a young, pliable looking
specimen, tho if the plant is older, the top
few inches may still be tender.
        I clear an area on the stalk of prickers
with my pocket knife, cutting down, towards
the base of the plant, and not
worrying about conserving edible
tissue. Then I "fell" the brute
with a horizontal cut at the bottom
of the defenseless area. I can now
hold the prickerless part with one
hand and cut and peel off the rind
with my knife hand. (It's easier to
work on the plant when it's horizontal, and in my hand where I can
rotate it.)
        Now, to conserve edible tissue,
I peel thinly. Once the knife starts the cut, the rind on some
plants peels off as easily as strings off some stalks of celery.
But more often the job requires quite a bit of cutting - sort
of like stripping stubborn-to-get-off bark from a twig.
        I keep peeling with the knife and pulling with my fingers
(careful to avoid getting pricked) as close to the very tip as
possible, because that's the tenderest morsel. (Tho tougher
parts may be chewed on, and the residue spit out, or only the
pith eaten.)
        Before chomping on the stalk I inspect for overlooked
prickers - it's easy to miss fine downy ones; but also easy to
spot them by proceeding slowly and cautiously.
        I don't eat plants likely to have been treated with
pesticides, or within about 20 yards of roads (I've read that
lead contamination drops off beyond that).
        Thistles are of the composite (Sunflower) family. Canad-
ian thistle, Cirsium, is one common genera. (The globe artichoke, cultivated for its succulent flower heads, is of the
same family, but of the thistlelike genus Cynara.)
        In Edible Native Plants of the Rocky Mountains (U. of NM
Press, 1967), Harrington says "As far as we know any species
of thistle can be used as food if taken in the right stage and
suitably prepared." (Tho I've heard that some thistles may
contain toxic levels of nitrates in their roots. I don't know
if this might apply to all of a certain species, or only to
plants under certain growing conditions such as where much
urine is deposited (barnyards) or where nitrogen fertilizers
are used.   ?)
        As well as eating raw stems, I've eaten cooked leaves,
after first cutting off the stickers with a scissors. Lots of
work. I don't plan on it again. Harrington ate "young leaves
raw as a kind of salad and they were just fair." He also ate
cooked roots and crowns and tho the older roots were a bit
fibrous, he found the crowns mild and pleasant tasting. He
said the flowers were "rather fuzzy or cottony tasting when
eaten raw," tho he said horses nip off the flowers of some
species. He ate the seedlike fruits raw and found them
bitter - less so if roasted.
        Next time you walk into a thistle, instead of cursing it,
eat it!   Julie Summers, Oregon, July 1985

Harvesting and Eating Thistle Roots

In October I experimented with thistle (Cirsium) roots. Towards the end of the month I dug up some roots of plants that had died back. The leaves were brown and withered and the dried flower stalks were still standing. After washing the roots, which were hard, I chewed one; it was like trying to eat a stick. I didn't cook any because I doubted that would improve them. I felt discouraged and wondered what was wrong.

Fortunately I didn't give up. The next morning I dug up plants that showed a rosette of green leaves and no flower stalks. (Superficially they resemble foxglove and ragwort which are poisonous, but close up their spines are visible - not to mention palpable.) These plants were more like it! Some had roots as big as a finger, tho most were smaller - more like crayon size. I cut off the leaves, then with a vegetable brush, scrubbed the roots (which are fortunately without prickers). I ate about five, raw. They were white, crisp and tasted to me somewhat like an insipid carrot.

After washing the roots I noticed my fingers were stained dark where there were any nicks or scratches, similar to what happens when I hand squeeze apple juice.

The next day I steamed some of the thistle roots on top of some diced potatoes I happened to be cooking. The thistle roots got tender in the same amount of time as did the potatoes. I ate them plain. I neither especially liked nor disliked them. They were only slightly reminiscent of artichoke heart. They had a cooked carrot texture, viz., not as mushy as the potatoes but I imagine with more cooking they would get softer, just as long-cooked carrots do. Julie Summers, Oregon, April

Desert Super Foods and Medicine Plants

As the trace element values in soils drop, as hybrid seeds produce inferior nutritional value in plants, and as toxic chemicals contaminate our usual foods, some are turning back to nature. Early American desert cultures had a well stocked larder and medical supplies for the taking. Indians of North America had respiratory and arthritic ailments, but due to an active life and natural food seldom suffered from cancer, heart problems, and nutritional disorders. A few of the plants they used included:

YUCCA was favored for rheumatoid and osteoid arthritis.

JIMSON WEED (moon flower) is widespread in desert areas and was used by most early cultures as a soothing drug. The leaves were smoked to treat asthma and epilepsy. (However Harrington, Edible Native Plants of the Rocky Mountains, writes "All parts of this plant contain several poisonous alkaloids in rather high concentrations, particularly the seeds. This is a good plant to leave strictly alone.")

MESQUITE. Seeds and pods were used as food.

JO JOBA has beans producing high quality oil. I use it to lubricate small motors and devices, and add a little to VW auto engines in summer. It assures lubrication under high heat conditions. In cosmetics and waxes it's worth ±$8 a pound. But as an appetite depressant it must have a toxic chemical removed before use.

ALOE VERA varieties furnish the well known healing qualities useful on burns and for rheumatic problems. Since the plant efficiently takes up trace minerals from soil it also has great potential for a super food.

BUFFALO GOURD. Seeds have food value similar to squash seeds. The roots grow to huge dimensions. Slice and soak in salt water to remove bitterness. They are 50% starch. (Article about Buffalo Gourd in MP#12 p.3.)

GRASS SEEDS of many varieties are easy to spot and gather. (Harrington suggests shaking or beating over a cloth or flat rock surface, a seed head that's about ready to shed naturally. He also suggests collecting seed heads just before they are ready to shed, and stowing them away in large cloth or paper sacks to dry out. Later on these sacks can be shaken or beaten and the harvest collected in the bottom.)

BEAN PODS of several varieties are often obvious in the desert and provide Indians with nutritious bread meal. (Some plants with bean-like seeds are very poisonous. Identify positively before eating.) A. Fry, Calif., Dec.1984

Composition of Montia perfoliata

Miner's lettuce, a member of the purslane family, is a smooth, succulent, low annual with numerous basal leaves and several erect stems 10 to 30 cm (4-12") tall. The basal leaves are long and narrow, broadening at the tip; the leaves farther up the stem are very character- istic in that they are fused to form a disk from which flower clusters with small white or pink flowers emerge.

The plant grows in moist ground, usually in partial shade, and has become a common weed in orchards and vineyards throughout California. The stem and leaves of miner's lettuce, when young, may be eaten raw as salad greens or, when more mature, as a pot herb, cooked and prepared in any of the many ways that spinach is used.

For this study, nine samples of miner's lettuce were obtained from two sites, one to three times a month, from February through July 1976. The samples were collected early in the morning and usually reached the laboratory within 2 to 3 hours. For analysis, the edible portions - leaves, stems, and blossoms - were combined, unless otherwise noted ....

As with many leafy vegetables, the moisture concentrat- ion was high, 92.4%, and consequently, the energy value low - 20 kcal per 100 grams. Proximate composition of the solids was: protein, 37.1%; fat 3.3%; carbohydrate 42.4%; and ash, 17.2%. Crude fiber comprised 12.4 per cent of the solids. Minerals (mg. per 100 grams): calcium, 52; phosphorous, 79; iron, 3; magnesium, 40; potassium, 317; sodium, 18. The lettuce had a moderate amount of ascorbic acid (vit. C) and carotene (vit. A), 29mg and 656 ug per 100 gm., respectively. A small amount of oxalic acid (14 mg per 100 gm) was present, with a calcium:oxalic acid ratio of 8.34:1, stoichiometric. No phytic acid was detected.

One cup raw, chopped miner's lettuce would provide about 33% of the ascorbic acid, 10% of the iron, and 6% of the magnesium of the U.S. RDA. It would provide 22% of the vitamin A but only 0.7% of the niacin.

A comparison of the composition of miner's lettuce with that of 21 other green leafy vegetables showed considerable similarities. Of particular nutritional importance is the calcium:oxalic acid ratio. A high ratio is desirable, so that free oxalic acid will be bound by the calcium, with sufficient calcium remaining for metabolic utilization. Miner's lettuce had a ratio of 8.34:1, indicating an excess of calcium in relation to oxalic acid. (Collars, mustard greens, kale, and cabbage had the highest ratios - between 90:1 and 45:1. Swiss chard, spinach, purslane, beet leaves, poke, rhubarb, and lambs-quarters had the lowest ratios - between 0.45:1 and 0.20:1.) Marc Schelstraete and Barbara Kennedy, PhD (condensed from Journal of the American Dietetic Association, July 1980)

More About Removing Hulls from Hominy
A little info on past history, namely the hull corn mentioned in MP#18 (also MP#19 & #20). First, the corn used in our family was field corn, not sweet, nor popcorn. Second, lye was used; namely wood ashes, preferably from hard wood. The ashes were put in a cloth bag, the corn added, and boiled until, when a spoonful was blown on, the hulls would curl back. The corn was then washed in two or more waters, rubbing between the hands in the process. I don't remember whether my mother soaked it overnight or not. Orrissa Rines, New Hampshire, April

Father Firma's Instructions for Lye Hominy
The (now defunct) Survival Food Storage Newsletter #25, says: "Put 8 quarts of water in an enamel or stainless steel kettle. Add 6 teaspoons of lye while stirring with a stainless spoon or a wooden stick - until the lye is dissolved. Heat this lye water until boiling and then slowly add 12 cups of clean dry field corn - at a rate that will allow the water/lye solution to continue boiling. Keep boiling this corn until the dark tips of the corn kernels can be removed easily by rubbing. Test one or two kernels as the boiling progresses. Boiling time (depending on the corn) is about 30 to 40 minutes. When the tips remove easily, take the kettle from the fire, pour off the cooking water through a wire screen strainer. Then rinse in cold water (2 changes). Then, under running water, with your hands, rub the (now) hominy to remove the dark tips. The running water will float these away as well as any remaining hulls." Lye is caustic stuff. If you use it please be careful of your eyes.

To Double the Taste Pleasure of Seeds, Roast a Portion
Use a frying pan or whatever will brown them. Mix one-third roasted seeds with around two-thirds unroasted raw seeds, and grind. That makes a puree or spread as good as peanut butter - even better if honey is added. I have used sesame seed butter for years on my waffles. Other seeds can work out well, depending on their oil content, etc.
Since scorching seeds kills enzymes, I only use a portion of roasted seeds to maintain flavor.
I once visited the infamous Professor Aviles in Guadalajara. He used flax seed to cure cancer. I always try to add a little flax seed to my diet, although straight flax is not really great by itself - even roasted. A. Fry, Calif., Nov.

Collapsible Water Bottles
I recently obtained two U.S. Army surplus folding water bottles which hold one U.S. gallon. They have to be two of the best water bags I've ever seen. A. Kelley, Ontario, May

Harnessing the Night's Cold for Refrigeration

Even tho days may be hot, in many regions nighttime temperatures dip to or below the 40's. By exposing food to the night's cold, and insulating it during the day, it can be kept relatively cold at all hours. I have been able to keep meat this way a number of days.

The coldest place to put food at night is directly under the open sky. Put there, food actually became four degrees colder than air temperature, one time I measured. For protection from animals, I put the food in a tightly-closing container and hang it from a limb or pole, preferably where there's no foliage above.

In the morning, before the temperature begins to rise, I wrap the food in whatever insulation is available. Sleeping bags and fluffy clothes are good. Before wrapping I remove whatever portion I will be using soon. I am also careful that the food is sealed so it won't drip on the insulation.

Because greater mass will maintain its temperature longer, if the amount of food I have is small, I may cool down a gallon jug or two of water at night along with the food, and insulate the water with the food.

Because of the nuisance I minimize the amount of food that needs cooling. I avoid leftovers, by cooking only what will be eaten immediately - which is also best from a nutritional standpoint.

Other ways of refrigerating without a machine or ice include cold brooks and evaporation (described in MP#12   ) and burying (MP#13   ). Tho I haven't tried it, a combination of methods might be most effective. Julie Summers, Apr.

Free Napkins and Paper Towels - from Paper Bags

I use bags of various sizes, but mostly the larger ones, which 25 to 100 pounds of rice and beans come in. Bulk food stores discard them. They are made of multiple layers so if the outer one is soiled I can discard it (or use it for pattern making). I cut the bags into pieces about 8x11" or smaller. They are not as soft or absorbent as the "real thing" but I find them adequate for wiping greasy fingers and other tasks where great absorbancy isn't necessary. Julie

Bush-Built and High-Tech Pack Frames Each Have Advantages

We have three pack frames. One, which we recently purchased, is welded out of aluminum tubing. Two, which we built out of sticks and twine, are A frames patterned after traditional Korean and American Indian designs.

For moving a lot of cargo a short distance, we prefer the high-tech frame. It loads faster; especially so if there are boxes and pails, because the back bands keep the load from digging into your back.

However, for carrying a single load a long distance, we prefer the "primitive" A frame. It's lighter. How, some may wonder, can a few branches lashed together surpass what's manufacturered out of modern alloys? The secret is the shape; the A frame's members needn't be as strong because they form a triangle (self bracing), and because there are no back bands to bend them.

The lack of bands is a limitation. The load must be carefully arranged so that soft things rest against your back. If that is done, the A frame is as comfortable as the high tech. (The straps are interchangeable.) (Plans for the bush-built frame are offered by the Light Living Library.) Holly & Bert, editors of this issue.

Message Post

Portable Dwelling Info-letter
6 issues(2 yrs)$5. Sample $1
Number 22   September 1986   POB 190, Philomath, OR 97370

Situating a Camp for Best Microclimate

Seek wind in high temperatures and avoid it in low temperatures. In wet, windy, cold weather seek thick stands of trees to break the wind and seek out protected valleys and south facing hills, slopes and cliffs. A windy exposure in the summer lessens the harassment of flies and mosquitoes.

In winter use an easterly, southerly and westerly exposure for the full day, preferably with a clearing (lake or wide river) fifty to a hundred meters wide to the south to provide added warmth from the reflection of the sun off the snow. Avoid cold-collecting depressions or basins. Stay out of the bottoms of valleys where the natural flow of air might intensify the cold.

In the summer use an easterly exposure with westerly protection for morning warmth and afternoon shade. To avoid morning mists and undue dampness, camp at least five meters above the surface of a lake, river or stream.

In seeking protection from strong wind, camp well away from open spots but never close to big trees that may be blown over or have branches broken off. In strong winds of about 150 to 200 km/hr an occasional tree is heard to come down every hour. In this case move to a clearing or amongst trees that are too small to kill (wrist thick).

Wind direction becomes important with respect to smoke and sparks, and the placement of the latrine. Winds should be parallel to the front of an open shelter to carry away smoke and sparks, and tents should be set up so that there is no danger from spark damage.

If there is no wind at the time and you are setting up on level terrain, you might put your camp up with respect to the prevailing winds in your particular area (generally from the northwest). If camping in a valley, set up (the front of an open shelter) parallel to it, as the winds will move up and down the valley.

(In a valley, wind is expected to blow up the valley during the day, and down the valley at night.) Least wind may be expected 10 to 11 a.m. and 9 to 10 p.m. Most wind is to be expected from 3 to 4 p.m and 4 to 5 a.m.

In non-mountainous terrain in the west the time to expect the least wind is from 3 to 6 in the early morning. The most wind is to be expected from 2 to 4 in the afternoon.

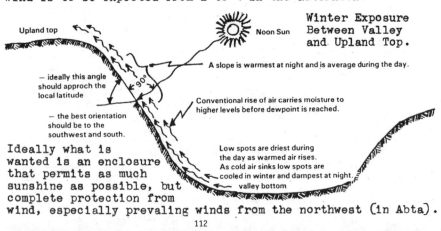

Upland top

Noon Sun

Winter Exposure Between Valley and Upland Top.

A slope is warmest at night and is average during the day.

— ideally this angle should approch the local latitude

90°

Conventional rise of air carries moisture to higher levels before dewpoint is reached.

— the best orientation should be to the southwest and south.

Ideally what is wanted is an enclosure that permits as much sunshine as possible, but complete protection from wind, especially prevaling winds from the northwest (in Abta).

Low spots are driest during the day as warmed air rises. As cold air sinks low spots are cooled in winter and dampest at night. valley bottom

Where there are no clouds, all radiation will be outwards at night with no return, and will be coldest at night, hottest in daytime. Low clouds and rain will produce some warmth retention at night. High clouds are not as effective. Thick trees may act somewhat like clouds.

Large bodies of water tend to keep a more constant temperature. Breeze tends to flow towards the warmer areas - inshore by day, offshore by night.

Anything reflective such as a wall, big rocks, or the edge of a grove of trees , creates a warmed mini-environment between it and the sun. The closer to the reflector the more warmth is intercepted. Mors Kochanski, Alberta

(This is a portion of "The Campsite" from Wilderness Arts and Recreation, V3 N2 March 1979. No longer published, to our knowledge. Copyright by Big Bear Wilderness Services Ltd., POB 2640, Edson, Alberta TOE OPO. Reprinted with permission. Several illustrations of the original article have not been reprinted, but their legends have been incorporated into text.)

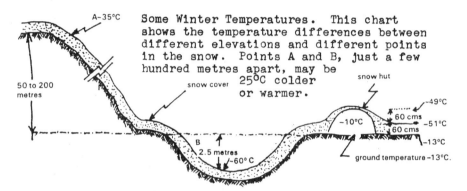

Some Winter Temperatures. This chart shows the temperature differences between different elevations and different points in the snow. Points A and B, just a few hundred metres apart, may be 25°C colder or warmer.

Wintering in a Tleanto - Feedback

In one long day we put up most of the tleanto (see MP#19 p.1&2) - including roof, ceiling, front wall, outer end walls - enough to give us rain and bug protection. (We had previously cut the poles and leveled the site.) In two more days we fitted the inner end walls. Then we spent many days gathering leaves for ceiling insulation.

Another problem with the leaves is, whenever we bump the ceiling the leaves shift and collect in sags of the plastic between the rafters, leaving bare spots without insulation, requiring redistributing the leaves or adding more. If we move this tleanto or build another, we'd like to insulate the ceiling some other way. (Ideas?)

We occupied the tleanto continually from early November until March, and occasionally since - moving out for warm sunny days and back in when the weather turns cool rainy. The tleanto stood up to winds, except for one corner of the fly (top tarp) which a gust ripped loose. We retied it using a bigger ball and it held. The tleanto did buffet a lot - sounding like it might blow away any moment.

A greater concern was flooding. During the heavy rains, there were rivulets every few feet. The ditch around the tleanto wasn't big enough to take the flow, and Craig had to enlarge it - in the middle of a downpour! He also dug a ditch around the floor inside (not shown in MP#19) which was

fortunate because springs developed in the back wall.
    The tleanto is quite balmy when sunny <u>and</u> <u>calm</u> even on
cold days, but chilly when there's a cold wind. A few days
we didn't want to leave the sack, but for most of the winter
the inner room was warm enough to do things like sew. The
coldest might have been 10 or 20 outside and 35 or 40 inside
(forgot to bring a thermometer, but ice never formed on
water in the inner room).
    We soon moved most of the kitchen activities (food prep-
aration, dish washing, sprouting) into the inner room, which
crowded it. We left the stove (butane) in the outer room
because of concern about fumes, but put it close enough to
the inner room to reach out to it. The aladdin (lamp) too
we kept in the outer room. Enough light shines through the
walls (4 layers of plastic).
    How do you dispose of human wastes during bad weather?
One heavy snow fall covered the ground and bushes deep enough
we couldn't even see where the latrine had been.
Craig & Wanda, California, April & June

<u>Ball Ties Can Be Used To Suspend Liners Within Tents</u>
    In MP#20 p.1, Bob Gillis of Shelter Systems
mentioned that their clips could be used to
suspend liners within tents. Ball ties can
also be used for that.
    Make a big bulky knot in one end of a piece
of twine (or alternatively, if you have a big
bead, string that on the twine). Use the knot
as a ball of a ball tie, wrapping the plastic
over it. Leave the loose end of twine hanging
through the tie, and tie it around the neck of
the next ball tie. Etc. Bert, Oregon, May

big
knots

<u>In Aladdin Lamp, Don't Use Diesel Fuel</u>
or low grade yellow kerosene. They'll leave bad odor and soot
up worse. Get lamp grade, or water white kerosene. Jack, NH

<u>Emission of Carbon Monoxide is One of the Greatest Dangers</u>
in sleeping with heat, especially with the newer tents of
impervious airtight fabric. (Also see reports MP#8 p.2)
I find that a gasoline (or propane) lantern will do an excellent job of heating in daytime, leaving a small opening in tent
for fresh air, etc. At night, the ordinary oil lantern will
keep temperature well above freezing, BUT frankly I am afraid
of the excess carbon dioxide and carbon monoxide when sleeping. But as a compromise, I have experimented with the use of
candle lanterns - the old favorite, Stonebridge folding candle
lantern of either aluminum or more sturdy (and heavier) metal
- available from camp supply houses. Swung from the peak of
the tent a single candle will last approximately four hours,
keeping temperature well above freezing. Then as it goes out
and temperature drops, I roll over and insert a fresh candle
without getting out of my sleeping bag. This will last until
daylight. Major Lyman F. Barry, New York, September

<u>Reflector Increases Lamp Light on One Spot</u>
    For Julie's lamp (MP#16   ), an old reflector, mirror,
or round stainless bowl can double the light put on one
desired place. Many hand spotlights (especially the cheapies)
have a fine bowl reflector and when they are broken it can be
salvaged. Paul Doerr, Pioneer, California, Feb. 85

Living Partly in Yurt. Want to Move from City.

We have three boys (ages 9, 6, 1½) and are living partly in a yurt and partly in a house in a big city. The yurt is in the backyard and we are transfering more and more functions outside. When we have enough confidence we're planning to leave the area. For now we sleep outside. We do "baths" and part of the cooking outside, but we're not completely free of the refrigerator. We still use the washing machine and the toilet. (No hot water in the house since we have our gas turned off. Also no regular stove or heat. We're allergic to the gas.)

Our big question is where are we going and what will we do for money? My husband has a good business of his own here doing gardener-handyman-tree work, etc. It will be hard to leave that "easy" money. We teach our kids at home so schools are no problem. Does anyone live in a tent with children?
Anne Callaway, California, June

Large Cardboard Boxes Provide Portable Shelters in Cities

There is a mention of cardboard housing in Julie Summers' review of "Re/Uses ..." (MP#21   ) which reminds me of one thing I saw in my tenure as an urban paramedic: Detroit General Hospital used to have some vents on the street, through which would come drafts of heated air. In the winter this spot became prime turf among the street population, and one or two enterprising souls would discover and transport a cardboard box from a refrigerator, etc, and set up housekeeping there on the street. This would trap the heat exhausted from the hospital, and thereby help the resident survive the Michigan winter nights. The more elaborate would drape plastic over to improve weatherproofness of the structure.
Jon,   Michigan, August

Some Buckets Better for Long Storage; Some Better for Access

I use plastic buckets for water and for dry good storage (beans, grains, etc). Some types are definitely better -- the lids are what make the difference.

The type with the harder lids, the ones with the slit around about ten places, are best for longer term storage, where you won't be opening them hardly ever. They're a pain to open, because they were designed to be pryed up with a "lid lifter", a small hand tool that makes the task MUCH easier. Opening them without it, is hard on the fingers.

The type of lids which are softest and have no rubber gasket, are made to be opened easily, by hand. But they don't seal as well as the gasketed ones, thus are not as good for dry foods (except in or near the kitchen, where the 'turnover' is reasonably often). They are fine for water hauling.

I keep a bucket in the car with a change or so of clothes, some quick foods, matches, a knife, and various small 'survival' items. In winter, I also have a down bag and a sleeping pad, a spare coat, mittens, and the like. A person with a car breakdown could be stuck for the night, and with temps occasionally below zero and deep snow drifts .... A bucket keeps the assorted stuff in one neat easy package that will thwart mice and bugs.

Plastic septic tanks are only good in 'stable' soils. The walls will not take the pressure/load if the soil is muddy or is unstable. They need to be surrounded with several inches of soft sand during installation. They would make a good underground water tank, if kept full most of the time.
Rick, Idaho, July

Foraging in the Woods to Make Money

People who find something lucrative, generally keep quiet about it. They don't want to encourage competition. People who are willing to talk about what they do, are most likely doing ordinary work that doesn't pay much. That includes us.

At various times Holly and I have made money (not a whole lot) by gathering mushrooms (chanterelles), cascara bark, floral greens, and berries. Other things which are gathered and sold in various places, are seed cones, moss, resin, antlers, various herbs, shell fish, and gem stones.

The past few falls chanterelle mushrooms have been popular with many people going into the woods for them. We've found them under douglas fir where the trees are fairly large and dense, with not much undergrowth. Mushrooms grow fastest when there's a period of warm weather following heavy rains. Chanterelles are golden colored, solider looking than most mushrooms, with wavy edges (but there are other yellow mushrooms, so before gathering look at some a buyer has, or see a mushroom book).

Two years ago local buyers were paying $2 a pound. We gathered maybe 20 pounds, but didn't connect with a buyer, so we ate some and gave the rest away. Last fall we did find a buyer, but he was far from where we were camped and foraging, and the price had dropped to $1 a pound, so making special trips (by bike or hitching - don't have a car) wasn't worth it. We gathered and sold only a few pounds.

Mushrooms, berries, floral greens, and some herbs are perishable and must be sold soon after picking. Chanterelles will keep a few days if kept cool and loose in net bags so they can breathe, but they lose weight fast and they're paid for by the pound.

Most pickers have cars, which enables them to go out picking in the morning and sell their harvests the same day. But much of their earnings go to support their cars. The only way to really make money is for a large family to share one car.

Some pickers we talked with fondly remembered an occasion when they found $50 worth in a few hours. But the day we talked they hadn't found many nor had we.

Cascara bark, moss, and some herbs are sold dry, so it's possible to accumulate a big load. But best to have a heated place for drying and storage - northwestern weather isn't dependable.

We'd rather forage in the woods than work on farms (which we've done more of), but so far we haven't made much foraging.

With any kind of work, if it's money you're after, the important thing is how much you clear. For example, if a job pays $100 a day, but holding down that job costs $95 a day (including rent, commuting, restaurants and convenience foods (because there's not time or energy left to fix meals), taxes, licenses, special clothes, training (time and tuition) needed to land the job, medical expenses and time incapacitated (because of stress, pollution, or hazards at work), time and expenses hunting the job, etc.) then you are really working for $5 a day! Bert, Oregon, July

Eye Damage by Heat

Ken (in MP#18) may have the clue to the cause of dammage. I now remember that glass blowers have eye problems. In the lab it's recommended that special yellow eye glasses be worn when working glass. I don't know if it's the sensable heat, or rather some other radiation that comes from the glow that causes the problem. Robin, Oregon, August 1985

Bears Are Not Very Fast When Going Down Hill

I have hiked alone and unarmed in bear country, but haven't seen any bears yet. I have a bell on my pack and blow a whistle now and then, so they know where I am. I have seen fresh bear shit but the bears have been long gone.

People have told me that I was walking in grizzly bear country, but I don't eat meat or carry butter, which I understand may attract them.

I understand that bears are not skilled at going downhill, as they have shorter front legs and tend to roll. So, if a bear is behind you, best to climb down the steepest hill you can find.

Also here's (a Canadian Press clipping. A man planting trees near Mackenzie BC was charged by a black bear. To escape he climbed a small tree, but the bear knocked him out of it. He outran the bear for 220 metres "across rough terrain" (doesn't say if down hill) where he climbed a taller tree. The bear circled the base of that tree, but was scared off a little later when the foreman arrived in an ATV. (Why didn't the bear climb the second tree? Are bears not good at climbing certain kinds of trees such as slender ones with thin bark? Or are they afraid to climb in the face of an enemy?))
Aarran, BC, June & July

Wilderness Self Defense Without Firearms

We have been portable dwelling full time for nearly ten years and recreationally backpacking for several years before that, and our persons have never been threatened by any animal larger than a hornet. Have we just been lucky? Several other long-time campers have reported no problems (accounts in MP#7 and #8 and #9). But we also read of attacks, not only by bears but recently (in Signpost) by cougars. One attacked a 12-year-old boy; another attacked a ten-year-old girl. In both cases the cougars were driven off by unarmed women.

We don't have a firearm and have mixed feelings about getting one. It would be one more thing to carry around and take care of. But we wonder how much of a chance we're taking.

Sometimes we sharpen sticks and keep them handy for use as spears, especially if bivying near a river, main game trail, or lush berry patch. (We don't put a camp where we expect to stay long,in such places.) We've talked with other people who arm themselves with spears, but no one who has had to use one.

Chal mentioned (in MP#21) throwing rocks to repel dogs. We've done that too. Would brandishing and throwing be effective against a bear? I've read about apes driving off enemies that way. Bert, Oregon, July

Florida is Antagonistic to Camping

In my letter, May/June issue (of the Advocate) I extended an invitation to RV travelers to stop at my place in north Florida.... That's still valid. But, I am getting lots of letters asking about tenting, camping, picking oranges. It is not tropical Florida here! In January and February, temperatures go down in the 20's, and on the Gulf edge it's damp, windy, stormy; no sun and no fish! Florida as a whole is antagonistic to camping; no overnight parking permitted at roadside parks. What is wanted are people to fill the motels and spend money! Ruth (reprinted from Rural Network]

(2007 update) Florida still is hostile, I've heard quite recently. So are LA, TX, WY. (Other states ?) Please avoid such places, both for your own safety and to help discourage such behavior. Esp, don't spend $s. BOYCOTT !!

Steamed Bread

For the past several months I have been steaming most of my breads in a pot-within-a-pot, rather than using a frying pan. (I have no regular oven.) I like the steaming method primarily because it avoids crust formation (browned food may be carcinogenic). Also I save handling time because I can make a larger size bread all at once; and there's no turning over required. Another bonus is I can cook other foods at the same time (such as beans), thus saving on fuel.

I grind five cups of wheat kernels into flour (which gives about 7½ cups flour). I make a sponge with half of the flour and most of the recipe's water (about 3½ cups). I let this "work" (ferment) at room temperature (about 65° at time of writing) all day. In the evening I knead in the other half of the flour. I let the resultant dough work over night. (In warmer weather I reduce fermentation times.) The next morning I punch down the dough and make it into a ball. I dust it generously with flour by rolling it around in a pan of flour. I then place the dough into a handleless 1½ quart stainless steel pot. I push the dough down to fit against the sides of the pot. It comes flush with the top of the pot.

Next I place the 1½ quart pot within a 4 quart pot (also stainless steel). The larger pot has a cup of water in it and three teaspoons lying in a triangle to form a trivet to keep the smaller pot elevated off the bottom of the larger pot, for even heat flow. A domed cover fits tightly on the larger pot. The smaller pot is uncovered. (The dough doesn't seem to need any cover, and anyway it would push off a cover as it rose.)

I put the pot-within-a-pot over high heat until the water comes to a boil. Then I reduce heat to a simmer for an hour and ten minutes. After that time I insulate the pot-within-a-pot under sweaters and blankets for two to four hours.

I cook the dough immediately after putting it in the pot. I.e., I don't let it pre-rise after I put it in its pot, because I have found doing so results in the dough's falling down upon cooking. Whereas cooking without pre-rising results in rising during the first part of cooking, without falling.

There's no need to duplicate my size pots. Expect some trial and error in the beginning. Some of my first steamed breads weren't done enough. I simply sliced them and cooked them further on my frying pan.

When cooking beans at the same time as the bread, first I soak one to two cups (dry measure) beans. After they are fully plumped, I drain them and place in the larger pot, adding fresh water to cover. (The soak water contains indigestable trisaccarides, and is thus discarded. See MP#12 p.2.) Directly on top of the beans (no spoons) I place the smaller pot, containing the dough. I rock the smaller pot and push it down, to sort of nest it in the beans, so there's enough room above it to accomodate rising. I bring the water to a boil and cook the same as above. Julie Summers, March

The Three Minute Timer Approach to Councils

(passing it from member to member around the circle, allowing each to speak three minutes) is a simple easy solution to group communication. It has proved to me to be one of our most valuable assets. I highly recommend it along with decentralized councils of 12 or less. Forest, Hawaii, July

From the Editors (Holly and Bert again this issue)

How might Message Post be more useful to you? What unusual equipment or services are you seeking? Know of?

Clothespins Provide Bulletin Board
where tacks and magnets are inappropriate
in such places as tents. Feed the line
around each clothespin's metal spring,
and loop it around and thru a second time
to anchor. Julie Summers, Oregon, April

Going on the Road with Bicycles
We live in a small primitive cabin on
a pond in Maine, but are thinking of
selling it and going on the road with
bicycles for a year (perhaps to New
Zealand!). Martha, Maine, November

Firearm Safety
Reference the ongoing discussion of firearms for back
country campers (MP#19 , MP#20 , MP#21 , MP#22):
I am a gunowner, and as both a paramedic and ER nurse have
had experience with accidental, malicious, and self-defense
usage of firearms (thus far, all by proxy - via my patients.)
As a gun owner, I am always aware of the "fool quotient".
That is to say, some damned fool is going to get his macho
up and through some stupid stunt, injure an innocent bystand-
er. Everybody in this culture thinks he "knows about guns",
but fails to realize 1) that TV is not an educational medium,
and 2) watching some dope act a fool does not constitute an
education on safe, responsible firearm handling.
There are four rules that I keep maniacally in my mind
at all times when near guns: a) No gun is unloaded ... even
if I just unloaded it myself. Treating any weapon as loaded
helps prevent shootings by "unloaded" guns. b) Never point
any firearm at anything you have any objection to putting a
hole in. Particularly people. This rule saved me from a
tragedy in my early hunting days, when an accidental
discharge went harmlessly into the air. c) Make certain that
you do not discharge your gun if there is any chance that a
missed shot will strike a non target. That means make sure
that you have a secure backstop. In the city, that pretty
much rules out use of rifles as self defense tools, because
any miss will all too likely result in injury to an
innocent. A handgun may cause injury at a distance of a mile
or more. Consider the implications of discharging a firearm
(handgun) inside a typical city home, and finding that the
bullet has penetrated the wall to injure a neighbor, or child.
Finally, d) any consumption of alcohol makes handling of any
weapon out of the question. I do not take a single drink
of any sort if I expect to handle a gun (target shoot, etc.).
Then there are the game laws of your state. In Michigan
you can be presumed to be in violation of the game laws if
afield out of season while armed, or armed and without
hunting license.
And, in concert with Bert's comments re: something else
to drag around, there is the security aspect to firearms
ownership to consider. Guns are very, very popular as break-
in booty. How do you lock up a weapon in a tent, if you are
not to go about armed? Jon, Michigan, September

<u>Hints</u> <u>for</u> <u>Living</u> <u>High</u> <u>at</u> <u>Low</u> <u>Cost</u>
     Take time to reflect on what you're doing with your life.
I find it helpful to make believe I'm dying and asking myself
"Did I really do the things I wanted to?" Then I can try to
change my life so I <u>am</u> doing what I want to (and will die
without regrets). Also periodically ask yourself if you've
become caught up in someone else's costly, irrational trip.
     Get out of the status game arena. Look at the clothes
you wear, transportation you take, sports you play, etc., and
ask yourself if there aren't less costly, equally satisfying
alternatives. Associate with people who don't judge status by
amount of money spent.
     Be patient. I have found many things come to those who
wait. E.g., instead of rushing out to buy it new, I give it
a chance to turn up used. In the mean time, while doing
without, I remind myself:
     If there is something you think you absolutely must have,
consider that there are probably millions of people in the
world who routinely get along without it.
     Remind yourself there are always alternatives, even tho
they may not always be easy to discover.
     Know that everything has its costs. Figure out what they
are and decide if you really want to pay. E.g., the purchase
price of a car is just one of its costs. There's also license,
gas, maintenance, pollution, parking, etc.
     Play productively, work playfully. I.e. get rid of the
work-play dichotomy. E.g., a hike (play) can be made productive by picking berries or wild greens at the same time.
Washing the dishes (work) can be made playful by having someone read out loud to you.
     Improvise. Make one thing serve the function of two or
more. Or use an inexpensive, readily available object in
place of what's costly and hard to get. Improvising comes
easily once one gets over the aversion to unconventional
appearances. E.g., use a jar for a rolling pin.
     Think long, hard and creatively (don't censor your imag-
ination) about alternative shelter. Rent is the key that
kept me imprisoned for a long time. The need for hundreds a
month to pay rent forced me to work steadily and that
incurred additional espenses -- besides leaving me too exhausted to explore for a way to break out. There isn't one
solution that will work for everyone. Many approaches are
needed. (Buying a house may be no real solution since it
merely substitutes mortgage payments and taxes for rent.)
     The meaning of life is the enjoyment of it.   Julie, 1980

<u>Why</u> <u>We</u> <u>Like</u> <u>Camping</u>
     Camping offers many advantages (along with disadvantages,
of course) compared to building a house or cabin or bringing in a mobile home. Attractions for us include easy changes
of scene, more choice of locations, more natural surroundings,
and more privacy. But the bottom line is - <u>very</u> <u>low</u> <u>cost</u>.
We need to work only ten hours a week about (total for the
two of us) to pay all our expenses. (That's averaged over a
year. Actually we work only one or two months a year, usually,
but put in 40-50 hours a week then.)
     Many people try camping and have an unpleasant time
because of insufficient or inappropriate equipment, or
inexperience, and conclude that camping necessarily means
hardships, discomforts and inconveniences. Not so. We've
been as comfortable camping as we ever were living in

apartments. There have been unpleasant moments, such as an
unexpected rain while moving. But every dwellingway has its
problems. In a house, the electricity may go off, the
furnace break down, the pipes freeze, the frame get eaten by
termites, etc. Bert, Oregon, December 1985

Another Clue to Cordial Camping
When companions don't put things away, and I have to deal
with them before I can proceed with my own activity, it bugs
me. I used to wonder how I could be so pusilanimous as to
begrudge a friend a few seconds of my time.
Perhaps the annoyance being out of proportion to the
time imposition comes from my considering putting-away to be
part of the task and therefore the responsibility of the
task's initiator. If I wasn't asked and didn't agree to finish
the job, but end up having to, I feel roped into it, even if
due to another's forgetfulness and not manipulativeness.
Julie Summers, Oregon,   1983

What is Householding?
If you open it, close it. If you turn it on, turn it off.
If you unlock it, lock it. If you break it, repair it.
If you can't fix it, call for help. If you borrow it, return
it. If you use it, take care of it. If you make a mess, clean
it up. If you move it, put it back. If it belongs to somebody else and you want to use it, get permission. If you don't
know how to operate it, leave it alone. If it doesn't concern
you, don't mess with it. (Sent by Mycall Sunanda, 1982)

Edible Every Time
Even if your cooking efforts aren't rewarded with exactly
what you had in mind, you can take steps to insure the end
result will at least be edible. Too much salt, pepper or hot
spices won't pose a problem if you simply omit them during
cooking - they may be added at the table if desired. Under-
doneness is remedied by further cooking. Overdone parts may
be trimmed off. About the only way to ruin something entirely
is to burn it. Here are some hints to help avoid that:
When learning to cook, or cooking something unfamiliar,
give it your undivided attention. Stay near the stove, so
you'll be able to hear and smell what's happening. It's
possible to hear when something is boiling dry, for example,
and add more water before it burns. One may also be able to
smell when food starts to get overdone and catch it before
completely ruined.
Use a timer. The cost of the gadget will be repaid many
times over in unspoiled food.
Slow down. Use a lower flame. Turn it down even more as
cooking progresses and the initial moisture that prevents
burning at first gets driven off. When cooking over a
campfire use coals, not a roaring blaze!
Cook with easily burned ingredients sparingly, if at all.
These include oil and fats, honey, molasses, corn syrup and
sucrose (table sugar). Like salt and pepper, they may be
added after cooking.
Use double pot cooking. This works well for oatmeal,
for example: Place oatmeal and boiling water in a small pot,
stirring while adding the oatmeal to the boiling water.
Then place the small pot within a larger covered pot that
contains a few inches of water in the bottom. Keep the
smaller pot off the bottom of the larger pot with a few
spoons, pebbles, or a rack. Bring the water in the larger

pot to a boil, then turn down the heat to a simmer. No further stirring is needed.

Use "insulative" cooking. It used to be called hay box cooking. But hay is only one of many materials that insulate. Towels, blankets, sleeping bags and clothes are other possibilities. The food is cooked over flame as usual by bringing to a boil and simmering. However the simmering time is cut by half or more. Then the pot is covered with insulation, and retained heat finishes cooking. Nest the pot in the insulation so there are no large air spaces around it. Add insulation until there are four or more inches of it all around the pot. When using this method for short grain brown rice, for example, I bring water and rice to a boil, simmer seven minutes, then insulate about an hour and it's ready to eat. I do practically all my cooking this way now.
Julie Summers, Oregon, February 1986

Living Lightly in City. Making Thatched-Roofed Root Cellar.
I count myself fortunate to have lived for a while near Tipi Village in Isla Vista, California. I barely got to know the people there, but since I left and returned to my native Kentucky, I find that my life wants to resemble the lifestyle I witnessed at Tipi Village - based on gardening, bicycle transport, and "Light Living".
My next project here is to make a thatched roof, layered for shedding water, over my root cellar/granary. I'll use organic straw from last year's rye crop as far as it goes and then weeds, bundled and applied to roof sheathing like shingles.
I live in a garage, in the older, more arboreal part of a typical city. It is well-built as go garages, block walls and poured concrete floor. I pay $60/month rent - inexpensive for mid city. I cleared weeds off of 30' by 30' waste ground beside garage, and raise tree seedlings. There is shade. No running water so two rain barrels collect roof water for bathing, etc., and I must buy drinking water at the nearby store. All waste is recycled into compost pile or buried in tree nursery. Urine collected in gallon jug, goes on compost. Feces, deposited on newspaper laid on floor, until buried air-dries in newspaper sacks within wire cage (to keep out dogs) beside tree nursery, and out of sight behind woodpile. I was worried, when I started depositing feces and urine outside, that odors would alert neighbors to what I was doing. But surprisingly little odor occurs, and no one has complained in five years. I guess the neighbors think that there is a bath-room in the upstairs part of the building, reserved for land-lord. I am vegetarian, which may reduce odor and danger of disease.
No heat in winter, unless I build an external, masonry chimney for my idle wood stove. It will remain idle, because I've other things to do now than build a chimney for my land-lord. I have learned to accept cold, dress warm, keep warm by shoveling snow for neighbors, always working on something or sleeping. This winter I may travel for a pleasant change.
I have electricity, so cook fairly conventionally on hot plate, have electric lights, etc. No refrigerator.
Improvement for me was digging of small root cellar, so that food would not freeze in winter. I had already made an 8' by 8' square platform, one foot above ground, for storing grain which I grow on a rented one-quarter acre. I raise vegies summers, grain in winter. I dug out, under granary, for root cellar, so stored grain, covered with fabric tarp-aulin, sheds water and insulates cellar. Steve, KY, August

Message Post

April 1987   Next in June

Portable Dwelling Info-letter
of the   Light Living Library
POB 190, Philomath, OR 97370

Toothwart or Pepperroot - Dentaria Species

The leaves and stems add a sharp flavor to a wild spring salad. The taste is strong so use sparingly. The small, white underground tubers are reported also edible.

Donald R. Kirk describes pepperroot as "perennials rising from thick, fleshy, stout rootstocks or tubers. The stems are erect, nearly hairless, usually unbranched, leafless below, with a few leaves on the upper stem. The leaves are basal, rising directly from the rootstocks. The white to rose or purple flowers are borne in a raceme." Typically a few inches high around here. "The various species are found on shady banks, rocky slopes, and in moist places, generally in mountain and coastal areas of the Pacific Coast states."

The flowers are among the first to bloom in the spring. This year they appeared here in March, ahead of anything else we noticed.

Meals Need Not Be Elaborate

Whereas other peoples of the world have feasts a few times times a year, North Americans seem addicted to at least one every day, and feel deprived if they don't get it. I have finally discarded this notion. I eat fewer meals and plainer meals. Thus I'm not constantly tempted to overeat, have more time for other activities, and am not jaded. So when I want a feast it doesn't take much to satisfy me. Julie Summers,'86

Earth-Sheltered Tents

Some of our tent sites have been earth sheltered - banks on three sides - for less wind and greater warmth, but I have neve excavated a cave. I make the site enough larger than The Thing (our dwelling) so there is a ditch and crawlway between the sides of The Thing and the banks. Using this crawlway I can remove dirt and leaves which fall in.

There hasn't been much coming loose of dirt even from streight up and down banks, except near the top which gets fros Sometimes the top tarp over The Thing extends beyond the ditch, and this keeps off rain and reduces frost heaving, and so reduce the amount of dirt that gets loosened and falls.

From the little digging we've done at camping sites, it seems to me that the soil would make much difference in the equipment and techniques needed. Where we've been, digging is generally easiest when the soil is damp but not soaking wet. This is soil with considerable clay. Bert, Oregon, May 1983

Excavating Caves for Storage & Housing is a Prize Idea

Myself I store food and have a place to hide it. I use a CO_2 regulator 5 psi for 5 min. per gallon. Dry grains only. One gallon jugs, such as apple juice, wine, etc. come in. Worl okay. I buy some cork and wax to seal them.

Back to caves. Texas has a lot of limestone caves. Just to find one no one knows about. Nevada has thousands of old shafts. Utah has a lot of sand stone mountains. They make the best caves (man made). A cave is a good fall out shelter. When the bombs come it will save a fellow. George, Louisiana,

To Find a Soil That's Strong Enough, Look For Clues in Landscape

Earthsheltered housing has become one of my favorite hobbies. According to "the engineering profession", there isn't any stable soils or rock that doesn't need bracing. All rocks have some type of cracks or fissures, and soil does not have long-term cohesive properties (compressive strength only, no strength in tension).

Anything is possible, though, depending on how "crazy" you are. I do know of an English professor in central Illinois who is raising a family in a tipi and an unbraced dirt cave.

Soil testing is done to classify soil so that engineers from different areas know they are talking about the same thing. To find a soil that is strong enough for your cave, look for clues in the existing landscape that you are considering building at. If there are steep hills or cliffs existing, then this would suggest a stable soil. Usually, though, these cliffs are held up by layers of rock or intertwined roots of trees and brush.

Sinkholes reveal the existance of limestone layers and possible natural caves. If you live in an area that is underlayed by limestone, you might luck out and find an undiscovered natural cave. The Appalachian mountains and many other areas have caves and sinkholes caused by rain seeping through cracks and dissolving the limestone through the years. Rainwater is naturally acidic, even before industrial smog adds to the acidity. The Chinese are taking advantage of their natural caves, using them as train tunnels, warehouses, factores and parks.

My earth-shelter philosophy: I think there are two main reasons for earthsheltered housing that should govern your housing solution. One goal is to burrow in deep to seek the constant internal heat of the earth and avoid the 24 hour cycle of temperature fluctuations on the earth's surface. You can accomplish this simply by digging straight down 2 to 4 feet and insulating the excavation. The Jansonite commune did this in Illinois in the 1830's, but they had a moisture problem. Line your excavation with plastic to avoid this. Make sure surface runoff (rainwater) is drained away from your hole, also.

The other feature of earthsheltering is that the dirt will protect your shelter from decomposing by ultra-violet rays and drafts from penetrating wind. Plastic becomes brittle and paint peels when exposed to the sun. For a simple shelter with this goal in mind, I would build a lean-to or a dome and cover it with plastic for waterproofing and then just put enough dirt on the structure to keep the plastic protected from the wind & sun.

Don't try relying on dirt as an insulator, it is a poor insulator and it weighs so much that a structure capable of supporting a couple feet of dirt would put you in debt to a bank for twenty years. Greg Stoewer, Illinois, April 1983

Where Cave Living is Practical

Living in a cave is practial only in a dry climate (if natural cave) or in a man-made cave (damp climates). Natural caves are usually too damp, irregular, and difficult of access. Abandoned mines would be practical, sometimes. Refer to several old National Geographic issues (before 1940) for articles on cave dwellers in Asia and the Near East - these usually are artificial caves and are in fairly dry climates. I've seen artificial sandstone caves in the midwest that are suitable, given forced ventilation (?). Some sandstones are soft enough to (work with hand tools when) first exposed. It hardens on(exposure to the air.) James H., May 1980 (reprinted from Living Free)

The $50 & Up Underground House Book, by Mike Oehler
"A boom in private underground shelter construction is clearly
trying to happen, and still none of the major publishers have
come up with a comprehensive how-to guide for the do-it-yourself-
er. Oehler flatly doesn't like concrete, and at the structural
core of his sub-surface dwellings is what he calls the "PSP
system" (post-shoring-polyethylene), which admittedly flunks
most Code requirements. Nevertheless, it sounds like the very
best low-cost outlaw home going. Even if you're holding out for
a guide on concrete underground construction, Oehler's book
provides many times its cost in perceptive tips on sub-surface
design, philosophy, living, and underground building in general."
(Review by Lewis Watson in The Next Whole Earth Catalog, First
Edition.) 1978, 112 pages, $7 postpaid from Mole Publishing Co.,
Rt 1 Box 618, Bonners Ferry, ID 83805 (1980 price)
"We will be dealing primarily with underground houses on
hillsides. Hillsides are preferred building sites for a number
of reasons. For one, the drainage is better. For another, you
stand a better chance of getting a sweeping view. Still another
is that hilly land is traditionally less expensive than flat
land, and is what most back-to-the-landers usually wind up with.
Sewage disposal is greatly simplified when there is indoor
plumbing. Then there are the terrain advantages of building on
the warm, sunny south slopes in cold climates and on the cooler
northern slopes in hot climates. Finally, and perhaps most
important, flat land is usually prime agricultural land and
should be left as such."
"While wood is the basic component of the PSP system, polyethylene is the secret of its success. Polyethylene is inexpensive, easy to work with, and readily available. It is an
absolute moisture barrier and is what keeps the wooden walls
from rotting. While it is true that this plastic deteriorates
quickly when exposed to the ultraviolet rays of sunlight, it
lasts indefinitely underground."   April 1987

Fenders Easy to Install and Remove
    Bicycle mud fenders can be made
from thin wooden slats, say ¼" x 4"
x 16". Some commercial produce
crates offer slats of useful
dimensions. Fenders can be easily
removed, thus reducing wind resistance when unnecessary during dry
weather. The fenders require no
struts of their own, because they
attach to bike frame: onto the
diagonal member behind the front wheel; onto vertical member
in front of rear of rear wheel; and under luggage rack over
rear wheel. If no luggage rack is there (unlikely if cyclist
is practical and environment-minded), maybe two struts could
be added to support upper, rear fender.
    Each fender slat receives a bored hole and a notch in its
edge, in pairs, some 2" from each end. Strip of inner tube,
about 1" x 4", is knotted at end, pushed thru each hole, and
then knotted at the other end. Attach fenders to frame, or
to luggage rack, by stretching rubber around member, and
hooking knot in notch. Steve Price, Kentucky, August

notch   c.17"   hole→
c.3½"   knot   insert rubber strip thru hole

How to Avoid Rousing Fido's Ire

Nikki was a beautiful long-haired, tan-colored dog at a shelter I worked at. He was friendly when let outside and he loved to go for walks. One day, he was tied out at one of the dog houses. His chain got caught under the wooden palate the house rested on. Dotty, a shelter worker, walked over to free him. As she grabbed the chain and freed it, Nikki growled. Before Dotty could stop him Nikki sank his teeth into her arm. Another worker got the dog off of her, but the damage was already done.

Thousands of people each year are bitten by dogs. It can be one of the most frightening experiences for anyone. It is also one of the most avoidable experiences for anyone. Very few people are bitten by vicious dogs. Very few people are bitten for no reason. Most people are bitten for one reason: they do not do unto dogs as they would do unto humans. ....

The key to avoiding getting bit by a dog is to treat a dog stranger the same way one would treat a human stranger. Approach the dog slowly or not at all - let the dog do the initial investigation. Let him do the touching also. If he wants to get acquainted he will make the first move. If he does not want to be friends, he will ignore you or run away.

Forcing yourself on a dog that does that will most likely result in the dog's biting you. Do not stare at him. He will think you mean him harm. Instead, glance at him often and keep your head bowed. This is the behavior dogs exhibit when they meet a strange dog or human. It is their way of saying they are not going to hurt anyone. Above all, let the dog have its "space". Let the dog decide whether it wants to be friends or not. Many dogs bite people because people force themselves on dogs and leave dogs no way out. ....

There are cases in which following these rules will do no good. The dog will still bite. But follow these rules and most of the people bitten by dogs will be spared the shock, the pain, and the medical bills. The dog will be spared his life. Carolyn Gossman, Pennsylvania (condensed from Calli's Tales, V6 N3 Winter 1987. Copyright 1987. Sample $2 from

Try to Collect the Plastic One Liter Sized Pour Bottles
used for irrigation solutions (saline, sterile water), if you are working in a hospital or know someone who is. The screw caps make them relatively watertight for resealing, and the price is right - most hospitals throw them out! The fact that any hospital must be considered to be a hotbed of pathogens may be dealt with by you washing the bottles out with dilute household bleach solution, and letting it set a while to maximize the germicidal effect. I use them for backpacking all the time, and I am mighty pleased. As an added bonus, most have a loop or hook on the bottom for hanging. Jon, MI, Aug.

Additional Use for Flip-In Safe Pocket
Instead of keeping my usual pocket items (knife, compass, lighter, adhesive tape and foam (for blisters), whistle, and plastic bags) loose in my pants pocket, I keep them in a safe pocket (Light Living Library). This way the items are less likely to get lost, and when I change pants it's easier to transfer pocket-contents.

I fasten the safe pocket to my belt, but instead of flipping it within my pants (as I'd do if carrying money or passport in populated areas), I just keep it within my pants pocket. Or, if I'm not wearing clothes with pockets, I can wear my safe pocket from my neck. Julie Summers, OR, June

Message Post

Portable Dwelling Info-letter
Six issues for $5.   Sample $1
June 1987   Number 23   POB 190, Philomath, OR 97370

For Better Simple Showers

Use jugs/bottles with <u>narrow</u> mouths, such as milk or bleach comes in, for easiest control of flow (rather than bowls or wide-mouth containers).

Use several small plastic bottles (rather than one big jug) for easier handling - for your first few showers at least. No larger than quart or liter size. (We don't like glass because it's heavier, slipperier when wet, and breakable. We'd like to try gourds some time.)

Allow yourself at least 1½ gallons total if soaping and rinsing; half a gallon if only rinsing - for your first showers. As you gain experience you'll need less water. (We use 3/4 to 1 gallon to soap and rinse. The colder the air the more water (hot) we like, so we can pour it liberally for faster rinsing.)

When soaping, wet and lather your lower portions first, to conserve body heat and to conserve water. (When you later wet your upper body, that will start rinsing your lower regions.)

When rinsing, rinse your top portions first and position yourself so that the drainage off of your top is onto your lower portions (rather than directly onto the ground). Examples: When rinsing your face, hold your chest out and your head back (as shown above), so that water running off of your chin helps rinse your body. When rinsing the back of your head, bend forward a little so that the flow goes down your back. When rinsing your left arm, touch your left fingers to your left thigh, so the water will continue on down your leg. Etc.

Shower over a different spot of ground each time (and away from any stream/lake) to spread the soap and water, so that no one plant gets too much soap. (A little may be good.)

Like most anything, simple showering improves with practice. For us, showering from bottles is now easier and better than showering from pipes (which we still do sometimes when visiting city people who lack secluded outdoor space).

(Imagine someone who, after growing up in a simple shelter without plumbing, visits a house and takes a shower - turning on faucets for the first time in her/his life. He first scorches himself, then chills himself - and drenches the bathroom - and comes out still soapy. Ever after he tells about those weird house-dwellers who insist on doing things the hard way.)

Appreciation to Julie Summers for the Light Living Library paper, "The Simple Shower". Also, articles about showering are in MP#3 p.1; MP#13 ; MP#16   . Holly &Bert

Comfortable in Tipi at 50 Below Zero

My tipi was made with a friend from Reginald & Gladys Laubin's design. With lining and ozan I've been able to adapt it to comfortable living at 50 below. Rugs and two feet of sawdust insulate me from the ground. The wood heater and cookstove sit back to back on a bed of rock and join into the same (smoke) pipe. It's a great glowing home to come home to after running dogs.   Lois, Yukon, September

Enjoy Long-Distance Horseback Travel With Children

Before starting our magazine, we spent most of our time living out of a tent, traveling extensively. We've spent a lot of time in Alaska (19 years) and four of our five children were born up there.

We live in a huge house now, and feel somewhat out of touch, even though we still havea wood cookstove, solar heating, and wash our clothes in an old Maytag wringer washer.

Our horses are our only connecting link - we all dream of the day we can saddle them and ride off knowing we won't be coming home until we're good and ready! (We'd love a correspondence with anyone experienced with long-distance horseback travel - especially with children.) Helen, Home Education Magazine, POB 1083, Tonasket, WA 98855,   February

Backpacking in the Deserts and Canyons of South Utah

Over the last 5-8 years I've probably done 700-800 miles there. The climate is high desert and needs to be treated as such. Here are some common-sense things experience has taught me:

Don't hike into any canyons with water in May in south Utah. Deer flies are vicious and overwhelming. They usually die off by mid July.

Mid July to mid August is very very hot, but if you can stand the heat you will have places such as the Pariah Fork Canyon of the San Rafael Forest to yourself.

Utah hunting season (last two weeks in Oct.) is the best fishing time in Utah of the entire year. Great weather, no people fishing, hungry fish. Malcolm Walden, Utah, April

Tips for Camping Near Towns

In response to Julie's inquiry (MP#22   ): I haven't as yet found a way that I feel is safe, to sleep in a heavily-trafficed area. In the northwest though, I haven't found any problems with sleeping near towns in parks and other densely vegetated areas often within city limits, but at sites which do not allow motorized access and have conditions which discourage foot travel.

Using a bicycle greatly expands the number of sites within a short time period of travel from town, makes carrying things easier and much less conspicuous.

Camauflage I feel is important when camping where people travel more frequently. I use a camauflage-printed mosquito net for the bike, since the chrome renders it so conspicuous. I sleep in a place as concealed by vegetation as possible. A few bracken ferns or other leafy vegetation can go a long way towards concealment.

Bus lockers are good for a very short term place to amass items bought, but must be paid for daily. Some towns such as Portland have large bicycle storage lockers for rent or for free, intended for commutors. These are large enough to store a lot in. They seem large enough to sleep in, but I doubt they could be locked from inside, and would be noisy.

I've made small storage areas with a green plastic garbage bag cut open and put over an A frame of sticks,and camauflaged.

I've also made camauflage nets using jute twine and with strips of green cloth and burlap tied at intervals, although I haven't used them. These seem ideal because you can attach parts of local vegetation to the net to blend with whatever surroundings you're in. A finer twine or string could be used also for less bulk and without a lot of cloth strips, using local vegetation instead. Dennis, CA, Sept.

Mesquite Beans Are Good to Eat

Sap may be chewed like gum. Sap is on tree trunk. Leaves can be used to make tea. Inner bark may be used to tan (leather) skins. Wood makes good handles for knives, picks, etc. Wood shavings are good to smoke meat while being grilled. (Kirk, in Wild Edible Plants, adds: "The long, sweet pods may be ground into a meal which may be prepared as cakes, mush etc.... Mesquite is found chiefly along streams and in areas from southern Kansas west to southeastern California and northwestern Mexico where the water table is relatively high. The plant is a shrub or small tree and grows to 25 feet; it usually has spines. The small greenish-yellow flowers are rather fragrant and are borne in cylindrical spikes....") George, Louisiana, December

Water Cress Adds Tang to Salads or Sandwiches

All across our continent there are small springs and creeks filled with the most delicious and healthful plant we could ask for. Water cress is brimming with vitamins and one of the very best liver tonics available. Once gathered, it can be kept for days and even weeks - simply by plopping it in cool water.

I usually gather some from a nearby spring here in southern California. My supply sits near my sink in a container of water - just waiting to be used in whatever meals I am cooking up. (Caution: water cress can absorb pollution from water.)   Al Fry, California, April

Tsuga Versus Taxus

Recently I came upon a tree that - from its needles - I took for a hemlock (Tsuga), but then I noticed its bark: papery, and quite red under the peeling parts. Sort of like madrone (Arbutus). I sent a branch tip to Oregon State U. Herbarium and they identified it as Western Yew, Taxus brevifolia (ranging from Alaska to California, east to Montana). I mention this because whereas hemlock isn't poisonous, and its needles may be steeped for tea; yew contains poison. So it is important not to confuse the two. (The tree called hemlock is in the pine family, whereas the extremely poisonous water hemlock (Cicuta maculata) and poison hemlock (Conium maculatum), are herbaceous plants, in the carrot family.) Julie Summers, Oregon, February

Fireless Cookery: Safety and Nutrition

Perishable foods should not be left at temperatures that promote bacterial growth (40 to 140°F) for longer than 2 to 3 hours. Monitor with a thermometer. I agree that "foods left in the cooker for more than 24 hours should be discarded." The maximum time is probably much less....

If the food is kept hot enough to prevent bacterial growth, I guess the losses might be comparable to a cafeteria steam table. In your example about a brown-rice/chicken mix, I doubt there would be much difference between simmering for a short time and then insulating, versus simmering for longer and not insulating. These foods are not a good source of vitamin C, the nutrient most sensitive to destruction by heat. Carolyn Raab, Nutrition Specialist, OSU, June (in reply to Julie Summers)

<u>Harvest</u> <u>and</u> <u>Preparation</u> <u>of</u> <u>Land</u> <u>Snails</u>
        So the snails are eating your vegetables. No <u>problem</u>
but an <u>opportunity</u> to apply the Permaculture principle of
using things that are in abundance. New Zealand snails are
similar to those eaten by the French and other Europeans.
        Wait until dark, turn off the tele and turn on the torch
and explore your garden while gathering snails.
        Initial preparation: One dozen large snails per person.
Put in covered dish full of warm water for 10 minutes. Use
only those that partly emerge from the shell. Put in covered
dish full of salty water for two hours. Wash in cold water,
scrub shells, wash again. Simmer for 30 minutes, wash off
any white material (edible but not attractive). Remove from
shells by twisting out with a tooth pick. Remove bits of
green, cut off heads and tails, wash.
        Poached snails: To prepared snails, add chopped carrot,
onion, celery, parley and flavouring herbs. Simmer about two
hours until snails are tender. Serve hot on toast or let
cool first. Ian Fielding, New Zealand, January

<u>Bears</u> <u>Can</u> <u>Run</u> <u>Downhill</u> <u>As</u> <u>Well</u> <u>As</u> <u>Up</u>
        Any moving bear, grizzly or black, I've seen, travelled
surprisingly quickly, up hill and down, if it saw me. Those
that didn't see me (a grizzly and two half-grown cubs on one
occasion; a lone grizzly on another occasion) kept eating
berries. A leading authority on bears, Stephen Herrero (book
review on p.5) says bears can run downhill, uphill or on the
level, equally well and fast (30 miles per hour!).
        I offer two possible explanations why the bear (MP#22
did   not climb the second tree. Perhaps the climber had
climbed higher in the second tree and more effort would have
been required by the bear. Also, the second tree was likely
further from the point of confrontation and the bear felt less
threatened. There may have been a carcass or other food or
cubs nearby which the bear wanted to protect. Thelma, BC, Jan.

<u>Can</u> <u>a</u> <u>Human</u> <u>Climb</u> <u>Down</u> <u>a</u> <u>Steep</u> <u>Slope</u> <u>Faster</u> <u>Than</u> <u>Can</u> <u>a</u> <u>Bear</u>?
        I have in mind slopes so steep that the human has to grab
bushes (or fall) and the bear has to brake with its claws (or
fall). Can a bear climb down a tree (or steep slope) head
first (as can squirrels), or does it have to back down (as
does a cat)?   Bert, Oregon, February
        A bear, being heavy, has to go down a tree tail first.
Not all cats go down tail first - we had one which often went
down head first. The chances of encountering a bear in
terrain too steep for the bear to give chase are remote, I
think. Nearly all bears will avoid humans, given the chance.
Thelma, British Columbia, March

<u>Camping</u> <u>Close</u> <u>to</u> <u>Large</u> <u>Trees</u> <u>is</u> <u>Dangerous</u>
        I had a close call while bicycling through the Five Rivers
area near Alsea last December. It was nearly dark when I
stopped and set a tarp near a tree that looked still alive.
It rained steadily all night but with almost no wind. Then
about 3 a.m. I heard a crack, sat up and moved closer to the
tree the rope was attached to. All of a sudden a large branch
smashed down across where I'd been lying. If I hadn't moved
it would have come down across my chest. The tree was a
medium sized moss covered alder, but more branched than most
as it was the only large tree around. I now try to avoid
alders entirely and won't sleep under any over a certain height
especially if branched. Dennis, Oregon, March

Bear Attack

"On September 1, 1976, a ten-year-old girl was attacked and injured by a black bear about 40 miles northeast of Williams Lake, B.C." writes Stephen Herrero. "The girl was carrying a water bucket back to a lonely hut from a nearby creek. When the bear approached her, she dropped the bucket and grabbed an axe laying nearby on the ground, hit the bear twice, then ran for the house. The bear followed and swatted the child, (breaking several ribs) and knocking her down. She managed to reach the door of the cabin. The bear attempted to follow her inside. With a good presence of mind and in spite of her injuries, she managed to reach and throw a pot of boiling water into the face of the bear. The bear fled. This young girl did everything right once she was attacked by the bear, which was probably attempting to prey on her...."

"During the night of July 25, 1971, (a couple) were sleeping in a mountain tent near the Holzworth Ranch steak-fry area of Colorado. At about 1:55 A.M. a bear attacked them", but bit the woman on her right buttock, then dragged the man 150 feet. The woman woke Gus Wedell, who was sleeping nearby in a motor home with his family. Gus grabbed a frying pan, ran to the man, and beat the bear with the pan, causing it to flee. The man was dead.

"On July 4, 1979, Karen Austrom was hiking alone in Mt. Robson Park, B.C. She "was confronted at close range by a 125-pound young, male black bear. The bear showed considerable vacillation before attacking. It even climbed a tree as if to escape. Once it attacked, Austrom played dead and repeatedly offered the bear one of her arms to protect her vital areas. When a large party arrived 45 minutes later, the bear had mauled and eaten much of her arm but her other injuries were minor. The bear retreated into the bush...."

"Rarely, however, do black bears use their power to injure or kill people. I have records of 20 people who were killed by black bears from 1900 through 1980.... Ten of the victims were age 18 or under. Five were younger than 10.... Nine were adult males.... Predation appeared to be the motive for 18 of the ... deaths.... 93% of the fatal attacks took place during the day...."

"What should a person do if attacked ...? (That) depends on the reason why the attack occurred.... In any place where many bears appear to be habituated to people, then the first assumption should be that ... you have gotten too close to it and it wants more space, or it is trying to get at food that you have. In the first instance simply backing away and watching the bear should end the attack. In the second case ... it is best to give up the food...."

"The most dangerous black bear appears to be one that attacks a person who has been hiking, walking, berry picking, fishing, or playing during the day in a rural or remote area.... If predation is the motive for an attack, the attack typically continues until the bear is forced to back down, or the person gets away, or the bear gets its prey. People who run away, unless they have somewhere to go, or people who act passively or play dead, are simply inviting the bear to continue the attack.... If a person climbs a tree ... they may have to fight the bear in the tree.... People have successfully kicked black bears in the head and have knocked them out of trees, but sometimes black bears have grabbed people by the foot and pulled them out of trees."

"Heavy objects such as axes, stout pieces of wood, or rocks are possible weapons. They can be used to hit a bear on the head, with the hope of stunning it and causing it to leave. Other aggressive actions by a person might include kicking, hitting with a fist, yelling or shouting, or banging objects, such as pots, together in front of a bear's face. This is an action plan of last resort - in close combat a bear has the advantage over an unarmed person. But in the rare situation in which a person might face such a black bear, fighting off the bear could save that person's life."

Black bears live in areas with dense trees or shrubs, and usually stay within several hundred yards of them. "Black" bears come in shades from black to blonde. So do grizzlies.

Grizzly bears (the author includes Alaskan "brown" bears) are generally much more aggressive than are blacks. Grizzlies have killed or seriously injured over twice as many people as have black bears, even though there are only one-tenth as many of them, and few live near people. South of Canada, grizzlies are found only around Glacier and Yellowstone Parks, MT, ID, WY - though an adult male may range 100 miles. Grizzlies frequent more open habitat than do black bears.

Most grizzly attacks, unlike black bear attacks, result from sudden encounters while hiking. Most attacks are by females with cubs, or by bears with carcasses to defend. "... most sudden encounters leading to injury have occurred when the person was not aware of the grizzly until it was less than 55 yards away...."

"Try to detect bears when they are distant. If the country is open enough ... use binoculars.... If you see a grizzly (or any bear), your response depends on how far away it is and whether you think it has sensed you. If the bear is unaware of you, try to detour quietly yet quickly downwind and away from the bear. Use cover if it is available. If you do this, chances are the bear won't sense you. Watch for the bear anyway, and remember that tree climbing is also a possibility", especially with grizzlies which, though they can climb, aren't as agile in trees as are black bears, and haven't been seen higher than 33 feet.

"If the grizzly is aware of you ... then my recommendation isn't so clear.... Avoid staring directly at the bear, which threatens it, but watch it closely.... A bear rearing onto its hind legs ... is trying to sense what is happening. Normally this is not an aggressive posture... The farther back the ears are, and the more they are flattened to the neck, the more the grizzly is aroused...."

When hiking where visibility is restricted, such as through dense brush, the author makes loud _low_-pitched noises (small bells not recommended) to avoid suddenly surprising a bear. However noise may _attract_ some bears. "Young adult grizzlies are particularly curious. ... Each bear is an individual...."

Bears are most likely to be found near their food. "Bears normally eat the above-ground portions of green, herbaceous plants when the plants are in early growth stages.... During summer bears prefer to feed at high elevations (where) plants grow very rapidly, and (therefore contain more protein)... Where available, berries and mast" (acorns/nuts) are relished. Black bears have killed young children who were berry picking. Early spring and late fall, grizzlies may feed on underground roots, bulbs, tubers, and corms. (Blacks do seldom if ever.)

"Absence of garbage with no signs of scavenging by bears is the first criterion for choosing a backcountry campsite. ... One of the worst possible campsites is in the middle of or just off a trail through dense brush...."

"... Cook downwind and well away from where you will sleep. Plan your meal quantities so that what is cooked is eaten.... Wash your dishes and pots thoroughly, and ... hike several hundred yards before emptying the dishwater.... After cooking ... wash yourself to remove any lingering food odors or even the odor of insect repellents or cosmetics... and change your clothes if you think they are odor-impregnated...."

"... Store your food well away from where you will sleep." If hanging it, at least 20' off the ground and 10' away from anything climbable. (There are several pages of diagrams.) Use trees/limbs/poles at least 4" in diameter. (A bear can bite through smaller timber.) "Where there are no trees ... big boulders and cliffs offer interesting challenges... Most people are better rock climbers than are bears...."

"... Sleep in a tent rather than without shelter.... I like to have a foot or two between me and the tent wall. Curious or garbage-addicted bears will sometimes bite or claw the sides of a tent as if testing to see if something edible is inside."

"Because of the limited amount of information available, I recommend no repellents except caution and understanding of bears, acting aggressively toward black bears, electrical fencing for specific uses, chemical sprays in some circumstances (of those tested, capsaicin containing "Phaser" was the most effective), and proper firearms in the hands of experts."

Bears are among the least of the dangers faced by most tourists. Even in Glacier Park, MT, "only 6 of the 150 fatalities ... through 1980 were caused by grizzly bears. Most deaths resulted from falls, auto accidents, drownings, and hypothermia." However "injury rates to backcountry visitors are higher - (as high as) one injury per 2620 backcountry use days in Mt. Revelstoke and Glacier Parks, Canada...."

Because most MP readers live/camp/hike in remote or rural areas where only black bears occur, this review draws chiefly from just two chapters: "The Predaceous Black Bear" and "Avoiding Encounters". _Six_ chapters are devoted to grizzly attacks and how to respond to them; and seven chapters to characteristics of bears including identification, sign, evolution, and food preference.

Stephen Herrero, a professor of environmental science and biology at the University of Calgary, has been studying bears, often in the field, since 1967.

We highly recommend this book, especially to those who frequent grizzly country. _Bear Attack_, 1985, 287 pages 6x9 hardbound, Nick Lyons Books, NY. Distributed by Winchester Press, 220 Old New Brunswick Rd, Piscataway, NJ 08854. $15.95 (ppd?)   Review by Bert & Holly

Europe Through the Back Door

"You can travel anywhere in Europe (and the world) for $25 a day plus transportation costs. Money has little to do with enjoying your trip. In fact, spending more money builds a thicker wall between you and what you came to see.... A tight budget forces you to travel 'close to the ground,' meeting and communicating with the people, not relying on service with a purchased smile", writes Rick Steves.

"Pack light!... Limit yourself to 20 pounds in a 'carry-on' sized bag (9" x 22" x 14" fits under the airplane seat). ... When you carry your own luggage, it's less likely to get lost, broken, or stolen. It sits on your lap or under your seat on the bus, taxi and airplane. You don't have to worry about it, and when you arrive, you leave - immediately...."

"Europe is casual. I have never felt out of place at symphonies, operas, plays, etc. wearing a new pair of jeans and a good-looking sweater.... Bring dark clothes that wash and dry quickly and easily. Minimize by bringing less and washing more often...."

"Camping is the cheapest way to see Europe and every camper I've talked to gives it rave reviews. Every town has a campground with enough ground for the average middle class European to pitch his tent or plop his "caravan" (trailer), good showers and washing facilities, a grocery store and restaurant, and a handy bus connection into town, all for three or four dollars per person per night...."

"There are still people traveling in Europe on $5 a day - and less. The one thing they have in common is that they sleep free.... Europe has plenty of places to throw out your sleeping bag.... Some cities enforce their 'no sleeping in parks' laws only selectively. Away from the cities, in forests or on beaches, you can pretty well sleep where you like. It's best to keep a low profile...."

This book includes chapters on planning, packing, transport, sleeping, eating, money, foreign phrases, health, the woman alone, photography, and museums; plus descriptions of 38 "back doors" - from the Dingle Peninsula of Ireland to the Samaria Gorge of Crete.

1987, 395 p.5x8, $13.60 ppd. John Muir Publicatns, POB 613, Santa Fe, NM 87504

Lives in Camper: Six Months in Woods; Six Months Traveling

I have a problem similar to Julie's (MP#22   ). I live in a camper. I park by a lake in the woods for six months of the year. While there, I have to go to town for supplies, laundry, etc. every few weeks.

I have a lot of friends in town. I stay with different ones each time, so I don't become a pest. I try to make my-self useful, like helping around their house. I keep where I sleep picked up and use a sleeping bag so I don't leave any dirty laundry behind.

Most of my friends work so I do my things while they are working. Of course I don't get much sleep as we sit up at night and gab, but I only stay in town each trip for two or three days and I can catch up on sleep when I get home. We always have fun and I get everything done I need to. At the end of our visit I'm ready to go back to the woods.

The other six months of the year, or when it gets cold, I travel a great deal. I still stay with family or friends, and still try to be helpful.

Of course my friends are always welcome at my place during summer, if they want to camp out. Some of my relatives from Florida come up and stay with relatives in town but they come out to my place for picnics and swimming.

I own my land. One time there was a cottage on it, but I had it torn down. My husband died before he could fix it up, and the taxes are much cheaper just paying on the land. I have water and use propane gas.

I love living alone but I also need friends around, so I have the best of two worlds. Gloria Orr, New York, Oct & Dec

Man Lives 19 Years in Plastic Wigwam in Woods near Boston

The state has the right to evict a hermit living in a makeshift wigwam on public land, but it must find him a home where he can be close to nature and preserve his independence, a judge ruled Wednesday. "... jail is not the answer," Housing Court Judge E. George Daher said. "A shelter is not the answer. He'd probably expire in a jail or a shelter."

Britt, 50, was in court fighting the state's 17-month effort to evict him from the mattress and plastic-sheet wig-wam in the woods he calls home. "I'm not a homeless person. I'm in the 19th year in my wigwam at the Chestnut Hill Reser-voir," said Britt, hitching up his pants, which were held up by a bicycle inner tube.

The state says Britt broke a Sept. 1985 agreement to leave the public land. Britt counters that the state and its housing specialists ignored him until the City of Boston decided to expand a cemetery and encroach on his home. (from Living Free #38; originally from The Buffalo News (AP), February 12, 1987)

Paper, the Poor Man's Multi-Use Material

If there is one thing that people on the street or road learn quickly, it is the thermal benefits of paper and card-board. As the homeless in larger cities got stuck on the street in the 80's, one could see whole rows of cardboard boxes serving to shelter them during colder nights. News-papers and cardboard served also to insulate them from the cold earth and cement. The same secrets served hobos and migrants during the hard times of thepast of course. The only difference today, is that we also have thin cheap plastic to help in this insulation procedure - and a lot more crazies to

make street life much more dangerous. Today, there are also
cheap tapes to allow the cardboard and paper to be made into
more efficient thermal aids.

Many shacks over the globe are just about as comfortable
as larger expensive houses, thanks to cardboard. By mixing
some wall paper paste in wet wadded up newspaper sludge, you
get paper mache. This can chink drafty holes in any structure.
You can add a little tobacco or other repulsion solution to
keep away the pests from such 'filler'.

If you ever get stuck in a bad situation and are cold,
remember to get some newspapers under your outer clothing.

A friend of mine once made several hundred dollars a
week by gathering cardboard and paper in his truck. Prices
vary from year to year of course, but at any given time a
little paper scrounging can help pay for running-to-the-city
gas. A Fry, California, April

Light Weight Outdoors Wood Stove Keeps Fire Off Ground

Solo Stove is made of stainless steel,
weighs just 19 ounces, and folds to the size
of a thin paperback book. "It burns twigs
and small branches safely and efficiently."
It "gives a camper the freedom and aesthetic
qualities of cooking over a wood fire without ... leaving an ugly fire scar."

The burning twigs set on a perforated
bottom, which is supported an inch or so
above the ground, allowing a good draft
and keeping the fire off the ground. (However hot ashes may
drop through, so to avoid all fire sign it will be necessary
to set the stove on something non-combustable.) Slanted
sides "focus heat onto pot". "Fuel is easily added thru
space" between pot and sides.

The Solo Stove has no chimney, and so is strictly for
use outside - not in a tent. It is lighter and, at $32.45
postpaid, is less expensive than a similar stove of another
brand reviewed in MP#14   . "It is available from your local
dealer,"or MTS Designs, Inc, 504 Sharon Road, Chapel Hill,
NC 27514 (919)929-9429   Review by Bert & Holly

Lighter Flints Can Rust

"Flints" are really a metal. Unfortunately it oxidizes.
This can take place in the plastic lighter, or even in the
plastic or glass phials in which you buy spare flints.

Not all flints oxidize. Back in the "good old days" one
could buy sets of flints that were coated with a red skin. I
still have some, and they do not oxidise. Bill Tarplee
(from Australasian Survivor, V6 N2, November 1986)

Check Foam Pads Carefully Before Buying

Not all pads that appear to be closed cell foam actually
are. This I found out through hard (and damp) experience
after purchasing a "High Country" sleeping pad this winter.
It looks like closed cell on the front and back sides, but the
the cut sides on close examination reveals its actual open
cell construction. The pad soaks up water on damp ground and
has flattened to a fraction of its original depth after four
months use. Dennis, Oregon, March

How Do You Deal With Ground Wetness?

In many areas there just isn't any spot that's not fully
saturated after heavy rains.

Report on Aladdin Kerosene Lamp

I've recently purchased an old Model "C". It costs about 3½¢ an hour to run, using pearl kerosene at $2.25 a gallon. That's close to what I spend on propane (at $1/gal) for both cooking and light in winter months, so the Aladdin seems rather expensive to use.

In use the lamp is kind of fiddly. When first warming up (5-10 min.) the mantel will carbon up if not adjusted properly. Once hot and properly adjusted it burns nicely without further attention. If the wick is uneven the mantel won't glow evenly.

The chimney puts out a lot of heat, enough to ignite paper within a foot of the top. I've been keeping it about two feet from overhead combustables, I think one could reduce this distance with a pie pan heat shield.

When operating properly the light is very nice - steady, bright, adjustable illumination, silent, and no fumes that I've noticed except when starting up and cooling off.

For packing, the fragile mantel ($2.79) and chimney ($7.69) could add a lot to the expense of the light. Also the tank leaks around the top if tipped over, adding to the fire hazard and requiring emptying when carrying a long distance.

At this point I think it's a light that will withstand long storage and provide a brighter, less fumey light than candles or wick-only kerosene so I may keep it as a back up....

In one letter I wrote about the Aladdin having fumes. It now seems to have been an anomaly. I can detect no smell after it warms up. I've tried "Klean Strip" paint thinner and it seems to work just fine. Next try diesel fuel. Do you know of additives to diesel that might produce toxic fumes?

Have you had any more information on radioactivity of gas lamp mantels? (report in MP#13) I live with one every day and, more, it's over the cook stove and eating table, so I probably ingest dust from it. It shure doesn't sound good.

I've recently tried the preformed mantel. I was told by a camper supply dealer that they wouldn't turn black as soon as the others. I blew up two when I first lit them. The third time I turned the gas on slowly after the initial burn and it was okay. These preformed mantels are made in Malta. The light from them is very bright. I wonder if they are more radioactive than the soft mantels. Robin, Oregon, Dec, Apr, May

Skunk Cabbage -- Is It Edible?

Towards the end of last March I came upon a marshy area with numerous yellow skunk cabbage plants, Lysichitum americanum (which is a close relative of the eastern skunk cabbage, Symplocarpus foetidus). Because the flower spikes and their surrounding colorful yellow spathes (modified leaves) were present, I'm positive of the plant's identity. (I've read that young leaves might be confused with false hellebore, Veratrum viride, which can be deadly.)

Although the plants had not been eaten right down to the leaf stalks, as had the ones I'd seen in August, some leaves had pieces missing, appearing to have been torn off. The plants didn't look savaged enough to be the work of bear; I wonder if deer might have been responsible.

I sampled a thumbnail-sized piece of raw leaf, chewing and spitting out. After some minutes I noticed a slight burning of my tongue.

I collected young leaves, some not yet unfurled. (The larger leaves are enormous, some easily spanning two feet.)

Upon returning home I tore leaves (mostly the unfurled ones) into coarse pieces (so they would fit into the pot). I covered a few cupfulls of them with water, brought to a boil, then simmered five minutes. Then I drained off the water, replaced it with fresh, and repeated the five minute cooking. I did the same with a third, final water.

I sampled a tablespoonful of leaves after draining the second water. A slight burning was noticable a few minutes after eating. (The irritation reminds me somewhat of the soreness following eating a lot of raw pineapple.) After the third cooking I ate about 1/8 cup. It was perhaps slightly less irritating than the previous taste.

The characteristic odor was somewhat diminished after cooking, but still noticable. I don't find it the kind of smell I would seek out and savor, but neither do I find it truely sickening.

The next day, noticing no after effects, I sampled another 1/8 cup, from what was left over from the previous day's cooking. Similar story. Slight irritation. Tho somewhat less than the day before. Probably because the cumulative effect (of the raw and less-cooked samples) was not present. A few hours later I tried another 1/8 cup, from the same leftovers, and got more irritation than any previous time, noticing it on the inside of my cheeks as well as on my tongue. Uncomfortable, but not extremely bad.

I suppose cooking with repeated water changes might further reduce the irritating quality, but I didn't care to expend the time. (And I wonder what food value would be left.) Only if I had excess time and fuel would I bother with this plant. (In which case I'd try the roots also.)

Nancy J. Turner, in Food Plants of British Columbia Indians - Coastal Peoples (review forthcoming) says: "Skunk cabbage was rarely used as food by British Columbia Indians, although in western Washington the leaf-stalks were roasted and eaten by the Quinault, the flower-stalks were steamed and eaten sparingly by the Cowlitz, the young leaves by the Skokomish, and the roots by the Quileute and Lower Chinook. In no case were they highly prized. ... The Kwakiutl dried and powdered the leaves and used them as a thickening agent for boiled currants (Ribes bracteosum) before these were formed into berry cakes. The Haida considered the plants to be poisonous, and recalled instances of children being killed by eating the leaves. However, they mixed the leaves with salmon eggs as a preservative. The Lillooet ... formerly ate the roots in small quantities....

"Whenever skunk cabbage leaves were available, they were used as 'Indian wax paper,' for lining berry baskets, berry-drying racks, and steaming pits. They apparently did not impart any unpleasant flavour to the food."

In A Field Guide to Rocky Mountain Wildflowers, John and Frank Craighead, and Ray Davis say: "Yellow Skunkcabbage is eaten by black bears throughout the warmer months. All of the plant - leaves, roots, and fruit - is consumed. Crystals of calcium oxalate, in all parts of this plant, produce a stinging, burning sensation in the mouth when chewed raw. Heat breaks or rearranges crystals in the starch so that the plant can be eaten with no unpleasant effect. By roasting and drying the root the Indians were able to use this plant, as well as the eastern Skunkcabbage ... for food. A flour

was prepared from the starch. The young green leaves
(cabbages) usually can be eaten after being boiled in several
changes of water. At times even repeated boilings will not
remove the stinging property. This plant is related to taro,
the staple food of the Polynesians. Like the Skunkcabbage,
taro contains crystals of calcium oxalate. Native peoples
throughout the world use members of the Arum family for food,
and quite independently they have discovered that drying or
heating removes the stinging properties."

Indian Gardens Mostly Untended
The Mohave and Yahi had gardens of corn, squash and beans
that were mostly let alone. They planted them (deep, in a
stick hole) in spring and left them until harvest, mostly
untended. The corn, for example, several seeds in a "hill",
several inches deep, the "hills" placed wherever ....
   Millet grows in thick-seeded heads; proso is a type.
Amaranth seeds heavily, is easily picked, hardy, disease/
insect resistant, drought resistant. Plant in fall or early
spring to use the abundant rain; finish before summer dry.
Paul Doerr, California, July

Alder Trees Especially Dangerous to Fall
   I read with interest the book review by Julie Summers, in
June 1989 MP#25, of Professional Timber Falling.
   Proper technique is of practical concern for people
living in the woods: cutting firewood, home logs, etc; most
especially the safety aspects. I've done a small amount of
falling for firewood and thinning, and was the wedge man when
we felled old growth cedar snags which had been killed by
forest fire.
   Professional tree fallers who coached me always emphasized that there is danger in falling those soft deciduous
trees: the cottonwoods and, most especially, those alder
trees. The sometimes severe lean and the easy splittability
of those trees may combine to cause an occurence known as a
"barberchair". This occurs when the tree begins to split
before your backcut is complete, thus causing that portion of
the butt to kick back, possibly hitting sawyer or saw, sometimes with fatal results. This is due to the weight of the
tree putting heavy pressure at the point where you're cutting.
   Although basic technique is the same as in falling
conifers, there is a critical point to remember. When
falling alders, you do not want to lollygag on your backcut.
This precludes the use of a wedge. If you wish to turn the
tree in a certain direction, do so by means of the shape of
your hinge, i.e. leaving more meat at the end of the hinge in
the direction you wish the tree to swing. Do not cut through
this hinge, for it is the means by which you control the tree.
I know of two people, one a personal friend, who were killed
while falling alder trees. In both cases they were attempting to wedge the tree over to the side, and were killed by
the resulting barberchair.
   To prevent this from occuring, make your backcut quickly and efficiently. Also, make sure your backcut is not much
above your facecut. A high backcut contributes to the
barberchair. Make sure your escape path is clear and not
180° from the direction of the fall. Wear a hardhat. It will
only take one near miss from a broken tree top to convince
you as it did me. Alders are especially prone to breaking.
   When falling conifers, use plastic wedges and save your
metal wedge for splitting wood. Hitting a metal wedge with
your chain saw can be very expensive. Gary R. Cropper,

Message Post

June 1988   Number 24

Portable Dwelling Info-letter
Six issues for $5. Sample $1
POB 190, Philomath, OR 97370

We Have Lived in Our 18' Diameter Yurt for Eight Years Now

It still has the original canvas (Pyrotone - 50/50 poly/cotton) roof, which we waterproofed by painting with exterior latex house paint (this doesn't work on untreated cotton canvas by the way). We need to replace our 100% cotton walls, and maybe we will this year - otherwise I'll patch the rot spots.

I wouldn't live in any other kind of structure. Even with the paint the yurt is very light. It is round, it uses space much better than a tipi, and it's beautiful.

Last year we were in northern Arizona for six months and lived in a 10' yurt. We used a white parachute over 4 mil plastic for the roof and we really enjoyed the light - especially the light of the stars. It was not a durable arrangement for the high desert sun, and we had to cover it with a blue plastic tarp after three months. Incidentally, we had an outdoor kitchen, so the yurt was primarily sleeping space.   Anne Schein, California, June 1987

Tipis Can Be Comfortable but are Not Very Light

You need an inside lining to keep comfortable in a tipi in really cold weather. The tipi is the only type of tent shelter in which you can have an open fire for winter warmth. But they are large and heavy and need long poles. A tipi is not a backpack tent and not cheap. It is pretty much a two man job to pitch. It's the only type of tent I have not slept in, though I have spent many afternoons in friends' tipis.

There is one best book on the tipi. Try your local library for The Indian Tipi by Reginald & Gladys Laubin, U of Oklahoma Press, Norman, OK 73019. Price $21.95.   Ernest Thompson Seton also wrote on tipis. Lyman Barry, NY, March

There is Much Good Camping in Northern California

The river canyons are largely empty and beautiful. I've been mining for gold on the North Fork American between Truckee and Sacramento. Pretty good gold at end of summer. Paul Rinne

My Three Children and I Enjoy Sled-Dog-Team Winters

And camper-backpacker summers. I spent much of my childhood on pack horses in the high Sierras. Joni, Alaska, March

Shelter Systems' New Portable Domes Have Shingled Covers

I've completed work on a new dome - The LightHouse (TM). The 18' diameter size is 9' tall, and has four doors and four clear vinyl triangular windows. It weighs 60 pounds. Packed size is 5'x18"x18". It will sell for $560 but I've a kit complete except for poles and stakes for $390. The kit can be assembed in under five hours.

Because all panels are shingled and clipped (no sewing) it is 100% leak proof and yet breathes. Bob Gillis, Dec

Shelter Systems also has a 12' diameter LightHouse, shown in the picture. 6½' high, weight 38 pounds, packed size 4'x12"x12". Assembled, it sells for $389.

The LightHouse goes up in 30 minutes without tools, according to the info sheet. You simply insert interchangeable poles into connectors spaced evenly over the cover. The poles are bent slightly when inserted and this tightens the cover. Once up, the LightHouse is free standing and can be moved. It comes down in five minutes.

The sidewalls are of a 5.5 oz polyester canvas, colored light tan. The translucent skylight above the sidewalls is constructed of a woven, ripstop, UV resistant film. A sunshade of silver and black ripstop covers the top of the dome. The frame is PVC tubing. Lexan clips join the covering without puncturing or weakening. In tropic weather the sidewalls can be rolled up to provide unsurpassed ventilation - net sidewalls are an option. Shelter Systems, Box 67, Aptos, CA 95001 (408)662-2821. Catalog $1.

<u>Domes</u> <u>Or</u> <u>Tunnels</u>?   <u>Shingles</u> <u>Or</u> <u>Big</u> <u>Sheet</u>?

I wonder about shingling. If the overlapping pieces lay snug together, how do they breathe? If there are gaps between them, will insects or rain get through? I was told that a wooden shingled roof must be steep, else it will leak.

The thought came to me that shingling was invented when there were only natural materials in small pieces (bundles of thatch, skins). Now that fabrics are made long and wide, the arc or tunnel shape (like the greenhouse plans you sent previously) or the shed shape (like the tleanto in MP Sept. 1986 p.1, or the Woodland Tent in LLL) seems simpler to make and a more efficient use of material. Also all the vents, doors and windows can be on the ends of the shelter under the overhanging roof, rather than on surfaces that must shed rain.

On the other hand, with shingling if one piece gets holed only it needs replacement, rather than the whole cover. (A patch on plastic doesn't hold up long in our experience.) Also a dome-shape frame is stronger for the same weight (or lighter for the same strength) than an arc-shaped or shed-shaped frame, because the poles brace each other in more different directions. Bert, Oregon, January

It's true that large sheeting lends itself to tunnel and cone shapes. However, I've found that with the same amount of strength of poles, I achieve more stiffness (i.e. strength) with domes than with tunnel shapes because of cross bracing (as you pointed out). Domes also fit into the environment more pleasingly, some feel. Many people like the looks of domes better than the tunnel shapes I make. Plus domes provide more headroom near the walls than do shed or cones. And domes use shorter poles and are thus more portable.

Besides allowing creation of dome shapes, shingling allows use of woven 6' wide material (which is much stronger than plastic film, though more expensive and not as available except as blue tarps). Shingling also lends itself to combining a variety of materials. E.g., the LightHouse has a top of silver/black to produce shade; upper side walls of translucent for lighting; clear vinyl windows for visibility; fabric sidewalls for doors and privacy. The shingling allows for extensive upper venting without leakage.

The shingled overlapped edges are pulled tight between the clips and this creates ridges which make the seams water tight even on a ridge point. My understanding of "why

shingling must be steep" is because of cracks and nail holes
in the shingles that will leak if not steep enough. With the
LightHouse, the clips used for joining do not puncture the
covering, so no leakage. Bob Gillis, California, February

(Other articles regarding merits of various shapes for
portable dwellings are in MP Sept.1983   , Sept. 1985
and   Sept. 1986   .)

Dealing With Wet Ground
Before pitching the tent, I place a (4-10 mil) plastic
ground sheet over the spot where the tent will nest on.
Thus I don't worry about a wet bottom come morning.
Wildflower, Connecticut, March

Reusing Cinders Saves Wood and Avoids Pot Black
I've learned a lot about cooking with wood, and
especially charcoal, embers and cinders in the past 8 years.
I save cinders from my wood fires by putting them in an old
cook pot with a tight lid. Then when I need to cook I can
relight them with a newspaper or kindling fire - that's
mighty handy on hot days. Plus, no pot black, no propane.
Plus I get two fires out of one piece of wood. We use
embers for heating too. I use less than half as much firewood as we did before, plus we're more comfortable.
Anne Schein, California, June 1987

Dome Up the Shrouds Over Storage Pails
In MP June 1985, Hank Schultz described how he shallowly buried plastic pails to use for storage. He suggested
wrapping a piece of plastic over the pail as a shroud, to
help keep moisture out in case the lid cracks or doesn't
seal tightly. He wrote, "Even the shrouds are rarely holed."
We have started storing some things of ours in buried
pails and have also unearthed several pails of MP supplies
that Hank put down. Some of the shrouds had holes.
Usually small holes such as by a slug or insect, rather than
the chewings or rippings of a mouse or other animal.
We now shroud with several layers of plastic and dome
them up in the middle by putting leaves or moss (dry if
possible) or folded up newspaper under them. This way the
water will tend to run off the shroud, and not puddle, and
therefore much less will go through any small hole.
In the few years we've been using pails this way, no
noticable moisture has gotten in. Make sure the lids are
pushed down and on tight all the way around. (Also see
articles in MP June 1986 p.1 and Sept. 1986   ) Bert & Holly

A Substitute for "D" Rings
I use "D" rings often when making or repairing camping
gear. (E.g., on shoulder straps.) I have found that buckles
(which turn up often in my scroungings) with their tongues
removed, substitute well for "D" rings (which don't often
turn up).   Julie Summers, Oregon, August

Plastic Bag Under Outer Shirt Provides Lightweight Rainwear
For light going in wet but mild weather, especially when
bicycling, I use a variation of what Jon described in MP
April 1986 p.9. I wear one or more short-sleeved T-shirts or
sweaters, and shorts. Then over that a plastic bag, long
enough to reach a little below my shorts, with holes cut for
neck and arms. Then, on top, an ordinary shirt - the lighter

the fabric the better. The top shirt gets wet but protects
the bag from ripping on bushes. The under shirts remain
fairly dry. My legs and arms get wet but that's tolerable if
it's not too cold. I protect my head with a rain hat or else
with several knit caps (fairly warm even when wet).
For working in dense brush, or when it's colder and I
need more clothes, I wear a complete rain suit (Holly made
from LLL's plans). It has proven durable but is heavy and
somewhat stiff - good for outside work but not for bicycling.
Bert, Oregon, January

Are the Spines of Devil's Club (Oplopanax horridum) Poisonous?
I had heard from various sources that they are. So the
day I lost my footing and inadvertently grabbed one of these
vegetable porcupines I was worried. I immediately removed the
spines, using a flame-sterilized twisty-tie wire - the best
implement I could come up with at the time. The pain subsided
rapidly, and healing occurred without any complications.
I've since read in Food Plants of British Columbia
Indians, by Nancy Turner, that some people are "highly
allergic" to the spines. (Likewise for swamp gooseberry
(Ribes lacustre) she says.) This would explain why some
people consider the spines poisonous while others don't.
Julie Summers, Oregon, February

Eating Too Much Poison Oak Causes Permanent Injury
With regard to eating small amounts of poison oak to
become immune (in MP Sept. 1986   and June 1987   ).
A friend of a friend ate too much and was never totally up to
par after that. I have often heard of people drinking the
milk of poison oak eating goats. I think I would prefer to
try that if I am ever in poison oak country again.
Nancy and Andy, New Mexico, January

Poison Oak Feedback
According to Sandra Baker, author of Poison Oak and
Poison Ivy (review in MP#9 May 1982 p.5), to develop a tolerance it is necessary to introduce the antigen (e.g., by eating
a piece of leaf a fourth the size of one's little fingernail,
which is what Sandra does) every 10 to 12 days. I wonder if
Robin had been. Also, according to Dr. Albert M. Klingman,
U Penn. Med. School, quoted in The Medicine Show, by the
editors of Consumer Reports (1955&1974), "Complete desensitization of highly sensitive persons is not possible with any
dosage. All that can be expected is a reduction in sensitivity (briefer, less generalized, less intense attacks ..)."
"... Dr. Kligman recommends oral dosage (rather than injections) with a potent poison ivy extract (Rhus oleoresin) if
treatment is undertaken."
Poison ivy/oak extracts, to be taken orally, are
available over the counter (at least they were a few years
ago). If anaphylactic shock were a problem, I wonder if
manufacturers would risk law suits by offering this product
over the counter. This is not to deny possible dangers. But
I just wonder how much riskier it is to eat a small quantity
than it is to blunder through a patch of the plant and thus
experience heavy exposure to it. If doing that doesn't cause
anaphylactic shock, would eating a small amount be any more
likely to? Julie Summers, Oregon, August

Economics Out of the Woods

With any kind of work or business, if it's money you're after, the important thing is, not how much you **earn**, but how much you **clear** after all expenses.

Seems obvious, doesn't it. Yet a small business person who publishes treatises on money and economics (no less) recently wrote us:

"Do you consider a very useful machine (a microfiche reader) overly priced when it costs you, second hand, $100; i.e. at most 10 hours of labour in a conventional job?"

Let's think about that. $100 for 10 hours labour assumes income of $10 an hour. Is that realistic?

When we work on farms we make more like $2 or $3 an hour. But $10 an hour isn't extraordinary these days. We might be able to earn that much in a big city. (Bert has done surveying and drafting; Holly typing and bookkeeping.)

But what do such jobs **cost**? We would need to rent an apartment, not only while working but while **looking** for work (which could take months). Bert would probably need a car to get to the various job sites. (Holly mightn't, but waiting for and riding buses is at her own time and expense.) We'd often be eating at fast-food joints or buying convenience foods, because we'd be too tired or short on time to prepare meals from low-cost bulk foods. We (Holly especially) would need more expensive clothes. And, though each of us might **earn** $10 an hour, after taxes and insurance we'd **collect** much less.

Furthermore, consider that most "nine-to-five" jobs are more like **six-to-six**, when you include dressing and commuting. Often there is training or retraining required at your own time and expense, **especially** for high pay jobs. There may be social obligations, such as after-work beers-and-gossip; neglect them and you may be first to be laid off and last to be rehired. Counting the stresses, worries and restrictions (can't travel far or devote an uninterrupted week to something you like), a demanding job (and high pay jobs **are** demanding) really takes up most of the 24 hours in a day. Putting it another way: any day that I work I'm not good for much else. Add the health hazards of a more polluted environment and higher accident risks (especially if commuting, or working with power tools).

I doubt that even a CPA with a super computer could calculate **all** the costs of a job. But no need to. Just ask ---

1. How much money and valuable goods did I have when I **started** looking for work (or setting up my business)?

2. How much money and valuable goods do I have at the **end** of the job (or season, or year)?

The difference is how much you **cleared**. Divide that by the number of days spent working or looking for work (or resting up from work, or recovering from illnesses or accidents), and that's how much you **cleared each day**.

This way of figuring is especially useful for portable/mobile dwellers whose pay and expenses fluctuate widely.

For example. Suppose I had left $200 cash when I started job hunting. A hundred days later after working a while I get laid off. Suppose I now have $1700 cash, plus a $100 microfiche reader and $400 worth of bulk foods I bought to take back to the woods. (I **don't** count anything I bought **and consumed** while employed, such as food eaten, clothes worn out, or videos rented (or booze or drugs taken) to get my mind off of work.) So I now have (1700 + 100 + 400 =) $2200 total. I started with $200. So I **cleared** (2200 - 200 =) $2000. Divide by the 100 days I worked (or searched, or recovered). Result: I cleared **$20 a day**.

That's it. Whether my pay rate was $2 an hour, $10 an hour, or $200 an hour isn't important. The money I spent while working is **gone**. Conceivably I **could** have saved more. But the fact is, I **didn't**.

So that $100 microfiche reader would actually cost me, not 10 **hours** of labour, but 5 **days** of labour ($100 divided by $20/day equals 5 days. If I could build an equally good one in 4 days while camped out in the woods, I'd save myself a day. Holly & Bert, Oregon, January

Indian Scout Craft and Lore

The author was a fullblooded Sioux, "raised as a young warrior in the 1870's & 80's," according to the back cover. The book contains a mix of questionable info ("... lightening does not strike in the water"); clichés ("In the great laboratory of nature there are endless secrets yet to be discovered"); and hints ("The best way to sleep in camp is feet toward the fire" because the feet are sensitive and will awaken you if the fire escapes). The how-to sections (e.g., making a canoe) are **not** detailed. The gesture-language chapter suffered badly from no illustrations (and there were only a few elsewhere). I'd say read it if an easy opportunity arises, but I wouldn't go out of my way.

"In the event of sudden danger, I was taught to remain perfectly motionless - a dead pause for the body, while the mind acts quickly yet steadily, planning a means of escape. If I discover the enemy first, I may pass undiscovered. This rule is followed by the animals as well.... and they (the hidden young) are made to close their eyes also. The shining pupil of the eye is a great giveaway."

A trick characteristic of deer and rabbit families: "at the end of the trail they make two loops, and conceal themselves at a point where the pursuer must, if he sticks to the trail, pass close by their hiding place and give timely warning...."

The author says salt is not needed for jerking (drying) meat, and my experience coincides with this.

Regarding camp sites: "In the case of a small party or solitary traveler, concealment is the first principle to be observed. Seclusion gives a sense of security...." When blazing trails: "You should not disfigure the tree.... It should be just enough guide for your friends, neatly done, and courting no unnecessary publicity."

Chas.A.Eastman (Ohiyesa), 1914,

I've Been Living on the Road for Almost Ten Months Now

Not in a fancy schmancy motorhome, but in my extremely basic truck. All it took to get me started were some blankets, curtains for the windows (I'm using old towels, actually), a Coleman stove, ice chest, and some homemade bookshelves. The investment so far has been about $500 (I already had the truck), and the payoff has been well worth it: an exponential increase in peace of mind.

I've never had any hassle about sleeping at the interstate rest areas (in Washington state). I've probably slept a hundred nights there. The badgers pull through once or twice a night, looking to break up beer parties 'n such, but if you're quietly eating, sleeping, cooking, reading, etc., they won't give you a second glance.

Road living, for those open-minded enough to consider it, is the easiest way I know to break from the vicious circle of jobs, rents, taxes, and bills. For anyone who has a vehicle, the expense of living in it is hardly more than the expense of owning it. Brick Pillow, WA, Dec. (condensed from *Living Free* #42, Stumm, Box 29-mp, Buffalo,NY 14223, sample $1)

Islands of Opportunity in the Pacific

Back in the mid 70's, the Mariana Islands just north of Guam entered into a covanent with the U.S. and since then have had handouts like nowhere on earth. Some ten thousand people receive   millions. As a result, unharvested fruits simply fall off trees and rot. The large lush island of Rota sits fertile and untended.

Most of the islanders hang out on Saipan where the glitter is. Some hundred thousand Japanese tourists keep the local glitter going and there is a lot of potential for 'go gitter' Americans. It's difficult to buy land but leasing is easy and all kinds of concessions are open to encourage small businesses. You can set up a business for $50 without all the zoning nonsense. Although the islands don't have the typical South Seas beauty adventurers expect, Americans are welcomed and given priority treatment. Local laws are very much like the states and mail is the same rate and fast. I have had a bank in Saipan paying me 18% interest for some time. You can check it out in person by taking a flight out of Guam. If you can't come up with data in your local library, I'll be happy to zerox a pile of background and current facts for $3. Al Fry, 9237 Craver, Morrongo Valley, CA 92256, Nov.

Dwells in Tree Houses in Central Park for Eight Years

A modern-day Tarzan lived rent free in the heart of Manhattan. When New York City officials finally brought him to earth, Tarzan turned out to be 22-year-old Bob Redman, who gave up life with mom in an apartment to commune with nature in the treetops.

The park's managers marveled at his final creation, a five-room, split-level dwelling more than 40 feet up a towering beech tree with a breathtaking skyline view. They were so impressed they dropped charges and gave him a job as a tree pruner at $300 a week.

Bob built his first tree house in the 850-acre park when he was 14, followed by 12 others, each more elaborate than the one before. He built them with precision and care, the way birds build nests. He'd scrounge around for used lumber, then haul the wood to the park at night and hoist it up board by board with ropes. "We marveled at his spectacular

workmanship. His last house had floors strong enough to hold
a truck, and with not one nail driven into the tree."
 Bob went to great lengths to conceal his creations -
choosing trees in out-of-the-way places, camouflaging them
with branches and green paint. But at no time did he break a
branch or harm the trees. Over the years, park workers would
discover Bob's houses and dismantle them. He'd simply start
over again in another tree.
 Friends came to visit at night, bringing sandwiches,
books, flashlights and radios. "I'd live in my houses for
weeks at a time, coming down only for food and to visit my
mother," says Bob. "I like to be in trees ... I like the
solitude and I can't find it anywhere else in the city."
(condensed from undated clipping in Living Free #42)

More About Plastic Pails and Drums for Storage

 The plastic pails with snap-on lids (1, 5, 10 gallon),
as well as the 55 gal garbage cans, can be used for above/
underground storage if they are kept clean (no spilled food).
Mice, etc. usually will not try to gnaw through, except sometimes at the lid-edge if they can reach it.
 Olives are shipped to this country in big 60 gallon
plastic drums with screw-on rims and inner sealing lids.
They are also good for storage. Let set in the sun to get
hot and drive out all moisture, add moth balls, and seal
while still hot. Paul Doerr, Luna Ventures, POB 398,

Nettle Patch Harvested Repeatedly

 This spring I've been picking nettles from a small
nearby patch. When picking from older plants I usually
harvest only the top 6 or 8 inches (leaves, stems, flowers) -
the tender part. I leave the rest of the plant in the ground.
The convenience of this patch brings me back and I find that
after a couple of weeks the plants previously pruned have
each sprouted three or four new tops from the old stalks.
By now, mid May, the old lower leaves are ragged but the new
tops are fresh and tender. I am on my third picking from
these same plants. (Also see "A Green for Most Seasons", LLL)
Robin, Oregon, May 1987

Hints for Making Bread from Coarse Flour

 Sometimes I have to use a flour mill that grinds only
coarse flour. I have found I can still get a tasty, tender,
nicely textured bread, if I make the dough as moist as possible
and soak the flour long (which helps to develop the dough's
stretchiness). I soak, overnight, half the flour mixed with
all the recipe's water and yeast. Or, if the weather is warm
and souring is a problem, I soak only a few hours - until
bubbly. (I use water that's around 60° F - a cool room
temperature, because hotter water would speed up fermentation
time.) Then I knead in the other half of the recipe's flour.
I let the dough rise once (maybe a couple of hours), punch
down, let rise again, and punch down a second time. Then I
put the dough in a pan and bake it. (Because I bake without
a regular, preheated oven I do not let the dough rise in the
pan before baking. I have found that to do so results in the
dough ultimately falling. Julie Summers, Oregon, August

Since Writing My Article About Lime-Hominy and Masa Tortillas

I've learned that it's easier to get rid of lumps if the lime
is first made into a thick paste, using only a little water,
then the paste may be stirred into the larger quantity of
water that the corn is soaking in. Julie Summers, August

Lightweight Cookstove Made from Large Tin Can

For most of my camping years, a #10 can
with a salvaged grill provided my cooking
needs quite well. And, if lost, replaced by
scrounging another can from a restaurant
dumpster. Punch holes along bottom of can.
Wildflower, Connecticut, March

Eating Allergenic Substances May Cause Severe Reactions

I would urge caution for anybody thinking about taking
any amount of poison oak/ivy/other in any way/shape/form.
Especially if they have had a bad reaction to the stuff in
the past. The possibility that they might develop a severe,
severe allergic reaction, possibly fatal (called anaphylactic
shock) cannot be discounted. Folks who take the bee sting
desensitization shots (which are controlled in strength, and
standardized in preparation, as raw leaf/stems are not) do
experience this and are under close supervision, and a carefully planned regimen for this very reason. I'm glad Robin
doesn't report any major problems (MP#22), but consider
the possibility that "taking a vacation" from the program
might allow your body's immune system to develop a "memory"
of the urushiol and subsequently over-react, with potentially
lethal results. Careful!! Jon, Michigan, September

Sleeping Bare May Not Be Best

I must strongly object to Major Lyman F. Barry's
comments on page 4 of MP#20 about sleeping nude in a sleeping
bag, and especially his references to that long discredited
1940 Arctic manual, which has embarassed the Air Corps for
too long. That "study" and manual was done solely to "prove"
that sleeping nude was best, and Eskimos were "studied" as
the extreme example. But the conclusions were arrived at
before the study and all the facts found totally contradict
the study.

The major problem is mixing up conditions; trying to
apply ideas for handling sweat from overheat to ways to stay
warm. Thus a hatred of clothing will lead one to be too cold
or overheated and sweaty: When the bag is too warm for outside conditions you will naturally open it to vent and cool
you. But, if you are then nude, the chill of cold air
directly on your skin will be so uncomfortable that you will
close it back up, prefering sweat to chill. Adding an
absorbent bag liner to soak up the sweat won't do a thing to
solve the problem causing the overheat and sweating, but will
make your bag heavier and add washing problems, plus result
in more harmful sweat loss as you make sweating more tolerable. Also, without vapor barrier in the bag, you will thus
greatly increase condensation in the outer insulation of the
bag as well as soaking inner insulation with your sweat.
Thus you will need much more drying time for the bag daily,
and will have to wash the whole bag often.

When practical, sleeping nude, as well as going nude
during the day, is far more comfortable than wearing clothes.
But clothes are needed at times for protection and warmth.
Generally when it is too cool out of your bag to go nude

you will find it <u>necessary</u> to wear some sort of clothing (at least shirt) in your bag, adequate to allow you to open and vent the bag without excessive chill on exposed upper torso. That clothing can be your spare shirt, shirt and jacket, PJs, sweat suit top, or even clothes you were wearing during the day. I got a real laugh over Lyman knocking flannel pajamas cause "they add no warmth", but then saying the same light flannel is ideal as sleeping bag liner! The only significant differences between using the flannel for PJs or liner is that the liner is heavier, harder to wash, not useful for anything else, and won't protect your upper torso from chill when you open top of bag to cool off. Thus the harder-to-wash liner will promote more sweating and more frequent washing.

The liner that <u>should</u> be in every cold weather sleeping bag is a vapor barrier liner, and that should be sewn right in, since it is <u>always</u> needed. Condensation and sweat soaking of the insulation is as much, or more of a problem in mild conditions above freezing up to 70 degrees, as in below freezing conditions. In <u>no</u> case do you want your insulation to be acting as a sponge to soak up sweat from overheat! Instead, avoid the overheat by selecting proper insulation thickness and ventilation. If you get cold, and have a vapor barrier liner in yourbag, you can get up to 20 degrees more warmth if you tightly close the bag up over your shoulders and around your neck. Without being snugly closed up, a VB liner will not addany direct warmth to your bag, but does always protect the insulation so you always have <u>all</u> the insulation you started with. Without VB liner you may start the night, when it's still warm, with full insulation, sweat from overheat and not notice it as it wets insulation, and wet outer insulation with condensation. Thus as the night gets colder, your insulation gets less and eventually you wake up cold but soaked with sweat! This makes you fear being cold the next night so you may throw an extra cover over the bag, or wear more clothes, eventually maybe finding an arrangement that merely leaves you sweat soaked but not cold in the morning.

When the outside temperature is about 65 degrees or higher you can tolerate the air directly on you, so can and should then sleep nude (and in fact go nude during the day). Then it is nice to have the bottom inner surface of your bag made with a fast wicking fabric so any sweat can wick <u>across</u> the <u>surface</u> to exposed area where it can evaporate (this is assuming you have VB so sweat doesn't go into insulation and ruin it). Altho cotton flannel is nice for that function, we have found an even better material: brushed knit Nylon. By having that laminated to a tough urethane VB film we have a VB liner material that has the desired wicking surface on it! Compared to cotton it's far more durable, lighter weight, easier to clean, drys much faster, and wicks faster! We're so pleased with it that we now use it on bottom interior of all our sleeping bags, and for all our VB clothing. We also list it for sale for $6.50 per yard (43 to 50" wide) but will sell it to readers of Light Living for $4.50 per yard.

Below 50 to 65 degrees, proper use of sleeping bag takes a bit more thought. Use all the insulation you have for a fast warmup, but <u>don't</u> go to sleep with all that extra insulation over you. When you finally feel <u>very</u> warm, remove excess insulation and adjust venting and thickness of clothing worn so you are not overheated nor chilled.

Then you won't sweat, and as the night gets cooler will naturally close the bag more, maintaining just the warmth you need. If you are really chilled before going to bed, try doing some vigorous exercises for a quick warmup and a better sleep. Jack Stephenson, Warmlite, RFD 4 Bx 145 - Hook Rd., Gilford, NH 03246 (603)293-8526; June

Single Blade Disposable Razors Work Fine for Haircuts.
Two or three razors are required as they dull quickly. Remove the safety guard with a pair of pliers, being careful not to touch the blade. In front of a mirror use very light strokes from the top of head down. With light pressure the top layers of hair are cut only, resulting in a more or less uniform length of hairs. Don't try to cut too much at once, rather make many light strokes, checking progress continually in the mirror. When a blade begins to get dull switch to a new razor as this method requires a very sharp blade and it's easier to make mistakes with a dull blade as they require greater pressure to cut.
The method does require some finesse, but much less than using scissors. Cutting your own hair with scissors is very awkward; using a razor requires much the same motions as a comb. There used to be a device sold that had a razor contained in a comb which would be an improvement over this method if it's still available. Results are never perfect, but each time you get a little better. It's not a good method for very short hair as variances in hair length are more apparent. The main advantages are that you can do it yourself, cost is low, it's quick, there's no waiting involved, and it does not require great skill. Dennis, Mar87

Economical Substitute for Commercial Toilet Paper?
Outside I use leaves. But inside they are impractical (if brought in damp they stick together and mold upon getting warm; and dry they are bulky). I've heard of people using the Sears catalog or newsprint. But I'm reluctant to rub myself with inked paper. (Might ink be carcinogenic?) Rinsing with water is a possibility (which I've read is used in various places around the globe) but what to dry with? A reused towel is a breeding ground for disease microorganisms. Neither do I find moss suitable because it contains debris, and sheds. Julie Summers, Oregon, June

Arranging Shelter When in Town With Friends
Julie - can you stay with friends who are away during the day - work, school, whatever? Then you can do your thing during the day, too, and socialize in the evening. Because your time wouldn't be as structured as theirs, you could do some chores or errands in lieu of reciprocal invitations. Thelma, British Columbia, January 1987

A Caravansarai Hostel?
I dreamed up this business for someone. Preferably underground for better temperature. A room of concrete with 2x7' conc shells/walls about 2' high. Bolt down plywood top. Plastic covered sleeping pad. 2' walks between. Traveler has own padlock for grill-door under bed, own sleeping bag, towel, mess kit, etc. Sleep rooms open into wash room, and wash room opens into dayroom with picnic tables and benches. Low rent, low costs, small profit. Paul Doerr, Luna Ventures, POB 398, Suisun, CA 94585; Jan.

<u>How to Camp Longer?</u>
This has been asked by several readers who camp a few days at a time. Without knowing the details, specific advice isn't practical. But in general, notice what limits your stay and try to make improvements.
Too cold at night? Bring more sleeping bags.
Too hot during day? Find shade. Or rig shade. Or camp nearer to water and take frequent Simple Showers.
Bed too hard? Bring more foam. Or build a mattress out of whatever local plants are springy and abundant/renewable.
Too much traffic? Get off the worn trails and look for spots most people don't go.
Not enough food? Bring more.
Too heavy to carry? Bring only concentrated foods such as rice, flour, nuts (remove shells), peanut butter, margarine, honey, raisins, granola, etc. Forage or sprout your salads.
To someone with no experience at all, our council is: Find a vacant spot that's <u>near</u> your room or car (or whatever shelter you're experienced with) and that's <u>not</u> in/by big trees, water (might rise), dry washes, trails, cow pastures, steep snow fields, or other potential hazards. Bring two (for back up) flashlights so you can return in the dark. Stay out until you start becoming uncomfortable. Return to your room or car. Note why you were uncomfortable. Next time try to improve. Expect to abort your first few campouts.
Many neophytes have unpleasant times because, for their first campout, they hike many miles to some remote scenery, without having fully tested their equipment or themselves.
Until well experienced: keep it close; keep it simple; keep it cautious; keep it cheap. Costly equipment that might have worked dandy for the sporting-goods clerk or outdoors writer, may not be what <u>you</u> will need where <u>you</u> will be. H & B

<u>Simple Shower During Warm Weather; Basin When Cold</u>
In response to the question about bathing: I use the Simple Shower in warm weather. I have a couple of bleach jugs that I've painted black to speed heating in the sun. On a clear sunny day the water is almost too hot by 3 or 4 p.m. I find one gallon is a good quantity for a pleasant hot shower if I'm not shampooing my hair.
In cold weather I heat water on the cook stove and bathe indoors with a basin and washcloth. Except for my hair and hands, I usually do not use soap with the Simple Shower or wash basin. Robin, Oregon, October

<u>Use a 55 Gallon Drum for a Japanese Bath</u>
We're the right size people. Six footer folks need to squash a 55 gallon drum to oval shape (between a pickup and a tree, for example) to fit in. The Japanese part is that we take water out for washing and use the tub for soaking and relaxing. It's a very efficient tub and we don't have to cut wood to stove length to burn them.
I've been busy with mountain life - basic wife and mother activities - and lots of other projects. Anne Schein, CA

<u>Storage Containers Bigger Than Drums</u>
Around fishing ports, and maybe other food handling areas, various plastic bins are used the same way that bushel baskets used to be. These are sized up to approx 3-4 foot cubes and may be available used cheap, or new. I'd look in <u>National Fisherman</u> for ads. Dave Stewart, New Jersey, July

Uses Water Instead of Toilet Paper

In the March 1988 MP, Julie Summers posed a question that I might be able to answer. It was about toilet paper substitutes and the use of water. On a global scale, more humans don't than do use toilet paper. I've been around the world so I speak from personal observation and experience. Most humans use water. Water is more hygenic. Feces dissolves quite readily in water and washes off your skin quite easily. Conversely, paper will smear the excreta over your skin plus leaving small deposits of paper and cellulose - that leads to chapping and itching. Personally, I've used water by preference for about eight years.

The technique is to: a) use only the left hand; b) use two fingers dipped in the water can to wash and wipe; c) dip the fingers back into the water can and use the thumb of the same hand to wash the stuff off your fingers; d) use the two fingers again to wash some more; e) repeat this until there is no more stuff on either your anus or fingers; f) throw the water away. Drying (with a towel for example) is not necessary. There are a few drops of water on you, sure, but it's no worse than the effect of a little sweat in the same place and cotton underwear will "wick" away the small amount of water in a minute. Even using snow in sub-zero outdoors in the wind at night I've never experienced any discomfort from not drying myself. On the other hand I find toilet paper irritating. Snow is even better   than water for washing with; use the same technique.

Where water is not available the alternatives are: a) a piece of rag - preferably cotton; b) newspaper or newsprint first crumpled up and then smoothed out in order to soften it and make it less slick. I don't think newspaper can harm you even though printers ink probably contains synthetic chemical poisons. That ink would have to make its way into your bloodstream to do damage - and how would it do that. If you're on the road you can always find discarded rags or newspapers. "Bridge" Peter DeNevai, HC#2 Box 5, Duchesne, UT 84021; March

Wipe First, Then Rinse With Stream from a Squeeze Bottle

When defecating outdoors, I wipe with newspaper first to get rid of most of the feces (which I'd just as soon touch as little as possible - I find the odor unpleasant and tenacious). Then I squirt a stream of water from a squeeze bottle, between my legs, from in front, while rubbing clean with my hand. This way no feces gets into the water container.

Because of all the diseases (some very serious) that can be spread by feces, I would not want to use anything that was touched by it without having been very well cleaned afterwards. I wonder if people sharing the same water container (as they do in water closets (public toilets) in some countries) which they dip their hand into, might be responsible for spreading much disease. A mere casual rinsing of the container undoubtedly leaves some microorganisms. A stream of water, with the stream pointing down so that no feces can fall into the source, sounds a lot more hygenic.

When I pee indoors into a pee jug, it's difficult to rinse with water (it tends to get all over the floor). I scavenged some blank newsprint and use that. When that is gone, maybe I'll try water and figure out how to cope with the drips.

Hemmorhoids would be one avenue for anything toxic in the ink (on newspaper used to wipe with) to enter the bloodstream. But a break in the skin is not necessary for substances to cause damage. I have read that used motor oil (for example) contains poisons that can be absorbed thru the skin, into the blood. It may also affect the skin itself, without entering the blood, just as do lye, bleach, strong acids, etc. Julie Summers, Oregon, April

When Painting or Pouring Fuels, Do It Downwind from Children. Keep the fumes out of their lungs. Wildflower, CT, September

Cataracts Among Glassblowers
Robin's comment in February 1987 MP reminds me. My Merck Manual, 14th Edition (a medical textbook), tells me that causes of cataract (opaqueness of the lens of the eye) include xrays, infra-red radiation (heat waves), trauma (blows to the eye) and other problems (like diabetes). Sooo - staring into the fire, regularly, for long times, when the fire is very hot, may help develop cataracts. Jon, Michigan, June

Shock Treatment for Snakebites and Insect Stings
One of the greatest medical breakthroughs for the back country wanderer has come about as a simple electrical device that can be carried in a duffle. For reasons still not clear, electricity in the form of high voltage, low amp shocks from stun guns is effective on practically all snake bites and insect stings. All across the world there are now people treating the most deadly snake bites with these devices or auto ignition voltage. 20 thousand volts or more seems to be effective. Lesser voltage will usually work fine on bee stings and ant bites. The only rules seem to be that the treatment be performed reasonably soon after the bite and that persons with pacemakers use special stun guns (such as the Nova unit: 2207 Braker Lane, Austin, TX 78758).
The June & July 1988 Outdoor Life went into some depth on such therapy. It told of one doctor in Ecuador who has successfully treated 60 cases of snakebite with electric motor spark plug wire voltage and stun gun shocks. Only one patient died; evidently because he waited too long after being bitten to get shocked. The doctor simply adds a short length of ignition wire to one of the stun gun wires. Placing one wire on the puncture mark and the other opposite to the wound seems to work best.
I and my family used some of the older electrical devices for as long as I can recall. Headaches and joint pains are usually simple to get rid of with a mild tingle. My current girl friend has spent hundreds of dollars going to hospitals with little relief for her migranes. A few minutes of electricity and the problem is virtually gone. According to some, the action of electricity on proteins is such that it can knock out viruses as well as venoms. Some ancients kept electrical eels and fish for treating patients. This article is meant to educate and does not advocate a treatment. Al Fry, Incredible Inquiries, 9237 Craver, Morongo Valley, CA 92256; (sheet from "Poor Man's Medicine Report" ($7.95))

Poison Oak More Dangerous On Skin or In Gut?
Julie Summers (in June 1988 MP) asked about the risk of a small dose by mouth, compared to the risk of rolling around in the stuff by accident. On the other hand, A) you can wash off

the oil from your skin; B) through-skin absorption is
unreliable (that's why docs and nurses give shots and pills);
and C) once you've swallowed the capsule, and its through the
stomach, it's nearly irretrievable. My point? I'm concerned
about the danger of absorbing 100% of a 2 gram dose taken by
mouth, versus 1% of a 100 gram exposure to your skin. Yeah,
skin exposure should itch a lot more, but anaphylactic shock
is a systemic reaction, not local, whereas the itching is
local. Compounding this is my "Jon-as-old-maid-nurse"
concern that somebody out in Buhungaland, miles from roadway
and more miles from hospital, may get into trouble and die
en route to help. I may well be overly cautious, but then,
that is (after all) part of my job. You all have got to do
what you see as best - but you oughta know something of the
risks you face. Jon Seaver, POB 21546, Detroit, MI 48221;June

New Herbs Book Describes Plant Uses in Great Detail
        Put out by Rodale Publishing, it is an exhaustive treat-
ment of plants as food, medicine, dyes, etc - how to cook and
eat - also possible toxicity. I must have a score of books
on wild plant foods, etc., but I consider this one the best.
Available from Rodale's Organic Gardening, Emmaus, PA 18099.
A bit expensive - $20 or so, but try a library.
        Regarding mayapple (mandrake), the book says handling the
roots (fresh, dried, or powdered) is extremely dangerous as
poison may be absorbed through skin. Says Indians ate young
shoots to commit suicide! Says seeds are poisonous! I wonder
how many I have eaten when I munched the fruit. Raw fruits
I have found delicious, but more than half a dozen very
laxative. But when made into a jelly, very delicious and not
laxative. Mayapple is Podophyllium pelatum.
        The common Jack in the Pulpit (by the way, IF it has red
berries in fall, it is not "Jack" but "Jane" - as only female
plants bear fruit) is of course a real poison when raw (as is
tapioca), but after baking, grinding, washing and rewashing to
remove poisonous acid, etc. can be made into flour. Catlin,
the great Indian author and painter, says it was the principle
bread source of western Indians and bulbs grew as large as a
pumpkin. Ones around here I never saw larger than a tulip
bulb. I made some flour out of it once and some flapjacks,
but had to add   much regular flour to the batter to make it
stick. It wouldn't pay, except as an emergency food source.
        At last warm, sunny weather. I must get down to enjoy
the pond and get more tan! Next week I am going to an Elder
Hostel program at Roberts Wesleyan College, Rochester, for a
course on Iroquois Indians. I hope to meet some interesting
folk. I am leading one of their day trips to Letchworth Park.
Lyman F. Barry, POB 331, Dansville, NY 14437;   June

I Tried Some Young Skunk Cabbage Leaves in January.
        I changed water two times. Same result as described in
March 1988 MP. I wonder if soda in the cooking water would
help. I haven't tried it yet. Maybe mashed up it would
release the calcium oxalate quicker.
        I've also been experimenting with planting or encouraging
useful plants in the forest where I spend much of my time.
So far, my efforts in cultivation have not been beneficial,
but I am just learning about some of the special requirements
for germination of some seeds. Rob, Oregon, May

Working and Traveling Since Leaving Oregon Three Years Ago

Much of the travel was to find work. Now, for a couple of months, we've been camped on Barb's parents' land, helping out since her dad died. Here we've reversed our usual arrangements. We have the tent set up, but use it mostly for storage and live mostly in the canopy (on the pickup) because the canopy is warmer (smaller and better insulated).

I strung together several extension cords and have a 60-watt light-bulb in the canopy, which we burn day and night during cold weather (shading it when we want to sleep). Besides providing light, it has kept us toasty - so far.

In a situation like this we really appreciate having our own mobile shelter. The sister with four kids has moved here, which helps financially, but she and her mother (living together in the house) frequently quarrel. I can imagine what it would be like if we lived in there too! ....

We aren't staying much longer. Barb's mother has to make some hard decisions which she has been unwilling to make, and our being here simply encourages her not to make them. She would rather cling to a dream that someday her kids will return and take over the farm, even tho all of them (5) have made it very clear they aren't interested. (One grand-kid is but he's only nine. He's a good worker for his age - worked for his grandparents the past two summers. He and his grand-mother might make a go of it if there weren't so many expenses. No mortgage, fortunately, but there are taxes, equipment upkeep (most of the equipment is old), fuel, etc.)

This is not a good area for budget back-to-the-landers. The land is expensive, both because it's rich cropland and because it's near the outer tendrils of suburbopolis. (Environmentally and economically, most of Chicago should move several hundred miles north, out of the prime agricultural zone - maybe to Lake Superior where it could still be a port.) Hank Schultz, Illinois, December & February

Living and Teaching Gardening in New York City

Today I am writing from Brooklyn in an unfurnished three-story house that I have had the luck to be housesitting. I moved here to work as a childrens and adult instructor at the Brooklyn Botanic Garden (BBG). This house seems to be very peaceful - a safe, spacial retreat from the mass of hyper NYC humanity. Living in NYC is different than any other city I've lived in or been to in America. It's almost like being in another country - except most of the people can speak English. It amazes me how almost every square foot of land is either built on or concreted over. People who are lucky enough to own or rent a home live stacked up on top of each other - some without windows. NYC has a terrible reputation to most folks outside it - more of a rotten apple than a big one. It's not as bad as some people say, although to newly move in from any other place in most of America, it can be extremely frustrating, time-consuming, and tiring, to just do daily chores - like shopping, post-office, bank, laundry, etc. I bought a small black-&-white TV for the first time in my life. So now I along with many others here can pretend to escape from the reality of this concrete jungle.

I don't know any of my neighbors. I'm fortunate to live about three blocks from Brooklyn's largest park - Prospect Park, although some would say I'm on the "bad" side because I am a minority living among (seemingly) black (stable)

families. I don't know if their culture is Black American, Caribbean, or African, etc., but I'm quite comfortable.

When I first came here the noise level everywhere was very loud. People talk loud, often interrupt, and don't hear as well. After only a month or so I didn't seem to notice. My bedroom, which at first seemed loud because the windows are right over the street noise below, now seems like a peaceful haven. I fear I may be a bit deaf when I leave here.

I have to wash my clothes more often because of the soot in the air. I'm not sure which is healthier - to breathe shallow or deeper. There are many NYC people who have never been outside the urban city, who think the world revolves around NYC, and that someone might get you if you went out in the country and walked down an empty road alone.

I've heard kids call the ground in the garden "the floor" and the tops of trees "the ceiling", and trees without leaves (in the winter) are "dead". The kids are great fun to be with - they are excited by the most simple natural things you show them. Most of them live their life going from one square box to another - and only walk on concrete. The school windows all have bars on them. Most streets are lined with litter, even though the street sweepers come twice a week.

During the fall and winter, I and three other BBG instructors either go to the schools or have a class come here for a hands-on lesson in botany. I am looking forward to the spring and summer when the Childrens Garden Program will begin - then we'll be teaching in a living outdoor hands-on setting - and I will be able to see the same children every week.

There are a lot of educational opportunities here. Most are expensive unless you are a NY resident. I often go to the programs at the Museum of Natural History. Occasionally I attend the Quaker-Friends Sunday worship which I'm familiar with, but miss being with those friends and groups who express our common spirituality, and the spirit, more vocally in an atmosphere of celebration. I have started volunteering at a Monday night community soup kitchen.

During the 4-day presidents weekend I'll be sharing a home in upper-NY ski country with two work friends and their Brooklyn friends. It is so wonderful to step out of the car after driving two+ hours away from NYC and to hear and feel silence!! Heather, New York, January 1988

Co-Gardening in the Bush During the Summer of 1987

We did much as we'd planned to do (Feb'87 MP). Harvests generally poor-to-fair. Peas and pole beans did best. We ate all we could green, then let many go to maturity (dry) for future seed or food. Why did peas/beans do better than other vegies? Because they are legumes and able to extract nitrogen? Or because we planted them in lower, moister spots with better(?) soil, thinking they could climb into the sun? (Did.)

Pests weren't much of a problem. We kept the mice trapped out. At each little patch we rigged a miniature lean-to of bark and put a snap-trap under it (so birds would not get caught - one did anyway so we ate it - tasted okay).

After this experience we're more interested in native-plant permaculture (Will Ross suggested, Mar'83 MP), and in "naturculture"(?) - learning how to utilize whatever grows naturally rather than trying to force our pet plants on the environment. Seems like, with a little high tech, humans could eat at least as many plants as can deer. (I've heard of pilot-industrial-scale work along this line, but not of any backpack-able equipment.) Bert, Oregon, Apr'88

Message Post

Portable Dwelling Info-letter
POB 190, Philomath, OR 97370
June 1989 #25   One issue $1   Six issues $5 cash; $5½ check

A Green in Many Places

Cleavers are usually small and inconspicuous,
and scattered amongst other growth. But I've
found Cleavers more often and in more habitats
than I have any other wild salad plant.

Even during winter I see small shoots of
Cleavers, in among the grass and vines, on
steep open slopes with southern exposure.

On hikes I nibble Cleavers raw. I like
them best when young and tender. Older plants
I may chew for the juice and spit out residue.
Flavor and succulency varies with place and
plant; some are much tastier than others.

If a plant has square stems, 6 to 8 narrow
leaves per whorl, and soft little bristles on
its leaves and stems, it's probably Cleavers
(Galium aparine), also called bedstraw or
goosegrass. It's continent-wide. Often it grows
reclining. Tiny 4-petaled flowers on slender stalks in leaf
axils are followed by tiny 2-lobed dry bristly "seeds".

Cleavers is of the madder family (Rubiaceae), along with
quinine and coffee. In fact, Cleavers' seeds are a recommended coffee substitute, tho I've never found them in enough
quantity to be inspired to collect them - voluntarily, and I
haven't discovered an easy way to liberate the ones that
stick to my socks.   Julie Summers, Oregon, January

Here's An Essene (Sprouted) Bread Recipe:

Soak 3 cups soft spring wheat in a one gallon jar for 24
hours. Sprout for 2 days or until tails are the same size as
grains (no rinsing necessary). Grind in a meat grinder (or
manual greens juicer). Knead into flat cakes ½" to 2" thick.
Place in cold frame in direct sun. Ideally frame box would be
black. In 3 to 6 hours, depending upon thickness, you've got
yummy "bread". If you can, use organic wheat and pure spring
water. Add any seasonings you like: poppy or seseme seed,
garlic flakes, etc. Plain is also just fine. Costs about 40¢
for 1½ pounds.   Laura Pierce & Mike Kolodny, NH, June'88

After 12 Years Storage, 76% of Wheat Germinated

The hard red wheat, bought from Fisher Mills of Portland
in 1977, was stored with no special atmosphere in sealed metal
drum lined with clear plastic, outside in a shady area.

A two-phase germination test was conducted this spring,
at room temperature, inside in daylight.

During phase I the wheat was sprouted as it would normally
be for eating. It was soaked for 12 hours in a jar, drained,
then twice a day rewet and promptly drained. After 5 days, of
564 grains: 298 showed sprouts over 1/8" long (1/8+); 75 showed sprouts under 1/8" long (1/8-); 66 showed white protrusions
at the sprout end (0+); and 125 showed nothing (0-).

The 1/8+ grains were eaten raw and tasted normal. During
phase II the other grains were kept swathed in damp newspaper
for 7 additional days. Of the 1/8-, 64 became 1/8+ (all but 7
were much longer than 1/8"), 9 remained 1/8-, and 2 became
mushy (presumed dead and decaying). Of the 0+, 33 became 1/8+
and 33 became mushy. Of the 0-, 16 became 1/8+, 10 became 1/8-
and 99 mushy. So 430 total out of 564 sprouted to some degree.

We have been grinding this wheat into flour and using for various baking, and it has tasted normal. Carl DeSilva, March

Meat-Tray Foam Makes Smooth Water-Proof Liners for Lids
I have found that it seals against the top of the jar or bottle. I have used it to replace paper liners in the lids. I don't know about the health hazards. I don't like to use plastic next to oily foods. Rob, Oregon, November

Embedded Clay Pots or Milk Jugs Create Mini-Oases
In some arid regions of northern India, farmers have been defying the odds for centuries by raising melons and other moisture-loving crops. The farmers prepare the soil in the usual way, then dig a hole and bury the pot so that only the neck protrudes above the soil line. The pot is then filled with water and a stone or stopper is placed on top. The crops, usually deep-rooted vining plants, are then sown around the buried clay pot. Because the pot is unglazed, water slowly seeps through the walls into the surrounding soil, where it nourishes the nearby plants. Water gets into the soil slowly and steadily, and none of it drains away before it can be used by the plant. The pots are filled periodically.

In the west, people improvised using plastic bottles and came up with a system that can be used as a liquid fertilizer as well as a water dispenser. Any size will do, but used milk jugs are ideal. Punch holes about knitting-needle size in the sides of the bottle or jug. Start at the base and punch the holes about two inches apart - half to all the way up depending on how deep you intend to set the bottle. Don't punch any in the bottom, as most of the liquid will drain straight down.

Now bury the bottle in the soil a fraction deeper than you have punched the holes. After filling the bottle, screw the cap on loosely and check to see how quickly the water drains into the soil. If it is draining faster than you want, screw on the cap a little more tightly. If too slowly, loosen the cap some more. Peter Tonge (from Christian Science Monitor, Apr.29,88; sent by Richard Stanewick). Seems useful for mini-gardens in the bush, or for encouraging favorite wild plants.

Using Human Wastes as Fertilizer
In Dec'88 MP, Anna asked how to sterilize human wastes for compost. Feces and urine need to be considered separately.

Feces can pass some contageous diseases, e.g., typhoid fever, if not properly used. I'd recommend digging a trench about one foot deep and then burying the feces starting at one end until the trench is completely filled in, making sure there is about 4" of regular soil on top of the feces. After a year it will have decomposed and be safe to plant over.

Urine, on the other hand, is sterile out of the bladder (if there's not hepatitis or other disease passed by urine) and can even be used to wash dirt out of wounds if other fluids are not available. It is high in nitrogen and can be poured around the base of plants. The ammonia smell disappears quickly. At home I pee in a bleach bottle and pour it over the compost pile. Ken Scharabok, Box 33399, Dayton, OH 45433; Mar.

I Store Books in Large Heavy-Duty Zip-Lock Bags
They work fine for me in the field. Glue tags to the bags and have a "med bag", "car bag", "biv bag", etc. A notebook on which bag contains what eases your search. Wildflower,CT,Mar

Portable Living Quarters Plus Underground Storage

I'm enthusiastic about portable dwelling (or maybe just dismayed with alternatives I see). But, in my experience, the actual living space, be it a tent, dome, camper, or whatever, is only a small part of the total system. Also needed is considerable storage space, and while that may be portable in the sense that everything can be taken apart and backpacked, it's not going to move often (unless you're Paul Bunyon).

I'm talking about portable dwelling that's also comfortable, efficient, and self-reliant - a way a family would want to live for many years. Some guy on the road hitching from hostel to hostel, may be very portable but is very dependent of people much less portable than himself.

I like the system Hopping Mole wrote about in MP #19 and #20, except that living underground seems to me unnecessarily difficult, requiring more high tech (for illumination, ventilation and access) than does comparable living space on the surface. And I don't see major advantages in most situations.

The system I'm working toward (and already have in part) uses portable living quarters and underground storage. I prefer that storage be underground (or low, at least) for concealment and protection. Storage doesn't need as much illumination, ventilation or access as does living space.

The living quarters may move several times a year, but will remain within an hour's travel of those storage units that are entered frequently. (The actual distances will depend on the means of transportation and difficulty of traverse.)

The dwelling system as a whole may become fairly large and complex, but I'd like each component (tent, storage container, conveyance, etc.) to be relatively small, simple, and easy to replace - which means, either inexpensive and durable so that spares can be stored, or else simple and quick to handcraft. I want enough redundancy and decentralization so that failure or loss of one or a few components will not jeopardise the system as a whole or its users.

(Dependency of the whole on parts is something I don't like about live-aboard boats. One serious malfunction or mistake and the entire boat, representing many years of labor, may sink, burn, or be seized. Ditto houses. Ditto most other dwellings.) Dave Drake, Oregon, January

What Storage Structures are Available?

Right now storage is the weakest portion of my system. I'm using various plastic barrels and pails, and a sheet-metal shed. The barrels and pails have been satisfactory so far except, of course, they won't hold anything big, and opening up many of them gets tedious. The shed had many problems when first purchased: phillips-head screws (difficult to unscrew); condensation on the underside of roof; cracks mice could squeeze thru; tall and white (visible a long distance to potential thieves); flimsy; no built-in floor. With effort I've overcome most of the problems but I wouldn't buy another.

I'm looking for storage structures lower and sturdier than the shed but larger than the barrels (some 50 gal.), and portable (at least initially), and mouse-proof, rust-proof, rot-proof, weather-proof. Do you know of anything available? Or do you have any ideas? Any experience?

I've been thinking about arches able to fit snuggly together to form a tunnel. The arches could be molded out of plastic. An arch is an easier shape to mold than a can, and so should be no more expensive in quantity than are trash cans

($5-$10 each in quantity). The arches would stack together for shipping (an advantage compared to large diameter pipes). I'll buy several hundred if the price is reasonable. Minimum size: 3' high, 2' wide, 2' long - maybe somewhat higher. Strong enough to withstand shallow burial. Light enough to backpack easily (50# max). Colored dark grey, brown or drab green (not white). Preferably rough textured (not shiny). Who might make them or be able to economically?

The tunnel could be closed on the ends with panels cut from PT plywood (pressure treated with chemicals to resist rot). The floor might also be PT plywood, or simply smoothed packed earth covered with a plastic vapor barrier (if burrowers aren't much of a problem). The tunnel could be buried. Or, if on the surface, made to look like an old log.

Incidentally, with any closed storage, the best time to open it is when the air outside is <u>cold</u>. If colder outside than inside, condensation won't form inside. Very early morning is usually the best time of day. Dave Drake, OR, Sept. & Jan.

Getting a Living from the Woods

Thirteen years ago, taking a rifle, a handful of beaver traps, and about $200 in bulk food, I headed into the woods. Except for a brief interval (which I'd like to forget), I've been in the woods ever since. For the most part, I've gotten my living from the woods: cutting cedar shake bolts, firewood, thinning trees, and running a small winter trapline for winter meat and needed cash.

At present, I'm being paid to camp out, watching equipment for various outfits. Such jobs are available if you look for them. Though there are drawbacks, the monetary remuneration has been very good in comparison with doing farm labor, and you don't give up your time, just your freedom of movement.

I would like correspondence with other folks who live in the woods. Gary R. Cropper, POB 864, Snoqualmie,WA 98065; Apr.

The Bivouac Buddy is a Portable Outdoor Shower

Weighing 13 pounds, it comes completely assembled. Suspend from a tree limb, or cantilever fashion from a camper. Fill the 8-gallon reservoir with water heated over a campfire or stove, and your shower is ready.

The Bivouac Buddy can also be used as a dressing room or a space for your portable potty. When not in use, it stows in a 34" diameter by 12" space.

Top and bottom are hi-molecular polyethlene with crack resistance and impact strength. Curtain is water repellent, 200 denier, oxford nylon. $159 each (ppd in 48 states). Teresa Harris, President, Dream Enterprises, Inc., 453 Hickory Hill Road, Sapulpa, OK 74066; 1988 (918) 224-9683

(Comments by Holly)   We had unkind words for Sunshower (Apr'
87 MP) which, in most situations, we feel is inferior to a
Simple Shower (hand-held plastic bottles or jugs) and a need-
less complication. So why are we mentioning something that's
much larger and more expensive than a Sunshower? (No, Dream
didn't buy an ad, or even subscribe.) Because Bivouac Buddy
might be better in some situations.
     1) In extremely cold/windy weather. After filling the
top tank with the hottest water tolerable, I might pour a
little water, even hotter, into the bottom and let the steam
preheat the inside before removing my clothes and getting wet.
     2) In places where water must not drain onto the floor
or ground, such as in a city rental garage. Unfortunately
Dream's press release doesn't specify the capacity of the
bottom piece, or whether it has any capacity at all. (It
might be just a grate.) It doesn't look able to hold 8 gal.
     Dream seems to be pitching their shower to people who
must bathe where nudity is risky (many campgrounds) or who are
afraid that, even in the wilds, someone might wander by and
(horrors!) see them naked. However, I've taken hundreds of
Simple Showers while wearing a bathing suit (two-piece best)
or shorts and halter, in all kinds of places, even in city
parks (repeatedly refilling my bottle from a drinking fount-
ain). And I've seen hundreds of others shower in swimsuits
(especially at ocean beaches). Of course I'd rather shower
nude, but not so much I'd buy a $159 device. How many will?
     A problem that Bivouac Buddy shares with Sunshower: tree
limbs capable of supporting the filled weight (±70 pounds),
which are also at a convenient height and clear underneath,
are scarce.   Holly, Oregon, February

Fiber Cement is Easy to Mold and Cure
     Fiber cement is used in the form of flat sheets for walls,
and ripply panels for ceilings, in South America as well as
other parts of the world. When it comes off the machine, it
has the character of wet leather. As such it can be pressed
into any simple mold. It sets up like concrete, is cured, and
is then ready for use. When dry it has flexibility reminiscent of plywood, and a similar strength. A standard ripply
roofing panel is set between roof joists three feet apart.
A man can stand on it and it will not break. This panel is
less than 1/8 of an inch thick. A high-V-profile panel is
made which spans over 20 feet, and is only 3/8 of an inch
thick. You can see that this material, which has been in use
for many years, is very strong and flexible.
     Fiber cement panels 1/8 inch thick cost about $3 a square
yard at retail (in Chile), and would be about $1 a square yard
purchased as a wet, leather-like product at the factory. It
will require one or two days for a workman to cut it and press
it into molds (if building a 40' diameter dish). One major
problem is that the fiber cement made in South America has
asbestos in it, which will soon be illegal to import into the
USA. With alternative fiber in it, it is either weaker or
more expensive. A recent sample of USA-made is weaker. Also
it would be nice to be able to produce the stuff without a
$300,000 machine as large as a mobile home. Michael Meredith
(from "The Espejo Parabolico": preliminary plans for a simple,
home-made, solar-powered steam turbine-generator; 11p.8x11;'88)
$5 from Michael Meredith,8941 Victoria Rd,Springfield,VA 22151

Wild Edible Plants Have High Nutritional Values

The word "vegetable" has only existed in the English language for about 200 years. Prior to this all edible plants were known as herbs. Modern vegetables have all been developed from these herbs, but are grown for their looks and size rather than nutritional and medicinal values. When using wild edible plants less are needed than vegetables because of their concentrated nutritional value.

These plants are sometimes known as weeds. "What is a weed?" A plant whose virtues have not yet been discovered." (Ralph Waldo Emerson) Some common wild edible plants whose leaves are edible raw or cooked are: chickweed (Stellaria media), cleavers (Galium aparine), dandelion (Taraxacum officinale), lambsquarters (Chenopodium album), fennel (Foenicucus vulgaris), mallow (Malva sylvestris), nasturtium (Trapacolum majus), plantain (Plantago), purslane (Portulaca oleracea), sow thistle (Sonchus oleraceus), redroot (Amaranthus). All plants should be positively identified before eating as some may contain toxic substances. Soil Assoc. of New Zealand, POB 2260, Auckland (sent by Ian Fielding)

More About the "Bivouac Buddy" - an Enclosed Portable Shower

Thank you for your review (in Mar'89 MP) of our product. The bottom piece has a capacity of 8 gallons. It is made of polyethylene - same as the top section - and is shaped like a saucer. If the Bivouac Buddy is hung outside you could tip one end and the water will spill out. If the water had to be drained away from the shower area, we have a drain kit available (or you could make your own). Simply, drill a hole in the bottom section along the side and insert gromet and tubing.

Answering your comment about support: Any limb that is larger than 5" in diameter and not dead should hold the weight of the shower plus eight gallons of water. Also, the tree limb doesn't have to be low. You can tie a rock or piece of wood to the end of your rope and that will help you throw it up and over a high limb. Teresa Harris, President, Dream Enterprises, Inc., 453 Hickory Hill Rd, Sapulpa, OK 74066; Apr. (918)224-9683 (13#, packed size 34x34x12", $159 ppd in 48 sts)

Simple Mukluks Cut From Innertube

Early this winter I had difficulty keeping my feet warm when working outside around camp. I needed footwear I could put on and off quickly, because I was frequently popping in and out of tents and wanted to keep their floors clean.

Thongs had been fine during warm weather, but are difficult to put on and keep on over socks. The ground was often wet and muddy, and if I wore tennies my socks and feet soon became muddy too.

So I cut two sections out of a car (or small truck?) inner-tube. Each is 29" long on road side, 17½" long on rim side, and 8" across when pressed flat. I folded over one end and lashed it very tightly with large rubber bands (cut from remainder of tube). That was all the fabrication needed.

I wear them over several pairs of socks. Elegant they ain't, but simple they are. And waterproof - until punctured, and then easily replaced. They go on quicker than tennies, and quicker than thongs over socks, but not as quickly as thongs on bare feet. They don't stay on well and aren't good for hiking (kaplop, kaplop, kaplop). But they're okay for going a few yards over familiar turf. Dave Drake, OR, Jan.

Primitive Life Skills

This one-hour VHS color video, featuring Robert Earthworm, was filmed unrehearsed at a primitive gathering in an arid area of eastern Washington, and covers: fire making with the bow drill; cordage from sinew or plant fibers; bread from flour and water; jerky dried over open fire; and medicinal plant use.

When making cordage, Robert holds two bundles of fibers between thumb and forefinger of one hand. The bundle furthest from your body is twisted with the other hand (around the bundle's axis) so the top of the bundle rotates away from your body. That bundle is then brought towards you, over the second bundle. The holding hand moves up and the second bundle, which is now furthest from you, is worked as was the first.

After two viewings and a little practice, I made cordage with ease. Previously, with only books, I had trouble splicing in new fibers. (Robert lets them stick out and trims later.)

With fire-making I succeeded too. But tho the video did inspire action (which written directions hadn't) only after 12 hours of dogged trial and error (over several days) did I get an ember.

Robert tells about plantain's ability to draw out poisons, and shows chewing up some of the leaf and applying it to an injured toe, securing it with a strip of soft leather. He also shows/ discusses St.John's wort, yarrow, mint, wood betony, and Juneberries.

(This is the first how-to video I have seen. I was impressed with its capacity to inspire, and to teach a relatively simple skill, such as cordage making. To teach a complex skill well (such as bow-drill fire-making) maybe a whole video would have to be devoted to it. In which case a whole book on the skill would be cheaper and maybe as good at least for those able to follow written directions. For plant identification, good color photos give sharper images and are easier to refer to than video. Neither book nor video can clarify what puzzles you, or watch you and correct you, as can a personal tutor. But such isn't always available.)

Producer Dale Nelson, 1986, $38 ppd in'88, Northwest Video, POB 251, Roseburg, OR 97470. Review by Julie Summers

Professional Timber Falling

Intended for both novices and veterans, this book by D. Douglas Dent advises how to fall and buck trees safely and for greatest utilization.

Improper gripping of the chain saw is the commonest cause of losing control. Wrap the thumb under the handle bar, opposite the direction of the fingers, so together they encircle the handle.

"Standing to one side of the saw prevents injuries if the saw should kick back." Ballistic-nylon leg protectors recommended. Unintentionally stubbing the saw's tip causes the majority of kickbacks. Be wary of any objects the tip might touch. (However, boring with the tip is sometimes recommended, tho no advice was given for doing so safely.)

The falling sequence(my summation):

STRIP LAYOUT. Plan the sequence and directions in which trees will be felled.

CHECK FOR SNAGS - dead/dying trees still standing. The slightest disturbance may topple them at any time in any direction. Douglas says fall them first.

SWAMP OUT. Clear brush and debris from around tree to be felled.

OBSERVE THE TOP for other trees hung up, or loose limbs (widow makers).

SIZE UP THE TREE. With plumb line or axe, determine which way it leans (which may not be how you want it to fall) and check base for irregularities or rot which might affect fall.

PLAN ESCAPE ROUTE back and to one side of direction of fall, 20' or more.

WALK OUT THE LAY. Check for hidden obstructions on which the tree could shatter, or catapult them at the faller.

FACE THE TREE. The "face" (a.k.a. undercut) "allows the tree to fall freely and helps direct where the tree will fall." It requires a horizontal cut (usually 1/3 or more the tree's diameter) plus a sloping cut which together remove a wide-angled wedge of wood.

THE BACKCUT, "the third and final cut required", is opposite the face, horizontal, and 2" or more above the horizontal cut of the face (to stop a tree that tries to jump back over the stump). Plastic or metal wedges should be driven into the kerf of the backcut as soon as space is available. "A narrow strip" (no exact width given) of holding (also called hinging) wood is left directly behind the face, because if the holding wood is cut thru completely, "the tree would fall in any direction because it hasn't had time to settle into the directing face."

ESCAPE. "Once the tree is committed to fall, don't hesitate at the stump."

This book made me realize the danger when falling even skinny trees, of dislodging widow makers in adjacent big trees. I'm looking up more these days.

I don't recommend falling trees with no instruction other than this review. At least read Douglas's book, which includes how to avoid common mistakes, how to control direction of fall, how to fall problem trees (such as hang ups), and how to buck into logs. 1974, 181 pages (including 86 diagrams & photos), $13½ pbk $16½ hbk in'88 ppd. D.Douglas Dent, POB 905, Beaverton OR 97005. Review by Julie Summers

Tracking Dog: Theory and Methods

"Very little in-depth study has been made in regard to the olfactory powers of the dog...." writes Glen R. Johnson. Nevertheless, a dog can be trained to follow the track left by a person, animal, vehicle tire, or other object moving thru vegetation, dirt, sand, snow, plowed field (retains scent better than short-cropped pasture), or other unpaved surface (not on pavement). Glen distinguishes three types of scent:

BODY ODOR is left on anything a person contacts. It dissipates in as little as two hours "in a hot sun with lots of air circulation...."

AIRBORNE SCENT is body odor carried by the air. Its rate of dissipation depends on wind characteristics.

TRACK SCENT. Vegetation crushed or soil disturbed smells differently than undisturbed surroundings. The track scent may linger as long as several days in lush vegetation when calm, cool, humid and overcast. "A light rain or heavy dew will freshen the track...."

In tests Glen conducted, a dog intercepting a trail less than 30 min. old, could soon tell the tracklayer's direction. With a track over 3 hours old, a dog couldn't tell direction.

With tracks less than 30 minutes old, a dog could tell one person's tracks from another's. With tracks over 3 hours old, a dog could only tell apart people appreciably different in weight.

"All breeds of dogs can be taught to track.... Dogs that receive punishment or scolding when learning to track, soon realize that as long as their nose is pointed down they are safe from abuse and they will take their masters for a merry walk...." Glen usually recommends 30' of line between dog and handler.

Glen gives detailed directions (74 p.) to train (1 hour, 6 days/wk, 10 wks) for the TD (Tracking Dog) test; plus 7 weeks more (43p.)for TDX(Excellent)test.

1975, 213 pages, $18.75 ppd in 1988 Arner Publications, 100 Bouck St., Rome, NY 18440. Review by Julie Summers

The Chernobyl Syndrome

This book by Dean Ing is a hodge-podge, seemingly put together hurriedly in the wake of the nuclear disaster to cash in on public concern. A reprint of Cresson Kearny's home-made fall-out-meter plans take up 82 of the 330 pages. Other how-to's include: plans for an air pump with fall-out filter; plans for a fuel-efficient 32-ounce coffee-can wood stove; tips for 12-volt electric system, unsticking vehicles, engine oil from castor beans, cleaning a chimney, and choosing backpackable saws.

"Don't use a battery to run a heat-element. (That) really squanders electricity. (Better to use)a candle for heat."

"To produce (methyl) alcohol, you will need a big metal drum or equivalent to contain the wood to be heated. An airtight lid is essential. For condenser a long water-cooled pipe is much easier to clean out (than a coil). Water, acids, wood tars and turpentine are all recoverable, along with alcohol and acetone..."

"For strong wood glue, boil and stir shavings of horn or hoof in water until you have a sticky gum. Use it while hot and wet." Sun dry for a day.

"A simple fire-carrier (can be) made from a big juice can, for travelers without matches. Punch ten spaced holes around the side of the can next to its bottom, and cut its top completely out. Add a long wire handle, borrow some fire, and keep a small bed of coals glowing as you hike along. For a fast fire, drop in a few hunks of wood and kindling and swing the can around in a circle; and the forced draft does the rest...."

"Why did primitive plant gatherers seldom live past forty? For one thing, grit from their stone grinders wore their teeth down to the gumline by that age.... Get the hand grinder! ...."

"A wire rope or cable is often cheaper per foot (than a nylon tow strap) but has its hazards.... Even a small chain or cable, under enough tension to snap it ... can cut you in two, or at least sever an arm or leg, before you can react...."

Some topics are only remotely related to disaster survival: e.g. how to train kids to handle money better.

As a survival handbook, I rate this inferior overall to several others. But with a $3.50 cover price, it provides cost-effective self-reliance reading.

Publisher:Baen, NY, 1988. Distributer: Simon&Schuster,1230 Ave. Americas, New York,NY 10020. Review by Chal Long

Northern Flights

"Nowhere in Alaska has progress less touched bush flying than here in Southeast. Ubiquitous mountains limit the use of the modern electronic navigational aids that help more northern pilots ... in the much flatter Interior and Arctic. Southeast's rugged terrain also inhibits construction of airports, and its thick forests and spongy muskeg leave few natural landing sites for wheelplanes. Since virtually all habitation is by salt water anyway, the floatplane continues to dominate here..."

Gerry Bruder, bush-pilot and author of this book,entertainingly and candidly describes Southeast's geography,weather, airplanes, flying techniques, pilots, passengers, communities and wildlife.

"Winter ... slips in and out of the archipelago like an inept invader. The prevailing oceanic air currents that bring Southeast its notorious rainfall also keep the region mild. Even in January precipitation is more likely to fall as rain than snow at sea level...."

"Subtle, unintentional pressure to get thru pervaded every air service .... Instinct told me to turn back. But the two bearded fishermen on board the Cessna 185 were impatient to get to Sitka.... A lucrative, two-day herring fishery would begin next morning, and the men had to catch a 4 A.M. sailing... They had already paid the $550 fare...."

"Thick rainfog hangs across the mouth of the valley. Not a solid curtain, which would simplify the go/no go decision, but a misty, shroudy one, creating a marginal situation. You circle several times, squinting out the windows. (Still uncertain, you decide to try.) So, you throttle back, lower the flaps twenty degrees, and enter. The world around you blurs...."

"My fellow pilots and I gave many 'tours' in visibility that restricted us to weaving along the shorelines of fjords at 200 feet; the passengers saw nothing of the magnificent valleys, lakes, and peaks. But the company made money...."

1988, 165 p.5x8,Pruett Publishing, 2928 Pearl St.,Boulder, CO 80301-9989; $11 ppd. Review by Holly & Bert

Vagabond Globetrotting: Revised Edition

The original edition was reviewed in Feb'85 MP(#17) p.5. M.L. Endicott, 1989, 176p.5x8, $9 ppd from Enchiridion International, Cullowhee,NC 28723-2589

Plastic Pails for Storage - Feedback

Two pails that I'd been using for several years, developed small leaks this spring. Both had lids of the kind in which notches are cut around the rim when they are first opened. Repeated opening had caused fine cracks to spread beyond the rim. Those pails had not had shrouds on them. I am now putting shrouds over all pails. (See MP#18 p.1)

Fortunately I had put old correspondence in the bottoms of the pails, outside of the plastic bags (holding back issues of MP, etc.) and that's all that got damp. I'm now doing that with all pails.

Also I am now inspecting all notched rims, and if there are sharp knife cuts or cracks starting, I use a hot nail to melt the plastic a little and round the end of the cut/crack, to try and keep it from spreading. Hank, Oregon, May

Plastic Septic Tanks Are Junk

An installer here put one in. Come rainy season, it collapsed. The installer had to put in another, a concrete one, at his expense. Paul Doerr, California, April (Septic tanks had been discussed as storage containers.)

Clean Enough to be Healthy; Dirty Enough to be Happy

Many cleanliness "problems" can be solved by relaxing standards. Paraphrasing Che Guevera: 'cleanliness beyond what's needed for health is a bore.' Maintaining a floor clean enough to eat off of, and furnishings shiny enough to see a reflection in, costs, most of all - time.

In Unschoolers Network (addr. on Page B) #19, Winter 1986, Nancy Plent said about John Holt, "Our conversations often centered on setting priorities .... He simply chose to eliminate movies, TV watching and other activities that ate up time and get right to the things most important to him. He endeared himself to me forever when he once stated matter of factly that he kept a dirty apartment. (I would have fudged on a statement like that, maybe saying 'cluttered' or 'untidy', but John called it the way he saw it.)

"He said that while he greatly enjoyed nice surroundings and would much rather live in elegance, keeping the 'dust tigers' away was just not as important to him as other things. With time so short, the vacuuming had to wait indefinitely."

I sweep my floor often; it's small, so sweeping doesn't take long. But I no longer wash it as frequently as I used to, because it's not necessary for health, and it takes a considerable amount of time. So now I have that time free for other pursuits, which I find more rewarding. When I'm expecting company I clean more thoroughly, which I can do quickly because my quarters are small. (Unexpected visitors aren't a problem for me far out in the boonies.)

In winter I also wash clothes less frequently. Ditto for my body. (I've read that Europeans think everyday bathing odd.) But tho I don't bathe my whole body often in winter, I do rinse off crotch and armpits frequently. (Doing it outside, using a squeeze bottle of water, makes it easy.) Julie Summers, Oregon, April

I Live On an Old 36-foot Power Boat

We heat it with a small "Jotul" stove; have a 12-volt electrical system; no running hot water. It's like camping on water. I would love to get more info from anyone in a similar living situation. Christina, Oregon, June

Coping With Blisters - 2nd Skin Product Report

Spenco says its product, 2nd Skin, "will remove all friction between two moving surfaces, clean wounds by absorbing secretions and relieve pain and itching of burns and rashes." For an idea of its appearance imagine the skin that forms on jello. A 3"x13" piece sold for $2 a few years ago at athletic stores.

It is not adhesive and requires tape to be held in place. It is 96% water and 4% polyethylene oxide, and mine, which I stored in the original plastic bag and tube, started to dry up after a number of months. It also got dirtier each time I took it out to cut off a small piece. (Cutting numerous assorted sizes all at once on a clean surface could alleviate that problem.) There are no claims for sterility on the package and my query letter to Spenco received no reply.

I was able to test it on a large scald burn which covered about 1/3 of the inside of my forearm. I covered half the burn with 2nd Skin and left the other half without it. I detected no difference in pain nor healing between halves.

It helped shield blisters on my feet, but not noticably better than my usual, less expensive taping procedure: I place something such as clean plastic or paper directly over the blister to avoid the tape sticking to it, and where called for I use a donut of flexible foam around the blister to relieve pressure on it. Julie Summers, Oregon, May

Accessory Boot Zipper

Boots can be adapted so they go off and on as easily as slippers. If there's about 1 5/8" space on your boots between the rows of lace holes - to accomodate a zipper and two pieces of stiff, narrow webbing (5/8" wide or less) - here's how it's done:

1.) Sew 1/8" diameter nylon cord to the webbing, at intervals about equal to the distance between lace holes. The webbing should be about as long as the lace-up length of the boots. (I used a sewing machine; tho at times I have done this kind of thing by hand.) I used nylon cord in lieu of eyelets, because I didn't have eyelets, and because I find eyelets tend to pull out. But if you prefer, use eyelets.

2.) Install a strong zipper approximately equal in length to the webbing. (I sewed webbing onto the zipper - instead of sewing the cord directly to the fabric of the zipper - because most zippers aren't made with stiff enough fabric to hold their shape when laced onto a boot. The more a zipper zigzags - instead of remaining relatively straight - the harder it is to zip.) I was able to machine stitch; I used the machine's zipper foot attachment.

3.) With the boot on and the zipper closed, lace the zipper to boot, using the gaps between the cord similarly as you would eyelets. To take off boot, simply unzip. When putting boot on, simply zip up. (If the feet swell, or if a different thickness of socks is worn, change the lace tension. Julie Summers, Oregon, July 1986

(2007 update) Julie later reported that uneven pull of the lacings made zipping difficult. But she was zipping ankle-length shoes. This might work well on some other garments.

Buses, Trailers, and an Acre of 'Junk'

In 1914 my grandfather had had enough of northwest winters and headed to sunny Southern California in his Model T. He and my parents never spent a winter in snow from that time. Each spring they headed back north to the family homestead.

In the 50's I read books called How to Retire Without Money and The Freedom Way and these along with Henry David Thoreau took away most of my fears of "Security". Thereafter I tried to enjoy myself and forget about depending on the many Systems.

Simplicity is a key but a person would be simple minded to pass up the many benefits of technology and money if the price is right and slavery doesn't result. I live in the 'cracks' that show up. I haven't punched a clock any longer than to set myself up in an independent lifestyle.

I have lived for years in trailers, motorhomes and buses by choice. I have an acre of 'junk' to add to my enjoyment and enough visitors to keep up my social life.

Today I got enough mail $ to cover overheads and fun, soaked in my hot tub long enough to study the moon and stars to enjoyment, and in a couple of weeks I may hop over to Manila to spend some time with my favorite little lady.

Life is great and all it takes is a little independent thinking and action. We are all different and so there are no formulas, only application of our own individual knowledges and a little perseverence toward our goals. Al Fry

Tips for Keeping Warm in Winter

While there are many new insulation materials now available, there are a lot of us that simply can't afford the latest breakthroughs. Some underwear now has thin layers of foam between the nylon covering layers. Others have quilted synthetic fibers. Over the years I have found wool hard to beat in winter clothing, and if purchased in thrift shops it's well within any budget. If you can't locate GI long-john woolies, you can tighten up the legs on wool suit pants and use them under your regular pants. Sometimes ski outfits can be picked up cheaply in the summer and this is a good way to go if you put comfort above looks in really cold weather.

If you ever see silk hanging on a thrift-store rack, grab it even if it's a lady's blouse. You wear it next to the skin on the body or feet. It wicks up the perspiration.

Down is very hot if you are active at all and you need ventilation and something to absorb the moisture. This is why wool is so great. It grabs the 'wet' and keeps you warm while it does so.

Many synthetic fibers are an abomination. If you have more than 20% polyester in a cloth you will wind up with a stinky, sticky covering that your body detests. Rayon (which was made from wood) is the only synthetic your skin will probably enjoy.

If you make clothing or sleeping bags, down and foam can be within your budget. A sharp knife will slice foam castaways up, and cheap surplus GI sleeping bags and pillows are usually not that hard to find. Common sense and a sewing machine can do wonders.

Keep your head and feet warm and it reduces the need for clothing. If you ever get hypothermia, remember not to thaw out your hands and feet too fast before your body. 'After drop' as it's called can be fatal. Al Fry,

INDEX

radioactivity and, 56, 105
reflectors and, 114
without fire, 92

Large gatherings, meeting people at, 86

Leather, see: Materials

Lighting, see: Heat and/or Light

Lost objects, finding, 45

Matches
  moisture resistant, 19
  waterproof, 1

Materials
  fiber cement, molding, 158
  Foam
  checking before purchase, 134
  healthfulness of, 70
  lids from, 155
  sewing, 4
  Innertubes
  as brakes, 52
  hat holder, 33
  mocassins from, 9, 60, 80, 106
  muluks from, 159
  storage containers, 33
  storing bedding in, 10
  Leather
  care of, 18
  free, 5

Mice, see: Pests

Miscellaneous Items
  binoculars, 32
  bottle collecting, 126
  bulletin board, making, 86, 119
  canteen fixing, 70
  clothespins, 58
  napkins, free, 111
  paper, 133, 134
  pencil stubs, reusing, 47
  razors, single blade, 147
  sunglasses, selecting, 68
  toilet paper substitute, 147,149, 150
  toothbrush case, 2
  towels, half, 58
  utensils, Lexan, 39

Natural living, teaching, 100

Nuclear fallout, 161

Paper, uses for, 133, 134

Pests
  mice, about, 60

mosquito repelling, 13, 18
mouse proofing, 3

Poison ivy/oak, see: First Aid

Polypropylene as fabric, 58, 59, 66, 67

Pressure cookery, see: Cooking

R/Vs, living in, 87, 88, 103, 133, 164

Salt tablets, about, 85

Search and rescue, wilderness, 82

Septic tanks, 162

Shelter, other
  boats, 162
  cardboard, 115
  caves, digging, 51, 123, 124
  D-rings for repairs, 140
  dampness, reducing, 19, 20, 24
  garage, 122
  greenhouses, living in, 64
  root cellar, 122
  underground, see: Underground Shelter
  wigwam, plastic, 133

Shower
  55 gallon drum for bathing, 148
  bivoauc buddy, 157, 158, 159
  conversion, 1
  dry-camp, 57
  simple, 78, 79, 127, 148

Small spaces, living in, 81

Solar stills, 2

Sprouting
  alfalfa, 89
  in rainwater, 61
  mustard seeds, 84
  seeds, 22, 154

Storage
  bedding, 10
  food, 54
  innertubes as, 10, 33
  organizing, 51, 156, 157
  plastic bags, 155
  plastic bottles, 126
  plastic drums, 31, 51, 144
  plastic pails, 84, 85, 115, 140, 144, 148, 162
  underground, 122, 156
  urban, 128

Stoves
  Alaskan, 92